THE ROUTLEDGE COMPANION TO MEDIA AND FAIRY-TALE CULTURES

From Cinderella to comic con to colonialism and more, this companion provides readers with a comprehensive and current guide to the fantastic, uncanny, and wonderful worlds of the fairy tale across media and cultures. It offers a clear, detailed, and expansive overview of contemporary themes and issues throughout the intersections of the fields of fairy-tale studies, media studies, and cultural studies, addressing, among others, issues of reception, audience cultures, ideology, remediation, and adaptation. Examples and case studies are drawn from a wide range of pertinent disciplines and settings, providing thorough, accessible treatment of central topics and specific media from around the globe.

Contributors: B. Grantham Aldred, Leah Claire Allen, Natalia Andrievskikh, Cristina Bacchilega, Meredith A. Bak, Balaka Basu, Lauren Bosc, Ian Brodie, Lindsay Brown, Milbre Burch, Molly Clark Hillard, Allison Craven, Anne E. Duggan, Bill Ellis, Danishka Esterhazy, William Gray, Pauline Greenhill, Lynda Haas, Naomi Hamer, Martine Hennard Dutheil de la Rochère, ku'ualoha ho'omanawanui, Rebecca Hutton, Vanessa Joosen, Michael Joseph, Maria Kaliambou, Anna Kérchy, Mikel J. Koven, Anne Kustritz, Vivian Labrie, John Laudun, Ming-Hsun Lin, Carl Lindahl, Martin Lovelace, Tomasz Z. Majkowski, Jodi McDavid, Lynne S. McNeill, Mayako Murai, Sadhana Naithani, Emma Nelson, Cynthia Nugent, Vanessa Nunes, Jessie Riddle, John Rieder, Jill Terry Rudy, Patricia Sawin, Jennifer Schacker, Veronica Schanoes, Ann Schmiesing, Claudia Schwabe, Karen Seago, Sue Short, Amanda Slack-Smith, Joseph Sobol, Victoria Tedeschi, Andrew Teverson, Catherine Tosenberger, Shaina Trapedo, Francisco Vaz da Silva, Brittany Warman, Olivia Weigeldt, Emma Whatman, Christy Williams, Jenny Heijun Wills, Ida Yoshinaga, Katharine Young, Csenge Virág Zalka, Agata Zarzycka

Pauline Greenhill is Professor of Women's and Gender Studies at the University of Winnipeg, Canada.

Jill Terry Rudy is Associate Professor of English at Brigham Young University, USA.

Naomi Hamer is Assistant Professor of English at Ryerson University, Canada.

Lauren Bosc is a Research Coordinator and Managing Editor for *Jeunesse* at the University of Winnipeg, Canada.

THE ROUTLEDGE COMPANION TO MEDIA AND FAIRY-TALE CULTURES

Edited by
Pauline Greenhill, Jill Terry Rudy,
Naomi Hamer, and Lauren Bosc

NEW YORK AND LONDON

First published 2018
by Routledge
711 Third Avenue, New York, NY 10017

and by Routledge
2 Park Square, Milton Park, Abingdon, Oxon OX14 4RN

Routledge is an imprint of the Taylor & Francis Group, an informa business

© 2018 Taylor & Francis

The right of the editors to be identified as the author of the editorial material, and of the authors for their individual chapters, has been asserted in accordance with sections 77 and 78 of the Copyright, Designs and Patents Act 1988.

All rights reserved. No part of this book may be reprinted or reproduced or utilized in any form or by any electronic, mechanical, or other means, now known or hereafter invented, including photocopying and recording, or in any information storage or retrieval system, without permission in writing from the publishers.

Trademark notice: Product or corporate names may be trademarks or registered trademarks, and are used only for identification and explanation without intent to infringe.

Library of Congress Cataloging-in-Publication Data
A catalog record for this book has been requested

ISBN: 978-1-138-94615-6 (hbk)
ISBN: 978-1-315-67099-7 (ebk)

Typeset in Bembo
by Apex CoVantage, LLC
Printed and bound by CPI Group (UK) Ltd, Croydon, CR0 4YY

CONTENTS

List of Figures		xi
Introduction and Acknowledgments		xiii
PAULINE GREENHILL, JILL TERRY RUDY, NAOMI HAMER,		
AND LAUREN BOSC		

PART I
BASIC CONCEPTS   1

1   **Overview of Basic Concepts (Folklore, Fairy Tale, Culture, and Media)**   3
    JILL TERRY RUDY

2   **Definition and History of Fairy Tales**   11
    CARL LINDAHL

3   **Constructing Fairy-Tale Media Forms (Texts, Textures, Contexts)**   20
    VANESSA NUNES AND PAULINE GREENHILL

PART II
ANALYTICAL APPROACHES   29

4   **Formalism**   31
    JILL TERRY RUDY

5   **Psychology**   40
    VERONICA SCHANOES

6   **Marxism**   47
    ANDREW TEVERSON

7   **Performance**   56
    PATRICIA SAWIN AND MILBRE BURCH

8   **Feminism**   65
    ALLISON CRAVEN

9   **Postmodernism**   74
    CRISTINA BACCHILEGA

CONTENTS

10 Colonialism, Postcolonialism, and Decolonization 83
CRISTINA BACCHILEGA AND SADHANA NAITHANI

PART III
ISSUES: POLITICAL AND IDENTITY ISSUES 91

11 Activism (Folktales and Social Justice: When Marvelous
Tales From the Oral Tradition Help Rethink and Stir the
Present From the Margins) 93
VIVIAN LABRIE

12 Disability 104
ANN SCHMIESING

13 Gender 113
ANNE E. DUGGAN

14 Indigeneity (*E Hoʻokikohoʻe iā Peʻapeʻamakawalu* [Digitizing
the Eight-Eyed Bat]: Indigenous Wonder Tales, Culture,
and Media) 122
KUʻUALOHA HOʻOMANAWANUI

15 Orientalism (Excavation and Representation: Two Orientalist
Modes in Fairy Tales) 133
JENNY HEIJUN WILLS

Thematic Issues Raised by Fairy-Tale Media 143

16 Adaptation and the Fairy-Tale Web 145
CRISTINA BACCHILEGA

17 Advertising 154
OLIVIA WEIGELDT

18 Convergence Culture (Media Convergence, Convergence
Culture, and Communicative Capitalism) 161
IDA YOSHINAGA

19 Crime/Justice 171
SUE SHORT

20 Disney Corporation 178
LYNDA HAAS AND SHAINA TRAPEDO

21 Hybridity 188
FRANCISCO VAZ DA SILVA

22 Intellectual Property 196
JOHN LAUDUN

CONTENTS

23 Pornography   205
    CATHERINE TOSENBERGER

24 Storyworlds/Narratology   213
    KATHARINE YOUNG

Issues of Intersection With Other Study Areas   223

25 Animal Studies   225
    PAULINE GREENHILL AND LEAH CLAIRE ALLEN

26 Children's and Young Adult (YA) Literature   235
    ANNA KÉRCHY

27 Fandom/Fan Cultures   245
    ANNE KUSTRITZ

28 Fat Studies ("Where Everything Round Is Good": Exploring and
    Reimagining Fatness in Fairy-Tale Media)   252
    LAUREN BOSC

29 Language   263
    B. GRANTHAM ALDRED

30 Oral Tradition   272
    MARTIN LOVELACE

31 Pedagogy   281
    CLAUDIA SCHWABE

32 Sexualities/Queer and Trans Studies   290
    PAULINE GREENHILL

33 Translation (Written Forms)   299
    KAREN SEAGO

PART IV
COMMUNICATIVE MEDIA   309

34 Print   311
    WILLIAM GRAY

35 Pictorial ("Such Strange Transformations": Burne-Jones's *Cinderella*
    and Domestic Technologies)   320
    MOLLY CLARK HILLARD

36 Material Culture (Fairy-Tale Things: Studying Fairy Tales From a
    Material Culture Perspective)   328
    MEREDITH A. BAK

vii

CONTENTS

37 **Theater** 337
JENNIFER SCHACKER

38 **Photographic** 348
MAYAKO MURAI

39 **Cinematic** 357
PAULINE GREENHILL

40 **Broadcast (Radio and Television)** 367
JILL TERRY RUDY

41 **Digital ("Blood and Glitter": Fairy Tales as Text, Texture, and
Context in Digital Media)** 376
LYNNE S. McNEILL

**PART V
EXPRESSIVE GENRES AND VENUES** 389

42 **Anime and Manga ("You Love Your Father, Don't You?": The
Influence of Tale Type 510B on Japanese Manga/Anime)** 391
BILL ELLIS

43 **Anthologies and Tale Collections** 399
JESSIE RIDDLE

44 **Autobiography** 408
MARTINE HENNARD DUTHEIL DE LA ROCHÈRE

45 **Blogs and Websites (Narrativizing the Daily "Once Upon
a Time": Re-Envisioning the Fairy-Tale Present With
Fairy-Tale Blogs)** 418
LINDSAY BROWN

46 **Chapbooks** 426
MARIA KALIAMBOU

47 **Children's Museums** 435
NAOMI HAMER

48 **Children's Picture Books and Illustrations** 443
BALAKA BASU

49 **Children's Television** 451
JODI McDAVID AND IAN BRODIE

50 **Cinema Science Fiction** 460
JOHN RIEDER

viii

CONTENTS

51 **Classical Music**   466
PAULINE GREENHILL AND DANISHKA ESTERHAZY

52 **Comics and Graphic Novels (Fairy-Tale Graphic Narrative)**   474
EMMA WHATMAN

53 **Comic Cons (Fairy-Tale Culture and Comic Conventions: Perpetuating Storytelling Traditions)**   483
EMMA NELSON

54 **Contemporary Art**   492
AMANDA SLACK-SMITH

55 **Criticism**   501
VANESSA JOOSEN

56 **Fan Fiction**   508
ANNE KUSTRITZ

57 **Fantasy**   515
MING-HSUN LIN

58 **Food (Sugar-Coated Fairy Tales and the Contemporary Cultures of Consumption)**   525
NATALIA ANDRIEVSKIKH

59 **Horror**   532
SUE SHORT

60 **Mobile Apps**   539
CYNTHIA NUGENT

61 **Music Videos and Pop Music**   548
REBECCA HUTTON AND EMMA WHATMAN

62 **Musicals**   556
JILL TERRY RUDY

63 **Novels**   565
CHRISTY WILLIAMS

64 **Opera**   572
PAULINE GREENHILL

65 **Poetry (Fairy-Tale Poems: The Winding Path to *Illo Tempore*)**   580
MICHAEL JOSEPH

66 **Reality Television**   590
VANESSA NUNES

CONTENTS

67 **Romance (The Transmedial Romance of "Beauty and the Beast")** 598
TOMASZ Z. MAJKOWSKI AND AGATA ZARZYCKA

68 **Storytelling (Fairy Tales in Contemporary American and European
Storytelling Performance)** 607
JOSEPH SOBOL AND CSENGE VIRÁG ZALKA

69 **Traditional Song** 616
PAULINE GREENHILL AND JILL TERRY RUDY

70 **Television Drama (Fairy Tales and American TV Drama)** 625
MIKEL J. KOVEN

71 **Video Games** 634
EMMA WHATMAN AND VICTORIA TEDESCHI

72 **YouTube and Internet Video** 642
BRITTANY WARMAN

List of Contributors 649
Index 655

FIGURES

11.1	The emblem of the *"Nuit des taons qui piquent"* in 1997, which built on *Crotte mon âne* (drawn by author)	96
11.2	One of the images found in the account of a 2007 session where *Le conte des trois princes* was shared in a workshop on popular education	98
11.3	Drawing made in reference to the tale by Nancy Beauseigle, who was responsible for the project on employment and activity	99
11.4	Danielle's bird, as photographed by the group (Carrefour de savoirs sur les besoins essentiels), at the meeting featuring a version of ATU 707 at the end of a two-year project with persons living in poverty in June 2005	100
28.1	Puss from *Shrek Forever After* (2010)	257
28.2	*Fat Princess: Piece of Cake* (2014)	259
35.1	Edward Coley Burne-Jones, *Cinderella*, 1863, watercolor on paper	321
38.1	*Agnes Weld as "Little Red Riding-Hood,"* A(I): 24	349
38.2	Chan-Hyo Bae, *Existing in Costume_Cinderella*, 230cm × 180cm, C-Print, 2008	354
41.1	A Tumblr post from the Swan Queen fandom, in response to the 50 Days of SQ challenge	378
41.2	A Tumblr post, highlighting the way that fans can speak to contemporary events through and with their fandoms	379
41.3	A Tumblr post, featuring fan-made material culture; the rhetorically redacted note about wishing for canon Swan Queen indicates that the user knows the hope is unlikely to be fulfilled, but wants to share it anyway	380
41.4	A sampling of Instagram posts that feature Tim Manley's published book, *Alice in TumblrLand*, in visual compositions that bring the offline text back into a user-controlled, digital space	382
46.1	*Cinderella; Or, the History of the Little Glass Slipper* (Chapbook), circa late 1700s, printed for Wilson, Spence and Mawman, York, UK	431
46.2	Walker, William, N.d., *The History of Valentine and Orson* (Chapbook), Beinecke Rare Book and Manuscript Library, Yale University	432
53.1	Comic-con fan Olivia McLaughlin dressed as hipster Ariel	488
53.2	Artist Karen Hallion with fans wearing her design on T-shirts	489
60.1	Locked screen of Tab Tales' *Little Red Riding Hood*	542
60.2	The four sprites of the parrot's flying cycle are played in a looping sequence of 1, 2, 3, 4, 3, 2; the flying cycle plays as long as the bird is touched	542
60.3	First story screen, *The King's Ears*	543
60.4	Story screen 2, *LittleRed App*, Gabriela Mistral and Paloma Valdivia	545

FIGURES

60.5	Two vignettes, *Caperucita Roja* codex, Gabriela Mistral and Paloma Valdivia	546
70.1	*Beauty and the Beast*'s (1987–1990) Linda Hamilton and Ron Perlman	626
70.2	*Beauty and the Beast*'s (2012–2016) Kristin Kreuk and Jay Ryan	627
70.3	*Once Upon a Time*'s (2011–) Robert Carlyle as Rumpelstiltskin	629
70.4	Members of the *Grimm* (2011–2017) cast	630

INTRODUCTION AND ACKNOWLEDGMENTS

*Pauline Greenhill, Jill Terry Rudy,
Naomi Hamer, and Lauren Bosc*

In 2014, Routledge's Erica Wetter contacted Pauline Greenhill to say that Jack Zipes had recommended her as a possible editor for a new *Companion* on fairy-tale media. The request corresponded, coincidentally, with a Partnership Development Grant on the topic, of which Greenhill was Principal Investigator, funded by the Social Sciences and Humanities Research Council of Canada, 890-2013-17, called "Fairy Tale Cultures and Media Today." Accordingly, it looked like an offer Pauline could not refuse![1] The research project drew together an international interdisciplinary team of co-applicants: Cristina Bacchilega, Steven Kohm, Anne Kustritz, Martin Lovelace, Sadhana Naithani, Jill Terry Rudy, Catherine Tosenberger, and Jack Zipes. All have contributed ideas and perspectives, and most have also written chapters for this *Companion*.

With work also being underway at the time of the Routledge request for *Channeling Wonder: Fairy Tales on Television* (Greenhill and Rudy 2014) and *Fairy-Tale Films Beyond Disney: International Perspectives* (Zipes, Greenhill, and Magnus-Johnston 2016), Greenhill felt unprepared to take on the *Companion* without substantial help. Rudy came on board immediately; she and Greenhill invited Naomi Hamer because of her expertise in children's cultures and media; Lauren Bosc as managing editor became so central to the intellectual direction of the work that she joined also. The process has been highly collaborative.

The resulting *Routledge Companion to Media and Fairy-Tale Cultures* provides a comprehensive and current guide to fairy tales as realized across media and cultures. It offers a clear, detailed, and expansive overview of contemporary themes and issues throughout the intersections of the fields of fairy-tale studies, media studies, and cultural studies. Moreover, this interdisciplinary *Companion* draws on perspectives from folkloristics, ethnology, and ethnography, as well as film studies, television studies, and media studies. Distinct from other volumes on fairy tales and popular cultures, this *Companion* is not organized around national textual histories but rather focuses on common issues and on media forms and genres, reflecting the transnational flows of fairy tales and cultures.

Fairy tales historically developed as oral traditions (told by people in different geographical locations and at various historical times up to the present) and literary stories (written by known authors). Throughout its history, however, the form has involved a variety of media, engaging the visual and/or auditory senses, sometimes resulting in new narrative forms. The fairy tale has inspired formal innovation over centuries, from chapbooks and the novel to reality TV formats, generating and moving new genres and new media. Our understanding of media comprises the current vernacular sense of relatively recent digital forms to include mobile applications and social media platforms, as well as older forms such as television, film, music, visual arts, writing, and oral communication. We understand culture in the anthropological sense of behaviors, beliefs, ideas, traditions, and materials of human collectivities. Though we focus on European fairy tales, and media originating in North America and Europe, many contributors extend internationally and cross-culturally to acknowledge the local and global reach of these stories and media and their effects on individuals, communities, nations, and empires.

The volume is structured in five sections. **Basic concepts** introduces fundamental ideas implicating the study of fairy tales, cultures, and media. It demarcates the field for our readers, with a brief history of fairy tales, a look at how fairy-tale practices change across media and cultures, and an examination of how fairy-tale structures function as creative and scholarly devices. **Analytical approaches** outlines theories and ideas that have strongly influenced how academics in particular understand the intersection of fairy tales, cultures, and media from ongoing historical views like feminism to newer areas like decolonization. The section is arranged to show the historical emergence of these perspectives.

Issues addresses sociocultural concerns problematized by and in fairy-tale cultures and media, including broadly political developments like dis/ability and gender, thematic and social issues like crime/justice and convergence culture, and both older and newer intersecting research areas like animal studies and copyright/intellectual property. **Communicative media** explores how fairy tales have been articulated through specific forms and combinations of visual, sound, and material media. It is again arranged in order of the historical emergence of these forms. Finally, **expressive genres and venues** addresses cross-cutting media forms and issues, such as contemporary art and fan fiction, influenced by and influencing fairy-tale plots, characters, and ideas, from classical music to anime and comic cons.

This *Companion* offers cutting-edge scholarship with both accessibility and academic sophistication; chapters seek to open their topic, rather than summing it up. This is not an encyclopedia, and thus readers should not expect a simple survey of what has been done in the field or area. In fact, many contributions are among the first to address the intersections of fairy tales, culture, and media with respect to their topics, and that is as it should be. Aiming for a sophisticated readerly audience, contributors give the detailed complexity that researchers and teachers seek in trying to enrich themselves and their students, a balance of specialist and general material. They define terms and concepts but then move on, take positions, and make connections—often international and interdisciplinary. Chapters include references to materials readers may consult for further information and also include mediagraphies to make applicable creative works more accessible. With the exception of the basic concepts and analytical approaches sections, which interweave in complex fashion with most of the other areas, each chapter also offers links to other entries in the *Companion*.

Contributors answered our call in their own distinct ways, too numerous to mention, but meriting a few hints. Some focus on particular media examples, as when Sue Short draws on a variety of horror films, some of which might not immediately strike the reader as fairy tales, to argue the apparent paradox of common underlying themes. Some locate transmedial links to demonstrate cultural politics, like Allison Craven's look at the commercialization of feminism in fairy-tale media. Others examine the manifestations of a specific tale or tale type, like Bill Ellis's exploration of "Peau d'Asne" (ATU 510B, an incest-inflected relative of "Cinderella," ATU 510A), in Japanese manga and anime. Some look at cross-cutting themes, like Natalia

INTRODUCTION AND ACKNOWLEDGMENTS

Andrievskikh on the gendered sex and violence associated with fairy-tale food. Position-taking along with critical argumentation manifests in Cristina Bacchilega and Sadhana Naithani's chapter, which not only describes colonialism and postcolonialism, but also advocates for decolonization in the world as well as in fairy tales.

And while readers would probably expect a *Companion to Media and Fairy-Tale Cultures* to include entries on children's and young adult literature (Anna Kérchy) and the Disney corporation (Lynda Haas and Shaina Trapedo), work on activism with fairy tales (Vivian Labrie) and fat studies (Lauren Bosc) may be more unexpected. Our contributors include creative artists (filmmaker Danishka Esterhazy, storyteller Milbre Burch, and app designer Cynthia Nugent) and a curator (Amanda Slack-Smith) as well as academics at levels from graduate students to emeritus professors. Insiders' perspectives on Indigenous stories from kuʻualoha hoʻomanawanui appear with considerations of classic elite European forms, like Pauline Greenhill on opera. Some of the entries exemplify cross-disciplinary work such as Naomi Hamer's research on mediated fairy-tale exhibits within children's museums, drawing together museum studies, cultural studies, and children's media studies. Others examine the intersections of popular culture, scholarship, and the culture industry, as in Jill Terry Rudy's chapter on fairy-tale musicals.

Sometimes it seems that fairy tales move, fully formed, in some superorganic way through a wide variety of cultures. Yet fairy tales also seem elemental, fragmentary, and strange. Either way, they are brought forth through distinctive social conventions and forces, including media. Oral primacy and intermedial mingling, therefore, must be combined in a folkloristic approach to tales. Holding these perspectives, or being held by them, requires thinking of fairy tales in relation with cultures and media.

Staying attuned to tradition requires us to insist on recognizing human beings as *communicative omnivores* whose expressive media overlap and expand rather than supersede and replace. While a history of communicative media may seem linear and progressive rising from speech to modern technologies, human beings use all available means to share dilemmas and insights about dealing with recurring life situations: oral storytelling, writing, printing presses, photographic imaging, moving and talking pictures, audio and audiovisual broadcasting, digital computing, and handheld devices. Folklore scholarship for some decades now has focused on how people in groups select and perform traditional expressions in specific, informal, close interactions. More recently, folklorists have examined how traditional expressions morph into the folkloresque and inform, and transform, with popular culture. Thinking of fairy-tale cultures and media leads to remembering, critiquing, and honoring cultural and communicative differences while holding oral communication as prime and investigating the consequences and pleasures of intermedial mingling.

We are happy to acknowledge the encouragement and assistance of Katharine Atherton and especially our editor Erica Wetter at Routledge; project manager Sheri Sipka; Laura Larsen for her light and deft hand at copy editing; all the contributors for their inspiration, diligence, and timely responses; Jack Zipes for his ongoing commitment to supporting scholarship on fairy-tale media; Matthew Somoroff for editorial support; research assistants Allison Norris and Alexandria van Dyck; and Kristy Stewart for her work as indexer.

Pauline is grateful to online streaming opera on CBC Music and Ici Musique for providing an appropriately dramatic sound track to her work. She thanks her fabulous co-editors, her colleagues in the Women's and Gender Studies Department at the University of Winnipeg (Best. Department. Ever!), and, as always, the long-suffering John Junson.

Jill expresses appreciation to Pauline for the heavy lifting, to Naomi for sharing the load, and to Lauren for organizational wizardry. Our contributors displayed patience and goodwill, as do her family members, always. She thanks Brigham Young University for Mentored Environment Grants to support student research and maintain the Fairy Tales and Television project; her fine English department, Office of Digital Humanities, and College of Humanities colleagues; and members of the SSHRC Partnership Development Grant, "Fairy Tale Cultures and Media Today."

Naomi extends her great thanks to her awesome co-editors for their patience, time, and editorial labor as well to colleagues (at the University of Winnipeg and beyond) and family who supported the completion of this project. She also expresses gratitude to Pauline Greenhill, Jill Terry Rudy, Jack Zipes, and the other esteemed scholars of the SSHRC Partnership Development Grant who warmly welcomed her into their meetings and enthusiastically participated in various jointly hosted keynotes and roundtables in the lead up to this publication.

Lauren would like to thank her co-editors for their incredible mentorship and for the opportunity to be included in such an exciting project. Her ability to assist an endeavor such as this could not have been possible without the brilliance and tirelessness of the editorial team and the support and encouragement from her ever-loving partner.

Note

1. Greenhill intends here all the horror-filled implications from that filmic reference, but assures all that no horse's head appeared on her bedcover.

Part I

BASIC CONCEPTS

1
OVERVIEW OF BASIC CONCEPTS
Folklore, Fairy Tale, Culture, and Media

Jill Terry Rudy

Folklorists, as experts trained in the study of traditional expression, think again and again about narrative, communication, and media. Primarily, folklorists think that oral expression matters, even advocating for understanding the primacy of words spoken in face-to-face interaction, because they study those expressions that involve tradition and groups, the lore and the folk. They specialize in studying expressions and performances that bring the past into the present, that follow and vary a familiar formula, that happen recognizably over new times and spaces as they are communicated between people who share at least one thing in common (Dundes 1965; Toelken 1996). Speaking and sharing artful knowledge in close groups, but also between them, remains a concern for tradition and a central component of folklore study. Folklorists assert traditional oral expression is crucial to being human. By extension, this posits the human body as the primary medium of expression and emphasizes mouths and ears as key producers and receptors of communication. Inherently, this involves people gathering close enough together to speak and be heard.

Yet because folklorists follow where traditional expressions lead, they must recognize the revolution toward other media, especially as new media evolve. They concede that the inclination to communicate using the voice and the spoken word has turned, and sometimes quickly, toward other media that inscribe and project communication. The hands and eyes and tools (technologies) that extend embodied capabilities become important in producing and receiving written, printed, photographed, and filmed expressions, including traditional ones. They also allow for participation by differently abled people, for example those who are hearing impaired. As communication and media connect with and beyond bodies to artifacts, machines, and airwaves, folklorists' preferred assumption of artistic communication in small groups speaking together (Ben-Amos 1972) morphs toward an admission of, perhaps even fascination with, intermedial mingling.

A history of communicative media may seem linear and progressive rising past such folklore to modern technologies—from human speech into a succession of writing implements, printing presses, photographic imaging, moving and talking pictures, audio and audiovisual broadcasting, and digital computing and handheld devices. Yet staying attuned to tradition requires us to insist on recognizing human beings as *communicative omnivores* whose expressive media overlap and expand rather than supersede and replace. This point cannot be overstated and bears repeating: folklorists have come to see human beings as using all available means to share dilemmas and insights about dealing with recurring life situations. Mostly, they call those insights tradition; some associate them with stories. Marina Warner, in her wise guide to fairy tale, claims this as a pleasure and power of the genre: "The stories face up to the inadmissible facts of reality and promise deliverance. This honest harshness combined with the wishful hoping has helped them to last" (2014, 95). Thinking of humans as communicative omnivores allows the apparently linear progression of media to turn into a kind of recursive arc where social media communities seem not so distant or different from neighbors gathered around a hearth. Indeed, much of the rhetoric of the World Wide Web talks about its power to bring together individuals and groups separated by oceans and continents (Mosco 2000).

Yet these are very different communicative situations as well, for the physical, cultural, emotional, intellectual, spiritual distances, and technological mediations are real. People in the Global North learn this when the electricity goes down, the signal goes out, or the batteries die; those in the Global South have daily reminders. Critical disjunctures manifest in the various forms of transmitting and receiving media, traditional expressions, and folk narratives—differences in attention, presence, virtuality that have not yet been studied enough for participants to know how, or if, to mitigate their consequences. And it can be all too easy to forget the impositions of mediation in the felt immediacy, even magic, of face-to-face, printed, broadcast, online, and mobile interacting and communicating. Participants tend to overlook that necessary energy of being present, owning devices, plugging in, and accessing service providers. And yet, people may bracket some media as lesser and others as advanced; they make, and forget that they made, a split that divides the oral from the literate, the analog from the digital, the haves from the have-nots. Media distinctions so often turn into unrecognized geopolitical, socioeconomic, cultural, even interpersonal gulfs. So, not surprisingly, folklore's founding and continuing practice remains enmeshed in these assumptions of social division which also happen to be imbricated in the rise of colonialism, modernity, imperialism, socialism, capitalism, and globalization.

Hearing, seeing, and knowing someone else's situation, their very different situatedness, may yet allow for their very similar humanity and life situations. This is one great reason for keeping and sharing the fairy tale, to acknowledge and transform social division. As Maria Tatar astutely observes, "Fairy tales register an effort on the part of both women and men to develop maps for coping with personal anxieties, family conflicts, social frictions, and the myriad frustrations of everyday life" (1999, xi). No wonder people around the world love them and tell them over and over in every available communicative technology and semiotic mode. Thus, holding the seemingly incongruous assumptions of oral and face-to-face communicating as prime while allowing for communicative omnivoraciousness takes scholars somewhere quite interesting.

The ideas and patterns associated with traditions, and expressed as stories, sayings, songs, customs, celebrations, objects, and artifacts, sometimes seem to have such a life of their own that scholars at one time thought of these expressions as superorganic entities. Traditions have appeared to be forces with their own volition, crossing social and technological divides, flowing, and insinuating themselves in human conversations, situations, institutions, communities, and nations through any means available (Ranke 1967; El-Shamy 1997). Fairy-tale scholar Jack Zipes (2006) considers fairy-tale motifs as memes, a cultural equivalent of DNA that, rather like the earlier superorganic assumptions, replicates itself in opportunistic ways throughout cultures and communities. Advocating a more situated and close view of tradition, folklorist Barre Toelken, also using biological terminology, recognizes folklore as a "species of learning and expression which uses culture-based interactive codes and formulas" (1996, 47).

Toelken is mostly interested in how people in groups select and perform traditional expressions in specific, informal, close interactions. He allows that it's best to think of such expressions as occurring "with or without literacy" and therefore "we might say that folklore is often *aliterate*" ([1976] 1996, 47). So, folklorists' incongruous assumptions of the oral as prime and the intermedial as inevitable both apply in sharing traditional expressions in general and traditional stories particularly. Thinking of fairy tales as *amedial* may challenge, or at least acknowledge, the constructedness of oral/literate splits and have/have not divides. Thinking of fairy-tale cultures and media leads to remembering, critiquing, and honoring cultural and communicative differences while holding oral communication as prime and investigating the consequences and pleasures of intermedial mingling.

And now, for a case in point. "Cinderella" (ATU 510A) continues as a perennial fairy-tale favorite whose various iterations perpetuate the intermedial mingling of communicative omnivores. In his casebook on the story, Alan Dundes addresses the teeter-totter tendencies of universalism and particularism with fairy tales. He acknowledges that people assume these stories have a primeval meaning and universal reach that explains all humanity or have such peculiarity that a tale perfectly establishes one nation's soul. Dundes, more moderately, encourages the recognition that "the item will not be limited to a single culture nor will it be worldwide" (1982, vi). This reminder is helpful especially with "Cinderella" because even browsing the children's folklore picture book aisle reveals stories from around the world: Chinese, Egyptian, North American Indigenous, Mexican, Russian. It seems that the story has been told worldwide and that it speaks to universal longings for acceptance, for social wealth, and for relief from drudgery and abuse.

By 1893, Marian Roalfe Cox annotated and published 345 variants of the story noting medieval analogues. Over 100 years later, this fairy tale still captured popular interest, with *Ella Enchanted* by Gail Carson Levine being a 1998 Newbery Honor book and 2004 film adaptation (dir. Tommy O'Haver), while *Ever After* (dir. Andy Tennant 1998) is a fondly remembered, and slightly realist and not-so-feminist, film adaptation (Williams 2010). As of spring 2016, the International Fairy Tale Filmography (IFTF) listed 132 "Cinderella" versions, with *Cendrillon* the earliest (dir. Georges Mèliés 1899). And the digital humanities project Fairy Tales on Television Visualizations (FTTV) finds "Cinderella" the most frequently televised fairy tale from the 1950s to the present, as indicated by a database of mostly North American, but some Japanese, British, and European, television shows. In 2015, Disney revisited its animated classic with the Kenneth Branagh–directed, live-action *Cinderella*. Each retelling situates the tale in specific contexts while adding to its intertextual and intermedial resonances.

Such retellings and remediations in the era of broadcast and spreadable (even conglomerate) media involve oscillating shifts of reality and fantasy, constitutive of the fairy tale and a key element of its intermedial proclivities, but a matter of controversy for fairy-tale scholars. Jessica Tiffin asserts that the tale denies reality (2009, 4), though a total denial would make any story incomprehensible. Warner questions not only if fairy tales reflect experience but asks, "Do they interact with reality and shape it?" (2014, 81). An oscillation between the two might involve accepting the magical event or character as natural yet unexplained, and then shift to highlighting the wondrous as an anomaly. Disney's *Enchanted* (dir. Kevin Lima 2007) exemplifies the mainstream, popular working through of these oscillations, produced by the company most associated with late-capitalist workings of magic and wonder. The movie's use of animation and live action not only signals the shift between fantasy and reality but plays with the consequences of blurring lines, and lives, between imagined and real worlds.

When the animated lead character, Giselle, falls through a well and comes out of a New York City manhole cover in her ridiculous hyperbolically poufy wedding dress, an early twenty-first-century iteration of fairy-tale fiction and reality manifests. With Disney's Cinderella as one visual cue to identify Giselle's princessness, the fairy tale itself becomes the parodic, and still metatextual, message that these stories are problematic but are not going away in the contemporary imagination.[1] Evidently, intertextual and intermedial associations with oral and print fairy-tale characters and their filmed, televised, and digital counterparts, and their requirement to negotiate shifts between fantasy and reality, still matter to powerful communications conglomerates and to those who make and view tales.

Consider these shifts in context of the politics and poetics of magic and wonder limned by Cristina Bacchilega in relation with modernity and coloniality. She traces the consequence that "the means of wonder, that is, magic, became a trick or childlike make-believe rather than the outcome of a way of knowing and being in the world" (2013, 194). In a few intermedial "Cinderella" retellings, this struggle over magic and wonder becomes a way of knowing and being rather than a mere trick or make-believe. The "Fractured Fairy Tales" segment of the *Rocky and Bullwinkle Show* (1959–1964) exemplifies how broadcast media in a droll tone can portray magical tricks *and* wondrous knowing. In one of several versions of the tale, Cinderella must sell pots and pans under contract to the fairy godmother, whose greater knowledge of contract law ends up winning the day. Megan Armknecht (2014) has analyzed how several "Fractured Fairy Tales" oscillate toward American Cold War values and frequently reward the character who can most realistically think about and manipulate contractual agreements. While the animation invokes something fantastic, the adapted plots and characters espouse realistic 1960s American mores.

Thought, and especially imagination, cannot be removed from this process of sharing traditional narrative, and so folklorists, throughout the discipline's history, have also thought again and again about thinking—and about the relationship of thinking with speaking and other forms of expression. Folklorists hold some paradoxical assumptions about traditional stories being situated communication. One long-held Euro-American idea about the relationship of thinking and expressing suggests that thoughts are universal, fully formed, mental things that expression merely exteriorizes. This concept suggests that stories just wait in people's brains for the moment when a skull metaphorically splits open and the expression springs forth, as Athena from Zeus's head. If thoughts are already fully formed in people's heads, then a specific situational context (Oring 1986) may be the wedge that splits it all open to let the expression out at an apt place and time. Additionally, if these pre-formed thoughts seem particularly symbolic, they may appear as archetypes, as in Jung's assertions of a collective unconscious which depends on, and interprets, fairy-tale characters, images, and situations as intuitive representations of the Self (Dundes 1982, 200–202). Yet if thoughts themselves are constructed through a medium of expression, like language or affect or imagery, then stories may be held in individual human memory not as whole expressions but as collectively constructed forms that emerge in specific performance situations.

With fairy tales, cultures, and media, these paradoxical assumptions of fully formed thoughts and socially constructed expression relate with where stories might come from, how they act, and what they do. Sometimes it seems that fairy tales move, fully formed, in some superorganic way through a wide variety of cultures. While tales shape-shift, transform, and adapt as they land in new situations, they seem recognizably whole and familiar—sometimes even psychic, as if tapping into some deeply human condition. Yet fairy tales also seem recognizably elemental and strange—sometimes even daft, as if stacking up building blocks of some other world to explain humanity. Either way, fairy tales exemplify that stories themselves are shared in specific times, places, and situations that may be long ago and far away, right now, or next year. They are brought forth through distinctive social conventions and forces, including media. Oral primacy and intermedial mingling, therefore, must be combined in a folkloristic approach to tales. And the ambiguous traits of fully formed and socially constructed thought and imagination constitute key qualities of traditional expression itself. Holding these perspectives, or being held by them, requires thinking of fairy tales in relation with cultures and media.

Always an expertise attuned to the traditional learning and arts of nations, communities, and groups, folklorists' scholarship trends toward the collective, the common, the mass, the popular forms of expression and, thus, includes specific ways of thinking about culture. The interest in tradition links culture with literature and with collective ways of knowing and living. Around the world, the Grimm brothers' publications and beliefs about the folk, language, tales, and legends directly influenced scholarly interests in these expressions as an elemental source of national and human experience (Warner 2014; Bauman and Briggs 2003; Bendix 1997). They focused on collecting traditional songs and stories in Native languages and rhythms, but their impetus was to validate what they understood as ancient, specifically German, ways of knowing and being in the world. These traditional expressions encapsulate beliefs and values of the people.

Though folklorists dispute traditions as uniquely national, they share the Grimms' idea that culture offers the base of group values and beliefs, the unseen but central tenets of collective identity and organization. This concept is not the Matthew Arnold version of cultivated taste for the rarefied best that has been thought or said (1875), but it is not entirely divorced from that ideal. Significantly, both views (culture and Culture, as it were) figured in Britain as the word "folklore" was coined in 1846 and remain operative today in understanding fairy tales, cultures, and media. So does the assumption that culture comes forth in and through traditional expressions, as through long-told tales, broadly forms of literature, which folklorist William A. "Bert" Wilson defines as "artistic expression in words of significant human experience" (2006, 16).

Certainly fairy tales deal in momentous social and cultural issues, with often clueless and shallow, yet engaging and fortunate, characters and with miraculous births, treacherous journeys, family betrayals, intimate desires, reversals of fortune, violent retributions, and so much more. Since Wilson's definition is *amedial*, it allows for artistic expression to be spoken, written, printed, filmed, recorded, screened, and so on. But fairy tales also expand and combine that potentially logocentric mediality because they so frequently invite illustration, imaging, in the sketch, the ballet, the painting, the panto, the play, the picture book, the movie set, the show, the YouTube video, the photo shoot, the toy, and the haute couture. And thus, the impetus of this *Companion*, to describe and analyze these junctures of fairy-tale cultures and media and more.

The history of these junctures offers a venue to better consider the connection of fairy tales and cultures. Equally with the literary and linguistic folklorists' drive to collect and classify tales, the newly emerging position of anthropologist in the mid-nineteenth century involved a scholarly sense of group life, especially allegedly "primitive" or "barbarous" groups—that is, those who did not share the colonizing groups' ideals and worldviews—informed by commonly held values and often expressed through traditional stories including myths and tales. Folklore was thus conceptualized as that specific part of culture, or group values, that gets expressed as stories, sayings, songs, superstitions, rituals, and ceremonies that stand out as unusual in the contemporary time period.

Nineteenth-century British scholars with a folkloristic bent grappled with an oral/literate divide that led some to tout evolutionary stages of human development leading from the primitive to barbarous to civilized (Meek 1976; Stocking 1992; Bauman and Briggs 2003). Traditional expressions, including tales with their spells, enchantments, mutilations, and wishes, appeared to colonial societies as what Edward B. Tylor termed "survivals" of an earlier phase of human development that had its own rationality given earlier beliefs but became odd and illogical when inserted in contemporary situations ([1871] 1958). Beliefs about "Ring around the Rosies" referring to the plague, or blessing someone who sneezes to prevent the soul's escape, exemplify a lingering (mis)application of Tylor's views on survivals, and the concept may still operate in some contemporary fairy-tale interpretations.

Problematic at the time and eclipsed by a functionalist approach to anthropological study by the early twentieth century, the idea of folklore as survivals waned. Still, Tylor's definition of culture as "that complex whole that includes knowledge, belief, art, morals, law, custom, and any other capabilities and habits acquired by man as a member of society" remains generally applicable and useful (1958, 1)—absent its non-inclusive language referring to only half the human race. A tinge of social constructionism can be sensed in Tylor's observation that these cultural "capabilities and habits" are acquired "as a member of society" (1). This anthropological impulse in folklore history still considers the oral traditional expression shared among close groups as prime while allowing that the "complex whole" of culture would be acquired through intermedial mingling because communication is vital to societal membership. Understanding better how the fairy tale reflects, even constructs, the complex whole of cultural capabilities in specific times and places and examining where media facilitates, or even impinges on, this process are interlocking and key purposes of this *Companion*.

Given that folklorists remain interested in traditional expression that brings the past into the present and happens recognizably in new times and places, it isn't surprising that collection and comparison have long been their methodological impulse and that anonymous creation is a presumed folkloric origin. Fairy tales seem to have been there before any specific encounter with them, and with the discovery of another version comes the often pleasurable frisson of similitude and dissimilitude, to borrow William Wordsworth's words for repetition and variation ([1800] 1950). Before and as folklore formalized as an academic endeavor, compilers of *The Ocean of Story* in the eleventh century CE and *Alf Layla wa-Layla* starting in the eighth century CE, and collectors Gianfrancesco Straparola, Giambattista Basile, Geoffrey Chaucer, Charles Perrault, and the Grimms in the fifteenth through nineteenth centuries followed this impulse to combine and compare through their various fairy-tale anthologies.

In all this collecting, the storyteller, not an author, has been the assumed source of the tale, a position that certainly shapes *The 1001 Nights*, framed by a life-saving telling by a gifted narrator, as well as the sometimes raucous storytelling scenes and structure of many tale collections. While authoring their literary tales for salons and courtly audiences, the French *conteuses* at the turn of the eighteenth century often positioned themselves as intermediary, not originating, tellers as well (Zipes 2012, 22–37). Madame Marie-Catherine d'Aulnoy, attributed with naming the genre from her work *Les Contes des fées* (1697), frequently embedded, or intercalated, her tales in novelistic fictions and credited the fairies themselves with inventing and sharing them.

If fairy tales are indeed stories of the people gifted from supernatural beings or collectively created and shared, then the printed compilations may only have been a boost, a hedge, or an aid to their sharing and spreading. On the other hand, if they are instead stories made up by gifted individuals and created and shared by artistic performers, then still the intermedial telling and showing of tales has also proven to assist in the sharing and spreading of fairy tales (Zipes 1999). So folklorists, while claiming a delineated expertise in the traditional, surely cannot be territorial about fairy-tale fields, or realms, or worlds. They might be insistent about the importance of oral transmission, but they ought to remain mightily curious about how, what, where, when, why, and whom fairy tales move. The genre, again, insists on intertextual resonances, intermedial instances, and interdisciplinary investigations (Warner 2014; Zipes 2012, xi; Haase 1999).

OVERVIEW OF BASIC CONCEPTS

Coming from a variety of scholarly disciplines and fields including folklore, women's studies, media studies, literary studies, criminology, cultural studies, disability studies, anthropology, language and linguistics, narratology, gender studies, queer and transgender studies, fat studies, and children's literature studies, contributors to this volume ask and sometimes even answer questions guided by their scholarly conversations. Each sets up a task or a test or explores an unfamiliar world by detailing, describing, analyzing, and interpreting particular intersections of tales, cultures, and media across time and place. Written for this particular time and place, contributions ponder the (inter)medial presence and implications of fairy-tale ubiquity in homes, museums, salons, books, media platforms, online communities, fandoms, popular culture, Indigenous nations, and personal lives.

Guidelines for contributors delineated the editors' intentions and the bracing tasks set for writers that we invite readers to accept as well. A primary challenge includes approaching fairy-tale cultures and media as a longstanding and ongoing scholarly conversation and as a puzzle or game where various parts come into play, pieces fit together, and players make exchanges to create new levels of understanding and even new worlds to imagine and experience. That challenge informs this invitation: "Ideally, your contribution would open the topic, rather than just summing it up. [. . .] In fact, [it] may be the first to address the intersections of fairy tales, culture, and media with respect to your topic, and that's as it should be."

The editors' imagined audience of both contributors and readers depends on not only a previous familiarity with the fairy tale but on an intellectual and affective engagement with tales, cultures, and media that borders on at least a mutual attachment and at times may feel like some sort of enthrallment itself. Our invitation establishes the parameters and tasks that contributions will exemplify including "the detailed complexity that researchers and teachers seek in trying to enrich themselves and their students" and a mandate to "take positions. Make connections—international and interdisciplinary. If appropriate, you would include a historical overview of your topic and references to materials readers may consult for further information." Our purpose is not only documenting current issues but also "critically discussing the leading views" and establishing future directions.

Note

1. The scene where the father presents the biography of important women to his daughter and her remaining fascination with Giselle and her princessness overtly addresses this concern about fairy-tale messages. The movie answers on the side of the tale's seemingly inescapable grasp on Morgan—an androgynous name with its own fairy-tale associations of Arthurian sorceress Morgana le Fay. In this case, a binary between real women and fairy-tale princesses is enacted and resolved in favor of the fantastic. See Greenhill and Matrix (2010a); Bacchilega and Rieder (2010); and Pershing and Gablehouse (2010) for more discussion and more nuanced workings of its feminist and fairy-tale messages.

References Cited and Further Reading

Armknecht, Megan. 2014. "'Fractured Fairy Tales' and Rocky and Bullwinkle for a Cold War Generation." American Folklore Society annual meeting, Santa Fe, New Mexico, November 8.

Bacchilega, Cristina. 2013. *Fairy Tales Transformed? Twenty-First Century Adaptations and the Politics of Wonder*. Detroit: Wayne State UP.

Bacchilega, Cristina, and John Rieder. 2010. "Mixing It Up: Generic Complexity and Gender Ideology in Early Twenty-First Century Fairy Tale Films." In *Fairy Tale Films*, edited by Greenhill and Matrix, 23–41.

Bauman, Richard, and Charles L. Briggs. 2003. *Voices of Modernity*. Cambridge: Cambridge UP.

Ben-Amos, Dan. 1972. "Toward a Definition of Folklore in Context." In *Toward New Perspectives in Folklore*, edited by Américo Paredes and Richard Bauman, 3–15. Austin: U Texas P.

Bendix, Regina. 1997. *In Search of Authenticity*. Madison: U Wisconsin P.

Dundes, Alan. 1965. "What Is Folklore?" In *The Study of Folklore*, edited by Alan Dundes, 1–3. Englewood Cliffs: Prentice Hall.

———. 1982. *Cinderella, a Casebook*. New York: Garland.

El-Shamy, Hasan. 1997. "Psychologically-Based Criteria for Classification by Motif and Tale-Type." *Journal of Folklore Research* 34 (3): 233–43.

Greenhill, Pauline, and Sidney Eve Matrix. 2010a. "Envisioning Ambiguity." In *Fairy Tale Films*, edited by Greenhill and Matrix, 1–22.

———. 2010b. *Fairy Tale Films: Visions of Ambiguity*. Logan: Utah State UP.

Haase, Donald. 1999. "Yours, Mine, or Ours?" In *The Classic Fairy Tales*, edited by Maria Tatar, 353–64. New York: Norton.

Levine, Gail Carson. 1997. *Ella Enchanted*. New York: HarperCollins.

Meek, Ronald L. 1976. *Social Science and the Ignoble Savage*. Cambridge: Cambridge UP.

Mosco, Vincent. 2000. "Webs of Myth and Power: Connectivity and the New Computer Technopolis." In *The World Wide Web and Contemporary Cultural Theory*, edited by Andrew Herman and Thomas Swiss, 37–60. New York: Routledge.

Oring, Elliott. 1986. "Folk Narratives." In *Folk Groups and Folklore Genres*, edited by Elliott Oring, 121–45. Logan: Utah State UP.

Pershing, Linda, and Lisa Gablehouse. 2010. "Disney's *Enchanted*: Patriarchal Backlash and Nostalgia in a Fairy Tale Film." In *Fairy Tale Films*, edited by Greenhill and Matrix, 137–56.

Ranke, Kurt. 1967. "Einfache Formen." *Journal of the Folklore Institute* 4 (1): 17–31.

Stocking, George W. 1992. *The Ethnographer's Magic and Other Essays in the History of Anthropology*. Madison: U Wisconsin P.

Tatar, Maria. 1999. *The Classic Fairy Tales*. New York: Norton.

Tiffin, Jessica. 2009. *Marvelous Geometry: Narrative and Metafiction in Modern Fairy Tale*. Detroit: Wayne State UP.

Toelken, Barre. (1979) 1996. *The Dynamics of Folklore*. Logan: Utah State UP.

Tylor, Edward B. (1871) 1958. *Primitive Culture*. New York: Harper.

Warner, Marina. 2014. *Once Upon a Time: A Short History of Fairy Tale*. Oxford: Oxford UP.

Williams, Christy. 2010. "The Shoe Still Fits: *Ever After* and the Pursuit of a Feminist Cinderella." In *Fairy Tale Films*, edited by Greenhill and Matrix, 99–115.

Wilson, William A. 2006. "The Deeper Necessity: Folklore and the Humanities." In *The Marrow of Human Experience*, edited by Jill Terry Rudy, 9–22. Logan: Utah State UP.

Wordsworth, William. (1800) 1950. "Preface to Lyrical Ballads." In *Selected Poems, Wordsworth*, edited by George W. Meyer, 1–24. Arlington Heights: Harlan Davidson.

Zipes, Jack. 1999. "Breaking the Disney Spell." In *The Classic Fairy Tales*, edited by Maria Tatar, 332–52. New York: Norton.

———. 2006. *Why Fairy Tales Stick*. New York: Routledge.

———. 2012. *The Irresistible Fairy Tale*. Princeton, NJ: Princeton UP.

Mediagraphy

Cendrillon. 1899. Director Georges Méliès. France.

Cinderella. 2015. Director Kenneth Branagh. USA.

Ella Enchanted. 2004. Director Tommy O'Haver. USA/Ireland/UK.

Enchanted. 2007. Director Kevin Lima. USA.

Ever After: A Cinderella Story. 1998. Director Andy Tennant. USA.

The Rocky and Bullwinkle Show (TV). 1959–1964. Creator Jay Ward. USA.

2
DEFINITION AND HISTORY OF FAIRY TALES

Carl Lindahl

"Fairy tale" is a term that provokes strong but bewilderingly diverse responses, a label laden with multiple and often contradictory associations. "Fairy-tale ending" is usually an upbeat way of naming a perfect conclusion, but a person inhabiting a "fairy-tale world" is typically the victim of hopeless delusions. To some, "fairy tale" refers exclusively to works of literature, while others regard such tales as essentially oral in nature. To certain storytellers, fairy tales are ageless, "so old that no one knows if anyone ever invented them" (Massignon 1968, 12); to certain readers, they are the invention of early modern Europeans and belong only to certain times, classes, and sensibilities.

A name that can mean so many diverse things to so many different people needs unpacking. It is much easier to chart the history of the term than to try to grasp the countless phenomena to which it has been applied. "Fairy tale" is a translation of the French *conte de fées* ("story about fairies"), and it is anything but timeless: it comes from the writings of a French aristocrat, Marie-Catherine Le Jumel de Barneville, Baroness d'Aulnoy, whose first *conte de fées* appeared in 1690. *L'Ile de la félicité* ("The Isle of Happiness") was a literary creation filled with allusions to classical mythology. A Russian prince seeking shelter from a storm encounters the god Cupid, who tells him about a magical island; Zephyr, the wind spirit, conveys him there, where the hero finds a jeweled palace and a fairy princess who becomes his lover. Although magic helpers and otherworldly princesses are well-known fairy tale fixtures, they are also rife in literary romance. At first glance, Madame d'Aulnoy's tale seems to rest entirely upon an aristocratic literary tradition.

Yet, beyond the page, Madame d'Aulnoy's fairy tale world possessed notable oral and servant-class dimensions. The circle of well-heeled French writers who created the stories derived only some of their art from ancient aristocratic texts and contemporary literary fashion. They credited many of their plots to the oral tellings of their nurses and grandmothers. The most famous of the salon writers, Charles Perrault, ascribed some of his tales to "Mother Goose" (*Ma Mère l'Oye*), a title proverbially given to old female storytellers in seventeenth-century France. His *Histoires ou contes du temps passé* (1697) presented polished updates of tales with long oral histories: for example, his "Cinderella, or the Little Glass Slipper" (*Cendrillon ou la petite pantoufle de verre*, ATU 510A) had surfaced in Italy more than sixty years earlier; a less closely related version written down from a servant's telling in China dates back another 800 years to around 850. Perrault and the other storytellers of Madame d'Aulnoy's salon read and performed their tales for one another before publishing them (Simonsen 1992, 17–18). In this social setting, an oral tale would give rise to a written story and vice versa. Thus, the term "fairy tale" was born in a milieu where established literary precedent, age-old oral tradition, and current fashion merged. Looking back at the history of those stories most often labeled "fairy tales" today, it is hard to find a time when those same three threads are not present.

What, then, is a fairy tale? Folklorist Stith Thompson offered a thumbnail characterization: "a tale of some length involving a succession of motifs or episodes. It moves in an unreal world without definite locality or definite characters and is filled with the marvelous. In this never-never land humble heroes kill adversaries, succeed to kingdoms, and marry princesses" (1946, 8). But to address this question more fully, it is necessary to survey the collections of Jacob and Wilhelm Grimm, whose work has been more influential than any other in shaping current readers' and listeners' perceptions of the form. The Grimms' first collection appeared in two volumes in 1812 and 1814, about a century and a quarter after Madame d'Aulnoy's first fairy tale. Notably, the brothers did not title their opus "Grimms' Fairy Tales," as pop culture now knows it, but rather *Kinder- und Hausmärchen*, "Children's and Household Tales." Although the Grimm anthology presents German versions of several of Perrault's tales (e.g., "Cinderella" appears as "Aschenputtel" ["Ash Girl," no. 21][1] and "Donkey Skin" as "Allerlei-rauh" ["All Kinds of Fur," no. 65, ATU 510B]), their collection also embraces other kinds of stories: animal tales like "The Wolf and the Kids" (no. 5, ATU 124), moralizing legends like "The Bright Sun Will Bring It to Light" (no. 115), and comic narratives like "Clever Else" (no. 34, ATU 1450) that are judged by many to lie outside the definition of fairy tale. *Märchen* may mean "little story," but in the Grimms' eyes it was not just any kind of story.

About half of the Grimms' tales fall within the parameters of the *Märchen* as commonly understood: a story set at least partially in a world distant in time or space from the narrator's, and featuring magical, transformative characters, forces, and events. The poetry of *Märchen* is manifest in its clear, sparse, and sometimes violent bright imagery, presenting a world of glass slippers and glass mountains, a princess's golden ball (no. 1) and the devil's golden hairs (no. 29), dresses "as golden as the sun, as silvery as the moon, and as bright as the stars" (Grimm and Grimm 2003, 239 [no. 65]), and faces envisaged in terms of elemental contrasts:

> [A] queen was sitting and sewing at a window with a black ebony frame. And as she was sewing and looking out the window, she pricked her finger with the needle, and three drops of blood fell on the snow. The red looked so beautiful on the white snow that she thought to herself, If only I had a child as white as snow, as red as blood, and as black as the wood of the window frame!
>
> (181 [no. 53])

The queen's daughter, Snow White, would grow to possess these selfsame features. Such sharp, bright images are part of the *Märchen*'s "abstract style," according to Max Lüthi, the most insightful explicator of the Grimms' poetics (1983, 24–36). This style, in turn, arises from the "one-dimensionality" of the *Märchen*: its giants, witches, and dragons appear magical to the tale's tellers and listeners, but in the eyes of the *Märchen* hero they appear normal because "the numinous excites neither fear nor curiosity" in him (7). The *Märchen* clearly differentiates the real world from the otherworld, yet the hero rarely shows awe in encountering magic. When the devil's grandmother changes the hero into an ant and tells him to crawl into her shawl, he simply answers, "All right [. . .] that's fine" (Grimm and Grimm 2003, 104 [no. 29]). *Märchen* characters typically lack depth; we experience them as stereotypes—wicked stepmothers, fairy godmothers, poor but kindly youngest sons.

This special kind of *Märchen* is what is most often known as a fairy tale, a *Zaubermärchen* ("magic tale"), or a wonder tale. A fairy tale is, by most accounts, a story 1) that unfolds in a time long ago and a place far away, 2) features magic or marvels and 3) symbolic objects that possess the power of poetic images, 4) presents stereotypical characters representing 5) extremes of good and evil, and 6) ends most often happily and always justly.

Thus the Grimms' "Snow White" (no. 53; ATU 709) opens, *"Once upon a time."* Within five sentences, the *good queen* has died and the *wicked stepmother* appears. The stepmother's *magic mirror* tells her that she is no longer "the fairest of all"; Snow White has replaced her. The defining fairy-tale elements of setting, magic, and character are in place. As the tale progresses the forces of good and evil contest, as the evil stepmother stalks and kills Snow White, but the heroine returns to life, and her stepmother is forced to dance herself to death in red-hot shoes. "Snow White," like so many *Märchen*, ends very happily for the protagonist and very badly for the villain. Yet some of the staples of the fairy tale repertoire do not end happily for their protagonists: in "The Fisherman and His Wife" (no. 19, ATU 555), a poor man catches a magic fish that grants his every wish in return for its freedom; for the man's wife, no wish is ever good enough; even after her wish to reign as emperor is granted, she demands to be pope—and then "to be like God" (Grimm and Grimm 2003, 72). This last wish is too greedy: her papal palace evaporates and the couple are back in the hovel they'd inhabited before their first wish was granted.

There are some additional elements that, if not definitive of fairy tales, are extremely common: 7) the form centers on young people: children, like "Little Red Riding Hood" (no. 26, ATU 333) and "Hansel and Gretel" (no. 15, ATU 327A), or adolescents, like Snow White and Cinderella. Typically, 8) the central figures, like Cinderella, first appear as adolescents, but become married adults by the tale's end. Finally, 9) fairy tale plots most commonly move from a real world, to a magical world, and then back to the real world. Thus, "Hansel and Gretel" begins and ends in the home of a poor woodcutter, but the bulk of the tale unfolds in the magic-haunted woods, in the gingerbread house of the witch. "Jack and the Beanstalk" (ATU 328) begins in the home that Jack shares with his mother but shifts to a magic world as Jack climbs into a sky-realm where he finds the giant and steals magic objects. At the end the son returns to his mother: "Jack and his mother became very rich, and he married a great princess, and they lived happy ever after" (Jacobs 1892, 67).

Fairy tales, then, tend to feature children who grow into adulthood by leaving home, conquering magical adversaries, and/or passing special tests. This fact has led folklorists to note that the fairy tale possesses the form and content of a *rite of passage*, a three-part ritual marking a person's transition from one state to another—from childhood to adulthood, for instance, or from single to married life. First, the initiate undergoes a *separation* from everyday society, enters a period of ritual *liminality* (marginality) marked by inversions and testing, and then ultimately returns to experience *reincorporation* in the everyday world as a "new person" with a new station in life (van Gennep 1960).

Traditional Euro-American weddings are rites of passage: 1) on the eve of the wedding, bride and groom *separate* and must not see each other; 2) while separated, they practice *marginal and inverted behavior* at bachelor/ette parties (isn't it a bit marginal to indulge sexual fantasies with strangers the night before wedding one's life partner?); and 3) they do not see each other again until the moment of *reincorporation*, when they exchange rings in front of assembled friends and family, marking themselves as a "new couple" in the eyes of their social group.

Similarly, the fairy tale is a kind of magic sandwich that begins in a recognizable world and then moves to the margins as the protagonists enter the magic forest or climb to the sky; finally, after meeting magical challenges, the heroes exit that magic world and reincorporate into their society at a new status: no longer helpless children, they are adults, spouses, providers. For some, the similarities of structure and content between fairy tales and rites of passage are too close to be coincidental: *Märchen*, argued Vladimir Propp (1946), must have originated in the rituals of primitive societies.

Although the term "fairy tale" is relatively young and confined to Europe, accounts of tales told to children by nurses and grandmothers—like so many of the tales heard and transformed by Perrault and the Grimms—are ancient and widespread. In the fourth century BCE, Plato mentioned "stories told by nurses." Nearly 1,900 years ago, Apuleius referred to "old wives' tales" (*anilis fabula*). In his satire, *The Golden Ass*, he depicts an old crone telling the tale of "Cupid and Psyche" (ATU 425B) to console a young woman held captive. In their first fairy tale collection, the Grimms identify the "The Singing, Springing Lark," a Beauty-and-the-Beast tale, as a descendant of "Cupid and Psyche" (Grimm and Grimm 2014, 505; ATU 425C).

Some fairy tale plots stretch back farther than the oldest references to old wives' tales. The Hebrew *Book of Tobit* (600–200 BCE) contains a version of "The Grateful Dead" (ATU 505); the Egyptian "Tale of Two Brothers" (ATU 318) is estimated to be 3,200–3,400 years old (Thompson 1946, 275). Although these narratives arguably bear an important historic relationship to fairy tales, are they fairy tales? Or, are they, rather, legends or myths? No plot, in itself, is inherently fairy tale. For example, the plot of "The Dragon-Slayer" (ATU 300), featuring a hero who kills a monster that is about to devour a princess, appears as a Greek myth (Perseus and Andromeda), a Christian legend (St. George and the Dragon), and a *Märchen*/fairy tale (the Grimms' "The Two Brothers" [no. 60]). Fairy-tale scholarship has long been bound up with the question of their age and the riddle of their relationship to ancient myth and other similarly plotted tales from around the world.

Although many people view fairy tales as diverting children's fare, nineteenth-century readers and collectors treated them extremely seriously, for they regarded *Märchen* as relics encoding knowledge about humanity's earliest beliefs and thinking patterns. The Grimms were among the most knowledgeable and impassioned early theorists. Jacob Grimm's sprawling *Deutsche Mythologie* ([1835], translated as *Teutonic Mythology* [1882–1883]), used *Kinder- und Hausmärchen* as evidence for reconstructing the Germanic tribal, pre-Christian religion. He and Wilhelm saw the tales as expressions of German national character and values, remnants of an ancient oral tradition that would be lost forever if not preserved. They considered *Märchen* essentially oral in nature: the greater the extent of their oral character, the greater their value as evidence of ancient German culture. In part 2 of their first edition (1814), they singled out one of their sources, Dorothea Viehmann, as a model narrator who retained "old stories clearly in mind, a gift which she says is not given to everyone." Her narration "was taken down verbatim and no one will fail to recognize its authenticity" (Tatar 1987, 212). Her stories bore proof that ancient oral art was still alive.

But the Grimms encountered criticism for failing to pretty up their tales. Poets and scholars found their texts stylistically raw and demanded that they be edited to do justice to their content. So the Grimms changed the wording of their tales in every subsequent edition; as a result, the seventh (1857), now the standard edition, differs greatly from the first. In their second edition (1819), the Grimms dropped the description of Viehmann and described their editing methods as follows:

> We did not embellish any events and features of the story itself. Instead we tried to relate the content just as we had heard it; we hardly need emphasize that the phrasing and filling in of details were mainly our work. [. . .] Only with time does one acquire the kind of attentiveness and tact required to sort out what is pure, simple, and yet intact from what is inauthentic.
>
> (Tatar 1987, 220)

Here the Grimms proclaim themselves arbiters of what constitutes an authentic oral tale. They did not change the source *content*, yet in taking control of the "phrasing" they became literary stylists. Thus, *Kinder- und Hausmärchen*, with its enormous influence over innumerable collectors and readers, became the most important historical landmark for defining *both* the oral *Märchen* and the literary fairy tale. Their world-famous work is at once a *Märchen* collection *and* a fairy tale collection.

From the Grimms' time through the twentieth century, there was a tendency to name a tale a *Märchen* when oral or oral-derived and a "fairy tale" when presented in literary or storybook style. The Grimms were major scholars of linguistics, history, and literature, and they applied their scholarly knowledge to *Kinder- und Hausmärchen*, which was originally published with notes comparing their texts to tales from earlier times and other cultures. The worldwide distribution of plots like those of "Beauty and the Beast" and "The Dragon-Slayer" convinced the Grimms and other folklorists that the stories were ancient, dating back to the hypothesized pre-historic root language of most European languages, Indo-European. Later, the Grimms reasoned, as Indo-European divided into Celtic, Germanic, Indic, Romance, and other branches, the stories stayed with the languages. Thus, tales collected in the Grimms' time from throughout Europe, the Middle East, and South Asia could be traced back to their origins. Early *Märchen* scholars devoted themselves to the bare bones of plot and symbol, ignoring stylistic flourishes. Their research goal was not aesthetic or semantic, but something more concrete: a time and place of origin, and a story structure: the *Urform*, or original plot, of the tale (Thompson 1946, 396–400, 430–439).

This search for origins possessed nationalistic motives. The Grimms first published *Kinder- und Hausmärchen* as Napoleon's armies occupied their native Hesse; the collection began more as an attempt to unite Germany than as a gesture to entertain children. In 1859, shortly after the Grimms' final edition appeared, Theodor Benfey published his study *Pantschatantra*, an attempt to prove that many European oral tales came originally from India. This claim ignited intense nationalistic reactions in Europe, with scholars of various nations attempting to establish that the tales of *their* country were the oldest, purest, and best. Occupied or oppressed nations were particularly invested in this approach. Finland, dominated by Russia and Sweden throughout the nineteenth century, soon took the lead in developing and practicing the Historic-Geographic Method (also known as the Finnish Method) to trace the "life history" of folktale plots. Scholars assembled as many variants of a plot as possible, grouped orally recorded variants by languages, arranged written versions by date, and weighed plot similarities and differences to reconstruct the tale's original form, age, and birthplace.

In pursuing this method, European folklorists created catalogues to classify tale plots. The Finn Antti Aarne published the first, *Verzeichnis der Märchentypen*, in 1910; the American Stith Thompson later revised, enlarged, and translated it into English as *The Types of the Folktale* (1927: revised 1961); and the German Han-Jörg Uther published *The Types of International Folktales*, a three-volume revision, in 2004. Scholars use the abbreviation ATU (for Aarne, Thompson, and Uther) to identify a folktale plot. A general plot is known as a *tale type*: thus, ATU 327, "The Children and the Ogre," covers a number of related plots in which children visit the home of a devil, witch, or monster. Many types possess specific variant plots, known as *subtypes*. Thus, Perrault's "Cendrillon" and "Peau d'Asne" belong to the same broad type, ATU 510. "Cendrillon" and the Grimms' "Aschenputtel" represent subtype 510A, "Cinderella"; and "Peau d'Asne" and the Grimms' "Allerleirauh" are subtype 510B, "Peau d'Asne." As is often the case with subtypes, the two major branches of the Cinderella story have been shaped by different social situations and appeal to different audiences. The heroine of 510B flees her home to avoid having to marry her father; the incest theme has restricted its circulation to children in many parts of the world. In contrast, 510A, focusing on a girl's mistreatment by a stepmother and stepsisters, is far more popular in children's storybooks and animated features like the 1950 Disney film.

The historic-geographic methodology is now discredited. Critics note that for every written or audiorecorded folktale performance, there are countless oral versions that have been lost forever; surviving evidence is insufficient to lead us back to an *Urform*, date, or site of origin (Thompson 1946, 440). Nevertheless, the catalogues remain useful because the great majority of complex tales of a given type are, in fact, historically related, and through close comparison of texts, researchers learn a great deal about the cultural similarities and differences of tale-telling communities. If we cannot find a tale's *Urform*, stated Carl von Sydow, we can still identify its *oikotype*, a national or regional subtype inflected with the local culture of the tellers (1948, 11–43). We can also learn something of what is, and what is not, universal about these stories.

For example, the most popular Perrault and Grimm tales are set in a feudal world of castles, kings, and princesses and are infused with magic. Many people consider these atmospheric fixtures to be defining properties of fairy tales. Yet most of the tales of the same ATU type, when told, for example, in the Appalachian Mountains, replace castles with farmhouses and kings with rich farmers, and they tamp down the magic. In American Jack Tales, Jack often faces magical adversaries, but he needs less magic to defeat them than his European fairy-tale counterparts do (Lindahl 1994, 2001). American Jack Tales deviate from stereotypical fairy tales in ways that correlate with distinctive aspects of Appalachian culture: modest rural dwellings, a history of democracy rather than monarchy, and a determination to survive without outside help. African American tales deviate even further from the stereotype. In the Grimms' "Juniper Tree" (no. 47, ATU 720), a boy murdered by his mother turns into a bird who kills the mother and comes back to life; in Alfred Anderson's version of the same tale type, the bird reveals the murder, but it is up to the father to kill the mother, and the boy does not return to human life. Magic is less effective and rewards are smaller in African American tales, which reflect a world of hardship in which survival alone may constitute the only victory (Lindahl, Owens, and Harvison 1997, 126–135).

During the twentieth century, scholars listened intently to tale performances and identified many differences between oral *Märchen* and literary fairy tales. They found, for example, that many oral tales that at first appear to be fantasy narratives are in fact belief stories performed during rituals to express spiritual and moral truths. Some Afghani Muslim women perform a version of "Cinderella" in the course of ritual supplication (Mills 1982), and Hindus in the Himalayan foothills tell stories that outwardly resemble fairy tales as part of their worship observances (Narayan 1997), so there are indeed some modern cases in which the relationship between myth, ritual, and *Märchen* appears as close as the Grimms and Propp imagined.

The nature of the storytellers and their audiences was also found to vary from the early stereotypes. According to Perrault and the Grimms, fairy tales were told primarily by old women to young children. Oral cultures do, of course, possess similar traditions of domestic, female-adult-to-child storytelling, but they also embrace a public tradition in which the narrators are typically male and the audience is adult and often large. The artistry of these public performances is substantial. In the twentieth century, folklorists recorded tales from master narrators like Éamonn a Búrc of Ireland and Zsuzsanna Palkó of Hungary, who could spin out one story to last an entire night from sundown to dawn (Zimmermann 2001; Dégh 1989).

In other ways, however, recent research finds the realm of the fairy tale more closely linked to the oral *Märchen* world than many had supposed. Interestingly, as the twentieth century progressed, authors of literary fairy tales, like Anne Sexton (1971) and Angela Carter (1979), imitated longstanding oral tradition by shaping their tales to address adults. Nevertheless, few literary fairy tales reach the length and complexity of oral performances by folk masters recorded in the first half of the twentieth century.

Also in spite of great differences from one culture to another, the literary fairy tale and the oral folktale are often very similar in form and expression, thanks to the influence of the Grimms, whose literary flourishes influenced oral as well as literary communities. In Siberia and Germany, narrators often preferred telling the Grimms' versions of folktales instead of long-established local forms (Morewedge 2001, 86; Neumann 1974).

One of the hottest areas of contention in contemporary fairy tale scholarship remains the tales' origin and essence: are they first and fundamentally oral or written in nature? There are extremists on both sides, as illustrated in the recent debate over whether the sixteenth-century Italian writer Straparola "invented" the fairy tale (see Ben-Amos 2010). Some participants insist upon oral origin without producing evidence; others examine only literary evidence to "prove" the fairy tale's literary nature. To determine the extent of literary versus oral influence in a tale, it is essential to examine the context of its creation, and we seldom do so without finding closer relationships than once assumed. Recent, context-based analyses of Straparola reveal the total interpenetration of oral and literary influences in his life and art (Straparola 2012; Masoni 2015).

The more closely we examine storytelling contexts, the more closely intertwined oral and literary communities appear. The great Hungarian narrator Zsuzsanna Palkó could not read, yet she received the plot of one of her most famous stories from a five-page chapbook tale that was read to her. She memorized the plot but elaborated it to the point that her oral performances spanned several hours and became thoroughly her own, imbued with her personal style (Dégh 1996, no. 1). At the other extreme, all members of the Muncy family of the Kentucky Appalachians were thoroughly literate, yet they also preserved a multigenerational tradition of oral *Märchen*. As a young girl in the 1940s, Jane Muncy listened to her grandmother's stories every night. Her grandmother's tales "were not always folktales handed down from generation to generation, but sometimes found in fairytale books, sometimes [. . .] Arabian Nights stories" (Lindahl 2004, 286, volume 1).

It would be absurd to argue that Zsuzsanna Palkó told her tales in an exclusively oral world or that Jane Muncy's literacy prevented her from participating fully in an oral tradition. When the storyteller and audience, no matter their education or background, relish oral storytelling, oral storytelling will occur. Whether literate or illiterate, people familiar with *Märchen* performance recognize the distinctions between oral and literary delivery even as they recognize the interrelated nature of the two traditions. A. K. Ramanujan (1989) grew up in an Indian household where printed Grimm tales graced the family library and local tales with similar plots lived on the lips of the family servants. Ramanujan loved them both, but as a lover of oral artistry, he favored the servants' tales. The relationship between literary fairy tale and oral *Märchen* is complex, in some ways closer than perceived by scholars just decades ago, yet distinct in profound ways that we are just beginning to appreciate.

This survey has treated fairy tales as performed in their historic home media of speech, writing, and ritual. But George Peele's play *The Old Wives' Tale* attests that drama has embedded fairy tales since the sixteenth century, and visual images of *Märchen* date back at least to the wooden misericords of medieval times (Jones 2003). Among the myriad media manifestations of fairy tales addressed throughout this *Companion*, it is the various forms of visual representation, from storybook illustrations to video games, that have done the most to transform the fairy tale. Fairy tales were once identified with their formulaic verbiage: "once upon a time," "mirror, mirror, on the wall," and "fee fie fo fum." In oral communities, the sharp, violent, and sparse imagery presented by the narrator created only the roughest outline of a picture. It was up to each listener to fill in the details herself and create a private *Märchen*-scape invisible to others (Lindahl 2001, 84–89). But from the nineteenth century, with George Cruikshank's illustrations of the Grimms and Gustave Doré's of Perrault, fairy tales have been associated with increasingly iconic images: the silhouette fairy godmother of Arthur Rackham's *Cinderella* (Evans 1919) and the speaking mirror of Disney's *Snow White* (1937), the living statues of Jean Cocteau's *Beauty and the Beast* (1946) and Jacques Demy's *Peau d'Âne* (1970), the cartoon princess with the conical hat, and the confectionary castle at the entrance of Disneyland. As the power of its word magic has diminished, the fairy tale's pictorial presence has grown.

Note

1. The numbering of the Grimm tales is based on the order of their seventh edition (1857), which most major translations follow.

References Cited and Further Reading

Aarne, Antti. 1910. *Verzeichnis der Märchentypen*. Helsinki: Suomalainen Tiedeakatemia.

Apuleius. 1999. *The Golden Ass*, translated by P. G. Walsh. New York: Oxford UP.

Ben-Amos, Dan, ed. 2010. "The European Fairy-Tale Tradition between Orality and Literacy." Special Issue of *Journal of American Folklore* 123 (490).

Benfey, Theodor. 1859. *Pantschatantra: fünf Bücher indischer Fablen, Märchen, un Erzählungen*. 2 vols. Leipzig: F. A. Brockhaus.

Carter, Angela. 1979. *The Bloody Chamber*. London: Gollancz.

Dégh, Linda. 1989. *Folktales and Society: Storytelling in a Hungarian Peasant Community*. 2nd ed. Bloomington: Indiana UP.

———. 1996. *Hungarian Folktales: The Art of Zsuzsanna Palkó*. Jackson: UP Mississippi.

Evans, C. S. 1919. *Cinderella*, retold by C. S. Evans and illustrated by Arthur Rackham. London: William Heinemann.

Georges, Denis. 2001. *The Irish Storyteller*. Dublin: Four Courts.

Grimm, Jacob. 1882–1883. *Teutonic Mythology*, translated by James S. Stallybrass. 4th ed. 3 vols. London: George Bell & Sons.

Grimm, Jacob, and Wilhelm Grimm. 1857 (2003). *The Complete Fairy Tales of the Brothers Grimm*, translated by Jack Zipes. 3rd ed. New York: Bantam.

———. 2014. *The Complete Folk and Fairy Tales of the Brothers Grimm*, translated by Jack Zipes. Princeton, NJ: Princeton UP.

Jacobs, Joseph. 1892. *English Fairy Tales*. 2nd ed. London: Strand.

Jones, Malcolm. 2003. *The Secret Middle Ages: Discovering the Real Medieval World*. London: Praeger.

Krohn, Kaarle. (1926) 1971. *Folklore Methodology*, translated by Roger L. Welsch. Austin: U Texas P.

Lindahl, Carl. 1994. "Jacks: The Name, the Tales, the American Traditions." In *Jack in Two Worlds*, edited by William B. McCarthy, xiii–xxxiv. Chapel Hill: U North Carolina P.

———. 2001. *Perspectives on the Jack Tales and Other North American Märchen*. Bloomington: Indiana UP.

———. 2004. *American Folktales: From the Collections of the Library of Congress*. Armonk, NY: M.E. Sharpe.

Lindahl, Carl, Maida Owens, and C. Renée Harvison. 1997. *Swapping Stories: Folktales from Louisiana*. Jackson: UP Mississippi.

Lüthi, Max. (1947) 1983. *The European Folktale: Form and Nature*, translated by John D. Niles. Philadelphia: ISHI.

Masoni, Licia. 2015. Review of *The Pleasant Nights*, ed. Donald Beecher. *Marvels & Tales* 29 (1): 147–9.

Massignon, Geneviève, ed. 1968. *Folktales of France*. Chicago: U Chicago P.

Mills, Margaret. 1982. "A Cinderella Variant in the Context of a Muslim Women's Ritual." In *Cinderella: A Casebook*, edited by Alan Dundes, 180–92. Madison: U Wisconsin P.

Morewedge, Rosmarie Thee. 2001. "Orality, Literacy, and the Medieval Folktale." In *Varieties and Consequences of Literacy and Orality*, edited by Ursula Schaefer and Edda Spielmann, 85–106. Tübingen: Narr.

Narayan, Kirin, with Urmila Devi Sood. 1997. *Mondays on the Dark Night of the Moon: Himalayan Foothill Folktales*. New York: Oxford UP.

Neumann, Siegfried. 1974. *Eine mecklenburgische Märchenfrau*. Berlin: Akademie-Verlag.

Perrault, Charles. (1695; 1697) 1880. *Les Contes de Perrault d'après les textes originaux*. Paris: Alphonse Lemerre.

Propp, Vladimir. (1946) 1983. *Les Racines historiques du conte merveilleux*, translated by Lise Gruel-Apert. Paris: Gallimard.

Ramanujan, A. K. 1989. "Telling Tales." *Daedalus* (Fall): 239–62.

Sexton, Anne. 1971. *Transformations*. Boston: Houghton Mifflin.

Simonsen, Michèle. 1992. *Perrault: Contes*. Paris: PU de France.

Straparola, Giovanni Francesco. (1550–1553) 2012. *The Pleasant Nights [Piacevoli Notti]*, translated by Donald Beecher. Vol. 1. Toronto: U Toronto P.

Tatar, Maria. 1987. *The Hard Facts of the Grimms' Fairy Tales*. Princeton, NJ: Princeton UP.

Thompson, Stith. 1946. *The Folktale*. New York: Dryden.

———. 1961. *The Types of the Folktale: A Classification and Bibliography*. 3rd ed. Helsinki: Suomalainen Tiedeakatemia.

Uther, Hans-Jörg. 2004. *The Types of International Folktales: A Classification and Bibliography*. 3 vols. Helsinki: Suomalainen Tiedeakatemia.

van Gennep, Arnold. (1909) 1960. *The Rites of Passage*, translated by M. B. Vizedom and G. L. Caffee. Chicago: U Chicago P.

von Sydow, Carl. (1932) 1948. "On the Spread of Tradition." In *Selected Papers in Folklore*, edited by Laurits Bodker, 11–43. Copenhagen: Rosenkild and Bagger.

Zimmermann, Georges Denis. 2001. *The Irish Storyteller*. Dublin: Four Courts.

Mediagraphy

Beauty and the Beast. 1946. Director Jean Cocteau. France.

Cinderella. 1950. Directors Clyde Geronimi, Wilfred Jackson, and Hamilton Luske. USA.

Peau d'Âne (Donkey Skin). 1970. Director Jacques Demy. France.

Snow White and the Seven Dwarfs. 1937. Director David Hand, William Cottrell, Wilfred Jackson, Larry Morey, Perce Pearce, and Ben Sharpsteen. USA.

3
CONSTRUCTING FAIRY-TALE MEDIA FORMS
Texts, Textures, Contexts
Vanessa Nunes and Pauline Greenhill

"Just as we know, almost intuitively, that a particular narrative is a fairy tale when we read it, it seems we know immediately that a particular film is a fairy tale when we see it" (Zipes 1996, 1). In the more than twenty years since he suggested that recognizing fairy-tale media can take place intuitively, Jack Zipes, along with a number of other scholars, has spent considerable time elucidating their constituent elements. But even well before that time, those who examined fairy tales in all their myriad forms often sought to clarify what makes them the kinds of texts—understood in the broadest sense to encompass all audio, visual, and audiovisual forms—that they are. In particular, and for many years, folklorists and fairy-tale scholars have sought the distinctive elements, structures, and contexts that produce traditional fairy tales, as opposed to apparently similar texts like fantasies (see e.g. Butler 2009) or, for that matter, arguably dissimilar ones like documentaries. To borrow from Alan Dundes's construction, fairy tales have some characteristic texts, textures, and contexts (1980, 20–32)—specifying exactly what those might be, though, has long been a challenge. Most explorations of those aspects are based on traditional narratives, but they have also been applied to literary fairy tales with known creators.

Some fairy-tale scholars and folklorists approach the definitional task by describing the particular elements that make up fairy tales, like motifs and archetypes; others look to distinctive parts but also their connections in broader and more encompassing structures, like functions, binary oppositions, memes, or scripts. More rarely, scholarship goes outside the actual content to consider fairy tale's performative environments. However, we begin by describing Aarne-Thompson-Uther (ATU) tale types, since contributors to this volume use them where possible when referring to traditional narratives.

Aarne-Thompson-Uther (ATU) Tale Types

Using ATU numbers to identify different tale types refers to *The Types of International Folktales: A Classification and Bibliography*, an index published in 2004 by Hans-Jörg Uther, revising and amplifying previous works by Antti Aarne (1910) and Stith Thompson (1928, 1961). As well as adding new sources, Uther's update worked within the original system's constraints, but rationalized the numbers and names where possible. The index organizes about 2,500 tale types under different categories, not only fairy tales (the latter identified as tales of magic; ATU numbers 300–749), but also animal tales, religious tales, realistic tales, anecdotes, jokes, and other folktales. Broadly speaking, a **tale type** is a narrative structure presenting a brief plot indicating motifs, settings, characters, and actions shared by a similar group of stories. As Dundes explains, "a tale type is a composite plot synopsis corresponding in exact verbatim detail to no one individual version but at the same time encompassing to some extent all of the extant versions of that folktale" (1997, 196).

In addition to offering tale-type descriptions, the index includes references to sources for its variants. The ATU organization system is thus a useful tool to locate different versions of the same tale and to compare them historically, culturally, and geographically. But the index has also been criticized. One complaint is that stories that share motifs and other significant elements may not be classified together under the same tale type. Further, oral tellers' versions may combine tale types, or may indeed be unclassifiable while nevertheless being very clearly fairy tale (see Lovelace, Best, and Greenhill forthcoming). Writing in 1997, before Uther's revisions and expansion of the index, Dundes notes that even though this system is not perfect, "the identification of folk narratives through motif and/or tale type numbers has become an international sine qua non among bona fide folklorists" as an aid for comparative analysis (195).

Constitutive Elements

One of the less systematic modes for describing folktale elements (and thus traditional, oral fairy tales) is by **motif**. Stith Thompson, who developed the *Motif-Index of Folk-Literature* (1932–1935; revised 1955), saw motifs as recurring characters, locales, occurrences, and actions "worthy of note because of something out of the ordinary, something of sufficiently striking character to become a part of tradition, oral or literary" (1955, 19). Even within a single subcategory, like the (clearly impressionistic) "J. The wise and the foolish," those striking "somethings" range from J427 "Association of cow and tiger: tiger eats cow as soon as she is hungry," to J621 "Destruction of enemy's weapons," to J1380 "Retorts concerning debts." Clearly, motifs comprise very different kinds and levels of activities and involve very diverse personae. While Thompson assumed that analysis of folktales (but also of ballads, myths, fables, medieval romances, exempla, fabliaux, jest books, and local legends) would comprise a search for and elucidation of motifs, current fairy-tale scholarship avoids such practices, finding the thinking behind the index flawed and dated and the categories inconsistent. Nevertheless, scholars often invoke the idea of motifs as constituent elements of fairy tales, or note particular motifs in their studies, because they are striking and traditional.

Another vague term, **archetype**, which also includes different levels and forms, comprises emblematic characters, acts, or situations often presumed to represent aspects of human nature. It has been used mainly by Jungians to suggest fairy tales' psychological relevance. For example, Marie-Louise von Franz explained the archetype as "not only an 'elementary thought' but also an elementary poetical image and fantasy, and an elementary emotion, and even an elementary impulse toward some typical action" (1996, 8). Understanding fairy tales as "mirror[ing] the basic patterns of the psyche" (1), she explores archetypes like the shadow, anima, and animus as expressed in particular tales (114–197). In Walter Rankin's *Grimm Pictures: Fairy Tale Archetypes in Eight Horror and Suspense Films* (2007), the archetypes can be discovered only by implication. For example, in linking Jonathan Demme's *The Silence of the Lambs* with "Little Red Riding Hood" (ATU 333), Rankin discusses cannibalism, the forest path, and emerging from the wolf's belly. The latter is distinctive to the story, but the other two recur in many fairy tales.

Probably the most (justifiably) famous mode for understanding the constituent elements of fairy tales, applied and misapplied across various genres and forms (see Bordwell 1988), is Vladimir Propp's formalist concept of **functions**. His *Morphology of the Folktale* (1968) sought to systematize the characteristics of ATU 300–749, the traditional oral "Tales of Magic" that comprise the classic fairy tales (Uther 2004, 174–396). Propp derives a syntagmatic (that is, sequential, the horizontal axis of the tale) narrative structure common to Russian traditional oral wonder tales, numbers 50–150 of Aleksandr Afanasyev's *Russian Fairy Tales* (1945). Propp contends that these folktales contain a particular series of thirty-one "recurrent constants" comprising actions which have a "particular place in the course of narration" and are "stable constant elements in a tale, independent of how and by whom they are fulfilled" (1968, 20–21).

Those functions are absentation; interdiction; violation; reconnaissance; delivery; trickery; complicity; villainy or lack; mediation, the connective incident; beginning counteraction; departure; donor first function; hero's reaction; provision or receipt of a magical agent; spatial transference between two kingdoms, guidance; struggle; branding, marking; victory; misfortune or lack liquidated; return; pursuit, chase; rescue; unrecognized arrival; unfounded claims; difficult task; solution; recognition; exposure; transfiguration; punishment; and wedding. The functions are undertaken by seven categories of characters/dramatis personae—villains, donors, helpers, princesses (sought-for persons), dispatchers, heroes, and false heroes—in the aforementioned fixed sequence.

This system has obvious advantages in being relatively concrete and evocative while avoiding the inappropriate combination of different levels and forms evident in the motif index. Not all functions or dramatis personae appear in all fairy tales, of course, and their specific manifestations and combinations vary from one to another. Propp himself used the example of "The Swan-Geese" (ATU 451) and clearly expected that folklorists and fairy-tale scholars would apply his system to various tales, analyzing them in terms of their specific manifestations of the thirty-one functions and seven personae. Some have taken up the challenge, often outside the fairy-tale form, for example combining it with Syd Field's (e.g. 1994) much more rudimentary system (first act set up; second act confrontation; third act resolution) to apply to film screenplays (Murphy 2015b). Terence Patrick Murphy offers the **plot genotype** as a "much more flexible interpretation of Propp morphology" (2015a, 161–162), explaining:

> In evolutionary biology, the genotype refers to the inherited instructions an organism carries within its genetic code; these instructions may be used to understand how a particular organism is specialized within the group to which it belongs. By extension, the plot genotype represents the functional structure or compositional schema of a particular fairytale.
>
> (2)

Murphy rejects Propp's view that all fairy tales follow one structural type and argues that the functions are not limited to thirty-one and they do not have identical sequences. Much European and North American scholarship has taken other routes, with researchers such as Murphy modifying or drawing quite selectively upon Propp's system. Some have criticized the schema's obviously gendered prescriptions, noting for example that the sex of characters can change from version to version. The emphasis on functions also limits the meaning to be taken from the tales. Consider, for example, that figures such as dragons or Baba Yaga take roles not only of villains but also of donors and helpers in Afanasyev's fairy tales. Based on a formalist analysis, their ambiguous nature would not be relevant because what matters is the chain of events and the character function in the tale, an approach that fails to recognize that who the character is also affects the story's perception.

Systems not necessarily developed specifically for fairy tales often prove useful in analyzing them in their many mediated forms. Proppian in its focus on personae (called **actants**) and interest in their relations (called **axes**) is Algirdas Julien Greimas's **actantial model** (1983). Though developed for narratives in general, arguably the facets and axes manifest in particular forms in fairy tales:

> (1) The subject (for example, the Prince) is what wants or does not want to be joined to (2) an object (the rescued Princess, for example). (3) The sender (for example, the King) is what instigates the action, while the (4) receiver (for example, the King, the Princess, the Prince) is what benefits from it. Lastly, (5) a helper (for example, the magic sword, the horse, the Prince's courage) helps to accomplish the action, while (6) an opponent (the witch, the dragon, the Prince's fatigue or a suspicion of terror) hinders it.
>
> (Hébert)

The subject and object form the axis of desire, the helper and opponent that of power, and the sender and receiver that of knowledge. Since the axes and actants do not manifest in any specific sequence, this structure, however, can be seen as paradigmatic (the vertical axis of the tale) rather than syntagmatic. Greimas did not intend this model to apply only to fairy tales, though it well evokes some of their most recognizable characteristics.

French anthropologist Claude Lévi-Strauss (1955) saw underlying paradigms of **binary oppositions** which apply across different tales (in contrast to Propp and others' ideas that considered sequences unfolding within individual tales). Though Lévi-Strauss was less concerned than most folklorists about distinctions between myths (usually thought to be sacred and true), legends (usually thought to be secular with questioned truth claims), and folktales (usually thought to be secular and fictional), he applied the concept of binary oppositions to fairy tales. Lévi-Strauss's idea that dualistic, divergent contrasts, for example, between male and female, life and death, day and night, are universal human ways of conceptualizing the world has come under severe conceptual and practical criticism. Yet some folklorists have found it compelling.

For example, anthropologist Bengt Holbek (1987) applies implicitly Lévi-Straussian paradigms to the collection of Evald Tang Kristensen (1892) of tales from Denmark: youth or age; low or high social status; and male or female. Holbek argues that fairy tales by definition, unlike other forms of folktales, always end with a marriage. Fairy tales, for him, are about the progress of young protagonists (female or male; low or high status) into adulthood via a series of specific moves, including leaving home, sharing (illicit) love, separation and/or trial of the protagonists, and—as already indicated—a resolution in matrimony and maturity. Somewhat controversial is Holbek's identification of particular tales as masculine or feminine in plot based on their primary protagonists, and his assertion that these types would necessarily be applicable to particular tellers, with men being mainly interested in masculine tales and women in both. Risto Järv (2005) points out empirical and ideological issues with these distinctions, finding historical shifts in tellers' gendered interests in particular tale types. He also notes that Holbek's definition of a tale like "Bluebeard" (ATU 312) as "masculine," based on its primary high status older male protagonist marrying a low status young woman, obviates its presentation of women's points of view.

In yet another system, Zipes applies Augustin Eugène Scribe's concept of the "well-made" (theatrical) play to Disney films. The common structure of Scribe's plays consists of six prescriptive elements that have been employed by dramatists to make their stories effective (Zipes 2016, 7–8). Zipes argues that Walt Disney "became the Scribe of animated fairy tale films" by finding "the recipe for a universal appeal" (8). Disney's **"well-made" flexible fairy-tale film structure** consists in the following: 1) traumatic and unfortunate incidents; 2) songs of woe and joy; 3) banishment and isolation; 4) quest, conflicts, and comic relief; 5) peripeteia (sudden reversal of fortune); and 6) miraculous resolution (Zipes 2016, 8).

Equally cross-genre is the idea that fairy tales and fairy-tale media involve particular **scripts**. Sung-Ae Lee (2016) borrows from the field of cognitive narratology to explain that

> A script in everyday life is a stereotyped sequence of actions that is part of a person's knowledge about the world [. . .] comparable to the stereotypic plot structures that readers call upon to anticipate the unfolding story logic of creative works [. . .] such as the suffering and triumph of an innocent persecuted heroine.
>
> (207–208)

This script may involve "a pattern of action sequences [. . .] or [. . .] a single action sequence within a larger pattern" (208). Lee recognizes that "a script may also blend different tales" (208) as she further connects it to Zipes's discussion of fairy-tale hypotexts.

Hypotext and related concepts from semiotics can be helpful in thinking about the relation between oral and literary fairy tales and media. In his study of transtextual relationships, Gérard Genette (1997) explains that "hypertextuality refers to any relationship uniting a text B (which I shall call the hypertext) to an earlier text A (I shall, of course, call it the hypotext), upon which it is grafted in a manner that is not that of commentary" (5). Thus a fairy-tale hypotext could be understood as a pre-existing narrative on which a film adaptation, for example, is based. However, as Zipes (2011) writes about fairy-tale films, "the hypotext is more a notion than anything else, somewhat like a meme carried about in our brains" (8). Zipes seeks to account for the fact that fairy tales appear in multiple versions in terms of content and form. Even when filmmakers are taking a very specific fairy-tale variant as a starting point, the story ends up changing based on readings, hearings, viewings, and even childhood memories of all the artists involved in the production and reception process (8).

Zipes's use of the term **meme** to talk about fairy-tale dissemination requires further unpacking. Drawing upon Richard Dawkins's concept (1976), Zipes (2006) explains that a meme is "an information pattern contained in a human brain (or in artifacts such as books or pictures) and stored in its memory, capable of being copied to another individual's brain that will store it and replicate it" (15). Zipes uses the term "to denote a particular fairy tale that has been canonized in the Western world and become so memorable that it appears to be transmitted naturally by our minds to communicate information that alerts us to pay attention to a specific given situation on which our lives may depend" (15). He thus claims that some classical fairy tales have become memes that have stuck in people's minds and replicated themselves. The fairy tale establishes a non-static symbolic order that "is certainly marked continually by recognizable recurring motifs, topoi, and conventions" (15).

Zipes seeks to address the way that fairy tales sometimes unconsciously structure other narratives. In one well-known example, David Slade's film *Hard Candy* (2005) as "Little Red Riding Hood," the filmmakers identified links only after the movie was complete. Recognizing the value of that connection, the producers used it to merchandise the film, including a poster of a girl wearing a red hoodie. And yet even more puzzling, given the relative unfamiliarity of the fairy-tale sources, is Vivian Labrie's (2014) compelling argument for elements of "The Three Golden Children" (ATU 707) in Joss Whedon's *Serenity* (2005), of "The Faithless Mother" (ATU 590) in Michael Caton-Jones's *This Boy's Life* (1993), and of "The Prince Whose Wishes Always Come True" (ATU 652) in Steven Soderbergh's *Solaris* (2002). Labrie's analysis does not rely on basic plot elements or common syntagmatic structures. It is transversal, connected at different narrative levels, and often linked to real life issues. Labrie's arguably memetic perspective differs from that of Zipes, who underlines that not all fairy tales actually are memes—only those which have really grabbed the popular imagination.

Labrie's focus on why lesser-known tale-type structures appear in films connects them, as did the work of historian Jan Vansina (e.g. 1985) and literary scholars Albert Lord (1960) and Milman Parry (e.g. Parry and Lord 1954) and their successors, to memory processes in oral transmission wherein narrators use common structures that foster storytelling. Lord, following Parry, proposed oral-formulaic composition for Homeric and medieval epic, using the example of Serbo-Croatian bards, who sang lengthy, complex tales in rhymed verse from memory. These non-literate bards would orally/aurally learn themes and structures of the tales as well as poetic meter and essentially recompose the epics each time they sang them. Labrie similarly notes the folk basis of fairy tales even in the twenty-first century because most people encounter and explore folktales and fairy tales, at least initially, outside formal education. However, unlike memetic theorists, Labrie sees fairy-tale meaning, rather than being hardwired into human brains, as crucially addressing human experience.

Meme theory has not been entirely well received by folklore scholars. For example, Ruth B. Bottigheimer considers Zipes's notion of the viral spread of motifs and plots to be "unreal," and she criticizes what she sees as his tendency to anthropomorphize abstract concepts and attribute agency to them (2009, 369). According to Bottigheimer, "a 'cultural trait' is not a real-world entity but an abstraction, a result of thought processes based on observations of what people habitually do. Not being persons, abstractions are not capable of volition and intention. And yet Zipes repeatedly injects volition and intention into memes and fairy tales" (369; see also Schrempp 2014).

Another systematic approach comes from Kevin Paul Smith (2007), drawing on Genette's theories to identify eight categories of **intertextual use** of fairy tales within mass-produced fictions:

1. Authorised: Explicit reference to a fairytale in the title
2. Writerly: Implicit reference to a fairytale in title
3. Incorporation: Explicit reference to a fairytale within the text
4. Allusion: Implicit reference to a fairytale within the text
5. Re-vision: putting a new spin on an old tale
6. Fabulation: crafting an original fairytale
7. Metafictional: discussion of fairytales
8. Architextual/Chronotopic: "Fairytale" setting/environment

(10)

Smith labels these eight as "elements," a choice of term seeking to reinforce that these categories might be thought of as parts of a complex whole and arranged in different combinations (10). Intertextuality is also in operation even when fairy tales are evoked in an adjectival sense. As Marina Warner (2014) puts it, "The term 'fairytale' is often used as an epithet—a fairytale setting, a fairytale ending—for a work that is not in itself a fairy tale, because it depends on elements of the form's symbolic language" (xviii). In this case, the reference seems to rely on a set of implicit expectations about fairy tales, whatever they might be.

Texture and Context

Scholars have also employed the notion of describing fairy tales in terms of their **texture**. Jessica Tiffin (2009) argues that fairy tales display a distinctive quality "in the sense of a characteristic, instantly recognizable feel or style [. . .] recognizable in the level of structure and content as much as language" (6). According to her, in the realm of fairy tales, "event, psychology, and cause and effect [. . .] are subordinate to the expectations of narrative shape and outcome rather than internal motivation," contending:

> By identifying fairy tale by texture, I am [. . .] invoking a range of characteristics which rely heavily on clean lines, deliberate patterning and a geometry of structure and motif, but also include style, voice, and some aspects of content and mimetic approach. This attribute of texture, rather than language or motif, renders a fairy tale intrinsically familiar and identifiable even through literary manipulation, and it is precisely this quality of identifiability which allows the form to provide such a rich ground for metafictional play.
>
> (8)

Tiffin is ultimately concerned with mediated forms of fairy tales—what patterns and structures are retained in (post)modern literary forms and in filmic narratives. Tiffin makes the point that it is precisely "the extreme adaptability shown by fairy-tale structures across the centuries, and its ability of continually reinvent its voices, settings, and message as well as its medium of expression," that makes film adaptation easy (179).

The notion of entanglement and rearrangement between constituent parts further resonates with Labrie's use of **topological analysis** to describe "a form of symbolic investigation which combines levels of character, function, place, and movement" (1997, 153). In particular, Labrie compares the presence of bureaucratic power in both folktales and films that "share a common topology linked somehow to everyday life" (2014, 153). Labrie's work literally maps the trajectories of characters as they move through stories—the locations in which they find themselves and the routes they take there.

Fairy-tale contexts do not need to narrate the place in which its telling is physically set, or magical and imagined locales would be impossible. Katharine Galloway Young (1987) calls the **Taleworld** "a realm of events not present to the storytelling occasion at all but conjured up for the occasion by the story" (211). Fairy tales invoke the presence of the Taleworld by using well-recognized framing formulae like "once upon a time" to open and like "and they lived happily ever after" to close. Openings can be simply "There was once" while closings tend to be more diverse, including "They remained happy and content/While we still don't have a cent," "They remained rich and consoled, and we're just sitting here and getting old," "And those who tell this tale and whoever caused it to be told/Will not die a terrible death whenever they grow old," and many more (Zipes 2013, 75, 238, 511).

But the presence of such openings and closings, and of particular kinds of structures, characters, situations, and acts, indicates what Young calls a **Storyrealm**. That is, the listeners understand that whatever the other circumstances of the performance context may be, what is being narrated is a *story*—rather than another genre of speech like a lecture, a sermon, or even a conversation. The Storyrealm sets up a series of discursive expectations. The time of the Storyrealm is arguably the here and now, the time when the story is being told. The Taleworld could be the present (and it often is in fairy-tale films), but it need not be, and it is always in some sense radically other than the Storyrealm. Parallels can be seen in written fairy tales, including literary tales. A written publication is paratextually located with a publisher and publishing location (a kind of literary Storyrealm). Again, almost invariably literary fairy tales specifically narrate another space, often one that is imaginary and/or in literal terms nowhere.

Context is also important because, as Elliott Oring notes, folk narratives "must be re-created with each telling" (1986, 123). Folk narratives—a category that includes traditional fairy tales—are "reflections of the societies and individuals which create and transmit them; consequently, they reflect a wide range of human ideas and emotions" (133). Alessandro Falassi's case study of environment's centrality in making sense of fairy tales discusses the **performative context** of the Tuscan *veglia*, "the ritualized evening gathering of family and friends by the fireplace" where social events such as fairy tales were performed (1980, xviii). As Roger Abrahams (1980) explains, Falassi employed a method that looks at "the structure of context, in which elements of time, place, and occasion of enactment are brought to bear in the analysis of significant actions and events" (xi). By examining structure of context, for instance, "it has become known that certain times and spaces are endowed with significance by a community" (xi).

Ultimately, there is no such thing as an authoritative magic potion strong enough to encompass all fairy tales into a single formulation. This is a malleable form, after all. And given that fairy tales have been defined in so many ways, it should be no surprise that scholars have likewise employed different methods and approaches in thinking about what makes them, from tale types, functions, and archetypes to memes, textures, and Storyrealms. To trace their distinctive elements and ways of operation seems a step forward from understanding first what a fairy tale is—and that is another equally complicated question.

References Cited and Further Reading

Aarne, Antti. (1910) 1971. *The Types of the Folk-Tale: A Classification and Bibliography*. New York: B. Franklin.

Abrahams, Roger. 1980. "Foreword." In *Folklore by the Fireside: Text and Context of the Tuscan Veglia*. Austin: U Texas P.

Afanasyev, Aleksandr. 1945. *Russian Fairy Tales*, translated by Norbert Guterman. New York: Pantheon Books.

Bordwell, David. 1988. "ApProppriations and ImPropprieties: Problems in the Morphology of Film Narrative." *Cinema Journal* 27 (3): 5–20.

Bottigheimer, Ruth B. 2009. "Why Fairy Tales Stick: The Evolution and Relevance of a Genre (Review)." *Journal of American Folklore* 122 (485): 367–70.

Butler, David. 2009. *Fantasy Cinema: Impossible Worlds on Screen*. London: Wallflower.

Dawkins, Richard. 1976. *The Selfish Gene*. Oxford: Oxford UP.

Dundes, Alan. 1980. *Interpreting Folklore*. Bloomington: Indiana UP.

———. 1997. "The Motif-Index and the Tale Type Index: A Critique." *Journal of Folklore Research* 34 (3): 195–202.

Falassi, Alessandro. 1980. *Folklore by the Fireside: Text and Context of the Tuscan Veglia*. Austin: U Texas P.

Field, Syd. 1994. *Screenplay: The Foundations of Screenwriting*. New York: Dell.

Genette, Gérard. 1997. *Palimpsests: Literature in the Second Degree*. Lincoln: U Nebraska P.

Greimas, Algirdas Julien. 1983. *Structural Semantics: An Attempt at a Method*. Lincoln: U Nebraska P.

Hébert, Louis. N.d. "The Actantial Model." *Signo: Theoretical Semiotics on the Web*. www.signosemio.com/greimas/actantial-model.asp.

Holbek, Bengt. 1987. *Interpretation of Fairy Tales: Danish Folklore in a European Perspective*. Helsinki: Suomalainen Tiedeakatemia.

Järv, Risto. 2005. "The Gender of the Heroes, Storytellers and Collectors of Estonian Fairy Tales." *Folklore: Electronic Journal of Folklore* 29: 45–60.

Kristensen, Evald Tang. 1892. *Danske sagn, som de har lydt i folkemunde*. Århus: Århus Folkeblads Bogtrykkeri.

Labrie, Vivian. 1997. "Help! Me, S/he, and the Boss." In *Undisciplined Women: Tradition and Culture in Canada*, edited by Pauline Greenhill and Diane Tye, 151–66. Montreal: McGill-Queen's UP.

———. 2014. "*Serenity* (ATU 707), *This Boy's Life* (ATU 590), *Star Wars* (Lacourcière 305A), *Solaris* (ATU 652)? About Extending the Aarne-Thompson-Uther Tale-type Identification Insight to Movies." In *Narratives Across Space and Time: Transmissions and Adaptations*, edited by Aikaterini Polymerou-Kamilaki, Evangelos Karamanes, and Ioannis Plemmenos, 295–314. Athens: Academy of Athens, Publications of the Hellenic Folklore Research Centre.

Lee, Sung-Ae. 2016. "The Fairy-Tale Film in Korea." In *Fairy-Tale Films Beyond Disney: International Perspectives*, edited by Jack Zipes, Pauline Greenhill, and Kendra Magnus-Johnston, 207–21. New York: Routledge.

Lévi-Strauss, Claude. 1955. "The Structural Study of Myth." *Journal of American Folklore* 68 (270): 428–44.

Lord, Albert Bates. 1960. *The Singer of Tales*. Cambridge, MA: Harvard UP.

Lovelace, Martin, Anita Best, and Pauline Greenhill. Forthcoming. *'The Maid in the Thick of the Well': Gender and the Magic Tales of Alice Lannon and Pius Power Senior*. Logan: Utah State UP.

Murphy, Terence Patrick. 2015a. *The Fairytale and Plot Structure*. New York: Palgrave Macmillan.

———. 2015b. *From Fairy Tale to Film Screenplay: Working with Plot Genotypes*. Basingstoke: Palgrave Macmillan.

Oring, Elliott. 1986. *Folk Groups and Folklore Genre: An Introduction*, edited by Elliott Oring. Logan: Utah State UP.

Parry, Milman, and Albert B. Lord. 1954. *Serbocroatian Heroic Songs*. Cambridge, MA: Harvard UP.

Propp, Vladimir. (1928) 1968. *Morphology of the Folktale*, translated by Laurence Scott. Austin: U Texas P.

Rankin, Walter. 2007. *Grimm Pictures: Fairy Tale Archetypes in Eight Horror and Suspense Films*. Jefferson, NC: McFarland.

Schrempp, Gregory Allen. 2014. *Science, Bread, and Circuses: Folkloristic Essays on Science for the Masses*. Logan: Utah State UP.

Smith, Kevin Paul. 2007. *The Postmodern Fairytale: Folkloric Intertext in Contemporary Fiction*. Basingstoke: Palgrave Macmillan.

Thompson, Stith. (1928) 1961. *The Types of the Folk-Tale: A Classification and Bibliography: Antti Aarne's Verzeichnis der marchentypen (FF communication)*. Hensinki: Suomalainen tiedeakatemia, Academia scientiarum fennica.

———. (1932–1935) 1955. *Motif-Index of Folk-Literature: A Classification of Narrative Elements in Folktales, Ballads, Myths, Fables, Mediaeval Romances, Exempla, Fabliaux, Jest-Books, and Local Legends*. Bloomington: Indiana UP.

Tiffin, Jessica. 2009. *Marvelous Geometry: Narrative and Metafiction in Modern Fairy Tale*. Detroit: Wayne State UP.

Uther, Hans-Jörg. 2004. *The Types of International Folktales: A Classification and Bibliography, based on the System of Antti Aarne and Stith Thompson*. 3 vols. Helsinki: Suomalainen Tiedeakatemia, Academia Scientiarum Fennica.

Vansina, Jan. 1985. *Oral Tradition as History*. Madison: U Wisconsin P.

von Franz, Marie-Louise. 1996. *The Interpretation of Fairy Tales*. Boston: Shambhala.

Warner, Marina. 2014. *Once Upon a Time: A Short History of Fairy Tale*. Oxford: Oxford UP.

Young, Katharine Galloway. 1987. *Taleworlds and Storyrealms: The Phenomenology of Narrative*. Dordrecht: Nijhoff.

Zipes, Jack. 1996. "Towards a Theory of the Fairy-Tale Film: The Case of *Pinocchio*." *The Lion and the Unicorn* 20 (1): 1–24.

———. 2006. *Why Fairy Tales Stick: The Evolution and Relevance of a Genre*. New York: Routledge.

———. 2011. *The Enchanted Screen: The Unknown History of Fairy-Tale Films*. New York: Routledge.

———, ed. 2013. *The Golden Age of Folk and Fairy Tales: From the Brothers Grimm to Andrew Lang*. Indianapolis: Hackett Publishing Company.

———. 2016. "The Great Cultural Tsunami of Fairy-Tale Films." In *Fairy-Tale Films Beyond Disney: International Perspectives*, edited by Jack Zipes, Pauline Greenhill, and Kendra Magnus-Johnston, 1–17. New York: Routledge.

Mediagraphy

Hard Candy. 2005. Director David Slade. USA.

Serenity. 2005. Director Joss Whedon. USA.

The Silence of the Lambs. 1991. Director Jonathan Demme. USA.

Solaris. 2002. Director Steven Soderbergh. USA.

This Boy's Life. 1993. Director Michael Caton-Jones. USA.

Part II

ANALYTICAL APPROACHES

4
FORMALISM
Jill Terry Rudy

Situating formalism in relation with fairy-tale culture and media evokes the ongoing specter and implications of twentieth-century literary theory. This perspective involves early twentieth-century Russian and Slavic literary scholars, folklorists, and linguists; inklings of structuralism and New Criticism; and semiotics and narratology, as well as aesthetics, attention, and affordances. In addition to systematizing literary scholarship, formalism involves teachable, publishable practices of close reading accompanied by attentiveness to textual and performance acoustics, semantics, and architectonics (Thompson 1971, 138). Purist approaches strictly focus on the artistic work, eliding issues of history, production, reception, and meaning. Still, the study of form lends itself, by extension, to textures, contexts, expressivity, and interpretations as an artistic work persists recognizably over time and conveys knowledge. Easily referenced back to Platonic Forms and Aristotelian treatises, a more mundane, vernacular formalism begins with speech acquisition and scribbles, with early investigations of word play, rhyme, rhythm, line, color, pattern, repetition, and framing—in our particular purview, with "Once upon a time."

Formalism is not only a literary movement but a way of attending to poetics, or the message itself according to Roman Jakobson's functions of language (1960). This turn then conjures distinctive ways of reading and viewing that require, and often reward, the learning and employment of detailed terminology, keen observation, and some crucial concepts. Fredric Jameson asserts that the formalists' insistent, systematizing focus on the "intrinsically literary" makes their work the starting place for twentieth-century criticism (1972, 43). Intermediality also works as an ongoing formalist consideration since several Russian scholars studied traditional literature such as *bylina*, similar to the ballad, and *skazki*, wonder tales, by putting print collections and compositions in relationship with oral expressive forms. Later moves toward structuralism and semiotics further expanded these studies toward all sign systems while still emphasizing the intrinsic workings of texts and considering cultural and social implications. So, formalism offers a practical, applicable toolbox for critically approaching fairy-tale cultures and media to the degree they involve literariness and to greater degree in acknowledgment of how fairy tale sheds pivotal light on artistic making and creative imaginings. Tracing the merit of formalism and related critical movements toward fairy-tale scholarship, this chapter also posits ways that fairy-tale cultures and media presage and attain formalist impulses and concludes by considering how fairy-tale form draws attention while it affords narrative, and sociocultural, ultimacy.

This chapter advocates attentive study of formal features involved with fairy-tale cultures and media because the fairy tale rewards such attentiveness with its persistent recognizability amidst intermedial and intertextual shapeshifting. Jessica Tiffin astutely observes that the fairy tale's ability to "find convivial company in genres as disparate as horror, science fiction, and radical postmodern literature points rather emphatically towards its status as an archaic and familiar form" (2009, 7). How else does one recognize a fairy tale in general, or in a specific story, unless one attends to its form? And, this chapter advocates more attention and work on the as yet understudied issues and venues that associate fairy-tale form with media—as compositional materials (spoken words, paper, ink, celluloid, digital 0s and 1s, human bodies), sensory channels (auditory, visual, kinesthetic), and communications technologies (human bodies, printing presses, cameras, projectors, broadcast microphones, radios, and televisions, screens, smart phones). Tiffin amends Alan Dundes's concept of texture to delineate some salient formal features: "clean lines, deliberate patterning and a geometry of structure and motif, but also [. . .] style, voice, and some aspects of content and mimetic approach" (2009, 7). Indeed, formalist study is a good starting point to answer the question consistently put to fairy-tale scholars: why do fairy tales persist? In good measure, they persist because of a flexible, resilient form that requires attention and allows compelling personal and collective affordances.

Russian Formalism, Structuralism, and Anglo-American New Criticism

This section introduces and explores some of the critical history, terminology, and concepts applicable for formalist analysis in connection with fairy-tale cultures and media. Prone to description and specialization, analytical approaches in the vein of Russian Formalism, structuralism, and New Criticism focus on *literary* expression by starting with the text and its constituent elements. These movements share key inclinations toward valuing literariness and scholarly rigor by delineating the verbal facts of a poem, ballad, novel, or tale (Thompson 1971, 149). They remain distinctive critical endeavors, however, by diverging in some basic assumptions about scholarship, literature, and art. New Criticism, the most influential British and American movement of literary criticism of the mid-twentieth century, attends to language and form as a non-paraphrasable unity that must be studied using techniques such as close reading in order to then interpret and appreciate cognitive messages.

Taking intrinsic literariness at face value, formalists attend more to the systemic aspects. Ewa Thompson concludes that "precise description of the literary fact is the objective of this group" and that interpretation remains beyond scholarship because it "cannot be ultimately validated logically" (1971, 149). Russian Formalism flourished among a scholarly group in St. Petersburg and Moscow from approximately 1915 to 1930. Its scholars adapted to or dispersed from Soviet life some instigating work known as the Prague Linguistic Circle which more overtly developed structuralist aspects relevant not only to literature but to all sign systems and to meaning. Victor Erlich notes the move toward structuralism allows that "ideological or emotional content was a legitimate object of critical analysis, provided that it is examined as a component of an esthetic structure" ([1955] 1980, 159). While New Critics focus more on modernist poetry and intricate works such as those of Henry James or William Faulkner, Russian Formalists and structuralists from that movement prominently feature folk literature and issues of oral traditional expression.

Important for the study of fairy-tale cultures and media, the shift from an insistent focus on literature to consideration of other sign systems still depends on an analytical perspective centered on the artistic work itself. Jameson attributes this focus to Ferdinand de Saussure's distinction of the *synchronic* from the *diachronic*, or the structural and systemic from the historical and contingent. Diachrony is the study of change over time, while synchrony considers linear association. According to Jameson's reading of Saussure, synchrony sees that "language as a total system is complete at every moment, no matter what happens to have been altered in it a moment before" (1972, 5–6). Diachrony, though, admits that "sounds have their own history and that meanings change" (6). Saussure asserts that the "basic components of the system are somehow self-defining," and scholarly focus shifts to the function of these units in relationships, as part of the system (Jameson 1972, 17).

Saussure also then differentiates the *langue*, "linguistic possibilities or potentialities at any given moment," from the *parole*, the "individual act of speech" (Jameson 1972, 22). In fairy-tale terms, langue is similar to the general possibilities of producing a Baba Yaga story, or any other tale, while parole would be a particular telling such as the Soviet televised story *Vanya from the Pioneers' Club* (1981, dir. Eduard Uspensky and Gennadiy Sokolskiy). Distinctions, such as synchrony and diachrony or langue and parole, apply to analyzing fairy-tale cultures and media by keeping focus on their systemic capacities. Where sometimes formalism may appear decontextualized and wholly intrinsic, many formalist concepts and terms emphasize the associative and relational elements that apprehend the fairy tale in its ever-present possibility but also its ongoing, specific enactments.

The focus on form not only applies to individual literary works but to genres and literary history because the contrastive formalist and structuralist methods apply not only to texts as multilevel systems but to literature as a distinctive system, at times a dominant expressive pattern but still one among other patterns and systems. In a way, genre serves as a pivot between the specific work, literature, and other social systems. According to Uri Margolin, formalist study of genre serves as "a basic category for the study of literary-historical changes" because "the Formalists made the genre a variable in a larger equation" (2005). Because anthologies, mash-ups, and genre mixing remain important contemporary practices involving the fairy tale, a formal analytic approach helps both to distinguish tales from other expressive forms while also relating or juxtaposing them to each other and to changes in literary history and other sociocultural forms.

Still, Caroline Levine distinguishes forms from genre to conceptualize and highlight the powerful properties of form broadly considered. Defining forms as "patternings, shapes, and arrangements," Levine explores how they "can organize both social and literary objects, and they can remain stable over time," and concludes that "forms thus migrate across contexts in a way that genres cannot" (2015, 13). In studying literature as a system, criticism becomes more systematized. And in expressly studying forms, literature and criticism in Levine's purview become more socially consequential, "expanding our usual definition of form in literary studies to include patterns of sociopolitical experience" (2). Since folklorists have long considered the transmission of tales, recognizing their historical-geographic nimbleness *and* romantic-nationalizing stability, this contemporary approach to form rings familiar on both the textual and contextual levels.

Literary study from previous centuries, including philology as the study of literary language and history and *belle lettres* as the study of fine literature, also attends to language and textual explication in order to better understand and appreciate literary works and their cultural implications, but literature before the nineteenth century was an unprofessionalized study object. Moves toward system and synchrony brought Russian Formalists to literariness as their study object, as Jameson admits their unique claim "is their stubborn attachment to the intrinsically literary," which leads to "the isolation of the intrinsic itself" (1972, 43). Much previous literary study emphasized speculations on authorial intent and biographical connections or investigation of sources and analogues (see Graff 1987). Distinguishing the material of literature from its devices, and recognizing the devices as a dominant feature, marks formalist study. Such scholarship also involves the narrative distinction between the *fabula* (story), or representational and chronological story elements, and the *sujet* (plot), or rearrangement according to compositional principles such as threefold repetition, "circular construction," and other reordering devices that draw attention to themselves (Margolin 2005). The proliferation of terms and concepts in connection with such scrutiny of literary form requires descriptive acuity and risks low-stakes conceptual payoff but brings energy and rigor by making literary study a more critical, and thus intellectually beneficial, endeavor.

The Most Famous Case of Propp's *Morphology of the Folktale*

In his introduction to the second edition of Vladimir Propp's first book, *Morphologiia Skazki*, published in Russia in 1928 and first translated and published in the United States in 1958, Alan Dundes assesses the impact of the translation along with the book's drawbacks and contributions to folklore, linguistics, and literary study. He writes, "One can only regret that there was a thirty-year time lag" (1968, 1). Dundes also regrets that Propp's version of formalist study does not attend to context, and therefore culture. As a folklorist attuned both to the group (folk) and the expression (lore), Dundes insists, "The form must ultimately be related to the culture or cultures in which it is found" (1968, 2). And so, he considers Propp's book a starting point for analysis, identifying the sequential approach to narrative functions as a *syntagmatic* type of chronological study in comparison with Claude Levi-Strauss's *paradigmatic* type of pattern study, "usually based upon an a priori binary principle of opposition" (1968, 1). While Levi-Strauss's work has "bravely attempted to relate the paradigm(s)" to "the world at large," Dundes finds no reason for a syntagmatic approach to avoid context and cultural commentary as well (1968, 1).

For his part, Propp took morphology as his starting point, studying formal and structural features, believing that "as long as there is no correct morphological study there can be no correct historical study" because scholars first must understand the relationship and function of component parts before delving into history or comparative study (Steiner 1984, 83). Famously, the book identifies thirty-one sequential functions that make up the Russian wonder tale, delimited as stories collected by Alexander Afanasyev and categorized as Aarne type index numbers 300 to 749. For Propp, the fairy tale was "a narrative about actions performed by certain characters" with the emphasis on the consistency of the actions rather than the variability of the characters. Propp sought the minimal narrative unit not for its own sake but for its part in the story as a whole: "the elements do not exist in isolation but are interlocked in a configuration—the compositional scheme of the fairy tale" (Steiner 1984, 84).

Propp's accomplishment of discovering not only the component parts of the Russian wonder tale, but also their specific order, facilitates descriptive study while, as Dundes notes, leaving cultural commentary and implications to be determined. The *Morphology*'s translation invigorated humanistic scholarship with its own implications for increased understanding of not only the fairy tale but narrative in general. More dense and nuanced than its common reduction to the thirty-one functions, Propp's work as an analytical approach may be well-known and utilized by students as a primer for identifying and describing fairy tale's component parts. Eva Thury's "A Proppian Analysis of *The Wizard of Oz*" applies the functions to the 1939 movie version, giving a thoughtful, intermedial example of the analytical possibilities aimed toward undergraduate students (2016).

Propp published other influential works on folklore and Russian literature, but his *Morphology* for at least six decades has remained a quintessential and quirky exhibit of how formalism and related critical movements relate with fairy-tale scholarship. Jameson's *The Prison-House of Language* (1972) offers a richly conceptualized assessment of formalist and structuralist projects with some pages on Propp's folktale analysis, and Stephen Benson's *Cycles of Influence* (2003) gives a thoroughly developed examination of the fairy tale's involvement in twentieth-century literary theories after Propp. Benson traces how Levi-Strauss, A. J. Greimas, and Claude Bremond critique and interact with Propp's premises and conclusions.

Levi-Strauss sees that Propp reintroduces "content in the guise of form" and therefore creates a schema that is both too abstract and not abstract enough, especially in comparison with Levi-Strauss's penchant for binaries (Benson 2003, 30–31). Greimas refines Propp's numerous functions into the "now famous semiotic square" to find the paradigmatic possibility in Propp's syntagmatic design. This then also sees cultural commentary in Propp's work since Greimas's structural analysis "logically account[s] for the existence within a single tale of contradictory elements" that both confront and support an "existing social order" (Benson 2003, 36). Bremond also develops his own schema from Propp's functions by grouping them into triads and allowing more narrative choice and omissions (Benson 2003, 37). Not only does Benson examine the theoretical implications of fairy-tale scholarship, he also turns to the stories and collections themselves to further explicate the influence of story cycles as theoretical design.

Semiotics, Narratology, and Fairy-Tale Cultures and Media

Fairy-tale cultures and media foreground and attain their own impulses toward system, schema, and structure; this accomplishment is well considered, in part, through formalism's relationships with structuralism, semiotics, and narratology. Adaptation studies also enters the picture here because of fairy tale's innate and persisting replication and variation. Fairy-tale versions have synchronic and diachronic dimensions since any one text or performance involves both the langue and parole. Any discrete utterances and iterations of fairy tale involve form and media while happening over time and often across space. Additionally, the storytelling session, cycle, collection, and anthology anticipate structuralist dimensions. As Benson observes, "The folk-tale cycle [. . .] manipulates narrative in a manner which anticipates the basic procedures and conceptions of structuralist narrative poetics." His point is that not only does folktale inform important twentieth-century formalist theories but that its form offers a "combinative, generative model of narrative" that precedes these theoretical formulations (2003, 44). Fairy tale is an exemplary form.

Whereas Russian Formalists and Anglo-American critics keep a focus on literature as specially marked language, the structuralist moves of the Prague Circle draw on and extend the Saussurean interest in all sign systems to the formal study of signs known as semiotics and the study of story called narratology. This semiotic view, according to Ann Jefferson, "meant seeing forms of expression as signs whose meanings depend on conventions, relations and systems, rather than on any inherent features" (1986, 93). Not only language but all forms of expression, such as cooking, photography, story, and mass media, may be considered as signs dependent on social convention and systems (Chandler N.d.). Attuned to formalism's interest in oral and print expressivity, these later twentieth-century theoretical moves extend literary study to issues of form and media that involve fairy tale with compositional materials, sensory channels, and communication technologies. This leads to the variety of studies and issues undertaken for this *Companion*.

Fairy-tale form, thus, prefigures these analytical configurations and theoretical interests involved with language, literary composition, literariness, signs, and, as Peter Steiner considers it, the ultimate goal of understanding "what brings together all the disparate human activities of a particular historical moment" (1984, 113). Benson's study of three folktale cycles considers some of these contributions to theorizing: "Narratives are [. . .] combining simple units to build a complex whole, generating narratives out of frames that in turn act as generative units themselves. The whole cycle acts as a sort of narrative mechanism" (2003, 63). Further, Benson asserts that fairy tale itself serves as a crucial forebear to narrative and literary criticism more generally, especially that a folktale cycle "*manipulates* narrative in a manner which anticipates the basic procedures and conceptions of structuralist narrative poetics" (44). Russian Formalist Viktor Schklovsky, writing early in the movement, frequently uses machine metaphors to investigate literary materials and especially literary devices. Steiner observes that "by focusing on the nuts and bolts of poetic texts [. . .] mechanistic Formalism radically reversed the value of content" (1984, 47). One could quite easily observe that the same is true for the fairy tale in that content usually is diminished as attention is drawn to the "nuts and bolts" of the storytelling, or perhaps that the content actually *is* the storytelling's nuts and bolts in the form of motifs or functions (depending on the analytical starting point) in generative combination, as the smallest units of composition or meaning organized into tales and narrative cycles. This would relate to the metafictional tendencies of fairy tale, and especially postmodern tales, as Tiffin analyzes (2009).

Awareness of fairy-tale poetic devices and mechanisms also suggests investigation, even construction, of structure and schemas. Propp's morphology does not follow mechanistic formalism, but rather, according to Steiner, an organic formalism (1984, 80–85). Dundes, after replicating Propp's work in his own *The Morphology of North American Indian Folktales* (1962), recognizes the elegance and conceptual utility of Propp's analytical approach. Although he faults Propp for leaving off with cultural commentary and only creating his functional schema, Dundes recognizes his approach relates not only to Russian literature and folk narrative forms. He surmises that "if there is a pattern in a culture, it is by no means necessary that it be limited to only one aspect of that culture," and then suggests that Proppian analysis applies to a variety of cultural forms including "comic books, motion picture and television plots, and the like" (1968, 3–4). The point, though, is not merely to overlay the functions onto other forms but rather to use the deeper observation of structure and organization to link expressivity with social life.

The issue of content resurfaces, and is diminished, as Dundes realizes that Proppian analysis "suggests that there can be structural borrowings as well as content borrowings." To suggest ways of overcoming Propp's failure to consider cultural implications, Dundes mentions his morphology could address issues of marriage, "thinking and learning processes," cultural "success stor[ies]," "the acquisition of folklore," and the generation of "new tales" (1968, 4). Far from the early formalist focus on literariness, these suggestions of applying Proppian analysis to a wide array of cultural patterns and media indicate the generative possibilities and wide applicability, and influence, of fairy-tale structures on the social world.

This brings up the pedagogical and institutional applicability of formalist analytical approaches because they are highly patterned and therefore imminently teachable and open to evaluation. Here, the formalist inclinations of the Anglo-American New Criticism particularly come to the fore, although, as previously mentioned, Proppian analysis may be practiced on a continuum of ability levels from rote identification of functions to nuanced textual and sociocultural analyses. Prominent features of a New Critical analytical approach include trying to explain how "the elements of a poem [literary work] fit in the total design of it, how the internal coherence of a poem is reached, how the symbol (to use the New Critical vocabulary) is structured" (Thompson 1971, 111). Searching for, describing, and interpreting these features became a primary practice in U.S. secondary English education in the last half of the twentieth century, while analyzing such features also works well in journal-length articles that for a time, before book expectations, helped professors merit tenure and advancement. In a scientific age, as with philological methods of the nineteenth century, formalist analysis systematizes literary criticism in recognizably rigorous ways.

Formalism involves attentiveness to the text itself, and its literariness and sign systems, as a starting point. The introductions to Jennifer Schacker and Christine Jones's anthologies exemplify formalist close reading of Perrault's "Little Red Riding Hood," featuring Jones's own translation, and guide students to read fairy tale in ways that avoid restating moralistic messages. The authors start with elements fitting into a total design—specific words from the original French and then attendant textual patterns, as well as contextual insights from the French seventeenth century (2012, 21–40; 2015, 1–17). Jones and Schacker's sociohistorical insights and pedagogical inclinations concur with the ideological concerns that emerged in later literary and cultural theorizing of the twentieth century. For, while the explicit focus on literariness and the text professionalizes humanistic study, leaving off on cultural commentary, or more commonly not attaining an analytical "so what," remains a formalist pitfall. Analyzing forms rather than following a formalist agenda may helpfully keep together the pleasures of formal analysis and close reading with the ways people employ literature, media, and traditional expression to comment on, challenge, and even create social worlds through the fairy tale's own compositional imperatives.

Fairy-Tale Forms and Affordances

Just as Russian Formalism and its extensions in structuralism, semiotics, and narratology could not avoid eventually relating literariness with other expressive forms and media, fairy-tale forms are best considered in relation: motif, function, cycle, variant, structure, style. And yet, as most who know (and love) the fairy tale recognize, there is a uniqueness to this form that merits discrete attention. Writers and other producers of fairy tale make a good starting place for identifying this form. In an epigraph to Kate Bernheimer's "Fairy Tale Is Form, Form Is Fairy Tale," Italo Calvino passes by nationalist and nostalgic reasons to assert that his attraction to tales came "because of my interest in style and structure, in the economy, rhythm, and hard logic in which they are told" (2009, 61). As Levine's comments indicate, forms persist in ways genre and other conventions do not. Bernheimer admits, "[Fairy-tale] form survives mutation. It is also adaptable to a diverse range of narrative styles and shapes" (2009, 62–63). She posits four elements that to her comprise Calvino's *hard logic* of fairy tale: "flatness, abstraction, intuitive logic, and normalized magic" (64). Bernheimer wisely observes, "Fairy tales are the skeletons of story, perhaps" (65). Other writers, critics, fans, and producers would select different elements, but most admit that fairy tale itself offers an elemental form that not only rewards critical attention but that also accomplishes social work.

A realm of form and formalism is aesthetics, which may be defined as "a study of value in the plastic, visual, conceptual, auditory and performance arts" (Mayo 2012, 359). Notice how media appears integrally in this definition. Fairy-tale forms, as much as any other, merit aesthetic scrutiny because while they so readily adapt and appear in almost every conceivable medium, as Bernheimer notes, they survive mutation. Considering aesthetics and the epistemological branch of philosophy, Stephen Mayo attributes retaining form through adaptability to something that seems rather like Saussurean langue: "The work of art exists between the materials used by the artists or the performers and the consciousness of the audience or viewers. Without the pattern recognition aptitudes of our minds there would be no work of art" (2012, 361). While some forms like plays, operas, and dance retain their form because of some type of notation or script (361), traditional expressions like the folktale also accomplish this but more often with structural schema, Mayo's "pattern recognition aptitudes of our minds," that have the combinatory and generative capacities noted by Benson's study.

Folklorists have studied these issues for almost two centuries and conceive of tradition as this human aptitude for pattern recognition—and pattern adaptation and performance. Dorothy

Noyes finds this "life of form in time and space" to be what folklorists study as tradition (2016, 132). With the Grimms and their fairy-tale collections as crucial contributors to the conceptualization and practices of folkloristics (Bauman and Briggs 2003), fairy-tale forms presage this aptitude. So in place of ahistorical, decontextualized formalist study, Noyes attributes social work to form: "Forms coordinate social attention both to themselves and to the actors who collaborate to realize them" (2016, 133). She also sees that forms "mediate between attention and inattention" because the mind eagerly registers newness, but quickly consigns it to the familiar, and thus appreciates new forms and adaptations of recognizable ones (133). Noyes reiterates Jakobson's communications schema that associates the poetic with the message itself to assert that "some forms are more aesthetic," returning us in a way to the Russian Formalists' insistence on isolating the literary from other expressions (134).

These more-aesthetic forms are more likely to draw attention to themselves, which rewards study focused intrinsically on them but also affords these aesthetic forms more social efficacy because of that attention. Noyes creates a schema of folkloristic forms and their social impact—art, occasion, news, and surround—and concludes that one important work of form is "coordinating us [by drawing our attention in the first place] but keeping us out of one another's way [. . .] [providing] a salutary distraction and reorientation" (168). Perhaps this is why and how the analysis of storytelling in all its guises relates with formal analysis because there is a processual component to listening, reading, and viewing related to the fact that forms must be somehow apprehended—as epistemological aesthetics admits.

This also brings us to the realm of affordances. With their distinctive form, fairy-tale cultures and media may accomplish certain things. Levine borrows the concept of affordance from design theory because it relates form with "potential uses or actions," but only to certain ones. She gives examples of how glass affords "transparency and brittleness" and a fork "stabbing and scooping," relating affordance to form (and material) by pointing out that "patterns and arrangements carry their affordances with them as they move across time and space" (2015, 6). As mentally aesthetic and aesthetically mental material, fairy-tale form affords the social work discussed by Noyes, coordination and mediation, and also the salient point of Proppian morphology, lack and lack liquidated (Thury 2016). This form affords materialization and transformation into numerous media. Fairy-tale form involves the instantaneously recognizable "once upon a time" with "and they lived happily ever after," in its generalizable conception and its actual utterances and performance. As this *Companion* champions, fairy-tale form affords cognitive and affective wonder and delight, perhaps even happiness, even as the frame relates the contingency of "once" with the ultimacy of "ever after."

References Cited and Further Reading

Bauman, Richard, and Charles L. Briggs. 2003. *Voices of Modernity: Language Ideologies and the Politics of Inequality.* Cambridge: Cambridge UP.

Benson, Stephen. 2003. *Cycles of Influence: Fiction, Folktale, Theory.* Detroit: Wayne State UP.

Berkheimer, Kate. 2009. "Fairy Tale Is Form, Form Is Fairy Tale." In *The Writer's Notebook: Craft Essays from Tin House*, edited by Aimee Bender, Dorothy Allison, and Susan Bell, 61–73. Portland: Tin House Books.

Chandler, Daniel. N.d. "Semiotics for Beginners." http://visual-memory.co.uk/daniel/Documents/S4B/sem01.html.

Dundes, Alan. 1962. *The Morphology of North American Indian Folktales.* Bloomington: Indiana UP.

———. 1968. "Introduction to the Second Edition." In *Morphology of the Folktale*, edited by Vladimir Propp, 1–6. Bloomington: Indiana UP.

Erlich, Victor. (1955) 1980. *Russian Formalism.* 4th ed. Berlin: De Gruyter.

Graff, Gerald. 1987. *Professing Literature: An Institutional History.* Chicago: U Chicago P.

Jakobson, Roman. 1960. "Closing Statement: Linguistics and Poetics." In *Style in Language*, edited by Thomas A. Sebeok, 350–77. Cambridge, MA: MIT Press.

Jameson, Fredric. 1972. *The Prison-House of Language: A Critical Account of Structuralism and Russian Formalism*. Princeton, NJ: Princeton UP.

Jefferson, Ann. 1986. "Structuralism and Post-Structuralism." In *Modern Literary Theory: A Comparative Introduction*, edited by Ann Jefferson and David Robey, 92–121. London: Batsford.

Jones, Christine A., and Jennifer Schacker, eds. 2012. *Marvelous Transformations: An Anthology of Fairy Tales and Contemporary Critical Perspectives*. Toronto: Broadview.

Levine, Caroline. 2015. *Forms: Whole, Rhythm, Hierarchy, Network*. Princeton, NJ: Princeton UP.

Lieberman, Anatoly. 1984. "Introduction." In *Theory and History of Folklore*, translated by Ariadna Y. Martin and Richard P. Martin, ix–lxxxi. Minneapolis: U Minnesota P.

Margolin, Uri. 2005. "Russian Formalism." In *The Johns Hopkins Guide to Literary Theory and Criticism*, edited by Michael Groden, Martin Kreiswirth, and Imre Szeman, N.p. 2nd ed. Baltimore: Johns Hopkins UP. http://litguide.press.jhu.edu/cgi-bin/view.cgi?eid=227&query=margolin.

Mayo, Stephen T. 2012. "Aesthetics: What Is Art?" In *The Problems of Philosophy*, edited by Michael S. Russo, 359–63. New York: SophiaOmni P.

Noyes, Dorothy. 2016. "Aesthetic Is the Opposite of Anaesthetic: On Tradition and Attention." In *Humble Theory: Folklore's Grasp on Social Life*, 127–76. Bloomington: Indiana UP.

Propp, Vladimir. (1928) 1968. *The Morphology of the Folktale*. Bloomington: Indiana UP.

———. 1984. *Theory and History of Folklore*, translated by Ariadna Y. Martin and Richard P. Martin. Minneapolis: U Minnesota P.

Schacker, Jennifer, and Christine A. Jones. 2015. *Feathers, Paws, Fins, and Claws: Fairy-Tale Beasts*. Detroit: Wayne State UP.

Steiner, Peter. 1984. *Russian Formalism: A Metapoetics*. Ithaca, NY: Cornell UP.

Thompson, Ewa M. 1971. *Russian Formalism and Anglo-American New Criticism*. Berlin: De Gruyter.

Thury, Eva M. 2016. "A Proppian Analysis of *The Wizard of Oz*." In *Introduction to Mythology: Contemporary Approaches to Classical and World Myths*, edited by Eva M. Thury and Margaret Kopfle Devinney, 665–75. Oxford: Oxford UP.

Tiffin, Jessica. 2009. *Marvelous Geometry: Narrative and Metafiction in Modern Fairy Tale*. Detroit: Wayne State UP.

Mediagraphy

"Vanya from the Pioneers' Club" (*Ivanushka iz Dvortsa Pionerov*, TV). 1981. Directors Eduard Uspensky and Gennadiy Sokolskiy. USSR.

5

PSYCHOLOGY

Veronica Schanoes

Fairy tales and psychoanalytic theory have long occupied the same psychic space. Indeed, Kenneth Kidd traces out a complex, deliberate, and largely successful attempt by psychoanalysts to join the two genres. As Alan Dundes put it, "almost every single major psychoanalyst wrote at least one paper applying psychoanalytic theory to folklore" (2003, 21), and Kidd notes that Sigmund Freud actively sought out folklorists who "could demonstrate the power of psycho-analysis through analysis of folklore" (Kidd 2011, 5). Psychoanalysis's concerns—childhood, sexuality, the family romance—became the focus of those who studied fairy tales and vice versa. In this chapter, I examine the ways psychoanalysis and clinical psychology as disciplines have made use of fairy tales and how contemporary fairy-tale retellings in turn make use of psychological thought and psychoanalytic theory. I examine the beginning of this relationship and then look at case studies from popular media culture. I consider two extraordinarily popu-lar and influential examples of psychoanalytic theory that used fairy tales to make connections with a broad audience: Bruno Bettelheim's *The Uses of Enchantment* (1976) and Clarissa Pinkola Estés's *Women Who Run With the Wolves* (1995), and then two recent popular feminist versions of fairy tales, Disney's *Maleficent* (2014) and Universal Studios' *Snow White and the Huntsman* (2012).

In many ways, the stage was set for the convergence of fairy tales and psychology by the comparative folklore practiced by folklorists of the nineteenth century. Just as Sir James Frazer's *The Golden Bough* proposed a common human path through myth, nineteenth-century folklorists collected tales across the world, often editing them in order to present a univer-sal human set of fairy tales. Excellent work has been done on the imperialist ideology of nineteenth-century folklore studies by Sara Hines (2010) and Sadhana Naithani (2010). Fairy tales were thought to represent the "childhood of the species," just as the so-called "primi-tive" cultures of Africans and North American Indians did. Individual human development was thought to recapitulate and accurately represent collective human cultural development. Thus, when psychological thought came to emphasize the formation and development of the psyche in childhood, the turn to fairy tales as representative of that childhood made a certain amount of sense.

Freud addressed fairy tales specifically in his 1913 essay "The Occurrence in Dreams of Material from Fairy Tales." Unsurprisingly, he finds in dreamers' use of fairy-tale material more or less what he tends to find in most material: phallic symbols, vaginal symbols, references to father figures. But about halfway through, he suggests that "if we carefully observe from clear instances the way in which dreamers use fairy tales and the point at which they bring them in, we may perhaps also succeed in picking up some hints which will help in interpreting remaining obscurities in the fairy tales themselves" (1997, 104). The line between dream and fairy tale, personal unconscious and public narrative, had already begun to blur. Carl Jung would erase that line completely, arguing for the existence of a "collective unconscious," a set of archetypes and referents shared by all people and expressed in narratives such as myths and fairy tales. This justified analyzing fairy tales using the same mechanisms Freud brought to dream analysis, although Jung rejected Freud's focus on sexuality as the driving force for these dreams. Marie-Louise von Franz, an early Jungian analyst, wrote several volumes about fairy tales, employing the Freudian dream-mechanisms as part of her studies (see for example 1996).

Kidd argues persuasively that psychoanalysis and our understandings of fairy tales have been in continuous dialogue for over a century. Certainly both genres have long been focused on childhood; while the first edition of the Grimms' collection was originally meant for scholars, it proved so popular for children that all subsequent editions were re-edited with that readership in mind. And in an era where the "folk" and "primitive peoples" were often taken metaphorically and literally to be at the same stage of psychological development as White European children of allegedly "advanced" civilizations, it is easy to see how the equation between folktales and children would be made. As Kidd writes, "[Freud and his colleagues saw] parallels among primitive people, children, and young nations, likening folklore to children's 'researches' and to national legends" (2011, 4). Kidd goes on to note that fairy-tale analysis was also a route for the popularization of psychoanalysis, one that Freud and his colleagues took to both consciously and cannily.

Early childhood experience—the Oedipus complex, for example, in Freudian theory, and the mother-child relationship in object-relations theory—is considered formative for the developing psyche and personality in practically all fields of psychoanalytic thought. It is perhaps unsurprising, then, that psychoanalytic theorists also take fairy tales to be formative for the developing psyche and personality. This assumption, an essentially psychoanalytic one, that fairy tales are deeply influential on the child's developing psyche and thus on the adult continued to inform much criticism involving fairy tales in any number of debates. Just one example is the second-wave feminist discussion around the effects of fairy tales on girls' sense of self. Alison Lurie writes, "To prepare children for women's liberation, therefore, and to protect them against Future Shock, you had better buy at least one collection of fairy tales" (1970). Marcia R. Lieberman could not disagree more with Lurie's conclusion, but she accepts the premise that fairy tales shape the child's psychology:

> A close examination of the treatment of girls and women in fairy tales reveals certain patterns which are keenly interesting not only in themselves, but also as material which has undoubtedly played a major contribution [sic] in forming the sexual role concept of children. [. . .] Millions of women must surely have formed their psycho-sexual self-concepts [. . .] in part from their favorite fairy tales.
>
> (1972, 384–385)

Almost thirty years later, Jerilyn S. Fisher and Ellen S. Silber concur, writing that "no less truthful now than it was in 1979 is Karen Rowe's recognition that the potency of fairy-tale characterizations and plot in *forming the female psyche* is 'awesome'" (1998, 67; italics added). None of these writers adduces any evidence for this formative effect they all assume: it is self-evident from the intertwined genres of psychoanalysis and fairy tales.

No surprise, then, that the formative effect of fairy tales is assumed by both Bettelheim and Estés. Their books represent versions of Freud's and Jung's theories filtered through popular conceptions of fairy tales. They have many differences; Bettelheim elides and denies gender difference while Estés essentializes it; Bettelheim follows Freud while Estés follows Jung; Bettelheim uses fairy tales to explain the child's psyche while Estés uses stories to heal the woman's. But they share both the conviction that fairy tales serve a therapeutic purpose and a common mythology of psychoanalysis and the fairy tale.

The Uses of Enchantment was a blockbuster, an international bestseller that took over not only the academic world but also the popular imagination. It won the National Book Award and the National Book Critics Circle Award. In 1995, almost twenty years after its initial release, it made the New York Public Library's list of the 159 "most influential and frequently requested 'Books of the Century'" (1996). And it promotes a very particular approach to understanding fairy tales. Fairy tales, Bettelheim argues, are honed by generations of folk wisdom into vehicles for working out various childhood intrapsychic problems and complexes. Only by hearing the Grimms' tales over and over again can the child best work through such universal experiences and problems as heterosexual relations and psychological independence from parents, through "id pressures" and "ego and superego requirements" (1989, 6). In Bettelheim's words, "this book explicates why fairy tales make such great and positive psychological contributions to the child's inner growth" (12).

Bettelheim released this book when the propriety of fairy tales for children seemed under attack. Feminists such as Lieberman were finding in the genre the source of patriarchal roles for women, on the one hand, and on the other, a new round valorizing realism in children's and teen's literature was in play. *The Uses of Enchantment* was written to justify the importance of fairy tales, and it found a readership more than willing to listen. Despite his partisanship on the side of fairy tales, Bettelheim's book has received highly justified criticism from fairy-tale scholars and betrays a strange, self-contradictory understanding of the genre itself.

Bettelheim touts the importance of "the story in its original form," always a dicey proposition when it comes to fairy tales rooted in folklore, which have variants spanning assorted cultures and times (1989, 19). He seems to mean the Brothers Grimm versions, ignoring the extensive editing process their works underwent. Yet, at the same time, he speaks of the tales' effectiveness as therapeutic devices because of centuries of refinement (6). Despite this acknowledgment of tales' variability, Bettelheim goes on to ascribe universal psychological significance to precisely those elements that often change—the number of swan or raven brothers in a given story, for instance. He ignores any question of the historical context of a tale, thus eliding much of the fairy-tale scholarship he might have benefitted from. And he is so committed to seeing the tales as dramatizations of intrapsychic issues that he asserts quite without evidence that "the unrealistic nature of these tales [. . .] is an important device, because it makes obvious that the fairy tales' concern is not useful information about the external world, but the inner processes taking place in an individual," thus ignoring the newness of the realist mode in literature and storytelling (25). He cannot even contemplate the possibility that the abuses children suffer in fairy tales are meaningful specifically because children suffer such abuse in their lives. Just as Freud could not accept his patients' memories of having been raped by their fathers and so transposed their stories into the Oedipus complex, whereby the child wants and tries to seduce the parent of the opposite sex, so Bettelheim ascribes all the wickedness enacted by adult antagonists in fairy tales to children themselves.

These criticisms have been made by a long line of critics, including the most illustrious, such as Jack Zipes and Maria Tatar. Tatar eloquently notes that Bettelheim's book was and is popular because it "capture[s] more accurately than any other volume what our own culture has wanted to find in fairy tales" and that despite Bettelheim's proclaimed sympathy for and insight into children's psyches, his book is deeply partisan on the side of the adult and exonerates adults of all wrongdoing (1992, xvii). In other words, *The Uses of Enchantment* is deeply invested in blaming the child-reader for the wrongs done in the tale by adults. As an example, in his discussion of "Donkey Skin" (ATU 510B), a tale in which a king attempts to force his daughter to marry him, rather than seeing a story about incestuous abuse, Bettelheim sees the Oedipal fantasy of a young girl who desires her father (248). "Hansel and Gretel" (ATU 327A) may start out as a tale about starving children abandoned by their parents, but in Bettelheim's hands it becomes the story of children stuck in the oral stage and motivated by greed who need to learn self-control and psychological maturation (159–166).

This deficiency model of childhood, whereby children are defined by their disturbances and shortcomings as compared to an idealized version of adulthood, is a model heavily invested in the progressive hypothesis of Bettelheim's version of psychoanalysis, whereby the child must work through and resolve a variety of complexes and psychological challenges before arriving at an adulthood defined by its psychic wholeness and integration. This stroking of the adult ego, this model of adult perfection and childhood disarray (as opposed, for example, to the romantic notion of childhood as the idyllic state from which we adults have fallen), is part of Bettelheim's appeal, Tatar has argued; he tells us what we want to hear.

Estés is also convinced of fairy tales' therapeutic value. *Women Who Run With the Wolves: Myths and Stories of the Wild Woman Archetype*, published originally in 1992, was also wildly popular, spending 145 weeks on the *New York Times* bestseller lists. Whereas Bettelheim takes Freud as his model, Estés is a Jungian psychoanalyst, and her book presents itself as an effort to uncover, reconstruct, and reclaim a "natural" Wild Woman archetype in order to heal contemporary women's "flagging vitality" (1995, 1). Bettelheim sees in fairy tales stories in which gender matters not at all; for Estés, gender is the essence of self, an essence that can best be found in fairy tales and other traditional stories.

Estés explicitly marks herself as deviating from "traditional psychology," which she claims "too soon runs out for the creative, the gifted, the deep woman" and is "silent about deeper issues important to women" (1995, 4). But instead of acknowledging the vast amount of work that had been done by feminist psychoanalysts and clinicians as diverse as Nancy Chodorow (1974) and Luce Irigaray (1981), Estés conducts her own "psychic-archeological digs" into women's "natural, instinctive psyche" (1995, 1). Changing her metaphor from that of an archeological dig to that of a tracker trying to find a path in a forest, she claims that fairy tales, myths, and other such stories provide traces of that route, allowing contemporary women to reconnect with the archetype of the Wild Woman and so, she says, unraveling life's difficulties and challenges and resolving insecurities. Fairy tales not only provide a trace of the proper path, but also, in her view, can provide all the model a woman needs for her life: "Most times, we are able, over time, to find the guiding myth or fairy tale that contains all the instruction a woman needs for her current psychic development. These stories comprise a woman's soul drama" (13). Whereas Bettelheim saw fairy tales as tools for children's development, to be used and passed through, Estés sees finding a guiding fairy tale as a goal appropriate for an adult's psychological health. Like Bettelheim, Estés extols the virtues of "unvarnished, uncorrupted stories of eld [sic]"—but when extant stories do not fit her vision of what a story of old ought to be, she remakes them into that vision (14–15). She relies not on collectors of stories, but on her own sensibilities.

As noted prior, this book was wildly popular, and it clearly struck a chord with its contemporary female readership; despite its many differences from Bettelheim's work, the two share a resonant mythology of fairy tales and psychoanalysis, a mythology of universalization and naturalization, of fairy tales as therapy. The language is different. Estés often collapses the divine/mystical and the psychological. Bettelheim speaks of "universal human problems" while Estés refers to the "natural, instinctive psyche," but both dismiss the historical/cultural specificity of the various tales they employ in favor of an essential truth. For Estés, the Wild Woman archetype "is the prototypical woman [. . .] no matter what culture, no matter what era, no matter what politic, she does not change. Her cycles change, her symbolic representations change, but in essence, *she* does not change" (1995, 8). For Bettelheim, the Grimms' tales *are* the true tales, transcending any kind of historical context. Estés speaks of instincts (1) and Bettelheim of drives (1989, 101), but again, fairy tales and psychoanalysis intertwine in a universalized, naturalized therapy for a universalized, naturalized subject. Is this the secret of their popularity? Against a world in which multiple peoples are insisting on historical and cultural specificity, in which people of various races and cultural backgrounds are claiming the situatedness and provisionality of experience and knowledge, Bettelheim and Estés use psychoanalysis and fairy tales as shields that reassert the universal, transhistorical, transcultural human subject, thus comforting the dominant readership with the illusion of connection across time, space, and culture.

This mythology was also to be found in academic journals contemporaneous with Estés, as Richard P. Sugg's review of Jungian approaches to fairy tales and popular culture describes fairy tales as "genuinely naïve expressions of folk feeling, unaltered by the Media, Madison Avenue, or Market Research. [. . .] [I]f there ever will be a global village on this planet [. . .] the content of fairy tales might provide for its cross-cultural unity" (1990, 156). Bettelheim and Estés also both hold out the promise of perfectability: if a child can use fairy tales to successfully navigate maturation's psychological challenges, if a woman can only reconnect with the Wild Woman archetype, life's difficulties and insecurities will be smoothed away. This fantasy—we could call it the fantasy of "happily ever after"—is a powerful one.

If psychoanalysts have ascribed such power to the fairy tale that one would suggest them as the basis for global unity, the popularity that fairy tales have brought to psychoanalytic work may be one reason why psychoanalytic theory has made so much of fairy tales. But so have fairy tales made much of psychoanalytic theory. Elsewhere (Schanoes 2014), I analyze the relationship between feminist fairy-tale retellings and feminist psychoanalytic theory from the 1970s through the 1990s, finding that each genre addressed the same sets of concerns, using the same tropes, the mother-daughter relationship and the mirror. I argue that these texts must be read in relation to each other in order to understand the feminist projects they undertake. Nancy Chodorow's (1974) analysis of mother-daughter relationships, for example, as well as Luce Irigaray's (1981) multivalent use of the mirror in her writing, are poetically echoed and commented on in Tanith Lee's *White as Snow* (2001) and Angela Carter's *The Bloody Chamber* (2015). Vanessa Joosen (2011) has studied fairy-tale responses to *The Uses of Enchantment*, finding again and again writers and illustrators both adopting Bettelheim's work and taking issue with it. Fairy tales are thus not a passive modality to be exploited by psychoanalysts, but active participants in the construction of psychological discourse about them, and well able to employ that discourse in the service of telling and retelling their stories.

I turn next to two recent popular cinematic versions of fairy tales, 2012's *Snow White and the Huntsman* and 2014's *Maleficent*. Both were commercial successes, with the latter being the highest-grossing film Angelina Jolie has ever starred in, and both were pop-feminist retellings of fairy tales, the former retelling the Grimms' version of "Snow White" (ATU 709) and the latter retelling Disney's version of "Sleeping Beauty" (ATU 410) as the story of that movie's villainess.

Both movies seek psychological depth for their villainesses by reaching to their childhoods, much as do the earlier psychoanalytic assumptions linking fairy tales to personality formation. The wicked queen, here named Ravenna, remains the antagonist of *Snow White and the Huntsman*, but sympathy is created for her by a flashback to her childhood living in squalor and danger; her mother tells her that her beauty is her only "power and protection" and constructs a spell that will allow her to keep her beauty forever, provided she drains the life-force and youth of young women. The child is then ripped from her mother's arms by an invading army. This scene is paralleled with Snow White's creation when Queen Eleanor pricks her finger on a rosebush and three drops of red blood fall onto white snow, thus illustrating the famous beginning of the fairy tale when the queen is struck by the beauty of the blood on the snow; the spell cast on Queen Ravenna involves her mother letting fall three drops of blood onto milk. Thus the sympathy itself closely connects mothers and daughters, stepmother and stepdaughter, even while contrasting Ravenna's trauma and misery to Snow White's happy and privileged childhood, and, as I argue extensively in my book (Schanoes 2014, Chapters 1 and 2), that connection is one pivot on which contemporary feminist psychoanalytic theory turns.

Similarly, *Maleficent* opens with a prologue about the title character's childhood, which is happy but lonely until she meets Stefan, a young human boy from a neighboring kingdom. Maleficent, a fairy and guardian of the magical realms in which she lives, and Stefan become close, providing a psychological backstory to Maleficent's hatred for him. In order to win the throne of his kingdom, Stefan drugs Maleficent and cuts off her wings in a scene that Jolie and the writer, Linda Woolverton, as well as numerous critics, call a metaphor for rape (Holmes 2014). Thus Maleficent's hostility toward Stefan and his infant daughter is justified in the narrative by the same kind of formative experiences that push Ravenna to evil in *Snow White and the Huntsman*.

The resemblance does not end there. Maleficent's descent into evil is redeemed through her connection to Aurora, Stefan's daughter, the title character of Disney's *Sleeping Beauty*. She develops a maternal relationship with the young girl, and it is revealed that it is Maleficent, not Flora, Fauna, and Merriwether (the good if ineffectual fairies also from *Sleeping Beauty*), who preserves Aurora's life and health throughout childhood. She and the girl become closer as Aurora enters adolescence, a relationship that culminates in Maleficent waking Aurora from her sleep with a maternal kiss; Aurora restoring Maleficent's wings to her, which allows her to defeat Stefan once and for all; and Maleficent adopting Aurora as her heir. Both movies thus deepen sympathy for, and the psychology of, aggressive, hostile women by demonstrating their early traumas and emphasizing maternal and daughterly connections, two essential pieces of contemporary feminist psychological theory; both mother-daughter relationships and trauma theory play important roles in current psychological models of feminine subjectivity.

Other contemporary fairy-tale retellings, such as ABC's *Once Upon a Time* (2011–), make use of a major commonality between the fairy-tale form and Freudian theory: the family romance, or the fantasy that one's mother and/or father are not one's true parents. The series begins as the biological daughter of Snow White and Prince Charming, Emma Swan, is found by the young son she gave up for adoption and who is currently being raised by Snow White's evil stepmother. Thus the fairy-tale tradition of parental and stepparental malfeasance is maintained, as is the Freudian fantasy that one's "true" (biological) parents are far and away superior to those one is being raised by and that they will one day come to reclaim their child.

Psychoanalytic theory and fairy tales, as genres, have much in common. As Kidd notes, both involve the metamorphosis of an oral text into a literary one: the oral folktale to the written fairy tale, and the patient's oral discussion to the analyst's written analysis and case study (2011, 28). As currently constructed, they indulge many of the same fantasies and tropes: the family romance, the mother-daughter relationship, and the centrality of the child figure. It is no wonder, then, that Bettelheim's and Estés's books achieved such popularity. Indeed, one need only search for "fairy tale" in Amazon's self-help section to find a rich confluence of material—"fairy tale" has become code for "happily ever after," and readers are eager to find psychological pathways to achieving it.

References Cited and Further Reading

Bettelheim, Bruno. 1976. *The Uses of Enchantment: The Meaning and Importance of Fairy Tales*. New York: Vintage Books.

Carter, Angela. (1979) 2015. *The Bloody Chamber and Other Stories*. New York: Penguin Books.

Chodorow, Nancy. 1974. "Family Structure and Feminine Personality." In *Women, Culture, and Society*, edited by Michelle Zimbalist Rosaldo and Louise Lamphere, 43–66. Stanford, CA: Stanford UP.

Dundes, Alan. 2003. *Parsing through Customs: Essays by a Freudian Folklorist*. Madison: U Wisconsin P.

Estés, Clarissa Pinkola. (1992) 1995. *Women Who Run With the Wolves: Myths and Stories of the Wild Woman Archetype*. New York: Ballantine Books.

Fisher, Jerilyn S., and Ellen S. Silber. 1998. "Fairy Tales, Feminist Theory, and the Lives of Women and Girls." In *Analyzing the Different Voice: Feminist Psychological Theory and Literary Texts*, edited by Jerilyn S. Fisher and Ellen S. Silber, 67–95. Lanham, MD: Rowman & Littlefield.

Frazer, Sir James. 1890. *The Golden Bough: A Study in Comparative Religion*. New York: Macmillan and Co.

Freud, Sigmund. (1913) 1997. "The Occurrence in Dreams of Material from Fairy Tales." In *Writings on Art and Literature*, translated and edited by James Strachey, 101–8. Stanford, CA: Stanford UP.

Hines, Sara. 2010. "Collecting the Empire: Andrew Lang's Fairy Books (1889–1910)." *Marvels & Tales* 24 (1): 39–56.

Holmes, Sally. 2014. "Angelina Jolie Says Violent *Maleficent* Scene Is a Metaphor for Rape." *Elle*, June 12. www.elle.com/culture/celebrities/news/a15426/angelina-jolie-maleficent-scene-metaphor-for-rape/.

Irigaray, Luce. 1981. "And the One Does Not Stir Without the Other." Translated by Helene V. Wenzel. *Signs* 7: 60–7.

Joosen, Vanessa. 2011. *Critical and Creative Perspectives on Fairy Tales: An Intertextual Dialogue between Fairy-Tale Scholarship and Postmodern Retellings*. Detroit: Wayne State UP.

Kidd, Kenneth B. 2011. *Freud in Oz: At the Intersections of Psychoanalysis and Children's Literature*. Minneapolis: U Minnesota P.

Lee, Tanith. 2001. *White as Snow*. New York: Tor Books.

Lieberman, Marcia R. 1972. "'Some Day My Prince Will Come': Female Acculturation through the Fairy Tale." *College English* 34: 383–95.

Lurie, Alison. 1970. "Fairy Tale Liberation." *New York Review of Books*, December 17, N.p.

Naithani, Sadhana. 2010. *The Story-Time of the British Empire: Colonial and Postcolonial Folkloristics*. Jackson: U Mississippi P.

New York Public Library. 1996. "The New York Public Library's Books of the Century." *NYPL.org*. www.nypl.org/voices/print-publications/books-of-the-century.

Schanoes, Veronica. 2014. *Fairy Tales, Myth, and Psychoanalytic Theory: Feminism and Retelling the Tale*. Burlington VT: Ashgate P.

Sugg, Richard P. 1990. "Fairy Tales and Popular Culture: Some Jungian Approaches." *Journal of Evolutionary Psychology* 11: 156–62.

Tatar, Maria. 1992. *Off with Their Heads: Fairy Tales and the Culture of Childhood*. Princeton, NJ: Princeton UP.

von Franz, Marie-Louise. 1996. *The Interpretation of Fairy Tales*. Boston: Shambhala P.

Mediagraphy

Maleficent. 2014. Director Robert Stromberg. USA

Once Upon a Time: Season 1 (TV). 2011. Creators Adam Horowitz and Edward Kitsis. USA.

Sleeping Beauty. 1959. Director Clyde Geronomi. USA.

Snow White and the Huntsman. 2012. Director Rupert Sanders. USA.

6

MARXISM

Andrew Teverson

The *fairy tale* [. . .] designates revolt; [. . .] It is for all times a childlike
story of war about cunning and light against the mythical powers.
Ernst Bloch, quoted in Zipes (1988, xxxviii)

Everything that has ever been called folk art, has always reflected domination.
Theodor Adorno (1974, 204)

Marxist approaches to fairy tales, in common with all Marxist approaches to literary and cultural works, are conditioned by the overarching political objectives of the theoretical discipline:
its struggle to understand how material realities, in particular the social and economic, have
shaped culture's development in the past, and its determination to show how culture can contribute to, or retard, the attainment of Marxist political goals in the present and in the future.
As a tool of analysis, therefore, Marxist-influenced criticism of fairy tale has both retrospective
and anticipatory functions. It is retrospective to the extent that it looks back at the developing
canon of the fairy tale and asks, at each stage, how the genre has reflected, and in some cases
either contributed to or contested, the interests of the dominant classes;[1] it is anticipatory to the
extent that one of Marxist criticism's habitual enquiries concerns the usefulness, or otherwise,
of the fairy tale as a tool for facilitating resistance to alienating forms of social and political
domination and for precipitating unified action toward socially and economically progressive
change.

So much at least can be said for Marxist approaches to fairy tales in general; any further
account of the critical field must necessarily become more subtle, for there is little consensus
in Marxist criticism about the ideological perspectives that fairy tales have typically reinforced
or about the genre's value as a vehicle for encouraging revolutionary resistance to capitalist
alienation. Indeed, the history of Marxist criticism of the fairy tale has been characterized
more by disagreement than by accord. These divergences focus upon a set of critical problems
that I will explore in this chapter. They revolve around two central questions: whether or not
fairy tales may be regarded as forms that continue to express (or indeed have ever expressed)
the outlooks of the lower social orders; and whether these stances, if they do survive in fairy
tales, can be of any practical value in the process of securing Marxism's revolutionary goals.

From within the Marxist critical camp, some more affirmative assessments of the political value of traditional tales are offered by Walter Benjamin (1892–1940) and Ernst Bloch
(1885–1977). In his 1936 essay, "The Storyteller: Reflections on the Works of Nikolai Leskov,"
Benjamin makes the influential argument that the fairy tale as a narrative form mediates the

ancestrally communicated "counsel" (*Rat*) of the common people and can, therefore, assist humankind in its imaginative struggle against dehumanizing systems of power imposed from above (1999, 86, 101).[2] In Benjamin's now well-known formulation, the fairy tale characteristically expresses the "cunning" (*List*) and "high spirits" (*Übermut*) of the oppressed and powerless, and through representation of these forms of popular imaginative defiance, it teaches humankind how to resist the forces of the "mythical world" (101).

In a similar vein, Bloch, in "The Fairy Tale Moves on Its Own Time" ([1930] 1988) and "Better Castles in the Sky at the Country Fair and Circus, in Fairy Tales and Colportage" ([1954] 1988), presents the genre as, at source, a product of a rebellious and resistant popular culture that "does not allow itself to be fooled by the present owners of paradise" and so is capable of arousing hopes for social change that may become politically mobilizing (Bloch 1988, 169).[3] In the fairy tale, Bloch observes, "smart Hans [. . .] practices the art of not allowing himself to be intimidated. The power of the giant is painted as power with a hole in it through which the weak individual can crawl [. . .] triumphantly" (170).

These ideas have become familiar to readers of fairy-tale criticism in English as a result of the scholarship of Jack Zipes, who has translated Bloch's major writings on aesthetics from German (Bloch 1988) and provided commentaries on the work of both Bloch and Benjamin, notably in *Breaking the Magic Spell* (2002, 146–178) and *Happily Ever After* (1997, 129–142). Writing from the perspective of folklore as much as from Marxist theories, Zipes has expressed some reservations about the conceptions of folk and fairy tale employed by both Bloch and Benjamin. For instance, he criticizes Benjamin's assumption that storytelling is in decline in contemporary culture because the forms of communal engagement that supported and generated it have been eroded in the process of industrialization and urbanization. Arrayed against this assumption, Zipes suggests, is the "renascence of storytelling" in literature, film, television, and new media, as well as the widespread storytelling practices that remain current in diverse cultures throughout the world that Benjamin, as a European intellectual, was perhaps not familiar with (1997, 135). Zipes also has misgivings about the assumption made by both Benjamin and Bloch that because fairy tales "speak in the name of the common people" they are easily aligned with demands for greater social justice (1986, 240). Instead Zipes argues for a more nuanced historical understanding of the development and significance of the fairy tale; one that is attentive to the complex cultural evolution of the genre and that does not obscure the fact that some manifestations of popular narrative tradition, far from being socially progressive, can perpetuate "gender and racial stereotypes or [. . .] feudal notions of power" (2015, 193–194).

Despite his concerns, however, Zipes's own approach to fairy tales broadly speaking develops the line of thought established by Bloch and Benjamin in the 1930s and elaborated or modified by post-war German Marxist scholars such as Bernd Wollenweber, Dieter Richter, Johannes Merkel, and Jens Tismar.[4] In particular, Zipes derives from Bloch the argument that, although the fairy tale has been co-opted by a pervasive culture industry that seeks to appropriate popular aesthetic forms and use their utopian potential to advance the interests of capital, the form nevertheless retains a "germ" of its original capacity to express popular dissatisfaction with authority and so stimulate a demand for a different order of society (2002, 21). So pervasive has been the influence of Zipes's scholarship upon contemporary analysis of the fairy tale that this approach to the genre is now a common one, both in criticism and in various cultural "reutilizations" of fairy tales that seek to emphasize and recover their radical potential.[5]

The current popularity of this approach to fairy tales, however, should not obscure the innovative force, and theoretical urgency, of Bloch's ideas when they were first articulated between the 1930s and 1950s. When Bloch began writing, Marxist theory and political practice, broadly speaking, promoted realism as the most appropriate, and for some the only, viable literary and cultural means of showing things as they are and therefore of revealing how the world should and could be changed. Karl Marx and Friedrich Engels, as the founders of the theory, had themselves proposed that Marxist objectives were most effectively supported in literature through "truthfulness of depiction" combined with "a concrete historical approach to the events described and personages" (Krylov 1976, x), and in Bloch's own time, his friend and intellectual sparring partner, Georg Lukács, had argued that *avant-garde* forms of art such as Expressionism and Surrealism could not advance the Marxist cause because they failed to show "man in the whole range of his relations to the real world" (Adorno et al. 2007, 48).[6]

Bloch, along with Benjamin and Bertolt Brecht, were among the first Marxist thinkers to contest this viewpoint systematically by arguing that forms of representation that did not conform to conventional models of realism had the capacity to challenge and disrupt settled perceptions and so could serve an important role in the contestation of established (bourgeois) notions of what is real. Because they are not enslaved to established models of reality, the "unused dreams" of non-realist art, as Bloch expresses it in an essay on Marxism and poetry, are capable of expressing "reality plus the future within it" (1988, 162). The widely current notion today that fantastical narratives such as fairy tales may be used in literature to disrupt settled expectations about the real, and to promote speculation about what more just and egalitarian forms of social organization are possible, owes a great deal to such interventions in the Marxist debate about the political functions of art.[7]

These arguments, however, also invite a degree of critical skepticism. To what extent do the vague, and often highly selfish, instances of wish fulfillment found in the fairy tale really encourage proactive forms of political mobilization? Is it not more accurate—more intuitive— to describe fairy tales as escapist fictions that encourage a retreat from the struggles of reality? And is it naive of us to believe that fairy tales, even if they originate as articulations of imaginative resistance, can still express dissatisfaction with authority in the market-driven consumer economy that now mediates them? This more skeptical note is sounded in the work of Bloch's younger contemporary, the Marxist critic Theodor Adorno (1903–1969), who questions both the description of fairy tales as narrative forms that can be identified with historic resistance and the view that they, or indeed any form of mass culture, can have present significances outside the pervasive culture industry that now determines them.

These arguments are made in Adorno's short essay on fairy tales and films, "Wolf als Großmutter" ("Wolf as Grandmother"), published in his collection of aphorisms *Minima Moralia* in 1951, in which he rejects the notion, implicit in the work of Bloch and Benjamin, that the materials of folk culture maintain a relative autonomy from authoritarian determination. He argues, on the contrary, that fairy tales, like popular films, have come to serve the interests of the dominant classes by fortifying the dividing practices that authority uses to secure and perpetuate its hegemonic control.[8] This they have done in the past, according to Adorno, by using "lying stereotypes" to buttress an agrarian social structure that depended upon the polarization of masters and servants (although at the pre-capitalist stage traditional tales are "not yet encompassed by the total structure") (1974, 204).

In the present, moreover, "the barbaric cruelty" of the fairy tale "that divides the world into good and evil" operates as a blueprint for the modern film in which social relations have become "wholly objectified." Because they surreptitiously serve the cause of "socialization" (Adorno 1974, 204), furthermore, the capacity of these cinematic fairy tales to transport readers and viewers into a dream-like state becomes additionally pernicious: they are narratives that peddle dreams for profit while helping ensure that their dreamers remain in a state of political stupefaction. Thus Adorno concludes: "The fairy-tale dreams, appealing so eagerly to the child in man, are nothing other than regression organized by total enlightenment, and where they pat the onlooker most confidentially on the shoulder, they most thoroughly betray him" (206).

Zipes, in his recent study of the fairy tales of the Brothers Grimm, recognizes the force of many of Adorno's arguments. Bloch, he concedes, "placed much too much faith" in "commodified art to offer a glow of possible change" (2015, 194). Adorno, meanwhile, has good reason to argue that "many fairy tales" function to "divert audiences" from "enlightenment": for Zipes "[t]here is no light in the Disneylands spread across the globe, only darkness and banality" (194). In the final analysis, however, Zipes allies himself with the arguments of those who remain optimistic about the continuing political value of fairy tales as a genre, and he does so on the basis that the hopefulness expressed in fairy tales, however corrupt its applications have been, persists and remains capable of articulating a radical demand for change. In Zipes's words:

> Whether a fairy tale is progressive—illuminates contradictions in a fictitious realm and tendentiously sides with the oppressed—or regressive—reinforces conservative notions of the status quo by furthering elitist ideas of hegemony [. . .] the genre continually brings out what is missing in most people's lives. The constant repetition of the fairy tale maxims is not always and necessarily what Adorno asserted it to be, a banalization of utopia or homogenization of daily life, but rather represents a persistent refusal to accept life as it is and a demand that utopian longing be fulfilled.
>
> (2015, 194)

The key problem with this defense, however, is that it insists that utopias need have no contents in order to be politically enabling. In effect, Zipes argues that it does not matter what a utopian anticipation of a better life looks like in traditional tales, the mere fact of its being utopian is enough to make it politically viable; hence fairy tales *as a genre*, as opposed to fairy tales in individual manifestations, can be regarded as a positive political force. But how persuasive is this argument? Its problematic element is in evidence in Bloch's celebration of the utopian yearnings found in a story (he calls it a "dream fairy tale") by Rudyard Kipling called "The Brushwood Boy" (1895), in which the central character, a colonial official in South Asia, dreams of an India that is "the land of his wishes" (Bloch 1988, 177).

This dream manifests in the appearance of a woman, The Brushwood Girl, with whom the protagonist falls in love and claims as his own—an act of reconciliation with India that allows the lovers to "discover themselves as real and rediscover their India in a real love mysticism." The story, for Bloch, is thus about the enabling power of a "wish geography." What Bloch fails to observe in this analysis, however, is that the "wish dreams" (1988, 177) of Kipling's story are by no means politically innocent or egalitarian: they support the cause of European domination of India by projecting India as a legitimate space for the realization of the expansionist fantasies of Europeans. Europe's utopianism thus becomes India's nightmare of domination.

Of course, Zipes would also critique Kipling's imperialist fairy tale along these lines, but what, then, does it mean to say that the utopian impulse in fairy tales, or fictions deriving from fairy tales, can remain politically valuable, even if we disagree politically with the uses to which utopianism are being put? If the utopian dream itself has the function of securing repression—if one nation's utopian projection is another nation's enslavement—how can this utopianism be assimilated into demands for progressive social change? And what precisely can this kind of utopianism, directed as it is toward domination and oppression, tell us about the steps we ought to take to secure greater social justice in the world?

It is this lack of clarity about how the conceptualization of utopia contributes to activism, toward securing better social organization, that scholars critical of Bloch's and Zipes's form of

Marxism draw attention to. Boria Sax, for instance, in a long review of Zipes's translation of Grimms' tales, argues that the Marxism found in Zipes's work, "as in that of many contemporary Marxist thinkers," can only serve "as a means of understanding the past" because it fails to offer a coherent account of what a society of the future might look like or what the "mechanism" for achieving it might be (1990, 49).

José Limón, likewise, in a more substantial critique made in the course of an exchange with Zipes about Marxism and folklore in the *Journal of American Folklore*, expresses concerns about the level of historical generalization and imprecision involved in attributing an "inherently oppositional character" to the materials of tradition purely on the basis of their "association with precapitalist modes of production or with 'underdeveloped' sectors" (1983, 48). Instead Limón offers a more cautious formulation:

> We should carefully understand folklore as a conditional expressive repertoire of residual and emergent practices implicated in a not intrinsically benign social matrix. [. . .] Such an understanding would free folklore from its "decline" characterization in Western Marxism while not ignoring its vulnerable yet resistive character in the contemporary world.
>
> (1983, 48)

To illustrate the limitations of Marxist thinking that needs only an alleged utopianism to identify progressive political orientations in the genre, we might look to the uses made of the fairy tale as a motif in *Nervous Conditions* (1988) by the Zimbabwean writer Tsitsi Dangarembga. This novel concerns the development and education of a young black Rhodesian girl, Tambudzai, known as Tambu, who starts her life in a state of poverty and deprivation but gains a prestigious scholarship to a convent school as a result of missionary education granted to her by her wealthy uncle after the untimely death of her brother. Conditioned, through her education, to understand her experiences by reference to the European fictions that are celebrated in her uncle's house and in the Mission School, Tambu initially sees her progress away from poverty toward social establishment in terms of a Romance or a fairy tale. Like Cinderella, she has left behind the "smoky kitchen" (59) in which she has to sleep at home, been rescued by a "prince" (36), and at the end of the novel is poised for social success. This state, in Tambu's mind, constitutes her "reincarnation"—her rightful journey away from her peasant self and toward "another self, a clean, well-groomed, genteel self" (58).

Increasingly, however, the novel begins to trouble the assumptions in this Romantic paradigm. Tambu has pursued her own dreams of success, but once this attainment is grasped she begins to perceive that there is a hollowness to her fairy-tale ending: she is still a second-class citizen, segregated from her White contemporaries in a dormitory for (Black) Africans, because the broader social inequalities that determine her life remain in place. In pursuing her European Romance, moreover, she has accepted a Europeanized model of individualistic self-realization at the expense of a more collective solution to the problems of her brothers and sisters: she has changed her own condition, but she has done nothing to challenge social conditions more broadly. The fairy-tale dreams, in this respect, have not liberated her; rather they have contributed to her ongoing oppression by misdirecting her aspirations for change. They have also served the interests of a White patriarchal social order that uses education to neutralize threatening forms of collective resistance.

Suddenly in this scenario the contents of utopian dreams become very important: the private and self-orientated utopia of the Romantic European fairy tale has entrapped Tambu; it was, in a sense, the wrong dream for her to dream. A more enabling vision, she starts to realize, would have been one that harbored hopes, not just for herself, but for the transformation of the system that placed her, and others like her, in a position of permanent inferiority. It is Tambu's more politically astute cousin, Nyasha, a budding historical materialist, who sees the situation most clearly. Tambu, she observes, has read "too many fairy-tales" about her own centrality, and her own right to happiness, and is bound to be disillusioned and disappointed (94–95). Nyasha by contrast is "going through a historical phase" that involves reading books about "the condition in South Africa [. . .] about Nazis and Japanese and Hiroshima and Nagasaki." "She had nightmares about these things," Tambu recalls, "but she carried on reading all the same, because, she said, you had to know the facts if you were ever going to find the solutions" (94–95).

In light of such a representation, is it sustainable to argue that it doesn't matter what the utopian hope expressed in fairy tale is, so long as it is indeed utopian? Implicit in Dangarembga's *Nervous Conditions* is the notion that the very form of the hopes raised by European fairy tales are profoundly antithetical to collectivist politics. This apprehension seems to be reinforced by many prominent European traditions: Cinderella almost always dreams about the improvement of conditions for herself, not about social revolutions that will bring about the improvement of conditions for all young women in situations of domestic slavery and persecution. Such individualistic fantasies are also widely apparent in applications of fairy tale in the popular media.

Most of the films produced by Disney or influenced by him, and indeed many of the films that set out to satirize the cinematic conventions established by the corporation, uphold individualistic self-fulfillment as a social (more properly anti-social) ideal. Perhaps the most naked expression of this is to be found in the 1991 Disney film *Beauty and the Beast*, which opens with its protagonist, Belle, caroling her distrust for the "little town full of little people" in which she and her father have come to live and proceeds to describe a journey that removes her from the village and installs her in a mansion in which the "little people" (in the form of Mrs. Potts, Lumiere, and Cogsworth) are securely identified as her loyal servants and inferiors.

The film justifies this narrative trajectory in part by presenting both Belle and the Beast as outsiders who have been shunned by conventional society and who therefore have to find a place apart from the crowd. In this respect, the film might be said to offer a progressive moral about the need to tolerate difference and marginality. Its appeal to viewers, however, also rests upon the idea that each individual watching the film has the same quality of *difference from the crowd* that Belle and her Beast do; that we are all, in effect, outsiders from one another and that any endeavor to transcend this will lead in the direction of mindless conformism and mob rule.

Such representations, of course, are on one level a reflection of the political individualism of North America in the era of the first George Bush (president from 1989–1993), but they also emerge consistently from the narrative tradition upon which the film relies, that of the European fairy tale, in which happiness is identified with individual fulfillment rather than with communal well-being. For Zipes, as for Bloch, such uses of fairy tale entail a "banalization of utopia," a betrayal of the original radical impulses of the genre. But there is another point of view available: that the film of *Beauty and the Beast* expresses dominant trends in European fairy tales that can be traced back to their earliest articulations and that the very form of utopian hope that is expressed in them—for personal elevation at the expense of collective identification—is the one that survives in these commercial applications of the genre.

This is not to say that fairy tales have not been or cannot be used to further egalitarian political agendas. The film that Disney's *Beauty and the Beast* in part responds to, Jean Cocteau's masterpiece *La belle et la bête* (1946), is a profound anti-fascist parable that expresses guilt and remorse at France's complicity with the dehumanizing regime of the Nazis. Likewise, numerous works of literature use folk and fairy tales to project forms of social organization that are non-hierarchical and collective. The stories of Ethel Carnie Holdsworth, for instance, described by Patricia E. Johnson as fictions that "appropriate the fairy-tale genre for anti-capitalist and communitarian ideals" (2016, 252), reject the unearned privilege of hereditary rule ("The King's Fool"), promote the dignity of collective work ("Lazy-Land"), and satirize those forms of authority that depend upon social polarization and the demonization of difference ("Little Blue Cloak").[9] In a different vein, the short Shona-language films of Tsitsi Dangarembga *Kare Kare Zvako* (Mother's Day, 2004) and *Nyaminyami amaji abulozi* (Nyami Nyami and the Evil Eggs, 2011) respond to, and in some respects moderate, the argument about tradition offered in *Nervous Conditions* by using folk traditions as the basis for a visual critique of self-interested behavior and patriarchal authoritarianism.[10]

Kare Kare Zvako, for instance, adapts a Shona folktale to tell the story of a selfish man who conceals food from his family in time of famine and ultimately, in a grotesque embodiment of compulsive egotism, kills and devours his wife and corrupts his children by making them complicit in his cannibalism. The abused wife refuses this act of assimilation, first by singing to her children from within the body of the husband, and finally by emerging, fully formed and alive, from her husband's distended stomach. The film has been seen, variously, as a parable about political corruption (Oyinsan 2014, 402), as the expression of a woman's demand to be "written [. . .] into the national discourse" (Veit-Wild 2005, 137), and as a spectacular rejection of the victimization of women in patriarchal societies (Veit-Wild 2005, 136; Lee 2006).

What is perhaps most significant for our present purposes, however, is the fact that the films' libertarian objectives are articulated in sympathy with the folk narratives upon which the film is based, not in conflict with them as is the case in *Nervous Conditions*. This affirmation of the transformative power of storytelling is reinforced at the close of the film when the resurrected mother is shown telling the Shona folktale upon which it is based to her children, a tale that begins with the film's title, "kare kare zvako"—"long long ago." The performance of story-telling, Dangarembga is suggesting, and the capacity of stories to caution against self-interest and reinforce in the young a sense of communal responsibility, can be a powerful social and educational tool and, hence, a valuable political weapon.

In each of the aforementioned fictions and films, traditional narratives become a foundation for modern works that advocate resistance to illegitimate power and the transformation of existing social relations. The extent to which these radical applications of tradition derive their critical orientations from tradition, however, remains a matter for debate. According to the school of thought established in the work of Bloch and Benjamin and elaborated by Zipes, radical political applications of the genre take their lead from the historical tradition of the fairy tale and its ancient expressions of resistance to authority and hope for change. As this chapter has shown, however, there is an alternative approach to the historical legacy of the fairy tale that resists the assumption that the optimism of the genre is innately radical and proposes instead that the forms of hope it endorses can be self-interested, socially divisive, and easily conscripted to serve the cause of capitalist consumerism and imperialist domination. According to this latter school, the political transformation of the genre must depend, not upon acts of return and recovery, but upon the unprecedented innovation of revolutionary departure.

Notes

1. This materialist approach to the history of the fairy tale was pioneered by Vladimir Propp in his later writings. For analysis of the Marxist dimensions of Propp's thought see Liberman (1984, xliv–lii) and Zipes (1986, 240–241).
2. The German title is "Der Erzähler: Betrachtungen zum Werk Nikolai Lesskows."
3. Respectively, Bloch's German titles are "Das Märchen geht selber in der Zeit" and "Bessere Luftschlösser in Jahrmarkt und Zircus, in Märchen und Kolportage."

4. For Zipes's account of these latter influences, and of the ways in which these writers modify earlier Marxist approaches to fairy tale, see 1986, 239–240.

5. Zipes employs the concept of "reutilization" of fairy tales in a number of works. The word is his translation of the German term *umfunktioniert* used by Bloch (see Zipes 1988, xxviii).

6. Later in the same article, written in direct response to the arguments of Bloch, Lukács presents the "sturdy realism of folk art" and "the popular realistic literature of the German past" (Adorno et al. 2007, 55) as antidotes to the mutilation of cultural heritage practiced by *avant-garde* artists. Although he does not make the claim directly, this idea implies that he also regards the forms of popular fantasy celebrated by Bloch as modes of aesthetic expression that are not representative of "the life and history" of the "people" (54).

7. For an example of contemporary applications of this set of ideas see Merrifield (2007). "Magical Marxism," Merrifield maintains, "means creating another fantasy in light of the ruling fantasy; its critical power doesn't come from criticism but from an ability to disrupt and reinvent, to create desire and inspire hope" (18).

8. It is perhaps not entirely coincidental that *Minima Moralia* was published in the same year as Louis Snyder's essay "Nationalistic Aspects of the Grimm Brothers' Fairy Tales" in which the prevalence of the tales of the Brothers Grimm in German households is presented as one of the cultural roots of Nazism (1978, 35–51). Grimms' tales, because of their representations of cruelty, their frequent expressions of anti-Semitism, and their seeming endorsements of hierarchical social structures and hero cults, were widely regarded as proto-fascist fictions in the period immediately following WWII. It was not until West German Marxist scholars and writers began to re-evaluate the stories in the 1960s that consistent arguments emerged for their socially progressive potential.

9. These stories were published in the collection *Lazy Land and Other Delightful Stories* in 1911 under the name of Ethel Carnie (see Johnson 2015, N.p).

10. "Kare Kare Zvako" is the conventional opening formula for Shona folktales and translates literally as "a long time ago," though Dangarembga gave it the English title *Mother's Day*. It was first shown at the Harare International Film Festival in September 2004 but is generally credited as having been released for its showing at the Sundance Film Festival in 2005. *Kare Kare Zvako* is the first in a trilogy of short films including *Nyami Nyami and the Evil Eggs* and a third film yet to be made (see Veit-Wild 2005; Lee 2006).

References Cited and Further Reading

Adorno, Theodor. (1951) 1974. "Wolf as Grandmother." In *Minima Moralia: Reflections from Damaged Life*, translated by E. F. N. Jephcott, 203–6. London: NLB.

Adorno, Theodor, Walter Benjamin, Ernst Bloch, Bertolt Brecht, and Georg Lukács. 2007. *Aesthetics and Politics*. London: Verso.

Benjamin, Walter. (1968) 1999. *Illuminations*, translated by Harry Zohn, edited by Hannah Arendt. London: Pimlico.

Bloch, Ernst. 1988. *The Utopian Function of Art and Literature: Selected Essays*, translated by Jack Zipes and Frank Mecklenburg. Cambridge: MIT P.

Dangarembga, Tsitsi. (1988) 2004. *Nervous Conditions*. Banbury: Ayebia Clarke.

Holdsworth, Ethel Carnie. 1911. *Lazy Land and Other Delightful Stories*. London: Books for Bairns.

Johnson, Patricia E. 2016. "Ethel Carnie Holdsworth's New Fairy Tales for the Working Class." *Marvels & Tales* 30 (2): 251–267.

Krylov, B., ed. 1976. *Marx and Engels on Literature and Art*. Moscow: Progress Publishers.

Lee, Christopher J. 2006. "Desperately Seeking Tsitsi: A Conversation with Tsitsi Dangarembga." *The Power/Money/Sex Reader: Online Exhibition*. http://powermoneysex.org.za/desperately-seeking-tsitsi-graeme/.

Liberman, Anatoly. 1984. Introduction to *Theory and History of Folklore*, edited by Vladimir Propp, ix–lxxxi. Manchester: Manchester UP.

Limón, José E. 1983. "Western Marxism and Folklore: A Critical Introduction." *Journal of American Folklore* 96 (379): 34–52.

Merrifield, Andy. 2007. *Magical Marxism: Subversive Politics and the Imagination*. London: Pluto.

Oyinsan, Bunmi. 2014. "Orature as a Site for Civil Contestation: Film and the Decolonization of Space and Place in Tsisti Dangarembga's *Kare Kare Zvako* (*Mother's Day*) 2005." In *The Handbook of Civil Society in Africa*, edited by Ebenezer Obadare, 399–413. New York: Springer.

Sax, Boria. 1990. "A Marxist Perspective on Grimm." *Children's Literature Association Quarterly* 15 (3): 149–50.

Snyder, Louis L. 1978. *The Roots of German Nationalism*. Bloomington: Indiana UP.

Veit-Wild, Flora. 2005. "Tsitsi Dangarembga's Film *Kare Kare Zvako*: The Survival of the Butchered Woman." *Research in African Literatures* 36 (2): 132–8.

Zipes, Jack. 1986. "Marxists and the Illumination of Folk and Fairy Tales." In *Fairy Tales and Society: Illusion, Allusion and Paradigm*, edited by Ruth B. Bottigheimer, 237–43. Philadelphia: U Pennsylvania P.

———. 1988. "Introduction: Toward a Realization of Anticipatory Illumination." In Bloch, xi–xliii.

———. 1997. *Happily Ever After: Fairy Tales, Children and the Culture Industry.* New York: Routledge.

———. 2002. *Breaking the Magic Spell: Radical Theories of Folk and Fairy Tales.* Revised and Expanded. Lexington: UP Kentucky.

———. 2015. *Grimm Legacies: The Magic Spell of the Grimms' Folk and Fairy Tales.* Princeton, NJ: Princeton UP.

Mediagraphy

Beauty and the Beast. 1991. Directors Gary Trousdale and Kirk Wise. USA.

Kare Kare Zvako (Mother's Day). 2004. Director Tsitsi Dangarembga. Zimbabwe.

La belle et la bête. 1946. Director Jean Cocteau. France.

Nyaminyami amaji abulozi (Nyami Nyami and the Evil Eggs). 2011. Director Tsitsi Dangarembga. Zimbabwe.

7

PERFORMANCE

Patricia Sawin and Milbre Burch

Performance as an approach to the study of folk and fairy tales investigates what happens when someone tells a story orally to an immediately present audience. Performance theory encourages attention to storytelling as communication; to the teller's creative process, rhetorical goals, and means for achieving them; to the social and cultural context in which the story is told; to the effects of the story on the audience; to the audience's manifest and internal responses; and to the reciprocal efforts of the teller to anticipate, satisfy, and possibly transform the audience's expectations. A performance approach emphasizes that a story is more than words or text. A storytelling experience derives significance from the teller's vocal and bodily expression, from the interaction of tale elements with a particular context, and from the impact on an audience of a story well told.

Two main strands of folklore performance theory emerged starting in the 1970s: in one strand scholars studied performers rooted in specific cultures' tale-telling traditions; in the other artist/ scholars ventured into telling traditional tales themselves and discovered the power of performance through their own practice and audience reactions. Performance scholar/artist Dwight Conquergood characterizes the first approach as conforming to "the dominant way of knowing in the academy, [. . .] empirical observation and critical analysis from a distanced perspective," while the second is "grounded in active, intimate, hands-on participation and personal connection, [. . .] anchored in practice and circulated within the performance community" (2002, 146).

Formalist/Functionalist Performance Theory

Richard Bauman's *Verbal Art as Performance* (1977) grounds the first strand, drawing together scholarship from several disciplinary traditions and articulating a synthetic and cross-culturally applicable definition of art. This approach liberates folklore study from cultural chauvinism by identifying artistry in the performance interaction rather than in any culture-specific genre or set of aesthetic standards and challenges the assumption that artistic language is less true than plain or unmarked speech.

Along with folklorist Roger Abrahams (1968) and literary theorist Kenneth Burke (1969), who elaborated the idea of "literature as equipment for living," Bauman emphasizes a functional view of cultural expression, depicting storytelling as an act that accomplishes something for teller and listeners. Following sociolinguist Dell Hymes, he stresses that the communicative capacity of utterances in use depends upon discursive and metalingual elements beyond their grammatical or referential qualities (1981). Drawing on the work of sociologist Erving Goffman (1974) and anthropologist Gregory Bateson (1972), he highlights how framing marks a segment of discourse or interaction as having certain functions or meanings. For example, "once upon a time" alerts listeners to expect a fairy tale with attendant characters and action.

Following linguist and semiotician Roman Jakobson (1960), Bauman focuses on a formalist definition of poetics, arguing that artistry resides in the work's calling attention to its form in addition to its content. Artistry so conceived need not conform to notions of beauty or to particular stylistic canons. Bauman draws upon the ethnographic work of classicists Albert Lord (1960) and Milman Parry with Yugoslavian epic singers to recognize that gifted performers tailor their performances to their immediate audiences, who thus influence story text. Bauman also emphasizes Russian literary theorist M. M. Bakhtin's (1981, 1986) concept of the "dialogic" ways in which speakers envision multiple interlocutors, past, present, and future, and any utterance—of which a story text is one example—serves as a link in a chain of communication (Bauman and Briggs 1990).

Bauman's formalist and functionalist definition encourages analysts to consider what the storytelling experience does for teller and listeners, yet focuses attention on the formal features of the story itself and on the teller's manipulation of them. Several scholars have criticized or expanded his approach. Katharine Young's phenomenological approach emphasizes how listeners are moved out of their usual life space and transported into the "taleworld" by a well-told story. Reading and listening are experientially distinct because authors close the border between taleworld and ordinary reality while storytellers play back and forth across an open boundary (1987). Patricia Sawin critiques Bauman's lack of attention to the evocation of emotion (2002). Deborah Kapchan insists that performance is also participatory (engaging the audience's attention and energies), transformative (potentially moving audiences to new social and affective states), and appropriable (requiring interpretation, through which its meaning may be further transformed) (2003).

While fairy tales retain an aura of essential orality, only a few scholars captured or analyzed the tales as performances prior to the 1970s. Taking down tales by hand meant requiring tellers to dictate slowly or recording only the outlines of a story. Nineteenth-century collectors prized the tales as components of national or cultural patrimony, often regarding current tellers as mere conduits (Wilson 1973), and sought to render tales into versions effective on the printed page (Zipes 1987). From the late nineteenth through the mid-twentieth centuries, historic-geographic research focused on textual variation and attempts to trace transmission of tale variants. Resources like *The Types of the Folktale* (published by Antti Aarne in 1910 and expanded by Stith Thompson in 1961 and Hans-Jörg Uther in 2004) and Johannes Bolte and Georg Polívka's synopses of Grimm variants (1913–1932) promoted further comparative study.

Another strand of folktale research, however, explored the relationship between the individual and tradition. Walter Anderson articulated the law of self-correction, arguing that community response would check an individual teller's tendency toward innovation or error (1923), while Carl von Sydow emphasized the role of community taste in stabilizing local variations or *oikotypes* (1948). Mark Azadovskii analyzed the influence of personality, psychology, and gender on Natalia Vinokurova's storytelling (1974 [1926]). Gyula Ortutay fostered attention to the skills of individual tellers, an approach elaborated by Linda Dégh in *Folktales and Society* (1969).

Ironically, access to new compact recording technologies that enabled the capture of story performances coincided with social changes that diminished the telling of traditional fictional tales, often replacing them with mediated entertainment. The formally elaborated wonder tales proved more vulnerable than less performative conversational genres (Dégh 2001). Thus scholars produced extensive studies of traditional folktale performance in social and cultural context in the Bahamas (Crowley 1966), South Africa (Scheub 1998, analyzing stories he collected in the 1960s), Hungary (Dégh 1969), and in the islands of the Southwest Indian Ocean (Haring 2007), but relatively little on the most widely known European fairy tales. In *Folklore by the Fireside* Alessandro Falassi contextualizes recently collected verbatim texts with memories from his childhood, explaining that fairy tales were told during the first hour of the family *veglia* because they were beloved by children but also appealed to adults when shaped to allude to local social conflicts (1980).

Conversely, most scholarship that reveals the power of the formalist performance approach analyzes verbal artistry in informal conversational genres. Bauman uses the example of tall-tale teller Ed Bell to explicate the features a teller can deploy to produce longer and more elaborated tales for new audiences (1986). Kapchan shows how a Moroccan market woman negotiates her gender identity and authority by appropriating men's speech forms in her banter with customers (1996). Bauman and Sawin focus on reported speech, demonstrating respectively how a quoted punch line stabilizes tellings of a humorous anecdote (Bauman 1986) and how a marginalized teller establishes her social value by quoting authoritative speakers (Sawin 2004). Ray Cashman suggests how local character anecdotes told at wakes restabilize community values challenged by the loss of key members (2008).

Features and processes identified in conversational storytelling may have existed in the traditional performing of fairy tales, but extant texts rarely provide full evidence. The formalist performance approach may, however, help contemporary students of the folktale recognize that the efforts of earlier collectors and literary retellers (usually seen as flattening performance into text) can themselves profitably be regarded as a certain kind of performance. The Grimms, for example, were experts at intersemiotic translation, transmuting tales from one symbol system (oral telling, possibly in dialect) to another (written texts suitable for reading silently or out loud). Wilhelm Grimm's revisions for successive editions reveal his attention to the tastes and values of German readers and increasing awareness that "childlike" peasant tales were expected to inculcate middle-class values in actual child readers (Zipes 1983).

Hymes's study of the Clackamas Chinook "Seal and Her Younger Sister Lived There," published by Melville Jacobs in 1959, exemplifies the interpretive power of attention to details of implied performance. Hymes, focusing on the impertinent voice of the younger sister and the scolding voice of the elder, recognizes that this story described less a treacherous murder than how compliance with propriety (not mentioning that her uncle's supposed wife sounds like a man when s/he urinates) endangers families and communities (1981). Bauman recasts the work of Henry Rowe Schoolcraft, an early collector of Native American stories decried for his "heavy handed editing," arguing that "Schoolcraft's textual practice and framing rhetoric represent the very work of decontextualization and recontextualization by which folklore is carried from the interaction order to the national and international spheres" (1993, 251).

Indeed, this dimension of Bauman's theory suggests that any version of a fairy tale in film, television, novel, poetry, and so forth might profitably be regarded as a performance. How do the work's creator(s) deploy formal resources in light of (or to challenge and stretch) cultural standards of artistry, how is the product aimed at the tastes of a particular audience, and what rhetorical goals do the creators have in mind? Live oral performance crucially differs from mediated (written and visual) forms in that in the latter the "teller" is rarely present to perceive the audience's reception and must rely upon similarly mediated and delayed report or communication of what the audience liked and didn't like. Thus the creators of mediated works usually cannot respond in the course of the performance but only in subsequent works, with the possible exception of serialized creations like serial novels and contemporary long-arc television series with their accompanying websites, Facebook pages, and fan Wikis (see Hay and Baxter 2014 on fan involvement in ABC's *Once Upon a Time* [2011–] and Barndollar and Schorn 2002, 159 on Dickens's celebrated practice of shaping later portions of his serial novels in response to audience reaction).

Contemporary tellers of folk and fairy tales and scholars who participate in the festival-based storytelling revival have thus been best able (through practice, performance, and participation) to recognize and document the influence of performed fairy tales on physically present audiences.

Fairy-Tale Performance Through a Teller/Listener's Lens

In *Teaching Oral Traditions* John Miles Foley reminds us:

> If we superimpose the history of our species on an annual calendar, the advent of writing occurs only in the month of December. [. . .] [The oral tradition has] served as the exclusive vehicle for verbal art through the first eleven months of our "species year" and [. . .] remains the principal channel for artistic discourse for most of the world's inhabitants.
>
> (1998, 2–3)

On this same calendar, then, electronic communication arrived on December 31 at 11:59:59 pm. Print publications have enjoyed a privileged place in Western civilization for 500 years. Digital media's evolving platforms and ever-changing tools will likely have a good long run in human communication. But even within a culture that is shifting its media consumption from page to screen, and continuously preferring fixed forms over face-to-face communication, oral storytelling endures as a disruptive technology. Fairy tales in performance are especially potent vehicles for disruption.

Oral storytelling's emergent nature and the interactive teller-listener relationship provide much of verbal art's power to disrupt expectations, to engage listeners, to alter understanding, to embody the im/possible, and to linger in memory. In an organized storytelling event, the lights stay up, theater's fourth wall is dismissed, and the teller addresses the audience straight on, responding to the acuity of the listeners and the nuances of the setting. Marie-Laure Ryan writes: "Since face-to-face interaction constantly renegotiates the role of the participants, every listener is, at least in principle, a potential storyteller" (2004, 41). Indeed, from the storyteller's point of view, the listener's verbal or nonverbal response is fully half of a co-creative conversation; it is the story's embodied echo told back to the teller. More than that, Laura Simms argues:

> A story [. . .] is lived between teller and listener. [. . .] The text alone, separated from the enlivened experience, can be analyzed, but the result is different. It is not a transformative event [. . .]. The meaning and the power of the story do not reside in the content alone; rather, they unfold in the dynamic process of listening/creating.
>
> (2011, 52)

Therefore, Simms concludes, storytelling "is not a solo performance. The narrative urges the listener out of self-consciousness and into the story. As the imaginative response becomes more and more vivid, the listeners participate in a heightened awareness of the event, as in ritual" (2011, 52). Both the dynamic process of listening/creating and the heightened awareness created in the oral telling of fairy tales require interrogation.

William Bernard McCarthy and Ruth Stotter provide a context for this study, reminding us: "A quiet revival in storytelling has been going on in the United States for at least half a century, but during the 1980s the revival produced an explosion of professional storytellers and storytelling festivals" (1994, 153). Revivalist storytellers—also called platform, professional, nontraditional, and neotraditional tellers—often build their repertoire from original and published sources rather than from stories learned within an oral community setting. McCarthy and Stotter explain: "Professional and nontraditional tellers assume complete autonomy in story selection and delivery style, limited only by their experiences, imagination, and availability of audiences willing to provide performance opportunities." They conclude, "In a revivalist storytelling context as in a traditional context [. . .] the experience of an audience listening to a narrator remains remarkably consistent" (155). The emergent quality, the listening/creating interactivity, and the heightened awareness are consistently present in storytelling revival events.

Winnipeg-based storyteller and folklorist Kay Stone has written prolifically about the North American storytelling revival (1986, 1993, 1998, among others) with particular regard to fairy-tale performance. Bearing witness to the emergent and interactive elements within revival storytelling performances, she writes: "Many urban storytellers [. . .] have developed an understanding of the creative dynamics of oral composition. They do not merely repeat tales, they re-create them at each performance" (1993, 250). Stone continues, "The *Märchen* seems to have returned to a full existence in adult audiences who respond positively to the transformational and cathartic powers of this sort of narrative" (251). Next she references the heightened awareness mentioned earlier: "Wondertales [sic] offer a way of deepening reality rather than escaping from it; disbelief is transformed rather than simply suspended" (243). Of the conjuring of this deepened reality, she concludes, "Narrating as an oral, face-to-face event is a powerful and immediate experience [. . .]. In some cases the actual experience can put listeners into a state of trance in which they are so caught up in the story that teller and tale disappear as external realities" (248).

Simms comes close to capturing the liminality of the trance when she writes, "Many contemporary researchers believe, as do all traditional peoples, that the realm of dreaming is not limited to sleep [. . .]. Every time a story is told and heard, the channel to the realm of dreams is opened and the dreamer within is summoned" (2011, 18). And she asserts: "The secret of the power of story is the essential realization that what happens to the character in the story is not important. What is of value is what happens to we who listen" (2011, 55). Stone agrees, "The old *Märchen* (and other types of tales) have offered direct and indirect models for a personal, face-to-face artistic exchange that has the potential for simultaneously transforming tellers, tales, and listeners" (1993, 266–267). She also contends:

> The wondertales offer a path into the woods of inner vision and creativity; one returns to the external world with new wisdom and new vision, paralleling the journey of the protagonist of a folktale. The wedding feast that concludes so many of the wondertales symbolically marks this union of inner and outer realities.
>
> (1998, 250)

This union begins when a storyteller finds a traditional narrative that enables her to speak in the authentic voice of her knowing about the world. Thus even a fairy tale in a storyteller's repertoire can be read as a kind of auto/biographical performance piece. As tellers or listeners, we may go back to the same story at different stages of our lives because we find new nourishment each time we drink of that particular well. The emergent nature of oral storytelling allows for the performance of a story to develop and grow in repeated tellings and listenings.

But the story that captures one listener may lull another into slumber. Why? For every tale told, there are at least as many versions heard as there are individuals in the audience. Each listener has a mental and emotional "screen"—woven of gender, age, race, ethnicity, interest in a given genre, language fluency, personal experience, individual and family biases, cultural beliefs, religion, and so on—through which the story images and narrative must pass. Through this screen, some stories pass deeply and unforgettably into the mind of the listener, while others are barely admitted entry and dwell on the doorstep of fading memory. The listener's readiness and willingness to be entranced by a particular tale or telling are keys to experiencing the dual realities of a storytelling trance. Ryan writes: "Through narrative we [. . .] explore alternate realities and expand our mental horizon beyond the physical, actual world—toward the worlds of dreams, phantasms, fantasy, possibilities, and counterfactuality" (2004, 2–3).

Before there were formal studies of the storytelling-event-induced trance state, storyteller Fran Stallings wrote about it (1988), drawing on research in psychology, hypnotherapy, education, and medicine, as well as on anecdotal evidence. She notes: "Psychologists studying the traits of highly hypnotizable subjects found high capacity for deep absorption, expanded responsiveness and awareness, greater childhood involvement in reading and fantasy play, and high levels of imagination and creativity. They sound like an ideal storytelling audience" (1988, 7).

Stallings examines the contributions of the teller, listener, tale, and context of any storytelling event—as well as aspects of a tale's delivery—to try to identify elements conducive to the trance. She remarks, "Not all stories have equal hypnotic power [. . .] but it seems that emotionally meaningful story *content* may help to focus our concentration inward [. . .] [and] 'Magic' plays an important part in many of our entrancing stories" (1988, 7). Like a hypnotherapist, the fairy-tale teller often begins with a paradoxical opening statement (for instance, "once there was and was not") and closes with a tagline meant to return the listener to the external reality of the everyday world (for example, "snip, snap, snout, this tale is out"). Stallings concludes, "Trance is an intense, actively focused attention state. Everything the teller does to hold our attention and focus it inward will help spin the web of silence" (18), but also notes: "It is very likely we listeners [. . .] entrance ourselves" (16). In later work, she argues succinctly: "Trance is a skill of the listener" (1993, 10).

Stallings notes that the return of our attention to the real world from this altered state takes the listener through liminal territory in ways not well served by a quick exit, a jump into discussion, or a mood-changing joke. "When a story has been especially powerful, many tellers are reluctant to jolt listeners with an abrupt shift" (1988, 8). Of this transition, she quotes storyteller Finley Stewart, "This kind of story leaves people quiet [. . .]. They don't want to come out" (1988, 8).

In further examining the impact of stories on listeners, Stallings asserts that "a story not only makes sense to us. It makes us care" (1988, 9). Another participant-observer of the American storytelling revival community, Kendall Haven, explicates why told stories make sense to us and why they make us care. He surveys the findings of prominent cognitive scientists and developmental psychologists and concludes: "Human minds do rely on stories and on story architecture as the primary roadmap for understanding, making sense of, remembering, and planning our lives—as well as the countless experiences and narratives we encounter along the way" (2007, vii). He goes on to state: "Evolutionary biologists confirm that 100,000 years of reliance on stories have evolutionarily hardwired a predisposition into human brains to think in story terms. We are programmed to prefer stories and to think in story structures" (2007, 4).

Within his research on the impact of told stories on listeners Haven attempts to identify the elements of an effective story. He created test stories with variations that would "isolate and shift individual elements or combinations of those elements" (2014, 66); then he told the different versions to different audiences and used brain activity scans to measure the effect of the alterations on the listeners. Haven concluded that an effective story has eight essential elements, identified in bold:

> A **character** that is of **interest** to the intended audience has a **goal** that is both important to that character (**motive**) and relevant to the audience. However, reaching that goal is blocked by [. . .] **problems and conflicts** that create real **risk and danger** for the main character. Still, this main character **struggles** [. . .] to achieve that important goal. This story must, then, be presented in sufficient relevant **detail** to make it seem real, vivid, and compelling.
>
> (2014, 67)

These elements are found in any tale with a dramatic arc—that is, those that start with exposition and move through rising action, climax, falling action, and denouement—but the constellation is particularly true for fairy tales from Western cultures.

Haven also found that the main character's motive was the key element for evoking empathy and identification on the part of the listener, writing that he "could induce an audience to either identify with a story character or to reject her and treat her as the story antagonist by shifting only a few bits of character motive information" (2014, 85). This is exactly the technique that contemporary fantasy and fairy tale writers have used in crafting feminist fairy tale revisions. So, through contemporary brain research, Aristotle's theories—long applied to dramatic literature—are confirmed to be true of told stories as well. Dramatic narratives engage the listener's sense of empathy. But how does it work exactly?

Neuroscientist Paul Zak has quantified the ways in which dramatic narratives change our brain chemistry and potentially influence our behavior. In a series of experiments, Zak studied brain imaging, the physiological changes (in respiration, heart rate, skin conductivity, etc.) and emotional changes (from interest to anxiety to empathy) experienced, and confirms that the listener's brain releases certain chemicals in response to the unfolding events in a story. The first of these chemicals—cortisol—registers the listener's distress concerning the plight of the protagonist. The second—oxytocin—floods the brain with a feeling of empathy for, identification with, and attachment to the characters. He concludes:

> Stories are powerful because they transport us into other people's worlds. But in doing that, they change the way our brains work, and potentially change our brain chemistry. And that's what it means to be a social creature: to care about others, to connect with others, even complete strangers, and [. . .] dramatic stories cause us to do that [. . .] they uplift us and we feel connected to others around us.
>
> (2012)

In fact, listening together—that is, witnessing characters taking risks and overcoming their struggles in a story world—may also result in a sense of fellow-feeling with others in the audience. So oral narratives with a dramatic arc can connect us (1) with the story's protagonist, (2) with others in the same audience, and (3) with others in the world beyond the parameters of a storytelling event. That is a powerful effect in a world of divisive, competing, and often fractured narratives.

Oral stories have the power to enter listeners' consciousness and linger there, mixing with other remembered narratives, and often moving listeners to action. In a survey of studies on the brain's processing of narrative, Heather Forest concludes:

Oral stories are a powerful and complex form of metaphor [. . .]. By offering listeners an imaginative virtual experience, stories can, as metaphor, link abstract ideas presented in the form of a plot, to concrete embodied experience and contribute to learning. Listeners can gain wisdom from stories through vicarious experience. At the neurological level, *imagined* stories are stored in the spatial memory center of the brain where *actual* lived experience is also stored.

(2007, 34)

Thus we may draw from the entire storehouse of observations—based on the remembered and imagined playing-out of choices and consequences—within the brain's narrative treasury. We may examine the lessons contained in any tale regardless of its provenance and apply their logic and their wisdom to our everyday lives. Accessing an array of stories can enrich us beyond the limitations of one culture or one lifetime by widening our arc of understanding and impacting our consciousness, our emotions, our physiology, and our behavior. For, as Simms has already reminded us, "What happens to the character in the story is not important. What is of value is what happens to we who listen" (2011, 55).

References Cited and Further Reading

Aarne, Antti. 1910. "Verzeichnis der Märchentypen." *Folklore Fellows Communications* (3).

Abrahams, Roger D. 1968. "Introductory Remarks to a Rhetorical Theory of Folklore." *Journal of American Folklore* 81: 143–8.

Anderson, Walter. 1923. *Kaiser und Abt: die Geschichte eines Schwanks*. Helsinki: Academia Scientiarum Fennica.

Azadovskii, Mark. (1926) 1974. *A Siberian Tale Teller*, translated by James R. Dow. Austin: U Texas P.

Bakhtin, Mikhail M. 1981. *The Dialogic Imagination*, translated by Caryl Emerson and Michael Holquist, edited by Michael Holquist. Austin: U Texas P.

———. 1986. "Problems of Speech Genres." In *Speech Genres and Other Late Essays*, translated by Vern W. McGee, edited by Caryl Emerson and Michael Holquist, 60–102. Austin: U Texas P.

Barndollar, David, and Susan Schorn. 2002. "Revisiting the Serial Format of Dickens's Novels: Or, *Little Dorrit* Goes a Long Way." In *Functions of Victorian Culture at the Present Time*, edited by Christine Kruger, 155–68. Athens: Ohio UP.

Bateson, Gregory. 1972. *Steps to an Ecology of Mind*. New York: Ballantine.

Bauman, Richard. 1977. *Verbal Art as Performance*. Rowley, MA: Newbury House.

———. 1986. *Story, Performance, and Event: Contextual Studies of Oral Narrative*. Cambridge: Cambridge UP.

———. 1993. "The Nationalization and Internationalization of Folklore: The Case of Schoolcraft's 'Gitshee Gauzinee'." *Western Folklore* 52 (2/4): 247–69.

Bauman, Richard, and Charles L. Briggs. 1990. "Poetics and Performance as Critical Perspectives on Language and Social Life." *Annual Review of Anthropology* 19: 59–88.

Bolte, Johannes, and George Polívka. 1913–1932. *Anmerkungen zu den Kinder- und hausmärchen der brüder Grimm*. Leipzig: Dieterich'sche Verlagsbuchhandlung.

Burke, Kenneth. 1969. *A Rhetoric of Motives*. Berkeley: U California P.

Caine, Renate N., and Geoffrey Caine. 1991. *Making Connections: Teaching and the Human Brain*. Alexandria, VA: Association for Supervision and Curriculum Development.

Cashman, Ray. 2008. *Storytelling on the Northern Irish Border: Characters and Community*. Bloomington: Indiana UP.

Conquergood, Dwight. 2002. "Performance Studies: Intervention and Radical Research." *The Drama Review* 46 (2): 145–56.

Crowley, Daniel J. 1966. *I Could Talk Old-Story Good: Creativity in Bahamian Folklore*. Berkeley: U California P.

Dégh, Linda. 1969. *Folktales and Society: Story-Telling in a Hungarian Peasant Community*. Bloomington: Indiana UP.

———. 2001. *Legend and Belief: Dialectics of a Folklore Genre*. Bloomington: Indiana UP.

Falassi, Alessandro. 1980. *Folklore by the Fireside: Text and Context of the Tuscan Veglia*. Austin: U Texas P.

Foley, John Miles. 1998. "Introduction: An Audience for Oral Traditions." In *Teaching Oral Traditions*, edited by John Miles Foley, 1–9. New York: Modern Language Association.

Forest, Heather. 2007. "The Inside Story: An Arts-Based Exploration of the Creative Process of the Storyteller as Leader," unpublished dissertation, Antioch University.

Goffman, Erving. 1974. *Frame Analysis: An Essay on the Organization of Experience.* New York: Harper Colophon.

Haring, Lee. 2007. *Stars and Keys: Folktales and Creolization in the Indian Ocean.* Bloomington: Indiana UP.

Haven, Kendall. 2007. *Story Proof: The Science behind the Startling Power of Story.* Westport, CT: Libraries Unlimited.

———. 2014. *Story Smart: Using the Science of Story to Persuade, Influence, Inspire, and Teach.* Santa Barbara, CA: Libraries Unlimited.

Hay, Rebecca, and Christa Baxter. 2014. "Happily Never After: The Commodification and Critique in ABC's *Once Upon a Time.*" In *Channeling Wonder: Fairy Tales on Television,* edited by Pauline Greenhill and Jill Terry Rudy, 316–35. Detroit: Wayne State UP.

Hymes, Dell. 1981. *'In Vain I Tried to Tell You': Essays in Native American Ethnopoetics.* Philadelphia: U Pennsylvania P.

Jakobson, Roman. 1960. "Closing Statement: Linguistics and Poetics." In *Style in Language,* edited by Thomas A. Sebeok, 350–77. Cambridge: MIT P.

Kapchan, Deborah. 1996. *Gender on the Market: Moroccan Women and the Revoicing of Tradition.* Philadelphia: U Pennsylvania P.

———. 2003. "Performance." In *Eight Words for the Study of Expressive Culture,* edited by Burt Feintuch, 121–45. Urbana: U Illinois P.

Lord, Albert B. 1960. *The Singer of Tales.* Cambridge, MA: Harvard UP.

McCarthy, William, and Ruth Stotter. 1994. "The Tellers and the Tales: Revivalist Storytelling." In *Jack in Two Worlds: Contemporary North American Tales and Their Tellers,* edited by William McCarthy, 153–67. Chapel Hill: U North Carolina P.

Ryan, Marie-Laure. 2004. *Narrative across Media: The Languages of Storytelling.* Lincoln: U Nebraska P.

Sawin, Patricia E. 2002. "Performance at the Nexus of Gender, Power, and Desire." *Journal of American Folklore* 115 (455): 28–61.

———. 2004. *Listening for a Life: A Dialogic Ethnography of Bessie Eldreth through Her Songs and Stories.* Logan: Utah State UP.

Scheub, Harold. 1998. *Story.* Madison: U Wisconsin P.

Simms, Laura. 2011. *Our Secret Territory: The Essence of Storytelling.* Boulder: Sentient Publications.

Stallings, Fran. 1988. "The Web of Silence: Storytelling's Power to Hypnotize." *National Storytelling Journal* 5 (2): 6–19.

———. 1993. "Journey into Darkness: The Story-Listening Trance." www.franstallings.com/pmwiki/uploads/Fran/Journey.pdf.

Stone, Kay. 1986. "Oral Narration in Contemporary North America." In *Fairy Tales and Society: Illusion, Allusion, and Paradigm,* edited by Ruth B. Bottigheimer, 13–31. Philadelphia: U Pennsylvania P.

———. 1993. "Once Upon a Time Today: Grimms Tales for Contemporary Performers." In *The Reception of Grimms' Fairy Tales: Responses, Reactions, Revisions,* edited by Donald Haase, 250–68. Detroit: Wayne State UP.

———. 1998. *Burning Brightly: New Light on Old Tales Told Today.* Peterborough, ON: Broadview P.

Sydow, Carl Wilhelm von. 1948. "Geography and Folktale Oikotypes." In *Selected Papers on Folklore,* 44–59. Copenhagen: Rosenkilde and Bagger.

Thompson, Stith. 1961. *The Types of the Folktale: A Classification and Bibliography, Antti Aarne's Verzeichnis der Märchentypen, Folklore Fellows Communications No. 3, Translated and Enlarged.* Helsinki: Academia Scientarum Fennica.

Uther, Hans-Jörg. 2004. *The Types of International Folktales: A Classification and Bibliography, Based on the System of Antti Aarne and Stith Thompson.* Helsinki: Academia Scientiarum Fennica.

Wilson, William A. 1973. "Herder, Folklore, and Romantic Nationalism." *Journal of Popular Culture* 6 (4): 819–35.

Young, Katharine Galloway. 1987. *Taleworlds and Storyrealms: The Phenomenology of Narrative.* Boston: Kluwer Academic Publishers.

Zipes, Jack. 1983. *Fairy Tales and the Art of Subversion: The Classical Genre for Children and the Process of Civilization.* New York: Wildman P.

———. 1987. *The Complete Fairy Tales of the Brothers Grimm.* New York: Bantam.

Mediagraphy

Once Upon a Time (TV). 2011–. Creators Adam Horowitz and Edward Kitsis. USA.

Zak, Paul. 2012. "Empathy, Neurochemistry and the Dramatic Arc: Paul Zak at the Future of Storytelling 2012." *YouTube,* October 3. www.youtube.com/watch?v=q1a7tiA1Qzo.

8
FEMINISM

Allison Craven

Fairy tale has proliferated in media forms since the advent of cinema and television and in multiple earlier technologies and performance modes (see Greenhill and Rudy 2014, 3 4). The coverage here of some feature-length animation and live-action motion pictures, and long-arc seasonal television series produced by major studios for transnational distribution, is but a slim selection of the range of "fairy tale films" (Greenhill and Matrix 2010) and fairy-tale phenomena in network and cable television (see Greenhill and Rudy 2014). It glosses, too, the convergent online extensions of fantasy worlds (Hay and Baxter 2014) and the myriad new species of fairy-tale forms uploaded and streamed on the Internet. These range from the hypercondensed adaptations in short films and music videos, to the plethora of fairy-tale paratexts in fan mash-ups and folk-feminist appropriations of fairy tale, uploaded on YouTube and social media, in artful dodges of copyrights, or interactively, and legally, devised for private immersion through packaged apps from iTunes.

The diversity emerges from the technology paradigm shift from analog broadcast systems to the niche and mass digital and online media that has been underway since the 1980s. If a term of enchantment might be applied, then transformation, that magical and marvelous element of fairy tale, suggests the scale of the resulting changes in media forms as well as frameworks of production, distribution, and consumption. This transformed media sphere is often termed synonymous with the globalized culture of postmodernity, in which the ubiquity of media and the aesthetic postmodernization of their produce blends almost seamlessly with social reality.

The period of change corresponds to that since the second wave of feminism, which extended roughly from the 1960s to the 1980s. A third wave, emerging in the early 1990s, is sometimes seen as a shift from modern to postmodern feminist epistemologies. But the enchanted metaphor of transformation does not so readily apply, and the model of waves of feminism is contentious. It assumes linearity and elides the complex and situated nature of feminist knowledge. Formulations of intersectional theory might more characterize the range of cultural, queer, and transgender perspectives that diversely constitute contemporary feminist critiques of power.[1] Second and third wave, nevertheless, remain prevalent terms in critical commentary on fairy-tale media. I use these terms advisedly to highlight some correspondence with the media paradigm shift. The feminist gaze on fairy tale, stemming from the second wave, is canvassed in the following, as well as crosscurrents in third-wave approaches to media and culture. Then the frame is tilted toward the postmodern cultures of contemporary media industries with the problem of resident giants in the global media landscape, especially Walt Disney Studios, regarded in terms of the fluctuating critical feminist reception of their productions.

ALLISON CRAVEN

Looking for Fairy Tale in Feminist Media Analysis

A debate in the 1970s, in which Alison Lurie (1970) argued for the empowering potential of little-known fairy tales and Marcia Lieberman ([1972] 1993) responded by protesting
the patriarchal stereotypes of women in fairy tales, is now much cited as an opening to the
second-wave feminist critique of fairy tale. This debate, along with other second-wave commentary on the assumed misogyny of fairy tales (such as that of Daly 1978; Brownmiller 1976;
Dworkin 1974), is posed by Donald Haase (2004) as evidence that "feminist scholarship and
modern fairy-tale studies emerged in tandem during the early 1970s" (31). While this claim
is debatable, it has gained a degree of acceptance. Lieberman's essay, in particular, has become
a touchstone for its account of stereotyping passive fairy-tale heroines and the paradigm of
the "beauty contest" in many tales (1993, 187). Vanessa Joosen (2011) discusses Lieberman's
essay, and the analysis of "Snow White" in *The Madwoman in the Attic* (Gilbert and Gubar
1979), which Joosen suggests is now canonical in both feminism and fairy-tale studies (215),
as the bases of "dialogical" intertextual networks of fairy-tale retellings and criticism. Equally
influential is Angela Carter's literature of fairy-tale retellings, including the nigh-canonical
The Bloody Chamber (1979), and she is recognized as having generational influences on both
feminist and more general approaches to fairy tale (Benson 2008).

The aforementioned works are not directly associated with what is known as feminist
media criticism in the same period, nor was it so attentive to fairy tale. This praxis was more
concerned with the technology of media, particularly film, and scrutiny of women's images
in a range of media texts. Sue Thornham argues that such image analysis has been a focus
of feminist media criticism since the 1960s. She highlights the semiotic and psychoanalytic
approaches in critique of the highly illusory properties of media texts that exposed the "disjunction" experienced by women in relation to "Woman-as-image" (2007, 53). To greatly
condense this body of theory and practice (see Thornham 1998 for a detailed explanation),
feminist critical analysis revealed the social structures implied and universalized by texts with
the political aim to disrupt the systems of meaning and representation.

These interests gained influential expression in Laura Mulvey's (1975) now landmark, if
much contested, account of the dialectic of narrative and image in cinema and her argument
as to how the apparatus of Hollywood cinema contrives to manipulate the visual pleasure of
the gaze upon the on-screen spectacle through the intersecting gazes of camera, audience, and
actors. These processes were organized around the male gaze and corresponded, she argued, to
forces in a culture based on sexual difference. The tendencies of film, she maintains, are, either,
to voyeurism (inviting the gaze) or fetishism (disavowing the gaze) in framing the "to-be-
looked-at-ness" of the woman (as spectacle).

Feminist theory of spectatorship both derived from, and intervened in, earlier debates in
both feminism and film study and was largely concerned with cinematic realism, rather than
fantasy modes that were neither as dominant nor as technologically subtle as today. This body
of theory was also oppositional to some forms of popular culture and drew on models of ideology, which, as Joanne Hollows and Rachel Moseley (2006) argue, are less influential today and
posed a more immediate connection between mass culture and the social real (3–6). Feminist
film/media theory in the second wave was allied with a secondary area of engagement with
women as filmmakers (Thornham 1998). Annette Kuhn (1994) emphasizes that the politics of
these dual quests was to analyze "the social/historical position of women as subordinated [. . .]
within dominant modes of production (such as capitalism)" or the social relations of "patriarchy" or "male domination" (4).

By comparison, third-wave media critics seem more engaged, on the whole, with television and new media than with film and cinema. Fairy-tale media is not conspicuous in their

debates, even if girl-power politics (also debated) is visible in the doll-puppetry of MTV's *Girl Code* fairy-tale retellings (2014). For example, their "Cinderella" dissolves into a girl-fight over a shoe and triumph by Cinderella: "I conquer all." The doll puppets and the puppeteers, a simulation of hand-made media, broadcast in branded MTV montage that circulates globally on MTV Online and YouTube, also imply questions about the assumptions of spectatorship, if the gaze on YouTube is seen as "gawking," as Teresa Rizzo (2008) terms it. *Girl Code* poses a youthful spectacle of casual hyperfamiliarity with both feminism and fairy tale. It is a playful and perhaps parodic take on the politics of pleasure and spectatorship, which are queried in third-wave approaches to media (Johnson 2007).

More in contention in third-wave feminism is "postfeminism," and some see slippage between the two (Genz and Brabon 2009). In many accounts, postfeminism is seen as a cultural discourse, or set of representational practices in media, rather than a political movement. It prioritizes individual interests within a rhetoric of empowerment with the aim of suppressing or disavowing feminist politics (McRobbie 2009). Alternatively, the regard for feminism in postfeminist discourse might be attributed to the perceived success of feminism (Tasker and Negra 2007). Stephanie Genz, instead, sees postfeminism as a form of agency or political subjectivity in neoliberal ideology. Celebrity subjects demonstrate "successful" femininity through acts of choice, empowerment, and transformation (Favara 2015; Genz 2015). A case study is Angelina Jolie, whose "successful" postfeminist femininity, according to Jeremiah Favara, is attained through choices. He compares the mature Jolie and her "global motherhood" to the youthful Jolie who was more "scary" (637). Jolie's "successful femininity" emerges, he argues, "because her choices result in the right kind of transformation" (636–637).

Her life transformation coalesces with her appearance among the hyperfeminine masquerades of heroines in recent fairy-tale films, namely her lead role in the eponymous *Maleficent* (2014), which Jolie also executive produced. A retelling of *Sleeping Beauty* (1959), the once flagship animated production of Walt Disney Studios, a theme of sexual violence (pertaining to Maleficent) in *Maleficent* has been widely noted. Jack Zipes, a longtime critic of Disney fairy tales, argues that this theme, and the reconfiguring of the former heroine, Aurora (Elle Fanning), as a political force in the plot of unification of kingdoms, represents a feminist turn in Disney films (Zipes 2016). Notwithstanding the potential power of *Maleficent* in communicating the disturbing horror of sexual violence, it is a curious twist in Disney's story, as Maleficent was the source of violence, or evil magic, against Aurora in the earlier film. The redemption of Maleficent poses crossing paths in second- and third-wave feminist approaches to media and a question about whose story is really redeemed.

The confronting fairy-glare of Jolie as Maleficent[2] signifies Disney's defiant retelling of the story. It is deceptively contextualized as addressed to (girl) children in a fairy-tale adaptation but is effectively no different from her *Lara Croft* (2001) masquerade. The to-be-looked-at-ness of horned Maleficent is supplemented by the postfeminist rhetoric of empowerment through Jolie's off-screen persona of successful femininity and her dual role as star and producer of the film. The appearance of Aurora, the heroine of the parodied earlier film, is subordinate, even submissive, to Maleficent, in a benevolent restaging of their former relationship. A key look between them at the conclusion of the film, as Aurora is revealed as the (admiring) narrator of Maleficent's story, suggests the continuing pertinence of Mulvey's matrix of gazes whereby audience complicity is secured.

In a contrasting yet no less seductive spectacle, in *Cinderella* (2015), a live-action remake of Disney's earlier animated *Cinderella* (1950), the historical morals of Charles Perrault's "Cinderilla; or the Little Glass Slipper" (2009), chastity and obedience, are coyly implied in the deflective allure of Ella (Lily James) gazing resolutely away and toward her (fetishized) oceanic blue ball gown.[3] Also deflected is the makeover of Cinderella's glamorous fairy godmother (Helena Bonham Carter), who is transformed from the frumpy cartoon figure while her signature song, "Bibbidi, Bobbidi, Boo," is played over the closing credits of the film. In contrast again, *The Princess and the Frog* (2009), a debut for an African American princess character, Tiana (voiced by Anika Noni Rose), is neither remake nor makeover, but instead a belated addition to the gallery of conventionally animated princesses nearly fifteen years into the era of the digital medium. Her appearance sparked a vigorous critical discussion of the character in a regime of representation that "normalizes" Whiteness (Gregory 2010), and the empowering or subversive potential of animation (Barker 2010), and as indicative of Disney's capacity or otherwise to render intersectionalities of class, race, and gender in their fairy tales.

Without conflating the specific cultural politics of each film or character, these films are all emblematic of the way the cinematic discourses of fantasy and enchantment are layered in the deflection of the woman/Woman-as-image disjunction: the idealized image is a fantasy character, a Disney fantasy character, at that, and Maleficent and Ella are derived from the superseded technology of hand-drawn animation only shortly after Tiana first appeared in it. It is not an optimistic scenario in which to ponder the politics of feminism and popular culture. The shift of perspectives on media between the second and third waves gains further angles in responses to signs of feminism in fairy-tale films and television.

Looking for Feminism in the Culture of Wonder

Attention to Disney media persists in spite of encouragement to look beyond Disney and to alternative and independent media (Zipes, Greenhill, and Magnus-Johnston 2016; Greenhill and Rudy 2014). Scrutiny of Disney productions rarely yields satisfaction to the critic in the sense of finding feminist outcomes, and the objectives of feminist action for social change are unlikely to be in tune with the profit-making aims of media corporations. But there are outcomes worth comparing in three fairy-tale films that have attracted feminist commentary for the ways they appear to represent feminism. To adapt Cristina Bacchilega (2013), who says (although not specifically of all these films) that they "interpellate" audiences as "consumers *and* producers of transformation" (3), similarly, some interpellate audiences as aware of feminism, or some version of it.

Beauty and the Beast (1991) has attracted feminist commentary since its release until the present, partly toward the (unsuccessful) feminism of the heroine, Belle (Cummins 1995), although Marina Warner (1994) saw Belle as cannily crafted to appeal to audiences of the time who were knowledgeable about second-wave feminism (313). The hero, the Beast, is also discussed; he is seen, variously, as violence prone (Gray 1992); or in a pattern of redemption narratives of masculine types (Jeffords 1995); or as a pro-feminist allegory of changing to a "better man" (Short 2015, 69). To date, the live-action remake of *Beauty and the Beast* (2017) has not led to new commentary about the Beast.

More cynical outcomes have resulted from the highly parodic remixes of tales produced by Disney and other studios in the twenty-first century, which routinely combine multiple tales and genres. A case study is Disney's *Enchanted* (2007), which is criticized for the cynicism of its genre remixing and the flagrant self-promotion in its convergent *mise-en-scene* (Bacchilega 2013; Cecire 2012). Like other pastiche tales, it is seen to parody then celebrate "enchantment" such that the parodies "[disavow] [. . .] belief in fairy tale fantasies," which, in turn, "opens up a space for rehearsing these same fantasies" (Bacchilega and Rieder 2010, 31–32). Meanwhile the views of the "feminism" of *Enchanted* range from reinforcement of heteropatriarchal values (Short 2015) to "faux feminism" or "anti-feminism" (Pershing 2010, 152–153).

Long after its 1998 release, *Ever After: A Cinderella Story* (1998) remains an object of persistent consideration as a feminist version of "Cinderella." Christy Williams (2010) sees it as reversing the heroine's passiveness, and Ella is "smart," "strong," "assertive," and does not rely on the prince (109). But Ella's feminism is "personal and individually centered," not a "radical" critique of "systemic" inequality (101), and thus it "fails" as feminism (114). Cathy Lynn Preston (2004) argues that *Ever After* directly responds to the "aftermath/afterglow" of second-wave feminism in placing romance into a feminist setting (200). She examines the use of the frame narrative as a device in the "shape-shifting" of postmodern forms of fairy tales, showing how the parodic reframing occurs across genres (from folktale to "legend/history") through the narrative gimmick of the film, "to set the record straight" on the origin of the Grimm brothers' tale of Cinderella (200–201). She places *Ever After*, along with other disparate adaptations of fairy tales in fiction and public media, within a multivocal network of the "accumulated web of feminist critique," including "academic discourse, folk performance, and popular media," that contest the "surface monovocality" of fairy-tale tradition (199). Preston's reading of *Ever After* therefore not only yields a perspective on postmodern culture, but reflexivity of the ways in which feminism is also implicated in the postmodernization of culture (210). In neither account of *Ever After*, however, is the maker, Twentieth Century Fox Film, targeted for the same corporate cynicism as so readily occurs with Disney productions.

Following the Money? Industry, Technology, Culture

> I always wanted to do a period piece and these costumes are couture, I mean they're wearing art.
>
> (Lily Collins, actor, on her role as Snow White in
> *Mirror Mirror*, quoted in Relativity Media 2012)

Many media consumers may know all the Disney fairy-tale films of the last ten years or DreamWorks' productions. More will be challenged to name one of the other major studios'. On television, recognition that Disney's ABC Studios is behind *Once Upon a Time* (2011–) is encouraged by the self-referential content in a way that may not readily occur in *Grimm* (2011–2017, GK/Hazy Mills/Universal Television) or *Supernatural* (2005–, Kripke/Warner Brothers/Wonderland).

The mainstream trade in fairy-tale media is dominated by "American conglomerates" (Bacchilega 2013, 1), and Disney is a powerful player, with vast profits, although its dominance in popularity is not exclusive,[4] and Stuart Cunningham, Terry Flew, and Adam Swift (2015) advise against assuming correspondence between company size and market dominance (32). They cite Janet Wasko's case that Disney cultivates a unique aura in the marketplace through its classic themes that secures its prominence (Cunningham, Flew, and Swift 2015, 58). Even so, its strategy of industrial "synergies," or conglomeration, the integration of its core business through "controlling a diverse portfolio of businesses" in related activities, is well-known (83; Levine 2005). The wryly coined, heteronormative "princess-industrial complex" (Hay and Baxter 2014, 329) alludes to this complex integration of the entertainment industries in which femininity and fairy tale are dual commodities.

While there is growing interest in feminist studies of media political economy (see McLaughlin and Carter 2013), it is not as prominent as other modes of media analysis by feminists, and women have traditionally been unwelcome in these domains (Riordan 2002, 3). A notable exception is Wasko's study of Disney political economy (2001). Similar attention might be paid to Disney's outperforming competition, such as Warner Brothers, or Summit

Entertainment—the producer of *The Twilight Saga* (2008–2012)—and its parent since its acquisition in 2012, Lions Gate Entertainment. Alternatively, "feminist political economy," in distinction from conventional approaches, applies feminist theory to political economic constructs. Such is the characterization of the discursive force of globalization as a "language of domination" (Gibson-Graham 2006, 120), which might in part account for why certain giants sustain their dominance, in spite of evidence to the contrary.

Disney scholarship has its own momentum, perhaps, owing to the length and dedication of its history in production of fairy tales and the now large critical literature. The princess-industrial complex also resonates with Disney's place in the writings of the Frankfurt School cultural critics and the views of Theodore Adorno and Walter Benjamin about the early cartoons which, Miriam Hansen (1993) highlights, appeared amidst their metonymic evocation of the fascist (aestheticization of the) military-industrial complex. Disney films "became emblematic of the juncture of art, politics, and technology" (28). Mickey Mouse and Donald Duck became fetishistic figures par excellence in posing, for Benjamin, an encounter between the human subject and technology, and thus the "industrially changed environment" of the time (Hansen 1993, 28–30).

Fairy-tale media, not only Disney's, continues to pose this challenge of confronting technology and change due to the historic juncture in which it has proliferated in the twenty-first century and the transition of technology paradigms from analog to digital platforms and the associated profound social, aesthetic, and industrial implications. The churning out of fairy tale at this time poses many questions, not least whether the reissue of these stories really concerns a message of change or of stability, or whether fairy tale, through—falsely—assumed universality, encodes some profitable illusion of the global value of media. The technologies are sometimes visible at the textual level and represent convergences of industries as well, as the innovation-based, Silicon Valley IT industries colonize the content-driven Hollywood film industries, and their co-evolution equalizes past disparities in revenues (Cunningham, Flew, and Swift 2015, 140–142).

As second-wave media theorists understood, subtler scrutiny is needed to understand the participation of women in these systems, what roles they play, and what power they wield. Lily Collins does not speak of taking over the princess-industrial complex when she took the job as Snow White because of the costumes in *Mirror Mirror* (2012). Aside from the profile of directors like Jennifer Lee from *Frozen* (2013) and Catherine Hardwicke from *Red Riding Hood* (2011), scrutiny of production crews reveals hubs of fairy-tale media expertise. Take *Red Riding Hood*, where Hardwicke had also directed *Twilight* (2008); editor Nancy Richardson worked on *Twilight* and *Eclipse* (2010); co-editor Julia Wong on *Tangled* (2010); and the lead cinematographer, Mandy Walker, on *Beastly* (2011). These women and their knowledge are unlikely to be overly identified with production companies because of the ephemeral contract and project arrangements in which they work. Scrutiny of productions beyond the text empowers knowledge of women's participation in the industry, and of the micro-cultures of productions, whatever traces of feminist knowledge may emerge in the texts.

Feminist Fairy Force One

Looking forward, Disney seems to be resurrecting its male action heroes in remakes of *The Jungle Book* (2016) and the touted *The Sword in the Stone* (in development) and various animated titles—apparently undeterred by Warner Brothers' relative flop with *Pan* (2015). The profusion of fairy-tale media in the twenty-first century is not an isolated swarm in the swarming worlds of popular culture. Fairy tale, with its history as a channel of conservative gender ideology, has a particular attraction for feminists, while the giants have cultivated enchantment, as if in homage to their own sense of power in the transformed media era. But their vulnerabilities are on show: the greater the variety of media, the lesser the range of tales, or so it seems with the reissuing of so many old titles in new formats. Fortunately, feminists are well practiced in the criticism of "Cinderella."

Undoubtedly, the predominance of feminist commentary still concerns representational discourses of fairy-tale media and the politics of spectatorship, and this remains a vital area of engagement, perhaps more than ever in the image-laden media sphere. The counter-strategy, to look beyond the mainstream, is, also, as pertinent as ever. But dislodging giants from their globally dominant comfort zones also demands vigorous scrutiny of their financial and structural processes and critique of the means by which they maintain the appearance of power as much as their actual dominance. Greater attention to the micro-cultures of productions—who writes, directs, produces, and edits the shows, and how autonomous or constrained the decisions they make, and where women are involved in these processes—is potentially as insightful into the feminist intelligence in the productions as analysis of the narrative and images screened. A feminist fairy force in swarm formation, with a range of tactics in the handling of giants, may tilt the balance of power and lead to less parody, more magic, and more sharing of the cultural wealth in feminism and folklore.

Notes

1. For a discussion of the trans-Atlantic application of this concept in twenty-first-century gender research, see, for instance, Carbin and Edenheim (2013).
2. See "Angelina Jolie and Elle Fanning" (2014).
3. See "The Official Poster" (2014).
4. See "Animation—Fantasy" and "Fantasy—Live-Action."

References Cited and Further Reading

"Animation—Fantasy." N.d. *Box Office Mojo.* www.boxofficemojo.com/genres/chart/?id=animatedfantasy.htm.

Bacchilega, Cristina. 2013. *Fairy Tales Transformed? Twenty-First Century Adaptations and the Politics of Wonder.* Detroit: Wayne State UP.

Bacchilega, Cristina, and John Rieder. 2010. "Mixing It Up: Generic Complexity and Gender Ideology in Early Twenty-First Century Fairy Tale Films." In *Fairy Tale Films,* edited by Greenhill and Matrix, 23–41.

Barker, Jennifer L. 2010. "Hollywood, Black Animation, and the Problem of Representation in *Little Ol' Bosko* and *The Princess and the Frog.*" *Journal of African American Studies* 14: 482–98.

Benson, Stephen, ed. 2008. *Contemporary Fiction and the Fairy Tale.* Detroit: Wayne State UP.

Brownmiller, Susan. 1976. *Against Our Will: Men, Women and Rape.* New York: Bantam.

Carbin, Maria, and Sara Edenheim. 2013. "The Intersectional Turn in Feminist Theory: A Dream of a Common Language?" *European Journal of Women's Studies* 20 (3): 233–48.

Carter, Angela. 1979. *The Bloody Chamber and Other Stories.* London: Victor Gollancz.

Cecire, Maria Sachiko. 2012. "Reality Remixed: Neomedieval Princess Culture in Disney's *Enchanted.*" In *The Disney Middle Ages: A Fairy-Tale and Fantasy Past,* edited by Tison Pugh and Susan Aronstein, 243–60. New York: Palgrave Macmillan.

Craven, Allison. 2017. *Fairy Tale Interrupted: Feminism, Masculinity, Wonder Cinema.* Bern: Peter Lang.

Cummins, June. 1995. "Romancing the Plot: The Real Beast of Disney's *Beauty and the Beast.*" *Children's Literature Association Quarterly* 20 (1): 22–8.

Cunningham, Stuart, Terry Flew, and Adam Swift. 2015. *Media Economics.* London: Palgrave Macmillan.

Daly, Mary. 1978. *Gyn/Ecology: The Metaethics of Radical Feminism.* Boston: Beacon.

Dworkin, Andrea. 1974. *Woman Hating.* New York: Dutton.

"Fantasy—Live-Action." N.d. *Box Office Mojo.* www.boxofficemojo.com/genres/chart/?id=liveactionfantasy.htm.

Favara, Jeremiah. 2015. "A Maternal Heart: Angelina Jolie, Choices of Maternity, Hegemonic Femininity in *People Magazine.*" *Feminist Media Studies* 15 (4): 626–42.

Genz, Stephanie. 2015. "My Job Is Me: Post-Feminist Celebrity Culture and the Gendering of Authenticity." *Feminist Media Studies* 15 (4): 545–61.

Genz, Stephanie, and Benjamin Brabon. 2009. *Postfeminism: Cultural Texts and Theories.* Edinburgh: Edinburgh UP.

Gibson-Graham, J. K. 2006. *The End of Capitalism (As We Knew It): A Feminist Critique of Political Economy.* 2nd ed. Minneapolis: U Minnesota P.

Gilbert, Sandra M., and Susan Gubar. 1979. *The Madwoman in the Attic: The Woman Writer and the Nineteenth-Century Literary Imagination.* New Haven, CT: Yale UP.

Gray, Elizabeth Dodson. 1992. "Beauty and the Beast: A Parable for Our Time." In *Women Respond to the Men's Movement: A Feminist Collection,* edited by Kay Leigh Hagan, 159–68. San Francisco: Pandora.

Greenhill, Pauline, and Sidney Eve Matrix, eds. 2010. *Fairy Tale Films: Visions of Ambiguity.* Logan: Utah State UP.

Greenhill, Pauline, and Jill Terry Rudy, eds. 2014. *Channeling Wonder: Fairy Tales on Television.* Detroit: Wayne State UP.

Gregory, Sarita McCoy. 2010. "Disney's Second Line: New Orleans, Racial Masquerade, and the Reproduction of Whiteness in *The Princess and the Frog.*" *Journal of African American Studies* 14: 432–49.

Haase, Donald, ed. 2004. *Fairy Tales and Feminism: New Approaches.* Detroit: Wayne State UP.

Hansen, Miriam. 1993. "Of Mice and Ducks: Benjamin and Adorno on Disney." *South Atlantic Quarterly* 92 (1): 27–61.

Hay, Rebecca, and Christa Baxter. 2014. "Happily Never After: The Commodification and Critique of Fairy Tale in ABC's *Once Upon a Time.*" In *Channeling Wonder,* edited by Greenhill and Rudy, 316–35.

Hollows, Joanne, and Rachel Moseley, eds. 2006. *Feminism in Popular Culture.* Oxford: Berg.

Jeffords, Susan. 1995. "The Curse of Masculinity: Disney's *Beauty and the Beast.*" In *From Mouse to Mermaid: The Politics of Film, Gender and Culture,* edited by Elizabeth Bell, Lynda Haas, and Laura Sells, 161–72. Bloomington: Indiana UP.

Johnson, Merri Lisa, ed. 2007. *Third Wave Feminism and Television: Jane Puts it in a Box.* London: IB Taurus.

Joosen, Vanessa. 2011. *Critical and Creative Perspectives on Fairy Tales.* Detroit: Wayne State UP.

Kuhn, Annette. 1994. *Women's Pictures: Feminism and Cinema.* 2nd ed. London: Verso.

Levine, Elana. 2005. "Fractured Fairy Tales and Fragmented Markets: Disney's Weddings of a Lifetime and the Cultural Politics of Media Conglomeration." *Television New Media* 6 (1): 71–88.

Lieberman, Marcia K. (1972) 1993. "'Some Day My Prince Will Come': Female Acculturation through the Fairy Tale." In *Don't Bet on the Prince: Contemporary Feminist Fairy Tales in North America and England,* edited by Jack Zipes, 185–200. Aldershot, UK: Scolar P.

Lurie, Alison. 1970. "Fairy Tale Liberation." *New York Review of Books,* December 17: 42–4.

McLaughlin, Lisa, and Cynthia Carter, eds. 2013. *Current Perspectives in Feminist Media Studies.* New York: Routledge.

McRobbie, Angela. 2009. *The Aftermath of Feminism.* London: Sage Publications.

Moen, Kristian. 2013. *Film and Fairy Tales: The Birth of Modern Fantasy.* London: IB Taurus.

Mulvey, Laura. 1975. "Visual Pleasure and Narrative Cinema." *Screen* 16 (3): 6–18.

Perrault, Charles. 2009. "Cinderilla; or the Little Glass Slipper." In *The Project Gutenberg eBook, The Fairy Tales of Charles Perrault, by Charles Perrault, et al,* translated by Robert Samber and J. E. Mansion. www.gutenberg.org/files/29021/29021-h/29021-h.htm#Cinderilla_or_The_Little_Glass_Slipper.

Pershing, Linda. 2010. "Disney's *Enchanted*: Patriarchal Backlash and Nostalgia in a Fairy Tale Film." In *Fairy Tale Films,* edited by Greenhill and Matrix, 137–56.

Preston, Cathy Lynn. 2004. "Disrupting the Boundaries of Genre and Gender: Postmodernism and the Fairy Tale." In *Fairy Tales and Feminism,* edited by Haase, 197–212.

Relativity Media. 2012. "Looking Through the Mirror: Special Features." In *Mirror Mirror,* directed by Tarsem Singh. USA.

Riordan, Ellen. 2002. "Intersections and New Directions: On Feminism and Political Economy." In *Sex and Money: Feminism and Political Economy in the Media,* edited by Eileen R. Meehan and Ellen Riordan, 3–15. Minneapolis: U Minnesota P.

Rizzo, Teresa. 2008. "YouTube: The New Cinema of Attractions." *Scan Journal* 5 (1). http://scan.net.au/scan/journal/display.php?journal_id=109

Short, Sue. 2015. *Fairy Tale and Film: Old Tales with a New Spin.* Basingstoke: Palgrave Macmillan.

Tasker, Yvonne, and Diane Negra, eds. 2007. *Interrogating Postfeminism: Gender and the Politics of Popular Culture.* Durham, NC: Duke UP.

Thornham, Sue. 1998. "Feminist Media and Film Theory." In *Contemporary Feminist Theories,* edited by Stevi Jackson and Jackie Jones, 213–31. Edinburgh: Edinburgh UP.

———. 2007. *Women, Feminism and Media.* Edinburgh: Edinburgh UP.

Warner, Marina. 1994. *From the Beast to the Blonde: On Fairy Tales and Their Tellers.* London: Chatto and Windus.

Wasko, Janet. 2001. *Understanding Disney: The Manufacture of Fantasy.* Cambridge, UK: Polity P.

Williams, Christy. 2010. "The Shoe Still Fits: *Ever After* and the Pursuit of a Feminist Cinderella." In *Fairy Tale Films,* edited by Greenhill and Matrix, 99–115.

Zipes, Jack. 2016. "Beyond Disney in the Twenty-First Century: Changing Aspects of Fairy-Tale Films in the American Film Industry." In *Fairy-Tale Films Beyond Disney*, edited by Zipes, Greenhill, and Magnus-Johnston, 278–93.

Zipes, Jack, Pauline Greenhill, and Kendra Magnus-Johnston, eds. 2016. *Fairy-Tale Films Beyond Disney: International Perspectives.* New York: Routledge.

Mediagraphy

"Angelina Jolie and Elle Fanning in Maleficent (2014)." 2014. Film poster. www.imdb.com/media/rm2488531712/tt1587310?ref_=tt_ov_i.

Beastly. 2011. Director Daniel Barnz. USA.

Beauty and the Beast. 1991. Directors Gary Trousdale and Kirk Wise. USA.

———. 2017. Director Bill Condon. USA.

Cinderella. 1950. Directors Clyde Geronimi and Wilfred Jackson. USA.

———. 2015. Director Kenneth Branagh. 2015. UK/USA.

Eclipse. 2010. Director David Slade. USA.

Enchanted. 2007. Director Kevin Lima. USA.

Ever After: A Cinderella Story. 1998. Director Andy Tennant. USA.

Frozen. 2013. Directors Chris Buck and Jennifer Lee. USA.

Grimm (TV). 2011–2017. Creators David Greenwalt, Jim Kouf, Stephen Carpenter. USA.

The Jungle Book. 2016. Director Jon Favreau. USA.

Lara Croft. 2001. Director Simon West. USA/UK/Japan/Germany.

Maleficent. 2014. Director Robert Stromberg. USA/UK.

Mirror Mirror. 2012. Director Tarsem Singh. USA/Canada.

MTV. 2014. "Girl Code to Fairy Tales: Cinderella." *YouTube*, December 5. www.youtube.com/watch?v=Ucol0oFtuDU.

"The Official Poster of Disney's 2015 Live-Action Film Cinderella." 2014. Film poster. https://en.wikipedia.org/wiki/Cinderella_(2015_Disney_film)#/media/File:Cinderella_2015_official_poster.jpg.

Once Upon a Time (TV). 2011–. Creators Adam Horowitz and Edward Kitsis. USA.

Pan. 2015. Director Joe Wright. USA/UK/Australia.

The Princess and the Frog. 2009. Directors Ron Clements and John Musker. USA.

Red Riding Hood. 2011. Director Catherine Hardwicke. USA.

Sleeping Beauty. 1959. Director Clyde Geronimi. USA.

Supernatural (TV). 2005–. Creator Eric Kripke. USA.

The Sword in the Stone (in development). Writers Bryan Cogman. USA.

Tangled. 2010. Directors Nathan Greno and Byron Howard. USA.

Twilight. 2008. Director Catherine Hardwicke. USA.

9
POSTMODERNISM
Cristina Bacchilega

In the late twentieth century, "postmodernism" became both a critical keyword and a fashionable buzzword internationally. The term has conflicting genealogies and usages, depending on whether postmodernism is identified as historical period, condition, philosophy, or aesthetics. Furthermore, postmodernism's critical cachet has depended to some degree on its slippery and overlapping definitions. Is postmodernism what comes *after* what is modern and/or modernist? Is postmodernism a critique, in theory and practice, of modernity as a grand culture of progress? Is postmodernism a skepticism about how we construct what is truth, or history, or the stability of the human subject? Is postmodernism a style that, in response to modernism, privileges flatness, pastiche, parody, and self-reflexivity?

The answer to all of these is yes to the extent that these definitions have been concurrently at play in academic and popular discourses. Thinking of postmodernism in relation to fairy-tale culture and media, then, can raise issues of periodization (Are the seventeenth-century tales by the French *conteuses* or Tex Avery's *Red Hot Riding Hood* 1943 cartoon postmodern ante litteram?), aesthetics (What do Angela Carter's highly literary collection of fairy-tale retellings, *The Bloody Chamber*, and the kitsch filmic adaptation of some of its stories, *The Company of Wolves*, have in common to possibly identify them both as postmodern?), and definition (How is the television show *Once Upon a Time* postmodern?).

Aiming to provide a framework for addressing such issues, this chapter asks a broader set of questions: What constitutes the intertextual appeal of the fairy tale in postmodern culture? How does thinking of fairy-tale culture and media impact our understanding of postmodern? And has the critical value of postmodernism changed over time in relation to both the production and reception of fairy tales across media? Leading up to the specifics of postmodern fairy tales and fairy-tale culture and media in postmodern times, the next section is a brief orientation to postmodernism and postmodernity in relation to one another and with a focus on their relevance to the study of narrative and culture.[1]

Postmodernism, Postmodernity, and Narrative Traditions

Starting in the 1960s, philosophers, social scientists, and cultural theorists have, by championing one definition of postmodernism over another, shaped an ongoing multidisciplinary, international debate as well as brought about scholarly self-reflexive shifts in fields such as anthropology, sociology, and literary studies (Anttonen 2005). For Jean Baudrillard ([1981] 1994), postmodernism is a culture of simulation where media-produced *simulacra* replace reality in an unending and dulling procession. For Jean-François Lyotard (1979), the postmodern condition is both characteristic of globalized social life and marked by skepticism toward the "master narratives" of Christianity, science, and socialism. For Fredric Jameson (1984), postmodernity is to be understood temporally as an economy of late capitalism that supersedes modernity and also as a set of practices that empties out history in favor of cultural consumption. For Linda Hutcheon (1988), postmodernism is a cultural project that is not synonymous with the social problems of postmodernity and one that, far from forgetting history, actively engages it through metafiction and parody. For David Harvey (1989), modernity and postmodernity are interpenetrating, opposed tendencies within capitalist society, which as a whole is marked by an oscillation between intensive (Fordist) and extensive (flexible) strategies of accumulation that push cultural production and consumption in distinctively different directions.

Not only is the definition of postmodernism to postmodernity conflicted, but its relationships to "modernity"—as social product of European industrial revolution and colonialism—and to "modernism"—as experimental, high art in the 1890–1940s period—are represented as overlapping and ambivalent. Especially in the 1980s and 1990s, scholars made much of taking a stand against the postmodern (Jameson and Baudrillard) or in defense of its potential as social and aesthetic critique (Lyotard and most strongly Hutcheon).

Generally speaking, several aspects of postmodernism and postmodernity are significant to the production, reception, and study of fairy tales and other genres associated with folk narrative as retooled in late-twentieth-century and more contemporary Euro-American culture (Warshaver 1991; Preston 1995; Lau 1999). Lyotard's focus on localized and contingent *petit récits* (small-scale stories) as postmodernism's alternative to failed grand narratives (such as History and Progress) implicitly valorizes the folktale, legend, and rumor. Typical of postmodern poetics is also a rejection of the hierarchical opposition of high/low culture, which on the one hand resulted in postmodernism's engagement with mass culture and on the other hand has brought renewed attention within literary traditions to so-called pre-modern or pre-modernist narrative forms. Within the discipline of folk-narrative studies, a postmodern turn has meant an understanding of performance as emergent event, a reflection of the politics of representation (Mills 1990), and a consideration of how—while enabling the transmission of stories from one context to another—decontextualization and entextualization impact the politics and poetics of culture (Bauman and Briggs 2003). These moves have also brought about a postmodern, self-reflexive style that blurs the distinction between scholarship (Haring 2007; Bendix 2000) and creative storytelling (de Caro 2008).

Twenty-first-century approaches have overall been much less focused on producing generalized definitions of the postmodern and more attentive instead to the specific politics and poetics of cultural texts operating within what is generally perceived as a globalized, postmodern world. As a result of economic and cultural globalization, local narrative traditions are increasingly performed and consumed across media all over the world in often fragmented and tourist-oriented form (Kirshenblatt-Gimblett 1998; Fife 2004; Bendix and Hemme 2004). And yet we should not underestimate the power of folklore's multivocality in postmodern popular culture (Preston 2004) or of grassroots' remediation in what Henry Jenkins calls "convergence culture" (2008). While postmodern remakes of, and conversations with, folk narrative traditions are not inherently conservative or progressive, attending to practices of representation, appropriation, and commercialization in these encounters is necessarily a scholarly responsibility in folklore and fairy-tale studies.

Postmodern Fairy Tales

Parody and pastiche, which are different forms of narrative self-reflexivity or re-visitation, are two of the most discussed postmodern strategies for the artistic articulation to a self-conscious, never unmediated relationship to history, subjectivity, language, and storytelling. Notably, the parodic recycling and fragmentation of fairy tales or tales of magic in postmodernity and in postmodern form are particularly prevalent. What constitutes the intertextual appeal of the fairy tale in postmodern culture? There is no one satisfying answer, but it is understood that "the fairy tale, as a well-known, culturally familiar body of texts with an almost canonical status within children's literature, is a ripe site for" reflection and rewriting (Makinen 2008, 148) that are both playful and critical. Furthermore, for many postmodern writers, the multiplicity of fairy-tale versions and the multivocality of the genre offer a fertile opportunity for intervening in an already multilayered reflection on story, social practices, and cultural values.

English-language writers famously associated with postmodernism have offered a range of reasons for turning to the fairy tale as choice intertexts. As theorized in his manifesto articles, originally published in 1967 and 1980 respectively, John Barth in *Chimera* (1972) and other fictions—along with other American literary authors in the 1970s and 1980s—reached back to tales from the Euro-American and "Arabian Nights" traditions and self-consciously rewrote them in order to replenish the modernist "literature of exhaustion." For Barth, the fairy tale's "once upon a time" was less of a formula and more of an occasion for literary storytelling to renew itself in a cycle of narrative citations that decenter the author. Robert Coover (see 1969) articulated his interest in fairy tales differently in 2004:

> Fairy tales, religious stories, national and family legends, games and sports, TV cartoons and movies, now video and computer games—it's a metaphoric toy box we all share. Sometimes all this story stuff feels like the very essence of our mother tongue, embedded there before we've even learned it, so much a part of us that we forget it didn't come with the language, but that someone made it up and put it there. The best way to expose that and free ourselves up is to get inside it and play with it and make it do new things.
>
> (Hudson 2004)

Recognizable in this statement and in Coover's literary practice is the reflection on how fairy tales have been naturalized as building blocks for storytelling and for normative plotting of (Euro-American) imaginations and lives, as well as that in postmodern fashion it is only by playing with these stories that we can work against being played by them and possibly change their shared uses and resonance.

A similar critical sensibility, but one strongly focused on women and gender, animated British writer Angela Carter as she revisited fairy tales in order to explode their mythic or normative weight while reactivating the pleasure principle and specific experience at work in their metaphors. Most influential is Carter's collection of short stories, *The Bloody Chamber* (1979): while she did not self-identify as a postmodern writer, Carter's tongue-in-cheek twists on the tales' sexuality and gender dynamics as well as the intertextual narrative strategies she employed to multiply the tales' meanings made her the poster author for "postmodern fairy tales." A few anthologies exemplify (Mieder 1985; Bernheimer 2010) this multigenre phenomenon, which several critics have also discussed (Bacchilega 1997; Hennard Dutheil de la Rochère 2006; Smith 2007; Benson 2008; Makinen 2008; Tiffin 2009; Bobby 2009; Joosen 2011; Kérchy 2011).

For Bacchilega, whose focus is on gender and narrative strategies, postmodern fairy tales are characterized by a double movement of exposure: one that reveals the ideological framing of women in the most popular fairy tales and another that makes visible or activates unexploited or forgotten possibilities in these well-known stories (1997, 22–23). With chapters organized around specific tale types—"Snow White" (ATU 709), "Little Red Riding Hood" (ATU 333), "Beauty and the Beast" (ATU 425C), and "Bluebeard" (ATU 312)—Bacchilega draws on a wide range of traditional versions as well as postmodern retellings to underscore both the multivocality of the fairy tale and the multiple ways in which postmodern revisions question and remake the powerful connection that fairy tales have with subjectivity, especially women's.

Providing readings of postmodern literary fairy tales by Margaret Atwood, Donald Barthelme, Robert Coover, Tanith Lee, and most prominently Carter, this study makes a foray into discussing postmodern fairy-tale film (*The Company of Wolves*), television series, and musical theater; while the analysis sticks to narrative aspects of postmodern fairy tales regardless of the media, it emphasizes the ideological drive of postmodern investments in fairy-tale culture and postmodern writers' approach to the fairy tale as multivocal: "Angela Carter's postmodern rewritings are acts of fairy-tale archaeology that release [a] story's many voices. [. . .] Carter tells tales that reactivate lost traditions, trace violently contradictory genealogies, and flesh out the complex and vital workings of desire and narrative" (Bacchilega 1997, 58, 59).

Kevin Paul Smith's approach in *The Postmodern Fairytale* (2007) has the distinction of addressing postmodern interrogations and uses of "fairytale" as a genre (rather than individual tales) and of presenting itself as broadly applicable to "mass-produced fictions" (10). This is how he introduces his study:

> In last three decades (1975–2005), [. . .] there has been a perceptible shift in the use of the fairytale by novelists and filmmakers. Rather than being something that underlies a narrative and informs its structure, or a handy metaphor, the fairytale has become central to the work [and] is being intertextually used for ends which can be called "postmodern."
>
> (1)

Analyzing works by Salman Rushdie, Carter, Kate Atkinson, and Terry Pratchett, Smith identifies eight different ways in which fairy tale works as an intertext in postmodern fictions: either explicit or implicit references in the title of the postmodern work; either explicit or implicit references in the work; re-vision, or "putting a new spin on an old tale"; fabulation, or "crafting an original fairytale"; metafictional discussion of fairy tales; and fairy tale as setting or chronotope (10). While none of these intertextual elements is "postmodern" per se, Smith's selection of texts ensures that they work to such ends.

Focusing on the substantive, two-way conversation between fairy-tale retellings and scholarship that began in the 1970s, Vanessa Joosen draws on a specific legacy of postmodernism: the blurring of boundaries between fiction and criticism, a blurring that depends both on intertextuality and self-conscious reflexivity (2011). Joosen's refreshing approach has at least two significant implications for future studies. First, postmodernism functions for her as a method rather than an object of study: her project is to tackle the dialogic relationship between fairy-tale retellings and scholarship, both of which *reflect on* the fairy tale in dynamic and often ambivalent ways. While most of Joosen's critical examples are interpretations no longer central to fairy-tale studies (Bettelheim's *The Uses of Enchantment* and Gilbert and Gubar's *The Madwoman in the Attic*), they remain broadly influential, as her readings show, in the popular and artistic imaginary. Also published in 2011 and further corroborating Joosen's approach is a brilliant example of parodic intertextual dialogue with the "Arabian Nights" tales as well as their critical interpretations: Andrei Codrescu's hypertextual novel, *Whatever Gets You through the Night: A Story of Sheherezade and the Arabian Entertainments*.

Second, proclaiming the interpretive function of fairy-tale illustrations, Joosen also explores their intertextuality and critical function as visual retellings. Her discussion of Jon Scieszka and Lane Smith's *The Stinky Cheese Man and Other Fairly Stupid Tales* (1992) as a "postmodern picture book" (19) foregrounds the use of fairy-tale citations in the collage that visually represents the disorderly tale told by the "Jack and the Beanstalk" (ATU 328A) giant after he's ingested parts of a book. She also reads illustrations of "Sleeping Beauty" by Michael Foreman (Carter 1982) as not only resexualizing the fairy tale in children's books, but also visually citing Freudian interpretations of the tale and possibly critiquing their patriarchal assumptions (180–182).

Fairy Tales Across Media in a Postmodern Culture

Focusing primarily on literary postmodernism or on the fairy tale as purely verbal narrative in the early-twenty-first century is problematic since postmodern strategies inform many a fairy tale in popular culture. Metanarrative play and ironic self-consciousness characterize Neil Gaiman's multimedia fairy tales (e.g., *MirrorMask* 2005; *Stardust* 1999), metafictional children's books like David Wiesner's *The Three Pigs* (2001), animated films as different as *Shrek* (2001) and *Ponyo* (2008), television series *Once Upon a Time* (2011–), *Fables* comic series (Willingham 2002–2015), fairy-tale photography by Dina Goldstein (2011) or Chan-Hyo Bae (2008–2010), and Donna Leishman's "after Angela Carter" digital fairy tales (2000, 2003). And increasingly significant are the cultural practices of recycling fairy tales, or fairy-tale fragments, and mixing them with other genres across media (Preston 2004; Ryan 2004; Haase 2006; Jorgensen 2007; Lau 2008; McAra and Calvin 2011; Greenhill and Matrix 2010; Cavallaro 2011; Zipes 2012; Ellis 2012).

To discuss fairy-tale culture and postmodernism today, then, it helps to ask if what makes the fairy-tale genre a prime candidate for popular remakes across media is different from what has interested literary authors from the 1970s on. Even the early postmodern art-house fairy-tale film *The Company of Wolves* (1984), which drew on Carter's screenplay and wolf-trilogy in *The Bloody Chamber* collection, depended for its success on B-movie kitsch, special effects, and genre mixing to become a cult movie—that is, its postmodern self-consciousness is played in a different key.

Circulating in postmodern popular cultural memory (Kukkonen 2008) as decontextualized motifs or iconic images, tales like "Cinderella" inform the discourse of advertisements (Dégh 1994) as much as journalism (Conrad 1998) and entertainment. While some filmic postmodern fairy tales engage the history and multivocality of the genre, in many cases and increasingly so, fairy-tale fragments and Disneyfied stereotypes are at play in popular films. "These fragments," Jeana Jorgensen writes, "whether fairy-tale motifs, characters, or plots are the building blocks of new media texts," which she identifies as "fairy-tale pastiches [. . .] to privilege their schizophrenic instrumentalization of fairy tale matter" (2007, 218). Compared to the intertextual exploration of more parodic postmodernism, these pastiches are flat, making use of the fairy tale and postmodern strategies as a gimmick or currency. Along these lines, Jessica Tiffin (2009) develops a sharp comparison between A. S. Byatt's "sophisticated and sensitive use of embedded tale and a simulated oral voice" in "The Djinn in the Nightingale's Eye" and Disney self-awareness in framing "*Aladdin* as both oral narrative and commodity" (222). However, functioning "almost as some kind of watershed in cinematic fairy-tale awareness," *Shrek* (2001) leads Tiffin and several other scholars to complicate this contrast.

Exemplifying the postmodern impulse in animated American film at the turn of the twenty-first century, *Shrek* applies irony to Disney tropes that, like the heroine's singing to birds and Beast's transformation, have been long naturalized in filmic fairy tales, but its fairy-tale hodgepodge also results—via its innovative digital animation and construction of a happy ending for those who refuse to fit the beauty myth of consumer culture—in the creation of a renewed fairy tale firmly rooted in the genre's tradition of culture-specific magic and social interventions. Furthermore, *Shrek's* parodic critique of Disney extends to representing on screen the very real conflicts within the culture industry (Zipes 2002, 229). Skepticism and optimism are both at play, and the transformative power of the fairy tale is renewed.

But not for long. As consumer culture demands, *Shrek 2* (2004) and *Shrek the Third* (2007) followed, along with imitators like *Happily N'Ever After* (2006) and *Puss in Boots* (2011). In these films and in live-action ones such as *Mirror Mirror* (2012), the pastiche of fairy-tale characters and tropes exploits and reduces the fairy-tale's cultural capital to a source of comic relief that requires genre remixing to continue to be viable. Further containing the subversive potential of *Shrek*, the Disney corporation's *Enchanted* (2007) applies similar postmodern techniques to poke fun at its own tropes—pastel two-dimensional animation, the heroine's naivety, true love's kiss—only to reestablish the power of its romance formula, harnessing it to that of credit-card magic and Disney "princess" commodities (Bacchilega and Rieder 2010).

Because postmodern irony and reflexivity are almost a given in contemporary fairy-tale culture, evaluating their ideological currency in popular entertainment is an important critical task; furthermore, postcolonial, queer, and Indigenous poetics and politics bring their own approaches to self-reflexivity and fragmentation. Bacchilega's (2013) study de-centers postmodern pop-culture retellings by approaching them in a broader geopolitical and analytical fairy-tale web of self-conscious and activist adaptations. The ideological power of postmodern fairy-tale parody, pastiche, and mix thereof across media holds more promise when we move away from big-money and Euro-American productions. The popular anime series *Revolutionary Girl Utena* (1977), "often described as the quintessential postmodern fairy tale," destabilizes gender categories (Lezubski 2014, 164); the originally made-for-television *Red Riding Trilogy* "refers to the traditional [Red Riding Hood] tale in order to engage and sometimes shock audiences into reflecting on how social and environmental corruption can insidiously become part of everyday life" (Greenhill and Kohm 2014, 191). Contemporary visual artists like Paula Rego, Kiki Smith, and Miwa Yanagi offer critical reflections on fairy tales that collide with sanitized and uplifting fairy-tale mythology (Zipes 2012) as well as, in the case of Yanagi, with a Euro-American centered perspective (Murai 2015).

Postmodern Fairy Tales and History

Overall, as Merja Makinen argues (2008), a significant distinction is to be made between postmodern approaches to fairy tale as a single, predictable pre-text and those that work with the already perpetually adapted and multivocal textuality of individual fairy tales and the fairy-tale genre:

> Knowledge of twenty-first-century conceptions of the fairy tale places huge pressures upon postmodern criticism of fiction that uses the fairy tale as an intertext. Postmodern fiction cannot really be said to rewrite the fairy tale as a previous, given, static text to be commented upon through parody. All it can do is re-engage contemporaneously with an already multilayered polyphony, adding a further critical layer to the plurality.
>
> (151)

Is the fairy tale, then, pre-postmodern? And if so, how? For some, there is striking similarity between postmodern narrative techniques and those of Giambattista Basile and French aristocratic women in the seventeenth century (Harries 2001); the same can be said of Tex Avery's cartoons (e.g., *The Bear's Tale* [1940] and *Red Hot Riding Hood* [1943]) and the U.S. television series *Fractured Fairy Tales* (1959–1964). However, isolating narrative strategies from the social context in which fairy-tale culture is produced de-historicizes both postmodern fairy tales and postmodernity: it does not do justice to the intertextuality of postmodern fairy tales, like Carter's, that could not have been produced without twentieth-century feminism and socialism, or to the dependence of postmodern fairy-tale films, like *Shrek*, on globalization's technological innovations and neoliberal economy. While historically there have been fairy tales about fairy tales—to the extent that in *A Flowering Tree and Other Oral Tales from India* folklorist and poet A. K. Ramanujan suggests there should be a tale type, Story about Stories (1997)—generally speaking this kind of self-reflexivity is not common in a genre that is generally recognized as building on the suspension of disbelief.

What can be understood as postmodern is that the fairy tale is a genre that is always already a hybrid, a "shape shifter and medium-breaker" (Greenhill and Matrix 2010, 3). But this too is hardly a definitive answer. Rather, if we recognize it as symptomatic of a postmodern critical sensibility, "such an image of the fairy tale is a period performance, one that may well be viewed as a historical oddity by subsequent generations" (Benson 2008, 13) and one that provides a necessarily partial lens for the analysis of specific social functions and impact that fairy tales across media have.

Note

1. The first part of this chapter draws on the German-language entry on postmodernism that I published in the *Enzyklopädie des Märchens* (Bacchilega 2014).

References Cited and Further Reading

Anttonen, Pertti J. 2005. *Tradition Through Modernity: Postmodernism and the Nation-State in Folklore Scholarship.* Helsinki: Finnish Literature Society.

Bacchilega, Cristina. 1997. *Postmodern Fairy Tales: Gender and Narrative Strategies.* Philadelphia: U Pennsylvania P.

———. 2013. *Fairy Tales Transformed? Twenty-First-Century Adaptations and the Politics of Wonder.* Detroit: Wayne State UP.

———. 2014. "Postmodernes Erzählen." *Enzyklopädie des Märchens: Handwörterbuch zur historischen und vergleichenden Erzählforschung,* edited by Rolf Wilhelm Brednich et al.: 1794–1800. Göttingen: de Gruyter.

Bacchilega, Cristina, and John Rieder. 2010. "Mixing It Up: Generic Complexity in Early 21st-Century Fairy-Tale Film." In *Fairy Tale Films,* edited by Greenhill and Matrix, 23–41.

Barth, John. 1967. "The Literature of Exhaustion." *The Atlantic,* August: 29–34.

———. 1972. *Chimera.* New York: Random House.

———. 1980. "The Literature of Replenishment: Postmodern Fiction." *The Atlantic,* January: 56–71.

Barthelme, Donald. 1967. *Snow White.* New York: Atheneum.

Baudrillard, Jean. (1981) 1994. *Simulacra and Simulation,* translated by Sheila Faria Glaser. Ann Arbor: U Michigan P.

Bauman, Richard, and Charles L. Briggs. 2003. *Voices of Modernity: Language Ideologies and the Politics of Inequality.* Cambridge: Cambridge UP.

Bendix, Regina. 2000. "The Pleasures of the Ear: Towards an Ethnography of Listening." *Cultural Analysis* 1: 33–50.

Bendix, Regina, and Dorothee Hemme. 2004. "Fairy Tale Activists: Narrative Imaginaries Along a German Tourist Route." *Tautosakos Darbai* 21: 187–97.

Benson, Stephen, ed. 2008. *Contemporary Fiction and the Fairy Tale.* Detroit: Wayne State UP.

Bernheimer, Kate, ed. 2010. *My Mother She Killed Me, My Father He Ate Me: Forty New Fairy Tales.* New York: Penguin.

Bettelheim, Bruno. 1976. *The Uses of Enchantment: The Meaning and Importance of Fairy Tales.* New York: Random House.

Bobby, Susan Redington, ed. 2009. *Fairy Tales Reimagined: Essays on New Retellings.* Jefferson: McFarland.

Carter, Angela. (1979) 2006. *The Bloody Chamber and Other Stories.* London: Vintage.

———, ed. 1982. *Sleeping Beauty and Other Favourite Fairy Tales,* illustrated by Michael Foreman. London: Gollancz.

Cavallaro, Dani. 2011. *The Fairy Tale and Anime: Traditional Themes, Images and Symbols at Play on Screen.* Jefferson, NC: McFarland.

Codrescu, Andrei. 2011. *Whatever Gets You through the Night: A Story of Sheherezade and the Arabian Entertainments.* Princeton, NJ: Princeton UP.

Conrad, JoAnn. 1998. "The Fracture in the Fairy Tale: Discursive Space in Rupture." *Tradisjon* 28: 25–36.

Coover, Robert. 1969. *Pricksongs & Descants, Fictions.* New York: Dutton.

de Caro, Frank, ed. 2008. *The Folklore Muse: Poetry, Fiction, and Other Reflections by Folklorists.* Logan: Utah State UP.

de Caro, Frank, and Rosan Augusta Jordan. 2004. *Re-Situating Folklore: Folk Contexts and Twentieth-Century Literature and Art.* Knoxville: U Tennessee P.

Dégh, Linda. 1994. *American Folklore and the Mass Media.* Bloomington: Indiana UP.

Ellis, Bill. 2012. "Fairy Tales as Metacommentary in Manga and Anime." *Marvelous Transformations*, edited by Christine Jones and Jennifer Schacker, 503–8. Toronto: Broadview P.

Fife, Wayne. 2004. "Penetrating Types: Conflating Modernist and Postmodernist Tourism on the Great Northern Peninsula of Newfoundland." *Journal of American Folklore* 464: 147–67.

Gaiman, Neil. 1999. *Stardust,* illustrated by Charles Vess. New York: HarperCollins.

———. 2005. *MirrorMask,* illustrated by Dave McKean. New York: HarperCollins.

Gilbert, Sandra, and Susan Gubar. (1984) 2000. *The Madwoman in the Attic: The Woman Writer and the Nineteenth-Century Literary Imagination.* New Haven, CT: Yale UP.

Greenhill, Pauline, and Steven Kohm. 2014. "Criminal Beasts and Swan Girls: The *Red Riding Trilogy* and Little Red Riding Hood on Television." In *Channeling Wonder: Fairy Tales on Television,* edited by Pauline Greenhill and Jill Terry Rudy, 189–209. Detroit: Wayne State UP.

Greenhill, Pauline, and Sidney Eve Matrix, eds. 2010. *Fairy Tale Films: Visions of Ambiguity.* Logan: Utah State UP.

Haase, Donald, ed. 2004. *Fairy Tales and Feminism.* Detroit: Wayne State UP.

———. 2006. "Hypertextual Gutenberg: The Textual and Hypertextual Life of Folktales and Fairy Tales in English-Language Popular Print Editions." *Fabula* 47: 222–30.

Haring, Lee. 2007. *Stars and Keys: Folktales and Creolization in the Indian Ocean,* with translations by Cladie Ricaud and Dawood Auleear. Bloomington: Indiana UP.

Harries, Elizabeth W. 2001. *Twice Upon a Time: Women Writers and the History of the Fairy Tale.* Princeton, NJ: Princeton UP.

Harvey, David. 1989. *The Condition of Postmodernity.* Cambridge, MA: Blackwell.

Hennard Dutheil de la Rochère, Martine. 2006. "Modelling for Bluebeard: Visual and Narrative Art in Angela Carter's 'The Bloody Chamber'." In *The Seeming and the Seen: Essays in Modern Visual and Literary Culture,* edited by Beverly Maeder, Jürg Schwyter, Ilona Sigrist, and Boris Vejdovsky, 183–208. Bern: Peter Lang.

Hudson, Gabe. 2004. "Notes on Craft: Some Instructions for Readers and Writers of American Fiction: An Interview with Robert Coover." www.mcsweeneys.net/articles/notes-on-craft-some-instructions-for-readers-and-writers-of-american-fiction-an-interview-with-robert-coover.

Hutcheon, Linda. 1988. *A Poetics of Postmodernism: History, Theory, Fiction.* New York: Routledge.

Jameson, Fredric. 1984. "Postmodernism, or the Cultural Logic of Late Capitalism." *New Left Review* 146: 53–92.

Jenkins, Henry. 2008. *Convergence Culture: Where Old and New Media Collide.* Revised ed. New York: NYU P.

Joosen, Vanessa. 2011. *Critical & Creative Perspectives on Fairy Tales: An Intertextual Dialogue between Fairy-Tale Scholarship and Postmodern Retellings.* Detroit: Wayne State UP.

Jorgensen, Jeana. 2007. "A Wave of the Magic Wand: Fairy Godmothers in Contemporary American Media." *Marvels & Tales* 21 (2): 216–27.

Kérchy, Anna, ed. 2011. *Postmodern Reinterpretations of Fairy Tales: How Applying New Methods Generates New Meanings.* Lewiston, NY: Edwin Mellen P.

Kirshenblatt-Gimblett, Barbara. 1998. *Destination Culture: Tourism, Museums, and Heritage.* Berkeley: U California P.

Kukkonen, Karin. 2008. "Popular Cultural Memory: Comics, Communities and Context Knowledge." *Nordicom Review* 29 (2): 261–73.

Lau, Kimberly. 1999. "Folklore and Theories of Globalization." *Folklore Forum* 30: 55–71.

———. 2008. "Erotic Infidelities: Angela Carter's Wolf Trilogy." *Marvels & Tales* 22 (1): 77–94.

Lezubski, Kirstian. 2014. "The Power to Revolutionize the World, or Absolute Gender Apocalypse? Queering the New Fairy-Tale Feminine in *Revolutionary Girl Utena*." In *Channeling Wonder: Fairy Tales on Television,* edited by Pauline Greenhill and Jill Terry Rudy, 163–85. Detroit: Wayne State UP.

Lyotard, Jean-François. (1979) 1984. *The Postmodern Condition: A Report on Knowledge,* translated by Geoff Bennington and Brian Massumi. Minneapolis: U Minnesota P.

Makinen, Merja. 2008. "Theorizing Fairy-Tale Fiction: Reading Jeanette Winterson." In *Contemporary Fiction and the Fairy Tale,* edited by Stephen Benson, 144–77. Detroit: Wayne State UP.

McAra, Catriona, and David Calvin, eds. 2011. *Anti-Tales: The Uses of Disenchantment.* Cambridge: Cambridge Scholars.

Mieder, Wolfgang. 1985. *Disenchantments: An Anthology of Modern Fairy Tale Poetry*. Lebanon, NH: UP New England.

Mills, Margaret. 1990. "Critical Theory and the Folklorists: Performance, Interpretive Authority, and Gender." *Southern Folklore* 47: 5–16.

Murai, Mayako. 2015. *From Dog Bridegroom to Wolf Girl: Contemporary Japanese Fairy-Tale Adaptations in Conversation with the West*. Detroit: Wayne State UP.

Pratchett, Terry. 1991. *Witches Abroad*. London: Victor Gollancz.

Preston, Cathy Lynn, ed. 1995. *Folklore, Literature, and Cultural Theory: Collected Essays*. New York: Garland.

———. 2004. "Disrupting the Boundaries of Genre and Gender: Postmodernism and the Fairy Tale." In *Fairy Tales and Feminism*, edited by Haase, 197–212.

Ramanujan, A. K. 1997. *The Flowering Tree and Other Oral Tales from India*. Berkeley: U California P.

Ryan, Marie-Laure. 2004. "Introduction." In *Narrative across Media: The Languages of Storytelling*, edited by Marie-Laure Ryan, 1–40. Lincoln: U Nebraska P.

Scieszka, Jon. 1992. *The Stinky Cheese Man and Other Fairly Stupid Tales*, illustrated by Lane Smith. London: Penguin.

Smith, Kevin Paul. 2007. *The Postmodern Fairytale*. New York: Palgrave Macmillan.

Tiffin, Jessica. 2009. *Marvelous Geometry: Narrative and Metafiction in Modern Fairy Tale*. Detroit: Wayne State UP.

Warshaver, Gerald E. 1991. "Postmodern Folklore." *Western Folklore* 50 (3): 219–29.

Wiesner, David. 2001. *The Three Pigs*. New York: Houghton Mifflin Harcourt.

Willingham, Bill. 2002–2015. *Fables*. New York: Vertigo DC Comics.

Zipes, Jack. 2002. *Breaking the Magic Spell: Radical Theories of Folk and Fairy Tales*. Revised and Expanded ed. Lexington: UP Kentucky.

———. 2012. *The Irresistible Fairy Tale: The Cultural and Social History of a Genre*. Princeton, NJ: Princeton UP.

Mediagraphy

Bae, Chan-Hyo. 2008–2010. *Existing in Costume: Fairy Tale Project*. Photograph Series. Korea/UK. www.mc2gallery.it/public/Chan-Hyo%20Bae.pdf.

The Bear's Tale. 1940. Director Tex Avery. USA.

The Company of Wolves. 1984. Director Neil Jordan. UK.

Enchanted. 2007. Director Kevin Lima. USA.

Fractured Fairy Tales in *Rocky and Bullwinkle Show* (TV). 1959–1964. Creators Jay Ward, Alex Anderson, and Bill Scott. USA.

Goldstein, Dina. 2011. *Fallen Princesses*. Photograph Series. USA. www.dinagoldstein.com/fallenprincesses.com.

Happily N'Ever After. 2006. Director Paul J. Bolger and Yvette Kaplan. USA.

Leishman, Donna. 2000. "red." Digital Fairy Tale. www.6amhoover.com/redriding/red.htm.

———. 2003. "The Bloody Chamber." Digital Fairy Tale. www.6amhoover.com/chamber/index_flash.htm.

MirrorMask. 2005. Director Dave McKean. UK and USA.

Mirror Mirror. 2012. Director Tarsem Singh. USA.

Once Upon a Time (TV). 2011–. Creators Adam Horowitz and Edward Kitsis. USA.

Ponyo on the Cliff by the Sea (Gake no ue no Ponyo). 2008. Director Hayao Miyasaki. Japan/USA.

Puss in Boots. 2011. Director Chris Miller. USA.

Red Hot Riding Hood. 1943. Director Tex Avery. USA.

Red Riding Trilogy. 2009. Directors Julian Jarrold, James Marsh, and Anand Tucker. UK.

Revolutionary Girl Utena (Shōjo Kakumei Utena, TV). (1997) 2011. Director Ikuhara Kunihiko. Japan/USA.

Shrek. 2001. Director Andrew Adamson and Vicky Jenson. USA.

Shrek 2. 2004. Director Andrew Adamson, Kelly Asbury, and Conrad Vernon. USA.

Shrek the Third. 2007. Director Chris Miller and Raman Hui. USA.

Stardust. 2007. Director Matthew Vaughn. USA.

10

COLONIALISM, POSTCOLONIALISM, AND DECOLONIZATION

Cristina Bacchilega and Sadhana Naithani

The definition of fairy tale stands to change the moment we connect it with colonialism, since the emergence and consolidation of fairy-tale cultures all over the world owe much to colonialism and its ideological buttresses, Orientalism and coloniality. While we know how *The Arabian Nights* were a European cultural production that, thanks to Antoine Galland's incredibly popular publication of *Le milles et une nuit* (1704–1715), fashioned an "Eastern" or "Oriental" tale characterized by opulence, sensuous women, genies, deceit, and magic, which went global in twentieth-century film (Butler 2009; Marzolph 2007a; Marzolph 2007b; Nurse 2010; Samatar 2015; Warner 2012), the impact of colonialism on the collection, translation, distribution, appeal, and study of fairy tales in the nineteenth and twentieth centuries is less discussed.

This lack depends on the international perception of the fairy tale being dominated by the European contours of this genre of storytelling, first named *conte de fées* in 1697 for a collection of French literary tales. In academic discourse the awareness of this domination and limitation of the term is acknowledged, and the genre has also been called wonder tale, tale of magic, *conte merveilleux*, and the like; in other words, the fairy tale is broadly understood as referring to narratives that deploy magic and wonder as important tools of storytelling. Thus, the fairy is not the only wondrous element that makes a tale a fairy tale; there are other animate and inanimate forms of magic and wonder. In spite of this broader definition, the European fairy tale's hegemony in common perception is unmistakable, and it is deeply and insidiously connected to colonialism and postcolonialism. This connection has spanned several centuries and informs contemporary global and capitalist media cultures. We would say that it is not possible to understand fairy tales' place in media cultures today without considering these stories' place in the colonial world.

To analyze the place of fairy-tale media and cultures today with reference to colonialism, postcolonialism, and decolonization is to reconsider colonial fairy-tale scholarship and practices, postcolonial predicaments, and actual and emerging processes of decolonization. It is also desirable to steer clear of certain popular binaries like colonizer/colonized, center/periphery, and local/global because the cultural processes under discussion here are more complex than can be contained in these binaries. Indeed, enclosing the fairy tale's circulation and appeal within simplistic notions has always proven difficult, and that is why the question of *Why Fairy Tales Stick* (Zipes 2006) remains relevant. While Jack Zipes has attempted to unearth the causes for the persistence of the pre-modern fairy tale in the postmodern realities of the Western world, fairy tales' trajectory in other parts of the world remains under-theorized. This intellectual lacuna means that the journey of the fairy tale in other parts of the world through modernity to contemporary times has been under-conceptualized. Although this gap has been recently addressed in some writings (Naithani 2010; Haase 2010; Do Rozario 2011; Briggs and Naithani 2012), much more extensive research and analysis are required to bring about change in the way the general understanding of fairy tale is shaped by the European contours of this narrative genre.

In order to rethink the definition of fairy tale we need to revisit colonial folklore scholarship and get an overview of how the fairy tales of non-European peoples were treated by European colonizers. On the one hand, in the colonial British Empire alone, the variety of folk narrative genres was immense. To identify and discuss the fairy tale—in relation to other emic genres (that is, those recognized by and relevant within the communities) of Africa, Asia, Australia, New Zealand, and Canada within the British Empire—was and is unfathomable without the knowledge of hundreds of languages and cultures. On the other hand, folklore collectors were limited as men and women from the European continent, who were White, literate, and employed by the colonial establishment. Sadhana Naithani (2010) has shown in detail how different kinds of colonial officers collected, translated, and published the folk narratives of different British colonies. In spite of the huge variety of folk narrative forms, these colonial collectors' methodologies, perceptions, and policies remained significantly similar. Created by Romantic understandings of the fairy tale and other oral narrative genres prevalent in Europe through the nineteenth century, British collectors' notions of genre in the colonies were based on imported, or etic, European folk narrative genres, namely fairy tale, folktale, legend, saga, fable, and so on.

The moment a British collector recognized an element of any of these genres in the narratives s/he was trying to gather in a colony, s/he fixed it into the European category. This fixing led to more serious problems, the most consequential being the colonial erasure of emic and Native categories of genre. Cristina Bacchilega (2007) has shown this process also taking place at the turn of the twentieth century, following the forceful annexation of the Hawaiian Kingdom to the U.S., in relation to Hawaiian *mo'olelo* (place-based stories and histories) that were translated into printed and photographically illustrated volumes of fanciful, exotic tales for Americans. These tales were not, from an emic perspective, fictional or tales of magic, and these collections—in addition to mistranslating—contributed to the infantilization and commodification of *both* Hawaiian knowledge and more generally fairy-tale culture.

The intimate relationship of narrative, place, and culture in non-European contexts was jeopardized when the narratives were disconnected from their Native generic identification and categorized as fairy tales. In *The Story-Time of the British Empire* (2010), Naithani discusses how this "cultural disjunction" (115) influenced the place of non-European wonder genres in the British colonial world. For example, calling narratives that played a role in the dispensation of legal justice "fables" not only changed the term of identification, but also the status of those narratives for international readers. Across the British Empire, collectors interpreted narratives of wonder as signs of backwardness, primitivism, ignorance, and worse in the worldview of the people who narrate them. The element of wonder convinced the British collector that people were superstitious, and the element of magical strategies to win a fight was viewed as reflective of the people's malicious nature. "Colonial folkloristics is a global theory of disjunctions" (Naithani 2010, 128) that failed to understand the philosophical perspectives behind the narratives of different cultures.

It is likely that these presumptive disjunctions between tradition and modernity, or folklore/orature and literature, were enacted within early modern Europe as well, and that such disjunctions are but part of the modern experience of culture. The dominant paradigm says Europe experienced modernity first and then took it to the colonies, which then followed suit under the influence of Europeans. Challenged by postcolonial thinkers (Chakrabarty 2007), this paradigm is in accordance with the colonizer-colonized binary. Further countering this Eurocentric paradigm, Walter D. Mignolo (2000) argues that colonialism was *the* catalytic factor in the creation of the modern world, constitutive of capitalism rather than vice versa: Europe experienced modernity after building colonial empires, or rather, colonial experience exposed Europeans and others *simultaneously* to cultural difference, causing their review of notions about the self in the light of the Other. As the joke goes: Columbus made a *great* discovery when he saw the first Indian, while the Indian who first saw Columbus made a *terrible* discovery! Mignolo's term "coloniality" applies to this *simultaneity* in an unprecedented historical moment, not containable in binary opposition; "coloniality" also applies to the ideology of colonialism that sets a standard of humanity and trajectory for progress whereby orality is necessarily inferior to literacy, a relevant point for scholars of narrative (Mignolo and Tlostanova 2007).

In its classical form, "colonialism" refers to nineteenth-century European political and economic control over other continents and involves exploitation of labor and resources in the colonies. Mignolo (2000) argues decisively that colonial exploitation began with the arrival of Columbus in the Americas in 1492, and its specific forms, such as the Spanish colonization of the Americas and the British colonization of South Asia, vary enormously from each other. In Africa, Australia, and North America, colonialism played itself out in different ways. Defined by Patrick Wolfe (2006) and applying specifically to Australia and the U.S., "settler colonialism" seeks not so much to exploit the labor and resources of the colonized, but to eliminate the Native, whether this structurally occurs via spatial removal, mass killings, or biocultural assimilation. Hawaiian historian and folk singer Jonathan Kay Kamakawiwoʻole Osorio cogently writes of how settler colonialism "through a long, insinuating invasion of people, ideas, and institutions [. . .] literally and figuratively dismembered the *lāhui* (the people) from their traditions, their lands, and ultimately their government" (2002, 3).

This story of violence is also enacted in the misrepresentation, deracination, and instrumentalization of *moʻolelo*. Bacchilega now sees the production of fairy-tale-like collections of Hawaiian stories at the turn of the twentieth century as contributing more specifically to the logic of *settler colonialism* and the replacement of Native Hawaiians with an "indigenous aura" (2015). Following the annexation of Hawaiʻi to the U.S. in 1898, stories connecting Hawaiian generations, land, and specific places were translated into English-language "fairy stories," presented as collected from a "vanishing" people, and offering a preview of the fragrance-filled paradise that settlers and tourists were being invited to experience. To refute the "vanishing Native" narrative, it is also important to note that such stories were also countered by auto-ethnographic anticolonial printed collections; Jill Terry Rudy has analyzed this uneven power struggle in a parallel process occurring with U.S. colonial collections of Native American tales in the early twentieth century (2013).

The differences between processes and experiences of colonialism are extremely significant, and yet an element connects them all, namely, the experience of disjunction of people and their stories from land, history, homegrown genres, and way of life. These disjunctions make establishing the relationship between wonder tales and reality most difficult. Within the European context, Lutz Röhrich wisely wrote: "The relationship between folktale and reality is [. . .] different in every historical epoch, it takes new shape again and again, and must be interpreted anew" (1991, 215). We proceed next to look for the fairy tale in the colonial and postcolonial realities of India in order to sketch one of many non-European scenarios concerning the changing uses and value of the genre.

While in the nineteenth century the European fairy tale was trickling into the Indian subcontinent in the forms of books and oral narration among the British populace, it was also entering the widening circle of Indians educated in the English language. And yet, its circulation was very limited. In contrast, local tales of magic and wonder seem to have been so abundant that even the British residents became aware of them, and a few became their collectors. Not only were local tales plentiful, they were also transforming under the influence of colonial reality. This alteration is not unique to India, but inflected differently in a highly literate nation such as nineteenth-century Hawai'i, where the change also involves the active translation by Hawaiians of tales from the *Arabian Nights* (Bacchilega and Arista 2007) as well as from the Grimms' (Schweizer 1988) and Perrault's collections (Kuwada 2009).

In South Asia, stories involving British gentlemen as ghosts offer a pertinent example of how this genre was so alive to the contextual reality that it changed the very image of Indian ghosts (Naithani 2001). That the British collectors did not categorize them as collectable ghost stories, seeing them instead as evidence of the superstitious nature of the Natives, is not surprising. A ghost in India was understood to be the soul of a person who died unsatisfied or had unfinished business, thus making the spirit unable or unwilling to leave the world of the living. But the Indian ghost stories of the late nineteenth century involving the British were not centered on death and the soul's desire to depart to its holy abode. Ghosts that appeared in the form of British gentlemen had several other purposes: they were either doing the work of the colonial state in a ghostly manner—killing children, chopping off heads of Native travelers, and the like—or else British officers who had lived in an area and were still seen by Native staff as ghosts in the form of cats and dogs. Indeed, some of these tales are still told in postcolonial India. And they do not all reflect poorly on the colonizer, as in the case of a ghost in a Veterinary Research Institute atop a Himalayan mountain of whom people are not afraid because they recognize him as a British veterinary scientist credited for creating major vaccines against diseases in cattle and horses.

These ghost stories are not fairy tales in the standard definition of the genre, but in India's colonial and postcolonial contexts, they point to how narratives of wonder speak to situated realities and to how what many call the supernatural is a way of grasping history. Whereas "magic"—as a sudden and mysterious means of wish fulfillment that is often now associated with the happily-ever-after attainment of riches and power—has become the prevalent association with the genre, "wonder" in a range of narrative genres, including fairy tales, elicits "attraction and recoil, producing a thrill, the shudder of pleasure and of fear. It names the marvel, the prodigy, the surprise as well as the responses they excite, of fascination and inquiry; it conveys the active motion towards experience and the passive stance of enrapturement" (Warner 2004, 3). Thinking of fairy tales in the context of colonialism, postcolonialism, and decolonization invites us to decouple the genre from wands and sparkles and to reflect more on its wondrous elements in relation to non-European wonder genres and realities.

Postcolonial reality is essentially different from colonial reality, but the impact of colonialism still defines it. In India, the dominant form of fairy tale in the media today is European. This ascendancy is expressed in books and textbooks, multimedia programs, films, games, television channels for children, and the popular fiction films often associated with Bollywood (Naithani 2015). Where is the Indian fairy tale?

Publications by A. K. Ramanujan (1997) and Kirin Narayan (1997) represent postcolonial collections that circulate internationally and within academia. In India, Indian fairy tales circulate in niche markets: as a series of comics called *Amar Chitra Katha* (1967—), an iconic publication that represents all its stories as reflective of "ancient Indian culture"; as thin volumes under broad titles based on regional identification such as *Folklore of Assam* (2012) published by the state-funded National Book Trust; and as products of a few alternative publishers and non-governmental organizations (NGOs) printing narratives of various tribal groups. *Amar Chitra Katha* is the most popular of these three projects, with no claim to authenticity or science. The National Book Trust series has limited circulation and is supposed to be dependable but has never been analytically cross-checked. The NGO publications have an articulated or implicit potential for decolonization, but none emphasize the local terminology used to categorize these narratives because the tradition of Indian fairy-tale scholarship has not yet decolonized itself. It is easier to use Euro-American categories familiar to urban educated people in India, as they are the prime consumers of these narratives.

Perhaps the British colonial collectors gave themselves the same kind of justification, as their target readers were Europeans (Sundmark 2007), and for them using European categories across the world provided a key to world folklore (Hines 2010). This practical consideration contributed at the time to make fairy-tale scholarship myopic, and the disjunction between stories and genre perpetuates today the notion that (previously) colonized people have stories, but not a tradition of abstraction in terms of genre, aesthetics, or poetic norms. The colonial portrayal of subaltern peoples as illiterate and ignorant killed expectations that they would theorize their own lives and genres. Within this colonial framework, scholars would tend not to worry about their defining categories, interpretive frameworks, or aesthetics; their narratives are meant to entertain us.

None of these Indian fairy tales, including the popular comics, occupy much space in contemporary Indian media culture when compared with the commercially oriented film industry, which has made a romantic notion of fairy tale its essential paradigm (Naithani 2015). Only a few films, such as *Bhavni Bhavai* (1980) and *Paheli* (2005), are based directly on Indian fairy tales. We should be on the lookout, however, for new cinema emerging from the northeastern parts of India, in the local languages and for the first time based on local fairy tales.

Even now, larger than the space occupied by popular cinema is that retained by oral narration in India. Tales of wonder and magic are narrated in formal and informal gatherings of people, by individuals and communities of performers, and by parents to their children. In this space, local categories continue to function. These forms are indigenously oriented: *doha dhani*, a term used by performers in Alwar, Rajasthan, for their narratives, refers to its structure of couplets; *riturain*, used by performers in the west Himalayan region, denotes the season of monsoon when these narratives are performed; and North Indian *katha* specifies both the narrative form and its performance event. Wonder tales in India often contain a religious element, but that does not make them myths. The appearance of a god in a story does not determine its genre.

However, most stories identified as fairy tales in Indian postcolonial society and media come from Disney; in fact, the old productions of Disney Studios have found a new market with globalization and through digital television networks. In contrast, the Indian fairy tale on public television is rendered in archaic style and idealized rural setting. Today's children are bound to feel alienated from this set of conventions and instead relate more strongly to Disney's slick productions. In the international context of media cultures today, wielding cutting-edge technology has become not only a crucial factor in a product's success, but the very magic by which a narrative is valorized. The Disney and Hollywood productions of fairy tales are more numerous, better distributed internationally, and richer in their picture, sound, and edit structures than those fairy tale films produced in Asia (minus Japan), Africa, the Pacific, or Latin America. This power imbalance sustains the old colonial paradigm. While educated elites understand local folklore as making children superstitious and un-modern, the global success of Disney princesses and fairy tales marks the continuation of a colonial model in postcolonial forms aimed to reproduce cultural hegemonies.

This sketch of how, in colonial and postcolonial India, the fairy tale and other wonder genres have changed in response to history seeks to suggest the complexities in using these categories in an international context and to encourage further situated studies such as those of Katrina Gutierrez and Tran Quynh Ngoc (in Stephens 2012). While thinking more flexibly of wonder across variously situated narratives may result in weaker genre boundaries and definitions, it may also begin to address the implicit hierarchy that in contemporary thought privileges the Euro-American fairy tale over the folktales of the far more extensive rest of the world.

Native and Indigenous Studies scholars in general have been suspicious of the postcolonial framework, which can ignore the claims of Indigenous people in postcolonial nations and generally seems to imply that colonialism is only in the past (Teves, Smith, and Raheja 2015). In Native and Indigenous Studies, "decolonization"—whether it is political, cultural, institutional, or all of the above—has more traction as it seeks the overturning of existing settler colonial states and emphasizes the methods of resistance and self-determination that Native peoples must engage with in the process (Ngũgĩ wa Thiong'o 1986; Tuhiwai-Smith 1999). Processes of decolonization, as well as discourses, emerge within former and currently colonized societies. In fairy-tale studies, Donald Haase called for "decolonizing" the discipline by denouncing approaches to the genre that, perhaps unwittingly, in effect "perpetuate colonialist perspectives": on the one hand, universalizing "traditional narratives at the expense of their specific historical and sociocultural contexts"; and, on the other hand, identifying "the fairy tale as a worldwide phenomenon" without doing justice "to the specifics of distinct culture" or the "differences that distinguish the European fairy tale from traditional narratives in many non-European cultures" (2010, 29). Alternatively, a transcultural approach to the genre, Haase suggests, is challenging but promising, especially if translations, edited collections, and the notion of national or cultural identity are problematized, rather than naturalized, in the process.

We agree, especially when it comes to the importance of mapping the work of translation in fairy-tale studies (Bacchilega 2015) and in urging fairy-tale scholars, whatever our location, to put non-Euro-American and Euro-American theorizations of folk-narrative genres in conversation with each other and, in doing so, to seriously consider the people's own understandings of stories and storytelling. But we also want to stress that multiple paths to decolonizing fairy-tale studies have been traced and continue to be made. Decolonizing the Disneyfied fairy-tale imaginary has informed feminist and queer approaches to the fairy tale (Turner and Greenhill 2012). Taking Native or emic genre systems as a starting point or framework for research leads to important understandings of the philosophy, knowledge system, and politics of culturally emplaced narratives (hoʻomanawanui 2014; Seifert 2002). Turning our critical attention to postcolonial and decolonizing uses of fairy tales or wonder tales in literature, film, popular culture, and social struggles can also help decenter the Euro-American fairy tale: reflecting on Nalo Hopkinson's speculative fiction (2001), the Jamaican "Cinderella" film *Dancehall Queen* (1997), and the transmedial *Sinalela* narratives by American Samoan Dan Taulapapa McMullin (2001, 2003) takes us on this path in Bacchilega's *Fairy Tales Transformed?* (2013). "Rooted in Wonder" (Yamashiro and Kuwada 2016) features wonder tales in the Pacific and North America as part and parcel of Indigenous activism and community organizing. These are not mainstream cultural products, but wonder tales, and their visionary potential are also deployed by world-renowned writers deserving of further attention, such as Salman Rushdie (Teverson 2001), Amos Tutuola, Albert Wendt, and Leslie Marmon Silko. The point of decolonizing fairy-tale studies, however, is not to expand its scope, but to change power relations within it and restore situated histories to the fantastic, in part by putting a different spin on the question of "why fairy tales stick" in order to register to whom and for what purposes non-realist tales are culturally alive as wondrous stories that are not coerced into the stronghold of fantasy as fiction only.

Extending his *Decolonising the Mind* (1986) work, award-winning novelist and scholar Ngũgĩ wa Thiong'o's *Globalectics* (2012) investigates the role of orature and the imagination in the process of de-linking the world's future from imperialism and coloniality. "Decoloniality" is not necessarily achieved at the same time of decolonization; it is rather an epistemic transformation that requires an intellectual, emotional, embodied, emplaced, and activist knowledge, a transformation that stories mobilize (Simpson 2011). Complementing or replacing Mignolo's high theory (2011), Ngũgĩ wa Thiong'o's "poor theory" is the outlook of stories that in his native Kenya mapped the interconnectedness of human bodies, land, nature, spirit, and art forms; orature—encompassing interlinked narrative genres and in alliance with literature and even "cyborature," rather than in opposition to them—is characteristic for him not of media but of a conception of the world, just as for Thomas King (2005) the distinction of Native literatures lies not in their themes but in their ways of knowing the world. We suggest that fairy tale as wonder tale connects with orature, as it takes place "in an animistic landscape, in which everything is animated" (Warner 2014, 20), and that in its making "the impossible possible" (Hopkinson and Nelson 2002, 98) lies its decolonial potential.

While "fairy tale" when applied to the folk narratives of the rest of the world is a colonial concept that continues to be useful in the work of international classification and communication, particularly for media and state institutions, it is time to focus on what makes a fairy tale, past or present, decolonial and on how this may change our definition of a genre that is not *the* wonder tale, but one among numerous wondrous genres.

References Cited and Further Reading

Amar Chitra Katha. 2015. "Stories Alive: Since 1967." *ACK Media.* www.ack-media.com/AmarChitraKatha.aspx.

Bacchilega, Cristina. 2007. *Legendary Hawaiʻi and the Politics of Place: Tradition, Translation, and Tourism.* Philadelphia: U Pennsylvania P.

———. 2013. *Fairy Tales Transformed? 21st-Century Adaptations and the Politics of Wonder.* Detroit: Wayne State UP.

———. 2015. "Narrative Cultures, Situated Story Webs, and the Politics of Relation." *Narrative Culture* 2 (1): 27–46.

Bacchilega, Cristina, and Noelani Arista. 2007. "The Arabian Nights in the Kuokoa, a Nineteenth-Century Hawaiian Newspaper: Reflections on the Politics of Translation." In *Arabian Nights in Transnational Perspectives*, edited by Ulrich Marzoph, 157–82. Detroit: Wayne State UP.

Briggs, Charles L., and Sadhana Naithani. 2012. "Coloniality of Folklore. Towards Multiple Genealogies." *Studies in History* 28 (2): 231–70.

Butler, David. 2009. *Fantasy Cinema: Impossible Worlds on Screen.* London: Wallflower P.

Chakrabarty, Dipesh. 2007. *Provincializing Europe.* Revised ed. Princeton, NJ: Princeton UP.

Das, Jogesh. 2012. *Folklore of Assam.* New Delhi: National Book Trust, India.

Do Rozario, Rebecca-Anne C. 2011. "Australia's Fairy Tales Illustrated in Print: Instances of Indigeneity, Colonization, and Suburbanization." *Marvels & Tales* 25 (1): 13–32.

Haase, Donald. 2010. "Decolonizing Fairy-Tale Studies." *Marvels & Tales* 24 (1): 17–38.

Hines, Sara. 2010. "Collecting the Empire: Andrew Lang's Fairy Books (1899–1910)." *Marvels & Tales* 24 (1): 39–56.

hoʻomanawanui, kuʻualoha. 2014. *Voices of Fire: Reweaving the Literary Lei of Pele and Hiʻiaka.* Minneapolis: U Minnesota P.

Hopkinson, Nalo. 2001. *Skin Folk.* New York: Warner Books.

Hopkinson, Nalo, and Alondra Nelson. 2002. "Making the Impossible Possible: An Interview with Nalo Hopkinson." *Social Text* 20 (2): 97–113.

King, Thomas. 2005. *The Truth about Stories: A Native Narrative.* Minneapolis: U Minnesota P.

Kuwada, Bryan Kamaoli. 2009. "How Blue Is His Beard? An Examination of the 1862 Hawaiian-Language Translation of 'Bluebeard'." *Marvels & Tales* 23 (1): 17–39.

Marzolph, Ulrich. 2007a. "Arabian Nights." In *EI: The Encyclopaedia of Islam Three Preview*, edited by Kate Fleet, Gudrun Krämer, Denis Matringe, John Nawas, and Everett Rowson, 30–40. Leiden: Brill.

———, ed. 2007b. *The Arabian Nights in Transnational Perspective.* Detroit: Wayne State UP.

McMullin, Dan Taulapapa. 2003. "The One-Eyed Fish." *Spectator* 23 (1): 113–15.

Mignolo, Walter D. 2000. *Local Histories/Global Designs: Coloniality, Subaltern Knowledges, and Border Thinking.* Princeton, NJ: Princeton UP.

———. 2011. *The Darker Side of Western Modernity: Global Futures, Decolonial Options.* Durham, NC: Duke UP.

Mignolo, Walter D., and Madina Tlostanova. 2007. "The Logic of Coloniality and the Limits of Postcoloniality." In *The Postcolonial and the Global*, edited by Revathi Krishnaswamy and John Charles Hawley, 109–23. Minneapolis: U Minnesota P.

Naithani, Sadhana. 2001. "An Axis Jump: British Colonialism in the Oral Folk Narratives of Nineteenth Century India." *Folklore* 112 (2): 183–8.

———. 2008. "Colonialism." In *The Greenwood Encyclopedia of Folk and Fairy Tales*, edited by Donald Haase, 222–6. Westport: Greenwood.

———. 2010. *The Story-Time of the British Empire: Colonial and Postcolonial Folkloristics.* Jackson: UP of Mississippi.

———. 2015. "'It's All a Fairy-Tale': A Folklorist's Reflections on Storytelling in Popular Hindi Cinema." In *Fairy Tale Films Beyond Disney: International Perspectives*, edited by Jack Zipes, Pauline Greenhill, and Kendra Magnus-Johnston, 196–206. New York: Routledge.

Narayan, Kirin, with Urmila Devi Sood. 1997. *Mondays on the Dark Night of the Moon.* London: Oxford UP.

Ngũgĩ wa Thiong'o. 1986. *Decolonising the Mind: The Politics of Language in African Literature.* London: Heinemann.

———. 2012. *Globalectics: Theory and the Politics of Knowing.* New York: Columbia UP.

Nurse, Paul McMichael. 2010. *Eastern Dreams.* Toronto: Viking.

Osorio, Jonathan Kay Kamakawiwo'ole. 2002. *Dismembering Lāhui: A History of the Hawaiian Nation to 1887.* Honolulu: U Hawai'i P.

Ramanujan, A. K. 1997. *A Flowering Tree and Other Oral Tales from India*, edited by Stuart Blackburn and Alan Dundes. Berkeley: U California P.

Röhrich, Lutz. 1991. *Folktales and Reality*, translated by Peter Tokofsky. Bloomington: Indiana UP.

Rudy, Jill Terry. 2013. "American Folklore Scholarship, *Tales of the North American Indians*, and Relational Communities." *Journal of American Folklore* 499: 3–30.

Samatar, Sofia. 2015. "Spectacle of the Other: Recreating *A Thousand and One Nights* in Film." In *Fairy Tale Films Beyond Disney: International Perspectives*, edited by Jack Zipes, Pauline Greenhill, and Kendra Magnus-Johnston, 34–47. New York: Routledge.

Schweizer, Niklaus R. 1988. "Kahaunani: 'Snow White' in Hawaiian: A Study in Acculturation." In *East Meets West: Homage to Edgar C. Knowlton, Jr.*, edited by Roger L. Hadlich and J. D. Ellsworth, 283–9. Honolulu: U Hawai'i P.

Seifert, Lewis C. 2002. "Orality, History, and 'Creoleness' in Patrick Chamoiseau's Creole Folktales." *Marvels & Tales* 16 (2): 214–30.

Simpson, Leanne. 2011. *Dancing on Our Turtle's Back. Stories of Nishnaabeg Re-Creation, Resurgence and a New Emergence.* Winnipeg: Arbeiter Ring Publishing.

Stephens, John, ed. 2012. *Subjectivity in Asian Children's Literature and Film: Global Theories and Implications.* New York: Routledge.

Sundmark, Björn. 2007. "In the Hope White People Will Like Them: Andrew Lang and the Colonization of Fairyland." In *Expectations and Experiences: Children, Childhood, and Children's Literature*, edited by Clare Bradford and Valerie Coghlan, 111–21. Lichfield, Staffordshire: Pied Piper.

Teverson, Andrew S. 2001. "Fairy Tale Politics: Free Speech and Multiculturalism in Haroun and the Sea of Stories." *Twentieth Century Literature* 47 (4): 444–66.

Teves, Stephanie Nohelani, Andrea Smith, and Michelle H. Raheja. 2015. "Colonialism." In *Native Studies Keywords*, edited by Stephanie Nohelani Teves, Andrea Smith, and Michelle H. Raheja, 271–83. Tucson: U Arizona P.

Tuhiwai-Smith, Linda. 1999. *Decolonizing Methodologies.* London: Zed.

Turner, Kay, and Pauline Greenhill, eds. 2012. *Transgressive Tales: Queering the Grimms.* Detroit: Wayne State UP.

Warner, Marina, ed. 2004. *Wonder Tales: Six French Stories of Enchantment.* Oxford: Oxford UP.

———. 2012. *Stranger Magic: Charmed States and The Arabian Nights.* Cambridge, MA: Harvard UP.

———. 2014. *Once Upon a Time.* Oxford: Oxford UP.

Wolfe, Patrick. 2006. "Settler Colonialism and the Elimination of the Native." *Journal of Genocide Research* 8 (4): 387–409.

Yamashiro, Aiko, and Bryan Kamaoli Kuwada, eds. 2016. "Rooted in Wonder." Special issue, *Marvels & Tales* 30 (1).

Zipes, Jack. 2006. *Why Fairy Tales Stick: The Evolution and Relevance of a Genre.* New York: Routledge.

Mediagraphy

Bhavni Bhavai. 1980. Director Ketan Mehta. India.
Dancehall Queen. 1997. Directors Rick Elgood and Don Letts. Jamaica.
Paheli. 2005. Director Amol Palekar. India.
Sinalela. 2001. Director Dan Taulapapa McMullin. Samoa/USA.

Part III

ISSUES

Political and Identity Issues

11

ACTIVISM

Folktales and Social Justice: When Marvelous Tales From the Oral Tradition Help Rethink and Stir the Present From the Margins

Vivian Labrie

> Humankind's adventure realises itself simultaneously in the singularity of each of our lives and in its collective capacity to constitute itself from now on into a positive subject of its own history. The relationship between personal and collective transformation is no more coined by the old opposition between reforms of mentalities and reforms of structure. Both approaches to transformation should be comprised and conducted as complements within a dynamic tension. To dream that another world is possible is not enough. We must also recognize and sustain other ways of being in this world that are already there though not seen by us.
>
> (Viveret 2005, 39–40)

Can marvelous tales, or *Märchen*, typical of the Aarne-Thompson-Uther (ATU) classification, collected from oral tradition and kept in formal folklore archives, help rethink and stir present-day issues from the margins of society? As singular as it is, this has been my experience in Quebec for almost forty years. I cannot step aside from my personal history to reflect on folktales and activism or, alternately, civic action for social justice. So I'll tell what I know, present some tales and how they interacted with real life issues. This should suffice to open the discussion about what might be learned from this unusual path of research-plus-quest for further adventures between reality, fiction, and the world to be.

Typology and Topology: What Does Humankind Tell Itself Through *Märchen*?

This story started on the research side in the 1970s while I was doing fieldwork with my colleague Robert Bouthillier. We collected an immense number of folksongs and folktales in Quebec and Acadie (Acadia), now archived at the Laval University Folklore and Ethnology

Archives. My personal focus was on marvelous folktales: I wanted to understand from the tale tellers themselves how they had learned and shared the extended and complex tales we were collecting from them. Among other things, they presented these tales of magic as tales of hardships (*contes de misères*) and tales of going through (*contes de traverses*) and explained that they more or less memorized them as journeys. Some responded with intricate designs when I asked them to map a tale on paper. I made a connection with the ancient method of *loci*, described by Cicero, of memorizing speeches by mentally spreading parts of them along a known path. This was far from the textual mechanisms of the written word, but close to a visual, vivid, figurative, metaphorical representation of meanings organized in a significant path that could be called, followed, and recalled (Labrie 1980, 1983).

In the 1980s, I started mapping tales myself and was astonished by their beautiful and somewhat unexpected topologies and arrangements of motifs. Some of these maps popped up when I looked for theoretical frames of reference to make sense of results from a research project about the bureaucratic culture of welfare recipients, agents, and managers. This led to links with movies sharing similar topologies and to new questions about what humankind tells itself through *Märchen* and their paths of cognition and transmission (Labrie 1984, 1990).

In the early 1990s, research on transitions—the "going through" aspect of tales—and helping others/being helped in real life and in folktales gave me the occasion to collect actual stories of help and to study and map a substantial corpus of *Märchen* collected in Quebec and Acadie. The mapping technique helped me grasp the tales' systemic organization in ways that would echo various concerns in human and social ecology (Labrie 1994b).

The results of this topological approach questioned some received ideas about folktales (Labrie 1999). Although the so-called hero could be approached as the figure who linked the greatest quantity of territory, in fact, quite often, other figures took on the story's relay and could be called heroes for the spatiotemporal portion where they were in charge. This folk repertoire offered imaginary worlds with specific space/time portions that could be mapped and studied with tools similar to those used in the social sciences. Mapped versions of a same type were consistent, as if they were modeling some kind of dynamic, just as theories try to present a model of the real world. The difference resided in the fact that in tales these models arrive already built, polysemic, incomplete although in unlimited numbers of versions. They give no cues to what they model, except that specific constellations of meanings can be studied as such and can sometimes be linked to similar configurations in fiction or real life. Are folktale types and their constellations of meanings theories per se? And if so, theories of what and for whom (Labrie 2004, 2014b)?

Let's transfer now to the quest side.

Aiming at a Society Free From Poverty

While still pursuing research, I became more socially engaged. By the end of the 1980s, I took jobs with popular education tasks in the low-income community where I lived in Quebec. I worked with groups involved in various social justice issues: literacy, poverty, inequalities, social policy, and international solidarity, for example. The posture and inspiration came from Paulo Freire's *Pedagogy of the Oppressed* and his approach to conscientization (1970, 1973): we learn from each other, and we can experiment and propose the changes we want for our world. Those who are excluded by the dominant neoliberal ideology must be part not only of the action, but also of the forums where the thinking is done. My workplace became a meeting place where ideas were shared with individuals living in poverty, others in solidarity with them, and various other actors and groups. The coalitions we took part in gathered people from workers' unions, student unions, community groups, feminist groups, religious groups, and cooperatives. With the Bread and Roses March of Women in 1995, and the International Year for the Eradication of Poverty, we started dreaming of a Quebec free from poverty. As "one must dream logically"—an expression from Yvette Muise, a woman living in poverty—our work led to the formation of the Collectif pour une loi sur l'élimination de la pauvreté (Collective for a Law on the Elimination of Poverty) in 1998 (Labrie 2008). In this context, many of my tasks consisted of teamwork where we devised events, sessions, and meetings during which we opened a specific issue and facilitated reflections and exchanges around it. This is where the folktales, which were at hand for me from my folk research background, come in on the quest side of my narrative.

Short forms, like ATU 1548, "The Stone Soup," where a meal for all is cooked with the addition of everyone's contribution to a stone starting the soup in a pot of boiling water, were of great help as starters for a group discussion (Labrie 1997b). However, unexpectedly, *Märchen* from Laval University's folklore archives proved themselves good theories to apply to some social justice issues. Without losing their polysemic potential to bear meaning on other levels, they provided fresh frames of reference that allowed thinking outside the box and helped personal and collective long-lasting appropriations of these issues. I'll give four examples: one about the economy; the next about politics; the third about the workplace; and the last about utopia. While all four tales joined the struggle in the 1990s, they remain alive, and they have become part of the theoretical apparatus I use on various occasions. Some of them have even found new lives in France.[1]

Crotte mon âne (ATU 563):[2] About the Economy

I first used this version of ATU 563, "The Table, the Donkey, and the Stick," in 1975, in an experiment for research on memorization (Labrie 1998c). Another chapter of its adventures happened in 1996 when we used it as a framework to introduce a group of adult participants of Atout-Lire, a literacy group, to economics. They had taken part in an anti-poverty event, the *Jeûne à relais du refus de la misère* (Relay Fast Against Poverty), organized with many groups in Quebec (Labrie 1997b). This two-week rotating fast sought the inclusion of an engagement from the government not to further impoverish the poorest fifth of the Quebec population with zero deficit measures in the agenda of the upcoming Summit on Economy and Employment. This fast had raised questions about the economy among some Atout-Lire members, and the group asked me for a series of three workshops to address them.

I suggested we could use this tale version in which an old sick man is sent to work in the woods by his wife. He is given a donkey that craps money on order. En route, a squall has him stop at a house for the night. Requested not to say "Crotte mon âne" ("Crap, my donkey"), his hosts uncover the trick and substitute a normal donkey. A similar scheme happens with a towel that provides food. The third time, when released from a tobacco container, a horsefly stings the villain hosts until the old man recovers the donkey and the towel.

During the first workshop, we evoked the etymology of the word "economy," *oikos-nomos*, or "house in order." This elicitation led us to determine that there is a lot of disorder in this tale's houses! Each episode revealed connections to the economy: with that of the donkey, we reviewed how money comes and goes in our lives; with that of the towel, we checked how food and other goods move from one table to another, using the proximity in French between "table" and "accountability"; and with the horsefly, we asked who rendered justice in the

Figure 11.1 The emblem of the *"Nuit des taons qui piquent"* in 1997, which built on *Crotte mon âne* (drawn by author)

economic system and if the government was a host taking goods from others or a stinging insect helping people receive their due. This ended up some months later in a *"Nuit des taons qui piquent"* (Night of Stinging Horseflies), an event attended by 200 people within the community (see figure 11.1). Songs were composed, workshops were held, and at dawn a joyful delegation brought a letter mentioning the tale in a call for economic justice to the prime minister of Quebec, leaving his early morning swim (Labrie 1997a).

While developing these events, an independent confirmation of our use of this tale's metaphor of the horsefly came when I got a copy of a local university bulletin about socioeconomy that cited as its motto this statement attributed to Socrates: *"Je suis le taon qui trouble votre quiétude"* (I am the horsefly bothering your complacency). This story has helped in various contexts to approach the economy in a concrete, justice-minded way. More recently, when I told the tale, and its adventures, which have become part of the telling, to a group of elders, I asked them what they would do if they had such a horsefly at their disposal. One said she would open the tobacco box and it would know whom to sting. Another one said he would free the horsefly, which would have offspring to feed, because it was unfair that it be detained. That won the consensus. Quite revolutionary for tranquil elderly individuals, many with significant losses of capacity.

Les trois princes (ATU 551):[3] About Politics

This version of ATU 551, "Water of Life," has inspired various analogies since I proposed it around 1992 as a sort of strategy manual for marginalized groups: Machiavelli had his Prince, why not the poor? The Prince of the Poor is the youngest of three princes. Being attentive to the well-being of a poor woman who works hard to feed her many children helps him find the water that cures every sickness to cure his father's eyes when his elder brothers fail. When he brings back the bottle, he meets his brothers, who take the water while he rests and pretend they found it. This works until a princess arrives at the harbor with her infant son and asks for the Prince of the Poor. The brothers can't explain how they got the water, and the Prince of the Poor is brought back from exile. He correctly explains how he found and collected the water and stirred the princess sleeping in the same castle, leaving her his location for when she would wake up. To his dismay, the father now sees the events otherwise.[4]

A book, events, and sessions led me to explore this tale's potential (Labrie 1994a). It was influential in releasing personal motivations to engage further and deeper in resolute collective actions to organize, convince, and make gains in the anti-poverty agenda. We linked it with a metaphor of salmon swimming upstream. Once, we reviewed it for its sequence of obstacles and how, when, and by whom they were countered (Labrie 1998a). These adventures with *Les trois princes* strengthened my hold on real politics. Political and economic decisions are often built along similar hardcore strategic and tactical interactions, generally interested, often brutal and ruthless, exceptionally transcending. They have vital impacts on people's lives, in particular for those at the margins who do not manage to win the game of the strongest over better equipped co-citizens. This tale also helped us become more aware of a less noble part of collective action: power games within the ranks of so-called brothers and sisters. How do you cultivate a clear vision and a posture of caring and kindness while still being strategic?

However meaningful at this level, this tale could not be limited to a manual for social strategy. On a very different level, in 2001, while walking the pilgrimage of the *grande troménie* (great pilgrimage/procession) of Locronan in Brittany, I was struck by many parallels between the *troménie*'s path and the topological features of *Les trois princes*. I explored another level in 2007, this time about popular education and how we could see it at work in the tale, during a meeting with Quebec groups involved in community action (see figure 11.2). As with *Crotte mon âne*, this tale was presented to various groups in a study about elders and social participation. Unexpectedly, the elders did not identify with their counterparts in the tale, but with the Prince of the Poor, and this led them to tell stories of indiscipline, including calls received from their own grandparents to rebel against injustice (Pelchat et al. 2010).

Le bateau qui va sur terre et sur mer (ATU 513):[5]
About the Workplace

This version (ATU 513A, "Six Go Through the Whole World," and ATU 513B, "The Land and Water Ship") served as a metaphor about employment and activity for a project in 1997–1998 with persons living in poverty and civil servants from the employment and welfare ministry in Quebec (Carrefour de savoirs sur les finances publiques and Labrie 1998). The youngest of three brothers, left out and disregarded by the rest of his family, builds a ship that goes on land and sea with the help of an old woman he was kind to whereas his brothers weren't. He leaves his family and travels with his ship. On his quest, he meets companions with extraordinary skills: Grugeon, who has no end to what he can eat; Bon Coureux, who runs fast; BrasseMontagne, who is preternaturally strong; Grand Souffleux, whose nostrils can launch hurricanes. Challenged by a king to a series of contests, they beat his men and his athletic princess, win huge amounts of bounty, leave with the princess, escape the king's ships, and pursue their own lives.

This tale provided metaphorical space to wonder whether regular jobs under the king's rule are the sole way to earn a living. It explored what happens to those in society who are excessively good at one thing but are left aside from standard life and normal nine-to-five paid work schedules until they are called to serve aboard a "land and water ship" (see figure 11.3)! During our project, we asked some questions: Do you remember a situation where a marginalized

Figure 11.2 One of the images found in the account of a 2007 session where *Le conte des trois princes* was shared in a workshop on popular education

and immoderate person contributed to solving a problem? What would be needed to ensure everyone has a function to his/her measure in society? Does it happen that we are useful only at precise moments, but then *very* useful? Government work programs were seen by the group as perilous quicksand between land and water, which called for a land, air, and water ship. In 2002, the inspiration of this project was not far when, during an event in front of the Quebec National Assembly, a group of artists issued competence cards based on free-form declarations of skills. There was a Great Singer, a Teller of True Stories, a Philosopher of the Low Seasons, an Accomplished Citizen, a Poetic Retailer, a Small Doer, and so on. Since then, this tale has found its way into the work of a French association, AequitaZ, about everyone's capacity to serve his/her crew.

Figure 11.3 Drawing made in reference to the tale by Nancy Beauseigle, who was responsible for the project on employment and activity

La barrière verte (L'eau qui bouille, l'arbre qui chante et le z-oiseau qui dit tout) (ATU 707):[6] **About Utopia**

This tale is a version of ATU 707, "The Three Golden Children." Two boys and a girl born to a queen and king are replaced in their crib by two dogs and a cat. They are put in a basket and launched in a river where they are found and raised by foster parents. The mother, accused of sorcery, is exiled. The foster parents die, but the children stay together. One day, the girl finds an old woman at the edge of the wood who says their fine garden could be even more beautiful if they had the bubbling water, the singing tree, and the bird of truth found in the garden of the end of the world.

We have here a good example of a three world topology (Labrie 1999). In the first world, the family is broken by half-truths and misdirection from the mother's siblings. In the second world, the children are raised peacefully in a coexisting territory with no idea of their origin. The truth is revealed when the children bring back the bird of truth from the third world. Resting on the shoulder of the girl, during a large feast which includes the royal family, the bird tells what happened, and the wrongdoings are exposed. This version, coupled with another that was part of my research corpus, has helped open various discussions on social control, non-violent action, and the quest for utopia (Labrie 1998b).

Utopia comes from the Greek roots *u*, not existing, and *topos*, place. Somehow the tale's progression opens up possibilities after the terrible deeds in the first world. It could be possible to maintain the unresolved state of coexistence. However, when the children are prompted

Figure 11.4 Danielle's bird, as photographed by the group (Carrefour de savoirs sur les besoins essentiels), at the meeting featuring a version of ATU 707 at the end of a two-year project with persons living in poverty in June 2005

to a quest for a better garden, they do not know where to find the end of the world. They discover that it is protected by a frightening space where they hear terrible cries which make them want to turn their heads, although they must not, or they will be changed into stone. The boys, who are first on the quest, do turn their heads. Only the girl finds the attention, resolve, and means to go through. With the help of an old man, she is bound to her horse, blindfolded, and ears stuffed, so she can keep her posture and find herself at last in the not-yet-existing—at least for her—garden.

The condition for justice to be re-established, this passage in u-topia, becomes the occasion for a truthful and more just integration of the three territories into one single, better informed universe. Not bad for a folktale.[7] At times the marvelous happens in real life too. It did in June 2005, during the final meeting of a two-year project, which involved a group of persons living in poverty. Participants had mentioned the importance of animal companions in their lives. Many had birds at home. So when preparing the agenda, the other moderator and I decided that I would tell this tale. The surprise came when Danielle, a participant, arrived with her lovebird in her T-shirt. She did not know I would tell the tale. Who brings birds to meetings? That's how I found myself telling the tale of the "bird of truth" in front of a bird resting on Danielle's shoulder (see figure 11.4). It was as if I had really met the girl in the tale.

Discussion and Issues for Future Work

These are only a few examples among the possibilities of an immense repertoire. Nonetheless we can learn from them and from their contribution to actual episodes of collective action for social justice.

Open, multilevel, evolving, yet singular constellations of meanings are perceived, nourished, and mediated between reality and fiction. I was a conscious facilitator. However, what transposed from research to quest with those tales was part of their own substance, including what was ingrained in them from their transmission through oral tradition—from folks to folks. Similarly, they were enriched, as were their subsequent narrations, by how other folks made sense of them for present-day issues they were confronting. These moments of sense-making and their anecdotes became part of their evolving yet singular constellations of meanings. Now, when I tell those tales, I can also bring up their travelogues, either briefly or extensively.

Inspiration is (re)gained from self-contained, short-lived representations of real problems and their possible resolutions from the margins. Although unusually mediated from research to quest, these interactions between reality and fiction took place and could happen again. They provided fresh and unusual emic (insiders') theories about hardships and their resolution from the margins to other people experiencing similar marginal situations. As do theories and models on a metaphorical level, the tales brought self-contained representations of problematic situations, with their components and possible moves, that could elicit inspiring parallels with equivalent situations in real life. They featured fixed and oppressive worldviews which produce exclusion and showed how they could be transcended or returned, through a succession of often improbable moves empowered by those who are left out and their allies, into a more satisfying state of the world for the remaining time of this story, which is short. As one tale teller I met in the 1970s said: "they are happy only five minutes at the end!"

A humble folks-to-folks posture is needed. An influential mainstream approach to *Märchen* claims the oral branches emanate from the published corpuses (Bottigheimer 2009). Although there is no beginning or end to an origins debate, this assumption is of no avail in the context described here, where tales moved from well-identified oral sources to the brouhaha of everyday life. Although mediated by an ethnographer who happened to be an activist as well, what happened here proceeded from a folks-to-folks posture, where unconsidered knowledge helped empower unconsidered persons, just like when, in tales, the key to the story's advancement resides not in the golden, gilded axe, but in the rusty one. In *Les trois princes*, the healing water must be collected in an old mossy bottle, not in the nicer ones. Other tales also show that the scheme at stake will not function if used for glorious or malevolent purposes. It works only within a humble posture.

Cues are given toward a possible epistemology of path making from the margins. This issue raises questions about the ways and characteristics of marvelous tales as genuine contributions to an epistemology of path-making from the margins. These tales need to be approached as such to deliver their potential. Michel Foucault's reflections about dominant knowledge, buried or subservient knowledge, and *le savoir des gens* (literally folk-lore) could be invoked here (1997). What I learned from traditional tale tellers about memory, transmission, and the semi-automatic, ever-evolving, collaborative way of living tradition on the research side was quite far from some predicaments of academic knowledge about folktales but proved quite close to the requirements of thinking/acting together for personal/collective transformation, or praxis, on the quest side.

These tales were not magic wands nor power tools, which, I venture, could lead to propaganda or social control. In fact, just as the first brothers will not share their snack with the old woman, and hence never build a land and water ship, they were easily disregarded by those with fixed ideas. But they acted as re-minders for the already re-minded, as clue givers for clue seekers, as theoretical tools for those trying to imagine ways through.

If humankind is depositing cues and clues about its immemorial adventures through the type-specific paths of marvelous tales, what it is thus telling itself remains open for further research. In a more general, meta-analytical way, what can be learned from the variety of quests in marvelous tales for the variety of quests in real life opens possibilities for further explorations on the research side as well as on the quest side. Here the scholar returns and draws on what could be observed while mapping a more extensive corpus and checking it for how one is helped or of help during the transitions and transactions in these stories (Labrie 1999, 2014b). In the studied corpus, there was no evidence for such polarized statements as one path fits all, or all paths are unique. What was found was a variety of type-related topologies with specific arrangements of worlds and recognizable path configurations across those universes.

Various events, movies (Labrie 2014a), and stories in real life would come, exemplify, and populate these still quite uncharted territories at one level or another (biological, cognitive, psychological, interpersonal, social, political, cosmic, metaphysical, spiritual, and so on) of their constellation of meanings; it would make sense, and at times long-lasting and enlightening sense. This is per se a very compelling aspect: if a given topology, say *Les trois princes*, can make sense at various levels, it tells something about how we humans think, explore, interact, wander, wonder, and solve problems. These hide-and-seek, almost geocache-like tribulations between levels of similar topologies could be documented to inform the research side, or the quest side, or both. The challenge is tailor-made for socially engaged ethnographers.

The method calls for rigorous and open minds. Although the links are unpredictable, a suitable attitude in this pursuit could include the following precepts. Access collected materials as they are and pay attention to their topology. Build a repertoire of stories and motifs. Listen to the real world and its stories and pay attention to their topology. Allow polysemy. Notice when links and associations are made. Superimpose the stories and check for their common grounds and common denominators without over-imposing. Keep it light, share, and have fun. Notice what speaks to you when it does. Check for chains of links when a link is found, including the equivalents in other registers of the supernatural aspects in the tale.[8] Enjoy the awesome. And know some will say it's all lies.

Related topics: Animal Studies; Oral Tradition; Traditional Song

Notes

1. Given the space and language factors that keep the full narrations in French out of reach, I must limit this presentation to the plot as the center of attention.
2. Told by Hermel Tremblay, Saint-Joseph-de-la-Rive, QC, 1947. Laval University Archive of Folklore and Ethnology (LUAFE), collected by Luc Lacourcière and Félix-Antoine Savard, 303–305.
3. Told by Mrs. André Blanchard, seventy-four years old, Hauterive, Saguenay, QC, June 30, 1955. LUAFE, collected by Luc Lacourcière, 2357.
4. I cannot present here the many details in the tale that could be read, from a sociopolitical level, as sound strategic advice for the Princes of the Poor of this world.
5. Told by Hilaire Benoit, seventy-two years old, Tracadie, NB, September 30, 1977. LUAFE, collected by Robert Bouthillier and Vivian Labrie, 3531.
6. Told by Mrs. Pierrot Haché, seventy-three years old, Le Goulet, Shippagan, NB, November, 1951. LUAFE, collected by Dominique Gauthier, 25.
7. I must express gratitude here for the inspiration gained, not only by me but by family, friends, and other companions, in this motif of the so-frightening, yet possible if one stays still, crossing of a mined field, just before some not-yet-existing liberation becomes possible. It has accompanied our own quests in various instances, like a voice recalling an immemorial truth to frightened ears.
8. Curiously enough, it was precisely the marvelous features of a long tale we were exploring together that a group of persons living in poverty in France one day saw as the most lifelike features of the tale!

References Cited and Further Reading

Bottigheimer, Ruth B. 2009. *Fairy Tales: A New History*. Albany: SUNY P.

Carrefour de savoirs sur les finances publiques, and Vivian Labrie. 1998. *Des concepts économiques pour tenir compte du problème de la pauvreté et de l'exclusion: Les plus pauvres et les finances publiques—1998–1999*. Québec: Carrefour de pastorale en monde ouvrier.

Foucault, Michel. 1997. *Il faut défendre la société: Cours au Collège de France—1976*. Paris: Gallimard-Seuil.

Freire, Paulo. 1970. *Pedagogy of the Oppressed*. New York: Herder and Herder.

———. 1973. *Education for Critical Consciousness*. 1st ed. New York: Seabury P.

Labrie, Vivian. 1980. "How Can We Understand the Retention of a Folktale?" In *Folklore from Two Continents: Essays in Honor of Linda Dégh*, edited by Nikolai Burlakhof, Carl Lindahl, and Harry Gammerdinger, 286–92. Bloomington: Trickster P.

———. 1983. "The Itinerary as a Possible Memorized Form of the Folktale." *ARV Scandinavian Yearbook of Folklore* 37: 89–102.

———. 1984. "Cartographie et analyse graphique de l'univers physique du conte à odyssée." In *Le conte, pourquoi? Comment?*, edited by Geneviève Calame-Griaule, Veronika Görög-Karady, and Michèle Chiche, 545–79. Paris: Éditions du CNRS.

———. 1990. "D'une histoire de galère à une rêverie mathématique: réflexion sur le lien entre la vie et les contes." In *D'un conte . . . à l'autre: la variabilité dans la littérature orale*, edited by Veronika Görög-Karady, 439–60. Paris: Éditions du CNRS.

———, ed. 1994a. *Les Trois Princes: Y voir plus clair à partir des pauvres, Collection Interactions*. Montréal: Novalis.

———. 1994b. "Topologie, contes et écologie humaine et sociale: des convergences épistémologiques." *Canadian Folklore Canadien* 16 (2): 59–87.

———. 1997a. "La pauvreté et les assistés sociaux." In *La crise de l'emploi. De nouveaux partages s'imposent!*, edited by Gilles Laflamme, Paul-André Lapointe, Alain Larocque, Jacques Mercier, Sylvie Morel, and Fernand Morin, 27–43. Québec: P de l'U Laval.

———. 1997b. "Let's Do It and It Will Get Done." In *Stone Soup: Reflections on Economic Injustice*, edited by Conférence religieuse canadienne and Jesuit Centre for Social Faith and Justice, 41–70. Montréal: Paulines.

———. 1998a. "Impasses: pourtant on passe et ça nous dépasse!" In *Intervenir à contre-courant: De nouvelles pratiques solidaires*, edited by Michel Beaudin, Monique Dumais, Guy Paiement, and Michel Rioux, 173–96. Montréal: Fides.

———. 1998b. "Intervenir en terrain miné: contrôler ou [se] désarmer?" In *Petite enfance, jeunes familles et prévention: Actes du colloque de printemps, Montréal, du 20 au 22 mai 1998*, edited by Club de pédiatrie sociale. Montréal: Ministère de la santé et des services sociaux, Gouvernement du Québec.

———. 1998c. "Les aventures immémoriales d'une version de l'âne qui crotte de l'argent." *Cahiers de littérature orale* 43: 163–85.

———. 1999. "Going through Hard Times: A Topological Exploration of a Folktale Corpus from Quebec and Acadie." *Fabula* 40 (1/2): 50–73.

———. 2004. "Traverses et misères dans les contes et dans la vie: Essai de systématisation d'un réflexe de chercheure." *Ethnologie* 26 (1): 61–93.

———. 2008. "Faisons-le et ça se fera! Histoire d'une affiche et d'un mouvement citoyen vers un Québec sans pauvreté." In *Tenir Parole! Trajectoires et paroles citoyennes autour d'une affiche*, edited by Collectif pour un Québec sans pauvreté, Marie-Claude Rose, Johanne Chagnon, Vivian Labrie, Micheline Belisle, Sophie Dupéré, France Fournier, Élisabeth Germain, Michel O'Neill, and Ian Renaud-Lauzé, 18–31. Québec: P de l'U Laval.

———. 2009. "Un siècle ou la suite du monde." In *Bretagnes: Du cœur aux lèvres: Mélanges offerts à Donatien Laurent*, edited by Fanch Postic, 389–99. Rennes: P U de Rennes.

———. 2014a. "Serenity (ATU 707), This Boy's Life (ATU 590), Star Wars (Lacourcière 305A), Solaris (ATU 652): About Extending the Aarne-Thompson-Uther Tale-Type Identification Insight to Movies." In *Narratives across Space and Time: Transmissions and Adaptations: Proceedings of the 15th Congress of the International Society for Folk Narrative Research (June 21–27, 2009 Athens)*, edited by Aikaterini Polymerou-Kamilaki, Evangelos Karamanes, and Ioannis Plemmenos, 295–314. Athens: Academy of Athens, Publications of the Hellenic Folklore Research Centre.

———. 2014b. "Twelve Märchen and Their Maps Go as Theories into the Real World." In *Narratives across Space and Time: Transmissions and Adaptations: Proceedings of the 15th Congress of the International Society for Folk Narrative Research (June 21–27, 2009 Athens)*, edited by Aikaterini Polymerou-Kamilaki, Evangelos Karamanes, and Ioannis Plemmenos, LV–XCI. Athens: Academy of Athens, Publications of the Hellenic Folklore Research Centre.

Pelchat, Yolande, Vivian Labrie, Lucie Gélineau, and Julie Descheneaux. 2010. *La participation sociale, les âges vieux et la suite du monde: Des aînéEs, des intervenantEs, des gestionnaires, des chercheures et des contes: Recherche exploratoire menée en 2010*. Québec: Centre de santé et de services sociaux de la Vieille Capitale.

Viveret, Patrick. 2005. *Pourquoi ça ne va pas plus mal?* Paris: Fayard.

12

DISABILITY

Ann Schmiesing

—BEHIND THE DOOR—DAY. *Elsa sits at the window looking out, long-*
ingly. Suddenly, her icy hands freeze the windowsill.
—LATER. *The King slips leather gloves onto Elsa's hands.*
KING: The gloves will help.
He pats her gloved hand.
KING (CONT'D): See? You're good [. . .]. Conceal it.
—*Frozen* (Lee 2013, 9)

"You may be forsaken by the whole world, but I shall not forsake you,"
said the king.
He took her with him to his royal palace, and since she was so beautiful and
good, he loved her with all his heart, had silver hands made for her, and
took her for his wife.
—"The Maiden Without Hands" (Grimm and Grimm 2003, 111)

"All narratives operate out of a desire to compensate for a limitation or to reign in excess,"
David T. Mitchell and Sharon L. Snyder observe with regard to the frequent dependence of
narratives on disability and related forms of physical difference to propel the plot or delineate
character (2000, 53). Mitchell and Snyder theorize this dependence as "narrative prosthesis," a
concept that Disney's animated film *Frozen* (2013) and the Grimm tale "The Maiden Without
Hands" exemplify in a particularly concrete manner: the maiden in the Grimm tale receives
silver hands to compensate for the ones that her father chopped off, while Elsa in *Frozen* is
given gloves to curb and conceal the ice-making powers with which she was born. The silver
hands and gloves are not only narratively but also literally prosthetic, as aids meant either to
substitute for a missing body part or to supplement or correct a problematic or malfunction-
ing one. In both narratives, moreover, the state of apparent normalcy that the prosthetic aid is
intended to restore or approximate appears more important to the giver of the prosthesis than
to its recipient, for Elsa did not request the gloves and the maiden did not ask for silver hands.

Frozen was of course inspired not by the Grimms' tale (or other variants of ATU 706, "The
Maiden without Hands") but, as its credits state, by Hans Christian Andersen's "The Snow
Queen," to which it nevertheless bears little resemblance. Having abandoned initial plans to
depict Elsa as malevolent, Walt Disney Animation Studios created a character who shares the
Snow Queen's ice-making abilities but not her demonic nature. Although *Frozen* is not an
adaptation of the "The Maiden Without Hands" and differs greatly from it in terms of plot, the

film's thematic similarities to the tale with respect to (dis)ability are particularly notable in light of the media response to *Frozen*, which included several articles in news venues and the blogosphere (Ali 2014; Clapp N.d.; "E" 2013; Feder 2014; "InkGypsy" 2014; Shelley 2014; Sweatt Orsborn 2014; Zare 2014) that interpreted Elsa's super-ability as (or as akin to) a disability.

These articles were overshadowed by media coverage of pastor and right-wing radio host Kevin Swanson's allegation that *Frozen* would "teach kids to be gay and is the work of the Devil" ("Disney's 'Frozen'" 2014), as well as by concerns that Elsa as depicted in her ice palace becomes too sexualized and that Disney failed in *Frozen* to present a racially diverse cast of characters. The critiques about disability and super-ability in *Frozen* nevertheless merit closer attention, both because Disney princess films have become virtually synonymous with the fairy-tale genre in current popular consciousness, as Jack Zipes points out (2011, 17), and because these posts and articles raise significant issues concerning the (lack of) depiction of disability in mainstream contemporary fairy-tale media. Because it is impossible here to provide a comprehensive account of disability in fairy-tale media, in this chapter I use media interpretations of *Frozen* as a vehicle through which to probe key issues, and I do so from a disability studies perspective.

Disability Studies and Fairy Tales

Disability studies scholars reject as "ableist" the centering of nondisabled views and the marginalization of disabled people, as well as assumptions that all disabled individuals aspire to a nondisabled norm and that an individual's characteristics are determined by his or her disability (Linton 1998, 9). Without rejecting medical intervention, disability studies scholars challenge the view of disability as a bodily defect to be remedied only through medical practice (the "medical model") and instead emphasize disability as a social construct requiring change in the body politic to ensure access (the "social model" of disability) (Couser 2002, 112). "Impairment" in the social model refers to the physical aspect of, say, being blind, whereas "disability" refers to the social conditions that impede access for sight-impaired people and in so doing make their impairment into a negative (Davis 2010, 303).

As Simi Linton has observed, popular representations of disability often reveal preoccupations with "overcoming" disability; this typically entails not an actual physical overcoming of impairment, but an overcoming of stigma and of the implicit expectations of what a disabled person can and cannot do or achieve (1998, 17). This stigma may lead some disabled individuals to attempt to "pass" as nondisabled. Nondisabled discourse also frequently portrays disabled people either as objects of pity or in effect as "supercripples" (or "supercrips"). Supercripple narratives go to such great lengths to show that the disabled person has "overcome" his or her disability that they portray him or her "as possessing talents and abilities only dreamed about by able-bodied people" (Siebers 2008, 111; see also Alaniz 2014, 31–32). Because in this manner they emphasize (super)ability, these narratives tend by nature to marginalize disability and reinscribe an ableist paradigm.

Although disability in the popular consciousness might often be conceived in terms of rigid categories (e.g., blindness, deafness, impaired mobility), disability studies views its subject as an unstable and expansive term that may include many diseases and conditions. The Americans with Disabilities Act (ADA) defines disability as "a physical or mental impairment that substantially limits one or more major life activities, a record of such an impairment, or being regarded as having such as impairment" ("Disability"). When applied to the fanciful realm of fairy tales, this description yields numerous examples of disabled characters. Those who populate European fairy tales include thumb-sized children, dwarfs, blinded stepsisters, wounded soldiers, characters temporarily paralyzed by a spell or put into a coma-like sleep, "Dummy" characters who may represent intellectual impairments, mute maidens, animals born to human parents, and the many human-animal hybrids who, as Rosemarie Garland-Thomson observes, may offer "mythical explanations" for the anomalous human body (1996, 1).

Most frequently, disability in fairy tales serves as a punishment for malevolent behavior or as a condition that amplifies the adversity against which a protagonist must struggle and prevail. For the protagonist, then, disability can function as the "lack" that, in Vladimir Propp's formulation, must frequently be "liquidated" in fairy tales for a happy ending to be achieved (1968, 53–55). This happy ending usually includes a magical restoration to physical normalcy or a figurative overcoming of the problem. The Maiden Without Hands, for example, has biological hands restored by God toward the tale's end. In *Frozen*, Elsa learns to control her ice-making super-ability, and two other characters whose bodies experience physical injury are restored to their original states: the white streak in Anna's hair that Elsa's powers accidentally caused is gone after her frozen body comes back to life, and the melting snowman's body is reconstituted when Elsa creates a snow flurry above his head.

Scholars have long examined the psychic injury and/or social marginalization that disability in fairy tales is so often used to symbolize, but this has typically involved mentioning disability itself only in passing and focusing instead almost entirely on its metaphorical meanings. By contrast, Susan Schoon Eberly (1988) examined disability in folklore and fairy tales from a medical perspective, arguing that changelings and hybrid characters exhibit signs of specific syndromes and deformities. Surveys of disability in fairy tales include Hans-Jörg Uther's book on disabled characters in popular literature (1981), as well as his more recent entry "Disability" in *Folktales and Fairy Tales: Traditions and Texts from Around the World* (2016). In addition, the *Enzyklopädie des Märchens* (Ranke and Brednich 1999) includes entries on various disabilities.

Since the turn of the millennium, several scholars have examined disability in specific tales or tale collections from a disability studies perspective. Beth Franks (2001) surveys portrayals of disability in the first 100 tales in the Grimms' collection, and Ann Schmiesing (2014) examines disability in the Grimms' tales with an emphasis on the manner in which the brothers' editing over seven editions affected how disability is portrayed. In their seminal study *Narrative Prosthesis*, Mitchell and Snyder analyze a retelling of Andersen's "The Steadfast Tin Soldier" (2000, 47–57); more recently, Vivian Yenika-Agbaw (2011) has studied representations of disability in several of Andersen's tales, and Lori Yamato (2017) has used disability studies theory to explore Andersen's "The Little Mermaid." Scholars have also begun to explore the intersectionality of disability and other identities in fairy tales: for example, Santiago Solis (2007) analyzes four "Snow White and the Seven Dwarfs" (ATU 709) picture books from a queercrip perspective to "examine and challenge the social construction of the homosexual and disabled body as defiantly shameful, abnormal, and pathological" (117).

Elsa: Super-Ability as Disability?

In both "The Maiden Without Hands" and *Frozen*, (dis)ability and gender intersect: although Elsa lives with a congenital superpower and the Grimms' maiden with an acquired disability, the agency of female hands is problematized in both narratives. Elsa's hands have supernatural abilities that her protective father determines must be constrained, controlled, and hidden, and after her capture by the duke's men her hands are even shackled with iron gloves to the walls of a dungeon. As for the maiden, her father promises to give the Devil whatever is behind his mill in exchange for wealth, not realizing that his daughter is standing there. She uses her biological hands to purify herself with water and to draw a chalk circle around herself so that the Devil cannot claim her. These actions, and the divine protection that they magically confer, lead the Devil to instruct her father to cut her hands off so that she can no longer protect herself, after which she sheds so many purifying tears on her maimed arms that the Devil still cannot come near her. But, whereas *Frozen* portrays Elsa's father as perhaps over-protective, "The Maiden Without Hands" depicts the father as physically abusive, and the history of the Grimm tale suggests that the physical abuse is a symbolic stand-in for sexual abuse (Schmiesing 2014, 85–89). Although with far more violence in "The Maiden Without Hands" than in *Frozen*, male characters in both narratives attempt to control the ability, disability, or super-ability of female hands, whether by cutting them off, gloving them, shackling them, or replacing them.

It is significant, however, that Elsa in *Frozen* is portrayed not as a supercripple whose "overcoming" of disability leads her to exhibit what nondisabled people might regard as super-abilities, but instead as a person whose super-abilities arguably prove in certain respects disabling. She thus differs from many comic superheroes: Marvel Silver Age comics, as José Alaniz notes, put "'overcompensation' for physical defect literally at the center of the action [. . .]. In case after case, a super-power 'overcompensates' for a perceived physical defect, difference, or outright disability" (2014, 35–36). Elsa is instead rather more like the mythical King Midas, whose ability to turn anything he touches into gold becomes akin to an impairment, insofar as even the food he touches turns to gold and cannot be consumed.

Indeed, Elsa's hands are "defective" in the sense that they do not function as human hands are supposed to, and throughout most of the film she cannot control their ice-making ability. Nevertheless, the film explicitly describes her as having "powers," not a disability (Lee 2013, 6). Bloggers and columnists who have interpreted her superpower as (or as like) a disability include "E" (2013) and Jeffery Zare (2014), two bloggers with autism who trace the parallels between other characters' treatment of Elsa and social attitudes toward autistic people; Nadia Ali (2014), a psychologist who reads *Frozen* as a story about mental illness; Shira Feder (2014), who also reads *Frozen* as about mental illness and specifically interprets Elsa as having an anxiety disorder; Sarah Sweatt Orsborn (2014), the mother of a daughter with spina bifida who sees *Frozen* as portraying "disability as superpower"; Daniela Clapp (N.d.), the mother of a daughter with Down syndrome who suggests that *Frozen* sends the message that we are "joined by our differences" and that disability is a "supernatural blessing"; Maureen Shelley (2014), who writes that *Frozen* offers "the glimmer of a more enlightened view of people with disabilities for Disney"; and InkGypsy (2014), who interprets Elsa as disabled and laments the paucity of disabled fairy-tale characters in mainstream films. In contrast to the many bloggers who interpret Elsa's superpower as (or as similar to) a disability, Keston Ott-Dahl (2014), the parent of a child with Down syndrome, writes that "Disney's next movie should have a disabled princess."

Bloggers such as "E" and Sweatt Orsborn observe that early in the film Elsa's powers bring her closer to her younger sister because she employs them to create a snowman and snowbanks that she and her sister can use for play. As Elsa's powers grow, however, she finds it difficult to control them, a situation that "E" regards as similar to the development of children with autism. Indeed, when Elsa's magic accidentally harms her sister, her exasperated father exclaims, "Elsa, what have you done? This is getting out of hand!"—an idiomatic statement that is also literally true with regard to her hands' ice-making abilities (Lee 2013, 5). After soliciting advice and a cure for Anna from the troll leader, her father places the gloves on Elsa's hands and isolates her from her sister and the world around her. As Sweatt Orsborn and Zare suggest, this seclusion leads Elsa to view her physical difference as something that she must hide from others and as a barrier to full participation in the social and family sphere, a view that neither she nor Anna originally had, but that instead is learned. Clapp similarly observes that disabled children are frequently regarded as "a danger to society" (N.d.) and that as a result they are often segregated from others.

Because the troll removed (and thus *dis-abled*) Anna's memories of Elsa's magical abilities and of the physical injury her abilities caused, she cannot understand why Elsa no longer plays with her. In one scene, Elsa sits on the floor of her darkened room, slumped against her bedroom door, while on the other side of the door Anna begs her to come out and play. Zare notes that Anna finds Elsa rude and cannot comprehend why her sister is rejecting her, just as "it is common for autistic people to unintentionally come off as rude"; as a result, Elsa acquires what Zare describes as a "social disability." Similarly, Ali interprets this scene as "a powerful metaphor for understanding how individuals and families grapple with mental health."

Elsa's isolation is briefly interrupted years later when, after the deaths of her parents at sea, she is to be crowned queen of Arendelle. Some bloggers see the coronation ceremony as a classic instance of "passing." "E," for example, insightfully notes that when Elsa must remove her gloves during the ceremony she has to "muster every tiny ounce of self-control she has, so that her hands will work the way 'normal' people do." Zare likewise finds that Elsa's predicament shows that the question of "whether to reveal or not to reveal" is difficult. For Elsa, passing proves impossible: although she manages to get through the coronation ceremony, she fails to control her powers when her sister grabs her hand at the coronation ball, causing her glove to slide off. With her hand ungloved, Elsa inadvertently makes icy spikes form on the floor, turns a staircase to ice, and freezes an outside fountain and even the fjord. She flees to the mountains as a crowd of villagers panic and the duke cries out, "Monster [. . .]. Monster!" (Lee 2013, 32).

His words not only recall similar charges of monstrosity in "The Mob Song" from Disney's *Beauty and the Beast*, but also bring to mind many other fairy-tale portrayals of reactions to physical difference. Elsa's allegedly monstrous nature manifests itself in her superpower and is not a visible part of her body, but she is nevertheless shunned and regarded as nonhuman in a way that is not entirely dissimilar to how the many nonhuman or human–animal hybrid characters in fairy tales are typically viewed by those around them, as for example Hans My Hedgehog in the Grimm tale of the same name (ATU 441) (and in the adaptation of the tale in Jim Henson's *The StoryTeller*) and the ogre in *Shrek*; moreover, although the king in "The Maiden Without Hands" does not find the main character monstrous, on first seeing her he cannot tell whether she is a spirit or a human. In all of these cases, "normalcy" is regarded as human, whereas disability and super-ability implicitly are not. Clapp compares the duke's exclamation that Elsa is a monster to the ugly names that disabled children are called and suggests that Elsa runs from those who shun and fear her just as disabled children often do.

Elsa lives in an ice palace that she magically builds on the highest mountain peak, where she sings the hit song "Let It Go." Several bloggers see aspects of their own experience of disability in the song's lyrics, observing that the "kingdom of isolation" of which Elsa sings captures the social reality faced by many disabled people (Zare 2014; Ali 2014). Ali sees the "swirling storm inside" that Elsa says she has failed to hide as a metaphor for mental illness but observes that Elsa accepts and empowers herself when she sings, "Let it go! Let it go! And I'll rise like the break of dawn! Let it go! That perfect girl is gone" (Lee 2013, 36). Such self-acceptance nevertheless still entails isolation for Elsa, who refuses to return to Arendelle when Anna comes to her ice palace. Elsa insists that she must remain alone in her palace, "where I can be who I am without hurting anybody" (66), but later in this conversation she inadvertently strikes Anna in the heart with a sharp snowflake, which causes Anna to gradually freeze in the scenes that follow. Elsa meanwhile remains in her ice palace until the duke's guards capture her, throw her into a dungeon, and shackle her hands—a scene that Ali compares to the institutionalizing of people with mental illness in asylums.

By the film's end, Elsa has escaped from the dungeon and manages to revive her frozen sister. The power of sisterly love enables her to control her powers, which she uses to create a skating rink for the villagers' amusement and skates made of ice for Anna. Just as she created the snowman and snowbanks at the beginning, at the end her powers are likewise employed in creating entertainment, and thus they could be read as a reference to Disney's establishment of amusement parks and/or to the "magical" ability of computer-generated animation to entertain. If we compare Elsa's super-ability to disability, however, we might note that disabled people have throughout history been seen as objects and creators of pleasure for nondisabled people, as for example as jesters or in freak shows (Linton 1998, 52). Although Elsa is not objectified in the same manner, her difference is nevertheless portrayed in rather ableist terms at the end, insofar as it becomes acceptable because it now amuses instead of offends.

Whereas the Grimms' Maiden Without Hands is restored to physical normalcy at the end of the tale and marries the king in a second wedding, Elsa retains her now-controllable powers and does not marry. Some commentators applauded Disney for emphasizing sisterly love in *Frozen* instead of the heterosexual marriage that happy endings in fairy tales and Disney princess films so often entail. Blogger Shelley, however, suggests that this ending could also be ableist: the absence of a wedding at the end mirrors the experience of many disabled women, for whom "the disability may be tolerated when they are children but when they become women the disability needs to be dealt with more strictly" (2014). To Shelley, the fact that Elsa does not receive "the ultimate Disney prize" of a fairy-tale wedding implies that her physical difference still marginalizes her. Although Disney's motivation in emphasizing sisterly love may largely have been to break away from the outdated fairy-tale endings that associate happiness for female protagonists with marriage, and not to marginalize Elsa, it is true that characters who experience a restoration to normalcy typically marry at the end of fairy tales (e.g., animal characters who become human in form), whereas those who do not shed their physical difference typically do not wed (e.g., Thumbling, ATU 700).

Alone among the bloggers considered here, Shelley insightfully points out that Disney packaged *Frozen* in movie theaters with a screening of the Mickey Mouse cartoon "Get a Horse!" Reworked in part from old footage, "Get a Horse!" depicts the villainous Peg-Leg Pete, whose very name points to his disability. Shelley contrasts the negative depiction of Peg-Leg Pete with Elsa, whom she describes as a "character with a disability that is both a 'power' and a 'curse'" (2014). Shelley is certainly right that Elsa is portrayed more sympathetically than Peg-Leg Pete, but the cartoon and the feature film may be read together as reinforcing ableism, insofar as the cartoon presents disability as negative and the feature ultimately exalts super-ability. The only instance in the feature where impairment is directly invoked appears in the song "Fixer Upper," where the trolls humorously refer to Kristoff as "socially impaired" (Lee 2013, 84)—an allusion that further precludes any serious engagement with actual impairment and disability. In addition, just as Maleficent's wings are restored in Disney's *Maleficent*, and Ariel is fully human at the end of *The Little Mermaid* (in contrast to Andersen's tale) and gets her voice back, the ending of *Frozen* follows typical fairy-tale patterns by fixing Anna's white-streaked hair and Olaf's melting snowman body.

Although disabled people (including this author) might indeed find that Elsa's experience in some respects can be related to their own experience, she is overtly depicted not as disabled but as extraordinarily *abled*. The bloggers considered here center disability and destabilize nondisabledness, and their readings of *Frozen* as a metaphor for disability present a refreshing alternative to its still-too-common presentations as a marker of psychic or social deviance, such as that which Peg-Leg Pete embodies. Disability and super-ability may share in common a deviation from constructions of normalcy, as the many thematic parallels between

Frozen and the Grimms' "The Maiden Without Hands" suggest. But the principal problem with reading super-ability as disability (or, in supercrip fashion, with reading disability as super-ability) is that the overarching frame of reference when we consider super-ability is still that of able-bodiedness.

Several bloggers comment directly or indirectly on this problem. For example, "E" writes, "I'm not saying that autism is a superpower like the magic in the animated film" (although autism is frequently depicted, in a supercrip-like manner, as both disability and super-ability in popular representations such as the film *Rain Man*). Similarly, Ali acknowledges that the parallels she draws between Elsa and a person with mental illness were "not what Disney [. . .] had in mind," and InkGypsy worries that although Elsa can be read as a child with "special needs," "she wasn't portrayed as such specifically and I have a feeling it's gone right under the radar of anyone who might like to feel it represents them." InkGypsy also observes that the paucity of disabled characters in fairy-tale films has led Italian artist Alexsandro Palombo to depict Disney fairy-tale princess characters as disabled; for example Palombo depicts Snow White in a wheelchair and Cinderella as an amputee (2014).

Palombo's work points to the lack of fairy-tale characters who simply happen to have disabilities (and are not defined by them), a lack that is typical of media representations of disability in general (see Riley 2005) and against which social media such as the blog posts examined here have pushed back. "There are no princesses like Delaney," Ott-Dahl quotes her daughter Jules as saying after the child watched *Frozen* with her sister Delaney. "And it's true," Ott-Dahl writes, "Delaney has Down syndrome." After mentioning that Disney's *Finding Nemo* presents Nemo as having a gimpy fin and Dory as having memory issues, a commenter on InkGypsy's blog observes that Disney typically presents the "other" as animal in form. Indeed, from Dumbo to Dory, the tendency to portray animal characters as recognizably disabled or physically different implicitly dehumanizes disability.

Some lesser-known films nevertheless incorporate fairy-tale motifs in portraying human characters with disabilities: although somewhat overwrought in its presentation of the "love is blind" cliché, Tamar van den Dop's *Blind*, for example, draws on Andersen's "The Snow Queen" in depicting the relationship between a blind young man and an albino woman. Too often, Hollywood fairy-tale films that portray human characters with physical differences have failed to represent this difference in an accurate, affirming, or inclusive manner. Rupert Sanders, director of *Snow White and the Huntsman*, was criticized for using computer-generated graphics to shrink regular-sized actors instead of casting little people to play the dwarfs (Rosenfeld 2012; Knopper 2012). By contrast, Tarsem Singh, director of the Snow White adaptation *Mirror Mirror*, was commended for not only employing little-people actors but for portraying the dwarfs in a manner that breaks with or directly challenges stereotypes. For example, when the prince mocks the dwarfs for being "minuscule," one responds, "That's the best you got?" (Knopper 2012). It is a question that could be asked generally of depictions of disability and related forms of physical difference in mainstream fairy-tale media.

Related topics: Blogs and Websites; Cinematic; Disney Corporation; Gender

References Cited and Further Reading

Alaniz, José. 2014. *Death, Disability, and the Superhero: The Silver Age and Beyond.* Jackson: UP Mississippi.
Ali, Nadia. 2014. "What Disney's 'Frozen' Can Teach Us about Mental Illness." *The Washington Post*, May 13. www.washingtonpost.com/blogs/she-the-people/wp/2014/05/13/what-disneys-frozen-teach-us-about-mental-illness/.
Clapp, Daniela. N.d. "Disney's Frozen Redefines True Love and Demonstrates That We Are Joined by Our Differences." *Music Transforms You.* http://danielaclapp.com/piano/disneys-frozen-redefines-true-love/.

Couser, G. Thomas. 2002. "Signifying Bodies: Life Writing and Disability Studies." In *Disability Studies: Enabling the Humanities*, edited by Sharon L. Snyder, Brenda Jo Brueggemann, and Rosemarie Garland-Thomson, 109–17. New York: The Modern Language Association of America.

Davis, Lennard J., ed. 2010. *The Disability Studies Reader*. 3rd ed. New York: Routledge.

"Disability." N.d. *ADA National Network: Glossary of ADA Terms*. https://adata.org/glossary-terms#D.

"Disney's 'Frozen' Will Teach Kids To Be Gay and Is the Work of the Devil: Kevin Swanson." 2014. *Huffington Post*, March 11. www.huffingtonpost.com/2014/03/11/frozen-disney-kevin-swanson-gay-_n_4937192.html.

"E." 2013. "Disney's Frozen and Autism." *The Third Glance: A Peek into My (Autistic) Mind*, December 21. https://thethirdglance.wordpress.com/2013/12/21/disneys-frozen-and-autism/.

Feder, Shira. 2014. "College Feminisms: Slamming the Door: An Analysis of Elsa (Frozen)." *The Feminist Wire*, October 16. www.thefeministwire.com/2014/10/slamming-door-analysis-elsa-frozen/.

"InkGypsy." 2014. "Disabled Disney Princesses." *Fairy Tale News*, January 31. http://fairytalenewsblog.blogspot.com/2014/01/disabled-disney-princesses.html.

Franks, Beth. 2001. "Gutting the Golden Goose: Disability in Grimms' Fairy Tales." In *Embodied Rhetorics: Disability in Language and Culture*, edited by James C. Wilson and Cynthia Lewiecki-Wilson, 244–58. Carbondale: Southern Illinois UP.

Garland-Thomson, Rosemarie, ed. 1996. *Freakery: Cultural Spectacles of the Extraordinary Body*. New York: NYU P.

Grimm, Jacob, and Wilhelm Grimm. 2003. *The Complete Fairy Tales of the Brothers Grimm*, translated by Jack Zipes. 3rd ed. New York: Bantam.

Knopper, Steve. 2012. "Winning a Little Dignity." *The Wall Street Journal*, March 30. www.wsj.com/articles/SB10001424052702304636404577291393994531090.

Lee, Jennifer. 2013. *Frozen: Final Shooting Draft*. Burbank: Walt Disney Animation Studios.

Linton, Simi. 1998. *Claiming Disability: Knowledge and Identity*. New York: NYU P.

Mitchell, David T., and Sharon L. Snyder. 2000. *Narrative Prosthesis: Disability and the Dependencies of Discourse*. Ann Arbor: U Michigan P.

Ott-Dahl, Keston. 2014. "Disney's Next Movie Should Have a Disabled Princess." *The Washington Post*, November 12. www.washingtonpost.com/posteverything/wp/2014/11/12/disneys-next-movie-should-have-a-disabled-princess/.

Palombo, Alexsandro. 2014. "Humor Chic Equal Rights—Disabled Disney Princesses 'Which Princess Are You?'" *Humor Chic*, January 27. http://humorchic.blogspot.it/2014/01/humor-chic-equal-rights-disabled-disney.html.

Propp, Vladimir. 1968. *Morphology of the Folktale*, translated by Laurence Scott, revised by Louis A. Wagner, introduction by Alan Dundes. 2nd ed. Austin: U Texas P.

Ranke, Kurt, and Rolf Wilhelm Brednich, eds. 1999. *Enzyklopädie des Märchens: Handwörterbuch zur historischen und vergleichenden Erzählforschung*. 6 vols. Berlin: de Gruyter.

Riley II, Charles A. 2005. *Disability and the Media: Prescriptions for Change*. Lebanon, NH: UP New England.

Rosenfeld, Everett. 2012. "Little People Angry Over Dwarves in *Snow White and the Huntsman* . . . But Not for Reasons You Might Think." *Time*, June 6. http://newsfeed.time.com/2012/06/06/little-people-angry-over-dwarves-in-snow-white-and-the-huntsman/.

Schmiesing, Ann. 2014. *Disability, Deformity, and Disease in the Grimms' Fairy Tales*. Detroit: Wayne State UP.

Schoon Eberly, Susan. 1988. "Fairies and the Folklore of Disability: Changelings, Hybrids and the Solitary Fairy." *Folklore* 99 (1): 58–77.

Shelley, Maureen. 2014. "Disney, Disability and *Frozen*." *The Word*, January 9. http://thecopycollective.blogspot.com/2014/01/disney-disability-and-frozen.html.

Siebers, Tobin. 2008. *Disability Theory*. Ann Arbor: U Michigan P.

Solis, Santiago. 2007. "Snow White and the Seven 'Dwarfs'—Queercripped." *Hypatia* 22 (1): 114–31.

Sweatt Orsborn, Sarah. 2014. "Watching Frozen with My Daughters: Disability as Superpower and the Power of Sister Love." *The Huffington Post*, April 7. www.huffingtonpost.com/sarah-sweatt-orsborn/watching-frozen-with-my-daughters_b_5105525.html.

Uther, Hans-Jörg. 1981. *Behinderte in populären Erzählungen: Studien zu historischen und vergleichenden Erzählforschung*. Berlin: de Gruyter.

———. 2016. "Disability." In *Folktales and Fairy Tales: Traditions and Texts from around the World*, edited by Anne E. Duggan and Donald Haase, 266–9. Westport, CT: Greenwood.

Yamoto, Lori. 2017. "Surgical Humanization in H. C. Andersen's 'The Little Mermaid.'" *Marvels & Tales* 31 (2).

Yenika-Agbaw, Vivian. 2011. "Reading Disability in Children's Literature: Hans Christian Andersen's Tales." *Journal of Literary and Cultural Disability Studies* 5 (1): 91–108.

Zare, Jeffery. 2014. "An Autistic's Reflection on Disney's *Frozen*." Autism Support Network. www.autismsupportnetwork.com/news/autistics-reflection-disney-frozen-elsa-3251111.

Zipes, Jack. 2011. *The Enchanted Screen: The Unknown History of Fairy-Tale Films*. New York: Routledge.

Mediagraphy

Beauty and the Beast. 1991. Directors Gary Trousdale and Kirk Wise. USA.

Blind. 2007. Director Tamar van den Dop. Netherlands.

Finding Nemo. 2003. Directors Andrew Stanton and Lee Unkrich. USA.

Frozen. 2013. Directors Chris Buck and Jennifer Lee. USA.

The Little Mermaid. 1989. Directors Ron Clements and John Musker. USA.

Maleficent. 2014. Director Robert Stromberg. USA.

Mirror Mirror. 2012. Director Tarsem Singh. USA.

Rain Man. 1988. Director Barry Levinson. USA.

Shrek. 2001. Directors Andrew Adamson and Vicky Jenson. USA.

Snow White and the Huntsman. 2012. Director Rupert Sanders. USA.

The StoryTeller (TV). 1988. Creator Jim Henson. USA.

13

GENDER

Anne E. Duggan

Whether taking the form of literary texts, film, comic books, or painting, fairy tales often center their attention on the heroine. Feminist theorists like Marcia Lieberman (1972) take for granted that the passive Disney princess exemplifies the heroine of fairy-tale tradition.[1] Others, including Lewis Seifert, Jack Zipes, Elizabeth Wanning Harries, Shawn Jarvis, and Jeannine Blackwell, point to a more complicated history. They do so in part by resuscitating women's lost voices and pre-1900 fairy-tale narratives that provide a dynamic and multifarious view of gender as it relates to the form throughout history.[2] The realization that Giovanni Francesco Straparola makes his sixteenth-century Puss in Boots female troubles our contemporary reception of the tale, in which Puss is decidedly male. Knowing that in 1697 Marie-Catherine d'Aulnoy produced a very active Cinderella figure in her tale "Finette-Cendron" (ATU 510A) challenges our assumptions about what the story can communicate about gender norms. Such examples foreground the problematic nature of gender representations within what has become the classical fairy-tale canon (select tales by Charles Perrault, Hans Christian Andersen, and the Brothers Grimm), which, with the exception of Jeanne-Marie Leprince de Beaumont's "Beauty and the Beast" (ATU 425C), does not include tales by women authors or those antecedents to Perrault's now canonical variants of popular fairy tales.[3] Already at the inception of the literary fairy-tale tradition in sixteenth- and seventeenth-century Italy and France, authors of fairy tales gendered heroines and heroes in ways that prove much more supple than we might imagine, anticipating much of the gender play that occurs in later periods and different media forms.

We can understand how gender functions within the fairy tale across different media from the perspective of 1) the editorial and publication history of fairy tales and canon formation; 2) revisions of what have become the "classical" fairy tales (notably "Little Red Riding Hood" ATU 333, "Cinderella," "Snow White" ATU 709, and "Sleeping Beauty" ATU 410) in which the heroine often plays a passive role, but which do not represent the fairy tale in general; and 3) hybrid media forms (i.e., fairy tale and comic book; fairy tale and painting), which allow for intermedial explorations of the possibilities of gender. Indeed, heteronormative constructions in fairy tales have always coexisted and competed with gender-bending ones, just as contemporary fairy tales articulated through different media maintain continuities and discontinuities with the canon. This speaks to the continued need to critique gender constructions that limit the scope of female as well as male agency and identity in the various forms the fairy tale can take.

There has been a significant history of scholarship on gender and fairy tales, from early modern studies (Seifert 1996) and postmodern studies (Bacchilega 1997) to interdisciplinary collections (Haase 2004). Inspired by these approaches, I situate my discussion of gender and the fairy tale in relation to canon development within print and media cultures, which in turn

ANNE E. DUGGAN

impacts both the history of revisionist fairy-tale texts and that of hybrid media forms. I focus on the French and Anglo-American traditions of fairy tales, all the while realizing that we see similar patterns and tensions between progressive and conservative representations of gender in other national language traditions.

Textual Histories

One way to approach gender in fairy tales is to uncover gender biases in the construction of the contemporary fairy-tale canon. When we examine the history of the form, we often find multifarious routes a character might take that problematize contemporary perceptions of how heroism and heroines get gendered. We also uncover the existence of fairy-tale canons that have since faded into oblivion, in which works by a woman author like d'Aulnoy successfully competed with those by Perrault or the Brothers Grimm. Peeling away these layers also points to ways in which the Disney corporation arguably helped construct the contemporary canon of classical tales, favoring rather subservient and domesticated heroines—at least until the 1990s[4]—which is not a reflection of either fairy-tale or folktale history. As Kathleen Ragan insists, "the low percentages in most current folk and fairy tale collections belie the fact that remarkable heroines can be found in folktales from all over the world. The subtle and pervasive power of editing has been severely underestimated" (1998, xxiii).[5]

The evolution of "Puss in Boots" (ATU 545B) illustrates the ways in which the fairy-tale canon eventually gets reshaped within patriarchal, heteronormative lines in print culture. In the earliest known written iteration of the tale by the sixteenth-century writer Straparola, the hero, Constantino Fortunato, is given a *female* cat (*una gatta*), who is a fairy in disguise, by his mother. The cat brings a gift of a hare to the king, and, as wily as her future incarnations, she manages to acquire for her master noble lands as well as the throne. By the early seventeenth century, Giambattista Basile replaces the mother with a father, but maintains the gender of the cat, who brings fish and fowl to the king, eventually assisting in her master's rise in fortune and scolding him at the end of the tale for his ingratitude.

In his rewritings of tales by Straparola and Basile, Perrault often deemphasizes the agency of female characters, and his now canonical version of "Puss in Boots" is exemplary of this. Like in Basile, it is the father who endows his son with the clever cat, who is now gendered masculine. The tale began as one that empowered the mother to offer a cunning female cat to her son and became one that eliminates all female characters except for the very passive daughter of the king. With the introduction of the character in *Shrek 2* (2004), voiced by Antonio Banderas, Puss is fully codified as a swashbuckling, Zorro-like male figure for international audiences. His association with Banderas—who played Zorro and incarnates "excessive masculinity" for American and global audiences—only strengthens the cat's relation to masculinity, and Puss's female past becomes almost unthinkable.[6]

A contemporary of Perrault, d'Aulnoy published a story influenced by the Italian cat tales called "The White Cat," maintaining the female gender of the feline who, in this version, rules as queen. D'Aulnoy also penned an alternative version of "Cinderella," in which her heroine, Finette-Cendron, brings together the wit of Little Thumbling (ATU 700) and the finesse of Puss in Boots to win back her family's kingdom. From the seventeenth to about the mid-nineteenth century, d'Aulnoy's plucky heroines attained popularity in France, traversed the Channel, and made their way across Europe. Indeed, d'Aulnoy was the most published French author in England between 1700 and 1739.[7] Although translations of the Grimms' tales began to appear in France as early as 1823, d'Aulnoy's tales were more popular than the Grimms' until the end of the century, although not as popular as those by Perrault.[8] By the turn

114

of the century in France, publishing history changes as tales by the Grimms begin to overtake those penned by d'Aulnoy and grow exponentially over the course of the century, particularly after the release of Disney's *Snow White and the Seven Dwarfs* (1937).[9] The French *Bibliothèque Nationale* held eight total versions of "Snow White" published between 1900 and 1936. But over the course of the next thirty-six years, the number rose to 148 published copies in the form of either individual or anthologized tales. Clearly, Disney's *Snow White* impacted the reception of the Grimms' tale among French readers.

So what does this print and media history have to do with gender? First, the feminocentric aristocratic salons that gave rise to d'Aulnoy's tales had been on the decline since the French Revolution and especially with nineteenth-century industrialization; in essence, the readership of her tales—the social class and milieu at their emergence—was disappearing. In some respects, the fate of d'Aulnoy's tales also follows that of what Joan DeJean calls "worldly anthologies" (2000, 57), developed for the tastes of aristocratic adults. DeJean argues that when the target audience for anthologies was (elite) adult readers, works by women were included at much higher rates than anthologies designed according to "the new literary pedagogy of the Enlightenment" (58), which targeted boys in the *collèges*. Since works by women writers were deemed "soft," a "threat to 'vigorous' male Christian standards," and thus "a direct threat to church and state" (66) due to their apparently dubious morality, they had to be eliminated from the canon. But underlying this exclusion is the position of women with respect to the universal: they and their works cannot be exemplary, at least within a patriarchal society whose notions of masculinity are opposed and viewed as superior to all that is associated with the feminine. Fairy tales by Perrault and the Grimms communicated more effectively the values of the now dominant bourgeoisie, with its emphasis on female domesticity and patriarchal authority. The global reach of Disney's *Snow White*, *Cinderella* (1950), and *Sleeping Beauty* (1959), which capitalized (quite literally) on the appeal of Perrault and the Grimms, only solidified this hegemony across national borders.

Revisionist Tales

One way of troubling gender in the fairy-tale tradition is to peel back the hidden layers of fairy-tale print history, resuscitating those popular female and male authors of times past who gave us active heroines and more complex gender relations than those found in the contemporary canon. Another is to provide new narratives for the passive heroines of the contemporary canon that emphasize the gender prejudices of source tales or empower heroines in unprecedented ways. Already nineteenth-century women in Britain, France, and Germany were challenging the patriarchal narratives of Perrault's tales. Post-revolutionary French writers like Stéphanie Félicité, comtesse de Genlis (1805) and Félicité de Choiseul-Meuse (1818) cast Prince Charmings who might have been noble at birth, but not at heart, and gave their heroines more agency than those of Perrault's tales. Indeed, nineteenth-century women writers often depicted failed princes, thus challenging the myth of the male hero who saves his princess that in fact underpins heteronormative, patriarchal ideology. English poet Christina Rossetti depicts a prince who fails in his quest to save the sleeping princess, thus destabilizing and challenging—in a manner similar to Genlis and Choiseul-Meuse—the potency of the hero upheld in the source tale. As Shandi Wagner argues, well before the postmodern feminist rewritings that emerged in the 1970s and 1980s, nineteenth-century British women writers rejected "the 'happily ever after' matrimonial conclusion" (2015, 10) typical of classical fairy tales.

In a similar manner, Julie Koehler (2016) looks at the ways in which nineteenth-century German women writers put into question the gender norms communicated through versions of "The Kind and the Unkind Girls" (ATU 480) by the Brothers Grimm. Unfortunately, even the history of fairy-tale revisions has been eclipsed by the persistence of the traditional canon and trio of Perrault-Grimm-Andersen. However, continual print and cinematic challenges to gender in the fairy tale eventually find a larger audience in the second half of the twentieth century, notably when women attained an unprecedented level of equality in Europe and North America, among other global regions.

Critics have written extensively about the ways in which writers like Angela Carter, Emma Donoghue, and in film Catherine Breillat have radically rewritten classical fairy tales, challenging their assumptions about gender and sexuality.[10] One strategy used by Carter and Breillat in particular is, to borrow Lisa Coulthard's words, the "desublimation of romance or perfect love" (2010, 63). In her discussion of Breillat's sexually challenging films, Coulthard argues that female desire must be sublimated within the paradigm of courtly love, which, like canonical tales such as "Snow White" and "Sleeping Beauty," concerns the abstraction and postponement of desire. Direct female desire must remain repressed in order to uphold ideal femininity, the pure lady from whom the male suitor maintains distance in order to sustain his desire. Both Carter and Breillat perturb such constructions.

In "The Tiger's Bride," for instance, Carter first de-idealizes the exchange of the heroine between father and beast, foregrounding the crude exchange of women within patriarchal society underlying the canonical tale. Carter exposes patriarchy and then undermines it by freeing up the heroine's desire, in part by challenging the male gaze: the heroine allows the beast to view her naked body only after she is allowed to gaze upon his naked, feline one. The gaze, which initiates the sexual encounter, is reciprocal, and the heroine, rather than "civilizing" the beast, becomes animal herself.

In the case of her film *The Sleeping Beauty* (2010), Breillat, as Maria Garcia argues, "consistently reimagines the much-celebrated rites of passage often reserved, in literature and cinema, for boys" (2011, 32). The film is structured like a quest, as the narrative of "The Snow Queen," which concerns a girl's search for her beloved and is the focus of the film, is grafted onto that of "Sleeping Beauty," thus effacing the male quest associated with the canonical tale. Moreover, the main character, Anastasia, is sexually awoken by the Romany woman of her dream quest, while her sexual encounter with the so-called prince is less than liberating. Garcia explains: "Breillat sets out to overturn the male fantasy that forms the subtext of nearly all the romantic fairy tales upon which young girls are weaned—that men awaken the virgin to her sexuality and, by extension, to her identity" (2011, 33).

In these texts, women writers and filmmakers subvert gender norms by 1) undermining the male gaze; 2) explicitly representing female desire; 3) providing female quest narratives; and 4) queering the heteronormative sexual awakening implicit in the resurrection kiss found in Disney versions of classical tales. While the focus here has been on rewriting the passive heroine, contemporary tales that trouble heteronormative masculinity exist as well. One notable example is Michael Cunningham's "The Wild Swan," a rewriting of the Grimms' "The Six Swans" (ATU 451), already a lesser-known tale in the Grimms' corpus. In his version, Cunningham focuses on the social stigma of the brother who did not regain both of his human arms, forced to live with one wing. Although marginalized because of his wing, failing to incarnate an ideal masculinity that would lead to heteronormative marriage, the brother nevertheless "loved his wing, helplessly" (2015, 11). Later we learn that his brothers "are on their second or third wives" (12); as such, Cunningham undermines the notion of marital bliss and suggests, in the end, that the normative brothers are no better off than their one-winged brother who embraces his difference. The hero does not quite live happily ever after—no one does—but it's "not the worst of all possible lives" (13).

GENDER

Hybrid Media Forms

In media forms such as the comic book, television series, and painting, characters from various classical fairy tales are extracted from their original narrative context and recontextualized within new narratives in which characters from different tales coexist, or are represented in unanticipated ways that trouble our understanding of a particular character. Here I focus on Bill Willingham's comic book series *Fables* (2002–15), which anticipates some of the tropes of ABC's *Once Upon a Time* (2011–), and the fairy-tale paintings of José Rodolfo Loaiza Ontiveros, which challenge the marketing strategies of the Disney brand from the perspective of gender and sexuality.

In both *Fables* and *Once Upon a Time*, characters such as Snow White, Prince Charming, and Sleeping Beauty coexist in a world resembling twentieth- or twenty-first-century society, and they maintain a tenuous relation with their magical homeland. Regarding the question of gender in *Once Upon a Time*, Charlotte Trinquet du Lys remarks: "The series presents several strong female characters, and if some of them have masculine attributes, they are nevertheless living in a patriarchal, heterosexual world that reflects traditional values reminiscent of Walt Disney's films" (2016, 738). To some degree, the same could be said about Willingham's *Fables*, which moves between liberating and heteronormative representations of femininity and masculinity.

In some respects, displacing fairy-tale characters into the universe of the comic book makes perfect sense. Rebecca Anne Do Rozario (2012) and Neta Gordon both remark upon the ways in which both forms privilege "formulaic portrayals of hypermasculine men and excessively sexualized and vulnerable women" (Gordon 2016, 3). Already often associated with things superhuman, it should come as no surprise that fairy-tale characters in *Fables* resemble superheroes. In the case of female characters, this hybridization "reinvigorate[s] the representation of the [Disney] princesses by drawing on superhero iconography, which is largely masculine in nature" (Do Rozario 2012, 193). There is certainly a level of female empowerment in *Fables*: Snow White is the "director of operations" in Fabletown, Cinderella fences with Bluebeard and is a secret agent, and Goldilocks is a Marxist revolutionary. Snow White, Cinderella, and Briar Rose are all ex-wives of Prince Charming, and, in "Cinderella Libertine," (2004) they express nothing but contempt for his womanizing ways. And while it might be viewed as a difficult task to empower Sleeping Beauty, as Gordon argues, "Briar Rose's sleeping enchantment is figured as a kind of superpower" (2016, 23).

Nevertheless, the series also conveys more traditional notions of gender. Snow White moves to the Farm to raise her cubs, giving up her position as director of operations. As is the case in *Once Upon a Time*, motherhood often intervenes to reposition women in more traditional roles. Gordon remarks upon the tensions between the purer Snow White and Rose Red, who, for all of her "wit, sensuality, bravery, and personal vision, in the *Fables* universe [. . .] is necessarily marginal" (2016, 95). In his discussion of gender in *Fables*, Mark Hill convincingly argues that Bigby embodies ideal masculinity:

> [T]here are no *overt* attempts to construct manhood in blatant opposition of the feminine [. . .]. Instead of building manhood in opposition to a femininity seen as weak, the men of *Fables* return to nineteenth-century models of masculine identity that are formed in opposition to boyhood [. . .]. Childishness, impulsiveness, and cowardliness are the hallmarks of the "boys"—Jack, the Frog Prince, and Bluebeard—and Bigby is the first to openly scorn those characters for their failings.
>
> (2009, 188)

Hill goes on to contend that although Snow White is able to exercise her authority over many of the male characters, she does not dominate in her relation to the hypermasculine Bigby, whose character ends up "systematically questioning the power of women" (191). Much like *Once Upon a Time*, *Fables* simultaneously unsettles and reinforces the type of gender configurations found in the classical canon.

With respect to the representation of gender in the fairy tale, at times it can feel as though we take one step forward and two steps back. As Libe García Zarranz (2007) has argued, the Disney heroine has become more complex since the 1990s due to the transformation of women's roles in society. However, Disney marketing strategies end up reifying the image of the passive princess, basically promoting, in Do Rozario's words, "representation over narrative" (2012, 193), that is, passivity over any agency the narrative might give her. This cannot be better exemplified than in examining the marketing techniques used by Disney to target adult women. Desiring to expand their marketing scope beyond young girls, Disney created the Disney World Fairy Tale Wedding Department in 1991, which went hand in hand with the construction of Disney's Wedding Pavilion in Orlando and the Disney-ABC-Lifetime show *Weddings of a Lifetime.*[11]

On the Bridal Boutique Website one can view wedding dresses, bridesmaid dresses, and flower girl dresses, the latter all themed around Disney princesses. On the media link, one can access a short video, "Watch the Fairy Tale Come to Life." In it we see seven adult models, each representing a different Disney princess. Despite the fact that the models are being filmed, the video looks like a string of still shots due to the models' lack of motion. The models incarnating Snow White, Tiana from *The Princess and the Frog*, and Sleeping Beauty are all reclined as the camera scans over their all-but-motionless bodies. As passive in the water as seaweed gently moving to the almost-still sea, the model embodying the Little Mermaid has a ribbon tied to her arm that makes her look like a prisoner in an aquarium. All the models seem to offer their agency-less bodies up to the gaze of the (male) viewer. Although writers and filmmakers such as Carter, Breillat, and Donoghue have seriously challenged the reified image of a pure and passive femininity, it remains intact in other domains of global media.

Just as writers and filmmakers have subverted gender in fairy-tale texts, so have painters. Exhibitions such as *Glass, Cinder, and Thorns* (2014) featuring artists like Mab Graves ("Snow White in This Black Forest") and Mimi Yoon ("Once Upon a Time No More") rework the canon in ways that free up female agency. The pop art of José Rodolfo Loaiza Ontiveros is particularly illustrative of how idealized, abstracted characters can be recontextualized to infuse them with an agency, sexuality, and corporeality denied them in the canonical and Disney traditions. In "Cinderella Revenge" (2014a), the heroine gives the finger to her stepmother's portrait, upon which she has written: "You fucking bitter old bitch." A painting with Cinderella's stepsisters, looking with marvel at a dildo, is titled "The End of Bitterness" (2013).

Several paintings introduce queer relations between characters: Cinderella's and Snow White's stepmothers embrace in "Sweet Poison" (2015); in another, one fairy-tale prince is about to place a sneaker with wings on another, suggesting a queer version of "Cinderella." At times Ontiveros integrates aspects from Mexican culture. In his painting "Paloma Negra," Snow White, Belle, and Cinderella are getting drunk with Frida Kahlo, referenced in other paintings as well.[12] "Paloma Negra" is a famous Mexican song that was sung by, among others, the queer Costa Rican–born Mexican diva Chavela Vargas (who may have been a lover of Kahlo) and used in the film *Frida* (2002, dir. Julie Taymor). The song can be read as expressing the heroine's tensions toward her unfaithful lover, whom she wishes to find but hopes she doesn't so that she can be free. In the painting, the effect of male betrayal is felt passionately when tying the image to the song, and it brings about female camaraderie in the face of despair. Whether it happens with a kiss, a dildo, or a bottle of booze, Ontiveros often undermines the female rivalry that typifies relations between female characters in the classical tale and Disney.

Looking across time, media forms, and national boundaries, the representation of gender in fairy tales is often ridden with tension. It is important to relativize the contemporary fairy-tale canon, which tends to privilege the passive heroine, by examining the diverse ways gender has been represented in earlier periods where there may have been a broader fairy-tale terrain, before the hegemonic hold of Disney. Particularly evident in twenty-first-century media, fairy-tale series and graphic novels can simultaneously uphold and subvert contemporary gender norms, while Disney marketing strategies continue to privilege the passive princess. As the work of Ontiveros and other artists makes clear, we must continue to question, subvert, and recreate fairy-tale narratives of all kinds in order to open up the possibilities of gender within and through the form.

Related topics: Cinematic; Contemporary Art; Disney Corporation; Hybridity; Pictorial; Sexualities/Queer and Trans Studies

Notes

1. Lieberman notes: "Most of the heroines in [Andrew Lang's] *The Blue Fairy Book* [. . .] are entirely passive, submissive, and helpless. This is most obviously true of the Sleeping Beauty, who lies asleep, in the ultimate state of passivity, waiting for a brave prince to awaken and save her" (1972, 388). Lieberman, however, does not discuss the tradition of the 1690s *conteuses*, whose works were indeed popular in their period, and which would have added nuance to her overall arguments.
2. See for instance essays in Canepa (1997) as well as books by Seifert (1996) and Harries (2001). In the same period, Jarvis and Blackwell edited the important collection *The Queen's Mirror* (2001), which resituates women writing in German within the field of fairy-tale collections and studies that had come to be dominated by the Grimms. This anthologizing work likely was sparked by Zipes's *Beauties, Beasts and Enchantment* (1989), which brought to English audiences the tales by the 1690s French women fairy-tale writers.
3. Shippey discusses this canon in terms of "core" tales, which include "Bluebeard" (ATU 312), "Snow White" (ATU 709), "Cinderella" (ATU 510A), "Little Red Riding Hood" (ATU 333), "Sleeping Beauty" (ATU 410), "Rapunzel" (ATU 310), and "Beauty and the Beast" (ATU 425C) (2003, 261).
4. See for instance Zarranz's discussion of the increasingly complex heroines in Disney's films starting in the 1990s. In her conclusion she notes that these are not "successful feminist representations" but do provide "complex female characters" (2007, 63).
5. See also Lurie's introduction to *Clever Gretchen and Other Forgotten Folktales* (1980).
6. Gabilondo notes that Banderas "embodies 'excessive masculinity,' a hypersexualized masculinity forbidden to normative American maleness. The Latin lover vicariously represents the sexual excess that Anglo-Saxon or Protestant masculinity desires for itself" (2006, 212).
7. Palmer asserts that "Professor McBurney's *Check-List of English Prose Fiction, 1700–1739* [. . .] has more listings for Mme d'Aulnoy than for any of her French contemporaries" (1975, 238).
8. See Appendix 1 and 2 in Duggan (2014, 282–285). For a summary of the statistics comparing d'Aulnoy to Perrault, see Duggan (2014, 264).
9. In a broad search of the catalogue at the *Bibliothèque Nationale*, from 1850 to 1900, 458 publications are listed of works by Perrault, 54 total works by d'Aulnoy (47 works of her individual or anthologized tales), and 53 by the Grimms (20 individual or collected tales in French; 3 tale collections in German). From 1901 to 1950, the numbers shift: Perrault is at 622, d'Aulnoy 108, and the Grimms 181. From 1951 to 2000, some 1,714 works are listed for Perrault, 107 for d'Aulnoy, and 1,021 for the Grimms.
10. On Angela Carter, see essays in Roemer and Bacchilega (2001); Bacchilega (1997), especially chapters 3 and 4; and, most recently, Lau (2014). On Donoghue, see Dutheil de la Rochère (2009) and Orme (2010). On Breillat, see Bacchilega (2013, 86–99) and Duggan (2016, 199–203).
11. See Levine's (2005) fascinating analysis of the cross-promotional synergies of Disney marketing strategies.
12. Ontiveros imitates Kahlo's "The Two Fridas" (1939) in "The Two Snow Whites" (2014).

ANNE E. DUGGAN

References Cited and Further Reading

Bacchilega, Cristina. 1997. *Postmodern Fairy Tales: Gender and Narrative Strategies*. Philadelphia: U Pennsylvania P.

———. 2013. *Fairy Tales Transformed?: Twenty-First-Century Adaptations and the Politics of Wonder*. Detroit: Wayne State UP.

Basile, Giambattista. 2007. *The Tale of Tales, or Entertainment for Little Ones*, translated and edited by Nancy Canepa. Detroit: Wayne State UP.

Benson, Stephen. 1998. "Angela Carter and the Literary *Märchen*: A Review Essay." *Marvels & Tales* 12 (1): 23–51.

Canepa, Nancy. 1997. *Out of the Woods: The Origins of the Literary Fairy Tale in Italy and France*. Detroit: Wayne State UP.

Carter, Angela. 1978. *The Bloody Chamber*. New York: Harper & Row.

Choiseul-Meuse, Félicité de. 1818. *Le Retour des fées*. 2 vols. Paris: Blanchard.

Coulthard, Lisa. 2010. "Desublimating Desire: Courtly Love and Catherine Breillat." *Journal for Cultural Research* 14 (1): 57–69.

Cunningham, Michael. 2015. *A Wild Swan and Other Tales*. New York: Farrar, Strauss and Giroux.

DeJean, Joan. 2000. "Classical Reeducation: Decanonizing the Feminine." *Yale French Studies* 97: 55–70.

Donoghue, Emma. 1997. *Kissing the Witch: Old Tales in New Skins*. New York: HarperCollins.

Do Rozario, Rebecca-Anne C. 2012. "Comic Book Princesses for Grown Ups: Cinderella Meets the Pages of the Superhero." *Colloquy* 24: 191–206.

Duggan, Anne E. 2014. "The Reception of the Grimms in Nineteenth-Century France: *Volkspoesie* and the Reconceptualization of the French Fairy-Tale Tradition." *Fabula: Journal of Folklore Studies* 55 (3/4): 260–85.

———. 2016. "Binary Outlaws: Queering the Classical Tale in François Ozon's *Criminal Lovers* and Catherine Breillat's *The Sleeping Beauty*." In *New Approaches to Teaching Folk and Fairy Tales*, edited by Christa C. Jones and Claudia Schwabe, 191–205. Logan: Utah State UP.

Dutheil de la Rochère, Martine Hennard. 2009. "Queering the Fairy Tale Canon: Emma Donoghue's *Kissing the Witch*." In *Fairy Tales Reimagined: Essays in New Retellings*, edited by Susan Redington Bobby and Kate Bernheimer, 13–30. Jefferson, NC: McFarland.

Gabilondo, Joseba. 2006. "Antonio Banderas: Hispanic Gay Masculinities and the Global Mirror Stage (1991–2001)." *Studies in 20th & 21st Century Literature* 30 (1): 209–33.

Garcia, Maria. 2011. "Rewriting Fairy Tales, Revising Female Identity: An Interview with Catherine Breillat." *Cineaste* 36 (3): 32–5.

Genlis, Stéphanie Félicité, comtesse de. 1805. *Nouveaux contes moraux*. 2 vols. Paris: Maradan.

Gordon, Neta. 2016. *A Tour of Fabletown: Patterns and Plots in Bill Willingham's* Fables. Jefferson, NC: McFarland.

Haase, Donald, ed. 2004. *Fairy Tales and Feminism: New Approaches*. Detroit: Wayne State UP.

Harries, Elizabeth Wanning. 2001. *Twice Upon a Time: Women Writers and the History of the Fairy Tale*. Princeton, NJ: Princeton UP.

Hill, Mark C. 2009. "Negotiating Wartime Masculinity in Bill Willingham's *Fables*." In *Fairy Tales Reimagined: Essays on New Retellings*, edited by Susan Redington Bobby, 181–95. Jefferson, NC: McFarland.

Jarvis, Shawn, and Jeannine Blackwell. 2001. *The Queen's Mirror: Fairy Tales by German Women 1780–1900*. Lincoln: U Nebraska P.

Koehler, Julie. 2016. "Kind Girls, Evil Sisters, and Wise Women: Coded Gender Discourse in Literary Fairy Tales by German Women in the 19th Century." Dissertation. Wayne State U.

Lau, Kimberly. 2014. *Erotic Infidelities: Love and Enchantment in Angela Carter's* The Bloody Chamber. Detroit: Wayne State UP.

Levine, Elana. 2005. "Fractured Fairy Tales and Fragmented Markets: Disney's *Weddings of a Lifetime* and the Cultural Politics of Media Conglomeration." *Television & New Media* 6 (1): 71–88.

Lieberman, Marcia. 1972. "Someday My Prince Will Come: Female Acculturation Through the Fairy Tale." *College English* 34: 383–95.

Lurie, Alison. 1980. *Clever Gretchen and Other Forgotten Folktales*. New York: Thomas Y. Crowell.

Orme, Jennifer. 2010. "Mouth to Mouth: Queer Desires in Emma Donoghue's *Kissing the Witch*." *Marvels & Tales* 24 (1): 116–30.

Palmer, Melvin D. 1975. "Madame d'Aulnoy in England." *Comparative Literature* 27 (3): 237–53.

Ragan, Kathleen, ed. 1998. *Fearless Girls, Wise Women & Beloved Sisters: Heroines in Folktales from around the World*. New York: W.W. Norton.

Roemer, Danielle M., and Cristina Bacchilega, eds. 1998. "Angela Carter and the Literary Märchen." Special issue of *Marvels & Tales* 12 (1).

———, eds. 2001. *Angela Carter and the Fairy Tale*. Detroit: Wayne State UP.

Seifert, Lewis. 1996. *Fairy Tales, Sexuality, and Gender in France 1690–1715: Nostalgic Utopias*. Cambridge: Cambridge UP.

Shippey, Tom. 2003. "Rewriting the Core: Transformations of the Fairy Tale in Contemporary Writing." In *A Companion to the Fairy Tale*, edited by Hilda Ellis Davidson and Anna Chaudhri, 253–74. Cambridge: D. S. Brewer.

Straparola, Giovanni Francesco. 2012. *The Pleasant Nights*, edited and introduction by Donald Beecher. 2 vols. Toronto: U Toronto P.

Trinquet du Lys, Charlotte. 2016. "Once upon a Time (Television Series, 2011–)." In *Folktales and Fairy Tales: Traditions and Texts from around the World*, edited by Anne E. Duggan, Donald Haase, with Helen Callow, 737–8. 2nd ed. 4 vols. Santa Barbara: ABC-CLIO.

Wagner, Shandi Lynne. 2015. "Sowing Seeds of Subversion: Nineteenth-Century British Women Writers' Subversive Use of Fairy Tales and Folklore." Dissertation. Wayne State U.

Willingham, Bill. 2002. *Fables: Animal Farm*. New York: DC Comics.

———. 2003. *Fables: Storybook Love*. New York: DC Comics.

———. 2004. *Fables: Cinderella Libertine*. New York: DC Comics.

———. 2010. *Fables: Legends in Exile*. New York: DC Comics.

Zarranz, Libe García. 2007. "Diswomen Strike Back? The Evolution of Disney's *Femmes* in the 1990s." *Atenea* 27 (2): 55–65.

Zipes, Jack. 1989. *Beauties, Beasts and Enchantment: Classic French Fairy Tales*. New York: New American Library.

Mediagraphy

Cinderella. 1950. Directors Clyde Geronimi, Hamilton Luske, and Wilfred Jackson. USA.

Disney's Fairy Tale Weddings & Honeymoons. 2016. www.disneyweddings.com/disney-boutique/.

Frida. 2002. Director Julie Taymor. USA/Canada/Mexico.

Glass, Cinder, and Thorns (Art Exhibit). 2014. Inner State Gallery. Detroit, USA. http://innerstategallery.com/glass-cinder-thorns/.

Graves, Mab. 2015. "Snow White in This Black Forest." Painting.

Kahlo, Frida. 1939. "The Two Fridas." Painting.

Once Upon a Time (TV). 2011–. Creators Adam Horowitz and Edward Kitsis. USA.

Ontiveros, José Rodolfo Loaiza. 2013. "The End of Bitterness." Painting.

———. 2014a. "Cinderella Revenge." Painting.

———. 2014b. "The Two Snow Whites." Painting.

———. 2015. "Sweet Poison." Painting.

———. 2016a. "Profanity Pop." *La Luz de Jesus*. Painting Series. http://laluzdejesus.com/jose-rodolfo-loaiza-ontiveros-profanity-pop-the-laluzapalooza-jury-winners/#more-2860.

———. 2016b. "Wonder Pop." *La Luz de Jesus*. Painting Series. http://laluzdejesus.com/jose-rodolfo-loaiza-ontiveros-j-a-w-cooper/#more-15059.

"Paloma Negra" (Song). 1988. Artist Tomás Méndez, album *Su Voz Y Sus Canciones*. Mexico.

———. 1991. Artist Chavela Vargas, album *Piensas en mi*. Costa Rica.

The Princess and the Frog. 2009. Directors Ron Clements and John Musker. USA.

Shrek 2. 2004. Director Andrew Adamson and Kelly Asbury. USA.

Sleeping Beauty. 1959. Director Clyde Geronimi. USA.

The Sleeping Beauty. 2010. Director Catherine Breillat. France.

Snow White and the Seven Dwarfs. 1937. Directors David Hand, William Cottrell, Wilfred Jackson, Larry Morey, Perce Pearce, and Ben Sharpsteen. USA.

Weddings of a Lifetime. 1995–1998. Disney/Lifetime. USA.

Yoon, Mimi. 2015. "Once Upon a Time No More." Painting.

14

INDIGENEITY

E Ho ʻokikoho ʻe iā Peʻape ʻamakawalu (Digitizing the Eight-Eyed Bat): Indigenous Wonder Tales, Culture, and Media

ku ʻualoha ho ʻomanawanui

> Do you ever wonder how it is we imagine the world in the way we do, how it is we imagine ourselves, if not through our stories. And in the English-speaking world, nothing could be easier, for we are surrounded by stories, and we can trace these stories back [. . .] to the beginnings of language. For these are our stories, the cornerstones of our culture.
>
> Thomas King (2008, 93)

In a 2012 article on Indigenous decolonization and sustainable self-determination, Jeff Corntassel (Cherokee) shares the story of three Canadian Mohawk who traveled to Bolivia to attend a conference on climate change. While there, they were confronted by other Indigenous people who questioned their Indigeneity because they were from the sprawling metropolis of Montreal. The men admitted it was a struggle to maintain the expectation of Indigenous peoples, whom many see as "examples of living healthy and sustainably with the[ir] environments" (Greg Horn in Corntassel 2012, 87). Corntassel's essay focuses on the challenges of decolonization and of sustainable self-determination, real-world politics, and economics.

How is this issue related to Indigenous wonder tales, culture, and media? In part because the real world is where culture is born and shaped; because stories are an important part of culture that carry culture, the worldviews, knowledge, and values of the people; and because media is a vehicle that both transports and transforms story across time and space. Colonialism, however, has disrupted Indigenous peoples' relationships with their traditional lands and environment, which in turn have disrupted all aspects of culture, including traditional stories, from the languages they are told in, to the media used to record, reproduce, and transmit them. Corntassel argues it is essential to "address the legacies of ongoing, contemporary colonialism [. . .] and re-vision [. . .] everyday acts of resurgence" (88).

A United Nations fact sheet on Indigenous peoples notes there are over 370 million people that make up 5,000 identified Indigenous (alternately called Native, First Nation, Tribal, and

Aboriginal) peoples spread across ninety countries worldwide. Each has its own distinct language, culture, and customs (United Nations N.d.). Thus, it is impossible to write about transmission of *Indigenous* stories, in part, because defining and constructing meaning is incredibly varied. Furthermore, the multiple generations and configurations of *media* are equally diverse, as is what constitutes the Native *wonder tale*. Therefore, I focus on a few selected examples of "everyday acts of resurgence" by Indigenous peoples in and around the Pacific Ocean in re-claiming, re-visioning, and decolonizing Indigenous wonder tales across various modes of modern media.

I argue that storytelling is a fundamental mode of Indigenous cultural continuity and that modern media genres are simply new ways for us to tell and represent our traditional stories, including wonder tales. There is a misconception that Indigeneity and modernity are antithetical and that Indigenous peoples do not (and cannot) represent ourselves and our stories utilizing media and related technologies. But we do, in infinite, celebratory ways.

I intentionally refrain from using the term "fairy tale," which specifically traces to post-seventeenth-century Europe. Because of its particular etymology, Indigenous literature scholars do not employ it to describe our non-European traditional narratives. What constitutes a European fairy tale, however, is more universal, and "wonder tale" is an apt description of the characteristics of traditional oral stories from non-European cultures. While the two terms are synonymous, "wonder tale" does not have specific roots or connotations that point specifically to Europe. As Cristina Bacchilega writes, "It is no accident that fairy tales are also known as 'wonder tales.' As an effect, wonder involves both awe and curiosity" (2013, 5). She quotes Marina Warner, who posits:

> Wonder has no opposite [. . .] [it is] compounded of dread and desire at once. [. . .] It names the marvel, the prodigy, the surprise as well as the responses they excite, of fascination and inquiry; it conveys the active motion towards experience and the passive stance of enrapturement.
>
> (2004, 3)

While "fairy tale" colloquially connotes a fabrication, a falsehood, something that isn't believable, the concept of "wonder tale" is useful in considering the elements of magic or wonder without the associated negative connotation.

Media, the plural of medium, refers to myriad genres of mass communication that vary from local to global and include electronic or broadcast (radio, television, film, recorded music, such as albums, CDs, video games) and digital (mobile, texting, e-mail, Internet, apps, social media, music and video streaming, etc.). It also incorporates older technologies, such as print (newspapers, books), which have evolved over time since the invention of the first printing press through the digital print age, to include relevant genres such as comic books and graphic novels. Indigenous storytelling and wonder tales are represented across these media, to varying quality and degrees.

Digitizing the Eight-Eyed Bat: Indigenous Wonder Tales in the Twenty-First Century

Indigeneity and *modernity* are not considered often enough together in a positive, proactive way. And why not? Storytelling is the core of all media content. Storytelling is integral to Indigenous cultural practice. However, first world, mainstream mass media culture often relegates the Indigenous to the margins, stereotyped as pre-industrial, pre-technological people with little, if any, capability. Yet, in all its forms, media is thought of as a first world, Euro-American invention, a tool of capitalism, popular culture, and entertainment. This attitude has led to rampant appropriation of Indigenous stories, including wonder tales, in a variety of media by global corporations such as Disney (*Moana*, released in November 2016, being just one recent example). In writing about cultural misappropriation of Native American culture and the fashion world, Jessica Metcalfe (Turtle Mountain Chippewa) defines cultural appropriation as a "loose idea of borrowing, sharing, and being inspired by other cultures" that allows for learning and growth, while "cultural misappropriation is [. . .] a place where one culture (most often one that has an historical record of oppressing other cultures) engages in the unauthorised taking of some aspects of another (most often a minority) culture" (2012). What distinguishes the two, Metcalfe continues, are the "power factors [that] shape the definitions of these two categories. Sharing is great. Unauthorised taking is not. Being inspired by an artist is great. Copying an artist and writing it off as your own is not" (Metcalfe 2012).

But Indigenous peoples use various media to tell our own stories in our own ways, wonder tales being one genre. Using digital media to disseminate ancient, traditional tales offers acts of cultural resurgence. Within the field of fairy-tale studies, Bacchilega writes about activist (or proactive) adaptations that remap worldly wonder tales that "contest the hegemony of Euro-American fairy-tale magic" (2013, 53–54). In examining Indigenous wonder tales and representations in new media, key questions of such mapping include *what is working* and *what is at stake* (for Indigenous people, culture, and knowledge)? *What is misrepresentation* and *why does it matter?* In considering such questions, I am reminded of the Polynesian hero figure, demigod, and ancestor Māui, whose adventures and exploits have been told and retold by Pacific peoples for millennia. In one Hawaiian version, Māui must rescue his mother, Hina, from Peʻapeʻamakawalu, a fearsome eight-eyed bat god. Peʻapeʻamakawalu is a particularly formidable adversary who can stay constantly awake, resting all but one eye at a time. Subsequently, *makawalu* (*lit.* eight eyes) is a Native Hawaiian concept of multiple perspectives, as much as vigilance. In the context of multiple media format (re)presentations, the "digitized" (or digital) eight-eyed bat is an appropriate metaphor to describe the myriad media Indigenous people use to tell and represent our stories and cultures in acts of resurgence, resistance, and insistence. It also suggests the need for vigilance against misrepresentation and abuse of our sacred, traditional tales of wonder in the greedy, capitalist hands of the multinational settler colonial Other.

Moʻolelo Kamahaʻo i Moana Nui (Indigenous Wonder Tales in the Pacific): Paikea

Whale rider legends are found in many cultures across the Pacific, but Māori versions are most familiar, at least in the English-speaking world. Whale rider tales provoke a sense of wonder at the communication and cooperation between humans and the most powerful, mystical beasts on the planet. In the Māori language, whales are *tohorā* and humpback whales are *paikea*, the most common species in Aotearoa (New Zealand). They are also *taniwha*, water spirit monsters, dangerous or powerful creatures. In addition, they can be a "chief, powerful leader, something [. . .] awesome," and can "take many forms [logs, reptiles, whales]," typically living in water (lakes, streams, or the ocean) (*Te Whanake* N.d.). Taniwha "are often regarded as guardians by the people" of a specific region, but they "may also have a malign influence on human[s]" (*Te Whanake*).

That anyone would even think of climbing aboard a whale, a creature of the deepest, most dangerous part of the ocean, one who can plunge to great depths deadly to humans in an instant, is in and of itself sublime. That the whales would not harm the person, but rather foster a collaborative relationship of adventure and discovery, is magical. Surely, non-Pacific writers like American novelist Herman Melville recognized such power and tried to capture it in *Moby Dick* (1851). But Melville's Ahab is representative of the colonization of the Pacific, a man obsessed with destroying the powerful leviathan, a metaphoric representation of Western colonization (Ahab) destroying the Pacific native (the white whale).

There are numerous whale rider stories across Aotearoa, many of which are specific to individual Māori *iwi* (tribes) and associated with specific locations. One of the most well-known is Paikea, an "epic character" and "key ancestor" of the Ngāti Porou of the East Coast of the North Island (Reedy 2015, 1).

Kahutia-te-rangi is the son of Uenuku, a prominent Māori ancestor from Hawaiki (the ancient Māori homeland). He takes the name Paikea after being rescued by the whale when his half-brother Ruatapu lures him out to sea to kill him. Kahutia-te-rangi chants a *karakia* (incantation) to the whale, who then carried him from Hawaiki safely to shore near Whāngārā, north of Gisborne (Te Maire Tau 2015). The small islet at Whāngārā, Te Motuopaikea ("the island of Paikea"), is the whale's fossilized remains, and the ancestor Paikea is believed to be buried there. It is a common practice in Indigenous cultures to name geological features to commemorate and remember such history, and in this case, it demonstrates the reverence Ngāti Porou have for Paikea and for whales.

Traditional Māori cultural arts, including storytelling, carving of ancestors, and composition of *haka* (a traditional Māori dance), continue to represent, remember, and demonstrate respect and reverence for Paikea. For example, *tekoteko* (carved figures set atop the gable of a meeting house) of Paikea adorn *whare nui* (meeting house) on *marae* (Māori community meeting place), such as Whitirēia in Whāngārā and Takahanga, a Ngāi Tahi marae at Kaikōura. A haka commemorating the whale-riding ancestor, "Paikea," was composed by Mikaera Pewhairangi, a farmer from Tokomaru Bay north of Turanga (Gisborne), in the 1870s. An undated Turanga *oriori* (song), "Pō! Pō!", was composed by Enoka Te Pakaru (Te Aitanga-a-Mahaki) (M.O. 1965, 19).

Yet perhaps one of the reasons Paikea's legend is particularly well-known outside of its specific Ngāti Porou context is because of Māori writer Witi Ihimaera's (1987) novella *Whale Rider*, one of the first modern interpretations of the tale. Ihimaera (Te Aitanga-a-Mahaki) was born near Gisborne, the region of North Island where Paikea lived. Set in Whāngārā, Ihimaera's novel focuses on Kahu, a young girl descended from Paikea. Kahu is "the first born to the eldest son of the whanau [family]," and as a girl, she "has broken the male line of descent," the first child of the family to do so (McCoy 2010). Kahu's paternal grandfather, Koro Apirama, is unable to accept that she can be the next leader of the people, and Kahu struggles to prove herself. When a pod of whales is stranded on the beach at Whāngārā, Kahu proves herself as the next leader of the tribe. Ihimaera creates a powerful narrative that imagines a modern Paikea negotiating modern struggles, using ancient wisdom and wonder to overcome them. He also interweaves key elements of contemporary Māori identity and threats to it, including nuclear testing in the Pacific by Euro-American powers (France, the United States), that are harming the oceans, symbolized by the whale stranding due to the degradation of their natural habitat, Moana Nui (the Pacific Ocean), the largest geological feature on earth.

Māori scholar Alice Te Punga Sommerville notes as well the diasporic movements of Māori across the Pacific, represented by Kahu's uncle Rawiri. She sees an important theme in the novella as making broader kinship connections that recontextualize Indigenous Pacific identities as more intimately linked by the ocean. This argument was first articulated in Sāmoan writer and scholar Albert Wendt's (1976) essay "Towards a New Oceania" and Tongan writer and scholar Epeli Hau'ofa's essay "Our Sea of Islands" (1994). From this perspective, Ihimaera's positioning of his Māori characters within a larger web of kinship connections across the

Pacific reflects Paikea's arrival from Hawaiki atop the back of another migratory Pacific species. This action symbolically represents this web of relationships between people, animals, and nature in physical and spiritual ways, an act of cultural resurgence forwarding an Indigenous worldview.

While *Whale Rider* is set in contemporary New Zealand, wondrous elements of the original tale are retained within the storyline: like her illustrious ancestor, Kahu is able to communicate with the whales, and the leader of the pod allows her to mount him. But in a clever plot twist to the original tale, where the whale saves the man from drowning, Kahu saves the whales from suffocating on the beach when they strand. In both cases, the "magical" communication between the two is what propels the action and results in a happy ending.

Multiple versions of the original publication followed, including an American edition and children's picture books, some available in different formats (hard cover, paperback, audio book, eBook). A major motion picture, based on Ihimaera's novel (which changes the main character's name to Pai [rather than Paikea]), *Whale Rider* (dir. Niki Caro) was released in 2002 to international acclaim. Several children's picture books by Māori artists visually depicting Paikea's story have appeared before and after the movie release. Picture books geared toward young children (Kindergarten through third grade) are a popular media for sharing wonder tales. Māori artist Robyn Kahukiwa published one of the first modern retellings in this format, *Paikea* (1993).

Māori visual artist Warren Pohaku's (Ngāi Tāmanuhiri) book *Traditional Maori Legends, Nga Tai Korero* (2000) features Paikea riding a whale on the cover. Ihimaera also released a children's picture book version of *The Whale Rider* (2005), gorgeously illustrated by Bruce Potter; Yan Peirsegale (Tahitian) translated it into French as *Kahu, Fille des Baleines* (Au Vent des Isles, 2009).

Visual art has always been an important media in representing and retelling wonder tales. Digital media allows Indigenous artists to create and recreate their traditional wonder tales and share them more broadly. For example, Māori artist Terangi Roimata Kutia-Tataurangi (Ngāti Porou) is from Whāngārā and a descendant of Paikea. She shares aspects of her art, culture, and ancestral land on her blog, *Ariaaariki*. She uses multiple art media to portray the story of Whāngārā and Paikea and published these on her blog. Her blog features photos of Whāngārā, where the movie *Whale Rider* was filmed, the little islet of Temotuopaikea a prominent, symbolic landmark clearly visible in key scenes. She also includes personal scenes of her grandparents' home and other special and symbolic images that connect the lives of Paikea's descendants to their homeland, continuing to document their presence on the land of their famous ancestor, his story still respectfully shared and kept at the forefront of communal memory. For her senior art thesis, completed in 2012, Kutia-Tataurangi included a series of paintings representing her cultural values as a Māori woman and included two paintings that represent her *whakapapa* (genealogy). In a March 31, 2013, post, she describes one of the paintings, "Whangara," as "a homage to my ancestor Paikea and the lime trail left by the Tohora (whales) when they migrate along the East Coast of Aotearoa. [. . .] This was the first painting I did when I started at Toihoukura. [. . .] It was the first time i used four Niho Taniwha [whale teeth] as a reference to Whangara" (Kutia-Tataurangi 2012–2014).

Web pages and blogs have been important media to cultivate wider audiences. In addition, they can be built and maintained by individuals with some technical assistance or who seek out technical training. Overall, they are quicker and require much less capital to develop for distribution than books or films and do not require the same kind of distribution network. Many, for educational use and to facilitate reader interest, can incorporate text, visual, audio, and digital components. One example is the blog *Ngā Maunga Kōrero o te Tairāwhiti* (stories about the Tairāwhiti mountains) by Wananga Te Ariki Walker (Ngati Porou), designed "to sketch a map of settlement of the district from its earliest known inhabitants through to contact with Europeans" (Walker 2014b). Walker is the former head of the Humanities department at Tairāwhiti Polytechnic Institute in Gisborne. "Paikea Ariki Moana the Original Whalerider" is the focus of issue 8, although a brief mention of Paikea as "the one and only whale rider" is first brought up in issue 5 (July 2014).

Similarly, digital media has become a platform to represent old stories in new ways. One example is Pewhairangi's haka "Paikea," which has a new digital life on the Internet. The Māori words, an English translation, history, background, notes, critical analysis, links to YouTube performances, and multiple Polynesian versions of Paikea from outside of Aotearoa, including Tahiti and the Cook Islands, are provided on a page of the website *New Zealand Folk Song* (2016).

Kisima Innitchuna (Never Alone)

Indigenous peoples have always worked and been represented in the electronic games industry. *Kisima Innitchuna*, or *Never Alone* (2014), however, is a video game that marks a new era of Indigenous communities representing themselves using traditional legends imbued with Indigenous knowledge as the foundation for collaboratively overcoming obstacles for players to advance. Game reviewer Xav de Matos (2014) describes the award-winning video game as an "atmospheric puzzle platform" game. It is divided into eight chapters that focus on different aspects of a traditional Inupiat (Inuit, Alaska Native) wonder tale, *Kunuuksaayuka*. In the original, Kunuuksaayuka, an Inupiaq boy, seeks to discover the source of a powerful, eternal blizzard that threatens the survival of his people. *Never Alone*'s main character, Nuna, is an Inupiaq girl who is accompanied on her quest by an unnamed Arctic fox. Single gamers can choose to play as Nuna or Fox, and can switch back and forth between them, while a multiple-player mode allows for cooperative play between family members or friends. Unlike many games which focus on competition, destruction, and violence, the emphasis of *Never Alone* (reflected in its title as well) is cooperation. To be successful, Nuna and Fox use their different but complementary skills and work together for their mutual survival and, in extension, the survival of their species.

Indigenous peoples recognize nature as sentient and themselves a part of a larger organized system; as Beth Brant (Mohawk) writes, "We do not worship nature. We are part of it" (1990, 119), an understanding Thomas King (Cherokee) describes as "the territory of Native oral literature" (2008, 114). This is reflected in *Never Alone*, as the story shows the intimate relationship between the Inupiat people and their natural environment. Nuna and Fox act to restore balance to their native environment, encountering various ancestral spirits of the land, both malevolent and helpful. Spirit animals appear in the different chapters and assist Nuna and Fox in overcoming obstacles, from strong winds, to crossing open water, to ascending steep cliffs, so they may continue their journey across the Arctic landscape.

Never Alone was released in November 2014 on multiple platforms. It is produced by a partnership between the Cook Inlet Tribal Council (CITC), a non-profit tribal organization that created Upper One Games, the first Indigenous-owned video game company, and E-Line Media in 2012. Their collaboration with the CITC created a powerful and timely model for successful partnership with Indigenous peoples and appropriate representation of Indigenous cultures, stories, and voices far too often ignored or blatantly misappropriated by multinational entertainment juggernauts such as Sony and Disney.[1]

Based in Anchorage, CITC serves an Alaska Native population of 12,000, working on diverse social, educational, and economic concerns. The board sought out opportunities to provide additional support to federal funding. In looking at diverse industries, CITC president and chief executive officer Gloria O'Neill shared, "we asked ourselves [. . .] what is the greatest asset of our people? And we said, our culture and our stories" (quoted in Parkinson 2014). In the same interview, E-Line Media CEO Alan Gershenfeld notes that "people think video games have disconnected youth from their heritage, from their storytelling and their culture. But why not use this incredibly powerful medium to fire imagination and reconnect youth with other cultures, with their own cultures and with their elders?" (quoted in Parkinson 2014).

A colonial approach to Native cultures has traditionally been, as de Matos succinctly notes, to "lock the [. . .] most important works behind glass" in museums and other institutions "to preserve their memory" (2014). Instead of seeing technology and new media as global, settler colonial tools only capable of erasing or misappropriating cultural stories, the producers of *Never Alone* "are using video games to help *preserve* the legends of a people," to more widely share traditional tales of wonder, and to "help reignite passion and preserve the legends within native communities throughout Alaska" and beyond (de Matos 2014, emphasis mine). The game allows players to "live out the legends and stories passed down for generations," doing so in a way that brings Indigenous culture and media together, bridging the artificial and negative stereotype that Indigenous cultures and technology aren't complementary (2014).

The *Never Alone* website notes that "nearly 40 Alaska Native elders, storytellers and community members contributed to the development of the game," an additional layer of collaborative work integral to many Indigenous cultures. The community-minded focus of *Never Alone* at multiple levels is an important model of Indigenous cultural ethics expanding into new mediums. As O'Neill says in De Matos's (2014) review:

> We really want to engage our community at all levels [. . .] when Upper One Games are [successful], it's the success of the community. [. . .] Our main goal is to take our stories to the world and invite people [to understand] who we are [. . .] games [are] a great way of [. . .] sharing [and] keeping our culture alive.

The *Never Alone* trailer frames the digitized version of the story within the context of Inupiaq oral tradition, where passing down culture knowledge and wisdom about the elements and environment is crucial for survival. The website also describes the video game format as a new way to share old stories:

> For thousands of years, we told stories from one generation to the next. Our stories help us to understand how the world is ordered and our place within it. But what good are old stories if the wisdom they contain is not shared? That's why we're making this game. We've gathered an amazing group of people, each bringing something special from different cultures but with the same purpose.

The website describes how story is incorporated, through separate video segments of "elders, storytellers, and other members of the Alaska Native community" who "share stories and wisdom about their culture, values and the amazing Arctic world encountered by players in over 30 minutes of interviews." Hyperlinks allow players to access or unlock these video segments, which are outside of gameplay. The video segments of live Indigenous people the game represents are critical to more successful gameplay because they allow players to see and experience the Inupiat as a real people who are not simply fictional, mythologized, or appropriated Other.

Reviewer Megan Farokhmanesh notes that one of the wondrous aspects of the tale is that it is set "in a place where survival shouldn't be possible." Through interaction with the harsh conditions of an Arctic landscape consumed by a fierce blizzard, "the game [explores] what it means to be human" (2014) through stories of traditional Indigenous knowledge based on generational experience. The Inupiat recognition of nature as sentient contributes to the sense of wonder and magic. Nuna cannot survive without Fox, and vice versa, and neither can survive without communication with or help from the spirit beings and wondrous elements they encounter.

The critical response to *Never Alone* by the gaming industry has been overwhelmingly positive, and the game has been viewed as a necessary intervention into the heavily mythologized world of the gaming genre. Luke Karmali (2014) describes it as "[bringing] together a beautiful aesthetic with stories, characters and folklore [. . .] long [. . .] circulated in Alaska Native cultures." E-Line CEO Gershenfeld describes it as "the start of a worldwide games movement" (quoted in Parkinson 2014).

Washington Post games reviewer Christopher Byrd (2014) has expressed cautious support. He acknowledges that "for smaller communities," such as Indigenous peoples overall, or perhaps the Inupiaq in particular,

> storytelling can mean the difference between vitality and cultural irrelevance. If the stories a community tells itself about its history and its purpose are not enough to bind its members to a common cause, it stands to reason that its membership could ultimately be assimilated into neighboring communities capable of advancing more pervasive counterclaims.

Because of the long history of settler colonialism in places like the United States, small Indigenous communities and their stories don't simply get assimilated into neighboring (Indigenous) communities. Rather, they get swallowed, erased, or appropriated into the dominant discourse of Western hegemony. Such hegemony is often thought of as solely White. But those who work within the industries of media and technology, for example, regardless of their own ethnic, cultural, and perhaps even Indigenous backgrounds, can be subsumed by the dominant discourse and perspectives of White patriarchy and consciously or unconsciously contribute to the mainstream narrative that diminishes or misappropriates Native stories.

Byrd, who is not White, recognizes that "the notion that video games can bolster the traditions of indigenous populations while vaulting over the pitfalls of cultural appropriation seems logical enough" (2014). Yet he also admits it is still not something he has ever considered. And why should he? In a larger world where Indigenous peoples, our cultures, and our stories are often ignored or misappropriated, such lack of consideration is par for the settler colonial course. Byrd writes,

> Until recently, the most that I had hoped for from the game industry, with respect to the subject of diversity, was that it would expand its outreach efforts to lure more women and minorities into game development and offer players a broader set of avatars and NPC's (non-playable characters) with which to interact.
>
> (2014)

Yet his caveat, "until recently," signals that at least some critics are pausing to consider that there are alternative options to mainstream White, male, settler colonial visions, storylines, and misrepresentations of Indigenous people and cultures.

The point that Indigenous stories told from Indigenous perspectives are valuable cannot be stressed enough. This is a point made in a different context by Zoe Todd (Métis) (2016) in reference to a lecture by Bruno Latour she attended in London, where Latour completely ignored Inuit concepts of the environment and causes of climate change, presenting such important ideas as exclusive to White Western European men. Todd was incensed at Latour's disregard for Inuit activists who first brought issues of climate change to the international stage, particularly through their understanding of climate as *Sila*, "an incredibly important organizing concept for many actors in Inuit territories [. . .][that] is both climate *and* life force" (2016, 5–6).

As an Indigenous woman, Todd experiences anthropology as "white public space [. . .] that distorts or erases or homogenises distinct Indigenous voices" (12). The same can be said for other kinds of engagements with Indigenous voices, such as video games or movies, which far too often misrepresent, distort, erase, or homogenize distinctive Indigenous voices, replacing them with stereotyped, settler colonial caricatures.

Ha'ina 'ia mai ana ka puana

Ha'ina 'ia mai ana ka puana (the story has been told) is a common refrain in Hawaiian songs that signals a conclusion. It functions as a narratological cue much in the same way "once upon a time" signals the start of a fairy tale. In *The Truth about Stories*, King discusses the devastating tragedies that occurred when the Aztec libraries and those of Alexandria were burned down, because in both cases,

> stories were lost. And, in the end, it didn't matter whether these stories were oral or written. So much for dependability. So much for permanence. Though it doesn't take a disaster to destroy a literature. If we stopped telling the stories and reading the books, we would discover that neglect is as powerful an agent as war and fire.
>
> (2008, 94)

Indigenous peoples have suffered through unbearable genocides and losses of our lands, languages, and cultures. Yet we are resilient, and we are still here. We still strive to preserve, protect, and regrow these things, and we innovate in the process. Despite exasperating losses, new media technologies, such as digital technology, smart phones and apps, and the World Wide Web are important tools in (re)telling, (re)creating, broadly sharing, and also preserving our stories, which represent us; celebrate our cultures; offer sage, timeless advice; and perpetuate our aesthetic practices and intellectual genealogies. Using new media facilitates everyday acts of resurgence that should also be read as acts of insistence and resistance—insistence of cultural continuity, as well as resistance to assimilation into settler society, their values and worldviews, particularly in regards to land and environment, and acceptance of their misrepresentations of us as Indigenous peoples, our cultures, and our stories.

Criticizing Disney's *Moana*, Healani Sonoda-Pale (Native Hawaiian) (2016) concludes that despite such exploitation of Hawaiian (and other Indigenous) traditions,

> Hawaiians have long been awakened to the call of aloha aina or love for the land, who is our mother, Papahanaumoku. [. . .] Those who aloha aina know our place in the universe and our kuleana [responsibility] to our land, our kupuna [elders and ancestors] and our communities. We are in the canoes, tapping kapa [traditional cloth], writing our own histories, creating art, [. . .] and protecting what is sacred.

As Indigenous peoples, our storytelling as acts of everyday resurgence help us celebrate our cultures and ourselves, to continue to remind ourselves and others that we are still here, visible, creative, intelligent peoples critically and artistically engaged with the world, ever vigilant as an eight-eyed bat. We carry our stories into the twenty-first century and beyond in digital *vaka* (canoes) traversing new currents and tides, navigating our wondrous futures through wonder tales from our past.

Related topics: Activism; Animal Studies; Blogs and Websites; Cinematic; Disney Corporation; Intellectual Property; Oral Tradition; Video Games

Note

1. For an in-depth discussion on different critical positions on Disney's *Moana*, see the Facebook page "Mana Moana: We Are Moana, We Are Maui" (2016–).

References Cited and Further Reading

Bacchilega, Cristina. 2013. *Fairy Tales Transformed?: Twenty-First-Century Adaptations and the Politics of Wonder*. Detroit: Wayne State UP.

Brant, Beth. 1990. "Recovery and Transformation: The Blue Heron." In *Bridges of Power: Women's Multicultural Alliances*, edited by Lisa Albrecht and Rose Brewster, 118–21. Philadelphia: New Society Publishers.

Byrd, Christopher. 2014. "In 'Never Alone' Native Alaskans Explore the Future of Oral Tradition." *Washington Post*, December 29. www.washingtonpost.com/news/comic-riffs/wp/2014/12/29/never-alone-review-native-alaskans-explore-the-future-of-oral-tradition/.

Corntassel, Jeff. 2012. "Re-Envisioning Resurgence: Indigenous Pathways to Decolonization and Sustainable Self-Determination." *Decolonization: Indigeneity, Educations & Society* 1 (1): 86–101.

de Matos, Xav. 2014. "Sharing Legends with the World in *Never Alone*, a Game Inspired by Alaskan Native Communities." *Engadget*, March 19. www.engadget.com/2014/03/19/sharing-legends-with-the-world-in-never-alone-a-game-inspired-b/.

Farokhmanesh, Megan. 2014. "*Never Alone's* First Trailer Explains the Importance of Passing Along Wisdom." *Polygon*, May 9. www.polygon.com/2014/5/9/5700434/never-alone-first-trailer-upper-one-games.

Hau'ofa, Epeli. 1994. "Our Sea of Islands." *The Contemporary Pacific* 6 (1): 147–61.

Ihimaera, Witi. 1987. *Whale Rider*. Auckland: Heinemann.

———. 2005. *The Whale Rider*. Auckland: Reed.

Kahukiwa, Robyn. 1993. *Paikea*. Auckland: Penguin Books.

Karmali, Luke. 2014. "Never Alone Is an Atmospheric Puzzle Game Exploring Culture and Folklore." *IGN*, May 8. www.ign.com/articles/2014/05/08/never-alone-is-an-atmospheric-puzzle-game-exploring-culture-and-folklore.

King, Thomas. 2008. *The Truth about Stories*. Minneapolis: U Minnesota P.

McCoy, Marion. 2010. "*The Whale Rider* Summary." *New Zealand Picture Book Collection*, November 30. www.picture books.co.nz/2010/11/the-whale-rider/.

Melville, Herman. 1851. *Moby Dick*. New York: Harper and Brothers.

Metcalfe, Jessica. 2012. "Native Americans Know That Cultural Misappropriation Is a Land of Darkness. *The Guardian*, May 18. www.theguardian.com/commentisfree/2012/may/18/native-americans-cultural-misappropriation.

M. O. 1965. "A Famous Oriori from Tauranga." *Ao Hou, the Maori Magazine* 53: 19–21. http://teaohou.natlib.govt. nz/journals/teaohou/issue/Mao53TeA/c12.html.

New Zealand Folk Song. 2016. http://folksong.org.nz/.

Parkinson, Hannah Jane. 2014. "Alaska's Indigenous Game *Never Alone* Teaches Co-Operation through Stories." *The Guardian*, September 29. www.theguardian.com/technology/2014/sep/29/never-alone-alaskas-indigenous-game-never-alone-teaches-cooperation-through-stories.

Piersegale, Yan, trans. 2009. *Kahu, Fille des Baleines [The Whale Rider]*. Pape'ete: Au Vent des Isles.

Pohatu, Warren. 2000. *Traditional Maori Legends: Nga Tai Korero*. Auckland: Raupo Publishing.

Reedy, Tamati Muturangi. 2015. "Ngāti Porou—Ancestors." *Te Ara, the Encyclopedia of New Zealand*, February 10. www.TeAra.govt.nz/en/ngati-porou.

Sonoda-Pale, Healani. 2016. "Disney's Commodification of Hawaiians." *Civil Beat*, October 7. www.civilbeat.org/2016/10/disneys-commodification-of-hawaiians/.

Te Maire Tau. 2015. "Ngāi Tahu—Early history." *Te Ara, the Encyclopedia of New Zealand*, February 10. www.TeAra.govt.nz/en/photograph/1621/the-ancestor-paikea.

Te Whanake Online Māori Dictionary. N.d. https://maoridictionary.co.nz/.

Todd, Zoe. 2016. "An Indigenous Feminist's Take on the Ontological Turn: 'Ontology' Is Just Another Word for Colonialism." *Journal of Historical Sociology* 29 (1): 4–22.

United Nations. N.d. *Fact Sheet: United Nations Permanent Forum on Indigenous Issues.* www.un.org/esa/socdev/unpfii/documents/5session_factsheet1.pdf.

Warner, Marina. 2004. *Fantastic Metamorphoses, Other Worlds: Ways of Telling the Self.* Oxford: Oxford UP.

Wendt, Albert. 1976. "Towards a New Oceania." *Mana Review* 1 (1): 49–60.

Mediagraphy

Kisima Innitchuna (Never Alone) (Video game). 2014. E-Line Media. http://neveralonegame.com/.

Kutia-Tataurangi, Terangi Roimata. 2012–2014 . . . *ariaaariki* . . . https://ariaaariki.wordpress.com.

———. 2013. "Graduate Exhibition 2012: . . . akoranga. . . ." . . . *ariaaariki* . . . March 31. https://ariaaariki.wordpress.com/2013/03/31/graduate-exhibition-2012-akoranga/.

"Mana Moana: We Are Moana, We Are Maui." 2016–. *Facebook Community Page.* www.facebook.com/manamoanawearemoanawearemaui/.

Moana. 2016. Directors Ron Clements and Don Hall. USA.

Walker, Wananga Te Ariki. 2014a. *Ngā Maunga Kōrero o te Tairāwhiti.* www.ngatiporou.com.

———. 2014b. "Paikea Ariki Moana the Original Whalerider." *Ngā Maunga Kōrero o te Tairāwhiti.* July 2014.

Whale Rider. 2002. Director Niki Caro. New Zealand.

15

ORIENTALISM

Excavation and Representation: Two Orientalist Modes in Fairy Tales

Jenny Heijun Wills

Orientalism, which Edward Said famously defined as "a style of thought based upon an onto-logical and epistemological distinction made between 'the Orient' and (most of the time) 'the Occident'" (1994, 2), both relies on and perpetuates a fictional, fantastical image of Asia, result-ing in a continued "dominating, restructuring, and having [of] authority over the Orient" (3). Thus, Orientalism depends on Western (mostly European and American) *ideas* about people, places, and practices in Asia, but these ideas, not necessarily informed by reality, are instead tools of Western self-definition. The Orient (hereafter always used ironically) is that which the Occident is *not*. Predictably, in European and American Orientalists' imagination, the Orient is inferior: crowded, antiquated, culturally non-complex, immoral, dirty. Paradoxically, some traits aligned with this imagined space are presented as complimentary; the Orient might also be exotic, beautiful, spiritual, pastoral. But these features belie a (White) supremacist approach: the Orient can be controlled, consumed, and fetishized by the Occidental subject. Regardless of the tone with which the Orient is described, it is fashioned in an ideological laboratory by Westerners *for* Westerners: what Stuart Hall has spiritedly termed "the west and the rest" (2007, 56).

Orientalism is inextricably bound to colonialism, since as Said insists, "The Orient is an integral part of European *material* civilization and culture" (1994, 2). A crucial part of anti-Orientalist criticism is to challenge the ways that the Orient is treated as a resource from which peoples, objects, and practices can be extracted and used at whim. Clothing, spices, and animals are just a few of the *things* fetishized and taken from the Orient and consumed by people in the West. Movements like Chinoiserie in Britain, Japonism in France, and Imagism in the United States exemplify the ways that aesthetic inspiration can also be extracted from the Orient. Narrative and myth are also valuable resources extracted by Western authors/translators who are celebrated for introducing readers to these foreign texts, modifying and reducing them for European and American audiences, and even conceiving new versions of the Orient based on their own imaginations.

Thus there are two approaches for considering relationships among fairy tales, media, and Orientalism. In the first part of this chapter I explore the ways that translators intro-duced Western audiences to foreign, Oriental fairy tales like "1001 Nights." I will consider how filmmakers and animators have delivered the Oriental fairy tale of "Aladdin" (ATU

561)—one of the most recognized additions to that earlier collection. This section focuses on the Orientalist act of appropriating, or extracting, narratives and the ways those texts are reformulated through a Western lens. The second part addresses the ways the Orient is constructed in different Western texts. How do Western authors and artists imagine and represent the East in fairy tales, and what are the impacts of those representations? Which stereotypes and assumptions are constructed and reiterated by these Orientalist works? Representations of the Orient are explored in both the literary text and various illustrations to the many editions of Hans Christian Andersen's "The Nightingale." I will conclude by considering how the Orient has become a paradox for Western authors and audiences: at once contained as antiquated or pre-modern, uncivilized, archaic, *and* hypertechnological, cyborgian, and dangerously unnatural. This paradox is represented in "The Nightingale" through the trope of techno-Orientalism.

But First, Some Background . . .

> The literary fairy tale has become an established genre within a process of Western civilization that cuts across all ages.

> (Zipes 2007, 1)

In 1859, German scholar Theodor Benfey argued that "the genre of the fairy tale originated in ancient India as an oral wonder tale and spread first to Persia and then to the entire Arabic-speaking world" (Zipes 2006, 46). In his introduction to *Panchatantra*, an anthology of fables and tales originally written in Sanskrit, Benfey coined the "theory of Indian origins," which imagined "some material travelling through Tibet, via Buddhist channels, to the Mongols, and then carried by the Mongols to Europe at a later date (in the thirteenth and fourteenth centuries)" (Belcher 2008, 116). This train of argument, by imagining the Orient as the force behind these narrative migrations, means European scholars like Benfey could simultaneously romanticize the genre's trajectory and understand their uses of these texts less as appropriation or plunder, and more as another addition in the text's impressive migratory genealogy. Stuart Blackburn and Alan Dundes explain of one particular story that "Theodor Benfey [. . .] used it to illustrate the way in which tales from India are taken over into Mongolian literature and through this intermediary carried to Europe" (1997, 250). I bring up this history because it reflects precisely what Said describes when he notes that one of Orientalism's driving gestures is the taking of resources—be they objects, people, and land or more abstract things like philosophies and aesthetics—as part of Western self-fashioning. Again from *Orientalism*: "Whereas Renaissance historians judged the Orient inflexibly as an enemy, those of the eighteenth century confronted the Orient's peculiarities with some detachment and with some attempt at dealing directly with Oriental source material, perhaps because such a technique helped a European to know himself better" (Said 1994, 117).

First, note that the Orient has always existed within the imagination of the Occidental (Western) subject, although its character (and usage) changes to reflect non-Oriental needs and the ebb and flow of colonial and political relations between those worlds. Second, this notion of Oriental source material links acts of colonial resource extraction that we mostly associate with goods, labor, and people with more abstract things like literary narrative and other modes of expression that are also seized by the European imagination. It is no coincidence that Orient-inspired and adapted fairy tales gained momentum at this time, led by notorious French Orientalist and archeologist Antoine Galland, who translated *Les mille et une nuit* (known in English as *1001 Nights* and/or *The Arabian Nights*—to which I shall return later), in addition to German scholars like Benfey. The fantastical elements of these fairy tales play into the exotic and strange illusion of the Orient while the universality of their themes make them excellent fodder for European self-recognition.

Indeed, the Orient provided ample fodder for Western writers to allegorize European social and political issues. In his survey of classical fairy tales and their history, Jack Zipes summarizes this movement:

> The infusion of the Oriental tales into the French literary tradition enriched and broadened the paradigmatic options for Western writers during the course of the eighteenth century. It became a favorite device (and still is) to deploy the action of a tale to the Orient while discussing sensitive issues of norms and power close to home.
>
> (2007, 16)

He goes on to suggest that in France the printing and distributing of simplified fairy tales as chapbooks were a perfect complement for the literary extraction of Oriental source material: "the fairy tales were often abridged; the language was changed and simplified; and there were multiple versions, which were read to children and nonliterates [. . .] As a result [. . .] the literary fairy tale for children began to be cultivated" (2007, 16). In other words, the Orientalist act of extracting source material from the Orient does not just overlap with this hugely important shift in the history of the fairy tale, when the intended audience became young people and the masses, it in some ways prompts it. The reduced, simplified translations of Oriental texts were in perfect company and ideal specimens for the chapbooks that revolutionized fairy tales in the eighteenth century. The popularity of these translations inevitably fostered a growing interest in the Orient and led to representational fabulations that still exist today. Consider, again, what the Orient has to offer the fairy tale: it is otherworldly, strange, uncanny in its concurrent similarities and differences. It is a place to which one might escape, although just temporarily, where danger is expected, and where fantastic imagery and goings-on are to be anticipated. In sum, the Orient is a fascinating metonym for the lands and people of fairy tales.

Moreover, as Said notes in *Culture and Imperialism*, colonialism, Orientalism, and the Global South are always present in European literature even when not visible; they exist as subtext below the surface of plot and in the margins of characterization. As Mark Rifkin would put it, they are part of the common sense of colonialism. Speaking of canonical nineteenth-century British texts, he explains that "even where colonies are not insistently or even perceptibly in evidence, the narrative sanctions a spatial moral order" (2014, 79). Thus, whether we are discussing the literary genealogy of the genre or the thematic harmony of the figures and settings they represent, Orientalism is always already present in any discussion about fairy tales.

Orientalist Excavation: The Complex History of *1001 Nights* and Disney's *Aladdin* (1992)

When eighteenth-century Europeans turned their gaze to the aesthetics and ideologies of the Orient, there were two strategies at hand. The first aim, as noted prior, was to better understand the European subject as opposite (and superior) to its Eastern counterpart; the second was to uncover the secrets of the Orient, indeed to master it, as a tactic of dominating trade relations already established through various colonial and non-colonial practices. The spirit behind these studies was not necessarily sinister, but rather reflected a growing curiosity with Asia and the Middle East, which eventually transformed into celebration and fetishization. Scholars of the Orient—or Orientalists—studied language foremost, but also examined other cultural behaviors including literary and artistic production. Paralleling archeological practices that go hand in hand with colonial exploration—that is excavation, so-called discovery, and display in the metropole—Orientalists and translators adopted texts including fairy tales and presented them to European audiences.

Some tales, like those in Benfey's collection or "Aladdin" from *1001 Nights*—which was delivered to European readers in many incarnations—were translated from various languages, including Persian, Sanskrit, and Arabic, and have ambiguous, multiple, or unknown origins. Both collections use frame stories that weave the various tales together. *1001 Nights*, for instance, features the protagonist, Shahryar, a cruel and embittered Oriental king who daily marries and executes a young virgin, causing the storyteller, Scheherazade—the king's next lover—to defer her death by distracting him with a nightly, never-ending story. Originally assembled in Arabic during the Islamic Golden Age, *1001 Nights* consists of ten volumes with multiple (although not consistent) stories in each. Volume 1 contains the well-known detective story "The Three Apples" about a man tasked with uncovering the truth behind a grisly murder, while Volume 6 features a seven-sectioned cycle about Sinbad the sailor who travels to magical lands via the tumultuous waters off the coast of East Africa and South Asia. Some of what have become the most popular stories were in fact supplements added by Galland in his French translation of an Arabic version. These include the magical story of Aladdin and his lamp as well as the tale about Ali Baba (ATU 954), who falls upon the hideaway of forty thieves when he inadvertently utters the secret phrase: "open sesame." Although Galland likely came upon these (and the several other) supplementary tales via oral storytellers, they are often credited to him as they do not appear in earlier versions of the collection.

1001 Nights is not just a prime example of Orientalist excavation, it also deployed as Oriental synecdoche, referenced in texts by numerous authors, including "Dickens and Nabokov, as well as in those of South African André Brink and the Japanese Mishima Yukio" (Yamanaka and Nishio 2006, x). As the editors of *The Arabian Nights Encyclopedia* put it, "Dickens's work is spiced with Oriental influences, mainly derived from the *Arabian Nights*" (Marzolph, van Leeuwen, and Wassouf 2004, 539).

In his analysis of the so-called unfaithful translations of the collection from Arabic to French and later English and other European languages, Robert Irwin makes a provocative claim: "Neglected until modern times in the Near East," he announces, "the *Arabian Nights* has been so widely and frequently translated into Western languages that, despite the Arab antecedents of the tales, it is a little tempting to consider the *Nights* as primarily a work of European literature" (2005, 9). While Irwin himself is critical of this kind of co-optation, in this statement we see both the colonialist urge to stake claim—to occupy, possess, and appropriate—the Orient as well as the rationale that justifies it: that is, the trope of the White man's burden manifested in the belief that Orientals wastefully neglect or fail to properly use a particular resource, making it necessary for Europeans to co-opt it and demonstrate the correct conduct.

But Irwin is in fact partially correct. Translated and recreated over and over again, *The Arabian Nights* has become a European invention, at least insofar as the Orient too is not a real space but a Western fantasy. Rana Kabbani explains with subtlety, "The *Nights* in many respects is a Western text, a manufactured product of Orientalism, still as much in currency today as at the beginning of the eighteenth century, when the *Nights* first made their appearance in the guise of a 'translation' into a European language" (2004, 26). Kabbani astutely suggests that we consider these stories less as accurate translations and more as Orientalist ideology and European self-invention and that the French versions were original creations molded by European Orientalism and stereotyping of the East.

This would certainly account for many anti-Arab figures in these texts that indeed seem to shore up Orientalist stereotypes and myths. From another perspective, Yuriko Yamanaka and

Tetsuo Nishio think through layers of Orientalism, exploring the ways *1001 Nights* "played a decisive role in forming the general image of the Islamic Middle East in Europe, which in turn influenced the Japanese view of the Middle East" (2006, xv). And in a move to connect the social realities and material consequences of Orientalism in folk and fairy tales, Somaya Sami Sabry thinks about the collection (and particularly the frame story's female protagonist storyteller) in relation to what she calls "the race over representation which [insists that Arab-American] women are running against a history of vilification and dehumanization [. . .] in which they transfigure and disrupt prevalent representations of themselves and their Arab culture" (2011, xiii–xiv).

Irwin, one of the foremost scholars on the topic, notes that *1001 Nights* has been translated and retranslated, expanded upon, adapted, and re-mediated time after time, including in works by notable writers and Orientalists like Jacques Cazotte, Thomas-Simon Gueulette, Jonathan Scott, Edgar Allen Poe, and Salman Rushdie as well as visual artists such as Eugene Delacroix and Edouard Frederic Wilhelm Richter and filmmakers including Fritz Lang and John Rawlins (see Samatar 2016). One incarnation that gained significant commercial attention in recent years is, of course, Disney's 1992 animated film, *Aladdin*, which prompted various additional texts, including a Broadway show, two sequels, a television program, a video game, and extensive merchandise. It is, of course, the story of a young and charismatic thief who, upon coming into possession of a magical ring and lamp, frees a genie who was trapped within the latter. The genie in turn grants Aladdin three wishes, and, fixated on wedding the sultan's beautiful daughter, Aladdin elects to have the genie transform him into (faux) royalty in order to be an adequate suitor.

Throughout the story, various villains attempt to claim the lamp, and with it the power of the magical genie; Aladdin must fend off competition for both the sultan's daughter and the genie, all the while disguising his class origins from the princess and her father. In the Disney version, magical elements that appear in Benfey's supplement, including the enchanted ring and of course the genie and the lamp, are coupled with additional charmed elements—a personified flying carpet and various anthropomorphized animal companions (such as the monkey, Abu; the princess [in the film, called Jasmine]'s protective pet tiger, Raja; and the villain Jafar's parrot, Iago). Brilliant colors, ethereal settings, innovative animation methods (including the use of computer graphics, less common in the 1990s [Sito 2013, 232]), robust and multilayered humor, and an Academy Award–winning score enhance what Roger Ebert termed the "basic fairy tale" (1995).

The film was a box office success, earning over $500 million in ticket revenues, but several critical thinkers saw it as one of many texts perpetuating bigoted prejudices about Arabs, including what Lee Wigle Artz and Mark A. Pollock call the "derogatory stereotypes of Arabs as double-dealing and sinister" (1995, 123). Indeed, while the Disney movie makes liberal alterations on its source texts (such as exaggerating the personality and presence of the genie to highlight the film's most recognizable star, Robin Williams), it maintains not just the villainy of the antagonists, but also Aladdin's own untrustworthiness. Jack Shaheen breaks down the four mythical portrayals of Arab-ness in the West—"the wealthy, oil-rich sheik; the uncultured barbarian; the sex-maniac harem owner; and the ruthless Arab terrorist" (quoted in Artz and Pollock 1995, 123)—and, indeed, all these figures make an appearance in the Disney adaptation in one way or another, from images of Aladdin as an uncivilized, "riff raff, street rat" ("One Jump Ahead" 2004) to the nefarious Jafar, who uses his magical powers to take over the palace. Each of these archetypes reflects a particular aspect of Orientalist imagination: the East is immoral, uncivilized, sexually perverse, and dangerous. Irwin cites even more directly problematic aspects:

[T]he film attracted a lot of criticism in some quarters when it was released. It was accused of racism and stereotyping. The lyrics of the opening song had to be rerecorded, as originally they included the lines: "I come from a land, from a faraway place where caravan camels roam./Where they cut off your ear if they don't like your face/ It's barbaric, but hey it's home."

(2004, 24–25)

The original lyrics speak wonders even if they were replaced: the Orient is distant and alien, Orientals are dangerous and ferocious, and Western readers find those qualities not just acceptable but comfortable.

Some critics point out the strategic timing of *Aladdin*'s release, linking it to American interests in the Middle East in an argument similar to that made by Christina Klein (2003). Timothy R. White and J. Emmett Winn, for instance, note:

Aladdin is one more successful attempt by Disney to Westernize, and even Americanize, an artistic product of another culture. As we saw in the Gulf War, other cultures tend to be valued in the West in relation to their usefulness to the West; the Arabic fairy tale of Aladdin became raw material for the Disney machine, which produced not an authentic depiction of an Oriental culture and its products, but an American cartoon depicting the Arabic world and its people as both exotic and humorous.

(1999, 62)

White and Winn are in ample company when they characterize the film as a watered-down version of an Arabic text. But what they infer by linking this construction with the Gulf War is a repeat of earlier colonial Orientalisms where other cultures (and their texts) are delivered, now in a neocolonial context, to Westerners in order to uphold particular ideological perspectives to either celebrate or vilify other nations based on complex trade relations. Indeed, with *Aladdin* and its various accouterments, we recognize that earlier Orientalist perspectives are not just echoed in twentieth- and twenty-first-century texts, they are repeated and sustained. Although the political goals may have changed to reflect the differently globalized world, the Orient continues as fodder for Western (re/self-)invention.

Imagining the "Orient": Narrating and Illustrating Hans Christian Andersen's "The Nightingale"

Even in instances of so-called translation or adaptation, we might read the new version as an original text premised more on the context of its production than that of its source material. In conversations about Orientalism and representation this is especially true, since many Westernized, translated, or adapted Oriental fairy tales reflect more the anti-Arab, xenophobic, and Eurocentric paradigms of their producers and consumers than celebrated and informative images of a recognizable East. In the context of newly invented Orientalist texts—that is, works that do not purport to be based on source materials but are instead self-acknowledged Western imaginings of Asia and the Middle East—the relationship manifests between fantasy, creation, and Orientalism. In the remaining pages I will look at two versions of Orientalist fairy tales that are not credited to a distant Oriental source, but are admittedly fabrications and fictionalizations set in Asia but created and consumed by Western subjects.

First, consider Hans Christian Andersen's popular story about a magical robotic bird owned by an obsessive and vulnerable Chinese emperor, "The Nightingale." Written in 1844, this fairy tale follows the emperor, who becomes transfixed by the beautiful singing voice of a wild bird—so much so that when the nightingale moves into the palace as a royal entertainer, he keeps her in a gilded cage and has silk strings tied to her legs so that she cannot fly away. Everyone knows about the emperor's affection for the nightingale and her song. One day, a package arrives with a wind-up mechanical nightingale, programmed to sing waltzes and move like an animatronic bird. The true nightingale flees the palace, but the emperor and his Chinese subjects are so pleased with the robotic nightingale that they do not mourn her departure. Predictably, the robotic nightingale one day breaks from overuse, and eventually the aggrieved emperor finds his health deteriorating. One evening when Death arrives to claim the emperor's life, the real nightingale returns to the palace and sings in hopes of revitalizing the emperor's health. Death is so impressed by the nightingale's song that he is banished, and the emperor returns to good health.

The Orientalist representation in Andersen's fairy tale is apparent throughout, particularly considering the potential universality of its plot; it might have taken place in any kingdom or land. But Andersen's decision to set the tale in China invites consideration of how the Orient is imagined as well as how themes of the tale are inspired by—and perpetuate—particular Orientalist stereotypes. From its opening lines, readers are aware of an Orientalist tone:

> In China, you know, the emperor is a Chinese, and all of those about him are China-men also. The story I am going to tell you happened a great many years ago, so it is well to hear it now before it is forgotten. The emperor's palace was the most beautiful in the world. It was built entirely of porcelain, and very costly, but so delicate and brittle that whoever touched it was obliged to be careful.
>
> (Andersen 2015)

Andersen's narrator mimics the Orientalist act of excavation, of bringing the Orient to the West, paralleling the recuperative and preservationist tones we have seen elsewhere. The Orient is also pictured as a place not just geographically foreign but also temporally distant, contained, and pre-modern. This passage also reveals a particular Orientalist aesthetic prevalent in Europe during Andersen's lifetime: the Orient as a place of ornamentation and excess to the point of fragility. The emperor's porcelain palace is not just impractical, it connotes delicacy, vulnerability, and most strikingly here, Asia itself (porcelain is one of the items European colonizers exported from China; the term "fine china" still used).

The images that accompanied Andersen's original fairy tale, as well as those adapted, bespeak the ways that European and American illustrators surveyed Oriental art. They range from English illustrator Edmund Dulac, who also illustrated an edition of *Arabian Nights* with Japonism-inspired paintings with their rich but matte colors and limited shading in 1911, to Kay Nielsen's watercolor illustrations, published in 1924 and appearing in collections like Robert Irwin's *Visions of the Jinn*, that are, in the words of Chris Albury and Dominic Winter, "wonderfully translucent/vellucent and dripping in Chinese influence" (quoted in Flood 2015). Perhaps referring to the whimsical, fantastical, and purportedly feminine mode of Chinoiserie—made popular in Europe in the eighteenth century but regaining popularity during the first half of the American twentieth century—Albury and Winter evoke typical Orientalist language to describe a multilayered set of representations on par with what Jean Baudrillard might call the simulacrum (2005). One of the most arresting representations is a print by stained glass artist Harry Clarke whose 1914 illustrations include an etching of the emperor and his nightingale in a style reminiscent of another Orientalist artist, Aubrey Beardsley. Clarke's black-and-white print showcases both the Oriental opulence of the Chinese emperor and his palace as well as his fragility; slight and pointed fingers hold a long, willowy branch upon which the delicate bird sits singing.

Andersen's story implicates how the Orient becomes both dangerous and subordinate because it is antiquated or pre-modern, but it is also threatening and its people nonhuman because of what has come to be known as techno-Orientalism David Morley and Kevin Robins explain:

> It seems that [. . .] the franchise on the story of the future is perceived to be passing into Oriental hands (a recurrent theme in contemporary popular culture, from *Blade Runner* through *Black Rain* to the *Ninja Turtles*, and in political journalism—in Europe and in America). The traditional equation of the West with modernity and of the Orient with the exotic (but underdeveloped) past is thrown into crisis in this new scenario, as the dynamic hub of the world economy is increasingly perceived to have moved from the Atlantic to the Pacific Rim.
>
> (1995, 6)

The Orient is threatening because it represents both past and future in dangerous ways. The West can fashion itself in opposition to the Orient's so-called barbaric religious and social ideologies as well as what it sees as its radical technological culture—contributing to what Lisa Nakamura calls "cybertyping" (2002, xvii). Although typically centering its gaze specifically on Japan, imagining Asia as a techno-orientalist place coincides with a post-WWII anxiety over Oriental technological power both in connection to online modes of globalization (particularly in the 1970s onward) and military advancement. Rachel C. Lee and Sau-Ling Cynthia Wong explain the dangerous consequences of techno-Orientalist thinking. "Asians," they argue, "have been contradictorily imagined as, on the one hand, machine-like workers, accomplishing 'inhuman' feats of 'coolie' manual labour, and on the other, as braniac competitors whose technological adeptness ranges from inventing gunpowder to being good with engineering and math" (2003, xiv).

Thus the theme in Andersen's tale of the natural versus the technological, with the Chinese emperor's foolish preference for the robotic nightingale, bespeaks more than the typical nineteenth-century fascination with technology and science, with the literary celebration of the pastoral over the industrial. In Andersen's fairy tale the robotic bird arrives as a gift from none other than the emperor of Japan when the Chinese emperor expected a book about his nation's "celebrated bird." The narrator details:

> But instead of a book, it was a work of art contained in a casket, an artificial nightingale made to look like a living one, and covered all over with diamonds, rubies, and sapphires. As soon as the artificial bird was wound up, it would sing like the real one, and could move its tail up and down, which sparkled with silver and gold.
>
> (2015)

The Chinese emperor is entranced by the robotic bird, and the Japanese emperor's gift not only undermines the real-life nightingale but also is a substitute for the expected non-technological book gift. When it inevitably breaks, the Chinese emperor is foiled, falling into such profound grief that he nearly dies. The danger of Japanese technological advancement is clear. Andersen's fairy tale reflects European curiosity and anxiety over the Orient—a paradox that almost always informs its representations. On the one hand, the archaic quaintness of China is fetishized and exoticized; on the other, the dangerous futurity and technological passion of

Japan is vilified and presented as perilous. Curiously, this framework later is mirrored in the twentieth century when Chinese and Chinese Americans are considered allies and good in contrast to Japanese and Japanese American foes who are deemed so threatening that Americans enforce a nationwide internment policy.

Although these two examples of Orientalism involve fairy tales, Orientalism can be seen in the production and consumption of too many works to detail here. Consider, for instance, the North American fascination with Japanese fairy-tale films like Hayao Miyazaki's *Spirited Away* (2001), a film that has gained global popularity (and an English-language dubbed version distributed by Disney) or Korean horror like Pil-Sung Yim's *Hansel & Gretel* (2007). Or think about the reliance on folk and fairy stories in canonical Asian American literature, like Maxine Hong Kingston's *The Woman Warrior* or Larissa Lai's *When Fox Is a Thousand*. There are numerous ways to continue to think about Orientalism and fairy tales in today's globalized context, recalling, as Said reminds us, that Orientalism is the subtext that undergirds all literatures, whether they directly address colonialism and imperialist histories/presents or not.

Related topics: Adaptation and the Fairy-Tale Web; Cinematic; Disney Corporation; Fantasy; Language; Opera; Photographic; Pictorial; Sexualities/Queer and Trans Studies; Storytelling; Translation

References Cited and Further Reading

Andersen, Hans Christian. 2010. *Fairy Tales by Hans Christian Andersen Illustrated by Harry Clarke*. London: Pook P.

———. 2015. *The Fairy Tales of Hans Christian Andersen Illustrated by Kay Nielsen*. London: Pook P.

Artz, Lee Wigle, and Mark A. Pollock. 1995. "Limiting the Options: Anti-Arab Images in U.S. Media Coverage of the Persian Gulf Crisis." In *The U.S. Media and the Middle East: Image and Perception*, edited by Yahya R. Kamalipour, 119–36. Westport: Praeger.

Baudrillard, Jean. 2005. *Simulacra and Simulation*, translated by Sheila Faria Glaser. Ann Arbor: U Michigan P.

Belcher, Stephen. 2008. "Theodor Benfey." In *The Greenwood Encyclopedia of Folktales and Fairy Tales*, edited by Donald Haase, 116. Vol. 1. Westport, CT: Greenwood.

Benfey, Theodor. 2009. *Panchatantra*. Charleston, SC: Bibliolife.

Blackburn, Stuart, and Alan Dundes, eds. 1997. *A Flowering Tree: And Other Oral Tales from India*. Berkeley: U California P.

Dulac, Edmund. 2016. *Sinbad the Sailor and Other Stories from* The Arabian Nights. Mineola, NY: Calla Editions.

Ebert, Roger. 1995. "*Aladdin*." Roger Ebert Reviews. www.rogerebert.com/reviews/aladdin-1992.

Flood, Alison. 2015. "Very Rare Hans Christian Andersen Illustration Sold at Auction." *The Guardian*, December 17. www.theguardian.com/books/2015/dec/17/very-rare-hans-christian-andersen-illustration-up-for-auction-watercolour.

Galland, Antoine. 2004. *Les Milles et Une Nuit: Contes Arabes*. Paris: Flammarion.

Hall, Stuart. 2007. "The West and the Rest: Discourse and Power." In *Race and Racialization: Essential Readings*, edited by Tania Das Gupta, Carl E. James, Roger C. A. Maaka, Grace-Edward Galabuzi, and Chris Andersen, 56–60. Toronto: Canadian Scholars P.

Hong Kingston, Maxine. 1989. *The Woman Warrior: Memoirs of a Girlhood among Ghosts*. New York: Vintage.

Irwin, Robert. 2004. "*The Arabian Nights* in Film Adaptations." In *The Arabian Nights Encyclopedia*, edited by Marzolph, van Leeuwen, and Wassouf, 22–5. Vol 1.

———. 2005. *The Arabian Nights: A Companion*. London: Tauris.

———. 2011. *Visions of the Jinn: Illustrators of* The Arabian Nights. Oxford: The Arcadian Library.

Kabbani, Rana. 2004. "*The Arabian Nights* as an Orientalist Text." In *The Arabian Nights Encyclopedia*, edited by Marzolph, van Leeuwen, and Wassouf, 25–9. Vol. 1.

Kennedy, Philip F., and Marina Warner, eds. 2013. *Scheherazade's Children: Global Encounters with the Arabian Nights*. New York: NYU P.

Klein, Christina. 2003. *Cold War Orientalism: Asia in the Middlebrow Imagination, 1945–1961*. Berkeley: U California P.

Lai, Larissa. 2004. *When Fox Is a Thousand*. Vancouver: Arsenal Pulp P.

Lee, Rachel C., and Sau-Ling Cynthia Wong, eds. 2003. *AsianAmerica.Net: Ethnicity, Nationalism, and Cyberspace*. New York: Routledge.

Marzolph, Ulrich. 2007. *The Arabian Nights in Transnational Perspective.* Detroit: Wayne State UP.

Marzolph, Ulrich, Richard van Leeuwen, and Hassan Wassouf. 2004. "Charles Dickens." In *The Arabian Nights Encyclopedia*, edited by Ulrich Marzolph, Richard van Leeuwen, and Hassan Wassouf, 538–9. Vol. 2. Santa Barbara: ABC-CLIO.

Morley, David, and Kevin Robins. 1995. *Spaces of Identity: Global Media, Electronic Landscapes, and Cultural Boundaries.* New York: Routledge.

Nakamura, Lisa. 2002. *Cybertypes: Race, Ethnicity, and Identity on the Internet.* New York: Routledge.

Rifkin, Mark. 2014. *Settler Common Sense: Queerness and Everyday Colonialism in the American Renaissance.* Minneapolis: U Minnesota P.

Sabry, Somaya Sami. 2011. *Arab-American Women's Writing and Performance: Orientalism, Race and the idea of* The Arabian Nights. London: Tauris.

Said, Edward. 1993. *Culture and Imperialism.* New York: Vintage.

———. 1994. *Orientalism.* 2nd ed. New York: Vintage.

Samatar, Sofia. 2016. "The Spectacle of the Other: Recreating *A Thousand and One Nights* in Film." In *Fairy-Tale Films Beyond Disney: International Perspectives*, edited by Jack Zipes, Pauline Greenhill, and Kendra Magnus-Johnston, 34–47. New York: Routledge.

Sito, Tom. 2013. *Moving Innovation: A History of Computer Animation.* Cambridge: MIT P.

Warner, Marina. 2013. *Stranger Magic: Charmed States and the Arabian Nights.* Cambridge, MA: Harvard UP.

White, Timothy R., and J. Emmett Winn. 1999. "Islam, Animation, and Money: The Reception of Disney's *Aladdin* in Southeast Asia." In *Themes and Issues in Asian Cartooning: Cute, Cheap, Mad, and Sexy*, edited by John A. Lent, 61–76. Bowling Green, OH: Bowling Green State U Popular P.

Yamanaka, Yuriko, and Tetsuo Nishio. 2006. *The Arabian Nights and Orientalism: Perspectives from East and West.* London: Tauris.

Zipes, Jack. 2006. *Why Fairy Tales Stick: The Evolution and Relevance of a Genre.* New York: Routledge.

———. 2007. *When Dreams Come True: Classical Fairy Tales and Their Tradition.* New York: Routledge.

Mediagraphy

Aladdin. 1992. Directors Ron Clements and John Musker. USA.

Hansel & Gretel. 2007. Director Pil-Sung Yim. South Korea.

"One Jump Ahead" (Song). 2004. Artist Brad Kane, album *Aladdin: Special Edition Soundtrack.* USA.

Spirited Away. 2001. Director Hayao Miyazaki. Japan.

THEMATIC ISSUES RAISED BY FAIRY-TALE MEDIA

16

ADAPTATION AND THE FAIRY-TALE WEB

Cristina Bacchilega

Like "fairy tale," adaptation is pervasive and not easily definable, for reasons that in both cases have to do with their complex intertextuality. It is thus productive to think through how focusing on "fairy-tale adaptations" raises questions of multimediality that impact both adaptation and fairy-tale studies and how understanding adaptation in relation to cultural change informs the fairy-tale web as framework. But first some grounding concepts with rather contemporary examples.

What Is an Adaptation?

Possibly the most widely influential answer to date is Linda Hutcheon's in *Adaptation* ([2006] 2012), which approaches the question by breaking it down into chapters about the what, who, why, how, where, and when of adaptation as both product and process. For Hutcheon, adaptation as product is

> an announced and extensive transposition of a particular work or works. This "transcoding" can involve a shift of medium (a poem to a film), or genre (an epic to a novel), or a change of frame and therefore context: telling the same story from a different point of view, for instance, can create a manifestly different interpretation.
>
> (2006, 7)

Georges Méliès's short film *Cinderella* (Cendrillon 1899), which remediates Charles Perrault's tale (1697); Anne Sexton's poem "Cinderella," which plays on the Grimms' tale (1971); and Sara Maitland's first-person "Cinderella" short story, "The Wicked Stepmother's Lament" (1987), all versions of tale type ATU 510A, would all fit the bill as fairy-tale adaptations since they announce their relationship to a specific tale, or the genre, and develop it through repetition with a difference in medium, genre, or frame. When approaching adaptation as process, Hutcheon distinguishes between its production, which "involves both (re-)interpretation and then (re-)creation," and its reception, whereby "we experience adaptations as palimpsests through our memory of other works that resonate through repetition with variation" (2006, 8). Examples of adaptation resulting from the interpretation and re-creation of fairy tales abound, ranging from the classic novel *Jane Eyre* that extensively reworks various fairy tales including "Cinderella" and "Bluebeard" (ATU 310) (Auerbach and Knoepflmacher 1992) to visual artifacts as different as Gustave Doré's illustrations of Perrault's tales (1867),

Dina Goldstein's dystopic photographs reimagining Disney princesses (2011), and Shaun Tan's artwork inspired by the Grimms (2015) as well as U.S. television series like *Beauty and the Beast* (1987–1990)/*Beauty and the Beast* (2012–2016) and *Once Upon a Time* (2011–). As for reception, the 2014 film *Into the Woods* is a good example, as it will be processed as fairy-tale adaptation by those who are familiar with the Broadway musical *Into the Woods* (1987) live or via TV or home video productions of the show, with the various fairy tales that mingle in the two productions, or both.

While Hutcheon's parameters are clear, their application to studying (fairy-tale) adaptations is not so straightforward. For instance, as Kamilla Elliott notes (2004), *what* is adapted when a novel is transposed on to the screen may be "the spirit of the text" (psychic concept of adaptation), its essence (genetic transfer), its reproduction in another medium (ventriloquism), relationship to other cultural texts (de[re]composing), or incarnation (use of less abstract signs). This means that, in adapting the ATU 425C tale type, films as varied as *Beastly* (2011), *La belle et la bête* (1946), Disney's *Beauty and the Beast* (1991), *Tie Me Up! Tie Me Down!* (Átame! 1990), and *Shrek* (2001) each take on very different elements of the story to be their core hypotext. And, given the powerful and extended re-visitation of fairy tale in *Pan's Labyrinth* (El laberinto del fauno 2006), it would also seem appropriate to extend the *what* of adaptation to genre rather than restrict it to individual tales. *Who* does the adaptation matters as well, as seen in Pauline Greenhill's discussion of "Snow Queen" filmic adaptations by male and female directors (2015, 2016), the heavily Disney-inflected *Once Upon a Time* (2011–) television series produced by the Disney/ABC Television Group, or the independent film *Dancehall Queen* (1997), a Jamaican dancehall-culture "Cinderella" filmed in Kingston and featuring a Jamaican cast. And connecting the *what*, *who*, *where*, and *when* is not only the poetics, but the politics, of adaptation, which leads to thinking about *for whom* as well.

Most crucially, does an adaptation have to be recognized as such in the process of reception in order to be one? Hutcheon posits it does. But what if most audiences don't perceive it as a palimpsest because its intertexts are not that popular, as in the case of Giambattista Basile's seventeenth-century collection of fairy tales on which the 2015 film *Tale of Tales* draws? Or the intertexts have powerful meanings for specific audiences or subcultures only, as Jennifer Orme argues about David Kaplan's *Little Red Riding Hood* 1997 film? Isn't there an experiential difference between immediately recognizing a text's invitation to be read as adaptation because we are so familiar with its intertexts we can do nothing but and accepting the invitation because reviewers or others in the know make us aware of it? And what is the import of this difference in the affective power of an adaptation in different knowledge communities? While the impact of the adaptation depends on the audience's awareness of this relationship (Cartmell and Whelehan 1999), that awareness and impact need not be universal or equally intense across the board. As I have argued before, a lot depends not only on where cultural production is located but also on where and from which knowledge systems, cultural habitus, and critical agendas the reader or interpreter accesses any fairy-tale adaptation (Bacchilega 2013).

At the same time that Hutcheon would require that producers and receivers engage knowingly with an adaptation as such, she draws little distinction among adaptation, translation, and appropriation. "What Isn't an Adaptation, and What Does It Matter?" asks Thomas Leitch, one of the leading and highly reflective figures in adaptation studies (2012). When discussing fairy-tale film specifically, Jack Zipes has emphasized that, like translation and appropriation, adaptation is an interpretive and transformative set of operations—selecting, updating, concretizing, amplifying, contextualizing, critiquing, and more; what Hutcheon sums up as "repetition without replication" (2006, xvi); in doing so he develops Robert Stam's understanding that "adaptations redistribute energies and intensities, provoke flows and displacements"

(2005, 46), therefore always resulting in change. Like appropriation and translation, adaptation is imbricated with matters of property and propriety in that making a story one's own often involves expropriation, which in turn raises "ethical responsibility to the source, hypotext, and audience" (Zipes 2011, 12). While for Julie Sanders it is useful to define appropriation as a wholesale rethinking of the hypotext, something like Adrienne Rich's "re-vision" (1972), Phyllis Frus and Christy Williams call attention to "radical transformations" in films and graphic novels that go "beyond adaptation" (2010). Zipes takes various distinctions into account, but makes it a point to show how filmic and other adaptations of fairy tales today rest on the centuries-long and cumulative appropriation, translation, and adaptation of the oral folktale as well as of so-called "classic" fairy tales.

In the end, what is gained by identifying a cultural product and process as adaptation is to understand it within the broader framework of intertextuality, whereby all texts to some degree invoke and rework other texts (Kristeva [1969] 1986; Genette 1982); to highlight the importance of "the protocols of a distinct medium" (Stam 2005, 45); and to take into account how cultural economy shapes the production and reception of adaptations. Simone Murray's work is in this respect a significant complement and corrective to adaptation studies that privilege intertextual interpretation, proposing to conceptualize "adaptations as the outcome of a vast, transnational, constantly mutating, and frequently internally conflicted socioeconomic system with tremendous influence in shaping the contours of contemporary culture" (2012b, 123) and to study how they are shaped by economics and institutions.

This sociological approach goes beyond Stam's considerations of how "studio style, ideological fashion, political and economic constraints, auteurist predilections, charismatic stars, cultural values, and so forth" (2005, 45) impact filmic adaptations. Murray's focus is on "industrial structures, interdependent networks of agents, commercial contexts, and legal and policy regimes within which adaptations come to be" (2012a, 6), and she discusses the role of book fairs, screen festivals, and prizes; the cross-promotion of related products in different markets; and the impact of an adaptation on the sales of its hypotext as well as, increasingly, on the production of amateur adaptations by "produsers." This approach, which contextualizes the intertextual one, has enormous potential for better understanding the phenomenon of fairy-tale filmic adaptations in the early twenty-first century, and Zipes's work on "hyping" in contemporary fairy-tale films is only the start of it (2015).

To approach fairy tales in print, film, comics, theater, television, blogs, YouTube videos, photographs, and other forms as adaptations, then, demands some attention to how their story power draws upon their "mediality"—the semiotics of each media, the senses they address, their "spatio-temporal extension," their signs' materiality, and their "cultural role and methods of production/ distribution" (Ryan 2004, 18–19)—and their circulation in a broader cultural economy. So in contrast to "retelling," which emphasizes narrative reoccurrence, and "revision," which points to interpretation, (fairy-tale) "adaptation" invites a consideration of transformative interpretation as grounded in the materiality, codes, experience, and promotion of a (fairy) story's move across media—and thus into new contexts, audiences, markets, and potential for further adaptation.

There is one caveat. In adaptation studies, much of the discussion has been weighed down by questions of fidelity to high or canonical literature; its preferred domain, as suggested by my examples so far, has for the most part been film, and the fairy tale, with its relatively low symbolic capital, or prestige, and its incorporation into the larger category of fantasy film, has rarely been a focus. Sue Short's film-studies book *Fairy Tale and Film* (2015) is an exception, but it assumes that scholars of fairy tales have not been engaging popular culture, which is amply disproven by ongoing work (see Rankin 2007; Greenhill and Matrix 2010; Zipes 2011;

Bacchilega 2013; Greenhill and Rudy 2014; Warner 2014; numerous essays in *Marvels & Tales: Journal of Fairy-Tale Studies*; and two important databases, the *International Fairy-Tale Filmography* and *At the Crossroads of Data and Wonder: Algorithmic Visualizations of Fairy Tales on Television*). Cultivating a conversation between fairy-tale studies and adaptation studies holds promise as long as it is a two-way learning process.

Fairy-Tale Multimediality and Adaptation

Thinking about fairy tales as adaptations is a particularly fertile site of inquiry into how their intertextuality is inflected by their multimedial history, a versatility across media that makes them exemplary as what John Bryant calls "fluid" texts (2002). Significantly, we need not limit the fairy tale's historical multimediality to the orality and print combination; rather, the fairy tale's multimediality includes, from the moment of a tale's conception, the visual.

Writer Italo Calvino wrote in the late 1950s about his own fantastic tales that their point of departure was an image, and this can apply to the genre more generally: "The tale is born from the image, [. . .] and the image is developed in a story according to its internal logic. The story takes on meanings, or rather, around the image extends a network of meanings that are always a little uncertain" ([1959] 1998, ix). Snow White (ATU 709) "red as blood, white as snow," Red Riding Hood (ATU 333), Sleeping Beauty (ATU 410), and Cinderella are powerful and multivalent images at the same time that they are stories and fairy-tale characters. Images or mental pictures are also at work in a storyteller's experience as s/he recalls elements of a story and in the listeners' as they take the story in, suggests Canadian folklorist Vivian Labrie (1980) based on her ethnographic work. So broadsides, illustrations, films, picture books, YouTube videos, and comics are just *some* visualizations of fairy tales. Furthermore, theater and dance performances played a part in the French fairy-tale vogue during Louis XIV's reign, just as pantomime (Schacker 2007) and later musicals (Cutolo 2014) have contributed to the popularity of the fairy tale in the United Kingdom and the United States respectively. Whether announcing its status as adaptation or not, the fairy tale proliferates multimedially (in various media at the same time) and intermedially (making connections across media boundaries), and has done so for centuries.

Angela Carter (1940–1992), whose intervention in the genre of the fairy tale was momentous and continues to inspire today, worked the multimediality of the genre in her own fairy tales about fairy tales. Carter adapted fairy tales most famously in print (*The Bloody Chamber* 1979), but also in other media, and these adaptations did not consistently originate as tales for print. The 1984 fairy-tale/horror film directed by Neil Jordan, *The Company of Wolves*, for which Carter wrote the screenplay, was an expansion of a 1980 homonymous radio play that replayed her story in the 1979 collection with a strong dramatization of interactive storytelling between Granny and Red Riding Hood (Croft 2003). And her short story "The Lady of the House of Love" in *The Bloody Chamber* (1979) reworked the 1976 radio play *Vampirella* (Hennard Dutheil de la Rochère 2011).

Intimately familiar with the technical possibilities of radio for producing acoustic images, Carter asserted, "I write for radio by choice," "as an extension and amplification of writing for the printed page," which Croft sees as "literally an extension of [Carter's] published work," her reaching "a wider, more diverse audience than the literary public" (2003, 37), as well as the amplification of orality and voice—especially women's voices in the plural. While intertextually and intermedially linked, *The Company of Wolves* print, audio, and filmic adaptations have no center of origin or fixed message; rather as they each exploit the singularity of medium and genre, they powerfully reenact the traditional multimediality of fairy tales, and they put it to work toward transformative performances of sexuality and gender.

A legitimate question that follows is whether a fairy-tale text, in whatever medium, is always already an adaptation since there is no "original" that speaks to all audiences and the tale itself is processed across media. I maintain that there isn't an essential difference between fairy-tale "version" and "adaptation" and that they operate in an intertextual and intermedial continuum; however, there may be reasons methodologically or in practice to distinguish between them that have to do with both processes of story production and reception.

Here are two examples of how the difference is not one of essence. When the Brothers Grimm wrote and published their seven editions of the *Kinder- und Hausmärchen* collection, their work involved not only a shift in medium from oral to print, but serious editing that resulted in ideological and aesthetic changes. They definitely changed the tales they had heard, and as such it is understood that the Grimms adapted and appropriated the folktale and that translations of the Grimms continued to adapt it further into children's literature.

However, it is also the case that—while it paradoxically involved their ongoing redaction of the tales they received—their project was to record and present German tales as authentically as possible, and not to change them, and they did comparative work to legitimize their tales as traditional (see Zipes 2015 for a synthesis of this complex process and the critical debates about it). Similarly, with Italo Calvino's collection *Italian Folktales* (*Fiabe Italiane*) ([1956] 1980), we have a writer translating and editing tales from various regional folktale volumes, not to make his mark on them (which of course he did, as did the folklorists whose work he translated), but rather to make a variety of "their" folktales more available to Italians. Calvino perceived himself in that project as one in a chain of storytellers, enjoying and participating in the rhythms of repetition and variation that animate folk/fairy tales' circulation; only later and in a different key would he wink at the fairy tale in his novel *The Nonexistent Knight* (1959) and revisit the genre's qualities from the perspective of a modern creative writer in his *Six Memos for the Next Millennium* (1988).

When ventriloquizing identifies a kind of filmic adaptation (Elliott 2003), it is a trope; for folklorists and other collectors of tales of magic, it is more of a practice that speaks to their motivation: the stories they circulate in print or other media are intended to speak for their oral tellers and their culture, not that of the collectors. Does that mean we should take their claims at face value? These claims need to be scrutinized, even more so when the collectors are, as colonizers for instance, not of the culture whose stories they want to record (Naithani 2010; Bacchilega 2007). However, it is also important to acknowledge that in the larger picture, today, the Grimms' and Calvino's tales are processed as "versions," providing historical and situated examples of the multivocality of the folk/fairy-tale genre. And even Perrault's highly literary tale "Red Riding Hood" is not a "one-off" but a story that shares symbolic affinities with the oral tradition and thus in a way adapts to it even as it popularizes the genre in print (Vaz da Silva 2016).

So within fairy-tale studies, which developed in the late 1970s and in conjunction with a proliferation of fairy-tale adaptations (Joosen 2011), it is pragmatic if nothing else to approach the genre's history and circulation by distinguishing—both on the basis of the producers' relationship to fairy-tale traditions and the receivers' experience—between versions that are not limited to the oral tradition and aim to ventriloquize, even replicate, and adaptations that not only actively seek to intervene in the tradition—whether to make the tales more marketable in a new context, protest their unsuitability for a given audience, or put them to radically different aesthetic and ideological uses—but are also perceived by audiences in Hutcheon's terms as "repetition, without replication." Once again, then, the situatedness of the production and reception of adaptations matters and renders the distinction between version and adaptation productively fuzzy.

Reading Fairy-Tale Adaptations in the Fairy-Tale Web

Grappling, as we must for most fairy tales, with the absence of an original text calls for a sharp turn away from adaptation as the result of a one-way transfer from its given source (e.g., tale to film) and an approach to fairy-tale adaptations as fluid texts that are produced and processed, in this century perhaps even more than before, in a web of connections that are "hypertextual," in that they do not refer back to one center (Haase 2006). While every fairy tale and fairy-tale adaptation presupposes antecedents and anticipates prospective intertexts, we as scholars and the culture industry as transmedia storytellers cannot fully predict or control which stories mingle with, influence, anticipate, interrupt, take over, or support one another in the fairy-tale web because every teller and recipient of a tale brings to it, hypertextually, her or his own texts. The hypertextual links we make to fairy-tale adaptations are not only multimedial, intermedial, and ideologically multivocal; they are dependent on popular cultural memory as well as, more unpredictably, on culturally located knowledges and non-hegemonic desires that adapters and audiences alike bring to the experience of fairy-tale adaptations.

Methodologically, approaching adaptations in such a fairy-tale web opens up possibilities for recognizing multiple traditions within the history of the fairy-tale genre: considering how the circulation of the genre relates to the spread of capitalism and colonialism, exploring the ties between the fairy tale and non-Euro-American wonder genres, rethinking the promiscuous relationship between fairy tales and other genres of the fantastic, and recognizing how the genre serves differently located artists and audiences. In other words, as an interpretive practice, the fairy-tale web helps us critically rethink the history of fairy-tale adaptations and relocate the genre geopolitically; and it offers us a significant point of entry into understanding how the fairy tale works in what Henry Jenkins has called convergence culture, "where old and new media collide, where grassroots and corporate media intersect, where the power of the media producer and the power of the media consumer interact in unpredictable ways" (2008, 2). How do producer and consumers in convergence culture deploy the multimediality and hypertextuality of fairy tales? As the power of conglomerate transmedia storytelling increases, are there also more opportunities for new storytellers and stories to wield the powers of wonder?

Bryant reminds us that collective and individual memory plays a role in what and how we perceive adaptations (2002), and I would add that we are witnessing an interesting development in the relationship between popular cultural memory and fairy-tale adaptations today. If we think with Karin Kukkonen (2008) of "popular cultural memory" as a transmedia repository of conventions and imagery that are continually reconstructed in relation to one another and in the experience of communities of recipients, it is clear that Disney continues to pervade popular cultural memory of fairy tales. However, since the 1970s the image of the fairy tale in popular cultural memory has also become both more fragmented and more expansive thanks to the confluence of several factors, including feminist critiques and revisions of fairy tales, the emergence of fairy-tale studies as a discipline, and the electronic accessibility of a wide range of fairy tales; the filtering of feminist and other social critiques into children's education and fairy tales in literature and popular culture so that, whether individuals identify with feminism or not, there is a widespread sensibility to issues of gender in fairy tales; and greater possibilities for reader response to become production and be shared in new media.

At play, then, in the currency of twenty-first-century fairy-tale adaptations is a, perhaps paradoxically, fertile (mis)match between the economy of profit, which makes stories that are not protected by copyright and come in (un)familiar versions particularly attractive to cultural conglomerates and adapters, and what can be described as a new economy of knowledge, whereby today's young adult and adult publics have acquired, or at least have the potential to easily access, a more complex and expansive sense of the "fairy tale" than what was generally available some thirty years ago. There is more awareness in the production and reception of fairy-tale adaptations of the multivocality of the genre, a pleasure in reaching for the pre-sanitized not-for-children-only tales, even a demand to redirect the "what if?" possibilities of the fairy tale. Increasingly, the culture industry can depend on being challenged by adult audiences who want fairy-tale "family" films to incorporate contemporary values that challenge the "happily ever after" heteronormativity of Disneyfied fairy tales; increasingly, the culture industry responds, albeit for the sake of profit, as seen in *Brave* (2012) and *Frozen* (2013). Popular fairy-tale themed songs range from Sara Bareilles's "Fairytale" (2004) to Misono's "Vs" (2006) and *Frozen*'s "Let It Go" (2013), all also circulating in official *and* fan-produced unauthorized YouTube videos. In convergence culture, the "high level of coordination and creative control" required in franchising and other forms of transmedia storytelling (Jenkins 2011) interacts—sometimes supporting, and others reigning it in—with the multiplicity of the fairy tale.

What's different is not that fairy-tale adaptations are all around us. Rather, "fairy-tale culture" has once again shifted and relies—to different extents and purposes, in conglomerate productions, genre fiction, audience expectations and interpretations—on rather complex and *competing* senses of what fairy tales are and do. Children in the first decade of the twenty-first century may very well have been exposed to *Shrek* films, that is, DreamWorks' parodies of Disney, before viewing what baby boomers would consider fairy-tale "classics" (Poniewozik 2009). Postcolonial, queer, Black, and Indigenous artists such as Nalo Hopkinson, Yousry Nasrallah, Emma Donoghue, Helen Oyeyemi, Dan Taulapapa McMullin, and Karlo Mila are adapting the fairy tale, tapping into the genre's transformative powers and links that the hegemony of the heteronormative and Euro-American fairy tale left behind. African American speculative-fiction author Octavia Butler's unfinished *Parable of the Trickster* epigraph reads, as reported by Gerry Canavan: "there is nothing new under the sun, but there are new suns" (2014). Not only are there new media platforms, but new adapters of fairy tales to connect with and learn from. Thinking of fairy tales and their transformative possibilities in a hypertextual web raises the stakes of exploring the what, who, why, how, where, when, and for whom of adaptation.

Related topics: Anthologies; Broadcast; Cinematic; Comic Cons; Convergence Culture; Criticism; Fan Cultures; Fan Fiction; Fantasy; Language; Material Culture; Orientalism; Print; Sexualities/Queer and Trans Studies; Translation; YouTube

References Cited and Further Reading

Auerbach, Nina, and U. C. Knoepflmacher, eds. 1992. *Forbidden Journeys: Fairy Tales and Fantasies by Victorian Women Writers.* Chicago: U Chicago P.

Bacchilega, Cristina. 2007. *Legendary Hawai'i and the Politics of Place: Tradition, Translation, and Tourism.* Philadelphia: U Pennsylvania P.

———. 2013. *Fairy Tales Transformed?: Twenty-First-Century Adaptations and the Politics of Wonder.* Detroit: Wayne State UP.

Bryant, John. 2002. *The Fluid Text: A Theory of Revision and Editing for Book and Screen.* Ann Arbor: U Michigan P.

Calvino, Italo. (1956) 1980. *Italian Folktales.* New York: Harcourt Brace Jovanovich.

———. (1959) 1962. *The Nonexistent Knight.* New York: Harcourt Brace Jovanovich.

———. (1959) 1998. *Our Ancestors*. London: Vintage Books.

———. 1988. *Six Memos for the Next Millennium*. Cambridge, MA: Harvard UP.

Canavan, Gerry. 2014. "'There's Nothing New/Under the Sun,/But There Are New Suns': Recovering Octavia E. Butler's Lost Parables." *Los Angeles Review of Books*, June 9. https://lareviewofbooks.org/article/theres-nothing-new-sun-new-suns-recovering-octavia-e-butlers-lost-parables/.

Carter, Angela. (1978) 1985. "Vampirella." In *Come Unto These Yellow Sands*, 83–116. Newcastle upon Tyne: Bloodaxe.

———. (1979) 2006. *The Bloody Chamber and Other Stories*. London: Vintage.

Cartmell, Deborah, and Imelda Whelehan, eds. 1999. *Adaptations: From Text to Screen, Screen to Text*. London: Routledge.

Croft, Charlotte. 2003. *'Anagrams of Desire': Angela Carter's Writing for Radio, Film and Television*. Manchester: Manchester UP.

Cutolo, Raffaele. 2014. *Into the Woods of Wicked Wonderland: Musicals Revise Fairy Tales*. Heidelberg: Universitätsverlag Winter.

Donoghue, Emma. 1999. *Kissing the Witch: Old Tales in New Skins*. New York: HarperCollins.

Elliott, Kamilla. 2003. *Rethinking the Novel/Film Debate*. Cambridge: Cambridge UP.

———. 2004. "Literary Film Adaptation and the Form/Content Dilemma." *Narrative across Media*, edited by Marie-Laure Ryan, 220–43. Lincoln: U Nebraska P.

Frank, Arthur W. 2010. *Letting Stories Breathe: A Socio-Narratology*. Chicago: U Chicago P.

Frus, Phyllis, and Christy Williams, eds. 2010. *Beyond Adaptation: Essays on Radical Transformations of Original Works*. Jefferson, NC: McFarland.

Genette, Gérard. 1982. *Palimpsestes: La littérature au second degré*. Paris: Seuil.

Greenhill, Pauline. 2015. "'The Snow Queen': Queer Coding in Male Directors' Films." *Marvels & Tales* 29 (1): 110–34.

———. 2016. "Team Snow Queen: Feminist Cinematic 'Misinterpretations' of a Fairy Tale." *Studies in European Cinema* 13 (1): 32–49.

Greenhill, Pauline, and Sidney Eve Matrix, eds. 2010. *Fairy Tale Films: Visions of Ambiguity*. Logan: Utah State UP.

Greenhill, Pauline, and Jill Terry Rudy, eds. 2014. *Channeling Wonder: Fairy Tales on Television*. Detroit: Wayne State UP.

Haase, Donald. (1993) 1999. "Yours, Mine, or Ours? Perrault, the Brothers Grimm, and the Ownership of Fairy Tales." In *The Classic Fairy Tales: A Norton Critical Edition*, edited by Maria Tatar, 353–64. New York: Norton.

———. 2006. "Hypertextual Gutenberg: The Textual and Hypertextual Life of Folktales and Fairy Tales in English-Language Popular Print Editions." *Fabula* 47: 222–30.

Hennard Dutheil de la Rochère, Martine. 2011. "Conjuring the Curse of Repetition or 'Sleeping Beauty' Revamped: Angela Carter's *Vampirella* and *The Lady of the House of Love*." *Études de lettres* 3–4: 337–58.

Hopkinson, Nalo. 2001. *Skin Folk*. New York: Warner Books.

Hutcheon, Linda. (2006) 2012. *A Theory of Adaptation*. New York: Routledge.

Jenkins, Henry. 2008. *Convergence Culture: Where Old and New Media Collide*. Rev. ed. New York: NYU P.

———. 2011. "Transmedia 202: Further Reflections." The Official Weblog of Henry Jenkins, August 1. http://henryjenkins.org/?s=Transmedia+202.

Joosen, Vanessa. 2011. *Critical and Creative Perspectives on Fairy Tales: An Intertextual Dialogue between Fairy-Tale Scholarship and Postmodern Retellings*. Detroit: Wayne State UP.

Kristeva, Julia. (1969) 1986. *Sémiótiké: Recherches pour une sémanalyse*. Paris: Seuil.

Kukkonen, Karin. 2008. "Popular Cultural Memory: Comics, Communities and Context Knowledge." *Nordicom Review* 29 (2): 261–73.

Labrie, Vivian. 1980. "How Can We Understand the Retention of a Folktale?" *Folklore on Two Continents: Essays in Honor of Linda Dégh*, edited by Nikolai Burlakoff and Carl Lindahl, 286–92. Bloomington: Trickster P.

Leitch, Thomas. 2012. "Adaptation and Intertextuality, or, What isn't an Adaptation, and What Does It Matter?" *A Companion to Literature, Film, and Adaptation*, edited by Deborah Cartmell, 87–104. Chichester: Wiley-Blackwell.

Maitland, Sara. 1987. *A Book of Spells*. London: Michael Joseph.

Mila, Karlo. 2005. "Leaving Prince Charming Behind." *Dream Fish Floating*. Wellington, Aotearoa: Huia.

Murray, Simone. 2012a. *The Adaptation Industry: The Cultural Economy of Contemporary Literary Adaptation*. New York: Routledge.

———. 2012b. "The Business of Adaptation: Reading the Market." *A Companion to Literature, Film, and Adaptation*, edited by Deborah Cartmell, 122–39. London: Blackwell Publishing.

Naithani, Sadhana. 2010. *The Story-Time of the British Empire: Colonial and Postcolonial Folkloristics*. Jackson: UP Mississippi.

Poniewozik, James. 2009. "The End of Fairy Tales? How Shrek and Friends Have Changed Children's Stories." *Folk & Fairy Tales*, edited by Martin Hallett and Barbara Karasek, 394–7. 4th ed. Peterborough, ON: Broadview P.

Rankin, Walter. 2007. *Grimm Pictures: Fairy Tale Archetypes in Eight Horror and Suspense Films*. Jefferson, NC: McFarland.

Rich, Adrienne. 1972. "When We Dead Awaken: Writing as Re-Vision." *College English* 34 (1): 18–30.

Ryan, Marie Laure. 2004. "Introduction." *Narrative across Media: The Language of Storytelling*, edited by Marie Laure Ryan, 1–40. Lincoln: U Nebraska P.

Sanders, Julie. 2006. *Adaptation and Appropriation*. New York: Routledge.

Schacker, Jennifer. 2007. "Unruly Tales: Ideology, Anxiety, and the Regulation of Genre." *Journal of American Folklore* 120 (478): 381–400.

Sexton, Anne. 1971. *Transformations*. Boston: Houghton Mifflin.

Short, Sue. 2015. *Fairy Tale and Film: Old Tales with a New Spin*. New York: Palgrave Macmillan.

Stam, Robert. 2005. "The Theory and Practice of Adaptation." *Literature and Film: A Guide to the Theory and Practice of Adaptation*, edited by Robert Stam and Alessandra Raengo, 1–52. Malden, MA: Blackwell.

Tan, Shaun. 2015. *The Singing Bones*. Sydney: Crows Nest, Allen & Unwin.

Vaz da Silva, Francisco. 2016. "Charles Perrault and the Evolution of 'Little Red Riding Hood'." *Marvels & Tales* 30 (2): 167–190.

Warner, Marina. 2014. *Once Upon a Time: A Short History of the Fairy Tale*. New York: Oxford UP.

Zipes, Jack. 2011. *The Enchanted Screen: The Unknown History of Fairy-Tale Films*. New York: Routledge.

———. 2015. *Grimm Legacies: The Magic Spell of the Grimms' Folk and Fairy Tales*. Princeton, NJ: Princeton UP.

Mediagraphy

Átame! (Tie Me Up! Tie Me Down!). 1990. Director Pedro Almodovar. Spain.

At the Crossroads of Data and Wonder: Algorithmic Visualizations of Fairy Tales on Television. 2014–. Creators Jill Terry Rudy, Jarom McDonald, Kristy Stewart, and Jessie Riddle. http://fttv.byu.edu.

Beastly. 2011. Director Daniel Barnz. USA.

Beauty and the Beast. 1991. Directors Gary Trousdale and Kirk Wise. USA.

——— (TV). 1987–1990. Creator Ron Koslow. USA.

——— (TV). 2012–2016. Creator Gary Fleder. USA.

Brave. 2012. Directors Mark Andrews, Brenda Chapman, and Steve Purcell. USA.

Cendrillon (Cinderella). 1899. Director Georges Méliès. France.

The Company of Wolves. 1984. Director Neil Jordan. UK.

Dancehall Queen. 1997. Directors Rick Elgood and Don Letts. Jamaica.

Doré, Gustave. 1867. *Le contes de Perrault*. Illustration. France.

Ehki ya shahrazade (Scheherazade, Tell Me a Story). 2009. Director Yousry Nasrallah. Egypt.

El laberinto del fauno (Pan's Labyrinth). 2006. Director Guillermo del Toro. Spain/Mexico/USA.

"Fairytale" (Song). 2004. Artist Sara Bareilles, album *Little Voice*. USA.

Frozen. 2013. Directors Chris Buck and Jennifer Lee. USA.

Goldstein, Dina. 2011. *Fallen Princesses*. Photograph Series. USA. www.dinagoldstein.com/fallenprincesses.com.

International Fairy-Tale Filmography. 2013–. Creators Jack Zipes, Pauline Greenhill, and Kendra Magnus-Johnston. http://iftf.uwinnipeg.ca.

Into the Woods (Musical). 1987. Music and Lyrics by Stephen Sondheim. Broadway. USA.

———. 2014. Director Rob Marshall. USA.

Into the Woods: Stephen Sondheim (DVD). 1997. Director James Lapine. USA.

La belle et la bête (Beauty and the Beast). 1946. Director Jean Cocteau. France.

"Let It Go" (Song). 2013. Artist Idina Menzel, album *Frozen Soundtrack*. USA.

Little Red Riding Hood. 1997. Director David Kaplan. USA.

Once Upon a Time (TV). 2011–. Creators Adam Horowitz and Edward Kitsis. USA.

Shrek. 2001. Directors Andrew Adamson and Vicky Jenson. USA.

Sinalela. 2001. Director and writer Dan Taulapapa McMullin. Samoa/USA.

Tale of Tales. 2015. Director Matteo Garrone. Italy/France/UK.

Vampirella (Radio Play). July 1976. Writer Angela Carter. BBC Radio 3. UK.

"Vs" (Song). 2006. Artist Misono, album *Never+land*. Japan.

17

ADVERTISING

Olivia Weigeldt

The fairy tale has long been such a mainstay in advertising that the fictional Don Draper, a successful 1960s Manhattan advertising director in the television series *Mad Men* (2007–2015), dismisses a proposed commercial for a shoe featuring Cinderella as "cliché" (Wittwer 2016). Cliché or not, the advertising industry has long used fairy-tale narratives, motifs, images, and signs to promote its products and messages, for the simple reason that "they work" (Odber de Baubeta 1997, 37). Fairy tales' recognizability and popularity (Zipes 2015) make it possible for these stories to represent a "world of desire, hope, and perfection" (Mieder 2015, 3). More importantly, though, fairy tales successfully integrate into all kinds of advertising because "elements like magic, transformation, and happy endings lend themselves perfectly to the advertiser's pitch that the featured product will miraculously change the viewer's life for the better" (Zipes 2015, 610; see also Bacchilega and Rieder 2014).

The possibility of the transformation which fairy tales so often project is a crucial tool within North American advertising rhetoric. As a form of mass communication, commercials seek to promote or sell messages, products, or services to their audiences to bring to the foreground—or more accurately to *create*—their consumer audience's desire for transformation. As Patricia Anne Odber de Baubeta highlights, advertisers must "convince us that our desires can be satisfied in reality, not merely in dreams or daydreams" (1997, 39). The dynamic between what is real and/or possible, and what is fantasy, opens up space for advertisements to productively engage fairy-tale narratives by manipulating the transformative tropes contained within them.

Ads work to position their intended audience as potential consumers and employ tactics and strategies of persuasion or manipulation to achieve this end. However, as Cristina Bacchilega points out, "Fairy tales interpellate us as consumers *and* producers of transformation" (2013, 3). Therefore, although advertising promotes consumption, it also creates the conditions required for individuals to desire to consume, thus upholding the consumer capitalist system. Commercials communicate social information beyond the product itself, with merchandise serving "as markers and communicators for interpersonal distinctions and self-expression" (Leiss et al. 2005, 5). Moreover, Raymond Williams suggests that the objects of ads—the advertised products—"are not enough" in themselves but "must be validated, if only in fantasy" (2000) with symbolic meanings. Critical examinations of the content and methods of advertising yield insights into how fairy tales communicate meanings about and beyond the products themselves, engage with individual and collective desires, and drive consumerism and its underlying ideologies and behaviors. But as this chapter shows, advertisements conversely "reflect back on [fairy tales], coloring our view of them" (Bacchilega 2013, 32), thus preserving and developing their cultural pervasiveness.

Advertising and Fairy-Tale Magic

Studies of fairy tales and advertising tend to focus on television commercials, originating with Tom Burns's marathon nineteen-hour television-watching spree in 1969 when he recorded all material relating to folklore observed on screen, a total of 101 instances in programs and commercials (Dégh 1994, 37), followed by Priscilla Denby's study of "folkloristic" traits on the small screen (1971, 114). While the sheer prevalence of fairy-tale elements makes it difficult to uniformly characterize their role in television advertising, "it is still beneficial to examine and catalogue the wonder and storytelling operating within these artifacts when possible." Further, commercials are "by nature temporary and ethereal" (Wittwer 2016), so an archive of commercials is not readily accessible as it may be for other kinds of media. Ads traditionally exist in the in-between spaces of network TV, and their fleeting nature makes them suitable for repetitive narrative devices. Because viewers are usually not in control of which ads they watch, deliberate comparison is at best difficult.

Critical cultural studies often incorporate semiotic analysis to understand how advertisers depend on signs to effectively communicate with consumers. Roland Barthes examines how commercials convey intended meanings by both the linguistic message, which focuses or adds meaning through text, and the connoted image, comprised of the visual elements' signified meanings (1977). For Barthes (1991), the myth as sign *already* has intentional meaning, suggesting a pattern of repetition not unlike those of motifs and narratives used by the advertising industry. Since the fairy tale operates in the realm of myth as Barthes views it, it is ripe for intentional employment in advertising. Any semiotic reading of fairy tales within advertisements, however, must also take into account how the creators' assumed hegemonic interpretation strategically propagates a dominant or normative and desired ideology. The crucial difference between fairy tales and ads in this semiotic realm is that "fairy tales try to change attitudes covertly, whereas advertisements advise the audience openly about what should be done and what should not" (Järv 2013, 100). The semiotic message of the ad is overt, whereas the fairy tale's meaning is not. When fairy tales are incorporated into ads, their messages become less covert, harnessing the magical transformations that are integral to so many of these narratives.

Critical advertising studies address how ads function as markers, communicators, and re-producers within capitalist systems of power (see Leiss et al. 2005). Fittingly, Williams describes the "system of market-control" as being "*magic*" or "a highly organized and professional system of magical inducements and satisfactions" (2000). That the idea of magic infiltrates academic discourse surrounding ads, even work not explicitly about their relation to fairy tales, showcases how easily collapsible the two areas are. Magic and advertising sometimes seem inseparable.

Williams's view that the product on its own is insufficient to motivate consumerism means that a washing machine, for example, is rarely advertised solely on the promise it will effectively clean clothing. Instead, the appliance is marketed as "an indication that we are forward-looking or an object of envy to our neighbours" (2000). The ad's basis is conversion; the consumer's life will improve if she buys the washing machine. However, the ad does not *show* this transformation; rather, the ad *is* the transformation. Thus, advertisements function by employing a desire (to be forward-looking or the envy of one's neighbors), which consumers link back to the product through their contextual reading of its ad. The product advertised thus stands in for the fulfillment of desire; the ad creates both the desire and its fulfillment. Not only are ads magical when infused with fairy-tale elements, ads are already magical in their process. In Marshall McLuhan's famous words, the "message is the medium" (Dégh and Vázsonyi

1979, 61). To achieve material fulfillment, to be *transformed*, resists a world where magic is fiction or illusion; the fairy-tale world and the advertisement both thrive on the impossible.

Ads work well with fairy tales by "creating a world where magic and reality can meet in harmony at least once in a while" (Mieder 2015, 3). This fantasy of merging fiction with actuality, at the very least, plays into a desire for the impossible. Both ads and fairy tales seem to be "mediators of a desirable world" (Järv 2013, 100). But when each form depends on stereotypes in their message delivery, especially with regards to gender (see Goffman 1979), one can ask whom, and whose needs, that realm serves. Constructing a positive transformation in a woman's life on the basis of her consumption and use of a washing machine renders her existence primarily in terms of a domestic role, in contrast to the realities of most women's actual experience. Tying a man's self-esteem to his vehicle's power may obviate his lack of actual control within capitalist patriarchy, but also suggests that power is what he should seek—rather than, for example, connection, spirituality, or intellectual growth. Fairy tales support these readings by, for example, giving Cinderella a washing machine so she can attend the ball, or transforming a car into a magic carpet that whisks its owner into any situation he desires. When the magic in ads functions successfully, it convinces, persuades, or manipulates consumers into accepting and enacting what its creators deem desirable—not only the purchase of a specific product, but also the maintenance of a world safe for gender hierarchy and capitalism.

In the realm of commercials, not only is magic desirable, but advertising's adoption of magic illustrates its significant role in upholding consumerist society and its associated behaviors. In their comprehensive study on fairy tales in TV commercials, Linda Dégh and Andrew Vázsonyi state, "magic is merchandise of prime necessity. Magic is in demand. People who travel by airplane still cannot do without the magic carpet. Let us see where the magic carpet is for sale" (1979, 49). Magic's adaptive nature may allow its application within a wide range of advertising contexts, but multiple subject positions read or consume magic. Dégh and Vázsonyi point out that the magic carpet, the princess, or any other visually recognizable fairy-tale motif or element can call on consumers' fragmented memories, without necessarily possessing any wider narrative information. As they state:

> A fairy princess appears on the television screen. She is a fairy and she appears; this is the whole tale. Who knows which tale was her original home environment? As a matter of fact, this cannot be known, because the fairy in question—offering margarine, floor wax, hair conditioner, or coffee—does not originate from one specific tale but from the tale in general.
>
> (57)

The fairy princess who stands in for one or many tales exemplifies the particular ability of these stories to be reduced to singular visual/conceptual elements that yield a powerful impact. It doesn't matter that viewers do not know that particular fairy princess's history; she is at once displaced from her context while living exactly where the ad purports she belongs, fully associated with domesticity.

Dégh and Vázsonyi highlight the fairy tale's particular ability to circulate without necessarily referencing an original "because the fairy tale circulates as a text that is already plural" (Bacchilega 2013, 32). Indeed, the actual number of fairy tales that most Euro North Americans know is quite small to begin with (Dégh 1989). Within advertising's mass-communication context, the tales' disconnected elements continue to spread freely and widely, perpetuating their existence as common knowledge and as part of a shared "cultural repertoire" (Leiss et al.

2005, 3), often lacking a concrete reference point. As Alessandro Falassi and Gail Kligman point out in their analysis of Volkswagen ads, connecting folklore to a product facilitates it being perceived as "within everybody's means" and "inclusive" (1976, 79). Since advertising seeks to increase consumption, appealing to a broad cross-section of people can make good marketing sense, and this is one of the reasons that fairy tales are so effective and powerful when mobilized to capitalist ends.

Fairy tales are not just adapted by the advertising industry; they are reproduced over and over again in and by commercials. That advertising figures in fairy-tale transmission itself ensures that narratives and motifs continue to be well-known, albeit sometimes in quite altered states. Advertising *uses* fairy tales strategically and purposefully to achieve its goals of consumer buy-in. By linking magical desire to craving a product, advertisements can successfully delink a fairy tale from its hypotext—the narrative idea which is the story's basis—while simultaneously preserving it. Whether or not an ad references a fully elaborated tale, it draws on the appeal that the story brings, even in a fragmented form. Ads function as "sites of storytelling" that "can provide insight into cultural desires and anxieties *and* affect the experiences and actions of the people who encounter them" (Bock 2014, 229).

To offer an example of these processes, Ines Imdahl analyzes the German gummy-bear manufacturer Haribo's invocation of the desire for a fairy-tale "happily ever after" in their marketing slogan, "*Haribo macht Kinder froh—und Erwachsene ebenso*" (Haribo makes kids and grown-ups happy). Imdahl suggests that the ad provides an entire story structure by using only a most basic narrative element—the formulaic closing "and they lived happily ever after" (2015, 12–14). Moreover, the slogan positions adults reading the ad on the same level as children being told a fairy tale while recognizing that, almost always, adults hold the buying power. The ad speaks to (and about) the adult, even as it simultaneous speaks to (and about) the child.

The Washing Machine Advertisement: Transformations and Displacements

Much fairy-tale advertising promotes cleaning products or tools (see Williams 2000; Odber de Baubeta 1997; Dégh and Vázsonyi 1979). Imdahl posits cleaning in advertising as "*Der Kampf gegen den Schmutz*"—the fight against uncleanliness—placing that act in a story arc pitting good against evil (2015, 5). The washing machine is often the object by which fairy tales meld with product persuasion, often with layered social meanings pertaining to gender roles. In its practical yet seemingly magical liminality, the washing machine literally transforms clothing from dirty to clean, with magically minimal labor. Although ads may not persuade most people to buy a washing machine as long as theirs continues to function, commercials relay other social information. One of the central questions asks who is performing the labor, and the answer shows that ads too often perpetuate sexism and gendered stereotypes. I read three ads featuring washing machines in order to tease out how they use the fairy tale.

A 2002 print advertisement for a Zanussi washing machine features a young girl in the kitchen with her mother and the appliance. Sequential images show the girl excitedly reading a party invitation, then sadly holding a bundle of stained pink fabric, the material going into the machine, and the mother embroidering butterfly wings. Finally, the girl happily wears a princess dress with the wings sewn on the back and a crown on her head while her mother stands satisfied in the distance next to the washing machine. The caption reads, "Create memories. You never know when you might have to be mum to a fairy princess. But when you do, it helps to know a little magic [. . .] Not to mention plenty of time to conjure up those magic wings" (Pongratz 2003, 70).

The washing machine doesn't just clean—it *transforms* by creating a memorable story. The Zanussi advertisement suggests that this memory, like the fairy-tale world it implicitly references, will be remembered by both mother and daughter. Yet as with the Haribo slogan, the ad is directed to the adult woman, who may or may not need to purchase a washing machine, but who nevertheless is encouraged to benefit from the reminder to share such domestic moments with her daughter. Zanussi's ad illustrates how cultural knowledge—including the fairy princess alluded to by Dégh and Vázsonyi—is learned and passed from one generation to another. The fairy tale is an opportune site for teaching domestic and gendered knowledge as the washing machine, in the kitchen, invites both girl and woman to participate in domestic activities. As "mum to a fairy princess," the mother possesses magical traits, reflected especially in her ability to "conjure" the finishing touches on the princess dress. The girl *becomes* a fairy princess when she performs this role through her costume. Like the magical washing machine, the mother's work is magic, so much so that using it cannot even be termed labor. The girl and woman are engaged in both labor *and* pleasure; the ad posits the two as inseparable. Feminine work is effectively depicted as satisfying and pleasurable, but also transformative. In the world of this fairy-tale advertisement, the mundane tasks of everyday domestic life are not boring, repetitive, and stressful, but instead marvelous, creative, and endlessly fulfilling for all involved.

Another ad that connects domestic labor, costume or disguise, and magic is a television commercial for the Samsung Ecobubble washing machine. It depicts a photography shoot for the appliance underway in the snowy wilderness of British Columbia, Canada. A grizzly bear suddenly approaches the photo set. The group backs away and assurances are heard that "he's gonna move on in a minute, just let the bear be" (Samsung Home Appliances 2013). The bear, however, closely examines the washing machine and suddenly stands upright, taking off an outer layer of fur. Standing in boxer shorts, he stuffs the fur into the machine and remains on set while his laundry is being done. When the wash cycle finally finishes, the bear takes out his fur, now completely white. "It got that clean on a cold cycle?" a woman asks off camera. The bear dresses, morphs into a polar bear, and leaves the scene.

This ad references elements of "The Bear" (ATU 510B), which also includes "Donkey Skin" and "Catskin." In it, a princess uses an enchanted bearskin as a disguise to elude her father who has imprisoned her. When she escapes to the forest, a hunter-prince hunts her, thinking that she is a bear. She manages to call off his hunting dogs, so surprising him that he asks her to return home with him. Still disguised as a bear, the princess astounds everyone by fully performing household duties. She changes her bearskin to a gown and attends a ball where the prince falls in love with her, then returns and changes back into her bear disguise. Eventually, her true form is revealed, and when she tells how her father had imprisoned her, the prince marries her (Lang 1900).

Although most viewers of the Samsung ad may not be familiar with the specifics of "The Bear," both contain recognizable fairy-tale elements. Like the Zanussi fairy princess, the bear *is* the story. It does not matter from whence he lumbers onto the photo shoot; only when he is documented—by the shoot, by the ad—does his story becomes important. While the Samsung ad draws on the element of bear-disguise, two things are surprising about who performs the domestic labor of laundry: first, that it is a bear, and second, that the bear is male, so characterized by the astonished photo set people anxiously watching and by its undressed appearance in boxer shorts. The bystanders' reactions clarify that it is that a *male* bear performs this household chore that makes the scene fantastical. The bear's activity is already magical; the washing machine only magnifies the enchantment when it transforms the fur into a white coat reminiscent of royal ermine, subtly echoing the position the princess in "The Bear" re-obtains after shedding her disguise and marrying the prince.

Although a bear doing laundry is clearly intended to be strange in and of itself, the ad employs documentary-style cinematographic techniques to convey a feeling of contrasting reality. The tension between the fantastical bear and the realist handheld camera and frame-breaking crew talk extends the washing machine not only beyond the realm of an interior, domestic house into nature, but also from a conventionally female domain into a conventionally male one. The interiority referenced by the washing machine has been displaced outside to nature so that it can be accessed by the masculinized figure of the bear. Both he and the camera-operator are male; the world is transformable for those who wield narrative control.

Further, Samsung situates its Ecobubble washing machine outside, reinterpreting its utility as an environmentally conscious product and therefore beneficial in a broader, global framework. Samsung seeks to fulfill a consumer desire to *feel* like the world can be saved, suggesting that consumers can do so by the mundane act of washing clothes. The reuse of positive values, like sensitivity to ecological destruction, but also of more problematic ones, like racism, can be discernable through advertising, reframed by their very overt and explicit visibility. In 2016, a commercial on Chinese television promoting the laundry detergent brand Qiaobi was widely condemned as racist (Daily Nation 2016). It depicts a Chinese woman flirting with a black man before sensually placing a capsule of detergent into his mouth and pushing him into the washing machine. When the cycle is complete, he emerges a light-skinned Chinese man, much to the woman's delight. The detergent's kiss transforms the man into a figure who is deemed more desirable by the ad's gaze, not unlike a frog prince (ATU 440); the twinkle in the newly transformed Chinese man's eye further explicitly connects the ad to wonder and magic.

While the transformative narrative of this ad is not unlike those used by Zanussi and Samsung, the Qiaobi ad's execution demonstrates the ability of fairy-tale narratives and motifs to bring to the fore problematic kinds of hegemonic and oppressive discourses. The fairy tale's "remarkable surface-flexibility" (Dégh and Vázsonyi 1979, 49) means it can be imbued with overtly racist ideologies as well as with progressive ones. This (negative) by-product of fairy tales' characteristically flexible qualities is in part integral to the traditional form's working, always already displaced from any and all primary sources.

The Qiaobi example also illustrates the global movement of elements of wonder and their redeployment in multiple contexts and with varying meanings. However, its overt use of racist ideology in conjunction with the transformation narrative actually mobilized condemnation and, ultimately, an apology from the firm "for the harm caused to the African people because of the spread of the ad and the over-amplification by the media [. . .]. We sincerely hope the public and the media will not over-read it" ("Chinese" 2016). Spread and (over)amplification are, of course, primary goals of the advertising industry; ironically, the firm blames what it actively seeks, as if these processes are external to their aims, rather than what they could only have hoped would happen. In this ad, the fairy tale of the princess's transformation of her frog suitor invokes a kind of Trojan horse of innocence and beneficence. However, it's worth remembering that in some traditional texts the transformation result happens not when she kisses him but instead when she violently throws him against the wall in disgust. Fairy tales, like commercials, offer endless variety and highly variable contents. So when the firm asks viewers not to "over-read" their meaning, it has never been more clear that the use of the fairy tale in advertising should be in fact systematically analyzed, queried, and critiqued.

Related topics: Broadcast; Fantasy; Gender; Material Culture; Photographic

References Cited and Further Reading

Bacchilega, Cristina. 2013. *Fairy Tales Transformed?: Twenty-First-Century Adaptations of Politics and Wonder*. Detroit: Wayne State UP.

Bacchilega, Cristina, and John Rieder. 2014. "The Fairy Tale and the Commercial in *Carosello* and *Fractured Fairy Tales*." In *Channeling Wonder: Fairy Tales on Television*, edited by Pauline Greenhill and Jill Terry Rudy, 336–59. Detroit: Wayne State UP.

Barthes, Roland. 1977. "The Rhetoric of the Image." In *Image Music Text*, translated by Stephen Heath, 32–51. London: Fontana P.

———. 1991. *Mythologies*, translated and edited by Annette Lavers. New York: The Noonday P.

Benjamin, Walter. 2008. "The Work of Art in the Age of Its Technological Reproducibility: Second Version." In *The Work of Art in the Age of Its Technological Reproducibility and Other Writings on Media*, translated by Edmund Jephcott, Rodney Livingstone, and Howard Eiland, edited by Michael W. Jennings, Brigid Doherty, and Thomas Y. Levin, 19–55. Cambridge, MA: Harvard UP.

Bock, Sheila. 2014. "'What Happens Here, Stays Here': Selling the Untellable in a Tourism Advertising Campaign." *Western Folklore* 73: 216–34.

"Chinese Firm Apologizes over Qiaobi Race-Row Advert." 2016. *BBC News*, May 29. www.bbc.com/news/world-asia-china-36407651.

DailyNation. 2016. "Racism in a Chinese Laundry Detergent Advertisement." *YouTube*, July 30. www.youtube.com/watch?v=Few8kJ0zfnY.

Dégh, Linda. 1989. "Beauty, Wealth, and Power: Career Choices for Women in Folktales, Fairy Tales and Modern Media." *Fabula* 30: 43–62.

———. 1994. *American Folklore and the Mass Media*. Bloomington: Indiana UP.

Dégh, Linda, and Andrew Vázsonyi. 1979. "Magic for Sale: Märchen and Legend in TV Advertising." *Fabula* 28: 47–68.

Denby, Priscilla. 1971. "Folklore in the Mass Media." *Folklore Forum* 4 (5): 113–25.

Falassi, Alessandro, and Gail Kligman. 1976. "*Folk-Wagen*: Folklore and the Volkswagen Ads." *New York Folklore* 2: 79–86.

Goffman, Erving. 1979. *Gender Advertisements*. New York: Harper & Row.

Imdahl, Ines. 2015. *Werbung auf der Couch: Warum Werbung Märchen Braucht*. Freiburg im Breisgrau: Herder.

Järv, Risto. 2013. "A Hen Who Doesn't Lay Golden Eggs?! Fairy Tale Advertisements and Their Strategies." In *Estonia and Poland 2: Perspectives on National and Regional Identity*, edited Liisi Laineste, Dorota Brzozowska, and Władysław Chłopick, 99–120. Tartu, Estonia: ELM Scholarly P.

Lang, Andrew. 1900. "The Bear." In *The Grey Fairy Book*, 269–74. New York: Longmans, Green, and Co.

Leiss, William, Stephen Kline, Sut Jhally, and Jacqueline Botterill. 2005. *Social Communication in Advertising: Consumption in the Mediated Marketplace*. 3rd ed. New York: Routledge.

Mieder, Walter. 2015. "Advertising and Fairy Tales." In *The Oxford Companion to Fairy Tales*, edited by Jack Zipes, 3–4. 2nd ed. Oxford: Oxford UP.

Odber de Baubeta, Patricia Anne. 1997. "Fairy Tale Motifs in Advertising." *Estudos de Literatura Oral* 3: 35–60.

———. 1998. "Fairy Tale Motifs in Advertising (2)." *Estudos de Literatura Oral* 4: 23–53.

Pongratz, Gerda. 2003. *Female Stereotypes as Reflected in English Advertising*. Hamburg: Diplomica.

Samsung Home Appliances. 2013. "Huge Bear Surprises Crew on EcoBubble Photo Shoot in BC." *YouTube*. www.youtube.com/watch?v=eryxAcsTcOA.

Williams, Raymond. 2000. "Advertising: The Magic System." *Advertising & Society Review* 1 (1).

Wittwer, Preston. 2016. "Don Draper Thinks Your Ad Is Cliché: Fairy Tale Iconography in TV Commercials." *Humanities* 5 (2): 1–17.

Zipes, Jack. 2015. "Television and Fairy Tales." *The Oxford Companion to Fairy Tales*, edited by Jack Zipes, 609–14. 2nd ed. Oxford: Oxford UP.

Mediagraphy

Mad Men (TV). 2007–2015. Creator Matt Weiner. USA.

18

CONVERGENCE CULTURE

Media Convergence, Convergence Culture, and Communicative Capitalism

Ida Yoshinaga

In an era when transnational media corporations wield data-analytic tools to refine methods of fairy-tale "monetization" or "commodification,"[1] fairy-tale scholars have had to step up their analytical game. Drawing from William Merrin's phrase "media studies 2.0," which dared the twentieth-century-mired field of media scholarship to find new approaches to evaluate new forms (2014, 6), researchers of fairy tale and folktale are developing theories and methods that might characterize a "fairy-tale studies 2.0," to contend with the hypermediacy (multiplication of forms; see Bolter and Grusin 2000) of their object of study. In the process, they engage issues raised by the convergence culture discourse, which focuses on the controversy around whether the digital mass-communication technologies of the millennium facilitate public education and social justice or marginalize and exploit working-class and poor populations already threatened by the global advance of neoliberalism and its stratifying political-economic policies. This discourse divides liberal, libertarian, and conservative researchers, who generally value the work of leading proponent Henry Jenkins, from media scholars working in Marxist, cultural studies, and critical theory traditions, who view Jenkins's analyses as dangerously naive. Although it has little direct engagement in these convergence culture debates, fairy-tale studies, in historicizing the relationship between media and meaning, contributes a powerful set of tools with which to address the gap between these two oppositional perspectives.

Originating in simple, albeit polysemic, oral forms, fairy tales' and folktales' permeability with other media—enabled by their "structural recognition" or "nostalgic familiarity" for diverse audiences (Tiffin 2009, 1–2)—allows them to animate complex, modern stories told in developing technological platforms. Fairy-tale research has thus entered the media convergence era with structural concepts that highlight the tales' intermediation into digital-era sites: fairy-tale "fragments" (Preston 2004, 210), "pastiches" (Jorgensen 2007, 218), "texture(s)" (Tiffin 2009, 5), and "memes" (Zipes 2012, 17–20). Fairy tales and folktales exemplify an ideal research subject for media convergence, which Jenkins defines as the "flow of content across multiple media platforms, the cooperation between multiple media industries, and the migratory behavior of media audiences who will go almost anywhere in search of the kinds of entertainment experiences they want" (2006, 2). Intertwining agency with structure, fairy-tale

161

studies constitutes a nuanced middle ground for debates pitting Jenkins's notion of convergence culture against critical media scholars' emphases on communicative capitalism.

In Jenkins's Habermasian ideal, twenty-first-century citizens' increased media activity affords them optimal expressive agency via membership in "knowledge communities" (2006). These communities (such as fan or advocacy groups) are propelled by members' "collective intelligence," which serves as a counter-balancing force against institutional power. The result is a modern, "participatory culture" of heightened public expression, fueled by information-sharing systems that expedite extensively distributive, highly interactive connections, especially "Web 2.0"–type platforms driven by "user-generated content" (2006; e.g., social media sites, "smart" technologies, Internet sites/blogs/videos, mobile device applications).

This paradigmatic shift in communications was enabled by a transformation in material forces: mass media evolved from a distribution-centered, top-down model, where people were passive vis-à-vis transnational conglomerates and nation-states, to a "spreadable" (Jenkins 2013, 3) or "hybrid" model emphasizing content circulation, "where a mix of top-down and bottom-up forces determine how material is shared across and among cultures in far more participatory (and messier) ways" (1–2). Global firms thus must factor into their decision making the increasingly knowledgeable, vociferous, and tactical participation of ordinary people within the marketplace. For instance, "citizen journalists" employ video/blog/mobile posts or feeds toward critical or counter-hegemonic witnessing/testimony/declaration in the public sphere if they are unhappy with a company's products or actions (Jenkins 2007).

On the other hand, detractors point to citizens' false consciousness in the de-valuing of their own (and others') labor. Proponents of oppositional perspectives believe that Big Media socializes people to attribute the informational *power* of convergence mainly to "innovative" global capitalism, which has progressively monopolized the tools of communication, rather than to acknowledge contributions of workers and consumers. These groups collectively forge information and knowledge into valuable commodities (e.g., stories/storyworlds) that multinational corporations sell at great profit. Disturbed by citizens' susceptibility to "communicative capitalism" (Dean 2005), this perspective notes barriers to civic engagement, community expression, and progressive social change (Kubitschko 2012).

Communicative capitalism is "the common-place idea that the market, today, is the site of democratic aspirations" (Dean 54). It tricks citizens into believing that the volume of information surfacing in new communication venues generates real institutional transformation, political resistance, and democratic outcomes. Although today's citizens are densely interconnected and technologically organized, their ability to influence government policies remains limited by the unequal societal (expressive) power between themselves and Big Media conglomerates.

Often skeptical of the phrase "convergence culture," this position contends that digital-era capitalist propaganda—circulated by the mainstream media's "cybertarian chorus" (Maxwell and Miller 2011, 595) that sings pro-business ideologies of "technology fetishism" (Dean 2005, 51)—masks the sharply stratified, global economy. Media conglomerates and their government allies own and control the very "means of communication" (Hebblewhite 2016, 213) during an era when capitalism's accumulative reach extends toward knowledge itself. The trumpeting of convergence culture—"where old and new media collide, where grassroots and corporate media intersect, where the power of the media producer and the power of the media consumer interact in unpredictable ways" (Jenkins 2006, 2)—underestimates the political-economic vulnerability of the populace. They can use digital networks to amplify their voices, but they are rarely heard by political or corporate elites who still dictate the distribution of societal resources, including capital and the information and communications technology (ICT) infrastructure.

The latter position urges scholars to research anti-hegemonic, "alternative media" practices rather than accept that millennial communication platforms automatically empower citizens (Fuchs 2012, 392–394). Critical media scholars must reject grand pronouncements of participatory culture and instead ground their work in historically and geographically specific patterns of "audience commodification," the corporate extraction of profit from people's participation in mass-informational systems (Fuchs 2016, 536–548). Researchers should explore theoretical developments that recast citizens' so-called "participation" in (and "interactivity" with) ICT platforms within the larger framework of media ownership and control: unequal production relations; uneven distribution systems; and globalized divisions of labor.

Media convergence specialists on either side of this debate might ask fairy-tale scholars: How might we evaluate whether digital fairy tales and folktales, "reassemblies of fragments on loan" (Zipes 2012, 4), truly support the expressive needs of story audiences, or whether they serve the profit-seeking agendas of communicative capitalism? Under what social conditions can these fairy-tale reassemblies facilitate media literacy, democratic education, and critical community movements toward equality, reconciliation, justice? How can we tell when these reassemblies lull citizens into leisure practices that preclude socioemotional functions of fantasy "for spiritual regeneration and [. . .] to contemplate alternatives to our harsh realities," but instead furnish mere escapism, ostensibly to "compensate for dull lives" (Zipes 2008, 2)? Does digital fairy tales' expressive power simply lubricate consumer purchases, erasing the undercompensated labor of real storytellers upon which mass-produced corporate fairy-tale products are dependent? Or might millennial, fairy-tale reassemblies—if interactive—guide participants to practice mindful, courageous, healing, ethical actions in the everyday world?

Fairy-tale studies confounds simplistic, binary perspectives on media convergence by situating digital intermediation within the larger crucible of wonder-tale history. Scholarship into fairy tales and folktales investigates how these storytelling forms are shaped as much by older, communitarian practices of intertextuality, intermediality, and remediation as by the modern, corporate strategy of entertainment franchise–driven transmediation. Fairy-tale studies centralizes the larger stakes of community expression and human informational exchange, returning the discourse to the notion of how (wonder) tales replicate as cultural-communicative forms—whether or not facilitated by the dizzying technological media offered by capitalism. Three approaches of fairy-tale studies to convergence culture are the global fairy-tale web, community-inclusive models for transmedia storytelling, and commercialized fairy-tale creolization.

Mapping the Field of Forces/Struggles:
The Global Fairy-Tale Web

Fairy-tale studies in the millennium has evaluated the intermediation of these tales within—and without—platforms owned by global media corporations. Fairy-tale texts are viewed as "medium-breakers" that resist the homogenization engendered by industrial production and monetization because jumping from one to another mass-communication system "failed to limit the texts to a single form" (Greenhill and Matrix 2010, 3). As a "medium *maker*," the genre historically helped legitimize nascent, commercial, story forms (e.g., movies and comic books), thus proving both an "early and persistent mode for successive communication technologies" (Greenhill and Rudy 2014, 15). Weaving between community and commodity, fairy tales operate "as shape-shifters, morphing into new versions [. . .] as they are retold and [. . .] migrate into other media" (Tatar 2010, 56). How to assess community-based fairy-tale and folktale expressions, in conversation with those produced within the global fantasy factory, remains a key challenge to fairy-tale studies.

One starting point has been to envision the greater ideological "field of forces"/"field of struggles" (Bourdieu 1993, 30) in which fairy-tale texts operate, including unequal relations between fairy-tale types, teller/audience positions, media platforms, and production modes. For instance, the diverse, global phenomena of storytelling practices that draw upon fairy tales, folktales, wonder tales, and numinous/spiritual tales constitute what Cristina Bacchilega calls the "fairy-tale web"—a discursive, intertextual formation with no originating point, comprising intercutting pathways—whose contemporary power relations she maps with particular attention to counter-hegemonic, "activist" retellings (2013).

Bacchilega's examples include fairy-tale texts from media platforms such as plays, graphic novels, retail window displays, comic strips, TV shows, animation, artwork, book illustrations, and cinema. Her project maps a worldly practitioners' network of fairy-tale plenitude, inviting cross-disciplinary conversations with media scholars of convergence. Bacchilega identifies major axes shaping the tales' rhetorical context, including historically old or new media (Angela Carter's literary fiction as opposed to *Fables* comic books, respectively) and the field of restricted production/autonomy or the field of large production/heteronomy (YouTube videos and blogs compared with commercial publishers' Grimm books and Hollywood film/TV adaptations). She broadly classifies the structures of power that influence fairy tales' reception yet honors the diversity of the texts without de-valuing those lacking in such discursive power. The fairy-tale web allows room both for the focus on stratification in modern fairy-tale practice that characterizes critical media approaches and for the possibility of audience agency foregrounded by proponents of the convergence culture thesis.

Transmedia Storytelling: Integrating Commercialized Wonder With Community Expression

Like other critical scholars of intermediality and narrative, researchers of fairy tales and folktales complicate the conceptual model of transmedia storytelling that dominates the marketing, entertainment industry, and communication studies literature on today's cross-media narrative phenomena. Transmedia storytelling refers to the "storyworld" movement of integrated (i.e., world-building) franchise-oriented, multi-platform entertainment, in which the marketing and creative divisions of media corporations "synergistically" coordinate the characters, visual styles, settings, and plots of a single storyverse across multiple media (see Norrington 2010). Narratologically, transmedia tales engage many media channels, which allows them to "take the audience on an emotional journey that goes from moment-to-moment" as they migrate from platform to platform (Pratten 2015, 2). Frequently, this migration involves audience interaction, such as the immersive storytelling found in theme parks and video games. The transmedia storytelling model reflects the optimistic assumptions of Jenkins and his supporters, who assess each step by its potential for greater audience choice, rather than by how it furthers profit extraction.

Rebecca Hay and Christa Baxter seek to nuance and deconstruct this transmedia model. Their research balances the convergence culture and communicative capitalism perspectives by illustrating how commodification processes shape knowledge communities, but also how fairy-tale fans in these communities sometimes resist top-down, marketing directives. Hay and Baxter examine ABC TV's multi-platform narrative strategies to build audiences for the fantasy series *Once Upon a Time* (*OUaT* 2011–). They also study viewer identification with the show's characters, as reflected in corporate- and fan-run social media. Hay and Baxter's transmedial approach captures the complex "cycle of presentation, identification, and commodification" that characterizes viewers' relationships to *OUaT* (2014, 317). A feminist example cites a fan's Facebook post entreating the producers to "OH PLEASE remember that Peter Pan was always played by a woman. OH PLEASE don't ruin him, like the movies have done and let a boy be the lead role" (321). Although Hay and Baxter unearth several examples of fans' expressive agency and collective intelligence, as critics of communicative capitalism would predict, ultimately, this attempt was futile. The showrunners cast yet another male performer to play the lead lost boy.

The transmedial storyworld model is also reconceptualized by folklorists to emphasize fairy tales' persistently polysemic, polyphonic nature in the digital era. Some fairy-tale and folktale scholars assess commercialized fairy tales, but reject the capitalistic directive of singular, franchised storyworlds, which—to keep company brands profitable—minimizes explicit, intertextual references to other (non-commodified) tale versions. These researchers theorize multiverses of story, networking tale variants together, whether company or community based. For example, Jeana Jorgensen discusses how mass-media, postmodern fairy tales, such as the film *Shrek 2* (2004) and Mercedes Lackey's novel *The Fairy Godmother* (2004), reframe the "helper" type of the fairy godmother through intertextual narrative techniques referencing aspects of that type in oral folktales, print literary versions, and even Disney variants. Jorgensen praises the reflexive, intermediating work of these two capitalistic and mass-produced, yet critically oriented, millennial fairy tales, which unearth "power structures and multivocality in the tales we tell, in addition to the tales we tell about those tales" (2007, 225). Jorgensen foregoes the corporate, narrative journey of platform-to-platform profit-extraction (e.g., a single-storyverse-based voyage from the *Shrek* movies and TV specials, to Universal Parks and Resorts' *Shrek 4-D* ride, to the inevitable ogre plush toys) in favor of a Shrek-inclusive multiverse of fairy-tale helper history; she visits commercial storyworlds but does not reify their exclusivist logic.

Future fairy-tale scholarship focused on cross-medial storyfication could investigate subversive, small producers within capitalism who take commodified forms, then redeploy them transmedially to engage public issues. One example, digital filmmaker/performer Todrick Hall, offers lush, defiantly hopeful, fantasy storyworlds working to encourage young, LGBT, and people of color audiences to consider social concerns like same-sex unions and transgender rights ("Todrick Hall" 2012). His music video storyworlds mix dance, costumes, film, musical theater, romantic comedy, and urbanized/queered Disney fairy-tale tropes, which he transmediates across both small (e.g., YouTube) and large (MTV) channels. As progressive-media organization Media That Matters demonstrates through its activism (Hughes 2011), cross-platform narratives do not require the fictive universe of a corporate brand; they can be marshaled to portray the storyworlds of an artisan/craftsperson or a political community/advocate.

Other fairy-tale and folktale researchers theorize cross-mediation within fairy-tale storyworlds beyond the monetization models established by communicative capitalism. Turning to the realm of alternative and community media, they focus upon grassroots intermediation practices that Jenkins would see as "spreadable" (bottom-up) rather than "sticky" (top-down) (2013, 4). In the communitarian spirit of fairy-tale content websites *The Journal of Mythic Arts* and *SurLaLune*, Judy A. Teaford and Tina Hanlon's *AppLit* website offers articles, fiction, poems, music, lesson plans, and multimedia (mostly film and stage play) links pertaining to Appalachian storytelling, including southeastern U.S. adaptations of European folktales and fairy tales, as well as wonder tales largely derived from working-class and poor rural communities of the U.S. Southeast (2000). *AppLit* represents a storyworld-development practice in stark contrast to Disney's transmedia narratology. It traverses multiple media, not to combine characters, settings, and storylines into a viewer-ready brand, but to broadcast an ongoing universe of richly layered, time-tested community stories in the diverse media forms that those tales have taken.

Similarly, instead of evaluating texts such as *Moana* (2016), an animated film that appropriates Pacific Islander and Native Hawaiian religious traditions and voyaging folklore to expand the Disney princess commodities market into the Pacific Rim, fairy-tale scholars might follow Bacchilega's (2013, 29, 44, 47–49, 196–202) recommendation to feature creolizing (rather than only hybridizing), alternative media projects around the world. This approach may function to further what Donald Haase (2010) refers to by the title "decolonizing fairy-tale studies." By studying the narrative strategies, formal techniques, and sociocultural/spiritual functions of folk, wonder, and numinous stories from Indigenous and Global South cultural communities, scholars widen core notions of the fairy tale. Faye Ginsburg's (2008) research on Indigenous new media expressions, along with Anishinaabe/Métis transmedia scholar and video game designer Elizabeth LaPensée's work on how Native people's twenty-first-century intermediations of their folk stories—in social impact games (2014) and machinima (LaPensée and Lewis 2013), among other platforms—typify the "aesthetics of survivance" (Vizenor 2008), conjoining communicative capitalism with the greater dictates of living communities.

Commercial Fairy-Tale Creolization for Women of Color and Urban Female Workers/Professionals: Remediating the Disney Paratext

Last, fairy-tale scholars of media convergence might study a particular creolization of mass-produced fairy tales: commercial, scripted TV stories that test the idealized, "Disney paratext" against socioeconomic conditions of women of color and female workers/professionals in urban communities. Rather than condemning the Disney fairy-tale formula outright, as critical media scholars might, this approach urges researchers to explore women's agency, lying somewhere between the female/feminist, creative-industry artists of modern-day fairy tales and the diverse ethnic, professional, and working-class women viewers whose socioeconomic lives the stories seek to depict. By connecting production with reception—even within the confines of communicative capitalism—this theoretical model views media convergence not as a monolithic or unidirectional given. Rather, it explores convergence for tensions, flows, reversals, contradictions, and other dynamics between various expressive platforms that enrich content across channels.

The "Disney paratext" (Greenhill and Matrix 2010, 5–8) in question refers to the pervasive (collectively) canonical intertext generated by The Walt Disney Company's control of mass-produced, audiovisual fairy-tale representations from the twentieth century onward. This paratext famously closes with an "HEA" ending (Bacchilega's shorthand for "happily ever after" [2013, 28]) to a formulaic plot: a young girl encounters a prince or articulates a dream before being threatened by a malicious older woman or other malevolent force, then gets captured/immobilized by the crone/force, provoking rescue by the prince or other (often magical) helpers, resulting in the HEA of newly acquired riches/status or reaffirmation of/ joining with royalty (Zipes 2010, xi). The Disney paratext dominates the field of forces/ struggles for corporate creative artists working as fairy-tale adapters, who know that various knowledge communities subscribe to its (gendered, sexualized, raced, classed) expectations.

One such adapter is African American television writer-producer Shonda Rhimes. In her season 5 premiere of *Grey's Anatomy* (2008a), Rhimes's titular narrator, Meredith Grey, tells the hospital drama's prime time audience, "The person who invented 'happily ever after' should have his ass kicked so hard!" ("Dream a Little Dream of Me, Part 1"). From within the corporate storytelling context of the ABC-Disney empire itself (her training ground as well as longtime employer), feminist Rhimes rigorously tests the Disney paratext against modern women's "reality." In the episode, two wealthy best friends arrive at the hospital's emergency room, wearing bloodied and torn ballgowns, having saved their driver in a limousine accident. As the drama unfolds, they discover that one friend had conducted a long affair with the other's husband. In another arc, cantankerous surgeon Cristina Yang is impaled by a falling icicle at the hospital's entrance. She gets literally swept off her feet by trauma specialist Major Owen Hunt, who carries her inside and removes her clothing to assess the icicle's damage, much to her dismay. The anti-HEA trope of two embittered, middle-aged princesses quarreling over failed dreams competes with the heteronormative, pro-HEA trope of the rugged military veteran who seduces the show's most career-oriented, female doctor by rescuing her within minutes of their first meeting.

Rhimes resembles her cynical, scientific narrator, who tells viewers in the episode's second part, "Fairy tales don't come true. Reality is much stormier. Much murkier. Much scarier. Reality. It's so much more interesting than living happily ever after" ("Dream a Little Dream of Me, Part 2" 2008b). Like her protagonist, Rhimes proves skeptical about modern-day wonder, even while experimenting with viewer expectations of its uses. Her dramatic, televisionary remediation of the Disney paratext departs from referencing specific fairy tales or folktales, in contrast with explicit intermediations within fantasy TV shows like *OUaT* (2011–) and *Grimm* (2011–2017). Rhimes practices what scholars of the new adaptation studies might consider a sophisticated intertextual and intermedial narrative artistry (see Leitch 2008). But she also operates within the heart of communicative capitalism—rather than the "artistic" realms of independent film or small producer–created literary books/graphic novels, media favored by many progressive fairy-tale scholars—and her scripts showcase physicians as innovative scientists, usually avoiding iconographies of enchantment, magic, or wonder.

Recent commercial remediations of the Disney paratext include MTV's short-lived *Happyland* (2014), a young adult–oriented series. *Happyland* follows Lucy Velez, a working-class Latina in her late teens raised by a single mother in a mobile-home community. It depicts her work as a low-level, under-appreciated events coordinator at Happyland, a Disneyland stand-in. In this romantic dramedy, Lucy tangles with her "prince," the spoiled, White, under-achieving son of the company founder, alongside diverse working-class members of Florida's service economy. The show's single season realistically portrays work in dead-end, fantasy-industry jobs: drug use, anonymous hook-ups, homelessness, fetishistic colleagues, racist/classist bosses, even visitors who die inside the park (whose bodies workers must secretly remove). In episode 4, Happyland management decides that Elena, Lucy's middle-aged mother, is too old to play Princess Adriana in park skits, a role she's labored at her whole adult life. Elena becomes depressed when assigned the role of the evil witch. The intelligent and capable Lucy becomes equally mortified when financial circumstances force her to play Adriana and wear ridiculous princess costumes.

Lucy dreams of fleeing Happyland, being able to afford college, and starting a career in environmental non-profit management, thus avoiding her mother's fate of lifelong, pink-collar work. Over the season, Lucy navigates among the prince's privileged circle, negotiating better park jobs while trying to remain loyal to her service-labor colleagues. Although the series finale reverts to the Disney paratext—Lucy kisses the prince with the park's fireworks show in the background—*Happyland* otherwise presents a generally realistic journey through the emotional, mental, and physical labor of working-class, tourism-industry employees while discursively dismantling the HEA formula on nearly every front.

Shows like *Happyland* and the more globally intertextual Americanized *telenovela Jane the Virgin* (2014a–) creolize the televisionary fairy tale with Latin-diasporic and service-class narratives. *Jane* similarly focalizes a multigenerational, single-parent household of financially struggling, working-class Latinas; its heroine, Jane, also works in Florida's pink-collar economy. Although *Jane*—postmodern, feminist, and reflexive—calls itself a "fairy-tale *telenovela*," ("Chapter 3" 2014b), its intermedial adaptation practice foregrounds the original Venezuelan precursor (*Juana la Virgen*), rather than lineages of European print/folkloric sources. However, it noticeably engages the Disney paratext by weaving animated fantasy motifs into a prime time, live-action, dramedic narrative. Such culturally and economically specific stories of working-class heroines weathering the tough, globalized economy produce fairy tales for the digital era of narrowcasting,[2] well deserving of new approaches to fairy-tale-and-feminism scholarship.

Happyland's and *Jane the Virgin*'s episodes function as experiments, departures, and innovations (Greenhill and Matrix 2010, 17–21) in fairy-tale topoi and form that accumulate into a "retranslation" (Bacchilega 2013, 130) or "(radical) transformation" (Frus and Williams 2010, 3; 7). Perhaps Jenkins's knowledge communities should be reconceptualized, not as groups of consumers who engage in commodifiable, participatory cultures, but as everyday workers seeking stories to reflect meaning in their experiences—whatever media platform or cross-medial journey they choose. Like Lucy and Jane, the U.S. working class—about 66% of the labor force—will be mostly people of color by 2032 (Wilson 2016). Wage stagnation and economic inequality are critical issues to this demographic. Mass-medial, fairy-tale creolizations aimed at its members, like Disney's *The Princess and the Frog* (2009), increasingly depict heroines who seek financial empowerment and career achievement.

As global corporations such as The Walt Disney Company draw upon regional and spiritual folklore to create commercialized fairy-tale texts, analytical challenges arise. With the Disney film *Moana*, producers initially developed this mass-produced wonder tale by consulting with an "Oceanic story trust" of Indigenous Pacific Islander cultural practitioners and scholars about their musical, performance, linguistic, craft/work, and visual forms (Sciretta 2016). This expropriative tactic caused tremendous controversy among Native Pacific communities, as seen in Facebook posts by Native Hawaiian and Pacific Islander scholars, artists, and teachers of *Mana Moana: We Are Moana, We Are Maui* (2016). Fairy-tale studies, which favors sophisticated approaches to intermediation, helps researchers untangle such complex, twenty-first-century, corporate moves—capitalistic strategies that extract storytelling information from Global South knowledge communities, then remediate these traditional treasures within the profitable, transnational, fantasy industry. Pacific Islander and Native Hawaiian responses to *Moana*, expressed over Internet petitions and social media, have been both critical and complicated (see Yiin 2016; Kaiʻili 2016). With theoretical frameworks forged in folkloristics and feminism, fairy-tale scholars are well equipped to study diverse digital expressions of Indigenous and other community storytellers, as these cultural practitioners weigh possibilities of commodification and of agency, when their stories get adapted into modern technological forms and thus enter realms of media convergence.

Related topics: Activism; Adaptation and the Fairy-Tale Web; Blogs and Websites; Broadcast; Cinematic; Disney Corporation; Gender; Hybridity; Indigeneity; Storyworlds/Narratology; TV Drama

Notes

1. "Monetization" is a business-based term, embraced by convergence culture scholars, that paints global capitalism as complex, routine, and negotiable—in contrast with the exploitation-focused "commodification" preferred by critical media theorists (see De Rosa and Burgess 2014).

2. John D. Jackson, Greg M. Nielsen, and Yon Hsu define the new media trend of "narrowcasting" as "individualized, focused dissemination," as opposed to "older media of *broadcasting* for wide, public dissemination" (2011, 103).

References Cited and Further Reading

Bacchilega, Cristina. 2013. *Fairy Tales Transformed?: Twenty-First Century Adaptations and the Politics of Wonder.* Detroit: Wayne State UP.

Bolter, Jay David, and Richard Grusin. 2000. *Remediation: Understanding New Media.* Cambridge, MA: MIT P.

Bourdieu, Pierre. 1993. *The Field of Cultural Production*, edited by Randal Johnson. New York: Columbia UP.

Dean, Jodi. 2005. "Communicative Capitalism and the Foreclosure of Politics." *Cultural Politics* 1 (1): 51–74.

DeRosa, Maria, and Marilyn Burgess. 2014. *Monetizing Digital Media: Trends, Key Insights and Strategies that Work.* Communications CDR/Canadian Interactive Alliance. http://bellfund.ca/PDFS/FINAL%20Monetization%20report-%20November%207%202014.pdf.

Frus, Phyllis, and Christy Williams. 2010. "Introduction: Making the Case for Transformation." In *Beyond Adaptation: Essays on Radical Transformations of Original Works*, 1–18. London: McFarland.

Fuchs, Christian. 2012. "Towards a Marxian Internet Studies." *tripleC: Open Access Journal for a Global Sustainable Information Society* 10 (2): 392–412.

———. 2016. "Dallas Smythe Today: The Audience Commodity, the Digital Labour Debate, Marxist Political Economy and Critical Theory: Prolegomena to a Digital Labour Theory of Value." In *Marx and the Political Economy of the Media*, edited by Christian Fuchs and Vincent Mosco, 522–600. Leiden: Brill.

Ginsburg, Faye. 2008. "Rethinking the Digital Age." In *The Media and Social Theory*, edited by David Hesmondhalgh and Jason Toynbee, 127–44. New York: Routledge.

Greenhill, Pauline, and Sidney Eve Matrix. 2010. "Introduction: Envisioning Ambiguity: Fairy Tale Films." In *Fairy Tale Films: Visions of Ambiguity*, edited by Pauline Greenhill and Sidney Eve Matrix, 1–22. Logan: Utah State UP.

Greenhill, Pauline, and Jill Terry Rudy. 2014. "Introduction: Channeling Wonder: Fairy Tales, Television, and Intermediality." In *Channeling Wonder: Fairy Tales on Television*, edited by Pauline Greenhill and Jill Terry Rudy, 1–21. Detroit: Wayne State UP.

Haase, Donald. 2010. "Decolonizing Fairy-Tale Studies." *Marvels & Tales* 24 (1): 17.

Hay, Rebecca, and Christa Baxter. 2014. "Happily Never After: The Commodification and Critique of Fairy Tale in ABC's *Once Upon a Time.*" In *Channeling Wonder: Fairy Tales on Television*, edited by Pauline Greenhill and Jill Terry Rudy, 316–35. Detroit: Wayne State UP.

Hebblewhite, William Henning James. 2016. "'Means of Communication as Means of Production' Revisited." In *Marx and the Political Economy of the Media*, edited by Christian Fuchs and Vincent Mosco, 470–89. Leiden: Brill.

Hughes, Lynn. 2011. "'Media that Matters' Conference Explores the Future of Storytelling." International Documentary Association. www.documentary.org/feature/transmedia-new-black-media-matters-conference-explores-future-storytelling.

Jackson, John D., Greg M. Nielsen, and Yon Hsu. 2011. *Mediated Society: A Critical Sociology of Media.* Don Mills, ON: Oxford UP.

Jenkins, Henry. 2006. *Convergence Culture: Where Old and New Media Collide.* New York: NYU P.

———. 2007. "Video Blogging, Citizen Journalism, and Credibility." *Confessions of an Aca-Fan: The Official Weblog of Henry Jenkins*, March 1. http://henryjenkins.org/2007/03/videoblogging.html.

———. 2013. "Introduction: Why Media Spreads." In *Spreadable Media: Creating Value and Meaning in a Networked Culture (Post-Millennial Pop)*, 1–46. New York: NYU P.

Jorgensen, Jeana. 2007. "A Wave of the Magic Wand: Fairy Godmothers in Contemporary American Media." *Marvels & Tales* 21 (2): 216–27.

Kaiʻili, Tēvita O. 2016. "Goddess Hina: The Missing Heroine from Disney's *Moana.*" *The Huffington Post*, December 6. www.huffingtonpost.com/entry/goddess-hina-the-missing-heroine-from-disney%CA%BCs-moana_us_5839f343e4b0a79f7433b6e5.

Kubitschko, Sebastian. 2012. "Critical Media Studies in a Time of Communicative Capitalism: An Interview with Jodi Dean." *PLATFORM: Journal of Media and Communication* 4 (1): 39–44.

Lackey, Mercedes. 2004. *The Fairy Godmother (Tales of the Five Hundred Kingdoms, Book 1).* New York: Luna.

LaPensée, Elizabeth. 2014. "Survivance among Social Impact Games." *Journal of Canadian Game Studies Association* 8 (3): 43–60.

LaPensée, Elizabeth, and Jason Edward Lewis. 2013. "Call It a Vision Quest: Machinima in a First Nations Context." In *Understanding Machinima: Essays on Filmmaking in Virtual Worlds*, edited by Jenna Ng, 105–77. London: Bloomsbury.

Leitch, Thomas. 2008. "Adaptation Studies at a Crossroads." *Adaptation* 1 (1): 63–77.

Maxwell, Richard, and Toby Miller. 2011. "Old, New and Middle-Aged Media Convergence." *Cultural Studies* 25: 585–603.

Merrin, William. 2014. *Media Studies 2.0.* New York: Routledge.

Norrington, Alison. 2010. "Harnessing 'e' in Storyworlds: Engage, Enhance, Experience, Entertain." *Publishing Research Quarterly* 26: 96–105.

Pratten, Robert. 2015. *Getting Started in Transmedia Storytelling: A Practical Guide for Beginners.* 2nd ed. North Charleston, SC: CreateSpace Independent Publishing Platform/Amazon.

Preston, Cathy Lynn. 2004. "Disrupting the Boundaries of Genre and Gender: Postmodernism and the Fairy Tale." In *Fairy Tales and Feminism: New Approaches*, edited by Donald Haase, 197–212. Detroit: Wayne State UP.

Sciretta, Peter. 2016. "How Disney Formed the Oceanic Story Trust to Make 'Moana' More Authentic." *Slashfilm*, September 7. www.slashfilm.com/moana-oceanic-story-trust/.

Tatar, Maria. 2010. "Why Fairy Tales Matter: The Performative and the Transformative." *Western Folklore* 69 (1): 55–64.

Tiffin, Jessica. 2009. *Marvelous Geometry: Narrative and Metafiction in Modern Fairy Tale.* Detroit: Wayne State UP.

"Todrick Hall's 'CinderFella,' a Pro-Gay Take on a Disney Classic." 2012. *HuffPost Queer Voices*, July 7. www.huffin gtonpost.com/2012/07/25/todrick-halls-cinderfella_n_1702228.html.

Vizenor, Gerald. 2008. "The Aesthetics of Survivance: Literary Theory and Practice." In *Survivance: Narratives of Native Presence*, edited by Gerald Vizenor, 1–24. Lincoln: U Nebraska P.

Wilson, Valerie. 2016. "People of Color Will be a Majority of the American Working Class in 2032: What This Means for the Effort to Grow Wages and Reduce Inequality." *Economic Policy Institute*, June 9. www.epi.org/publication/the-changing-demographics-of-americas-working-class/.

Yiin, Wesley. 2016. "Is Disney's Portrayal of Maui, a Polynesian Demigod, in 'Moana' Culturally Insensitive?" *The Washington Post*, June 28. www.washingtonpost.com/news/morning-mix/wp/2016/06/28/is-disneys-portrayal-of-maui-a-polynesian-demigod-in-moana-racially-insensitive/.

Zipes, Jack. 2008. "Why Fantasy Matters Too Much." *CLC Web: Comparative Literature and Culture* 10 (4/3). 1–12.

———. 2010. "Foreword: Grounding the Spell." In *Fairy Tale Films: Visions of Ambiguity*, edited by Pauline Greenhill and Sidney Eve Matrix, ix–xiii. Logan: Utah State UP.

———. 2012. *The Irresistible Fairy Tale: The Cultural and Social History of a Genre.* Princeton, NJ: Princeton UP.

Mediagraphy

AppLit: Resources for Readers and Teachers of Appalachian Literature for Children and Young Adults. 2000. Creators Judy A. Teaford and Tina Hanlon. http://www2.ferrum.edu/AppLit/.

Grey's Anatomy (TV). 2005–. Creator Shonda Rhimes. USA.

———. "Dream a Little Dream of Me, Part 1." 2008a. Episode 5.1. 25 Sept.

———. "Dream a Little Dream of Me, Part 2." 2008b. Episode 5.2. 25 Sept.

Grimm (TV). 2011–2017. Creators Stephen Carpenter, David Greenwalt, and Jim Kouf. USA.

Happyland (TV). 2014. Creator Ben Epstein. USA.

Jane the Virgin (TV). 2014a–. Creator Jennie Snyder Urman. USA.

———. "Chapter 3." 2014b. Episode 1.3. 27 Oct.

The Journal of Mythic Arts: Winner of the World Fantasy Award. 1997. Creators Terri Windling and Midori Snyder. http://endicottstudio.typepad.com/jomahome/.

"Mana Moana: We Are Moana, We Are Maui." 2016–. *Facebook Community Page.* www.facebook.com/manamo anawearemoanawearemaui/.

Moana. 2016. Directors Ron Clements, John Musker, Don Hall, and Chris Williams. USA.

Once Upon a Time (TV). 2011–. Creators Edward Kitsis and Adam Horowitz. USA.

The Princess and the Frog. 2009. Directors Ron Clements and John Muster. USA.

Shrek 2. 2004. Directors Adam Adamson, Kelly Asbury, and Konrad Vernon. USA.

SurLaLune. 1998–. Creator Heidi Ann Heiner. www.surlalunefairytales.com/.

19

CRIME/JUSTICE

Sue Short

The fairy tale's attitude to crime is not necessarily consistent with notions of "justice," with many seemingly reprehensible acts either going unpunished or explicitly rewarded. One reason is that certain forms of conduct were not officially deemed "crimes" when these stories first emerged, yet an additional factor is that fairy tales tend to dispense with rules—and regard officialdom with some suspicion also. There is consequently no concept of an effective police force that will investigate and arrest wrongdoers, a reliable legal system to try them, or any guarantee of an appropriate punishment if found guilty (and miscarriages of justice—where any such trial occurs—engender little faith in such a system). Instead, great flexibility is shown in terms of "outlawed" or illicit conduct, and any form of retribution is often either supernatural or non-existent. Frequently, those we would regard as victims of crime are simply presented as unlucky, often receiving no recompense, despite experiencing behavior that we would now deem to be unlawful.

We might consider examples such as "Perceforest" and "Sun, Moon and Talia," precursors to "Sleeping Beauty" (ATU 410), in which young women are sexually violated as they sleep, or equally unsavory tales featuring daughters "romantically" pursued by their fathers, none of which culminate in the respective males being punished for what we would clearly consider to be criminal acts today. (Indeed, spurious means are used to mitigate any responsibility, blaming Venus for sexually assaulting an unconscious woman, while cases of "unnatural love" are explained as being tempted by the devil or driven by devotion for the girl's deceased mother.) The outcomes of such acts are especially jarring. Daughters who are driven from their homes by amorous fathers are often happily reconciled with them in time (a fate conspicuously denied to abusive mothers) while tales of comatose women unwittingly impregnated by intruders have a still more problematic denouement: not only accepting these men as their husbands when they awake, but proving remarkably steadfast in their devotion. Evidently, the very idea of "consent" is deemed immaterial in such tales, with no crime seemingly committed and thus no need for perpetrators to be punished (in fact, in a perversion of contemporary mores, rapists are even deemed to be saviors in these scenarios, rousing women from an enchanted sleep and thereby breaking the curse they were under).

Cases of child abuse often have an equally odd conclusion (similarly granting male parents a reprieve). Hansel and Gretel (in ATU 327A) may be abandoned in the woods by their father (twice), yet he is not deemed to be the real antagonist. Killing the witch provides an apparent means of dispatching their mother (co-conspirator in the abandonment plan), who is conveniently deceased once they arrive home again, with no recriminations for Dad. Equally, the father in "The Juniper Tree" (ATU 720) enjoys a pleasant meal with his resurrected son, once the wicked stepmother is killed, despite unwittingly eating his body earlier in the tale! Such tales evidently need to be understood in the context of their time, their culture, and their prevailing attitudes. In fairy-tale lore cruelties and hardships must be endured and overcome, and any form of retribution is deemed a personal (and somewhat arbitrary) matter, rather than an offense to be reported, tried, and punished. Before the days of political campaigning led to cases of sexual abuse and child cruelty being officially made crimes that were punishable by law, there was no recourse to external agencies, leaving protagonists without any official sanction. Maidens taken advantage of in their sleep take solace in the children that are conceived as a result, while abused or endangered children are forced to either leave the family home or hope for supernatural salvation (with a paternal ideal also saved in the process!).

Modern variations in film provide an illuminating take on such scenarios. For example, if sexual assault is problematically treated in folklore, sometimes scarcely even considered to be a criminal act, this stance has been significantly modified. Two contrasting takes on the violation of an incumbent woman each vilify the act while presenting divergent responses. *Rosemary's Baby* (1968) is especially discomfiting because it situates rape in the marital bed, while the wife slept, the husband explaining the next morning that he didn't want to miss "baby night." Sure enough, she discovers she is pregnant, and, in a manner akin to the aforementioned tales, she accepts her situation. The devil himself is to blame (using Rosemary to conceive his own child), leaving her a hapless victim. A radically different example is offered in *Kill Bill* (2003–2004). The heroine (initially billed only as "the Bride") is pimped out by hospital orderlies as she lies in a coma. Waking during the assault, she murders both assailants and sets about finding her former lover—the man responsible for putting her in a coma, whose child she was carrying at the time—finally killing him too. The contrast between a meek wife (exploited by her husband in the worst way imaginable) and a woman who takes lethal revenge against her abusers highlights dramatically different responses to an equally abhorrent act. Feminist protest evidently informs the sexual politics of director Quentin Tarantino's film (made three decades on and notably co-written with its star, Uma Thurman), as well as accompanying legal and cultural changes that deem the Bride's vengeance to be just, while Rosemary's plight—and her comparative powerlessness—attests to conditions that led to such protest in the first place.[1]

If sexual assault is problematically treated in some folktales, murder is regarded as a serious crime, often demanding fatal repercussions for perpetrators, especially where children are concerned. Mining ideas reminiscent of "The Juniper Tree," horror cinema is populated with various mistreated children who acquire untold power in death (including hit franchises like *The Ring* and *The Grudge*). Dispensing with any notion of a protective maternal spirit,[2] such figures take vengeance for themselves and seem incapable of being appeased. Even when murderous parents have been eliminated, more people are killed in seemingly random fashion, as if all the living are somehow to blame for failing to protect them, resulting in an endless and unbreakable curse. In other cases the dead are able to find closure through killing those responsible and form interesting alliances in doing so. The murder of innocent women by husbands and suitors—a motif popularized in the likes of "Bluebeard" (ATU 312) and "The Robber Bride" (ATU 955)—has been interestingly revised on screen, allowing female victims the means to secure justice. In *The Gift* (2000) and *What Lies Beneath* (2000) murdered women warn endangered counterparts about the men they are involved with and finally kill their assailants. Although set in the modern world, there is no sense of any official means of retribution available, necessitating a supernatural solution instead. Their killers are so ostensibly respectable that the police are unlikely to trace their crimes to them, let alone secure a conviction in court, making vigilante justice seem to be the only form available. In all such cases we are reassured that, while evil figures seemingly get away with murder, the truth will emerge and justice will eventually be served. Those formerly denied any rights or status in society—namely women and children—achieve an unprecedented degree of power in death, and while child spirits are often fairly random in their targets (unleashing their fury at innocent parties), this is not the case with victims of duplicitous men, who single out their killers for revenge, while protecting other women from sharing their tragic fate.

As Maria Tatar has noted (2006), similar examples of female kinship and camaraderie predate these supernatural thrillers (including the sister in "Bluebeard" who alerts her brothers about the murderous fiend threatening his new bride, the female cook in "The Robber Bride" who warns a young bride-to-be about her fiancé's murderous ways, and the youngest sister in "Fitcher's Bird" [ATU 311], who risks her life to find and resurrect her murdered siblings, returning them home and securing their killer's death). Such examples set important narrative precedents, depicting violent men thwarted by females who unite to put an end to their crimes. Although these heroines tend to rely on male intervention when it comes to taking violent reprisals against such men, modern variants make a woman fully responsible for defending herself, uniting with other females who were formerly considered rivals, an outcome that suggests the influence of progressive sexual politics (even as it points to continued failings in terms of official protection for women).

By the same token, if vigilante justice often appears to be the only recourse available, this situation also enables greater agency for victims of crime, who thus assume the role of avenging heroes. *Kill Bill*'s Bride undergoes this dramatic transition, taking direct vengeance on her attackers (and wasting no sentiment seeking to preserve any ideals of family unity when she realizes she is now a mother, dispatching the child's father, along with all the enemies he rallied against her). Modern narratives are obviously at liberty to grant protagonists greater freedom than tales of old—the woman in question is a trained assassin, with skills that enable her to take revenge against those who have wronged her—one that is bloody, brutal, and very much outside the bounds of the law.

This last point is a crucial one because it demonstrates the kind of ambivalence often seen in the fairy tale's depiction of crime and justice. By dispatching with any ideas of a legal process to be followed, a story can be told with heightened risk and added drama. A hero may be placed in greater peril, having to take on enemies single-handedly, yet in overcoming unlikely odds their success is granted mythic proportions. The result may not be believable, but this is scarcely the remit of such narratives, permitting a level of wish-fulfillment in dramatic reversals of fortune and astonishing feats of bravery. We might also note that justice, in such instances, is frequently hinged on meting out extreme violence, favoring an "eye for an eye," regardless of what any laws may dictate. This is evidently intended to satisfy the blood lust of audiences, providing a denouement commensurate with hard times and equally tough outlooks. As is frequently suggested in fairy tales (and their more brutal folkloric predecessors), life is harsh, often cruel and unfair, and a degree of ruthlessness is necessary to survive.

This is especially true, it seems, when it comes to property rights, with poverty-stricken protagonists often radically redistributing the assets of wealthier citizens. The pint-sized hero of "Hop o' my Thumb" (ATU 327B) swindles riches from a slumbering giant, while the equally diminutive hero of "Tom Thumb" (ATU 700) also advances himself by thievery, joining a gang of robbers to steal from the king's coffers. In such cases we are invited to applaud criminality and champion "deserving" perpetrators. Stealing is sanctioned as a means of getting ahead, rewarding conniving and duplicity for those on the lower rung of the social ladder (provided their targets are comparatively rich and/or villainous). If fairy-tale audiences are reassured by heinous crimes being punished in the aforementioned examples, narratives where vast riches are attained, without work, place us on a different side of the law—in league with perpetrators of crimes that are evidently taken less seriously—albeit with some morally tenuous results.

Aladdin (in ATU 561) acquires limitless wealth through theft, stealing magical artifacts (after swindling the stranger who informs him of their whereabouts) and thereafter getting whatever he wishes for. His crime may be explicable on the grounds of need rather than greed, with a widowed mother to provide for, yet he is also quite a dubious character, and we might note that in early versions of the tale he takes to stealing women too, using the genie's power to abduct his princess, rather than wooing her with treasure or winning her father over. As with similar scenarios involving wastrels on the make, and given to capturing females rather than courting them, we are invited to applaud such daring and presume that their love interests will feel the same way.[3] Theft, in all these scenarios, is deemed a legitimate means of advancement in an otherwise unequal world and is thus rarely reprimanded, making such figures the recognizable precursors of modern-day antiheroes who rely on their wits to get by, with corporations and casinos substituting for kings' coffers and fabulous treasure in contemporary scenarios. Notably, beyond presenting a frivolous escapade, a continued sense of injustice and inequality often motivates theft on screen, a point readily made with examples like *Blood Diamond* (2006) and *Three Kings* (1999), both of which allow evident underdogs to profit through theft yet applaud this act as a necessary evening of unequal odds, affirming the injustice and corruption that led to the acquisition of diamonds and gold in the first place.

The fairy tale's attitude to law-breaking is clearly based on who we are invited to sympathize with, rather than strictly observing the letter of the law. Even murder is sanctioned, in some cases, as justifiable homicide if the assailant is personally threatened. Hansel and Gretel are thus permitted to kill the cannibalistic witch intent on devouring them—and are even rewarded with her treasure—while their victim is seen to get her just desserts. The hero in "Jack and the Beanstalk" (ATU 328A) is on shakier moral grounds. Although also on the brink of starvation before he resorts to theft and murder, his crimes seem more premeditated, repeatedly entering the ogre's home to steal his belongings until he is eventually discovered and pursued. He may have a mother to look after (like Aladdin), yet he makes her an accessory to murder (instructing her to bring the weapon), and although we are asked to justify this act on the grounds of self-defense (with the ogre additionally claimed as responsible for killing and stealing from Jack's father, according to some versions), this motive would not hold much water in a court of law! Some argue that these tales are empowering for children, who identify with the diminutive protagonists able to outsmart oversized oppressors (often read as figurative parent figures) while Zipes perceives a politically subversive message proffered in the stark inequalities shown—and the suggestion that they can be overcome.[4]

We might ask if social injustice is truly countered, however, or if these tales simply promote ruthless self-interest? (In the same vein, when underdog characters succeed to the throne, deposing dishonest kings, we have no reason to assume that their rule will be any fairer, often having advanced through equally dishonest means.) Wish-fulfillment is an understandable pleasure, yet a discrepancy often arises when we look at the underlying message of such narratives and ask if the values promoted are necessarily positive (and if we would really want our lives to be governed by a similar laissez-faire attitude). An additional inconsistency arises in narratives that remind us to be careful what we wish for. Despite numerous tales designed as consolatory fantasies (concocting feasts for the famished and vast riches for the impoverished), an equivalent number warn against their consequences, from overflowing porridge pots that threaten to destroy a village to "ill-gotten gains" that prove to be equally destructive.

If vast wealth is often promoted as the solution to life's troubles, a number of tales warn that material pursuit at all costs will only invite danger and death. This cautionary message is apparent from some of our oldest tales to more familiar incarnations in modern crime drama. The story of "Ali Baba and the Forty Thieves" (ATU 954) resembles a heist-gone-wrong plot,

CRIME/JUSTICE

bringing apparent good fortune followed by calamity when the owners of stolen treasure seek reprisals, murdering Ali's brother, Kassim, and lying in wait outside his own home. Fortunately, his female servant, Morgiana, is willing to murder to save his household, putting an end to the threat, although the message remains that there is no such thing as easy money and that in entering the world of criminals you are liable to forfeit your life. Kassim's fatal flaw is not simply in forgetting the password needed to get out of the thieves' lair but his desire to go there alone, despite being wealthy already. Greed is invariably corrupting, such narratives assert, reprimanding the desire for wealth as divisive and destructive.

In the tale type known as "The Treasure Finders Who Murder One Another" (ATU 763), money simply brings out the worst in people, allowing no one to prosper ultimately. Films that rework this plot include *The Treasure of the Sierra Madre* (1948), *Shallow Grave* (1994), *A Simple Plan* (1999), and *No Country for Old Men* (2007). In each case protagonists come across money that does not belong to them and pay a heavy price trying to keep it. Pursued and threatened by the rightful owners (a plot twist akin to "Ali Baba"), they ultimately lose everything they have. Such "accidental" wealth is not a boon for those who find it, but fosters murderous rivalries, resulting in a situation where no one manages to keep their hoard in the end. In some cases this failure seems just (the yuppies in *Shallow Grave* are smug and crucially do not need the money they find), yet we genuinely want more deserving characters to succeed and cannot help but feel pity when they fail, some dying pointlessly for an empty dream.

Is a sense of cosmic irony at work in such denouements, affirming the old adage that "cheats never prosper"? Is the intended message that the pursuit of wealth is inimical to social relations and that we should not place such value on material possessions? If so, there are a significant number of conflicting tales that are only too happy to peddle dreams of instant fortunes without the toil. Such fantasies are no less diverting today than they were in the past, offering the vicarious pleasure of seeing unlikely heroes prosper. Interestingly, although fairy tales have often been wary of female covetousness and wrongdoing (see Tatar's *Off with Their Heads!* [1993] for a sobering list of female "sins" curtailed), some films have rewritten these rules, presenting females who take a lead role in the crime stakes and rob themselves a fortune. From the gang of women who hold up a bank in *Domino* (2005), the female couple who steal from the mob in *Bound* (1996), or the eponymous heroine who gets away with a haul of drug money in *Jackie Brown* (1997), new avenues of criminality are being explored by female characters, some of whom prove to be as wily as Morgiana (the crucial force behind Ali Baba's rise in fortunes) and able to profit more directly from their daring.[5]

We are even seeing new takes on "Red Riding Hood" (ATU 333) where male predators are dispatched by their victims, rather than any third party (see Kohm and Greenhill 2013, 2014). *Freeway* (1996) provides a salient lesson about the flawed legal system that makes vigilante justice seem as much a necessity today as it was deemed in pre-modern times: the only permissible route to take against wrongdoers. Our adolescent heroine, Vanessa, fights back against the middle-class pervert intent on raping and killing her and is rewarded with a custodial sentence for seriously injuring him (her background and prior record making her more easily criminalized in the eyes of the law). By the time two police officers discover the truth (finding evidence in his garage of past "trophies"), her grandmother has been killed by the same culprit, yet our heroine is also at the scene, having broken free of her correctional facility, and finishes the predator off. As modern versions of the "huntsman," the police clearly prove wanting, leaving it to an extraordinarily tough young woman to effectively do their job. A similar outlook is consequently presented as tales of old, suggesting that when it comes to survival we are on our own and that any means are justified to defend ourselves. *In the Cut* (2003) revises "Bluebeard" to offer a comparable lesson: the law proves incapable of apprehending the

175

perpetrator (who happens to be a policeman), requiring an imperiled woman to take the law into her own hands to dispatch him.[6]

The fairy tale's ambivalence with regard to criminality is thus apparent in modern incarnations, approving a degree of irreverence with regard to the law, especially when measures are taken in the interest of justice. Even so, rooting for law-breakers (as we sometimes will) does not necessarily mean they will succeed, while some extremely unpleasant felons may evade capture or censure, despite being ripe for a fall. Fairy tales have a long history of such inconsistencies, allowing (and even approving) some seemingly reprehensible acts. Ruth Bottigheimer's conception of fate as a "wheel of fortune" in medieval tales, stressing "the uncertain tenure of earthly goods and success" (1987, 127), is a useful way to make sense of the somewhat amoral disposition still to be found in some versions (and the often haphazard fortunes granted protagonists).

As Tatar has pointed out (2003), fairy tales were never ideal lessons in moral instruction, not only because of their marked inconsistency but because many seemingly heroic protagonists do not behave particularly well, frequently flouting the rules of everyday good conduct. Then again, these were never intended as *everyday* narratives; they are larger-than-life tales, and we do not consequently expect to see mundane or even believable events portrayed, but dramatic extremes. Transformation (of one's form or fortune) is the key imperative in such tales and virtually any means used to achieve this. The same is true of the narratives that draw from fairy tales, offering us murders and malevolent ghosts, heists and hold-ups, and all manner of excursions into what we would now call "criminality," yet without any guarantee of "justice" necessarily being served. Ultimately, life is still presented as fickle and unfair, the world is rife with wrongdoers (including those you might least suspect), officials still prove inept and untrustworthy, and—in lieu of a fairy godmother, benevolent genie, or handy hunter offering protection from mortal woes—there is no external force to rely on but oneself. The letter of the law may not always be obeyed, and we may well cheer protagonists who flout such rules, yet survival—making it to the end credits—is often the best we can hope for in terms of a happy end.

Related topics: Broadcast; Cinematic; Gender; Horror; Sexualities/Queer and Trans Studies; TV Drama

Notes

1. It is worth noting that marital rape was only deemed a criminal act in the last few decades, a law that is by no means universal still. Although it is never made explicit whether Rosemary is truly the victim of a satanic cult or experiencing post-partum hysteria, she is still impregnated when asleep and thus either raped by her husband or he facilitates the devil in doing so. Either way, she is as powerless as her folkloric predecessors. Curiously, in the TV mini-series made in 2014, although the modern-day Rosemary eventually leaves her husband, she similarly seems to suffer from a lack of choices in other respects. Impregnated while she is passed out, she sees the pregnancy to full-term (with no apparent option available) and proudly deems her son "perfect" in the end, apparently reconciled to the circumstances that created him. Almodovar's *Talk to Her* (2002) makes an interesting comparison on the theme of non-consensual sex and resulting pregnancy, with the act criminalized in this instance (by hospital authorities) and punished—the suspect is imprisoned and eventually kills himself. The fact that the victim wakes from her coma while giving birth offers a pointed contrast to the likes of "Perceforest," although the child in this case is stillborn. See Novoa (2005) for further discussion of the film's relationship to fairy tales.
2. The motif of the maternal spirit who watches over her children may have served a dual psychological role, employing a belief in the afterlife to comfort bereaved children while also warning resentful stepparents to take good care of their non-biological charges, suggesting reprisals may be taken if they are harmed. See Warner's *From the Beast to the Blonde* (1995) for further suggestions about the psychosocial role tales may have played, both for listeners and tellers.
3. The *Arabian Nights* tales include other instances where women are abducted, acts that are similarly not criminalized or narratively censured. Modern versions tend to efface this aspect of "Aladdin," including Disney's film, which has Princess Jasmine directly choose him as her husband.

CRIME/JUSTICE

4. Zipes has made this assertion about the progressive sociopolitical ramifications of fairy tales throughout his career; see especially his early work, including *Breaking the Magic Spell* (1979) and *Fairy Tales and the Art of Subversion* (1983).

5. Morgiana is the unsung, and often unnamed, hero of "Ali Baba" who does all the heavy lifting in terms of violently defending the household. A remarkable female character, she might be equated with the female assassins and bodyguards we have since seen on screen.

6. Campion's TV drama *Top of the Lake* reprises this theme of female vigilantism against male violence, partly necessitated by corruption in the police force. A twelve-year-old girl is raped and impregnated by her father after being drugged with Rohypnol. Any conviction seems unlikely as he is protected by a senior police officer who is guilty of the same crimes. Both men are eventually shot by their victims, killed in the first case, left a paraplegic in the second (as the sequel reveals), and intent on manipulating the law to prosecute his "assailant" (a twist reminiscent of *Freeway*).

References Cited and Further Reading

Bottigheimer, Ruth B. 1987. *Grimms' Bad Girls and Bold Boys: The Moral and Social Vision of the Tales.* New Haven, CT: Yale UP.

Kohm, Steven, and Pauline Greenhill. 2013. "'This Is the North, Where We Do What We Want:' Popular Green Criminology and 'Little Red Riding Hood' Films." In *Routledge International Handbook of Green Criminology*, edited by Nigel South and Avi Brisman, 365–78. New York: Routledge.

———. 2014. "'Little Red Riding Hood' Crime Films: Critical Variations on Criminal Themes." *Law, Culture and the Humanities* 10 (2): 257–78.

Novoa, Adriana. 2005. "Whose Talk Is It? Almodovar and the Fairy Tale in *Talk to Her.*" *Marvels & Tales* 19 (2): 224–48.

Short, Sue. 2006. *Misfit Sisters: Screen Horror and Rite of Passage.* London: Palgrave.

———. 2015. *Fairy Tale and Film: Old Tales with a New Spin.* London: Palgrave.

Tatar, Maria. 1993. *Off with Their Heads! Fairy Tales and the Culture of Childhood.* Princeton, NJ: Princeton UP.

———. 2003. *The Hard Facts of the Grimms' Fairy Tales.* Princeton, NJ: Princeton UP.

———. 2006. *Secrets beyond the Door: The Story of Bluebeard and His Wives.* Princeton, NJ: Princeton UP.

Warner, Marina. 1995. *From the Beast to the Blonde: On Fairy Tales and Their Tellers.* London: Vintage.

Zipes, Jack. 1979. *Breaking the Magic Spell: Radical Theories of Folk and Fairy Tales.* London: Heinemann.

———. 1983. *Fairy Tales and the Art of Subversion: The Classical Genre for Children and the Process of Civilization.* New York: Wildman.

Mediagraphy

Aladdin. 1992. Directors Ron Clements and John Musker. USA.

Blood Diamond. 2006. Director Edward Zwick. USA.

Bound. 1996. Director The Wachowskis. USA.

Domino. 2005. Director Tony Scott. USA.

Freeway. 1996. Director Matthew Bright. USA.

The Gift. 2000. Director Sam Raimi. USA.

The Grudge. 2004. Director Takashi Shimizu. USA.

In the Cut. 2003. Director Jane Campion. USA.

Jackie Brown. 1997. Director Quentin Tarantino. USA.

Kill Bill. 2003–2004. Director Quentin Tarantino. USA.

No Country for Old Men. 2007. Directors Joel and Ethan Coen. USA.

The Ring. 2002. Director Gore Verbinski. USA.

Rosemary's Baby. 1968. Director Roman Polanski. USA.

——— (TV mini-series). 2014. Director Agnieszka Holland. USA.

Shallow Grave. 1994. Director Danny Boyle. UK.

A Simple Plan. 1999. Director Sam Raimi. USA.

Talk to Her. 2002. Director Pedro Almodovar. Spain.

Three Kings. 1999. Director David O'Russell. USA.

Top of the Lake (TV). 2013. Director Jane Campion. New Zealand.

The Treasure of the Sierra Madre. 1948. Director John Huston. USA.

What Lies Beneath. 2000. Director Robert Zemeckis. USA.

20

DISNEY CORPORATION

Lynda Haas and Shaina Trapedo

What do *Snow White and the Seven Dwarfs* (1937), *The Muppets* (2015), *My Neighbor Totoro* (1988), *Winnie the Pooh* (2011), *Star Wars* (2015), and *The Avengers* (2012) all have in common? They are properties of The Walt Disney Company (hereafter Disney)—a highly diversified, multinational mass media and entertainment conglomerate, considered one of the most influential brands in the world and valued by Forbes (2015) at approximately $180 billion. More than any other entity, Disney is responsible for Western culture's basic perceptions about the fairy-tale genre—the company borrows, appropriates, and revises the tales and then, with global distribution channels in every conceivable medium (print, film, television, Internet, music, radio, live performances, retail stores, theme parks, and cruise ships), makes their version pervasive.

For example, Disney Publishing Worldwide is the world's largest producer of children's books and magazines with over 700 million products sold each year; its subsidiaries (including Hyperion Press, ESPN Books, Disney Learning, and Marvel Press) publish books, magazines, comics/graphic novels, and digital products in eighty-five countries in seventy-five languages. Disney Interactive, the company's online/digital arm, offers multi-platform video games and online/mobile gateways; the studio entertainment division, the empire's foundation, includes Walt Disney Studios (live-action films), Walt Disney Animation, Disney Nature, Pixar, Industrial Light and Magic, Marvel, and Touchstone. Disney is also pervasive in TV programming, with subsidiaries Disney Channels Worldwide, Disney Family, ABC, ABC Family, and ESPN and, in partnership with Hearst, the History Channel, A&E, and Lifetime (The Walt Disney Company 2015). For almost a century, and with a very wide reach, Disney has been telling and retelling their versions of fairy tales to generations of children and their parents.

The company began with Walt Disney (hereafter Walt), whose own rags-to-riches story, a realized American Dream, became a core motif of the Disney version, expertly embedded in their early fairy-tale adaptation films such as *Snow White and the Seven Dwarfs* (1937), *Pinocchio* (1940), and *Cinderella* (1950), and the foundation for the Disney empire even today. In most Disney fairy tales, the dream motif is presented as one of "true love," and the protagonist, who generally starts in a humble position, has realized, by the story's end, a carefree "happily ever after" existence. "True love" and "happily ever after" do appear in some classic fairy tales—but not the majority; Disney either focuses on tales that include these elements or adds them to tales that do not, amplifying and Americanizing the dream motif and, at the same time, narrowing perceptions of what "fairy tale" means.

The Disney signature is a mega-brand logo that appears with a sprinkling of fairy dust as part of the opening credits of every film. It's a common misperception that this is Walt's signature and that he was an artist, animator, writer, and/or director—in reality, he began as a cartoonist, but learned early on that his real talent was facilitating and innovating. He wasn't the only, or even the first, Hollywood producer to make use of classic fairy tales, but his versions have become a staple of our cultural consciousness. Like his fairy-tale storytelling predecessors, Walt grasped the magical power of narrative and used that gift to charm patrons and delight audiences. In his role as producer—who had a hand in everything that the writers, cartoonists, animators, and directors were creating—he left his unique imprint (Schickel 1968, 33). This is Walt's true signature, more important than the stylized Disney logo: he taught his team how to delight audiences and reflect their values; it is this signature that remains a vital part of the company today as Disney continues its role of culture's magic mirror.

Because Disney has been a pervasive and consistent reflection of culture, the study of its versions provides insight into how preferences, ideals, and values have changed through the years. Also, because the empire began by appropriating fairy tales that speak to both children and parents, Disney learned early how to attract this dual audience: children and parents alike have come to equate all fairy tales with Disney. Most parents consider Disney products kid-friendly, and thus rarely question their children's consumption, and children, who watch the films multiple times, learn their implicit lessons. Thus, Disney's impact on the cultural imaginary, which begins in childhood, becomes what Henry Giroux (2004) has called "public pedagogy" (59).

Establishing the Disney Empire: The First Princess Films

Walt Disney Productions began making animated shorts in 1928 by adapting classic fairy tales and setting them to music. Between 1929 and 1939, the Disney team created 75 Silly Symphonies (often featuring Mickey Mouse) and seven times won Oscars for Best Animated Short Film. One of the best-received, *Three Little Pigs* (1933), established practices responsible for Disney's current popularity. First, Disney's talent for innovation: *Three Little Pigs* was the first film to use the now standard storyboard process (Gabler 2007, 415) and introduced "personality animation," in which each character is created to focus on one main trait; this became a foundational practice in Disney feature films starting with the dwarf characters in *Snow White and the Seven Dwarfs* and may be one reason they resonate with young viewers. Although considered an innovation in film, personality animation parallels character conventions in classic fairy tales: characters are usually flat, simple, and focused on one trait, completely good or entirely evil, and easy to identify.

Another aspect of *Three Little Pigs* that grounded future films and contributed to Disney's continuing popularity was the musical score. It included the song "Who's Afraid of the Big Bad Wolf?" by Frank Churchill and Ann Ronell, which became a best-selling hit that had a significant impact on American history and culture, as Brandie Ashe (2012) explains:

> [W]ith some encouragement from United States President Franklin D. Roosevelt, who called the cartoon his favorite film, [the song] became the unofficial anthem of the Great Depression, a way for people to thumb their noses at the dire state of the economy. [. . .] And as the United States entered World War II in the next decade, "Big Bad Wolf" found new life as a musical "screw you" to Nazi Germany.

Tracking the development of fairy tales from their oral tradition, Jack Zipes argues that the change in media to written tales in the nineteenth century "violated the communal aspects of folk tale" that brought people together and that, by transforming text into animated image, Disney secured a "cultural stranglehold on the fairy tale" (1996, 21) that perpetuates single versions of the once mutable tales that were customized to reflect the values of various communities. However, through the studio's unique investment in developing music and lyrics to enhance the stories, Disney has arguably restored some oral and communal properties of the fairy tale that were compromised by the rise of print culture. In perfecting the genre of the musical fairy tale, Disney has demonstrated its commitment to promoting "communal harmony" for its increasingly global audience by delivering messages that resonate in story, song, and social relevance.

Walt was not one to rest on his laurels, and after *Three Little Pigs* famously said, "You can't top pigs with pigs" (Gabler 2007, 415). In mid-1934, he announced the studio's newest project: the first animated feature film, *Snow White and the Seven Dwarfs*. Although most Hollywood insiders called the project "Disney's Folly," and even his brother, Roy, and his wife, Lillian, tried to talk him out of moving forward, Walt was convinced that feature-length animated films would be the studio's future and would increase its revenues, so he mortgaged his house to pay for production costs (Thomas 1991, 66). When it was released nationwide in 1937, the film's success sealed the Disney brand and instituted conventions that became standard in future productions.

The success that Disney now enjoys and its significant impact as creator and purveyor of culture began with the animated feature films, and more specifically with the early princess films. Although other films in the early days helped crystallize the animated feature film as a genre, the features based on tales from the Brothers Grimm and Charles Perrault formed a foundation and inaugurated the "Disney Princess," even though at the time the company didn't market the characters in this way. It wasn't until 2000 that Andy Mooney, chair of Disney's Consumer Products Division, patented the young heroines of Disney fairy-tale adaptations as a group and aggressively marketed the Disney Princess brand, which is now a multibillion dollar franchise with over 25,000 different consumer products; as Peggy Orenstein (2006) in the *New York Times* writes, "To call princesses a 'trend' among girls is like calling Harry Potter a book. [. . .] [It's] not only the fastest-growing brand the company has ever created, [. . .] it is on its way to becoming the largest girls' franchise on the planet."

The first Disney princess was drawn by Grim Natwick, who was famous for his creation of Betty Boop for Fleischer Studios; after auditioning over 150 girls, the team settled on the voice talent of Adriana Caselotti, who provided the high-pitched tone of Snow White (Smith 1996, 92); and to capture her movement, the animators filmed live-action footage of fifteen-year-old ballet dancer Marjorie Celeste Belcher. Revising her age in the Grimms' tale from seven to fifteen, and giving her the voice of a child, the body and movement of a dancer, and just a hint of heteronormative sex appeal lingering from her predecessor, Betty Boop, made Snow White another paradigm for all that followed. No matter how much they have changed over the decades as new artists, technologies, and attitudes contributed to the creation of Disney princesses, the combination of innocence and sexuality in a teenaged body has prevailed.

Snow White and the Seven Dwarfs was an instant blockbuster that established a number of firsts: it was the first feature-length animated film, thus establishing the now popular genre; it was the first animated film to use the multiplane camera (invented by Disney artists); and it was the first film to release an accompanying soundtrack. Building on the successful marriage of animation and music in the Disney shorts, the soundtrack became a bestseller and was nominated for Best Musical Score. Since then, Disney has produced fourteen feature-length animated films based on fairy tales, and ten have been nominated for, or won, Oscars for music (Kaufman 2012, 51).

The opening shot features a white leather-bound storybook that opens to reveal an illuminated manuscript beginning with the words "Once upon a time"; this scene signals the film's allegiance to its fairy-tale source, the Brothers Grimm tale "Schneewittchen" ("Little Snow White" ATU 709), and at the same time creates a frame around the story—the film ends with "happily ever after" and the closing of the book. This framing device was replicated in several Disney fairy tale films over the next two decades. However, the Disney storyline sanitizes the Grimms' tale, leaving out anything that would not play well with the film-going audiences of the late 1930s. For example, the stepmother's cannibalism is removed, as she does not eat the organs brought to her by the huntsman (which she thinks are Snow White's). Nor does she meet her death at Snow White's wedding according to the gruesome Grimm ending by being forced to dance in red-hot shoes. Instead, she falls from a high cliff with an off-screen scream all the way down into silence.

Although often criticized for sanitizing darker aspects such as these, the Disney team changed elements in much the same way as did the Brothers Grimm in their successive editions to make them more suitable for children and more in line with the dominant values of their Christian, middle-class audience. In the introduction to his translation of the 1812 edition of the tales, Zipes writes: "Wilhelm, who became the major editor from 1816 onward, [. . .] could not control his desire to make the tales more artistic to appeal to middle-class reading audiences." In the later editions, he writes, the brothers "vaccinated" the tales "with their sentimental Christianity and puritanical ideology" (2014, xx). For example, the evil biological mother in several tales from the 1812 edition was revised to an evil stepmother in later editions, and dialogue like "God will not forsake us" was added (Grimm and Grimm 2011).

Since they began as orally transmitted stories told by storytellers who no doubt embellished each telling with unique dramatic elements, traditional fairy tales have never had one fixed form. Snow White's story was in circulation long before it was written down by the Grimms, and Disney's version could be considered just another retelling with unique embellishments meant to cater to a specific audience. The problem most critics have is not that Disney changes the classic tales, but rather, that the Disney version has become, for most of the population, "the" version—a problem exacerbated by the company's aggressive trademarking practice, which shuts down other voices and secures ownership and authority for the Disney empire. Even the words "Snow White" are trademarked by Disney (U.S. Trademark 2013). In fact, Disney takes ownership of its properties so seriously that it has twice been able to change U.S. Patent Laws so that "Steamboat Willie," the first appearance of Mickey Mouse, would not become part of the public domain—an incident that patent lawyers have named "the Mickey Mouse Curve" (Schlackman 2014).

Some critics have more trouble with original elements that Disney's early fairy tales leave in rather than what they take out—most notably, the patriarchal view of the world and implicit lessons about gender roles. As Kaitlin Ebersol (2014) suggests, all Disney's early princess adaptations share the same basic plot: "a beautiful woman suffers because of circumstances out of her control and ultimately finds salvation in the love of a powerful man." The passivity of the female role is established by the first words Snow White sings: "I'm wishing for the one I love to find me today. I'm hoping and I'm dreaming of the nice things he'll say" ("I'm Wishing/ One Song" 1937). That Disney did not attempt to update the female role in the early films is not surprising since the goal was to make films that would bring the company popular acclaim, and the passive female role was the mainstream perception at the time.

Post-Walt Princesses, Old Tales, and New Directions

For almost three decades following Walt's death in 1966, the animation studio primarily produced films based on anthropomorphized animal characters that did not reach the levels of the earlier work. Competing interests like the growth of Disney's live-action feature films and the expansion of theme parks worldwide caused the animation department to slip into the role of the neglected stepchild—gradually driven out of the central corporate headquarters in Burbank into nearby trailers and drab office parks. Fifty years after *Snow White*, Disney's animation department was in danger of being disbanded and outsourced entirely. To Walt's nephew, Roy E. Disney, it must have seemed like the studio was losing its magic when he launched the "SaveDisney" campaign, claiming that he "felt creatively the company was not going anywhere interesting" (Schneider 1999).

In 1989, the help Disney so desperately needed would not come from air or land, but from sea. The release of *The Little Mermaid* (1989) signaled Disney's return to fairy-tale classics, initiating a decade that came to be known as the studio's "Renaissance" period. Under the new visionary direction of Roy E. Disney and Michael Eisner, the Disney films of the 1990s not only demonstrate the verve of the fairy-tale genre, but also Disney's developing awareness of its brand and cultural clout.

Unlike its cinematic predecessors, *The Little Mermaid* does not signal allegiance to its source by opening with a close-up of a leather-bound storybook, but rather, it employs the studio's newly developed Computer Animation Production System (CAPS) to put the audience eye level with dolphins jumping through the surf in its opening frames. Although Hans Christian Andersen's tale of the mermaid princess who falls in love with a human prince was one of the first film concepts Walt explored in the 1930s, it took two "waves" of feminism before Ariel—Disney's plucky and defiant ingénue—came ashore. Ron Clements and John Musker not only gave Andersen's mermaid a name, they also gave her a voice that challenged the patriarchal power structures of her father's kingdom. Laura Sells (1995) argues that in adapting the tale for its modern audience, Disney shifts the thematic focus of Andersen's plot from class struggle to gender privilege. Staying true to established Disney practice, the film bypasses the suffering and death of the heroine—not to mention the fairy tale's preoccupation with Protestant theology—and instead provides the "happily ever after" ending its audience expects. Although the film's rebellious and somewhat gawky princess swims against the tide, feminist critics still fault the studio for furnishing its impressionable viewers with yet another female role model whose only motivation is to find her prince.

Two years later, Disney replicated the formula of classic fairy tale plus modernized heroine plus Broadway musical to even greater critical and fiscal success with *Beauty and the Beast* (1991). Due to the musical talents of Alan Menken and Howard Ashman, the film not only won Oscars for Best Song and Best Score, it was also the first Disney animated feature to employ a female screenwriter, Linda Woolverton (who later wrote screenplays for several other Disney films, including *The Lion King* [1994] and *Maleficent* [2014]). Jeanne-Marie Leprince de Beaumont's 1756 French fairy tale ends happily, but Woolverton still had to "Disneyfy" the rest by dropping the sibling rivalry subplot and expunging the supplications to God and sexual tension laced throughout the original. Although possibly inspired by Jean Cocteau's character Avenant in his 1946 French film adaptation, Woolverton introduces an updated version of the classic Disney villain in the figure of Gaston, whose misogyny and egocentrism position him as the quintessential antagonist for the film's late-twentieth-century predominantly female viewers. Similar to Cinderella, Disney's Belle is a commoner, but that is where the comparisons end. Fashioned to mirror the cultural sensibilities of her 1990s audience, Belle is literary and outspoken. While she is adventurous like Ariel, her ambitions lie far beyond romance. Belle dreams of finding fulfillment outside of her provincial existence and expresses angst over the pressure to meet social expectations, singing, "I want so much more than they've got planned" ("Belle (Reprise)" 1991).

In addition to providing a role model for young audiences of whom parents and critics approved, the film offered another Disney first. While earlier adaptations uphold the "love at first sight" trope, *Beauty and the Beast* portrays the *process* of falling in love (largely contained to a montage sequence during the musical number "Something There" 1991). Initially praised as a progressive portrait of femininity, for all her resilience and compassion, ultimately Belle "marries a batterer" (Sun et al. 2002), and critics like June Cummins (1995) insist Belle perpetuates stereotypes about female domesticity and courtship consistent with Disney's earliest works.

Disney's continued effort to respond to cultural trends is visible in the last two princess projects that rounded out the Disney Renaissance. The third wave of feminism that hit in the early 1990s criticized earlier proponents for focusing on "problems of straight, white, upper- and middle-class women while ignoring issues specific to different races, classes, and orientation" (Ebersol 2014). *Aladdin* (1992) and *Mulan* (1998) feature non-European heroines whose stories are derived from Middle Eastern and Chinese folklore. Animators and writers again purged the darker elements of each story and embedded classic fairy-tale tropes, animal sidekicks, and "happily ever afters," although both films received critical attention for perpetuating stereotypes and Westernizing cultural icons. Still, with each new release during the 1990s, "Disney's influence" became "an almost inescapable part of growing up" (Jackson 1996) as its role transformed from reflecting to projecting social values for their young audience. The critical acclaim and financial gains received for their updated takes on fairy-tale classics were enough for the animation department to earn its very own happy ending, at least for the time being. By 1995, Walt Disney Feature Animation was restored to a "castle" all their own at the newly constructed Roy E. Disney Animation Building in Burbank.

In the early 2000s, the studio's focus shifted toward tween TV programming, live-action films, and "sci-fi excursions [which] reflected a search for a new identity for Disney," according to Andrew Osmond, to whom Disney producer Don Hahn admitted, "if the studio stuck to fairy tales, 'the animated form [would] wither and die'" (2011, 31). Creative differences, corporate restructuring, and significant competition from Pixar led the studio into a second decline. It was almost a decade before Disney returned to its fairy tale foundations and hand-drawn style with the release of *The Princess and the Frog* in 2009. By now, the Disney Princess franchise had grown into a cultural phenomenon, which is gestured toward in the opening sequence of the film. To the mothers in the theater, young Charlotte's bedroom might look all too familiar: scattered all about are dress-up gowns in various shades of pink, crowns, cone-shaped hats, slippers, dolls, toy castles, and coaches, as well as a tea party set that closely resembles Mrs. Potts and Chip from *Beauty and the Beast*. Tiana's mother makes a living producing the material goods that enable children like Charlotte Le Bouff to entertain the fantasy of being a fairy-tale princess.

Unlike the Grimms' "The Frog Prince," the film does not begin "once upon a time" in a faraway land, but in the gritty streets of New Orleans during the Roaring Twenties. More importantly, the studio broke new ground by creating its first African American princess. Assuming the studio understood the power of visual representation and the fact that adolescent viewers "tend to believe that Disney's version of the fairy tale is the real story rather than the 'classic' version" (Hurley 2005, 222), animating the nineteenth-century German tale with a Black heroine was a significant creative decision.

But more than Tiana's skin tone separates her from her royal cartoon cohort. Tiana's strong work ethic and fiscal acumen posture her as a sensible princess for the twenty-first century. Seventy-two years after Snow White trills, "I'm wishing for the one I love to find me today" ("I'm Wishing/One Song" 1937), Tiana belts out, "Fairytales can come true/You gotta make 'em happen, it all depends on you/So I work real hard each and every day [. . .] Look out boys I'm coming through" ("Almost There" 2009). Disney also updates (and at the same time downgrades) the status of the fairy-tale prince; while Prince Naveen might be charming, he is also spoiled, lazy, and reliant. Although it strays far from its source text, the film maintains fairy-tale tropes such as wish fulfillment, retributive justice, and a romance realized; however, it also subtly works against tradition by embedding socially responsible messages like independence is power, success doesn't come easily, and relationships take work.

The following year, *Tangled* (2010) signaled a more pronounced departure from fairy-tale conventions with a title that makes no overt reference to its traditional origins. Director Nathan Greno explains the film essentially outgrew its working title "Rapunzel" (ATU 310) as the story became increasingly invested in Rapunzel and Flynn Ryder as a duo (Markovitz 2010). Subsequent films including *Frozen* (2013) likewise use adjectives as titles, marking an investment in exploring the complexity of the human condition through fairy-tale narratives rather than the conditions of humanity as memorialized in those tales.

Rapunzel, the studio's first computer-animated princess, was originally considered as a follow up to *Snow White*, but the prince's clandestine visits and the resulting teen pregnancy in the Grimms' version proved too controversial to proceed. In addition to cutting the sexual content and liberating Rapunzel from her tower, *Tangled* builds in a backstory for Mother Gothel that aligns her with earlier Disney antagonists driven by vanity and envy like Snow White's stepmother, Cinderella's stepsisters, and Maleficent in *Sleeping Beauty* (1959), as well as the live-action diversion *Maleficent*. More poignantly than in previous films, *Tangled* holds up the mirror at a slightly skewed angle to reflect its cultural context. In an allegedly postfeminist setting in which women have achieved a degree of equality, the harmful effects of patriarchal order are overshadowed by the damage of women and girls tearing each other down. To this end, the writers offer a moment of uncomfortable humor as Mother Gothel sings a list of Rapunzel's supposed "faults" (i.e., "Gullible, naive, positively grubby, ditzy and a bit, well, hmm vague, plus, I believe, gettin' kinda chubby" ["Mother Knows Best" 2010]). In light of recent campaigns against body-shaming and the girl empowerment movement, Rapunzel is transformed from a damsel in distress into an independent young woman who "uses her intellect and sense of right and wrong to challenge the notion her mother pushes on her" (Stephens 2014, 99).

Disney's animated blockbuster, *Frozen*, breaks conventions in both art and life. Jennifer Lee, who co-wrote and co-directed the film based on Hans Christian Andersen's "The Snow Queen," is the studio's first female director. According to producer Peter Del Vecho, "'Inspired by' means exactly that. There is snow and there is ice and there is a Queen, but other than that, we depart from it quite a bit" (Connelly 2013). But *Frozen* borrows more from Andersen's tale than just its winter motif. For instance, the evil trolls are repurposed to find the good in everyone (singing "Fixer Upper"), and both versions reach their dramatic climax when an act of love thaws a frozen heart.

In addition to including a romantic subplot between Anna and Prince Hans that exposes "love at first sight" as a dangerous ideal, Disney's writers recast the two female figures of Andersen's classic—Gerda/Anna and the Snow Queen/Elsa—as sisters. As one of the few animated films that passes the "Bechdel-Wallace Test" (Garber 2015) by having at least two women protagonists speak to each other about something other than a man, *Frozen* drew critical acclaim for its representation of sisterhood while offering a definition of love that requires acceptance and sacrifice. Unlike Disney's Snow White, who admits to the forest animals she feels "ashamed" for feeling afraid, *Frozen* revamps the princess archetype by depicting the anxiety and self-doubt implicit in meeting social standards and holding positions of authority. In "Let it Go" (2013), the film's musical apex, Elsa departs from her princess predecessors by rejecting the fairy tale notion that the best way to achieve a "happy ending" is by trying to please everyone.

There is, however, an area of social concern that Disney has been reluctant to address: perpetuating an unrealistic standard of beauty through their alluring heroines at the height of sexual maturity. As Idina Menzel's Broadway voice comes warbling out of Elsa's flawless Barbie frame, the lyric "that perfect girl is gone" loses some of its credibility. Disney's Moana is the studio's first Polynesian princess and the first with a realistic body type, revealing that the corporation's creative teams may finally be moving away from animated female bodies whose eyes are set wider than their waists (Boozan 2015).

The dreams and wishes of Disney's twenty-first-century fairy-tale figures have become realistic to the point of banality: to be self-employed (*The Princess and the Frog*), to travel (*Tangled*), and to reconcile with a family member (*Frozen*). Yet, from the standpoint of a modern audience, these ambitions require no less courage, ingenuity, and persistence than outwitting a witch or slaying a dragon. Such fairy-tale refinishings remain true to the genre in helping children learn how to navigate adulthood. With several waves of the wand of cultural history, Disney's fairy-tale princess has been transformed from domesticated object of desire to independent ingénue—reaping billions in merchandising along the way. "Going off script" seems to be the new Disney formula for remaining synonymous with the genre while at the same time reimagining the genre itself, as they've begun to do in recent live-action films such as *Enchanted* (2007), *Into the Woods* (2014), *Maleficent, Cinderella* (2015), and *Beauty and the Beast* (2017), whose British cast transports the tale a long way from Anaheim in both dialect and creative direction. As form follows function, Disney's migration from cartoon animation to live-action and transmedial storytelling befits a company whose social function continuously transforms in order to accommodate the artistic intersection of fairy-tale fantasy and the limitations of reality.

Related topics: Advertising; Cinematic; Convergence Culture; Gender; Musicals

References Cited and Further Reading

Ashe, Brandie. 2012. "Who's Afraid of the Big Bad Wolf?" *True Classics Blog*, July 28. http://trueclassics.net/2012/07/28/whos-afraid-of-the-big-bad-wolf/.

Boozan, Glenn. 2015. "11 Disney Princesses Whose Eyes Are Literally Bigger Than Their Stomachs." *Above Average*, June 22. http://aboveaverage.com/11-disney-princesses-whose-eyes-are-literally-bigger-than-their-stomachs/.

Connelly, Brendon. 2013. "Inside the Research, Design and Animation of Walt Disney's Frozen with Producer Peter Del Vecho." *Bleeding Cool Comic Book, Movie, TV News*, September 25. www.bleedingcool.com/2013/09/25/inside-the-research-design-and-animation-of-walt-disneys-frozen-with-producer-peter-del-vecho/.

Cummins, June. 1995. "Romancing the Plot: The Real Beast of Disney's *Beauty and the Beast*." *Children's Literature Association Quarterly* 20 (1): 22–8.

Ebersol, Kaitlin. 2014. "How Fourth-Wave Feminism Is Changing Disney's Princesses." *Highbrow Magazine*, October 23. www.highbrowmagazine.com/4388-how-fourth-wave-feminism-changing-disney-s-princesses.

Forbes. 2015. "#11 Walt Disney." October 12. www.forbes.com/companies/walt-disney/.

Gabler, Neal. 2007. *Walt Disney: The Triumph of the American Imagination.* New York: Vintage Books.

Garber, Megan. 2015. "Call It the 'Bechdel-Wallace Test'." *The Atlantic*, August 25. www.theatlantic.com/entertainment/archive/2015/08/call-it-the-bechdel-wallace-test/402259/#article-comments.

Giroux, Henry. 2004. "Cultural Studies, Public Pedagogy, and the Responsibility of Intellectuals." *Communication and Critical/Cultural Studies* 1 (1): 59–79.

Grimm, Jacob, and Wilhelm Grimm. 2011. "Hansel and Gretel." In *Folklore and Mythology Electronic Texts*, translated by D. L. Ashliman. www.pitt.edu/~dash/grimm015.html.

Hurley, Dorothy J. 2005. "Seeing White: Children of Color and the Disney Fairy Tale Princess." *Journal of Negro Education* 74 (3): 221–32.

Jackson, Kathy Merlock. 1996. "Walt Disney: Its Persuasive Products and Cultural Contexts." *Journal of Popular Film & Television* 24 (2): 50.

Kaufman, J. B. 2012. *The Fairest One of All: The Making of Walt Disney's Snow White and the Seven Dwarfs.* San Francisco: Walt Disney Family Foundation P.

Markovitz, Adam. 2010. "How Did Rapunzel Become 'Tangled'? Directors Nathan Greno and Byron Howard Set the Record Straight." *EW.com*, November 24. www.ew.com/article/2010/11/24/tangled-rapunzel-nathan-greno-byron-howard.

Orenstein, Peggy. 2006. "What's Wrong with Cinderella?" *New York Times*, December 24. www.nytimes.com/2006/12/24/magazine/24princess.t.html?pagewanted=all&_r=0.

Osmond, Andrew. 2011. "Disney after Disney." *Sight & Sound* 21 (2): 30–1.

Schickel, Richard. 1968. *The Disney Version: The Life, Times, and Commerce of Walt Disney.* New York: Simon and Schuster.

Schlackman, Steve. 2014. "How Mickey Mouse Keeps Changing Copyright Law." *Art Law Journal Online*, February 15. http://artlawjournal.com/mickey-mouse-keeps-changing-copyright-law/.

Schneider, Mike. 1999. "Nephew Is Disney's Last Disney." *The Seattle Times*, November 4. http://community.seattletimes.nwsource.com/archive/?date=19991104&slug=2993263.

Sells, Laura. 1995. "Where Do the Mermaids Stand?: Voice and Body in *The Little Mermaid*." In *From Mouse to Mermaid: The Politics of Film, Gender, and Culture*, edited by Elizabeth Bell, Lynda Haas, and Laura Sells, 175–92. Bloomington: Indiana UP.

Smith, Dave. 1996. *Disney A to Z: The Updated Official Encyclopedia.* Burbank: Disney Editions.

Stephens, Jena. 2014. "Disney's Darlings: An Analysis of *The Princess and the Frog, Tangled, Brave,* and the Changing Characterization of the Princess Archetype." *Interdisciplinary Humanities* 31 (3): 95–107.

Sun, Chyng-Feng, Miguel Picker, Monique Fordham, Linda Mizell, Rhonda Berkower, and Nancy Inouye. 2002. *Mickey Mouse Monopoly.* Northampton, MA: Media Education Foundation.

Thomas, Bob. 1991. *Disney's Art of Animation: From Mickey Mouse to Beauty and the Beast.* New York: Hyperion.

United States Patent and Trademark Office. 2013. "Snow White." USPTO: United States Patent and Trademark Office. http://tsdr.uspto.gov/#caseNumber=77618057&caseType=SERIAL_NO&searchType=statusSearch.

The Walt Disney Company. 2015. "Disney Consumer Products." *Walt Disney.* https://thewaltdisneycompany.com/disney-companies/disney-consumer-products.

Zipes, Jack. 1996. "Breaking the Disney Spell." In *From Mouse to Mermaid: The Politics of Film, Gender, and Culture*, edited by Elizabeth Bell, Lynda Haas, and Laura Sells, 21–42. Bloomington: Indiana UP.

———. 2014. "Introduction: Rediscovering the Original Tales of the Brothers Grimm." *The Original Folk and Fairy Tales of the Brothers Grimm: The Complete First Edition.* Princeton, NJ: Princeton UP.

Mediagraphy

Aladdin. 1992. Directors Ron Clements and John Musker. USA.

The Avengers. 2012. Director Joss Whedon. USA.

Beauty and the Beast. 1991. Directors Gary Trousdale and Kirk Wise. USA.

———. 2017. Director Bill Condon. USA.

"Belle (reprise)" (Song). 1991. Artists Alan Menken and Howard Ashman, album *Beauty and the Beast: Original Motion Picture Soundtrack.* USA.

Cinderella. 1950. Directors David Hand, Wilfred Jackson, and Hamilton Luske. USA.

———. 2015. Director Kenneth Branagh. USA.

Enchanted. 2007. Director Kevin Lima. USA.

"Fixer Upper" (Song). 2013. Artists Kristen Anderson-Lopez and Robert Lopez, album *Frozen: Original Motion Picture Soundtrack.* USA.

Frozen. 2013. Directors Chris Buck and Jennifer Lee. USA.

"I'm Wishing" (Song). 1938. Artists Frank Churchill, Larry Morey, and Leigh Harline, album *Songs from Walt Disney's Snow White and the Seven Dwarfs.* USA.

Into the Woods. 2014. Director Rob Marshall. USA.

La belle et la bête. 1946. Director Jean Cocteau. France.

"Let It Go" (Song). 2013. Artist Idina Menzel, album *Frozen: Original Motion Picture Soundtrack.* USA.

The Lion King. 1994. Directors Roger Allers and Rob Minkoff. USA.

The Little Mermaid. 1989. Directors Ron Clements and John Musker. USA.

Maleficent. 2014. Director Robert Stromberg. USA.

"Mother Knows Best" (Song). 2010. Artists Alan Menken and Glenn Slater, album *Tangled: Original Soundtrack.* USA.

Mulan. 1998. Directors Tony Bancroft and Barry Cook. USA.

The Muppets. 2015. Directors Randall Einhorn, Matt Sohn and Bill Barretta. USA.

My Neighbor Totoro. Director Hayao Miyazaki. 1988. Japan.

DISNEY CORPORATION

"One Song" (Song). 1938. Artists Frank Churchill, Larry Morey, and Leigh Harline, album *Songs from Walt Disney's Snow White and the Seven Dwarfs*. USA.

Pinocchio. 1940. Directors Hamilton Luske and Ben Sharpsteen. USA.

The Princess and the Frog. 2009. Directors Ron Clements and John Musker. USA.

Sleeping Beauty. 1959. Director Clyde Geronimi. USA.

Snow White and the Seven Dwarfs. 1937. Director Clyde Geronimi. USA.

"Something There" (Song). 1991. Artists Alan Menken and Howard Ashman, album *Beauty and the Beast: Original Motion Picture Soundtrack*. USA.

Star Wars: The Force Awakens. 2015. Director J. J. Abrams. USA.

Tangled. 2010. Directors Nathan Greno and Byron Howard. USA.

The Three Little Pigs. 1933. Director Burt Gillett. USA.

Winnie the Pooh. 2011. Directors Stephen J. Anderson and Don Hall. USA.

21

HYBRIDITY

Francisco Vaz da Silva

The musical *Into the Woods*, recently adapted into a film (2014), describes how the characters from various fairy tales go into the woods in order to fulfill various needs and wishes. In the forest, the characters trespass into each other's plots and establish unexpected relationships; as Cinderella's Prince sums it up, "Anything can happen in the woods [. . .] Foolishness can happen in the woods [. . .] Right and wrong don't matter in the woods." *Into the Woods* draws attention to fairy-tale hybridity on two levels. First, the differences between plots are less important than the shared feature that everyone enters the woods, hence inter-plot hybridity is a given. Second, a blurred period of open-ended possibilities in relationships and identities unfolds in the woods before patterns are set anew, which matches the fact (noted by Vladimir Propp 1983, 63–74) that going into the woods launches betwixt-and-between phases of transformation in fairy tales.

This chapter is not concerned with inter-plot hybridity, which is largely a function of our tendency to think about tale types as fixed texts (for a discussion of this sort of hybridity, see Haring 2008, 464). Rather, it explores the hybridity that pervades into-the-woods spells, also known as enchantments, in fairy tales. I argue that the core of fairy tales is enchantment, which is a phase ruled by cyclic time, and I submit that cyclic time breeds hybridity. Therefore, I take it that examining hybridity in fairy tales requires addressing the cyclic logic "of 'ordeals,' 'deaths' and 'resurrections'" that fairy tales share with initiation rites (Eliade 1998, 202). I wish to do so at the simplest possible level. Propp (1996, 114; 1983, 16, 63) famously argued that the basic form of the fairy tale is about a hero who grabs magical powers in the forest, then slays a monster and liberates a princess. But, clearly, this androcentric model both supposes and obfuscates the princess's prior enchantment. Therefore, I take it that a feminine enchantment is the simplest fairy-tale form, and I address hybridity at this basic level.

In a recent essay I pointed out that feminine enchantments often comprise a blood connection with an older woman as well as a sexual experience (Vaz da Silva 2015, 107–113). In this discussion I focus on the feminine connection. I examine stories in which a witchy fairy shuts a girl in a tower in the woods, and I discuss hybridity in light of this basic strand in fairy tales.

Discrete Outlines Versus Hybridity in Fairy-Tale Models

For a start, let me state the obvious. Something hybrid is a heterogeneous piece, a complex unit. Therefore, being on the lookout for hybridity involves heeding complexity, nuance, and ambiguity. Acknowledging the transmedial metamorphoses of tales in the modern culture is of the essence. Overall, the following discussion challenges a longstanding consensus on the need to foreground the homogeneity, purity, and simplicity of fairy tales.

The consensus on the purity of fairy-tale outlines is so pervasive as to be almost invisible. For instance, the founder of the standard folktale classification, Antti Aarne, assumed that "originally" (whatever that means) each tale type was a fixed text with its own set of motifs; therefore, in accordance with this assumption, Aarne used texts from the Grimm collection and the Copenhagen archives as templates for the tale types he devised (see Thompson 1977, 417, 439). But the assumption that tales are fixed texts is simplistic. As Propp pointed out, "Tales possess one special characteristic: components of one tale can, without any alteration whatsoever, be transferred to another" (1996, 7). Alternatively, Propp proposed, "The entire store of fairy tales ought to be examined as a chain of variants" (114).

Yet, although Propp rejected Aarne's assumption that one could define discrete tale types containing their own motifs, he did share with Aarne the aim of defining clear-cut units in fairy tales. So he proposed to drop the "amazing multiformity, picturesqueness, and color" of the attributes of fairy-tale characters in order to focus solely on the characters' abstract actions, which he called functions (1996, 20–21, 87). Thus he defined the axis of all fairy tales in terms of a string of discrete functions: "none will fall out of order, nor will any one exclude or contradict any other" (22). But Propp himself noted that various anomalies complicate the seductive simplicity of his discrete-units model. He acknowledged cases of "the double morphological meaning of a single function" (69), which implies that functions overlap; and he recognized that the *dramatis personae* may hold opposite functions, which entails they are hybrid too. For instance, the witch often "begins as an antagonistic donor and then becomes an involuntary helper" (81). Eleazar Meletinsky and collaborators developed this point: "Almost every personage can perform temporarily some opposite functions. To consider such cases as mechanically superimposed is incorrect. [. . .] [I]t is obvious that functional fields are continuous, and that they form a cyclical structure" (Meletinsky et al. 1974, 117). The following discussion draws on this insight.

Max Lüthi is another case in point. He submitted that the style of fairy tales aims "for clarity, exactness, positiveness, and precision. There is no 'if' and no 'perhaps'" (1979, 57). His model stresses the "isolation of the characters" (50) and their "depthlessness"—hence, he wrote, "[i]nstead of different modes of behavior being combined in a single person, we see them sharply separated from one another and divided among persons who stand side by side" (1982, 14–15). Such isolated characters "have no inner life, no environment, no relationship to past or future generations, no relationship to time" (37). Hence, "there are no aging persons, and no aging otherworld beings either" (19).

Yet, Lüthi noted:

> Mircea Eliade once said that the hearers of fairy tales [. . .] experience a sort of initiation not entirely unlike that in the customs of some primitive peoples. "The folk tale transposes the initiation process into the sphere of imagination." [. . .] How correct this scholar's assertion is can be shown in any folk fairy tale.
>
> (1979, 59–60)

Lüthi himself remarked that "Rapunzel" (ATU 310) portrays the sort of process of "development and maturation" in which "every step forward involves a dying," like in "[p]rimitive [. . .] rites of passage" (113). And he noted that "Dornröschen" (ATU 410) "tells of death and resurrection" regarding a girl who "is fifteen years old when she comes under the spell: the time of transition from childhood to maidenhood" (24). But Lüthi adds, "[O]ne instinctually conceives of the princess as an image of the human spirit: the story portrays the endowment, peril, paralysis, and redemption of not just one girl, but of all mankind" (1979, 24). Alas, the "instinctive" preconception that fairy tales are spiritual allegory brushes aside physical maturation, which misses the point that fairy tales are *about* cosmic and physiologic time.

Maturation in Fairy Tales

Both "Rapunzel" and "Dornröschen" feature a disquieting fairy (whom the Grimms take to calling, respectively, an "enchantress" and a "wise woman"; Grimm and Grimm 2014, 37, 163; see François 2011; see Tatar 2012, 57, 241) who shuts a pubertal girl in a tower. A fascinating description of the tower enclosure is offered in Mademoiselle de la Force's "Persinette," the literary ancestor of the Grimms' "Rapunzel" (Lüthi 1979, 118; Tatar 2012, 56). This seventeenth-century variant recounts how a fairy grants parsley from her enclosed garden to a pregnant woman in exchange for her child. At the child's birth, the fairy names her *Persinette* (from *persil*, parsley) and makes her the most beautiful creature in the world. And before Persinette turns twelve, "since the fairy knew her fate, she decided to spare her to her destiny" by enclosing Persinette in a tower in the heart of a forest (La Force 1698, 104). But the girl eventually becomes pregnant in her tower, and the fairy belatedly recognizes that "destiny cannot be avoided, and my foresight was to no avail" (116).

To grasp what the girl's destiny is, consider the acts of the fairy. She names the girl after an herb reputed for inducing feminine hemorrhages (just as rampion was recommended for regulating the menstrual cycle; Warner 2008; Bricout 2005, 47), and she shuts the girl in the tower at the outset of puberty. Moreover, the fairy acknowledges the ineluctability of the girl's fate after the latter becomes pregnant. So Persinette's inevitable fate is her maturation and sexual initiation, taken together.

Consider the locus of Persinette's maturation. It is a doorless silver tower, brightly lit inside by "the fire of carbuncles [*escarboucles*] as though the sun shone there" (La Force 1698, 105). A silver tower secluded in the dark forest, suffused with a red glow, strongly suggests the lunar dwelling of a pubertal girl—a point that resonates with a leitmotiv in comparative folklore. James Frazer, in a section of *The Golden Bough* called "The Seclusion of Girls at Puberty," quotes many instances worldwide of the custom of keeping menarcheal girls secluded from the sun for a spell. Frazer notes, "[A] superstition so widely diffused as this might be expected to leave traces in legends and folk-tales. And it has done so" (1913, 70). Indeed, both the tales ATU 310, "The Maiden in the Tower," and ATU 410, "Sleeping Beauty," feature the seclusion of girls at puberty.

Cyclic Time, Hybridity, Queer Time

Arguably, the structural parallel of fairy tales and rites of passage hinges on the representation of maturation in cyclic terms. Rites of passage mark the separation from an old phase or status, through a liminal transition, into a new status. Arnold Van Gennep, who proposed this model, pointed out that in the liminal stage the "idea of a renewal, a periodic death and rebirth," often finds expression in lunar symbolism (1961, 180). Anthropologist Victor Turner developed this insight as he noted that the liminal phase features processes of "[u]ndoing, dissolution, decomposition [. . .] accompanied by processes of growth, transformation and the reformulation of old elements in new patterns" (1977, 99).

Which brings us to hybridity. In such ontological transformations, Turner notes, "logically antithetical processes of death and growth may be represented by the same tokens," as happens in lunar symbolism because "the same moon waxes and wanes," in snake symbolism because "the snake appears to die, but only to shed its old skin and reappear in a new one," and in bear symbolism because "the bear 'dies' in autumn and is 'reborn' in spring" (1977, 99). This point on the hybridity of "logically antithetical" processes applies to fairy tales as well, which is why—as Meletinsky et al. noted—in fairy tales "almost any personage can perform temporarily some opposite functions" (1974, 117).

Alan Dundes quoted Ruth Benedict to the effect that we "do not see the lens through which we look," which, Dundes argues, is shaped by "the combination of 'line,' 'straight,' and 'square'" (2007, 200). While Dundes acknowledges some formulations that contemplate escaping "the vise of linearity," he submits that such attempts confirm "the boundaries imposed by lines and boxes" (206). In light of these cultural constraints, the cyclic logic of fairy tales does look queer, and queer studies have taken notice. Kay Turner and Pauline Greenhill point out that queer studies have an interest in the fairy-tale form, which "invites ambiguity and ambivalence" (2012, 6). In the same trend, Lewis Seifert (2015, 23) argues that the queerness of the fairy-tale form stems from its narrative uses of time.

Hybrid Fates, Cycling Girls

In such narrative uses of time, the prevalence of moon symbolism is quite remarkable. The moon conspicuously features death-and-rebirth cycles every month, which precisely match feminine cycles (Shuttle and Redgrove 1999, 127–129); hence, it is hardly surprising that the hybrid fairies bear lunar attributes even as they bring girls to start cycling along with the moon.

Indeed, the Märchen fairies who fate girls are close relatives of the ancient Fates who spin individual destinies, such as the Latin *Fata*, the Greek *Moirai*, and the Germanic *Nornir* (Grimm 1880, 405; Hennard Dutheil de la Rochère and Dasen 2011, 16). The old Fates occasionally appear as a single woman, and their numbers do vary, but usually they are three (Grimm 1880, 405–410; Kerényi 1998, 32–33). Carl Kerényi pointed out that the Moirai "actually *are* real trinities, sometimes almost forming a single Threefold Goddess" (1998, 31). Robert Graves stated that "[t]he Three Fates are a divided form of the Triple Goddess" (1961, 225), and Kerényi associated the tripartition of the Fates with the usual division of the lunar month into three parts (1998, 31–32). Likewise, the modern fairies act in three steps. In "Persinette," as we saw, the single fairy grants beauty to the girl, then she imposes on her the name bearing her fate, and finally she tries to attenuate the girl's fate. Likewise, in Perrault's "La Belle au bois dormant" and in the Grimms' "Dornröschen" the group of seven or twelve invited fairies grants the girl brilliant social graces, then the uninvited fairy imposes a hard fate on her, which finally one invited fairy softens.

This ternary pattern is recognizable in modern films as well. Take the two retellings by the Disney studios. In the first film, *Sleeping Beauty* (1959), two fairies grant beauty and song to the little princess, then Maleficent (the uninvited fairy) curses her to prick her finger and die, but the third fairy attenuates the foretold death into sleep. The second film, *Maleficent* (2014), focuses on the eponymous fairy. At the christening, the fairies still grant beauty and grace to the princess. Maleficent confirms this beneficent spell but also curses the princess into a death-like sleep and then allows that the girl might reawaken by the effect of true love's kiss. Moreover, beyond this tripartite action on the girl's christening, Maleficent acts on the girl's fate in three steps. First she utters the fatal curse, then she tries in vain to revoke it before the girl's sixteenth birthday, and finally Maleficent herself kisses the girl with true love and revives her. The princess is nothing if accurate when she calls "fairy godmother" the hybrid fairy who shapes her destiny in three steps.

Ultimately, the fairies' ternary fating boils down to antithetical gifts. In "Persinette" the fairy grants the girl utmost beauty and a spell in the tower. In Perrault's "La Belle au bois dormant," seven young fairies grace the girl with "all the perfections imaginable" whereas an "old fairy" curses her to die the moment she touches a spindle. In the Grimms' "Dornröschen," twelve fairies grant the girl splendid things while the thirteenth fairy decrees she will prick herself with a spindle. Disney's *Sleeping Beauty* sharply contrasts the good-fairies' gifts and the dark curse, and, one step ahead, *Maleficent* casts and describes the eponymous fairy as "both hero and villain." Even so, the binary traits of the fairies belong in the ternary tempo of lunar cycles. Remarkably, in the film, Maleficent has horns like the crescent moon (on the horned moon in folklore, see Vaz da Silva 2008, 19–22, 68–70, 116–119). Also, her trichromatic image conveys the contrast of black and white, with a splash of red, which evokes lunar phases along with women's cycles. And the point is that Maleficent resonates with all the hybrid fairies who bring girls to maturity according to the lunar rhythms of death and rebirth. Like the moon goes through bright and dark phases, and springs anew out of darkness, so all the motley fairies grant social graces *and* a death curse from which cycling girls emerge to accrued life.

To his credit, Bruno Bettelheim noted that a curse concerning a fifteen-year-old girl, uttered by a thirteenth fairy, likely conveys a menstrual theme (1978, 232–233). The rub of the matter is that a solar year fits twelve moon cycles plus a small residue. Therefore, as anthropologist Chris Knight explains, as long as people reckon with moon cycles in the frame of the solar year, there is "no way in which the number '13' could be avoided." The modern Gregorian calendar features twelve months adjusted to the solar year, but in folklore the number thirteen is often relevant for traditions that reckon with the moon (2004, 3). Indeed, the Grimms' contrast between the twelve fairies who receive golden plates and the one who does not suggests that the thirteenth fairy represents an attribute beyond the pale of solar time.[1] Moreover, Perrault's parallel between the *vieille Fée* secluded in her tower (who utters the curse) and the secluded old spinner in a tower (who makes the curse come true) hints that they both impersonate the ancient Fate who fates girls to seclusions in a tower. From another angle, Cyrille François mentions Jacob Grimm's acknowledgment (a propos of "Dornröschen," Grimm 1880, 419) that spindles are an essential characteristic of German wise women as a reason to think that the *weise Frau* who curses the girl is the selfsame fairy as the old spinner who makes the curse come true (François 2011, 268). Certainly, in "Sleeping Beauty" Maleficent herself lures the girl to the spinning wheel.

In sum, the old Fates who take possession of young girls in the tower cause them to bleed. As the young girls spin a spindle they start cycling with the moon; as they prick a finger, they mark with blood the thread of their lives.

It remains to note that the contrasting gifts of the fairies delineate the hybridity of girls who meet cyclic time. Dornröschen's father would want a dazzling daughter, all social graces, unhindered by the dark curse—but the tale recounts that the daughter must tap the lunar sphere before she becomes a bride. For the sake of comparison, consider one Italian namesake of Dornröschen, Rosina, whom the fairies fate to shine like the sun *and* to turn into a snake the minute she sees the sun, before she can at last turn into a radiant bride (Nerucci 1880, 280–285; see a translated adaption in Calvino 1982, 225–229). In a Sicilian variant, the girl turns into a *black* snake before she turns into a radiant bride (Zipes and Russo 2009, 279–287). Going under the dark skin of a snake matches being enclosed in the lunar tower, which accords with Robert Briffault's point that snakes have in common with the moon "the gift of immortality through perpetual renewal," hence they "play the same part in regard to the functions of women as the moon" (1977, 312, 315). Regardless of the broadly equivalent images in use, the constant factor is that each girl is a hybrid who endures a dark phase before she shines forth in bridal fulfillment (see Cardigos 1996, 129–139).

This stable pattern allows for creative twists and turns. Consider how the film *Tangled* (2010) transforms the theme of "The Girl in the Tower" (ATU 310). In this tale, the secluded girl impersonates an herb associated with lunar bleedings; contrariwise, in the film, the girl impersonates a solar flower that grants the healing power of incorruptible life. This shift puts the situation in the tower on its head. Instead of a fairy who helps a girl grow into lunar time, the film depicts an aging woman who taps the girl's golden hair to keep herself young. The charm she devises to tap the glow in Rapunzel's hair includes the lines: "Bring back what once was mine [. . .] Change the Fates' design." The golden entanglement in the tower keeps Rapunzel mired in immaturity, secluded from lunar cycles. Hence, her golden hair must go if the girl is to come of age on her eighteenth birthday. Rapunzel's sweetheart does cut her hair, and this momentous act releases lunar time: the old woman totters into dust, and Rapunzel (now an eighteen-year-old brunette) learns that her sweetheart has "a thing for brunettes." Having reverted to "the Fates' design," she has matured and is ready for love.

Tangled offers a useful thought experiment as it twists the tale of a girl cursed to lunar darkness into the story of a girl trapped in solar light. Rapunzel entangled in her own golden hair is like Dornröschen hypothetically not cursed by the dark fairy, like Rosina not turned into a black snake, and like Persinette never dwelling in her tower. *Tangled* makes the point that a girl who would take only the golden spells would remain tangled in immaturity. Like the other variants, it assumes that girls must tap the lunar sphere—they must take up the dark aspect as well as the golden attributes of the fairies' fating.

Two-in-one, One-in-two

The point, again, is that hybridity is of the essence of fairy-tale characters. We saw that one fairy who yields antithetical attributes is equivalent to one aggregate unit of (two or more) antithetical fairies. Now I wish to point out that, likewise, a hybrid girl bearing antithetical attributes can split into two interdependent characters. Another tale ("The Kind and the Unkind Girls," ATU 480) externalizes the hybridity of the cyclic girl fated by the fairies into two halves—one girl gets only the golden attributes and marries, the other gets only the dark attributes and is cast aside. In such stories the fairy's curse comes closer to the demeaning sense of "the curse" in colloquial speech—an irritant to be discarded (Delaney, Lupton, and Toth 1988, 116). Perrault's "Les Fées," for instance, features one fairy who appears in two contrasted guises to two sisters who impersonate the split dimensions of the pubertal girl. One guise of the fairy fates one girl to expel flowers and precious stones when she speaks—and this girl becomes a bride—whereas the other guise of the fairy curses the other girl to expel serpents and toads—and this girl dies, like a tossed rag, in a corner of the woods.

Even though the split of the menarcheal girl makes it trivial to treat the lunar curse like an irritant to be discarded, the cyclic framework and the attendant hybridity persist. Another variant of ATU 480, the Grimms' "Frau Holle," associates the contrasting girls with, respectively, gold and pitch. Kay Turner points out the unusual fact that Frau Holle's abode is "a sun-drenched realm," and she helps explain this queer detail as she notes that Holle "owns a solar underground even as she controls the weather above" (2015, 52). The point is that the "good" girl who finds sunshine in the netherworld then takes to shaking the feathers in Holle's bed so as to make snow in the upper world. This mirror-inverted correlation between netherworld sunshine and a snowy winter on earth is surely one particular instance of the widespread notion that "the otherworld is an inverted image of this world" (Eliade 1974, 205; Vaz da Silva 2002, 40). And note that the girl who provides for a snowy winter up on earth then returns to the upper world covered with gold. The emergence of the golden girl after winter likely marks the merry season (and, conversely, the emergence of the black girl marks the return of winter). The implication is that the two girls—like the contrasting seasons—are the mirror-like halves of a single cycle: one goes down when the other goes up, one becomes black after the other becomes golden. Still, this seasonal coding coexists with the usual lunar imagery: in a variant from Thuringia, the golden girl is welcomed back home by a yellow cock while the other crosses a gate of pitch into a misty abode of snakes and toads (Grimm and Grimm 1884, vol. 1, 371–372).

A Basic Thread, and Beyond

I reiterate that the foregoing discussion is very basic. It covers but a tiny number of tales; and, even so, important issues—such as Frau Holle's winter/lunar traits, Sleeping Beauty's enchanted sleep, and Rapunzel's childbearing and exile—are left unexamined. But recall that I focus on fairy-tale hybridity as a structural feature. I argue that hybridity stems from the cyclic pattern that fairy tales share with rites of passage, and I chose to examine this feature at the simplest possible level—the same-sex thread in which an old woman transmits moon blood to a young girl—and to spell out the most obvious lunar imagery in place. Please take this chapter as a teaser. I hope it might yet be developed, corrected, and taken in unexpected directions by your own research.

Related topics: Animal Studies; Anthologies; Autobiography; Cinema Science Fiction; Convergence Culture; Criticism; Gender; Musicals; Sexualities/Queer and Trans Studies; Storyworlds/ Narratology

Note

1. Likewise, Perrault's contrast between seven fairies and the eighth fairy recalls that a lunar month comprises four weeks averaging seven days plus a remainder, which again yields the same dichotomy between accredited time and liminal time as in Grimm.

References Cited and Further Reading

Bettelheim, Bruno. 1978. *The Uses of Enchantment: The Meaning and Importance of Fairy Tales.* London: Peregrine.

Bricout, Bernadette. 2005. *La clé des contes.* Paris: Seuil.

Briffault, Robert. 1977. *The Mothers*, edited by Gordon Rattray Taylor. Abridged ed. New York: Atheneum.

Calvino, Italo. 1982. *Italian Folktales*, translated by George Martin. 2nd ed. Harmondsworth: Penguin.

Cardigos, Isabel. 1996. *In and Out of Enchantment: Blood Symbolism and Gender in Portuguese Fairytales.* Helsinki: Academia Scientiarum Fennica.

Delaney, Janice, Mary Jane Lupton, and Emily Toth. 1988. *The Curse: A Cultural History of Menstruation.* Urbana: U Illinois P.

Dundes, Alan. 2007. "As the Crow Flies: A Straightforward Study of Lineal Worldview in American Folk Speech." In *The Meaning of Folklore: The Analytical Essays of Alan Dundes*, edited by Simon J. Bronner. 200–10. Logan: Utah State UP.

Eliade, Mircea. 1974. *Shamanism: Archaic Techniques of Ecstasy*, translated by Willard R. Trask. Revised and enlarged ed. Princeton, NJ: Princeton UP.

———. 1998. *Myth and Reality*, edited by Willard R. Trask. Prospect Heights, IL: Waveland P.

François, Cyrille. 2011. "Fées et *weise Frauen*. Les faiseuses de dons chez Perrault et les Grimm, du merveilleux rationalisé au merveilleux naturalisé." *Études de lettres* 3–4: 259–728.

Frazer, James George. 1913. *The Golden Bough: A Study in Magic and Religion.* 3rd ed. Vol. 10, *Balder the Beautiful: The Fire Festivals of Europe and the Doctrine of the External Soul, I.* London: Macmillan.

Gennep, Arnold van. 1961. *The Rites of Passage*, translated by Monika B. Vizedon and Gabrielle L. Caffee. Chicago: U Chicago P.

Graves, Robert. 1961. *The White Goddess*. London: Faber and Faber.

Grimm, Jacob. 1880. *Teutonic Mythology*, translated by James Steven Stallybrass. Vol. 1. London: Sonnenschein & Allen.

Grimm, Jacob, and Wilhelm Grimm. 1884. *Grimm's Household Tales, with the Author's Notes*, translated and edited by Margaret Hunt. 2 vols. London: Bell.

———. 2014. *The Original Folk and Fairy Tales of the Brothers Grimm: The Complete First Edition*, translated and edited by Jack Zipes. Princeton, NJ: Princeton UP.

Haring, Lee. 2008. "Hybridity, Hybridization." In *The Greenwood Encyclopedia of Folktales & Fairy Tales*, edited by Donald Haase, 463–7. Vol. 1. Westport, CT: Greenwood P.

Hennard Dutheil de la Rochère, Martine, and Véronique Dasen. 2011. "Des *Fata* aux Fées: Regards croisés de l'Antiquité à nos jours." *Études de lettres* 3–4: 15–34.

Kerényi, Carl. 1998. *The Gods of the Greeks*. New York: Thames and Hudson.

Knight, Chris. 2004. *Decoding Fairy Tales*. London: Lionel Sims/Radical Anthropology Group. http://radicalanthropology group.org/sites/default/fifiles/pdf/class_text_020.pdf

La Force, Mademoiselle de. 1698. *Les Contes des contes*. Vol. 1. Paris: Benard.

Lüthi, Max. 1979. *Once Upon a Time: On the Nature of Fairy Tales*, translated by Lee Chadeayne and Paul Gottwald, edited by Francis Lee Utley. Bloomington: Indiana UP.

———. 1982. *The European Folktale: Form and Nature*, translated by John D. Niles. Philadelphia: Institute for the Study of Human Issues.

Meletinsky, Eleazar, S. Nekludov, E. Novic, and D. Segal. 1974. "Problems of the Structural Analysis of Fairytales." In *Soviet Structural Folkloristics*, translated by Terrell Popoff and Helen Milosevich, edited by Pierre Maranda, 73–139. The Hague: Mouton.

Nerucci, Gherardo. 1880. *Sessanta novelle popolari montalesi*. Firenze: Successori Le Monnier.

Propp, Vladimir. 1983. *Les racines historiques du conte merveilleux*, translated by Lise Gruel-Apert. Paris: Gallimard.

———. 1996. *Morphology of the Folktale*, translated by Laurence Scott. 2nd ed. Austin: U Texas P.

Seifert, Lewis C. 2015. "Queer Time in Charles Perrault's 'Sleeping Beauty'." *Marvels & Tales* 29 (1): 21–41.

Shuttle, Penelope, and Peter Redgrove. 1999. *The Wise Wound: Menstruation and Everywoman*. London: Marion Boyars.

Sondheim, Stephen, and James Lapine. 2014. *Into the Woods*. New York: Theatre Communications Group.

Tatar, Maria, ed. 2012. *The Annotated Brothers Grimm*, translated by Maria Tatar. The Bicentennial ed. New York: Norton.

Thompson, Stith. 1977. *The Folktale*. Berkeley: U California P.

Turner, Kay. 2015. "At Home in the Realm of Enchantment: The Queer Enticements of the Grimms' 'Frau Holle'." *Marvels & Tales* 29 (1): 42–63.

Turner, Kay, and Pauline Greenhill. 2012. "Introduction: Once Upon a Queer Time." In *Transgressive Tales: Queering the Grimms*, edited by Kay Turner and Pauline Greenhill, 1–24. Detroit: Wayne State UP.

Turner, Victor W. 1977. *The Forest of Symbols: Aspects of Ndembu Ritual*. Ithaca, NY: Cornell UP.

Vaz da Silva, Francisco. 2002. *Metamorphosis: The Dynamics of Symbolism in European Fairy Tales*. New York: Peter Lang.

———. 2008. *Archeology of Intangible Heritage*. New York: Peter Lang.

———. 2015. "Fairy-Tale Symbolism." In *The Cambridge Companion to Fairy Tales*, edited by Maria Tatar, 97–116. Cambridge: Cambridge UP.

Warner, Marina. 2008. "Rapunzel, Parsley & Pregnancy." *The New York Review of Books*, July 17. www.nybooks.com/ articles/archives/2008/jul/17/rapunzel-parsley-pregnancy/.

Zipes, Jack, and Joseph Russo, eds. 2009. *The Collected Sicilian Folk and Fairy Tales of Giuseppe Pitrè*, translated by Jack Zipes and Joseph Russo. 2 vols. New York: Routledge.

Mediagraphy

Into the Woods. 2014. Director James Lapine. USA.

Maleficent. 2014. Director Robert Stromberg. UK/USA.

Sleeping Beauty. 1959. Director Clyde Geronimi. USA.

Tangled. 2010. Directors Nathan Greno and Byron Howard. USA.

22

INTELLECTUAL PROPERTY

John Laudun

Many critics of current intellectual property regimes in general and copyright laws in particular argue that they have unfairly extended the term, and reach, of copyright in service of industry in general and the Disney corporation in particular, even going so far as to deride contemporary copyright law in the U.S. as "Mickey's law." As unfortunate as such an outcome may be, it is important for those interested in the study of fairy tales to understand that copyright and the interest in, and formalized study of, fairy tales came of age in parallel; their natures and, perhaps, their destinies are intertwined.

Before embarking on any such history, however, I define some terms involved and some principles that lie behind them. While intellectual property is an abstraction capable of covering ideas and practices that reward creativity and invention, the phrase itself is an awkward pairing of two things that seem to have inverse value propositions. The term arose at the end of the eighteenth century and gained currency in the nineteenth century as various nations attempted to limit, first, internal trafficking and, later, international trafficking of inventions and texts. Through much of the nineteenth and decidedly in the twentieth centuries, most intellectual property regimes divided into three main branches: patents, trademarks, and copyright. While copyright is the central concern for texts, it is part of a larger network of ideas and laws, and the boundaries between various practices are quite fuzzy. This ambiguity can especially be seen in the movement toward the end of the twentieth century and the beginning of the twenty-first century to expand the reach of intellectual property to cover a wider array of materials and methods, such as trade secrets, trade dress, business processes, and software processes. These are not easily specified by diagrams and a list of parts nor simply as a text on file somewhere. The same can be said for the extensive commodity-producing machines of contemporary media companies that establish franchises that produce movies, publish books, manufacture toys, release music, and so on.

Focusing more narrowly on copyright, rights in most European political philosophies precede the state and are considered to structure governments and laws. In contrast to rights, privileges are produced by the state as a representative of the will of the people. In this view, as Siva Vaidhyanathan (2001) argues, copyright is really copyprivilege and is an attempt by a government to find an equitable balance that rewards an author for creation and a publisher for distribution. The result is a monopoly for a limited period of time at the end of which not only do the facts and ideas in the work become public domain but also their particular expression in the given work. Monopoly, as a term, is not incidental. The purpose of both patent and copyright is to limit competition, and both terms arose in the industrial era. As Vaidhyanathan notes, "Patents and copyrights are the only constitutionally mandated monopolies, created with the recognition that unfettered competition would drain creators of their financial incentive to create" (2001, 87).

At present, Western nations have largely standardized the term of copyright to be the creator's life plus seventy years. For much of the history of copyright, however, the term was significantly shorter. In the U.S., the original term was fourteen years from the moment of creation of the work. In 1831, it was extended to twenty-eight years, renewable for another fourteen years. In 1909, it became twenty-eight years with another twenty-eight years available for renewal. In 1976, the term was set in the form known today, extending over the author's life plus fifty years to benefit the author's estate. In 1998, the U.S. aligned with the European standard of life of the author plus seventy years.[1]

The notion of an international standard raises, of course, the problem of international enforcement. Initial efforts focused on treaties that promised reciprocal granting of copyrights. Books by English authors, in English and easily read by American audiences, were more cheaply produced, and thus priced, than those by American authors. American publishers copied texts of works popular in England and republished them in the U.S. without paying royalties and vice versa (including in Canada, with Canadian publishers appropriating American work). Both English and American authors suffered under such practices. Reciprocal copyrights halted this practice and became the foundation for the complex network of international treaties that have, in the current moment, sought simplification under a variety of regional pacts with names like "Trans-Pacific Partnership."

As important as who can copy, as will be discussed in the following, is what can be copied, and much of that relies upon a couple of seemingly commonsensical distinctions that can quickly become complicated. For example, common sense would suggest that facts are not copyrightable, and indeed they are not, although particular compilations of facts, as in a reference work, are. Ideas are not copyrightable, but particular expressions of ideas are. Finally, common sense suggests that the rights at stake are those of an author and that his (and gender presumption matters here) ability to assign copyright is foundational to imagining intellectual property. As shown by the place of fairy tales in the development of ideas about what is and is not copyrightable, the role of the independent, individuated subject "distinguishes the creativity produced by an individual from the rest of society" (Ploman and Hamilton 1980, 7).

The first copyright laws were mostly concerned with restricting the growth of the emergent printing industry. As printing presses became widely available, European monarchies and the Papacy sought to restrict who could legally produce books. These state-sanctioned guilds were further restricted, in many instances, by lists of approved and banned books. The practice that eventually emerged was that particular presses were given the rights to make copies of particular books, and thus books were distributed among the presses, without their having to worry about competition.

Copyright arose out of a particular moment in the publishing industry's history when, as the legacy safeguards fell away and a more open market emerged, publishers freely created their own versions of popular works. Such publishing was profitable in two dimensions: first, and perhaps foremost, the book was already established as successful, lowering the risks associated with setting up a print run, and, second, the secondary publisher could undercut the initial publisher and sell at a lower price. This happened precisely because they had only the costs of printing and distribution and none of the costs associated with creation, like paying an author, including the ongoing remittance of a royalty.

In England, this exclusion eventually resulted in getting a number of authors involved in re-establishing copyright, such that both William Wordsworth and Thomas Carlyle were instrumental in the passage of the Copyright Act of 1842 in the United Kingdom, which defined copyright as belonging to the author who then granted it to a publisher. The term of copyright was set at the author's life plus seven years or forty-two years after the work's initial publication, whichever was longer: this was the first-time that copyright was extended post-mortem.

American copyright law at its inception was concerned not only with protecting the profitability of creation but also with balancing that protection against the rights of others to discuss, criticize, or extend copyrighted material. One particular dimension of this concern was manifested in the notion of a limited term for copyright, the understanding being that creators should enjoy the privilege "just long enough to create more, but the work should live afterward in the public domain as common property of the reading public" (Vaidhyanathan 2001, 21). Thus the granting of monopoly was conceived as a tax paid by the public for the creation of original expressions of ideas and facts, but a tax with its end built in.

The founding view of copyright in the U.S. was as a means to encourage the creation of novel ideas, facts, and expressions for the sake of enriching a body politic, as George Washington imagined it. However, copyright does not, within the marketplace of ideas, which was the way James Madison preferred to think of it, guarantee anyone will be interested enough in ideas, facts, or expressions to want to copy them. However, once an idea can be conceived of as "intellectual property" a powerful metaphorical regime has been invoked, and thus ideas, as property, give their owners a collection of rights. Indeed, perhaps the most fundamental shift is that ideas can now have owners.

The problem with the notion of intellectual property is that the two things that it seeks to hold together often have inverse value propositions. Tangible property, arguably made more solid by being the noun in the phrase, typically increases in value the less there is in relationship to demand. Ideas, however, gain in value as a function of social power, as they are possessed by more people—something Thomas Jefferson argued in his attempts to keep copyright out of the U.S. Constitution. Jefferson feared that, thanks in part to this contradiction, any copyright provision would encourage the development of state-sanctioned entities that would exercise unnecessary, if not deleterious, effects on the flow of ideas for the sake of power and/or self-enrichment.[2]

Jefferson's concerns were, over the course of the nineteenth century, eventually worn away by cases like *Stowe v. Thomas* (1853)[3] that goaded American authors to pursue a formalized intellectual property regime. The leading advocate for the expansion of copyright protection in the United States was Mark Twain, and his concern was the work of Charles Dickens. The American reading public was exploding, thanks chiefly to cheap imports. Many English books were cheaper in the U.S. than they were in their native land: *A Tale of Two Cities* sold for the equivalent of $2.50 in London at the same time that is was available on the streets of Manhattan for 6 cents (see Clark 1960).

As Vaidhyanathan observes, Twain's thirty-year pursuit of copyright reform, especially in his steadfast use of "property" in such discussions, was a double-edged sword. On the one hand, Twain, as both Clemens the businessman and Twain the author, lobbied hard in magazine articles and in appearances before the U.S. Congress for legislation that would end this theft of texts. On the other, as an author Twain was himself a thief:

> Many of the devices, characters, and events that he used in his fiction were unapologetically lifted from others. Twain was not hung up on originality. In his work, he frequently alluded to other authors and works, and even to his own previous works, to signify on what had come before and to satirize flaws in literature and society. Mark Twain was firmly embedded in storytelling tradition that lay outside the romantic assumptions of authorial distinction that informed the philosophical tenets of copyright law.
>
> (Vaidhyanathan 2001, 57)

Perhaps the most clear-cut case is Twain's "A True Story, Repeated Word for Word as I Heard It." Published in 1874 in *Atlantic Monthly*, the text claims to be nothing more than a transcription of a story told by a woman Twain calls "Aunt Rachel" but whom we now know was Mary Ann Cord. Despite the story's title, Twain copyrighted the work. In doing so, he followed an unfortunate practice that emerged from a larger belief that certain materials were, by definition, unauthored. These materials were increasingly termed "folklore" or "traditional," and in many instances the sources were women in peasant households or men and women of non-European societies who to this day are too often labeled "primitive," a word that developed its particular meaning in the nineteenth century.

Twain's use of Cord's text, whether or not it was "word for word," foregrounds a tension at work in arenas adjacent to "local color" literature, as the texts that focused on distinctive cultures of American regions in the latter half of the nineteenth century came to be called. A literature of regions, of nations, had developed, nurtured by both scholars and writers. Twain, a member of the American Folklore Society, was not alone in, ostensibly, collecting such stories. Others engaged in similar activities, and not too dissimilar texts regularly appeared in the pages of the *Journal of American Folklore*, among other periodicals. Prefaces framed the texts with notes like, "The following tale was obtained, about 1890, from Aunt Cindy, a very old negress, who could remember events that happened some seventy years ago, and who had at her tongue's end the history of every family and plantation" (Jamison 1905, 250). Moreover, the texts were often rendered in eye dialect, whereby "I" becomes "Ah" and gerunds are spelled "-in'," alienating the narrator's spoken words from the common literary language assumed to flow readily between authors and readers.

Obviously, the collection and publication of folk cultural expressions has implications for fairy tales. One question that arises, especially given Twain's explicit use of "word for word" and its implicit use elsewhere, is authorship. While early collectors left many of their processes under-considered, the Grimms in an early publication, the *Circular Concerning the Collection of Folk Poetry* of 1815, were rather clear that they did not consider themselves authors of the texts they published, only editors, and they did not claim exclusive rights to the tales (Haase 1993, 394). As a matter of course, the Grimms insisted upon constructing the tales as being in the public domain and thus available for collection. While the Brothers focused their own work on producing complete editions—which were quite expensive—they never pursued copyright claims against the publishers who reused their materials in broadsides, posters, and single-story editions, suggesting they were fully committed to the idea that the materials they collected were public.

The Grimms helped establish a way of conceiving of the verbal production of some individuals as belonging to that individual and the verbal production of others as belonging to "the nation" or the common good—what we now call the public domain.[4] The regime they established regularly privileged the expressions of men like themselves, often middle or upper class, as the kind of material that could be considered intellectual property, and the expressions of other individuals, often women and folks of other classes and ethnicities, as not claimable as intellectual property. One central figure in the Grimms' textual enterprise, as Valdimar Hafstein notes, was Dorothea Viehmann:

> One of those happy pieces of good fortune was the acquaintance with a peasant woman from the village of Zwehrn near Kassel. Through her we acquired a good part of the tales published here along with a number of additions to the first volume. They can therefore be counted as genuinely Hessian. This woman, still vigorous and not much over fifty, is called Viehmann. She has a firmly set, pleasant face with bright, clear eyes and was probably beautiful when she was young. She has these stories

clearly in mind, a gift which she says is not given to everyone. Many people cannot memorize anything at all. She narrates carefully, confidently, and in an unusually lively manner, taking great pleasure in it.

(quoted in Hafstein 2014, 25)

This description leaves out the fact that Viehmann was the wife of a tradesman, a tailor, that she was from a Hugenot family, and that she was not atypical for the women that the Grimms consulted in making their collection. Viehmann and the others were conduits for folklore, bearers of tradition as they would come to be called.

Hafstein's assessment of the figuration of these women as passive conduits to a process that must be actively created, not only elsewhere but also elsewise, extends the archeology of knowledge begun by Michel Foucault among others and continued into the domain of folkloristics by Richard Bauman and Charles Briggs (2003). Bauman and Briggs focus on the creation of a new kind of authority, and thus of a new kind of author, a specialist whose job is to report back to modernity the various states of nonmodernity—typically the peasants of a modern nation or the natives of a nonmodern one. Hafstein discusses the development of a new kind of material, what he describes as *nonauthored*: "the Grimms helped give a shape to these regimes by devising an instrument (sharper than a letter opener, duller than a scalpel) for carving up the discursive field into authored works on the one hand and nonauthored texts on the other" (2014, 20). In this way, the Grimms helped establish a paradigm that continues to this day and haunts all discussions of not only folk culture, with the complex moniker of "intangible cultural heritage," but also of intellectual property itself, which has an uneasy relationship with the thing that cannot exist as property, namely the public domain (see Rikoon 2004).

Ideas of the public domain did not pre-exist the emergence of copyright, but emerged simultaneously with, and as its necessary twin, as Hafstein notes:

Folklore, in fact, came to be defined as such only with reference to norms of originality and ownership intrinsic to authorship and the intellectual property regime. A critical genealogy allows us to understand folklore as a constitutive outside of authorship. Folklore is the nonauthored. Better yet, it is the antiauthored. It circumscribes the discursive domain of authorship and defines the criterion of originality.

(2014, 22)

Thanks to the particularities of the moment in which copyright arose, folklore's placement in the public domain, as common knowledge, gave it a timeless quality: it's not a matter of *when* but *how* folk narrative was created. Folklore became a convenient way for the aspiring middle classes to refer to texts, including fairy tales, circulating among the non-literate common people. The former had access to authored literature; the latter to nonauthored folklore. Peasant culture was imagined, and taken, as a common heritage available, and belonging, to all. Collecting their culture, their tales, was collecting our culture. Thus, a wide variety of travelers embarked upon missions to save culture, as they sometimes imagined it, or as some would have it to mine it like gemstones from the earth. They saw themselves as excising something that only a skilled craftsman, aware of market values, could polish and publish as the transformed work, still somehow reflecting the original.

Literary aspirations and/or dimensions entered. The Grimms remained firmly in the middle, seeking to have their work variously understood as quintessentially German or, later, quintessentially human, and thus have it remain part of a collective *ours*, as Donald Haase (1993) terms it. But Hans Christian Andersen was adamant that his work was *his*. When a version of

"The Princess on the Pea" found its way into the work of the Grimms, he was furious. While he admitted to taking inspiration from folk materials, Andersen felt he used stories that simply circulated among ordinary people and gave them, as Hafstein notes, "poetic truth": "These I have told in my own way: where I thought it fitting, I have changed them and let imagination freshen the colors in the picture that had begun to fade" (quoted in Hafstein 2014, 13). In believing he was reviving tales in some ways dead (but still moving—akin to zombies one supposes), Andersen anticipated later considerations of folklore as largely circulating among the unlettered (and thus?) un-creative classes. In 1926 Kaarle Krohn assumed that "it is a misconception to seek the collective in artistic creations. [. . .] [A]ny unified composition, large or small, presupposes an individual composer" (25). Only a few years later in 1929, Roman Jakobson and Petr Bogatyrev argued that, for innovation in language, and thus in linguistic artifacts like folk narrative:

> we can examine those cases where language transformations take place as a result of a kind of socialization or generalization of individual speech errors (lapsus), individual emotional states, or aesthetic deformations of speech. [. . .] But with the usual changes for linguistic change in effect we can speak of the "birth" of a language innovation only from that moment when it constitutes a social fact, i.e., when the community of speakers has adopted it as its own.
>
> (1980, 4)

The function of "the folk" under such a model is selection: by choosing to repeat a change, whether a purposeful or accidental act of an individual, they make it folk. The most extreme version of this logic is what Alan Dundes (1969) termed the devolutionary premise: that much of what was, and is, folklore began life as the creative products of members of the refined classes and that its continuance among the masses is one of, literally, unwitting repetition, rendering texts shard by shard. In this view, one assumes, folklore collection closed a loop, re-capturing materials by refined individuals of materials that had once belonged to them, or people like them. Whether the devolutionary premise was at work in any given individual effort is less the issue than the fact that the nonauthored nature of folktales made their collection and publication by an author a ready, and welcome, possibility. In particular this meant that the stories told by peasants or merchants in general, and women in particular, could be collected in the public domain and then shifted, through editing and other magical authorial activities, into intellectual property. Since the default for all publications is copyright, any given work's availability in the public domain was largely a matter of authors and publishers not pursuing possible claims of infringement, as was the case with the Grimms.

The result overall of this dynamic was that folk narrative collectors, and authors like Andersen and Twain inspired by folk narratives, emerged as the names on the spines of books, and on the transaction lines of checks, while the individuals who had told the stories, many of whom were elderly and a significant proportion of whom were women, would find themselves, quite literally, unnamed. On both sides of the Atlantic, published authors now found themselves on the receiving end of fame and fortune. The result was an impoverishment of the commons for the sake of a limited set of producers. New books now cost more because authors were more assured of getting paid, but the class of authors had been narrowly defined to the advantage of a small set of human verbal productivity.

However the tides turned in favor of authors, publishers, and/or the public, and however the battles were framed, in terms of common law or creativity, by the beginning of the twentieth century a celebrity culture (as we now imagine it) benefited both authors and publishers.

This joining of two sides that had for so long been in opposition meant that the focus on the author, as an individual genius whose work must be protected against those who would seek to deny him, or occasionally her, a well-earned reward, had become important to publishers as well, as they realized that a strong author capable of granting a monopoly strengthened their own position in the marketplace. Complicating this alliance, however, were the unintended consequences of a change in the 1909 copyright law in the U.S. as well as the rise of media industries, first film and then television.

The Copyright Act of 1909[5] raised the issue of private corporate ownership. In particular, Section 3 introduced the idea of composite works owned by the sponsoring entity:

> [T]he copyright provided by this Act shall protect all the copyrightable component parts of the work copyrighted, and all matter therein in which copyright is already subsisting, but without extending the duration or scope of such copyright. The copyright upon composite works or periodicals shall give to the proprietor thereof all the rights in respect thereto which he would have if each part were individually copyrighted under this Act.
>
> (1076)

Where before copyright could only be bestowed upon a named individual, the new law, introduced primarily for the publishers of encyclopedias and newspapers, created a new category of creativity: work for hire. The emergent film industry was quick to adapt the law to their own ends, hiring writers to crank out countless short stories during the period that stories fell under copyright but films did not. This particular gap in the Act was corrected three years later in 1912, but the utility of studio writers to feed the production schedule with content was sufficiently established, and, more importantly, the value of a producer or publisher owning the copyright to a work was immediately clear.

The desire to own as much of the production process as possible was established from the outset: the film industry's first steps took place under the watchful eye of Thomas Edison, who was keen to capture the profit in the promising new entertainment sector through a dense web of patents on film equipment, legal contracts for distribution, and copyrights on works. Edison's pecuniary system led many aspiring entrants to set up as far from Edison and his headquarters in Menlo Park, New Jersey, as possible: they chose Los Angeles, California. Larger histories of copyright during this time reveal how first Edison, then D. W. Griffith, and then a host of others not only developed the studio system but also the network of shell companies that exercised control over any intellectual property generated anywhere within the system.

Because of the money involved, many early cases that helped shape subsequent law, either through statute or precedence, emerged from wrangling between authors of published works and potentially, or actually, derivative films. Many appeared before, and some of the most interesting decisions were written by Judge Learned Hand. In attempting to maintain the idea/expression dichotomy, he often engaged in extended textual comparative analyses seeking to discern any pattern that may be the signature of a unique expression of an idea. Hand's assumption was that such patterns, stories told in a distinctive way, were protectable under copyright (Gunther 2011, 280). The judge's conclusion in the case of *Sheldon v. Metro-Goldwyn* was that the defendants had indeed infringed:

> True, the assault is deferred in the picture from this scene to the next, but it is the same dramatic trick. Again, the poison in each case is found at home, and the girl talks with her betrothed just after the villain has left and again pledges him her faith.

Surely the sequence of these details is pro tanto [to that extent] the very web of the authors' dramatic expression; and copying them is not "fair use."[6]

The phrase "web of the authors' dramatic expression" is oft quoted in discussions of copyright, especially when trying to unravel the dense tangle of works that may or may not be derivative.

While the judge's conclusion focused on matters of expression, its status as expression largely rested on nineteenth-century ideas about who gets to author. Folk culture's status as conventionally in the public domain, or in a quasi-legal limbo of "intangible cultural heritage," has made it largely available to media companies for use and reuse, with the results themselves beneficiaries of the privileged status of intellectual property. It is no accident that, having mined and copyrighted a subset of European folktales, the Disney Corporation has embarked upon a campaign of similarly treating folktales from around the world. One point of view is that the company is bringing balance in representations of folk culture. Another suggests it is simply engaging in the now centuries-old practice of mining other people's minds for material that it can claim exists in the public domain but, having traveled through a dense network of individuals and shell companies, is now very much an intellectual property. And as most media companies now recognize, the possibilities for commodification of an expression, in the form of toys, costumes, books, and much more, seem limitless.

The complexities of copyright in particular and intellectual property in general have not, of course, diminished with the introduction of the Internet, which has lowered the barriers to quotation, pastiche, and reproduction. The legal tangles continue, especially with the extension of patents to include software, business processes, and designs (which can also be copyrighted). So many complexities have arisen that some legal scholars and intellectual property (IP) activists have called upon a rethinking of the IP regime (see, for example, Lawrence Lessig's *Free Culture* [2004] or Eric Raymond's *The Cathedral and the Bazaar* [1999]). Certainly one attempt to do so has been undertaken under the auspices of the World Intellectual Property Organization, which has specifically organized a committee on Intellectual Property and Genetic Resources, Traditional Knowledge, and Folklore. Where such extensions, revisions, or refutations lead will be an interesting question.

Related topics: Classical Music; Convergence Culture; Disney Corporation; Fan Fiction; Indigeneity; Language; Novels; Print; TV Drama; YouTube and Internet Video

Notes

1. Sonny Bono Copyright Term Extension Act of 1989. Public Law 105-298—Oct. 27 1998. 112 Statute 2827–2834.
2. Jefferson expressed his concerns in a letter to Isaac McPherson in 1813 (Lipscomb and Bergh 1905, Vol. 13, 333–335).
3. *Stowe v. Thomas*, 23 F. Cas. 201 (C.C.E.D.Pa. 1853).
4. For a brief discussion of "Cinderella" (ATU 510A) as media public domain, see Haynes (2005, 131–133).
5. Copyright Act of 1909. 1909. Public Law 349. Sixtieth Congress, Second Session, 4 March. www.legisworks.org/congress/60/publaw-349.pdf.
6. *Sheldon v. Metro-Goldwyn Pictures Corporation*. 1936. Circuit Court of Appeals, Second Circuit. 17 Jan. 81 F.2d 49.

References Cited and Further Reading

Bauman, Richard, and Charles L. Briggs. 2003. *Voices of Modernity: Language Ideologies and the Politics of Inequality*. Cambridge: Cambridge UP.

Clark, Aubert. 1960. *The Movement for International Copyright in Nineteenth Century America*. Washington, DC: Catholic U America P.

Dundes, Alan. 1969. "The Devolutionary Premise in Folklore Theory." *Journal of the Folklore Institute* 6 (1): 5–19.

Gunther, Gerald. 2011. *Learned Hand: The Man and the Judge.* Oxford: Oxford UP.

Haase, Donald. 1993. "Yours, Mine, or Ours? Perrault, the Brothers Grimm, and the Ownership of Fairy Tales." *Merveilles & Contes* 7 (2): 383–402.

Hafstein, Valdimar. 2014. "The Constant Muse: Copyright and Creative Agency." *Narrative Culture* 1 (1): 9–48.

Haynes, Richard. 2005. *Media Rights and Intellectual Property.* Edinburgh: Edinburgh UP.

Jakobson, Roman, and Petr Bogatyrev. 1980. "Folklore as a Special Form of Creation." Translated by John M. O'Hara. *Folklore Forum* 13 (1): 1–21.

Jamison, C. V. 1905. "A Louisiana Legend Concerning Will o' the Wisp." *Journal of American Folklore* 18 (70): 250–1.

Krohn, Kaarle. (1926) 1971. *Folklore Methodology.* Austin: U Texas P.

Lessig, Lawrence. 2004. *Free Culture: How Big Media Uses Technology and the Law to Lock Down Culture and Control Creativity.* London: Penguin.

Lipscomb, Andrew A., and Albert Ellery Bergh, eds. 1905. *The Writings of Thomas Jefferson.* 20 vols. Washington, DC: Thomas Jefferson Memorial Association.

Ploman, Edward, and Clark Hamilton. 1980. *Copyright: Intellectual Property in the Information Age.* New York: Routledge and Kegan Paul.

Raymond, Eric. 1999. *The Cathedral and the Bazaar.* Sebastopol, CA: O'Reilly Media.

Rikoon, J. Sanford. 2004. "On the Politics of the Politics of Origins: Social (in) Justice and the International Agenda on Intellectual Property, Traditional Knowledge, and Folklore." *Journal of American Folklore* 117 (465): 325–36.

Tatar, Maria. 2004. *Annotated Brothers Grimm: Bicentennial Edition.* New York: Norton.

Twain, Mark. 1874. "A True Story, Repeated Word for Word as I Heard It." *The Atlantic Monthly* (November): 591–4.

Vaidhyanathan, Siva. 2001. *Copyrights and Copywrongs: The Rise of Intellectual Property and How It Threatens Creativity.* New York: NYU P.

23
PORNOGRAPHY
Catherine Tosenberger[1]

In the Erotic Museum, located in the Red Light District of Amsterdam, there is a vivid testament to what Cristina Bacchilega calls "the libidinal power of fairy tales" (2008, 14): an entire room dedicated to a mural depicting pornographic fairy tales. In an idyllic sylvan landscape, a prince drools upon a grinning Sleeping Beauty; a wolf flashes an enormous penis at a perplexed and intrigued Little Red Riding Hood; and Snow White, in dominatrix gear, presides over the cavorting, horny seven dwarfs. Pornographic animated films play on a continuous loop, and viewers are invited to sit upon toadstools and watch or contemplate carved figures of Disney's Snow White and the seven dwarfs.

Fairy tales and pornography would seem at first glance to be diametrically opposed: fairy tales are popularly conceived of as the ultimate innocent childhood fantasies, while pornography is proverbially the benchmark for adult depravity. In addition, fairy tales have actual plots, ones that are usually more complex than that of the stereotypical mainstream porn film (i.e., "Here's your pizza ma'am, with *extra sausage*"). However, both tend to take place in fantasy universes, where flat, one-dimensional characters move through a series of pre-ordained plot incidents to an imposed happy ending; both negotiate in a variety of ways with the concept of utopia; and both are intimately concerned with desire and the fulfilling of desire. Unsurprisingly, a large number of hardcore pornographic films borrow the plots and imagery of fairy tales. Jeana Jorgensen remarks:

> [T]here is little explicit sex to be found in most literary fairy tales, especially the classic tales of the Grimms, Charles Perrault, and the French conteuses. The overt sexuality of eroticized fairy tales, however, could be viewed as a carnivalesque inversion, making the implicit explicit. Since so many fairy tales end in marriage—to the extent that Vladimir Propp has marriage as the fairy tale's ultimate function—sex is an underlying concern of fairy tales, though it rarely comes to the forefront as it does in erotic [material].
>
> (2008, 28)

Fairy tales and pornography are both gendered: fairy tales are in general associated with a female audience, and pornography with a male audience. Fairy-tale porn, in addition to invoking the frisson of the allegedly innocent stories of childhood, plays with assumptions about the perceived audience of the texts. However, as Linda Williams notes, even prior to the mainstreaming of the Internet, which made the most esoteric fetishes visible and available for wide consumption, pornography was always varied and complex. Pornographic films parallel movie musicals: all the action stops for the "number," whether song-and-dance or sexual. Moreover, "feature-length hard-core films [. . .] closely resemble musicals structurally in their tendency to

Pornography and Parody

Fairy-tale porn is a subtype of the broader category of the porn parody. While many (including some fairy-tale porn) limit their reference to the title (i.e., *Snow White Loves Black Pole* [2008] or the *Da Vinci Load* [2006]), other films engage more closely with the object of parody, addressing the sexuality that Hollywood films often erase or elide (Cindy Patton, quoted in Penley 2004, 328). Paul Booth argues that "[p]orn parody films highlight an undercurrent of sexuality within all mainstream texts by providing negotiated readings of mainstream media" (2015, 128). Nina K. Martin remarks that porn parodies often take on male-identified genres, such as Westerns and sci-fi (2006, 196). At least some of the films directly or indirectly court a female audience.

Fairy tales, with their linear plots and flat characters, lend themselves quite easily to the pornographic film structure. Fairy-tale pornography has an obvious Hollywood referent in Disney—indeed, there are many amateur works of fan fiction and fan art featuring the Disney versions of fairy-tale characters in a variety of pornographic scenarios. But more broadly, fairy-tale porn invokes what Eric Tribunella, echoing Jorgensen, calls "the carnivalesque pleasure in adult nostalgia, revelry in the taboo, and exertion of adult agency over the artifacts of childhood" (2008, 136).

A key feature of many adult-oriented reworkings of fairy tales is an engagement with broader cultural understandings. Since the late nineteenth century, fairy tales have increasingly become associated with children. In opposition to this narrative, we have the "recovery story"—a narrative about the fairy tale that has in the past been most effectively mined by postmodern writers and filmmakers, horror auteurs, and, yes, pornography. In opposition to the Disneyfied popular view, fairy tales are "really" dark, bloody, and sexual. The collections of Perrault, the Brothers Grimm, and other early fairy tale writers certainly provide much material that does not meet post-Romantic standards of appropriateness for children.

Pornography has addressed the issue in overt and self-conscious ways. Laura Kipnis argues that "one of pornography's large themes is that we're adults who were once children, in whom the social has been instilled at great and even tragic cost" (1998, 168). The presence or absence of sexuality is one of the primary factors in whether a given text is designated as being for adults or for children (Tribunella 2008). Booth states that "[h]ard core pornography is always about juxtaposition"—the most private and intimate human acts with spectacle, the "reality" of the bodies and acts onscreen with the "unreality" of a film production, and, in the case of porn parodies, the disjuncture between mainstream Hollywood and the more "cultish and shadowed" world of pornographic filmmaking (2015, 127–128). When pornography tackles fairy tales, that juxtaposition becomes the ultimate form of the recovery story: fairy-tale porn *requires* that the audience bring its concept of fairy tales as children's texts in order to make the most of its titillating spectacle. The Disneyfied view of fairy tales functions exactly the way that James R. Kincaid (1998) argues broader constructs of childhood innocence do: enticing primarily in the threat of its violation.

Fairy tales do in fact already contain plenty of violence, the majority are concerned with romance and desire, and numerous scholars articulate the tensions surrounding gender and sexuality that exist within the fairy tale. Pornography takes those tensions and hyperbolically expands upon them. For example, several pornographic films use "Beauty and the Beast" (ATU 425C), an extremely popular point of reference within mainstream romance.

Eroticizing the Other: Beauty and the Beast

Linda J. Lee (2008) points out that along with "Cinderella," "Beauty and the Beast" has the most common plot in romance. According to Betsy Hearne, folk and literary iterations of ATU 425C "reveal more clearly than any other [tale] the interweaving of social custom and law with fantasy narratives" (1989, xxi)—specifically, the social reality of young women forced to marry unappealing older men and the necessity that these women accommodate themselves to their fate. Laurence Talairach-Vielmas says it deals with "the violence of male sexuality, which the heroine must learn to tame—and accept—and which marks the main stage of her education into womanhood" (275). Lee concurs: "Typical interpretations of 'Beauty and the Beast' focus on the transformative power of love or on a shift in the female protagonist's attitude toward sex from revulsion to pleasure" (2008, 59). However, the majority of pornographic films that invoke "Beauty and the Beast" focus instead on a spectacle of an encounter with the eroticized Other. The four movies under consideration here do not engage extensively with the plot of the fairy tale; each consists of a series of unconnected vignettes of sex between a conventionally attractive performer (usually a normatively feminine White woman) and a performer marked as (freakishly) Other, by virtue of age (old), race (non-White), or gender identity (non-cisgender).

Beauty and the Beast (2004) is a Spanish-language film with very little dialogue, written and directed by "Sonia H." This film equates beastliness with the elderly body: except for the final scene, each pornographic encounter (all heterosexual) is between a young and old performer— three old men and two old women. The camera lingers upon the spectacles of old and young flesh together and eroticizes the issues faced by elderly bodies—the older male performers often resort to dildoes to penetrate their female companions, when erections cannot be sustained. The final episode is between two young performers.

In the other films, "beastliness," following the fairy tale, is figured specifically as an exaggerated, potentially threatening masculinity. *Beauty and the Butch* (2008), produced by L Factor Productions ("Made for Women Who Love Women"), is the most playful; the film is an amateurish production, with refreshingly average-looking performers who actually talk and engage with each other. In this film, "butch" does not just refer to women whose self-presentation is masculine, but also to femme women who adopt a dominant role over their more submissive (and always conventionally femme) partners. By replacing "beast" with "butch," the film pokes fun at mainstream heterosexual porn's distaste for non-normatively feminine women; the "beastliness" of the butch is not a threat to their enthusiastic femme partners, but rather to the primacy of the usual assumed porn audience of heterosexual men with conventional tastes.

In the 1982 *Beauty and the Beast* the bulk of the movie takes the form of a pseudo-anthropological "documentary," featuring "Dr. Dick Richards, M.D." introducing, in quasi-scientific language, scenes of sexually "deviant" behavior and non-normative bodies. Trans and intersex people are a particular focus, and the film treats them with a mixture of prurience and sympathy; Richards's narration highlights the gender transgression as having immense erotic power. The film includes extended interviews with a trans woman and an intersex woman; these performers are given space to discuss their histories and relationship to notions of gender and sexual identity, which allows them rather more dignity than most mainstream films, never mind pornographic films. However, little people having sex with average-sized women and men who have sex with blow-up dolls are treated with mockery; these scenes are presented as comedy interludes rather than titillating erotic spectacles.

The other form of "beastliness" on display is exaggerated masculinity, in the form of an enormous penis. There are several scenes featuring a photo shoot of a White man with a penis that hangs down to his knees; however, the majority center around the legendary Black performer Long Dong Silver. Long Dong appears as himself in a couple of scenes as part of a burlesque act introduced by Richards and in a porn scene; but he, and the female performer Seka, are the stars of the apparently entirely separate second film that has been stitched into the "pseudo-documentary." This story features Southern woman Seka eagerly awaiting the return of her Black lover Long Dong from the Civil War (!); when he appears, he is wearing a Confederate uniform (!!!) and proceeds to deflower Seka's innocent belle.

This portion of *Beauty and the Beast* (1982), as well as the next, fall into the problematic genre of interracial porn. Williams argues that this genre, which usually features Black men and White women, can function in a subversive and progressive manner, citing the films' "complex flirtation with the now historically proscribed stereotype operating on both sides of the line. Thus the very taboos that once effectively policed the racial border now work in the service of eroticizing its transgression" (2004, 286). However, Daniel Bernardi points out that these films trade on "a racialized attraction that reduces people of color [. . .] to abnormal or hyperfeminized body parts and phenotypes while constructing interracial sex as fetishistic perversions for the 'pleasure' of spectators coded as white" (2006, 224–225). They make the ithyphallic Black man into a "kink" and code the threatening specter of Black male sexuality as savage and "beastly." A specifically racialized masculinity relies upon racist social-evolutionary rhetoric of the Black man—as represented by an iconographically enormous, engorged penis—as both ultimate ideal and threat to the White women in the films and to the "the white male [audience, who] [. . .] remains present ideologically even if absent from the mise-en-scene" (Bernardi 2006, 233).

The "threat" is most apparent in the 1982 *Beauty and the Beast*, in which Seka's angelic blonde southern belle in virginal white is ravished by Long Dong Silver; Long Dong's partners seem to be in as much pain as pleasure. In contrast, *Beauty and the 14" Beast*, from West Coast Productions, which specializes in interracial films, comes across as rather good-natured. Despite the DVD cover, which features a shot of a large penis (the fourteen-inch beast!) and a visibly disconcerted woman, each of the sex scenes—between a number of different performers, all well-endowed Black men and skinny White women—appears happy, with one or two being rather romantic, and others as giddy and giggly. This film doesn't cater quite as overtly to an assumed normative White male audience; the friendly cheerfulness of the sex scenes undercuts the titular position of the Black male performers as "beastly."

"We All Live in a House of Candy": Hansel and Gretel

At first glance, the Grimms' "Hansel and Gretel" (ATU 327A) is not the most obvious choice to receive a pornographic film treatment. "Little Red Riding Hood" (ATU 333) is the only other well-known non-romantic fairy tale that regularly appears in porn films, but that story, as Zipes (1993) and others demonstrate, contains a very obvious narrative of sexual threat that "Hansel and Gretel" appears to lack. However, the overriding theme in "Hansel and Gretel" is disrupted and disruptive eating. The tale opens with a scene of starvation, passes through several episodes of unwholesome surfeit (the house of candy, the witch's cannibalism, and the witch being cooked in her own oven), and ends with satisfaction. Williams argues that porn films follow this same pattern, with bad sex in the beginning signaling lack (1999, 166). The discourses of food and sexuality are, of course, deeply intertwined, and with them their concomitant anxieties about the appropriate conditions for satisfying these base bodily needs. "Hansel and Gretel" reflects social realities and depicts, in fantastic form, the terror and desire surrounding them. Modern American versions, in keeping with the surfeit of resources in the West (dependent upon the exploitation of and theft from poorer cultures), often preach moderation and caution against greed and excessive eating.

Pornography itself is, of course, often characterized as a dangerous, unwholesome pleasure: not the respectable, acceptable broccoli of nutritious highbrow art, but a toxic tooth-rotting indulgence in the lowest form of empty calories that will ultimately poison and destroy the consumer. Pornographic films that take "Hansel and Gretel" as their target text invoke this discourse of excess and indulgence; the films I examine here treat the witch's cottage as the transformative space of terror and desire, but approach the motif in radically different ways.

The 2011 *Bread Crumbs*, directed by Mike Nichols,[2] is not hardcore pornography, but a straightforward condemnation of excessive sexuality, in stereotypical horror movie style. The actors and crew of an adult film travel to an isolated cabin in the woods, where they are menaced and murdered by a bizarre adolescent brother-and-sister pair. The victims, however, are not the usual horny teenagers, but jaded members of the porn industry. As per the usual slasher formula, several characters emerge as sympathetic, notably Angie, an aging star and recovering alcoholic on what she plans as her final shoot. When two unsettling orphaned adolescents (Henry and Patti) appear from the woods, almost causing the crew's van to crash, Angie speaks kindly to them; when Patti shows up at the cabin later, dragging her creepy doll, Angie attempts to connect with her, and she tries to protect her later. Even though not a virgin—Angie is the oldest and most experienced porn star—her kindness and maternal instincts situate her as the "Final Girl," Carol J. Clover's term for the slasher movie heroine who invites the audience's sympathy and identification (1992).

The film engages extensively with discourses of innocence: after Henry attacks and murders several members of the cast and crew, Angie tries to protect Patti, whom she believes is a victim. It turns out, however, that Patti is the mastermind and directs the mentally challenged Henry to kill. Henry insists that "we all live in a house of candy" as he stuffs sweets down his victims' mouths; the meaning is never made clear, but the fact that they attack a porn shoot is suggestive. When Henry rips open the blouse of one of the women, Patti admonishes him, shouting, "We don't play that way." Further, despite Angie's plan, Eddie, the malicious director (played by Nichols himself), informs her that he will never allow her to leave the industry.

Here, the pornography industry—and, on a broader level, sex itself—is positioned as the seductive, toxic "house of candy" that lures in innocents and disrupts and perverts family ties. Vi says she wishes she hadn't stopped speaking to her mother, and Angie says she's leaving because she wants to have a family and doesn't want to raise a child in this environment. At a key moment, Angie buys herself some time by convincing Henry that she is his and Patti's mother; when she takes the opportunity to flee, Henry's anguished howls of "Mommy! Mommy!" provide a genuinely chilling moment. While the overall narrative is rather confused and silly, the fairy tale and its anxieties about family and abandonment give this Z-grade film a little more depth than it might otherwise have.

Hansel and Gretel and the Horny Witch (N.d.) is vintage cartoon pornography; the animation style appears to be that of the 1960s. It's a highly condensed version, concentrating on the interlude in the forest. The whole film is wildly phallic and takes full advantage of the freedoms offered by animation. Hansel and Gretel, naked in the forest like Adam and Eve, have sex with each other while a bunch of Disney-esque woodland creatures, inspired by their example, do the same. After this scene of happy fucking, Hansel and Gretel encounter the witch, watering her garden of penises with milk squirting from her breasts. She captures the pair, imprisons Hansel, and sets Gretel to work (pumping water, polishing knickknacks) in her house full of phalluses; she and Gretel also penetrate each other with a variety of objects. Hansel is hit with a magic spell that causes his penis to grow to gargantuan proportions; he uses it to bust out of prison, pole-vault to the witch's house, and fuck the witch until the head of his penis comes out through her mouth. Gretel then lures the exhausted witch to the open oven door, and a bunch of bunnies push her in. Hansel's penis goes back to normal, and they have missionary-position sex surrounded by their woodland friends. Unlike in *Bread Crumbs*, nature—woodland creatures and sentient trees—is benevolent. Hansel and Gretel are at one with the woods; the witch, with her cultivated garden of phalluses and unnatural breast milk, is the threatening interloper who must be defeated and destroyed by Adam/Hansel and Gretel/Eve and their Disney-esque animal companions.

Hansel and Gretel (2001, directed by Paul Thomas for Vivid, one of the largest American porn studios) concentrates its energies on fairy tale and porn conventions, to surprisingly successful effect. While comedic scenes in porn films are common, Martin has observed that humor is rarely allowed to intrude upon the actual sex scenes, which she attributes to straight cismale–oriented porn's need to "[maintain] the awe and drama surrounding the representation of the penis" (2006, 193). However, *Hansel and Gretel* does not always insist upon a strict dichotomy between comedy and sex scenes. The overall effect is quite charming; the fairy-tale plot and the presence of the young, handsome Dale DaBone (an actor known for his comic performances) as Hansel may be an attempt by Vivid to broaden their consumer base.

The film opens with "Mother Goose" (Gwen Summers) teasingly asserting fidelity to the fairy tale: "We got an expert to translate from the original German. [. . .] Not to worry—they still get lost in the woods and find an edible cottage." But, she adds, "We made up a lot of stuff too." The film retains this metafictive framework throughout; although Mother Goose doesn't show up again until the end, the narrative voice, usually in the form of title cards, continues to comment on the action. Hansel, son of Helmut Hugencock, "not the brightest porch light on the block," has showbiz aspirations: he can't master juggling, so he invents "mime juggling." His other talent is absolutely terrible Brando and Cagney impersonations (to which the title cards respond, "Yikes").

The film has a lot of fun with fairy-tale conventions. The story begins, "Once upon a time in the fairy-tale section of the medieval German countryside," and Ava, Helmut's new wife, introduces herself to Hansel as "your evil stepmother" (to which he responds, "Oh fuck! An evil stepmother!"). The "Hansel and Gretel" plot lacks only the final triumphant return to the father's house: this Hansel and Gretel are fully aware and annoyed that Helmut has abandoned them. Additions include extended sex scenes (during which all action pauses, just as in a musical song-and-dance number) and a brief exchange with a Robin Hood–like traveler who gives the pair directions to the enchanted cottage (in exchange for sex with Gretel).

Hansel and Gretel reach the witch's cottage, where after a number of groanworthy puns about cannibalism, Gretel engages in enthusiastic sex with the witch and a male guard; during the requisite money shot, the guard giggles, "Ja, die Spritzen ist gut!" This film is also a romance. Gretel is Ava's daughter, making her and Hansel stepsiblings, as Hansel takes great pains to remind us on several occasions. The climax of the film comes when she and Hansel declare their love for one another and have sex in the final scene. The fairy tale does not just provide a framework for the plot; this film has interpreted the themes by featuring an unusually large and extended number of cunnilingus scenes for a mainstream heterosexual porn movie.

The obsession with consumption and its discontents in "Hansel and Gretel" not only suggests a variety of potential pornographic expansions, but also provides an opening for examining the discourse of pornography itself.

Fairy-tale porn films marry the historical sociocultural narratives of desire and anxiety to the contemporary iterations of those same issues through the lens of explicit sex. While pornographic films are often dismissed as proverbially worthless, these narratives—like the similarly marginalized forms of romance and, indeed, the fairy tale—provide crucial insights into discourses of sexuality.

Related topics: Cinematic; Gender; Musicals; Sexualities/Queer and Trans Studies

Notes

1. The research for this chapter was made possible thanks to Social Sciences and Humanities Research Council of Canada grant 410-2011-29 (Pauline Greenhill, principal investigator). I would also like to thank my research assistants Angela Sylvester, Murray Gordon, Calley Gresham, and Kendra Magnus-Johnston for their invaluable support.
2. *Not* the acclaimed Mike Nichols who directed films like *Closer* (2004) and *Angels in America* (2003).

References Cited and Further Reading

Bacchilega, Cristina. 2008. "Preface to the Special Issue on Erotic Tales." *Marvels & Tales* 22 (1): 13–23.

Bernardi, Daniel. 2006. "Interracial Joysticks: Pornography's Web of Racist Attractions." In *Pornography: Film and Culture*, edited by Peter Lehman, 220–43. New Brunswick, NJ: Rutgers UP.

Booth, Paul. 2015. *Playing Fans: Negotiating Fandom and Media in the Digital Age*. Iowa City: U Iowa P.

Clover, Carol J. 1992. *Men, Women and Chain Saws: Gender in the Modern Horror Film*. Princeton, NJ: Princeton UP.

Hearne, Betsy. 1989. *Beauty and the Beast: Visions and Revisions of an Old Tale*. Chicago: U Chicago P.

Jones, Sarah Gwenllian. 2002. "The Sex Lives of Cult Television Characters." *Screen* 43: 79–90.

Jorgensen, Jeana. 2008. "Innocent Initiations: Female Agency in Eroticized Fairy Tales." *Marvels & Tales* 22 (1): 27–37.

Kincaid, James R. 1998. *Erotic Innocence*. Durham, NC: Duke UP.

Kipnis, Laura. 1998. *Bound and Gagged: Pornography and the Politics of Fantasy in America*. Durham, NC: Duke UP.

Kooistra, Lorraine Janzen. 1997. "*Goblin Market* as a Cross-Audienced Poem: Children's Fairy Tale, Adult Erotic Fantasy." *Children's Literature* 25: 181–204.

Lee, Linda J. 2008. "Guilty Pleasures: Reading Romance Novels as Reworked Fairy Tales." *Marvels & Tales* 22 (1): 52–66.

Martin, Nina K. 2006. "Never Laugh at a Man with His Pants Down: The Affective Dynamics of Comedy and Porn." In *Pornography: Film and Culture*, edited by Peter Lehman, 189–205. New Brunswick, NJ: Rutgers UP.

Mendoza, Victor Roman. 2006. "'Come Buy': The Crossing of Sexual and Consumer Desire in Christina Rossetti's *Goblin Market*." *English Literary History* 73 (4): 913–47.

Penley, Constance. 2004. "Crackers and Whackers: The White-Trashing of Porn." In *Porn Studies*, edited by Linda Williams, 309–32. Durham, NC: Duke UP.

Talairach-Vielmas, Laurence. 2010. "Beautiful Maidens, Hideous Suitors: Victorian Fairy Tales and the Process of Civilization." *Marvels & Tales* 24 (2): 272–96.

Tatar, Maria. 1993. *Off With Their Heads! Fairy Tales and the Culture of Childhood*. Princeton, NJ: Princeton UP.

Tribunella, Eric L. 2008. "From Kiddie Lit to Kiddie Porn: The Sexualization of Children's Literature." *Children's Literature Association Quarterly* 33 (2): 135–55.

Warner, Marina. 1995. *From the Beast to the Blonde: On Fairy Tales & Their Tellers*. London: Oxford UP.

Williams, Linda. 1999. *Hard Core: Power, Pleasure, and the "Frenzy of the Visible"*. Berkeley: U California P.

———. 2004. "Skin Flicks on the Racial Border: Pornography, Exploitation, and Interracial Lust." In *Porn Studies*, edited by Linda Williams, 269–308. Durham, NC: Duke UP.

Zipes, Jack. 1993. *The Trials & Tribulations of Little Red Riding Hood*. New York: Routledge.

———. 1997. *Happily Ever After: Fairy Tales, Children, and the Culture Industry*. New York: Routledge.

———. 2006. *Why Fairy Tales Stick: The Evolution and Relevance of a Genre*. New York: Routledge.

Mediagraphy

Angels in America (TV). 2003. Director Mike Nichols. USA/Italy.
Beauty and the 14" Beast. 2006. Director James A. USA.
Beauty and the Beast. 1982. Director Dr. Dick Richards. USA.
————. 2004. Director Sonya H. USA.
Beauty and the Butch. 2008. Producer L Factor Productions. USA.
Bread Crumbs. 2010. Director Mike Nichols. USA.
Closer. 2004. Director Mike Nichols. USA.
The Da Vinci Load. 2006. Director Jerome Tanner. USA.
Hansel and Gretel. 2001. Director Paul Thomas. USA.
Hansel and Gretel and the Horny Witch. N.d. www.redtube.com/62504.
Snow White Loves Black Pole 1. 2008. Director anonymous. USA.

24

STORYWORLDS/ NARRATOLOGY

Katharine Young

Suppose you inhabited a reality in which every now and then your fellow inhabitants conjured up alternate realities for you out of thin air. As you go around, little ruptures burst through the surface of the ordinary and other worlds show up. These alternate realities pelt you frequently, soliciting your sympathy and engagement, or alternatively evoking your repugnance or resistance, or leave you in a state of indifference. But there they are, hovering, awaiting your attention. Your fellow inhabitants cast forth these alternate realities for your interest, amusement, instruction, illumination, deception, arousal, provocation, and contemplation. When you are fascinated, amused, even offended, the little worlds elaborate themselves ever more vividly for you, but as soon as you turn away from them, they disappear, *fffft*.

My contention is that you do inhabit such a reality. Every time somebody tells a story, reads a book, or sees a film, she cracks open a little world. As long as the teller speaks and you listen, you can be transported into that other reality. You take in the antics of the inhabitants of the storyworld; you find yourself moved or disturbed, sometimes to the point of tears or laughter; you follow out the consequences of the people's actions; you are sensitive to their moods: what happens there counts for you. You perceive a world replete with topologies, formations, installations; with paths, buildings, objects; with phenomena, acts, and consequences. It is real.

But the reality is only sustained by your attention. If you get distracted, lose interest, drift off, the reality collapses. As William James famously put it: "Each world *whilst it is attended to* is real after its own fashion; only the reality lapses with the attention" ([1890] 1910, 293). We inhabit what the phenomenologist Alfred Schutz calls "multiple realities" (1970, 245). Peter Berger and Thomas Luckmann suggest:

> Different objects present themselves to consciousness as constituents of different spheres of reality. I recognize the fellowmen I must deal with in the course of everyday life as pertaining to a reality quite different from the disembodied figures that appear in my dreams. [. . .] Put differently, I am conscious of the world as consisting of multiple realities. As I move from one reality to another I experience the transition as a kind of shock. This shock is to be understood as caused by the shift in attentiveness that the transition entails. Waking up from a dream illustrates this shift most simply.
>
> (1966, 21)

Curiously, we are not, in fact, shocked by our shifts from realm to realm. We are, it turns out, extraordinarily competent at realm shifting, so competent that we hardly notice what it takes to do it.

We extract our perceptual attention from the realm of the ordinary and invest it in another reality, and we do it frequently, sometimes distractedly, sometimes fascinatedly, every time we read a story, watch a film, or play a game, for instance. From our anchorage in everyday life, we are available to the solicitations of other realities. They beguile us, fleetingly, insistently, inconsequentially, or consequentially.

> To be sure, those experiences of shock befall me frequently amidst my daily life; they themselves pertain to its reality. They show me that the world of working in standard time is not the sole finite province of meaning but only one of many others accessible to my intentional life.
>
> There are as many innumerable kinds of different shock experiences as there are different finite provinces of meaning upon which I may bestow the accent of reality. Some instances are: the shock of falling asleep as the leap into the world of dreams; the inner transformation we endure if the curtain in the theater rises as the transition into the world of the stage-play; the radical change in our attitude if, before a painting, we permit our visual field to be limited by what is within the frame as the passage into the pictorial world; our quandary, relaxing into laughter, as, in listening to a joke, we are for a short time ready to accept the fictitious world of the jest as a reality in relation to which the world of our daily life takes on the character of foolishness; the child's turning toward his toy as the transition into the play-world; and so on.
>
> (Schutz 1970, 254–255)

We might include the player's heightened awareness as she projects agency from her body into her avatar as her entry into the world of the game; the child moving his gaze from his surroundings to the illustrations in a book when he hears his father's voice animating its figures as his absorption in the fictitious reality; or the relinquishment of our own projects in the world in favor of an engagement in the adventures of a character as our passage into the world the film illuminates on the screen. Each reality holds together constellations of meaning that are particular to it: "all these worlds—the world of dreams, of imageries and phantasms, especially the world of art, the world of religious experience, the world of scientific contemplation, the play world of the child, and the world of the insane—are finite provinces of meaning" (Schutz 1970, 255). The constitution of each province sustains the meaningfulness of the events taking place in it, but that meaning does not necessarily translate from one reality to another.

The world of "imageries and phantasms" is a special sort of alternate reality, one I may perceive vividly even though I cannot act in it.

> Living in one of the many worlds of phantasy we have no longer to master the outer world and to overcome the resistance of its objects. We are free from the pragmatic motive which governs our natural attitude toward the world of daily life, free also from the bondage of "interobjective" space and intersubjective standard time. No longer are we confined within the limits of our actual, restorable, or attainable reality. What occurs in the outer world no longer imposes upon us issues between which we have to choose nor does it put a limit on our possible accomplishments.
>
> However, there are no "possible accomplishments" in the world of phantasms if we take this term as a synonym of "performable" [. . .] the imagining self does not transform the outer world.
>
> (Schutz 1970, 257–258)

The world of a tale—which I call the Taleworld and narratologists now call the storyworld (Young 1987; Ryan and Thon 2014)—is real in this way. It takes up my attention without affording me any motor projects in it. Although I bestow the accent of reality on whichever world has engaged my attention, I cannot enter into the storyworld to change it. It would come nearer to say the storyworld changes me.

Imagining is not the creation of images in the mind. The root word "image" has misled us here, as if imagined objects were insubstantial visualizations. Imagining is the creation of perceptual experiences whose objects are virtual rather than actual. Imagined objects solicit my senses just as actual objects do: I touch, taste, smell, and hear as well as see them. But instead of the imagined objects delivering perceptual experiences to me, I lend them my perceptual senses. As Elaine Scarry writes, "Imagining is an act of perceptual mimesis," not because it imitates perception but because it instructs us on how to do so (2001, 6). But "the imagined object lacks the vitality and vivacity of the perceived one; it is in fact these very attributes of vitality and vivacity that enable us to differentiate the actual world present to our senses from the one that we introduce through the exercise of the imagination" (3). In imagining, I re-enact perceiving in attenuated form.

Storytellings in all media guide the imagining self in the act of conjuring up a storyworld. Scarry describes this process as imagining under "authorial instruction" (2001, 99). In the interactive form of tellings and hearings, or in the displaced interactive forms of writings and readings or representings and viewings, I am conducted through a reality making its appearance in my imagination as I move. In hearings, readings, and viewings, I export part of the effort of imagining to the text. In consequence, although imagining under authorial instruction is never quite like perceiving, it attains a vitality and vivacity the spontaneous imaginings of everyday life do not. Because of the imagined world's solicitations of the senses, I am drawn toward motor projects I cannot enact. My body participates perceptually in the storyworld. Insofar as hearers, readers, or viewers are absorbed in these solicitations of their senses, their attention is deflected from the reality in which the act of narration takes place and turned toward the storyworld opening before them. They are in thrall to an alternate reality. Brian Sturm describes this effect as "storylistening trance" (1999).

Once hearers, readers, or viewers are released from their enthrallment, they turn back to the storyworld from their footing in the realm of the ordinary and accord it an ontological status. If the story is true, the storyworld is understood to be or to have been continuous with the reality in which the story is being told. If it is fiction, the two realities are understood to be discontinuous. The storyworld of the fairy *legend* takes the first ontological status; the storyworld of the fairy *tale* takes the second.

In the fairy tale, the storyworld *is* the world but an enchanted one. Tzvetan Todorov describes it as the pure marvelous (1973, 57). Phenomena that would be supernatural if they occurred in the realm of the ordinary are natural in the fairy-tale world. As Todorov writes, "The supernatural events in fairy tales provoke no surprise: neither a hundred year's sleep, nor a talking wolf, nor the magical gifts of the fairies" (1973, 54). The supernatural is simply constitutive of the fairy-tale world and no longer evokes the awe, horror, or fear it would in the ordinary world. The fairy-tale world is one of "a group of otherwise most heterogeneous finite provinces of meaning, none of them reducible to the other. This group is commonly known as that of fancies or imageries and embraces among many others the realms of daydreams, of play, of fiction, of fairy-tales, of myths, of jokes" (Schutz 1970, 256–257).

Hearers, readers, and viewers recognize the specific constitution of the fairy-tale world by what Schutz calls its *metaphysical constants*, ways of being that are particular to that reality

(Natanson 1970, 198). Maurice Natanson described the metaphysical constants of the realm of the ordinary:

> These universal features of daily life [are] "metaphysical constants" for human existence. Being born into a world, being born of mother's unique to us, being born into a world already inhabited as well as interpreted by others, having to grow older in this world and having to die in it are all inescapable realities.
>
> (94)

For alternate realities, the metaphysical constants are different. Non-carbon-based life forms might exhibit signs of intelligence in science fictions; after an enchanted night in fairyland, mortals might return to the paramount reality to find that a year has elapsed; the inhabitants of the realm of the dead might emerge in this realm as diaphanous apparitions.

The metaphysical constants of the fairy-tale world include the following:

- Stepmothers are wicked
- There are no coincidences
- Very few people have names
- Animals talk
- People, animals, and objects can be enchanted
- Spells, curses, and transformations always work
- Magical transformations are commonplace: objects, animals, and humans turn into each other
- Most magical objects only work once
- Untoward things happen in the forest
- It is possible to fly
- It is possible to sleep for extraordinarily long times
- The third son or daughter is always better than the first two
- Things happen in threes
- Always follow the advice of strangers
- Punishments are cruel:

  - beheading, burning, blinding, drowning, pushing out a tower window, poisoning, stabbing, rolling in a barrel spiked with nails, cutting off hands

- There are only two classes: nobles and peasants
- Death is sometimes reversible
- Cannibalism and incest occur; murder is pretty frequent
- Fairy tales are all family stories
- Disguises always work
- Guilty secrets are always revealed
- Villains often demand first-born children
- Pairs of siblings are always loyal to each other, triads in competition
- The only surgery is slitting open the stomach
- Getting devoured is a major risk
- Fairies are morally ambiguous
- Curiosity is dangerous
- Interdictions are always violated
- Prophecies always come true

- Challenges are always accepted
- Curses are always fulfilled but have escape clauses
- Women's and men's desire for a child causes trouble
- Thefts have disproportionate consequences
- Unfair bargains always turn out well
- Heroes never die
- Heroines are always beautiful; heroes, not necessarily
- Noble heroes are always brave and handsome, peasant heroes stupid and plain
- Princesses are always beautiful but passive
- Princesses are always rescued
- It's better to be lucky than smart
- Marriage is usually the end, not the beginning
- Kindness is always rewarded; unkindness is always punished
- Wit, cunning, and tricks can substitute for magic
- Girls are often struck either silent, still, or (apparently) dead
- Giants and dwarves are amoral
- Witches, wizards, and fairies are natural to this realm; gods and demons are not
- Cooks and tailors are consequential characters
- Hair is either black or blonde
- Alchemy is pervasive
- Tokens prove stories
- Spinning is a dangerous practice
- Everybody wears a cloak

Tales do not need to specify all the metaphysical constants of the world they invoke. Following what literary theorist Marie-Laure Ryan calls "the principle of minimal departure," alternate realities will follow the rules of the ordinary one, unless otherwise specified (1991, 51). To the extent that all fairy tales share a storyworld, tellers can rely on hearers', readers', and viewers' familiarity with the form to grasp its metaphysical constants without detailed instruction. But each tale must specify the metaphysical constants that are unique to it.

The opening "Once upon a time" and the closing "And they lived happily ever after" or "The end" announce entry into and exit from the shared storyworld of the fairy-tale form. "The Story of the Three Bears" in Robert Southey's (1837) version begins:

> Once upon a time there were Three Bears, who lived together in a house of their own, in a wood. One of them was a Little, Small Wee Bear; and one was a Middle-sized Bear, and the other was a Great, Huge Bear. They had each a pot for their porridge, a little pot for the Little, Small, Wee Bear; and a middle-sized pot for the Middle Bear, and a great pot for the Great, Huge Bear. And they had each a chair to sit in; a little chair for the Little, Small, Wee Bear; and a middle-sized chair for the Middle Bear; and a great chair for the Great, Huge Bear. And they had each a bed to sleep in; a little bed for the Little, Small, Wee Bear; and a middle-sized bed for the Middle Bear; and a great bed for the Great, Huge Bear.

With the opening phrase, hearers or readers are entered into the fairy-tale world, which discloses a house, porridge, chairs, and beds. We know what these are by the principle of minimal departure. Their possession by bears introduces a metaphysical constant specific to the fairy-tale world: bears who behave as only humans would in the ordinary world. When the bears discover that the little old woman has been eating their porridge, they speak:

> "Somebody has been at my porridge!" said the Great, Huge Bear, in his great, rough, gruff voice. And when the Middle Bear looked at his, he saw that the spoon was standing in it too. They were wooden spoons; if they had been silver ones, the naughty old Woman would have put them in her pocket.
>
> "Somebody has been at my porridge!" said the Middle Bear in his middle voice.
>
> Then the Little, Small, Wee Bear looked at his, and there was the spoon in the porridge-pot, but the porridge was all gone.
>
> "Somebody has been at my porridge, and has eaten it all up!" said the Little, Small, Wee Bear, in his little, small, wee voice.
>
> (Southey 1837)

Speaking animals are one of the metaphysical constants of the fairy tale, but because not all animals speak, the tale must specify this departure from the ordinary world. In Jacob and Wilhelm Grimm's "The Goose Girl," this departure is specified explicitly. "Now the princess's horse was the fairy's gift, and it was called Falada, and could speak" (Taylor 1826). In contrast to the bears, who speak as humans do, the horse's capacity to speak is both restricted and enhanced. It speaks only in gnomic utterances but does so even after its head is severed from its body. Speaking here is treated as a magical transformation worked by the fairies on an otherwise inarticulate creature. The interpolation of the fairy gift turns what hearers or readers would have supposed to be an ordinary horse into one of the constitutive elements of the fairy-tale world: a talking animal.

In the Grimm brothers' "Puss-in-Boots," the cat whose speech is as articulate as humans seems to have come by that faculty without magical intervention but never to have bothered to use it until the miller's son complains of inheriting nothing but a cat.

> "A cat! What am I going to do with that?"
>
> But the cat heard his words and said, "Don't worry, Master. What do you think? That I'm worth less than a half-ruined mill or a mangy donkey? Give me a cloak, a hat with a feather in it, a bag and a pair of boots, and you will see what I can do."
>
> The young man, by no means surprised, for it was quite common for cats to talk in those days, gave the cat what he asked for, and as he strode away, confident and cheerful, the cat said, "Don't look so glum, Master. See you soon!"
>
> (Grimm and Grimm 1853)

This is one of the few tales to remark upon an animal's ability to talk, and then only to note it as a commonplace of that reality. It is the unremarkableness of talking animals that marks the fairy-tale form.

Sometimes the ontological status of animal speech is ambiguous. In both the Grimms' "The Juniper Tree" (ATU 720) and Joseph Jacobs's "The Rose Tree" (1890) a dead child is transformed into a bird who sings about how he or she was murdered. Although the tale hearer understands the words of the song, the characters in the fairy tale hear only birdsong. When the bird speaks instead of singing, the characters understand it perfectly well. In "The Rose-Tree," the bird sings the following verse:

> My wicked mother slew me,
> My dear father ate me,

My little brother whom I love
Sits below, and I sing above
Stick, stock, stone dead.
(Jacobs 1890)

But the watchmaker hears only the birdsong: "'Oh, the beautiful song! sing it again, sweet bird,' asked the watchmaker." But when the bird speaks, the watchmaker obeys:

"If you will give me first that gold watch and chain in your hand." The jeweler gave the watch and chain. The bird took it in one foot, the shoes in the other, and, after having repeated the song, flew away to where three millers were picking up a millstone.

(Jacobs 1890)

Whereas the principle of minimal departure pares down what the teller has to describe, imagining under authorial instruction opens out what the tellers may describe. Fairy-tale descriptions are typically spare. The bears are wee, middle-sized, or huge; the bird's song in "The Rose Tree" is beautiful. Each description endows the character with a distinctive trait.

In the Grimm brothers' "All Fur" (ATU 510B), the princess tries to avoid marrying her father by obliging him to get her three dresses before she will consent to his proposal: "'Before I fulfill your wish, I must have three dresses, one as golden as the sun, one as silvery as the moon, and one as bright as the stars'" (Zipes 2001, 47). The description invites the reader to imagine what a sun, moon, or star dress might look like. But even the lush descriptions of the three dresses in Perrault's version of the tale, "Donkey Skin," spark perceptual imagination:

The most beautiful blue of the firmament, even when it is encircled with large clouds of gold, is not a deeper azure. [. . .] When night unfurls its veils in the skies, the moon, whose brilliant voyage makes the stars turn pale, was no more majestic than this dress. [. . .] It was so beautiful, vibrant, and radiant that the blonde lover of Clymene, who drives his chariot of gold along the arch of the heavens, was not dazzled by a more brilliant light.

(Tatar 1999, 110–111)

Tellers' descriptions of the animal skin cloaks invite hearers, readers, or viewers to counter their imagining of the beautiful dresses with their imagining of the ugly disguise: "The hide of the donkey will be the perfect disguise to make you unrecognizable. Conceal yourself carefully under that skin. It is so hideous that no one will ever believe it covers anything beautiful" ("Donkeyskin," Tatar 1999, 112); "There's a strange animal lying in the hollow tree. We've never seen anything like it. Its skin is made up of a thousand different kinds of fur, and it's lying there asleep" ("All Fur," Zipes 2001, 48).

All descriptions are inherently incomplete. They are completed by the hearer's, reader's, or viewer's imagining under authorial instruction. Although Perrault's description provides hearers or readers more perceptual material to imagine with, in a sense it requires them to imagine more. Story makers select the elements of the fairy-tale world that hearers, readers, and viewers take up to animate their perceptual mimesis. The undescribed recedes into the background.

In contrast to narratives, illustrations appear to be spatially replete but temporally incomplete. They invite the viewer to imagine what brought about the state of affairs represented or what might happen next. The unrepresented recedes into the background. The appearance of spatial repleteness is deceptive. All images frame off the reality in which they are embedded and foreground those aspects to which they direct the viewer's attention. The figures in the foreground are themselves incomplete, simplifying, stylizing, or intensifying some qualities over others. So the surround, the background, and the under-represented also recede. Film curates both sound and image to arouse the viewer's tactile-kinesthetic, olfactory, and gustatory imagination by perceptual mimesis. But neither the audible nor the visible world of the film is replete. As always, what can be seen and heard both under- and overdetermines what is audible and visible in the film world. In all media, what gets represented implies what does not so that hearers, readers, and viewers imagine what is not specified there as well as what is.

Description incites not only perceptual imagination but also aesthetic affect. If "All Fur" and "Donkeyskin" arouse the aesthetic question of beauty and ugliness, "The Prince and the Dragon" arouses the affective question of terror and awe. The eldest prince chases a hare who hides in a mill by a river:

> The prince followed and entered the mill, but stopped in terror by the door, for, instead of a hare, before him stood a dragon, breathing fire and flame. At this fearful sight the prince turned to fly, but a fiery tongue coiled round his waist, and drew him into the dragon's mouth, and he was seen no more.
>
> (Lang 1903, 80)

By these practices, hearers, readers, and viewers participate in the alternate reality of the fairy-tale world. Its inhabitants cannot enter the realm of the ordinary, nor can inhabitants of the realm of the ordinary enter it. From the perspective of the inhabitants of the enchanted world, our world cannot be imagined; from our perspective in the realm of the ordinary, their world can *only* be imagined. The only way to enter into the fairy-tale world is the way James suggests, by a turn of attention. This is the case with all fiction: the alternate reality has no separate existence. It is conjured up by the storyteller for the story hearer, or by the writer for the reader, or by the filmmaker for the viewer, and lasts only as long as the pair of them keep the machinery going.

Fairy tales transport us to the marvelous as an elsewhere. We are offered a temporary pass to an alternate reality, but we can be recalled from it at any time by the insistences of everyday life. But while we are there, the fairy-tale world gathers itself together around us and enfolds us in its reality.

Related topics: Animal Studies; Oral Tradition; Print; Storytelling

References Cited and Further Reading

Berger, Peter, and Thomas Luckmann. 1966. *The Social Construction of Reality: A Treatise on the Sociology of Knowledge.* New York: Anchor.
Grimm, Jacob, and Wilhelm Grimm. 1853. *Household Stories.* London: Addey and Company.
———. 1987. *The Complete Fairy Tales of the Brothers Grimm,* translated and edited by Jack Zipes. New York: Bantam.
Jacobs, Joseph. 1890. *English Fairy Tales.* London: David Nutt.
James, William. (1890) 1918. *The Principles of Psychology.* Vol. 2. New York: Dover.
Lang, Andrew. 1903. "The Prince and the Dragon." *The Crimson Fairy Book.* London: Longmans Green & CO.
Natanson, Maurice. 1970. *The Journeying Self: A Study in Philosophy and Social Role.* Reading, MA: Addison-Wesley.
Ryan, Marie-Laure. 1991. *Possible Worlds, Artificial Intelligence, and Narrative Theory.* Bloomington: Indiana UP.
Ryan, Marie-Laure, and Jan-Noël Thon, eds. 2014. *Storyworlds across Media: Toward a Media-Conscious Narratology.* Lincoln: U Nebraska P.

Scarry, Elaine. 2001. *Dreaming by the Book*. Princeton, NJ: Princeton UP.

Schutz, Alfred. 1970. *On Phenomenology and Social Relations*. Chicago: U Chicago P.

Southey, Robert. 1837. *The Doctor*, edited by J. W. Warter. London.

Sturm, Brian. 1999. "The Enchanted Imagination: Storytelling's Power to Entrance Listeners." *School Library Media Research* 2.

Tatar, Maria, ed. 1999. *The Classic Fairy Tales*. New York: W. W. Norton.

Taylor, Edgar, trans. 1826. *German Popular Stories (from Kinder- und Hausmärchen, 1814)*. London: James Robins.

Todorov, Tzvetan. 1973. *The Fantastic: A Structural Approach to a Literary Genre*, translated by Richard Howard. Ithaca, NY: Cornell UP.

Young, Katharine. 1987. *Taleworlds and Storyrealms: The Phenomenology of Narrative*. The Hague: Martinus Nijhoff.

Zipes, Jack, ed. 2001. *The Great Fairy Tale Tradition*. London: W. W. Norton.

ISSUES OF INTERSECTION WITH OTHER STUDY AREAS

25
ANIMAL STUDIES
Pauline Greenhill and Leah Claire Allen

Animal studies is founded on the concept that humans are themselves animals, not superior, exceptional, enlightened beings who, unlike their nonhuman relatives, transcend their biology. Animal studies joins with related theoretical positions, such as posthumanism, an intellectual location seeking to destabilize conventional notions of the human and its discursive centrality (see Wolfe 2010), and transbiology, the exploration of interventions into human and nonhuman animal biology (Franklin 2006). Works from these perspectives offer fairy-tale studies ways of thinking about how human representations of different species create understandings—as well as misunderstandings—of what it means to be human and what it means to be animal. But conversely, traditional tales have destabilized and transformed notions of the human long before animal studies, posthumanism, and transbiology.

Fairy tales, folktales, and wonder tales have always included animal main characters who interact interspecifically—across alleged species boundaries—with humans and nonhuman animals. These stories also thematize transformations between human and nonhuman animal forms, including nonhuman animals dressing as humans and vice versa, as well as magical somatic transformations between human and nonhuman forms. Fairy tales extend transbiology to include transgenic magic, in which nonhuman and human biological characteristics combine. As fairy-tale media amply demonstrate, these narratives sometimes prefigure, implicitly or explicitly, animal studies' profound respect for nonhuman animals and advocacy for more balanced relationships with them. Fairy tales and fairy-tale studies echo posthumanism when they reject the rationalism of the European Enlightenment that dismissed nonhuman animals as debased, abject beasts. Instead, fairy tales attribute consciousness, power, and significance to nonhuman animals as they investigate human/nonhuman animal relationships.

Despite fairy tales' topical relevance to the interdiscipline of animal studies, they have not extensively intersected. In a significant exception, Lewis Seifert examines two French fairy tales in which animals do not "disappear before the human," but "almost always retain distinctive traits of their nonhuman beings" (2011, 244). Seifert argues that "Babiole" and "Prince Wild Boar" draw attention to the "nonhuman dimension" of "hybrid characters" but also unsettle "any certainty about exactly what boundaries separate humans from animals" (2011, 246; see also Hoffman 2005; Eichel-Lojkine 2013). With Seifert, we see fairy tales as sites from which to launch critiques of alleged human nature, including kinship relationships and the cultural construction of normative human bodies. As well, fairy-tale studies grounds interventions in ecological discourses via the inferred perspectives of animals and therefore participates in ecocritical discussions. Attending to how fairy tales and fairy-tale studies address these human/nonhuman relations contributes to animal studies by historicizing and reimagining issues included under its rubric.

225

Background and Perspectives

Animal studies emerged in part from animal rights activism in Australia, Europe, and North America in the 1970s (Wolfe 2003). Those movements questioned the ethics of conventional unidirectional relationships between nonhuman animals and humans that presumed humans could exploit, with impunity, all other creatures for food, clothing, research, and/or entertainment. Animal studies seeks to displace this unidirectionality and works to undermine speciesism, both in practice and in philosophical concepts of the self that rely on human exceptionalism. Recent work in animal studies, theoretically informed by Jacques Derrida's 1997 lecture "The Animal That Therefore I Am" (2008), critiques the anthropocentric presumptions that have informed ideas of the human self through the history of philosophy.

Over the last decade, animal studies has also drawn on Giorgio Agamben's *The Open: Man and Animal*, which traces how the human has been defined in opposition to the nonhuman or animal (2003; see also Weil 2012). Using this philosophical framework of decentering the human, animal studies shows not only how human presumptions have influenced studies of nonhuman animals, but also how sexism, heterosexism, racism, and ableism have influenced human understanding of nonhuman animal cultures. Dawn McCance points out that as French and Anglo-American feminisms began to reject "rights theory" in the 1980s, they became increasingly relevant to animal studies in moving "beyond subject-centered traditions of ethics, offering [. . .] critiques of anthropocentrism, speciesism, and the hierarchical (mind/body, man/woman, man/animal) dualism this subject inevitably reinstates" (2013, 93). Thus, "feminism approaches animal studies by first abandoning the humanist notion of the fixed and pregiven self" (96).

Critics working at the intersection of feminism and animal studies include Mel Y. Chen (2012), who explores how discourses on animals and toxicity implicate sexuality, race, and affect in diverse sites, from nineteenth-century newspaper ads to Hollywood cinema to contemporary art. Similarly, Annie Potts and Jovian Parry's feminist frameworks connect the negative media hype surrounding the concept of "vegan sexuality" and the term "vegansexual" to cultural anxiety over the possibility that "intimate rejection of carnism" might disrupt the "powerful cultural links between meat-eating, masculinity, and virility" (2014, 234). These studies share a desire to restructure categorical thinking about hierarchical relationships between humans as well as with nonhuman animals.

While fairy tales are replete with nonhuman animal protagonists and consistently disrupt conventional notions of proper species relations, fairy-tale scholarship has often used human-centered categories to describe these stories. For example, "Animal Tales" is the first category that appears in *The Types of International Folktales* (Uther 2004), a flawed but nevertheless useful standardized system numbering oral narratives, sometimes used by fairy-tale scholars. We employ it here because it reminds readers that the indexed tales are international and traditional. *The Types'* distinctions classify relationships between human and nonhuman animals as fundamental and primary, including dividing wild from domestic, thus pigeonholing animals on the basis of their interactions, or lack thereof, with humans. Thus, "Animal Tales" is subdivided into "Wild Animals," "Wild Animals and Domestic Animals," "Wild Animals and Humans," "Domestic Animals," and "Other Animals and Objects."

Numerous stories in the second index section, called "Tales of Magic," comprising the classic, mainly European-associated wonder/fairy tales (ATU numbers 300–749, Uther 2004, 174–396),[1] also implicate nonhuman animals and investigate myriad human/nonhuman relations and transformations. Those include what Kay Turner and Pauline Greenhill term "Animal Trans" (2012, 303–305), describing nonhuman animals turning into people and/

or people becoming nonhuman animals. As well, the fluid and typically gender-associated term "drag" fits "Animal Drag" stories of nonhuman animals dressing as people and/or vice versa. Because such tales have long circulated in oral tradition, as have literary fairy tales with known authors, they show an ongoing need to understand such interactions. Fairy tales are *already* species-queer, posthuman, and transbiological; their stories and characters destabilize and upend normative species relations. As such, when these stories appear in multiple media platforms, they continue to work through central animal studies concerns.

Familiar fairy tales brim with nonhuman animal characters interacting with, dressing as, and/or turning into humans and vice versa. Think of the male wolf in "Little Red Riding Hood" (ATU 333), who initiates an apparently unremarkable conversation with the title character. He follows by eating, dressing as, and masquerading as her grandmother. This gender and species cross-dressing wolf's dealings offer considerable complexity, as humans are typically expected to eat and costume themselves as nonhuman animals, not vice versa. Less well-known tales, too, enact interspecific relations in multiple guises. In "The Twelve Brothers" (ATU 451), a woman accidentally causes her brothers to turn into ravens. They do not become hegemonic masculine mammals, though men as "beasts" is a convention of Euro North American culture. The bird brothers may even care for the heroine's children, magically stolen at birth by her evil mother-in-law. Finally, their human shape is restored, but one brother sometimes remains with a wing in place of one of his arms. TV's *The StoryTeller*'s *The Three Ravens* (see Greenhill 2014) draws on this hypotext, which includes highly unconventional relationships of interspecific family and nurturance, as well as unusual embodiments. Animal helpers who are not transformed humans also abound in fairy tales, from the domestic horse Falada who, even when decapitated, continues to give advice and assistance to the "goose girl" princess (ATU 533), to the wild fish who grants wish after wish to the man who catches him in "The Fisherman and His Wife" (ATU 555). Perennial favorite "Puss in Boots" (ATU 545B; see Nikolajeva 2009), about a sartorially splendid trickster feline who manipulates all the humans and supernaturals in his vicinity, appears in storybooks, films, television, and video games.

Nearly every imaginable medium reprises fairy tales about animals and human/nonhuman animal interactions. For example, in the police procedural television show *Grimm* (2011–2017), the human hero, a "Grimm," must control fairy-tale creatures called "Wesen," who usually look human but can "woge" into an appearance incorporating a nonhuman animal, such as a mammal, insect, reptile, or bird. Fairy-tale media like *Grimm* say a great deal about cultural expectations for nonhuman animals and their interaction with one another and with humans even as they re-enact conventional ideas of proper relations. Such media can also offer a rich archive to the field of animal studies in its quest for critical and practical frameworks not necessarily centered on the exceptional human.

Animal Drag

A quintessential animal drag narrative, "Little Red Riding Hood," appears in numerous versions and languages from many different countries in a wide range of cinema—feature length and short; animated and live action; made for theatrical, television, video, and Internet release—as well as novels, short stories, poetry, music, plays, and musicals. Such adaptations may use the fairy-tale title, as does David Kaplan's short *Little Red Riding Hood* (see Orme 2015), or allude to it, like the feature *Une fille à croquer* (A Girl Good Enough to Eat). Though films including species transformation are not uncommon, as in *The Company of Wolves*, many trade on the notion that humans (usually but not exclusively men) are metaphorical beasts, such as *Freeway*,

Jin-Roh: The Wolf Brigade, or the made-for-TV Red Riding Trilogy, in particular *Red Riding: In the Year of Our Lord 1974* (see Kohm and Greenhill 2013).

Yet most "Little Red Riding Hood" versions narrate the story of a male beast who dresses not just as human, but as an *elderly woman*. In drag's best traditions, this wolf's cross-dressing incites questions about the relationships between gender and authority (see Garber 1992, 375–390). Has the wolf, a debased animal, obtained more power by crossing into human form, or diminished his standing by trading youthful male virility for the clothing and affect of an old woman? In simultaneously crossing gender, species, and age, the wolf forces his diegetic and extratextual audiences to confront the definitional limits of all three categories. In addition, his actions highlight how speciesism has framed gender as a presumptively human concern. To use the human-decentering perspective of animal studies, "Little Red Riding Hood" queries why gender differences among nonhuman animals do not carry the same critical traction as those between human animals.

This narrative of human/animal relationships and cross-dressing also finds its way into digital media. The children's interactive storybook *Happily Ever After Volume One* offers a conventional version of "Little Red Riding Hood," but more innovative contributions exploring the tale's drag narrative also appear in several game genres. *The Path*, a psychological horror art game, associates Red Riding Hoods with diverse ages, abilities, and genderings—sometimes femme, sometimes butch—with wolves of varying genders, forms, and relations to humanness. As in most versions, straying from the path motivates the action. *Little Red Riding Hood's Zombie BBQ*, an action rail-shooter game, recalls the *Buffy the Vampire Slayer* season four episode "Fear Itself," in which the title character, asked what is in her "Little Red Riding Hood" Halloween costume's basket, answers: "weapons." Playable character Red specializes in guns, but gamers may instead choose Momotarō ("Peach Boy," a transgenic character from Japanese folklore, magically born from a peach), who uses ninja stars. Although this tale offers deeply species-queer interactions, some versions nevertheless reproduce normative species relations. The hidden object adventure game *Dark Parables: The Red Riding Hood Sisters*, for example, mobilizes a stereotypical lupine-hating discourse of ravenous red-eyed beasts with giant fangs, emphasizing the wolf's nonhuman animal nature at the expense of his cross-species dressing. In the game, the Wolf Queen, a transgenic woman with wolf paws and ears, enforces the notion that (part)humans must lead other creatures and that even wild animals need people.

In other fairy tales, female humans, like their male counterparts, dress as animals. "Princess Mouseskin" combines the Cinderella variant "Peau d'Asne" (ATU 510B) with "Love Like Salt" (ATU 923). It relates the story of a king who seeks to murder his daughter for saying she loved him more than salt. The executioner who takes her to the woods spares her, giving her a mouse's skin to wear. This bodily masquerade, unlikely for reasons of scale and disguise, exemplifies for Joy Brooke Fairfield the girl's queer "sideways growth" as well as her "becoming-mouse" and "becoming-man" (2012, 223). Feature-film versions of the related "Donkey Skin" include *Peau d'âne*, a favorite of French children, and the Russian *Oslinaja schkura* (The Donkey's Hide, The Princess with the Donkey Skin), among others. Novels, short stories, poetry, and music deal with the same story, invoking animal drag as a complicated cross-gender and cross-species performance.

Sapsorrow, from *The StoryTeller* series, exemplifies the ATU 510B tale type's linkage of humanity and beastliness with the theme of paternal incest. The daughter threatened with marriage to her king father saves herself from this fate, rendering herself sexually unattractive by disguising herself and fleeing to another kingdom as Straggletag, a wild-haired, bearded person dressed in animal skins. Her interactions with the prince who employs her demonstrate her intelligence and quick wit. Her symbolic, literally impossible statements invoke Straggletag's transbiological position, such as when she states, "I live where hens catch mice and cats lay eggs." The interspecific relationship between beast-woman Straggletag and human prince is prefigured, compared, and contrasted with the princess's many friendships with animals. Straggletag does not eat geese because she likes them. Her animal friends care for her and bring her food, not vice versa. They are not her pets; by all appearances, she is theirs. Animals craft her Straggletag disguise and remove it at the crucial moment, re-dressing and coiffing her as the princess she is, rendering her more suitable for marriage to the prince (see Greenhill 2014).

A woman's bird disguise is similarly an essential element of her self-rescue in "Fitcher's Bird" (ATU 311; see Greenhill 2008). This "Bluebeard"-like tale (ATU 312) has a clever youngest sister betrothed to an evil sorcerer. To escape him she creates avatars, including rolling in honey and feathers to become Fitcher's Bird. In her avian form she encounters the bridegroom's friends and Fitcher himself and has friendly dialogues with them. As in other fairy tales, conversations between humans and (an apparent) nonhuman seem commonplace. The story also provides the basis for a book of photographs by Cindy Sherman (1992). The bird disguise image centers on her pelvic area, thus avoiding the perhaps more difficult-to-render head and upper torso.

The bidirectionality of fairy-tale animal drag—nonhumans dressing as humans and vice versa—offers a way beyond unidirectional speciesist thinking. In contrast to notions of appropriate relations in which humans use animals for food, labor, companionship, and so on, many fairy tales mobilize species itself to advantageous ends. The wolf uses human drag to deceive Little Red Riding Hood, whereas Princess Mouseskin uses animal drag to escape murder. In constructing species as a fluid and flexible category that can be assumed and then discarded, these fairy tales disrupt the apparent fixity of boundaries between species, making room for reciprocal relations between nonhuman animals and human animals. Their provocative claim that species is drag also lays the groundwork for conceptions of transbiology and animal trans.

Animal Trans

Animal trans fairy tales first reveal and then resist the normative social construction of species by transcending, altering, and/or performing it. Many fairy tales de-link hierarchical biological categories from innate human or nonhuman nature, making way for trans- and post-species conceptions of human and animal selves, implicating gender, sex, and sexuality. For example, "Beauty and the Beast" (ATU 425C) includes a double transformation from man to beast and then back to man. Popular media may mitigate the traditional tale type's species-queer elements where, for example, some popular films avoid the physical alteration and draw instead on the idea of men as metaphorical beasts who need a good woman to rescue and/or rehabilitate their nasty selves.[2] Yet other movies, live-action and animated alike, make the Beast transgenic in appearance, not a conventional nonhuman animal. The best-known "Beauty and the Beast" live-action film, Jean Cocteau's *La belle et la bête*, clearly influenced many subsequent versions including Disney's; in them, the beast is a leonine but beautifully dressed part-human.

The latter resemblance manifests in the 1980s romance/action American television series *Beauty and the Beast.* Beast Vincent lives in a supportive bookish community of mainly pacifist humans who reside in tunnels beneath New York City. He is often called upon to commit the violence necessary to rescue Catherine, his attorney Beauty, as well as his fellow underground dwellers. But his character can manifest differently. In the recent TV remake, Catherine is a homicide detective and Vincent a human soldier whose DNA has been mutated by the evil corporation Muirfield; he morphs into a still recognizably human, violent, yellow-eyed, zombie-like creature.

The tale's popularity has led to a plethora of themed television including episodes of *Fractured Fairy Tales*, Shelley Duvall's *Faerie Tale Theatre*, and made-for-TV movies and specials. But its many other formats demonstrate its ubiquitous malleability. *Mystery Legends: Beauty and the Beast*, another hidden-object game, has a horned, lion-headed beast. Its website narrates: "[o]nce upon a time, deep within the heart of a kingdom, a charming prince was cursed by a scorned enchantress. Entangled within her wicked spell, he lay dying until a fair maiden's love revealed the beauty within the beast. However, their happily ever after was not destined to last." Somewhat unusually, this game has the presumed female Beauty as the player, whose task is to "Save the charming prince!" As well, there are "Beauty and the Beast" themed novels, graphic novels, picture books, short stories, poetry, music, operas, ballet, and theatrical productions including plays, pantomime, and the stage adaptation of the Disney film.

Marriage is often the conclusion of ATU 425C, but many other oral narratives implicate "The Animal Bride" (ATU 402). (The bride need not be a mammal; she could be a reptile or bird.) Tales of seal wives are more common cross-culturally than ones about seal husbands.[3] Neil Jordan's film *Ondine* and Solveig Eggerz's novel *Seal Woman* (2008) both use these traditional "selkie narratives" metaphorically and, as Kirsten Møllegaard (2014) argues, offer postmodern reflections on transnational migration. Tomm Moore's animated feature *Song of the Sea* relegates the seal-to-man marriage to the backstory. Child heroine Saoirse engages in a magical quest to save the fairy world but needs access to the sea and being a seal, paradoxically, in order to survive as human.

The fairy-tale associations of men with large mammals, as in "The Two Girls, the Bear, and the Dwarf" (ATU 426), in which sisters disenchant a prince who has been turned into a bear, fit stereotypical hegemonic notions of large, hairy, commanding, and powerful men. "The Animal as Bridegroom" (ATU 425A) title character may also be a bear, as in the film *Kvitebjørn Kong Valemon* (The Polar Bear King), or a more abject domestic animal as in Charles Ludlam's play *The Enchanted Pig* (1989). Perhaps less hegemonic, "Hans My Hedgehog" (ATU 441) involves a human-animal hybrid who eventually becomes fully human. Much like "Princess Mouseskin," the story raises issues of scale in grafting a (tiny) hedgehog upper body onto a human lower body. *The StoryTeller's Hans My Hedgehog* (see Greenhill 2014) excises the rape of the princess bride's predecessor(s), found in some traditional versions, but adds a mother-blaming plot twist in which her mother misinforms the princess about the method for disenchanting the hedgehog-man and grafts on a "Search for the Lost Husband" (ATU 425) section. Other stories, like ATU 451 prior, raise considerably less macho possibilities. "The Frog King" (ATU 440), for example, has an amphibious title protagonist. This fairy tale appears in the expected literary, theatrical, film, television, and video game forms but also in popular songs, including Peter Gabriel's "Kiss That Frog."

In "The Juniper Tree" (ATU 720), a murdered boy becomes a vengeful bird. Many adaptations lack avian transformation, instead using realist conventions and metaphors. However, *Le piege d'Issoudun* (2003) incorporates a theatrical play-within-the-film of the Grimm version interspersed with its brutal neorealist narrative of a privileged mother who drowns her children in the family swimming pool before seeking to commit suicide. In the play, the dead child's bones transform into a bird and then into a living boy. This narrative demonstrates how the traditional tale makes the bird-boy an agent of the mother's justice, as well as a metaphor for the family's breakdown. The tale was made into an opera in 1985 by Philip Glass and Robert Moran and in the same year appeared as a novel by Barbara Comyns. Issue seventeen of the horror comic *Grimm Fairy Tales* (Tyler, Tedesco, and Rio 2007) is also titled and draws on "The Juniper Tree."

Sometimes transbiology replaces animal cross-dressing, as in *The Wolves of Kromer*, in which the hybrid wolves are gay male Little Red Riding Hoods and innocent victims. As in traditional versions, "the human and wolf societies in this film exist side-by-side, ambivalent and even hostile to each other" (Bernhardt-House 2008, 60). The "once upon a time, not so very long ago" opening voiceover by Boy George signals a fairy tale in the colloquial, often pejorative sense, making lycanthrophobia a metaphor for homophobia. In the film's otherwise realistic small English village setting, wolves live in the woods and wilds beyond. With pointed ears, claw fingernails, bare feet, and tails, they dress in fur coats and ragged clothing. Many villagers hate and fear these outsiders and periodically hunt and murder them; some of the most virulent community members are themselves closeted wolves. Recognizing and then subverting popular associations between wolves and predatory violence (often exploited in video games), the film uses fairy-tale narrative structure and characters to critically re-examine sensitive issues relating to crime and vengeance and their associations with lycanthro/homophobia.

Animal studies often asks what it would mean to transcend the human; fairy tales implicitly and explicitly offer some implications for a bidirectional model in refiguring species relations. Where the social needs of human and nonhuman animals organize narratives, as they do in fairy tales, survival of the fittest is no longer the organizing principle of kinship, and evolution fails as the justification for human domination of animals. Indeed, sometimes the animals triumph.

Human/Nonhuman Animal Kinship

Fairy tales concerning nonhuman animals and human/nonhuman hybrids often offer radically alternative views of kinship in terms of familial relations, as described prior, but also in terms of biological relations. Oral and written versions tend to best exemplify these overlaps, sometimes in relation to non-normative sexualities and embodiments. As Barbara Herrnstein Smith indicates:

> The problem of our kinship to other animals mirrors that of our relation to other problematic beings: for example, the unborn, the mentally disabled, the drunk, or the terminally comatose—beings, that is, who are recognizably our own kind but not yet, not quite, not just now, or no longer what we readily think of as *what we ourselves are*. [. . .] there are difficulties handling both sameness and difference, [and] difficulties framing the claims—either conceptual or ethical—of kinship.
>
> (2004, 1)

Kinship issues can be amplified when human and nonhuman animals join the same body. In "The Three Doctors" (ATU 660), animal parts replace amputated human parts and their integration leads to a blend of alleged characteristics, as in "The one with the cat's eye can see best at night [. . .], the one with the thief's hand steals, and the one with the hog's stomach is always hungry" (Uther 2004, 362). Fairy tales similarly involving animal prosthetics and/or partly animal bodies currently gain considerable attention from queer scholarship, including Hans Christian Andersen's "The Little Mermaid" as a text expressing transsexuality and transgender embodiment (see Padva 2005; Hurley 2014). In particular, the mermaid's willingness to transform her body to fit the person she feels she is, despite considerable ongoing pain, echoes how some transgender people describe medical and hormone interventions. As Leland Spencer points out, the Andersen story's sad ending resonates all too accurately with the experiences of many transsexual and transgender people. Even in the Disney film, the mermaid's father exhibits "patriarchal and borderline abusive behavior" that "is consistent with typical parental reactions upon discovery that their child's desired identity performance does not match his or her body" (Spencer 2014, 121). Issues of prejudice, ignorance, false presumption, and voice also demonstrate commonalities with transgender and transsexual experiences.

Recent films expand on the notion that supernatural animals or human/nonhuman transgenics know a great deal about ecology and can teach human beings about coexistence. The animated film *Heisei tanuki gassen pompoko* (Pom Poko) draws on folktale tradition about foxes (*kitsune*) and raccoon dogs (*tanuki*) shape-shifting into human and other forms. Construction of a suburb encroaches on their habitat and "the usually fun-loving *tanuki* [. . . use] their magical abilities to trick, bluff, cajole, terrify, and otherwise dissuade the humans from building the project" while bickering "among themselves about whether their war is aggressive or persuasive" (Ortabasi 2013, 255). The *tanuki* stage a giant magical ghost parade, but the human viewers see it as "simply a fun spectacle [. . .] and the tanuki must ultimately admit defeat" (Ortabasi 2013, 256). Sadly, many *tanuki* and *kitsune* choose to become human to survive; those who lack the ability to cross species live a dangerous marginal existence. Melek Ortabasi notes that *Pom Poko* exposes speciesism. Similarly, fairy-tale films from diverse locations and times, such as *Gake no ue no Ponyo* (Ponyo 2008) and *How to Train Your Dragon* (2010), explore supernatural creatures and how their relationships to each other and to the earth may teach humans viable alternatives to exploitation of both.

In conventional models of kinship, supernatural creatures, nonhuman animals, human-animal hybrids, trans animals, and animals in drag are clearly not "what we ourselves are," in Herrnstein Smith's words. And yet, fairy tales take place in worlds where these various identities and embodiments coexist with human animals in both the harmony and the strife that characterizes all kinship. These stories' genderqueer aspects have already attracted interest in queer studies. Their species-queer elements also merit attention from animal studies. Within their diegetic worlds, the fairy tales discussed here detach species from its hierarchical taxonomical meaning and treat the boundary between human and animal as fluid and permeable, deeply implicated with other human social relations. Critical analysis of these representations, then, will allow animal studies to see species as a flexible, not always divisive, category.

Related topics: Activism; Adaptation and the Fairy-Tale Web; Broadcast; Cinematic; Disney Corporation; Hybridity; Opera; TV Drama; Video Games

Notes

1. "ATU" reflects the index's history, developed in 1910 by Antti Aarne and updated by Stith Thompson in 1928 and 1961 and again by Hans-Jörg Uther in 2004 (Uther 2004, 7).
2. Indeed, as Sue Short (2015) indicates, this idea is a staple of American romantic comedies.
3. Though the shape-shifting Wesen on TV's *Grimm* (2011–2017) come in female and male forms, traditional fairy tales with human women who become nonhuman animals are relatively rare.

References Cited and Further Reading

Agamben, Giorgio. 2003. *The Open: Man and Animal.* Redwood City, CA: Stanford UP.
Bernhardt-House, Phillip A. 2008. "The Werewolf as Queer, the Queer as Werewolf, and Queer Werewolves." In *Queering the Non/Human,* edited by Noreen Giffney and Myra J. Hird, 159–83. Aldershot: Ashgate.
Chen, Mel Y. 2012. *Animacies: Biopolitics, Racial Mattering, and Queer Affect.* Durham, NC: Duke UP.
Comyns, Barbara. 1985. *The Juniper Tree.* New York: St. Martin's.
Derrida, Jacques. 2008. *The Animal That Therefore I Am,* translated by David Wills. New York: Fordham UP.
Eggerz, Solveig. 2008. *Seal Woman.* Denver: Ghost Road.
Eichel-Lojkine, Patricia. 2013. "De la dignité et excellence de l'animal: Faut-il voir dans la parole de la fable un discours dissident?" *Les Dossiers du Grihl* 1 http://dossiersgrihl.revues.org/5628.

Fairfield, Joy Brooke. 2012. "Becoming-Mouse, Becoming-Man: The Sideways Growth of Princess Mouseskin." In *Transgressive Tales*, edited by Turner and Greenhill, 223–43.

Franklin, Sarah. 2006. "The Cyborg Embryo: Our Path to Transbiology." *Theory, Culture & Society* 23 (7–8): 167–87.

Garber, Marjorie. 1992. *Vested Interests: Cross-Dressing and Cultural Anxiety.* New York: Routledge.

Greenhill, Pauline. 2008. "'Fitcher's [Queer] Bird': A Fairy-Tale Heroine and Her Avatars." *Marvels & Tales* 22 (1): 143–67.

———. 2014. "Wanting (To Be) Animal: Fairy-Tale Transbiology in *The StoryTeller*." *Feral Feminisms* 2: 29–45.

Herrnstein Smith, Barbara. 2004. "Animal Relatives, Difficult Relations." *differences: A Journal of Feminist Cultural Studies* 15 (1): 1–23.

Hoffman, Kathryn A. 2005. "Of Monkey Girls and a Hog-Faced Gentlewoman: Marvel in Fairy Tales, Fairgrounds, and Cabinets of Curiosities." *Marvels & Tales* 19 (1): 67–85.

Hurley, Nat. 2014. "The Little Transgender Mermaid: A Shape-Shifting Tale." In *Seriality and Texts for Young People: The Compulsion to Repeat*, edited by Mavis Reimer, Nyala Ali, Deanna England, and Melanie Dennis Unrau, 258–78. London: Palgrave Macmillan.

Kohm, Steven, and Pauline Greenhill. 2013. "'This Is the North, Where We Do What We Want': Popular Green Criminology and 'Little Red Riding Hood' Films." In *Routledge International Handbook of Green Criminology*, edited by Nigel South and Avi Brisman, 365–78. Abingdon: Routledge.

Ludlam, Charles. 1989. *The Complete Plays of Charles Ludlam.* New York: Perennial Library.

McCance, Dawn. 2013. *Critical Animal Studies: An Introduction.* Albany: SUNY P.

Møllegaard, Kirsten. 2014. "Global Flows in Coastal Contact Zones: Selkie Lore in Neil Jordan's *Ondine* and Solveig Eggerz's *Seal Woman*." In *Unsettling Assumptions: Tradition, Gender, Drag*, edited by Pauline Greenhill and Diane Tye, 93–111. Logan: Utah State UP.

Nikolajeva, Maria. 2009. "Devils, Demons, Familiars, Friends: Toward a Semiotics of Literary Cats." *Marvels & Tales* 23 (2): 248–67.

Orme, Jennifer. 2015. "A Wolf's Queer Invitation: David Kaplan's *Little Red Riding Hood* and Queer Possibility." *Marvels & Tales* 29 (1): 87–109.

Ortabasi, Melek. 2013. "(Re)animating Folklore: Raccoon Dogs, Foxes, and Other Supernatural Japanese Citizens in Takahata Isao's *Heisei tanuki gassen pompoko*." *Marvels & Tales* 27 (2): 254–75.

Padva, Gilad. 2005. "Radical Sissies and Stereotyped Fairies in Laurie Lynd's *The Fairy Who Didn't Want to Be a Fairy Anymore*." *Cinema Journal* 45 (1): 66–78.

Potts, Annie, and Jovian Parry. 2014. "Too Sexy for Your Meat: Vegan Sexuality and the Intimate Rejection of Carnism." In *Thinking the Unthinkable: New Readings in Critical Animal Studies*, edited by John Sorenson, 234–50. Toronto: Canadian Scholars' P.

Sherman, Cindy. 1992. *Fitcher's Bird.* New York: Rizzoli.

Short, Sue. 2015. *Fairy Tale and Film: Old Tales with a New Spin.* New York: Palgrave Macmillan.

Seifert, Lewis C. 2011. "Animal-Human Hybridity in d'Aulnoy's 'Babiole' and 'Prince Wild Boar'." *Marvels & Tales* 25 (2): 244–60.

Spencer, Leland G. 2014. "Performing Transgender Identity in The Little Mermaid: From Andersen to Disney." *Communication Studies* 65 (1): 112–27.

Turner, Kay, and Pauline Greenhill, eds. 2012. *Transgressive Tales: Queering the Grimms.* Detroit: Wayne State UP.

Tyler, Joe, Ralph Tedesco, and Al Rio. 2007. *Grimm Fairy Tales 17: The Juniper Tree.* Horsham, PA: Zenescope.

Uther, Hans-Jörg. 2004. *The Types of International Folktales: A Classification and Bibliography, Based on the System of Antti Aarne and Stith Thompson.* Helsinki: Academia Scientiarum Fennica.

Weil, Kari. 2012. *Thinking Animals: Why Animal Studies Now?* New York: Columbia UP.

Wolfe, Cary. 2003. *Animal Rites: American Culture, the Discourse of Species, and Posthumanist Theory.* Chicago: U Chicago P.

———. 2010. *What Is Posthumanism?* Minneapolis: U Minnesota P.

Mediagraphy

Beauty and the Beast (TV). 1987–1990. Creator Ron Koslow. USA.

——— (TV). 2012. Creators Sherri Cooper-Landsman, Ron Koslow, Jennifer Levin. USA.

Buffy the Vampire Slayer (TV). 1997–2003. Creator Joss Whedon. USA.

The Company of Wolves. 1984. Director Neil Jordan. UK.

Dark Parables: The Red Riding Hood Sisters (Computer Game). 2012. Creative Director Steven Zhao. www.bigfishgames. com/games/7447/dark-parables-the-red-riding-hood-sisters/.

Fractured Fairy Tales (TV). 1959–1962. Creators Jay Ward, Bill Scott. USA.

Freeway. 1986. Director Matthew Bright. USA.

Gake no ue no Ponyo (Ponyo). 2008. Director Hayao Miyazaki. Japan.

Grimm (TV). 2011–2017. Creators David Greenwalt, Jim Kouf, Stephen Carpenter. USA.

Happily Ever After Volume One (Video Game). 2010. Nintendo. www.nintendo.com/games/detail/0RrE4J0229n UAQZTB50N-0Vf-0awErPP.

Heisei tanuki gassen pompoko (Pom Poko). 1994. Director Takahata Isao. Japan.

How to Train Your Dragon. 2010. Directors Dean DuBlois, Chris Sanders. USA.

Jin-Roh: The Wolf Brigade. 1999. Director Hiroyuki Okiura. Japan.

The Juniper Tree (Opera). 1985. Music Philip Glass, Robert Moran: Libretto Arthur Yorinks. USA.

"Kiss That Frog" (Song). 1992. Artist Peter Gabriel, Album *Us.* UK.

Kvitebjørn Kong Valemon (The Polar Bear King). 1991. Director Ola Solum. Germany/Norway/Sweden.

La belle et la bête. 1946. Director Jean Cocteau. France.

Le piège d'Issoudun. 2003. Director Micheline Lanctôt. Canada.

Little Red Riding Hood. 1997. Director David Kaplan. USA.

Little Red Riding Hood's Zombie BBQ (Video Game). 2008. Designer/Producer Jose M. Iñiguez. www.nintendo.com/games/detail/5azEvG-3KHWZsBXLEiXRlEyU3j7W2qHK.

Mystery Legends: Beauty and the Beast (Computer Game). 2011. www.bigfishgames.com/games/6401/mystery-legends-beauty-and-the-beast/.

Ondine. 2009. Director Neil Jordan. Ireland/USA.

Oslinaja schkura. 1982. Director Nadeshda Koscheverova. Soviet Union.

The Path (Computer Game). 2009. Designer/director Auriea Harvey, Michaël Samyn. www.tale-of-tales.com/ThePath/.

Peau d'âne. 1970. Director Jacques Demy. France.

Red Riding: In the Year of Our Lord 1974. 2009. Director Julian Jarrold. UK.

Song of the Sea. 2010. Director Tomm Moore. Belgium/Denmark/Ireland/Luxembourg.

The StoryTeller (TV). 1987–1988. Creator Jim Henson. UK.

Une fille à croquer. 1951. Director Raoul André. France.

The Wolves of Kromer. 1988. Director Will Gould. UK.

26

CHILDREN'S AND YOUNG ADULT (YA) LITERATURE

Anna Kérchy

One of the most remarkable features of fairy tales is their affective narratological potential to stimulate wonder, to activate the "unconscious, intuitive, imaginative aspects of the mind" (Lüthi 1982, 12), to engage audiences in a fantastic vision of a fictional alternate universe that enchants by suspending natural physical laws and rational logic of ordinary consensus reality. Tales can nevertheless provide pragmatic assistance in understanding the perplexing complexity of human existence and the diverse thought systems attempting to make sense thereof.

According to Maria Tatar, while reading fairy tales, imagination can be put in the service of crafting a relational model of identity and sharing communal practices of crisis management: "less a refuge from life than a quiet sanctuary, [tales offer] a chance to *meet* characters worth observing and to witness how they manage conflict, peril, and adventure" (1987, 18). Jack Zipes and Marina Warner highlight the ideology-critical, ethical significance of tale's educative function grounded in fantasizing agency. Warner defines the wonder tale as a narrative "compounded of dread and desire, fascination and inquiry" (2004, 3), while Zipes asserts that tales challenge prevailing regimes of power and meaning, can "compensate for the lack of power, wealth, and pleasure that most people experience," and evoke "profound feelings of awe and respect for life as a miraculous process" alterable with a little imagination driven by a "hope for change" (2011, 21–22).

Wondrous stories about the wisdom of the ignorant, the unsuspected metamorphic powers of the overlooked, and the marvel of the mundane hold a particular appeal for marginalized minorities, including minors living in the shadows of grown-ups. Most children's stories, like fairy tales, embark on non-mimetically remapping "quirky or critical or alternative visions of the world designed to provoke that ultimate response of childhood 'Why?' 'Why are things as they are?' 'Why can't they be different?'" (Reynolds 2007, 3).

Just like fairy tales about quests, transformations, or magic can expand the experiences gained from lived reality and facilitate the integration of both vulnerability and empowerment within the self, children's and young adult literatures allow young readers to "negotiate the passage from the Real to the Symbolic"—as Karen Coats's (2004, 137) Freudian terminology suggests—by relying on textual compasses to create a coherent self in periods of identity crisis. Both the best fairy tales and children's/young adult (YA) fiction teach readers to think for themselves through stories that "make interest" beyond the colonizing narratives of normativity (Bruhm and Hurley 2004, xx).

Yan Wu, Kerry Mallan, and Roderick McGillis call the major feat of children's literature "education by fantasy" (2013, xi). An imaginative construction of non-existent but possible worlds opens up political vistas by urging the empathic consideration of others' perspectives and the recognition of collective memory's role in shaping our understanding of past and future. This "imaginative responsibility of confronting the world as we know it or as it might be or even as it might have been" allows "multiple ways of knowing: curiosity, creativity, pleasure, and imagination as the bedrock of reason in its most exalted form" (2013 xi–xii). This chapter reads fairy-tale cultures and children's/YA literatures as "magic mirror[s] of the imagination" (Bobby 2009, 11) to explore the changing meanings attributed to fantasy alternatively interpreted as a psychic automatism, a survival strategy, and a feat of solidarity.

Notions of childhood and the purposes and practices of children's literature have altered over time, along with the changing cultural evaluation of fairy tales, no longer seen as "static literary models to be internalized for therapeutic consumption" or corrective ends, but as live, fluid forms shaped by social interactions, and possible instruments of individual autonomy (Zipes 1979, 177). C. S. Lewis refused to treat children as "a strange species whose habits you have 'made up' like an anthropologist or a commercial traveler" (1994, 22); J. R. R. Tolkien and Maurice Sendak rejected the label "writing for children," while E. B. White famously proclaimed that writers of children's books "have to write up, not down" (Popova 2016). Mendlesohn and Levy pointed out an extension of age in children's fiction: while Victorian Lewis Carroll's Alice in Wonderland is barely over seven, by the 1930s twelve is an ideal age, by the 1950s and into the 1980s fourteen-year-olds regularly appear, and from the 1980s a new category develops—"first through appropriating the work of adult writers, later as new teen lists, until the emergence of Young Adult"—which features older child protagonists in their late teens (2006, 6).

The label "crossover fiction" (Beckett 2009)—in cinematic adaptations the category "family adventure"—has spread to denote the blurring of the borderlines between child, young adult, and adult interpretive communities. It evokes an archaic feature of folk/fairy tales by stressing how creative imagination can become the ground of intergenerational bonding since truly fine stories address all, enabling a time travel whereby mature readers can nostalgically travel back to forgotten childhoods when they rebelled against maturity's conventions and children can daringly activate futuristic or anachronistic scenarios at their own whim. The age-old interest in fairyland relates to a "curiosity about the World, a flexibility of response, and an ability to play" that Terry Pratchett associates with "neoteny" or juvenilization, the retaining of youth by the human "species, [. . .] forever sticking our fingers into the electric socket of the Universe to see what'll happen next" (1994).

This universal infantile open-mindedness serves the basis of the moral philosophical program organizing the deep structural foundation of fairy tales that G. K. Chesterton calls "The Ethics of Elfland" (1908). Fairy-tale logic, concomitant with children's social sensibility and resilience, can help us appreciate the unfulfilled possibilities lurking beneath the actualized realities of our world and invites all to relate compassionately toward non-normative alterities as potential sources of unpredictable magic.

Although many fairy tales teach children mature moral standards by allowing the good to triumph, yet an epistemology of uncertainty, akin with children's relatively limited knowledge of the world, guarantees the charm of the stories in which unpredictable chance called miracle or Providence is a predictable plot-organizing device. Therefore, the wisdom learned might eventually be the recognition of ignorance. The knowledge of the world's unknowability becomes a liberating experience reframed in terms of an "ethics of wonder," which feminist philosopher Marguerite La Caze defined as a generous respect and non-possessive "desire for what/who we cannot fully understand" (2013, 17).

Lewis also argued for the beneficial use of fantastic imagination in a metaphysical quest for meaning fueled by "a longing for the I know not what" (1994, 29), an affectively charged cognitive dissonance he identified, inspired by Tolkien's "On Fairy-Stories" (1947), as a major prerequisite of writing for children. In Lewis's view, unlike realist fiction likely to leave daily frustrations unresolved in young readers' psyches, "books inviting to fairylands"—an umbrella term for all quality children's literature—arouse a yearning for the unknowable and hence "far from dulling or emptying the actual world, give it a new dimension of depth." One "does not despise real woods because he has read of enchanted woods: the reading makes all real woods a little enchanted," the child "reading the fairy tale desires and is happy in the very fact of desiring"(1994, 29–30).

These ideas refute charges of regressive escapism in favor of the genre's therapeutic potential. They also offer an exciting reinterpretation of the Freudian psychoanalytical understanding of desire as a traumatic kernel of psychosexual development grounded in a futile compensation of an irredeemable sense of loss, an anxious yearning rendered insatiable by the compulsive reemergence of new objects of desire. Fantasizing, based on a surplus of proliferating meanings, ignites desire for enchantment and enchantment by a desire that leads, paradoxically through word-magic, to an unspeakable sense of a heterogeneous completeness embracing an insatiable curiosity, incertitude, vulnerability, and also hope against all odds as integral parts of the marvelous totality of being. Desire rooted in "hesitation" (Todorov 1970) as a productive force of enchantment is certainly a more liberating experience than the "monstrous duty to enjoy" the "idiotic pleasure of consumption" globally prescribed by unimaginative capitalist regimes that bombard us with promises of ready-made pleasures, yet ultimately deprive us of enjoying ourselves in our own inventive ways (Žižek 1989).

Lessons on imagination as an engine of resilience and the playful mockery of normative thinking and disciplinary ideology offer a more fertile ground for fairy tales' creative repurposings and critical investigations than repressive cautionary contents. Neil Gaiman's epigraph to his children's gothic fantasy novel, *Coraline* (2002), is paradigmatic of how postmodern fiction has recycled the fairy-tale tradition for the sake of youngsters' empowerment: "Fairy tales are more than true—not because they tell us dragons exist, but because they tell us dragons can be beaten."

Accordingly, tomboyish Coraline, assisted by a talking cat, defeats her monstrous Other Mother—an uncanny doppelganger who wants to replace her eyes with buttons and steal her soul. She accomplishes a quest for herself through boldly facing the Otherness lurking within the selfsame and denouncing her infantile desire for dependence as unreliable. Her subversive gender-bending performance (she pretends to play tea party with her dolls as she is setting a final trap for the witch) is in line with the girl's adventure story she authors herself. Gaiman's novel addresses over-eight-year-olds, but its metaimaginative "psychonarration" allows readers of all ages to get a glimpse at the girl focalizer's "transparent mind" (Nikolajeva 2002, 180) and to celebrate children's fantasizing agency. The "funcanny" (Mäkäräinen 2015) gothic adventures are both initiated and resolved by daydreaming Coraline's pretense play. She fights the villain in a game of hide-and-seek, makes the haunted house disintegrate flattened into a child-drawn sketch, and turns curiosity into a girlish strategy of survival based on an empowering awareness of fantasizing.

The novel's adaptations expand further the range of the target audience and facilitate a transmedia storytelling experience by dispersing integral fictional elements across multiple delivery channels where each medium makes its unique contribution to the unfolding of the story (Jenkins 2006). The different modes of dis/enchantment elicited prove to be both representative and formative of postmillennial fantasists' cultural anxieties, via a revisionary process that "affects people's sense of what is possible" (Bacchilega 2013, 7), imag(in)able. Craig Russell's (2008) graphic novel adopts a teenage Coraline to appeal to YA readers, while Henry Selick's

2009 animated film adaptation foregrounds adult fears about children's safety, combining Hollywood horror film tropes (full moon, zoophobia, madwomen, abduction) with the iconography of anti-child-abuse campaigns (the child as a defenseless ragdoll) and the visual frenzy of 3D CGI technology producing a photorealistic replica of what has never been.

In the film's stunningly colorful alternate reality reminiscent of a phantasmagorical theme park, Coraline's blue hair becomes her major personality marker. It facilitates her recognition in fan art and cosplay, popular YA means of creative transmedia storytelling, as well as in the toy market, making the fictional universe accessible in a commodified form for enthusiast collectors and their infants. Spin-off products marketed online are characteristic of the twenty-first-century production and reception of fairy tales conditioned by pressures of globalization and hyperconsumerization complicit in a gradual disenchantment process (Haase 2004). As Bacchilega puts it, they risk turning the subversive "politics of wonder" into a hegemonically contained "commercialized poetics of magic" (2013, 5).

However, they also promise an augmentation of magic via a transmediation enhancing our intimacy with the fictional universe due to everyday gadgets, applications, and relics facilitating the identification with its heroine, and they train even the youngest "to learn the need to deal with plurality, as they learn the basic conventions of how story works" (Mackey 1995, 44). These products promise interactive agency and intergenerational bonding conjoint with a metaimaginative celebration of fantasy—familiar from children's books like Michael Ende's *The Neverending Story* (1979) in which readers are prompted to give love and create stories for others to save the kingdom of Fantastica.

The major trope of putting fantasy to collaborative creative purposes in YA fiction is the amorous encounter between reader and fictional character. *Between the Lines* (2012), Jodi Picoult's romantic YA novel co-authored with her daughter Samantha Leer, tells the love story of teenage bookworm Delilah and a one-dimensional storybook prince dissatisfied with his predetermined literary existence who literally speaks to her from the pages of her favorite fairy tale, seeking her help to free him from the confines of the text. Emma Donoghue's *Kissing the Witch* (1997) dares readers to voice their own desires and decide about the witch's final declaration, a gift of choice. A sense of intimacy is established by the mouth-to-mouth passing of stories (Orme 2010, 128) and the direct metaleptic address that blurs the boundaries between the diegetic storyworld and the extradiegetic reality, suggesting that the fictional character and his flesh-and-blood reader belong to the same narrative. In Jennifer Orme's (2010) wording, the question is: "What will *you* do with the stories? Chew on them, swallow them, spit them out, or pass them along with stories and kisses?" (129). A metafictional enchantment is induced by the recognition that fairyland is a narrative product we are (de)constructing throughout the (post)modern experimentation with the variability of the traditional fairy-tale format (Tiffin 2009). Queering the narrative provokes wonder by opening up a "mesh of possibilities, gaps, dissonances and resonances, lapses and excesses of meaning, when constituent elements of [. . .] identity aren't made (or can't be made) to signify monolithically" (Sedgwick 1993, 8).

The metaimaginative pleasure of communally reinventing a shared narrative has been enhanced by Catherynne M. Valente's employment of new technological and social media strategies that reclaimed the interactive potential of fairy tales on launching her *The Girl Who Circumnavigated Fairyland in a Ship of Her Own Making* (2011)—about a girl named September spirited away from her average life to Fairyland—as a crowd-funded project, published serialized online. A new generation of reader-fans became involved in the development of the story through a "cyber-community tale-telling," updating for (post)millennial times the seventeenth-century *salons de fées*' agenda to provide solutions to the concerns and entertainment of a mostly female community of fantasists (Pilinovsky 2011, 26). The blurring of boundaries between our world and fairylands evokes metafictional dilemmas related to "questions of the battle over the narrative" that Zipes encapsulates as follows: "Can we humans who have become caricatures of humans in today's society of the spectacle in which commercials, advertisements, and other media influences invade our lives, determine the plot and narrative of our lives?" (2011, 302).

Postmillenial children's and YA fiction's repurposing of fairy-tale tropes specifically enables young readers to cope with these uncertainties and to make sense of incomprehensible "new monsters" including advanced information technology, financial crisis, environmental catastrophe, migration, or post-9/11 permanent threats of terrorism (Wu, Mallan, and McGillis 2013; Bradford et al. 2011). The key feature of YA fiction is its currency, its "absolute synchronicity with concerns of audience to whom it is marketed" (Coats 2004, 137); however, the core patterns of fairy tales—rites of passage, psychological and social journeys of self-discovery, traumatization by a lack, and quest for a remedy (Tiffin 2009, 12)—also overlap with the most common themes of YA "problem novels" centered on existential struggle, stories of healing and survival related to minor frustrations (anxiety over grades, body image, peer pressure) (Trupe 2006; Eccleshare 1996, 387), or major collective historical cataclysms.

Meg Fox's transmedia fairy-tale collages treat repressed memories of child abuse, while Jane Yolen's *Briar Rose* (1992) and Louise Murphy's *The True Story of Hansel and Gretel: A Novel of War and Survival* (2003) use classic fairy tales as allegories of the Holocaust, coded narratives of foremothers' wartime experiences that defy rational comprehension and mimetic modes of representation. As cultural materialist philosopher Slavoj Žižek (2002) argues, fantastification can place the traumatic unimaginable into comprehensible form. In Zipes's words, fairy tales portray the general human condition of being cast in a world we can neither fully understand nor view as a whole, yet the ritual healing power of storytelling helps to transcend the pain of meaninglessness by the power of metamorphosis and a compassionate embracing of Otherness (1996, 380)—motifs permeating YA fiction's empowering reinterpretation of vulnerability, too.

Confronting Otherness often discovered at the core of oneself, and breaking the silence and speaking out to voice fantasies deviating from the norm, are common themes of YA coming-of-age problem novels that focus on the identity crises and social challenges teenagers must face until they grow up and manage to develop adequate socialization skills (Trupe 2006). The leitmotif on the adolescent struggle for the acceptance of difference—crossing the boundaries to recognize who you are—resonates particularly well with the twisted versions of classic fairy tales that subversively rewrite canonized master narratives. YA textual revenge takes many forms in "anti-tales" (McAra and Calvin 2011) that reiterate the "hard logic" of the fairy tale (Bernheimer 2009, 64) only to defamiliarize a familiar set of codes like the conventionally happy ending that becomes systematically challenged as a clichéd guarantee of the contentment of the deserving characters by the reestablishment of the status quo.

The victimized can fight back aggressively as in the tellingly entitled teen horror film *Hansel & Gretel Witch Hunters* (2013) or the first-person-shooter computer game *American McGee's Alice* (2000) where the heroine must flee the madhouse and fight the Red Queen and her own inner daemons to save a nightmarish Wonderland by revindicating the powers of her imagination (Kérchy 2016). Magic can emerge as a "transformative site for politics of gender and sexuality" (Battis 2011, 315) when the protagonists embark on freely exploring their desires beyond wedded heterosexual bliss as in the emancipatory lesbian erotica of Jeanette Winterson's Twelve Dancing Princesses (1989) or Santiago Solis's queercrip, gay, and disabled rereading of the seven dwarves' bonding (2007).

Many YA retellings question the normative beauty ideal conveyed in classic fairy tales and maintained by contemporary post-industrialist consumer societies of spectacle by staging adolescents' physical and psychic vulnerabilities in a lookist society. In Marissa Meyer's debut YA science fiction novel *Cinder* (2012), a dystopian New Beijing connects the glass slipper motif to the footbinding tradition of ancient China (from where one of the earliest versions of Cinderella originates), yet the tiny feet are not eroticized fetish but prosthetic implants of the posthuman disabled heroine who ends up embracing her anomalous embodiment. She defines herself as a deformed cyborg, a lunar outcast, and a lower-class mechanic but refuses second-rate citizenship and rewires her own destiny. The YA romance film *Penelope* (2006) recycles the fairy-tale theme of humanimal transformation to delight with a similar punch line: a young woman distorted by a pig snout and ears is released from the curse when she is genuinely loved by one of her kind, who turns out to be herself.

Speculating about the psychic motivations of antagonists initiates complex ethical reflections on the status of evil in human characters as well as the scapegoating of difference in prejudiced society. The intimate focus on the neglected point-of-view of a seemingly villainous social outcast—originally marginalized in the storyworld and unanimously condemned by readers—provokes an enchantment by forbidden thrills fused with a trial of our "imaginative resistance" (Szabó Gendler 2000), a reluctance to empathize with immoral characters. Our notion of truth gets debased as just one possible way of freeze-framing in a subjective narrative the ungraspable essence of ever-changing, kaleidoscopic reality.

In Angela Carter's tale cycle (1979) big bad (were)wolves transform into humans (Granny and Wolf Alice in Wonderland among them) to meet wolfish Red Riding Hoods and bestial brides, brought to the silver screen by Neil Jordan's gothic horror-fantasy *The Company of Wolves* (1984) and adapted to shadow puppetry by Layla Holzer (2017). Although Gregory Maguire's novel *Wicked: The Life and Times of the Wicked Witch of the West* (1995), also turned into a Broadway musical hit (2003), was allegedly inspired by actual cultural traumas provoking collective moral panic—the Holocaust, the First Gulf War, and toddler James Bulger's horrifying local murder by ten-year-old boys—his recycling of Baum's Oz novel verges on moral relativization. Throughout the investigation of the causes of becoming monstrous, the green-skinned witch, resembling Margaret Hamilton from the 1939 film adaptation, is gradually revealed to be a brave fighter against a totalitarian regime, a defender of animal rights, and an idealistic victim ostracized because of her dermatological difference's disability and her dysfunctional family.

This relativization gets a troubling metafictional twist in *The Darkest Desire: The Wolf's Own Tale* by Anthony Schmitz (1999) where the first-person narrative of the wicked wolf (a metaphorical embodiment of the lowliest serial infant-killer or pedophile) tells the unhappy life of an addict tormented by his passion for children's flesh. The atonement of the wolf as a sympathetic criminal, the melancholy of a beast whose bestiality is in his nature against his will, and its philosophical speculations about possibilities of self-improvement are contrasted by the manipulative inhumanness of the fictional Brothers Grimm who parade as therapists to exploit the wolf's misery for literary inspiration. Artists are like wolves who seduce their curious prey into a story they will never be able to leave behind.

Instead of explicit intertextual references, a therapeutic fairy-tale logic might lurk in clandestine forms at the heart of the text. Some stories force us to climb to the top of a plum tree and refuse to come down until we find arguments against the meaninglessness of existence, like a character in Janne Teller's *Nothing* (2010), a controversial YA novel that revolutionized the genre by creating what critics coined a haunting existential fairy tale and a fantastic parable about human instability. The impossible comes true as a group of teens gather a hidden pile of precious objects—including a beloved bike, the coffin of dead brother, a lost virginity, and the head of a pet dog named Cinderella—to prove the worthiness of life to their classmate who proclaims that "nothing was worth doing, because nothing meant anything anyway" (2). In a brutally twisted game, the guarantee of the meaningfulness of things resides in the pain implied in sacrificially giving them up as the most significant constituents of their lives.

The deviant trickster on the tree top, much like Italo Calvino's (1977) Baron in the Trees, challenges all to take an unprecedented look at their habitual environment and to explore as fairy-tale philosophers the non-utilitarian, speculative, other side of things independent of common intellectual standards and customary trivial definitions. The novel recycles the wondrous-rational (il)logic of fairy tales in which incomprehensible happiness always rests upon incomprehensible conditions.

It is a matter of changing sociocultural evaluation whether the didactic instrumentalization or the deviant escapism of fantasy is seen to predominate. Whereas Lewis's portal quest fantasy saga *The Chronicles of Narnia* (1950–65) was criticized by fellow Inkling (an Oxford University literary group) Tolkien for being an all-too-obvious Christian allegory, young readers' of today's secularized era might entirely fail to decode the religious symbolism of Lewis's fantastic mythological mash-up, and postmillenial dogmatic critics express anxieties about the books' sacrilegious spreading of a lust for the occult.

Online fan fictions extend Lewis's fictional universe by celebrating the characters' rebellious imaginative agency. In Inky's widely reblogged 2013 sketch the older girl, Susan, does not lose Narnia when she "discovers lipstick" (Lewis's euphemism for sexual awakening), as the original suggests, but embarks on fabulous adventures in the real world. She becomes a nurse on the front in WWII, a lit graduate on the East Coast "kissing boys and kissing girls" and "helping smuggle birth control to the ladies in her dorm because Susan Pevensie is a *queen* and she understands the right of a woman to rule over her own body." She protests against Vietnam and matures into a storyteller who crafts tales about how "Rapunzel cuts off her own hair and uses it to climb down the tower and escape" (Inky 2013). In a secular reinterpretation of the spiritual and political function of fantasy, since the Lion forbade her magic, Susan made her own, she did not lose faith, she found it—in imagination, in herself.

Centered on the clash of black-and-white magic, the wizarding world of the *Harry Potter* series (1997–2007) represents the most vital backlash against the realistic fiction dominating children's literature from the 1970s to the 1990s. However, J. K. Rowling's socialism permeates imperceptibly the marvelous storyworld in which the orphaned boy-savior and his allies use magic spells, their wit, and the power of friendship to fight against the racism of pure-bloods, the oppression of house elves, warfare reducing children to collateral damage, and the totalitarian rule of the Dark Lord (Nel 2003).

Harry starts out as a male Cinderella, living in a cupboard under the stairs, a vulnerable everyboy readers can identify with, and ends up incorporating a historical trauma (Battis 2011, 316) in an increasingly war-ridden alternate reality. Rowling inoculates the conservative genre of the boarding school coming-of-age novel with fairy-tale themes for the progressive political purpose of creating the multicultural democratic institution of Hogwarts. Although the School of Witchcraft and Wizardry is contrasted with the petty world of mundane muggles, magic-less humanity still endlessly amazes the magically gifted enchanted by their Otherness through the ethics of wonder, the governing principle of the fairy tale. *Fantastic Beasts and Where to Find Them* (2016), a cinematic spinoff prequel centered on the adventures of magizoologist Newt Scamander, future author of a Hogwarts textbook, refreshes the Potter franchise by relocating the wizarding world from 1990s British school to 1920s jazz age Manhattan. Urban magic lure is revamped by dark fantasies about civilization's destruction, while beasts of nature represent precious persecuted minorities and sociocritical agents who call attention to environmental protection, trans-species solidarity, and the interdependence of all living things.

Online extensions of Rowling's fictional universe blur fantasy into lived reality by courtesy of the charity organization the Harry Potter Alliance, intent on making activism accessible through the power of storytelling to engage fans in work for equality, human rights, and literacy. This project shifts enchantment from the "passive stance of enrapturement" toward "the active motion of experience" (Warner 2004, 3) and puts into effect the pedagogical and political functions of wonder, which can "instill a sense of self-reflecting and self-critical community and demonstrate how the ordinary can become extraordinary" (Zipes 1995, 6) or, vice versa, how Otherness can be revealed as a part of the self/same. Hence, fairy tales as instruments of collective daydreaming (Greenhill and Matrix 2010, 4) and "subversive storytelling" can help schools and families become not just institutions of correction, discipline, and distraction, but ideal sites of "self-reflective enchantment," too (Zipes 1995, 6).

Advocating an imagination open to multiplicity and resistant to closure can propose "a transformed world order, one which reaches beyond a fear of the unknown to embrace new ways of being" and dreaming (Bradford et al. 2011, 3). Children's and YA literatures nurture the fairy-tale spirit as an effective method in developing imaginativeness and fostering resilience and empathy—helping young readers accept themselves and connect with Others with a thoughtful understanding that broadens the perspective on humankind's enchanting totality.

Related topics: Adaptation and the Fairy-Tale Web; Cinematic; Comics and Graphic Novels; Convergence Culture; Digital; Fan Cultures; Fantasy; Gender; Horror; Romance; Sexualities/Queer and Trans Studies

References Cited and Further Reading

Abate, Michelle, and Kenneth Kidd, eds. 2014. *Over the Rainbow: Queer Children's and Young Adult Literature*. Ann Arbor: U Michigan P.

Bacchilega, Cristina. 2013. *Fairy Tales Transformed? Twenty-First-Century Adaptations and the Politics of Wonder*. Detroit: Wayne State UP.

Battis, Jes. 2011. "Trans Magic: The Radical Performance of the Young Wizard in YA Literature." In *Over the Rainbow*, edited by Abate and Kidd, 314–29.

Beckett, Sandra L. 2009. *Crossover Fiction: Global and Historical Perspectives*. New York: Routledge.

Bernheimer, Kate. 2009. "Fairy Tale Is Form: Form Is Fairy Tale." In *The Writer's Notebook: Craft Essays from Tin House*, edited by Susan Bell, Dorothy Allison, Steve Almond, and Aimee Bender, 61–73. Portland: Tin House.

Bobby, Susan Reddington, ed. 2009. *Fairy Tales Reimagined*. Jefferson: McFarland.

Bradford, Clare, Kerry Mallan, John Stephens, and Robyn McCallum. 2011. *New World Orders in Contemporary Literature: Utopian Transformations*. Houndsmill: Palgrave.

Bruhm, Steven, and Natasha Hurley, eds. 2004. *Curiouser: On the Queerness of Children*. Minneapolis: U Minnesota P.

Calvino, Italo. 1977. *The Baron in the Trees*. Boston: Houghton Mifflin.

Carroll, Lewis. (1865) 2015. *The Annotated Alice: Alice's Adventures in Wonderland & Through the Looking-Glass*, edited by Martin Gardner and Mark Burnstein. New York: Norton.

Carter, Angela. 1979. *The Bloody Chamber*. London: Gollancz.

Chesterton, G. K. (1908) 2008. "The Ethics of Elfland." In *Orthodoxy*, 40–56. Rockville: Serenity.

Coats, Karen. 2004. *Looking Glasses and Neverlands: Lacan, Desire, and Subjectivity in Children's Literature*. Iowa City: U Iowa P.

Donoghue, Emma. 1997. *Kissing the Witch*. New York: Harper Collins.

Eccleshare, Julia. 1996. "Teenage Fiction, Realism, Romances, Contemporary Problem Novels." In *International Companion*, edited by Hunt, 387–97.

Ende, Michael. 1983. *The Neverending Story*. London: Allen Lane.

Gaiman, Neil. 2002. *Coraline*. London: Bloomsbury.

Greenhill, Pauline, and Sidney Eve Matrix. 2010. "Introduction." In *Fairy Tale Film: Visions of Ambiguity*, edited by Pauline Greenhill and Sidney Eve Matrix, 1–23. Logan: Utah State UP.

Haase, Donald, ed. 2004. *Fairy Tales and Feminism: New Approaches*. Detroit: Wayne State UP.

CHILDREN'S AND YOUNG ADULT LITERATURE

Hunt, Peter, ed. 1996. *International Companion Encyclopedia of Children's Literature.* New York: Routledge.

Jenkins, Henry. 2006. *Convergence Culture: Where Old and New Media Collide.* New York: NYU P.

Kérchy, Anna. 2016. *Alice in Transmedia Wonderland: Curiouser and Curiouser New Forms of a Children's Classic.* Jefferson, NC: McFarland.

La Caze, Marguerite. 2013. *Wonder and Generosity: Their Role in Ethics and Politics.* Albany: SUNY P.

Lewis, C. S. 1950–1965. *The Chronicles of Narnia.* London: HarperCollins.

———. (1952) 1994. "Three Ways of Writing for Children." In *Of Other Worlds: Essays and Stories,* 22–35. New York: Houghton, Mifflin, Harcourt.

Lüthi, Max. 1982. *The European Folktale: Form and Nature,* translated by John D. Niles. Bloomington: Indiana UP.

Mackey, Margaret. 1995. "Communities of Fictions: Story, Format and Thomas the Tank Engine." *Children's Literature in Education* 26 (1): 39–52.

Maguire, Gregory. 1995. *Wicked: The Life and Times of the Wicked Witch of the West.* New York: HarperCollins.

Mäkäräinen, Meeri. 2015. "The *Funcanny* Valley: A Study of Positive Emotional Reactions to Strangeness." *Academic MindTrek Conference Proceedings,* 175–81. Tampere: Aalto.

McAra, Catriona Fay, and David Calvin, eds. 2011. *Anti-Tales: The Uses of Disenchantment.* Newcastle upon Tyne: Cambridge Scholars Publishing.

Mendlesohn, Farah, and Michael Levy. 2006. *Children's Fantasy Literature: An Introduction.* Cambridge: Cambridge UP.

Meyer, Marissa. 2012. *Cinder.* New York: Macmillan.

Murphy, Louise. 2003. *The True Story of Hansel and Gretel: A Novel of War and Survival.* New York: Penguin.

Nel, Philip. 2003. *J. K. Rowling's Harry Potter Novels: A Reader's Guide.* New York: Continuum.

Nikolajeva, Maria. 2002. "Imprints of the Mind: The Depiction of Consciousness in Children's Fiction." *Children's Literature Association Quarterly* 26: 174–87.

Orme, Jennifer. 2010. "Mouth to Mouth: Queer Desires in Emma Donoghue's *Kissing the Witch.*" *Marvels & Tales* 24 (1): 116–30.

Picoult, Jodi, and Samantha Leer. 2012. *Between the Lines.* New York: Simon and Schuster.

Pilinovsky, Helen. 2011. "*Salon des Fées.* Cyber Salon: Re-Coding the Commodified Fairy Tale." In *Postmodern Reinterpretations of Fairy Tales,* edited by Anna Kérchy, 17–33. Lewiston, NY: Edwin Mellen.

Popova, Maria. 2016. "The Best Children's Books of 2016." *Brain Pickings Online,* December 12. www.brainpickings.org/2016/12/12/the-best-childrens-books-of-2016/.

Pratchett, Terry. 1994. "When the Children Read Fantasy." *SF2 Concatenation.* www.concatenation.org/articles/pratchett.html.

Reynolds, Kimberley. 2007. *Radical Children's Literature: Future Visions and Aesthetic Transformation in Juvenile Fiction.* New York: Palgrave Macmillan.

Rowling, J. K. 1997–2007. *The Harry Potter Series.* London: Bloomsbury.

Russell, Craig P. 2008. *Coraline.* New York: Harper Collins.

Schmitz, Anthony. 1999. *The Darkest Desire: The Wolf's Own Tale.* Hopewell: Ecco P.

Sedgwick, Eve Kosofsky. 1993. *Tendencies.* Durham, NC: Duke UP.

Solis, Santiago. 2007. "Snow White and the Seven Dwarves: Queercripped." *Hypatia* 22 (1): 114–31.

Szabó Gendler, Tamar. 2000. "The Puzzle of Imaginative Resistance." *Journal of Philosophy* 97 (2): 55–81.

Tatar, Maria. 1987. *The Hard Facts of the Grimms' Fairy Tales.* Princeton, NJ: Princeton UP.

Teller, Janne. 2010. *Nothing.* New York: Atheneum.

Tiffin, Jessica. 2009. *Marvelous Geometry: Narrative and Metafiction in Modern Fairy Tale.* Detroit: Wayne State UP.

Todorov, Tzvetan. 1970. *The Fantastic: A Structural Approach to a Literary Genre,* translated by Richard Howell. Ithaca, NY: Cornell UP.

Tolkien, J.R.R. (1947) 1964. "On Fairy Stories." *Tree and Leaf.* New York: Harper Collins.

Trupe, Alice. 2006. *Thematic Guide to Young Adult Literature.* Westport, CN: Greenwood P.

Valente, Catherynne M. 2011. *The Girl Who Circumnavigated Fairyland in a Ship of Her Own Making.* New York: Macmillan.

Warner, Marina. 2004. *Fantastic Metamorphoses, Other Worlds: Ways of Telling the Self.* Oxford: Oxford UP.

Winterson, Jeanette. 1989. *Sexing the Cherry.* London: Vintage.

Wu, Yan, Kerry Mallan, and Roderick McGillis, eds. 2013. *(Re)imagining the World: Children's Literature's Response to Changing Times.* New York: Springer.

Yolen, Jane. 1992. *Briar Rose.* New York: Thor Books.

Zipes, Jack. 1979. *Breaking the Magic Spell: Radical Theories of Folk and Fairy Tales.* London: Heinemann.

———. 1995. *Creative Storytelling: Building Community/Changing Lives.* New York: Routledge.

———. 1996. "Spells of Enchantment." In *Folk and Fairy Tales,* edited by Martin Hallett and Barbara Karasek, 370–92. Peterborough, ON: Broadview P.

——. 2011. *The Enchanted Screen: The Unknown History of Fairy-Tale Films*. New York: Routledge.

Žižek, Slavoj. 1989. *The Sublime Object of Ideology*. London: Verso.

——. 2002. *Welcome to the Desert of the Real! Five Essays on September 11 and Related Dates*. London: Verso.

Mediagraphy

American McGee's Alice (Computer Game). 2000. Developer Rogue Entertainment, Director American McGee.

The Company of Wolves. 1984. Director Neil Jordan. UK.

Coraline. 2009. Director Henry Selick. USA.

Fantastic Beasts and Where to Find Them. 2016. Director David Yates. UK/USA.

Hansel and Gretel Witch Hunters. 2013. Director Tommy Wirkola. Germany/USA.

Healing through Literary, Visual, Performance Arts. 2004–2015. Artist Meg Fox. www.megfoxart.com/.

Inky. 2013. "Untitled Narnia Fanfiction Sketch." *Tumblr*. www.ink-splotch.tumblr.com.

Penelope. 2006. Director Mark Palansky. UK/USA.

Wicked: The Untold Story of the Witches of Oz (Musical). 2003. Music by Stephen Schwartz, Script by Winnie Holzman. Broadway. USA.

The Wizard of Oz. 1939. Director Victor Fleming. USA.

Wondertales: Angela Carter's Theatre of Shadows (Shadow Puppetry). 2017. Artist Layla Holzer. Bristol. UK.

27
FANDOM/FAN CULTURES

Anne Kustritz

The difference between fairy-tale storytelling cultures and fan cultures is often a matter of perspective and interpretation, at times simply different names for the same practices, at other times a question of cultural value or academic discipline, and at still others intersecting but distinct groupings that could be represented as an overlapping set of Venn diagrams. In his landmark *Textual Poachers*, Henry Jenkins argues that the term "fan" does not really specify a fixed group of people or set of behaviors, but rather identifies a devalued and even abject intersection of taste, interactivity, and mass culture (1992). By this formulation, according to cultural norms, fans love things they shouldn't in ways that are generally deemed extreme. The definition of fans thus shifts as cultural values and tastes shift, across time and across cultures and subcultures, much in the same way that the audience and social status of fairy tales have shifted from common culture to children's culture (Stone 1975).

Jenkins also argues that practices of modern fan cultures descend from pre-industrial folk cultures, which normalized creative participation in cultural life. Fairy tales are intertwined with this older model of interactive, participatory storytelling, as even literary fairy tales quickly exceeded their original form to inspire numerous interconnected versions and retellings in multiple media, a phenomenon that Cristina Bacchilega terms the "fairy tale web" (2013, 1–30). Thus, determining the relevance of fan cultures in relation to fairy tales requires teasing apart the many different types of fans and fan cultures, the hierarchies of cultural value at stake in the term "fan," and whether fan culture is defined from the perspectives of scholars, mainstream culture, or fans themselves. Each of these decisions constructs a different understanding of what fairy tales have contributed to fan culture, how contemporary fan cultures interact with fairy tales, and the political ramifications of thinking through fans and fairy tales together.

Fandom and Fairy Tales Are Bad for You: Fan Taxonomies and (De)Valuation of Participatory Storytelling

To understand overlaps between fan cultures and fairy tales, one must acknowledge that there are many different types of fans, fan practices, and fan cultures. Focus on fan cultures immediately brings to light an initial theoretical distinction between organized groups of fans who interact, have a social and technological infrastructure, and think of themselves as a community versus individuals or those who share their fandom with only a few friends. Not all fans want to be part of, or have access to, a larger fan culture. Although isolated, individual fans are sometimes analyzed within fan studies by scholars like Matt Hills (2002), because they do not participate in a "fan culture" they are beyond the scope of this piece, which seeks to address the cultural practices, traditions, and social world of organized fans. Then, even within the category of organized fans, the practices and infrastructure of fans of celebrities, sports, musicians, and media vary dramatically (Coppa 2006). However, those who are not part of a fan culture may feel that they are fans, while others who participate deeply in fan cultures may shy away from so identifying (Kustritz 2015). Further, many people may act in ways that closely resemble fandom and yet are rarely identified as such by those involved or by outside observers. These complications suggest the need to consider how and why certain activities, groups, and people become labeled as fans by outsiders or mainstream culture and why some do or do not self-identify as fans. It also raises the contentious issue of the boundaries of fandom: who is a fan and who isn't.

Jenkins argues that the term "fan" derives from "fanatic" and largely names practices that mainstream culture deems excessive, oriented toward cultural objects that mainstream culture deems valueless and childish (1992); Joli Jenson would add that cultural objects beloved primarily by women, which thus become feminized, also often prompt use of the fan label (1992). Kay Stone (1975), Maria Nikolajeva (2003), and Linda Lee (2008) argue that a similar structural association between fairy tales, femininity, and childhood likewise reduce the cultural value of fairy tales. In other words, fans, and perhaps especially fairy-tale fans, have bad taste and exercise it far too enthusiastically. Other terms are used for people who are extremely passionate about activities and cultural objects generally deemed valuable, such as connoisseur, aficionado, collector, and expert. A Google image search on September 5, 2015, revealed a crowdsourced version of this cultural separation. The keyword "fans" resulted in images of a contraption for creating cool breezes, but also numerous images of large, tightly packed, homogenous crowds of people, often shouting, sometimes covered in body paint (Google 2015b). The search term "connoisseur," on the other hand, resulted largely in images of individual people alone, carefully studying their object of interest, frequently very expensive things, like wine, cigars, cameras, and fine art (Google 2015a).

The difference between these collections of images recalls Pierre Bourdieu's work on distinction (1984) and Peter Stallybrass and Allon White's work on bourgeoisie separation from the crowd (1986). Conversely, "fan," like its pre-industrial precursor folk culture, is generally attached to popular pleasures, available to everyone and historically associated with bodily interaction. Thus, John Fiske charts the histories of soccer and wrestling as popular pleasures repeatedly associated with spectacles of bodily excess, the threat of mindless mob behavior, and boisterous interaction including shouting, standing, costuming, and the possibility of the crowd usurping the distance between performer and audience by directly joining in (1989, 69–102). Barbara Ehrenreich, Elizabeth Hess, and Gloria Jacobs note similar references to bodily excesses and crowd mentality in news stories about female Beatles fans, who reporters often noted fainted, burst into tears, and produced other physical responses, en masse (1992 [1997]). Fairy-tale storytelling cultures might also be productively considered as interactive, asking teller and audience to involve themselves bodily and creatively in the narration process and to become, in a sense, part of the story, as each iteration of the tale adapts to suit the needs of particular individuals, communities, and historical moments.

In contrast, Bourdieu (1984) and Stallybrass and White (1986) argue that bourgeoisie distinction requires a theoretical separation from the crowd and its tastes, pleasures, and physicality, as well as an intellectual and analytical distance from the cultural object itself. Such detachment is achieved largely through consumption of cultural objects restricted by their expense and through practices and behaviors limited by education, gained via formal study and/or through the informal learning that leads to etiquette, manners, and what Michel Foucault might call bodily discipline (1978, 1979). Thus many of the connoisseur search images include a magnifying glass, emphasizing their intellectual appreciation of the object, a quality that distinguishes them from, rather than connects them with, the masses and the object itself (Google 2015a). Likewise, an academic who specializes in queer theory may engage in many fan behaviors, such as collecting books by theorist Judith Butler (ideally with her autograph), obsessively studying her every publication and utterance, following her career, attending her public appearances, and hoping for a chance to meet and interact with her in person. However, rarely will such an academic be dismissively called a Judith Butler *fan* and, instead, will rather aspire to the distinguished title of Judith Butler expert. Because these terms mark different statuses within hierarchies of social distinction, an insistence upon identifying as a fan can become a defiant act of affirmation, resistance, and solidarity against class-based power structures and prejudice.

Both industrial mass culture and folk culture are popular pleasures with a low bar to participation, although their positions within capitalism differ theoretically, if not always in practice. While people can spend a lot of money on these activities, there are very often low-cost or even no cost alternatives; the extreme expense of box seats at a professional sports game contrasts to a gathering of friends watching the same game on TV at home or in a public venue. Further, excessive consumption associated with such activities is often popularly deemed a "waste of money" due to their negligible cultural value; money spent on popular pleasures is not exchanged for greater distinction or cultural capital, appears to be exchanged for nothing but pleasure itself, and is thus squandered. As a result, fans are frequently accused of wasting their money on consumerist junk, while folk cultural objects can be deemed antiquated and thus valueless, or conversely artisan and highly valuable, but unappreciated in their culture of origin where they are not studied and displayed but "put to everyday use" (Walker 1967).

This distinction connects to another basic set of analytical categories for studying fan cultures, defined according to their level of interactivity; here the analytical categories of fan culture and folk culture diverge historically at the juncture of mass production, but converge again when the culture industry borrows from fairy-tale themes. While fans are culturally stereotyped for excessive interactivity and bad objects, in practice the intensity and qualities of interactivity vary significantly. Just as many fans are derided for spending too much money on popular pleasures, many also receive social scorn for applying the behaviors associated with connoisseurship to industrial mass cultural products. One form of this behavior is associated with what I have termed "as is" fandom (Kustritz 2011; Russo 2009, 126), and obsession_inc called "affirmative fandom," which treats the cultural object as a closed text of great value and high artistry that must be studied and collected, often with great reverence for the original author's intentions and authority (Russo 2009). At the other end of the spectrum lies what I have called "creative fandom," and obsession_inc and some theorists name "transformative fandom," which applies to fan practices that treat the cultural object as an open system that can be edited, expanded, and interacted with by anyone, in any way, with equal authority. These categories are of particular importance to understanding connections between modern fan culture, fairy-tale folk culture, and the copyright system, as discussed in greater detail in the following.

Thus fans may be thought of as isolated or part of a culture, affirmative or transformative. While these may be used by scholars as distinct analytical categories for separate fan cultures, in practice they form more of a spectrum, and individual fan activities may incorporate both, while individual fans often participate in activities all across the spectrum. Nevertheless, from an academic perspective, it can be helpful to note that some fan cultures fall more clearly toward one or another end of this continuum. Trivia and collectables, for example, fit much more clearly within the affirmative end, while fan fiction, original stories based on a previously published narrative, fits more comfortably in the transformative end. Although activities like collecting can certainly be part of modern fairy-tale cultures, especially when commoditized by the modern mass culture industry, highly interactive, transformative fan activities have much more in common with the collective, multi-authored history of fairy-tale storytelling.

Fans, Fairy Tales, Storytelling, and the Market

The line between normative consumer activities and excessive consumption has shifted in recent years as the Internet makes interactivity with popular culture easier and an increasingly mainstream part of everyday life. As a result, many fan activities with roots in the pre-industrial history of folk culture and collective storytelling have slowly garnered greater social recognition, increased attention from the industry, and a modicum of respectability. This shift can be charted in the theoretical distance between Jenkins's two landmark books; while *Textual Poachers* (1992) was largely occupied with documenting and recuperating fan activities in an age when fan behaviors were seen as obscure and often ridiculous, *Convergence Culture* (2006) documents producers' deliberate cultivation of fan communities, the growing cultural power and influence of networked fan communities, and the centrality of fan behaviors like participation and interactivity across cultural registers, from education, to news, to politics. Yet, while the social consensus regarding the legitimacy of participatory popular culture has changed, the influence of the market and intellectual property laws including copyright prevent a wholesale return to pre-industrial shared culture. The interactions between fan cultures and fairy-tale cultures are thus also colored by international legal systems. The longevity of fairy-tale storytelling cultures, as they cross over and intermingle with fan storytelling cultures, offers an ideal example for tracing transformations in participatory storytelling over time.

Traditional fairy tales (as opposed to literary fairy tales with known authors like Hans Christian Andersen) originate and/or recirculate in oral storytelling traditions, wherein the notion of an original makes little sense, and every tale is adapted by each storyteller to suit the audience, the occasion, and the cultural context. This process of borrowing from and building upon other cultural objects pervaded oral and written expression in pre-copyright society, and this principle applies both to the arts and the sciences. As implied by the Sir Isaac Newton adage, "If I have seen further, it is by standing on the shoulders of giants," discoveries in science, and movements in art and literature, are dependent upon a lineage of works and knowledge that came before (Bartlett 1994; Lenthem 2007). In addition, many forms of art and literature contain not only the traces of earlier works' influence, but direct call-and-response patterns, as well as a history of adaptation and sampling (Barthes 1977; Krauss 1986). Shakespeare's history plays and modern historical fiction like Tracy Chevalier's *The Girl with the Pearl Earring* (1999) and Philippa Gregory's *The Other Boleyn Girl* (2002) are examples of the numerous stories renarrating historical events. Stock or archetypal characters like the fool, the Don Juan, the corrupt politician, and the nagging housewife are constantly re-appropriated and reused in new stories ranging from *commedia dell'arte*, to opera, to modern sitcoms. Further, many stories much more directly comment upon, reproduce, and adapt other stories, including Dante's *Divine Comedy* (Alighieri 2003 [1320]), which adapts and expands the plot, characters, and settings of the Bible, and Jane Austen's *Northanger Abbey* (2003 [1803]), a critique of gothic romances, specifically Ann Radcliffe's *The Mysteries of Udolpho* (2001 [1794]). In both pre-industrial and mass-mediated fairy tales one may similarly consider not only the practice of retelling, but also repetition of characters and archetypes, including the abused apprentice, the noble or vain prince, the wicked stepmother, and the innocent or precocious young girl.

Yet all this borrowing comes into question legally and philosophically under copyright law, which prohibits the reproduction of a protected work, but also its adaptation into another medium and the creation of derivative works, all means by which the vibrant fairy-tale tradition survived for centuries before the era of mass reproduction. Thus Lawrence Lessig describes copyright as creating a "read-only" society, wherein media is supplied to the population by a small group of professionals in a fixed state, much like a read-only DVD, and interactivity is forbidden (2008). Lessig, like other scholars, activists, and philosophers of the copyleft, advocates a "read-write" society, in which the participatory and interactive activities that were normative before copyright, and which have become increasingly widespread due to convergence culture, should become the legal standard. The irony of fairy tales' interaction with the history of copyright is that despite their origin as collaboratively authored collective culture, many were also made into fixed forms of property and taken out of common circulation, most notoriously by Disney (Hendenkamp 2002; Litman 1993; Sprigman 2005).

As the latter cited works detail, while anyone could comment upon, adapt, and add to the legacy of fairy tales in the pre-copyright era, once corporations began to make fairy tales into property, adding to, retelling, or critiquing their versions of fairy tales became illegal. The case of fan fiction based on fairy tales brings these processes into sharp relief, as it extends and replicates the practices of collective authorship common to many earlier fairy-tale cultures. Corporations allege copyright infringement primarily through cease-and-desist letters, rather than defending it formally through actual court cases, often because the threat of action by an entity with substantial resources is sufficient to deter creators (many of whom are not, in actual fact, contravening copyright legislation, see Greenhill 2006). The difference lies largely in semantics and the intervention of copyright law. Because works of fan fiction predominantly reinterpret mass media cultural properties, they become doubly tainted, first through association with the market, and second as a form of theft and unoriginality, as if Disney versions of fairy tales were wholly novel, rather than standing on the shoulders of the many folk storytellers who came before.

Thus, transformative fan cultures share much with fairy-tale cultures in their modern form, and that includes a troubled relationship with the market and an ironic tension with copyright. In the absence of intellectual property law, creative fan cultures essentially replicate many key characteristics of earlier folk practices, including the storytelling cultures that spread and nurtured fairy tales. Because both fairy tales and fan cultures currently exist in a cultural landscape dominated by corporate media, fairy tales sometimes seem to have one fixed or specific version, and fan creativity is derided as merely derivative, as though any culture, or any part of culture, were wholly cut off from history. Transformative fandom refers to more than just fan fiction; like the fairy-tale web, which includes adaptations and retellings in multiple media, fan creativity involves numerous forms like spoken word recordings, essays, art, costuming, and a lively process of audience response and feedback. The term "transformative" also connects back to copyright and serves as a mixed defense and apologia for transformative fan culture's collaborative and interactive model of cultural engagement. In the United States, although copyright forbids unlicensed derivative works, it currently provides an exception for transformative works in the doctrine of "fair use." Many lawyers, activists, and artists debate the precise dividing line between transformative and derivative, due to its critical importance in defining the scope within which people have the right to co-create their own cultural life (Katyal 2004; Tan 2013; Tushnet 1996; Wong 2008). By claiming the title transformative, fan infrastructure, like the non-profit Organization for Transformative Works, founded in 2007, stridently claims that authority over creative works must remain with, or be restored to, the people, and if the sweeping popularity of remix, file sharing, and memes are any indication, the cultural zeitgeist is with them. The term "transformation" also brings fan cultures full circle back to fairy tales, not only due to their shared history as transformative works of art, performance, and literature, but also due to their central focus on transformation through magic and wonder. Transformative fan cultures thus overlap and intertwine with the history and spirit of fairy-tale cultures.

Cultures of Transformation

Transformative fan cultures and fairy-tale storytelling cultures name different cultural positions and remarkably similar activities. Although increasingly imbricated in the modern industry, fairy tales hearken back to the pre-industrial past, while fan culture is born of mass production. Yet both describe folk practices with an interactive, collective approach to cultural production and reproduction. This irreverent attitude to cultural objects often conflicts with modern copyright and intellectual property regimes, which seek to isolate the historical flow of ideas by making one snapshot in the development of human imagination into private property. Transformative fan cultures and fairy tale storytelling cultures place precedence on all people's ability to become authors of their own culture and insert themselves into the ongoing narrative flow that makes sense of and shapes the world around us. In fairy tales the term "transformation" often connects to moments of wonder, when magic unseats everyday assumptions and the impossible becomes possible. Transformative fan cultures likewise challenge the limits of the possible by inserting the pleasures and demands of everyday people back into mass culture narrative products, opening space for the unexpected to emerge.

Related topics: Adaptation and the Fairy-Tale Web; Comic Cons; Convergence Culture; Fan Fiction; Intellectual Property; Sexualities/Queer and Trans Studies; Storytelling

References Cited and Further Reading

Alighieri, Dante. (1320) 2003. *The Divine Comedy (the Inferno, the Purgatorio, the Paradiso)*. London: Penguin.

Austen, Jane. (1803) 2003. *Northanger Abbey*. London: Penguin.

Bacchilega, Cristina. 2013. *Fairy Tales Transformed? Twenty-First Century Adaptations and the Politics of Wonder*. Detroit: Wayne State UP.

Barthes, Roland. 1977. *Image, Music, Text*. New York: Hill and Wang.

Bartlett, Andrew. 1994. "Airshafts, Loudspeakers, and the Hip Hop Sample: Contexts and African American Musical Aesthetics." *African American Review* 28 (4): 639–52.

Bourdieu, Pierre. 1984. *Distinction: A Social Critique of the Judgment of Taste*. Cambridge, MA: Harvard UP.

Chevalier, Tracy. 1999. *The Girl With the Pearl Earring*. London: Penguin.

Coppa, Francesca. 2006. "A Brief History of Media Fandom." In *Fan Fiction and Fan Communities in the Age of the Internet: New Essays*, edited by Karen Hellekson and Kristina Busse, 41–60. Jefferson, NC: Mcfarland & Company.

Ehrenreich, Barbara, Elizabeth Hess, and Gloria Jacobs. (1992) 1997. "Beatlemania: A Sexually Defiant Subculture?" In *The Subcultures Reader*, edited by Ken Gelder and Sarah Thornton, 523–36. London: Routledge.

Fiske, John. 1989. *Understanding Popular Culture*. New York: Routledge.

Foucault, Michel. 1978. *History of Sexuality*. Vol. 1. New York: Pantheon Books.

———. 1979. *Discipline and Punish*. New York: Vintage.

Google. 2015a. "Images Search 'Connoisseur'." https://images.google.com/.

———. 2015b. "Images Search 'Fans'." https://images.google.com/.

Greenhill, Pauline. 2006. "Natalka Husar and Diana Thorneycroft versus the Law: A Critical Feminist Consideration of Intellectual Property and Artistic Practice." *Canadian Journal of Women and the Law/Revue Juridique La Femme Et Le Droit* 18 (2): 439–78.

Gregory, Philippa. 2002. *The Other Boleyn Girl*. New York: Pocket Star Books.

Hendenkamp, Douglas A. 2002. "Free Mickey Mouse: Copyright Notice, Derivative Works, and the Copyright Act of 1909." *Virginia Sports and Entertainment Law Journal* 2: 254–278.

Hills, Matt. 2002. *Fan Cultures*. New York: Routledge.

Jenkins, Henry. 1992. *Textual Poachers: Television Fans and Participatory Culture.* New York: Routledge.

———. 2006. *Convergence Culture.* New York: NYU P.

Jenson, Joli. 1992. "Fandom as Pathology." In *The Adoring Audience: Fan Culture and Popular Media*, edited by Lisa A. Lewis, 9–29. London: Routledge.

Katyal, Sonia K. 2004. "Privacy vs. Piracy." *Yale Journal of Law & Technology* 7: 222–345.

Krauss, Rosalind E. 1986. *The Originality of the Avante-Garde and Other Modernist Myths.* Cambridge, MA: MIT P.

Kustritz, Anne. 2011. "Acafandom and Beyond: Week One, Part One (Anne Kustritz, Louisa Stein, and Sam Ford)." *Henry Jenkins*, June 13. http://henryjenkins.org/2011/06/acafandom_and_beyond_week_one.html.

———. 2015. "Homework and the Digital Field: Reflections on Fan Identity and Identification." In *Technology, Scale, and Difference in Contemporary Anthropology*, edited by Tom Boellstorff, Bill Maurer, Jacinthe Mazzocchetti, and Olivier Servais, 95–116. Paris: Academia-L'Harmattan.

Lee, Linda J. 2008. "Guilty Pleasures: Reading Romance Novels as Reworked Fairy Tales." *Marvels & Tales* 22: 52–66.

Lessig, Lawrence. 2008. *Remix: Making Art and Commerce Thrive in the Hybrid Economy.* London: Bloomsbury.

Lethem, Jonathan. 2007. "The Ecstasy of Influence." *Harper's Magazine* 314 (1881): 59.

Litman, Jessica. 1993. "Mickey Mouse Emeritus: Character Protection and the Public Domain." *University of Miami Entertainment & Sports Law Review* 11: 429–435.

Nikolajeva, Maria. 2003. "Fairy Tale and Fantasy: From Archaic to Postmodern." *Marvels & Tales* 17: 138–56.

obsession_inc. 2009. "Affirmational Fandom vs. Transformational Fandom." Hosted by Livejournal. http://obsession-inc.dreamwidth.org/82589.html.

"Organization for Transformative Works." *Fanlore.* http://fanlore.org/wiki/Organization_for_Transformative_Works.

Radcliffe, Ann. (1794) 2001. *The Mysteries of Udolpho.* London: Penguin.

Russo, Julie Levin. 2009. "User-Penetrated Content: Fan Video in the Age of Convergence." *Cinema Journal* 48 (4): 125–30.

Sprigman, Chris. 2005. "The Mouse That Ate the Public Domain: Disney, the Copyright Term Extension Act and Eldred v. Ashcroft." *FindLaw.* http://writ.news.findlaw.com/commentary/20020305_sprigman.html.

Stallybrass, Peter, and Allon White. 1986. *The Politics and Poetics of Transgression.* Ithaca, NY: Cornell UP.

Stone, Kay. 1975. "Things Walt Disney Never Told Us." *Journal of American Folklore* 88: 42–50.

Tan, David. 2013. "What Do Judges Know about Contemporary Art? Richard Prince and Reimagining the Fair Use Test in Copyright Law." *Revista Forumul Judecătorilor* 2: 63–79.

Tushnet, Rebecca. 1996. "Legal Fictions: Copyright, Fan Fiction, and a New Common Law." *Loyola of Los Angeles Entertainment Law Review* 17: 651–686.

Walker, Alice. 1967. *Love and Trouble: Stories of Black Women.* New York: Harcourt.

Wong, Mary W. S. 2008. "'Transformative' User-Generated Content in Copyright Law: Infringing Derivative Works or Fair Use." *Vanderbilt Journal of Entertainment & Technology Law* 11: 1075–1139.

28

FAT STUDIES

"Where Everything Round Is Good": Exploring and Reimagining Fatness in Fairy-Tale Media

Lauren Bosc

As the (inter)disciplines of fairy-tale studies and fat studies grow, the gap of scholarship at their intersections widens. Despite the potential, little scholarship interrogates how fatness figures within fairy-tale media. This lack fails to reflect the vast array of relevant readings, retellings, and reimaginings. Here I demonstrate how fat bodies and fatness are evoked in ways that both stabilize and destabilize normative fairy-tale narratives. As fairy-tales "stick" in the popular imagination, their morals, ideals, and representations tend to be accepted and normalized while their antitheses are discarded and made invisible (Zipes 2006). In the fairy-tale imaginary, old women are hags and witches (not sweet and caring), princes are gallant saviors and heroes (not selfish or ugly), and princesses are helpless and *thin*. These characteristics do not bode well for fat bodies in a fairy-tale context, as they lack a space to be seen as anything other than Other, relegating fat fairy-tale possibilities to an impossible—and too often merely humorous—dystopia.

Through the lens of fat studies, fatness functions simultaneously as a fairy-tale failure, threat, and disruption. Fat bodies almost invariably present threats to an individual's "happy ending," where the "Cinderella" (ATU 510A) story rhetoric of "fat to fairy tale" in weight-loss regimes and news stories normalizes the thin body. Fairy-tale media encourage viewers to position fat bodies as objects deserving of destruction and revolution and/or as objects of humor and derision—abject subjects deserving degradation and dismissal. Yet fatness and fat bodies also offer a space of possibility. For example, some fat activists embrace disruptive potential by rewriting tales such as "Snow White" (ATU 709) (Noll 2014), calling for fat fairy-tale characters in online gaming communities, and reading fat fairy-tale princesses as sources of power and heroic potential (*Fat Princess: Piece of Cake*, Noll 2014). While Jane Yolen (1999) yearns for a world "where everything round is good: the sun, wheels, cookies, and the princess" (153), for space to redefine fat positively in a fairy-tale context, this chapter uncovers possibilities: in reimagining the intersection of fatness and fairy-tale norms to shift normative narratives away from the dominance of thin bodies in fairy tales and in celebrating the possibilities in fat fairy tales.

Background and Intersections

Embodiment theory and methodology take up the normative body as an object of analysis, and the research discipline of fat studies seeks to "address fatness as a cultural and social, power-entrenched phenomenon" (Kyrölä 2014, 9). Fat bodies, inscribed with characteristics such as repulsive, funny, unclean, and obscene (LeBesco 2004, 16), privilege thin bodies and thinness (see also LeBesco and Braziel 2001; Rothblum and Solovay 2009). In contemporary Western societies, the fat body that fails to obey the imperative to become thinner is presented as "gross, repugnant and ill [. . .] to be avoided at all costs" (Lupton 2013, 55). Fat studies opposes medical and/or health research on "obesity" and the "obesity epidemic," reclaiming the word "fat" to re-signify its negative connotations and celebrate it as a descriptor, not a discriminator (Lupton 2013). While "[t]here is no generic fat body in the sense that fatness would be universally identifiable to anyone and in any body under any circumstances," (Kyrölä 2014, 7), I avoid arbitrarily ascribing fatness to bodies and instead use "fat" as grounded from my social location and in the foundations of the fat studies field.

In Western fairy tales, fatness and the fat body have diverse meanings in different settings. For example, Charles Perrault features a "fat monkey" (2009, 94) in "The Sleeping Beauty in the Wood" (ATU 410) and a "fat coachman" (132) in "Cinderella" but does not use the descriptor in any other tales. Similarly, few Hans Christian Andersen fairy tales use the word "fat" to describe people and characters (e.g., a "fat water-snake" in "The Little Mermaid," 2016). Fat manifests more liberally in the Brothers Grimm, not only describing the secondary characteristics of toads (2014, 415), dead bodies (87), and literal jars of fat (16; 480), but also as a verb—"fattening up" of Hansel in "Hansel and Gretel" (ATU 327A)—and as the super-ability of a helper figure in "The Six Servants"/"How Six Made Their Way through the World" (ATU 513B). Fat bodies in "classic" fairy tales are rarely a feature of a main character or protagonist—when they are, fatness leads to their demise, such as in *Otesánek* (Erben, Němcová, and Lada 1996) and *The Three Fat Men* (Olesha 1964). And as Yolen describes, the fairy tale featuring a (positively viewed) fat prince or princess is "not yet written" (1999, 158)—a point I challenge in this chapter's final section.

Overcoming Fatness

Katariina Kyrölä notes that fatness within media often functions as "the necessary starting point for heroic transformations into proud and happy slimness" (2014, 2). This narrative, which follows a "fat to fit" journey, capitalizes simultaneously on the fat body's threat and the possibility of its transformation. The social and cultural perception that fat bodies pose a threat to health, both at the individual and communal levels (see Kyrölä 2014, 40), has been thoroughly disputed and reinscribed as a means of biopolitical control rather than a conclusion based on empirical evidence (Oliver 2006; Boero 2012; Harjunen 2017). The conflation of fatness and unhealthiness drives media to muster stereotypical fairy-tale narratives to exploit the "heroic transformations" Western society expects from fat individuals. Demonstrated by news articles (Winter 2013), weight-loss "success books" (Engebretson and Magnan 2008, 153), and dieting companies (see Atkins's "fairy tale cookies" in Eenfeldt 2012), capitalist industry thrives on marketing the goal of achieving a bodily "happily ever after." Generally, this narrative involves a villain (fatness) threatening the hero/princess (normatively thin man/woman), the heroic quest to defeat the villain (diet), and the protagonist's eventual triumph in reaching a happy ending (thinness).

This narrative is embraced in the news article "Too Fat for a Fairy Tale!" According to Katy Winter (2013), Clare Cunliffe-Saunders's life was ruined when she gained weight from an injury and a pregnancy and was accordingly prevented from working as a fairy-tale princess in a local children's theater in the United Kingdom. In what Winter calls a "Thin-derella" story, Saunders felt like more of a "fairy blobmother than a beautiful princess" and, unemployed, decided to "transform" her life through a fitness and diet regime in order to re-embody her princess persona (2013). Channeling the neoliberal, individualistic self-help narrative that many anti-fat people and organizations profess as the only path to "transformation," fitness and diet (Oliver 2006; Harjunen 2017) are situated as a magical combination, bound to win the prince/princess and secure the happy ending. By perpetuating the "fat to fairy tale ending" narrative, Winter participates in a production of knowledge that privileges thinness over fatness, shares this knowledge as fact with her readers, and fosters a fatphobic environment. Such works purvey falsely articulated fairy-tale narratives hinging on the "magic" of diet and exercise and simultaneously shame fat people for embracing the same rhetoric.

Films such as *The Cinderella Pact* (2010) and *200 Pounds Beauty* (Minyeo-neun goerowo, 2006) replicate this discourse. Both feature a female protagonist who, through diet and exercise (the former) or extreme plastic surgery (the latter), lose weight and live the "Cinderella" dream. They are transformed from ugly, undesirable, fat women by their fairy godmothers (a personal trainer/exercise regimen and a plastic surgeon) into thin, beautiful, desirable versions. With this transformation, the protagonists realize that they had always been beautiful "inside" despite their fat bodies. Nola, in *The Cinderella Pact*, ends the film declaring, "To all the beautiful women who brought me here tonight. Just know you're your own fairy-godmother. Keep dreaming your dreams and creating your magic and writing your own happy endings." Viewers' embracing of this ending positions fatness as a fairy-tale failure and as ultimately antithetical to the supposed "happily ever after" that all individuals are enjoined to seek.

However, a number of bloggers, journalists, and online writers challenge this "fat to fit" journey and fairy-tale narrative. In particular, Candice Russell (2014), Mary Elizabeth Williams (2016), and Maddie Crum (2016) call out the "happy" in the "happily ever after" as a false ending to the elusive, impossible fairy-tale weight-loss story. Crum suggests that the fairy-tale ending so consistently used to describe the "weight-loss journey" is both damaging and useless—a description echoed by Williams, who describes the internationally broadcast weight-loss television program *The Biggest Loser* as a "broken fairy-tale" (2016). Despite contestants of the show, along with countless others online, speaking out about the failure of the fairy-tale transformation from fat to thin and their inability to find a "happy ending" through the "magic" of diet and exercise,[1] the fairy-tale weight loss narrative persists.

Fearing and Fighting Fatness

Like the desire to overcome fatness, the injunction to fear it, and fight it and what it represents, is also present in fairy-tale media. Represented in examples from the villainous Ursula (*The Little Mermaid* 1989) to the blood-lustful Queen of Hearts (Carroll 1865), fear-inducing fatness is situated in the contexts of "fat as fatal"—a literal "killer" (Boero 2012)—a threatening form of embodiment manifesting individually and socially. Kyrölä posits that "if one part of the body image is always fixed as an object of fear that has to be carried around *and fought*, the body image may become centrally organized through that fear" (56, emphasis added). The fat body's alleged threat—to health, normative structures of thinness, "beauty" norms, and so on—justifies nearly any means to extinguish the threat and fear associated with it. Two examples here, *Little Otik* (2000, also known as *Greedy Guts* or *Otesánek*) and *The Three Fat Men* (1964) by Yuri Olesha, include fat characters who elicit fear and anger.

Little Otik offers a version of a story in Karel J. Erben's book of Czech folktales. Directed by Czech filmmaker Jan Švankmajer, the film begins when a childless couple discovers and animates a tree root in their desire for a baby. This child, whom they name Otik, is marked by his insatiable appetite. As he eats—everything from his mother's hair, large slabs of pork and bread, the postman, the social worker, his parents, the neighbor, to finally the landlady's bed of cabbages—he grows fatter and fatter. His fat child-body eventually, and predictably, becomes uncontrollable, and the film ends, as the tale does, with the implication of his death by gardening hoe. Otik's growth, characterized by some theorists as an allegory of capitalist greed and consumption (Smith and Jehlička 2007), is the central source of fear in film and tale. Initially, Otik is framed and treated by those around him as other babies are: he is pushed in a pram, he cries incessantly, and he needs to be fed often.

Only when Otik begins to digress from the normative constitution of a child, when he grows fat, does his intelligibility as child come into question. Paralleling the fear associated with fat children in the United States (Boero 2012), the film positions Otik's endlessly growing body as a result of his "weak willed father" and "overindulgent mother" (Erdman Farrell 2011, 79). With each ingestion Otik grows in size, although not in demeanor, embodying a monstrous creature with baby-like mannerisms. Initially, Otik's body fits within the frame; the lens shows him close-up and intimately. However, as he consumes and grows, the camera shifts from close-ups of Otik's face and mouth to featuring him in medium shot, towering over those around him, or looking over his shoulder at those below him. His body, uncontainable within the borders of the frame, forces the viewer to disassociate and expel any feelings for him—situating the fight as necessarily toward his fat body and not his person. As "fat people are often treated as not quite human" (Erdman Farrell 2011, 6; see also Wann 2009), Otik is destroyed because of what he has become: an uncontrollable, fat monster.

Similarly, Yuri Olesha's *Three Fat Men* (1964) centers on the Soviet proletariat's ultimate goal of overthrowing those in power and what they represent—the Three Fat Men and their overconsumption and gluttony—and embracing revolution. In Olesha's text—a "revolutionary fairy-tale" adapted from a novel into a play, an opera, a ballet, a film, a puppet show, and a radio drama—characters fall into two distinct groups: fat or thin. The fat population, aligned with the Three Fat Men, is wealthy and flippant, while the thin population is honest, well intentioned, and hard-working. The correlation of fatness with wealth, overindulgence, and gluttony is present in the "fat cat" business person (Erdman Farrell 2011, 18) and "the fat and undesirable ordinary person, who could not handle the riches and abundance of modernity" (18).

Amy Erdman Farrell (2011) suggests that during the nineteenth century in Europe and North America, "one had to have both wealth (meaning one had sufficient food and physical leisure) and health (meaning one was free of the diseases that wasted away bodily flesh) in order to maintain a hefty body," which led to the conflation between fatness and a "generalized sense of prosperity, distinction, and high status" (27). Since fatness was associated with wealth, fat individuals were often understood as greedy and gluttonous, wherein "their greed and avarice allowed their bodies to grow corpulent" (28). Overindulgence, or the perception of it, was the downfall of those who could afford it. In the case of *The Three Fat Men*, it is the precise reason the thin public wishes to overthrow them. Olesha uses mockery and comedy to position the Three Fat Men as deserving punishment: the first time they are introduced, one eats his napkin. When confronted with this reality, he responds, "Am I really? I didn't notice" (Olesha 1964, 48). When the Three Fat Men attempt to be serious, they seem to "grow a little thinner" (50).

Representing all things absurd, and arguably wicked—corpulence, gluttony, overindulgence—the fat bodies of the Three Fat Men become the site through which revolution is enacted.

Humorous Fatness

By far the most common representation of fatness within fairy-tale media is the fat, funny character meant to be laughed at and not with. While fatness is often positioned as a threat, many animated fairy-tale films (e.g., the *Shrek* series [2001–2010], *Red Shoes and the 7 Dwarfs* [2017]), video games (e.g., *Fat Princess* [2009]), and eBooks (e.g., Dweezel and Pallie 2015), among others, feature a fat character for comic relief. Kyrölä (2014) posits "fatness and comedy have been so repetitively combined that the presence of a fat actor in a film or television series does easily raise expectations of the genre being comedy" (97–98). She theorizes that because of the "internal dynamic of fear" (56) instilled in perceptions of fatness, laughter often works to mediate fear "when the fat woman or man is understood as a butt of jokes, someone to be laughed at, and when the viewers are assumed to automatically put themselves in a superior position in relation to the body they look at" (2014, 104; Hole 2003, 312). Similarly, laughing at a fat fairy-tale character dismisses fatness as a serious and productive part of that character's identity and again normalizes the thin body within these narratives.

Online forums are littered with images of fat princesses, many playing on the personas created by the Disney corporation, including a fat Ariel, fat Cinderella, and fat Belle (see Sumi K.), which ridicule and preclude the possibility of a fat, desirable princess. In some cases, this joke is degrading and shameful, such as in *The Big Fat Mermaid* (2015)—an eBook in a series of "funny stories for kids"—wherein the protagonist, Aria, looks "something like an overfilled water balloon, or a grocery bag filled with jello, or even a trash bag full of bacon grease. [. . .] Aria the mermaid was so fat that no joke could ever communicate her true massiveness" (Dweezel and Pallie 2015, 7–8). Ariel Peterson (2016) suggests fairy-tale godmothers are fat rather than "fit," and often incompetent and hilarious, a trend that also follows the slapstick comedy–driven, fat, clumsy character of Fairy Mary in Disney's recent *Tinker Bell* (2008–2015) film series.

The joke is exemplified in the video game *Fat Princess* (2009), created for the PlayStation 3 gaming system. Players role-play as a number of characters—a male mage, villager, warrior, worker, ranger, and healer—and the game is described on its website as:

> Frantic and fun, Fat Princess pits two hordes of players against each other in comic medieval battle royale. Your goal is to rescue your beloved princess from the enemy dungeon. There's a catch though: your adversary has been stuffing her with food to fatten her up and it's going to take most of your army working together to carry her back across the battlefield.
>
> (2009)

Critiqued by feminist bloggers and gamers Melissa McEwan (2008); Holly (2008); and Anita Sarkeesian (2013), the video game hinges on the idea that "the dashing hero thinks he's rescuing a beautiful damsel in distress, but the 'joke' is on him because it turns out she's larger than acceptable! And therefore unattractive and a horrible burden for him to rescue, of course" (Holly 2008). To add to the joke of rescuing a fat princess, the game design strips the princess of her femininity as she grows fatter; the fatter she gets the more she burps, farts, and her voice lowers (Sarkeesian 2013). Relying on the perception that since "[t]he fat female body [. . .] overflows its allotted space in signification that cannot be confined to the category of

'Woman,'" (Hole 2003, 318), fat women in popular culture are considered innately funny (315). Capitalizing on the normative fairy-tale princess as a desirable prize at the end of the journey to rescue her, *Fat Princess* is built around one big sexist fat joke (Sarkeesian 2013)—after all, "LOL who would want to rescue a fat chick?" (Holly 2008).

In the *Shrek* film franchise, ogres Shrek (Mike Myers) and Fiona (Cameron Diaz), although fat, are never explicitly described as such. Instead, while positioned as the endearing and comedic protagonists, they are described as horrible, ugly, terrible, gross, hideous, stupid, and big within the film. The character that most intrigues me is Puss in Boots (Antonio Banderas) in *Shrek Forever After* (2010). In a reality where Shrek makes a wish with Rumpelstiltskin, he creates an alternative universe where his quest companion and friend, Puss, is fat. Coming across Puss in this alternate reality, Shrek exclaims, "Puss! What happened to you? You got so fa . . . fancy" (2010), quickly correcting himself before he calls his friend fat. Once a quick, suave, Spanish-accented, boot-wearing "Zorro" character—with "cunning, agility, and hunting skills" (Nikolajeva 2009, 253) and voiced by an actor known for his "excessive masculinity" (Gabilondo 2006, 212), Puss now wears a bow around his neck. His only threat is, "Feed me, if you dare" (see figure 28.1). He is more interested in eating chimichangas and the gingerbread man than fighting, and at the penultimate comedic moment, when he decides to swing in and save the day, his signature boots split down the sides when he tries to put them on.

Puss thus serves as a central character to be laughed at, wheezing after running a few feet, and failing to clean himself with his tongue because his fat body prohibits any type of flexibility. His now feminized, pink-bow-wearing, fat male body threatens his hitherto hypermasculine persona. Kyrölä (2014) posits, "A fat male body is [. . .] coded as dangerously bordering on femininity with visible breasts and a protruding belly: the loss of rigid bodily boundaries would mean the loss of rigid, naturalized gender differences—in other words, the fat male body represents in some ways gender incongruity" (104). The *Shrek* films make fatness narratively and descriptively invisible in relation to the hypervisible, arguably fat bodies of ogres Shrek and Fiona, but then capitalize upon it as a central joke in the fat Puss in Boots. In this fairy-tale world, fatness only exists in the dystopic, alternate reality of Shrek's life; even then, it occurs for the sole purpose of encouraging laughter. This punch line is made clear in the credits of *Shrek Forever After*, where Puss—having returned to his former thin self—looks in a mirror only to

Figure 28.1 Puss from *Shrek Forever After* (2010)

see his fat alter-ego looking back, embodying the "unresolved tension between the 'inner' and the 'outer' self" (Kyrölä 2014, 101). Whereas fat individuals often strive to discover their (thin) "inner beauty," (thin) Puss is forever stuck with his hilariously fat inner self.

Disruptive Fatness

While the fat body often functions in fairy-tale media as antithetical to the fairy-tale dream, as a threatening figure to be fought and overthrown, and/or as the butt of a joke, it is also taken up by activists, feminists, and fat-positive groups as a site of potential disruption. Fat activists and scholars have spoken out against fat oppression and have called for an embracing of fat bodies (Burgard et al. 2009); for Allyson Mitchell, "fat activism is about doing something. It is about changing [. . .] [j]ust about everything you can think of when it comes to how fat and fat people are treated, thought about, and represented in our society" (2005, 212). Fat activism collides with fairy-tale media to raise awareness of how fatness is depicted, treated, and invisibi- lized in fairy-tale media, and it also makes space for positive representations of fairy-tale fatness.

Take, for example, "The Six Servants" (1812) and "How Six Made Their Way through the World" (1819, 1857) (ATU 513B) in the Grimms' collection.[2] This tale features a flawed hero aided by heroic helpers, including a man who "was immensely fat and really a small moun- tain," who can expand his body "three thousand times as fat" (Zipes 2013, 463). This figure—a hero *because of* his fat abilities—disrupts normative representations of heroes or helpers in fairy tales. Unfortunately, the powerful and useful fat man is erased from the tale in most adap- tations: the fat helper is absented from Shaun Tan's book *The Singing Bones* (2015); the films *Jason and the Argonauts* (1963 and 2000), *Sechse kommen durch die ganze Welt* (Six Make Their Way through the World, 1959 or 1972), and *Sprookjesboom de Film* (The Fairy Tale Tree, 2012); and the TV episode *The Six Who Went Far* (1988). Fatness as disruptive, however, is not always invisible as many fairy-tale media enthusiasts demonstrate.

In her photography series *Fallen Princesses* (2009), Dina Goldstein features ten fairy-tale princesses where "the Disneyfied '. . . happily ever after' is replaced with a realistic outcome and addresses current issues" (Goldstein 2009a). Little Red Riding Hood is depicted as a fat "Not-So-Little Red Riding Hood," downing a soft drink and carrying a basket of McDonald's hamburgers. This photo elicited intense critiques and praise. While Jack Zipes directly links this image to Red's sexuality (2011, 3), Li Cornfeld argues that "Not-So-Little Red Riding Hood," no longer the sexually objectified little girl, is positioned as a woman who simultane- ously "struggles with control" and has the power to take control for herself (2011, 6). In her analysis, Little Red Riding Hood "falls" to a place where she eats in order to not be eaten.

For others, this image disempowers, representing fatness as the "ultimate downfall" (Mammen 2009; Smith 2009). Goldstein, in response, shares a forty-one-page e-mail, prefaced with "Brace yourself!" that consolidates a debate on the merits of "Not-So-Little Red Riding Hood" on JPG.com, and Goldstein herself comments "Now Now kids . . . relax . . its just my personal comment on today's fast food society. Art or not if it makes you think and dialogue then I'm happy" (sic, Goldstein 2009c). While this image clearly disrupts Little Red Riding Hood's fairy-tale trajectory, fatness still links to sickness, entrapment, and loss, discouraging fat positivity in a fairy-tale world.

Similarly disruptive, Katherine Noll's protagonist, Neve Bianca (Snow White), in *Mirror, Mirror* (2014) fulfills her "happily ever after" by embracing and accepting her "not skinny" (176) body. The first in Noll's *Fat Fairy Tales Series*, the novel presents "plus-sized women finding love and renewal [. . .] in modern day fairy tale format" ("The Fat Fairy Tales" 2011). It follows Neve leaving home and her narcissistic, fat-shaming stepmother to find herself—and

Figure 28.2 Fat Princess: Piece of Cake (2014)

her self-confidence—headlining a burlesque show at a traveling music festival. The trajectory of self-hating to self-loving hinges upon Neve "finding the 'princess' within herself" (2014) and being her own hero by embracing her body and her new life. It raises the question: was Neve's new-found happiness discovered because of her fat body, or in spite of it? In response to her own self-deprecating fat joke at the novel's conclusion, Neve declares, "Guys, I don't care. [. . .] I'm not skinny. It's okay. It's part of who I am. And I like me" (2014, 176). In this self-reclamation, Neve doesn't celebrate and accept her *fat* body: she clarifies that she likes herself and her "not skinny" body. Although Noll sidesteps a clear declaration for a fat "happily ever after," settling for a thinned-down message of body positivity, her attempt to rewrite and disrupt normative fairy-tale narratives shows how they can be reinterpolated, redesigned, and adapted. These adaptations take on many forms, such as through the reimagination of video games.

The mobile phone app for the *Fat Princess* (2009) video game franchise, *Fat Princess: Piece of Cake* (2014),[3] includes the army from the PlayStation 3 version but reorganizes an action, real-time-strategy multiplayer game to a strategic match-three game where three characters face off against three enemies. Each turn, players must match sets of three colored gems that correspond to battle moves. Once victorious, the army and their Fat Princess, who follows behind, beat the level and advance. Unlike *Fat Princess* (2009), *Fat Princess: Piece of Cake* (2014) uses the princess and her size to the battle's advantage: instead of immobilizing her by feeding her cake and making her fatter—as in the original—eating emboldens her. The more cake players feed her, the more powerful she becomes. The Fat Princess, the ultimate weapon, uses her body to slam into opponents and destroy them much more efficiently than the other characters. The message is clear: fatness is power, and eating cake only makes the Fat Princess stronger (see figure 28.2). While this game retains its stance that a fat princess is inherently funny, Sony and the game's developers "tak[e] the comic medieval battle royale to the next level" (2014) and (perhaps unintentionally) empower the Fat Princess to use her body to her team's advantage, redefining her from immobility and weakness to strength and empowerment. This renewal, albeit in a small way, not only disrupts the creators' original fat fairy-tale narrative, but also creates positive space for future fat fairy-tale possibilities.

Fat Futures

Taking Jane Yolen's (1999) call seriously, activists and fairy-tale media enthusiasts continuously redefine normative representations of the fat fairy-tale protagonist and envision a character "that is not yet written" (153). Confronted by negative depictions of fatness within numerous fairy-tale contexts—fat bodies as terrifying, humorous, and obstacles to the ideal body—these creators reject what they are fed and develop media, reveling in the possibility of fat fairy-tales. I hope, like Yolen, that these and future disruptions will continue to push the boundaries of how bodies are depicted and accepted within fairy-tales and create a new, fatter space for all bodies to be celebrated.

Related topics: Cinematic; Disability; Food; Gender; Mobile Apps; Reality TV; Video Games

Notes

1. For more on contestant backlash, see Lear (2017); Callahan and Fears (2016); and Mooney (2015).
2. The Fat Man is edited out of the 1819 and 1857 collections (Zipes 2013, 453–467).
3. Sony recently announced, without citing any particular reason, that as of January 1, 2017, *Fat Princess: Piece of Cake* would be retired.

References Cited and Further Reading

Andersen, Hans Christian. 1981. *Fairytales*, edited by Kay Rasmus Nielsen. New York: Metropolitan Museum of Art and Viking P.

Boero, Natalie. 2012. *Killer Fat: Media, Medicine, and Morals in the American "Obesity Epidemic"*. New Brunswick, NJ: Rutgers UP.

Burgard, Deb, Elana Dykewomon, Esther Rothblum, and Pattie Thomas. 2009. "Are We Ready to Throw Our Weight Around? Fat Studies and Political Activism." In *The Fat Studies Reader*, edited by Esther Rothblum and Sondra Solovay, 334–40. New York: NYU P.

Callahan, Maureen, and Danika Fears. 2016. "'Biggest Loser' Contestants Demand NBC Cancel Show." *The New York Post*, May 23. http://nypost.com/2016/05/23/former-contestants-want-to-put-an-end-to-the-biggest-loser/.

Carroll, Lewis. 1865. *Alice's Adventures in Wonderland*. London: Macmillan.

Cornfeld, Li. 2011. "Shooting Heroines: Sexual Violence and Dina Goldstein's Fallen Princesses Photography Series." In *Fallen Princesses*, edited by Dina Goldstein, 1–8. www.fallenprincesses.com/docs/essays/shooting_heroines.pdf.

Crum, Maddie. 2016. "It's Time to Stop Thinking about Weight Loss as a Fairy Tale Ending." *The Huffington Post*, February 29. www.huffingtonpost.com/entry/13-ways-of-looking-at-a-fat-girl_us_56d0d902e4b0871f60eb8613.

Dweezel, Dexter, and Parnassus Pallie. 2015. *Funny Stories for Kids: The Big Fat Mermaid*. Dweezel and Pallie eBooks.

Eenfeldt, Andreas. 2012. "Atkins, Greed and the Fairy Tale Cookies." *Diet Doctor*, April 4. www.dietdoctor.com/atkins-greed-and-the-fairy-tale-cookies.

Engebretson, Gail, and Robert Magnan. 2008. *Fat No More: Long Term Success Following Weight Loss Surgery*. Madison, WI: Erickson Publishing.

Erben, Karel Jaromír, Božena Němcová, and Josef Lada. 1996. *Folk Tales*. Prague: Albatross.

Erdman Farrell, Amy. 2011. *Fat Shame: Stigma and the Fat Body in American Culture*. New York: NYU P.

Gabilondo, Joseba. 2006. "Antonio Banderas: Hispanic Gay Masculinities and the Global Mirror Stage (1991–2001)." *Studies in 20th & 21st Century Literature* 30 (1): 209–33.

Grimm, Jacob, and Wilhelm Grimm. 2014. *The Original Folk and Fairy Tales of the Brothers Grimm*, translated and edited by Jack Zipes. Princeton, NJ: Princeton UP.

Harjunen, Hannele. 2017. *Neoliberal Bodies and the Gendered Fat Body*. London: Routledge.

Hole, Anne. 2003. "Performing Identity: Dawn French and the Funny Fat Female Body." *Feminist Media Studies* 3 (3): 315–28.

Holly. 2008. "Well, That was Bound to Happen." *Feministe*, July 23. www.feministe.us/blog/archives/2008/07/23/well-that-was-bound-to-happen/.

K, Sumi. N.d. "Chubby Disney Princesses." *Simple Thing Called Life*. www.simplethingcalledlife.com/stcl/fat-disney-princesses/.

Kyrölä, Katariina. 2014. *The Weight of Images: Affect, Body Image and Fat in the Media*. New York: Routledge.

Lear, Samantha. 2017. "11 Former 'Biggest Loser' Stars Who Have Spoken Out Against the Show." *Wetpaint*, May 8. www.wetpaint.com/biggest-loser-backlash-weight-gain-1589102/.

LeBesco, Kathleen. 2004. *Revolting Bodies? The Struggle to Redefine Fat Identity*. Boston: U Massachusetts P.

LeBesco, Kathleen, and Jana Evans Braziel. 2001. "Editors' Introduction." In *Bodies Out of Bounds: Fatness and Transgression*, edited by Jana Evans Braziel and Kathleen LeBesco, 1–18. Los Angeles: U California P.

Lupton, Deborah. 2013. *Fat*. New York: Routledge.

Mammen, Miranda. 2009. "Princess Fat Shaming." *Women's Glib*, June 19. http://womensglib.wordpress.com/2009/06/19/princess-fat-shaming/.

McEwan, Melissa. 2008. "I Write Letters." *Shakesville*, July 21. www.shakesville.com/2008/07/i-write-letters.html.

Mitchell, Allyson. 2005. "Pissed Off." In *Fat: An Anthropology of an Obsession*, 211–25. New York: Jeremy P Tarcher/Penguin.

Mooney, Paula. 2015. "'Biggest Loser' Secrets Exposed: 8-Hour Workouts, 1K Calories Daily, Severe Shin-Splints and Bloody Urine." *Inquisitr*, January 18. www.inquisitr.com/1767405/biggest-loser-secrets-exposed-8-hour-workouts-1k-calories-daily-severe-shin-splints-and-bloody-urine/.

Murray, Samantha. 2008. *The 'Fat' Female Body*. London: Palgrave Macmillan.

Nikolajeva, Maria. 2009. "Devils, Demons, Familiars, Friends: Toward a Semiotics of Literary Cats." *Marvels & Tales* 23 (2): 248–67.

Noll, Katherine. 2014. *Mirror, Mirror: The Fat Fairy Tales, Book One*. New York: Red Sky Presents.

Olesha, Yuri. 1964. *The Three Fat Men*, translated by Fainna Glagoleva. Moscow: Progress Publishers.

Oliver, J. Eric. 2006. *Fat Politics: The Real Story behind America's Obesity Epidemic*. New York: Oxford UP.

Perrault, Charles. 2009. *The Complete Fairy Tales*, translated by Christopher Betts. New York: Oxford UP.

Peterson, Ariel. 2016. "Fat Fairies: Stereotype, Body Type, and Personality of TV Godmothers." UC Berkeley: Western States Folklore Conference, April 8. http://scholarsarchive.byu.edu/cgi/viewcontent.cgi?article=1078&context=english_symposium.

Rothblum, Esther, and Sondra Solovay. 2009. *The Fat Studies Reader*. New York: NYU P.

Russell, Candice. 2014. "The Truth about 'before and after' Weight Loss Photos." *Huffington Post*, July 16. www.huffingtonpost.com/candice-russell/before-and-after-weight-loss-b_5332831.html?ir=Women.

Sarkeesian, Anita. 2013. "Damsel in Distress: Part 3—Tropes vs Women in Video Games." *Feminist Frequency*, August 1. https://feministfrequency.com/2013/08/01/damsel-in-distress-part-3-tropes-vs-women/.

Smith, Anastasia. 2009. "'Fallen Princesses:' Damsels in a Different Kind of Distress." *The Sister Project*, June 24. http://thesisterproject.com/smith/fallen-princesses-damsels-in-a-different-kind-of-distress/.

Smith, Joe, and Petr Jehlička. 2007. "Stories around Food, Politics and Change in Poland and the Czech Republic." *Transactions of the Institute of British Geographers* 32 (3): 395–410.

Tan, Shaun. 2015. *The Singing Bones*. New York: Arthur A. Levine Books.

Wann, Marilyn. 2009. "Foreword: Fat Studies: An Invitation to Revolution." In *The Fat Studies Reader*, edited by Esther Rothblum and Sondra Solovay, xi–xxvi. New York: NYU P.

Williams, Mary Elizabeth. 2016. "'The Biggest Loser' Is a Broken Fairy Tale: Our Reality TV Obsession with Radical Transformation Needs Limits." *Salon*, May 2. www.salon.com/2016/05/02/the_biggest_loser_is_a_broken_fairy_tale_our_reality_tv_obsession_with_radical_transformation_needs_limits/.

Winter, Katy. 2013. "Too Fat for a Fairy Tale! Actress Becomes Real Life Thin-derella after Shedding Five Stone to Fit Back in to Her Princess Costumes." *The Daily Mail Online*, January 18. www.dailymail.co.uk/femail/article-2264386/Too-fat-fairy-tale-Actress-real-life-Thin-derella-shedding-stone-fit-princess-costumes.html.

Yolen, Jane. (1999) 2003. "Fat Is Not a Fairy Tale." In *The Poets' Grimm: 20th Century Poems from Grimm Fairy Tales*, edited by Jeanne Marie Beaumont and Claudia Carlson, 158. Ashland: Story Line.

Zipes, Jack. 2006. *Why Fairy Tales Stick: The Evolution and Relevance of a Genre*. New York: Routledge.

———. 2011. "Subverting the Myth of Happiness: Dina Goldstein's 'Fallen Princesses'." In *Fallen Princesses*, edited by Dina Goldstein, 1–4. www.fallenprincesses.com/docs/essays/goldstein.pdf.

———, ed. 2013. *The Golden Age of Folk and Fairy Tales: From the Brothers Grimm to Andrew Lang*. Indianapolis: Hackett Publishing Company.

Mediagraphy

200 Pounds Beauty (Minyeo-neun goerowo). 2006. Director Yong-hwa Kim. South Korea.

The Cinderella Pact (Lying to be Perfect). 2010. Director Gary Harvey. USA/Canada.

Fat Princess (Video Game). 2009. Sony/PS3/TBC. www.playstation.com/en-ca/games/fat-princess-ps3/.

Fat Princess: Piece of Cake (Mobile App). 2014. Sony/PSVita. www.playstation.com/en-ca/games/fat-princess-piece-of-cake-psvita/.

Goldstein, Dina. 2009a. *Fallen Princesses*. Photograph Series. Canada. www.fallenprincesses.com/series/.

———. 2009b. "Fat Shaming and Not So Little Red Riding Hood." www.fallenprincesses.com/docs/conflictand controversy/red_and_fat_shaming.pdf.

———. 2009c. "Not So Little Red Riding Hood." *Fallen Princesses*. Photograph. Canada.

Grimm Masterpiece Theater (Gurimu meisaku gekijou, TV). "The Six Who Went Far." 1988. Episode 1.14. Jan 20. Directors Fumio Kurokawa, Hiroshi Saitô, Kazuyoshi Yokota, Shigeru Ômachi, Kerrigan Mahan, Jirô Saitô, Takayoshi Suzuki, Tom Wyner, and Murasaki Ômura. Japan/USA.

Jason and the Argonauts. 1963. Director Don Chaffey. UK/USA.

———. 2000. Director Nick Willing. USA/Turkey.

The Little Mermaid. 1989. Directors Ron Clements and John Musker. USA.

Little Otik (Otesánek). 2000. Director Jan Švankmajer. Czech Republic.

Red Shoes and the 7 Dwarfs. 2017. Director Sung-ho Hong. South Korea.

Sechse kommen durch die ganze Welt (Six Make Their Way through the World). 1959. Director Lothar Barke. East Germany.

———. 1972. Director Rainer Simon. East Germany.

Shrek Forever After. 2010. Director Mike Mitchell. USA.

Sprookjesboom de Film (The Fairy Tale Tree). 2012. Director Hans Walther. The Netherlands.

Tinker Bell (Film Series). 2008–2015. Director Bradley Raymond. USA.

29
LANGUAGE
B. Grantham Aldred

Beginnings

Once upon a time, there were four words so powerful that they could instantly define the form of a work. Any story beginning with these four words would be expected to feature magical turns of chance, formulaic plots, and happy endings. Any use of this phrase created a narrative frame so strong that it has become a near-universal signifier of the fairy tale, defining the very form. This phenomenon is not just a local turn of phrase; as Max Lüthi says, "The wonderful phrase 'Once upon a time' is found not only in German fairy tales; all European peoples know and love it" (1970, 47).

While this opening formula sets the stage, fairy tales frequently feature distinctive and characteristic turns of phrase that serve to identify fairy-tale texts. Over the years, folklorists and literary scholars have devoted considerable efforts to defining the fairy tale, but one aspect rarely discussed in fairy-tale scholarship is how language operates as a defining characteristic. While in recent years, some scholars have examined language use through specific lenses, such as Alessandra Levorato's (2003) work on word choices and gendered representations of power, the language of fairy tales is too often ignored, glossed over, or dismissed as lacking detail or distinction. This chapter seeks to address the larger use of language within fairy tales, especially in context of the wide variation between fairy-tale texts.

Individual adaptations of the same fairy tale feature dramatically different words, even when communicating the same content in the same form. Take for example the opening paragraphs to two well-known versions of ATU 333, "Little Red Riding Hood."

Jacob and Wilhelm Grimm:

> There was once a sweet little maid, much beloved by everybody, but most of all by her grandmother, who never knew how to make enough of her. Once she sent her a little cap of red velvet, and as it was very becoming to her, and she never wore anything else, people called her Little Red-cap.
>
> (1966, 132)

Charles Perrault:

> Once upon a time, in a village, there lived a little girl, the prettiest you could wish to see. Her mother adored her, and her grandmother adored her even more. This kind lady had a riding-hood made for her granddaughter; it was red, and it suited her so well that everywhere she went she was called Little Red Riding Hood.
>
> (2009, 99)

263

These two versions are near complete re-phrasings of the same content, even accounting for translational choices. However, within the text there are signifying phrases, which I will refer to as linguistic anchors, which connect a retelling to the familiar source text of a fairy tale as directly as structure or content. These linguistic anchor phrases are so directly tied to their tales that they become the central signifiers of the tale, tying adaptations to "source texts." In cases of extreme divergence, the linguistic anchors may be the only identifiable common link.

This process has an effect not only on adaptations but on tales in culture, with these linguistic anchors becoming shorthand for specific tales and for general fairy-tale concepts. Overall, the specificity and distinctiveness of language in fairy tales provides a direct connection to cultural communication in a manner that is very different from other folklore forms. Defining how a linguistic anchor becomes a summative excerpt requires several steps: first, understanding what defines fairy-tale language and how one can categorize language in a form that lacks definitive central texts; second, seeing how fairy-tale language plays out in adaptations and what that says about the stability and variability of fairy-tale texts; third, examining how this use of language has expanded beyond explicit retellings and what that tells us about the role of fairy tales in the popular imagination.

Linguistic Dynamism and Stasis

The language of fairy tales is often described as simplistic and sparse. As Lüthi wrote, "The absence of all desire to describe unessential details gives the European fairy tale its clarity and precision" (1970, 50). Most tales use simple descriptions without extraneous detail, providing only what is relevant to the story. Fairy tales rarely describe aspects of the world beyond a simple generic term, a cottage is just a cottage, a wolf is just a wolf, a spindle is just a spindle. This often extends to characters, many of whom are not given names or descriptions beyond a profession (e.g., woodsman) or single relationship (e.g., stepmother). This linguistic sparseness has led to fairy-tale language being described as artificial or stylized: "A major contributing factor to its artificiality is in the characteristic simplicity of fairy tale, the extent to which it resists detail. It is sufficient to know that a man has three sons; whether he is a farmer or a merchant may not even be important" (Tiffin 2009, 13).

However, while tales are told using simple language, individual revisions may use widely variable language. Fairy-tale retellings frequently vary in their language, with different versions of a specific text using very different words to tell the same story. Addressing this characteristic, Alan Dundes describes folktales as "free-phrase" in opposition to "fixed-phrase" folklore like proverbs, riddles, or tongue twisters, which require identical language between tellings to remain the same text (1980, 23). For many folktales, including fairy tales, this variability is partially due to the lack of an authoritative original text, as emphasized (even if not entirely truthfully) in early collections of texts such as the Grimms' and Perrault, which were framed as collections of circulating oral tales. In one description, Steven Swann Jones says this has given the texts a level of dynamic "fluidity." He observes, "Since the tales circulated orally at the start, there are no exact and established versions, no identifiable authors and no fixed titles [. . .] underlying the apparent fluidity of the texts is their surprisingly strict adherence to some basic structures characterizing the genre" (1995, 3).

While many of the words change in each telling, pockets of consistency exist, often emerging in specific phrases that are stable between different tellings. These phrases serve as linguistic anchors, creating a direct connection to either the fairy tale (in the case of framing anchors) or to a specific tale through recognizable phrases. These linguistic anchors partially enable the free-phrase nature of the fairy tale, rendering the highly variable tales recognizable despite variation.

LANGUAGE

Two of the most recognizable linguistic anchors occur at the beginning and ending of fairy-tale texts, providing a complicated linguistic frame around a tale. Between "once upon a time" and "they lived happily ever after," a tale can transcend the present context and establish the form's trappings.

> "Once upon a time," "In a certain country," "a thousand years ago, or longer," "at a time when animals still talked," "once in an old castle in the midst of a large and dense forest"—Such beginnings suggest that what follows does not pertain to the here and now that we know.
>
> (Bettelheim 1977, 62)

This frame sets the stage for the timeless past of the fairy-tale world encompassing the tale within the form's frame.

These framing anchors may define a form, but many tales have text-specific linguistic anchors within, as well. These come in a number of different arrangements, but there are three worth highlighting as examples. First, there are formulaic exchanges, statements by or between characters that use static identifiable phrasings. One well-known example of such an exchange would be declarations by the giant in the tale "Jack and the Beanstalk" (ATU 328A). In one popular variation, the giant loudly declaims, "Fee-fi-fo-fum,/I smell the blood of an Englishman/be he alive, or be he dead/I shall grind his bones to make my bread" (Tatar 2002, 136). This poetic phrasing is differentiated from the prose of the rest of the tale and is often repeated multiple times in an individual retelling in an identical format. Not all formulaic exchanges require poetic structure. The question and response sequence from "Little Red Riding Hood," "Why Grandmother, what big ___ you have" uses a repetitive structure, reiterating the question and response structure a variable number of times until the concluding question about teeth. Such formulaic exchanges occur in many fairy tales and fairy-tale adaptations and frequently remain markedly consistent across versions, serving to tie variations together.

A second form of linguistic anchor is the magical incantation. Fairy tales often use highly static, often poetic language for magical incantations. In some cases, the language is simple but repetitive; phrases such as "open sesame" or "clickity-clack, get into my sack" enact magical effects upon the world and are used to enact sequences of magical action. Other spells are much more poetic, as Marina Warner describes:

> Of all the charged, active, enchanted elements in the tales, it is the words of the story that possess charmed life. Spells are formed of repetition, rhyme and nonsense; when they occur in fairy tales, they're often in verse—riddles and ditties, and they belong to the same family of verbal patterning as counting out, skipping songs, and nursery rhymes.
>
> (2014, 41)

These magical poems, a notable example is the "mirror mirror on the wall/who is the fairest of them all" exchange heard in Disney's *Snow White and the Seven Dwarfs* (1937), are similar in manifestation to stories about Icelandic *kraftskalds* (magical poets) using poetic magic to transform the world or childhood oaths made serious by the use of rhyme, "cross my heart, hope to die, stick a needle in my eye." Specific magical incantations remain consistent across many different variations, with specific effects that are often tied to the tale's structure.

Third, there are static names or descriptions. Some characters or objects have variable names across different retellings or are defined simply by their role. But in some tales, names

265

or descriptions can serve as linguistic anchors. In a few narratives, the name of the main character is a linguistic anchor all by itself. Snow White retains a remarkably static name between versions, even as some of the reasons for the name are stripped from retellings. Little Snow White (*Schneewittchen*) becomes a proper name rather than a descriptive nickname. Some of these names emerge from translation. Little Red Riding Hood becomes a static whole phrase in the transition from the single German word *Rotkäppchen*; Rapunzel retains the Germanic term for her eponymous vegetable rather than the translated rampion in most variations. Some even maintain a specific name from a false etymology. The name Cinderella is presented as a derivation of the word "cinder" and the diminutive "ella," when it comes from the French *Cendrillon*, which speaks of ashes rather than cinders (Bettelheim 1977, 253). These static phrasings are not restricted to named characters, to human characters, or even to living things. Well-known linguistic anchors include Fairy Godmothers, Wicked Stepmothers, Big Bad Wolves, Magic Beans, and Glass Slippers.

While these phrases differ in their specific details, all of them have the same effect: to create static points of reference that anchor the free-phrase fairy tales to each other. Two different versions of "The Three Little Pigs" (ATU 124) may have very different phrasings of most of the tale, but retain the specific phrasing of the Big Bad Wolf's threat to "huff and puff and blow the house down." Set among the characteristic sparseness of these tales, these pockets of artful repetition attain a much more significant status.

Variation Through Playful Adaptation

Fairy-tale adaptations are incredibly common, with immense variation, and linguistic anchors often serve as the site of linguistic play in a way that highlights how variants often use such anchors as a tie when changing other fundamental aspects of a fairy tale. In short, the introduction of variation to the familiar linguistic anchor serves to highlight the connection to the original while inverting expectations in playful ways. Some aspects of this effect have to do with the nature of the revision. Jack Zipes identifies a specific aspect of adaptations of well-known or classical fairy tales: "The purpose of producing a revised fairy tale is to create something new that incorporates the critical and creative thinking of the producer and corresponds to changed demands and tastes of audiences" (1994, 9). In other words, revising a fairy tale can be about taking the familiar and adapting to local taste culture and may include significant variation. However, what connects different variations on a given tale are linguistic anchors that symbolize their shared connection to the source text.

Several patterns emerge in retellings that demonstrate the multiple uses of linguistic anchors to create fairy-tale connections. Faithful modernization is one type of retelling which seeks to maintain the tone of the source text, usually keeping the same story structure and characters, while conforming to contemporary storytelling techniques. These often use linguistic anchors verbatim or with minimal adaptation, emphasizing their similarities. Some use material within the retelling, emphasizing well-known linguistic anchors. For instance, Disney's 1933 animated *Three Little Pigs* has the wolf deliver his formulaic threat at each different house, pictured as increasingly modern in design. Others make use of linguistic cues to set the stage of their adaptations from the title. The film adaptations *Mirror Mirror* (2012) and *Snow White and the Huntsman* (2012) both use familiar linguistic anchors in their titles to frame their tonally different variations. *Mirror Mirror* uses the familiar opening refrain of the evil queen's magical incantation to re-center their tale around a magical tale with her at the center. Meanwhile, *Snow White and the Huntsman* makes use of the archaic term "Huntsman" to reframe the story around the relationship between the two titular characters.

LANGUAGE

Other playful adaptations also recontextualize individual tales for contemporary audiences, changing the tone or highlighting incongruous aspects of well-known stories. While creators may dramatically change the structure or meaning, they often make direct use of linguistic anchors to maintain their connections to the source text. The Warner Brothers cartoon *Little Red Riding Rabbit* (1944) crafts a complicated recontextualization. In this version, the wolf is more interested in eating Bugs Bunny, the rabbit that Red is bringing to her grandmother as part of her basket, than in anthropophagy. Once Red arrives at her grandmother's house, she is shuffled off without her basket as the wolf tries to devour Bugs. However, the cartoon maintains the parodic structure as Red, in this version an oblivious teenager, keeps returning to try and continue the formulaic exchange with the reluctant "Grandma" using the linguistic anchor to keep trying to drag the story back toward the familiar source text. A clear example comes early in the short film. As Red Riding Hood arrives, she opens with, "Hey Grandma! I brought a little bunny rabbit for ya. To have!" The wolf responds by visibly salivating with the phrase, "Rabbit, mmm." Red replies, "Hey Grandma, you almost forgot! Uhh, Grandma, what big eyes you got!" The wolf replies, "Yeah, yeah, I know. Alright, alright. Big eyes, big eyes, yeah, I know, goodbye," as he physically tosses Red out the front door in order to focus on eating the rabbit. This use of the familiar anchor presents the story as a rote script and further highlights the variations for humorous effect. It's funny that in a Red Riding Hood adaptation, the wolf doesn't want to go through the ritual exchange in order to eat the girl.

The 1959 musical *Once Upon a Mattress* uses variation on linguistic anchors to update "The Princess on the Pea" (ATU 708) for modern audiences, introducing suggestive sexual content to the apparently innocent narrative. The song "Happily Ever After" repeats the formulaic phrase while expressing significant skepticism over its promises.

> They all live happily, happily, happily ever after.
> The couple is happily leaving the chapel eternally tied.
> As the curtain descends, there is nothing but loving and laughter.
> When the fairy tale ends the heroine's always a bride.
> Ella, the girl of the cinders did the wash and the walls and the winders.
> But she landed a prince who was brawny and blue-eyed and blond.
> Still, I honestly doubt that she could ever have done it
> without that crazy lady with the wand.
> Cinderella had outside help!
> I have no one but me . . .
>
> (1959)

These shifts correspond to the needs of the storyteller in the same way that many of the elements of the originals match the needs of prior tellers. As Jones puts it, "The fantastic creations in fairy tales may be seen as metaphoric dramatizations of the thoughts and feelings audience members may harbor about their daily lives and the problems they face" (1995, 11). By using linguistic anchors to juxtapose the needs and practices of the past with the present, these versions make explicit their producers' and audiences' thoughts and feelings on classic tales.

Finally, linguistic anchors play a significant role in postmodern intertextual adaptations of fairy tales. Postmodern retellings often use elements from multiple fairy tales to construct an intertextual whole, as described by Jeana Jorgensen: "I have taken to calling these new texts 'fairy-tale pastiches,' which is not to deny that they can have parodic functions, but rather to privilege the schizophrenic instrumentalization of fairy-tale matter" (2007, 218). They often use explicit repetition of linguistic anchors to highlight their parodic subversion. This process can be done while remaining technically faithful to the text, using the lack of variation to highlight other differences.

An example comes from the movie *Shrek* (2001), in a scene in which the Gingerbread Man is being interrogated by the villain. It includes a textually faithful repetition of the English folksong "Do You Know the Muffin Man" split into a call and response interrogation with increased emphasis. While textually faithful to the folksong, the parodic use of the full text subverts the meaning of its inclusion. Other fairy-tale pastiches seek to subtly use specific linguistic anchors as a form of narrative play. The television show *Once Upon a Time* (2011–) uses synonymous character names as a gesture toward names as linguistic anchors. In the mundane world where fairy-tale characters at first did not know their magical connections, the Evil Queen goes by the name Regina and the Red Riding Hood analogue is called Ruby. These names gesture toward the static linguistic signs of the fairy-tale source texts while simultaneously distancing the show from those source texts.

This type of play can be self-conscious within the retelling itself. In Bill Willingham's comic book *Fables* (2002), while the characters are essentially the same as their namesakes, they are aware of the trappings of the tales. In the first story arc, fairy-tale character Rose Red is murdered, and her murder scene makes explicit references in a way that both connects and distances the narrative from the traditional tale.

> Next to the broken mirror in the upper right-hand corner of the panel, the words "No more happily ever after" drips red down the wall, lacerated with numerous bleeding cuts. [. . .] This morbid slash at the cliché of "happily ever after" is one of many discursive tactics Willingham employs to toy with a reader's assumption about what a fairy tale is.
>
> (Harris 2016, 4)

This metanarrative use of a linguistic anchor establishes that the characters know traditional tale structure, that they distance themselves from it, and that the audience's expectations should be attuned to that level of self-awareness.

Overall, the ways in which linguistic anchors are used points toward the use of the folk voice within fairy-tale narratives. Fairy-tale retellings frequently make use of small and large cues to connect to the linguistic techniques of folktales. Tiffin explores this process in the use of framing narratives and cues in fairy-tale film: "In keeping with film's apparently transparent offer of itself as a substitute oral and folk tradition, many fairy-tale films rely heavily on an explicit evocation of the folk voice in order to frame and contextualize their narratives" (2009, 185). These linguistic cues and this use of the folk voice become the way in which the source texts are ultimately reified, turned into discrete recognizable texts. And they also become the ways in which those tales exist and manifest within the popular imagination.

Fairy-Tale Language in the Popular Imagination

The relationship between fairy-tale texts and their linguistic anchors becomes especially interesting when one looks at the way those anchors are used beyond explicit tale tellings. Fairy tales are frequently referenced elements of cultural heritage, used as shorthand for meanings and messages found in the texts. However, tales are often invoked through the specific use of linguistic anchors rather than more circumspect or explicit references to tale texts. This reference ties into the way in which postmodern tellings blend different fragments of texts. Cathy Preston observes, "In postmodernity the 'stuff' of fairy tales exists as fragments (princess, frog, slipper, commodity relations in a marriage market) in the nebulous realm that we might most simply identify as cultural knowledge" (2004, 210). Instead of using summaries of texts or referencing titles, these linguistic anchors serve as signifiers of entire tales.

These signifiers are deployed in interesting and complicated ways. An excellent set of examples come from Wolfgang Mieder's examination of what he calls modern anti-fairy tales (1987). Mieder examines fairy-tale adaptations in humorous form in "movies, advertisements, comic strips, caricatures, cartoons, greeting cards, and graffiti" (1987, 7) and cites examples that use only recognizable fragments of fairy-tale texts. Some of his best examples come from the captions of *New Yorker* cartoons and reflect general fairy-tale phrases: "A little boy simply interrupts his father's fairy tale reading by stating "'Once Upon a Time . . .' You read me that one before so now it's TWICE upon a time, right?'" (9), or "they lived happily ever after until the children were grown and she decided to pursue a career and his masculinity was threatened" (10). Others use phrases from specific tales, such as a number of greeting cards that use the "mirror, mirror" sequence from "Snow White" (ATU 709): "One such greeting card, for example, has a ridiculous figure as, 'Mirror, mirror on the wall, who's the fairest of them all?' The response on the inside of the card is 'it's still Snow White, but keep trying, kid!'" (Mieder 1987, 23). These can even be varied while maintaining their recognizable language. One 1963 cartoon features a group of women in front of a large computer looking at a ticker tape print out. One says to the others, "It says *I'm* the fairest one of all! So there!" (25). These variants use enough of the language to be instantly recognizable as the characteristic linguistic anchors of the tales while eschewing all the other normal characteristics of fairy tales such as structure and magic.

These phrases have such a hold on the cultural imagination that they often appear outside of storytelling contexts as a way of referencing (and often refuting) tale content. Lüthi says generally speaking that "our attitude toward fairy tales is ambivalent. 'Don't tell me any fairy tales' we say, in the derogatory sense" (1970, 21). But our use of linguistic anchors often positions fairy tales as points of desire or aspiration. Books such as *The Cinderella Complex: Women's Hidden Fear of Independence* by Colette Dowling (1981), *Before You Meet Prince Charming: A Guide to Radiant Purity* by Sarah Mally (2006), or *Spinning Straw into Gold: The Art of Creating Money* by Frank W. Butterfield (2012) use fairy-tale linguistic anchors to promise help in everyday life. Self-help books and advertisements serving as a form of wish fulfillment is nothing new. Linda Dégh (1994) and Sandra Dolby (2005) explore how linguistic anchors invoked recall entire tales and create meanings independent of tale structure.

Fairy-tale phrases developed for certain versions can adopt broad cultural relevance. As Zipes describes:

> Disney released *The Three Little Pigs* in 1933 and followed it with *The Big Bad Wolf* and *The Three Little Wolves*, all of which involved fairy-tale characters and stories that touched on the lives of people during the depression. [. . .] *The Three Little Pigs* was acclaimed by the nation, the wolf was on many American doorsteps and "Who's Afraid of the Big Bad Wolf?" became a rallying cry.
>
> (1994, 86)

The phrase referenced the economic dangers of the Great Depression and invoked a hopeful tale against hardship. This reinforcing of the phrase led to it becoming a significant linguistic anchor for later versions of the tale, even being parodied by Edward Albee in his play entitled *Who's Afraid of Virginia Woolf?* (1962).

Endings

The distinctive elements of fairy-tale language survive in the (post)modern era as part of the still popular tales. Lüthi sees the language as surviving partially because of its artistic appeal: "If *Grimm's Fairy Tales* have lived on far past their era and have won the hearts of the world, if they also appeal to us today, and if not only the story, but the manner in which it is told delights us" (1970, 28–29). But the language also survives because in its distinctness, its very markedness, it opens up opportunities for linguistic play, for variable retellings, for postmodern pastiches, for fleeting references.

These anchors help fairy tales survive as an identifiable part of culture. As Tiffin asserts, "If metafictional play with fairy tale requires recognition, then it is important to establish precisely how fairy tale is identified, how it is different from any other kind of narrative" (2009, 5). Whether the linguistic anchors of fairy tales remain so static because people need them as signposts for recognition or if that persistence is simply what allows them to fill that needed linguistic role in culture and storytelling, the fact remains that so long as they continue to open the doors to this sort of creative linguistic play, we will all live happily ever after.

Related topics: Adaptation and the Fairy-Tale Web; Cinematic; Gender; Musicals; Oral Tradition; Pedagogy; Poetry; Traditional Song; Translation

References Cited and Further Reading

Bettelheim, Bruno. 1977. *The Uses of Enchantment: The Meaning and Importance of Fairy Tales.* New York: Vintage Books.

Butterfield, Frank W. 2012. *Spinning Straw into Gold: The Art of Creating Money.* Charleston: Create Space Independent Publishing Platform.

Dégh, Linda. 1994. *American Folklore and the Mass Media.* Bloomington: Indiana UP.

Dolby, Sandra K. 2005. *Self-Help Books: Why Americans Keep Reading Them.* Urbana: U Illinois P.

Dowling, Colette. 1981. *The Cinderella Complex: Women's Hidden Fear of Independence.* New York: Summit Books.

Dundes, Alan. 1980. *Interpreting Folklore.* Bloomington: Indiana UP.

Grimm, Jacob, and Wilhelm Grimm. 1966. *Household Stories.* Ann Arbor, MI: University Microfilms Inc.

Harris, Jason Marc. 2016. "We All Live in Fabletown: Bill Willingham's Fables—A Fairy-Tale Epic for the 21st Century." *Humanities* 5 (2): 1–21.

Jones, Steven Swann. 1995. *The Fairy Tale: The Magic Mirror of Imagination.* New York: Twayne Publishers.

Jorgensen, Jeana. 2007. "A Wave of the Magic Wand: Fairy Godmothers in Contemporary American Media." *Marvels & Tales* 21 (2): 216–27.

Levorato, Alessandra. 2003. *Language and Gender in the Fairy Tale Tradition: A Linguistic Analysis of Old and New Story Telling.* New York: Palgrave Macmillan.

Lüthi, Max. 1970. *Once Upon a Time: On the Nature of Fairy Tales.* New York: F. Ungar Publishing Company.

Mally, Sarah. 2006. *Before You Meet Prince Charming: A Guide to Radiant Purity.* Cedar Rapids: Tomorrow's Forefathers.

Mieder, Wolfgang. 1987. *Tradition and Innovation in Folk Literature.* Lebanon, NH: UP New England.

Perrault, Charles. 2009. *The Complete Fairy Tales.* New York: Oxford UP.

Preston, Cathy Lynn. 2004. "Disrupting the Boundaries of Genre and Gender: Postmodernism and the Fairy Tale." In *Fairy Tales and Feminism: New Approaches*, edited by Donald Haase, 197–212. Detroit: Wayne State UP.

Tatar, Maria. 2002. *The Annotated Classic Fairy Tales.* New York: Norton.

Tiffin, Jessica. 2009. *Marvelous Geometry: Narrative and Metafiction in Modern Fairy Tale.* Detroit: Wayne State UP.

Warner, Marina. 2014. *Once Upon a Time: A Short History of Fairy Tale.* Oxford: Oxford UP.

Willingham, Bill. 2002. *Fables: Legends in Exile.* New York: DC Comics.

Zipes, Jack. 1988. "The Changing Function of the Fairy Tale." *The Lion and the Unicorn* 12 (2): 7–31.

———. 1994. *Fairy Tale as Myth/Myth as Fairy Tale.* Lexington: UP Kentucky.

LANGUAGE

Mediagraphy

"Happily Ever After" (Song). 1959. Music by Mary Rodgers, lyrics by Marshall Barer, album *Once Upon a Mattress*. USA.

Little Red Riding Rabbit. 1944. Director Friz (Isadore) Freleng. USA.

Mirror Mirror. 2012. Director Tarsem Singh. USA.

Once Upon a Mattress (Musical). 1959. Music by Mary Rodgers, lyrics by Marshall Barer, and book by Jay Thompson, Dean Fuller, and Marshall Barer. Off Broadway, Phoenix Theater. USA.

———. 2005. Director Kathleen Marshall. USA.

Once Upon a Time (TV). 2011–. Creators Edward Kitsis and Adam Horowitz. USA.

Shrek. 2001. Directors Andrew Adamson and Vicky Jenson. USA.

Snow White and the Huntsman. 2012. Director Rupert Sanders. USA.

Snow White and the Seven Dwarfs. 1937. Directors William Cottrell, David Hand, Wilfred Jackson, Larry Morey, Perce Pearce, and Ben Sharpsteen. USA.

Three Little Pigs. 1933. Director Burt Gillett. USA.

Who's Afraid of Virginia Woolf (Play). 1962. Written by Edward Albee. Nederlander Theatre. USA.

30

ORAL TRADITION

Martin Lovelace

Before fairy tales were ever written they were told. Specifically when and where they began to be told, by whom, and to whom are questions that have absorbed folklorists and other scholars for more than two centuries. The study of folktales—stories told and accepted by audiences as fiction (Bascom 1965, 4)—demands knowledge of oral and literary versions of tales "from Ireland to India," as Stith Thompson put it in his still vital study *The Folktale* (1946). One must go back, he said, before the sixteenth century and much farther afield than Western Europe (22). Tale motifs and plots (or tale types) that appear in Western European tales appear in oral tradition in modern India, where some of them derive from the 2,000-year-old tale book *Panchatantra* (Thompson 1946, 15), but who put them into the *Panchatantra*, and who told them before they were written down? Their makers may not have been of any high social rank, or educated, or even literate; and to judge by the dismissive phrase that still falls readily from the mouths and keyboards of the "educated," many were "old wives."

Evidence for the oral existence of fairy tales in antiquity appears in classical narratives such as the tale of "Cupid and Psyche" inset within the frame story of Apuleius's *The Golden Ass* (ca. 160 C.E.). The novel's narrator describes a storytelling situation in which an old woman tries to divert a younger woman kidnapped by robbers by telling her "the pretty story of an old wife's tale" (Walsh 1994, 74). The story begins with a fairy-tale opening formula: "In a certain city there lived a king and queen with three notably beautiful daughters" (75) and continues in the pattern recognized in *The Types of International Folktales* (Uther 2004) as ATU 425B "Son of the Witch." The goddess Venus is the "witch" who resents the loss of her son Cupid to the younger and more beautiful Psyche and opposes their marriage until Jupiter raises Psyche to the heavens and grants her immortality, thereby removing the taint of an "unequal" marriage between a god and a mortal woman. Jan M. Ziolkowski, in *Fairy Tales from Before Fairy Tales* (2009), notes that the story is "often considered the first fairy tale in Western literature" (58). Alex Scobie argues that the presence in "Cupid and Psyche" of characteristic fairy-tale structure and motifs gives further evidence of its original orality (1983, 39), and the exhaustive study of the history and geographic diffusion of the Cupid and Psyche story by Jan-Öjvind Swahn destroys the arguments of Albert Wesselski and other doubters of the existence of folktales in the classical period (Swahn 1955, 397–398). Graham Anderson's *Fairytale in the Ancient World* (2000), and especially William Hansen's *Ariadne's Thread: A Guide to International Tales Found in Classical Literature* (2002), provide massive proof of the antiquity of many themes and motifs that continued to appear over centuries in folktales and eventually in their literary adaptations, fairy tales.

As a literary genre distinct from orally told folktales, the written fairy tale appeared in Italy in the sixteenth century. Maria Tatar has provided a chronology of fairy-tale production that begins with *The Pleasant Nights* by the Venetian Giovanni Francesco Straparola (1550–3), followed by Giambattista Basile's *The Tale of Tales, or Entertainments for the Little Ones*, also known as *The Pentamerone* (1634–6); in France Marie-Catherine d'Aulnoy's *Tales of the Fairies* was printed in 1697, and in the same year Charles Perrault published *Stories, or Tales from Times Past with Moralities* (Tatar 2015, xi–xii). In *Fairy Tales: A New History* (2009) Ruth B. Bottigheimer argues that Straparola invented the fairy tale, with its characteristic "rise" of a poor young man or woman to a glittering marriage, or the "restoration" plot in which a royal person loses their throne, endures trials, and finally regains happiness (10–13). Her thesis is that these elite-written stories sank down to the general population, even to the non-literate, who heard them read and then reproduced them, ultimately to be recorded by folklorists who called them examples of oral tradition. Her knowledge of the literary history of the European fairy tale is impressive: she is historically correct to argue that elite writers copied and recast earlier tales they had read, or that some stories in oral tradition began in literary sources (Thompson 1946, 176–187), but her tone grows unreasonably dismissive whenever "old women" and "unlettered folk" are mentioned as putative makers of tales (Bottigheimer 2009, 2–3).

This educated disdain is all too familiar—it can be heard in Apuleius's narrator calling the old woman storyteller a "crazy, drunken old hag" (Walsh 1994, 113)—and it reflects the traditional "literacentrism" to which historians and literary scholars remain oddly prone (Buchan 1989, 3). Bottigheimer is unwilling to admit the possibility that stories have ever been transmitted through space and time without the aid of print. Willem de Blécourt, following Bottigheimer, has also questioned "the assumption" of the orality of fairy tales (de Blécourt 2012, vii), but the opinion that oral transmission of fairy tales is a romantic construct, unsupported by documentary evidence, is not new but a restatement of ideas propounded in the 1930s by German folklorist Albert Wesselski. He believed that the folk "could only reproduce, not produce, and should be regarded neither as preparing, preserving nor disseminating stories" (de Blécourt 2012, 57). Wesselski (1871–1939) was writing well before the major twentieth-century collections and studies of field-recorded orally told fairy tales had appeared, most notably Linda Dégh's *Folktales and Society* (1962 in German; 1969 in English), and Herbert Halpert and J. D. A. Widdowson's *Folktales of Newfoundland: The Resilience of the Oral Tradition* (1996). Halpert and Widdowson were able to record more than 150 tales, of which a third were "wonder tales," *Märchen*, or fairy tales (ATU 300–749).

These modern folktale studies give attention to narrators and their aesthetics, audience responses, contexts for tale telling, and performance descriptions and treat storytelling as the complex social phenomenon that it is. Folklorists do not deny the possibility of interplay between printed versions of fairy tales and oral narration over the course of their long histories; nevertheless, the hypothesis that individual fairy tales first appeared in print, as the product of elite writers, then spread down the social register to oral performers, is an unlikely one, especially in print-starved and barely literate regions such as Newfoundland in the earlier twentieth century.[1]

For the most authoritative study of how tales have been made and transmitted, and a truly enlightening analysis of their social functions and meanings, turn to the work of Danish folktale scholar Bengt Holbek (1933–1992), whose *Interpretation of Fairy Tales* (1987) has been called "the best single monograph ever written on the fairy tale genre" (Dundes 2006, 69). Holbek had no doubt that fairy tales derived from oral tradition: "No word of any language and few pre-industrial artifacts had spread as far and wide as the haunting themes of these tales, despite their lack of physical substance, their total dependence on the faulty memories of men" (1987, 17). While recognizing that tales recorded in Europe and beyond had "counterparts in European and Oriental literatures of earlier centuries" (17), Holbek saw such literary versions not as sources used by tellers but as derivations from the original oral creations of "craftsmen"

(39–44) who had apprenticed themselves to masters of the art of tale telling. He defines fairy tale as "a category of tale in which a hero or heroine is subjected to a series of trials and tribulations characterized by the occurrence of 'marvellous' beings, phenomena, and events, finally to marry the princess or prince in splendor and glory" (1989, 40), and, more compactly, as "tales which end with a wedding or with the triumph of the couple who were cast out earlier in the tale because their marriage was a misalliance" (1987, 404).

Bottigheimer's "rise" and "restoration" plots recognize the same patterns, but Holbek's interpretation of their meaning accounts for their resonance as stories: they symbolize experiences common to most of us. They are about leaving the family of one's birth; being tested in kindness, courage, and endurance; finding and learning to trust a romantic partner; and succeeding in having the marriage approved by parents, thereby gaining an independence and means of livelihood for the new family. The stories are always of unlikely, socially unequal marriages in which the parents of the higher-status partner must be won over to give consent. It is the story of individual maturation but with a recognition that the principal obstacles facing the young couple are instigated by members of their own families: jealous siblings, clinging parents, hostile in-laws. Holbek argues that the characters in fairy tales are masks for figures in real-life family relationships in which tensions existed. The tales made it possible to think about, or hint about, oppressive or abusive family situations by throwing the contentious situations onto a screen of fiction where ogres, giants, wicked stepmothers, witches, kings, and queens enacted violence against well-meaning but disempowered youth. No matter whether the hero or heroine is of peasant or royal birth, the tales see life's conflicts from the perspective of the socially powerless.

Holbek based and tested his interpretation on one of the largest and most accurate nineteenth-century collections of orally told fairy tales, the recordings made (by dictation) by Evald Tang Kristensen (1843–1929) in Denmark between 1868 and 1907. From the 2,448 folktales recorded by Kristensen, Holbek selected those 770 that were fairy tales recorded from 127 narrators. As is usual with tellers of fairy tales, most of the narrators knew several stories: the average was over eleven (Holbek 1987, 87). They were predominantly men, although Kristensen recorded from women also, and they lived almost entirely in rural areas. Unlike Hans Naumann and other 1920s proponents of *gesunkenes Kulturgut*, who theorized that fairy tales and other folk literature spread "down" the social scale, after being invented at elite levels (Dow 2014), Holbek believed magic tales had *always* been told mainly among the poor (1987, 151). Dégh observed that in Hungary in the 1950s "well-to-do peasants" felt that the long magic tales, being "lies," were unworthy of their attention (1969, 81). Fairy tales in oral tradition see the social order from the bottom up. They were implicitly revolutionary in their natural contexts, but their subversive edge was blunted by writers who turned them into entertainments for courtiers (Perrault) or moral lessons for children (Grimm).

The fairy tale in oral transmission is also an aural tradition. Narrators of fairy tales have often told folklorists recording them that they "hear" the voice of the person they learned the tale from as they perform their own version and that they repeat some of the original narrator's turns of phrase. Opening and closing formulas, with their relatively fixed phrasing—"Not in my time, not in your time, but when the monkeys used to walk, talk, and chew tobacco"—are especially likely to be remembered whole. Storytelling has often run in families (Roberts 1974; Braid 2002), and many narrators have warm memories of hearing tales from close relatives. The Kentucky narrator Jane Muncy told folklorist Carl Lindahl of lying in bed next to her grandmother and "drifting off to sleep" after a couple of stories "with my ear at her back, because I liked to hear her heart beat" (Lindahl 2010, 255). Similarly, two Newfoundland tellers of fairy tales remembered from boyhood lying on a wooden floor next to a wood stove while an uncle told stories (Halpert and Widdowson 1996, 494, 501). As Dorothy Noyes has noted, the core meaning of "traditio" in classical Latin is to "hand over" ownership of some kind of valuable property in a person-to-person relationship (2009, 234–235).

The personal connection that the recipient has with the previous "owner" of a tale is important; a tale teller generally remembers the person from whom a tale was learned, and, while hard to document, it is likely that something of the original teller's performance is carried over into the re-creation of the story. Lawrence Millman, who traveled through the rural west of Ireland in 1975 searching for tellers of magic tales, observed that a tale "divorced from its teller" is "a mere outline of the real thing" and that a narrator *needs* the personal contact with another storyteller in order to be inspired to tell his own version:

> Mickey's inability to read prevents him from refreshing his memory at the local library, where he probably could collect dozens of stories with ease. No, he needs human contacts. [. . .] actual people to tell him stories. He once had these people, though sometimes at a cost: "I'd often work half a day wit' a farmer for nothing, just t' get a good story from him."
>
> (Millman 1977, 125)

Just because collections of tales exist in books does not mean they were influential or even accepted into local storytelling tradition. Pius Power Sr., a brilliant Newfoundland narrator, observed that he would not tell "Cinderella," although he knew it: it had no meaning for him (Best 1988). Stories are passed along networks of individuals who care more than the average person does about them; when they tell the tales they are remembering not merely words and a plot but also the sound of a voice and often, although not always, the warmth of a relationship.

A further detail that a literary understanding of fairy tales obscures is that tales were to a large degree regarded as the property of the oral teller. But aren't tales generously "shared" by benign storytellers? And aren't they communal property? Not necessarily. The ethnographic literature on the acquisition of stories in oral tradition shows stories being kept away from rival narrators since possession of a unique repertoire of tales was highly regarded (Dégh 1969, 89–90). Being able to perform a distinctive tale gave status, made the narrator welcome, and was even a means of livelihood in the case of wandering beggars such as the Siberian penal colonists described by Mark Azadovskii who drew out their tales long enough to be fed and given a bed for the night by the peasants whose homes they visited (1926; 1974, 19). Itinerant craftspeople, such as tailors in rural Scotland and Ireland, often added storytelling to their main handicrafts. David Thomson tells how a storyteller hid in the loft of an Irish cottage while another narrator told a story that he would never have told had he known his rival was listening: "from that night, he had the story, as good in every word as the words of the man of the house. And he told it after that wherever he went tailoring until the day he died. But he never dared go more to that house, that was all" (1965, 45–47). Those who have conducted fieldwork among traditional tellers of fairy tales recognize that there are many complex reasons individuals have for telling stories, from the sense of obligation to carry on tradition—"a job that must be done" (Noyes 2009, 248)—to an egotistical or economically driven motive. Along with "ownership" of a story, meaning the community's recognition of the "right" of the narrator to tell that tale, comes a sense of responsibility to maintain it as something too valuable to be lost.

In its original oral form, even more than in its literary versions, the fairy tale is an intensely visual genre. Storytelling sessions among the Haya people of Tanzania begin with the audience's invocation to the narrator "See so that we may see" (Seitel 1980, vii). "Seeing" the events of a tale as they unfold is vital to both tellers and audiences. For a storyteller the visual details of scenes and confrontations are essential to memorizing and structuring the tale. Vivian Labrie developed a persuasive theory of the connection between visualization and memorization through interviews with traditional storytellers in New Brunswick, Canada, in the 1970s. One of them, Ephrem Godin, observed: "When somebody tells you a tale, you keep your attention until the hero sets out for another place and then, you notice again where he stops if you want to be able to tell it back" (Labrie 1981, 101).

Labrie calls this "visual itinerary" "the very framework of remembering" and notes that it was a method used by orators in antiquity. "The task of the narrator," she says, "consists of depicting, for the blind audience, what he sees as it unfolds from his memory into his consciousness" (1981, 102). D. A. MacDonald's interviews with the Scottish storyteller Donald Alastair Johnson reveal just how detailed a narrator's vision could be: "I could see just, how . . . where . . . when he went up to the cauldron, I was just as if I were seeing the cauldron right there—rusty" (MacDonald 1978, 15). Johnson compared narrating to describing a succession of images that ran, left to right, like a film projected on a wall.

Full transcriptions of traditional tale tellers performing folktales often reveal the cues given by narrators to steer their audiences toward what the narrator is seeing. In the following passage Allan Oake, of Beaumont, Newfoundland, is telling his version of the swan maidens episode in ATU 313, "The Magic Flight." Through the speech of an old man advising the hero he tells the audience what to look for: "'you'll see, look away to the mountain tops you'll see a cloud' he said 'a little cloud risin. The once' he said 'you'll see three girls comin' down for a bathing'" (Halpert and Widdowson 1996, 160). The visual cueing is reinforced immediately as the hero follows the old man's advice, and the episode unfolds in the same sequence of images, from the distant cloud to the body of the naked girl. Seeing a light in darkness, which resolves into a lighted window, through which can be seen—giants, or whatever the story demands, is a similar device used by narrators to limit what is seen by the mind's eye as they carry their listeners forward to the next challenge of their hero.

Max Lüthi's "Aspects of the *Märchen* and the Legend" (1969) describes the distinctive visual design characteristic of each genre, with the fairy tale (or *Märchen*) typically using images that are linear (swords, staffs, feathers), or nested within other things (the ogre's heart in an egg, in a duck, on a pond), and strongly colored (black, red, white) or metallic (copper, silver, gold). The fairy-tale world is deliberately made to be out of and beyond everyday experience. Legend, by contrast, being a truth-oriented genre, emphasizes quotidian reality interrupted by an outlandish event.

The distinctive style of the fairy tale also owes much to what is possible, or necessary, in oral performance. One of the first to codify the traits of style of oral narrative was the Danish folklorist Axel Olrik in his 1909 essay "Epic Laws of Folk Narrative" (1909 [1965], 129–141). The "Law of Three" gives the tale its sequence of trials of the hero or the number of brothers or sisters. Characters appear "Two to a Scene" and always "Contrast": rich/poor, powerful/weak, honest/deceptive. People in the same role, "Twins," are not differentiated: Cinderella's sisters, for example. Olrik believed he had uncovered superorganic "laws" that governed all traditional narrating, but in reality his essay describes what is possible in the oral medium and the range of devices available to narrators as they create vivid scenes their audiences can readily imagine.

Olrik's proto-structuralist work anticipated *Morphology of the Folktale* by Vladimir Propp, which first appeared in Russian in 1928 (1968), the essential work for understanding how a fairy tale can be composed in oral performance, without recourse to memory of any particular fixed, or written, text. The teller, or maker, of such a story would have absorbed, through listening to other narrators, the "rules" for creating versions of fairy tales that would be acceptable to audiences, who also knew the conventions of the genre. Propp, after pulling apart 100 tales recorded by the nineteenth-century folklorist A. N. Afanasyev found there were potentially seven tale roles, or types of character defined by the actions they perform in a tale, and up to thirty-one kinds of events that the characters cause to happen. The tales move from the hero's separation from family, through testing encounters with characters who provide magic objects or become future helpers on the quest, to conflicts with dangerous adversaries, culminating in a glorious wedding of social unequals.

The flaw in Propp's schema is that his model is based on male-centered fairy tales, in which marriage is the end of the story for the male hero. He has won his princess and a kingdom and no more need be said. Female-centered fairy tales, however, begin at the wedding, after which events run badly downhill for the heroine bride. Her female in-laws plot against her, and the story follows her adventures as she struggles to restore her marriage and regain her happiness. This idea of the family as fraught with enmity could only be safely imagined and spoken of via the screen of fiction (Holbek 1989, 49). Holbek felt that the wedding was the crucial act in fairy tales: weddings showed that the young couple had won each other's trust and love; they had gained independence from the parental generation and secured their economic future when the old people had surrendered "the keys of the kingdom" to them.

Holbek's analysis shows that fairy tales are about generational conflict, finding a life partner, and the triumph of the "have-nots" over the "haves" (1989, 44). The giants, the witches, and the palaces of gold are aspects of the central relationships of life artfully reimagined, and disguised, through the conventions of the oral fairy tale. The weak, but clever, heroines and heroes defeat the strong and stupid ogres. The tales are coded, as feminist readings of other genres of oral literature, such as ballads, have shown (Stewart 1993; Wollstadt 2003).

Alan Dundes stated, in a riposte to purely literary understandings of fairy tales as texts consumed in private reading, "one cannot possibly read fairy tales; one can only properly hear them told" (1986, 259). This is because the oral performance of a tale is a much more multi-channeled experience than reading, or even listening to someone else read, a fixed text: "A vast chasm separates an oral tale with its subtle nuances entailing significant body movements, eye expression, pregnant pauses, and the like from the inevitably flat and fixed record of what was once a live and often compelling storytelling event" (259).

The oral tale in performance is flexible, creatively variable. Stage properties could be improvised out of immediate surroundings: a storyteller is remembered for acting out the throwing of a man into jail in his story by opening a little door and pushing one of his listeners into the cellar (Arsenault 2002, 4). A cockroach crawling across the floor could be brought into a tale as a character, a narrator's penknife could be passed around the audience as the very knife used to slay the giant (Crowley 1966, 28). The oral fairy tale, being an interplay between teller and audience, is never the same tale twice. Just how complex this interplay is, with its feedback from listeners to teller, was described by Robert A. Georges in his analysis of "storytelling events" (1969), which argues that the "text" of a story told is but one element in the whole event and far from the "static entity" it is tacitly assumed to be (327).

Georges looked forward to the use of "sound cameras" by folklorists to capture the "wholeness" of storytelling events (327). At minimum two video cameras, to record narrator and listeners, are necessary. In my own experience the storyteller Alice Lannon, whom I videotaped narrating magic tales at her home in Placentia, Newfoundland, with folklorist Barbara Rieti in 1999, delivered her stories to Barbara rather than me. Was this because she was placing gendered inflections in her tales best appreciated by another woman? Or because I was sitting next to the unblinking stare of the video camera? A second or third camera to register our responses might have helped interpret this, as well as forcing us as ethnographers to submit equally to the camera's gaze.

Regrettably none of the narrators tape recorded by Halpert and Widdowson in the 1970s were filmed, although a videotape is available of a tale performance by Emile Benoit, a brilliant narrator from the French-speaking Port-au-Port Peninsula of Newfoundland.[2] *Folktales of Newfoundland* nevertheless made a major advance in the way tale texts should be presented, as complete transcriptions of everything that can be heard on the sound recording. John Widdowson spent countless hours listening to the recordings and transcribing the tales exactly; he worked out a system that is both readable and reflective of the dynamics of actual speech (Halpert and Widdowson 1996, lxi–lxv). An alternative, and equally respectful, treatment of what storytellers actually said (as opposed to what editors emended to suit their idea of readability) was the ethnopoetic model employed by Pauline Greenhill in her re-transcription of stories, including magic tales, recorded in the Canadian Maritimes by Helen Creighton (Greenhill 1985). The use of audio and video recordings has enabled us to attend more closely to nuances in a teller's performance and to recognize, as Greenhill suggests, that "nothing is completely extraneous or meaningless in a story's telling" (227). This willingness by analysts to listen closely is, of course, very far from earlier ways of presenting tales in words scribbled down, perhaps half-heard, by a collector in "the field" or, worse, revised and turned into "fairy tale" style by an editor in a library.

Angela Carter was one of the few writers of fairy tales who took the trouble to read widely in collections of folktales and to show appropriate respect to their tellers. Her introduction to *The Virago Book of Fairy Tales* (1990) recognizes that literature, for the great majority of humanity, "has been narrated, not written—heard not read. So fairy tales, folktales, stories from the oral tradition, are all of them the most vital connection we have with the imaginations of the ordinary men and women whose labour created our world." These tales, she wrote, are "stories without known originators that can be remade again and again by every person who tells them, the perennially refreshed entertainment of the poor" (ix). Carter's own revisions of well-known fairy tales in *The Bloody Chamber* (1979) are subtle, original remakings. They are fine works of literature but neither superior, nor inferior, to the oral tales that influenced them. The fairy tale in literature and the fairy tale in oral tradition belong in separate categories of experience; both can be profound works of artful imagination.

The magic tale is not yet gone from oral tradition, especially when considered from a global perspective. In middle-class families in Calcutta, for example, grandmothers continue to tell the Bengali fairy tales that they learned aurally as children or young women, although their daughters-in-law prefer that they read the grandchildren European tales from Grimm, or Disney, the better to fit them for success in the international economy (Roy 2013). In Newfoundland it may be that the last narrators to have learned fairy tales solely from oral tradition have passed away, but the actor Andy Jones has so internalized and re-animated stories from the Halpert and Widdowson field recordings he listened to in MUNFLA, Memorial University's Folklore and Language Archive, that they are now "his" stories as much as they ever were for their original tellers (Jones 2003, 2009). His puppet play versions delight adults and children. In North America and Europe revival storytellers also lead individuals into the magic space of fairy tale through the power of the spoken word (McCarthy 1994).

Related topics: Adaptation and the Fairy-Tale Web; Language; Storytelling; Traditional Song

Notes

1. For further debate on the oral/print origin and transmission question see *The Journal of American Folklore* 123 (2010), a special issue introduced by Dan Ben-Amos in which Ruth B. Bottigheimer's *Fairy Godfather: Straparola, Venice, and the Fairy Tale Tradition* (2002) is trenchantly critiqued by Ben-Amos, Francisco Vaz da Silva, and Jan M.

Ziolkowski. Willem de Blécourt's *Tales of Magic, Tales in Print* (2012) is challenged as "Reductionist Scholarship" by Jack Zipes in his *The Irresistible Fairy Tale* (2012, 175–189).

2. Emile Benoit (1913–1992), one of the last narrators in Newfoundland to have learned his tales from oral tradition, can be seen telling "Black Mountain," his version of ATU 313, "The Magic Flight," in a video recorded in 1985 at Memorial University. His performance, which appears to be a combination of memory and improvisation, takes almost two hours; commendably the film crew show audience reactions as well as the narrator. For a full study of Emile Benoit, Blanche Ozon, Angela Kerfont, and other Franco-Newfoundland storytellers, see Thomas (1992), which explores "public" storytelling, as in Benoit's exuberantly dramatic manner, and the quieter "private" tradition of Ozon and Kerfont. The Folklore and Language Archive, MUNFLA, at Memorial University has the original field tapes of fairy tales recorded from oral tradition in the 1970s and later by Herbert Halpert, John Widdowson, Gerald Thomas, and others, which can be accessed by researchers.

References Cited and Further Reading

Anderson, Graham. 2000. *Fairytale in the Ancient World*. London: Routledge.

Arsenault, Georges. 2002. *Acadian Legends, Folktales, and Songs from Prince Edward Island*. Charlottetown: Acorn P.

Azadovskii, Mark. (1926) 1974. *A Siberian Tale Teller*, translated by James R. Dow. Austin: U Texas P.

Bascom, William. 1965. "The Forms of Folklore: Prose Narratives." *Journal of American Folklore* 78: 3–20.

Ben-Amos, Dan. 2010a. "Introduction: The European Fairy-Tale Tradition between Orality and Literacy." *Journal of American Folklore* 123: 373–6.

———. 2010b. "Straparola: The Revolution That Was Not." *Journal of American Folklore* 123: 426–46.

Best, Anita. 1988. "Female Characters in Newfoundland *Märchen*." Unpublished paper.

Bottigheimer, Ruth B., ed. 1986. *Fairy Tales and Society*. Philadelphia: U Pennsylvania P.

———. 2002. *Fairy Godfather: Straparola, Venice, and the Fairy Tale Tradition*. Philadelphia: U Pennsylvania P.

———. 2009. *Fairy Tales: A New History*. Albany: SUNY P.

Braid, Donald. 2002. *Scottish Traveller Tales*. Jackson: UP Mississippi.

Buchan, David. 1989. "Folk Tradition and Literature Till 1603." In *Bryght Lanternis: Essays on the Language and Literature of Medieval and Renaissance Scotland*, edited by Derrick McClure and M. R. G. Spiller, 1–12. Aberdeen: Aberdeen UP.

Carter, Angela. 1979. *The Bloody Chamber and Other Stories*. London: Gollancz.

———, ed. 1990. *The Virago Book of Fairy Tales*. London: Virago P.

Crowley, Daniel J. 1966. *I Could Talk Old-Story Good: Creativity in Bahamian Folklore*. Berkeley: U California P.

de Blécourt, Willem. 2012. *Tales of Magic, Tales in Print*. Manchester: Manchester UP.

Dégh, Linda. 1969. *Folktales and Society*. Bloomington: Indiana UP.

Dow, James R. 2014. "Hans Naumann's *gesunkenes Kulturgut* and primitive *Gemeinschaftskultur*." *Journal of Folklore Research* 51: 49–100.

Dundes, Alan. 1986. "Fairy Tales from a Folkloristic Perspective." In *Fairy Tales and Society*, edited by Ruth B. Bottigheimer, 259–60. Philadelphia: U Pennsylvania P.

———. 2006. "Towards a Theory of Fairy Tales as In-Law Confrontations." In *Toplore: Stories and Songs*, edited by Paul Catteeu. Trier: Wissenschaftlicher Verlag.

Georges, Robert A. 1969. "Toward an Understanding of Storytelling Events." *Journal of American Folklore* 82 (1969): 313–328.

Greenhill, Pauline. 1985. *Lots of Stories: Maritime Narratives from the Creighton Collection*. Ottawa: Mercury Series, National Museums of Canada.

Halpert, Herbert, and J. D. A. Widdowson, eds. 1996. *Folktales of Newfoundland: The Resilience of the Oral Tradition*. New York: Garland.

Hansen, William. 2002. *Ariadne's Thread: A Guide to International Tales found in Classical Literature*. Ithaca, NY: Cornell UP.

Holbek, Bengt. 1987. *Interpretation of Fairy Tales*. Helsinki: Academia Scientiarum Fennica.

———. 1989. "The Language of Fairy Tales." In *Nordic Folklore*, edited by Reimund Kvideland and Henning K. Sehmsdorf, 40–62. Bloomington: Indiana UP.

Jones, Andy. 2003. *Peg Bearskin: A Traditional Newfoundland Tale*. St. John's: Running the Goat Books and Broadsides.

———. 2009. *The Queen of Paradise's Garden: A Traditional Newfoundland Tale*. St. John's: Running the Goat Books and Broadsides.

Labrie, Vivian. 1981. "The Itinerary as a Possible Memorized Form of the Folktale." In *ARV: Scandinavian Yearbook of Folklore*, 37. Stockholm: Royal Gustavus Adolphus Academy.

Lindahl, Carl. 2010. "Leonard Roberts, the Farmer-Lewis-Muncy Family, and the Magic Circle of the Mountain *Märchen." Journal of American Folklore* 123: 252–75.

Lüthi, Max. 1969. "Aspects of the *Märchen* and the Legend." *Genre* 2: 162–78.

MacDonald, D. A. 1978. "A Visual Memory." *Scottish Studies* 22: 1–26.

McCarthy, William Bernard. 1994. *Jack in Two Worlds: Contemporary North American Tales and Their Tellers.* Chapel Hill: U North Carolina P.

Millman, Lawrence. 1977. *Our Like Will Not Be There Again: Notes from the West of Ireland.* Boston: Little, Brown.

Noyes, Dorothy. 2009. "Tradition: Three Traditions." *Journal of Folklore Research* 46: 233–68.

Olrik, Axel. (1909) 1965. "Epic Laws of Folk Narrative." In *The Study of Folklore*, edited by Alan Dundes, 129–41. Englewood Cliffs, NJ: Prentice-Hall.

Propp, Vladimir. (1928) 1968. *Morphology of the Folktale.* Austin: U Texas P.

Roberts, Leonard. 1974. *Sang Branch Settlers: Folksongs and Tales of an Eastern Kentucky Family.* Austin: U Texas P.

Roy, Purna. 2013. "Situational Storytelling for Children and Young Adults in Bengali Households: A Study of Texts in Contexts." M.A. Thesis. St. John's Newfoundland: Memorial University.

Scobie, Alex. 1983. *Apuleius and Folklore.* London: Folklore Society.

Seitel, Peter. 1980. *See So That We May See: Performances and Interpretations of Traditional Tales from Tanzania.* Bloomington: Indiana UP.

Stewart, Polly. 1993. "Wishful Willful Wily Women: Lessons for Female Success in the Child Ballads." In *Feminist Messages: Coding in Women's Folk Culture*, edited by Joan N. Radner, 54–73. Urbana: U Illinois P.

Swahn, Jan-Öjvind. 1955. *The Tale of Cupid and Psyche.* Lund: Gleerup.

Tatar, Maria. 2015. *The Cambridge Companion to Fairy Tales.* Cambridge: Cambridge UP.

Thomas, Gerald. 1992. *The Two Traditions: The Art of Storytelling Amongst French Newfoundlanders.* St. John's: Breakwater.

Thompson, Stith. 1946. *The Folktale.* New York: Holt, Rinehart and Winston.

Thomson, David. 1965. *The People of the Sea.* Cleveland, OH: World Publishing.

Uther, Hans-Jörg. 2004. *The Types of International Folktales.* Helsinki: Academia Scientiarum Fennica.

Vaz da Silva, Francisco. 2010. "The Invention of Fairy Tales." *Journal of American Folklore* 123: 398–425.

Walsh, P. G. 1994. *Apuleius: The Golden Ass. Translated with Introduction and Explanatory Notes.* Oxford: Clarendon P.

Wollstadt, Lynn. 2003. "A Good Man Is Hard to Find: Positive Masculinity in the Songs Sung by Scottish Women." In *The Flowering Thorn: International Ballad Studies*, edited by Thomas A. McKean, 67–75. Logan: Utah State UP.

Ziolkowski, Jan M. 2009. *Fairy Tales from Before Fairy Tales: The Medieval Latin Past of Wonderful Lies.* Ann Arbor: U Michigan P.

———. 2010. "Straparola and the Fairy Tale: Between Literary and Oral Traditions." *Journal of American Folklore* 123: 377–97.

Zipes, Jack. 2012. *The Irresistible Fairy Tale: The Cultural and Social History of a Genre.* Princeton, NJ: Princeton UP.

Mediagraphy

Black Mountain. 1985. Created by Emile Benoit. Memorial University Digital Archives Initiative, DELTS Video Collection. http://collections.mun.ca/cdm/ref/collection/extension/id/3052/rec/1.

31

PEDAGOGY

Claudia Schwabe

Pedagogy is the academic discipline that deals with the theory and practice of education; it thus concerns the use of teaching strategies and methods inside and outside institutional settings. In this chapter, pedagogy is used synonymously with teaching. Fairy-tale pedagogy (in German *Märchenpädagogik*) refers to how to best instruct with and about the genre. It comprises two crucial aspects: first, the use of the fairy tale as a tool to support instruction in academic subjects other than fairy-tale studies, and, second, the critical teaching of the genre, its history, and its development. As Donald Haase states:

> The fairy tale becomes a tool of pedagogy when it is deliberately used to teach values, norms, behaviors, skills, or other lessons [. . .]. The fairy tale has lent itself to pedagogical uses because of its association with children and because of its kinship with other didactic forms such as the exemplum, fable, parable, and cautionary tale.
>
> (2008b, 734)

This chapter provides an overview of fairy tales' employment as pedagogical instruments throughout different stages of history and debunks the prevailing misconception that fairy tales as educational means are only tied to children and that these stories' pedagogical use is limited to Kindergarten and primary school settings. Fairy-tale pedagogy includes college and university courses with a focus on authors, on the genre's development, and on adaptations, as well as teaching across various disciplines and incorporating the genre into pedagogical methodology. This chapter also highlights the pedagogical role of media culture. As Christa C. Jones and Claudia Schwabe (2016) reveal, we are currently at the threshold of rethinking the pedagogical paradigm of the fairy tale.

Early Traditions of Fairy Tales and Pedagogy

Viewed historically, fairy tales are rooted in oral storytelling traditions. Early antecedents were primal tales that educated audiences about valuable life lessons and universal truths. As Jack Zipes states, "once a plethora of stories began to circulate in societies throughout the world, they contained the seeds of fairy tales, ironically tales at first without fairies formed by metaphor and metamorphosis and by a human disposition to communicate relevant experiences" (2012, 4). Primal tales provided their listeners with concrete examples of human conduct and offered general "guidelines on how to overcome serious challenges, [survive] struggles, or master problematic interpersonal relations" (Jones and Schwabe 2016, 3). Other early predecessors of fairy tales with educational purposes are tied to major religions—Hinduism, Buddhism, Judaism, Christianity, and Islam—and cultures. Spiritual lessons, moral instructions, and sagacious teachings are an integral part of many religious texts and miracle tales, such as Bible tales, Jataka tales (telling about the lives of the Buddha in both human and animal form), or the epic Sanskrit poem Ramayana. Ancient fables (fictitious narratives giving the semblance of truth, with the moral at the beginning or end), including the *Panchatantra* (an Indian collection of interrelated animal fables) and Aesop's fables, can also be considered early antecedents. In ancient Greek and Roman education, fables were employed as teaching tools in training exercises (*progymnasmata*) to instruct boys in prose composition and public speaking. Students were required to memorize fables, amplify or abbreviate them, or create stories of their own. As a pedagogical device, the fable introduced students to a simple narrative form that could be used as persuasive examples in actual court cases and in deliberative settings (Ochs 1996, 640).

For centuries, folktales and fairy tales in Europe served the cause of adult entertainment (Tatar 2007, 285). Literary fairy tales were written first for upper-class audiences and mainly for adult readers (Zipes 1997, 78; Seifert 2006, 1), but it was not until the writings of the intellectual and witty French salon women (such as Charlotte-Rose Caumont de La Force, Marie-Jeanne L'Héritier de Villandon, Henriette-Julie de Murat, and Marie-Catherine d'Aulnoy) and a few men (such as Charles Perrault) in the late seventeenth century that the fairy tale became increasingly associated with children. Lewis Seifert observes, "it appears that the association of folk- and fairy tales with an archetypal storytelling for children was an integral part of the salon game" (2006, 45). As pedagogical aid, the genre is closely tied to the emergence of children's literature and the concept of childhood as a separate stage of life in the seventeenth and eighteenth centuries.

French literary fairy tales were translated, shortened, simplified, significantly altered, and ultimately published as a series of inexpensive chapbooks, known as *Bibliothèque Bleue*, which were then widely disseminated and read to children and the lower classes (O'Sullivan 2010, 95). Works by John Locke and Jean Jacques Rousseau vastly influenced the growing cultural consensus about childhood's importance (Popiel 2008, 52). With the invention of childhood, the child was gradually separated from adult society and delivered into the hands of new institutions such as schools, colleges, and the nuclear family. "The notion that children needed to be subjected to the civilizing process and to a system of education generated the need for pedagogical tools, and the fairy tale was soon enlisted in the service of teaching children" (Haase 2008b, 734). Early examples for the use of fairy tales as means to teach children morals and virtues include the didactic tales written by French Roman Catholic archbishop and theologian François Fénelon in the 1690s, Sarah Fielding's *The Governess; or, Little Female Academy* (1749), and Jeanne-Marie Leprince de Beaumont's *Magasin des enfants* (1756–1757) and *Magasin des adolescents* (1760) (Zipes 1999, 16–17).

While French literary fairy tales feature fairies as recurring pedagogues who emphasize the moral lessons of the story, the German collection *Kinder- und Hausmärchen* (Children's and Household Tales, 1812–1815) by Jacob and Wilhelm Grimm largely forgoes fairies as magical mentors. Instead, the Grimms considered their entire collection, which encapsulates fundamental educational and social values for adults and children alike, to be an "educational manual" (*Erziehungsbuch*) for the German folk (Grimm and Grimm 1815, VIII). Although less didactic in nature than the French moralistic tales, the Grimms' collection was conceived first and foremost as an instrument of national pedagogy to preserve German heritage, culture, and identity. Initially composing with an adult readership in mind, the Grimms later embellished, sanitized, and reworked their tales to tailor them to what they perceived to be of educational benefit for children. They eliminated profanity and sexual references, included Christian prayers and values, expanded on narrative, and added illustrations. By the second half of the nineteenth century, the Grimms' *Kinder- und Hausmärchen* had been incorporated as educational primers into the Prussian elementary teaching curriculum (Bottigheimer 1991, 199).

In Victorian England, Edgar Taylor and his cousin John Edward Taylor helped transform the Grimms' tales into classical fairy tales for children by adding humorous illustrations and making sentimental changes that appealed to young readers (Zipes 2014, 88). Along with other middle-class writers, educators, publishers, and parents, Edgar Taylor took an anti-Enlightenment stance, resisting the rigid exclusion of fairy tales and fictional works in the age of reason. In his introduction to *German Popular Stories*, a translation of some of Grimms' tales, he emphasizes imagination as an important part equal to the cultivation of reason for moral education (1823, v).

Although many publications of fairy tales contained didactic lessons intended for children, most Victorian writers also had in mind adult middle-class readers whose ideas could be challenged and reformed. Writers explored the potential of fairy tales as a form of literary communication to convey individual and social protest. Between 1840 and 1880 prominent fairy-tale writers, such as John Ruskin, William Makepeace Thackeray, and Frances Browne, used the genre as a socio-critical, educational instrument to raise public awareness about social inequality and the Industrial Revolution's negative effects. As Zipes elaborates:

> Numerous writers took a philanthropic view of the poor and underprivileged and sought to voice a concern about the cruel exploitation and deprivation of the young. It was almost as though the fairy tales were to instill a spirit of moral protest in the readers [. . .] so that they would take a noble and ethical stand against forces of intolerance and authoritarianism.
>
> (1987, xix)

International Responses to Fairy-Tale Pedagogy in the Nineteenth and Twentieth Centuries

Throughout the nineteenth and twentieth centuries, the pedagogical use of fairy tales, whether for children or adults, was frequently disputed. In nineteenth-century Britain, for instance, a leading figure of the anti-fairy-tale school was the prolific and devoutly evangelical writer of children's literature Mary Martha Sherwood. In *The Governess, or The Little Female Academy*, a revision of Sarah Fielding's work from 1749, Sherwood sharply criticizes fairy tales as "improper medium of instruction because it would be absurd in such tales to introduce Christian principles as motives of action" (1820, 88). In contrast, strong advocate German Egyptologist and novelist Georg Ebers saw the banishment of fairy tales from a child's life as "perverse and unjust" (*verkehrt und ungerecht*) (1893, 20). Driven by his own positive childhood experiences with fairy tales, he defended the genre with "voice and pen" (*Wort und Schrift*) against all opponents (20). He argued:

> A pedagogue who would banish fairy tales would [. . .] also condemn religion or anything else that could exercise any influence on the hearts and dispositions of children; for even religion is not of this world, having little to do with fact, and faith, its foundation, ceasing where knowledge begins.
>
> (1890, 253)

When the Grimms' stories were translated on a large scale in China during the early 1920s, Chinese scholars and translators valued their moral nature so highly that they referred to them as "educational fairy tales" (Hung 1985, 124). To some followers of the Chinese Folk Literature Movement (1918–1943), such as Zhao Jingshen, the tales' educational intention "gave an extra incentive to introduce the Grimm tales rather than other foreign fairy tales in China, as their pedagogical purpose coincided with the aim of reforming the existing traditional Chinese culture by educating the Chinese masses through popular literature" (Li 2014, 127). While numerous scholars praised the moralistic messages of the Grimms' fairy tales, others were more critical. Although inspired by the Brothers Grimm and their notions on folk literature studies, Chinese folklorist and writer Zhou Zuoren held an ambivalent attitude toward several of their fairy tales, especially those with substantial moral overtones. From his point of view, fairy tales should be free from any political indoctrination and moralistic instruction. If the tales were to play a role in children's education, they should have a literary rather than a moral function (Li 2014, 126).

In 1928, leading Soviet "pedologists" edited the anthology *We Are Against the Fairy Tale* (Balina 2005, 105–106). As a new educational approach in the study of children's behavior and development, pedology was intended to supersede the established pedagogy and was heralded as an "empirical, scientific discipline" (*Pedagogicheskaia entsiklopediia* 1928, 91). Pedologists' highly negative attitude toward folk and fairy tales stemmed from their belief that folk and fairy lore reflected the ideology of the ruling classes and reiterated aristocratic values. According to Felix J. Oinas, "A special Children's Proletkul't ('Proletarian Cultural and Educational Organization') sought to eradicate folktales on the basis that they glorified tsars and tsareviches, corrupted and instigated sickly fantasies in children, developed the *kulak* ('wealthy farmers') attitude, and strengthened bourgeois ideals" (1978, 77). Radical educators, such as Lenin's widow, Nadezhda Krupskaya, aimed to suppress the fairy tale as a relic of the former power structure. By 1924 Krupskaya's political influence had led to the exclusion of fairy tales from library shelves, and in an attack on the satirical writer Korney Chukosvky four years later she denounced his literary fairy tales as "bourgeois nonsense" (Dobrenko 1997, 173; Balina 2005, 106).

During the Third Reich, the Nazis abused the fairy tale as pedagogical instrument and pressed the genre into the service of National Socialist propaganda. To promote their racist ideology in Germany before and during WWII, the Nazis exploited and perverted the Grimms' tales in particular, chosen for close association with the idea of German nationalism, which the Nazis perceived as the stories' important Nordic cultural heritage. Used as instruction material and entertainment for the Hitler Youth, the tales were thoroughly politicized in print and film and conscripted into the German war effort (Haase 2008a, 457). After the war, politicians, scholars of literature, writers, and laypersons in the Allied occupation zones heavily debated the pedagogical value and educational purpose of the Grimms' tales. Considering the fairy tale's function as cornerstone of National Socialism's educational system, Anglo-American occupation forces in 1945 banned the publication of new fairy-tale editions and reduced fairy tales in teaching curricula (Bastian 1981, 186; Shen 2015, 8). At the initiative of the British military government, German reading books were scrutinized for "brutal" fairy tales because the authorities believed that the cruelty depicted in them was partially responsible for the atrocities of Nazism. Furthermore, British occupation forces criticized the folktales and accused them of providing children with the illusion of a "fantasy world" that does not correspond to reality (Bastian 1981, 186).

In the first years of the Federal Republic and the East German Democratic Republic (GDR), pedagogues continued to debate the role of fairy tales in education and children's literature. For East Germany, with its mission of molding people into proper citizens, the prime question was whether or not fairy tales would be suitable for socialism. "The popularity and folksiness of fairy tales in the end trumped their bourgeois editorial imprint and redeemed them to socialist advantage" (Shen 2015, 8). In 1952, a new, "improved" version of the Grimms' tales published in the GDR contained major revisions, more happy endings, no Christian prayers, and less violence (Jarvis 2008, 410). Following the Grimms' tales' rehabilitation in the divided German nation, the 1960s and 1970s saw a reevaluation of the fairy tale's pedagogical potential around the globe. While socio-critical scholars excoriated fairy tales for being violent, causing fear, and instilling in children a false sense of reality, Austrian-American psychoanalyst Bruno Bettelheim argued that children need fairy tales:

> The figures and events of fairy tales [. . .] personify and illustrate inner conflicts, but they suggest ever so subtly how these conflicts may be solved, and what the next step in the development toward higher humanity might be [. . .]. The fairy tale reassures, gives hope for the future, and holds out the promise of a happy ending.
>
> (1976, 26)

André F. Favat's *Child and Tale* (1977) also focuses on child psychology but explores why children are drawn to fairy tales. His research suggests that traditional tales appeal to very young children because many of the genre's characteristics correspond with those that Swiss psychologist Jean Piaget ascribed to pre-reading and early reading ages. Besides emerging discussions about the fairy tale's place in child development that drew on notable psychologists, including Sigmund Freud, Carl Jung, Bettelheim, and Favat, educators worldwide challenged conservative ideologies by reclaiming the stories in fresh and innovative ways. Gianni Rodari, one of the most original twentieth-century Italian pedagogues and writers of children's literature, based on his belief in the power of storytelling and the liberating force of the written word, developed a series of pedagogical techniques for teachers and parents to invent fairy tales and playful activities for children to collaborate in the creative process (Miele 2008, 810–812). His unique approaches and methods of empowering children to tap into their imaginative minds and to hone their skills in storytelling have earned Rodari an international reputation among schools and educators (Haase 2008b, 735).

Fairy-Tale Pedagogy and Higher Education in the Twenty-First Century

Between 1990 and 2010, little work addressed approaches to teaching fairy tales at the college and university level. Most focused mainly on Kindergarten, early childhood education, and the elementary classroom (e.g., Bosma 1992; Polette 2005). Angelika Kraemer (2008) and Kim Snowden (2010) have taken the vanguard, showing numerous reasons why the fairy tale in visual and print media offers an excellent pedagogical instrument in the higher education classroom.

For example, due to folk and fairy tales' plain language and compact form, instructors in foreign-language and translation courses frequently use them to teach vocabulary, grammatical principles, and other language-specific skills (Haase 2008b, 735). Of course, teachers are not limited to folktales but can draw on the often more complex and ambitious literary fairy tale, or *Kunstmärchen*. Yet traditional fairy tales often prove more challenging to interpret than longer texts that appear to lend themselves more readily to decoding. Due to the versatile themes imbedded in classical tales and the astonishingly diverse landscape of modern retellings in print and media, the genre is appropriate for various interdisciplinary fields, including literature and language studies, creative writing, linguistics, gender studies, queer studies, feminist studies, cultural studies, psychology, history, anthropology, film and media studies, and political studies. Particularly in cultural and media studies, the genre lends itself to pedagogical use across media.

Recently more scholars have engaged with fairy-tale pedagogy at the higher education level. Moving beyond the traditional fairy-tale canon—especially as represented by the Brothers Grimm, Charles Perrault, Hans Christian Andersen, and Walt Disney—Christine A. Jones and Jennifer Schacker's anthology (2012) challenges the common pedagogical strategy of organizing fairy-tale textbooks and courses according to motifs and countries. Instead, they assemble international texts chronologically, add new translations, and highlight contemporary critical approaches, from both literary scholars and folklorists, on key concepts. Not only are these editors reflexive about their own research and instruction, they also offer future fairy-tale scholars, students, and aficionados refreshing insights into new ways of thinking about and engaging with the genre. For example, Snowden elaborates how she incorporates fairy-tale films, in particular Neil Jordan's *The Company of Wolves*, into her Women's Studies course curriculum. Approaching the film through the lens of feminist pedagogy, Snowden teaches her students about representations of female archetypes in fairy tales, discussing socially constructed ideas of gender, femininity, sexuality, and beauty.

New Approaches to Teaching Folk and Fairy Tales (Jones and Schwabe 2016) is the first volume in fairy-tale studies to deal exclusively with pedagogical tactics, methods, and strategies in higher education and foreground new scholarly perspectives that expand the scope of courses beyond strict disciplinary boundaries. In this anthology, a group of sixteen international scholars provide invaluable information on the pedagogical uses of fairy tales and detail teaching strategies that help them reach their educational objectives and goals. By reading through a critical lens, scholars also demonstrate how the fairy tale can be used to help students increase critical thinking abilities, strengthen writing skills, and explore cultural values. At the post-secondary level, students may discover that exercising their critical faculties guided by fairy-tale pedagogy can lead to more sophisticated insights not only about the discipline of study but also about maxims and truths that apply to their own lives and reality.

Most students nowadays encounter fairy tales for the first time through film and television, especially the Disney versions. Born and raised in Western culture, for them Disney is synonymous with fairy tales. Scholars can seize this teaching opportunity to open students' eyes and minds to the genre's rich and diverse history. While fairy tales have often been positioned as escapist, distinguished fairy-tale scholars Maria Tatar and Christina Phillips Mattson stress that fairy tales and fantasy literature

> are less a way out than a way in, an escape into perils and possibilities. Moving in the optative mode, they tell us how things might be, should be, could be, or ought to be. These stories give us the great "what ifs?" and they introduce students to hypotheticals, giving them worlds that may not be real yet also characters that shape their identities in much the same way as people in real life.
>
> (2016, 23)

With more higher education classrooms equipped with instructional technology, teachers can draw on media as pedagogical aids to teach about the genre's cultural and historical foundations, to analyze why fairy tales continue to fascinate readers and viewers, to help students develop their analytical and critical thinking skills, to examine the relationships between mediated and printed fairy tales, or to inform students about sociohistorical, feminist, queer, and Marxist approaches to analyzing fairy tales. Kraemer describes the advantages of using media and technology as teaching tools in a fourth-year German-language course on fairy tales at Michigan State University. Fairy tales were selected because of their popularity among students, their short length, their level of vocabulary, their potential for teaching about culture, and their accessibility online (2008, 63). Through interactive online assignments about fairy tales, such as Web quests (online scavenger hunts) and the exploration of different websites (online books, audio files, and videos), Kraemer's students were able to read, listen to, watch, and learn about fairy tales and their cultural histories in new, creative, and fun ways (2008, 66–67). Pauline Greenhill and Jennifer Orme (2016) demonstrate the benefits and disadvantages of delivering a Women's and Gender Studies fairy-tale film course entirely online, concluding that taking best advantage of the mediated format means that the result is neither better nor worse than live courses. Several fairy-tale themed MOOCs (Massive Open Online Courses) are available, with quality ranging from the superb (e.g., Thomsen, Frandsen, Bøggild, and Möller-Christensen) to the abysmal. Potential students need to scrutinize the instructors' credentials; the topic's popularity means that some courses are prepared by instructors with only the most superficial understanding of the genre and are rife with misinformation, misconceptions, and blatant errors.

Thanks to fast-growing modern technologies and the rapidly expanding number of Internet forums, online newspapers, blogs, wikis, video-sharing websites, video games, and social media, educators are in an excellent position to benefit from these vast resources. The advancement of publicly accessible online fairy-tale research databases such as the International Fairy-Tale Filmography and the Fairy-Tale Teleography offer significant educational opportunities to teachers and students alike. Other helpful online resources for teaching fairy tales in the post-secondary classroom include privately owned websites, blogs, and social media pages. Heidi Anne Heiner's invaluable website *SurLaLune Fairy Tales* features hyperlinked textual annotations to numerous international fairy tales, guides for teachers and students, histories of tales, bibliographies, illustrations, modern interpretations of tales, a blog, and book galleries. Tracey A. Callison's research website *Folk and Fairy* offers a vast selection of print sources from literary traditions ranging from feminism to psychology to Marxism. Noteworthy blogs are Maria Tatar's *Breezes from Wonderland*, Kristin's *Tales of Faerie*, Tahlia Merrill Kirk's *Diamonds & Toads*, and Amy Kraft and Sophie Bushwick's *Tabled Fables*, which also features eight illuminating fairy-tale podcasts. Now that the first necessary steps have been taken to validate the use of folk and fairy tales in the higher education classroom, the way is paved for future generations of scholars and educators to explore the fairy tale's abundant possibilities and pedagogical potential.

Related topics: Blogs and Websites; Children's and Young Adult (YA) Literature; Children's Television; Cinematic; Gender; Language

References Cited and Further Reading

Balina, Marina. 2005. "Fairy Tales of Socialist Realism: Introduction." In *Politicizing Magic: An Anthology of Russian and Soviet Fairy Tales*, edited by Marina Balina, Helena Goscilo, and Mark Lipovetsky, 105–21. Evanston, IL: Northwestern UP.

Bastian, Ulrike. 1981. *Die "Kinder- und Hausmärchen" der Brüder Grimm in der literaturpädagogischen Diskussion des 19. und 20. Jahrhunderts.* Frankfurt am Main: Haag & Herchen.

Bettelheim, Bruno. 1976. *The Uses of Enchantment: The Meaning and Importance of Fairy Tales.* New York: Random House.

Bosma, Bette. 1992. *Fairy Tales, Fables, Legends, and Myths: Using Folk Literature in Your Classroom.* New York: Teachers College P.

Bottigheimer, Ruth B. 1991. "From Gold to Guilt: The Forces Which Reshaped Grimms' Tales." In *The Brothers Grimm and Folktale*, edited by James M. McGlathery, 192–204. Chicago: U Illinois P.

Dobrenko, Evgenii. 1997. *Formirovka sovetskogo chitatelia*. St. Petersburg: Akademicheskii proekt.

Ebers, Georg. 1890. "A Plea for the Fairy Tale." In *The Review of Reviews*, edited by W. T. Stead, 253. Vol. 2. London: Mowbray House.

———. 1893. *Die Geschichte meines Lebens: Vom Kind bis zum Manne*. Stuttgart: Deutsche Verlags-Anstalt.

Favat, André F. 1977. *Child and Tale: The Origins of Interest*. Urbana, IL: National Council of Teachers of English.

Fielding, Sarah. 1749. *The Governess, or, Little Female Academy*. London: Andrew Millar.

Greenhill, Pauline, and Jennifer Orme. 2016. "Teaching 'Gender in Fairy-Tale Films and Cinematic Folklore' Online: Negotiating Between Needs and Wants." In *New Approaches*, edited by Jones and Schwabe, 206–26.

Grimm, Jacob, and Wilhelm Grimm. 1815. *Kinder- und Hausmärchen. Gesammelt durch die Brüder Grimm*. Vol. 2. Berlin: Realschulbuchhandlung.

Haase, Donald. 2008a. "Fairy Tales, Hope, and the Culture of Defeat from the Postbellum American South to Postwar Germany." In *Kriegs- und Nachkriegskindheiten: Studien zur literarischen Erinnerungskultur für junge Leser*, edited by Gabriele von Glasenapp and Hans-Heino Ewers, 455–64. Frankfurt am Main: Peter Lang.

———. 2008b. "Pedagogy." In *The Greenwood Encyclopedia of Folktales and Fairy Tales*, edited by Donald Haase, 734–5. Westport: Greenwood Publishing.

Hung, Chang-tai. 1985. *Going to the People: Chinese Intellectuals and Folk Literature, 1918–1937*. Cambridge, MA: Harvard UP.

Jarvis, Shawn C. 2008. "German Tales." In *The Greenwood Encyclopedia of Folktales and Fairy Tales*, edited by Donald Haase, 404–13. Westport: Greenwood Publishing.

Jones, Christa C., and Claudia Schwabe, eds. 2016. *New Approaches to Teaching Folk and Fairy Tales*. Logan: Utah State UP.

Jones, Christine A., and Jennifer Schacker, eds. 2012. *Marvelous Transformations: An Anthology of Fairy Tales and Contemporary Critical Perspectives*. Peterborough, ON: Broadview P.

Kraemer, Angelika. 2008. "Happily Ever After: Integrating Language and Literature through Technology?" *Die Unterrichtspraxis/Teaching German* 41 (1): 67–71.

Leprince de Beaumont, Jeanne-Marie. 1756–1757. *Magasin des enfants, ou Dialogues d'une sage gouvernante avec ses eleves de la premiere distinction*. 4 vols. London: J. Haberkorn.

———. 1760. *Magasin des adolescentes, ou Dialogues d'une sage gouvernante avec ses eleves de la premiere distinction*. Lyon: Jean-Baptiste Reguilliat.

Li, Dechao. 2014. "The Influence of the Grimms' Fairy Tales on the Folk Literature Movement in China (1918–1943)." In *Grimms' Tales around the Globe: The Dynamics of Their International Reception*, edited by Vanessa Joosen and Gillian Lathey, 119–34. Detroit: Wayne State UP.

Miele, Gina M. 2008. "Gianni Rodari." In *The Greenwood Encyclopedia of Folktales and Fairy Tales*, edited by Donald Haase, 810–12. Westport: Greenwood Publishing.

Ochs, Donovan J. 1996. "Roman Rhetoric: The Progymnasmata." In *Encyclopedia of Rhetoric and Composition: Communication from Ancient Times*, edited by Theresa Enos, 636–43. New York: Routledge.

Oinas, Felix J. 1978. "The Political Uses and Themes of Folklore in the Soviet Union." In *Folklore, Nationalism and Politics*, edited by Felix J. Oinas, 77–97. Columbus, OH: Slavica.

O'Sullivan, Emer. 2010. *Historical Dictionary of Children's Literature*. Lanham, MD: Scarecrow P.

Pedagogicheskaia entsiklopediia. 1928. Vol. 2. Moscow: Rabotnik prosveshcheniia.

Polette, Nancy. 2005. *Teaching Thinking Skills with Fairy Tales and Fantasy*. Westport, CT: Libraries Unlimited.

Popiel, Jennifer J. 2008. *Rousseau's Daughters: Domesticity, Education, and Autonomy in Modern France*. Lebanon, NH: UP New England.

Seifert, Lewis. 2006. *Fairy Tales, Sexuality, and Gender in France, 1690–1715: Nostalgic Utopias*. Cambridge: Cambridge UP.

Shen, Qinna. 2015. *The Politics of Magic: DEFA Fairy-Tale Films*. Detroit: Wayne State UP.

Sherwood, Mary Martha. 1820. *The Governess, or the Little Female Academy*. Wellington: Salop.

Snowden, Kim. 2010. "Fairy Tale Film in the Classroom: Feminist Cultural Pedagogy, Angela Carter, and Neil Jordan's *The Company of Wolves*." In *Fairy Tale Films: Visions of Ambiguity*, edited by Pauline Greenhill and Sidney Eve Matrix, 157–77. Logan: Utah State UP.

Tatar, Maria. 2007. "Reading Fairy Tales." In *Crosscurrents of Children's Literature: An Anthology of Texts and Criticism*, edited by John Daniel Stahl, Tina L. Hanlon, and Elizabeth Lennox Keyser, 284–91. Oxford: Oxford UP.

Tatar, Maria, and Christina Phillips Mattson. 2016. "Fairy Tales, Myth, and Fantasy." In *New Approaches*, edited by Jones and Schwabe, 21–34.

Taylor, Edgar, trans. 1823. *German Popular Stories: Translated from the Kinder- und Hausmärchen; Collected by M. M. Grimm, from Oral Tradition*. London: Baldwyn.

Zipes, Jack. 1987. *Victorian Fairy Tales: The Revolt of the Fairies and Elves*. New York: Routledge.

———. 1997. *Happily Ever After: Fairy Tales, Children, and the Culture Industry*. New York: Routledge.

———. 1999. *When Dreams Came True: Classical Fairy Tales and Their Tradition*. New York: Routledge.

———. 2012. *The Irresistible Fairy Tale: The Cultural and Social History of a Genre*. Princeton, NJ: Princeton UP.

———. 2014. *Grimm Legacies: The Magic Spell of the Grimms' Folk and Fairy Tales*. Princeton, NJ: Princeton UP.

PEDAGOGY

Mediagraphy

At the Crossroads of Data and Wonder: Algorithmic Visualizations of Fairy Tales on Television. 2014. Creators Jill Terry Rudy, Jarom McDonald, Kristy Stewart, and Jessie Riddle. http://fttv.byu.edu.

Callison, Tracey A. N.d. "Sources for the Analysis and Interpretation of Folk and Fairy Tales." Folk and Fairy. www.folkandfairy.org.

The Company of Wolves. 1984. Director Neil Jordan. UK.

Heiner, Heidi Anne. 1999. *SurLaLune Fairy Tales.* www.surlalunefairytales.com.

International Fairy-Tale Filmography. 2014–. Creators Jack Zipes, Pauline Greenhill, and Kendra Magnus-Johnston. http://iftf.uwinnipeg.ca.

Kirk, Tahlia Merrill. 2007. *Diamonds & Toads.* www.diamondsandtoads.com.

Kraft, Amy, and Sophie Bushwick. 2012. *Tabled Fables: A Podcast about Fairy Tales.* http://tabledfables.tumblr.com.

Kristin. 2010. *Tales of Faerie.* http://talesoffaerie.blogspot.de.

Tatar, Maria. 2009. "Maria Tatar's Forum for Storytelling, Folklore, and Children's Literature." Breezes from Wonderland. https://blogs.harvard.edu/tatar/.

Thomsen, Torsten Bøgh, Johannes Nørregaard Frandsen, Jacob Bøggild, and Ivy York Möller-Christensen. N.d. "Hans Christian Andersen's Fairy Tales." Class Central. www.class-central.com/mooc/3487/futurelearn-hans-christian-andersen-s-fairy-tales.

32

SEXUALITIES/QUEER AND TRANS STUDIES

Pauline Greenhill

Fairy tales are prodigiously queer in every possible way, though, as Lewis C. Seifert notes, they are "overwhelmingly perceived as heterosexual" (2015a, 16). Fairy tales'—both oral and literary—strangeness, oddity, and/or bizarreness are indisputable. Much more controversial is their queerness as:

> designat[ing] those genders and sexualities that resist [. . .] normative constructions, including not only gay male and lesbian sexualities but also nonnormative heterosexualities and the range of gender expressions often classified as transgender. As forms of resistance to the heteronormative order, queer genders and sexualities aim to destabilize the binaries (such as masculine-feminine, heterosexual-homosexual, dominant-submissive, active-passive) that are so central to upholding normative categories.
>
> (16)

Seifert also notes "queer" as a verb, reading "against the grain so as to pick up signs and meanings neglected or obscured by heteronormative interpretations" (16). This chapter works thus—queering fairy tales, but also sexes, sexualities, and genders in fairy-tale media. "Sexes" refers to (outward physical indicators of) genetic distinctions between humans, including the conventional male and female, but also intersex.[1] "Sexualities" mean the multiple ways that human erotic life displays within relationships, including both feelings and actions. "Genders" designate social and cultural manifestations of the allegedly natural, biological distinctions of sex, including transgender "people whose gender identity, expression or behavior is different from those typically associated with their assigned sex at birth" (National Center for Transgender Equality 2014) and cisgender people whose gender identity and expression match their assigned sex. I explore these subjects through looking at how scholars have understood (queer) fairy tales and media and how media have constructed (queer) fairy-tale characters, closing with the example of Hans Christian Andersen's tale "The Snow Queen."[2]

Queer(ing) Fairy Tales

Fairy tales can also queer in the verb sense of spoiling or ruining. Despite their heteronormative reputation, fairy tales' traditional, literary, and mediated adapted forms resist attempts to constrain them within prescribed limits. Yet anyone giving public talks about fairy tales as queer texts often finds herself defending the very idea of sullying these allegedly innocent stories by suggesting they might not be always resolutely heterosexual. The experience recalls film scholar Alexander Doty's work interpreting beloved films as queer and the enthusiastic resistance encountered there: "Rarely do such battles produce more rancor than when you are trying to convince people, queer and straight, that a 'popular,' 'mass,' 'mainstream,' 'classic' text might be understood queerly" (2000, 4). Indeed, fairy tales can be profoundly threatening; Lithuanian censors in 2014 banned "a collection of fairy tales for children about minorities. At issue were two tales depicting same-sex love" (Seifert 2015a, 15). Seifert argues that "the magic of the fairy tales [. . .] was all too threatening and all too real because they had the power to reshape their readers' understanding of what constituted sexual relations, marriage, and family" (2015a, 15). Despite great resistance, however, fairy-tale scholars have outed—analyzed, explored, and revealed the queerness of—tales in various media.

We acknowledge Seifert as the first English-language scholar to consider non-mainstream, non-heteronormative sexualities in fairy tales (1996). Many since have examined non-heterosexuality, transgender, and non-binary sex in twentieth- and twenty-first-century literary rewritings (e.g. Hennard 2009). But with few exceptions until Kay Turner and Pauline Greenhill's anthology of critical essays (2012), traditional oral versions received scant attention. That work queered folktales including "Clever Gretel" (ATU 1741) and "Clever Else" (ATU 1450, Bacchilega 2012); "The Maiden Who Seeks Her Brothers" (ATU 451, Jorgensen 2012); "Princess Mouseskin" (ATU 923, Fairfield 2012); and "Frau Trude" (ATU 334, Turner 2012, 2015); as well as the complex, multi-ATU-type Canadian stories "Peg Bearskin" and "La Poiluse" (Greenhill, Best, and Andersen-Grégoire 2012). Other traditional tales queered include "Sleeping Beauty" (ATU 410, Seifert 2015b); "The Shift of Sex" (ATU 514, Greenhill and Andersen-Grégoire 2014); "Fitcher's Bird" (ATU 311, Greenhill 2008); and "Hans My Hedgehog" (ATU 441, Greenhill 2014). Rarely, fairy-tale scholars have addressed queer fairy-tale media, including Anne Duggan's (2013) study of queer director Jacques Demy's films, particularly *Donkey Skin* (1970), *The Pied Piper* (1972), and *Lady Oscar* (1979); Jennifer Orme's (2015) exploration of David Kaplan's film *Little Red Riding Hood* (1979); and Tison Pugh's (2015) work on the illustrations of the Wizard of Oz books.

Seifert points out that queering fairy tales often requires "paying closer attention to the journey fairy-tale characters make—and not letting ourselves get overly preoccupied with their destination" (2015a, 18). Too often the fairy-tale source provides an unshakeable alibi for the straight (and the narrow) despite inescapably queer content. Much queer fairy-tale scholarship simply points out the obvious—a character who begins as female and is magically transformed into a man as trans or two female characters kissing and declaring their undying love as lesbian—noting "erotic innuendo hiding in plain sight" (17), as Seifert describes Pugh's (2015) readings of the Oz illustrations.

Films about the Chinese character Mulan (see Li 2016) exemplify such actions. The tale may be a version of ATU 514**, involving a woman who dresses as a man and becomes a soldier—a familiar ballad trope (see Greenhill 1995). Mulan as a cross-dresser fits the broad definition of transgender, although the connection is rarely made, probably because of concerns about queering/spoiling. Recent American mediations are problematic. Mulan became bisexual on the television show *Once Upon a Time* (2011–; "Quite a Common Fairy" 2013), tiresomely conflating transgender (gender) with lesbian/bisexual (sexuality) (Stryker 2006). With expressions of her lesbian attraction to character Aurora confined to sad, depressed looks and the heterosexual alibi of previous attraction to men, this Mulan not only irksomely represents the tragic unhappy lesbian/gay/bisexual trope (see, e.g., Ahmed 2010; Love 2007),[3] but also demonstrates the exasperating practice of multiply othering characters of color—already extremely scarce in the show.

PAULINE GREENHILL

(Making) Fairy Tales (Im)Perfectly Queer:
"The Snow Queen" and More

Yet some media denote less closeted representations of same-sex relationships. "Cinderella" (ATU 510A) is the perhaps surprising subject for several, given the character's Disney princess credentials and her reputation. But in Venezuelan-born director Fina Torres's *Celestial Clockwork* (1995), Cinderella is Ana, a Venezuelan operatic mezzo soprano in Paris, with not one but three princes charming, male, female, and male respectively: producer Italo Medici, seeking the perfect singer to play "Cinderella" in his film of Rossini's opera; and her romantic partner, Alcanie, finally admitting her love when she shows up at Ana's marriage to her gay friend, Armand, so she can stay in France and he can satisfy his family's wish for a church wedding (see Soliño 2001; Lawless 2015). Samoan Dan Taulapapa McMullin's multiple adaptations of "Sinalela"—video short, poems, and short story—about (intersexual) *fa'afafine* relocates "Cinderella" to "a Samoan specificity" that calls "to decolonize lands, economies, and minds" (Bacchilega 2013, 69). McMullin's work joyously counters the homophobia and transphobia encountered by *fa'afafine* and intersex folks under conditions of coloniality and refuses presumptions about the impossibility of a happy ending for those who don't fit the hegemonic mainstream. From the U.S., among other fairy-tale themed music videos he has made, Todrick Hall's "Cinderfella" (2014), which concludes with the banner "Legalize Love," has the pop singer attend a ball where he meets "Prince Charming," out former boy-band member Lance Bass.

These queer media texts are sadly rare. However, in a queer reading, the plethora of straight fairy-tale interpretations indicates the extent to which installing heteronormativity in the hegemonic mainstream requires relentless repetition and, as Doty points out, intensive interpretation. To suggest some of this labor—and to exemplify queering processes—I use the Andersen literary fairy tale "The Snow Queen." It offers already promising analytical material. Though ostensibly based around heterosexual relationships (between the boy Kai and the Snow Queen and between Kai and his friend Gerda) and a heterosexual quest (Gerda seeks Kai, taken by the Snow Queen), a closer look reveals their unconventionality. Gerda and Kai "were not brother and sister, but they were as fond of each other as if they had been" (Andersen and Tatar 2008, 22), yet most live-action films render this quasi-sibling relationship romantic. Further, Kai and the Snow Queen instantiate intergenerational love between a young boy and an adult woman—by no means mainstream, though arguably not as tabooed as connections between older men and children (see, e.g., Kohm and Greenhill 2014 on "Little Red Riding Hood" [ATU 333] films dealing with pedophilia).

Further, "The Snow Queen" explores relationships between Gerda and the women helpers/hinderers she meets on her quest. One old woman is "determined to keep little Gerda around" (Andersen and Tatar 2008, 37), and the princess whose bedroom Gerda invades gives her a pair of boots and a fur muff. Maria Tatar notes that "the fetishizing of feet and hands, along with boots and muffs, is intriguing given the chaste and pious register in which the tale moves" (Andersen and Tatar 2008, 49). The Finn woman, who "was walking around with practically nothing on," "help[s] Gerda unbutton and take off her mittens and boots" (58). In particular, Gerda and the Little Robber Girl have provided grist for lesbian interpretations. The Robber Girl's sadistic/sexual tendencies implicating Gerda are multiple: the Robber Girl declares that she will not let the robbers chop Gerda to pieces "because I'd rather do it myself" (53); demands that Gerda kiss one of her doves; and takes her to bed where she "clasped Gerda's neck with one arm, gripped her knife with her other hand" and tells her to "'lie still and be quiet [. . .] or else I'll poke you in the stomach with my knife" (55) (see Greenhill 2015, 115–116). An

292

interspecific love relationship manifests between Gerda and the reindeer, who when he needs to leave the girl "kissed her on the lips, while big sparkling tears ran down his cheeks" (59).

In addition, the association with Andersen queers the tale. Although his sexuality is controversial and disputed, his diaries and self-descriptions make it clear that he was by no means uncomplicatedly heterosexual. Biographer Jackie Wullschlager concludes that Andersen's life included "intense erotic relationships with men" along with attractions to both sexes (2000, 94; see Greenhill 2015, 116–119).

Based on my ongoing research (Greenhill 2015, 2016), I draw on three live-action "Snow Queen" film/television adaptations available in English, feature length, intended for adult and/or family audiences. My final example, the animated Disney (family) blockbuster *Frozen* (2013), has a tenuous connection to Andersen's story. But it shows how the production and marketing of consumer goods associated with a successful film—arguably its paratexts, working to frame its interpretation—constrain its (closeted) associations with non-normative sex, gender, and sexuality. I draw on folklorist Jo Radner's theorizing on feminist and queer coding. Her work suggests that multiple hearers and potentially taboo topics—as with "Snow Queen" family films in particular—may lead to coding:

> a set of signals—words, forms, behaviors, signifiers of some kind—that protect the creator from the consequences of openly expressing particular messages. Coding occurs in the context of complex audiences in which some members may be competent and willing to decode the message, but others are not.
>
> (Radner and Lanser 1993, 3)

Considering the many individuals involved in the production of even the simplest film, source and intentionality of coding become a problem. Who is responsible? Are codes deliberate or unconscious? While some film theories identify the director as the most significant individual creator or auteur (see, e.g., Stam 2000), coding can enter a movie at almost any level. Directors, but also writers, wardrobe and make-up people, editors, composers, and actors, among others, may participate in coding. And given the careful production of professional film and television, while accidents do happen, creators deliberate extensively the form and content of any final cut. Most material, then, is intentional. I do not presume that only gay, lesbian, bisexual, trans (and so on) folks create queer films or make queer readings or that only adults can decode sexual readings. Even the "Snow Queen" film clearly aimed only at adults can presume its audience as heterogeneous in terms of gender, sex (normativity), sexuality, feminist and queer sensibilities, and so forth.

Snow Queen Films and the (Absent) Lesbian Text

Male directors' live-action films of "The Snow Queen" tend to simultaneously present and absent non-normative sexualities. Philip Saville's made-for-TV *Hans Christian Andersen: My Life as a Fairy Tale* (2003) constitutes many of Andersen's stories as reflections of their writer's life and experiences.[4] Unsurprisingly, given its production for the U.S. family-oriented Hallmark Entertainment, Andersen's queering is coded. Though actor Kieran Bew's twitchy and affected performance in the title role invokes the term "queer," the film locates the writer's infatuations as heterosexual. It makes singer Jenny Lind—one of Andersen's actual crushes—the Snow Queen after she refuses his proposal of marriage.[5] One possibility film offers, exploited here, allows character-linking via use of the same actor. In scenes representing the tale, directly following Lind's rejection, Bew (Andersen) is Kai, besotted with the Snow Queen/Lind (actor Flora Montgomery), and Jette Collin (actor Emily Hamilton), whose love for the writer is unrequited, is Gerda.

Somewhat different processes manifest in *Snow Queen* (David Wu, 2002), which Jack Zipes calls:

> a well-made American melodrama in the Disney tradition [. . .]. It has all the "feel-good" elements of a Hollywood narrative [. . .] young pull-yourself-up-by-the-boot-straps hero, highly erotic villainess, valiant black-and-white struggle between the erotic force of evil and the pure and honest American soul, reconciliation between father and suitor for his daughter's hand, happy ending.
>
> (2011, 273–274)

In this "family film" (described by executive producer Robert Halmi Sr. in DVD extras), another Hallmark Entertainment production, Kai and Gerda are young adults. With a plethora of coding around other relationships, it nevertheless offers a clear representation of a lesbian crush by the Robber Girl on Gerda while simultaneously coding the im/possibility of lesbian relationships via humor and misdirection toward Gerda's heterosocial/heterosexual quest. Their first meeting has the Robber Girl jumping on Gerda from a tree, with the unlikely result that the two end up in the missionary position, the Robber Girl atop Gerda, their lips separated by a fraction of an inch. Producer Halmi says, "there are social issues and moral issues that children wouldn't quite understand," commenting that the Andersen story is for adults as much as children. He says, "The Snow Queen represents the ultimate temptation"—yet she is not so for Gerda, again coding lesbian im/possibility.

Women writers and critics often interpret "The Snow Queen" against a backdrop of Andersen's apparently (hetero)sexist intentions. Many confess an early obsession with the story, often identifying with the Snow Queen rather than Gerda. Filmmaker Danishka Esterhazy says:

> I had a big children's storybook of "The Snow Queen." And it was absolutely one of my favorite storybooks by far. I read it all the time. And I think I kind of misinterpreted it as a child, because I thought the Snow Queen was awesome. I thought the fact that she was really powerful and untouchable was just great. [Laughs.] Like she was a superhero. I was Team Snow Queen! I was like, Gerda? Whatever! It was the awesome Snow Queen who lives in this great palace and she's so fantastic. How can I end up with a life like that? How can I be like her?[6]

Feminists like Esterhazy and Catherine Breillat deliberately read outside and beyond what Andersen wanted his contemporaries to take from his story—a parable about religion and emotion versus science and knowledge.

Breillat's *La belle endormie* (Sleeping Beauty, 2010) "turn[s] the story of a passive princess who waits to be saved by a prince into a queer feminist tale" by "setting up a dialectic between" "Sleeping Beauty" as the frame story and "The Snow Queen" (Duggan 2016, 71). No family film, it makes Andersen's tale part of the dream the helpful fairies grant to the frame story's heroine, Anastasia, during her 100-year sleep. Yet dream and reality overlap. Anastasia meets Peter, her Kai figure, in her dream-world journey, and his grandson in the closing section. When Peter is spirited away by the Snow Queen, Anastasia goes on a quest to find him and encounters, among others, her Romany "Little Robber Girl," who appears in the waking narrative as an adult. Indeed, just as six-year-old Anastasia is about to complete her search for Peter, sixteen-year-old Anastasia awakens to find Johan, his grandson, in her bedroom. Their relationship proves less than ideal, and the film ends with a modern, pregnant Anastasia disenchanted with her Prince Charming.

Anastasia before pricking her finger and falling asleep calls herself "Sir Vladimir," climbs trees and hangs upside down from a branch, and asserts, "I am a boy!" When her father disagrees, she says, "I'm a princess and I decide"—thus Anastasia (Gerda) problematizes her own gender. Further, unlike male directors, who tend to archly wink in the direction of a lesbian relationship between Gerda and the Robber Girl, Breillat includes an explicit sex scene between the two as teenager and woman—outside the "Snow Queen" narrative section.

Frozen (2013) is in very limited ways a "Snow Queen" story, with two princesses, one of whom possesses a magical gift to turn what she touches to ice, eventually finding their love for one another, sealed by a kiss between the two. That they are sisters does not preclude their relationship being coded lesbian. Blogger Steven D. Greydanus (N.d.) offers an inventory of queer elements, from Elsa's "born this way" "difference" to her indifference to men to the family in the sauna. But the media merchandise tells quite another story. On Amazon.ca, *Frozen* themed items for sale included: "board books" with storybook, twelve figurines, and playmat; DVDs; plastic "Summer Olaf" toys; piano and guitar songbooks of soundtrack music; pop-up books; stickers; headphones; language arts games; jewelry boxes; socks; hand soap; umbrellas; apps; games; temporary tattoos; water bottles; snow globes; digital cameras; clogs; shampoo; party supply packs (table cover, paper plates and cups, napkins, and wrapping paper); travel trunks with dresses and accessories; bike helmets; plastic cups; markers and coloring book; curtains; lip balm; pillow cases; eBooks; "Little Kingdom Arendelle Treat Shoppe[s]"; toy bins; board games; candy; cake toppers; sing-along DVDs; lanyards; vitamins; wrapping paper; arm floats; fishing kits; "Adventure Kit[s] with Camera, Flashlight and Binoculars"; puzzles; pool sets; and happy birthday banners.

Strong gendering of these items manifests with the characters represented on and with them. On Amazon.ca, "Frozen Elsa" got 22,024 items and "Frozen Anna" 50,107; in contrast, "Frozen Olaf" got 14,591 and "Frozen Kristoff" 4,768, only just beating "Frozen Sven" at 4,746. Nonhuman male-named figures numerically dominate the primary male character. Even including nonhuman figures only 25% are male identified; when nonhuman figures are excluded, just under 5% are male identified. Presumptively, the market is girls.

Only girls appear to be depicted with the materials. A search for "Frozen Kristoff Costume" showed only pictures of the cartoon figure and the outfit on a mannequin. Female embodiments predominate, with conventional femininity represented in items like the "Crystal Kingdom Vanity" in which "Anna & Elsa Magically Appear in Mirror!" It has "LIGHTS & SOUNDS Plays 'For the First Time In Forever'" and "INCLUDES 3 Beauty Accessories." The box depicts a little blonde girl wearing a party dress with snowflakes on it, a snowflake pendant, and a tiara with Elsa's image on it. She presses the button to make Anna and Elsa manifest in the mirror. Pictures of a ride-on Jeep show an African American girl (passenger) and a White girl (driver). Of course, cisboys and trans girls may also want and obtain these items (and clearly, many do), but representing them as specifically girls' toys overdetermines their location.

Elsa's associated materials are almost all strongly gendered female: "Sparkle Princess Elsa" dolls; Elsa styling doll heads, advertising that the child playing with them can "Wear & Share Accessories"; "Tiara Snowflake Wand Braid Hair Piece and Blue Gloves Set"; "Slipper with Snow Queen Snowflake Wand"; throw and canvas tote; dress-up long white braided hair wig; an "Enchanted Ice Scepter"; a "Singing Elsa Cuddle Pillow"; "Elsas [sic] Magical Musical Gloves"; a giant party balloon; a "Frozen Castle" toy; night light; rain boots; pet tag; iPod Touch case; phone case; and shoes. The majority of these items are clothing or accessories. Olaf the snowman, in contrast, has generally gender-neutral stuff: a ceramic mug; iced tea set; Nintendo game "Olaf's Quest"; "Melting Olaf the Snowman Kit" with book; chicken soup; and explicitly designated "boys" underpants.

Though Anna has a few of her own items, including singing dolls, costumes, and wall decals, she often appears with her sister. Anna and Elsa have "little girls" swimsuits; backpacks; athletic shoes; pajamas; luncheon napkins; watches; garden tool sets with purple gloves, fork, and shovel; wallets; thermoses; rain coats; duct tape; rolling suitcases; (girls') underpants; bathing suits; purses; slippers; diary sets; Jenga games; party hats; "Royal Closet Gift Set[s]"; and "Beauty Kit[s]" with lip balm, lip gloss, press-on nails, nail gems, nail stickers, "Strong Heart Nail File," and zippered case—again, mainly strongly gendered feminine.

Items picturing Anna, Elsa, and Olaf together are much more gender neutral: wall decals; toothbrush and toothpaste set to "Make brushing magical!"; karaoke sets; door posters; pencil cases; backpack and lunch box; "edible icing image cake decoration toppers"; "Kids Reversible Double Duvet Cover Bedding Set"; baseball caps; stationery set; growth charts; art sets; boom boxes; bandages; acoustic guitars; chairs; alarm clocks; photo booth props; party decorations; and swim rings.

Video games are notoriously heterosexist, but also notoriously princess-focused: "the original Donkey Kong (1981) game featured the player as the male plumber Mario attempting to rescue Princess Zelda from the giant male ape" (Consalvo 2003, 172). Princesses are not limited to fairy tales, but are strongly associated with them, thanks in large part to the Disney Princesses franchise, though neither Elsa nor Anna is "included in the official line-up" thereof ("List" N.d.). The games and apps associated with *Frozen* are highly sexist: Olaf gets to go on a quest or skating; Elsa and Anna get makeovers and cook. I note, however, thefrozengames.com, which includes several "hot" items including "Frozen Elsa Birth Care," "Elsa Frozen Flirting Realife," and "Spank Princess Elsa [sic] Butt."

As demonstrated, heteronormativity does not entirely rule the fairy-tale world. While traditional fairy tales often included same-sex romances, interspecific relationships, and other queer indices, those which did were not the best-known examples of the form. However, feminist and queer artists and their allies have begun creating alternatives, using recognizable figures like Cinderella or Rapunzel. One need only search the Internet for such materials, where lesbian princesses search for sex and love (see Tan 2016), interracial same-sex romances are celebrated, and all sorts of magical transformations are possible.

Related topics: Adaptation and the Fairy-Tale Web; Advertising; Cinematic; Disney Corporation; Gender; Material Culture; Music Videos and Pop Music; Video Games; YouTube and Internet Video

Notes

1. As described by the Intersex Society of North America,

> "Intersex" is a general term used for a variety of conditions in which a person is born with a reproductive or sexual anatomy that doesn't seem to fit the typical definitions of female or male [. . .]. Though we speak of intersex as an inborn condition, intersex anatomy doesn't always show up at birth. Sometimes a person isn't found to have intersex anatomy until she or he reaches the age of puberty, or finds himself an infertile adult, or dies of old age and is autopsied. Some people live and die with intersex anatomy without anyone (including themselves) ever knowing.

> (ISNA 1993–2008)

2. Segments of this chapter appeared in "'The Snow Queen': Queer Coding in Male Directors' Films" (2015), *Marvels & Tales* 29 (1): 110–34; and "Team Snow Queen: Feminist Cinematic 'Misinterpretations' of a Fairy Tale" (2016), *Studies in European Cinema* 13 (1): 32–47. I thank the publishers for their permission and cooperation. I thank Heather Milne for useful suggestions.

3. Excellent scholarship addresses pulp novels,

> in which the butch was usually killed off and the femme gets together with a man. Most such works drove home the message that lesbians are doomed to misery, that their identities and relationships are not viable, and that femmes are just confused straight women who need a man to show them the light. Lesbian pulp writers like Ann Bannon subverted this trope.
>
> (Heather Milne, pers. comm.; see, e.g., Walters 1989)

4. The biopic *Hans Christian Andersen* (directed by Charles Vidor, 1952) incorporates a ballet dancer who plays "The Little Mermaid" as the writer's unrequited love interest. Andersen is played by queer suspect actor Danny Kaye and his rival, the dancer's husband, by out gay actor Farley Granger.

5. Jenny Lind was reserved and distant, like the female main character in "The Snow Queen" (Andersen 2005, 310).

6. All quotations from Esterhazy are from my Winnipeg interview with her on March 9, 2012.

References Cited and Further Reading

Ahmed, Sara. 2010. *The Promise of Happiness.* Durham, NC: Duke UP.

Andersen, Hans Christian, and Maria Tatar. 2008. *The Annotated Hans Christian Andersen.* New York: W. W. Norton.

Andersen, Jens. 2005. *Hans Christian Andersen: A New Life*, translated by Tiina Nunnally. New York: Overlook Duckworth.

Bacchilega, Cristina. 2012. "Whetting Her Appetite: What's a 'Clever' Woman To Do in the Grimms' Collection?" In *Transgressive Tales*, edited by Turner and Greenhill, 27–47.

———. 2013. *Fairy Tales Transformed? Twenty-First-Century Adaptations and the Politics of Wonder.* Detroit: Wayne State UP.

Consalvo, Mia. 2003. "Hot Dates and Fairy-Tale Romances: Studying Sexuality in Video Games." In *The Video Game Theory Reader*, edited Mark J. P. Wolf and Bernard Perron, 171–94. New York: Routledge.

Doty, Alexander. 2000. *Flaming Classics: Queering the Film Canon.* New York: Routledge.

Duggan, Anne E. 2013. *Queer Enchantments: Gender, Sexuality, and Class in the Fairy-Tale Cinema of Jacques Demy.* Detroit: Wayne State UP.

———. 2016. "The Fairy-Tale Film in France: Postwar Reimaginings." In *Fairy-Tale Films Beyond Disney: International Perspectives*, edited by Jack Zipes, Pauline Greenhill, and Kendra Magnus-Johnston, 64–79. New York: Routledge.

Fairfield, Joy Brooke. 2012. "Becoming-Mouse, Becoming-Man: The Sideways Growth of Princess Mouseskin." In *Transgressive Tales*, edited by Turner and Greenhill, 223–43.

Greenhill, Pauline. 1995. "'Neither a Man nor a Maid': Sexualities and Gendered Meanings in Cross-Dressing Ballads." *Journal of American Folklore* 108 (428): 156–77.

———. 2008. "'Fitcher's [Queer] Bird': A Fairy-Tale Heroine and Her Avatars." *Marvels & Tales* 22 (1): 143–67.

———. 2014. "Wanting (To Be) Animal: Fairy-Tale Transbiology in *The StoryTeller.*" *Feral Feminisms* 2: 29–45. http://feralfeminisms.com/wp-content/uploads/2014/05/ff_Wanting-To-Be-Animal_Issue2.pdf.

———. 2015. "'The Snow Queen': Queer Coding in Male Directors' Films." *Marvels & Tales* 29 (1): 110–34.

———. 2016. "Team Snow Queen: Feminist Cinematic 'Misinterpretations' of a Fairy Tale." *Studies in European Cinema* 13 (1): 32–47.

Greenhill, Pauline, Anita Best, and Emilie Andersen-Grégoire. 2012. "Queering Gender: Transformations in 'Peg Bearskin' and Related Tales." In *Transgressive Tales*, edited by Turner and Greenhill, 181–205.

Greenhill, Pauline, and Emilie Andersen-Grégoire. 2014. "'If Thou Be Woman, Be Now Man!' The Shift of Sex' as Transsexual Imagination." In *Unsettling Assumptions: Tradition, Gender, Drag*, edited by Pauline Greenhill and Diane Tye, 56–73. Logan: Utah State UP.

Greydanus, Steven D. N.d. "So, How Gay Is Disney's *Frozen?*" *Decent Films.* http://decentfilms.com/blog/frozen-themes.

Hennard Dutheil de la Rochère, Martine. 2009. "Queering the Fairy Tale Canon: Emma Donoghue's *Kissing the Witch.*" In *Fairy Tales Reimagined: Essays on New Retellings*, edited by Susan Redington Bobby, 13–30. Jefferson, NC: McFarland.

ISNA. 1993–2009. "What Is Intersex?" Intersex Society of North America. www.isna.org/faq/what_is_intersex.

Jorgensen, Jeana. 2012. "Queering Kinship in 'The Maiden Who Seeks Her Brothers'." In *Transgressive Tales*, edited by Turner and Greenhill, 69–89.

Kohm, Steven, and Pauline Greenhill. 2014. "'Little Red Riding Hood' Crime Films: Critical Variations on Criminal Themes." *Law, Culture and the Humanities* 10 (2): 257–78.

Lawless, Cecelia Burke. 2015. "Inside-Out: A Socio-Spatial Reading of *Mecánicas celestes.*" In *Despite All Adversities: Spanish-American Queer Cinema*, edited by Andrés Lema-Hincapié and Debra A. Castillo, 111–24. Albany: SUNY P.

Li, Jing. 2016. "The Love Story, Female Images, and Gender Politics: Folktale Films in the People's Republic of China (PRC)." In *Fairy-Tale Films Beyond Disney: International Perspectives*, edited by Jack Zipes, Pauline Greenhill, and Kendra Magnus-Johnston, 180–95. New York: Routledge.

"List of Disney Princesses." N.d. Disney Princess Wikia. http://disneyprincess.wikia.com/wiki/List_of_Disney_Princesses.

Love, Heather. 2007. *Feeling Backward: Loss and the Politics of Queer History.* Cambridge, MA: Harvard UP.

National Center for Transgender Equality. 2014. *Transgender Terminology*, January 15. www.transequality.org/issues/resources/transgender-terminology.

Orme, Jennifer. 2015. "A Wolf's Queer Invitation: David Kaplan's *Little Red Riding Hood* and Queer Possibility." *Marvels & Tales* 29 (1): 87–109.

Pugh, Tison. 2015. "John R. Neill: Illustrator (and Author) of L. Frank Baum's Queer Oz." *Marvels & Tales* 29 (1): 64–86.

Radner, Joan N., and Susan S. Lanser. 1993. "Strategies of Coding in Women's Cultures." In *Feminist Messages: Coding in Women's Folklore Culture*, edited by Joan N. Radner, 1–29. Urbana: U Illinois P.

Seifert, Lewis C. 1996. *Fairy Tales, Sexuality, and Gender in France, 1690–1715 Nostalgic Utopias.* Cambridge: Cambridge UP.

———. 2015a. "Introduction: Queer(ing) Fairy Tales." *Marvels & Tales* 29 (1): 15–20.

———. 2015b. "Queer Time in Charles Perrault's 'Sleeping Beauty.'" *Marvels & Tales* 29 (1): 21–41.

Soliño, María Elena. 2001. "From Perrault Through Disney to Fina Torres: Cinderella Learns Spanish and Talks Back in *Celestial Clockwork.*" *Letras Femeninas* 27 (2): 68–84.

Stam, Robert. 2000. *Film Theory: An Introduction.* Malden, MA: Blackwell Publishers.

Stryker, Susan. 2006. "(De)Subjugated Knowledges: An Introduction to Transgender Studies." In *The Transgender Studies Reader*, edited by Susan Stryker and Stephen Whittle, 1–18. New York: Routledge.

Tan, Nigel. 2016. "A Lesbian Princess Hopes to Find True Love in Fairytale Web Series." *GayStarLoves*, April 25. www.gaystarnews.com/article/lesbian-princess-hopes-find-love-fairytale-web-series/#gs.InJNC24.

Turner, Kay. 2012. "Playing with Fire: Transgression as Truth in Grimms' 'Frau Trude'." In *Transgressive Tales*, edited by Turner and Greenhill, 245–75.

———. 2015. "At Home in the Realm of Enchantment: The Queer Enticements of the Grimms' 'Frau Holle'." *Marvels & Tales* 29 (1): 42–63.

Turner, Kay, and Pauline Greenhill, eds. 2012. *Transgressive Tales: Queering the Grimms.* Detroit: Wayne State UP.

Walters, Suzanna Danuta. 1989. "As Her Hand Crept Slowly up Her Thigh: Ann Bannon and the Politics of Pulp." *Social Text* 23: 83–101.

Wullschlager, Jackie. 2000. *Hans Christian Andersen: The Life of a Storyteller.* London: Allen Lane/Penguin P.

Zipes, Jack. 2011. *The Enchanted Screen: The Unknown History of Fairy-Tale Films.* New York: Routledge.

Mediagraphy

Celestial Clockwork. 1995. Director Fina Torres. Belgium/France/Spain/Venezuela.

Donkey Skin. 1970. Director Jacques Demy. France.

Frozen. 2013. Director Jennifer Lee and Chris Buck. USA.

Hall, Todrick. 2014. "Cinderfella by Todrick Hall." *YouTube*, May 5. www.youtube.com/watch?v=F9ZA7bn5ujk.

Hans Christian Andersen. 1952. Director Charles Vidor. USA.

Hans Christian Andersen: My Life as a Fairy Tale. 2003. Director Philip Saville. USA.

La belle endormie (Sleeping Beauty). 2010. Director Catherine Breillat. France.

Lady Oscar. 1979. Director Jacques Demy. Japan.

Little Red Riding Hood. 1997. Director David Kaplan.

Mulan. 1998. Directors Tony Bancroft and Barry Cook. USA.

Once Upon a Time (TV). 2011. Creators Adam Horowitz and Edward Kitsis. USA.

———. "Quite a Common Fairy." 2013. Episode 3.3. October 13.

The Pied Piper. 1979. Director Jacques Demy. UK/USA.

TheFrozenGames.com. N.d. http://thefrozengames.com/.

Snow Queen. 2002. Director David Wu. USA/Germany/Canada.

33
TRANSLATION
Written Forms
Karen Seago

In *Once Upon a Time*, Marina Warner uses a map metaphor to visualize the history of fairy tales, using famous collections as landmarks that chart and pinpoint the form's journey across the globe and across time (2014, xiii). The images of the map and journey capture a central feature of traditional fairy tales: stories marked by international dissemination. They have traveled along migration and trade routes in oral and print transmission to solidify eventually into print text collections with titles and authors (or collectors/editors) and a place and date of publication. At this last point of the trajectory we can start talking about translation—rendering an identifiable text from one language (and culture) to another. But the long history of fairy tales involves their circulation through languages and cultures, across varying audiences and formats—also processes of translation, even if it is impossible to trace any nuanced textual relations.

This chapter addresses historical and critical effects involving fairy tales and translation, tracking tales as stepping stones in a dissemination process initially shaped by oral dispersion across linguistic and cultural borders. It documents the contribution of prominent written collections and their translation to the genesis of this form and the international canon of fairy tales we are familiar with today. The chapter explores how translations of texts spark interest in storytelling to influence the textualization of fairy tales in various countries and times and considers how the interpretation of fairy tales as children's literature shapes content and form in line with what is deemed appropriate. Although films, TV shows, and serials offer creative interpretations for twentieth- and twenty-first-century audiences, and often involve movement from one language and culture to others, the processes of transcreation involved in adapting fairy tales to audiovisual formats of dissemination go beyond the scope of this chapter. For the early years, from the fourteenth to the seventeenth century, the image is impressionistic; orally transmitted, popular tales appear only through the traces they leave in manuscripts and contemporary accounts. But even with print collections, it is impossible to capture the full extent of their dissemination in translation. Research is patchy, only available in the libraries of the receiving cultures, or missing reception in many languages. The discussion is in chronological order of when the main collections were published, spanning the development from the fourteenth to the late nineteenth century.

The oldest written versions of fairy-tale-type stories are from the fifth-century Indian *Panchatantra*, also known in English as *The Fables of Bidpai* (Opie and Opie 1974, 23). Stories from this collection were translated into Persian in the late sixth century and via this text into Arabic in the late eighth century. It contains early variants of "Puss in Boots" (ATU 545B) and "The Three Wishes" (ATU 675) and by 1600 had been translated into many European languages, including Greek, Spanish, Italian, German, and English (Opie and Opie 1974, 23). But the most widely recognized collection of Asian tales that shaped European storytelling is *The 1001 Nights*. The earliest written collection of these tales is a fourteenth-century Syrian manuscript bringing together stories of varying antiquity and origin from India, Iran, the Arab world, and the Mediterranean (Mahdi 1995, 7–9). This edition was translated by Antoine Galland in the eighteenth century as *Les mille et une nuits* (1001 Nights) and, as discussed in the following in more detail, exerted a profound influence on European traditions.

Sixteenth-Century Italy: Straparola

Footprints of these tales can be traced in Mediterranean tradition. Stories from this collection circulated in oral form (evidenced in Spain through translations of individual tales from the twelfth century) and influenced one of the first European collections, Giovanni Straparola's *Le Piacevoli Notti* (1551–1553). Partly inspired by Giovanni Boccaccio's *Decameron* (1350s), it contains a mixture of material; its seventy-three tales were partly assembled from earlier collections of novellas and partly from contemporary oral storytelling traditions, including material from *The 1001 Nights* (Bottigheimer 2002, 9). Straparola's stories were lewd, rude, and told in Venetian dialect, which limited their influence in England. Only one story was translated in William Painter's very popular *Palace of Pleasure* (1566–1567) and then in nineteenth-century editions for adults.

But the collection was immensely popular in Italy, with twenty printings in its first fifty years, and abroad. Between 1553 and 1613, there were sixteen French translations, seven Spanish, and four German, until censorship from 1613 until the early 1700s stopped publications, although there were adaptations of Straparola's stories by, for example, Madame d'Aulnoy (Bottigheimer 2002, 123). An influential 1817 German translation *Maerchen des Straparola* by Schmidt published as volume 1 of a fairy-tale series served as the source text for a Danish translation in 1818 (Bottigheimer 2002, 123). The turn of the twentieth century saw W. G. Waters's (1894) accurate and Richard Burton's (1906) archaizing English translations.

Translations of Straparola were primarily aimed at an adult readership but, like Giovanni Basile's *Lo Cunti de li cunti* (The Tale of Tales), published in five volumes between 1634 and 1636, contained and influenced what would become staples of popular tales. Because Basile published his remarkable collection in a semi-archaic Neapolitan dialect, it had little impact until its translation into standard Italian in 1747, German in 1846, and English in 1848. Because of this late translation, Iona and Peter Opie argue that Perrault's *Histoires du temps passé, ou Contes de ma mère l'Oye* (1697) were not influenced by Basile, despite sharing five common versions (1974, 25).

Seventeenth-Century France: The Vogue for Fairy Tales

Perrault's *contes* were part of the vogue for fairy tales in late-seventeenth-century literary salons and contributed to the debate over the merits of ancient versus modern literature. But he published under his son's name and claimed that the tales were aimed at children, unlike the sophisticated, elegant, and witty stories by the leading aristocratic authors Marie-Catherine d'Aulnoy, Véronique Bernard, Charlotte-Rose Caumont La Force, Marie-Jeanne L'Héritier de Villandon, and Henriette-Julie de Murat, which were aimed at adults and argued for moral and literary renewal. Three fairy tales were published in 1695, two years before Perrault, by L'Heritier de Villandon in her *Oeuvres meslées* (Assorted Works): "L'adroite princesse" (The Discreet Princess, or the Adventures of Finetta: An Entertaining Story for the Amusement of Young Masters and Misses, trans. Robert Samber 1818) (ATU 510A), "Les enchantements de l'éloquence" (The Enchantments of Eloquence) (ATU 480), and "Marmoisan" (ATU 514**). Madame d'Aulnoy's *Contes des fées* were published in three volumes in 1697–1698 (and *Contes nouveaux, ou les fées á la mode* in 1698) and subsequently translated into English as *A Collection of Novels and Tales of the Fairies* (1699/1707); the English term "fairy tale" is traced to this publication.

In English translations, these elegant, ironic stories, expressive of seventeenth-century French cultural life, were adapted for children not only in style but also in content: the framing novellas and some of the stories were omitted, while other stories were included and erroneously attributed to d'Aulnoy (Buczkowski 2009, 60–61). Only in 1855 did a more accurate translation by James Robinson Planché come out that sought to render d'Aulnoy's distinctive style, figures of speech, and word play, but an 1892 translation by Annie Macdonell and Miss Lee, *The fairy tales of Madame d'Aulnoy, newly done into English*, notes that "the moralizing verses at the end of each story have been omitted" (Ritchie 1892, v). Anne Thackeray Ritchie, in her long introduction, asserts that "many of Madame d'Aulnoy's tales have been taken with scarce any variation from the *Pentamerone* of Basile and the *Nights* of Straparola" (xx).

The *conteuses* decisively contributed to the formation of the literary fairy-tale canon, but Ritchie's dismissive tone is typical of much of the reception of the *contes des fées*. The shift to children as the primary audience, signaled by Perrault's homely storyteller scenario depicted in the famous frontispiece to the first edition, further contributed to the marginal international reception of the literary *contes des fées* in translation. From the late twentieth century, however, they have received critical attention with scholarly editions and translations (many for the first time) that paid tribute to their cultural, literary, political, and contemporary allusions in critical introductions and translations of selected tales (Zipes 1989; Warner 1996; Seifert and Stanton 2010).

Perrault's (1697) *Contes* was first translated into English by Robert Samber in 1729 as *Histories, or Tales of Past Times* and advertised as "very entertaining and instructive for children" (Opie and Opie 1974, 30). Some doubt existed until 1951 whether there existed an earlier, 1719, version by G. M. Gent, *Histories or Tales of Past Times, told by Mother Goose, with Morals*, but the Opies showed the 1719 date to be an error with the edition actually published in 1799 (1974, 30). A parallel French-English text edition, published in 1785, translated by Samber and Guy Miège, contains two stories by Marie-Jeanne l'Héritier de Villandon and Madame d'Aulnoy. In 1888, *Perrault's Popular Tales* with an erudite introduction by Andrew Lang was published in Oxford with countless editions and translations since. Perrault was translated into German in 1790 by Friedrich Justin Bertuch as *Ammenmärchen* (Nurses' tales), unambiguously placing it in the nursery, while *Märchen der Mutter Gans* (Tales of Mother Goose), picking up on the English title, was first used in 1825 and is still available today. A Spanish translation by Teodoro Baro came out in 1883 in Barcelona under the title *Cuentas de Mamá Oca*.

Perrault's collection is taken as the moment when fairy tales became the province of children, and his treatment of some motifs found in popular French stories or in the Italian collections by Basile and Straparola demonstrates a child-appropriate expurgation of "gore, obscenity, and paganism" by, for example, removing Little Red Riding Hood drinking her grandmother's blood, her striptease, and her joining the wolf in bed (Ennis 2002, 284). In translation, Perrault's *contes* were received as "simple traditional stories" (Lang 1888, xvii). As was the case with the *contes des fées*, the textual, semantic complexity, the wit, and the cultural allusions were only rendered in twentieth-century translations, among them Angela Carter's (1977). The only French fairy-tale writer who expressly conceived her stories as children's literature with an explicit didactic intention was Madame Leprince de Beaumont. Her 1757 *Magasin des enfens* was written for her charges (she worked as a governess in England) and was translated into English as *The Young Misses Magazine* in 1761.

The *1001 Nights*

Sanitizing or omitting topics perceived as sensitive or offensive has always been a feature of translation, not only in texts aimed at children. The translation history of the *1001 Nights* exemplifies widely varying approaches ranging from adaptation, compilation, and creative writing, to scholarly rendering and redaction, to archaizing and erotic Orientalization. It also demonstrates the extensive practice of relay or indirect translation where the translator works from another translation rather than the original source text. Given the very different approaches outlined in the following, the relay translations via Galland conveyed a very specific, French eighteenth-century interpretation of the *1001 Nights*.

Galland's *Les mille et une nuits*, in twelve volumes, 1704–1717, consisted of a *mélange*: translations from the early Syrian and other manuscripts, stories from oral sources, and invented material, including the famous frame story (Makdisi and Nussbaum 2008, 13). Galland's translation approach is characterized by omissions (for example removing poetic passages), amplifications, and reorganization as well as a toning down of the erotic, imposing a unity of style adapted to French expectations of literariness (for example by removing repetition and enumerations), and adding explanations on plot and cultural detail (Seifert 2002, 232). His translation was enormously influential, seen as providing a true image of the Orient and generating a craze for Oriental fairy stories in France and abroad. His version was the medium by which *The Arabian Nights* first entered the English-speaking world.

Anonymous translations of early volumes were published by Grub Street in 1706 as *Arabian Nights' Entertainments* and the entire twelve volumes in 1721; both translations were popular in chapbook format and frequently adapted as children's texts (France 2000, 150). Jonathan Scott's six-volume translation in 1811 used Galland as its source text, but added translations from another manuscript and provided a critical introduction as well as numerous annotations explaining Muslim religion and customs (Ballaster 2013, 39). With Edward William Lane's 1838–1841 edition, a direct translation from the Arabic became available in English.[1] Lane provided extensive footnotes, eventually published separately as *Arabian Society in the Middle Ages: Studies from the Thousand and One Nights*. The third English translation directly from the Arabic was Richard Burton's archaizing and eroticizing ten-volume edition in 1885. As an in-depth review of all English translations noted: "The different versions [. . .] have each its proper destination—Galland for the nursery, Lane for the library, Payne for the study, and Burton for the sewers" (Reeve 1886, 184).

Indirect translation using French or English texts was also how *The Arabian Nights* arrived in other languages: into Russian by Alexey Filatev via Galland in 1763–1771, into Chinese as *Yi Qian Lin Yi Ye* by Guisheng Zhou via Burton in 1903 (Wang-Chi Wong 2014, 134), and into Japanese by Hideki Nagamine via Jonathan Scott (indirectly Galland) and Edward William Lane in 1875. Translation into German tended to be direct: Gustav Weil in 1839–1842 and Max Henning in 1895, except for August Ernst Zinserling in 1823 who used an 1804 French translation as source.

TRANSLATION

The Grimms and Their Impact: Asbjørnsen and Moe, Hans Christian Andersen

In 1812, Jakob and Wilhelm Grimm published the first volume of their *Kinder- und Hausmärchen* (Children's and Household Tales), with another seven editions of the complete collection and ten editions of a selected collection of a continually revised corpus of tales over the next forty-five years. The Grimms had first conceived a scholarly initiative, collecting stories from oral transmission to evidence a distinctive German cultural heritage, producing an extensive apparatus of notes on the tales' sources, variants, and "folk" storytellers. They claimed that the vernacular material had been noted without editorial (or writerly) intervention, although this was not the case. The impact of the Grimms' tales has been extraordinary: its programmatic intention of collecting, noting, and documenting orally transmitted material sparked folkloric interest and collecting initiatives in many countries. In 1841, Peter Christen Asbjørnsen and Jørgen Moe published *Norske Folkeeventyr*, translated by George Webb Dasent into English as *Popular Tales from the Norse*, into German by Friedrich Breesemann in 1847 as *Norwegische Volksmärchen*, and into French by Eugène Beauvois as *Contes Populaires de la Norvege, de la Finlande et de la Bourgogne* in 1859.

In Germany and in translation, the *Kinder- und Hausmärchen* were primarily received as children's literature, and editorial intervention and polishing produced the "Gattung Grimm," a recognizable fairy-tale style that greatly shaped expectations of the form. The first translation was into Danish in 1816 by Adam Oehlenschläger, followed by another nine translations by Johan Frederik Lindencrone (1821/1823, 1844) and various selections by Christian Molbech (1832, 1835, 1836, 1838, 1839, 1843) in the nineteenth century alone (Dollerup 1995, 100). The Grimm translations produced an interest in folk stories in Denmark (and in other countries); in this context Hans Christian Andersen produced his fairy tales in 1835: part literary, part inspired by folk motifs, part traditional stories. Andersen's *Fairy Tales* were translated into German in 1844, English in 1846, and French in 1848. An 1869 French translation presented Andersen "as the Scandinavian Perrault" (Cyrille 2014, 180).

The first English translation of the Grimms was a selection by Edgar Taylor and Francis Jardine in 1823 as *German Popular Stories*. This edition's success inspired Wilhelm Grimm to put together the "Kleine Ausgabe" of 1825, a selection of the most popular tales for a "small edition" framed as a children's book. In every decade of the nineteenth century new translations and varying selections appeared, always aimed at children; sensitive topics, uncouth language, and inappropriate religious references were omitted or amended and the style and narrative perspective adjusted to suit the emerging conventions of children's literature as instruction and entertainment. Some introduced a storyteller and framing device similar to Boccaccio, Basile, Straparola, and *The 1001 Nights*, and motifs or titles and names from Perrault found their way in as well. Margaret Hunt's scholarly translation in 1884 made a complete edition of all tales and the scholarly apparatus available in English.

The first French translation, *Vieux contes pour l'amusement des grands et des petits enfants*, in 1824, was a quite literal relay translation of Taylor's *German Popular Stories*, except for "Brier Rose," which followed the Perrault version of "Sleeping Beauty." Another five French translations appeared in the nineteenth century of varying selections, with one scholarly version in 1869. On the one hand, French translations were at pains to establish the differences between the Grimms and Perrault, framing the Grimms' stories as popular tales in contrast to Perrault's more literary tales, stressing the Grimms' scholarly intention as opposed to Perrault's entertaining one, and avoiding stories where the German and French versions were very similar. On the other hand, translators domesticated the German titles by choosing the French version, for example explaining "Fitcher's Vogel" as "the German Bluebeard" (Francois 2014, 185), and used a fairy-tale vocabulary established in the *Contes des fées* rather than lexis in general use: "cabinet" instead of "chambre" for room, "marâtre" rather than "belle-mère" for stepmother (Seifert and Stanton 2010, 44).

Critical Issues: Translation Effects

Didactic, moral, and educational considerations have always governed the acceptability of children's reading, and translations of children's texts demonstrably conform to the receiving culture's norms and expectations. These shape the selection of tales and their textual realization in the target language. In the didactic and morally charged context of English reception, key features that influence the selection of the Grimms' fairy tales are moral constraints, respect for authority figures, profanity, Christian religious characters acting in a non-religious context and being duped, and conformity to the fairy-tale format. Concern over profanity in the German collection is explicitly addressed in most prefaces. Stories about divine characters are either not translated at all or references to God and the devil omitted or altered. Particular areas of concern were matters of profanity, morality, depiction of the body and bodily functions, violence, and the maintaining of class markers.

In his 1823 translation, Taylor variously translated the devil as a giant, evil spirit, or diabolical agency. A consistent strategy transposed Christian references to classical or Nordic myth, rendering the devil as Pluto and his grandmother as Hecate, while God becomes Jupiter, the archangel is Mercury, and heaven is Olympus; hell has been translated as the Scandinavian hell or even a cave. Sensitivities manifest not only in explicit irreverence for religious topics or characters, but also in more general motifs that could be interpreted as blasphemy. So, for example, the dead Snow White's reawakening at the end of the story could be seen as a resurrection, which should only be performed by God or Jesus. Consequently, some translations add reassurances that the girl is not in fact dead or edit out passages that marvel at the fact that her body does not decay.

Moral objections lead to overt sexuality and references to conception, birth, and even death being omitted or paraphrased. In fact, most aspects relating to the body, its fluids, or its parts are censored in some way. Sleeping Beauty pricking her finger on the spindle, or Snow White coughing up the poisoned apple from her throat, are sometimes omitted. However, not all translations have a problem with the disenchanting kiss in Sleeping Beauty; quite a few texts eroticize the sleeping girl. Bodily functions including scatological matters are highly problematic. When not absolutely essential to the narrative any such references are omitted; if they are a central motif, they are paraphrased, often leading to narrative inconsistency. Sensitivities around the body's natural processes go so far that the "pisspot" in which a couple live in one story has only been translated in the twentieth century, and even here with stylistic shift, as a "chamber pot." In the nineteenth century, the pisspot is rendered as hut, hovel, ditch, or lowly chamber. Even a heap of dung is translated as a pile of hay or straw, while bird-droppings become falling leaves or hail. References to dirt, lice, fleas, or personal grooming are omitted or paraphrased. In "Sleeping Beauty," the association of crab with crab lice—sexual disease—is apparently so strong that the queen hears the prophecy of her pregnancy from a little fish.

There is a great reluctance in the translations to deal with intense emotion or base instincts: great joy, rage, envy, revenge, pride, or vanity are all tempered or even omitted. Great care is taken to show authority figures in non-compromising situations. For example, most translations exonerate the king in "Sleeping Beauty" from any carelessness in looking after his child; the blame is shifted onto servants, or his actions are presented in the passive voice or in an impersonal, abstract manner so that he cannot be identified as the responsible agent. The sanctity of the family is protected by obscuring characters' kin connections, as when the evil stepmother in "Snow White" is referred to only as the queen.

Gender norms and family roles are also inflected by cultural norms in the English translations. Many choices represent women as noticeably more flighty, irresponsible, and childish than in the German, while male authority and rational decision making is reinforced even where the German source text suggests emotional insecurity and paternal errors of judgment. Violence is usually edited out or reduced; for example, the cook caught boxing the kitchen boy's ear in "Sleeping Beauty" reaches instead for a spice box. By contrast, translations into Danish render or even increase the depicted violence, especially during periods of German political aggression. Translations in the 1940s noticeably select more stories with violent incidents and cruel punishments for translation than in the nineteenth century and later in the twentieth century; they visually foreground this "German cruelty" by including illustrations of these violent episodes (Dollerup 1999, 245–247).

Translation of the highly literary, complex tales of the seventeenth-century French *conteuses* pose quite different challenges involving social, cultural, and literary norms and ideals. Terms such as *agréable*, *bienséance*, *galant*, *négligence*, and *tendresse* are annotated in translators' footnotes in an attempt to provide nuanced context without disrupting the narrative. *Honnêteté* is singled out as an almost undefinable and untranslatable polysemous notion of "an ideal in seventeenth-century France that encompasses the social and the ethical, in varying combinations according to the inclinations of the user" (Seifert and Stanton 2010, 44). While names on the whole did not pose major challenges, they were usually translated if descriptive, in d'Aulnoy's "La princesse Carpillon," Prince Boffu is rendered as Prince Hunchback, but maintained if proper names, such as Isidore in "Don Gabriel." The difference between the two grammatical genders in French and biological gender in English posed problems in the use of the personal pronoun. For example, in a tale where a rosebush turns into a prince, in French, both are masculine, but in English a decision is required as to when the rosebush as "it" will be replaced by (Prince) Rosebush as "he."

All these issues complicate the fact that the fairy tale is "nomadic" (Warner 1994, xvii) and perceived as universal communal property (Haase 1993, 384), yet appropriated by each culture with little awareness of the differences between a story in translation and its source version in Arabic, French, Danish, or German. The fact that Basile's Italian sleeping beauty Talia is raped by a married king, woken from her deathly sleep by the children she bears, and persecuted by his outraged wife; the French Belle is wakened by the adoring presence of the Prince and is then persecuted by his mother, who turns out to be an ogre; and the German Dornröschen is kissed awake by her prince and they live happily ever after does not change the perception of an enduring notion or relevance of the Sleeping Beauty. Differences in translation are perhaps less dramatic, and yet they produce quite distinct nationally and culturally specific versions, a problem further exacerbated by relay translations that convey a story at two, sometimes three removes, thus multiplying the reinterpretation of features across a range of cultural and language traditions.

The impact of translation strategies on texts is an issue only rarely addressed in the literature on fairy tales in international reception. Many books on fairy-tale traditions do not mention translation in their index or do not address it beyond noting dates and sometimes publishers, often not even the translators. Pirated translations, in the nineteenth century in particular, produced collections with material from different cultural traditions, often using established titles associated with Grimm, Perrault, or Andersen. Titles of stories also migrate across culturally distinct versions hiding national tradition as source: the French Little Red Riding Hood can be gobbled up by the wolf, the German rescued by a woodsman, and, in an early Breton tale, the girl outwits the wolf and saves herself.

Translation is a step in the continuum of fairy-tale mediations, but it has also produced an international canon of the fairy tale that represents a small, and distinctly edited, selection of the many, many different models, versions, and voices of the rich tale traditions of Europe and the world. Research is needed to address this; we need more studies of the international reception of tale traditions, like Gillian Lathey and Vanessa Joosen's exemplary *Grimms' Tales around the Globe* (2014), which consider the inflections of a story in its varied translated shapes.

Related topics: Adaptation and the Fairy-Tale Web; Children's and Young Adult (YA) Literature; Language; Orientalism

Note

1. John Payne's 1820 direct translation was available in private circulation only.

References Cited and Further Reading

Andersen, Hans-Christian. 1835. *Eventyr, fortalte for Børn.* Copenhagen: C.A. Reitzel.
Anon., trans. 1706–1721. *Arabian Winter-Evenings' Entertainment or Arabian Arabian Nights' Entertainments.* London: Grub Street.
Anon., trans. 1824. *Vieux contes pour l'amusement des grands et des petits enfants.* Paris: Boulland.
Anon., trans. 1844. *H. C. Andersens Märchen.* Berlin: n.p.
Asbjørnsen, Peter, and Jørgen Moe. 1841. *Norske Folke-Eventyr, samlede ved Asbjørnsen & Moe.* Christiana: n.p.
Ballaster, Ros. 2013. "The Sea Born Tale; Eighteenth-Century Translations of the *Thousand and One Nights* and the Lure of Elemental Difference." In *Scheherezade's Children: Global Encounters with the Arabian Nights,* edited by Philip F. Kennedy and Marina Warner, 27–52. New York: NYU P.
Baro, Teodoro. 1883. *Cuentas de Mamá Oca.* Barcelona: Librería de Juan y Antonio Bastinos.
Basile, Giovanni. 1634–36. *Lo Cunti de li cunti.* 5 vols. Napoli: Camillo Cavallo.
Beauvois, Eugène, trans. 1859. *Contes Populaires de la Norvege, de la Finlande et de la Bourgogne.* Paris: Dentu.
Bertuch, Friedrich Justin. 1790. *Ammenmärchen. Die blaue Bibliothek aller Nationen.* Gotha: Ettinger.
Boccaccio, Giovanni. 1350s. *Decameron.* www.brown.edu/Departments/Italian_Studies/dweb/the_project/about.php.
Bottigheimer, Ruth. 2002. *Fairy Godfather: Straparola, Venice and the Fairy Tale Tradition.* Philadelphia: U Pennsylvania P.
Breesemann, F., trans. 1847. *Norwegische Volksmärchen.* Berlin: n.p.
Buczkowski, Paul. 2009. "The First Precise English Translation of Madame d'Aulnoy's Fairy Tales." *Marvels & Tales* 23 (1): 59–78.
Burton, Richard, trans. 1885–86. *The Book of the Thousand and One Nights: A Plain and Literal Translation of the Arabian Nights' Entertainments.* 10 vols. Benares [Stoke Newington]: n.p.
———, trans. 1906. *The Most Delectable Nights of Straparola of Carravagio.* Paris: C. Carrington.
Carter, Angela, trans. 1977. *The Fairy Tales of Charles Perrault.* London: Gollancz.
Cox, Marian Roalfe. 1893. *Cinderella: Three Hundred and Forty-Five Variants.* London: The Folklore Society.
Dasent, George Webb, trans. 1859. *Popular Tales from the Norse.* Edinburgh: Edmonston & Douglas.
D'Aulnoy, Marie Catherine. 1697–1698. *Contes des fees.* Paris: n.p.
———. 1698. *Contes nouveaux, ou les fées á la mode.* Paris: n.p.
———, trans. (1699/1707) 1728. *A Collection of Novels and Tales of the Fairies.* London: Brotheron.
Dollerup, Cay. 1995. "Translation as a Creative Force in Literature: The Birth of the European Bourgeois Fairy Tale." *The Modern Language Review* 90 (1): 94–102.
———. 1999. *Tales and Translation: The Grimm Tales from Pan-Germanic Narratives to Shared International Fairytales.* Amsterdam: Benjamins.
Dundes, Alan, ed. 1988. *Cinderella: A Casebook.* Madison: U Wisconsin P.
Ennis, Mary Louise. 2002. "Histoires ou contes du temps passé avec des moralités." In *The Oxford Companion to Fairy Tale: The Western Fairy Tale Tradition from Medieval to Modern,* edited by Jack Zipes, 2836–85. Oxford: Oxford UP.

TRANSLATION

Filatev, Alexey, trans. (1763–1771) 1774. *Тысяча и одна ночь: сказки арабс [One Thousand and One Nights: Arabian Tales]*. Moskva: pri Imperatorskom Moskovskom Universitete.

France, Peter, ed. 2000. *The Oxford Guide to Literature in English Translation*. Oxford: Oxford UP.

Francois, Cyrille. 2014. "Translating in the 'Tongue of Perrault': The Reception of the *Kinder- und Hausmärchen* in France." In *Grimms' Tales around the Globe: The Dynamics of Their International Reception*, edited by Gillian Lathey and Vanessa Joosen, 178–98. Detroit: Wayne State UP.

Galland, Antoine. 1704–1717. *Les mille et une nuits*. Paris: Barbin.

Gent, Robert Samber, trans. (1719) 1799. *Histories, or Tales of Past Times Told by Mother Goose, with Morals*. London: Montagu & Pote.

Grimm, Jacob, and Wilhelm Grimm. 1812. *Kinder- und Hausmärchen*. Vol. 1. Berlin: Reimer.

Haase, Donald. 1993. "Yours, Mine or Ours? Perrault, the Brothers Grimm and the Ownership of Fairy Tales." *Marvels & Tales* 7 (2): 383–402.

Hearne, Betsy. 1989. *Beauty and the Beast: Visions and Revisions of an Old Tale*. Chicago: U Chicago P.

Henning, Max, trans. 1895. *Tausend und eine Nacht*. Leipzig: Reclam.

Hosemann, Theodor, trans. 1848. *Contes choisi* [H. C. Andersen]. Berlin: Schröter.

Hunt, Margaret, ed., trans. 1884. *Grimm's Household Tales*. London: Bell.

Lane, Edward William, trans. 1838–1841. *A New Translation of the Thousand Nights and a Night: Known in England as the Arabian Nights' Entertainments*. London: Knight & Co.

———. 1883. *Arabian Society in the Middle Ages: Studies from the Thousand and One Nights*, edited by Stanley Lane-Poole. London: Chatto & Windus.

Lang, Andrew. 1888. "Introduction." In *Perrault's Popular Tales*, edited by Andrew Lang, vi–cxv. Oxford: Clarendon.

Lathey, Gillian, and Vanessa Joosen, eds. 2014. *Grimms' Tales around the Globe: The Dynamics of Their International Reception*. Detroit: Wayne State UP.

Leprince de Beaumont, Jeanne-Marie. (1757) 1798. *Magasin des enfans*. Lyon: Rusand.

———. 1781 [1761]. *The Young Misses Magazine*. Edinburgh: C. Elliot.

L'Heritier de Villandon, Marie-Jeanne. 1695. *Oeuvres mesleés*. Paris: Guignard.

Lindencrone, Johan Frederik, trans. 1821. *Folke-Eventyr samlede af Brødrene Grimm*. Copenhagen: Nøers Forlag.

Mahdi, Muhsin. 1995. *The Thousand and One Nights*. Leiden: E. J. Brill.

Makdisi, Saree, and Felicity Nussbaum, eds. 2008. *The Arabian Nights in Historical Context: Between East and West*. Oxford: Oxford UP.

Molbech, Christian, trans. 1832. *Dansk Læsebog i Prosa til Brug ved Sprogunderviisning i Modersmaalet*. Copenhagen: Reitzel.

———. 1835. *Julegave for Børn*. Copenhagen: Reitzel

———. 1836. *Julegave for Børn*. Copenhagen: Reitzel

———. 1838. *Julegave for Børn*. Copenhagen: Reitzel

———. 1839. *Julegave for Børn*. Copenhagen: Reitzel

———. 1843. *Udvalgte Eventyr og Fortællinger: En Læsebog for Folket og for den barnilge Verden*. Copenhagen: Reitzel.

Nagamine, Hideki, trans. 1875. *Arabiya monogatari: Kaikan kyōki*. Tokyo: Nihon Hyōronsha.

Oehlenschläger, Adam, trans. 1816. *Eventyr af forskiellige Digtere*. Copenhagen: Gyldendal.

Opie, Iona, and Peter Opie. 1974. *The Classic Fairy Tales*. London: Granada.

Painter, William. 1566–1567. *Palace of Pleasure*. London: Denham.

Perrault, Charles. 1697. *Histoires du temps passé, ou Contes de ma mère l'Oye*. Paris: Barbin.

Planché, James Robinson, trans. 1855. *Fairy Tales of the Countess d'Aulnoy*, illustrated by John Gilbert. London: Routledge.

Pocci, Franz von, trans. 1846. *A Danish Story Book*. London: Cundall.

Reeve, Henry. 1886. "The Arabian Nights." *The Edinburgh Review*, July: 166–99.

Ritchie, Anne. 1892. "Introduction." *The Fairy Tales of Madame d'Aulnoy*, translated by Annie Macdonnell and Miss Lee, ix–xxi. London: Lawrence & Bullen.

Samber, Robert, trans. 1729. *Histories, or Tales of Past Times with Morals. By M. Perrault*. London: J. Pote.

Samber, Robert [Guy Miège]. 1785. *The Histories of Passed Times, or the Tales of Mother Goose: With Morals . . . A New Edition, to Which Are Added Two Novels, viz. The Discreet Princess, and The Widow and Her Two Daughters. Adorned with Fine Cuts*. London: Pote, Brussels: n.p.

Schmidt, Friedrich W. F., trans. 1817. *Maerchen des Straparola*. Berlin: Duncker und Humblot.

Scott, Jonathan, trans. 1811. *The Thousand and One Nights: The Arabian Nights Entertainments*. Edinburgh and London: Ballantyne.

Seago, Karen. 2001. "Shifting Meanings: Translating Grimms' Fairy Tales as Children's Literature." In *Aspects of Specialised Translation*, edited by Lucile Desblache, 171–80. Paris: La Maison du Dictionnaire.

Seifert, Lewis C. 2002. "Galland, Antoine." In *The Oxford Companion to Fairy Tales, the Western Fairy Tale Tradition from Medieval to Modern*, edited by Jack Zipes, 231–3. Oxford: Oxford UP.

Seifert, Lewis C., and Domna C. Stanton, eds., trans. 2010. *Enchanted Eloquence: Fairy Tales by Seventeenth-Century French Women Writers*. Toronto: Iter Inc.

Straparola, Giovanni. 1551–1553. *Le Piacevoli Notti*. Naples: Bulifon.

Sutton, Martin. 1996. *The Sin-Complex: A Critical Study of English Versions of the Grimms' Kinder- und Hausmärchen in the Nineteenth Century*. Kassel: Brüder Grimm Gesellschaft.

Taylor, Edgar, and Francis Jardine, trans. 1823. *German Popular Stories*, trans. from the Kinder- und Hausmärchen Collected by M. M. Grimm from Oral Tradition. London: Baldwyn.

Uther, Hans-Jörg. 2011. *The Types of International Folktales: A Classification and Bibliography, Based on the System of Antti Aarne and Stith Thompson*. Helsinki: Finnish Academy of Science and Letters.

Wang-Chi Wong, Lawrence. 2014. "From 'Controlling the Barbarians' to 'Wholesale Westernization': Translation and Politics in Late Imperial and Early Republican China, 1840–1919." In *Asian Translation Traditions*, edited by Eva Hung and Judy Wakabayashi, 109–34. London: Routledge.

Warner, Marina. 1994. *From the Beast to the Blonde: On Fairy Tale and their Tellers*. London: Chatto & Windus.

———, ed. 1996. *Wonder Tales*. New York: Farrar, Straus and Giroux.

———. 2014. *Once Upon a Time: A Short History of Fairy Tale*. Oxford: Oxford UP.

Waters, W. G., trans. 1894. *The Nights of Straparola*. London: Lawrence and Bullen.

Weil, Gustav, trans. 1839–42. *Tausend und eine Nacht*. Stuttgart: Verlag der Klassiker.

Zinserling, August Ernst, trans. 1823–1824. *Der Tausend und Einen Nacht noch nicht übersetzte Mährchen, Erzählungen und Anekdoten*, 1–3. Stuttgart und Tübingen: n.p.

Zipes, Jack, ed., trans. 1989. *Beauties, Beasts and Enchantment: Classic French Fairy Tales*. New York: NAL Books.

———, ed. 2002. *The Oxford Companion to Fairy Tales, the Western Fairy Tale Tradition from Medieval to Modern*. Oxford: Oxford UP.

Part IV

COMMUNICATIVE MEDIA

34

PRINT

William Gray

Notwithstanding the impact of fairy-tale films and oral storytelling, most of us will probably have had formative early experiences of reading fairy tales in print. However, the relation of fairy tales to print culture is perhaps more complex and controversial than might commonly be expected. The assumption that there is a quasi-natural transition from the oral transmission of fairy tales to their subsequent collection in printed volumes has been radically challenged by two scholars in particular, Ruth B. Bottigheimer (2002, 2009) and Willem de Blécourt (2012), who argue that this "natural" order of things with respect to the origin of fairy tales is actually a kind of myth, propagated above all by the Grimms and their (more or less scholarly and more or less credulous) fan base over the next couple of centuries.

Of this myth of origins, Bottigheimer says: "Literary analysis undermines it, literary history rejects it, social history repudiates it, and publishing history (whether of manuscripts or of books) contradicts it" (2009, 1). Fairy tale as we now understand the term, specifically the so-called "rise tale," which "begins with a poor and lowly hero or heroine who rises dramatically up the social ladder" (13), Bottigheimer argues, began to circulate not in the immemorial past in oral form, but in a particular historical context and in the form of print: in sixteenth-century Venice in the collection *Le piacevoli notti* (Pleasant Nights) by Gianfrancesco Straparola (1550), Bottigheimer's "Fairy Godfather" (2002, 11–13). Jack Zipes has devoted two appendices of his magnum opus *The Irresistible Fairy Tale* (2012b) to demolishing the arguments not only of Bottigheimer but also of de Blécourt.

Valdimar Hafstein gives an important slant on this argument about the role of print in the origins of the fairy tale (2015). He argues that the very dichotomy on which the dispute between Bottigheimer and Zipes seems to rest, that is, folklore versus individual authorship in print, far from being a natural opposition, was actually created at a particular historical moment: the Romantic inauguration of the author as solitary genius (18). Hafstein's point is that it was not just that before the invention of the author everything was public domain "folklore" (20); rather, he insists, the very concept of "folklore" (anonymous, usually oral, public production) was co-created with its binary opposite, the isolated Romantic author/genius. And this is not a merely intellectual debate; it has to do with intellectual property. The invention of "folklore" and of the author as individual creative genius go hand in hand with the invention of something more practical and economically motivated: copyright.

Hafstein's argument seeks to undermine the received dichotomy of individual author versus folklore as non-authored, or, as he says, "anti-authored" (21), production. Rather than individual author and anonymous folklore being pre-established either/or options, they are actually at extreme ends of an always already existing spectrum of collaborative creative production. And somewhere near the middle of that spectrum come collector-editors, such as the Grimms (32). The ambiguity about where to draw a dividing line in the fusion of their shaping creativity with the material they received is only a *problem* if you start with the abstract premises of individual author versus anonymous folklore. This idea connects with Jerome McGann's idea of a social contract between author, editor, and publisher, which rejects privileging the holograph (handwritten by the author) manuscript—if it is extant—and proposes to take instead as copy text the first printed edition where it has authorial approval because much of our experience of creative agency is actually *collaborative* (1983).

As Hafstein points out, the difference of emphasis (not dichotomy) between the fastidious editor concerned with the faithful reproduction of received material, on the one hand, and the creative artistic elaboration of that given material, on the other, can be seen in the partnership of the Grimms themselves, with Jacob generally more concerned with scholarly accuracy and Wilhelm more willing to recreate the material with a degree of artistic license. But the recognition of difference does not necessitate division; the Grimms were (though Hafstein doesn't put it exactly this way) precisely a *team*. And such collaboration is less the exception than the norm in our experience of cultural production.

Recalling Alan Dundes's famous answer to the question: "Who are the folk?" [. . .]. "Among others, *we* are" (quoted in Bronner 2007, 231), Hafstein provocatively suggests as an answer to the question: "Who are the Grimms?"—"Among others, we are! But so is everybody else" (2015, 32). Challenging what Hafstein calls "the untenable dichotomy" of authorship in print and oral folk tradition can open up a more realistic and helpful perspective on creativity and the circulation of culture because story sharing involves a teller addressing various audiences whatever the medium. Especially with print fairy tales, authorship itself, whether attributed to a single writer, director, show runner, or corporation, still resembles a storyteller reaching a certain audience through timely morals and motivations.

Challenging the oral-print dichotomy may also shed light on what seems one of the more puzzling aspects of the Grimms' textual production: the paradoxical idea that by editing and rewriting one can get *closer* to the "authentic" voice of the storyteller. As Zipes (2015) points out, by comparing the different versions of the oral tales the Grimms claimed to be recording, for example a comparison of the 1810 Ölenberg manuscript with the 1812/15 editions of *Kinder- und Hausmärchen*, it is clear that the Grimms had to abandon any pretentions to exact verbal accuracy, so that in fact none of their tales could strictly speaking count as "pure," "authentic," or "original." Nevertheless, because the Grimms believed their tales bore the traces of a profound oral tradition, "they felt justified to proclaim that tales were 'genuine' and 'pure' because the changes they made were based on their understanding of the 'natural' poetics of oral storytelling" (Zipes 2015, 9). The creative literary representation of the folkloric voice can thus arguably take us not *away from*, but actually *toward* that "original" voice, since such "originality" is a kind of illusion produced by the performative process that may be conveyed orally, in print, and even through still and audiovisual images.

Rather than print culture being inimical to the flourishing of fairy tales, in fact both in the older form of chapbooks—already semi-canonized by the Romantics—and in the newer form of newspapers and magazines, it has provided a fertile context in which fairy tales of all shapes and sizes thrive. So, another important approach to the relation of print culture to fairy tales is Caroline Sumpter's (2008). She undercuts the conventional—though increasingly unstable— opposition between the (always already disappearing) tradition of "authentic" oral storytelling on the one hand and the "alien" invasion of print culture on the other. The "departure of the fairies" is an enduring literary theme that runs from Chaucer through Kipling to Tolkien. In Sumpter's discussion of this narrative, that itself almost amounts to a folktale, the role of the villain who symbolically drives away both the fairies and the authentic oral culture of storytelling is Print Culture (here capitalized in the spirit of such allegorical narratives).

This tale of lost origins reaches a climax in the Romantic period, and then in its Victorian afterlife, and has dominated most accounts until fairly recently. According to this version, print culture, and especially magazines and newspapers, metonymically represent the evils of modern civilization and increasingly sweep away the vibrant old traditions of storytelling. Jennifer Schacker analyzes the relationship and cultural implications of folklore, fairy tale, and print in nineteenth-century Britain (2003). Sumpter, and others, examine the way chapbooks become like a halfway house in which the authentic traditions of times past are represented not only by oral storytelling but in print. Once chapbooks have become replaced by more modern and more technologically sophisticated productions (and are therefore sufficiently outmoded and rare), they acquire some of the mystical glamor of "tradition."

Cathy L. Preston and Michael J. Preston study how ephemeral print such as chapbooks and broadsides transmitted much folklore, some of which went back to medieval times (1995). Chapbooks were controversial, not only in the eighteenth and early-nineteenth centuries but also in histories of children's literature (O'Malley 2003, 18–21); nevertheless, as Victor E. Neuburg puts it: "fairy tales were available to [young readers] only in chapbook form. The rich tradition of English fairy mythology survived in the eighteenth century almost entirely because of chapbooks" (1968, 15). This is the reading material famously lamented by Wordsworth in *The Prelude* (1979) ("Oh! Give us once again the wishing cap/Of Fortunatus, and the invisible coat/of Jack the giant-killer"), which literary histories routinely set alongside S. T. Coleridge's 1797 letter to Thomas Poole about his "early reading of Faery Tales, Genii &c &c." (1956–1971). Thus, print may take on a vernacular appeal, especially in conjunction with the fairy tale, confirming that an oral/print continuum is more conceptually productive, and empirically accurate, than a dichotomy.

But if chapbooks could be elevated into the venerable realms of "tradition," the new bogey was the arrival and pervasive circulation of newspapers and magazines, whose contemporary relevance and therefore ephemerality is the opposite of the supposedly eternal values of oral culture. Sumpter's wide-ranging and ground-breaking book begins with yet another "Alternative History of the Fairy Tale," where she contends that "fairy tales were clearly circulating in Britain before the 1750s: in newspapers and magazines as well as chapbooks. They evolved alongside, rather than cleared the way for, that newest of genres, the novel—a dialogue that was to continue throughout the nineteenth century" (2008, 13). Thus, Sumpter shows that even innovative print forms could facilitate the sharing of tales.

The newer print culture, especially of magazines, gave the first home to many fairy tales and fantasy works which are now mostly known in terms of their appearance in books. For example, Charles Kingsley's *The Water-Babies: A Fairy Tale for a Land Baby*, serialized 1862–1863 in *Macmillan's Magazine*, then published by Macmillan in 1863; George MacDonald's *At The Back Of The North Wind* (1868–70; 1871), *The Princess and the Goblin* (1870–1; 1872), and *The Princess and Curdie* (1877; 1883) all originally appeared in *Good Words for the Young* (which MacDonald edited 1869–1872). Robert Louis Stevenson's *Fables* (*Longman's Magazine*, 1895) first appeared in book form as *The Strange Case of Dr Jekyll and Mr Hyde with Other Fables* (1895). Laurence Housman's fairy tales "A Capful of Moonshine" and "How Little Duke Jarl Saved the Castle" first appeared in the *Dome* in October 1898 and October 1899 respectively, and were later included in *The Blue Moon* (1904). And the stories in Edith Nesbit's *Book of Dragons* (1900) first appeared in the *Strand Magazine* (1899–1900).

The original magazine context of fairy tales is important to understanding their reception history, argues Sumpter. Though pedagogically convenient, extracting the tales from that context, as Zipes does, is liable to skew the reader response to the fairy tale when abstracted from the accompanying material in the original serial publication (1987). The response in question here is not only that of the modern reader who will lose much of the situatedness of the historical telling of the tale when it is anthologized (no matter how good the contextualizing notes); also in question is the response of the historical magazine readers who often exercised considerable agency in the production of the tales they read.

Sumpter includes an interesting example when the purportedly juvenile readers of Keir Hardie's politically motivated magazine threaten to go on strike if the magazine does not regularly provide their staple fare because tales were relegated to the back page (or omitted altogether) if a political issue that the editor deemed more important came up (2008, 124–125). The *Labour Leader* featured Hardie's own fairy tale "Jack Clearhead" which included such messages as the maiden "Social-ism" being trapped in a dungeon with the fearsome "Press Curs" (88). Magazines linked writers and readers with fairy tales and such social commentary.

The explicit symbolic and allegorical motivation was by no means new to fairy tales and fables: the full title of Charles Perrault's fairy-tale collection was after all *Stories or Fairy Tales from Past Times with Morals*. However, for Charles Dickens the moralizing went too far in the overt promotion of teetotalism in George Cruikshank's fairy tales (Sumpter 2008, 28–29). Dickens's wrath in "Fraud on the Fairies" was published in October 1853 in his own weekly journal *Household Words*. The attack included a satirical teetotal version of "Cinderella." Nothing daunted, Cruikshank responded by publishing his own teetotal version of "Cinderella" in the 1854 *Fairy Book*. Sumpter also makes a strong case for the *implicit* or coded gay motivation of the fairy tales (for example by Laurence Housman) in decadent *fin de siècle* little magazines such as the *Dome* and the *Yellow Book* (2008, 131–140). Fairy tales (and fables) have always been retold, and every retelling, including these magazine versions, involves some kind of motivation, even if only the storyteller's need to keep the wolf from the door.

The New Chapbooks? Disney and Ladybird Fairy-Tale Storybooks

Disney and Ladybird fairy-tale storybooks are arguably comparable with historical chapbooks insofar as they are cheap, popular, strikingly illustrated, and often disdained by educationalists and sections of the literary elite. A brief examination and comparison of versions by Disney, Vera Southgate's stories published in the Ladybird series *Well-Loved Tales* (1964–1974), and the later Ladybird Disney tales again shows how motivations and values of writers and readers appear in print. Some discrepancies between the Disney print versions of "Snow White," "Cinderella," and "Sleeping Beauty" are particularly interesting since the original Ladybird versions of fairy tales retold by Vera Southgate in the "Easy Reading" *Well-Loved Tales* were replaced in the 1980s onward by the Ladybird Disney versions. The different versions suggest changing motivations in retelling tales by adjusting attitudes toward violence and women's roles and also indicate ways that corporations and media conglomerates may act, and be received, as authors and storytellers.

Walt Disney indisputably made the most influential intervention in the modern history of fairy tales. But while his major impact was undoubtedly through his animated films, to which much attention has been devoted, not least by Zipes (1994, 72–95; 2012a, 191–210), the lesser but still enormous impact of the Disney tie-in fairy-tale books seems relatively under-researched. This is not to underestimate the importance of other kinds of merchandising, sometimes in print, for example a special *Snow White* issue of the magazine *Hollywood* in May 1938 (Miller) and a coloring book (Hollis and Sibley 1987, 78–79). Before the advent of readily available home video versions of the Disney fairy-tale animations on VHS, DVD, Blu-Ray Disc, and now online streamed versions from Netflix and other providers, arguably the print retelling with the iconic Disney images of "Snow White" (ATU 709), "Cinderella" (ATU 510A), and "Sleeping Beauty" (ATU 410) became the major form of their dissemination outside the cinema.

From *Walt Disney's Snow White and the Seven Dwarfs: Adapted from Grimms' Fairy Tales* (1937), published soon after the release of Disney's eponymous animated film, tie-in Disney storybooks of this and other fairy tales have continued to be produced in tandem with Disney fairy-tale films. While certain key features, and indeed innovations, of the Disney films remain constant through the tie-in storybooks (for example Snow White always meets the Prince at the beginning of the Disney versions), there are discrepancies between the various Disney versions, with the consequence that while the animated film version is fixed, the printed editions differ, resulting in a more variable, and thus folkloric, text that further blurs an oral/print dichotomy. In many ways noted in the following, the Vera Southgate/Ladybird version aligns more closely with the Grimms' while still signaling awareness of Disney fairy-tale conventions and softening the harshness of the Grimms' and Disney's versions.

Ladybird books, originally a British phenomenon, gradually developed during the twentieth century; by the 1960s they were immensely popular, covering a huge range of topics and being widely used in British primary schools (Johnson and Alderson 2014). From October 2013, the original *Well-Loved Tales* series was reissued to mark the fiftieth anniversary of its first publication, with edited text by Vera Southgate, author of the entire series. *Snow White and the Seven Dwarfs*, with its title referencing Disney rather than the Grimms, who simply called the tale "Snow White," was retold first by Southgate in the Ladybird "Easy Reading" series (for ages twelve and up) in 1969. Despite the title's nod to Disney, however, the beginning of the fairy tale very much follows the Grimm versions—not only the 1812 and 1857 versions but also the urtext of 1808 in a letter from Jacob Grimm to Carl von Savigny (Zipes 2015, 552). This (not unimportant) backstory of how Snow White got her name when her mother pricked her finger while sewing by an ebony-framed window on a snowy day is entirely dispensed with in the Disney versions.

The 1969 Ladybird version—following the 1812 and 1857 Grimm versions, though not the 1808 version, which has the King off fighting in a war (Zipes 2015, 553)—says nothing about the King, while the later Ladybird Disney version lets him off the hook by saying that he was already dead by the time the action commences. Only the Disney versions have Snow White meet the Prince at the beginning of the story; the original Ladybird edition omits this episode (though it is later introduced into the Ladybird Disney version). While the original Ladybird version is in many respects closer to the Grimms than the Disney adaptations (including the Ladybird Disney edition), the book omits all mention of the huntsman substituting an animal's heart (let alone its lungs and liver, as in the Grimms) for Snow White's in the elaborate casket the Queen has given him for this gruesome purpose. However, all the Disney versions not only make reference to this detail, they also incorporate an illustration of the casket with its distinctive clasp, which features a sword-shaped pin penetrating a heart-shaped hasp.

In the original Ladybird version, the dwarfs' house is "small and neat" as in the Grimms; however, in the Disney versions (including the Ladybird Disney edition) everything is dusty, dirty, and untidy. Understandably tired out after dusting and cleaning the filthy cottage in the Disney adaptation (though no such housework is required in Grimm or the original Ladybird), Snow White lies down across three or more of the tiny beds and falls asleep. In Grimm and the original Ladybird version, Snow White tries all the dwarfs' beds but only the seventh is right. And when she awakes to find the dwarfs watching her, she is initially frightened in the original Ladybird version (as in Grimm 1857, but not 1812).

The original Ladybird version follows the Grimms by including the Queen's first two murder attempts, death by corset and death by poison comb, before moving onto the poison apple—or more accurately the poison (red) half of an apple. Disney's Queen is less subtle in this respect, and her apple is all red. As in the Grimms, the original Ladybird version has the poisoned Snow White laid to rest in a glass coffin; sometimes Disney has a glass coffin or a golden casket covered in glass, but in the Ladybird Disney edition it is "a special bed made of glass and gold" (Southgate 2003, 39). As in Grimm, Snow White's resuscitation is effected in the original Ladybird storybook by an accidental jolt to her coffin (1857)—and not by an irritable servant slapping her on the back (Grimm 1812)—thus dislodging the piece of poison apple stuck in her throat. In Disney of course it is all down to the Prince's kiss.

The original Ladybird version spares younger readers the gruesome spectacle of the evil Queen having to dance herself to death in red-hot iron slippers at Snow White's wedding (as in all Grimm versions, including the 1808 urtext); in this 1969 version she dies of sheer rage. The Disney storybooks mostly follow the film and have the Queen fall off a cliff amid thunder and lightning while trying to perpetrate a final murderous act (rolling a boulder onto the approaching dwarfs), though in some more recent Disney storybook versions she just falls off a cliff.

The beginning of Southgate's version of "Sleeping Beauty" in the Ladybird series *Well-Loved Tales* (1965) follows the Grimms' (1857) version of "Briar Rose" when a frog announces to the wife of a childless couple when she is bathing that she will give birth to a daughter (in the 1812 Grimms' edition a crab does the annunciation). In Disney (the film and the printed Ladybird Disney) we begin with the happy couple arranging the feast to celebrate the birth of their daughter, Aurora, which is the name of the Princess's *daughter* in Part II of Perrault's "Sleeping Beauty." Southgate's version borrows from Perrault some of the magic gifts the fairies bestow on the infant at her christening; the Grimms' list of the gifts of the "wise women" is much shorter. Both the Southgate versions (1990, 2012) follow the Grimms' list of creatures in the castle who fall asleep, including the flies on the wall.

Both Southgate versions omit the miserable deaths suffered by the princes who over the years have tried vainly to penetrate the hedge of thorns to reach the Sleeping Beauty (Briar Rose). After the century-old spell has elapsed, the thorns turn into beautiful flowers (roses, in Southgate) and let the prince enter, and the princess is awakened by his kiss. Life picks up again where it left off in the castle: horses, dogs, pigeons, and flies resume their normal activities.

After the prince and princess get married and start living happily ever after, the 2012 Southgate version offers a brief history of "Sleeping Beauty," mentioning not only Tchaikovsky, Disney, and Perrault, but also the much more obscure fourteenth-century Catalan tale *Frayre de Joy e Sor de Placer* and the sixteenth-century French romance *Perceforest*. However, while such literary references are undoubtedly worthy, and even impressive, in a Ladybird book, one cannot help wondering who exactly they are trying to impress and whether they are really appropriate to the *Well-Loved Tales* series. This paratextual information suggests that the long print history of the story affords the tale, and perhaps the series itself, more educational and economic status.

The initial backstory of *Sleeping Beauty* is omitted by the Ladybird Disney. Not only the princess's prospective spouse (Philip) but the fairy godmothers (Flora, Fauna, and Merryweather)—who rename the princess "Briar Rose"—are all named, as is the wicked fairy Maleficent, who will of course feature in a later Disney film all of her own. Unique to the Disney versions is Maleficent's ability to shapeshift into a huge and terrible black dragon. Apart from these far from minor alterations, the story of "Sleeping Beauty" remains broadly similar to the Grimms' "Briar Rose"—and of course totally omits the second part of Perrault's "Sleeping Beauty" (and of Giambattista Basile's "Sun, Moon and Talia") in which the princess's children face the threat of cannibalism from either the prince's ogreish mother (or his existing wife, in "Sun, Moon and Talia").

There is of course no Ladybird Disney version of "Rapunzel" (ATU 310) since there was no Disney film of this fairy tale until *Tangled* (2010), which is *very* loosely based on the traditional tale, as is the tie-in "Little Golden Book" of the film (*Disney: Tangled* 2010). There are, however, two Ladybird editions of Southgate's version of "Rapunzel": the original 1968 edition replicated in 2014 to celebrate the fiftieth anniversary of Ladybird's *Well-Loved Tales* series and the 2012 edition with different illustrations, but an identical text to the original 1968 Southgate version. This exact textual identity is interesting since (as we have seen) the various Ladybird editions by Southgate, for example of "Sleeping Beauty," do have textual differences.

The 2012 Ladybird edition does, however, contain "A History of *Rapunzel*," which after mentioning the films *Tangled* and *Shrek* (2001)—and the latter's sequels—goes on to cite not only the Grimms' "Rapunzel," but also "Persinette" (1697) by Charlotte-Rose de Caumont de La Force and Giambattista Basile's 1634 version "Petrosinella." Again, while such literary references are undoubtedly impressive in a Ladybird book, one cannot help wondering just how appropriate they really are to the *Well-Loved Tales* series. Perhaps Ladybird might be suspected of overcompensating for what some would see as the faux pas of embracing the Disney brand in the 1980s. Be that as it may, it is nevertheless surely a welcome move to reinstate the Southgate versions of the classic fairy tales, which were all but lost in the heyday of the Disney Ladybird editions.

Fairy-Tale Retellings in Print (By Literary "Celebs")

The Disney and Ladybird Disney imprints indicate that readers may embrace corporate authors as storytellers, while the continuing loyalty to Southgate versions also honors the individual author as storyteller. Fairy tales have always been tales for the (re)telling, for example by nineteenth-century literary celebs Charles Dickens and George Cruikshank in their respectively satirical and temperance versions of "Cinderella." As Disney suggests, celebrity may arise as much from successfully retelling fairy-tales, in print or film, as in some previous accomplishment.

The Fairies Return: Or, New Tales for Old, appearing originally in 1934 and edited by Peter Llewelyn Davies, who is the original of Peter Pan and adopted son of J. M. Barrie, is an early twentieth-century collection of fairy-tale retellings by nowadays rather less celebrated celebs. This book was republished in Zipes's important series "Oddly Modern Fairy Tales" with an introduction by Maria Tatar (Davies 2012). Other now less well-known storytelling celebs in this series include Naomi Mitchison (2014) and Walter de la Mare (2014), introduced by currently fêted fairy-tale writers Marina Warner and Philip Pullman respectively. Pullman (perhaps rather modestly) retells the Grimms' tales in his own voice in *Grimm Tales for Young and Old* (2012). This attribution to one tale teller also happens in other media such as when viewers and critics refer to the Kenneth Branagh (2015) *Cinderella* film or Joss Whedon's *Buffy the Vampire Slayer* (1997–2003).

Authors associated with retelling the fairy tale over the past few decades achieve cultural recognition that verges on celebrity. The number of more radical fairy-tale retellings in print has increased exponentially in the later twentieth and early twenty-first centuries through the tellings of such authors: writers include Margaret Atwood, Neil Gaiman, Tanith Lee, Kelly Link, Patricia A. McKillip, Robin McKinley, Jane Yolen, and of course Angela Carter in *The Bloody Chamber* (1979). Some of these writers have been anthologized in the many and varied fairy-tale collections of Ellen Datlow and Terri Windling, starting with *Snow White, Blood Red* in 1993. Another phenomenon is that of longer novellas or novel-length fairy stories, although such "faerie romances"—to use the subtitle of George MacDonald's *Phantastes* (1858)—go well back into the nineteenth century, arguably to Novalis's *Heinrich von Ofterdingen* (1800). Notable recent examples include Cornelia Funke's *Reckless* (Funke, Wigram, and Latsch 2010) and its sequels; Neil Gaiman's work, especially perhaps *Stardust* (Gaiman and Vess 1997) and *The Sleeper and the Spindle* (Gaiman and Riddell 2014); Robin McKinley's *Beauty: A Retelling of the Story of Beauty and the Beast* (1978) and *Spindle's End* (2000); and Catherynne M. Valente, *The Orphan's Tales: In the Night Garden* (2006) and *The Girl Who Circumnavigated Fairyland in a Ship of Her Own Making* (2012).

The celebrity associated with tale telling thus reinforces the importance of the author function while tying it directly with the storyteller role. While celebrity is not synonymous with scholarship, fairy-tale studies has produced well-regarded and recognized authors who themselves become important cultural tale tellers, such as Zipes, Tatar, and Warner. Print remains the crucial venue for constructing and sharing fairy-tale scholarship. Fairy-tale magazines and journals currently available in print include *Marvels & Tales* published by Wayne State University Press, which also produces Kate Bernheimer's *Fairy Tale Review* as well as the "Fairy-Tale Studies" series of critical monographs. See also *Gramarye*, the journal of the Sussex Centre for Folklore, Fairy Tales, and Fantasy. Rather than working to patrol borders between oral and print tale telling, scholars, writers, readers, and viewers benefit from the historical and contemporary continuum that is the heritage of this storytelling.

Related topics: Adaptation and the Fairy-Tale Web; Anthologies and Tale Collections; Chapbooks; Children's and Young Adult (YA) Literature; Convergence Culture; Disney Corporation; Intellectual Property; Novels; Material Culture; Oral Tradition; Pictorial; Poetry; Storyworlds/Narratology

References Cited and Further Reading

Bottigheimer, Ruth B. 2002. *Fairy Godfather: Straparola, Venice and the Fairy Tale Tradition.* Philadelphia: U Pennsylvania P.
———. 2009. *Fairy Tales: A New History.* New York: SUNY P.
Bronner, Simon. 2007. "Grouping Lore: Scientists and Musicians." In *The Meaning of Folklore*, edited by Simon Bronner, 229–31. Logan: Utah State UP.
Carter, Angela. 1979. *The Bloody Chamber and Other Stories.* Harmondsworth: Penguin.
Coleridge, Samuel Taylor. 1956–1971. *Collected Letters of Samuel Taylor Coleridge*, edited by E. L. Griggs. Oxford: Clarendon.
Cruikshank, George. (1854) 1910. *The Cruikshank Fairy Book.* New York: Putnam.
Datlow, Ellen, and Terri Windling. 1993. *Snow White, Blood Red.* New York: W. Morrow.
Davies, Peter Llewelyn. 2012. *The Fairies Return: Or, New Tales for Old*, edited by Maria Tatar. Princeton, NJ: Princeton UP.
de Blécourt, Willem. 2012. *Tales of Magic, Tales in Print: On the Genealogy of Fairy Tales and the Brothers Grimm.* Manchester: Manchester UP.
de la Mare, Walter. 2014. *Told Again: Old Tales Told Again.* Princeton, NJ: Princeton UP.
Dickens, Charles. 1853. *Frauds on the Fairies.* London: Bradbury & Evans.
Disney: Tangled. 2010. New York: Golden Books.
Funke, Cornelia, Lionel Wigram, and Oliver Latsch. 2010. *Reckless.* New York: Little, Brown.
Gaiman, Neil, and Chris Riddell. 2014. *The Sleeper and the Spindle.* New York: Harper.
Gaiman, Neil, and Charles Vess. 1997. *Stardust: Being a Romance within the Realms of Faerie, Book 1.* London: Vertigo.
Grimm, Jacob, and Wilhelm Grimm. 1812. *Kinder- und Hausmärchen (Children's and Household Tales).* 1st ed. Germany.
———. 1857. *Kinder- und Hausmärchen (Children's and Household Tales).* 7th ed. Germany.
Hafstein, Valdimar. 2015. "Fairy Tales, Copyright, and the Public Domain." In *The Cambridge Companion to Fairy Tales*, edited by Maria Tatar, 11–38. Cambridge: Cambridge UP.

PRINT

Hollis, Richard, and Brian Sibley. 1987. *Walt Disney's Snow White and the Seven Dwarfs & the Making of the Classic Film*. London: André Deutsch.

Housman, Laurence. 1904. *The Blue Moon*. London: John Murray.

Johnson, Lorraine, and Brian Alderson. 2014. *The Ladybird Story: Children's Books for Everyone*. London: British Library Publishing.

Kingsley, Charles. (1863) 1898. *The Water-Babies: A Fairy Tale for a Land-Baby*. New York: Maynard, Merrill, & Co.

MacDonald, George. 1858. *Phantastes: A Faerie Romance for Men and Women*. London: Smith, Elder.

———. (1868–1870) 1871. *At the Back of the North Wind*. London: Strahan & Co.

———. (1870–1871) 1872. *The Princess and the Goblin*. London: Strahan.

———. (1877) 1883. *The Princess and Curdie*. London: Chatto & Windus.

McGann, Jerome J. 1983. *A Critique of Modern Textual Criticism*. Chicago: U Chicago P.

McKinley, Robin. 1978. *Beauty: A Retelling of the Story of Beauty and the Beast*. New York: Harper Collins.

———. 2000. *Spindle's End*. New York: ACE Books.

Miller, Llewellyn, ed. 1938. "Snow White." *Hollywood* 27 (5).

Mitchinson, Naomi. 2014. *The Fourth Pig*. Princeton, NJ: Princeton UP.

Nesbit, Edith. 1900. *The Book of Dragons*. London: Harper.

Neuburg, Victor E. 1968. *The Penny Histories: A Study of Chapbooks for Young Readers Over Two Centuries*. London: Oxford UP.

Novalis. 1800. *Heinrich von Ofterdingen ein nachgelassener Roman; zwei Theile*. Berlin: Buchh. der Realsch.

O'Malley, Andrew. 2003. *The Making of the Modern Child: Children's Literature and Childhood in the Late Eighteenth Century*. London: Routledge.

Preston, Cathy L., and Michael J. Preston. 1995. *The Other Print Tradition: Essays on Chapbooks, Broadsides, and Related Ephemera*. London: Routledge.

Pullman, Philip. 2012. *Grimm Tales for Young and Old*. London: Penguin.

Schacker, Jennifer. 2005. *National Dreams: The Remaking of Fairy Tales in Nineteenth-Century England*. Philadelphia: U Pennsylvania P.

Southgate, Vera. 1964–1974. *Well-Loved Tales (Easy Reading Series)*. Loughborough, UK: Ladybird Books.

———. 1969. *Snow White and the Seven Dwarfs (Easy Reading Series)*. Loughborough, UK: Ladybird Books.

———. (1965) 1990. *Sleeping Beauty: Well-Loved Tales*, illustrated by Eric Winter. Loughborough, UK: Ladybird Books.

———. 2003. *Snow White and the Seven Dwarfs*. London: Ladybird.

———. 2012a. *Rapunzel*. London: Ladybird.

———. 2012b. *Sleeping Beauty*. London: Ladybird.

———. (1968) 2014. *Rapunzel: Well-Loved Tales*. Loughborough, UK: Ladybird Books.

Stevenson, Robert Louis. 1895. *The Strange Case of Dr. Jekyll and Mr. Hyde*. New York: Charles Scribner's Sons.

Straparola, Gianfrancesco. (1550) 2012. *Le piacevoli notti* (Pleasant Nights), edited by Don Beecher, translated by W. G. Waters. Toronto: U Toronto Press.

Sumpter, Caroline. 2008. *The Victorian Press and the Fairy Tale*. Basingstoke: Palgrave Macmillan.

Valente, Catherynne M. 2006. *The Orphan's Tales: In the Night Garden*. New York: Bantam Books.

———. 2012. *The Girl Who Circumnavigated Fairyland in a Ship of Her Own Making*. New York: Square Fish.

Walt Disney's Snow White and the Seven Dwarfs: Adapted from Grimms' Fairy Tales. 1937. New York: H.N. Abrams.

Wordsworth, William. 1979. *The Prelude of 1850*. New York: Norton Critical Edition.

Zipes, Jack, ed. 1987. *Victorian Fairy Tales: The Revolt of the Fairies and the Elves*. New York: Routledge.

———. 1994. *Fairy Tale as Myth/Myth as Fairy Tale*. Lexington: Kentucky UP.

———. (1983) 2012a. *Fairy Tales and the Art of Subversion*. New York: Routledge.

———. 2012b. *The Irresistible Fairy Tale: The Cultural and Social History of a Genre*. Princeton, NJ: Princeton UP.

———. 2015. *Grimm Legacies: The Magic Spell of the Grimms' Folk and Fairy Tales*. Princeton, NJ: Princeton UP.

Mediagraphy

Buffy the Vampire Slayer (TV). 1997–2003. Creator Joss Whedon. USA.

Cinderella. 2015. Director Kenneth Branagh. USA.

Maleficent. 2014. Director Robert Stromberg. USA.

Shrek. 2001. Directors Andrew Adamson and Vicky Jenson. USA.

Tangled. 2010. Directors Nathan Greno and Byron Howard. USA.

35

PICTORIAL

"Such Strange Transformations": Burne-Jones's *Cinderella* and Domestic Technologies

Molly Clark Hillard

The long nineteenth century was the golden era of fairy painting. From Henry Fuseli's and Joseph Noel Paton's darkly layered treatments of Shakespeare's fairies to the twee fairy processions of Richard Doyle, from the gothic dreamscapes of Richard Dadd and John Anster Fitzgerald to the saturated picture book illustrations of Edmund Dulac and Arthur Rackham, the century was awash in the visual fairy. One subset of this genre was the Victorian fairy-tale painting. These were painted from the mid-century onward, primarily by the Pre-Raphaelite Brotherhood and their circle. The fairy-*tale* painting is far less ubiquitous than the fairy painting, but those that remain to us are extremely interesting to fairy-tale and visual scholars alike. As with the fairy tale in print media, the fairy-tale painting speaks to some of the era's deepest, most abiding ideologies, fears, and desires.

Edward Burne-Jones's watercolor painting *Cinderella* (1863) captures a moment after Cinderella has returned from the ball, yet before the prince comes to seek her. She stands in the doorway of her stepmother's scullery, gazing out. One hand rests on her hair, the other plucks absent-mindedly at her apron. One foot is bare, the other still wears a glass slipper. Her bottle-green dress, patched and worn, is tucked up into her belt on one side. On the other dangles a formidable key ring. A rose in a bowl behind her picks up the pink of her skin and the green of the dress. A mouse, no doubt one of those that pulled the carriage the night before, scurries in and out of the pumpkin on the floor nearby. Lining the shelves and peeking out of the cupboards behind her is a sizable collection of willow-patterned plates. This last is seemingly an anomalous element in the painting: porcelain plays no part in any literary version of the tale. Contemporary commentators on the work don't even mention the porcelain as an element worth notice.[1] And yet, the willow pattern takes up over half of the painting's background and is hardly subtle. The question then becomes, what connections pertain between this fairy tale and the pattern of Chinoiserie so popular in Britain in the eighteenth and nineteenth centuries? This chapter suggests that both porcelain and fairy tales offer what I would call domestic technologies—that is, narratives for an emerging English bourgeois, imperial self. Indeed, the willow-patterned plate stands as an Anglicized narrative of transformation in precisely the same way and in the same time frame as "Cinderella" (ATU 510A). And as such, both the tale and the plate allowed a young Burne-Jones to speak to his emerging identity as a

PICTORIAL

Figure 35.1 Edward Coley Burne-Jones, *Cinderella*, 1863, watercolor on paper
Museum of Fine Arts Boston

solo artist. In this way, Burne-Jones's work can be situated in larger discourses of the Victorian fairy tale and the vast mediascape it occupied.[2]

Burne-Jones had a lifelong affinity for folklore. From his earliest paid work, drawings for Archibald Maclaren's *The Fairy Family* (1857), to his last acclaimed oil paintings, his art paid homage to the tales of Perrault and the Grimms, as well as to Arthurian legendry. Of course, the fairy tale would have absolutely saturated young Ned Jones's field of vision. As I (and others) have argued elsewhere, the fairy tale was ubiquitous to the mid-nineteenth-century print and visual art worlds (Clark Hillard 2014; Talairach-Vielmas 2014; Sumpter 2008; Schacker 2003; Bown 2001; Silver 1999). As a working artist from a comparatively poor background, Burne-Jones could scarcely have avoided immersion in the lucrative fairy-tale market. Nevertheless, his friends and family seemed to think his attraction to the tale was not just genuine, but second nature: upon first meeting him in London, Dante Gabriel Rossetti called Burne-Jones "one of the nicest young fellows in dreamland" (De Lisle 1906, 130). In *Memorials*, his wife Georgiana Burne-Jones characterized his fairy-tale work as "a welcome outlet for his abounding humor, and in this form the stories took at his hands as quaint a shape as they wear in the pages of the Brothers Grimm of blessed memory" (G. Burne-Jones 1904, 249). Nor was his interest uninformed: Burne-Jones was also a member of the Folk-Lore Society, founded in 1878, and later a member of the International Folklore Congress of 1891 in London, the first major conference of the Folk-Lore Society (Jacobs and Nutt 1892, ix).

The painting of "Cinderella" marked a crucial point in Burne-Jones's artistic career and personal life. In 1853, at the age of twenty, he enrolled at Exeter College, Oxford, as a divinity student, after four years at the Birmingham School of Art. There he met William Morris. Drawn together by a mutual interest in poetry, and in the artistry of Dante Gabriel Rossetti, the two formed a strong, lifelong bond. After orchestrating an introduction to Rossetti in 1856, Burne-Jones and Morris dropped out of school and moved to London to learn art full-time under Rossetti's tutelage. That same year Burne-Jones became engaged to fifteen-year-old Georgiana Macdonald, a frequenter of the Pre-Raphaelite art studios and an aspiring artist in her own right. The two married in 1860. By 1861, Georgie had given birth to their first child (and had, bitterly and reluctantly, given up artistry to full-time parenting[3]), and Burne-Jones had become a partner in Morris, Marshall, Faulkner & Co. (later Morris & Co.), Morris's decorative arts studio. He continued to produce for Morris throughout his life, contributing designs for tapestries, jewelry, ceramic tiles, stained glass, and woodcuts. But by 1863, Burne-Jones had also begun to paint prolifically on his own and to create a painterly "voice" distinct from his earliest work that was highly indebted to Rossetti. He was producing subjects in watercolor, but was also beginning to experiment with oils, the medium that would mark his mature production. The years 1856–1863, therefore, were a tumultuous time of training, emergence, and transformation.

The year 1863 was also a crucial pass in the history of "Cinderella."[4] The tale had entered European print tradition as "Cenerentola" in Giambattista Basile's *Pentamerone* (1634); as "Cendrillon" in Charles Perrault's *Histoires ou contes du temps passé* (1697); and as "Aschenputtel" in the Grimms' *Kinder- und Hausmärchen* (1812). But the tale has one of the oldest print histories of all fairy tales, with at least two versions dating to ninth-century China, the tale of "Ye Xian" or "Sheh Hsien" (Li 2016; Reed 2003, 70–71; Jameson 1982; Eberhard 1965). So, although most Victorians didn't know it, "Cinderella" represents the European appropriation of an Eastern tradition.

The tale was incorporated into Victorian England with the first translations of fairy tales. The tales of Perrault were first translated into English by Robert Samber as *Histories, or Tales of Past Times: With Morals* (1729). A few decades later, the work of the Brothers Grimm brought the German tale into prominence. It was first translated into English by Edgar Taylor in 1823 and throughout the century remained a staple of English reading. During the nineteenth century, these works enjoyed multiple re-printings and retellings, both in their entirety and as selections of tales. Some of the earliest English adaptations of the tale were pantomime theatricals. The story first appeared at the Theatre Royal, Drury Lane, in 1804 as part of the "New

Grand Allegorical Pantomime Spectacle"; by 1820, the tale was a staple of the pantomime genre ("The Origin of Popular Pantomime Stories" N.d.).

In the two versions most familiar to an English audience—Perrault and the Grimms—the girl's father is a gentleman, often a merchant. Cinderella's transformation does not just restore her to her rightful middle class, but ultimately elevates her into the ruling class. Perhaps for this reason, "Cinderella" became a useful allegory in Victorian England for the rise of the middle class, its transformation through imperial and industrial might into England's "princes of industry" (Carlyle 2000). This Victorian use for "Cinderella" can be seen, for example, in *Punch*'s illustrated poem on the Great Exhibition, "The Cinderella of 1851" (Anonymous 1851). Drawing upon one common nickname of the exhibition hall, the Fairy Palace, the poem views the hall through the eyes of two little pauper girls who are taken to see it. They think that a fairy godmother has transformed the building, just as Cinderella's fairy godmother transforms her. Small wonder that the anonymous poet should call "Cinderella" to mind when thinking about the Crystal Palace; that mid-century testament to England's middle-class prosperity, clothed head to toe with the glass and iron manufacture that made English factory owners wealthy, and stuffed with exhibits that revealed the lucre of English trade, surely evoked magical transformation.

In another telling example, shortly before Burne-Jones began work on his own *Cinderella*, Charles Dickens wrote and serially published *Great Expectations* (1860–61). The novel includes an extended "Cinderella" motif in which Dickens torques, inverts, and recasts the tale. While at first Pip sees Miss Havisham as fairy godmother to his Cinderella ("'This is a gay figure, Pip' said she, making her crutch stick play round me, as if she, the fairy godmother who had changed me, were bestowing the finishing gift" [157]), he later comes to recognize that Magwitch ("Magic Witch") in fact embodies an even grislier version of that role. Miss Havisham herself takes a turn as a stagnant Cinderella, ever limping in one shoe, with her clocks stopped at the moment that her intended deserted her. Although Pip would like to see cold Estella as "the Princess" of Satis House, "rescue[d]" and transformed into a loving bride (231), Estella is a false heroine compared to the real transformation of village girl Biddy as she comes under Joe's loving influence: "Imperceptibly I became conscious of a change in Biddy. [. . .] Her shoes came up at the heel, her hair grew bright and neat, her hands were always clean" (125). Pip comes to learn that his own "transformation," characterized by class climbing and familial erasure, and the "property" he accrues, with its ties to imperial and industrial abuses, is not "great," but actually toxic and filthy.[5] By 1863, then, "Cinderella" as a Victorian text was coming to have an acknowledged connection to middle-class accrual of wealth and the middle-class transformation into a ruling class. I would argue that Burne-Jones's interpretation of "Cinderella" takes full measure of this mid-century significance of the tale. While most critics and art anthologies dismiss the painting as merely fanciful or sweet, preferring to focus on Burne-Jones's medievalism of the same period, I see the painting as evocative of, and contributing to, various discourses integral to the period as a whole.

Central to mid-century ideologies, and to the painting, is the Victorian cult of domesticity. In *Cinderella*, the maiden stands on the verge of marriage, on the actual threshold of her stepmother's home, gazing into her future. Coventry Patmore's long narrative poem *The Angel in the House* (1854) had given a guiding metaphor to Victorian ideal womanhood: a deity of domestic virtue, order, and engagement. The poem was followed by John Ruskin's "Of Queens' Gardens" in *Sesame and Lilies* (1865), which argued that the home was the rightful sphere of influence and rule for women (whereas the marketplace was the male domain). Patmore and Ruskin were drawing on a model of separate gender spheres initiated as early as 1839 with Sarah Stickney Ellis's *The Women of England*. For these reasons, Cinderella's key ring is significant; if the pocket watch was fast becoming a literary and visual symbol of Victorian middle-class masculine power (the keepers of time, the holders of the twenty-four-hour clock and its regulatory function over industry), house keys were the corresponding symbol of the agency afforded to women (the chatelaines of domestic space).[6] In this picture, the very domestic work that degrades Cinderella in the tale marks Burne-Jones's version of *Cinderella* as the angel in the middle-class home.

Marriage and domestic space were certainly on Burne-Jones's mind in 1863: his own marriage had taken place only three years before, and the couple moved houses regularly (MacCarthy 2012, 111). And although there is no record that reveals the model for *Cinderella*, my research suggests that she was most likely one of the four Macdonald sisters. At this point in his career, Burne-Jones was only using various family members to sit for him. He may also have been using Pre-Raphaelite staple Fanny Cornforth (MacCarthy 2012, 208), but the face of Cinderella is almost certainly not Cornforth's. Louisa was apparently Burne-Jones's favorite of the Macdonald sisters (MacCarthy 2012, 191), and, at fifteen in 1863, she had not yet married MP Alfred Baldwin. Alice, then twenty-six, was living with the Burne-Joneses in 1863, shortly before her marriage to John Lockwood Kipling, but Cinderella's face more resembles Edward John Poynter's paintings of Louisa and Georgie. Aesthetically, it makes sense that Burne-Jones would favor the delicately featured Macdonalds over the more Rubenesque Cornforth for his Cinderella. But it makes thematic sense too. The Macdonald sisters—Agnes, Alice, Louisa, and Georgiana—all married between 1860 and 1866, women close to Burne-Jones, were crossing the very same threshold that he depicts in the painting. For many of the women in his circle—Georgie; Rossetti's wife, Lizzie Siddal; William Morris's wife, Jane Burden—marriage meant the end of a budding artistic career and the relegation to domestic duties, modeling, or full-time muse-work. Perhaps this fate can identify Cinderella's preoccupied, rather troubled expression not as dreaminess, but as concern for her future.

Another discursively aestheticized inhabitant of domestic space surrounds Burne-Jones's Cinderella: willow-patterned porcelain. The willow "china" pattern was an important component of Chinoiserie (the imitation or evocation of Chinese motifs and techniques in Western art in the eighteenth and nineteenth centuries). Of course, even porcelain produced in Asia was influenced by European trade requirements, at least as far back as the fifteenth century. But the willow pattern is an especially notorious example of English appropriation of Eastern visuality. The willow pattern emerged as part of the "blue and white" transfer pattern technique, where the pattern is printed onto the porcelain in a manner similar to etching, which enables the pattern to be reproduced in bulk. The pattern was called "Mandarin" by the Caughley studio in the 1770s. Spode created what is now considered the standard design of "willow pattern" in the 1790s, and soon many other studios had copied the design. In order to promote sales, a tale was invented and circulated that narrativized the various pictures making up the design (Chang 2010, 86–87).[7] Both the pattern and tale, then, are English and (in terms of its stylistic associations) have no connection to China other than an Orientalist one.

As Elizabeth Chang has argued, Chinese visuality is a mirror to the English self (2010, 98). She investigates the extensive porcelain collections of James Abbott McNeill Whistler and Dante Gabriel Rossetti—Burne-Jones's bosom friends—and draws important connections between collection and artistic production in the aesthetic tradition. The middle-class collection of porcelain, especially by bohemian artists, was imbedded in the international marketplace, despite the fact that these artists evinced a separation from bourgeois life. For them, porcelain stood as a symbol of their own creativity even as their purchase of it erased the difference between artist and buyer (Chang 2010, 104). Some of these artists were creating paintings that represented their porcelain collections at the time that Burne-Jones painted *Cinderella*: Whistler's *Purple and Rose: The Lange Leizen of the Six Marks* (1864) and *The Artist in*

His Studio (1865–1866) are notable examples, as is Poynter's *Portrait of Agnes Macdonald* (1867). For Chang, these artists' porcelain collections became a "feature of [. . .] intimate domestic space, [which] bridges three initially divided sites—the showroom, the studio, and the drawing room" (2010, 100).

The fairy tale gained popularity in England at roughly the same time as did porcelain. And even though Burne-Jones would not have known that "Cinderella" was a European appropriation of a Chinese tale, as the willow pattern was of porcelain technique, it would not have taxed his imagination to perceive similarities between tale and plate as the transfer of culture between nations, shaped and embellished by many invisible hands. That a tale accompanied the willow-patterned plate (however fabricated) may have prompted further connection between tale and material art. Both porcelain and the fairy tale are domestic forms, ones that share an importation history and a relationship to the home. The blank porcelain, on which an artisan paints, or transfers, designs, is not unlike the fluid and flexible fairy tale, which can absorb the design of many nations and eras. Porcelain and the fairy tale are both technologies of the home, of "intimate domestic space," and, as nominally household objects, are in fact *keys* to traditionally feminine spaces. They are also both forms that were subjects of male collection in Victorian England; one could conclude, then, that *Cinderella* shows a male artist objectifying women, the fairy tale, and the East and appropriating this trifecta as domestic ornamentation that signaled his arrival into bourgeois Victorian society.

On the other hand, as I have argued elsewhere, Burne-Jones routinely represented himself through the female figures in his paintings (Clark Hillard 2014, 122). Burne-Jones produced *Cinderella* at a time when he was making a movement from decorative art toward narrative painting. His art was transforming in the wake of other such narrative expansions, the rise of the novel and narrative poetry. Since Rossetti was known for his porcelain collection, and Morris was gaining fame for his own decorative arts, perhaps the figure of Cinderella symbolizes Burne-Jones as an artist emerging from Rossetti's influence and branching out from coterie work with Morris and toward original, solo production. Unlike Whistler's *Lange Leizen*, for example, which places the model in the midst of the blue-and-white porcelain that occupies the fore, middle, and background of the painting, Burne-Jones locates Cinderella in the foreground of the watercolor, with the porcelain to the rear. The single rose, her position on the threshold, and her authoritative bunch of keys would also support this reading. If Cinderella stands in for Burne-Jones, then perhaps her "strange transformations" speak to a transformative moment in his own history. Her story, in which she first labors, is then befriended by a fairy godmother, and is ultimately collected by a prince, resonates with his own dependence upon patronage. Unlike his wealthier friends Morris, Rossetti, and Whistler, Burne-Jones had to produce to earn a livelihood and relied upon being collected into a wealthy household, upon becoming—like porcelain or the fairy tale—a household name.

All in all, Burne-Jones's *Cinderella* contributes to the rich culture of the fairy tale in the Victorian period. Recent years have seen growth in Victorian fairy-tale scholarship, but there is more work to be done to connect the rise of fairy-tale print media with the explosion of visual culture in the nineteenth century. The rise of children's book publication, the changes in color printing techniques, and the democratization of gallery painting through the influence of the politically radical Pre-Raphaelites all contributed to this visual explosion, and the fairy tale was intimately connected to each of these innovations. Burne-Jones was enmeshed in these innovations, too, and is therefore a useful case study for broader concerns of Victorian fairy-tale "technologies." Later scholars and art critics have dismissed fairy tale art as quaint, sweet, childish, or picturesque—a view often encouraged by the Victorians themselves. But a close examination of the art itself reveals what all fairy-tale media reveals: that fairy tales are bound to the historical moment that adapts and shapes them. Mid-Victorian fairy-tale painting offers a fascinating glimpse into England's international market, capitalist practices, and aesthetic values. It contributes, in other words, to England's national narrative.

Related topics: Children's Picture Books and Illustrations; Contemporary Art; Gender; Orientalism; Photographic; Print

Notes

1. "It is the day after the ball, and in her worn and patched green gown, the little glass slipper on her foot, she leans there dreamingly playing with the corner of her apron; a pink rose is in a glass on the shelf, and, on the ground beside her, half lost in the shadow, are the pumpkin and the rat which have known such strange transformations" (De Lisle 1906, 68).
2. See, for instance, Bown (2001); Clark Hillard (2014); Schacker (2003); Silver (1999); Sumpter (2008).
3. "I remember the feeling of exile with which I now heard through its closed door the well-known voices of friends together with Edward's familiar laugh, while I sat with my little son on my knee and dropped selfish tears on him as 'separator of companions and the terminator of delights'" (G. Burne-Jones 1904, 236).
4. Late in the century, Marian Roalfe Cox would subdivide the tale into three closely related variants: "Cinderella," together with tale type 510B Peau d'Âne, in English versions "Catskin," and "Cap-O-Rushes" (1892, 1–80), in which the girl's father wishes to marry his daughter.
5. For the filthiness of money in *Great Expectations*, see, esp., Dickens (1996, 78–79 and 173). See also Meckier (2002); Ostry (2002); Stone (1979).
6. See, for instance, Agnes Wickfield in Charles Dickens's *David Copperfield* (1850) or Esther Summerson in his *Bleak House* (1853). The key is again connected to female agency in Lewis Carroll's *Alice's Adventures in Wonderland* (1865) and in Frances Hodgson Burnett's *The Secret Garden* (1911).
7. In sum: a woman defies her father's arranged marriage and escapes with her preferred lover. The pair is caught and put to death, but the sympathetic gods turn them into a pair of doves.

References Cited and Further Reading

Anonymous. 1851. "The Cinderella of 1851." *Punch* 21: 132–3.

Basile, Giambattista. (1634) 1893. *The Pentamerone (Il Pentamerone)*, translated by Richard Burton. London: Henry and Co.

Bown, Nicola. 2001. *Fairies in Nineteenth-Century Art and Literature*. Cambridge: Cambridge UP.

Burne-Jones, Georgiana. 1904. *Memorials of Edward Burne-Jones*. London: Macmillan.

Burnett, Frances Hodgeson. (1911) 2002. *The Secret Garden*. London: Penguin.

Carlyle, Thomas. (1843) 2000. "Past and Present." In *The Norton Anthology of English Literature*, edited by M. H. Abrams and Stephen Greenblatt, 1117. Vol. 2, 7th ed. New York: Norton.

Chang, Elizabeth. 2010. *Britain's Chinese Eye: Literature, Empire, and Aesthetics in Nineteenth Century Britain*. Palo Alto, CA: Stanford UP.

Clark Hillard, Molly. 2014. *Spellbound: The Fairy Tale and the Victorians*. Columbus: Ohio State UP.

Cox, Marian Roalfe. 1892. *Cinderella: Three Hundred and Forty-Five Variants*. London: David Nutt.

De Lisle, Fortunée. 1906. *Burne-Jones*. London: Methuen.

Dickens, Charles. (1849–1850) 1995. *David Copperfield*. London: Penguin.

———. (1852–1853) 2003. *Bleak House*. London: Penguin.

———. (1860–1861) 1996. *Great Expectations*. London: Penguin.

Eberhard, Wolfram, ed. 1965. "Cinderella." In *Folktales of China*, 156–61. Chicago: U Chicago P.

Grimm, Jacob, and Wilhelm Grimm. (1812). *German Fairy Tales (Kinder- und Hausmärchen)*, translated by Margaret Hunt, edited by Helmut Brackert and Volkmar Sander. New York: Continuum, 1985.

Jacobs, Joseph, and Alfred Nutt, eds. 1892. *International Folklore Congress 1891: Papers and Transactions*. London: David Nutt.

Jameson, Richard. 1982. "Cinderella in China." In *Cinderella: A Folklore Casebook*, edited by Alan Dundes, 71–97. New York: Garland.

Li, Jing. 2016. "Comparability and Distinctiveness of Chinese Folktales." In *Folktales and Fairy Tales: Traditions and Texts from around the World*, edited by Anne Duggan and Donald Haase, 203–4. 2nd ed. Westport, CT: Greenwood.

MacCarthy, Fiona. 2012. *The Last Pre-Raphaelite: Edward Burne-Jones and the Victorian Imagination.* Cambridge, MA: Harvard UP.

Maclaren, Archibald. 1857. *The Fairy Family: A Series of Ballads and Metrical Tales Illustrating the Fairy Mythology of Europe.* London: Longman.

Martineau, Jane, ed. 1997. *Victorian Fairy Painting.* London: Royal Academy of Arts.

Meckier, Jerome. 2002. *Dickens's Great Expectations: Misnar's Pavilion versus Cinderella.* Lexington: UP Kentucky.

"The Origin of Popular Pantomime Stories." N.d. Victoria and Albert Museum. www.vam.ac.uk/content/articles/t/pantomime-origins/.

Ostry, Elaine. 2002. *Social Dreaming: Dickens and the Fairy Tale.* London: Routledge.

Patmore, Coventry. 1854. *The Angel in the House.* London: Parker and Son.

Perrault, Charles. (1694) 1969. *The Fairy Tales of Charles Perrault (Histoires ou contes du temps passé),* translated by A. E. Johnson. New York: Dover.

Reed, Carrie Elizabeth. 2003. *A Tang Miscellany: An Introduction to Youyang Zazu.* New York: Peter Lang.

Ruskin, John. (1865) 2002. "Of Queens' Gardens." In *Sesame and Lilies,* 68–93. New Haven, CT: Yale UP.

Samber, Robert, trans. 1729. *Histories or Tales of Past Times . . . with Morals,* by M. Perrault. London: J. Pote.

Schacker, Jennifer. 2003. *National Dreams: The Remaking of Fairy Tales in Nineteenth-Century England.* Philadelphia: U Pennsylvania P.

Silver, Carole G. 1999. *Strange and Secret Peoples: Fairies and Victorian Consciousness.* Oxford: Oxford UP.

Stickney Ellis, Sarah. 1839 (2010). *The Women of England, Their Social Duties, and Domestic Habits.* Cambridge: Cambridge UP.

Stone, Harry. 1979. *Dickens and the Invisible World: Fairy Tales, Fantasy, and Novel-Making.* Bloomington: Indiana UP.

Sumpter, Caroline. 2008. *The Victorian Press and the Fairy Tale.* Basingstoke: Palgrave.

Talairach-Vielmas, Laurence. 2014. *Fairy Tales, Natural History and Victorian Culture.* Basingstoke: Palgrave Macmillan.

Mediagraphy

Burne-Jones, Edward. 1863. *Cinderella.* Watercolor on paper. Museum of Fine Arts Boston.

Poynter, Edward John. 1866. *Portrait of Agnes Macdonald.* Watercolor on Paper. Private Collection.

———. 1868. *Portrait of Louisa Baldwin.* Watercolor on Paper. Private Collection.

Whistler, James Abbott McNeill. 1864. *Purple and Rose: The Lange Leizen of the Six Marks.* Oil on canvas. Philadelphia Museum of Art.

———. 1865–1866. *The Artist in His Studio.* Oil on paper mounted to canvas. Art Institute of Chicago.

36
MATERIAL CULTURE

Fairy-Tale Things: Studying Fairy Tales From a Material Culture Perspective

Meredith A. Bak

In May 2015, a three-year-old Aboriginal girl named Samara Muir and her mother, Rachel, went to the Watergardens shopping center in Melbourne, Australia, to attend a Disney themed event. Clad in an ice blue gown in the style of *Frozen's* (2013) lead character, Queen Elsa, Samara waited in line for an attraction. There, they were approached by a White mother and her two young daughters, who launched into a racially motivated verbal attack, claiming that Samara did not belong in the costume because Queen Elsa isn't Black. Rachel Muir's post about the experience on social media was met with overwhelming support from around the globe, both celebrating Samara's inherent beauty and sense of self and defending her right to dress up as the Disney queen. In the wake of the harassment, communities both in and outside Australia rallied in Samara's support. The child received invitations to appear in a Disney on Ice show and in a music video for the Indigenous rapper Adam Briggs. Positive publicity often included images of an incredulously happy Samara in her Queen Elsa dress, clutching an Elsa doll close. Perhaps most complex of all, Samara also received a video message from an actress who plays Queen Elsa at Disney's Orlando, Florida, theme park. In the message, the actress reiterated Samara's self-worth, encouraging her to be herself and—echoing the film's signature refrain—to "let it go" (Keady 2015; Rose 2015; Wilford 2015), defending her right to pretend to be Elsa—an effort aided by licensed merchandise.

Taken as a whole, the incident begins to map out a complex network of identification, belonging, and affect all centered around Disney's *Frozen*. Although many factors are at play in this scenario, the blue dress that Samara wore and the doll she held affectionately both played a central role. For many, these objects might be regarded as enabling all children to engage in imaginary play and perform in the roles of beloved characters. For others, however, the objects seem to entrench a reductive idea about who, exactly, is entitled to such play—the "ideal" or intended user in this case specified by race and gender. The episode demonstrates the significant role of material culture in cementing or transforming the thematic weight of a fairy tale and its popular reception and interpretation. An adaptation of Hans Christian Andersen's "The Snow Queen," *Frozen* has widely been interpreted as a story about self-acceptance. On the level of narrative, it has been praised for celebrating love between sisters over the stereotypical heterosexual romance centered on a prince charming (Bartyzel 2014; Dalfonzo 2013; Song 2014).

Extending this interpretation, the film's hallmark song, "Let It Go," has been interpreted as a queer coming-out anthem, prompting polarized responses across the political spectrum. That the performative act of a little girl donning an Elsa costume received such a hostile response by some indicates the dogma and rigidity with which some regard fairy tales and their iconic characters. Simultaneously, the overwhelmingly supportive response by others also demonstrates the possibility that fairy tales' popular interpretations can be transformed, the messages associated with them flexible, capable of expansion, inclusion. As Samara Muir's dress signaled her pretend play as Queen Elsa, it also transformed the cultural imagination and broadened the popular interpretation of *Frozen* itself, now read as an allegory of tolerance as it intersects with race—an interpretation that Disney would likely be enthusiastic to absorb, given its fraught legacy charged with perpetuating problematic ideological positions with regard to race, gender, and cultural imperialism (Giroux 1994; Wasko 2001).

The longevity and broad cultural appeal of fairy tales are often attributed to the form's malleability, the ability of these tales to retain their identity even as versions change to reflect shifting social ideas and are adapted across different media such as the oral tradition, the written word, film, television, song, and game. They are at once slippery, dynamic forms, yet also anchored by particular themes, recurring tropes and characters. Each version of a tale concretizes or solidifies a specific inflection of that story, and certain adaptations will find surer purchase as canon for a range of reasons, from their cultural resonance at a particular point in time to the scope, scale, and intensity of their dissemination, as in the case of many Disney versions. These points of relative stasis and fluctuation can be traced at the level of text, iconography, and broader social interpretation and critical response, forming a network of innumerable intersections between fairy tales and media cultures.

However, the realm of material culture also represents a significant area in which the meanings and messages of fairy tales persist and vary across space and time. In ways distinct from oral tradition, the written word, visual iconography, or the moving image, material things structure and invite particular kinds of interactions from their users. Like many other media franchises—and particularly those aimed principally at children—fairy tales are kept aloft not only through reading, hearing, and seeing, but also through "doing," through acts of embodiment and performance that material objects can facilitate (Buckingham and Sefton-Green 2003, 379). In contemporary children's media culture, Buckingham writes, "characters are effectively the children's equivalent of brands, and they can be deployed across a wide range of products, from media and toys to food and clothing" (2011, 91). The objectification of fairy-tale elements into material objects thus provides occasion to observe how users animate fairy tales and, in so doing, can sustain or modify their meanings. Aspects of material culture are thus a crucial point from which new permutations of a tale are generated, in both sanctioned and unsanctioned ways. This chapter will consider a few key issues and approaches to the study of fairy tales from a material culture perspective. What follows is less a summary than a series of observations and provocations. I outline some core definitions, methodologies, and critical issues that surface in the intersection between fairy tales and material culture and highlight possible directions for future research.

Material Culture: Definitions and Historical Perspectives

The notion of materiality surfaces in relation to fairy tales in a few adjacent ways. Because fairy tales are a form that originated in the oral tradition, one critical position foregrounds the notion that textual incarnations of fairy tales, in themselves, constitute forms of material culture. In addition to the perception that a story's elements form its "source material," the material components of printed fairy tales, from their ink and paper to the binding and packaging of tales into collections, have played an important role in determining particular audience formations and have served to anchor specific story versions. Printed versions could be duplicated and disseminated without the variation associated with oral storytelling, thereby standardizing certain renditions in both text and image. The introduction of the printing press in the fifteenth century thus changed "the form, themes, production, and reception" of these tales (Zipes 1994, 11).

A second point concerns the thematic importance of things *within* fairy tales. As fairy tales are read and told, the language undergoes a process akin to transubstantiation; as Maria Tatar argues, "words become wands" (2014, 6). Fairy tales bear an interesting relation to material culture given their oscillation between weighty corporeality and ephemeral magic. "On the one hand," Tatar writes, "there is a drive to create substance, materiality, or thingness, and on the other hand, a compulsion to affirm the weightless charms of light, airy nothingness" (6). Likewise, fairy tales are full of magical and enchanted objects, which often play a central role in the story by transforming and reshaping the characters' fates. These function both as unalterable objects that testify to certain truths or inevitabilities (one might think of the evidentiary weight of Bluebeard's bloody key and the perfect fit of Cinderella's glass slipper), yet they also serve as placeholders or vessels that mark a range of possible transformations or reversals of fate (for example, the pumpkin that becomes Cinderella's coach or the gold that Rumpelstiltskin spins from straw). Just as so many fairy tales are dominated by objects that prompt shifts and transformations at the level of narrative, so too do the real-life objects inspired by fairy tales take on a significant and complex role in structuring and enacting cultural values and everyday practices.

While the concepts of the material and materiality writ large interface with fairy tales in a number of ways, an examination of consumer objects inspired by, or thematized around, fairy tales represents a particularly salient site of investigation, given the function of such objects in sustaining and shaping the tales' cultural importance. Fairy-tale objects, especially as they circulate in contemporary consumer culture, invite distinct methodological approaches and considerations that help expand scholarly conversation beyond literary, film, and media studies. Material culture is a multidisciplinary inquiry energized by fields as diverse as social history, design, decorative arts, folklore, art history, and cultural studies. It is guided by the fundamental premise that the material world offers a unique site of study and that objects have the capacity to yield distinct information in ways that text or image alone may not. Underpinning this inquiry is the assumption that artifacts reflect their cultural and historical contexts in both implicit and explicit ways and that these objects can shape and structure everyday human interactions (Garrison 2008). Focusing on material objects enables a shift in perspective, reframing questions about "how inanimate objects constitute human subjects, how they move them, how they threaten them, how they facilitate or threaten their relation to other subjects" (Brown 2001, 7). Given the ubiquity of physical objects across all cultural practices, objects theoretically have the capacity to aid in the reconstruction and circulation of a much wider range of histories than modes of cultural transmission linked only to particular social groups, such as the written word. However, the objects often deemed worthy of preservation and study nevertheless reflect cultural prejudices as well (Prown 1982).

Although it may seem apparent, the distinction between visual and material cultures is often difficult to discern; the two domains are closely related and overlap in many cases. Sally Promey suggests that the division between material and visual culture studies is problematic in that it frequently "serves to reinvent old sensory hierarchies, to reinforce an imperialism of the eye" and relegating the other senses to an afterthought (2008, 289). Part of the desire to validate and recognize the importance of the visual and iconographic emerges from the historical tradition, in which the written document has retained primacy as evidence, with the visual serving principally as supplementary or illustrative instead of as evidence in its own right. Nevertheless, articulating core distinctions between these categories helps facilitate discussion about how things operate differently than images.

Take, for example, two children's toothbrushes, one emblazoned with an image of *Star Wars* franchise hero Han Solo across its handle, the other a battery-operated model made of molded plastic to take the form of a lightsaber's hilt. Both are licensed merchandise, differentiating them in the marketplace from other toothbrushes and perhaps even motivating reluctant children to brush their teeth. Indeed, both are functional toothbrushes. However, whereas the first toothbrush is thematized by its Star Wars–related image, the second, in a sense, is transformed into a lightsaber itself. In addition to its distinct shape, the battery-operated example includes a working button that moves the brush and activates a light feature, simulating the activation of the saber's blade.

A similar distinction is readily observed in licensed clothing. Whereas some licensed apparel bears the image of familiar characters, like a child's shirt featuring *Frozen*'s Anna and Elsa, other clothing reproduces character costumes, such as princess dresses, and thus invites the wearer to inhabit a new persona. Whereas the first is used in everyday life to signify affinity with the characters, the second has the potential to turn its wearer *into* the character in play through performance. Both historically and contemporarily, fairy-tale images have been emblazoned on the surfaces of a wide range of products, from transferware dishes to children's bedroom furniture and textiles. Considering the thingness of things is a challenging enterprise in scholarly contexts that frequently privilege literary, discursive, or visual analyses, yet careful consideration of the material world can yield important knowledge including the transformative properties of objects.

Methods

The histories of children's literature and material culture have always been intertwined since the publication of John Newbery's *A Little Pretty Pocket-Book* in 1744, which was sold alongside pincushions and balls. Considering the literary in tandem with the material, Robin Bernstein argues, offers an opportunity to more fully consider how literature functions in children's everyday lives, where stories circulate alongside playthings, which can be used to enrich, subvert, or otherwise engage with narrative themes (2013). The study of material culture both necessitates and invites a diverse array of methodological approaches. Jules David Prown outlines one comprehensive methodological approach involving a systematic program of description, deduction, and speculation. In an exercise in slowed-down analytical thinking, Prown encourages scholars to scrutinize an object's physical properties and consider the modes of sensory engagement it seems to facilitate or encourage. From there, it is possible to develop hypotheses about the object's function, meaning, and users, which can then be checked. To be sure, many material culture approaches are sensory- and inquiry-based, exemplified by an exercise developed in a pedagogical document entitled "Twenty Questions to Ask an Object" (Andrews et al. 2015).

In an elaboration of Prownian analysis, Kenneth Haltman stresses that it is important to consider not only what objects signify, but also *how* they do so (2000). Material culture inquiry is thus also informed by design theory, which offers both a vocabulary and a conceptual framework through which to understand how things work. We tend to know how to operate and negotiate everyday objects as though their uses are natural and intuitive, yet this apparent ease built into an object's design is, in fact, the product of both careful engineering and a close consideration of human psychology (Norman 2013). Building upon the notion of "affordances," (Gibson 1979) an object's attributes that make possible particular actions (for example, a chair affords sitting), design scholar and practitioner Don Norman has developed a series of terms to further specify the design properties of an object, such as its constraints—what it *can't* do; its signifiers—those aspects that help specify what the user is *supposed* to do with it; and feedback—elements that indicate that an input has been received or that an object is being used as intended (Norman 2013). These methods and approaches can help illuminate the way that objects help support, challenge, modify, or even undermine the ideological underpinnings or thematic significance of a fairy tale. Considering a few brief case studies helps demonstrate such an application.

Certain children's playthings advance an understanding of the fairy tale as immutable, capable of being reproduced without adaptation or variation. Crayola's Picture-Tracer is a paradigmatic example. First introduced around 1911, the picture tracer consisted of a drawing tablet overlaid with a roll of tracing paper and a set of crayons. The tracer came with a series of twelve images featuring scenes from fairy tales, which the child was meant to slip under the tracing paper roll and trace with the crayons. The toy's packaging extolled the tracer's virtues as creative and educational, proclaiming that it was "everything a toy should be—and nothing it should not be," implying a tidy and perfect copy with no remainder, surplus, or deviation (Crayola Picture-Tracer ca. 1911). With it, the child was meant not to modify and adapt the fairy-tale scenes but to reproduce them faithfully, as indicated by the transparent tracing paper and the feedback of correlating drawn crayon lines precisely with the chromolithographed story scenes. Of course, in practice, the extent to which children actually used the tracer as specified is another question. It is possible—even probable—that children reveled in the opportunity to trace the basic contours of the scene but then modified shapes, colors, and other details.

In a second instance, the circumstances of an object's production, including the quality of its materials and construction, have the capacity to undo or radically reverse the narrative or textual meaning of a fairy tale. Disney's *Little Mermaid* Prince Eric's Castle Play Set is an ill-fated toy that exemplifies this possibility. The white and gold plastic castle features six play areas, such as a ballroom, dressing room, garden, and stables—spaces through which the child can navigate the figures of Ariel, Eric, Ursula, and others via a spiral staircase or manually operated elevator (*The Little Mermaid* N.d). Within the narrative of Disney's adaptation of Andersen's "The Little Mermaid," this is the place where Ariel, a former mermaid turned human with a pair of legs, lives happily ever after with her prince. Not only does the inclusion of an Ursula figure undermine this narrative (it is unclear why the evil sea witch who stole Ariel's voice now comfortably cohabitates with the happy couple), but even more fundamentally, the play set's material qualities frequently prevented play practices that would allow the film's happy ending to play out at all. Upon the toy's release, a string of customer complaints flagged the play set's flimsiness and, in particular, the tendency for Ariel's legs to almost immediately snap off of her body ("The Little Mermaid" 2014). That the character's legs—which bear enormous thematic significance within the narrative—are so indifferently rendered in plastic as to break suggests a disconnect between the story as narrative and its embodiment within material culture. The toy, meant to enable children to play out the story's happy ending, undercuts rather than facilitates the opportunity for this narrative to emerge, requiring the child to adapt accordingly.

Critical Issues: Voice and Agency in Material Consumer Culture

Although material culture invites numerous methodological approaches, some related critical issues arise in relation to such work. In particular, within material culture studies, there is a tendency to revert to metaphors concerning speech, voice, and enunciation when attempting to explain the means by which objects divulge information. It is convenient, although problematic, to ask how objects can "speak" to us. Such a characterization might seem apt in relation to cultural forms such as fairy tales, which largely originated in the oral tradition. The sentiment that things can metaphorically "speak" for themselves and on behalf of their cultural and historical contexts is a powerful trope within material culture studies, as well as within popular language. However, the use of voice as a governing metaphor proves problematic for at least two reasons.

First, the elevation of the "voice" above other sensory and expressive registers privileges a culture of orality and vocalization. In the case of fairy tales, this orientation has already been explored extensively, and thus its application to material culture represents a missed opportunity to explore other interpretive methods that are unique to objects and that have the potential to yield new interpretive findings. A second objection concerns the subjectivity and agency of children as presumed audiences, particularly in relation to film adaptations of fairy tales and the material objects produced as a result of franchised fairy-tale narratives. Within both popular and critical discourses, the child's voice is romanticized and evoked as a true or authentic expression, yet it is often simultaneously excluded from the very social and political arenas that are integral to children's advocacy (James 2007). Thus, asking what objects "say" when children—as frequent audiences for such tales—are, themselves, often denied the opportunity to speak is a point of political tension. The material offers an opportunity to trace out agency and meaning outside of written or iconographic language, but in order to capitalize upon this opportunity, it may be advisable to avoid metaphors of the voice and orality, which can be too closely subsumed by the hegemony of language.

A second critical issue within material culture emerges in relation to ascribing user agency within broader circuits of capitalist production. Material culture has long borne a close relationship to scholarly inquiry associated with consumer culture. Methods and materials of production, distribution, and circulation charge objects with significance and meaning. Consumption represents a valuable framework for considering material culture because things help reflect social status, can help trace or indicate the relationship between consumer demand and innovations in production, and allow us to see how users invest them with meaning (Martin 1993, 142). Consumer goods related to fairy tales thus represent a particularly fruitful intersection of folk and factory as popular stories and icons become commodified. It is impossible to inventory the extent to which fairy-tale elements have found their way into the realm of material culture. Within children's material culture alone, virtually every category of consumer good has been fashioned or thematized by fairy-tale icons and images, from clothing and playthings to home furnishings and food. As has been intimated, elements of material culture have the capacity to canonize or validate particular renditions of a character or tale. In a discussion of the many ancillary elements and paratexts that circulate around contemporary fairy tales, Michael Drout noted the primacy of the icon over text in defining the hegemonic version of particular characters. He writes, "I have a box in the basement filled with my daughter's Disney princesses; these dolls lock into place a particular look for fairy tale characters whose descriptions are not quite as fixed as the icon designed to sell merchandise to little girls" (quoted in Zipes 2014, 68).

Some scholars argue that individual social actors play a significant role in negotiating the meanings and messages inscribed in consumer objects. Daniel Miller's ethnographic work, for example, suggests that the global circulation of brands such as Coca-Cola might be understood less as an instance of cultural imperialism, but instead as a site at which the product is meaningfully appropriated within the local context and charged with unique meaning (1998). In her work on children's licensed media toys of the late twentieth century, Ellen Seiter similarly argues that elements of mass culture contribute to children's social and cultural worlds and that such toys can even be interpreted and employed in subversive or oppositional ways—a point about which Zipes is skeptical (Seiter 1995; Cook 2004; Zipes 2013). The extent to which the user exercises agency in relation to the object, then, remains open. In such work, it is vital not to foreclose any critical accounts of user agency, but perhaps equally advisable to be cautious about overly optimistic interpretations.

Considerations for Further Research

Fairy tales intersect with questions related to material culture in innumerable ways. The production, circulation, and consumption of consumer products inspired by fairy tales represents perhaps the most prominent way in which fairy-tale objects populate the contemporary mediascape, where they infiltrate everyday life and have the capacity to structure the quotidian experiences of the users who encounter them. There, these elements of material culture can reproduce, canonize, extend, and run counter to a tale's meaning and message as it is previously or popularly understood. As the opening example of Samara Muir suggests, even as a film entitled *Frozen* (and one made by a monolithic media conglomerate) might imply a certain ideological rigidity, the little girl's performance and the world's reaction instead suggest the degree to which the thematic undercurrents are flexible and adaptable, plastic and able to accommodate a broad range of experiences. Such reactions can, in turn, be interpreted broadly, as transformative signs of social or political change or, as Zipes might warn, as an instance of "calculated or contrived subversion" of a dominant ideological position, which can ultimately be recuperated and obscured by the logic of capital (2013, 19).

I conclude by gesturing toward some of the broader preoccupations and ongoing questions that might help shape the trajectories of future materialist explorations of folk and fairy tales. Several approaches and burgeoning traditions represent yet other opportunities for material culture–related research. Practitioners of object-oriented ontology, for example, offer a framework that radically repositions the anthropocentric frame of reference, which, in turn, opens up the scope of inquiry to include critical questions about the ontological and ecological dimensions of things (Bogost 2012; Bryant 2011). Such work might invigorate studies of objects according to temporalities and flows beholden to logics other than the human perspective. Likewise, there is abundant opportunity to consider fairy tales from the perspective of the built and natural environments, particularly as locations such as Iceland and New Zealand have been used and re-appropriated as fantasy landscapes in media productions. A further area of inquiry concerns the degree of disconnect between the aspirational themes of fairy tales as they are incorporated into iconography and merchandise and the conditions of the laborers responsible for producing them. In other words, how might material objects associated with fairy tales help articulate which social subjects have the liberty to incorporate the mythology of "happily ever after" into their conditions of possibility and which are excluded from such a formulation? Objects have the capacity to enlarge or restrict the sphere of political action, and the application of material culture questions and methods has much to offer in the study of fairy tales. Objects can serve as evidence in ways that are distinct from the textual and iconographic. In this way, material culture is capable of expanding the study of fairy tales in new directions, opening up the discussion to even broader multidisciplinary possibilities.

Related topics: Adaptation and the Fairy-Tale Web; Children's and Young Adult (YA) Literature; Comic Cons; Contemporary Art; Disney Corporation; Food; Language; Oral Tradition; Print

Acknowledgment

Research for this chapter was supported by the National Endowment for the Humanities Summer Institute in American Material Culture: Nineteenth-Century New York, directed by David Jaffee at the Bard Graduate Center in 2015.

References Cited and Further Reading

Andrews, Debby, Sarah Carter, Estella Chung, Ellen Garvey, Shirley Wajda, and Catherine Whalen. 2015. "Twenty Questions to Ask an Object." *Humanities and Social Sciences Online.* https://networks.h-net.org/twenty-questions-ask-object-handout.

Bartyzel, Monika. 2014. "Girls on Film: How Frozen Killed Prince Charming." *The Week*, January 17. http://theweek.com/articles/452811/girls-film-how-frozen-killed-prince-charming.

Bernstein, Robin. 2013. "Toys Are Good for Us: Why We Should Embrace the Historical Integration of Children's Literature, Material Culture, and Play." *Children's Literature Association Quarterly* 4: 458–63.

Bogost, Ian. 2012. *Alien Phenomenology, Or, What It's Like to Be a Thing.* Minneapolis: U Minnesota P.

Brown, Bill. 2001. "Thing Theory." *Critical Inquiry* 28 (1): 1–22.

Bryant, Levi R. 2011. *The Democracy of Objects.* Ann Arbor: MPublishing.

Buckingham, David. 2011. *The Material Child.* Cambridge: Polity.

Buckingham, David, and Julian Sefton-Green. 2003. "Gotta Catch 'Em All: Structure, Agency and Pedagogy in Children's Media Culture." *Media, Culture & Society* 25 (3): 379–99.

Cook, Daniel Thomas. 2004. "Beyond Either/Or." *Journal of Consumer Culture* 4 (2): 147–53.

Dalfonzo, Gina. 2013. "Frozen's Cynical Twist on Prince Charming." *The Atlantic*, December 10. www.theatlantic.com/entertainment/archive/2013/12/-em-frozen-em-s-cynical-twist-on-prince-charming/282204/.

Garrison, J. Ritchie. 2008. "Material Cultures." In *A Companion to American Cultural History*, edited by Karen Halttunen, 295–310. Hoboken: Wiley-Blackwell.

Gibson, James. (1979) 2014. "The Theory of Affordances." In *The People, Place, and Space Reader*, edited by Jen Jack Gieseking, William Mangold, Cindi Katz, Setha Low, and Susan Saegert, 56–60. New York: Routledge.

Giroux, Henry. 1994. "Animating Youth: The Disneyfication of Children's Culture." *Socialist Review* 94 (3): 23–55.

Haltman, Kenneth. 2000. "Introduction." In *American Artifacts: Essays in Material Culture*, edited by Jules David Prown and Kenneth Haltman, 1–10. East Lansing: Michigan State UP.

James, Allison. 2007. "Giving Voice to Children's Voices: Practices and Problems, Pitfalls and Potentials." *American Anthropologist* 109 (2): 261–72.

Keady, Cameron. 2015. "Bullies Tell Girl in 'Frozen' Costume That 'Elsa Isn't Black,' So Internet Steps In." *The Huffington Post*, June 26. www.huffingtonpost.com/2015/06/26/elsa-racist-comments_n_7665666.html.

"*The Little Mermaid*—Prince Eric's Castle Play Set Customer Reviews—Product Reviews—Read Top Consumer Ratings." 2014. *Disney Store.* http://reviews.disneystore.com/1928-en_us/1339938/disney-the-little-mermaid-prince-erics-castle-play-set-reviews/reviews.htm.

Martin, Ann Smart. 1993. "Makers, Buyers, and Users: Consumerism as a Material Culture Framework." *Winterthur Portfolio* 28 (2/3): 141–57.

Miller, Daniel. 1998. "Coca-Cola: A Black Sweet Drink from Trinidad." In *Material Cultures: Why Some Things Matter*, edited by Daniel Miller, 169–87. London: U College London P.

Norman, Donald A. 2013. *The Design of Everyday Things: Revised and Expanded Edition.* New York: Basic Books.

Promey, Sally. 2008. "Situating Visual Culture." In *A Companion to American Cultural History*, edited by Karen Halttunen, 279–94. Malden, MA: Wiley-Blackwell.

Prown, Jules David. 1982. "Mind in Matter: An Introduction to Material Culture Theory and Method." *Winterthur Portfolio* 17 (1): 1–19.

Rose, Rebecca. 2015. "Queen Elsa Stands Up for Little Girl After Bullies Make Racist Comments About Her 'Frozen' Costume." *Cosmopolitan*, June 24. www.cosmopolitan.com/politics/news/a42487/queen-elsa-stands-up-for-little-girl-after-bullies-make-racist-comments-about-her-frozen-costume/.

Seiter, Ellen. 1995. *Sold Separately: Children and Parents in Consumer Culture.* New Brunswick, NJ: Rutgers UP.

Song, Isabel. 2014. "Why We're Still Talking about 'Frozen'." *The Huffington Post*, May 7. www.huffingtonpost.com/isabel-song/why-were-still-talking-ab_b_4840545.html.

Tatar, Maria. 2014. *The Cambridge Companion to Fairy Tales*. Cambridge: Cambridge UP.

Wasko, Janet. 2001. "Challenging Disney Myths." *Journal of Communication Inquiry* 25 (3): 237–57.

Wilford, Denette. 2015. "This Little Girl Gets Her Own Fairy-Tale Ending." *The Loop*, June 24. www.theloop.ca/this-is-what-you-call-a-happily-ever-after/.

Zipes, Jack. 1994. *Fairy Tale as Myth/Myth as Fairy Tale*. Lexington: UP Kentucky.

———. 2013. *Relentless Progress: The Reconfiguration of Children's Literature, Fairy Tales, and Storytelling*. New York: Routledge.

———. 2014. *Grimm Legacies: The Magic Spell of the Grimms' Folk and Fairy Tales*. Princeton, NJ: Princeton UP.

Mediagraphy

Crayola Picture-Tracer. ca. 1911 (2002). Binney & Smith Co. Diana Korzenik Collection of Art Education Ephemera, Prints and Ephemera, Huntington Digital Library. Box 64. Set 3. http://hdl.huntington.org/cdm/ref/collection/p9539coll1/id/6885.

Frozen. 2013. Directors Chris Buck and Jennifer Lee. USA.

The Little Mermaid. 1989. Directors Ron Clements and John Musker. USA.

The Little Mermaid—Prince Eric's Castle Play Set. N.d. *Disney*. www.amazon.com/disney-The-Little-Mermaid-Prince/dp/B00I3MRPZA.

37
THEATER
Jennifer Schacker

When the James Lapine and Stephen Sondheim musical *Into the Woods* made its Broadway premiere in November 1987, *New York Times* theater critic Frank Rich noted that the show's fairy-tale characters—Cinderella, Little Red Riding Hood, Jack, various princes charming, a witch, and other "figures from children's literature"—were engaged in "the same painful, existential" journey undertaken by the adult characters in Sondheim's earlier musicals (1987). Rich's review acknowledged that the cultural resonance of *Into the Woods* depended on audience familiarity with several distinct phenomena: popular ideas about the maturation process (including "pubescent traumas" and adult dilemmas), the emergent conventions of a Sondheim musical, and a horizon of expectations regarding fairy tales. That fairy tales should be particularly well suited to exploration of social-sexual questions was an idea popularized by Bruno Bettelheim's 1976 *The Uses of Enchantment*—and Bettelheim has continued to serve as a touchstone in popular theorizing about the genre, despite decades of scholarship problematizing such a fundamentally ahistorical perspective. But the link between fairy tales and theater itself has received little critical attention in fairy-tale studies despite the fact that many storylines currently considered to be "classic" fairy tales have a long and varied history as theatrical performance. From the eighteenth century onward, forms of theater have played a significant role in the multimedial history of the fairy-tale genre. As in other media, fairy tales have been used onstage both to reinforce and to subvert dominant ideologies.

If the category of "fairy tale" is taken to encompass a broad range of secular, fantastical narrative traditions, then there are numerous modes of traditional performance to consider, spanning the globe—such as the Prince Panji stories performed in Javanese *wayang topeng* (mask and shadow theater), or the Kabuki treatments of Japanese *bakeneko* (supernatural cat) tales, to name just two examples. But even if we limit our scope to the relatively narrow body of story currently considered as "classic fairy tale" (predominantly European, dating from the fifteenth through the nineteenth centuries, recognizable to Sondheim's anticipated audience) and use English-language popular culture as a primary vantage point, various transnational forms of theater and performance play important roles in that history and in maintaining the genre's cultural currency. Understood in this way, the fairy tale has figured significantly in the emergence of many performance forms that remain current in Canada, the United States, Great Britain, and elsewhere—including ballet, Christmas pantomime, improv theater, and children's theater (or TYA/Theater for Young Audiences). Even a cursory survey of the histories of these theatrical forms demonstrates the centrality of fairy-tale material in theater history, both popular and elite, as well as the centrality of theatrical performance in fairy-tale history.

The origins of the English term "fairy tale" in print history, and specifically the history of translation, is very well-known: the term is generally traced to an elusive 1699 translation of Marie-Catherine Le Jumel de Barnville, baroness d'Aulnoy's *Contes de fées*—rendered in

English as "Tales of the Fairys." While that particular book is "regarded as a bibliographic ghost" (Palmer and Palmer 1974, 227), the term certainly gained currency, sometimes attached to narratives we might now classify as "fairy legends": stories about encounters with fairies or other supernatural figures. Less frequently noted, early British usage of "fairy tale" referenced forms of popular theater as often as it did narratives found in book form or in oral traditions. Importantly, no modifier was needed to reference fairy tales on stage: a survey of English periodicals of the eighteenth and nineteenth centuries reveals that a "fairy tale" was as likely to be a theatrical production (musical, comical, or melodramatic) as it was a story to be read or heard at hearthside. Apparently the term "fairy-tale play" would have been redundant.

In the 1760s, the popular dramatist George Colman used the indefinite article with the term "fairy tale"—entitling his abbreviated, farcical version of Shakespeare's *A Midsummer Night's Dream*, "A Fairy Tale." Colman took considerable liberties with the play, as he did with several other works by Shakespeare, while adapting them to current theatrical tastes. In *A Fairy Tale*, Colman focused almost exclusively on Shakespeare's fairy characters and the "mechanicals" (Bottom and company), re-envisioning these characters in terms that would have been familiar and appealing to London theatergoers: a "pantomime-inspired farce" (Marsden 1995, 80). The associations between "fairy tale" and spectacle, fantasy, satire, and farce were well established by this early date, both onstage and in print. For instance, fairy tales are one of many comedic forms included in the anonymous 1745 miscellany entitled *The Agreeable Companion; or, An Universal Medley of Wit and Good-Humour, Consisting of a Curious Collection of the Most Humourous Essays, Smart Repartees, Prudential Maxims, Familiar Dialogues, Epigrams and Epitaphs, Tales and Fables, Emblems and Riddles, Shining Epistles, and Beautiful Characters Both Fabulous and Real*. Appreciation of the fairy tale as a vehicle for humor, satire, and parody spans print and performance during this early period.

By the turn of the nineteenth century, British periodicals increasingly used the term "fairy tale" (lower case) to reference a host of spectacular and often amusing performance forms whose boundaries are fuzzy and whose histories overlap, all deeply influenced by Italian performers and performance styles—particularly those of Commedia dell'Arte. With its characteristic elements of mask, dance, pantomime, music, improvisatory and slapstick comedy, carnivalesque reversals, and bawdiness, Commedia dell'Arte left its mark on local theatrical practice in both early modern France and England—where it impacted Elizabethan drama (sixteenth century), the Stuart masque (early seventeenth-century), and then English interpretations of the *ballet d'action* by the early eighteenth-century dancing master John Weaver (Grantham 2015, 277–278). This occurred right alongside the development of the literary fairy tale, during the same time periods and through the same transcultural channels.

Commedia Dell'arte

In his survey of the supernatural in eighteenth-century forms of European musical theater, David J. Buch names Commedia dell'Arte "the first venue for fairy tales and the newer oriental fantasies adapted in the theaters of the Parisian fairs" (2008, xv). Popular with both mass and elite audiences, performed in both European fairgrounds and at court, Commedia dell'Arte could be considered "the visual theatre of everyday life" in the sixteenth through the eighteenth centuries (Goldsmith 2015, 321), and the most famous of Commedia's characters include the cheeky servants Arlecchino and Columbina (Harlequin and Columbine), the wealthy womanizer Pantalone, and the clownish Scaramuccia (Scaramouche). But Commedia often featured otherworldly themes and figures such as the *mago* (magician) and *negromante* (necromancer), as well as "astrologers, sorceresses, fairies, oracles, spirits, and ghosts" (Buch

2008, 17–18). Buch dubs this particular mode of theatrical representation of the supernatural as the "comic-marvelous," in which magic is used "not to bedazzle and inspire awe or admiration (a primary goal of the 'marvellous'), but to allow the lowborn to achieve powers that would otherwise be impossible for them." For Buch, the comic-marvelous mode of Commedia dell'Arte stands in contrast to the use of marvels and magic in "more serious court opera," where magic is the province of the powerful, reinforcing the connection between nobility and divinity (2008, 18). The carnivalesque elements associated with Commedia dell'Arte—the anarchic combination of comedy and violence, the reversals of power positions, the interrogation of dominant social, cultural, moral, and aesthetic standards—echo in the various performance forms that adopted and adapted Commedia conventions and that draw specifically on a repertoire of fairy tales.

In Italy, Carlo Gozzi's series of plays called *Fiabe Teatrali* (1761–65) stand as an interesting example. The history of the Italian term *fiaba* parallels that of "fairy tale": *fiaba* has long been used to designate not only folk and literary tales, but also a theatrical form that has close ties to Commedia dell'Arte traditions. Gozzi's *fiabe* drew inspiration from Giambattista Basile's "profoundly ludic text" *Lo Cunto de li Cunti* (Tale of Tales; Canepa 1999, 251). Gozzi also drew inspiration from the wave of "oriental tales" written in the wake of Antoine Galland's French translation/adaptation of *Alf Layla wa-Layla* (entitled *Les Mille et Une Nuits, Contes Arabes* [1704–17]), as well as the stock characters and performance style associated with Commedia dell'Arte. In Gozzi's *Fiabe Teatrali*, familiar character types (masks) from Commedia mingle with characters that were still considered novel on the Venetian stage: "witches, wizards, and the King of Hearts, a monarch of an imaginary kingdom costumed like the playing cards" (Griffin 2015, 334). Gozzi mobilizes such characters and fantastical settings, but combines these with references to contemporary Venice—including satirical and rather biting treatment of the Venetian theater world. For example, *L'Amore dell tre melarance* (known in English as "The Love for Three Oranges" [1761]—later the inspiration for Sergei Prokofiev's 1921 opera) is based on the last tale in Basile's *Lo Cunto de li Cunti*, but Gozzi adds a comic rivalry between a magician and a fairy, characters who represented his own rivals, Carlo Goldoni and Pietro Chiari (see Nicholson 1979, 468). In other of Gozzi's fairy-tale plays, the fantastical elements offer further opportunities for satire and social critique but also "imaginary, formal solutions to unresolvable social contradictions" that arose from Gozzi's position as both a member of the minor nobility and a playwright in need of patronage in a rapidly shifting socio-economic climate (see Emery 1997, 264–268).

Basile's *Lo Cunto de li Cunti* had no presence on the eighteenth-century London stage and would not be translated into English until 1848, but many of the French literary fairy tales that would eventually dominate English pantomime echo Basile's text (see Magnanini 2007). The first of Perrault's tales to gain notoriety in pantomime form was the highly Orientalized 1798 "grand dramatic [and musical] romance" of *Blue Beard, or Female Curiosity!*, by George Colman the Younger (son of the Colman discussed prior), largely inspired by André Grétry's 1789 opera *Raoul Barbe-bleue*. While Colman's *Blue Beard* was undoubtedly shaped by the popularity of English versions of Galland's *Les Mille et Une Nuits*, that work had made its mark in London theaters significantly earlier. For example, at least one serious drama of the early eighteenth century was based on Galland's version of the *1001 Nights'* frame story: Delarivier Manley's *Almyna, or the Arabian Vow* (1707; see Orr 2008, 108–111). There were also many Orientalized melodramas, including James Boaden's recasting of "Beauty and the Beast" as *Selima and Azor* (1776; see Allen 1981, 103; Orr 2008, 111), and afterpiece entertainments like *The Genii . . . An Arabian Nights Entertainment*, opening on Boxing Day 1752 and then running for a total of 207 performances at Drury Lane Theatre. English fairy tales, on the other hand, inspired or were referenced in a relatively small number of early eighteenth-century productions, and these tales were ones that were already well established in English chapbook form; examples include the 1730 farce *Jack the Giant Killer* at Little Haymarket Theatre (see Burling 1993, 136) and the 1733 opera parody *The Opera of Operas; or, Tom Thumb the Great* at Lincoln's Inn Fields (see Griffel 2013, 357).

British Pantomime

In contemporary British theater, the Christmas pantomime is the most significant venue for fairy-tale material, but pantomime itself has a complicated history. In early to mid-eighteenth-century England, pantomime was "considered as a form promising sheer entertainment," something that "seemed new and scandalous" (O'Brien 2004, 40), offering a distinctive and popular combination of music, dance and acrobatics, and slapstick comedy interspersed with some melo/dramatic story elements (mistaken identities, star-crossed romance, thwarted inheritance claims, etc.). Until the mid-nineteenth century, pantomime also regularly featured Commedia dell'Arte figures in a distinct section of the performance known as the "harlequinade," when the pantomime's main characters are transformed into Anglicized versions of stock characters: Harlequin, Columbine, Pantaloon, Clown. Drawing on continental forms and styles, pantomime nevertheless would come to be considered as uniquely English (see Schacker 2007, 391–395, 2012, 156–162), its concerns modern and increasingly urban. Eighteenth-century pantomime as a whole shared with Gozzi's *Fiabe* an engagement with the broader theater scene, recasting "the most notable features of the contemporary British stage: the plots of sentimental comedy, the scenery and diegetic material of Italian opera, the physical farce of Continental commedia dell'arte, and the elegance of dance" (O'Brien 2004, 10). Early pantomime productions anticipated audience familiarity with the range of current performance forms, frequently offering examples of meta-theatrical satire as well as social commentary.

Late eighteenth-century pantomime was greatly impacted by the London stage's most popular pantomime player, Joseph Grimaldi, "a London Clown, born, bred," known for his elaborate costumes, nimble footwork and acrobatics, and interactions with the audience (Booth 1991, 154). In the present context, Grimaldi is significant because some of his most successful pantomimes were fairy-tale themed. The most famous of Grimaldi's roles was Squire Bugle in *Harlequin and Mother Goose* (1806), which had a phenomenally complicated plot that bore no clear relation to a specific fairy tale, but secured Grimaldi's position as a star of the Georgian stage and made the figure of "Mother Goose" a standard in the pantomime repertoire (see Stott 2009, 172). Just two years earlier, Grimaldi had appeared in the first pantomime version of "Cinderella," staged at Drury Lane in 1804; he played a newly developed character, the stepsisters' servant Pedro. A reviewer for *The Times* praised this show for its "striking" transformations, such as the "changes of Cinderella's kitchen-table into a toilette; of a pumpkin into a pavilioned chariot; of the mice into horses" (quoted in Findlater 1978, 102) and so on—feats of stage magic that exploit and expand the varieties of magical transformation associated with the fairy-tale genre and with this tale, in particular. In 1820, Grimaldi appeared in another "Cinderella" pantomime, *Harlequin and Cinderella; or, the Little Glass Slipper*, this time cross-dressed as the Baroness/stepmother—anticipating what would become the most beloved modern panto role: the Dame.

By the end of the nineteenth century, the fairy-tale themed Christmas pantomime would be considered "an English institution" to such a great extent that a "Boxing Day without pantomime would be as empty as a Christmas Day without dinner" (Lancaster 1883, 12–13). Without question, pantomime had become a significant medium for the (playful) transmission and transformation of classic fairy tales. Indeed, a fairly stable set of tales has served as the basis for most panto productions of the past 150 years: these include the perennial favorites "Cinderella" (ATU 510A) and "Aladdin" (ATU 561), but also "Little Red Riding Hood" (ATU 333), "Sindbad," "Beauty and the Beast" (ATU 425C), "Puss-in-Boots" (ATU 545), "Dick Whittington" (ATU 1651), and "Jack and the Beanstalk" (ATU 328), as well as the once-popular, currently obscure pantomime tales of "Bluebeard" (ATU 312), "The Yellow Dwarf," and "The White Cat." A large proportion of this canon of tales associated with Victorian and modern pantomime is French in descent: stories from *Alf Layla wa-Layla* as it was introduced to European readerships by Galland in the early years of the eighteenth century, and stories first translated from the work of Perrault and d'Aulnoy during the same time period, but which took considerably longer to gain their stronghold on popular musical theater.

When panto entered the mainstream of mid-nineteenth-century theater, fairy-tale elements served its topical humor, broad satire, and slapstick comedy—as well as social commentary. For example, serious current events resonate in productions from 1830, the year of the "swing riots," in which agricultural workers in East Kent destroyed threshing machines and tithe barns. That December, the Adelphi Theatre's pantomime *Grimalkin the Great* featured actors dressed as Luddite cats whose services are threatened by the new technology of the mouse-trap (see Mayer 1969, 256). Beyond London, Christmas pantomime could also speak to local concerns, as did the Manchester Theatre Royal *Sleeping Beauty* of 1863, in which the spindle traditionally associated with the heroine's enchantment was displaced by stage depiction of a demonic factory, a spinning mill (see Sullivan 2011, 141). Many decades later, in the wake of what was known as "Black Week" (December 1899), when British forces in South Africa suffered three successive, staggering defeats and nearly 3,000 men were killed, the Drury Lane pantomime of *Jack and the Beanstalk* featured a comic and rousing enactment of British conquest. A troupe of child actors led by the pantomime's cross-dressed hero Jack (the "stunning" Nellie Stewart) felled a giant evocatively named "Blunderboer"—and the audience joined in a chorus of "Rule Britannia" (see Schacker 2013, 57, 61–62). Pantomimes are generally evaluated in terms of innovative costuming and set design, outrageous antics and physical comedy, novel feats of stage magic—all of which have the potential to contribute to a self-reflexive commentary on the dynamics of performance, the performativity of social identities, economies of desire, and the economics of theatrical production—the very processes in which performers and audience alike were engaged.

Ballet

From theatrical afterpiece to Christmas season entertainment, pantomime has long been cast as a form of popular culture, and classical ballet would seem to be at the other end of the spectrum of cultural value: ballet currently has the status of an elite and rarefied form, with its roots in Old Regime France, but most of its enduring and "exemplary choreographic themes" are also drawn from the fairy-tale tradition (Canton 1994, 2). Some of the best-known works in the slim canon of classical ballet were inspired by tales by Charles Perrault and are ones that had already been ensconced as English pantomime classics. Developed in late-nineteenth-century Russia by ballet masters from Italy, France, and Russia (Enrico Cecchettit, Marius Petipa, Lev Ivanov), these include the ballets known to English-speaking audiences as *Sleeping Beauty* (1890), *Cinderella* (1893), and *Bluebeard* (1896). "Classical ballet," as it endures today, might appear to be quite distinct from the fanciful, comical early eighteenth-century "pantomime-ballets" of John Weaver, as well as the popular *ballet d'action* and *féeries* (combining spectacle, magical stage effects, mime, and dance) that flourished in Paris, London, and elsewhere in the early nineteenth century. But the European ballets of that earlier period had also engaged fairy-tale themes, including versions of *Sleeping Beauty* (such as the one staged in Paris, 1829) and several *Cinderella* ballets (an all-child production in Vienna [1813] and adult productions in London [1822] and Paris [1823]).

The introduction of fairy-tale themes to Russian dance in the late nineteenth century brings the fairy tale's fraught position in a politics of culture squarely into view. As Jennifer Homans points out, "we like to think of [Tchaikovsky's] *The Sleeping Beauty* as an elevated artistic landmark, but at the time of its premiere in 1890 many critics and observers saw it as a sell-out to low popular taste" (2010, 273). That taste was one associated with the popular musical theater venues that were springing up all over St. Petersburg in the wake of the Czar's theatrical reforms and that were venues for elaborate *ballets-féeries* currently being performed by Italian troupes. The style of these *ballets-féeries* was generally considered inelegant and vulgar in comparison with that of *ballet du cour* (court ballet), and the productions were notable for their spectacular sets, costumes, and effects. The Russian ballet version of *Sleeping Beauty* (1890) invited comparison to the Italian productions current in St. Petersburg, as well as harking back to an earlier tradition of dance; it was undoubtedly its own kind of *ballet féerie*, but it could also be seen as "an astute counterattack designed to beat the Italians at their own game while at the same time affirming the aristocratic heritage of the Russian ballet" (Homans 2010, 274). In fact, the tradition of court ballet that czarist Russia inherited and adapted from France and Italy had its own lengthy legacy of spectacle and excess, burlesque and comedy, eroticism and exoticism, illusion and enchantment—from the lavish entertainments coordinated by Catherine de Medici in the late sixteenth century (exemplified by the five-hour extravaganza *Ballet Comique de la Reine* of 1581) through the "sheer magnitude of theatrical spectacle" that characterized *la belle danse* in the court of Louis XIV (Homans 2010, 31).

Unlike Victorian and Edwardian pantomime, the canon of fairy-tale ballet includes folk and literary tales from Germany, most notably Petipa and Ivanov's *The Nutcracker* (1892; inspired by E. T. A. Hoffmann's "Nussknacker und Mausekönig" [The Nutcracker and the King of Mice, 1816] by way of Alexandre Dumas's short story "Histoire du casse-noisette" [Story of the Nutcracker, 1845]) and Petipa's *The Magic Mirror* (1903; inspired by both the Grimms' "Snow White" and Alexander Pushkin's "The Tale of the Dead Princesses and the Seven Knights"). The origins of the plot of *Swan Lake* (1877; revived by Petipa and Ivanov in 1895) are more contentious, but likely combine German and Russian traditions: the Johann Karl August Musäus *volksmärchen* known in English as "The Stolen Veil" and the folktale known as "The White Duck," collected by Aleksandr Afanasyev. Russian folktales inspired later Ballets Russes productions like *Firebird* (1910), and tales by Hans Christian Andersen also generated ballets, such as the 1920 production of *The Song of the Nightingale* (with set design by Henri Matisse).

Critical reworking of classic fairy tales and the conventions of classical ballet have underpinned many experimental and *avant-garde* productions in recent decades, such as Pina Bausch's *Bluebeard* (1977) and the *cirque noir* (combining aerial arts, ballet, and shadow puppetry) of Sky Candy's *The Red Shoes* (2011). In a critical turn comparable to that in recent fairy-tale studies, dance historians have also offered radical reconsiderations of sex and gender in fairy-tale ballet. For example, Laura Katz Rizzo has challenged the master narrative of classical dance—which has tended to foreground the contributions of women only as ballerinas or anonymous members of the *corps de ballet*, seen as relatively passive vehicles for the work of male choreographers. Tracing the production history of Tchaikovsky's *Sleeping Beauty*, Rizzo recuperates the significant contributions of choreographers like Bronislava Nijinsky and Catherine Littlefield, artistic directors like Barbara Weisberger and Lucia Chase, and the agency of contemporary ballerinas like Arantxa Ochoa, Dede Barfield, and Martha Chamberlain (2015). Peter Stoneley

Fairy Tales in Twentieth- and Twenty-First-Century Theater

Pantomime, ballet, and Commedia dell'Arte remain vibrant, evolving traditions, with fairy-tale themes, characters, and plot elements essential to the fabric of each. But since the turn of the twentieth century, several other significant forms of fairy-tale theater have emerged, including the Broadway musical—which is certainly thriving in 2016. For example, Maya Cantu observes that the figure of Cinderella is pervasive in Broadway productions of the 2010s (the revival of Rodgers and Hammerstein's *Cinderella* [1957], musical versions of the films *Ever After* [1998] and *Pretty Woman* [1990]; Cantu 2015, 1). Cinderella figures also weave their way through the history of Broadway musicals, both those few that explicitly retell the Cinderella story and those that index "the Cinderella Paradigm, relying on strategies of adaptation that resonate with modern American myths and narratives of assimilation and upward mobility" (Cantu 2015, 3). Cantu suggests that a critical study of the Cinderellas of Broadway musicals reveals that they "have a long history of complicating and defying the stereotypes of feminine passivity that have long been associated with Perrault's (and later Disney's) heroine" (2015, 7–8). Seen in this light, fairy-tale paradigms in Broadway musicals resonate with many of the examples of fairy-tale theater discussed earlier, using latent potentialities of the fairy-tale genre to subvert dominant ideologies.

The vast majority of fairy-tale themed Broadway shows are currently marketed to audiences of both adults and children, and in this they revive a well-established tradition: children made up part of the audience for fairy plays, pantomimes, and puppet theater in earlier centuries, and private performances of fairy-tale plays figured in the education and entertainment of privileged children (Jarvis 2000, 139). In early twentieth-century America, Winthrop Ames's 1912 *Snow White and the Seven Dwarfs* was explicitly framed as a "play for the children" when it debuted at New York City's Little Theater, a production that was thought likely to "appeal to them as few productions ever have" ("Play" 1912, 13). Ames anticipated that he would produce "more fairy plays for children" ("Fairyland" 1912, x6), but in fact this play has a more significant place in film history than it does in theater history. The "perfectly child-like" Marguerite Clark played the title character, a role she reprised in the 1916 silent film—which in turn inspired Walt Disney's animated feature film. Ames's successful Broadway production for children had joined a range of American popular performance forms—vaudeville, wild west shows, musical theater—whose advertising strategies targeted youngsters in the early decades of the twentieth century, but this kind of "fairy play" had virtually disappeared from Broadway by the 1920s (van de Water 2012, 150). During the same period fairy tales became (and have remained) "staples" in another form of theater for children: the movement known as Theatre for Young Audiences, or TYA (Thompson 2000, 114).

TYA has its origins in philanthropic and often state-supported initiatives, with early examples including New York City's Children's Educational Theatre, established in 1903 by settlement worker Alice Minnie Herts, and the Moscow Central Children's Theatre, first championed by Nadezhda Kruoskaya (wife to Vladimir Lenin) and run by fifteen-year-old Natalya Sats (see van de Water 2012, 20–25)—at whose request and for whose theater Sergei Prokofiev composed *Peter and the Wolf* (1936). The work of organizations like these made a concerted effort to distinguish their uses of drama from those of the world of professional/"adult" theater; in this context, fairy tales were seen as useful tools in children's moral education and cultural assimilation (see Tuite 1998; van de Water 2012, 9–40). Reflecting in 1939 on the work of settlement workers like Herts, Winifred Ward wrote of "the picturesque beauty of the folk tale play" that served "children who live amid the ugliness of factory and slum districts" and filled "a far greater need than do the [. . .] plays for more fortunate children" (quoted in van de Water 2012, 13). By the late 1930s, folktales and fairy tales were thus embraced by practitioners of children's theater not because they promised spectacle, stage magic, topical comedy, and social critique, but because they were increasingly associated with escapism, transformation, moral elevation, and psychological self-expression.

A lineage of theater scholars and practitioners links the social and educational work of early TYA to current fairy-tale theater. Ward herself was a pioneering theater professor and progressive educator from Northwestern University who developed the field of "creative dramatics," a classroom practice of acting without scripts that focused more on the process and experience of children as players than on the performance as aesthetic product—and which drew heavily on canonical fairy tales as a shared repertoire of story. Ward's legacy extends into the development of drama therapy, especially through the work of her former student, Neva Boyd, but also the "theater games" and improvisational techniques developed by Boyd's student, Viola Spolin. Like forerunners Boyd, Ward, and Herts, Spolin worked for a time at the intersection of social work and theater, serving as the drama supervisor for the Chicago branch of the WPA's Recreational Project from 1939–1941. But fairy tales played an even stronger role in Spolin's theatrical innovations than they had in those of her teachers and colleagues: Spolin saw fairy tales and folktales as prime resources for the spontaneity, intuitiveness, and "meditation in action" she sought to develop in performers (adult and child) through improvisatory and problem-solving games. To unleash creativity, Spolin believed, players must be "liberated from what she calls the approval/disapproval syndrome that keeps us in the past and obscures the self" (Sills 1999, x). Spolin's *Improvisation for the Theatre: A Handbook of Teaching and Directing Techniques* has proven highly influential since its publication in 1963, not only in the fields of theater education and drama therapy, but also in forms ranging from experimental, political, and *avant-garde* theater to stand-up comedy and mainstream cinema (see Coleman 1990, 24). Particularly significant in this regard are Spolin's collaborations with her son, Paul Sills. Sills is best known as a founder of the Second City theater company in Chicago, but he also extended Spolin's work, developing "story theater," in which actors use song, dance, mime, spoken word, and minimal props to create plays based on tales from the Brothers Grimm and Aesop's fables. A Broadway version of "Paul Sills' Story Theater" premiered in 1970 (followed by a television version in 1971) and was hailed by *New York Times* reviewer Clive Barnes as "so pure and simple, so direct in its theatrical language, even unliterary," that it could both shock and delight (1970, 54).

Spolin's legacy—and especially her view of fairy tales and dramatic play as natural bedfellows, potentially liberatory and therapeutic, primal and universal—resonates with many current assumptions about the genre's form, function, meaning, and audience, as my opening example of *Into the Woods* suggests. Spolin valued fairy tales as pathways to immediacy, spontaneity, and creativity, a form that presumably exists outside the bounds of time and place. The irony here is that even that perspective demands historicization, being rooted in a particular conception of the fairy tale, particular social conditions and political projects, and a particular tradition of twentieth-century theater theory and practice. Nevertheless, current uses of fairy tale onstage continue to intersect in some compelling ways with a much longer tradition of the fairy tale as comic spectacle, with an edge of self-parody and social commentary.

Related topics: Broadcast; Cinematic; Musicals; Opera; Orientalism

THEATER

References Cited and Further Reading

Allen, Ralph G. 1981. "Irrational Entertainment in the Age of Reason." In *The Stage and the Page: London's "Whole Show" in the Eighteenth-Century Theatre*, edited by George Winchester Stone, Jr., 90–114. Berkeley: U California P.

Anon. 1745. *The Agreeable Companion; or, an Universal Medley of Wit and Good-Humour, Consisting of a Curious Collection of the Most Humourous Essays, Smart Repartees, Prudential Maxims, Familiar Dialogues, Epigrams and Epitaphs, Tales and Fables, Emblems and Riddles, Shining Epistles, and Beautiful Characters Both Fabulous and Real.* London: W. Bickerton.

Barnes, Clive. 1970. "The Stage: 'Story Theater' Opens at Ambassador." *New York Times*, October 27.

Basile, Giambattista. 1634–1636. *Lo Cunto de li Cunti: Il Pentamerone.* 5 vols. Naples: Beltrano and Scorrigio.

Bettelheim, Bruno. 1976. *The Uses of Enchantment: The Meaning and Importance of Fairy Tales.* New York: Knopf.

Booth, Michael R. 1991. *Theatre in the Victorian Age.* Cambridge: Cambridge UP.

Buch, David. J. 2008. *Magic Flutes and Enchanted Forests: The Supernatural in Eighteenth-Century Musical Theater.* Chicago: U Chicago P.

Burling, William J. 1993. *A Checklist of New Plays and Entertainments on the London Stage, 1700–1737.* London: Associated UP.

Canepa, Nancy L. 1999. *From Court to Forest: Giambattista Basile's Lo cunto de li cunti and the Birth of the Literary Fairy Tale.* Detroit: Wayne State UP.

Canton, Katia. 1994. *The Fairy Tale Revisited: A Survey of the Evolution of the Tales, from Classical Literary Interpretations to Innovative Contemporary Dance-Theater Productions.* New York: Peter Lang.

Cantu, Maya. 2015. *American Cinderellas on the Broadway Musical Stage: Imagining the Working Girl from Irene to Gypsy.* London: Palgrave Macmillan.

Coleman, Janet. 1990. *The Compass: The Improvisational Theatre that Revolutionized American Comedy.* Chicago: U Chicago P.

Dumas, Alexandre. 1845. *Histoire d'un casse-noisette.* Paris: J. Hetzel.

Emery, Ted. 1997. "The Reactionary Imagination: Ideology and the Form of the Fairy Tale in Gozzi's *Il re servo* [The King Stag]." In *Out of the Woods: The Origins of the Literary Fairy Tale in Italy and France*, edited by Nancy L. Canepa, 247–77. Detroit: Wayne State UP.

"Fairyland Busy Making Little Words of Big Ones: What a Visitor Behind the Scenes Discovered When He Called on Snow White and the Seven Dwarfs." 1912. *New York Times*, November 10: x6.

Findlater, Richard. 1978. *Joseph Grimaldi, His Life and Theatre.* 2nd ed. Cambridge: Cambridge UP.

Galland, Antoine. 1704–1717. *Les Mille et Une Nuits, Contes Arabes.* Paris: Claude Barbin and Florentin Delaulne.

Goldsmith, Elizabeth C. 2015. "Writing for the Elite: Moliere, Marivaux, and Beaumarchais." In *The Routledge Companion to Commedia dell'Arte*, edited by Judith Chaffee and Olly Crick, 321–8. London: Routledge.

Grantham, Barry. 2015. "Classical Ballet and the Commedia dell'Arte." In *The Routledge Companion to Commedia dell'Arte*, edited by Judith Chaffee and Olly Crick, 276–83. London: Routledge.

Griffel, Margaret Ross. 2013. *Operas in English: A Dictionary.* Lanham, MD: Scarecrow P.

Griffin, Mike. 2015. "Goldoni and Gozzi: Reformers with Separate Agendas." In *The Routledge Companion to Commedia dell'Arte*, edited by Judith Chaffee and Olly Crick, 329–37. London: Routledge.

Hoffmann, E. T. A. (1816) 2015. *Nussknacker und Mausekönig.* Hamburg: Severus.

Homans, Jennifer. 2010. *Apollo's Angels: A History of Ballet.* New York: Random House.

Jarvis, Shawn. 2000. "Drama and Fairy Tales." In *The Oxford Companion to Fairy Tales: The Western Fairy Tale Tradition from Medieval to Modern*, edited by Jack Zipes, 137–41. New York: Oxford UP.

Lancaster, George. 1883. "Notes on the Pantomimes." *The Theatre*, January 1: 12–20.

Magnanini, Suzanne. 2007. "Postulated Routes from Naples to Paris: The Printer Antonio Bulifon and Giambattista Basile's Fairy Tales in Seventeenth-Century France." *Marvels & Tales* 21 (1): 78–92.

Marsden, Jean I. 1995. *The Reimagined Text: Shakespeare, Adaptation, and Eighteenth-Century Literary Theory.* Louisville: UP Kentucky.

Mayer, David. 1969. *Harlequin in His Element: The English Pantomime, 1806–1836.* Cambridge, MA: Harvard UP.

Nicholson, David. 1979. "Gozzi's *Turandot*: A Tragicomic Fairy Tale." *Theatre Journal* 31 (4): 467–78.

O'Brien, John. 2004. *Harlequin Britain: Pantomime and Entertainment, 1690–1760.* Baltimore: Johns Hopkins UP.

Orr, Bridget. 2008. "Galland, Georgian Theatre, and the Creation of Popular Orientalism." In *The Arabian Nights in Historical Context: Between East and West*, edited by Saree Makdisi and Felicity Nussbaum, 108–30. Oxford: Oxford UP.

Palmer, Nancy, and Melvin Palmer. 1974. "English Editions of French *Contes des Fées* Attributed to Mme D'Aulnoy." *Studies in Bibliography* 27: 227–32.

"Play for Children at Little Theatre: With Marguerite Clark a Charming Snow White in the Well-Loved Fairy Tale." 1912. *New York Times*, November 8: 13.

Rich, Frank. 1987. "Stage: 'Into the Woods,' From Sondheim." *New York Times*, November 6.

Rizzo, Laura Katz. 2015. *Dancing the Fairy Tale: Producing and Performing* The Sleeping Beauty. Philadelphia: Temple UP.

Schacker, Jennifer. 2007. "Unruly Tales: Ideology, Anxiety, and the Regulation of Genre." *Journal of American Folklore* 120: 381–400.

———. 2012. "Fairy Gold: The Economics and Erotics of Fairy-Tale Pantomime." *Marvels & Tales* 26 (2): 153–77.

———. 2013. "Slaying Blunderboer: Cross-Dressed Heroes, National Identities, and Wartime Pantomime." *Marvels & Tales* 27 (1): 52–64.

Sills, Paul. (1963) 1999. "Introduction." In *Improvisation for the Theater: A Handbook of Teaching and Directing Techniques*, by Viola Spolin, x–xii. 3rd ed. Evanston, IL: Northwestern UP.

Spolin, Viola. 1963. *Improvisation for the Theatre: A Handbook of Teaching and Directing Techniques.* Evanston, IL: Northwestern UP.

Stoneley, Peter. 2007. *A Queer History of the Ballet.* New York: Routledge.

Stott, Andrew McConnell. 2009. *The Pantomime Life of Joseph Grimaldi: Laughter, Madness and the Story of Britain's Greatest Comedian.* Edinburgh: Canongate.

Sullivan, Jill Alexandra. 2011. *The Politics of the Pantomime: Regional Identity in the Theatre, 1860–1900.* Hatfield: U Hertfordshire P.

Thompson, Melissa C. 2000. "If the Shoe Fits: Virtue and Absolute Beauty in Fairy Tale Drama." *Youth Theatre Journal* 14 (1): 114–22.

Tuite, Patrick. 1998. "Assimilating Immigrants through Drama: The Social Politics of Alice Minnie Herts and Lillian Ward." *Youth Theatre Journal* 12: 10–18.

van de Water, Manon. 2012. *Theatre, Youth, and Culture: A Critical and Historical Exploration.* New York: Palgrave.

Mediagraphy

Almyna, or the Arabian Vow (Play). 1707. Writer Delarivier Manley. UK.

Ballet Comique de la Reine (Court ballet). 1581. Hôtel de Bourbon. France.

Blue Beard, or Female Curiosity! (Pantomime/melodrama). 1798. Libretto by George Colman the Younger, music by Michael Kelly. Drury Lane Theatre, London. UK.

Bluebeard ([Sinjaja boroda] Ballet). 1896. Music by Pyotr Schenk, choreography by Marius Petipa. Russia.

Bluebeard, while Listening to a Taped Recording of Béla Bartók's opea Duke Bluebeard's Castle, a Piece by Pina Bausch ([Blaubart, Beim Anhören einer Tonbandaufnahme von Béla Bartók's Oper Herzog Blaubarts Burg, Stück von Pina Bausch] Modern dance). 1977. Choreography by Pina Bausch. Tanztheater Wuppertal Pina Bausch. Germany.

Cinderella ([Aschenbrödel] Ballet). 1813. Choreography by Louis-Antoine Duport. Austria.

——— ([Cendrillon] Ballet). 1822. Choreography by François Albert Decombe. King's Theatre, London. UK.

——— ([Cendrillon] Ballet). 1823. Choreography by François Albert Decombe. Paris Opera. France.

——— (Pantomime). 1804. Music by Michael Kelly. Drury Lane Theatre, London. UK.

——— (TV musical). 1957. Music by Richard Rodgers, book and lyrics by Oscar Hammerstein. USA.

——— ([Zolushka] Ballet). 1893. Music by Baron Boris Fitinhoff-Schell, choreography supervised by Marius Petipa. Russia.

Ever After. 1998. Director Andy Tennant. USA.

A Fairy Tale (Play). 1763. Writer George Colman the Elder. Drury Lane Theatre, London. UK.

Fiabe Teatrali (Series of plays). 1761–1765. Writer Carlo Gozzi. Italy.

Firebird ([L'oiseau de feu] Ballet). 1910. Music by Igor Stravinsky, choreography by Michel Fokine. France.

The Genii . . . An Arabian Nights Entertainment (Pantomime). 1752. Director Henry Woodward. Drury Lane Theatre, London. UK.

Grimalkin the Great (Pantomime). 1830. Adelphi Theatre, London. UK.

Harlequin and Cinderella; or, the Little Glass Slipper (Pantomime). 1820. Covent Garden Theatre, London. UK.

Harlequin and Mother Goose, Or, the Golden Egg! (Pantomime). 1806. Covent Garden Theatre, London. UK.

Into the Woods (Musical). 1987. Music and lyrics by Stephen Sondheim and book by James Lapine. Broadway. USA.

Jack and the Beanstalk (Pantomime). 1899. Drury Lane Theatre, London. UK.

Jack the Giant Killer (Farce). 1730. Little Haymarket Theatre, London. UK.

L'amore dell tre melarance (Play). 1761. Writer Carlo Gozzi. Italy.

The Love for Three Oranges ([L'amour des trois oranges] Opera). 1921. Music and libretto by Sergei Prokofiev. USA.

The Magic Mirror ([Le Miroir Magique] Ballet). 1903. Music by Arsenii Koreschenko, choreography by Marius Petipa. Russia.

The Nutcracker ([Shchelkunchik, Balet-feyeriya] Ballet). 1892. Music by Pyotr Ilyich Tchaikovsky, choreography by Marius Petipa and Lev Ivanov. Russia.

The Opera of Operas; or, Tom Thumb the Great (Burlesque opera). 1733. Lincoln's Inn Fields, London. UK.

THEATER

Paul Sills' Story Theatre (Play). 1970. Director Paul Sills. Broadway. USA.

Peter and the Wolf ([Petya i volk] Symphonic tone poem with narration). 1936. Music by Sergei Prokofiev. USSR.

Pretty Woman. 1990. Director Garry Marshall. USA.

Raoul Barbe-bleue (Opera). 1789. Music by André Grétry. France.

The Red Shoes (Aerial Art Performance). 2011. Sky Candy, Austin, TX. USA.

Selima and Azor: A Persian Tale, in Three Parts (Melodrama). 1784.

Sleeping Beauty ([La belle au bois dormant] Ballet). 1829. Music by Ferdinand Hérold. France.

——— (Pantomime). 1863. Theatre Royal, Manchester. UK.

——— ([Spyashchaya krasavits] Ballet). 1890. Music by Pyotr Ilyich Tchaikovsky, choreography by Marius Petipa. Russia.

Snow White. 1916. Director J. Searle Dawley. USA.

Snow White and the Seven Dwarfs (Play). 1912. Writer Jessie Brahm White [pseudonym for Wintrop Ames]. Broadway. USA.

The Song of the Nightingale ([Le chant du rossignol] Ballet). 1920. Music by Igor Stravinsky, choreography by Leonid Massine. France.

Story Theatre (TV). 1971. Creator Paul Sills. Canada.

Swan Lake ([Lebedinoye ozero] Ballet). 1876. Music by Pyotr Ilyich Tchaikovsky, choreography by Václav Reisinger. Russia.

"The Tale of the Dead Princesses and the Seven Knights." ([Сказка о мёртвой царевне и семи богатырях] Poem). 1833. Writer Alexander Pushkin.

38

PHOTOGRAPHIC

Mayako Murai

Photographs based on or inspired by fairy tales can be regarded as a subgenre of tableau photography, a genre that combines the art form of the stage with still photography. In representing a scene from a fairy tale, a genre of narrative that does not claim verisimilitude, such photographs inevitably draw the viewer's attention to their staged and performed aspect, revealing the device often deliberately made invisible in documentary photographs intended as a realistic representation of the subject.

The performative aspect of fairy-tale photography can be seen clearly in Charles Lutwidge Dodgson's (Lewis Carroll, British, 1832–1898) *Agnes Weld as "Little Red Riding-Hood"* (1857; see figure 38.1), one of the earliest inspired by a fairy tale. When Dodgson took up photography in 1856, it was considered fashionable for gentlemen to try their hands at this latest symbiosis between science and art (Taylor 2002, 11). His portrait of an eight-year-old girl posing as "Little Red Riding Hood" (ATU 333) was taken a year before his now infamous portrait of *Alice Liddell as "The Beggar-Maid"* (1858). His photographs of the girl for whom the *Alice* books were written have caused more controversy over their sexually exploitative nature than the books, indicating one important aspect of this medium that inevitably involves the real body and life of the subject.[1] In embodying fairy-tale narratives using actual people, animals, objects, and places, fairy-tale photographs may render explicit the social, cultural, and political implications hidden beneath the assumed universality of canonized tales. After analyzing Dodgson's portrait of a prepubescent girl as Little Red Riding Hood, this chapter discusses the ways in which later photographers—mainly women—have drawn from as well as have subverted the Victorian conventions of representing the female body and portraying the fairy tale.

In his *Agnes Weld as "Little Red Riding-Hood,"* Dodgson makes Agnes Weld, daughter of Alfred Tennyson's sister-in-law, pose against a wall covered with thick ivy. The viewer can easily identify the girl as Little Red Riding Hood because of the hooded cape she wears over her dress and the basket of food in her hand. The whiteness of the dress and the napkin partially covering the basket can be seen as symbolizing the childlike innocence and purity that, as we know, are to be violated later. In this sense, the implicitly male photographer/viewer is placed in the position of the one who holds knowledge and power—in other words, the wolf.[2] The girl's gesture of pulling the cloak protectively across her body seems to predict the danger to come. This photograph captures the ambivalent notion of female sexuality dominant in Victorian society, representing Little Red Riding Hood both as innocent virgin and as seductress.[3] Encouraged by Tennyson's praise for the portrait of his niece, Dodgson felt confident enough to submit it to the prestigious Annual Exhibition of the Photographic Society in London (Taylor 2002, 48). His portraits of young girls have certainly influenced the way the prepubescent female body is staged, framed, and exhibited for the male gaze. His choice of Little Red Riding Hood in portraying his object of admiration and desire is also indicative

348

Figure 38.1 Agnes Weld as "Little Red Riding-Hood," A(I): 24
Lewis Carroll Photograph, Albums; undated; M. L. Parrish Collection of Victorian Novelists, Manuscripts Division, Department of Rare Books and Special Collections, Princeton University Library.

of the Victorian fetishization of that character such as is found in Charles Dickens's nostalgic passion for this iconic fairy-tale girl, who is always already lost since we know that she is to be devoured by the big bad wolf: "I felt that if I could have married Little Red Riding-Hood, I should have known perfect bliss. But, it was not to be" (Dickens 1850, 291).

As Dodgson's portrait of Agnes Weld as Little Red Riding Hood shows, fairy-tale photographs do not usually intend to represent real individuals and places but to typecast them to fit into the viewer's narrative expectations. At the same time, however, his photograph also reveals that the actual body of the model cannot be completely contained within the frame. Agnes Weld stares at the camera menacingly as if she were a wild animal; as Laurence Talairach-Vielmas observes, she "is the wolf, potentially emasculating the male photographer by mesmerizing him with her Medusa-like gaze" (2007, 89).[4] Like the ivy growing thickly in the background, the girl's potentially rampant sexuality may devour the male photographer/viewer, whose voyeuristic gaze Dodgson's portrait of Little Red Riding Hood exposes to light.

More than a century later, fashion photographer Sarah Moon (French, 1941–) re-appropriated this kind of sexualization of Little Red Riding Hood in order to problematize the pedophiliac gaze prevalent in modern society. Moon's *Little Red Riding Hood* (1983), one of the first uses of photography to illustrate a fairy tale in the form of a picture book, employs black-and-white photographs to recast Perrault's tale in a modern urban setting. She reimagines the encounter between a country girl and a wolf as the meeting between a fashionable schoolgirl and the driver of a large black car with glaring headlights. The camera angles place viewers in the position of the driver-wolf who remains invisible except when pictured as a menacing shadow. In doing so, Moon's photographs make viewers recognize their own potential complicity in the fetishization of young girls in contemporary visual culture. The disturbingly tactile image of rumpled bedclothes at the end of Moon's retelling suggests that the girl is finally consumed by the desiring gaze of the viewer, who looms over the absent victim, now reduced to a small dent on the sheet.

The use of photography to illustrate fairy tales is rarely found in picture books intended mainly for children. Although Moon's *Little Red Riding Hood* was awarded the Premio Grafice at the Bologna Children's Book Fair, it caused a controversy as to whether it was suitable for a child audience (Garret 1993). Perhaps the realism of photography as a medium that uses a flesh-and-blood girl renders too explicit the underlying implication that "Little Red Riding Hood" is, to use Susan Brownmiller's words, "a parable of rape" (1975, 310). This reading is emphasized by the stark realism of Moon's retelling, which follows Perrault's tale up to the point where the wolf eats up the girl but leaves out his tongue-in-cheek moral intended to frame this brutal tale in a more civilized context.[5]

Cindy Sherman's (American, 1954–) picture book *Fitcher's Bird* (1992) also seems to be intended more for adults than for children. Like Perrault's "Bluebeard" (ATU 312), the Grimms' "Fitcher's Bird" (ATU 311) tells the story of a girl who marries a rich and murderous husband who has already killed her two older sisters. In this story, the blood-stained item that reveals the heroine's disobedience to the sorcerer's injunction not to enter a certain room in his house is not a key but an egg, and the heroine tricks him by disguising herself as a bird and thereby succeeds in rescuing herself and her sisters.

Sherman is known for her self-portraits in which she appears in various guises reflecting cultural stereotypes of women. Her retelling of the Grimms' tale, however, uses wax dolls, and, unlike Moon's *Little Red Riding Hood*, which portrays a flesh-and-blood girl and a real car in an actual street, it consists almost entirely of artificial objects. Moreover, the artificiality of the dolls and other objects are emphasized with intense lighting and vividly saturated colors; the sorcerer's gray hair glistens with a nylon sheen, and his gold coins glitter too flashily for metal. Sherman thus undermines the realism usually expected of photography. Instead, her photographs' realism resides in their depiction of ugly feelings that may reside not only in the fairy-tale villain but also in all of us. In Sherman's photographs, the smooth, shining surface of the immaculate egg is echoed by the surfaces of the other objects fetishized by the sorcerer such as skulls, gold coins, and the dismembered bodies of young women.

The cold artificiality of the smooth skull decorated with colorful imitation flowers that Fitcher mistakes for his bride's head is contrasted with the warm sensuousness of the heroine's body covered with what appears to be real feathers and lit by sunlight from a bright blue sky behind her. Whereas the heroine's face remains invisible throughout the book, the sorcerer's is repeatedly shown close-up first from the standpoint of his victim who looks up at him through his abundant gray beard. However, as he is gradually forced to occupy the victim's position himself by the heroine's cunning, Sherman's visual retelling signals the reversal of the power relation between predator and prey by switching the camera angle. It now looks down on his face dripping with sweat as he carries a heavy basket containing gold coins and the sisters to his new bride's house. In the final image, he helplessly exposes a raw, pink nipple in the throes of death. While closely following the Grimms' text, Sherman's photographic restaging brings to light the morbid and excessive desires underpinning the fairy-tale romance.

The work of Anna Gaskell (American, 1969–) also focuses on the dark desires latent in fairy tales. Her photographs of Alice-like girls deconstruct the image of these innocent and seductive little children as those fetishized by Victorian male writers and artists. Her *hide* series (1998) is inspired by Perrault's "Donkey Skin" (ATU 510B), the story of a girl who disguises herself in a donkey's skin to escape her own father's marriage proposal. Gaskell's title plays on two of the available meanings of the word "hide," namely, the skin of an animal and the act of concealing oneself from view. In her recasting of "Donkey Skin," a darker branch of the Cinderella cycle (ATU 510), the heroine is multiplied, and the girls wearing Victorian middle-class clothes are shown performing apparently cruel and strangely erotic rituals upon one another in a candlelit old mansion evocative of gothic fiction. The close-up images of expressionless girls taken from oblique angles suggest that something sinister and destructive is going on, but the nature of the supposedly diabolical act remains hidden from the viewer's sight, just as Perrault's heroine conceals herself from her father's desiring gaze. Gaskell's photographic narrative of concealment and disavowal engenders the mixed feeling of pleasure and unease by evoking—and not showing—the return of the repressed.

In this sense, Gaskell's fairy-tale photography adopts a psychoanalytic approach in representing the invisible that contrasts to the kind of photography that contrives to give a concrete form to the invisible. The most famous as well as the earliest example of the latter would be the so-called Cottingley Fairies photographs. In 1917, Frances and Elsie Wright, aged nine and sixteen, took photographs of themselves accompanied by fairies. They captured the Victorian fascination with the images of enchanting fairies so ingeniously that a number of people, notably Sir Arthur Conan Doyle, believed in their authenticity. Their five photographs succeed in conveying the same feeling of enchantment as that created by the popular Victorian fairy paintings depicting winged girls in translucent dresses dancing in circles among flowers and toadstools. Even after having been proved to be fakes in the 1980s, the Cottingley Fairies have continued to inspire visual artists who similarly employ an elaborate artifice to create a fairy-tale atmosphere.

Carrie Mae Weems's (American, 1953–) *Mirror, Mirror* from the *Ain't Jokin'* series (1987–1988), on the other hand, disrupts this kind of fairy-tale magic by making visible its racist bias. Her recasting of the Grimms' "Snow White" (ATU 709), a black-and-white photograph, shows a Black woman holding a mirror from which a White fairy-godmother-like woman speaks to her. The caption reads: "Looking into the mirror, the black woman asked, 'Mirror, Mirror on the wall, who's the finest of them all?'" The mirror says, "Snow White, you black bitch, and don't you forget it!!!" *Mirror, Mirror* challenges the supposed universality of the equation of beauty with Whiteness in the classic tale about a girl whose skin is so white that she is named after it. It reveals the hidden hierarchical binary opposition between whiteness and blackness underlying many traditional European fairy tales. In Weems's photograph, the mirror frame that looks as black as the ebony window-frame, the color that Snow White's mother wishes for her daughter's hair, is foregrounded as the most striking—and the most beautiful—color.

Miwa Yanagi's (Japanese, 1967–) *Snow White* (2004; Yanagi 2007, 35), on the other hand, destabilizes the binary opposition between the young, beautiful princess and the old, ugly witch, a well-established topos in traditional European fairy tales. In her recasting, Snow White and the wicked queen are shown as mirror images of one another. The figure with her back to the camera appears to be the young Snow White, and the figure confronting the girl looks like her wicked stepmother. A closer look, however, reveals that the masked figure is the reflection of the girl in the mirror. In the Grimms' "Snow White," it is the wicked stepmother who sees not her own but her stepdaughter's face in the magic mirror. She then sets out to kill Snow White, whose youthful beauty has defeated her in an implicit contest that defines aging as a demeaning and fatal process for women. In Yanagi's photograph, however, the two stages of a woman's life are compressed into one figure in which the young self coexists with the old self, emphasizing their continuity, symbolized by the apple they give and receive at the same time.

As her recasting of "Snow White" shows, Yanagi's *Fairy Tale* series (2004–2006) subverts the conventional portrayal of the female body by reversing, blending, and dissolving the opposition between young girl and old woman (Yanagi 2007). Her reconfiguration of women's intergenerational relationship is ambiguous rather than simply either antagonistic or harmonious. The ambiguity is further intensified by the fact that all the models in *Fairy Tale* are girls aged between five and ten. Playing the parts of old women, the children wear masks with exaggerated wrinkles and the hooked nose typical of a fairy-tale witch, but their bodies are undisguised, with lacy chemises revealing their young, smooth, plump limbs. Instead of trying to make the disguise look natural, Yanagi deliberately emphasizes the disjunction between the withered crone mask and its wearer's girlish body. These images' uncanny yet often humorous hybridity destabilizes our naturalized notions of youth and old age, presented instead as arbitrary and therefore open to revision.

Yanagi also explores ideas about women and their lives in her *My Grandmothers* series (1999–), photographs of young women performing their self-images as old women. To create these pictures, the artist conducted a series of interviews with her models in which she asked them what they imagined they would be like fifty years later. She then staged and photographed the scenes. As a result, two stages of a woman's life are superimposed on one image in such a way that both are revealed as imaginary constructs. These photographs simultaneously expose the compulsory aspect of gender and age performance and point toward the possibility of performing differently. Some of the images of future selves in *My Grandmothers* reveal how old fairy-tale formulas may inform the ways people understand and imagine their life stories as far as half a century into the future. In *Yuka* (2000; Yanagi 2009, 54–55), for example, an old woman with bright red hair roars across the Golden Gate Bridge in the sidecar of a Harley-Davidson driven by her boyfriend, who looks fifty years younger than she is. This image seems to fulfill the standard fairy-tale wish that "someday my prince will come," apart from the fact that, here, "someday" is postponed half a century. That Yuka's dream must be deferred so long raises a question as to the social and cultural constraints imposed on her as a young woman living in contemporary Japan.

In *Mitsue* (2009; Yanagi 2009, 12–13), an extremely old woman—her neck overemphatically skeletal—wearing a witchlike black hood and dress and holding sprouting bulbs in her hands, lies on earth covered with moss and dead leaves; she looks up at the sky with a calm expression suggesting her embrace of her integration into the natural cycle of death and regeneration. *Mitsue* bears a striking thematic, compositional, and tonal resemblance to Kiki Smith's photograph *Sleeping Witch* (2000),[6] which also depicts a gray-haired woman—the artist herself, in this case—in a black hood and dress lying among fallen leaves with a black apple in her hand, suggesting that female artists across different cultures are telling new stories about women in old age, drawing on the shared sources of traditional fairy tales in mutually resonant ways (Murai 2015, 81–103).

Dina Goldstein's (Canadian, 1969–) *Fallen Princesses* series (2007–2010) also subverts conventional images of women and their lives in her parodic recasting of heroines from Walt Disney's fairy-tale animations in present-day realistic settings. *Snowy* (2008), for example, portrays a young woman in the iconic Disney Snow White outfit standing in a North American suburban living room and staring into the camera with an indignant expression on her lipsticked face. She holds two babies, one crying and the other sucking fingers, while another little girl pulls on her skirt demandingly. A fourth baby can be seen crawling among toys scattered around in the far corner of the room. Her husband, in a Disney prince's costume, apparently oblivious to what is going on, lounges in a chair with his legs propped on a footstool and watches a polo match on TV with a can of beer and a bag of potato chips. The ironic juxtaposition of the idealized fairy-tale marriage in Disney's film and the drab reality of middle-class family life problematizes the politics of gender and class underlying this ever-popular fairy tale; even if you marry a handsome man with a good income, problems will follow you as long as traditional gender roles remain the same.

Goldstein also plays with the cultural and racial stereotypes endorsed by Disney's adaptation of traditional stories of non-Western cultures. Her *Pocahauntas* (2010) portrays a fashion-model-like beauty with the same long black hair and exotic costume as Disney's eponymous heroine on a couch watching TV in a room full of conventional Native American souvenir goods, such as a banal painting depicting a large bear and various wooden and fabric crafts. The room is also littered with domestic cats—one is eating dried cat food spilled on the floor, and another lies on top of a cat tower made to look like a tree—and ornamental animal furs. In one corner stands a traditional European portrait of a handsome blond man, presumably the English explorer John Smith, whose life, according to Disney's retelling, is saved by Pocahontas, who has developed a romantic relationship with him. This emphatically kitsch portrayal of the Powhatan chief's nature-loving daughter critiques Disney's exoticization and commodification of non-Western culture on a global scale. Goldstein also emphasizes the cultural specificity of North American culture, which has increasingly come to be regarded as the global norm over the past century. In *Not So Little Riding Hood* (2008), for example, an obese girl walks through a forest drinking from a McDonald's large-size cup, the color of which matches her red hooded cape, carrying a basket heaped with hamburgers and French fries. This exaggeratedly McDonaldized—rather than Disneyfied as in Goldstein's other images—Little Red Riding Hood exposes another aspect of North American culture that purports to assume universality in its global marketing but is in fact a culture-and class-specific phenomenon.

The London-based photographer Chan-Hyo Bae's (Korean, 1975–) *Existing in Costume* series (2006–; see figure 38.2) exposes the cultural imbalance in the global fairy-tale culture in a more acute way. Bae's photographs restage well-known European fairy tales, such as "Cinderella" (ATU 510A), "Beauty and the Beast" (ATU 425C), and "Snow White," in the style of traditional European oil painting portraying powerful rulers. Pointing out that these fairy tales "contain tacit messages that the weak should obey the order designed by the strong in order to enjoy happiness," he draws an analogy between two influential traditions in the West, oil portraiture of royalty and fairy tales that end with royal marriage (Bae 2014). The twist in his photography is that he casts himself in the role of fairy-tale princesses in a way that recalls Cindy Sherman's self-portraits. While his reflexive re-appropriation of the conventions of European oil portraiture, such as strong color contrasts, symmetrical composition, and the posing of the central figure indicating power, denaturalizes the Eurocentric norm operating in the production and reception of art, his gender- and race-bending self-portrait critiques the West's feminization of the East discussed by Edward Said in *Orientalism* (1978). The image of an Oriental man wearing a dress and a wig of an eighteenth-century English lady works to

Figure 38.2 Chan-Hyo Bae, *Existing in Costume_Cinderella*, 230cm × 180cm, C-Print, 2008
Courtesy of the artist.

defamiliarize the privileged image of European royalty to which fairy-tale heroes and heroines continue to aspire even in recent Disney fairy-tale films. Bae's fairy-tale photographs give an insight into the way in which the fairy tale still works as a Eurocentric colonializing norm in today's globalizing culture.

Another recent tendency in fairy-tale photography is the reconsideration of the relationship between human beings and nature, especially wild animals, a motif central to many fairy tales across cultures. Amy Stein's (American, 1970–) *Domesticated* series (2005–2007) explores the changing boundaries between modern human society and the natural environment. *Watering Hole* (2005), for example, depicts a large erect standing bear facing a girl in a bathing suit—a modern-day Goldilocks—standing on the diving board of a swimming pool in a garden. The two are separated by a wire-mesh fence that looks as if it could be easily broken by the bear. Rather than evoking terror, however, the image makes the viewer recognize that it is staged, shown by the stiff postures of both the girl and the bear and the position of the camera right behind the bear. The picture also seems strange and unreal because it is set in a suburban garden, rather than in a wild forest as we would usually expect of such a fairy-tale-like encounter.

A further twist, however, is that, although the image looks fake, it *is* based on an actual event; Stein's *Domesticated* series re-enacts real encounters with wild animals about which she learned from residents of a small town bordering a forest in Pennsylvania. Her photographs give evidence to stories of human-animal encounters currently being told and circulated as humans continue to encroach upon nature. Her use of taxidermic animals also raises the question of what it means to "domesticate" nature. Taxidermy, an art of apparently lifelike preservation of animals after their death, complicates the boundaries between nature and artifact, wild and domesticated, and life and death. The irony is that the stiffness of the recreated life of an animal may not be recognizable in a photograph, a medium that can only capture an object as a still image. Stein's photograph is carefully staged so as to give both a momentary illusion of reality and a sense of disbelief in that realism at the same time, offering a new twist to fairy-tale photography's concern with the dichotomy between fantasy and reality. Another important element in her fairy-tale photography is that it consists of portraits of animals, characters that have been marginalized—unless they transform into humans—in the largely anthropocentric fairy-tale tradition in Euro-American culture.

Over the past century and a half, the fairy tale has provided photography with multiple performative possibilities. As a medium using material bodies and objects, photography, in turn, has contributed to the reassessment of the fairy tale from the perspectives of cultural, social, political, and environmental concerns such as gender, sexuality, class, race, ethnicity, and species. The examples discussed here demonstrate the potential of photography to help us understand the fairy tale's ever-renewable visual and aesthetic possibilities.

Related topics: Animal Studies; Children's and Young Adult (YA) Literature; Contemporary Art; Disney Corporation; Fat Studies; Gender; Hybridity; Orientalism; Pictorial; Sexualities/Queer and Trans Studies

Notes

1. Controversy over Dodgson's motivations for photographing young girls has intensified especially since the publication of Morton N. Cohen's *Lewis Carroll, Photographer of Children: Four Nude Studies* (1978). For a detailed analysis of *Alice Liddell as "The Beggar-Maid,"* see Susina (2010, 95–106).
2. See Laura Mulvey's analysis of the male gaze in cinema (1975).
3. Lynn Vallone contrasts the complex ambiguity of Dodgson's photographic representation of Little Red Riding Hood with the naivety of his poem inscribed on the facing page of Weld's photograph, in which "[Little Red Riding Hood's] innocent confidence is all that is needed to vanquish the wolf" (2005, 195–196). Dodgson's poem is reproduced in Taylor and Wakeling (2002, 140).
4. Carol Mavor also sees Weld's eyes as "the eyes of the wolf that has presumably just eaten her grandmother; we wonder whether she has eaten the wolf, and whether she is about ready to eat us up" (1995, 29).
5. Sandra L. Beckett compares Moon's *Little Red Riding Hood* with modern retellings using other media than photography that emphasize the sexuality and violence inherent in Perrault's tale such as Anne Ikhlef's 1985 film *La véritable histoire du Chaperon rouge* (The real story of Red Riding Hood) and Roberto Innocenti's 1988 illustration of the tale (Beckett 2008, 32–33).
6. Smith's *Sleeping Witch* appears on the cover of Posner and Smith (2001).

References Cited and Further Reading

Bae, Chan-Hyo. 2014. "Existing in Costume: Fairy Tale Project." www.mc2gallery.it/public/Chan-Hyo%20Bae.pdf.
Beckett, Sandra L. 2008. *Red Riding Hood for All Ages: A Fairy-Tale Icon in Cross-Cultural Contexts.* Detroit: Wayne State UP.
Brownmiller, Susan. 1975. *Against Our Will: Men, Women, and Rape.* New York: Fawcett Columbine.
Cohen, Morton N. 1978. *Lewis Carroll, Photographer of Children: Four Nude Studies.* Philadelphia: Rosenbach Foundation.
Dickens, Charles. 1850. "A Christmas Tree." *Household Words,* December 21: 289–95.
Frisch, Aaron. 2012. *The Girl in Red,* illustrated by Roberto Innocenti. Mankato, MN: Creative Editions.
Garret, Jefferey. 1993. "'With Murderous Ending, Shocking, Menacing . . .': Sarah Moon's *Little Red Riding Hood* 10 Years after." *Bookbird* 31 (3): 8–9.
Mavor, Carol. 1995. *Pleasures Taken: Performances of Sexuality and Loss in Victorian Photography.* Durham, NC: Duke UP.
Moon, Sarah. (1983) 2002. *Little Red Riding Hood.* Mankato, MN: Creative Editions.

Mulvey, Laura. 1975. "Visual Pleasure and Narrative Cinema." *Screen* 16 (3): 6–18.

Murai, Mayako. 2015. *From Dog Bridegroom to Wolf Girl: Contemporary Japanese Fairy-Tale Adaptations in Conversation with the West*. Detroit: Wayne State UP.

Posner, Helaine, and Kiki Smith. 2001. *Kiki Smith: Telling Tales*. New York: International Center of Photography.

Sherman, Cindy. 1992. *Fitcher's Bird*. New York: Rizzoli.

Susina, Jan. 2010. *The Place of Lewis Carroll in Children's Literature*. New York: Routledge.

Talairach-Vielmas, Laurence. 2007. *Moulding the Female Body in Victorian Fairy Tales and Sensation Novels*. Aldershot: Ashgate.

Taylor, Roger. 2002. "'All in the Golden Afternoon': Photographs of Charles Lutwidge Dodgson." In Taylor and Wakeling, *Lewis Carroll, Photographer*, 1–120.

Taylor, Roger, and Edward Wakeling, eds. 2002. *Lewis Carroll, Photographer: The Princeton University Library Albums*. Princeton, NJ: Princeton UP.

Vallone, Lynn. 2005. "Reading Girlhood in Victorian Photography." *The Lion and the Unicorn* 29 (2): 190–210.

Yanagi, Miwa. 2007. *Fairy Tale: Strange Stories of Women Young and Old*. Kyoto: Seigensha.

———. 2009. *Miwa Yanagi*. Kyoto: Tankōsha.

Mediagraphy

Bae, Chan-Hyo. 2008–2010. *Existing in Costume: Fairy Tales*. Photograph Series. Korea/UK. www.mc2gallery.it/public/Chan-Hyo%20Bae.pdf.

Dodgson, Charles Lutwidge. 1857. *Agnes Weld as "Little Red Riding-Hood."* Photograph. UK. http://libweb2.princeton.edu/rbsc2/portfolio/lc1/r00000009.htm.

———. 1858. *Alice Liddell as "The Beggar-Maid".* Photograph. UK. http://libweb2.princeton.edu/rbsc2/portfolio/lc2/00000014.htm.

Gaskell, Anna. 1998. "Anna Gaskell, Hide." White Cube. http://whitecube.com/exhibitions/anna_gaskell_hide_duke_street_1999/.

Goldstein, Dina. 2007–2010. *Fallen Princesses*. Photograph Series. Canada. www.fallenprincesses.com/.

Griffith, Frances, and Elsie Wright. 1917–1920. *The Cottingley Fairies*. Photograph Series. UK.

La véritable histoire du Chaperon rouge. 1985. Director Anne Ikhlef. France.

Smith, Kiki. 2000. *Sleeping Witch*. Photograph. USA.

Stein, Amy. 2005–2007. *Domesticated*. Photograph Series. USA. www.amystein.com/domesticated/.

Weems, Carrie Mae. 1987–1988. *Ain't Jokin'*. Photograph Series. USA. http://carriemaeweems.net/galleries/aint-jokin.html.

Yanagi, Miwa. 1999. *My Grandmothers*. Photograph Series. Japan. www.yanagimiwa.net/e/grandmothers/e/index.html.

———. 2000. *Yuka*. Photograph. Japan. www.yanagimiwa.net/e/grandmothers/e/project/02.html.

———. 2004. *Snow White*. Photograph. Japan. www.yanagimiwa.net/e/fairy/.

———. 2004–2006. *Fairytale*. Photograph Series. Japan. www.yanagimiwa.net/e/fairy/.

———. 2009. *Mitsue*. Photograph. Japan. www.yanagimiwa.net/e/grandmothers/e/project/25.html.

39
CINEMATIC

Pauline Greenhill

Cinema using fairy-tale stories, characters, names, images, motifs, and themes dates from film's earliest history, beginning with director Georges Méliès's 1896 *Le manoir du diable* (The House of the Devil). Short or feature length, animated and/or live action, made on film stock or in digital formats, fairy-tale films appear in movie theaters, on television, and on computer screens. Using Kevin Paul Smith's schema for understanding how fairy tales work in literary adaptation (2007, 10), their intertexts can include explicit reference in the title, as does Finnish director Päivi Hartzell's 1986 *Lumikuningatar* (The Snow Queen), after the Hans Christian Andersen tale. There can be implicit reference in the title, as in Mike Nichols's 2011 *Bread Crumbs*, recalling Hansel and Gretel's materials for marking their path through the woods. Explicit incorporation is found when the main character of Helma Sanders-Brahms's *Deutschland bleiche Mutter* (Germany, Pale Mother, 1980) narrates a version of "The Robber Bridegroom" (ATU 955) to her daughter. Inclusion of fairy-tale references can also be implicit in the content, as when the title character in *Carrie* (Brian De Palma, 1976) finally gets to go to her high school prom, just as Cinderella goes to the ball—though with much more dire results. Discussion of fairy tales appears in "Once Upon a Crime" (2012), an episode of the American television show *Castle*, when the writer and police dialogue about fairy tales' true meanings. Fairy-tale settings and/or environments, accessed from modern-day New York through a magic mirror, appear in *The 10th Kingdom* (David Carson and Herbert Wise, 2000). Filmmakers may re-vision a story, sometimes with new spin, as when *H & G* (Danishka Esterhazy, 2013) relocates "Hansel and Gretel" (ATU 327A) to Winnipeg, Manitoba, Canada, with two lost underclass children seeking shelter on a farm, or they may create an entirely new tale, like *The Fall* (Tarsem Singh, 2006), not based on any specific previous literary or traditional fairy tale.

Though the Disney Corporation's many highly successful adaptations are internationally recognized, they by no means encompass, delimit, or prescribe criteria for fairy-tale films. And even Disney fairy-tale films vary over time and from one story to another. Walt Disney's own bizarre 1922 short animation of *Little Red Riding Hood* begins with an extended scene of donut-making and incorporates Red's helpful dog, neither of which appears in most traditional versions. The 1937 (David Hand) animated feature *Snow White and the Seven Dwarfs* instantiated what Jack Zipes (2016) calls "the well-made fairy-tale film," a sequence of events, ditties, practices, clashes, and problems, with a magical resolution. The racist, sexist literary fairy-tale renderings of *Peter Pan* (Wilfred Jackson, Clyde Geronimi, and Hamilton Luske, 1953) and *The Little Mermaid* (John Musker and Ron Clements, 1989) gave way to a more-or-less successful effort at a strong heroine in *Beauty and the Beast* (Gary Trousdale and Kirk Wise, 1991). *Mary Poppins* (Robert Stevenson, 1964), among others, shows that Disney's work in live-action fairy tales predates its reflexive pastiches *Enchanted* (Kevin Lima, 2007) and *Into the Woods* (Rob Marshall, 2014). Also live action, the 2014 (faux) feminist re-vision *Maleficent* (Robert Stromberg) contrasts with the throwback *Cinderella* (Kenneth Branagh, 2015). Thus, the concept of a single, unified standard Disney version of fairy-tale films is more than somewhat suspect.

Many of Disney's recent live-action releases to cinema seriously address adult audiences—consider, for example, the rape subtext in *Maleficent* and the violence in *Into the Woods*. These works go beyond merely coding visual and verbal content for knowing, alternate readings by adults taking their children to the movies, while ostensibly speaking mainly to supposedly innocent child viewers. And internationally and historically, fairy-tale films in general do not posit that their viewers will chiefly or even largely be children. This chapter explores mainly live-action films for adults, which look at the more serious side of fairy tales. I use as examples two "Hansel and Gretel" films, but begin with an overview of the tale and variety of films using it. I conclude with reflections on how these dark fairy-tale films mess with and challenge normative gender assumptions and constructions. To demonstrate the malleability of the topic, however, I begin with "Little Red Riding Hood" films to demonstrate how multiple tales can be used by filmmakers to address similar areas.

Harms to Children and "Hansel and Gretel"

"Little Red Riding Hood" (ATU 333) has been the hypotext for a number of distinctly adult narratives exploring pedophilia (sex between adults and children) and other harms to children. The American horror movie *Little Erin Merryweather* (David Morwick, 2003) details consequences in adulthood of abuse in childhood, rendering a serial killer whose modus operandi replicates details of the fairy tale, the story her father read to her as he molested her. The British *Red Riding Trilogy*'s three postmodern film noir films (2009), *The Year of Our Lord 1974* (Julian Jarrold), *The Year of Our Lord 1980* (James Marsh), and *The Year of Our Lord 1983* (Anand Tucker), use the traditional narrative as a source for plot elements (such as girls venturing into everyday but dangerous places), visual images (such as the innocent red-coated girl), and metaphors (such as the wolf as predator linking to human sexuality). Regardless of linguistic, national, or cultural origins, filmmakers return to "Little Red Riding Hood" repeatedly to explore violence and crime. The French horror *Promenons-nous dans les bois* (Deep in the Woods, Lionel Delplanque, 2000) locates motives for murder within patriarchal control over women, children, and young men. *A Wicked Tale* by Singapore director Merwyn Tong Tzang (2005) surreally considers dangerous male and female sexualities. The Japanese anime *Jin-Roh: The Wolf Brigade* (Hiroyuki Okiura, 1999) explores a dystopian future in which a renegade police gang seek control over the society and underground resistance employs couriers called "Red Riding Hoods."[1]

Like "Little Red Riding Hood," "Hansel and Gretel" (ATU 327A) offers a brutal narrative of child abandonment, cannibalism, and murder. The subject of numerous filmic adaptations, those available in English include American, British, Canadian, Dutch, French, German/Polish, Israeli, and Korean.[2] Zipes's *The Enchanted Screen* (2011, 413) lists forty-one "Hansel and Gretel" films from 1909–2007. Zipes did not include movies that allude only obliquely to the tale, including *The Night of the Hunter* (Charles Laughton, 1955, discussed below), with implicit reference, and *The Last Butterfly* (Karel Kachnya, 1991), which incorporates a fairy-tale play. Even more "Hansel and Gretel" films have appeared since, including four English-language live-action features in 2013, from the campy fantasy horror *Hansel & Gretel: Witch Hunters* (Tommy Wirkola) to the campy comedy horror *Hansel & Gretel Get Baked* (Duane Journey). Not all these films offer valuable material for a cultural analysis of harms to children, though some relatively unlikely suspects—particularly works in the horror genre—do so. I consider two examples: live action (not animated, because of its conventional associations with family entertainment); present-day or recent setting (not located in a distantly historicized or science fiction chronotope, arguably displacing issues to another time and place);[3] realistic (with little or no recourse to supernatural creatures and happenings as modes to explain away causes and consequences);[4] aimed primarily for adult audiences (not child and/or family fare, therefore not censoring or mitigating harm); not based on the late-nineteenth-century Humperdinck opera (generically distinct); feature length (rather than shorter works, allowing more extended exposition); and not originally made as TV programming or serials.

The best-known traditional version of "Hansel and Gretel" concerns a father persuaded by his wife, the children's stepmother, to abandon his daughter and son in the woods. Twice they find their way home, but eventually they become lost and encounter a gingerbread house, wherein a witch lives. She tries to fatten Hansel and forces Gretel to do housework. The boy deceives the witch by proffering a stick or bone instead of his finger when she wants to test whether or not he is sufficiently plumped up for cooking. When she eventually decides to roast him anyway, Gretel tricks the witch and pushes her into the oven. The children take the witch's treasure and, sometimes with supernatural help, bring it home to their now (again) widowed father.

Even within Europe, traditional versions of ATU 327A vary extensively. For example, Zipes comments that in the manuscript on which the Grimms based their story:

> the children are not given lovely names; their mother is their biological mother; the children do not need the help of God to save themselves; they automatically return home with money that will guarantee a warm welcome. Indeed, the Grimms changed this oral tale [. . .] and in the process they demonized a stepmother, transformed the children into two pious innocents with cute names who trust in God, and added a silly duck that helps them across a pond to sooth a sobbing father, who does not show any grief about his dead wife, nor does he apologize for abandoning them.
>
> (2011, 194)

The cannibalistic figures include not only witches, but also "ogres, giants, [. . .] demons, and magicians" (Zipes 2013, 121). There may be one child protagonist, or three, male and/or female, who may be lost, not abandoned. The house in the woods may have conventional construction materials. In an Italian version, the boy Peppe drinks from a magical brook that turns him into a sheep and his sister Maria "more beautiful than the sun" (136). Maria grows up and marries a king. Her stepmother, jealous that Maria's success has exceeded her own daughter's, plots against the young queen. Both stepmother and stepsister are explicitly evil and receive gruesome punishments in the end, but their powers are not supernatural, and they are not cannibals. The stepmother as non-supernatural evil cannibal is also found in a Romanian version, in which (like the Italian story) the boy transforms, this time into a cuckoo (see 121–153). Recall these extreme variations in tradition when considering the relevance to ATU 327A of the films I discuss that stray as far from the familiar Grimm variant. Indeed, rather than drifting from a set original—folklorists deny the primacy of any single traditional text—filmmakers produce readings that are (ironically) closer to tradition than they may suspect.[5]

Zipes sees the story as fundamentally dealing with "abandonment and the search for home" (2011, 200), though filmmakers may not take up these themes. The tale incorporates striking images evoking appropriate and inappropriate food; many have become cultural clichés, like the breadcrumb trail, the gingerbread house, the imprisoned Hansel's bony "finger," and the witch shoved into the oven. Many adult film versions use these images (sometimes *only* these images). Zipes links "Hansel and Gretel" with "Tom Thumb" (ATU 700), "The Pied Piper" legend, "Donkey Skin" (ATU 510B), and "The Juniper Tree" (ATU 720, see Greenhill and Brydon 2010; Greenhill 2014) and says that cinematic adaptations of these works "comment metaphorically on modern attitudes toward the maltreatment of children, the causes of physical abuse and violence suffered by young people, and the trauma of incest" (2011, 193). Child disappearance, especially as motivated by stranger-danger/pedophilia fears, is remarkably absent, though child sexual abuse sometimes appears as an explanation for ambivalent or evil Hansel and Gretel characters' actions—as it does for some filmed Little Red Riding Hoods. Recurring themes and ideas include: lost, abandoned people; making the title characters teenagers or (young) adults; rendering them as vengeful/misbehaving rather than innocent; dealing directly with child abuse and violence; using the name Grimm; creating an identity/homology between stepmother and witch;[6] and playing with those characters' gender. Live-action films exploit their medium to enact and highlight the latter theme, also present in some traditional versions. Marking an identification between the (step)parent and the evil figure the children encounter, the same actor can take both roles.

The latter process takes place in "Hansel and Gretel" shorts and family films, as in Joan Collins's stepmother/witch in *Faerie Tale Theatre* (1983) and Delta Burke's stepmother occupying the witch's house at the close of Garry J. Tunnicliffe's 2002 movie. In the short *Hansel & Gretel: An Appalachian Version* (Tom Davenport, 1975), Marlene Elbin plays both, but the witch is voiced by Julian Yochum. A transgender (step)mother/witch (Michael Yama) also appears in Tim Burton's (1982) Disney TV version. The same processes take place in adult versions. In *Freeway II: Confessions of a Trickbaby* (Matthew Bright, 1999), Vincent Gallo plays Sister Gomez, a composite witch/stepmother. Danishka Esterhazy's neorealist *H & G* (2013) sets the story in present-day Winnipeg; stepparent and witch figures are male. This kind of play with expectations about the characters is also evident in other cinematic versions of well-known fairy tales.

Given the tale's horrific content, it is not surprising that "Hansel and Gretel" themed films aimed at adult audiences often invoke drama and/or horror. Yet what Zipes calls "the rationalization of abuse" (2011, 195) only manifests rarely in these movies. Such works lack the tendency

> to tell the story of child abuse and abandonment from an adult perspective that diminishes or excuses the consequences of adult actions harmful to children. Even if the tale may point to the parents as culpable, there is a certain amount of rationalization of guilt and responsibility that shapes the telling of the tale.
>
> (2011, 195)

Indeed, parents may be entirely absent, as in *Criminal Lovers* (François Ozon, 1999) discussed in the following, or their (ir)responsibility and blame quite obvious, as in *The Night of the Hunter*. Their treatment of the tale may in part be linked to the fact that both directors are recognized as queer. Homophobia may have prevented Laughton, who was relatively uncloseted for his time as bisexual, from obtaining support to direct other films, whereas Ozon's sexuality has definitely contributed positively to his bad-boy image.

The Night of the Hunter (Directed by Charles Laughton, 1955)

This moody American "lyrical horror film," "expressionist period piece," and "realistic fairy tale" (Couchman 2009, 134) alludes to "Bluebeard" (ATU 312) and "Little Red Riding Hood" as well as to "Hansel and Gretel."[7] Robert Mitchum plays psychotic serial femicidal preacher Harry Powell, whose Christianity tolerates murder but not sexuality. He seeks and marries

Willa Harper (Shelley Winters), widow of his hanged cellmate, Ben Harper (Peter Graves), whose two children, John (Billy Chapin) and Pearl (Sally Jane Bruce), have hidden the money from their father's bank robbery. John's suspicions about his stepfather are confirmed when Powell threatens the children. He murders Willa when she realizes that he has lied to her, then pretends she abandoned him and her children. Powell further reveals his evil when he withholds food from the children. When the preacher threatens to slit John's throat, Pearl reveals that the money is in her doll. The siblings escape with the doll and run away, taking a boat and floating down the river, watched by various animals. Powell follows.

Kindly widow Rachel Cooper (Lillian Gish) takes them into her home. Her Christianity, as fervent to Powell's, directs—unlike his—to forgiveness and to caring for orphaned and abandoned children. The preacher shows up at her house, claiming to be the children's father, but Cooper defends them with her shotgun, eventually shooting him. When the police come to arrest Powell, the scene recalls for John his father's arrest and he protests, revealing the doll with the money. John refuses to identify Powell as the man who killed his mother. A vigilante mob gathers, brandishing ropes and farm implements, but the police take Powell away. The concluding Christmas scenes with Cooper and the children suggest a happy-ever-after.

This "eccentric and weird" chiller (Bauer 1999, 614), an "oddball classic" (Vineberg 1991, 27), explores ideas around criminality and psychosis, using parental figures who, like Hansel and Gretel's father and stepmother, fail rather spectacularly to care for John and Pearl. The boy's empathy for Powell during his arrest and trial underline the link John traces between the preacher and his biological father and their intertwined fates. This connection stressed their common criminality, yet their distinctive motivations are notable. Ben robs a bank for a benevolent reason—caring for his family—but kills two men in the process. Evil stepfather Powell is also a thief and killer; Bluebeard-like, he is a serial wife-murderer who takes their money. And while Ben leaves his wife and family too soon, Powell relentlessly follows John and Pearl when they run away, refusing to relinquish hold.

Willa's death literalizes her seeming numbness and absence. She differs from vibrant, warm, and caring stepmother Cooper, no "Hansel and Gretel" witch, whose house is a refuge filled with good food. However, though arguably Powell is the stepfather/witch figure, he and Cooper seem equally obsessed with Christianity. Cooper repeats Bible stories to her charges, and when Powell threatens her house he sings his constant refrain, the hymn "Leaning on the Everlasting Arms," and she joins in. Perhaps director Laughton unconsciously chose this song to allude to the American right to bear arms; the good characters in the film—father Ben Harper and stepmother Rachel Cooper—both use firearms to defend their families, while the evil preacher Powell's weapon of choice is a switchblade.

Night's film noir visuals obscure its very non-noir emphasis on Christianity, clear judgments of good and evil, and happy conclusion. It fits the fairy tale, though many of those who describe it as such misrecognize the form as only being for children, always having a happy ending, and so on (e.g., Bauer 1999). Yet others have a more accurate understanding, calling the film "a fairy tale, with all the elements in place—a wicked step-parent, a pair of innocent, besieged orphans, a perilous journey, and even a fairy godmother" (Vineberg 1991, 27). As such, intertextuality resonates in the film. Not only echoing familiar fairy-tale motifs, characters, and ideology, *Night* also includes John telling an original fairy tale as a bedtime story to Pearl. Exegetical narrations like the latter clearly reference the youngsters' own situation. A haunting extradiegetic magical song, apparently reflecting Pearl's point of view, again alludes to the children's plight, as do Biblical storytellings by Cooper that open the film and punctuate significant moments.

This film, like many fairy tales, explores the problematics of family and community. Specific to several "Hansel and Gretel" films, including *Night*, is the notion that the family may not be sufficient to the task of raising children. Ideally, as in *Night*, unrelated community members take the role of caregiver to orphaned and/or abandoned children. Though clearly lacking a Christian perspective, *Les amants criminels* demonstrates similar processes.

Criminal Lovers (Les amants criminels) (Directed by François Ozon, 1999)

These two otherwise very different films not only use materials from "Hansel and Gretel," but *Criminal* consciously quotes ideas and materials from *Night*. Yet while *Night* has innocents for its Hansel and Gretel (or mainly innocent, since John's unwillingness to implicate Powell is arguably immoral/amoral), *Criminal* has perhaps inexplicably evil title characters. *Night* is black and white, *Criminal* color—in their judgments as well as the medium of production. *Night's* violence is usually obscured or off screen; *Criminal* has overt, explicit scenes of a literally bloody murder and its gory aftermath.

Multiple sexualities manifest in *Criminal*, by French "provocateur" Ozon (Schilt 2011, 32; see Rees-Roberts 2008, 31–35). Within its Hitchcockian structure (see Hain 2007, 279), sex, murder, and cannibalism motivate this film (as they do *Freeway II*, another adult "Hansel & Gretel" film), with great emphasis on their effects from the movie's very beginning. Teenaged Alice (Natacha Régnier) wants to have sex with her classmate Luc (Jérémie Renier), but he cannot get an erection with her. She persuades him to murder Saïd (Salim Kechiouche), who has expressed his sexual attraction to her. Alice and Luc rob a jewelry store and drive to a remote wood where they bury Saïd's body. As so many versions of ATU 327A, they mark their trail, but nevertheless become lost. They come upon a boat and float down the river (as do John and Pearl in *Night*). They reach a house where a large, foreign-accented "ogre" (Predrag Manojlovic) imprisons them. He releases Luc, has sex with him, and feeds him meat from Saïd's body. He lets the two escape; Luc has sex with Alice by a river, while various animals watch (recalling those in *Night*).[8] Anne E. Duggan notes, "This scene renders pornographic a typical Disney moment in which a virginal heroine and her prince encounter each other in the woods, surrounded by innocent woodland creatures" (2016, 70). The police arrive, kill Alice, and arrest Luc and the ogre. Again recalling *Night*, Luc protests the rough treatment of his ambivalent father figure.[9]

These amoral/immoral kids flout bourgeois morality, as do characters White Girl and Cyclona in *Freeway II*, but without the excuses/explanations given for the latter two, making them abused members of the underclass. Evidently middle or even upper class, Alice persuades Luc to murder Saïd by claiming that he organized and photographed her gang rape, but when she confesses that this is a lie, Luc does not stray from their plan. Complex repressions of sexual impulses of both Alice and Luc lead to Saïd's murder, but the choice of target seems racially motivated; he is Arab North African and they are White European. These are not *Freeway II's* arguably excusable homicides, motivated by abuse or abandonment. Mark Hain comments that "teenage anti-heroine Alice [. . .] initiates a murder out of a combination of sexual kicks, neurotic revenge for desiring/being desired by the Other (in the person of an Arab classmate), and for something new to do," calls her "a vapid, controlling, castrating high school femme fatale," and says that "the most disturbing aspect of her characterization is that she apparently longs for her own death as a form of sexual extreme" (2007, 282). While Ozon himself would probably not make the same judgment against his characters, mainstream Euro North American audiences might very well do so. There is little that makes Alice likeable.

Criminal Lovers follows the narrative sequence of well-known versions of "Hansel and Gretel" quite closely, clearly demonstrating how a filmmaker may be inspired by fairy tale without in any way succumbing to its conventional ethos of child-appropriateness and happy endings. The themes of murder and cannibalism are overdetermined in Ozon's film, while child abandonment takes on a new meaning, or perhaps a more open inflection. As in well-known versions of "Hansel and Gretel," main characters Luc and Alice go to the woods, but they do so because of their own horrific action—their need to conceal the murder of their classmate and his body. As in some European versions of "Hansel and Gretel," the evil householder/witch is an male ogre figure, taking the ambiguous role of stepparent. As does *Night*, *Criminal Lovers* disorders conventional gender expectations for the witch/stepparent.

"Hansel and Gretel" Films: Messing With Fairy Tales, Messing With Gender

Folklorist Bengt Holbek notes that "the witch's house is a parallel of the parents' house," but he suggests that ATU 327A "is dominated by a woman (who hides her cruel intentions behind a friendly appearance)" (1987, 393–394). For him, the story is about "contrasts: the house of the parents is *outside* the forest; that of the witch is *in* it; the former has no food, the latter has food in abundance," and also about "subtle correspondences [. . .] when the children return after having killed the witch, their mother, too, has died" (394). Holbek was discussing a specifically Danish series of traditional folktales, but his conclusions would probably seem self-evident to most Euro North Americans familiar with the conventional version. Filmmakers use the story with the sometimes quite explicit purpose of disturbing orthodox ideas of gender and sex. Whether as explicitly feminist readings, like Esterhazy, or to undermine heteronormativity, like the queer Laughton and Ozon, filmmakers drawing on fairy tales often have ideological motives for their dealings with gender and sexuality. Indeed, often fairy-tale films deal with their hypotexts by reversing conventional gender expectations, whether by making the "Hansel and Gretel" witch a man or using male Red Riding Hoods and female wolves. They thus address issues of family and community, including the very quotidian nature of harms against children, in ways that destabilize normative expectations not only for fairy tales, but also for society.

Related topics: Anime/Manga; Animal Studies; Adaptation and the Fairy-Tale Web; Cinema Science Fiction; Disney Corporation; Food; Gender; Horror

Notes

1. For discussion of how "Little Red Riding Hood" films explore criminality and harms to children, see Greenhill and Kohm (2013, 2014) and Kohm and Greenhill (2011, 2013, 2014).
2. See the *International Fairy Tale Filmography* for cinema and *At the Crossroads of Data and Wonder: Algorithmic Visualizations of Fairy Tales on Television* for television versions of "Little Red Riding Hood" and "Hansel and Gretel."
3. *AI: Artificial Intelligence* (Steven Spielberg, 2001), a science fiction ATU 327A film, offers a resolution where otherworldly beings offer comfort to the robot child.
4. We thus exclude *What Lies Beneath* (Robert Zemeckis, 2000; see Rankin 2007, 142–167), among others.
5. Most animated and live-action films for children closely follow the Brothers Grimm, though North American productions mitigate its horror. For example, in the *Faerie Tale Theatre* version (James Frawley, 1983), Gretel's witch murder resuscitates children who have been turned into a gingerbread fence, and the witch becomes gingerbread. *Hansel & Gretel* (Gary J. Tunnicliffe, 2002) includes lengthy interludes when the children meet the Sandman, played by comedian Howie Mandel in a multicolored coat and rabbit slippers, in addition to a comic bogeyman, a flatulent troll, and a helpful blonde wood faerie.

PAULINE GREENHILL

6. Much scholarship over determines the witch as female; for example:

> the witch is without exception old and evil; occasionally she appears integrated into the bourgeois family as the stepmother. Thus the potential for evil is lurking in every woman. It was even made formally implicit, as when Hänsel and Gretel come out of the enchanted forest, after having burned the witch, and find their stepmother dead.
>
> (Bovenschen et al. 1978, 114)

Many filmmakers resist this gendering, as do the two detailed here.

7. Davis Grubb, on whose book the film is based, "identified Hans Christian Andersen as one of his masters" though *Night* "seems more strongly connected to the darker stories of the brothers Grimm" including "Hansel and Gretel" (Couchman 2009, 43; see also 41–44).

8. *Night*'s animal sequence begins with a spider web, followed by a frog, owl, turtle, two rabbits, and a fox (twice); *Lovers* has hawk, rabbit, fox, deer, hedgehog, pigeon, hawk, and fox. Hain compares the film instead to Hitchcock's 1960 *Psycho* (2007, 286), which links with other "Hansel and Gretel" films via its themes of cannibalism (Walton 2004) and transgender. "Hansel and Gretel" themed *Whoever Slew Auntie Roo?* (Curtis Harrington, 1972) also plays with *Psycho*'s main idea in its title character, who "keeps her little daughter's decaying corpse entombed secretly in an attic nursery" (Morrison 2010, 134); thus a female—not male—character preserves her daughter—not mother—in the attic—not the basement.

9. Schilt says Ozon quotes *Night* "rather unabashedly" (2011, 53), and Asibong says the film is frequently "nodded to" (2008, 62).

References Cited and Further Reading

Asibong, Andrew. 2008. *François Ozon*. Manchester: Manchester UP.

Bacchilega, Cristina. 2013. *Fairy Tales Transformed? Twenty-First-Century Adaptations and the Politics of Wonder*. Detroit: Wayne State UP.

Bauer, Stephen F. 1999. "Oedipus Again: A Critical Study of Charles Laughton's *The Night of the Hunter*." *The Psychoanalytic Quarterly* 68 (4): 611–36.

Bell, Elizabeth, Lynda Haas, and Laura Sells, eds. 1995. *From Mouse to Mermaid: The Politics of Film, Gender, and Culture*. Bloomington: Indiana UP.

Bovenschen, Silvia, Jeannine Blackwell, Johanna Moore, and Beth Weckmueller. 1978. "The Contemporary Witch, the Historical Witch and the Witch Myth: The Witch, Subject of the Appropriation of Nature and Object of the Domination of Nature." *New German Critique* 15: 82–119.

Cavallaro, Dani. 2011. *The Fairy Tale and Anime: Traditional Themes, Images and Symbols at Play on Screen*. Jefferson, NC: McFarland.

Couchman, Jeffrey. 2009. *The Night of the Hunter: A Biography of a Film*. Evanston, IL: Northwestern UP.

Duggan, Anne E. 2013. *Queer Enchantments: Gender, Sexuality, and Class in the Fairy-Tale Cinema of Jacques Demy*. Detroit: Wayne State UP.

———. 2016. "The Fairy-Tale Film in France: Postwar Reimaginings." In *Fairy-Tale Films Beyond Disney*, edited by Zipes, Greenhill, and Magnus-Johnston, 64–79.

Greenhill, Pauline. 2014. *"Le piège d'Issoudun*: Motherhood in Crisis." *Narrative Culture* 1 (1): 49–69.

———. 2015. "'The Snow Queen': Queer Coding in Male Directors' Films." *Marvels & Tales* 29 (1): 110–34.

———. 2017. "Fairy-Tale Films." In *The Oxford Research Encyclopedia of Literature*, edited by Paula Rabinowitz. http://literature.oxfordre.com/view/10.1093/acrefore/9780190201098.001.0001/acrefore-9780190201098-e-83?rskey=VdsC74&result=1. DOI 10.1093/acrefore/9780190201098.013.83.

Greenhill, Pauline, and Anne Brydon. 2010. "Mourning Mothers and Seeing Siblings: Feminism and Place in *The Juniper Tree*." In *Fairy Tale Films*, edited by Greenhill and Matrix, 116–26.

Greenhill, Pauline, and Steven Kohm. 2013. "*Hoodwinked!* and *Jin-Roh: The Wolf Brigade*: Animated 'Little Red Riding Hood' Films and the Rashômon Effect." *Marvels & Tales* 27 (1): 89–108.

———. 2014. "Criminal Beasts: The *Red Riding Trilogy* and Little Red Riding Hood on TV." In *Channeling Wonder*, edited by Greenhill and Rudy, 189–209.

Greenhill, Pauline, and Sidney Eve Matrix, eds. 2010. *Fairy Tale Films: Visions of Ambiguity*. Logan: Utah State UP.

Greenhill, Pauline, and Jill T. Rudy, eds. 2014. *Channeling Wonder: Fairy Tales on Television*. Detroit: Wayne State UP.

Hain, Mark. 2007. "Explicit Ambiguity: Sexual Identity, Hitchcockian Criticism, and the Films of François Ozon." *Quarterly Review of Film and Video* 24 (3): 277–88.

Holbek, Bengt. 1987. *Interpretation of Fairy Tales: Danish Folklore in a European Perspective*. Helsinki: Suomalainen Tiedeakatemia.

Hubner, Laura. Forthcoming. *Fairytale and Gothic Horror: Uncanny Transformations in Film*. Basingstoke: Palgrave McMillan.

Kohm, Steven, and Pauline Greenhill. 2011. "Pedophile Crime Films as Popular Criminology: A Problem of Justice?" *Theoretical Criminology* 15 (2): 195–216.

———. 2013. "'This Is the North, Where We Do What We Want': Popular Green Criminology and 'Little Red Riding Hood' Films." In *Routledge International Handbook of Green Criminology*, edited by Nigel South and Avi Brisman, 365–78. London: Routledge.

———. 2014. "Little Red Riding Hood Crime Films: Critical Variations on Criminal Themes." *Law, Culture and the Humanities* 10 (2): 257–78.

Moen, Kristian. 2012. *Film and Fairy Tales: The Birth of Modern Fantasy*. London: I.B. Tauris.

Morrison, James. 2010. "Shelley Winters: Camp, Abjection, and the Aging Star." In *Hollywood Reborn: Movie Stars of the 1970s*, edited by James Morrison, 120–37. New Brunswick, NJ: Rutgers UP.

Pugh, Tison, and Susan L. Aronstein, eds. 2012. *The Disney Middle Ages: A Fairy-Tale and Fantasy Past*. New York: Palgrave Macmillan.

Rankin, Walter. 2007. *Grimm Pictures: Fairy Tale Archetypes in Eight Horror and Suspense Films*. Jefferson, NC: McFarland.

Rees-Roberts, Nick. 2008. *French Queer Cinema*. Edinburgh: Edinburgh UP.

Schilt, Thibaut. 2011. *François Ozon*. Urbana: U Illinois P.

Short, Sue. 2015. *Fairy Tale and Film: Old Tales with a New Spin*. Basingstoke: Palgrave Macmillan.

Smith, Kevin Paul. 2007. *The Postmodern Fairytale: Folkloric Intertexts in Contemporary Fiction*. Basingstoke: Palgrave Macmillan.

Tresca, Don. 2014. "Lost in the Woods: Adapting 'Hansel and Gretel' for Television." In *Channeling Wonder*, edited by Greenhill and Rudy, 64–81.

Vineberg, Steve. 1991. "Enchantment and Terror." *The Threepenny Review* 47 (Autumn): 27–9.

Walton, Priscilla L. 2004. *Our Cannibals, Ourselves*. Urbana: U Illinois P.

Zipes, Jack. 2011. *The Enchanted Screen: The Unknown History of Fairy-Tale Films*. New York: Routledge.

———, ed. 2013. *The Golden Age of Folk and Fairy Tales: From the Brothers Grimm to Andrew Lang*. Indianapolis: Hackett.

———. 2016. "The Great Cultural Tsunami of Fairy-Tale Films." In *Fairy-Tale Films Beyond Disney*, edited by Zipes, Greenhill, and Magnus-Johnston, 7–11.

Zipes, Jack, Pauline Greenhill, and Kendra Magnus-Johnston, eds. 2016. *Fairy-Tale Films Beyond Disney: International Perspectives*. New York: Routledge.

Mediagraphy

The 10th Kingdom. 2000. Directors David Carson and Herbert Wise. USA.

AI: Artificial Intelligence. 2001. Director Steven Spielberg. USA.

At the Crossroads of Data and Wonder: Algorithmic Visualizations of Fairy Tales on Television. 2014. Creators Jill Terry Rudy, Jarom McDonald, Kristy Stewart, and Jessie Riddle. http://fttv.byu.edu/.

Beauty and the Beast. 1991. Directors Gary Trousdale and Kirk Wise. USA.

Bread Crumbs. 2011. Director Mike Nichols. USA.

Carrie. 1976. Director Brian De Palma. USA.

Castle (TV). 2009–2016. Creator Andrew W. Marlowe. USA.

———. "Once Upon a Crime." 2012. Episode 4.17. February 27.

Cinderella. 2015. Director Kenneth Branagh. USA.

Deutschland bleiche Mutter (Germany, Pale Mother). 1980. Director Helma Sanders-Brahms. Germany.

Enchanted. 2007. Director Kevin Lima. USA.

The Fall. 2006. Director Tarsem Singh. India/USA.

Freeway 2: Confessions of a Trickbaby. 1999. Director Matthew Bright. USA.

H & G. 2013. Director Danishka Esterhazy. Canada.

Hansel & Gretel. 2002. Director Gary J. Tunnicliffe. USA.

Hansel & Gretel: An Appalachian Version. 1975. Director Tom Davenport. USA.

Hansel & Gretel Get Baked. 2013. Director Duane Journey. USA.

Hansel & Gretel: Witch Hunters. 2013. Director Tommy Wirkola. Germany/USA.

Hansel and Gretel. 1982. Director Tim Burton. USA.

Hansel and Gretel (Faerie Tale Theatre). 1983. Director James Frawley. USA.

International Fairy Tale Filmography. 2013–. Creators Jack Zipes, Pauline Greenhill, and Kendra Magnus-Johnston. http://iftf.uwinnipeg.ca.

Into the Woods. 2014. Director Rob Marshall. USA.

Jin-Roh: The Wolf Brigade. 1999. Director Hiroyuki Okiura. Japan.

The Last Butterfly. 1991. Director Karel Kachnya. France/UK/Czechoslovakia.

Le manoir du diable (The House of the Devil). 1896. Director Georges Méliès. France.

Les amants criminels (Criminal Lovers). 1999. Director François Ozon. France.

Little Erin Merryweather. 2003. Director David Morwick. USA.

The Little Mermaid. 1989. Directors John Musker and Ron Clements. USA.

Little Red Riding Hood. 1922. Director Walt Disney. USA.

Lumikuningatar (The Snow Queen). 1986. Director Päivi Hartzell. Finland.

Maleficent. 2014. Director Robert Stromberg. USA.

Mary Poppins. 1964. Director Robert Stevenson. USA.

The Night of the Hunter. 1955. Director Charles Laughton. USA.

Peter Pan. 1953. Directors Wilfred Jackson, Clyde Geronimi, and Hamilton Luske. USA.

Promenons-nous dans les bois (Deep in the Woods). 2000. Director Lionel Delplanque. France.

Psycho. 1960. Director Alfred Hitchcock. USA.

Red Riding: In the Year of Our Lord 1974. 2009. Director Julian Jarrold. UK.

Red Riding: In the Year of Our Lord 1980. 2009. Director James Marsh. UK.

Red Riding: In the Year of Our Lord 1983. 2009. Director Anand Tucker. UK.

Snow White and the Seven Dwarfs. 1937. Director David Hand, William Cottrell, Wilfred Jackson, Larry Morey, Perce Pearce, and Ben Sharpsteen. USA.

What Lies Beneath. 2000. Director Robert Zemeckis. USA.

Whoever Slew Auntie Roo? 1972. Director Curtis Harrington. UK.

A Wicked Tale. 2005. Director Merwyn Tong Tzang. Singapore.

40
BROADCAST
Radio and Television
Jill Terry Rudy

Radio and television since the early twentieth century have sent sounds and images by airwaves to receptive devices in a wide variety of locations. The achievement of listening and viewing at a distance was hailed as a significant, desirable accomplishment and also recognized as a potentially mesmerizing waste of time (Hubbell 1942; Sterling and Kittross 2002). While imagination, oral storytelling, and even silent reading can evoke what one author calls "audiovisual hallucination" (Langan 2001), radio and television bring actual audio and audiovisual programs into private and public spaces. Kendra Magnus-Johnston's teleography of fairy tales on television indicates that fairy tales haven't been broadcast newcomers, appearing since the earliest television programming—a history repeated from radio (2014). While fairy-tale programming has never been more than a small percentage of broadcasts, listeners and viewers have regularly found fairy tales by touching that dial.

When radio emerged as a popular medium for not only news and sporting events but live entertainment in the United States, shows like *Let's Pretend* (1934–1954) filled a Saturday morning or weekday afternoon time slot with fairy tales for families. Performed live each week for most of its run, the award-winning program included a neighborly announcer/narrator and an ensemble of young actors, live orchestra, and sound crew with production and scripts by CBS director of children's programs Nila Mack (Anderson 2004). Their wide repertoire included tales from Andersen, Perrault, d'Aulnoy, and the Grimms. Broadcasts eventually included a live studio audience of cheering children who, after the opening theme music, started the show chanting, "What about that story?" After opening banter and an orchestral interlude, the narrator said the magical words, "Once upon a time." Young actors would voice the various characters and creatures, while technicians created memorable sound effects. The stories would end, often with "happily ever after," with production credits and the closing theme music.

Whether with radio, television, or post-broadcast media such as podcasts and Internet streaming, broadcast media history tells of new storytelling techniques connecting to previous familiarity with fairy tales. The fairy tale thrives on such repetition and variation, what Barre Toelken calls the "twin laws of folklore" (1996, 39). Jessica Tiffin observes that "fairy tale becomes simply one of the oldest and most strongly marked of narrative structures" (2009, 3). She writes of the fairy tale's historical "self-consciousness about textuality" that operates "within a set of codes recognized by both writer and reader" (3). The recognizable codes align with what Jason Mittell calls poetics—the inner workings of texts (2015, 5). Fairy tale often announces its own fictionality while laying out its inner workings; thus, it not only familiarizes by making metafictional moves but by forecasting its own poetics. This metapoetics also attunes fairy tale to genre mixing (Bacchilega and Rieder 2010), such as in the dramas, special events, and children's shows emerging with radio and television.

Because of accessibility in everyday life and lingering resonance with seasonal schedules, broadcast stories create relationships that transform distances of time and space into the here and now. Fictional characters and their stories become part of the daily routine or calendar round. Even with significant changes between analog scheduling restrictions and nearly constant digital availability, broadcast tales refract Sidney Mintz's concepts of inside and outside meaning. Mintz focuses on making changes in consuming food products, but his ideas also work well with incorporating broadcasts into daily life. Inside meaning relates to "circumstances of daily domestic life and work," while outside meaning involves the "environing economic, social, and political (even military) conditions" (1996, 20). Broadcast media involve technological conditions, as well as these others, to make and keep stories on the air.

Once attaining access, people quickly incorporate listening and viewing into their lives. We look forward to a Sunday evening of *Wonderful World of Disney* (1968–79; 1983–86; 1991–), a late night of binge watching *Game of Thrones* (2011–), a weekend airing of *Selected Shorts* (1985–), or catching up during a morning run with the podcast of a radio or Internet personality who might speak of tales. Mintz celebrates the capacity "of our species to invest life with meaning on this intimate, immediate, and homely level," but he will not let us forget that such moments depend on the vagaries and powers of intense environing conditions (1996, 20–21). Fairy tales themselves teach much the same thing—that economic, social, and political stations in life make a difference and could possibly be transformed by a kind deed or swish of a wand. The metapoetics of the broadcast fairy tale support relationships at a distance by tuning in producers and audiences alike to the inner workings and implications of storied beginnings and endings.

Metapoetics and the Intermediality of Broadcast Fairy Tales

Although not all fairy tales begin with "once upon a time" or end with "and they lived happily ever after," it sometimes seems like they do. Along with the metafictional self-consciousness of fairy tale that signals unreality, the fairy tale displays a metapoetics, a hyperawareness of its inner workings that is recognizable whether tales are performed orally, printed, filmed, broadcast, or streamed. Mittell takes a poetics approach to complex television storytelling because he is interested in how texts work and because this approach links texts in contexts (2015, 5). Fairy tales on the radio and television afford some distinctive contextual implications, including the ability to reach mass audiences in real time and from a distance. And yet, in many ways broadcast tales refract other media capacities. This is not exactly Marshall McLuhan's concept that the "content of a medium is another medium" (1964, 1), but broadcast media that share fairy tales often mimic each other.

Radio and television broadcasts, as with early film productions, included tales because of their popularity across age spans, their familiarity in the midst of new programming formats, their accessibility in terms of copyright and public fair use, and their wondrous narrative appeal in audio and visual iterations. Broadcast media, also similar to film, split the storyteller role into collaborative teams of producers, directors, writers, actors, designers, and technicians while also involving marketing teams, industry executives, and government regulators. Thus, authorship pertains to broadcast tales as well as other media (see Jones and Schacker 2013, 523–537; Mittell 2015, 86–117). Broadcast fairy tales have offered *live* productions sent across significant distances, thus bringing audiences technologically mediated tales with the immediacy of theater or oral storytelling. Radio and television programming also simulates some rhythms of oral storytelling that depend on access to the best storytellers in times of leisure, or leisurely work, even though these media may at times replace community story sharing (Bruford and MacDonald 1994, 4–8). In a post-broadcast era of Internet streaming and YouTube channels, audiences may access fairy tales on demand, as they also can when owning books. And, similar to books, radio and television often present tales in anthologies where different stories are grouped into one series. Thus, broadcast tales emphasize the intermedial proclivities of the fairy tale, not only in terms of multiple sensory modes of listening and seeing at a distance but also with various communicative technologies.

Fairy tales over the airwaves work as advertisements, entertainment, and a public service often linked with education. Broadcast advertising has regularly employed tale motifs and plots in order to sell magic itself and products ranging from soap to cereal to mobile phones (Dégh 1994; Wittwer 2016). While the Soviet Union, Britain, and most Asian, African, and Latin American countries created centralized, state-controlled networks or corporations subsidized by license fees, the United States never imposed such fees because of the commercial model, but major national networks did offer unsponsored programs, and public-supported broadcasting eventually emerged. Good citizenship and education, therefore, have been components, and concerns, related to broadcast media that involves fairy-tale programming and implicates intermediality. Jennifer Schacker examines how printed tale collections since the nineteenth century both entertain and instruct about cultural norms and intercultural relationships. She critiques how printed and illustrated tale collections were conceived, in part, to distinguish supposedly modern readers from apparently illiterate tale tellers (2003). Owning and using technological devices like radios and televisions also has indicated modern progress for individuals and nations. The means of producing and receiving broadcast tales, therefore, symbolically comment on individual and group validity and presence in contemporary society (Hearne 2017). Additionally, as with other medial iterations, tales socialize and instruct about apt attitudes and behaviors for achieving one's place in society (Zipes 2008). Scholars and governments have questioned the influence of broadcast programming, especially on children's socialization, learning, and behavior (Shramm, Lyle, and Parker 1961). The power to shape expectations, even dreams, and provide social norms and scripts has been a lasting concern with fairy tales as well (Seifert 1996; Harries 2001).

This occurs, in part, because tales are performances in addition to being texts. Broadcast media highlight the performative aspects of fairy tale because they accept accountability to audiences for displays of communicative competence (Bauman 1984). Listeners and viewers maintain strong personal attachments to these programs, and the fairy tales' distribution by radio and television also creates global mass audiences (Tulloch 1990, 190–193; Dunleavy 2009). Broadcast media have kept many tales in circulation, reached wide audiences, and also mixed fairy tale with a range of other forms, from children's shows and mini-series to situation comedies, dramatic serials, and Monster of the Week appearances (Rudy and McDonald 2016). While maligned as mass, mindless entertainment, the continuing popularity and variety of broadcast media support tale telling and embed the fairy tale in everyday life for multiple purposes, not insignificantly for creating relationships at a distance (Williams 1974, 22–24).

Metapoetic Capacities of Broadcast Tales' Beginnings and Endings

Broadcast fairy tales enact relationships, in part, by turning familiar narrative keys that create a virtual intersubjectivity when literal relationships between fictional and real characters are not possible. Arthur Frank uses the term "capacities" to discuss these keys of "how stories do their work for people and on people" (2010, 28). Two capacities relevant to the metapoetics of broadcast tales involve *trouble* and *suspense*. Of trouble, Frank observes, "Stories have the capacity to deal with human troubles, but also the capacity to make TROUBLE for humans" (28). Of suspense he writes, "Stories make life dramatic and remind people that endings are never assured" (32). With tales' old and elemental narrative structure, broadcast media signal trouble and suspense to producers and viewers and invite relationships, particularly with the beginnings and endings of fairy-tale shows.

In consideration of cultural engagement and the poetics of beginnings, Mittell focuses on the television show's pilot where the narrative premise is introduced and established, yet he acknowledges there are many entryways into broadcast tales (2015, 5). In terms of production, the beginnings are pushed back to the conception of ideas for a show, the development of production partnerships, and the apparatus of preparing, pitching, and presenting the show.[1] These production elements may be shared with viewers in interviews, official websites, and fan conventions and may become part of a show's narrative and ritual aspects (Hay and Baxter 2014). The show's title also is an important beginning, a linguistic anchor that forecasts its inner workings with fairy tale. In October 2011, the television dramas *Once Upon a Time (OUaT)*(2011a) and *Grimm* (2011–2017) premiered on the major U.S. networks American Broadcasting Company (ABC) and National Broadcasting Company (NBC), signaling the fairy tale's high-profile return to the North American prime time weekly schedule. Both shows combine reality and fantasy elements, with *OUaT* developing parallel worlds and *Grimm* offering a distinctive world-within-a-world (Willsey 2014; Schwabe 2014). The Columbia Broadcasting System (CBS) network previously presented a dual-reality fairy-tale drama with its three-season crime procedural *Beauty and the Beast* (1987–1990). Using fairy-tale story titles, motifs, and associated names to initiate connections meta-poetically draws on familiarity with fairy tale.

While the pilot and the title may be crucial to a show's initial and continuing existence, the trailer has become an important beginning, condensing narrative introductions. The initial trailers of the 2011 NBC and ABC fairy-tale dramas involve production decisions, such as ambient sounds and soundtrack music, visual images, actors' characterizations, and printed words, to initiate not only stories, but also relationships with potential viewers. Although the trailers present familiar fairy-tale motifs, they also introduce new characters and unexpected troubling and suspenseful situations. Months before the shows premiered, a *Grimm* trailer was posted on YouTube on May 16, 2011, and a *Once Upon a Time* trailer on May 17, 2011.[2] The trailers link narrative trouble and suspense to a counter-metafictional claim that fairy tales are not fiction.

The *Grimm* trailer, with a run time of about four minutes, serves as a mini-pilot, following the attack on a sorority woman wearing a red hoodie and the abduction of a young girl. The counter-metafictional claim is given through an initial voiceover by a woman, Marie Kessler (Kate Burton), whom viewers eventually see in a hospital bed speaking to a man, Nick Burkhardt (David Giuntoli). He already has been seen as a detective investigating with his partner, Hank Griffin (Russell Hornsby), a mysterious attack by an animal who left boot prints, and he has experienced bizarre moments where people momentarily turn into creepy creatures. Interspersed with these images, soundtrack, and dialogue, three separate screenshots with words in a striking, linear font have announced, "We Know the Stories," "But There's One Thing," "They Didn't Tell Us." Then the woman's voice announces the narrative trouble, that the family misfortune is coming to the younger man and that "this is no fairy tale." After showing Nick and Marie in the hospital, the scene cuts to a letter carrier and a young girl in a red hoodie as the woman's voiceover continues, "These stories are real" (2011).

The metapoetic beginnings of the series become even more self-evident through authorship claims and more plot allusions to "Little Red Riding Hood." In a dream sequence of a woman running through a hazy forest, words appear on screen to give intertextual credentials and authorship to the show: first, it reads, "From the Executive Producers," and then "of *Buffy* and *Angel*" appear word by word on screen.[3] This intertextual connection with two popular supernatural series introduces potential viewers to the artistic pedigree of the show. Relationships are enacted here when Nick works on the crime scene with Hank, when viewers later learn that the hospitalized woman is Nick's aunt, when Nick follows a false lead and meets his first shape-shifting creature and future friend, Monroe (Silas Weir Mitchell), and when he and Hank search for the young girl in a forest cottage. Of central interest to later fans, the dream-woman in the hazy forest turns out to be Nick's girlfriend, Juliette Silverton (Bitsie Tulloch), who has a bizarre story arc that eventually will involve several fairy-tale transformations.

Less like an episode, the *Once Upon a Time* trailer works by montage, shifting between an apparently sleepy, stormy town named Storybrooke and the impressive production values of carriages, castles, and costumes in an enchanted forest land. The metapoetic connection with fairy-tale beginnings comes in an early scene with a young boy, Henry (Jared Mills), talking with Emma Swan (Jennifer Morrison) by her car. The fairy-tale motif Henry first mentions is an evil queen's curse. He tells an incredulous Emma, "Time is frozen here," and explains that bad things happen when people try to escape. The screen cuts to black with ominous background music, and the voice of Mr. Gold/Rumpelstiltskin (Robert Carlyle) announces, "It has begun," with a quick cut to a castle with distant storm clouds gathering. The jump cuts between Storybrooke and the Enchanted Forest speed up during the course of the two-minute trailer. Onscreen words later state that "There Are Two Sides" "To Every Story," and indeed, the suspense and trouble related in the trailer involve the dual identities of the characters who do not yet know what the young Henry later asserts—that their stories are already written in his fairy-tale book (2011b).

Once Upon a Time also introduces a potential challenge for these shows, the issue of the problematic metapoetics of fairy-tale endings. Cristina Bacchilega asserts that "in the culture industry, the signature mark of the fairy-tale genre continues to be its 'happily-ever-after' ending" (2013, 28). She finds plenty of trouble with what she abbreviates as the HEA (happily ever after), particularly the magic that leads to romantic suspense and inevitable weddings. Because fairy tale is an elemental and persistent narrative form, any broadcast ending, from sporting event to live production to reality show or sitcom, may be compared to an HEA. The phrase is both specific and general enough to remain provocatively indeterminate even as its long-term promises linger. The phrase actually evades endings with its "ever after" projections, a point that leads to parody (Bacchilega 2013, 11–12) as well as to narrative resolution. In terms of television, Mittell recognizes that endings especially remain a trouble. He notes, "Actual finales are quite rare for American television series" (2015, 319). The point is to keep being renewed for another season, and cancellations may come up unexpectedly. However, acclaimed scripted dramas of the new millennial golden age of television, such as those studied by Mittell and Gary Edgerton (2013), have reduced the suspense about endings, shifting many shows to a production schedule that includes season and series finales. As episodic drama has meshed with serialized stories, the increasing suspense about plot and character arcs put pressure on coming up with a finale. As fan fiction, convention attendance, and online comments attest, these endings often matter because of viewers' attachment and sense of relationship with the characters, actors, and even production facets including opening titles and theme songs that trigger memories and pleasant associations (Armknecht, Rudy, and Forrester 2017). Intertextually, each series finale calls out to all the others and brings a performative accountability to an audience to the fore.

Paradoxically there is a great deal of suspense associated with broadcast fairy-tale endings because fairy tale announces its metapoetics over distances of time and space and because so much is already known about characters and plots. This suspense involves not only how characters and situations may arrive at a happy ending but also the possibility that, this time, this story may end unhappily (as historically many tales do). By overtly indexing their fairy-tale connections, the trailers of *Grimm* and *Once Upon a Time* initiate such suspense. When the girl in the red sweatshirt is rescued by Nick and Hank, there is a happy ending. But *Once Upon a Time* viewers are enticed in that initial trailer by dialogue that reiterates, and negates, the HEA refrain. The first statement comes in an exchange between the evil queen/Regina Mills (Lana Parilla) and Snow White/Mary Margaret Blanchard (Ginnifer Goodwin), who holds her injured new husband Prince Charming/David Nolan (Josh Dallas) and asks, "Why did you do this?" The evil queen announces, "Because this is my happy ending." The scene then cuts to Storybrooke, where Mary Margaret tells Emma, "Believing in even the possibility of a happy ending is a very powerful thing." Rumpelstiltskin confirms the trouble and suspense when he says of the new place where the characters are going, "No more happy endings" (2011b). This sets a high bar for the series finale; will producers actually leave their audience with no happy endings?

Fairy-Tale Metapoetics and Relationships in the Flow of Broadcast Media

The attachment to characters, series, and their endings reiterates that the wonder tale is a narrative form enmeshed in cultural engagements. Marina Warner represents the concerns of numerous fairy tale scholars when she observes that "one of the things that fairy tale promises is an unbroken link with the past" (2014, 53). Although open to dispute, the intertextuality, and intermediality, of tales involves travel over centuries, from homelands through global migrations. Thus, fairy tales when they come to radio and television are already broadcasting from a long and far reach. This reach constitutes and delineates groups through its metapoetics. As Donald Haase presciently asserts, fairy tales belong to individuals and groups, from families to nations, even as their telling constructs and realigns such relations (1999, 2010). Attentiveness to community well-being often comes through keeping relationships of story, land, and peoples. Understanding these connections occurs best in light of a relational perspective involving a "subject/subject intersubjectivity" that includes reciprocity and multiple perspectives (Rudy 2013, 6–8). With the weight of HEA hanging over any fairy-tale episode, series, or special event, broadcast retellings offer suspense steeped in familiarity by including a wide range of tales and inviting viewer identification and attachment.

The metapoetic signals of fairy-tale beginnings and endings involve shows and stories with troubles that address coming of age, facing villains and tests, enjoying pretend worlds, and seeking a better life. The Fairy Tales on Television Visualizations (FTTV) database indicates a preference for classic tales in the most frequently televised tales: "Cinderella" (ATU 510A), "Snow White" (ATU 709), and "Little Red Riding Hood" (ATU 333). Yet the database includes many lesser-known tales and numerous references to a general fairy-taleness that does not identify with a particular tale type. While mash-ups and serial storytelling have been important narrative techniques in early twenty-first-century televised tales, anthologies remain important for transmitting an array of tales and expanding the possibilities of the form. From the *Rocky and Bullwinkle* "Fractured Fairy Tales" (1959–64) and *Shirley Temple's Storybook* (1958–1961) through *Shelley Duvall's Faerie Tale Theatre* (1982–87), *Jim Henson's The StoryTeller* (1987–89), and *Grimm's Fairy Tale Classics* (1987–1989) to *Lost Tales of the Brothers Grimm* (2006–2007), anthology production teams uniquely juxtapose tales to match a thematic arc, highlight certain celebrities, preserve literary heritage, and innovate and play while introducing viewers to lesser known stories.

Broadcast fairy tales associate trouble and suspense with the personal attachments made possible by viewing and listening to stories. Frank identifies "the capacity of stories to arouse people's imaginations" as a powerful way to explore different ways of living (2010, 42). The possibility of establishing and keeping relationships over distances pertains here because one can see in the trailers discussed prior the seeds of relationships between characters and between viewers, characters, production teams, and shows. While stories and series end, broadcast viewing and listening goes on. As Mittell indicates, television is not particularly well suited to endings (2015). This relates to Raymond Williams's observation that flow is most desirable with television (1974, 78–118). A show's continuing production and airtime are signs of growth in relationships and the attainment of inside meaning with viewers and listeners. Ratings and sponsors become precursors and supporters of these relationships. Emerging fan involvement through online activity and convention attendance may overcome the trouble of staying on the air or at least keep memories of shows alive and accessible. The cheering young voices in an Internet stream of a *Let's Pretend* (1934–1954) taping indicate the thrill of broadcast participation. Arthur Anderson (2004) writes about meeting the show's listeners decades later at old-time radio conventions, and through this he acknowledges the lingering, resonant attachments between the fairy tale, shows, actors, and audiences. Like fairy tales in other media, broadcast tales tussle with the issues of growing up, getting along, and surviving or thriving in a dangerous and wonderful world that is not quite our own. Broadcast tales enact such troublous and suspenseful transformations 24/7—while production, transmission, and reception continue and inside meanings last.

Related topics: Adaptation and the Fairy-Tale Web; Advertising; Anthologies and Tale Collections; Children's Television; Cinema Science Fiction; Convergence Culture; Crime/Justice; Fandom/Fan Cultures; Musicals; Opera; Reality TV; Storytelling; Theater; TV Drama

Notes

1. As part of the metafictionality, shows ranging from *Seinfeld* (1989–1998) to *As Time Goes By* (1992–2002) and several others reflexively include TV show beginnings when characters become involved in proposing new television productions.
2. Accessing the trailers on October 15, 2016, there were 2,252,609 views of the *Grimm* (2011–2017) original with 1,036 comments as recent as three weeks prior. The *Once Upon a Time* (2011–) trailer has 4,296,635 views with 2,125 comments with responses to previous comments as recent as seventeen hours previous.
3. While this association implies that Joss Whedon, the creator of *Buffy the Vampire Slayer* (1997–2003) and *Angel* (1999–2004), is involved in the project, the co-executive producer of *Grimm* (2011–2017) who has this credit is David Greenwalt.

References Cited and Further Reading

Anderson, Arthur. 2004. *Let's Pretend and the Golden Age of Radio.* Albany, Georgia: BearManor Media.

Armknecht, Megan, Jill Terry Rudy, and Sibelan Forrester. 2017. "Identifying Impressions of Baba Yaga: Navigating the Uses of Attachment and Wonder on Soviet and American Television." *Marvels & Tales* 31 (1): 62–79.

Bacchilega, Cristina. 2013. *Fairy Tales Transformed? Twenty-First Century Adaptation and the Politics of Wonder.* Detroit: Wayne State UP.

Bacchilega, Cristina, and John Rieder. 2010. "Mixing It Up: Generic Complexity in Early 21st-Century Fairy-Tale Film." In *Fairy Tale Films: Visions of Ambiguity,* edited by Pauline Greenhill and Sidney Eve Matrix, 23–41. Logan: Utah State UP.

Bauman, Richard. 1984. *Verbal Art as Performance.* Prospect Heights, IL: Waveland P.

Bruford, A. J., and D. A. MacDonald, eds. 1994. *Scottish Traditional Tales*. Edinburgh: Polygon.

Dégh, Linda. 1994. *American Folklore and the Mass Media*. Bloomington: Indiana UP.

Dunleavy, Trisha. 2009. *Television Drama: Form, Agency, Innovation*. Basingstoke, Hampshire: Palgrave Macmillan.

Edgerton, Gary R. 2013. *The Sopranos*. Detroit: Wayne State UP.

Frank, Arthur. 2010. *Letting Stories Breathe: A Socio-Narratology*. Chicago: Chicago UP.

Haase, Donald. 1999. "Yours, Mine, or Ours: Perrault, the Brothers Grimm, and the Ownership of Fairy Tales." In *The Classic Fairy Tales*, edited by Maria Tatar, 353–64. New York: Norton.

———. 2010. "Decolonizing Fairy Tale Studies." *Marvels & Tales* 24 (1): 17–38.

Harries, Elizabeth Wanning. 2001. *Twice Upon a Time: Women Writers and the History of the Fairy Tale*. Princeton, NJ: Princeton UP.

Hay, Rebecca, and Christa Baxter. 2014. "Happily Never After: The Commodification and Critique of Fairy Tale in ABC's *Once Upon a Time*." In *Channeling Wonder: Fairy Tales on Television*, edited by Pauline Greenhill and Jill Terry Rudy, 316–35. Detroit: Wayne State UP.

Hearne, Joanna. 2017. "'I'm Not a Fairy Tale': Indigenous Storytelling on Canadian Television." *Marvels & Tales* 31 (1): 126–46.

Hubbell, Richard Whitaker. 1942. *4000 Years of Television: The Story of Seeing at a Distance*. New York: G. P. Putnams.

Jones, Christine A., and Jennifer Schacker. 2013. *Marvelous Transformations: An Anthology of Fairy Tales and Contemporary Critical Perspectives*. Peterborough, ON: Broadview P.

Langan, Celeste. 2001. "Understanding Media in 1805: Audiovisual Hallucination in *The Lay of the Last Minstrel*." *Studies in Romanticism* 40 (1): 49–70.

Magnus-Johnston, Kendra. 2014. "A Critical Introduction to the Fairy-Tale Teleography." In *Channeling Wonder: Fairy Tales on Television*, edited by Pauline Greenhill and Jill Terry Rudy, 363–78. Detroit: Wayne State UP.

McLuhan, Marshall. 1964. "The Medium Is the Message." In *Understanding Media: The Extensions of Man*, 1–11. New York: McGraw-Hill.

Mintz, Sidney. 1996. *Tasting Food, Tasting Freedom: Excursions into Eating, Culture, and the Past*. Boston: Beacon P.

Mittell, Jason. 2015. *Complex TV: The Poetics of Contemporary Television Storytelling*. New York: NYU P.

Rudy, Jill Terry. 2013. "American Folklore Scholarship, *Tales of the North American Indians*, and Relational Communities." *Journal of American Folklore* 126 (499): 3–30.

Rudy, Jill Terry, and Jarom L. McDonald. 2016. "Baba Yaga, Monsters of the Week, and Pop Culture's Formation of Wonder and Families through Monstrosity." *Humanities* 5 (2): 40–57.

Schacker, Jennifer. 2003. *National Dreams: The Remaking of Fairy Tales in Nineteenth-Century England*. Philadelphia: U Pennsylvania P.

Schramm, Wilbur, Jack Lyle, and Edwin B. Parker. 1961. *Television in the Lives of Our Children*. Stanford: Stanford UP.

Schwabe, Claudia. 2014. "Getting Real with Fairy Tales: Magic Realism in *Grimm* and *Once Upon a Time*." In *Channeling Wonder: Fairy Tales on Television*, edited by Pauline Greenhill and Jill Terry Rudy, 294–315. Detroit: Wayne State UP.

Seifert, Lewis. 1996. *Fairy Tales, Sexuality, and Gender in France, 1691–1715: Nostalgic Utopias*. Cambridge: Cambridge UP.

Sterling, Christopher H., and John Michael Kittross. 2002. *Stay Tuned: A History of American Broadcasting*. 3rd ed. Mahwah, NJ: Lawrence Erlbaum.

Tiffin, Jessica. 2009. *Marvelous Geometry: Narrative and Metafiction in Modern Fairy Tale*. Detroit: Wayne State UP.

Toelken, Barre. 1996. *The Dynamics of Folklore: Revised and Expanded Edition*. Logan: Utah State UP.

Tulloch, John. 1990. *Television Drama: Agency, Audience, and Myth*. London: Routledge.

Warner, Marina. 2014. *Once Upon a Time: A Short History of Fairy Tale*. Oxford: Oxford UP.

Williams, Raymond. 1974. *Television: Technology and Cultural Form*. London: Fontana.

Willsey, Kristiana. 2014. "New Fairy Tales Are Old Again: *Grimm* and the Brothers Grimm." In *Channeling Wonder: Fairy Tales on Television*, edited by Pauline Greenhill and Jill Terry Rudy, 210–28. Detroit: Wayne State UP.

Wittwer, Preston. 2016. "Don Draper Thinks Your Ad Is Cliché: Fairy Tale Iconography in TV Commercials." *Humanities* 5 (2): 29–46.

Zipes, Jack. 2008. *Relentless Progress: The Reconfiguration of Children's Literature, Fairy Tales, and Storytelling*. New York: Routledge.

Mediagraphy

Angel (TV). 1999–2004. Creators Joss Whedon and David Greenwalt. USA.

As Time Goes By (TV). 1992–2002. Creator Colin Bostock-Smith. UK.

At the Crossroads of Data and Wonder: Algorithmic Visualizations of Fairy Tales on Television. 2014–. Creators Jill Terry Rudy, Jarom McDonald, Kristy Stewart, and Jessie Riddle. http://fttv.byu.edu/.

BROADCAST

Beauty and the Beast (TV). 1987–1990. Creator Ron Koslow. USA.

Buffy the Vampire Slayer (TV). 1997–2003. Creator Joss Whedon. USA.

Fractured Fairy Tales (Rocky and Bullwinkle Show) (TV). 1959–1964. Creators Jay Ward, Alex Anderson, and Bill Scott. USA.

Game of Thrones (TV). 2011–. Creators David Benioff and D. B. Weiss. Ireland.

Grimm (TV). 2011–2017. Executive producers David Greenwalt, Sean Hayes, Jim Kouf. USA.

——— (TV Trailer). 2011. www.youtube.com/watch?v=2rVy3RBJmNo.

Grimm Fairy Tale Classics (TV). 1989–1995. Directors Tom Wyner and Kerrigan Mahan. USA.

Grimm's Fairy Tale Classics (TV). 1987–1989. Director Hiroshi Saito. Japan.

Jim Henson's the StoryTeller (TV). 1987–1989. Creator Jim Henson. UK.

Let's Pretend (Radio). 1934–1954. Director Nila Mack. USA.

Lost (TV). 2004–2010. Creators Jeffrey Lieber, J. J. Abrams, Damon Lindelof. USA.

Lost Tales of the Brothers Grimm (TV). 2006–2007. Director Quinn Merkeley. Canada.

Once Upon a Time (TV). 2011a. Creators Adam Horowitz and Edward Kitsis. USA.

——— (TV Trailer). 2011b. www.youtube.com/watch?v=Rga4rp4j5TY.

Seinfeld (TV). 1989–1998. Creators Larry David and Jerry Seinfeld. USA.

Selected Shorts (Live Performance/Radio). 1985. Creator Isaiah Sheffer. USA.

Shelley Duvall's Faerie Tale Theatre (TV). 1982–1987. Creator Shelley Duvall. USA.

Shirley Temple's Storybook (TV). 1958–1961. Executive Producer William H. Brown. USA.

Wonderful World of Disney (TV). 1968–1979, 1983–1986, 1991. Creator Walt Disney. USA.

41

DIGITAL

"Blood and Glitter": Fairy Tales as Text, Texture, and Context in Digital Media

Lynne S. McNeill

> Rapunzel chopped off all her hair, and everyone was loving her new profile picture. But then she was like, *Wait, did everyone hate my long hair and they just weren't telling me?*
>
> (Tim Manley 2013)

Adaptable and malleable as they are, fairy tales have been slipping the confines of genre and medium for centuries, so it's no wonder that they would show up in even the most contemporary, technological settings of social media and blogging platforms. Fairy tales emerge in these spaces often less as text and more as texture or context, offering a culturally salient, if brief, setting of tone or mood. The vernacular web is inherently hybrid—presenting user-generated, quotidian content through the filters and frames of commercial, institutional forces (Howard 2008; Bronner 2009)—and fairy tales in digital media are no exception. Oral folktales and literary fairy tales alike are rendered in thousands of shades of gray in online spaces, with folk content and transmission blending with published, copyrighted material and mass broadcast. For any teller of contemporary fairy tales online, style and content are constrained by the medium's structure, but users nevertheless have a range of choices. The platform itself becomes a part of the tale's message. This chapter considers three fairy-tale themed Tumblrs in order to demonstrate the various ways in which fairy tales manifest in digital media.

Tumblr is a social network and microblogging service, founded in 2007 by then twenty-one-year-old web developer David Karp. The service is free, and bloggers can run as many Tumblrs as they wish, separating them by theme or interest. Users can follow others' blogs, can tag other users in their posts, can leave notes in the form of likes or reblogs, and can create their own folksonomies[1] through the use of hashtags. According to Amanda Brennan, one of Tumblr's content and community associates who has been working with its content team for three years, Tumblr users form one of the most passionate communities online.[2] Brennan is in charge of Tumblr's trending algorithm, tracking the kinds of communities that form and the topics those communities are talking about. Fandom is a major focus on Tumblr (although by

376

no means is fandom the only theme of the 340.7 million blogs) (Karp 2017), and according to Brennan, at least one fairy-tale themed production is consistently in the top twenty fandoms.

ABC's *Once Upon a Time* (*OUaT*, 2011–), a fantasy show that sets familiar fairy-tale characters in the "third reality" of a magical world where "the fantastical and the real partially converge" at "a specific place within the diegetical real world" (Schwabe 2014, 301), has one of the strongest fandoms on Tumblr. As is common within fandoms, the "[relation]shipping" of particular characters[3] is a strong theme; for *OUaT*, the "Swan Queen" ship, pairing protagonist Emma Swan and evil queen Regina Mills, is one of the most dominant on Tumblr. Fans not only generate their own narratives, creating new stories or filling in the narrative blanks the show's writers have left open with their own content, but also create multimedia displays using images and text from the show, sometimes of their own creation, or sometimes recontextualizing lines from the show that highlight the ship in the new format (see figure 41.1 and figure 41.2). And, of course, good old-fashioned fan swag is popular, too, as exemplified in figure 41.3, and is made more accessible by an abundance of affordable merchandise-design websites like Cafe Press, which allows users to upload their own art and order clothing and accessories featuring the images.

Fan creations and ships like Swan Queen are emblematic of how fairy tales and fairy-tale content often appear online, appropriated for users' own purposes.[4] More than desiring to tell a coherent tale, users seek *bricolage*, the construction of a personally relevant, pieced-together montage of meaning that invokes but does not replicate traditional tale telling. Cathy Preston observed this tendency in contemporary mass culture, noting,

> In postmodernity the "stuff" of fairy tales exists as fragments (princess, frog, slipper, commodity relations in a marriage market) in the nebulous realm that we might most simply identify as cultural knowledge. From an etic positioning the scholar may delineate among forms of transmission and impose genre classification on individual performances of the "stuff" for the purposes of analysis, but from an emic positioning it is free-floating cultural data that can be invoked conversationally, narratively, dramatically, or graphically as an e-mail message sent to an individual or a self-defined group, as a movie or a television special, or as a magazine advertisement, not to mention the many other forms it may take: a bed-time story told to a child, an edited text in a published collection, an authored short story or poem, a text in or of an academic article, a comic strip or cartoon, a television commercial, an item in the news or an item rumored to have been in the news, or a ritual enactment.

> (2004, 210)

Several years later, Preston's list of potential forms would certainly include the social media post and the blog. Far from showing any adherence to a purportedly "true" or "original" form of the tale (or the version presented by the show's writers), fans maintain the dynamism of the folk process and promote what they might call a "better" or "more relevant" version of a fairy tale.

The idea of a "true" form of the fairy tale has sometimes been promoted in popular culture. Catherine Tosenberger's study of fairy tales, ostension, and the television show *Supernatural* (2005–) considers the episode "Bedtime Stories" (2007), which she says "explicitly engages not just with the fairy tales themselves, but also with the stories we tell *about* fairy tales in our culture—the folklore about the folklore" (2010, 1.3). Tosenberger points out that one of the stories that we tell about fairy tales is that we need to get back to their "roots" as more violent, earthy, and genuine stories, not the sugary confections fed to us by Disney. As she says, "This story about fairy tales—we can call it the 'recovery story'—is a rescue operation, uncovering the 'real' fairy tale and liberating it from Disney oppression, and theoretically also recovering

Figure 41.1 A Tumblr post from the Swan Queen fandom, in response to the 50 Days of SQ challenge

Figure 41.2 A Tumblr post, highlighting the way that fans can speak to contemporary events through and with their fandoms

Figure 41.3 A Tumblr post, featuring fan-made material culture; the rhetorically redacted note about wishing for canon Swan Queen indicates that the user knows the hope is unlikely to be fulfilled, but wants to share it anyway

the 'true' voices of the 'original' tellers, usually figured as female" (2010, 5.1). Despite the popularity of the recovery narrative (which can manifest in both factual documentary forms and fictional ones, such as with the popular 1998 "Cinderella" recreation *Ever After*), fairy-tale content on Tumblr seems more intent on continuing the ongoing adaptation effort but moving it back into the hands of the folk.

Alice in Tumblr-Land (fairytalesfor20somethings.tumblr.com)

Some manifestations of fairy tales in digital media retain the classic form of narrative. This retention, combined with a diminishing interest in the preservation or "recovery" of earlier oral or literary versions of a fairy tale online, is perhaps best represented by a Tumblr that began in 2012, "Fairy Tales for Twenty-Somethings." Tim Manley, then a twenty-seven-year-old New York City high school teacher, began retelling classic fairy tales with a modern twist, setting the characters and their storylines in the context of a contemporary urban twenty-something's daily life. The form seemed a logical choice to Manley; as he explains, "Fairy tales were a big part of the way I made sense of the world as a child, and so it seemed logical to return to them as I try to make sense of it now" (quoted in Gray 2012). Manley's characters—familiar faces such as Snow White, Rapunzel, Peter Pan, and Beauty and the Beast, among others[5]—find themselves in distinctly modern situations: dating, dealing with technology and social media, trying to find meaningful employment, all while maintaining enough of their traditional identities to make the intertextual contrast striking:

> Little Red Riding Hood decided to walk home from her grandmother's house because she didn't want to waste money on a cab. But soon she was being stalked by a creepy wolf. He cornered her in the entryway to her apartment and started unzipping his pants, but then she was like, "oh *hell* no," and kneed him in the balls and shot him in the face with pepper spray. The next day, she borrowed money from her mother and moved to a safer neighborhood.
>
> The Ugly Duckling still felt gross compared with everyone else. But then she got Instagram, and there's this one filter that makes her look awesome.
>
> Cinderella divorced the Prince pretty quickly—no, he wasn't secretly gay, just kind of a prick—and moved back in with her stepmother. As a symbolic gesture, she vowed not to wear glass slippers, or any slippers, ever again. From here on out, all Crocs, all the time.
>
> Rumpelstiltskin tried his best to secure his identity, but every princess he stole a baby from guessed his name after a quick Google search. They also knew his date of birth, favorite movies, and the last ten restaurants he'd "checked in" at.
>
> Thumbelina never got much bigger, but she did get her own reality TV show, so that was cool.
>
> (Manley 2013)

The narratives are accompanied by illustrations that mimic the style of familiar versions of these characters and yet highlight the new context.[6] Manley made a strategic decision when he chose Tumblr as the platform for his project. As he explains,

> Digital media is very much a medium of the people. Many current protest movements are beginning now on social media, because most people can have access to it and find a voice in it. So, once again, the spreading of fairy tales has fallen into the hands of regular people. Anyone can rewrite a famous fairy tale on digital media right now. Anyone can manipulate the mainstream stories. When I began keeping a tumblr of fairy tales, I wasn't trying to be a writer. I was just having fun. There's no sign-up fee for Tumblr, and no laws on who can or can't post, and very few about what you can or can't post.
>
> (pers. comm.)

Unlike most Tumblrs, "Fairy Tales for Twenty-Somethings" has had a trajectory that defies expectations. Early on in the project, Manley struggled to get views. The power of folksonomies wasn't lost on him, though, and he intentionally tagged one of his first posts with "feminism," knowing that he'd draw an audience. From then on, he regularly used diverse tags to draw in an audience:

> Sometimes, I'd end up making this enormous list of tags on each post, hoping someone would happen to search for those words or phrases. [. . .] I do know that there

was always a spike in new followers after I posted a new fairytale. It makes sense: New, quality content led to more followers.

(omgstephlol 2013)

Once his work began getting attention, though, it wasn't long before he was offered a book deal, turning "Fairy Tales for Twenty-Somethings" into the published book *Alice in Tumblr-Land* (2013). Since the publication, the Tumblr has shifted focus to a general promotion of Manley's current projects. The move from the vernacular, user-driven medium of Tumblr to the mass-produced, elite realm of publishing was a definite change for his tales, but not one that Manley feels severed his work from its roots. He points out that books have their own magic: "A book is far more romantic than a website. There is some power in a physical object that a digital screen just cannot have" (pers. comm.). Books have long been a popular vehicle for fairy tales, and as Manley points out, the texture of fairy tales—the "romantic" elements—may be better reflected in a printed medium than on the screen. Of course, fans are at the ready to return his works back into a more egalitarian mode; shortly after the book came out, social media posts to Twitter and Instagram with the titular hashtag #AliceInTumblrLand began to appear, depicting readers' staging of their books in noticeably "romantic" tableaux, uniting the institutional power of the printed text and the user-generated power of social media (see figure 41.4).

Figure 41.4 A sampling of Instagram posts that feature Tim Manley's published book, *Alice in TumblrLand*, in visual compositions that bring the offline text back into a user-controlled, digital space

DIGITAL

"Fairy Tale Mood" (fairytalemood.tumblr.com)

In contrast to the textual nature of "Fairy Tales for Twenty-Somethings," Sarah Cross's Tumblr, "Fairy Tale Mood," doesn't focus on narrative retellings, contemporary or otherwise. Cross is the author of the modern fairy tale novels *Kill Me Softly* (2013), a retelling of "Sleeping Beauty" (ATU 410), and *Tear You Apart* (2015), a retelling of "Snow White" (ATU 709). Both are written for a YA audience and are recommended in editorial reviews for fans of *Once Upon a Time* (2011–). While there are advertisements for her books on the "Fairy Tale Mood" Tumblr, the focus isn't on posting tales themselves but, as the name suggests, creating a fairy tale *attitude*, emphasizing texture and context over text. Cross explains her goal in the "About" section of her Tumblr:

> I love fairy tales. I write fairy tale retellings (among other things) and this tumblr originated as an inspiration board I was making for myself. There's so much gorgeous fairy tale imagery out there, I wanted to collect it—and share it with people who love fairy tales as much as I do.
>
> Fairy tales are both magical and dark, and there's definitely a mix of blood and glitter here. I love the grim, twisted elements as much as I love the sparkly princess gowns and happily ever afters. Poison apples and bloody chambers, mad tea parties and mermaids, glass slippers and silver hands [. . .] I'll try not to leave anything out.
>
> (Cross 2011–)

The origin of this Tumblr in the genre of inspiration board—a popular online form[7] derived from the offline practice of a corkboard or bulletin board on which one gathers inspirational materials—makes sense. The format is more collage than text, "the physical juxtaposition of disparate materials, symbols, images, and voices" (Lindquist 2000, 55), and the creation of a particular inspirational ambience is more important than the communication of a particular story. Compared to Manley's Tumblr, Cross's blog far better exemplifies Preston's description of the postmodern fairy tale—fragmented pieces of shared textual awareness that recombine endlessly for new expressive purposes (2004).

Cross's description of fairy tales as paradoxically combining "blood and glitter" is a popular idea in the fairy-tale content that is regularly reblogged on Tumblr—the tag "fairy tales" gets appended to a wide range of posts that capture a combination of the grim and the fantastical, from architecture to interior design, fashion to food, quotations to paintings. In this context, "fairy tale" references not a story but an evocative sensory experience, a color palette, a feeling that combines the ethereal, the ancient, and, often, the subversive. Cross does at times use specific tales as tags, but like all tags the tale's name functions as metadata rather than data. What matters here isn't a coherent narrative, nor even an incoherent one; what matters is the overall tone that can perhaps be best described as folkloresque.[8]

As Michael Dylan Foster explains, the "folkloresque" is "popular culture's own (emic) perception and performance of folklore [. . .]. That is, it refers to creative, often commercial products or texts (e.g., films, graphic novels, video games) that give the impression to the consumer (viewer, reader, listener, player) that they derive directly from existing folkloric traditions" (2015, 5). Despite this appearance, a folkloresque product is rarely derived from any single piece of folklore, more often being an amalgamation of traditional motifs with newly created content. On Tumblr, the folkloresque reigns supreme; the technology itself (not only the networking capability of computer-mediated communication but also the creative design possibilities allowed by computer programs and mobile apps) creates a previously impossible opportunity to reconfigure existing textual and visual content into something that embodies any number of traditional elements in conjunction with original content. The sense that there is a fairy-tale quality to these productions—that they embody the paradox of blood and glitter—means that the creators have been successful in matching their work to the community's expectations of style and tone.

"Fairy Fables" (fairy-fables.tumblr.com)

In a strange mix of seeming narrative coherency and engaging modern nonsense, the Tumblr "Fairy Fables," a mirror of a Twitter account by the same name, produces new micronarrative fairy tales every three hours every day—that's eight tweets each day—all produced by a Twitter bot. This is perhaps the strangest of modern fairy-tale manifestations: puzzling narratives generated by an AI (Artificial Intelligence) that is programmed with a concise version of something resembling Vladimir Propp's morphology ([1928] 1968). Rather than the thirty-one functions that Propp uncovered in traditional Russian tales, the structure of Fairy Fables' narratives has only four component parts: an opening formula, an action involving two components, a closing phrase, and a narrative conclusion. As an example, here is a tweet from October 8, 2016: "Before the stars found their places [opening formula], a milkmaid was bitten by a shining magpie [action involving two elements], and as all feared [closing phrase] it rained for three days and nights [narrative conclusion]." Other examples follow a similar pattern, often repeating the formulaic elements:

> Once upon a time, a Tsarina was awakened by a monstrous sparrow, and as all hoped the fairies were restored.
>
> A long time ago, a goosegirl was given a message by an elven crow, and as was destined evil was vanquished.
>
> When the Mastermaid spun straw into copper thread, a farmer hunted a bear, and at last magic was saved.
>
> When the shepherdess wept for the sun, a witch wanted a dragon, and as was destined the snow melted away.
>
> A long time ago, a witch fought a magpie, and suddenly the fairies were restored.
>
> ("Fairy Fables" 2016–)

The narratives become repetitive quickly, and taken together, they lose any sense of meaning. But engaged with one at a time, the way they would appear contextualized in a follower's Twitter feed, embedded among other, unrelated tweets, they're quite appealingly enigmatic. Readers are inclined to make connections between disparate elements, wondering *why*, perhaps, everyone had feared that it would rain for three days and nights. The traditional-seeming nature of these micronarratives stands out, the formulas lending a distinctly folkloresque impression to the posts.

The bot that generates these tweets, created with a story-grammar generation library called Tracery, appears to be telling a story, but it's not, at least not in the traditional sense—any appearance of narrative intent is simply the result of an appropriate programming of the grammar. The perception of narrative agency, however, isn't something to dismiss simply because the force behind it is nonhuman. Rhetoricians have been expanding their understanding of agency to encompass not only human actors but also nonhuman components of communication, defining agency broadly as a "type of relational energy, persuadability, or affectability that emerges from the convergence of various factors, human and non-human, conscious and non-conscious, including the material conditions that make possible the emergence of a rhetorical event" (Shirley and Colton 2016, 1). In other words, the randomly generated output of a machine-based algorithm is just as likely a source of genuine meaning and communication as a person sitting in front of you telling you a story. There is perhaps little meaningful difference between an AI-generated text that engages its audience and a story crafted in a more conventional, culturally situated context.[9]

Here we see the technological prowess of communications media being put to a truly curious use. Far from providing a platform for everyday people to reclaim the folk status of fairy-tale content, "Fairy Fables" has replaced the human with the mechanical, the folk with the institutional. Implicit in almost all instances of fairy tales being shared online, whether as narratives or as textural tones, there remains a sense of a "teller," someone behind the manifestation of tradition within the technology. Is the AI the storyteller in these contexts? Do audiences actually require a teller in order for a story to have meaning?

Donald Haase, in his discussion of reception and fairy tales, notes that in typical fairy-tale analysis, "[t]he tendency to minimize or obscure the role of the actual tale teller is paralleled by the tendency to construct a stereotypical storyteller. Behind the idea of the anonymous fairy tale produced by collective voice, there is often the image of an ideal storyteller" (2012, 540). Haase notes that one of the functions of reception studies with regard to fairy tales has been to "reexamine the role and identity of the sender" (540), and the "Fairy Fables" Tumblr and Twitter accounts certainly prompt us to do just that. The anonymous teller here is in fact no teller at all, and yet audiences surely do their job of reception just the same.

Twitter, and in this case the Tumblr, too, as it is a mirror of the Twitter account, is constrained by length of posts: Tweets were limited to 140 characters, now doubled to 280. Any narrative shared through this platform will exhibit brevity, hence the common term "micronarrative" for stories shared via this medium. The constraint of length is one that challenges many people's perception of the viability of Twitter for any substantive communication; critics often point to the fact that many Twitter-based polemics go beyond a single tweet, often using a numbering system (1/7, 2/7, 3/7, etc.) to indicate how long the actual message is. But in reality, the micronarrative form can be quite expressive; one need only consider serious hashtags such as #WhyIStayed or #BlackLivesMatter (Thomas 2017) to see the impact that 140 characters can contain, and the inherent collectivity of the folksonomy guarantees that the narratives won't exist in a vacuum but rather will immediately become part of a larger narrative tradition. While individual tweets may seem fleeting, the addition of a popular hashtag increases the likelihood of retweets, which serve to perpetuate the narrative and also help ensure that the aggregated body of texts will likely be remembered.[10]

There are two ways to look at the brevity of tweets: either as rhetorically sound distillations of more complex points or as evidence that the teller doesn't have much to say. This is a judgment that all Twitter users are making every time they read through their feeds—assessing each tweet, considering its contextual markers and the user's aptitude with the format, noting framing elements such as hashtags and in-group terminology—to determine whether they're looking at a successfully distilled missive or at banal, unimportant content. Given this, "Fairy Fables" stands to be received as a genuine source of traditional narratives. Those users who track down the source of the narratives may learn otherwise, but users who scroll through a feed and simply glimpse the tales may end up imagining or assuming the very same stereotypical teller that Haase describes: an anonymous, wise woman, sharing ancient wisdom, even if she's using a contemporary medium to do so. Perhaps the programmer is simply a conduit for the anonymous tellers of the old tales that make up the formulaic grammar. If the meaning is in the reception, there may indeed be wisdom found in the stories told by an AI. As Preston found that the "free floating cultural data" (2004, 210) of postmodern fairy tales is no barrier to the emic process of storytelling, so the fragmented micronarratives of "Fairy Fables" can generate an authentic sense of the folkloresque or fairytalesque, even without any ties to actual folk.

Digital Media and Fairy Tales

The nature of digital media offers a complementary home for the diffusion that fairy tales have undergone in contemporary communication. Of course, the blending and mixing of fairy-tale elements isn't unique to digital media; many popular cultural forms such as film, literature, television, and comic books do very much the same thing. As Christine A. Jones and Jennifer Schacker note, the collective histories of literary tales and oral traditions have long been "tangled webs whose many tendrils interlock and whose pattern changes depending on the vantage point from which one looks at them" (2012, 37). What characterizes digital media in particular is that the people doing the remixing are usually non-professionals, everyday people retelling these familiar stories in all new ways, looking to engage their hobbies and fandoms, to generate a folkloresque atmosphere in which to conduct their work or play, to inject a sense of fantasy into their daily lives.

There's a satisfaction for fairy tale enthusiasts in knowing that fairy tales persist in the modern age, that technology hasn't curtailed the marvelous but has only served to give people new opportunities for creativity and reinvention. Whether tales are being recast and retold, used to create atmosphere or texture, or even generated by artificial intelligence, these ongoing processes stretch back into time, tying new manifestations diachronically to the past. The lure of the fairy-tale mood hasn't left us; for all our recontextualizing, it's astonishing how so many tales remain recognizable in fragmentation. As Tim Manley tells us of the Little Mermaid, "[She] was a human now, but sometimes at an upscale party someone would say to her, 'That's a very unusual accent. Where are you from?' Her past haunted her. She could never escape who she used to be" (2013).

Related topics: Adaptation and the Fairy-Tale Web; Blogs and Websites; Broadcast; Children's and Young Adult (YA) Literature; Cinematic; Convergence Culture; Fandom/Fan Cultures; Fan Fiction; Gender; Hybridity; Sexualities/Queer and Trans Studies; YouTube and Internet Video

Notes

1. A folksonomy is a grassroots, emic classification system, derived from user subject tags, which can give, as Coppelie Cocq explains, "an angle of approach to alternative voices compared to traditional media" (2015, 273).
2. Video call with the author, September 14, 2016.
3. "Shipping" is short for "relationshipping"—the fan process of imagining or depicting, often in art or narrative, a romantic relationship between two characters who are not explicitly depicted in the source material as being in a such a pairing. Popular ships often develop their own names or titles that become folksonomic categories. "Swan Queen" is sometimes written as "Swen," or "SwanMills," a reference to the two characters' last names. Hashtags connect to events or customs within the fandom, such as #50DaysOfSQ, in which content related to the popular ship would be posted for fifty days straight.
4. Fan fiction, as a genre, is often understood to be women centered, as are fairy tales.
5. The "others" highlight the broad definition of fairy tale that Manley uses, including literary figures such as Alice in Wonderland and Peter Pan, as well as legendary characters such as King Arthur and Robin Hood, and fable staples, like the Tortoise and the Hare.
6. The illustrations that accompany the early Tumblr posts are often general images of the characters, taken from the web. As the book project progressed, Manley's own illustrations began to appear more on the blog.

7. This is exemplified in Pinterest, the visual format of which is a digital corkboard where users can "pin" posts that they want to save and share.

8. Students working with Brigham Young University's "Visualizing Wonder" database use the term "fairytalesque" to describe this quality.

9. For further discussion of this idea, see Shirley and Colton's (2016) fascinating article on the Twitter account @Horse_ebooks. The account began as a bot, generating random-yet-enigmatic tweets drawn (unsurprisingly) from the texts of ebooks about horses, but was later taken over by an actual person who strove to mimic the appealing tone of the auto-generated tweets. When the handover was made public, fans, who had fully embraced the quirky twitter bot with fan fiction, art, and poetry, felt deeply betrayed to discover that their beloved account was actually run by a human being.

10. Andrew Peck (2015, 15) uses the term "aggregated volition" to describe the way that networked communication exhibits and reinforces communal practice.

References Cited and Further Reading

Bacon-Smith, Camille. 1992. *Enterprising Women: Television Fandom and the Creation of Popular Myth.* Philadelphia: U Pennsylvania P.

Blank, Trevor Ed. 2009. *Folklore and the Internet.* Logan: Utah State UP.

Bronner, Simon. 2009. "Digitizing and Virtualizing Folklore." In *Folklore and the Internet*, edited by Trevor J. Blank, 21–66. Logan: Utah State UP.

Cocq, Coppelie. 2015. "Indigenous Voices on the Web: Folksomonies and Endangered Languages." *Journal of American Folklore* 128 (509): 273–85.

Cross, Sarah. 2013. *Kill Me Softly.* Minneapolis: Egmont USA.

———. 2015. *Tear You Apart.* Minneapolis: Carolrhoda Lab.

Foster, Michael Dylan. 2015. "Introduction: The Challenge of the Folkloresque." In *The Folkloresque: Reframing Folklore in a Popular Culture World*, edited by Michael Dylan Foster and Jeffrey A. Tolbert, 3–36. Logan: Utah State UP.

Gray, Emma. 2012. "Fairy Tales for Twenty Somethings Tumblr Reveals the Truth about Growing Up." *The Huffington Post*, October 18. www.huffingtonpost.com/2012/10/18/fairy-tales-for-20-somethings-tumblr_n_1980186.html.

Haase, Donald. 2012. "Dear Reader." In *Marvelous Transformations: An Anthology of Fairy Tales and Contemporary Critical Perspectives*, edited by Christine A. Jones and Jennifer Schacker, 539–44. Toronto: Broadview P.

Howard, Robert Glenn. 2008. "Electronic Hybridity: The Persistent Processes of the Vernacular Web." *Journal of American Folklore* 121 (480): 192–218.

Jamison, Anne. 2013. *Fic: Why Fanfiction Is Taking Over the World.* Dallas: Smart Pop.

Jones, Christine A., and Jennifer Schacker. 2012. "Introduction: How to Read a Fairy Tale." In *Marvelous Transformations: An Anthology of Fairy Tales and Contemporary Critical Perspectives*, edited by Christine A. Jones and Jennifer Schacker, 21–40. Toronto: Broadview P.

Karp, David. 2017. "About." *Tumblr*, March 20. www.tumblr.com/about.

Lindquist, Danille. 2000. "Some Assembly Required: Collage, Creativity, and the Self in Everyday Life." *Folklore Forum* 31 (1): 55–77.

Manley, Tim. 2013. *Alice in Tumblr-Land: And Other Fairy Tales for a New Generation.* New York: Penguin Books.

omgstephlol. 2013. "Ever Wonder How Tumblrs Turn into Books? One Writer's Story." *Inklings*, November 19. http://inklings.kinja.com/ever-wonder-how-tumblrs-turn-into-books-one-writers-s-1465763927.

Peck, Andrew. 2015. "At the Modems of Madness: The Slender Man, Ostension, and the Digital Age." *Contemporary Legend* 3 (5): 14–37.

Preston, Cathy Lynn. 2004. "Disrupting the Boundaries of Genre and Gender: Postmodernism and the Fairy Tale." In *Fairy Tales and Feminism: New Approaches*, edited by Donald Haase, 197–212. Detroit: Wayne State UP.

Propp, Vladimir. (1928) 1968. *Morphology of the Folktale.* Austin: U Texas P.

Schwabe, Claudia. 2014. "Getting Real with Fairy Tales: Magic Realism in *Grimm* and *Once Upon a Time*." In *Channeling Wonder: Fairy Tales on Television*, edited by Pauline Greenhill and Jill Terry Rudy, 294–315. Detroit: Wayne State UP.

Shirley, Beth, and Jared Colton. 2016. "The Moral Act of Attributing Agency to Non-Humans." *Present Tense* 6 (1): 1–12.

Thomas, Jeannie. 2017. "#BlackLivesMatter: Galvanizing and Oppositional Narratives." In *Race and Ethnicity in Digital Culture: Changing Traditions, Impressions, and Expressions in a Mediated World*, edited by Anthony Bak Buccitelli. Santa Barbara, CA: Praeger Books.

Tosenberger, Catherine. 2010. "'Kinda Like the Folklore of its Day': *Supernatural*, Fairy Tales, and Ostension." *Transformative Works and Culture* 4: 1.1–10.1.

Mediagraphy

Cross, Sarah. 2011–. "Fairy Tale Mood." *Tumblr.* http://fairytalemood.tumblr.com.

Ever After. 1998. Director Andy Tennant. USA.

"Fairy Fables." 2015–. fairy-fables.tumblr.com.

harrus-corner. 2016–. "Harru's Little Corner." *Tumblr.* http://harrus-corner.tumblr.com.

Manley, Tim. 2012–. "Fairytales for Twenty-Somethings." *Tumblr.* http://fairytalesfor20somethings.tumblr.com.

mmisery. 2011–. *Tumblr.* http://mmisery.tumblr.com.

Once Upon a Time (TV). 2011–. Creators Adam Horowitz and Edward Kitsis. USA.

superfluous-stuckupitude. 2014–. "Press On." *Tumblr.* http://superfluous-stuckupitude.tumblr.com.

Supernatural (TV). 2005–. Creator Eric Kripke. USA.

———. "Bedtime Stories." 2007. Episode 3.5. November 1.

Visualizing Wonder. 2014–. http://fairytales.byu.edu/.

Part V

EXPRESSIVE GENRES AND VENUES

42

ANIME AND MANGA

"You Love Your Father, Don't You?": The Influence of Tale Type 510B on Japanese Manga/Anime

Bill Ellis

Psychosexual development, the emerging awareness of one's sexual identity, is a central topic in the folk and popular culture of childhood. In traditional Freudian theory, the first stages occur in very early youth, often during infancy or one's first years of self-consciousness. They are followed by a longer *latent* stage, during which sexual issues are hidden from consciousness, although they are expressed symbolically in other activities such as games, art, and storytelling. At puberty, individuals confront and resolve remaining conflicts with increased frankness. Freudian psychoanalysis has been used to discuss how fantasy stories express these conflicts, both symbolically and, at times, explicitly. Freud himself began the process by observing that dreams related by his patients often contained motifs and elements that had clearly been imported from well-known fairy tales ([1913] 1997). Bruno Bettelheim (1976) made a stronger and more inclusive case for fairy tales as communicating advice to youngsters on how to negotiate psychosexual conflicts. More recently folklorist Alan Dundes (1980, 1987) has proposed a number of Freudian readings of popular fairy tales.

These psychoanalytical explications have, however, been bedeviled by the cultural assumption that a healthy development results in a socially prescribed heterosexual relationship, a Prince Charming for every Princess. Queer studies has challenged the gender stereotypes such readings support and suggested that even canonical tales that were assumed to have uncontroversial social meanings could in fact be re-read in subversive ways to reveal decidedly queer meanings. Folklorists understand that a tale need not have a single authoritative meaning, even for its teller, and audience members may draw radically different conclusions from the same tale in context. Finally, recognition that many tales were rewritten during Victorian times has led scholars to notice and give due weight to lesser-known variants that addressed psychosexual issues much more frankly. Fairy tales thus have come to be understood as adventurous and often transgressive explorations of human sexuality.

This chapter draws on the insight of queer studies scholars in addressing the influence of ATU 510B (Peau d'Asne or "Donkey Skin") on recent Japanese manga and anime. As noted by Michiko N. Wilson (2013), patriarchal values still determine most heterosexual relationships, and opportunities for women in the job market remain severely limited. Accordingly, many plots in this emerging popular culture show female protagonists making culturally "appropriate" choices of mates and careers. But so-called "shōjo" manga/anime does not passively reflect the real world of Japanese readers and viewers. Susan J. Napier, drawing on the increasing attention these art forms are receiving from Japanese commentators, notes that the hallmark of the genre is a "potential for unfettered change and excitement" (2005, 149) that contrasts dramatically with a regimented system of cultural and workforce expectations. Indeed, Napier notes, the transformative power of female protagonists appeals to both genders for similar reasons.

"Donkey Skin" narrates the sexual maturation of a young woman who finds she is desired by her own father. Her flight and subsequent journey are marked by transformations, beastly and celestial, as she attracts a royal bridegroom. Margaret Yocom (2012) suggests that the story contains queered elements, marking the protagonist's ability to transgress social definitions of her sexual and indeed human identity. Such elements are also common to the Japanese "magical girl" tradition, as is the issue of a daughter's potentially incestuous feelings for her father. This chapter argues that a number of manga/anime series draw on this fairy tale, sometimes in a transgressive way that challenges the notion that the story's theme is unnatural. In fact, such tales concede, young girls' romantic fantasies about their fathers are a natural and healthy part of psychosexual growth.

Fairy Tales, Manga/Anime, and Incest

The intimately related art forms of manga (graphic novels) and anime (animated films or series) emerged as a vital popular culture in Japan during the 1970s and developed into a global phenomenon at the beginning of the twenty-first century. A number of scholars observe that the discursive mode of manga/anime is similar to that of the fairy tale. Dani Cavallaro argues that both are fantasy-imbued narratives that explore "the buried landscapes of the human psyche" and so comment on the process of identity formation (2011, 17). Napier likewise suggests that manga/anime embodies "a fundamental concern or even unease with the body and thus, implicitly, with identity itself" (2005, 115). Many series use animation as a potent metaphor to create protagonists who are multiply conflicted in identity, their bodies morphing fluidly into beastly or celestial variants of themselves (see Ellis 2015). This metaphor makes concrete the characters' quest for a stable psychosexual identity that, Napier argues, "transcends the categorizing nature of society" (2005, 115).

Indeed, the capacity of animation to challenge social norms of identity allows audiences, as Judith (Jack) Halberstam argues, "to explore ideas about humanness, alterity, and alternative imaginaries" (2011, 33). This critic suggests that animated fantasies are like fairy tales, which

> have always occupied the ambiguous territory between childhood and adulthood, home and away, harm and safety. They [. . .] open doors to alternative worlds and allow children to confront archetypal fears, engage in prepubescent fantasy, and indulge infantile desires about being scared, eaten, chased, and demolished.
>
> (44)

Halberstam's first points are supported by many critics of both fairy tales and manga/anime. Animation creates a narrative landscape where, in Napier's words, "both characters and viewers can explore the [. . .] possibilities of creating and encapsulating worlds" (2005, 115–116). However, when Halberstam turns to the psychosexual function of such fantasies, the "desires" specifically mentioned are *not* emotions young children seek to indulge. Children do find it enjoyable to learn to cope with fearful ideas through stories, but a more challenging argument would be that fantasy tales provide ways of fulfilling young peoples' *active* psychosexual desires, albeit in symbolic ways.

The taboo against parent/child incest is generally observed, yet Freudian psychology holds that it is deeply embedded in children's early development, as they become aware of their sexual identity and learn to negotiate their relationships with others. The Oedipus complex, or the stages by which a young boy negotiates his desire to retain his mother's affection and dispossess his father, has been foundational for Freudian analysis. The female parallel has been less prominent in psychoanalytic theory: Freud acknowledged that girls likewise crossed this phase of psychosexual development, feeling romantic longings for their fathers and resolving them in an analogous, if slightly different way. He thus referred to such childhood conflicts as "Oedipal" regardless of gender.

Bettelheim agreed, discussing "the Oedipal girl" and her conflicts. Like other psychoanalysts, Bettelheim stressed that children's Oedipal desires are not the same as adults' sexual urges. At this stage they are not explicitly erotic; rather, both young boys and girls wish simply to possess the parent's love exclusively in a self-indulgent world (1976, 112–113). Such a phase needs to be successfully resolved during childhood, or serious complexes will emerge when children develop into young adults, preventing them from entering into relationships with others and perhaps leading to mental illness. But during the latent phase of psychosexual development, such feelings can be safely indulged through private fantasies or collectively through fairy tales or manga/anime plots.

"Allerleirauh's" Emergence in Japanese Popular Culture

Because of its close relationship to the "Cinderella" cycle, ATU 510B has been intensively studied by folktale scholars (e.g., Goldberg 1997). The tale's common beginning tells how a king develops an uncontrollable desire for his daughter, who resembles his dead wife. The daughter rejects his advances, first by demanding a series of wonderful gifts (such as a coat made of every kind of animal fur), and then by leaving home, taking the gifts with her. The second half of this tale resembles the better-known "Cinderella" plot (ATU 510A): the girl works as a servant, wearing the coat of animal fur by day but using the wonderful gifts to disguise herself at night and attend a series of balls. Unlike the more passive Cinderella, she is, Christine Goldberg says, "an admirable, resourceful heroine" who "takes charge of her life" (1997, 29). Dundes argues that the tale is best understood not as relating a father's "unnatural" lust, but rather as a projection of the daughter's (psychosexually normal) passion for her father (1980, 217; 1987, 60). In this reading, the daughter has two choices: to cut her ties with her father and seek a father-substitute in the outside world or risk both internal and external disaster by staying and attempting to indulge it. Jacques Demy's musical film adaptation, *Peau d'Âne* (Donkey Skin, 1970), in fact shows the daughter initially agreeing to wed her father, a wish that the director described as understandable and innocent. While the film shows her instead going out into the world to seek a culturally legitimate mate, her underlying desire for her father is expressed when, in the final scene, her father appears at the wedding and marries her daughter's confidant, the Lilac Fairy (see Duggan 2013).

Or maybe there are other options for this clever, resourceful princess. As many scholars (e.g., Yocom 2012, 92; Ashliman 2016) note, the Grimms' first published version in 1812 suggests that the princess uses the disguises to dance with her father, and when she is finally unmasked, she marries him, and they "lived happily until they died." While later editions and retellings emphasize that the man the princess marries is *not* her father but a different king,

Yocom argues that the "two-king" version is also radically ambiguous, exploring "so many different kinds of physical attractions, liaisons, and appearances that the man–woman wedding can be seen as just one of several possibilities" (2012, 102). She develops an open-ended reading of "Allerleirauh" ("All Kinds of Fur") that focuses on the protagonist's tactical use of disguise, which she sees as exploring the human capacity of exploring multiple "skins," particularly gender identities.

No Japanese fairy tale provides a direct parallel to the incest motif, although one tradition is analogous, telling how an outcast girl uses an "old woman's skin" to disguise herself as a servant in a rich household and eventually marry the son of a rich family (Goldberg 1997, 35–36). As Mayako Murai (2015) shows, however, the Grimms' version, "Allerleirauh," became available during the 1920s as part of Kaneda Kiichi's Japanese edition of *Die Kinder- und Hausmärchen*. Jacob Grimm's bicentenary in 1984 resulted in a new burst of Japanese academic interest in these tales, and soon after, Nippon Animation produced an anime series titled *Grimm Masterpiece Theatre*. "Allerleirauh" was one of the tales included, as *Senbikigawa*, or "Thousand Furs." The anime version did not shrink from the incest issue; indeed, it is a central plot motif throughout the telling. The episode begins jarringly with the daughter's escape from her palace as the king, a grotesque figure with maniacal eyes and a long white beard, brutally tries to restrain her. As she flees into the wilderness, the castle behind her is destroyed by fire and bolts of lightning. The origin of the king's infatuation with his daughter then is told through a series of flashbacks, emphasizing its impact on the princess's emotions.

The plot continues much as the revised Grimms' story does, showing the princess arriving in a neighboring kingdom and working as a servant by day but attending royal balls in disguise at night. She quickly falls in love with the king, and as she dances with him, animated images of colorful flowers swirl around her. But this blissful scene changes to a threatening image of circling fireballs, out of which the image of her sex-crazed father, holding a torch (for her?), appears. So, in this version, she is unable to consummate her new love because her memories of her father produce terrifying moments of guilt, explaining her anxious disappearances from the ballroom. The second king has, however, already taken an interest in the mysterious new servant girl and quickly sees through the disguise. He unmasks her, then gallantly offers his support to help her overcome her memories of her father's advances (or, in Dundes's reading, the guilt she feels over her attraction to her father). In this way, the anime introduces both the tale and its Freudian psychosexual subtext to a broad popular audience.

Fairy Tales in Manga/Anime

As Murai (2015) documents, Western fairy tales became explosively popular in Japan in the following decade, thanks to a series of popular books that highlighted their covert psychosexual content. This burst of interest, called the *Gurimu būmu* ("Grimm Boom"), included psychoanalytical explications, translations of works by Western folklorists, and literary retellings. As Murai observes, all of these publications, which had high sales, emphasized the original violent and sexually charged details of the European versions. In Japan, where sanitized versions had previously held sway, these publications made the Grimm tales central in emerging works of protest literature and art that used the tales as sources for self-conscious Freudian symbols for sexual inequity (2015, 31). Given this growing awareness of psychosexual issues, then, it is not surprising that the creators of manga/anime series consciously used such themes in their works, expecting them to have latent effects on young audiences and to be recognized as embodying Freudian meanings by older, more sophisticated viewers.

And the *Grimm Masterpiece Theatre* adaptation links three motifs: the princess's multiple secret identities, an infatuation with an older fatherly male, and the threat of a personal or global catastrophe. In a psychosexual context, we could see the older male to whom the protagonist is attracted as a sexualized fantasy version of her father, while the secret identity and catastrophe relate to the protagonist's struggle to achieve a stable sexual identity and avoid the negative consequences of her incestuous impulses. These linked motifs are often found in "magical girl" series, which became extraordinarily popular at the same time as the Japanese Grimm Boom. The range of manga/anime titles in this subgenre is huge (see Napier 2005, 147), but this chapter will look closely at two examples, *Cardcaptor Sakura* (1996–2000) and *Sasami: Magical Girls Club* (2006–2007).

Ostensibly about a central character's secret quest to recapture and tame a set of enchanted cards that have gotten loose by accident, *Cardcaptor Sakura* actually explores the wide range of human love. Sakura feels love of different kinds for many people of both genders, particularly for her kind and loving father (who is, like the king in the fairy tale, a widower). In the social world around her, we catch glimpses of a number of unorthodox relationships, including intense same-sex partnerships and at least one Lolita-style affair between one of Sakura's classmates and a much older teacher. Among the international fan base that developed around this series, including a surprising number of older-teen and college-aged males, these same-sex affairs generated considerable discussion.

However, the most transgressive issue was hidden in plain sight. Sakura is emotionally drawn to two mature characters: one is Yukito, a preternaturally handsome high school student, and the other is Eriol, an equally mysterious exchange student from England. Like Sakura, each has a secret identity that links them with the magical card quest, but, much more importantly for our purposes, both share a disturbing resemblance to the ideal, kind, loving father whom she idolizes. Indeed, at one point Sakura suddenly notices the similarities among the three, and the manga artists helpfully include images behind her that point out the similarities (CLAMP 1999, Vol. 8, 14). The story also contains an enigmatic catastrophe theme: when the seal of the book containing the enchanted cards is broken, a prophecy holds, "disaster will befall this world." She asks her magical helper if this "disaster" would be "like the earth splitting in half or something," and she is reassured that the catastrophe is not global but personal in nature. "But for that person," the helper comments when Sakura is out of hearing, "it could be more painful than the earth splitting in half" (CLAMP 1997, Vol. 2, 105–107).

And indeed, we see what this means in one of the series climaxes, when she declares her love for Yukito, whom she has idolized from the beginning. "Well, you love your father, don't you," her idol kindly prompts her; then he adds, more pointedly, "Is the love you feel for me . . . kind of like what you feel for your father?" A painful silence ensues, and finally Sakura, pressed to examine her feelings more intimately than before, replies reluctantly, "It is." Chaos breaks out around the two of them, during which the magical girl senses that they are under attack from someone who is behind a nearby curtain. She dashes over and finds, logically enough, the other father-image, Eriol (CLAMP 1999, Vol. 10, 39–41). The ensuing episodes lead from this intense moment of insight to a happy ending. Yukito, the protective father figure, helps her see that her affections are dangerous and gives her the guidance to recognize and renounce them. At the same time, she recognizes that Eriol, her other idol, is a dark and dangerous father figure. Using her powers, she defeats him and averts a catastrophe. Her victory gives her male rival, who is a suitable mate although with lesser power, the courage to declare his love, which Sakura in time accepts. Thus the story, like the fairy tale, leads to a socially acceptable heterosexual happy ending, although tellingly the other unorthodox romances likewise continue and, tellingly, are not censured by the tale. Heterosexual marriage thus is presented as only one of several valid possibilities.

This more subversive implication is developed by *Sasami: Magical Girls Club* (2006–2007). The plot focuses on a grade-school girl who possesses a "wild talent"; however, her father insists that she keep her powers secret from everyone. The children's stories he writes for a living give his daughter access to a magical world through imagination, which she appreciates and enjoys. But this enchanted realm is only a fictional one, and when Sasami meets other girls with supernatural powers, she eventually travels with them on an overnight stay to a real world ruled by magic. There she wanders into a wood and meets a mysterious older man named Amitav, who invites her to dance beside a lake. Much like the princess in the anime "Allerleirauh," she finds the experience blissful, symbolized by a swirl of colorful flowers and lights. There is no shift to a fiery catastrophe, but at one point she notices that in the reflecting surface of the lake her partner looks the same, but she has transformed into a sexually mature woman. "Someday this is the Sasami you'll become," her partner says, with a smile (2006, "Hoshizora DANZU [Dance of the Star-Lit Sky]").

While the experience ends with no bad consequences, it haunts the young girl, and she finds herself dissatisfied with her father's fantasies and longs to return to a real magical world. At this point, we learn that Amitav is no stranger to Sasami's father, who has known him for many years; indeed, he himself has been to the same world of enchantment many times, and it is the inspiration for the stories he writes as fantasies. Her father also knows that Amitav has an evil twin whom the witch world has locked deep underground for fear that he will cause a cosmic disaster (thus the three connected motifs—fatherly love interest, secret identity, and catastrophe—appear together). After many adventures, the plot resolves when Amitav realizes that Sasami's attraction to him has become dangerous. He agrees to return to his own enchanted realm and remain there with his dangerous twin, leaving Sasami to develop safely in her own world. The girl consents, but only after giving the mysterious stranger a passionate "magical kiss," an intimacy rarely shown in anime intended for younger audiences.

So do traditional sexual norms win again, as with *Cardcaptor Sakura*? It's not so simple: the father's fantasy writings allow his daughter to continue to indulge her emotions in a pleasurable but safe way, much like "magical girl" anime itself. The last scene of the final episode of *Sasami* (2007, "AMI-chan no uta" [Amitav's Song]) underscores this lesson: we find Sasami in her father's study, musing alone over her adventures. She suddenly turns and finds Amitav, who had supposedly been left in the magical world, sitting asleep in her father's chair. Curiously, she reaches out a finger to touch him, but at that moment her mother calls her away to help in the kitchen. "I'll be back to play with you after supper," Sasami says cheerfully, and she leaves the room. A series of extreme close-ups of Amitav's face follow, fading in and out of images of the pages of the fantasy story her father is drafting. And then—an instant before the credits roll, Amitav's eyelids flicker!

An American reviewer called this series, "Predictable yet inoffensive," adding, "you should feel entirely safe allowing your six-year-old girl to watch it" (Brienza 2009). Perhaps, but fathers should expect uncomfortable questions, especially about those flickering eyelids. True, the conclusion affirms that Sasami and her friends are healthy grade-schoolers, in spite of their secret identities, negotiating the transition to sexual identity. But Sasami does not repress her fantasies about a sexualized father-lover so much as she domesticates them. In this way, Amitav remains a factor in her home routine, not as a psychic danger but as a romantic idea she can play with and use it to grow into whoever she is, really.

Domesticating Incest

Japanese culture, with its highly structured set of social rules, cannot be accused of encouraging young girls to violate deeply held social taboos in real life. And even with the multiple opportunities that animation provides for radical challenges to social norms, most anime plots in fact move toward conservative safe endings, with women choosing (or being chosen by) appropriate male partners. The alternative, the magical girl theme implies, is internal and perhaps external catastrophe. Or is it? In fact, both Sakura and Sasami, like many other characters in Japanese manga/anime, are allowed to entertain their incestuous fantasies and at the same time avoid disaster not by repressing these emotions but by accepting and playing with them in safe ways.

In much the same way, the Western fairy tale provides potent opportunities for both creators and their audiences to explore psychosexual emotions that are otherwise strongly repressed in ordinary life. Plots such as these affirm that potentially tabooed fantasies during the latent stage are common and normal. Girls (and boys) must of course move through the Oedipal stage to achieve full sexual maturity. Nevertheless, series like *Cardcaptor Sakura* and *Sasami* suggest that it is healthier to domesticate such longings in playful ways, rather than to try to pretend they do not exist.

Related topics: Cinematic; Comics and Graphic Novels; Fandom/Fan Cultures; Fantasy; Gender; Sexualities/Queer and Trans Studies

References Cited and Further Reading

Ashliman, D. L. 2016. "The Father Who Wanted to Marry His Daughter: Folktales of Aarne-Thompson-Uther Type 510B." In *Folklore and Mythology Electronic Texts*. University of Pittsburgh. www.pitt.edu/~dash/type0510b.html.

Bettelheim, Bruno. 1976. *The Uses of Enchantment*. New York: Alfred A. Knopf.

Brienza, Casey. 2009. "Review: *Sasami: Magical Girls Club* DVD—Season One." *Anime News Network*. www.anime newsnetwork.com/review/sasami/magical-girls-club/dvd-season-one.

Cavallaro, Dani. 2011. *The Fairy Tale and Anime: Traditional Themes, Images and Symbols at Play on Screen*. Jefferson, NC: McFarland.

CLAMP. 1996–2000. *Cardcaptor Sakura* [カードキャプターさくら] (Manga). Tokyo: Kodansha.

Duggan, Anne. 2013. *Queer Enchantments: Gender, Sexuality, and Class in the Fairy-Tale Cinema of Jacques Demy*. Detroit: Wayne State UP.

Dundes, Alan. 1980. *Interpreting Folklore*. Bloomington: Indiana UP.

———. 1987. "The Psychoanalytic Study of the Grimms' Tales with Special Reference to 'The Maiden Without Hands' (AT 706)." *Germanic Review* 62 (2): 50–66.

Ellis, Bill. 2008. "Sleeping Beauty Awakens Herself: Folklore and Gender Inversion in *Cardcaptor Sakura*." In *The Japanification of Children's Popular Culture: From Godzilla to Spirited Away*, edited by Mark I. West, 249–66. Lanham, MD: Scarecrow P.

———. 2012. "Fairy Tales as Metacommentary in Manga and Anime." In *Marvelous Transformations: An Anthology of Fairy Tales and Contemporary Critical Perspectives*, edited by Christine A. Jones and Jennifer Schacker, 503–8. Peterborough, ON: Broadview P.

———. 2015. "The Fairy-Telling Craft of *Princess Tutu*: Metacommentary and the Folkloresque." In *The Folkloresque: Reframing Folklore in a Popular Culture World*, edited by Michael Dylan Foster and Jeffrey Tolbert, 189–208. Salt Lake City: Utah UP.

Freud, Sigmund. (1913) 1997. *Writings on Art and Literature*. Stanford: Stanford UP.

Goldberg, Christine. 1997. "The Donkey Skin Folktale Cycle (AT 510B)." *Journal of American Folklore* 110 (435): 28–46.

Halberstam, Jack (Judith). 2011. *The Queer Art of Failure*. Durham, NC: Duke UP.

Murai, Mayako. 2015. *From Dog Bridegroom to Wolf Girl: Contemporary Japanese Fairy-Tale Adaptations in Conversation with the West*. Detroit: Wayne State UP.

Napier, Susan J. 2005. *Anime from Akira to Howl's Moving Castle: Experiencing Contemporary Japanese Animation.* New York: Palgrave Macmillan.

Taggart, James M. 1990. *Enchanted Maidens: Gender Relations in Spanish Folktales of Courtship and Marriage.* Princeton, NJ: Princeton UP.

Wilson, Michiko N. 2013. "Ōba Minako the Raconteur: Refashioning a *Yamauba* Tale." *Marvels & Tales* 27 (2): 218–33.

Yocom, Margaret R. 2012. "But Who Are You Really? Ambiguous Bodies and Ambiguous Pronouns in 'Allerleirauh'." In *Transgressive Tales: Queering the Grimms*, edited by Kay Turner and Pauline Greenhill, 91–118. Detroit: Wayne State UP.

Mediagraphy

Grimm Masterpiece Theater [グリム名作劇場, *Gurimu Meisaku Gekijō*] (TV). 1987–1989. Director Hiroshi Saito. Japan.

Peau d'Âne (Donkey Skin). 1970. Director Jacques Demy. France.

Sasami: Magical Girls Club [砂沙美☆魔法少女クラブ, *Sasami: Mahō Shōjo Club*] (TV). 2006–2007. Director Nobuhiro Takamoto. Japan.

———. "Hoshizora DANZU [Dance of the Star-Lit Sky]." 2006. Episode 1.6. May 25.

———. "AMI-chan no uta [Amitav's Song]." 2007. Episode 2.13. January 11.

43

ANTHOLOGIES AND TALE COLLECTIONS

Jessie Riddle

Stories, particularly fairy tales, are often shared more than one at a time. Such compilations help shape ideas about the kind of stories they include and the people associated with them. Fairy tales have held a particularly significant place in the history of these story groups—all forms of media that draw on fairy tales have produced compilations. Some of these groupings are "anthologies," assembling initially discrete texts. Seth Lerer (2003) describes anthologies as "volumes guided by a critical intelligence" (1255)—"an editorial, authorial, scribal, or patronal aegis"—in contrast to "miscellanies," compiled without a specific intention or planned structure (1265). These definitions highlight the fundamental duality of anthologies: they are the conjunction of disparate texts and a unifying editorial process or vision, simultaneously multifaceted and uniform.

Fairy-tale scholars have used a similarly dual structure to define fairy tales by simple plots and characters and their ability to inspire an infinite number of variations and re-creations (Zipes 2012, 9). This dual structure is integral to the way fairy tales have been used as an expression of national and individual identity. Tale collections and other kinds of anthologies have been used to represent specific pieces of a group's storytelling tradition and, by extension, the character of its people. Cristina Bacchilega (2013), Jack Zipes, and others note that as we retell or "transform" fairy tales, they can also transform us as individuals and as a group or "affect the making of who we are and the world we are in" (Zipes 2012, 2). This process is illustrated in part by the history of the tale collection, a specific kind of anthology that involves documenting and compiling orally told tales in a new medium. Those who produce tale collections have often assumed the role of the storyteller and de-emphasized the role of the editor, although the process of selecting which stories to include and how to translate them across genres of media is significant (Jones and Schacker 2013).

Donald Haase (1993) provides an overview of how fairy tales—often groupings of fairy tales—have been used as symbols and indexes for identity. He writes that fairy tales have often been used as didactic or nationalistic tools for teaching a specific set of social values through a simplistic perpetuation of canons and the uncritical association of fairy tales with group identity. He contrasts this compliant perspective with individual readings of tales, which can be a revolutionary act of creation. However, those individual readings are made possible in part by the otherwise normative perceived canon of fairy tales—for example, the many reimaginings of fairy tales that have been popularized by multinational companies like Disney. From this lens, while a single story can make a complex statement about a particular aspect of the human experience, a collection of narratives that people hold in common can simultaneously limit *and* resonate with individuals and can make possible new and creative interpretations of the information available.

Revisions or retellings of fairy tales often seek to add more perspectives, or voices, to our understanding of both the tale and the cultural ideology associated with it. Mikhail Bakhtin (1982) contrasts heteroglossia, or a text that represents a dialogue between multiple speakers, with authoritative discourse, or a text that represents the voice of a single speaker and does not allow for a conversation—engagement with other speakers' voices. Literary critics have explored this idea at length, with many concluding that heteroglossic texts provide a more resonant experience for the reader (Barthes 1974). This confluence of voices is made possible in anthologies by combining the ideas of multiple tales with those of the author/collector/editor/teller.[1]

Anthologies, however, seek to be authoritative as well as heteroglossic, as clarified in Roland Barthes's (1974) discussion of the similar concepts of readerly versus writerly texts. Barthes, like Bakhtin, describes two kinds of texts, each of which allows for a different kind of engagement with the reader. Readerly texts, like authoritative texts, countenance passive reading, while writerly texts require more effort from the reader and invite them to participate in the creation of meaning. In terms of critical intention, anthologies of fairy tales exhibit the intent to provide texts that are both readerly and writerly—authoritative and heteroglossic. Some degree of heteroglossia is present as the reader engages with the dialogue among the tales but also between the reader's previous understanding of the tales and the writers' perspectives, even as that dialogue is filtered through the authoritative act of the creator's selection and editing of texts. Both the reader and the writerly aspects of anthologies influence how readers shape their understanding of themselves and the tales.

While scholars seem to prefer the idea of heteroglossia to that of authoritativeness, the reality of both of these forces in fairy-tale anthologies becomes clearer through the lens of Barre Toelken's twin laws of folklore. Toelken (1996) proposes that folklore—a category whose exact boundaries are as contested as that of the fairy tale—exhibits the processes of conservatism and dynamism (39). In other words, for something to be defined as folklore it must have some elements that continue between people who enact it, but it must also have some element of variation in each performance. It is this duality that allows folktales, beliefs, and behaviors to be held in common in a group of people and yet hold a different significance for each member. In applying these ideas to fairy-tale anthologies, we can consider conservatism as an impulse toward consistency and simplicity: an established canon of stories, for example, or the prevalence of a particular interpretation of a single story. Dynamism can be thought of as an impulse toward change and complexity, or a desire to expand the canon of recognized fairy tales and challenge normative interpretations of their significance. In order for fairy tales and fairy-tale anthologies to continue to entertain and resonate, readers must both recognize a story or grouping of stories as familiar and see or read them in a new way.

The way that creators structure and edit anthologies, whether in print, audiovisually mediated, or shared orally, presents epistemological frameworks that shape audience responses to specific texts. However, fairy tales are heteroglossic and never entirely align with those frameworks. While the authoritative aspects of anthology may have contributed to allowing fairy tales to be used in normative and oppressive ways, as Haase (1993), Zipes (2012, 136), and others have stated, those elements also provide a framework with which to understand and remember the stories. Audience members and/or readers may agree or disagree with the creator's framework as they perceive it, but tale selection and editing allow them to more easily engage with the variety of stories presented. I examine how certain groupings or anthologies have changed the way people think about fairy tales. By considering these specific permutations, I identify how the changing face of fairy tales influences the way we group and identify ourselves.

Oral Repertoires and the Anthologizing Impulse

Current practices and cultural memories of oral storytelling play an important role in shaping fairy-tale anthologies. The roots of popular contemporary fairy tales in oral tradition are a source of debate (Bottigheimer 2009, 2–3); however, it seems clear that many of the stories adapted in literature and other media started as oral narratives. Precisely because these renditions were not written down, it is difficult to know with any certainty what role intertextuality and anthologizing played in such early storytelling traditions. What has remained from this "imagined history," however, is a visual idea of old women or men surrounded by family members and children, sharing the repertoire of stories they have learned and practiced telling throughout their life (Warner 2014, xii). Many editors of anthologies and tale collections use this image of "authentic" fairy tales: Perrault has Mother Goose on the frontispiece of his text, and the Grimms' first cover image is Dorothea Viehmann, who was a central source of their material. Storytellers often are associated with an oral repertoire, not for telling just one story, and traditional practices of group story sharing such as the British *ceilidh* and Italian *veglia* have different tellers presenting stories one after the other. Thus, fairy tales illuminate the intermedial possibilities of anthologizing as an act of putting distinctive stories in association with each other because of some common thematic thread or organizing principle.

Oral storytelling patterns are also related to later forms of anthology through Albert Lord's idea of the "formula" (1960). Although Lord describes oral sung epics rather than fairy tales, his analysis clarifies how consistent tropes can be used to tell new versions of stories. Lord explains that repeated concise verbal formulas aid singers in quickly re-composing a variety of longer verses. He writes that "the picture that emerges is not really one of conflict between preserver of tradition and creative artist; it is rather one of the preservation of tradition by the constant re-creation of it. The ideal is a true story well and truly retold" (29). As with the formulas, specific kernels of the tales alluded to—images, actions, phrases, or associated ideological structures—aid storytellers in creating stories that are simultaneously familiar and new, indicative of both the group and the individual.

Redefining Representations Through Print Anthologies and Tale Collections

The constant retelling of fairy tales in print anthologies has allowed similar tales to resonate with and index identity for a wide variety of readers. The earliest written records we have of what we would now refer to as fairy tales were used to facilitate oral performances. These brief written sketches implied that the stories would be retold and thus re-created in every performance—that certain key motifs or plot elements or characters would remain, but that each performance would be essentially new. Describing the storytellers who used such early texts, Warner (2014) writes, "Voicing was an art of living creators, and the voice of the storyteller was polyphonous; the stories created were all different and the same at one and the same time" (64). She also explains that the manuscripts themselves changed between performances: the records were fluid and the work constantly re-created as it was passed on. As written anthologies have increased in number, their use as indexes for identity has increased, even as this fluidity and constant transformation has continued. If critical intent shapes anthologies, it seems reasonable to assume that fairy-tale anthologies have always redefined what they purport to represent.

When Italian authors Giambattista Basile and Giovanni Francesco Straparola began writing and compiling what fairy-tale scholars identify as the earliest literary collections of fairy tales, what they included helped lay the foundation for contemporary fairy-tale anthologies. The kinds of stories they placed in conjunction were significant: according to Ruth Bottigheimer (2009), Straparola's writing and editing established the genre of "rise tales" (11–13). Nancy Canepa (1999) explains that Basile's *Tale of Tales, or Entertainment for Little Ones* (1932) used an ornate Baroque literary style to translate previously oral narratives like "Cinderella" (ATU 510A) and "Sleeping Beauty" (ATU 410) across the intermedial divide (11–12). Basile also used those stories to comment on contemporary sociohistorical issues, laying the foundation for later written collections to comment on or celebrate their own societies.

Perhaps equally significant, however, was the structure Basile and Straparola used to present their stories as a grouping. Like Boccaccio's *Decameron* (2003), published two centuries prior, Straparola's *Pleasant Nights* (2012) mimics the narrative structure of an oral storytelling session. He uses a single narrator as a framing device and link between a series of tales. His tales are ostensibly independent, discrete texts, and yet because of the single storyteller the reader expects them to be connected. This allowed Straparola to simultaneously appeal to the narrative authority and conservative tradition associated with oral storytelling, but also to retell the stories using uniquely heteroglossic combinations of courtly language and bawdy humor. This melding of oral and written narrative tropes set an important precedent for future compilers of fairy-tale collections. Basile also used a frame narrative, but involved ten old women as the storytellers of his five nights of stories. The frame tale of the false and true brides comments directly on personal identity that affects group identity as well. The use of frame narratives in Basile's and Straparola's texts also seems to have contributed to the tendency of later writers and readers to think of discrete tales as a cohesive group, which also increased their association with identity (Benson 2003).

Anthologies allowed early collectors of fairy tales and wonder tales to make a statement not only about a single story, but about a grouping of stories and the culture or group associated with those stories. This became more evident in the seventeenth century with the onset of the French salon writers, who wrote stories—often about fairies—that drew on oral narratives and posed a counter-narrative to the hegemonic power of religion and state they experienced. Unlike later works' emphasis on the rural, unpolished narrator, the French salon writers' works emphasized the literary ability of their creators. Given this, it is significant that some writers still chose to publish their works as a group and as embedded stories within stories. Catherine d'Aulnoy, whose collection *Les contes des fées* (2009) some scholars describe as the first to use the term *conte de fées*, or fairy tale, appears to have drawn on a variety of contemporary texts as well as oral legend when forming her particular style of fairy stories—eloquent language and other-worldly settings—and her collection directly addressed upper- and middle-class readers in order to critique French society (Bottigheimer 2009, 69–71). As with the Italian writers, however, d'Aulnoy's work was reprinted and popularized for a broader audience. Her use of multiple tales allowed her to create a coherent and pointed narrative that resonated with diverse audiences.

Charles Perrault also published fairy-tale collections in late-seventeenth-century France and drew on a variety of written texts and oral narratives in order to communicate with a specific audience. His choice of tales and presentation style is different than d'Aulnoy's, however: he claims oral narrative as his main source, and his selection of tales has an earthlier setting. Additionally, his texts were marketed primarily for children. Perrault's tale selections and presentation are perhaps closer than d'Aulnoy's to that of many contemporary collections of fairy tales. However, he also used the format of an anthology—introductory text, title, tale selection, and editing—to appeal to a specific demographic, only to see his collections (2009) popularized among a wider, international audience. This pattern clarifies the importance of heteroglossia in anthology—the multivocality of a collection of stories allows them to engage readers beyond those addressed in the creator's framework.

As with retellings of individual tales, structuring and editing an anthology or tale collection allowed creators to both address and critique specific cultural audiences. The way in which anthologies can magnify and transform that ability into a powerful and singular expression of identity became clear a century and a half later with Jacob and Wilhelm Grimm. For the Brothers Grimm, the act of compiling an anthology allowed them to describe a specific world-view and make a political point, but unlike d'Aulnoy and the salon writers, they claimed to be recording or clarifying a world and worldview that already existed, and the political themes of their collection supported the power and legitimacy of the German state rather than undermining it (Georges and Jones 1995, 37–40). They removed certain tales from later editions of their books because they did not seem "German enough" and heavily edited the tales they did include to more clearly reflect supposedly German values: for example, changing the queen in "Snow White" (ATU 709) from the protagonist's mother to a stepmother (Zipes 2016, xxxvii). For the Grimms, anthology was a rhetorical device, and a very successful one.

The popularity of fairy-tale anthologies after the Grimms' success was increased by many other writers who translated existing anthologies, collected tales from their own region, and wrote literary fairy tales. Although the Grimms' texts included oral legends and other kinds of folklore, the writers who responded to their work particularly emphasized fairy tales. Jennifer Schacker (2003) examines the trajectory and influence of tale-collection translators who aimed at nineteenth-century British audiences such as Edgar Taylor, George Dasent, Edward Lane, and T. Crofton Croker. Aleksandr Afanasyev, Elias Lönnrot, Peter Christen Asbjørnsen, Jørgen Moe, and many others compiled national collections of tales and other traditional materials after the Grimms' model. Other authors emphasized literary style and individual authorship, reminiscent of Basile and d'Aulnoy. Hans Christian Andersen, for example, drew from childhood memories of hearing tales for his early works, and thus his stories relate to Danish culture. Yet his tales gained more popularity and attention in translation, showing, like the Grimms', that the grouping of tales by nation need not constrain reaching an international audience (Joosen and Lathey 2014).

While many anthologies focus on characterizing a particular place or group of people, others attempt to represent something universal about the human condition. Like the Brothers Grimm, Andrew Lang's colored fairy books were meant to gather fairy tales and express the collective wisdom, or essential identity, of a group. However, Lang defined the group of people associated with fairy tales as humanity. He attributed fairy tales to the "universal imagination" and suggested that all people share a core set of values expressed in their stories. While scholars have criticized Lang's lack of cultural relativism (Hines 2010), his approach helped change how people conceptualize and use fairy tales as a group. Because Lang's stories were not structurally united by origin, it was important to provide another framing device. He accomplished this by editing his tales to reflect Victorian social norms, marketing his books to children and including vibrant illustrations. While many earlier anthologies of fairy tales also used images—including Taylor's translation of the Grimms with George Cruikshank illustrations (Schacker 2003, 13)—Warner (2014) notes that this period of history marked a rise in illustrated children's books and an increasing association of fairy tales with children and visual storytelling (104).

Questioning the Canon: Anthologies and Mash-Ups in Television

The framing devices that print anthologies use to connect stories and identify target audiences also appear in audiovisual fairy-tale anthologies. Most obviously, the emphasis on the visual aspect of fairy tales retains its importance in these media: audiences might recognize Little Red

Riding Hood or the Pied Piper by what happens in the plot, but they are more likely to notice a red hood or a musician followed by a line of people. Televised anthologies usually connect and simplify discrete tales by picking a specific way to alter the stories that remains consistent throughout the series—for example, changing their setting. The impulse toward complexity is also apparent in both the revision of popular stories and the inclusion of examples not generally considered part of the fairy-tale canon. This urge becomes more obvious when looking at the wide range of stories that screenwriters opt to include. Nevertheless, the premise of TV shows that present fairy tales in a grouping rests at least in part on the assumption that there is a common set of stories audience members will be familiar with and identify as fairy tales.

Starting with the onset of American television in the 1940s, *Shirley Temple's Storybook* (1958–1961) began presenting fairy tales as a grouping on the small screen. Like the Grimms' *Kinder- und Hausmärchen* (2014) and many collections that followed it, *Storybook* did not focus exclusively on fairy tales: instead, it provided a sampling of many popular stories familiar to audiences. However, many of the episodes involved well-known fairy tales. This use reflects one of the more important trends of fairy tales in television: while there are occasionally series that focus exclusively on "fairy tales," in TV as in literature, that term constantly evolves. Further, fairy-tale themes and ideas are often combined with stories or plot elements that most people would consider decidedly not part of the form. Such adaptation complicates an accepted narrative genre for audiences by allowing screenwriters to represent their vision of the cultural identity associated with this narrative legacy. While identifying clear patterns or trends is difficult, broad, overlapping categories of shows include "anthologies" and "mash-ups."

Many programs follow a format similar to that of literary anthologies: the show begins with a narrative framing device, such as a grandmother telling children stories from her childhood, and then moves into a serial recounting of one or more tales per episode. In such cases, tales are presented as discrete narrative arcs. These shows are more diverse than they might appear: while a select few focus on a specific grouping of fairy tales, such as *Kinder- und Hausmärchen*, a more common trend is to include many popular or well-known stories, often with a title that references "stories" rather than fairy tales specifically. Even shows that reference fairy tales in the title, however—like *Hello Kitty's Furry Tale Theatre* (1987)—may begin with the tales of Charles Perrault and the Brothers Grimm and quickly expand to include examples from cultures beyond Europe, from popular literature, and even from movies. TV anthologies that do not include new stories may instead make old stories new by changing crucial details of the plot or setting. Shows like *Fractured Fairy Tales* (1959–1961; 1961–1964) and *Happily Ever After: Fairy Tales for Every Child* (1995–2000) tend to use tales from well-known fairy-tale anthologies but change key details of each episode, expressing a worldview that differs from the one U.S. audiences typically associate with fairy tales.

This re-creation of otherwise familiar narratives is even more apparent in TV shows like *Once Upon a Time in Wonderland* (2013–2014) that weave multiple fairy tales together into a single narrative arc. Called "mash-ups," rather than telling a series of discrete stories from a new perspective, these shows create an entirely new story that reflects the authors' particular vision of fairy tales and the groups of people associated with them. The number of fairy-tale mash-ups seems to have increased in the last five to ten years, with shows like *Once Upon a Time* (2011–) and *Grimm* (2011–2017). These shows follow a serialized format, with characters from specific stories appearing in individual episodes, but they also have consistent characters and story arcs that continue throughout multiple seasons. Despite the fact that the latter two shows came out at the same time and draw from some of the same narrative traditions, their sources are manifestly different, as is their approach to adapting the fairy tale for contemporary audiences.

Once Upon a Time explores the genre boundaries of fairy tale by including a number of Disney properties with varying degrees of proximity to that category, including the Chinese legend of Fa Mulan, J. M. Barrie's *Peter Pan* (1980), and Mary Shelley's *Frankenstein* (2012). In contrast, *Grimm* draws primarily from the stories collected by the Grimms, all of which are clearly culturally marked as fairy tales. However, *Grimm* places these stories into a frame narrative of a cop procedural and emphasizes the gritty, "real," monstrous faces of creatures described in legend. A third, more abstract and integrative approach appears in several Japanese animes that reference fairy tales. *Ookami-San and Her Seven Companions* (2010) uses visual motifs from fairy tales including "Snow White," "Little Red Riding Hood" (ATU 333), and Aesop's fables to shape and complicate the audience's understandings of various characters. For example, one character is portrayed as both Little Red Riding Hood and the poisoned apple that killed Snow White. Mash-ups allow producers to rework fairy tales' expressions of identity more comprehensively, but it seems some creators choose to go the opposite way and use a more direct correlation with existing versions of tales. This process may evince a tendency toward simplifying tales in order to resonate more with audiences.

Characterization and Critique: Film Anthologies and (Re)Creating Identity

Serialized anthologies of fairy tales are more common in television than in movies, presumably because the episodic structure of television lends itself more easily to a series of discrete stories. However, some movies reference multiple fairy tales and use them to create a new story, as do the 2014 adaptation of the musical *Into the Woods* and the 2015 horror *Tale of Tales*. Both of these film adaptations focus on specific textual sources: *Into the Woods* on the tales of the Grimms and Perrault, and *Tale of Tales* on the stories of Basile. In that sense they, unlike some of the television anthologies, seem to further the association of a particular group of stories with a particular culture, time, and place. Both movies are set in fantastic worlds that parallel common ideas about medieval Europe: Germany and Italy, respectively. However, both movies also use the body of tales they reference to critique and undermine contemporary expectations of fairy tales having a happy ending.

Familiarity and innovation enable a third consistent impulse in fairy-tale anthologies: the desire to characterize and critique a worldview or culture associated with a set of stories. Fairy-tale scholars like Zipes, Schacker, and Christine Jones have repeatedly voiced their opposition to the idea that fairy tales are inherently simple and have demonstrated that they are complex and powerful tools used for more than didactic moral lessons and nationalist group identities. But it is the mutually constituting simplicity and heteroglossia in fairy tales that allows them to challenge the social norms they represent. Whether or not the creator of an anthology explicitly makes a critical argument about the group of people whose stories he or she is anthologizing, the rhetorical function of presenting fairy tales in a group is to make a statement about identity. To be clear, individual fairy tales have a similar function when they are shared, but by simultaneously engaging in a conversation between stories and defining the boundaries of that conversation, anthologies can be used as a powerful representation of a group. Television and film have not necessarily changed this process, but they provide a window into how quickly this process occurs and how often our definition of fairy tales and anthologies is in flux.

Related topics: Adaptation and the Fairy-Tale Web; Broadcast; Children's Television; Cinematic; Convergence Culture; Hybridity; Oral Tradition; Print; Storyworlds/Narratology

JESSIE RIDDLE

Note

1. All these titles reflect specific facets of the process of sharing fairy tales. I sometimes use the term "author" to refer to it. Henry Glassie notes that emic concepts of and terms for authorship vary, but he also describes similarities: "I would generalize that all narratives are simultaneously informational and artful, and that the more the artful prevails over the informational, the more likely are narrators to think of themselves as authors and to be taken as authors by others" (2013, 527).

References Cited and Further Reading

Andersen, Hans Christian. 2006. *Fairy Tales*, translated by Tiina Nunnally. New York: Penguin.

Bacchilega, Cristina. 2013. *Fairy Tales Transformed? Twenty-First Century Adaptations and the Politics of Wonder.* Detroit: Wayne State UP.

Bakhtin, Mikhail. 1982. "Discourse in the Novel." In *The Dialogic Imagination: Four Essays by Mikhail Bakhtin*, edited by Michael Holquist, 269–422. Austin: U Texas P.

Barrie, J. M. (1911) 1980. *Peter Pan.* New York: Simon and Schuster Children's Publishing.

Barthes, Roland. 1974. *S/Z: An Essay*, translated by Richard Miller. New York: Hill and Wang.

Basile, Giambattista. 1932. *The Pentamerone*, translated and edited by Norman Penzer. 2 vols. London: John Lane and the Bodley Head.

Benson, Stephen. 2003. *Cycles of Influence: Fiction, Folktale, Theory.* Detroit: Wayne State UP.

Boccaccio, Giovanni. 2003. *The Decameron*, translated and edited by G. H. McWilliam. London: Penguin Books.

Bottigheimer, Ruth B. 2009. *Fairy Tales: A New History.* Albany: SUNY P.

Canepa, Nancy. 1999. *From Court to Forest: Giambattista Basile's Lo cunto de li cunti and the Birth of the Literary Fairy Tale.* Detroit: Wayne State UP.

D'Aulnoy, Marie Catherine Baronne. 2009. *Fairy Tales*, translated by Annie Macdonell. Gloucester: Dodo P.

Georges, Robert A., and Michael Owen Jones. 1995. *Folkloristics: An Introduction.* Bloomington: Indiana UP.

Glassie, Henry. 2013. "Authorship in Oral Narrative." In *Marvelous Transformations*, edited by Christine A. Jones and Jennifer Schacker, 523–8. Peterborough, ON: Broadview P.

Grimm, Jacob, and Wilhelm Grimm. 2014. *The Complete First Edition: The Original Folk and Fairy Tales of the Brothers Grimm*, translated and edited by Jack Zipes. Princeton, NJ: Princeton UP.

Haase, Donald. 1993. "Yours, Mine, or Ours? Perrault, the Brothers Grimm, and the Ownership of Fairy Tales." *Marvels & Tales* 7 (2): 383–402.

Hines, Sara. 2010. "Collecting the Empire: Andrew Lang's Fairy Books (1889–1910)." *Marvels & Tales* 24 (1): 39–56.

Jones, Christine A., and Jennifer Schacker. 2013. "On Fairy Tales and their Anthologies." In *Marvelous Transformations*, edited by Christine A. Jones and Jennifer Schacker, 493–8. Peterborough, ON: Broadview P.

Joosen, Vanessa, and Gillian Lathey, eds. 2014. *Grimms' Tales Around the Globe: The Dynamics of Their International Reception.* Detroit: Wayne State UP.

Lang, Andrew. (1965) 1982. *The Green Fairy Book.* New York: Dover Publications.

Lerer, Seth. 2003. "Medieval English Literature and the Idea of the Anthology." *PMLA* 118 (5): 1251–67.

Lord, Albert B. 1960. *The Singer of Tales*, edited by Stephen Mitchell and Gregory Nagy. 2nd ed. Vol. 1. Cambridge, MA: Harvard UP.

Perrault, Charles. 2008. *The Fairy Tales of Charles Perrault*, translated by Angela Carter. London: Penguin.

———. 2009. *The Complete Fairy Tales*, translated Christopher Betts. Oxford: Oxford UP.

Schacker, Jennifer. 2003. *National Dreams: The Remaking of Fairy Tales in Nineteenth Century England.* Philadelphia: U Pennsylvania P.

Shelley, Mary. (1818) 2012. *Frankenstein: The 1818 Text, Contexts, Criticisms.* 2nd ed. New York: W.W. Norton & Company.

Straparola, Giovan Francesco. 2012. *The Pleasant Nights*, translated by W. G. Waters, edited by Donald Beecher. 2 vols. Toronto: U Toronto P.

Toelken, Barre. 1996. "The Folklore Process." In *The Dynamics of Folklore*, 31–54. Logan: Utah State UP.

Warner, Marina. 2014. *Once Upon a Time: A Short History of Fairy Tale.* Oxford: Oxford UP.

Zipes, Jack. 2012. *The Irresistible Fairy Tale.* Princeton, NJ: Princeton UP.

———. 2016. *The Original Folk and Fairy Tales of the Brothers Grimm: The Complete First Edition.* Princeton, NJ: Princeton UP.

ANTHOLOGIES AND TALE COLLECTIONS

Mediagraphy

The Bullwinkle Show: Fractured Fairy Tales (TV). 1961–1964. Creators Jay Ward, Bill Scott, and Alex Anderson. USA.

Grimm (TV). 2011–2017. Creators Stephen Carpenter, David Greenwalt, and Jim Kouf. USA.

Happily Ever After: Fairy Tales for Every Child (TV). 1995–2000. Directors Bruce W. Smith, Anthony Bell, and Edward Bell. USA.

Hello Kitty's Furry Tale Theatre (TV). 1987. Director Michael Maliani. Canada/USA/Japan.

Into the Woods. 2014. Director Rob Marshall. USA.

Ōkami-san to Shichinin no Nakamatachi (Ōkami-san and Her Seven Companions) (TV). 2010. Creator J. C. Staff. Japan.

Once Upon a Time (TV). 2011–. Creators Adam Horowitz and Edward Kitsis. USA.

Once Upon a Time in Wonderland (TV). 2013–2014. Creators Jane Espenson, Zack Estrin, Adam Horowitz, and Edward Kitsis. USA.

Rocky and His Friends: Fractured Fairy Tales (TV). 1959–1961. Creators Jay Ward, Bill Scott, and Alex Anderson. USA.

Shirley Temple's Storybook (TV). 1958–1961. Presented by Shirley Temple. USA.

Tale of Tales. 2015. Director Matteo Garrone. Italy/France/UK.

44

AUTOBIOGRAPHY

Martine Hennard Dutheil de la Rochère

Autobiography is a slippery genre that notoriously defies easy definition. Its codes, norms, and conventions are culturally and historically variable, and it encompasses a great variety of narrative forms such as memoirs, diaries, letters, testimonies, and personal essays in print and other media while also including more allusive or oblique types of life-writing like autobiographical fiction. Although autobiography extends to nonverbal forms of self-expression like illustration, photography, film, video, and performance art, I mainly focus on written narrative media.

Recording memories and experience in autobiographical form presupposes the notion of an individualized self, the possibility of assuming a personal voice, and a belief in the value and interest of rendering the story of one's life. It also implies that producing, circulating, and publishing such documents is a socially acceptable form of self-expression. It therefore postulates that identity is not merely determined by tradition, family, or community, but shaped in the interaction of individual self and social context, private life and public image—a complex process of self-fashioning and self-accomplishment. Autobiography was made possible by Enlightenment notions of selfhood and fostered by Romantic self-inquiry, self-actualization, and artistic self-creation and was popularized during the nineteenth century when fictional autobiography was the model for the European *Bildungsroman*; it was followed by more experimental forms of life-writing in the twentieth century to the present day.

Philippe Lejeune defines autobiography as a "retrospective prose narrative written by a real person concerning his existence, where the focus is his individual life, in particular the story of his personality" (1989, 4) in a novel, poem, diary, or essay. He emphasizes the genre's contractual and relational dimension premised on its documentary value (at once factual and subjective) and that it is usually written in the first person. And yet, many autobiographies explore the inevitable blurring of the boundary between life-writing and fiction-making, due to circumstances, subjectivity, the workings of memory, and the nature of language and narrative. Moreover, internal as well as external factors such as familial, social, cultural, religious, or political constraints have led some authors to resort to disguises, pseudonyms, indirection, and allegory to express more troubled, fluid, porous, or fragmented concepts of selfhood. Some draw on fairy-tale plots, motifs, or characters to capture the tension between individual trajectory and collective script. Because the fairy tale has long been a predominantly female form and provides suitable role models or masks, many women have represented their lives in fairy-tale terms throughout the centuries.

Although fairy-tale autobiography may seem contradictory, the combination is not so unusual or surprising. Because the fairy tale is associated with anonymous folklore and perceived as non-realistic, exhibiting its fictional status, this hybrid form complicates Lejeune's pact with the reader. And yet, ordinary people, writers, and fairy-tale scholars alike note the identificatory force and inspiring roles offered by the fairy tale and its impact on their self-image, career path, or worldview, and testify to its paradoxical appropriateness to articulate personal experience and intimate truths. Jack Zipes invites parallels with "Jack and the Beanstalk" (ATU 328A) as he half playfully compares his good luck to that of "the troubled and fortunate protagonists of fairy tales" (2016a, x). Pauline Greenhill takes her childhood reading of folktales and her identification with "Fitcher's Bird" (ATU 311) as a queer "self-creation" in adulthood as a starting point to investigate self-image and articulate a feminist critique of the psychoanalytical model of the mirror-stage (2008). Marina Warner, whose creative and critical work has long evolved in complementary and contrapuntal fashion, also develops these parallels in her autobiography in progress, *Inventory of a Life Mislaid*. In fact, many fairy-tale critics link their fascination for the fairy tale with a story read in childhood that captured their experience of the world in metaphoric fashion. The "my favorite story when I was young" rubric of the fairy-tale journal *Gramarye* includes (in order of appearance) contributions from Maria Nicolajeva, Martine Hennard Dutheil de la Rochère, William Gray, Jacqueline Simpson, Colin Manlove, Sadhana Naithani, Ruth B. Bottigheimer, Donald Haase, and Diane Purkiss.

Because autobiography requires storytelling skills and a capacity to organize individual life in structured narrative form, fairy-tale conventions provide familiar plots, patterns, images, and themes that give a recognizable shape to the biographical material and make it communicable to oneself and to readers. Moreover, from a psychological point of view, many writers comment that childhood acquires a fairy-tale dimension in the retrospective act of autobiography. Authors of fairy-tale autobiographies thus tend to revisit familiar tropes, playing with repetition and difference, endorsement and irony, and the tension between autobiography's factual claims and the fictionalizing effects of its textual and imaginative re-creation.

As "fables of the politics of experience" (Carter 1998, 452), fairy tales thus draw attention to the complex interrelations between individual life and collective script. Glossing Italo Calvino's claim that "folktales are real" (*le fiabe sono vere*), Warner observes that, in keeping with the form's utopian spirit, "The structures of wonder and magic open ways of recording experience while imagining a time when suffering will be over" (2014, 74). As such, first-person testimonies and fairy tales alike are driven by a common desire to share human-interest stories that contain useful life lessons or messages of hope.

It is therefore no strange paradox that the fairy tale has long served as a blueprint for telling one's life story in a more or less overt fashion. Because these age-old narratives are grounded in material history and experience, they speak of the dangers, opportunities, and possibilities of living in the world and provide ready-made scripts for imagining human life in narrative form: "From the beginning," says Zipes, "fairy tales were symbolic commentaries on the mores and customs of a particular society and the classes and groups within these societies and how their actions and relations could lead to success and happiness" (2000, xxi). Passed on by storytellers who lent them their own voice, the form's alleged anonymity granted narrators freedom to use, adapt, and reshape the material as they thought best. From the perspective of feminist folkloristics, Cristina Bacchilega discusses how women have long used folktales to voice their concerns and tell their life stories in oblique ways, often resorting to coding strategies to offer counter-narratives of female agency or resilience (1995; see also Radner and Lanser 1987).

Because fairy tales deal with basic human concerns, fears, hopes, and desires, they suggest that life-writing is bound up with fiction-making as a paradoxical condition for truth-telling. Thus, in the course of history, anonymous storytellers and published authors alike have drawn on the form to utter unpalatable truths or celebrate triumph over adversity in the guise of anonymous lore or children's stories. Warner insists on the crucial—if often hidden or encrypted—realistic dimension that only appears when these stories are read in context: "The experiences these stories recount are remembered, lived experiences of women [. . .] rooted in the social, legal and economic history of marriage and the family" (1994, 238), and Elizabeth Wanning Harries has unfolded its rich written history from the seventeenth to the late twentieth century (2003).

The fairy tale as a literary form, paralleling the advent of modernity in Europe, allowed for new experiments with fairy tales as authored texts written in a playful "double register" (Warner 2014, 147) allowing for satire, polemic, and sexual critique as well as disguised biographical commentary. Among other aristocratic *conteuses*, Marie-Catherine d'Aulnoy wrote memoirs of the French, English, and Spanish courts, but made more pointed comments on courtly life, arranged marriages, thwarted love, and female desire in her two fairy-tale collections (1697 and 1698) (see Seifert 1996). Unhappily married at sixteen and exiled after plotting against her husband, for d'Aulnoy the fairy tale provided a form of self-expression safer than memoirs or private correspondence to preserve their author's reputation.

It is no wonder that these women represented themselves as fairies and fairy godmothers in these subtly ironic tales, including Marie-Jeanne L'Héritier de Villandon, who "inscrib[ed] her autobiographical situation in a modernist version of the genre's female transmission" (Hannon 1998, 195). It is tempting to read Gabrielle-Suzanne de Villeneuve's and Jeanne-Marie Leprince de Beaumont's versions of "Beauty and the Beast" (ATU 425C) as disguised autobiographies, self-consciously invested with personal significance to reflect on patriarchal structures, social strictures, unhappy marriages, and monstrous husbands. The form thus offered recognizable plots that offered a free space to reflect on personal experience and explore utopian possibilities for artistic, emotional, or erotic fulfillment while providing the necessary disguise to ward off social reprobation and censorship. The form invited multilevel interpretation where informed readers could elicit critical and subversive commentary underneath the glitter of the mock-naive *contes merveilleux*.

Even the much tamer didactic tales for the nursery published in the eighteenth century, when the form was appropriated and reconfigured for children, such as those of the French governess Beaumont in her *Magasin des Enfants* (1756), contain autobiographical allusions and real-life settings. Beaumont's volume is organized around Melle Bonne, a fictional double for the author herself as a governess, pedagogue, and promoter of girls' education. The book is framed to reproduce the specific circumstances of its production, while the dialogues between the governess and her pupils are inspired by Beaumont's life models. Lewis Carroll adopted a similar strategy in *Alice's Adventures in Wonderland* (1865). From the late seventeenth century onward, the fairy tale should not be reduced to a futile literary fashion or "civilizing" tool to enforce morals and manners; it was used to make subtle social and political commentaries and reflect on the authors' own living conditions, experiences, concerns, and opinions.

"Autobiography is an inherently Romantic form," Frances Wilson argues (2014, 71), and the word was coined at the turn of the nineteenth century ("self-biography," "auto-biography"). The success of fictional memoirs and confessions was nevertheless accompanied by anxieties about the genre's instability, materialized in the proliferation of split selves and doubles in European fiction. Simultaneously, the revival of the literary fairy tale (*Kunstmärchen*) in Romantic literature served to criticize bourgeois values and beliefs and celebrate human creativity. It often represented singular men or women struggling against an oppressive social order that crushes imagination, feelings, desires, and artistic aspirations in the name of religious duty, social order, and conventional morality.

Jeannine Blackwell discusses the recasting of fairy tales as autobiography by women writers who used the form "for introspection, life narration, as metaphor for traumatic psychosocial events, social criticism, and—above all—entertainment" (2004, 74). Among others, she mentions Goethe's close friend and key figure of the movement, Bettina von Arnim, who adopted a fairy-tale structure for her childhood memories centering on the death of her mother in *Clemens Brentanos Frühlingskranz* (Clemens Brentano's Spring Wreath 1844). While Goethe's autobiographical *Dichtung und Wahrheit* (Poetry and Truth 1811–1833) sought to demonstrate the organic nature and universal significance of his intellectual and artistic development, Bettina's life-writing imaginatively reworks her memories and correspondence and traces her relationship with her brother from early intimacy to ultimate rejection of conventional female roles.

The weaving of fairy-tale patterns, motifs, and allusions in nineteenth-century novels of education with strong biographical resonances, such as Charles Dickens's *David Copperfield* (1849–50) and Charlotte Brontë's *Jane Eyre* (1847), also shows fairy-tale intertexts framing but also ironizing male and female destinies. Hans Christian Andersen's *Das Märchen meines Lebens ohne Dichtung* (The Fairy Tale of My Life: An Autobiography 1847) is one of three autobiographies, the last reinterpreting and reimagining his life to conform most fully to fairy-tale conventions. Andersen explored various literary forms (poetry, drama, novel, travelogue, autobiography) and experimented with hybridized genres to the point of considering his literary fairy tales as a type of life-writing, at once realistic and subjective: "Most of what I have written is a reflection of myself. Every character is from life" (quoted in Høyrup 2016, 34).

Andersen considered "The Ugly Duckling" (1843) a physical and psychological self-portrait that captured his remarkable life trajectory. The fairy tale reflects the Romantic view of individual talent as more powerful than the contingencies of social background and ungainly appearance, and Andersen uses it to celebrate his overcoming of adverse circumstances and self-transformation into a famous, admired, and influential author (Høyrup 2016, 33–37). The fairy-tale form thus served self-mythifying and/or self-ironizing purposes, bearing witness to exceptional or non-normative trajectories in oblique fashion and often hinting at the discrepancy between social image and intimate self.

The fairy tale indeed allowed for a mapping of personal experience onto wish-fulfillment fantasies while conveying an implicit critique of social norms, values, and conventions. Oscar Wilde revisited and parodied several stories by Andersen in his own symbolist fairy-tale collections, *The Happy Prince and Other Tales* (1888) and *A House of Pomegranates* (1891). Moreover, "It is a poignant irony, often noted, that the hauntingly tragic qualities of Wilde's fairy tales were to foreshadow many of the experiences of his own life" (Gavin 2016, 1102). The irony and melancholy, implicit critique of Victorian morality and social inequality, and mournful reflections on the artist's role, as well as the homoerotic undertones of "The Happy Prince," have been widely read in biographical terms. Bettina Kümmerling-Meibauer documents how Hugo von Hoffmannstahl (1874–1929), Robert Musil (1880–1942), and Alfred Döblin (1878–1957) also resorted to fairy-tale motifs and elements in their notebooks, letters, diaries, travel accounts, and memoirs and, conversely, how several of their *Kunstmärchen* have autobiographical sources.

In the twentieth century, the twin popularity of autobiography and fairy tale led to self-conscious experiments responding to historical events including two murderous world wars, the feminist movement, the development of psychological/psychoanalytical criticism, and the rise of literary theory in the post-war period, which led to countless retellings and the fairy tale's rebirth as a form for adults in book form and, increasingly, through mass media and new technologies. The writer, poet, ethnologist, and art critic Michel Leiris (1901–1990), who experimented with auto-ethnography in *L'Âge d'homme* (1939, Manhood), begins the first volume of his autobiography *La Règle du jeu*, entitled *Biffures* (1948, Scratches), with "Once upon a time" to foreground the form's fictive and reconstructive nature.

Several authors have drawn on the darker side of classic fairy tales to deal with traumatic historical events, memories, and cultural legacies (war, persecution, exile, accident, sexual abuse). The Holocaust, in particular, has been the subject of novels, fictionalized autobiographies, and memoirs that use fairy-tale/folktale structures and motifs to tackle traumatic experience and represent the unspeakable in metaphoric ways. The familiar stories allow the oblique expression and communication of intimate, secret, or taboo material (witnessed or co-witnessed) across generations while linking historical and personal events to collective memory.

Donald Haase underlines how autobiographies of war survivors draw on "the fairy tale's potential as an emotional strategy" (2000, 361) to maintain hope and a sense of human bond and thus become "a psychological survival tool" (372) to outlive concentration camp horrors. Extremities and atrocities find expression in striking fairy-tale imagery or motifs (fear, hunger, evil, violence, murder, captivity, abuse) that capture intimate and collective truths that could not be shared otherwise. In spite of its inevitable ambiguities, the fairy-tale intertext in autobiographical fiction communicates unspeakable experience, as Federica K. Clementi argues with regard to Ruth Klüger's autobiography, *Still Alive: A Holocaust Girlhood Remembered* (2001), seen as "a post-modern fairy tale" (2008, 44).

Co-witnessing has become a pressing issue as survivors disappear and historical memory is lost among younger generations. Maurice Sendak's allusive illustrations for the Grimms' "Dear Mili" ([*Liebe Milli*, 1816] 1988) are a testimony to his troubled youth as the son of Holocaust-haunted parents. Art Spiegelman's graphic novel series *Maus: A Survivor's Tale* (1986–1991) memorializes his father's experiences as a Polish Jew during the Holocaust in an animal fable/folktale and his sharing this traumatic legacy with his son: "Using a frame narrative within which his father tells his survivor's tale of Nazi persecution and internment in Auschwitz, Spiegelman also engages his own difficult relationship with his father, underlining that this graphic novel combines fiction, survivor's tale, and autobiography of a second-generation Holocaust artist" (Haase 2016, 461). Jane Yolen's young adult novel *Briar Rose* (1992) reworks biographical material in fictional form by centering on the passing on of traumatic Holocaust memories to third-generation American Jews (Hennard Dutheil de la Rochère and Viret 2011). In a private exchange (2016), Yolen drew my attention to a new Holocaust novel she is writing for young adults (2018), mobilizing "Hansel and Gretel" (ATU 327) to talk about the Lodz Ghetto, Polish partisans, and the labor camps. In this forthcoming book, she again merges historical fact and fairy tale to address co-witnessing, family legacy, and cultural memory.

As Elisabeth Wanning Harries shows (2000), women writers have responded to the fairy tale in diverse and contradictory ways to address issues of female identity, prescribed social roles and models, and self-representation, often using the magic mirror as a metaphor to narrate their life stories. Christa Wolf's childhood memories of a Nazi childhood in *Kindheitsmuster* (Patterns of Childhood, 1976) and Carolyn Kay Steedman's double biography/autobiography *Landscape for a Good Woman* (1986) exemplify modern uses of the fairy tale to address the problematic articulation of private and public selves, hidden and official identities, and children's sense of doubling, dilemmas, and distress as they grow up in deeply disturbing family environments and war time. Francesca Duranti's fictional autobiographies also mobilize fairy-tale conventions to reflect on female struggles for selfhood and self-expression, as in *Lieto fine* (Happy Ending, 1987).

Since the 1970s, the rise of critical studies investigating the psychological impact and socio-historical relevance of fairy tales has inspired many authors to represent their life in fairy-tale terms and has led to a veritable fashion for fairy-tale retellings in short fiction and novelistic form (see Joosen 2011). Bruno Bettelheim's hugely influential *The Uses of Enchantment* (1976) insisted on tales' importance in developing the human psyche and their therapeutic function in overcoming conflicts and crises. Taking their cue from Bettelheim (or quarreling with him like Angela Carter), many women writers have revisited the fairy-tale tradition to explore alternative life choices and depart from heteronormative plots. Olga Broumas in *Beginning with O* (1977) and Emma Donoghue in *Kissing the Witch* (1997), among others, use traditional stories to question fixed gender roles and inscribe their intimate and often painful experiences in poetry or prose. Although biographical readings of literary works are no doubt reductive and limiting, reading fiction as autobiography raises complex interrelations between reality and fiction in the shaping of identity.

Kate Bernheimer (1998) presents reflections on fairy tales shaping women's imagination and sense of self, starting with her memories of watching Disney's fairy-tale movies in her grandfather's basement. Her collection gathers autobiographical essays by twenty-eight women writers, including Julia Alvarez's self-portrait as a survivor of a cruel dictatorship, Margaret Atwood's association of her birth at the beginning of WWII with the Grimms' tales, A. S. Byatt's sense of isolation finding an echo in "The Snow Queen," and Maria Flook's finding in "Rapunzel" (ATU 310) the means to survive adolescence. Joyce Carol Oates reflects on the tension between the stereotypical images of fairy tales and the realities of women's lives, and Terri Windling poignantly tells about domestic abuse and the silence imposed on the victims in fairy-tale terms, in this collection, as well as in *The Armless Maiden and Other Tales for Childhood's Survivors* (1995). For these women, the fairy tale offers existential, psychological, and narrative resources with which to deal with traumatic or taboo material while offering a suitable aesthetic form to express it.

Fairy-tale autobiography also takes the form of children's literature, now recognized as an art form in its own right and addressing a crossover audience. The interplay of translation and encrypted autobiographical rewritings of fairy tales is exemplified in Yagawa Sumiko's work (1930–2002). A poet and translator of *Heidi, Alice's Adventures in Wonderland,* and the Grimms' tales, Sumiko is also a renowned writer of children's books. Following her translation of *Red Riding Hood* (Rotkäppchen) for a picture book (2001), her retelling *Omimai,* published the same year, is about a girl and her cat visiting an elderly woman in a wheelchair. The new version challenges stereotypes of old age and disability to emphasize a shared moment between girl and grandmother, blurring the boundaries between past, present, and future. As Tomoko Aoyama points out, Yagawa had planned an alternative (and more disturbing) ending that suggests the girl's sudden death (2015, 50). This darker narrative path, rejected by the editor and publisher, can be seen as foreshadowing the author's suicide the following year, drawing attention once again to the complex interweaving of life and storytelling.

The fairy tale has become a privileged mode for marginalized or persecuted artist figures threatened by censorship, hate campaigns, and state violence. Salman Rushdie's *Haroun and the Sea of Stories* (1990), addressed to his young son Zafar, offers a way of maintaining hope and keeping on writing despite the death sentence for "blasphemy" that had sent him into hiding in the aftermath of the publication of *The Satanic Verses* (1988). This thinly disguised fictional autobiography transmutes the persecuted writer's dire situation into an Oriental fantasy about the need to preserve freedom of imagination and storytelling and thus opts for fairy-tale allegorical writing for children to conjure fear, despair, and silencing.

Fairy-tale autobiography also pertains to non-literary or mixed artistic forms such as film, photography, and performance arts. The autobiographical resonances of Jean Cocteau's classic film version of *La belle et la bête.* (1946), starring the filmmaker's partner, Jean Marais, as the Beast, are implied in the director's making-of journal. Zipes (2011) mentions films based on Andersen's fantasized autobiography but finds the alleged autobiographical resonances of Disney's animated *Pinocchio* (1940, after Carlo Collodi's *Pinocchio*) "somewhat misleading (and yet compelling)" (305). In contrast, the autobiographical dimension of Jacques Demy's fairy-tale films, with their characteristic mix of fantasy and intimate biographical material, has been investigated by Anne Duggan, teasing out the queering of gender, sexuality, and class in such films as *Peau d'Âne* (Donkey Skin, 1979) and *The Pied Piper* (1972) as Demy's own self-construction against more domesticated or socially acceptable images (Duggan 2013, 8).

The traditional association of autobiography with writing needs expansion to encompass other modes of memorializing experience through the fairy tale in the twenty-first century. The democratization and segmentation of the book market (see DiBattista and Wittman 2014), the collapse of traditional distinctions between high and popular culture, and the growing success of mass media and celebrity culture have resulted in the proliferation of fairy-tale autobiographies ironically anticipated by Anne Sexton's retelling of "Cinderella" in *Transformations* (1971). The fairy tale remains a favorite mode for exploring life experience today in testimonial or inspirational books, in keeping with Zipes's understanding of the form as "providing a metaphorical means to step back and, for a brief moment, regard solutions or ways to strategize one's approach to daily existence" (Zipes 2016a, 6).

The fairy tale as a shared cultural reference with its familiar symbolic language, clear moral values and recognizable types, and characteristic mix of adventures, triumph over adversity, and romance, has an immediate appeal and commercial potential. It is thus mobilized to turn the lives of pop, rock, or media stars into easily marketable media fare, as in Jo Wood's *Hey Jo: A Rock and Roll Fairytale* (2013) or Fantasia's Cinderella-like tale as a school drop-out and teenage mother turned American Idol superstar in *Life Is Not a Fairy Tale* (2005).

TV programs also capitalize on the form to seduce audiences and invite identification. Linda Lee has shown how reality TV mobilizes fairy-tale elements and effects in programs like *Extreme Makeover* (2002–2007), *Who Wants to Marry a Multi-Millionaire?* (1999–2000), *The Bachelor* (2002–)/*The Bachelorette* (2003–), and *Beauty and the Geek* (2005–2008). These programs typically draw on "Cinderella" (ATU 510A), "Beauty and the Beast," and "The Ugly Duckling" to promote dominant cultural values and reinforce social norms like the heteronormative nuclear family, social status and wealth as synonymous with happiness, an uncritical embrace of commodity culture and dominant standards of beauty, and ruthless competition among women (and, more recently, men). The shows present supposedly unscripted situations and allegedly spontaneous autobiographical reflections or confessions by contestants. Explicitly or implicitly, they invite the audience to identify with a range of character types based on the kind and unkind girl prototype (ATU 480) while playing with unexpected twists and turns of the plot and manipulating expectations. Claudia Schwabe (2014) discusses the blurring of the boundary between fantasy and reality in fairy-tale series and identification of actors and viewers alike with fairy-tale characters.

Fairy-tale autobiography has also become ubiquitous in new media, and the boundary between reality and fiction is increasingly blurred in fairy-tale themed live TV shows, gaming, and self-representation as fairy-tale icons on social media and through cosplay. The growth in the cultural significance of games—role-playing, board, and computer—shows how pleasure and performance have become publicly linked through play, informing self-images and standing in for life itself. The Disney corporation encourages viewers to identify with fairy-tale princesses through video games like *Disney Princess: My Fairy Tale Adventure* (2012), as well as quizzes on social media, dressing up, and fairy-tale themed weddings at Disney World. Life and fairy tale have become so indistinguishable that the Disney corporation was sued for $250 million by an author claiming that *Frozen* (2013) was stolen from her autobiography in 2014 (Denham 2014).

New media not only revive reader or viewer identification with specific characters and situations, such as casting oneself as a fairy-tale character in games like *American McGee's Alice* (2000), but can be seen as a new form of life-writing and even lifestyle. Fostered by electronic media, fairy-tale communities invite prolonged identification with iconic characters through role-playing games (RPGs) and massively multiplayer online role-playing games (MMORPGs) such as *Fairyland Online*. They seek to absorb the player for hours, days, or weeks to the point that the avatar becomes inseparable from the player and the time spent on gaming activities and virtual worlds indistinguishable from real life.

The online dating application Tinder has generated the "Tinderella," and modern-day bios and blogs based on "Cinderella" or "Little Red Riding Hood" (ATU 333) abound. Blogs offer a modern-day equivalent of the memoirs or diaries of old, although mostly written by ordinary people and immediately accessible to thousands of readers online. They too suggest a continuum of fictional and situational constructs of life in the twenty-first century. Katherine Langrish's "Seven Miles of Steel Thistles" blog gathers pieces by fantasy writers discussing fairy tales that have deep personal resonances. Windling's inspiring weekly "Tunes for a Monday morning" blog also presents life-inspired essays on a personal theme, relevant topic, or aspect of folklore, fairy tale, or fantasy. She weaves together reflections based on traditional stories, illustrations, photography, arts, and crafts, focusing on how fairy tales enable us to reconnect with the essentials of life, writing, body, self, loved ones, and community, but also animals, the natural world, and our immediate environment. Fairy-tale autobiography today may therefore hint at possibilities for more fluid identities, and new ways of reconnecting with the self, as well as with more meaningful communities and modes of being.

Related topics: Blogs and Websites; Children's and Young Adult (YA) Literature; Cinematic; Criticism; Disability; Disney Corporation; Gender; Hybridity; Novels; Reality TV; Video Games

References Cited and Further Reading

Andersen, Hans Christian. 1843. *New Fairy Tales (Nye Eventyr)*. Copenhagen: C. A. Reitzel.

———. (1847) 2000. *The Fairy Tale of My Life: An Autobiography (Das Märchen meines Lebens ohne Dichtung)*. New York: Cooper Press Square.

Bacchilega, Cristina. 1995. "'Writing' and 'Voice': The Articulations of Gender in Folklore and Literature." In *Folklore, Literature, and Cultural Theory: Collected Essays*, edited by Cathy Lynn Preston, 83–101. New York: Garland Publishing.

Beaumont, Jeanne-Marie Leprince de. (1756) 2000. *Contes et autres écrits*, edited by Barbara Kaltz. Oxford: Voltaire Foundation Ltd.

Bernheimer, Kate, ed. 1998. *Mirror, Mirror on the Wall: Women Writers Explore their Favorite Fairy Tales*. New York: Anchor Books.

Bettelheim, Bruno. 1976. *The Uses of Enchantment: The Meaning and Importance of Fairy Tales*. New York: Knopf.

Blackwell, Jeannine. 2004. "German Fairy Tales: A User's Manual." In *Fairy Tales and Feminism: New Approaches*, edited by Donald Haase, 73–98. Detroit: Wayne State UP.

Brontë, Charlotte. (1847) 2006. *Jane Eyre*, edited by Stevie Davis. London: Penguin Classics, 2006.

Broumas, Olga. 1977. *Beginning with O*. New Haven, CT: Yale UP.

Carroll, Lewis. (1865) 1998. *Alice's Adventures in Wonderland and Through the Looking-Glass*, edited by Hugh Haughton. London: Penguin Classics.

Carter, Angela. (1976) 1998. "The Better to Eat You With." In *Shaking a Leg: Collected Journalism and Writings*, edited by Jenny Uglow, 451–5. London: Vintage.

Clementi, Federica K. 2008. "Re-Centering the Mother: Shoah Autobiography in Ruth Klüger, Edith Bruck, Sarah Kofman." Dissertation. New York: CUNY.

Denham, Jess. 2014. "Disney Sued for $250 Million after Woman Claims *Frozen* Is Stolen from Her Life Story." *Independent UK*, September 25. www.independent.co.uk/arts-entertainment/films/news/disney-sued-for-250-million-by-woman-claiming-frozen-is-stolen-from-her-life-story-9754862.html.

DiBattista, Maria, and Emily O. Wittman. 2014. "Introduction." In *The Cambridge Companion to Autobiography*, edited by Maria DiBattista and Emily O. Wittman, 1–20. Cambridge: Cambridge UP.

Dickens, Charles. 1850. *David Copperfield*, edited by Jeremy Tambling. London: Penguin Classics, 2004.

Donoghue, Emma. 1997. *Kissing the Witch: Old Tales in New Skins*. New York: HarperCollins.

Duggan, Anne E. 2013. *Queer Enchantments: Gender, Sexuality and Class in the Fairy-Tale Cinema of Jacques Demy.* Detroit: Wayne State UP.

Duranti, Francesca. (1987) 1991. *Happy Ending (Lieto fine),* translated by Annapaola Concogni. London: Random House.

Fantasia. 2005. *Life Is Not a Fairy Tale.* New York: Fireside (Simon & Schuster).

Gavin, Adrienne E. "Wilde, Oscar." In *Folk Tales and Fairy Tales: Traditions and Texts from around the World,* edited by Anne E. Duggan and Donald Haase, with Helen J. Callow, 1101–3. Santa Barbara: Greenwood.

Goethe, Johann Wolfgang von. (1811–1833) 1948. *Aus meinem Leben: Dichtung und Wahrheit.* Hamburger Ausgabe in 14 Bänden. Hamburg, 1948. www.zeno.org/Literatur/M/Goethe,+Johann+Wolfgang/Autobiographisches/Aus+meinem+Leben.+Dichtung+und+Wahrheit.

———. 1883. *The Autobiography of Goethe, Truth and Fiction: Relating to My Life,* translated by John Oxenford. Boston: Estes and Lauriat.

Greenhill, Pauline. 2008. "Fitcher's (Queer) Bird: A Fairy Tale Heroine and Her Avatars." *Marvels & Tales* 22 (1): 143–67.

Greenhill, Pauline, and Jill T. Rudy, eds. 2014. *Channeling Wonder: Fairy Tales on Television.* Detroit: Wayne State UP.

Haase, Donald. 2000. "Children, War, and the Imaginative Space of Fairy Tales." *The Lion and the Unicorn: A Critical Journal of Children's Literature* 24: 360–77.

———. 2016. "Holocaust." In *Folktales and Fairy Tales: Traditions and Texts from around the World,* edited by Anne E. Duggan, Donald Haase, with Helen J. Callow, 459–62. 2nd ed. Santa Barbara: Greenwood.

Hannon, Patricia. 1998. *Fabulous Identities: Women's Fairy Tales in Seventeenth-Century France.* Amsterdam: Rodopi.

Harries, Elisabeth Wanning. 2000. "The Mirror Broken: Women's Autobiography and Fairy Tales." *Marvels & Tales* 14 (1): 122–35.

———. 2003. *Twice Upon a Time: Women Writers and the History of the Fairy Tale.* Princeton, NJ: Princeton UP.

Hennard Dutheil de la Rochère, Martine, and Géraldine Viret. 2011. "'Sleeping Beauty' in Chelmno: Jane Yolen's *Briar Rose* or Breaking the Spell of Silence." *Etudes de Lettres* 289: 399–424.

Høyrup, Helene. 2016. "Andersen, Hans Christian (1805–1875)." In *Folktales and Fairy Tales: Traditions and Texts from around the World,* edited by Anne E. Duggan, Donald Haase, with Helen J. Callow, 33–7. 2nd ed. Santa Barbara: Greenwood.

Joosen, Vanessa. 2011. *Critical and Creative Perspectives on Fairy Tales: An Intertextual Dialogue between Fairy-Tale Scholarship and Postmodern Retellings.* Detroit: Wayne State UP.

Klüger, Ruth. 1992. *Still Alive: A Holocaust Girlhood Remembered.* New York: The Feminist Press.

Kümmerling-Meibauer, Bettina. 1991. *Die Kunstmärchen von Hoffmannstahl, Musil und Döblin.* Köln, Weimar, Wien: Böhlau Verlag.

Langrish, Katherine. 2010. "All the Fairytale Reflections." *Seven Miles of Steel Thistles.* http://steelthistles.blogspot.ch/p/about-fairytale-reflections.html.

Lee, Linda J. 2014. "Ugly Stepsisters and Unkind Girls: Reality TV's Repurposed Fairy Tales." In *Channeling Wonder,* edited by Greenhill and Rudy, 275–93.

Leiris, Michel. (1939) 1973. *L'Âge d'homme.* Paris: Gallimard.

Lejeune, Philippe. (1975) 1989. "The Autobiographical Pact." In *On Autobiography,* translated by Katherine Leary, edited by Paul John Eakin. *Theory and History of Literature,* Vol. 52. Minneapolis: U Minnesota P.

Radner, Joan N., and Susan S. Lanser. 1987. "The Feminist Voice: Strategies of Coding in Folklore and Literature." *Journal of American Folklore* 100 (398): 412–25.

Rushdie, Salman. 1990. *Haroun and the Sea of Stories.* London: Granta.

Schwabe, Claudia. 2014. "Magic Realism in *Grimm* and *Once Upon a Time.*" In *Channeling Wonder,* edited by Greenhill and Rudy, 294–315.

Schwalm, Helga. "Autobiography." In *The Living Handbook of Narratology,* edited by Peter Hühn et al. Hamburg: Hamburg U. www.lhn.uni-hamburg.de/article/autobiography.

Seifert, Lewis C. 1996. *Fairy Tales, Sexuality and Gender in France, 1690–1715: Nostalgic Utopias.* Cambridge: Cambridge UP.

Sexton, Anne. 1971. *Transformations.* Boston: Houghton Mifflin.

Spiegelman, Art. 1980. *Maus.* New York: Pantheon Books.

Steedman, Carolyn Kay. 1986. *Landscape for a Good Woman: A Story of Two Lives.* New Brunswick, NJ: Rutgers UP.

Tomoko, Aoyama. 2015. "The Girl-Grandmother Relation in Literature." In *Configurations of Family in Contemporary Japan,* edited by Tomoko Aoyama, Laura Dales, and Romit Dasgupta, 49–64. London: Routledge.

Von Arnim, Bettina. 1844. *Clemens Brentanos Frühlingskranz.* Charlottenburg: Egbert Bauer.

Warner, Marina. 1994. *From the Beast to the Blonde: On Fairy Tales and Their Tellers.* London: Chatto & Windus.

———. 2014. *Once Upon a Time: A Short History of Fairy Tale.* Oxford: Oxford UP.

———. Forthcoming. *Inventory of a Life Mislaid.*

Wilde, Oscar. (1888, 1891) 1990. *The Complete Fairy Tales of Oscar Wilde,* edited by Jack Zipes. New York: Signet Classics.

Wilson, Frances. 2014. "Romantic Autobiography." In *The Cambridge Companion to Autobiography,* edited by Maria DiBattista and Emily O. Wittman, 71–101. Cambridge: Cambridge UP.

Windling, Terri. 1995. *The Armless Maiden and Other Tales for Childhood's Survivors.* New York: Tor Books.

———. 2011. "Tunes for a Monday Morning." *Myth and Moor: Musings on Mythic Life and Art from Dartmoor Studio.* www.terriwindling.com.

Wood, Jo. 2013. *Hey Jo: A Rock and Roll Fairytale.* New York: HarperCollins.

Wolf, Christa. 1976. *Kindheitsmuster.* Berlin & Weimar: Aufbau Verlag.

Yagawa, Sumiko. 2001. *Omimai,* illustrated by Uno Akira. Tōkyō: Biriken Shuppan.

Yolen, Jane. 1992. *Briar Rose.* New York: Tor Books.

Zipes, Jack. 2000. "Introduction." In *The Oxford Companion to Fairy Tales: The Western Fairy Tale Tradition from Medieval to Modern.* Oxford: Oxford UP.

———. 2011. *The Enchanted Screen: The Unknown History of Fairy-Tale Films.* New York: Routledge.

———. 2016a. "Foreword." In *Fairy Tale Films Beyond Disney: International Perspectives,* edited by Jack Zipes, Pauline Greenhill, and Kendra Magnus-Johnston, x–xi. New York: Routledge.

———. 2016b. "The Great Cultural Tsunami of Fairy-Tale Films." In *Fairy Tale Films Beyond Disney: International Perspectives,* edited by Jack Zipes, Pauline Greenhill, and Kendra Magnus-Johnston, 1–17. New York: Routledge.

Mediagraphy

American McGee's Alice (Video Game). 2000. Designer/Publisher Rogue Entertainment and Electronic Arts. www.imdb.com/title/tt0251576/.

The Bachelor (TV). 2002–. Creator Mike Fleiss. USA.

The Bachelorette (TV). 2003–. Creator Mike Fleiss. USA.

Beauty and the Geek (TV). 2005–2008. Directors Brian Smith, Lisa Michelle Singer, Matt Jackson, and Hal Grant. USA.

Disney Princess: My Fairy Tale Adventure (Video Game). 2012. Published by Disney Interactive Studios. http://lol.disney.com/games/disney-princess-my-fairytale-adventure-video-game.

Extreme Makeover (TV). 2002–2007. Created by Howard Schultz. USA.

Fairyland Online (Online Game). Lager Network Technologies. http://fairyland.lagernet.com.

Frozen. 2013. Directed by Chris Buck and Jennifer Lee. USA.

La belle et la bête. (Beauty and the Beast). 1946. Director Jean Cocteau. France.

Peau d'Âne (Donkey Skin). 1979. Director Jacques Demy. France.

The Pied Piper. 1972. Director Jacques Demy. France.

Pinocchio. 1940. Director Ben Sharpsteen and Hamilton Luske. USA.

Who Wants to Marry a Multi-Millionaire? (TV). 1999–2000. Director Don Weiner. USA.

45

BLOGS AND WEBSITES

Narrativizing the Daily "Once Upon a Time": Re-Envisioning the Fairy-Tale Present With Fairy-Tale Blogs

Lindsay Brown

> Fairy tales are informed by a human disposition to action—to transform the world and make it more adaptable to human needs, while we also try to change and make ourselves fit for the world.
>
> (Zipes 2012, 2)

In *The Irresistible Fairy Tale*, Jack Zipes describes the fairy tale using the metaphor of a land whale, a mammal that "constantly adapted to its changing environment." He asserts that "[t]he fairy tale is no different [. . .] emanat[ing] from a wide variety of tiny tales that were widespread throughout the world and continue to exist in unique ways under different environmental conditions" (2012, 21). This flexible and dynamic quality also applies to the technological media by which information about fairy tales is shared. Just as the Internet and various social media platforms are undergoing almost constant change, so too are fairy tales themselves. As part of a "living tradition come down through the centuries" (Warner 2014, xvi), a defining characteristic of traditional fairy tales is their origin in oral custom that changes alongside the speaker. Similarly, in the online world, blogs in particular have emerged in the past two decades as a forum for the sharing of personal stories and for connecting people with similar interests. It seems a natural pairing, then, that fairy tales and the culture surrounding the tradition of telling these stories find a home on numerous blogs. Not only are both the content and context undergoing constant change, but the layout and construction of the blog *extend* the reader's experience of the stories and culture.

The Blog

Blog is a truncated iteration of the term *weblog*, a term coined by Jorn Barger in 1997 (Siles 2012, 415) that today takes many forms. The (we)blog is a webpage where a weblogger (sometimes called a blogger, or a pre-surfer) "logs" all the other webpages she finds interesting. The format is normally to add the newest entry at the top of the page, so that repeat visitors can catch up by simply reading down the page until they reach a link they saw on their last visit (Barger 1999).

In 2016, the immensely popular microblog—including platforms like Twitter, Facebook, and Tumblr—had a firm grasp on blog culture; however, I am especially interested in the personal blog (a weblog wherein one individual posts for the purpose of entertainment or to engage in a particular community). Although scholar Jodi Dean diagnosed that "as of the summer of 2007 the blog is dead"—"killed by boredom, success, and even newer media" (2010, 33)—the personal blog remains significant in the dissemination and discussion of fairy tales. Additionally, blogs like *Once Upon a Blog* and *Tales of Faerie* (which I examine in this chapter) make it possible for all manner of people to engage meaningfully in a wide range of discussions about the fairy tale while giving participants the means through which to reimagine their lives as a type of modern fairy tale.

Since the hosts of these blogs post information stretching from news releases about the newest fairy-tale film, to reading recommendations, to stories about fairy-tale-inspired fashion, fairy-tale fans may sink their teeth into the material or eventually become agents of production themselves. The accessibility of sites with content management systems like Blogger and Word-Press means that "mediated reflexivity [is] available to virtually anyone who wants to bother" (Dean 2010, 29). Not only are these platforms free and moderately user-friendly, the form itself allows for fans, scholars, and authors alike to engage in an ongoing process of immersion, without the obstacles of pay-walls or institutional access. One can "live inside a story by reading it over and over again" (Bernheimer 2009, 2) and can take that desire one step further by making regular posts and thus contributing to the ever-growing online discourse about the form.

Not only is the personal blog a way almost anyone can share their stories and engage with the world of fairy tales, but the physical layout and structure of the blog itself—a chronological, repetitive, predictable (and thus comfortable) form—encourages the writer to follow a thoughtfully curated path, one that bears a striking resemblance to the unfolding of many fairy tales. Kate Bernheimer speaks of the "flatness, abstraction, everyday magic, and repetitive forms" of the fairy-tale collections that she found in the library as a little girl (2009, 1). The specific descriptors that Bernheimer uses can be readily applied to the form and feeling of the blog. The "flatness" of the story—narratively speaking, the static and often formulaic unfolding of plot—is complemented by the literal two-dimensional presentation of the computer screen. The simple appearance of the blog conforms to a consistent structure: a title is displayed at the top of the page, a menu-bar guides the viewer through the blog's contents, and the posts follow a reverse-chronological structure.

Similarly, many fairy tales appear deceptively simple on the surface: they follow a basic and accessible narrative structure; feature simple, archetypal characters; present straightforward conflict(s), often framed as "good vs. evil"; and can convey a basic moral or lesson. However, closer examination reveals that these tales are much more than simply a means by which one may lull a child to sleep. Their complexity has made them persist over time; different audiences can read them differently yet still take something away from them. There are as many unique interpretations of these texts as there are individuals reading/viewing/hearing them. Similarly, the bloggers who write about fairy tales are multifaceted—with multiplicities of identities— and as such, each must choose and curate what they present in their online persona.

Fairy-Tale Blogs as Personal Fairy-Tale Identities

Bloggers control their own identity, and the option to create an online persona shifts editorial and creative power into their hands. Through the creation of a blog, people can select a facet of their lives (such as being a folklorist) to develop as their Internet persona. As with the world of fiction and fairy tale, authors have the ability to be who they want—to narrativize themselves.

In the same way that video game avatars give gamers the means to create and develop a virtual identity, blogs give this option to bloggers. Although it can be difficult to hide personal information during the registration process, bloggers have agency over the name they use in the public sphere of the blog.

Bloggers like Gypsy Thornton post using their username: in Thornton's case, InkGypsy, a "[[h]uman/zombie hybrid who wishes she had tastier brains to snack on while writing" ("About InkGypsy." InkGypsy 2010–). The use of a pseudonym is by no means new; a virtual identity is akin to a pen name, like Samuel Langhorne Clemens's "Mark Twain." These noms de plume may provide the author with the opportunity to start anew, to write without worry of retribution, to conceal or reveal chosen parts of their identity, or simply to be creative and have fun. Many fairy-tale blogs are also linked or connected to information about the various facets of the author's identity. Jeana Jorgensen's blog *Foxy Folklorist* is hosted on Patheos—"the premier online destination to engage in the global dialogue about religion and spirituality and to explore and experience the world's beliefs" (Patheos 2016). The decision to host her blog on this particular site's Atheist Channel indicates that Jorgensen belongs to a particular group associated with a skeptical view of religion, yet another aspect of her identity that is linked by context to her identity as a folklorist. *Foxy Folklorist* contains posts discussing feminism, sex education, consent, rape culture, and gender, in addition to posts about folklore. By making space for a wide range of topics on *Foxy Folklorist*, Jorgenson demonstrates a clear valuing of the discussion of many topics and recognizes their place in fairy-tale discourse.

Although there is room for many subjects to coexist on one blog, there often remains an uncertainty about whether or not it is possible or desirable to compartmentalize the multiplicities of the blogger's identity into separate spaces. In Jorgensen's case, a post on her personal site from March 22, 2016, demonstrates the dilemma that she faces about where to house her writing. She states, "I'm still deciding if I'm going to keep blogging here or not; maybe I'll use my personal site as a way to write about topics that aren't related to my career as a folklorist. [. . .] Then again, being a folklorist has irrevocably shaped how I think about and do things" (Jorgensen 2016–), revealing the interconnectedness of various aspects of her identity. The second and third posts on her blog at Patheos are titled "Why Have a Folklore Blogger at Patheos" and "On Being a Mostly-Atheist Folklorist," respectively, making it clear that the intersections of faith, scholarship, and blogging assemble to variegate her online identity.

Developing and maintaining a blog takes commitment and time. In addition to posting regularly and interacting with readers' comments, there are many complexities to negotiate on the Internet. With doxxing (the publishing of private and/or identifying information about someone online, usually with the intent to threaten or harm), a far too real crime committed against individuals online, with harassment more and more common, the appeal and desire to embrace a carefully curated online persona have practical aspects. For some, "[t]he anonymity of the Internet is the only reason I allowed my thoughts to be available to the public," as Kristin of *Tales of Faerie* explains in February of 2011, justifying her use of a pseudonym. As such, the cultivation of the persona puts control firmly in the hands of the blogger.

The power associated with naming immediately calls to mind the tale of "Rumpelstiltskin" (ATU 500, "The Name of the Supernatural Helper") wherein the title character's name is key to the narrative and moral. In the story, Rumpelstiltskin (or the little man) helps the protagonist complete an impossible task, spinning straw into gold, in exchange for her first-born child. The only recourse the protagonist has to avoid relinquishing her offspring is to guess her helper's (unlikely) name. At first glance, naming gives power to the protagonist; however, there is also power in the helper's withholding his name, similar to how bloggers may withhold or obscure significant parts of their identity. Although the little man is eventually named—and bloggers can be doxxed—both have a measure of agency in their anonymity in the literal sense of namelessness. Identity is fluid; online personas, whether using pseudonyms or actual names, give bloggers the power and control to shift their identity in ways that align with the vacillations of their interests, beliefs, and sense of self, just as Jorgenson (and many others) have done.

Relationship to Time

A central paradox inherent in fairy tales is their situation in the past, present, and future simultaneously. Many originated in oral tradition, which imbues them with a sense of timelessness; many were told much before they were first fixed in writing. Further, many people have enjoyed their presence for as long as they can remember. But the influence of the Brothers Grimm, Charles Perrault, and Hans Christian Andersen on modern European and North American storytelling is immense. The motifs of these early tales have persevered, finding a home in the stories of today, but their specific uses have shifted alongside social mores. The frameworks of the stories may have only changed slightly, yet the interpretations have expanded and will surely expand further as they move into the future. Likewise, blogs—a now ubiquitous part of the digital world—play an essential role in the discussion of fairy tales today, destined to evolve and shift in ways that will maintain their place in the future of the cybernetic landscape.

One classic fairy-tale circumstance that has extended into modern storytelling is the challenge to complete an impossible task, as in "Vasilisa the Beautiful" collected by Aleksandr Afanasyev (similar to ATU 510A, "Cinderella"). Vasilisa, the title character in this Russian fairy tale, receives a little doll from her dying mother, a doll that will provide counsel in any of Vasilisa's times of need. The doll assists Vasilisa by helping her cope with grief and assisting with tasks like weeding the garden, spinning a basket of flax, and fetching fire from the dreaded Baba Yaga. Vasilisa is able to successfully overcome the challenges that she faces, mostly with the help of the little doll. On the surface it appears that Vasilisa has little agency in this tale; however, one must not overlook the fact that Vasilisa's intelligence also contributes to her survival. For instance, Vasilisa "remembered what the Baba Yaga had said, that not every question led to good" (Wheeler 1912, 47), and kept her questions to a minimum.

When a character is assigned a seemingly impossible undertaking, the stakes increase—often failure literally means death—and consequently so does the dramatic tension. One particularly salient example appears in J. K. Rowling's *Harry Potter* series (1997–2007). In each novel, protagonist Harry and his friends are faced with one or more impossible missions. Like Vasilisa and the young woman in Rumpelstiltskin, Harry must find ways to succeed in the face of doom, whether it be through mystical intervention or sheer cunning. The repeated employment of the trope of the impossible task in today's most popular fiction speaks to its ability to remain relevant and effective over decades.

The unfolding fairy-tale narrative gets its efficiency from an audience's shared assumptions about a manufactured past. Readers have been exposed to variations of what the past looks like in a fairy tale: ostentatious castles nestled in dense, terrifying woods; small townships, peopled with working-class villagers; or the presence of, for instance, kings and queens, all acting as markers for a past unmoored from specificity. There may be kings and queens today, but these monarchs do not resemble the royalty of a fairy-tale world. Through repeated exposure, these images become simulacrums of what the past actually was: a copy of a copy of the actual past. The past "is thereby modified," having "itself become a vast collection of images" (Jameson 1984, 66). Frederic Jameson proposes many contemporary films as examples of this process, creating what he calls *the nostalgia mode*: the use of images from the past to create a past that is not *really* the past. It is here that, like the nostalgia film, the fairy tale "was never a matter of some old-fashioned 'representation' of historical content, but approached the 'past' through stylistic connotation, conveying 'pastness' by the glossy quality of the image" (1984, 67). Since these stories are not localized in a date or place—often, instead, taking place "once upon a time"—they can be readily transmitted and transmuted, creating what Zipes argues is a *counterworld*, which "gain[s] distance from our world of reality so that we can know it as well as ourselves" (2012, 20). Many fairy tales find efficiency in minimal exposition, a compilation of events linked together in a linear path.

Similarly, blog entries are linked together by time and time-stamps. On the homepage, the top-most post is the most recent, with subsequent posts stretching backward in time. The reverse chronological structure maintains immediacy without being beholden to the past: "Since blogs are what is said at the moment, they are also constantly open to revision" (Myers 2010, 66). Blog posts are not immutable, but still afford a conceptualization of the blogger's time: "The present moment, measured in clock time, and marked by the automatic time-stamp, is the default time of blogs, as placelessness is the default special orientation" (67). The first post is the most recent, giving a sense of presentness, so despite the time-stamps, the blog is always in the now, using language that maintains the present-tense.

In older, archived posts, phrases expressed in the present tense such as "I am absolutely LOVING this book" (Kristin, May 29, 2016) situate the ideas from the past in the present. The ability to constantly update information makes blogs "more dynamic than older-style home pages, more permanent than posts to a net discussion list. They are more private and personal than traditional journalism, more public than diaries" (Jenkins 2006, 179). Like the diary, the blog provides pleasure in the steady accumulation of a personal, present-tense narrative that, through digital archivism, will remain accessible far into the future

Fairy-Tale Blogs as Personal Fairy-Tale Narratives

Fairy tales are hyperbolically narrativized and schematized, whereas daily life is an unbroken line of incidents that apparently offer little content for stories. Although daily life can be atomized into units of measurement such as minutes, days, and weeks, these units do not inherently form a story, necessarily imposing a narrative onto time. The structure of a blog may capture daily incidents, turning what may seem to be banal moments of life into narrative elements, representing the desire to impose some order onto the seeming chaos of life. One appeal of the fairy tale is its oftentimes predictable narrative, the structure that provides a measure of comfort in its unfolding. Even though the blog post exists in the past, and even though the fairy tale is set in a past that is not the actual past, the digital world of the blog enables the fairy tale to persist into the present, thanks to the blogger's continued labor.

By examining the fairy-tale elements that bloggers see around them in their analog life, and subsequently posting about them digitally, they link fairy tales to the narrative that is their life. In effect, bloggers repurpose the fairy-tale-ness of what they see around them, which resembles what Zipes argues is the continued growth of the fairy tale as it "embrac[es], if not swallow[s], all types of genres, art forms, and cultural institutions, and adjust[s] itself to new environments through the human disposition to re-create relevant narratives" (2012, 22). The bloggers' process of narrativization extends their engagement with fairy tales, while fairy tales extend into new media.

Like those fairy tales that "rise to the fore in our minds and Western culture [. . .] and assume a specific status as classical or traditional" (Zipes 2012, 17), the world of the blog ascribes canonical status to its more popular and thorough sites. My two example English-language blogs, InkGypsy's *Once Upon a Blog* and Kristin's *Tales of Faerie*, have extensive followers, use intertextual references to one another, may continue frequent updates, appear on the first page of Google results (using the search terms "fairy tale" and "blogs"), and maintain aesthetic appeal.

A beautiful image from Max Eilenberg's 2006 retelling of "Beauty and the Beast" (ATU 425C), illustrated by Angela Barrett, is centered at the top of the homepage of *Tales of Faerie*, hosted by Kristin from Chicago. The illustration's focal point is the bodies of Belle and the Beast wrapped in an embrace, lying in the snow, on the bank of a body of water. Belle has her arms around the Beast's torso, and her face is contorted in pain or sorrow. The color scheme is comprised of shades of purple, grays, and stark white; juxtaposed together, the colors connote sadness and isolation and evoke the physical sensation of coolness. The mood reflects the darkness that exists in many fairy tales, including "Beauty and the Beast," a well-known European tale that has become a part of the collective memory of many people. By choosing this image as the header to her blog, Kristin draws on what is familiar (the tale) and acknowledges the allure of melancholic beauty (the header).

The header image on InkGypsy's *Once Upon a Blog*, in contrast, offers an array of newspapers, moveable type, a Polaroid image, and a fountain pen. Yet these artifacts elicit a sense of the past and mobilize the melancholic romanticizing of dying media. There is a certain nostalgic quality to the way that these antiquated objects are placed at the forefront of the blog. Their position in the header, appearing on every page of the blog, reinforces how important it is to consider fairy tales in the past, present, and future. It is her use of these images online that reinvigorates them into the present. Her blog thus becomes a space for the fairy tales of old to mingle with the culture of the present.

The physical layout and design schemes of both Kristin's *Tales of Faerie* and InkGypsy's *Once Upon a Blog* literalize a sense of the past. The background patterns call to mind Victorian wallpapers, adding to the overall sense of pastness. That the aesthetics of these blogs offer a sort of modernized antiquity underscores the ways that previous posts are archived, keeping the past relevant and easily accessible in the present.

The posts often use present tense: "Yes. I need a creek. Preferably many! So if I'm not here for stretches this Summer you now know: I'm looking for a creek" (InkGypsy, August 16, 2015); "So I want to know from you—what are your absolute favorite fairy tale books?" (Kristin, June 17, 2016). Regardless of when the reader comes across an archived post, despite its time-stamp indicating its original date, the conversation between author and reader remains in the present. The reader may comment on posts regardless of their original appearance, keeping the post in the here and now. By commenting, the audience extends themselves into the discourse of fairy tales, participating in the narrativization of the blog and, by extension, their own lives.

Both InkGypsy and Kristin demonstrate on their blogs that their engagement with fairy tales is inextricably linked to the perception of their own lives as fairy-tale narratives, going so far as to assert that "[a]fter having a fairy tale blog for years, it really starts to bleed into the rest of your life" (Kristin 2014). A tangible example of fairy-tale narrativization occurs when Kristin uses her blog to announce major life events. The first of these posts was written on May 1, 2013, and is titled "Happily Ever After Starts Here." In this post Kristin makes multiple references to "Prince Tony" who lives "in a distant kingdom," framing their relationship to one another in terms of fairy-tale roles and tropes. If Tony is Prince, Kristin is Princess, an understanding of herself that is firmly rooted in the tradition of fairy tales.

Another major life event that Kristin posts about is her pregnancy: "Tony and I are very pleased to announce that the Kingdom of Tales of Faerie will be getting a little bit bigger this winter—we will be welcoming a new little Prince or Princess in late February!" Again, Kristin makes reference to the people in her life in terms of their roles in her fairy-tale world. Additionally, Kristin reflects on the effect that pregnancy has had on her engagement with fairy-tales, stating, "I'm just too hormonal to read a really sad, dark book about a young boy [. . .] I usually love a good creepy look at fairy tales, but right now I'm reading fairy tales for comfort" (2016). Kristin's love for fairy tales informs how she conceptualizes her personal life, and it is the mediation between blog and fairy tale that helps her narrativize.

Similarly, InkGyspy uses fairy tales to narrativize her life. In one such post, "Back to School with Knights and Trolls," she uses the language of fairy tales and the personal update format of blogs to talk about her son and the "interesting creatures" he goes to school with. Anchoring the post is a watercolor, ink, and pencil image titled "Lena och riddaren dansa" (or "Lena dances with the knight") by John Bauer. By selecting this chaotically beautiful image, Ink-Gypsy draws a parallel between the fairy-tale story and the "busy, busy time" of going back to school. In addition to sharing general information about her family, InkGypsy also uses her blog to share specific, personal information about her life. On November 29, 2010, InkGypsy explains her absence from posting, disclosing:

> 2010 has been a rough year for me and my family. We've lost jobs, house, had financial issues, health issues (which turned out to be minor, thank goodness!) and problem after problem with computers and other supposedly-necessary equipment, just to keep the pressure on. Things are not resolved. We're not quite back on our feet and breathing easy yet but we are all together, safe and healthy.

Despite all these setbacks and challenges, InkGypsy's desire to remain connected to fairy tales and the blogging community is incredibly strong. In the same post, she states that she will continue posting as much as possible because, "I miss the fairy tale community. I miss sharing. I miss touching base with all the tales I know and discovering new variations. Fairy tales inform my life, my creativity and help me cope in my day-to-day with the truths of the stories" (Ink-Gypsy 2010). Not only does she enjoy being a part of the online community, she asserts that fairy tales *inform her life*. She draws inspiration and strength from fairy-tale narratives, making them an essential part of the way she navigates the typical and atypical.

Both blogs and fairy tales have "enabled humans to invent and reinvent their lives" (Zipes 2012, 4). The form of the blog and the fairy tale both provide the opportunity to narrativize lives and extend them into fairy tales, as well as for fairy tales to extend themselves into new media. In *Once Upon a Blog* and *Tales of Faerie*, a continued interest in the exploration of our oldest stories allows fairy-tales fans—bloggers and audience alike—to re-envision their own lives.

Related topics: Autobiography; Convergence Culture; Digital; Fandom/Fan Cultures; Language; Novel; Pedagogy; Storytelling; Storyworlds/Narratology; YouTube and Internet Video

References Cited and Further Reading

Bernheimer, Kate. 2009. "Foreword: The Affect of Fairy Tales." In *Fairy Tales Reimagined: Essays on New Readings*, edited by Susan Redington Bobby, 1–4. Jefferson: McFarland & Company.

Dean, Jodi. 2010. *Blog Theory: Feedback and Capture in the Circuits of Drive*. Cambridge: Polity P.

Eilenberg, Max, and Angela Barrett (Illustrator). 2006. *Beauty and the Beast*. Somerville: Candlewick P.

Jameson, Frederic. 1984. "Postmodernism, or, the Cultural Logic of Late Capitalism." *New Left Review* 146: 59–92.

Jenkins, Henry. 2006. *Fans, Bloggers, and Gamers: Exploring Participatory Culture*. New York: NYU P.

Myers, Greg. 2010. *The Discourse of Blogs and Wikis*. New York: Continuum International.

Patheos. 2016. About Us. http://www.patheos.com/about-patheos.

Rowling, J. K. 1997–2007. *Harry Potter* (Series). London: Bloomsbury.

Siles, Ignacio. 2012. "Web Technologies of the Self: The Arising of the 'Blogger' Identity." *Journal of Computer-Mediated Communication* 17: 408–21.

Warner, Marina. 2014. *Once Upon a Time: A Short History of Fairy Tale.* Oxford: Oxford UP.

Wheeler, Post. 1912. *Russian Wonder Tales with a Foreword on the Russian.* New York: The Century Co.

Zipes, Jack. 2012. *The Irresistible Fairy Tale.* Princeton, NJ: Princeton UP.

Mediagraphy

Ashliman, D. L. 2016. *Folklore and Mythology Electronic Texts.* www.pitt.edu/~dash/folktexts.html.

Barger, Jorn. 1999. Weblog Resources FAQ. http://robotwisdom.com/weblogs.

———. 2008. *Robot Wisdom Auxiliary.* http://robotwisdom2.blogspot.ca/.

Do Rozario, Rebecca C. 2013–. *Doc in Boots.* https://docinboots.wordpress.com/.

Fairy Tale Review Blog. 2008–. http://fairytalereview.com/blog/.

Heiner, Heidi Anne. 1998–. *SurLaLune Fairy Tales.* www.surlalunefairytales.com/.

Hoffman, Adam. 2014–. *Fairy Tale Fandom.* www.fairytalefandom.com/.

InkGypsy. 2010–. *Once Upon a Blog.* http://fairytalenewsblog.blogspot.ca/.

Jorgenson, Jeana. 2016–. *Foxy Folklorist.* www.patheos.com/blogs/foxyfolklorist/.

Kristin. 2013–. *Tales of Faerie.* http://talesoffaerie.blogspot.ca/.

R, Christie. 2012–. *Spinning Straw into Gold.* http://spinstrawintogold.blogspot.ca/.

Reichelt, Megan. 2012–. *The Dark Forest.* http://darkforestfairytales.blogspot.ca/.

Tatar, Maria. 2009–. *Breezes from Wonderland.* http://blogs.harvard.edu/tatar/.

Thompson, Christa. 2013–. *The Fairytale Traveller.* http://thefairytaletraveler.com/.

Visualizing Wonder. 2014–. http://fairytales.byu.edu/.

Wojtaszek, Kristina. 2012–. *Twice Upon a Time.* https://authorkw.wordpress.com/blog/.

Wolford, Kate. 2011–. *Enchanted Conversation: A Fairy Tale Magazine.* www.fairytalemagazine.com/.

46

CHAPBOOKS

Maria Kaliambou

In bibliographic terms, chapbooks are small, cheap books, with a wide variety of possible content, produced in Western Europe in the early modern era (ca. 1500–1800). They had few pages (eight, twelve, sixteen, twenty-four, or thirty-six), a small format (seven by five inches or smaller), and crude illustrations, were printed in large numbers, and were sold by itinerant merchants and peddlers (so-called chapmen). The word "chapbook" is a neologism of the nineteenth century, invented by librarians and bibliophiles who wanted to define popular cheap literature published in England since the invention of printing. The etymology stems either from the words "cheap" and "book" or from the words "chapman" and "book." Thus, one defining element is their low price; indeed, they were meant to be affordable to anyone.

Some believe small chapbooks first appeared in France (Weiss 1942, 10). However, almost everywhere after the beginning of print there has been production of cheap prints parallel with more elaborate publications. So, one can find printed chapbooks in many countries around the globe, such as England, France, Germany, the Netherlands, Italy, Spain, Greece, Bulgaria, the United States, Brazil, China, India, and parts of West Africa.

Chapbooks have different names in other European countries. In France, *bibliothèque bleue* (blue library) refers to the blue cover of small books, giving significance to their external appearance. In Germany, *Volksbuch* (the book of the people) underlines the social dimension of the readership. The Portuguese *literatura de cordel* (literature on a string) hints to the ways they were distributed, namely sold hanging on a rope. Other terms used by publishers are little books, small books, curious books, pamphlets, and ephemera, referring to various criteria such as the content, format, or use of these popular publications.

Their peak was in the late seventeenth and eighteenth centuries. From the nineteenth century onward, chapbooks were gradually replaced by other popular print forms, such as pulp magazines, dime novels, and graphic novels. Today the term refers mostly to modern collections of poetry, which range from very low- to very high-quality publications. The current circulation of numerous zines, self-published poetry booklets, and online publications of poetry (e-chapbooks) may be considered contemporary versions of the form.

Chapbooks contributed to the wide popularity of folktales and fairy tales. From the first years of their appearance they included these stories. Gradually chapbooks with folktales became children's readings (Roth 1979). Even today one can find small and thin chapbooks with fairy tales sold in kiosks and in markets.

Because of their cheap appearance, chapbooks were overloaded with many negative stereotypes and were thus dismissed by some academics as unworthy of study. With the exception of early research on British chapbooks by Harry Weiss (1942), the academic acknowledgment of the importance of chapbooks is a relatively recent phenomenon. After the 1960s, bibliographic and social historians, literature scholars, folklorists, and sociologists praised the power and value of chapbooks as important cultural artifacts (see Burke [1978] 2009; Chartier 1987; Neuburg 1972; Roth 1979; Roth 1993; Schenda 1970; Slater 1989; Spufford 1981; Watt 1995). Most scholars today agree that popular literature, including chapbooks, is a gateway to understanding and analyzing culture and society, in particular how they change. Yet there remains a considerable dearth of research analyzing chapbooks' value as a powerful means of knowledge and literature dissemination.

Despite their popularity, chapbooks are hard to find. First, because of their fragile construction, the majority could not last long. Second, until recently libraries were not interested in acquiring them. Yet some bibliophiles of the nineteenth century and other private collectors lovingly gathered and saved them from disappearance (Neuburg 1972, 11). The private collections by James Boswell and Samuel Pepys constitute two important sources for research of English chapbooks, now in libraries and university archives (Weiss 1942, 141). The Pepys collection from seventeenth-century England mirrors the literacy and reading tastes of English people at that time (see Spufford 1981). Today, ironically, chapbooks from previous centuries are recognized as valuable, and are sold at high prices in auctions, and thus are no longer "cheap books."

Contents

Chapbooks cover nearly every imaginable subject. Their wide range of genres, blurred with each other, a tendency "deeply ingrained in their very nature" (Duval 1994, 41), makes their classification difficult. The first bibliographic systematization of their vast material was done by bibliographers at the Harvard Library in 1905 and is printed in the *Catalogue of English and American Chap-Books and Broadside Ballads in Harvard College Library*. Its subjects are: 1) religious and moral: Sunday reading, 2) cheap repository tracts, 3) household manuals, 4) historical, political, geographical, 5) geographical description and local history, 6) travel and adventure, 7) odd characters and strange events, 8) prose fiction, 9) legendary romances, fairy stories, and folktales in prose, 10) dramatic, 11) metrical tales and other verse, 12) song books, 13) jest books, humorous fiction, riddles, etc. 14) humorous metrical tales, etc. 15) dream books, fortune telling, and legerdemain, 16) demonology and witchcraft, 17) prophecies, 18) crime and criminals: collections, 19) crime and criminals: trials, 20) crime and criminals: executions, 21) crime and criminals: dreadful warnings, 22) crime and criminals: individual criminals and persons accused of crime, and 23) miscellaneous, including social satire, chapbooks on matrimony, manners and customs, proverbs, etc. (Harvard Library 1905).

Victor E. Neuburg (1972) follows this organization, whereas Weiss reduces the categories to eighteen (1942, 30). Margaret Spufford divides the small books into three groups: merry books (courtship, sex, and songs), godly books (popular religion), and historical and chivalric novels (1981, 156–257). Klaus Roth, based on popular printed material from southeast Europe, offers a more minimalistic division of chapbooks into two generic categories: literature (prose, poetry, and drama) and manual literature (religious and secular) (1993, 19).

Chapbooks often have catchy titles with superlative forms (such as "The Most Beautiful Fairy Tales," "Exquisite Fairy Tales," and "Special Chosen Fairy Tales") in an effort to capture their audience's interest. Some have extremely long titles covering a full page, almost resembling a table of contents (Weiss 1942, 30). Chapbooks' titles usually refer to their genre. However, publishers' uses of genres were very elastic. In many cases, producers filled the pages with whatever material was available. For instance, a chapbook with folktales can also include short stories, myths, songs, and riddles (Kaliambou 2006, 124–130). Publishers' sources were oral and written (Neuburg 1972, 5), both traditional and literary works, autochthonous or in translation, often in a highly condensed, adapted, and transformed format.

Fairy tales in chapbooks could include a compilation of various translations intertwined with oral traditions. For instance, the unknown author of a Greek chapbook from the end of the nineteenth century borrowed motifs by Charles Perrault, the Brothers Grimm, and other sources to publish one of the first translations into Greek of "Little Red Riding Hood" (ATU 333) ("I Kokkinskoufitsa" N.d.). Some lines from the dialogue between the girl and the wolf are verbatim translations from Perrault; other passages go back to Grimm; the end resembles neither, with the girl screaming and thus alerting huntsmen to kill the wolf (see Kaliambou 2007b, 56).

Another translation and adaptation tactic was the domestication of the fairy tales to the audience's environment. Familiar localities with their traditions and customs make the set of the stories, as another example of "Little Red Riding Hood" in a 1914 Greek chapbook exemplifies. This version takes place in a Greek village of a minority ethnic group around Christmas time. Stylistic characteristics known from other genres of popular literature (popular novels, popular romances, crime stories, etc.) dominate. Linguistic elements (diminutives and superlatives forms, use of standard adjectives, direct speech, metaphors and comparisons, shifting from standard to everyday language, restricted vocabulary, use of colloquial expressions) and aesthetic characteristics (lengthy sentimental descriptions, gender stereotypes of the strong man and the submissive woman, polarization between good and bad characters, amplifications of narrative elements) make evident that chapbooks with folktales and fairy tales are in a constant dialogue with other genres of popular literature (see Kaliambou 2007a).

One striking characteristic of chapbook production from the fifteenth to the nineteenth century is the longevity of their texts. Based on trade lists and publishers' catalogues, Neuburg (1972, 75–81) and Spufford (1981, 258–261) could prove the continuing popularity of some titles printed throughout the centuries in cheap formats, such as "Valentine and Orson," "Fortunatus," "Guy of Warwick," and "The Seven Champions of Christendom." Similarly, "Jack the Giant Killer" (ATU 328), "Jack and the Beanstalk" (ATU 328A), "Cinderella" (ATU 510A), "Sleeping Beauty" (ATU 410), "Tom Thumb" (ATU 700), Charles Perrault's stories, and other folktales and fairy tales also circulated continuously. Thus, despite the stereotype that they are ephemeral, chapbooks could resist the obstacles of time.

Production

Various agents are involved in the production of chapbooks, including publishers, printers, illustrators, authors, translators, booksellers, and paper suppliers, forming what Robert Darnton calls "the communications circuit" (1982, 68). In order to keep production costs low, the same person could cover many jobs. For instance, a publisher could also be the printer, distributor, or even author of a chapbook. The majority of agents remained anonymous, and the date or place of publication were not always provided. Thus, very often we lack information about who wrote, translated, adapted, or edited the folktales and fairy tales in chapbooks.

The successful publishing companies were mostly family businesses; the involvement of different generations played a catalytic role for long-lasting success. For example, the biggest publisher in England in the eighteenth century was the Dicey family. In 1720 William Dicey started a publishing company with Robert Raikes in Northampton. In 1756, Cluer Dicey, William's son, took over and transferred the business to London (Neuburg 1972, 48). Similarly in France, the two family dynasties who dominated the market of the blue books were two generations of the Oudot family and three of the Garnier family (see Chartier 1987, 256).

The authors of those cheap publications remained in most cases anonymous. Some were authors of more respectable literature who accepted commissions for chapbooks for financial reasons and used pseudonyms to cover their true identity. Most creators were skillful and highly efficient adapters who at a very fast pace had to produce great numbers of chapbooks. The texts were changed, minimized, condensed, or prolonged to fit the format, size, and page length (Weiss 1942, 11). Characteristically, one Glasgow publisher/adapter reduced the Bible to fit twenty-four pages including illustrations. Similarly, the length of folktales and fairy tales could be very elastic. The same narrative could be longer or shorter depending on the available pages. For instance, in eighteenth-century chapbooks one can find both a twenty-six-page version of "Cinderella" and a seventeen-page one.

Illustrations, often crude woodcuts apparently executed carelessly, are an integral element. Chapbooks from the early modern era have an illustration (usually woodcut) on the title page and few if any within. They thus differ from broadsides, single sheets that contained posters, advertisements, proclamations, and (most relevant to folklorists) ballads, circulated parallel to chapbooks but targeted more to their readers' visual tastes. Chapbooks looked more serious than their contemporary broadsides, being more substantial than the even more ephemeral broadsides (Newcomb 2011, 482, 484).

In chapbooks with folktales and fairy tales, the title page, which functioned as the best incentive for readers to buy, was covered with an illustration. Gradually, the cover of the folktale chapbook became the symbol for the whole booklet. Illustrations circulated from one example to another or were reprinted for many years despite having faded. Images were not always relevant to the text and sometimes were used just to fill the page. The illustrators, like the authors, were mainly anonymous.

Distribution

Chapmen were the main distributors in the early modern era. These itinerant peddlers carried chapbooks, together with other merchandise, on their shoulders and sold them in open markets, in stores, in bookstores, in kiosks, or privately to houses. Through them, chapbooks, an urban-created phenomenon, could reach remote villages. Like ballad sellers, chapmen might have performed the content of the booklet to help sell it. They had an interactive relationship with their buyers, which helped them sense the recipient's taste. These peddlers established a network of communication and played a crucial role in the distribution of social, historic, political, and religious knowledge. Tessa Watt argues that we can better understand the chapbook phenomenon if we understand the social relations within which they circulated (1995). Further, chapbooks probably reached more hands when adults and children borrowed, resold, or rented them.

Affordability is one of the main characteristics of chapbooks. As their name implies (reminiscent of the later term "dime novel" for popular books in nineteenth-century America), chapbooks were accessible to almost anyone; prices were between two and six pennies, depending the number of pages. Chartier, examining the inventory of the Garnier bookshop for the year 1789, concludes that blue chapbooks were the cheapest of all ordinary books (1987, 256). Maria Kaliambou, comparing Greek nineteenth- and twentieth-century folktale chapbooks with other material goods, found that their price was equivalent to a piece of bread; even low-paid workers could afford them (2006, 68–70).

Although the information available is sparse, it appears that chapbooks were published in thousands of copies. For instance, French sixteenth- and seventeenth-century booklets of eight or sixteen pages were printed in editions of 1,250 to 2,500 (Chartier 1992, 280). A common strategy was the publication of a series, usually focused in one genre, such as short stories or folktales. However, publishers did not necessarily produce all the announced items.

Reception, Readership

Series subscribers' lists indicate the age, gender, and region of the readership; it is evident that the buyers of folktales were not only children but adults as well (Kaliambou 2006, 80–83). Yet it is notoriously difficult to find much detail about the actual readers, the real audience of the chapbooks. These cheap productions constituted a competitive business among publishers, which implies a considerable demand. But who actually read them? Literacy rates at the beginning of the sixteenth century were low, yet they increased significantly during the next centuries (Burke 2009, 342–352). Spufford sought to measure reading skills in English society in the second half of seventeenth century; she concluded that in East Anglia approximately 30 percent of the male population could read (but not write equally well) but fewer women acquired reading and writing skills (1981, 19–45).

Indirect sources provide information about reading skills. For instance, evidence of the participation of women in reading activities is the woodcut printed on the seventh page of the English chapbook *Cinderella; Or, the History of the Little Glass Slipper*, showing Cinderella reading a book (see figure 46.1). The accompanying text demonstrates her love of reading: "Her books were the only companions she had, and when her sisters went out, she used to take the opportunity of reading theirs" (N.d.). This eighteenth-century (fictional) woman reads in order to forget her sorrows and find an outlet for her interests. The chapbook was printed in York, priced one penny, and had thirty-two pages and nine unrefined woodcuts. The author or translator remains anonymous, but it is obviously a free translation of Perrault's version from 1697. Although it is not dated, based on a handwritten inscription, it must have been published at the end of the eighteenth century. On the last page, a list of published books provides helpful information on the preferences of publisher and audience. Titles from this list demonstrate that fairy tales and fairy-tale-like materials such as "Tom Thumb," "Enchanted Castle," "Fables," and "Tales of Past Times with Mother Goose" were printed alongside literary and legendary subjects such as "Robin Hood," "Robinson Crusoe," and "Gulliver's Travels" (*Cinderella* N.d.).

However, chapbooks did reach bigger audiences than literacy rates might imply. Reading aloud was an activity among family or community circles. One person who could read served as the pathway to the literary world for others. Chapbooks functioned as an educational tool: some readers practiced and developed their reading skills, and some listeners came into contact with literary texts that they memorized and reused in oral performance. Thus, chapbooks contributed to the interplay between oral and written literature; they have a role "in between" (see Roth 1993, 11–13).

Gradually, chapbooks with folktales became exclusively for children. On the last page of a 1950s Greek chapbook the publisher makes their significance for children explicit: "The most beautiful fairy tales. [. . .] With exquisite appearance and abundantly illustrated our fairy tales are the indispensable friend for every child. Chosen from the masterworks of the world literature they are the best nourishment for the child's mind and phantasy" (*Oi treis koutamares* N.d., 32). Publishers embellished them in order to appeal to young audiences and to have various practical and learning uses. Examples from the nineteenth and twentieth centuries had knowledge quizzes, tests, riddles, and painting games to entertain and educate. Some were combined with special offers: for instance, on the last page of the Greek chapbook *Modern Robinsons and Other Fairy Tales* (Monternoi Robinsones kai alla Paramythia N.d.), published in the mid-twentieth century, a knowledge quiz includes the inscription that if the child/reader finds the correct answer, she will have a discount on the next chapbook. All these strategies of publishers served the purpose of gaining bigger audiences.

(7)
the very neweſt faſhions. Her books were the only companions ſhe had, and when her ſiſters went out, ſhe uſed to take the opportunity of reading theirs.

The poor girl bore all patiently, and dared not to tell her father, who would have rattled her off; for his

A 4

Figure 46.1 Cinderella; Or, the History of the Little Glass Slipper (Chapbook), circa late 1700s, printed for Wilson, Spence and Mawman, York, UK

From Gale. Eighteenth Century Collections Online. © Gale, a part of Cengage Learning, Inc. Reproduced by permission. www.cengage.com/permissions

Significance

The importance of chapbooks, as well as of other popular publications, is now accepted and underscored by scholars. Particularly for fairy-tale studies, chapbooks constitute a significant research resource because they played a crucial role in the wide dissemination of folktales and fairy tales into the population. In some cases, chapbooks are the first written documentations of oral tales (see Rubini 2003, re: ATU 566, "The Three Magic Objects and the Wonderful Fruits" [Fortunatus]) or functioned as the vehicle for translations of Western European stories into the peripheries of Europe (see Kaliambou 2006 for Greece). Chapbooks testify to the reciprocal influences between oral and written sources and underline the ongoing exchange between orality and literacy.

Figure 46.2 Walker, William, N.d., *The History of Valentine and Orson* (Chapbook), Beinecke Rare Book and Manuscript Library, Yale University

Their power lies in the combination of easy and cheap pleasure with moral edification. At the end of the eighteenth century the publisher of one widely circulated chapbook (see figure 46.2) explains to the reader right away on the title page why its content is so important:

> Reader, thou'lt find this little book contains
> Enough to answer thy expense and pains;
> And if with caution thou wilt read it through,
> 'T will both instruct thee and delight thee too.
> (*The History of Valentine and Orson*, 1)

CHAPBOOKS

Related topics: Children's and Young Adult (YA) Literature; Children's Picture Books and Illustrations; Print

References Cited and Further Reading

Burke, Peter. (1978) 2009. *Popular Culture in Early Modern Europe*. 3rd ed. Burlington, VT: Ashgate.

Chartier, Roger. 1987. *The Cultural Uses of Print in Early Modern France*, translated by Lydia G. Cochrane. Princeton, NJ: Princeton UP.

———. 1992. "Reading Matter and 'Popular' Reading: From the Renaissance to the Seventeenth Century." In *A History of Reading in the West*, edited by Guglielmo Cavallo and Roger Chartier, 269–83. Amherst: U Massachusetts P.

Darnton, Robert. 1982. "What Is the History of Books?" *Daedalus* 111 (3): 65–83.

Duval, Giles. 1994. "Standardization vs. Genre: Conduct-Books and English Chap-Literature." In *The Crisis of Courtesy: Studies in the Conduct-Book in Britain, 1600–1900*, edited by Jacques Carré, 41–9. Leiden, The Netherlands: Brill.

Harvard Library. 1905. *Catalogue of English and American Chap-Books and Broadside Ballads in Harvard College Library*, edited by William Coolidge Lane, 56. Cambridge, MA: Library of Harvard U.

Kaliambou, Maria. 2006. *Heimat—Glaube—Familie. Wertevermittlung in griechischen Popularmärchen (1870–1970)*. Neuried: Ars Una.

———. 2007a. "Popularmärchen und popularer Roman: Ein 'Dialog' zwischen den Gattungen." *Fabula* 48 (1/2): 60–72.

———. 2007b. "The Transformation of Folktales and Fairy Tales into Popular Booklets." *Marvels & Tales* 21 (1): 50–64.

Lyons, Martin. 1997. "What Did the Peasants Read? Written and Printed Culture in Rural France, 1815–1914." *European History Quarterly* 27 (2): 165–97.

Mandrou, Robert. 1985. *De la culture populaire aux 17e et 18e siècles: La Bibliothèque bleue de Troyes*. 3rd ed. Paris: Éditions Imago.

Neuburg, E. Victor. 1972. *Chapbooks: A Guide to Reference Material on English, Scottish and American Chapbook Literature of the Eighteenth and Nineteenth Centuries*. London: The Woburn P.

———. 1977. *Popular Literature: A History and Guide: From the Beginning of Printing to the Year 1897*. London: The Woburn P.

———. 1989. "Chapbooks in America: Reconstructing the Popular Reading of Early America." In *Reading in America: Literature and Social History*, edited by Cathy Davidson, 81–113. Baltimore: John Hopkins UP.

Newcomb, Lori Humphrey. 2011. "Chapbooks." In *The Oxford History of Popular Print Culture: Volume One, Cheap Print in Britain and Ireland to 1660*, edited by Joad Raymond, 471–90. Oxford: Oxford UP.

Perrault, Charles. 1901. *The Tales of Mother Goose: As First Collected by Charles Perrault in 1696*, translated by Charles Welsh. Boston: D. C. Heath & Co.

Preston, Cathy Lynn, and Michael J. Preston, eds. 1995. *The Other Print Tradition: Essays on Chapbooks, Broadsides, and Related Ephemera*. London: Garland Publishing.

Rölleke, Heinz, ed. 1999. *Kinder- und Hausmärchen gesammelt durch die Brüder Grimm. Vollständige Ausgabe auf der Grundlage der dritten Auflage (1837)*. Darmstadt: Wissenschaftliche Buchgesellschaft.

Roth, Klaus. 1979. "Chapbook." In *Enzyklopädie des Märchens. Handwörterbuch zur historischen und vergleichenden Erzählforschung*, edited by Kurt Ranke, Hermann Bausinger, Wolfgang Brückner, Max Lüthi, Lutz Röhrich, Rudolf Schenda, 1232–40. Berlin: De Gruyter.

———. 1993. "Populare Lesestoffe in Südosteuropa." In *Südosteuropäische Popularliteratur im 19. und 20. Jahrhundert*, edited by Klaus Roth, 11–32. Munich: Münchner Vereinigung für Volkskunde, Südosteuropa-Gesellschaft.

Rubini, Luisa. 2003. "Fortunatus in Italy: A History between Translations, Chapbooks, and Fairy Tales." *Fabula* 44 (1/2): 25–54.

Schenda, Rudolf. 1970. *Volk ohne Buch. Studien zur Sozialgeschichte der populären Lesestoffe 1770–1910*. Frankfurt am Main: Vittorio Klostermann.

Shepard, Leslie. 1973. *The History of Street Literature: The Story of Broadside Ballads, Chapbooks, Proclamations, News-Sheets, Election Bills, Tracts, Pamphlets, Cocks, Catchpennies, and Other Ephemera*. Newton Abbot: David and Charles.

Slater, Candace. 1989. *Stories on a String: The Brazilian Literatura de Cordel*. Berkeley: U California P.

Spufford, Margaret. 1981. *Small Books and Pleasant Histories: Popular Fiction and Its Readership in Seventeenth-Century England*. Cambridge: Cambridge UP.

Watt, Tessa. 1995. "Piety in the Pedlar's Pack: Continuity and Change, 1578–1630." In *The World of Rural Dissenters, 1520–1725*, edited by Margaret Spufford, 235–72. Cambridge: Cambridge UP.

Weiss, Harry B. 1942. *A Book about Chapbooks: The People's Literature of Bygone Times*. Ann Arbor: Edwards Brothers Inc.

Mediagraphy

Cinderella; Or, the History of the Little Glass Slipper (Chapbook). N.d. (ca. late 1700s.) York, UK: Wilson, Spence and Mawman.

The History of Valentine and Orson (Chapbook). N.d. (ca. late 1700s.). Otley, UK: William Walker.

"I Kokkinoskoufi [Red Riding Hood]." 1914. In *Ta penintadio paramythia tou laou [The Fifty Two Fairy Tales of the People]* (Chapbook). Athens: Saliveros.

"I Kokkinoskoufitsa [Little Red Riding Hood]." N.d. (ca. 1880s). In *O papoutsomenos gatos kai i Kokkinoskoufitsa. Paramythia dia ta kala paidia [Puss in Boots and Little Red Riding Hood: Fairy Tales for the Brave Children]* (Chapbook). Athens: Anonymously Published.

Monternoi Robinsones kai alla Paramythia [Modern Robinsons and Other Fairy Tales] (Chapbook). N.d. (ca. 1950s.) Athens: Saliveros.

Oi treis koutamares [The Three Stupidities] (Chapbook). N.d. (ca. 1950s.) Athens: Daremas.

47

CHILDREN'S MUSEUMS

Naomi Hamer

Museums and art galleries have held numerous international exhibits over the past century pertaining to fairy-tale cultures, particularly as represented through fine art and picture book illustrations. However, fairy-tale exhibits at children's museums are a relatively new phenomenon. In the context of a children's museum, exhibits invite visitors to engage with fairy-tale narratives through a combination of traditional curatorial display conventions and the active play environments of science-oriented children's museums. Moreover, these exhibits often provide opportunities for young readers to engage with fairy-tale narratives through immersive designed spaces. The use of digital and mobile technologies has increasingly become a key mode for engagement with the material for young audiences at all museum sites. While spaces offer potential critical engagement with tales, recent mediated exhibits often continue to sustain nationalistic discourses and the prioritizing of literary fairy tales and fairy-tale authorship.

Fairy-Tale Museums and Houses

Museums, art galleries, and public libraries have often provided sites for thematic collections and exhibits focused on fairy-tale cultures. These exhibits have been diverse in scope and artifacts on display, ranging in recent exhibits from fairy-tale textiles and gowns (*Fairytale Fiesta* 2014, Witte Museum, U.S.) and designer haute-couture fashion (*Fairytale Fashion* 2016, Fashion Institute of Technology, U.S.) to children's book illustrations (*Once Upon a Time: Fairy Tales from the Osborne Collection of Early Children's Books* 2016, Toronto Public Library, Canada). Nevertheless, historically, fairy-tale-specific museums have offered specialized venues solely for interactive engagement with fairy-tale cultures for both adult and child visitors. The most well-known international museums include: the Hans Christian Andersen House and Museum (Denmark); the House of Fairytales "Zhili-Byli" (Russia); Bad Oeynhausen, German Fairy-Tale and Wesersagamsuem (Germany); Grimmworld Kassel (Germany); Miyazawa Kenji Dowa Mura (Village of Fairy Tales, Japan); and the Ghibli museum (Japan) dedicated to the work of Miyazaki Hayao's studio. Distinct from fairy-tale themed amusement parks and playground spaces, these museums pair creative engagement with fairy-tale narratives with curatorial displays of historical collections and landmark sites, often providing celebrations of specific national figures by focusing on the works and life experiences of fairy-tale authors/auteurs.

Over the last decade, many of these museums have updated and renovated their exhibit spaces to engage specifically with young visitors and families. The Hans Christian Andersen House and Museum at the site of Andersen's birthplace in Odense provides a key example of a specialized fairy-tale museum that has received a contemporary update. Designed to celebrate the Andersen Bicentenary in 2005, the renovations particularly reflect the roles played by fairy-tale museums as sites of nationalism. Moreover, Janne J. Liburd describes how the bicentenary celebrations were part of a broader tourism initiative by the Danish government "to making certain parts of the country more attractive as a tourist destination while striving to create new prospects for Danish citizens" (2009, 41).

The museum itself includes the birth-house of Andersen—refurnished with a mixture of original furniture and replica artifacts. Visitors are invited to walk through the house and physically experience a recreation of Andersen's early childhood. Manuscripts and memorabilia from Andersen's life (as well as a complete library of first editions of his work in translation) continue to be traditionally displayed in glass cases. However, renovations and new designs for the exhibition spaces have allowed for video installation art in the basement inspired by "The Little Mermaid"; interactive touch screens; a film that involves reenactments of events in the writer's life; and excerpts from his writings projected on the walls of the museum.

In addition, two mobile apps explore the museum in Odense as well as other sites of Andersen's life and inspirations across Denmark: the *Hans Christian Andersen Trail* (2016) and *H. C. Andersens Odense* (2015). These apps further extend the experience of the museum house, sustaining and cultivating a quasi-mythic narrative of Andersen as a creative genius/ fairy-tale author from modest origins and a celebration of the geographic site of his birth itself underlined by Danish nationalism. Jack Zipes describes the depiction of Andersen by biographers, photographers, and portrait painters as "the ugly duckling [. . .], the poor, gifted son of a cobbler who transformed himself into a successful, 'beautiful' writer through his magical, innate talents: Hans Christian Andersen as fairy tale" (2005, 2). Kendra Magnus-Johnston's examination of the representation of fairy-tale authors in popular cinema reflects this ubiquitous reading of Andersen's life as a fairy-tale narrative (2016).

For example, Magnus-Johnston observes that the television movie biopic *Hans Christian Andersen: My Life as a Fairy Tale* (2003), echoing the title of one of Andersen's own autobiographies, involves "[t]he arguably delusional protagonist repeats ad nauseaum variations on the film's title, assuring others—or perhaps even more, himself—that his life is a fairy tale" (2016, 22). Similar to the filmic representations, the Hans Christian Andersen House and Museum illustrates how "the author is fictionalized and made functional for profit" (Magnus-Johnston 2016, 19). While the museum reveals some of the harshness of his life and the conflicts between his public persona and his lived experience, most of the interactive, filmic, and mediated experiences function to support this fairy tale of Andersen. Moreover, both the exhibits and the apps move away from any exploration of the amalgam of folkloric narratives that may have inspired or informed Andersen's literary fairy tales.

The Hans Christian Andersen House and Museum is a key venue for touristic travel in Denmark (see Lyons 2012) but also is identified as a site for those interested in literary themed travels (see Literary Traveler 2002). A number of popular blogs review and provide advice about fairy-tale-related travel with a focus on museums and exhibits. While many of these sites, such as "Castles and Manor Houses from around the World" and "Deutsche Marchen Strasse: German Fairy Tale Route," provide detailed information and travel advice on particular touristic sites affiliated with fairy tales, other sites particularly engage across media with a focus on travel with children and families. These blogs indicate a shift in the emphasis from visitation to these sites primarily by scholars, adult tourists, and enthusiasts to specific niche sites focused on creative engagement with fairy-tale cultures by children and families. The most popular of these sites is a travel blog entitled "The Fairytale Traveler: Travel and Lifestyle Inspired by Books, Film, TV and Mythology" (Thompson 2016). This blog is hosted by Christa Thompson, who describes herself as a "wanderlusting nerdy mom with a serious commitment to discovering a real unicorn. When I'm not traveling the globe in search of fandom, film locations, legends, myth and lore, I'm doing normal mom stuff, nerd style" (2016). The blog particularly highlights family- and child-oriented fairy-tale sites with the contributions of Thompson's son under the persona of "The Little Fairytale Traveler." This blog also indicates an increased interest in hands-on offers of engagement with fairy-tale narratives at children's museums and in exhibits specifically targeting young audiences.

Fairy-Tale Exhibits at Children's Museums

Since the founding of the Brooklyn Children's Museum in Crown Heights, Brooklyn, New York, in 1899, the children's museum has evolved internationally as a non-profit public institution focused on informal family-oriented education and interactive play environments (Acosta 2000; Judd and Kracht 1997). The majority of these museums highlight science and environmental education with the originating aim to provide experiential learning about natural science for young urban visitors and their families (Allen 2004; Unrath and Luehrman 2009). While these institutions sometimes house and display collections of historical artifacts including children's books and toys, children's museums tend to be defined distinctly from historical museums of childhood such as the Victoria & Albert Museum of Childhood in Bethnal Green, London (UK), or rare children's book collections such as the Osborne Collection of Early Children's Books in Toronto, Canada.

Over the past two decades, children's story or book museums have emerged as new specialized institutions that concentrate on literacy education through exhibits and programs often related to children's literature, storytelling, picture book illustration, and fairy-tale narratives. Recent children's book exhibits at public libraries and art galleries have increasingly applied hybrid approaches and mediated experiences for young people to engage with these children's literature texts, affiliated artifacts, or the act of storytelling in itself. Many curators and education directors at these sites create interactive and immersive exhibits to engage with specialized library and archival collections such as Seven Stories: The National Centre for British Children's Books in Newcastle upon Tyne, UK. The Eric Carle Museum of Picture Book Art in Amherst, Massachusetts (U.S.), defines itself as an art museum for picture book art focusing on the role of art education and displaying the work as fine art. Other venues are primarily designed to offer literacy education to young people outside or in tandem with a school environment, such as the Discover Children's Story Centre in Stratford, East London (UK), that centers on an activity-oriented story trail through an indoor playscape with temporary installations. The Story Museum in Oxford (UK) defines itself distinctively as a museum focused on the concept of story rather than a particular collection or archive. Its programs encourage young people to write and create their own stories inspired by their exhibits and creative activities.

One of the Oxford Story Museum's first exhibits, *26 Characters: Celebrating Childhood Story Heroes* (2014), invited well-known authors for young people to choose their favorite heroes from children's stories. In the preface to the exhibit companion guide, one of the curators, Cambridge Jones, describes the motivation behind the exhibit:

> We decided to create an exhibition of the greatest storytellers. We concluded that just asking writers and storytellers to sit as my subjects was not sufficiently in keeping with the magic of the building and the big plans. So we decided to ask them all who their favourite character from childhood stories was [. . .] and then we would photograph them in character.
>
> (*26 Characters* 2014)

Each author's area in the exhibit included an immersive space dedicated to a portrait of the author photographed in a costume inspired by the character and affiliated story. For example,

Neil Gaiman chose to dress as Badger from Kenneth Grahame's canonical children's literature text, *The Wind and the Willows* (1908). The portrait was displayed in the context of a corner designed to look like Badger's home where visitors could sit in the character's armchair and listen to Gaiman read from the novel over a sound system.

While the focus of the museum and the basis of the exhibit were broadly defined as the heroes of childhood stories, this foundational exhibit primarily involved the celebration of canonical classics of British children's literature (using costumes from the National Theatre and Royal Shakespeare Company to add to the cultural capital). Other characters included Terry Pratchett as "Just William" from *Just William* by Richmal Crompton and Cressida Cowell as the title character in *Peter Pan*, all cultivating a nostalgic vision of the great narratives of children's literature and European fairy tales. Alongside these were three examples from folkloric traditions outside the British Children's literature canon: Jamila Gavin as Hanuman the Monkey God from the Ramayana, Benjamin Zephaniah as Anansi the Spider, and Michael Rosen as Till Eulenspiegel, a trickster character from medieval European folklore. While these characters broaden the notion of children's stories beyond the British national context, published authors (although some do perform as oral storytellers as well) continue to be celebrated and prioritized within the museum context.

These sites often promote traditional children's literature and literacies alongside new literacies. New literacies are defined as those practices that draw upon technical affordances of new media technologies but also cultivate a "new ethos" that is often defined as "participatory," "collaborative," and "distributed" (Knobel and Lankshear 2007, 9). While these characteristics are often connected to new technologies, these spaces illustrate the potential to offer interactive engagement across older and new media forms.

The Tinderbox Culture Centre for Children located next door to the Hans Christian Andersen House and Museum exemplifies shifts in fairy-tale museums toward new literacies and hands-on engagement. Distinct from the Hans Christian Andersen House and Museum itself, this art center provides engagement with fairy-tale narratives characteristic of children's museums directly aimed at young elementary school–age visitors. The site includes an art studio, a puppet theater, storytelling and performances, and an immersive "Fairytale Land" based on Andersen's "The Steadfast Tin Soldier" with the main aim to dress-up play and explore a castle. This site departs from the collection-oriented approach, reflecting discourses of creativity, experiential learning, and the role of storytelling through the creative arts. This museum reveals an emphasis on creativity as central to a young person's learning. Amy F. Ogata observes that "[s]uch awe at the child's apparently innate creativity has its roots in the romantic era, and has not only persisted but also expanded in our own age" (2013, ix). For example, the description of the Art Studio on the Tinderbox website includes: "Hans Christian Andersen drew, painted and made paper cuttings with as much enthusiasm as he wrote. In the Art Studio you will find activities and materials related to his creativity and to the fairytale unfolded in the Fairytale Land" (The Tinderbox 2016).

Despite the emphasis on the act of storytelling, the celebration of Andersen as a creative author of fairy tale is sustained. Similarly, Miyazawa Kenji Dowa Mura (Village of Fairy Tales) located in Iwate, Tohoku (Japan), consists of a large venue dedicated to the literary fairy tales of Japanese poet and children's author Kenji Miyazawa. The emphasis of this site is mediated engagement with literary fairy-tale narratives including video and soundscapes; objects such as plants, birds, and rocks from Miyazawa fairy tales; and a "Fairies' Trail" through a wild plant garden and fruit trees (Village of Fairy Tales 2016). The emphasis here is tactile and physical experience of the story elements. However, similar to the Tinderbox, the focus is on the figure and work of Miyazawa. These exhibits reflect an interest in educational discourses of play and experiential learning, while the selection of content remains close to the literary and artistic features of the literary fairy-tale texts themselves.

At a temporary exhibit entitled *Moving Stories: Children's Books from Page to Screen* (2014) at Seven Stories: National Centre for Children's Books (UK), young visitors are offered freedom to enter experiences from both so-called "Journeys of Adventure," based on fantasy-infused adaptations of published children's literature (e.g., Barrie's *Peter Pan* [1911], Brian Selznick's *The Invention of Hugo Cabret* [2007], and Shaun Tan's *Lost and Found* [2011]), as well as popular fairy-tale narratives (e.g., "Snow White," ATU 709, and "Cinderella," ATU 510A). As part of this exhibit, visitors are invited to engage with various cross-media texts including film stills, audio clips, and tactile and sensory experiences, including a ride in Cinderella's pumpkin-esque chariot to the ball. The exhibits are designed to be immersive but within carefully chosen sites from the tales that involve confined domestic spaces. Margaret Mackey observes:

> Most readers, viewers, and players are familiar with two associated phenomena. One is the sensation of being completely absorbed in a fictional world. A different form of involvement includes the capacity to move in and out of that absorbed attention in order to consider wider questions about the fiction, yet without entirely leaving the "fiction zone."
>
> (2007, 177)

This controlled design functions to both idealize the story worlds but also to ensure protective play and movement.

Within the context of an immersive exhibit, the visual and verbal elements of print texts are not only adapted across multiple media platforms, but the design of each affiliated text has the opportunity to meaningfully extend, inform, or potentially subvert the central discourses of the fairy tale or children's literature narrative. In her work on recreational play in relation to cross-media worlds and transmedia storytelling by Canadian young adults, Mackey (2007) observes that the participants in her study "expressed a preference for some kind of enlarged fictional universe that expanded beyond the limits of a single title" (182). She uses *The Lord of the Rings* (Tolkien 1954–55) as an example of what she has defined as the "Big World" phenomenon, namely that the fictional world is expanded beyond a single title to a trilogy of books and *The Hobbit* (1937), a prequel, as well as related stories, languages, histories, maps, and legends of Middle Earth in *The Silmarillion* (1973). Similarly, Henry Jenkins defines a "transmedia story" as one that "unfolds across multiple media platforms with each new text making a distinctive and valuable contribution to the whole" (2006, 95–96). Immersive fairy-tale exhibits provide experiences with the possibility to engage with transmedia narratives across geographic and cultural boundaries. Nevertheless, many of the fairy-tale immersive venues emphasize immersion in the story worlds rather than the experience of critical engagement, which requires moving in and out of the story-world space. They also continue to reinforce national contexts and celebratory discourses of authorship around fairy-tale narratives.

Young People as Co-Curators

Most of these exhibits geared at young people avoid the darker discourses articulated in fairy-tale narratives through the omission of textual representations of violence, death, and other controversial topics. However, there are some select exhibits that explicitly provide opportunities for young readers to engage with these contentious discourses in a creative manner. Commissioned as part of a broader exhibit curated by Araki Natsumi at the Mori Art

Museum (Tokyo, Japan) called *Go-Betweens: The World Seen through Children* (2014a), Takayuki Yamamoto's work "New Hell: What Kind of Hell Will We Go To?, Tokyo" was situated among a range of art pieces that aim to emphasize the subjectivity of young people's experiences using diverse media. The artwork relies heavily on magical realism blurring the boundaries between fantasy/fairy-tale elements as well as realistic documentary and photographic representations.

The curator's description of the *Go-Betweens* exhibit described their process as "[t]aking as key words the likes of play, dreams and memories, it also homes in on the diverse sensate nature of children, their creativity unconstrained by adult convention or the bounds of tradition" (2014a). This official discourse is that of childhood as sensory, creative, and boundary breaking. Yamamoto's work is about the practices of storytelling and story-world creation within Japanese spiritual and religious cultures as much as it is about young people's perceptions. Moreover, distinct from other exhibits, it posits young people as co-creators.

While the work has been reproduced in various international locations, this exhibit included the work of young people in Tokyo. In his workshops with young people, Yamamoto first introduces the participants to Buddhist *mandala*, or Japanese map-like paintings, from the Kamakura period (1185–1333) that depicted *jigokudo*, a stage of existence that people need to pass through in order to get to heaven. In an interview related to the Mori Art Museum exhibit, the artist explains how he describes these traditions to young participants: "The Buddhists used the mandala to give an idea of what happens to people in the six stages of existence. Hell is but one stage that we must go through, and once you have passed through you get closer to heaven" (quoted in Wakeling 2014). One example from the project is a video of a young female participant's depiction of a "hearts everywhere hell" through the creation of paper-mache and painted sculpted objects as well as recited written narrative. Her video performance of her story to accompany the art work details her creation:

> If you can't stop thinking about somebody you love and neglect work—you'll go there. All the hearts squash your body and soul. And you'll be a flat human. Once you're a flat human, you will be ice cream topping and the ogre will eat you. For 111 years, until the soft, the soft serve ice-cream spills. You'll be eaten as ice cream topping. When it spills you will be free to go. Everybody is happy but it is still painful to be in hell.
>
> (*Go-Betweens* "New Hell: What Kind of Hell Will We Go To?" 2014b)

This young person's hybrid composition illustrates engagement with various cultural contexts for storytelling and world-building, presenting a text that is at once subversive and normative in its dark material. While the content deals with issues not often situated in children's museum exhibits, the use of craft material and art style to depict the narrative involves those often associated with childhood play. In addition, the written narrative echoes folkloric elements from diverse cultural traditions, among them the curse or spell to be broken. The ice cream visual of excess is reminiscent of picture book adaptations of "Hansel and Gretel" (ATU 327A) or the anxiety of being eaten, a visual obsession of the internationally renowned children's book author Maurice Sendak. At another level of discourse, an interview on a Tokyo Art blog exemplifies an overriding discourse of the creative child, one that promotes the child's need to be given freedom within structure to channel their innate creativity. Yamamato says about the process:

> I grab their attention and direct it towards the project. Of course, if you leave kids to make whatever they want, they will probably just want to make Martians. As the

artist, I create the situation. I want to encourage them to channel their creativity into thinking about what is possible. They start by following me, but by the end, I've stepped back and they are in control.

(quoted in Wakeling 2014)

Despite positioning the child in a creator role to engage with taboo topics found in folkloric narratives, the intention of the artistic collaboration continues to be for an adult artist to instruct about cultural and art history through a creative process. While many of the exhibits and museum venues offer new potential through mediated engagement, there are still significant gaps in the ways these may become sites for critical pedagogy and participation with the subversive and critically empowering elements of both fairy-tale narratives and storytelling practices.

Related topics: Autobiography; Blogs and Websites; Children's and Young Adult (YA) Literature; Children's Picture Books and Illustrations; Contemporary Art; Digital; Material Culture; Mobile Apps

References Cited and Further Reading

Acosta, Teresa Y. 2000. "Parent-Child Social Play in a Children's Museum." *Family Relations* 49: 45–52.

Allen, Sue. 2004. "Designs for Learning: Studying Science Museum Exhibits That Do More Than Entertain." *Science Education* 88 (1): 17–34.

Andersen, Hans Christian. 1838. "The Steadfast Tin Soldier." *Fairy Tales Told for Children New Collection, First Version.* Copenhagen: Reitzel.

Barrie, J. M. 1911. *Peter Pan; or the Boy Who Wouldn't Grow Up.* New York: Charles Scribner's Sons.

"Castles and Manor Houses from Around the World." 2010–2014. www.castlesandmanorhouses.com.

Crompton, Richmal. 1922. *Just William.* London: George Newnes.

"Deutsche Märchen Strasse: German Fairy Tale Route." 2016. www.deutsche-maerchenstrasse.com/en/?lang=en_US.

Grahame, Kenneth. 1908. *The Wind in the Willows.* London: Methuen.

Henderson, Tara Zollinger, and David J. Atencio. 2007. "Integration of Play, Learning, and Experience: What Museums Afford Young Visitors." *Early Childhood Education Journal* 35: 245.

Jenkins, Henry. 2006. *Convergence Culture: Where Old and New Media Collide.* New York: NYU P.

Jones, Cambridge, and Alice Rochester. 2014. *26 Characters: Celebrating Childhood Story Heroes.* Oxford: The Story Museum.

Judd, Mary K., and James B. Kracht. 1997. "The World at Their Fingertips: Children in Museums." In *Learning Opportunities Beyond School*, edited by Barbara Hatcher and Shirley S. Beck, 18–24. Onley, MD: Association of Childhood Education International.

Knobel, Michelle, and Colin Lankshear. 2007. *A New Literacies Sampler.* New York: Peter Lang.

Kress, Gunther R., and Theo van Leeuwen. 2001. *Multimodal Discourse: The Modes and Media of Contemporary Communication.* London: Oxford UP.

Kücklich, Julian. 2003–2004. "Play and Playability as Key Concepts in New Media Studies." Report on Research Undertaken during Marie Curie Fellowship. Ireland: Dublin City University.

Liburd, Janne J. 2009. "Tourism and the Hans Christian Andersen Bicentenary Event in Denmark." In *International Perspectives of Festivals and Events: Paradigms of Analysis*, edited by Jane Ali-Knight, Alan Fyall, Martin Robertson, and Adele Ladkin, 41–52. London: Routledge.

Literary Traveler. 2002. "Hans Christian Andersen Travels Through Denmark." June 1. www.literarytraveler.com/articles/hans-christian-andersen-travels-through-denmark/.

Lyons, Colette. 2012. "Danish Delight: Fairytales, Fantasy and Food on Funen, Hans Christian Andersen's Island." *The Daily Mail Online*, November 7. www.dailymail.co.uk/travel/article-2229215/Denmark-holidays-Funen-fairy-tale-home-Hans-Christian-Andersen.html.

Mackey, Margaret. 2007. *Mapping Recreational Literacies: Contemporary Adults at Play.* New York: Peter Lang.

Magnus-Johnston, Kendra. 2016. "'My Life as a Fairy Tale': The Fairy-Tale Author in Popular Cinema." In *Fairy-Tale Films Beyond Disney: International Perspectives*, edited by Jack Zipes, Pauline Greenhill, and Kendra Magnus-Johnston, 18–33. New York: Routledge.

Ogata, Amy F. 2013. *Designing the Creative Child: Playthings and Places in Midcentury America.* Minneapolis: U Minnesota P.

Piscitelli, Barbara, and David Anderson. 2001. "Young Children's Perspectives of Museum Settings and Experiences." *Museum Management and Curatorship* 19 (3): 269–82.

Selznick, Brian. 2007. *The Invention of Hugo Cabret.* New York: Scholastic.

Simon, Nina. 2010. "The Participatory Museum." *Museum 2.0.* www.participatorymuseum.org.

Tan, Shaun. 2011. *Lost and Found.* New York: Scholastic.

Thompson, Christa. 2016. "The Fairytale Traveler: Travel and Lifestyle Inspired by Books, Film, TV and Mythology." http://thefairytaletraveler.com.

The Tinderbox. 2016. "Odense City Museums." http://museum.odense.dk/en/museums/the-tinderbox.

Tolkien, J. R. R. 1937. *The Hobbit, or There and Back Again.* London: George Allen & Unwin.

———. 1954–1955. *The Lord of the Rings.* London: George Allen & Unwin.

———. 1973. *The Silmarillion.* London: George Allen & Unwin.

Unrath, Kathy, and Mick Luehrman. 2009. "Bringing Children to Art—Bringing Art to Children: Museum Education Program Connects Preservice Teachers and Museum Visitors through 'Portable Children's Museums'." *Art Education* 62 (1): 41.

Village of Fairy Tales (Miyazawa Kenji Dowa Mura). 2016. "Japan National Tourism Organization." www.jnto.go.jp/eng/spot/thempark/miyazawa-kenji-dowa-mura.html.

Wakeling, Emily. 2014. "New Hell: Interview with Takayuki Yamamoto." *Tokyo Art Beat,* June 16. www.tokyoartbeat.com/tablog/entries.en/2014/06/new-hell-interview-with-takayuki-yamamoto.html.

Zipes, Jack. 2005. *Hans Christian Andersen: The Misunderstood Storyteller.* New York: Routledge.

Mediagraphy

26 Characters: Celebrating Childhood Story Heroes (Exhibit). 2014. Curator Cambridge Jones. Story Museum. Oxford, UK. www.storymuseum.org.uk/stories/26-characters-exhibition/.

Fairytale Fashion (Exhibit). 2016. Curator Colleen Hill. Fashion Institute of Technology. New York City, New York, USA.

Fairytale Fiesta (Exhibit). 2014. Witte Museum. San Antonia, Texas, USA. http://do210.com/events/weekly/mon/fairytale-fiesta.

Hans Christian Andersen: My Life as a Fairy Tale. 2003. Director Philip Saville. USA.

Hans Christian Andersen Trail (Mobile App). 2016. University of Southern Denmark, H. C. Andersen Centret/Destinationa Fyn. www.visitfyn.com/ln-int/fyn/follow-hans-christian-andersen-trail.

H. C. Andersens Odense (Mobile App). 2015. Odense Kommune, Odense Bys Museer. http://andersensodense.dk.

Go-Betweens: The World Seen Through Children (Exhibit). 2014a. Curator Araki Natsumi. Mori Art Museum. Tokyo, Japan. www.mori.art.museum/english/contents/go_betweens/about/index.html.

———. "New Hell: What Kind of Hell Will We Go To?" 2014b. Artist Takayuki Yamamoto.

Moving Stories: Children's Books From Page to Screen (Exhibit). 2014. Curator Claire Hampton. Seven Stories: National Centre for Children's Books. Newcastle upon Tyne, UK.

Once Upon a Time: Fairy Tales From the Osborne Collection of Early Children's Books (Exhibit). 2016. Toronto Public Library. Toronto, Ontario, Canada. www.torontopubliclibrary.ca/programs-and-classes/exhibits/once-upon-a-time.jsp.

48

CHILDREN'S PICTURE BOOKS AND ILLUSTRATIONS

Balaka Basu

The fairy-tale picture book is a strange object: by its very nature, it must pin down images, closing down the lacunae that the stories themselves leave open. Although developed from an oral tradition of storytelling, where narrators embellished and specified details as they pleased, in its written form, the fairy tale is commonly characterized by its skeleton plot, which is only intermittently fleshed out with sparse description. Not much time is spent describing the setting of these stories: they take place "once upon a time" or "in a faraway land," but we often have very little idea what these times and spaces are actually like. Whether intentional or not, the effect of this indeterminacy is to create greater accessibility; audiences and readers are, if not invited, then at least permitted to imagine themselves into the narrative. However, although visual representations of such stories can do important cultural work by creating common graphic vocabularies within nations and cultures, since the detailed specificity of an illustration limits the ability of readers to see their representations within it, pinning an image to an open-ended text can serve to foreclose some imaginative possibilities, with social, cultural, and political consequences to this foreclosure.

History of Word/Image in the Fairy-Tale Tradition

Almost all of the nineteenth-century European fairy tales appeared first in printed books or booklets with few or no illustrations. After the works achieved a certain degree of popularity, artwork was provided in order to make the stories more appealing to children. For example, when Jacob and Wilhelm Grimm published the first edition of their *Children's and Household Tales*, it was timed aptly for Christmas sales in 1812. In his letter of thanks for the dedication of the volume to his wife and child, German Romanticist Achim von Arnim wrote that while the volume made an impressive gift, he would advise the inclusion of illustrations:

> Have your brother draw a few pages for the tales, the lack of copper plates and the surrounding learnedness exclude it from the realm of children's books and prevent more widespread distribution. I wouldn't be surprised if a certain speculator in Leipzig did not extract the most entertaining tales and reprint them with accompanying pictures.
>
> (quoted in Freudenburg 1998, 267–268)

443

Von Arnim, in noting the lack of woodcuts and engravings, seeks to market the stories to child readers, who like Lewis Carroll's Alice see no use in books "without pictures or conversation" (2003, 9).

In the mid-nineteenth century, supplementary illustrations were often made using the technique of wood engraving. Here, after the artist has created the image, which may be drawn directly onto the block or transferred from a separate drawing, the engraver carves out the image from the surface of the wood. Ink is applied to the parts that have not been carved, leaving the gouges as white space. Such illustrations are sometimes referred to as cuts or woodcuts. With new color printing techniques making their appearance in the mid-nineteenth century, the toy book—a brightly colored picture book—became a popular gift for children and eventually evolved into the modern picture book, which usually comes in a standard length of thirty-two pages and around 500 to 600 words. In illustrated fairy-tale books, the words usually come first and the images follow. In the nineteenth century, this was undoubtedly because of the high expense associated with printing illustrations.

For example, Hans Christian Andersen's *Fairy Tales Told for Children* was published in installments between 1835 and 1837. Since they were not immediately popular, the stories were not released in an illustrated edition until 1849, when Andersen's German publisher decided that their increasing success merited such attention. Vilhelm Pedersen, a Danish naval officer, provided this first series of illustrations, which Andersen himself appreciated and endorsed. Like John Tenniel's illustrations of Carroll's *Alice's Adventures in Wonderland* (1865) and *Through the Looking Glass* (1871), for many readers Pedersen's detailed engravings embody Andersen's work, with Pedersen's soft lines and use of shadow underscoring Andersen's poignant melancholy. The collaboration between artist and writer in these cases comes together to form a text greater than the sum of its parts.

In *How Picturebooks Work*, Maria Nikolajeva and Carole Scott draw a distinction between an illustrated text and a picture book, which depends on the quantity and significance of the images. In an illustrated text, images are subordinate to the text and occur with lesser frequency, while the picture book's images are equally if not more important than its words (2006, 6). The picture book encourages reexamination because images frequently have considerable depth, offering more to see the longer one looks. Conversely, a narrative without illustration with its rush to find out "what happened next" does not encourage stopping. A successful picture book will be one where both modes—image and word—influence and inform each other, although not always in obvious ways (Nikolajeva and Scott 2006, 11). For instance, the words may provide counterpoint and contradiction to the images, rather than emphasis (Nodelman 1988, 199; Nikolajeva and Scott 2006). Whereas the illustrated fairy tale relies much more heavily upon the words, in the fairy-tale picture book, the images are essential to its reading because they shape the reader/viewer's understanding and experience, not just of the story, but of the world at large.

While artists like Pedersen and Tenniel had relatively amicable relationships with their authors, relationships between writers and illustrators were not always so friendly, especially since the hierarchy of word and image continued to be contested by both artists and writers. Collaborating with L. Frank Baum, W. W. Denslow (1856–1915) created twenty-four individual plates as well as headpieces, tailpieces, and other marginalia to illustrate the American literary fairy tale *The Wonderful Wizard of Oz* (1900). Both Baum and Denslow were copyright holders on this first Oz book, which as a new literary fairy tale required a high degree of visual imagination to create memorable iconography. However, arguments between writer and artist destroyed their partnership, with each individual believing his work was responsible for the success of the book.

Nationalism and Orientalism in Fairy-Tale Illustrations

The Western fairy tale achieved one of its golden ages during the rise of European nationalism in the nineteenth century, a time when the folk of Europe were attempting to create cultural motifs that would represent and unify their infant nations. Jacob and Wilhelm Grimm collected together their *Children's and Household Tales* in 1812, for instance, in order to codify a new German identity by curating a shared cultural heritage. The Grimms' fairy-tale world stands in for a cohesive national ideology and past. Nostalgia for this imaginary "once upon a time" suggests that readers of the *Tales* will attempt to recreate this cultural memory in their own present, an ultimately conservative project.

The second edition of the *Tales* was published in 1819, and its frontispiece was the only image. Drawn by Jacob and Wilhelm's brother, Ludwig Emil Grimm, it featured a portrait of one of the major contributors to the collection. Dorothea Viehmann differed from other contributors of stories; the Grimms described her as a peasant, and her portrait demonstrates an idealized version of one of the folk. Jack Zipes argues that "the Brothers Grimm sought to validate the genuine nature of their folk tales with her picture as a 'mythic' peasant woman" (2015, 15). Viehmann's image thus represents the every-teller, whose stories invent the nation's cultural history. Similarly, decades before Disney's cinematic colonization of the European fairy tale began with *Snow White and the Seven Dwarfs* (1937), L. Frank Baum and W. W. Denslow envisioned a "modern" quintessentially American fairy tale for the children of still another new nation, this time in the "new world." *The Wonderful Wizard of Oz* was specifically designed to belong to American children in a way that the fairy tales of the Brothers Grimm could not yet do before the age of Disney.

In addition to the fairy tale's relevance to nation building, it is also important to acknowledge its relationship with the exotic Other and the disturbing practice of Orientalism. Nowhere is this connection more apparent than in the Western translation and reception of *Arabian Nights* (as the Arabic collection *1001 Nights* is commonly known). Translated and published in France during the early eighteenth century by Antoine Galland, this collection, geared toward a primarily adult audience of readers, initially had no illustrations. Subsequent unauthorized editions possessed engraved frontispieces that make no effort to portray the Middle Eastern setting. Only when Edward William Lane began to publish his translation in 1838, first serialized in newspapers before being bound into volumes, did the illustrations begin to attempt to reflect at least a romanticized version of life in the Arab world. Lane was anxious that the text be educational and thus required his engraver, William Harvey, to adhere to a high standard of accuracy by copying authentic Egyptian and Moorish engravings, but even then, its exoticism of the culture is readily apparent.

Walter Crane (1845–1915), a hugely important figure in fairy-tale illustrations and picture books for children, completed the first colored illustrations for *Arabian Nights* in *Aladdin's Picture Book* (1876). Impressed by Japanese prints, Crane used the bold outlines and flat color of Japanese art to great effect. Not only did this style appeal to children, it also eased the printer's task, as shading was still particularly hard to convey. Crane was also a holistic or—as he termed it—a decorative artist: one who was concerned with the artistic effect of the book taken together and not just the individual pictures. In order to incorporate words and images together into a pleasing whole, Crane studied the techniques of illuminated manuscripts. He was also one of the first artists to truly consider what children might actually enjoy in terms of illustration. He writes:

> Children, like ancient Egyptians, appear to see things in profile, and like definite statements in design. They prefer well-designed forms and bright frank colour. They

don't want to bother with three dimensions. They can accept symbolic representations. They themselves employ drawing [. . .] as a kind of picture writing and eagerly follow a pictured story.

(1913, 85)

Probably the most famous of the *Arabian Nights* illustrators was early twentieth-century artist Edmund Dulac. His picture books, *Stories from the Arabian Nights* (1907) and *Sinbad the Sailor & Other Tales from the Arabian Nights* (1914), used motifs from Persian, Chinese, and Japanese art. Dulac's illustrations clearly left their imprint on Disney's *Aladdin* (1992), whose artists paid homage to his work in the towers and minarets of Agrabah. Successive illustrators of *Arabian Nights* did not feel the need to copy Crane and Dulac in their attempts to achieve authenticity. Kay Nielsen (1886–1957)—also famous for his illustrations of Andersen's works—found inspiration from all over Asia to create his *Arabian Nights* images, producing fantastical pictures that are stunningly surreal. Here, *Arabian Nights* functions as the Other, using iconography that reads as foreign and exotic to the Western world: turbans, odalisques, and key pattern borders.

Nielsen's impact on fairy-tale imagery was extremely significant. Not only was he an influential print artist, he also worked for Disney on films like *Fantasia* (1940). As Didier Ghez's book points out, Neilsen's concept art for a potential 1940s film of *The Little Mermaid* directly influenced the 1989 film when Disney director Ron Clements rediscovered it in 1985 (2016, 8). One particular image of the Little Mermaid, with flowing hair, wide eyes, and clasped hands, is a clear reference for the future Ariel. Since Disney and fairy tales are now practically synonymous in the contemporary Euro North American popular experience of fairy tales, to affect Disney's imagery is to affect the way contemporary young people envision the fairy tale itself.

One of the problems with Disney as a global brand, however, is that it both participates in this process of Orientalism while simultaneously overwhelming other interpretations. Many of the children whose experience is not reflected on screen and on the page are investing in franchises that do not include them. The visual tradition of fairy tales, which can bring people together to form cohesive nations, can also be incredibly alienating if seen by the numerous children whose experiences are not reflected therein. Dorothy Hurley discusses the troubling consequences of this for children of color. She writes:

> Since the invention of cinema, the visual representation of fairy tale characters has been dominated by the Disney version of these tales. Such is the power of visual representation that children tend to believe that Disney's version of the fairy tale is the real story rather than the "classic" version. [. . .] [Disney's] images [. . .] are then translated into beliefs children hold about status in particular group membership, in relation to notions of good, bad, pretty, and ugly as reflected in the films.
>
> (2005, 222)

Hurley begins to examine the role that Disney plays in enforcing systems of White privilege in the minds of children of color; she notes that *Aladdin* is the first fairy-tale film in the Disney canon to take place outside of Europe and feature people of color, and yet, even here, the essential "privileging of Western or White culture" is preserved (2005, 226). It seems as if this is diversity in name only; children of color do not see themselves reflected within the story—and since the imagery is so pervasive, they feel unwelcome in the Euro North American fairy-tale tradition.

If one hunts for contemporary fairy-tale picture books, many of the texts are produced by Disney, encompassing short versions of and sequels to the popular animated films, from *Snow*

White and the Seven Dwarfs and *Cinderella* (1950) all the way to *Frozen* (2013), including titles like *Princess Adventure Stories* (Disney Book Group 2013). It's intriguing to note that this text does not list an author, simply crediting the Disney Corporation. Contemporary iconography reflects the impact of the Disney brand, as we can see by charting the images of the Beast from "Beauty and the Beast" (ATU 425C). Early illustrations of this fairy tale varied the Beast's monstrosity, using wolves, boars, and even horned goats. Both the Columbia Broadcasting System (CBS) television show *Beauty and the Beast* (1987–1990) and the 1991 Disney film introduce a leonine element into the mix, and many subsequent picture books follow this trend.

Up until Disney's *Cinderella*, for example, cover illustrations for "Cinderella" (ATU 510A) picture books usually featured the protagonist in her humble beginnings: dressed in rags and patiently enduring hardship. The Little Golden Book that accompanied the film, however, showed Cinderella in her fancy ball gown. This image heavily influenced subsequent texts— the majority of which showed Cinderella resembling her Disney iteration (Robinson and Wildermith 2015, 64–65). In other words, the massive commodification of the Disney brand seriously affects the images that are allowed to persist in symbolizing Euro North American culture.

Modern Picture Books and Intertextuality

Perry Nodelman examines the role of intertextuality particularly in relation to the visual representations in picture books. He writes, "[I]ntertextuality even of nontexts—of the conventions of visual imagery—[. . .] make clear the extent to which even the most apparently simple of picture books exists in the context of the entire history of visual depiction" (1988, 124). Similarly, in *The Picture Book* (2006), Angus Hyland writes that "illustration [in children's books], rather than what we think of as fine art, forms the basis of our aesthetic education." As a personal example, he goes on to say that he can "trace [his] own appreciation of Picasso backwards via Hockney to Escher to Ardizzoni, to Arthur Rackham" (7). Rackham, of course, is one of the most famous fairy-tale illustrators of the late nineteenth and early twentieth centuries. His work with the Grimms' stories is macabre, filled with dark spaces, swirling lines, and unsaturated colors that evoke mystery and enchantment. While Hyland traces his understanding of fine art backward to Rackham, more contemporary illustrators often incorporate fine art motifs within their picture books, creating, in lieu of intertextuality, what might be called intervisuality, as when Paul O. Zelinsky interweaves classic motifs from Italian Renaissance art into his *Rapunzel* (2002). Young readers who encounter such visual semiotics first in the picture book will theoretically find them appealing when encountered within the walls of a museum.

A comparable history of fairy-tale illustration is exemplified in Maurice Sendak's illustrations for Lore Segal's translations of the Grimms' stories in *The Juniper Tree: And Other Tales from Grimm* (1973). While Sendak's artwork was surreally disproportionate and delightfully claustrophobic, his use of crosshatching nostalgically recalls those nineteenth-century woodcuts, suggesting that these drawings are part of an ongoing tradition. Other artists from the modern period participate in this sense of artistic continuity, incorporating other historical resonances: Trina Schart Hyman, for example, illustrates *Sleeping Beauty* (1977) and *Little Red Riding Hood* (1983) with a dark, lush style that uses light and shadow in ways reminiscent of early twentieth-century fairy-tale artists like Arthur Rackham and Edmund Dulac. Conversely, artists like Jack Kent utilize a different tradition within works like *Happily Ever After* (1976), drawing upon cartoon and newspaper lines and color blocking to bring a different perspective to the fairy-tale picture book.

Fairy Tales and the Postmodern Picture Book

Viewing fairy-tale illustration as an introduction to the "classic" canon of fine art is complicated by the picture book's potential for innovation. David Lewis suggests that the picture book is often a radical form, where "the promiscuous mixing together of words and images—is able to shake loose generic bonds and derail expectations" (2001, 68). This is especially apparent in the postmodern picture book, which is currently a popular vehicle for the fairy tale. This genre is often characterized by its consideration of the means of storytelling within the context of the narrative. David Weisner's *The Three Pigs* (2001) and Jon Scieszka and Lane Smith's *The Stinky Cheese Man and Other Fairly Stupid Tales* (1992) are excellent examples of this approach. Weisner's pigs travel outside the story's frame, appearing in the margins of the page to comment on the story with word balloons that reference comic book art. As the narrative unfolds, the expected images start to break and tilt, while the pigs escape into the page gutters (i.e., the white spaces between facing pages and between framed images and text on a single page). As they leave the story world to enter into ours, the pigs' stylized portrayal begins to look more and more three dimensional and realistic. In *The Stinky Cheese Man*, Scieszka and Smith use non-linearity to parody book design and layout, creating humor through its mixed-up and unrestrainedly anarchic versions of familiar fairy tales. Marilyn Singer's *Mirror Mirror* (2010) and its sequel *Follow Follow* (2013) are compelling in this arena as well; her invented poetic form, the reverso, conveys one meaning when read down the page and another when read in reverse, cleverly utilizing a different perspective in each direction. The mirror images reflect as well, using similar shapes that transform meaning across facing pages.

Eliza Dresang argues that the principles of radical change theory in picture books for the digital era are based on three fundamental principles: interactivity, connectivity, and access (2008, 294–295). Since the picture book's iconotext communicates meaning multimodally, it offers the opportunity to exploit these principles with digital technology. Applications (apps) like *Little Red Riding Hood* (2013) by Nosy Crow (and other fairy tale adaptations from Nosy Crow apps) allow images to come alive, providing readers/users with the ability to interact with and alter the narrative in a choose-your-own-adventure fashion. Apps are essentially interactive, so they permit users to experience play and storytelling simultaneously. The picture book has long been noted for its materiality, in other words, a profound concern with the book as physical object. In studying a picture book, therefore, one must pay careful attention to its paratextual elements, including but not limited to cover images, the page layout, the interplay between words and images on the page, and the way page turns are orchestrated. To all these possibilities, the fairy-tale picture book app adds other material considerations including the motions undertaken by the user and the inclusion of sound and music.

However, such innovations in text delivery are paralleled by a contemporary trend in contemporary picture books that privileges simplicity without sacrificing depth. Bethany Woolvin's *Little Red* (2016), for instance, uses only three colors, red, black, and white, and its minimalist text and art allow for plenty of negative space that highlights each mode. Nevertheless, Woolvin's words and images remain subversive: here, the wolf doesn't fool Little Red at all. When this subversive, radical vision of the picture book is taken together with the more conservative nature of the fairy tale, we meet with a startling juxtaposition of tradition and iconoclasm.

Opening the Fairy-Tale Picture Book

We generally expect both the fairy tale and the picture book to serve as vehicles for a child's unrestrained imagination. Each mode on its own has narrative gaps that work to invite the

CHILDREN'S PICTURE BOOKS AND ILLUSTRATIONS

reader in: white spaces and archetypical, undefined characters and places. Each mode is characterized by internationalism. However, both the fairy tale and the picture book can have didactic qualities: the fairy tale may seek to communicate cultural mores, while the picture book trains children to understand visual semiotics. Neither of these pedagogical projects is enhanced by ambiguity. Paradoxically, therefore, their juxtaposition works as a limiting force, where instability is made stable and the inherent conflicts of each remain muffled by the other.

Related topics: Chapbooks; Children's and Young Adult (YA) Literature; Disney Corporation; Mobile Apps; Orientalism; Print

References Cited and Further Reading

Andersen, Hans Christian. 1835–1837. *Eventyr, fortalte for Børn (Fairy Tales Told for Children).* Copenhagen: C.A. Reitzel.

Baum, L. Frank. 1900. *The Wonderful Wizard of Oz*, illustrated by W. W. Denslow. Chicago: Geo. M. Hill Co.

Beckett, Sandra. 2002. *Recycling Red Riding Hood.* New York: Routledge.

Carroll, Lewis. (1865; 1871) 2003. *Alice's Adventures in Wonderland and Through the Looking Glass.* New York: Penguin.

Crane, Walter. 1876. *Aladdin's Picture Book.* London: Routledge.

———. 1913. "Notes on My Own Books for Children." *Imprint:* 81–6.

Daniel, Noel, ed. 2012. *Fairy Tales of the Brothers Grimm.* Los Angeles: Taschen.

———. 2013. *Fairy Tales of Hans Christian Andersen.* Los Angeles: Taschen.

Disney Book Group. 2013. *Princess Adventure Stories.* New York: Disney P.

Dresang, Eliza T. 2008. "Radical Change Revisited: Dynamic Digital Age Books for Youth." *Contemporary Issues in Technology and Teacher Education* 8 (3): 294–304.

Dulac, Edmund, illus. 1907. *Stories from Arabian Nights.* London: Hodder and Stoughton.

———. 1914. *Sinbad the Sailor and Other Stories from the Arabian Nights.* London: Hodder and Stoughton.

Fièvre, François. 2013. *Le Conte et l'image: L'illustration des contes de Grimm en Angleterre au XIXe siècle.* Tours: UP François-Rabelais.

Freudenberg, Rachel. 1998. "Illustrating Childhood—'Hansel and Gretel'." *Marvels & Tales* 12 (2): 263–318.

Galland, Antoine. 1704–1717. *Les mille et une nuits, contes arabes traduits en Français (One Thousand and One Nights).* Paris: La Haye.

Ghez, Didier. 2016. *They Drew as They Pleased: The Hidden Art of Disney's Musical Years.* San Francisco: Chronicle Books.

Grimm, Jacob, and Wilhelm Grimm. 1812. *Kinder- und Hausmärchen.* Vol. 1. Berlin: Realschulbuchhandlung/G. Reimer.

———. 1819. *Kinder- und Hausmärchen.* Revised ed. Berlin: Realschulbuchhandlung/G. Reimer.

Hurley, Dorothy. 2005. "Seeing White: Children of Color and the Disney Fairy Tale Princess." *The Journal of Negro Education* 74 (3): 221–32.

Hyland, Angus. 2006. *The Picture Book: Contemporary Illustration.* London: Lawrence King Publishing.

Hyman, Trina Schart. 1977. *Sleeping Beauty.* New York: Little, Brown & Co.

———. 1983. *Little Red Riding Hood.* New York: Holiday House Publishing.

Irwin, Robert. 2011. *Visions of the Jinn: Illustrators of the Arabian Nights.* Oxford: The Arcadian Library.

Kent, Jack. 1976. *Happily Ever After.* New York: Random House.

Lane, Edward William. 1863. *Arabian Nights.* Boston: Little, Brown & Co.

Lewis, David. 2001. *Reading Contemporary Picturebooks: Picturing Texts.* New York: Routledge.

Nikolajeva, Maria, and Carole Scott. 2006. *How Picturebooks Work.* New York: Routledge.

Nodelman, Perry. 1988. *Words about Pictures: The Narrative Art of Children's Picture Books.* Athens: U Georgia P.

Op de Beeck, Nathalie. 2010. *Suspended Animation: Children's Picture Books and the Fairy Tale of Modernity.* Minneapolis: U Minnesota P.

Robinson, Linda, and Susan Wildermith. 2015. "From Rags to Splendor: The Evolution of Cinderella Cover Illustrations from 1800 to 2014." *Visual Communication* 15 (1): 54–70.

Scieszka, Jon, and Lane Smith. 1992. *The Stinky Cheese Man and Other Fairly Stupid Tales.* New York: Viking.

Segal, Lore, and Maurice Sendak. 1973. *The Juniper Tree: And Other Tales from Grimm.* New York: Farrar, Straus and Giroux.

Singer, Marilyn. 2010. *Mirror Mirror: A Book of Reverso Poems.* New York: Penguin.

———. 2013. *Follow Follow: A Book of Reverso Poems.* New York: Penguin.

Weisner, David. 2001. *The Three Pigs*. New York: Clarion Books.
Woolvin, Bethany. 2016. *Little Red*. Atlanta: Peachtree Publishers.
Zelinsky, Paul O. 2002. *Rapunzel*. New York: Puffin Books.
Zipes, Jack. 2015. *Grimm Legacies*. Princeton, NJ: Princeton UP.

Mediagraphy

Aladdin. 1992. Directors Ron Clements and John Musker. USA.

Beauty and the Beast. 1991. Directors Gary Trousdale and Kirk Wise. USA.

——— (TV). 1987–1990. Creator Ron Koslow. USA.

Cinderella. 1950. Director Clyde Geronimi, Wilfred Jackson, and Hamilton Luske. USA.

Fantasia. 1940. Directors Joe Grant, Dick Huemer, Samuel Armstrong, James Algar, Bill Roberts, Paul Satterfield, Ben Sharpsteen, David D. Hand, Hamilton Luske, Jim Handley, Ford Beebe, T. Hee, Norman Ferguson, and Wilfred Jackson. USA.

Frozen. 2013. Directors Chris Buck and Jennifer Lee. USA.

The Little Mermaid. 1989. Directors Ron Clements and John Musker. USA.

Little Red Riding Hood (Mobile App). 2013. Nosy Crow. http://nosycrow.com/apps/little-red-riding-hood/.

Nielsen, Kay. N.d. *Shenreddin and Nureddin in Egypt* (Gouache and Watercolor on Paper). Art Institute of Chicago.

Nielsen, Kay. 1941. "Little Mermaid Concept Art" (Watercolor on Paper). *Wikia: The Home of Fandom*. http://disney.wikia.com/wiki/File:Little-mermaid-concept-art-by-kay-nielsen-1941.jpg.

Snow White and the Seven Dwarfs. 1937. Directors William Cottrell, David Hand, Wilfred Jackson, Larry Morey, Perce Pearce, and Ben Sharpsteen. USA.

49

CHILDREN'S TELEVISION

Jodi McDavid and Ian Brodie

The presentation of fairy tales and traditional literature in children's television reflects both the best and the worst of the medium. In many respects it represents a logical extension of the infantilization of tale already present in the nineteenth century with the reframing of folktale as a children's genre. In this chapter, we consider how various programs have presented "Little Red Riding Hood" (ATU 333). The tale's prominence in the Western canon, in cross-cultural reinterpretations, and within the scholarly literature (Beckett 2008, 2013; Dundes 1989) offers a wealth of examples through its perennial adaptation by children's television producers. By focusing on the one tale, we allow ourselves room to consider how various producers choose to play with or to adhere to the type. As we discuss, fairy tale in children's television faces a triple-faceted "triviality barrier" (Sutton-Smith 1970): a maligned genre in a maligned medium for a maligned audience. However, we eschew the cynical approach and instead adapt a hermeneutic of openness, proceeding with the notion that children's television producers can (and often do) avail themselves of the possibilities of both medium and fairy-tale form. The screen's presence within the familiar confines of the family home and the small size of its audience at the time of viewing provide an intimacy closer to interpersonal communication than in other mediations like film and theater.

Canons of vernacular narrative comprise a store of public domain materials freely adaptable to generate inexpensive content for a captive and allegedly non-discerning audience. A tale's ongoing presence in multiple versions, through the child's (presumed) exposure to them through storytelling, literature (as read or read to), film, toys, or other television, provides a low entry point to the specific program: the story is recognizable to the child or the adult making viewing choices on behalf of the child. Fairy tale's formulaic nature—the deep structural patterns described by Vladimir Propp (1971) and built upon by Bengt Holbek (1989)—eases adaptation by making simple correlations between the characters of a tale type and a program's established characters (as we describe in the following for *Max and Ruby* [2002–2013] and *Sesame Street* [1969–]).

Unlike mediations for other audiences, however, producers often hedge on this presumption of exposure, and one can distinguish programs along a spectrum: at one end, no assumed familiarity is made, the version is self-contained, and all a child really needs to do is listen; at the other, familiarity not only with the tale but with a variety of cultural tropes is assumed, and as the child brings that fluency to the moment of reception the performance unfolds collaboratively. The former is authoritative, unidirectional, monologic, perhaps hegemonic, and integral; the latter is exploratory, collaborative, dialogic, perhaps subversive, and fragmented. The latter may be so fragmented and collaborative that one is no longer speaking of "the performance of a tale" at all: rather, the tale is invoked through metonyms and motifs and is background to the exercise of meaning-making between the television producer and the child. And familiarity with the narratives in multiple versions means that television producers often engage with parody and intertextual play, features of children's folklore.

Children's Television and Children's Folklore

Indeed, "play" is perhaps the most critical idea in our approach. Folklorists who study children's folklore distinguish the materials directed at children from the culture children share among themselves. The former closely aligns with William Bascom's ideas of folklore's functions within a society, namely validating culture, educating, maintaining conformity, and simply being amusing (1954). It operates well in a public model of performance with a rigid division between teller and audience and the additional social relations brought to the storytelling event (parent and child being the most obvious in this case). We see as much in the following examples that we identify most closely with storytelling, where a text is presented more or less *in toto* from an omniscient, authoritarian voice, and it operates on a model of child as "a simple adult," a thing to be civilized and not a subject with her own complex culture (Zumwalt 1999, 29).

The folklore children tell among themselves, however, is as much about challenging the regimented categorizations and assumptions that parents and other authorities present to them as it is about digesting and reaffirming them. Jay Mechling's (1986) delineation of the tensions folklorists have found in children's folklore serves us well: of hierarchy versus equality (which questions status and authority, including that given to privileged versions of a tale); of male versus female (which encourages and allows for queering of tales); of dynamism and conservatism (which builds on an initial impetus to replication and quickly moves to experimentation and recontextualization); and of order versus disorder (which subsumes the tensions before it and considers deconstruction alongside reconstruction).

We can similarly distinguish children's television from family television. Both comprise programming intended to be suitable for watching by all ages, containing negligible references to or displays of sexuality, violence, profanity, and so forth. However, family television is produced for (early) evening viewing in prime time (typically seven to nine in the evening) with the anticipation of a once-per-week schedule (or one-time specials and mini-series) for initial airing. With the expectation of adult viewership, it maintains a model of public performance. For example, productions like the 1965 Rodgers and Hammerstein version of *Cinderella* (see Sawin 2014), while suitable for all ages according to the broadcasting standards of the era, were intended as much for the adult viewer as for the child, programmed within times of leisure and ostensibly distinct from times of work (as defined by the adult male patterning of time).

Children's television, in contrast, is intended for airing outside prime time with the presumption of an exclusively child or child-centric audience, namely on weekdays during the daytime and Saturday mornings (see Mittell 2003b). The child may be alone with the program: if adults are present they are often acting as childminders, one of many tasks expected of them in the performance of domestic labor. Television serves both as a companion to household chores (Lull 1980) and specifically as a facilitator for childminding, in other words, the "electronic babysitter." The same differentiation of labor that privileges and allows for a clear demarcation between work time and leisure time for those who work outside the home, while blurring that distinction for those tied to the home, occasioned what Edward D. Ives referred to as the "two traditions" (1977), a public, male, "serious leisure" performance and a personal, female, marginalized one. Whereas Ives examined the consequences of the two traditions on song and story repertoires, we note its influence on audience: if an adult male is unlikely to be present, the material is largely trivialized.[1] Thus, children's television, never intended for prime time, joins soap operas, game shows, and daytime talk as trivialized genres (Allen 1995; Mittell 2003a; Whannel 2004).

Yet trivialization allows for subversion, and the interpersonal performances of children's television permit greater experimentation with the form. If "family television" echoes the folklore directed *at* children, "children's television" echoes folklore children share among themselves, beyond the adult gaze. Although of course children have no control over the televisual means of production, the increasing presence of the parodic and intertextual suggests a greater understanding of how children negotiate received texts. The use of fairy tales specifically demonstrates both conservatism and dynamism, a tendency toward creativity and the deliberate playing with forms, where the precedent becomes a framework for individual, and on occasion transgressive, performances, perhaps best exemplified by parody (Zumwalt 1999).[2]

The tales' very malleability coincides with the (seeming) disposability of the form, creating versions approaching the dynamism of ephemeral live storytelling as opposed to the (seeming) permanent achievement of film or printed text. We take seriously the folkloristic stance of each version of a tale being a performative storytelling event—wherein a teller draws from a received repertoire and re-creates a narrative according to the teller's understanding of both the medium and the specific audience's expectations at a particular time and place—to get a better sense of how the broadly encompassing category of "children's television" negotiates and presents fairy tale despite the triviality barrier.

Anthology and Storytelling

Anthologies do not suggest continuity between the protagonists from one episode to the other: each tale is presented as separate, connected through a framing device, whether a storyteller (established as such through the conventions of the program itself) explicitly structures what is to come as story and provides the televisual equivalents of opening and closing formulae and ongoing, omniscient narration, or a house style of animation or a repertory cast of actors. Intertextual referents for interpreting the tale exclude the series itself, and the story is presented in its entirety. Anthology series are analogous to a storyteller; producers select from a repertoire of narratives and present them in a particular, idiosyncratic style recognizable from story to story despite each episode's exclusive integrity.

Nippon Animation's *Gurimu Meisaku Gekijō* (Grimm Masterpiece Theatre, 1987–1989) retold the Grimms' and other European tales in a manner "faithful to the original storylines of these narratives, sometimes disturbingly so" (Ellis 2008, 513), bringing new content (for the Japanese audience) to the anime style of animation (see Jorgensen and Warman 2014). Presenting "Little Red Riding Hood" in its fifth episode (1987), the producers set it in an idealized pre-modern middle European countryside. Riding Hood's good character is shown through her instant willingness to accept the mission and warnings from her mother and her love of animals. Languorous depictions of fish in streams, rabbits in the field, and other scenes of nature highlight the animators' skills. The Wolf constantly and unsuccessfully uses trickery to feed himself, and all the information he gathers is through overhearing the other characters. He dons Grandmother's clothes because he cannot get away in time, and he attributes his appearance to illness. The Hunter intends to shoot the sleeping Wolf's bloated stomach when he hears Riding Hood's cries. He cuts the Wolf open and then sends Riding Hood for stones to fill up the now empty stomach. When Wolf awakens the weight of the stones sends him rolling down the hill. Riding Hood apologizes for not having obeyed her mother, and Grandmother forgives her.[3]

HBO's *Happily Ever After: Fairy Tales for Every Child* (1995–2000) again took tales primarily from the Western European canon and set them in various multicultural contexts with the express intent of being more inclusive of African American, Latino, and Asian American audiences (as using variants from those groups apparently did not occur to the producers).

> [The] simple idea behind the project works beautifully: Timeless stories *known to all children* should be opened up to speak to every child. Why not make these magical kingdoms ethnically diverse places in which all children can feel welcome? Changes are made but the tales, narrated by Robert Guillaume, remain remarkably intact.
>
> (O'Connor 1995, emphasis added)

For its third episode (1995), the producers placed "Little Red Riding Hood" in pre-modern China and named her "Little Red Happy Coat." Frequent and conspicuous references to stereotyped elements of Chinese culture include when she first meets the Wolf he suggests a visit to a teahouse rather than to a field to pick flowers and later when the disguised Wolf gives her pet names ("my little dumpling"/"my little eggroll"/"my little leechee nut"). Happy Coat has greater agency than the anime Riding Hood: she is inquisitive, plays with animals, and climbs trees. She volunteers to take the food to Grandmother despite her Mother's apprehension. Her attempts to run away from the Wolf are for naught yet sufficient to allow the Herbalist—replacing the Huntsman—to arrive. The latter prepares a treatment that causes the Wolf to hiccough and belch until Grandmother and Happy Coat are freed. Happy Coat apologizes to her Grandmother, and the Herbalist, who has hogtied the unconscious Wolf, takes him far away.

Both *Grimm Masterpiece Theatre* (renamed *Grimm's Fairy Tale Classics* when it aired in the United States starting in 1989) and *Happily Ever After* (1995–2000) premiered in once-a-week, prime time slots, were half an hour in duration, and fulfill their respective reputations for "disturbingly faithful" and "remarkably intact" tale renditions. The former's fidelity is a by-product of the assumption that this is a new story for its audience; the latter's variations from the received text are blatant and telegraphed (and, of course, the entire point of the exercise) but nevertheless require no foreknowledge to work. Both have a remarkable authority: they are presented as wholes, within an intact universe separate from our own, with all referents internally consistent, from a responsible adult voice.

Parody and Subversion

In contrast is *Wolves, Witches and Giants* (1995–1999), a ten-minute program originally created for daily syndication for ITV, narrated by Spike Milligan, who also voices all the characters. The "Little Red Riding Hood" episode's (1995) rustic setting is interspersed with motorcars, Australian soap operas, breath spray, and electric lighting. It is "in the excitement of chasing a moose" that Riding Hood loses herself in the woods, and when the Wolf offers to carry her basket she demurs, glad that "chivalry is not dead." The Wolf takes a short cut (by car) to the cottage and eats Granny. He grows tired of Riding Hood's "what big hands/ears/eyes you have" verbal dueling and attacks, but he is too tangled in bedclothes to be successful. Riding Hood barricades herself in the larder and calls out a window for help: a Woodcutter, whose sandwiches the Wolf had stolen the week before, rescues her. Riding Hood skips home while eating the cake and honey, the Wolf vows to eat her one day, and Granny's fate is unclear.

Fractured Fairy Tales, a recurring segment on Jay Ward's *Rocky and His Friends* (1959–1961), created originally for daytime television, presented three "Little Red Riding Hoods." Most approximating the Western European versions is "Ridinghoods Anonymous." Little Red is going to sell Grandmother "a membership in the PTA" when she encounters a Wolf struggling to "kick the Ridinghood habit" by referring to his recovery handbook. Every effort to greet her amiably is met with self-defensive violence until he convinces her of his sincere efforts to quit. He buys a PTA membership and offers to take the basket (the first of which is a decoy and explodes) but soon realizes that a Grandmother is a still-allowable lunch. Grandmother convinces him that she is a Ridinghood and Little Red the grandmother and that Ridinghoods actually sell DAR (Daughters of American Ridinghoods) memberships. Returning to the woods (with another exploding basket), he accuses Little Red of tricking him, but she shows in the handbook that grandmothers belong to the DAR. Rushing back, he poses as a photographer offering a free picture with a Shetland pony to Ridinghoods, and when Grandmother says she is in fact a grandmother he grabs her. Quick-wittedly, she says dispatches are needed at the front and he is the only one with a horse. Little Red arrives, and they feel safe having heard the basket of dispatches explode, but the Wolf somehow makes it back. He has quit Ridinghoods Anonymous and pursues them both. He believes he has lived happily ever after, as he is a member of the PTA and DAR and has acquired 200 baskets. They explode, and he ascends to heaven.

Both *Wolves, Witches and Giants* and *Fractured Fairy Tales* are gleefully irreverent toward their source material. Milligan's vocal gymnastics and the narration of Edward Everett Horton (described by Pauline Kael as "hollow-head-under-a-top-hat" [1985, 105]), the simplistic animation, fewer concerns with narrative symmetry, and the intersection of the mundane and modern world with the storyworld in which the events occur all contribute to versions closer to how a child would tell one (see Sutton-Smith 1981). Each version has sufficient integrity to work as a story, but, rather than the solemnity of "reinterpretation," the producers clearly aim at something closer to play. Cristina Bacchilega and John Rieder, writing on *Fractured Fairy Tales*, observe that the show's frequent use of the phrase "we all know" with respect to the tale's plot explicitly notes that this is but one of many versions known to the audience (2014, 352).

Enactment and Play

Series suggest continuity between the protagonists, and when they draw plot from fairy tales the characters within the established program narrative assume the tale roles. A number of children's television series revolve around a set of characters engaging in imaginative play, either as the central conceit for each episode (*The Backyardigans* [2004–2010], *Toopy and Binoo* [2005–]) or as one of the possible ways they interact. Whether or not there is a specific framing device (if the characters announce to each other that they are playing) or change in landscape (if the play occurs in the found universe of established sets, such as backyards or play rooms, or if a new setting is created), the roles are selected and performed in part as a consequence of the established personalities of the show's own storyworld, and the personalities are assumed (albeit not always fundamentally necessary) referents. The characters know that this is a story and that they are engaged in its performance.

Max and Ruby (2002–2013), an eight-minute animated program, serves both as interstitial daytime programming and, when three episodes are bundled together, as a half-hour program. In "Ruby Riding Hood," Ruby, the elder, responsible sister to the appetitive Max (who only ever says one word per segment, repeated throughout, and inevitably the last line), has packed a basket of cookies for her grandmother. After his furtive efforts at stealing them, Ruby sits Max down and tells him the story of "Little Red Riding Ruby and the Big Max Wolf": "Remember the story of Little Red Riding Hood? [Max nods] Well, it's exactly the same, only different." Her version depicts Max with false ears and nose repeatedly demanding cookies from a likewise minimally costumed Ruby (dressed in a hood) as she passes the landmarks of their real neighborhood: Max/Wolf overtakes her thanks to a chat with a Woodcutter, and when she arrives he is covered head to toe in a shawl. He reveals himself, exclaims "Cookies!", and Ruby ends her version with, "And he ate up all the cookies and Grandma didn't get to enjoy a single one! You don't want to be like the Big Max Wolf and eat up all of Grandma's cookies, do you? [guilty look] I didn't think so." Ruby sets off for her grandmother's, taking the same route as was shown in her story, stopping at all the same places but saying, "No Big Max Wolf here!" But Max sneaks past her, and she arrives to find him in the same shawl. She is momentarily confused, only to be interrupted by Grandma, delightedly surprised at the gift of cookies. Ruby catches on, Max reveals himself, and as there are plenty to go around they all enjoy the cookies. The show makes explicit reference to the tale as known before Ruby reshapes the narrative to meet the specific purpose of telling it at that moment to that audience, while the animators provide its simultaneous depiction. As narrator, Ruby is an established character, one half of a social identity pairing of elder and younger sibling, a relationship brought to and informing the storytelling event (Georges 1969). The narrated version then becomes the motivating text for the enactment that comprises the second half of the segment.

Intertextuality

Whereas anthologies and series present an entire narrative, however inflected by style or characterization, children's television also uses intertextual reference, wherein knowledge of a tale type is assumed and segments, elements, or motifs can be employed alongside other narratives and forms. The children's television staple *Sesame Street* was built on such postmodern approaches to narrative, where each episode features a "Street story" of human adults interacting with puppet characters (many of whom are nonhuman) interspersed with short films and animations, songs, variety-show sketches, and parodies. The structure assumes and informs both an understanding of television conventions and an implicit canon of traditional narrative. Segments are repeated and incorporated over the course of the series and dubbed for non-English international versions of the show (which also feature original content).

Rarely do the televised *Sesame Street* (1969–) iterations of "Little Red Riding Hood" present a full story: producers simply assume a viewer's familiarity with the motifs. In the show's first twenty years Little Red Riding Hood was confined to the non-Street stories: Kermit the Frog would report on specific scenes from the story in "News Flash" segments (1974; 1988a; 1988b) or Cookie Monster would re-enact scenes in "Monsterpiece Theatre," aping PBS's *Masterpiece Theatre* (1994). In later decades her story entered into the Street: first, with "Grandma's Day," Street characters (Big Bird and Snuffleupagus) engage in imaginative play, only for one of them to momentarily forget the line between fact and fiction (Big Bird's concern about the Wolf) followed by the surprise of indeed discovering a Wolf Grandmother (1992); later, Riding Hood and Wolf seamlessly and without explanation assume roles within the Street characters' imaginative play (2001); and finally Riding Hood and Wolf normally interact with the Street characters when she orders a basket at the local corner store (2013).

As the show's producers never set out to tell a complete version we can understand "Little Red Riding Hood" as a kernel narrative (Kalčik 1975), a story so well-known to a group that its full retelling would be superfluous and that can serve instead as a referent for common understanding and further communication. *Sesame Street* impels its viewers to bring that knowledge (along with the knowledge of its own established characters and tropes) to the performance, making them active collaborators in its creation. The presentation is not wholly esoteric: there is enough intelligibility for comprehension. But telegraphing that there are referents that would make comprehension fuller and thus more rewarding encourages the viewer to seek them out.

Assumptions of Canonicity

The use of fairy tale in children's television demonstrates two interconnected moments in narrative canonicity: the provision of a core of texts—"here are the stories you ought to know"—and the assumption of that same core—"this will make sense because of the stories you ought to know." We have used "Little Red Riding Hood" as our example, but we could have just as easily used "Goldilocks," "Sleeping Beauty," "Princess and the Pea," or "Jack and the Beanstalk," and little distinction is made between traditional narrative and that which has entered the public domain, such as *Kunstmärchen* and other examples from children's literature. The assumed canonical core is framed by the biases of producers, as "ought" is inherently subjective. When *Sesame Street* attempted the Efik-Ibibio "Why the Sun and Moon Live in the Sky" (1998), it was a complete narrative, appearing to make no assumptions about established familiarity and cleaving conservatively to Elphinstone Dayrell's version (1910) (which had been made into a popular children's book in 1968). On the other hand, and as we discuss elsewhere in greater detail (Brodie and McDavid 2014), the children's show *Super Why!*'s free adaptations of traditional narratives extend both to Western and non-Western alike, and the consequences of these reworked versions (of Japan's "Momotarō the Peach Boy" and "Tiddalick the Frog" from Australian Aboriginal mythology, as but two examples) being the first and perhaps only version a child may encounter are uncertain.

Children's television has emerged as one of the earliest introductions to fairy tale, if only as a consequence of producers basing content on public domain materials. From a top-down, monologic performance of tale to performances that increasingly demand more from the child until it is a collaborative, dialogic creation, television assumes, implies, and builds a de facto canon. The repetition both of structure—through the formulaic nature of tale and of the programs themselves—and of content—through the economics of syndication and reruns—can inform not only what stories are told but how stories can be told differently, an implicit schooling in the folkloristic concepts of type and version. These texts can be integral or splintered, solemn or subversive, and mirror both the functional aspects of folklore directed at children and the experimentation of the folklore children tell among themselves.

Related topics: Anime and Manga; Broadcast; Children's and Young Adult (YA) Literature; Children's Picture Books and Illustrations; Pedagogy; Storytelling; Storyworlds/Narratology

Notes

1. Ian Wojcik-Andrews (2000) makes a similar distinction between "family" and "children's" film, the latter of which was seen as untenable in an industry without state subsidies (17). Unlike cinema, however, there is a "need" to fill television airtime. We are grateful to Naomi Hamer for bringing Wojcik-Andrews's work to our attention.
2. Although new models of television distribution, including specialty cable channels with children's programming around the clock and on-demand streaming services (that further negate the context of scheduling), have dismantled this rigid division, the patterns set up by terrestrial television (broadcast through antennae) continue to wield influence.
3. When the show was presented on American television, some elements of the chase scenes, the eating, the Hunter's use of the gun, and the cutting and subsequent sewing up of the Wolf were edited out. The long scenes of nature were filled with voiceover narration.

References Cited and Further Reading

Allen, Robert C. 1995. "Introduction." In *To Be Continued . . .: Soap Operas Around the World*. New York: Routledge.
Bacchilega, Cristina, and John Rieder. 2014. "The Fairy Tale and the Commercial in *Carosello* and *Fractured Fairy Tales*." In *Channeling Wonder: Fairy Tales on Television*, edited by Greenhill and Rudy, 338–59.

Bascom, William R. 1954. "Four Functions of Folklore." *Journal of American Folklore* 67 (266): 333–49.

Beckett, Sandra L. 2008. *Red Riding Hood for All Ages: A Fairy-Tale Icon in Cross-Cultural Contexts.* Detroit: Wayne State UP.

———. 2013. *Revisioning Red Riding Hood around the World: An Anthology of International Retellings.* Detroit: Wayne State UP.

Brodie, Ian, and Jodi McDavid. 2014. "Who's Got the Power? *Super Why!*, Viewer Agency, and Traditional Narrative." In *Channeling Wonder: Fairy Tales on Television*, edited by Greenhill and Rudy, 25–44.

Dayrell, Elphinstone. 1910. *Folk Stories from Southern Nigeria, West Africa.* New York: Longmans.

———. 1968. *Why the Sun and Moon Live in the Sky*, illustrated by Blair Lent. New York: Haughton-Mifflin.

Dundes, Alan, ed. 1989. *Little Red Riding Hood: A Casebook.* Madison: U Wisconsin P.

Ellis, Bill. 2008. "Japanese Popular Culture." In *The Greenwood Encyclopedia of Folktales and Fairy Tales*, edited by Donald Haase, 513. Westport, CT: Greenwood.

Georges, Robert A. 1969. "Toward an Understanding of Storytelling Events." *Journal of American Folklore* 82 (326): 313–28.

Greenhill, Pauline, and Jill Terry Rudy, eds. 2014. *Channeling Wonder: Fairy Tales on Television.* Detroit: Wayne State UP.

Holbek, Bengt. 1989. "The Language of Fairy Tales." In *Nordic Folklore: Recent Studies*, edited by Reimund Kvideland and Henning K. Sehmsdorf, 40–62. Bloomington: Indiana UP.

Ives, Edward D. 1977. "Lumbercamp Singing and the Two Traditions." *Canadian Folk Music Journal* 5: 17–23.

Jorgensen, Jeana, and Brittany Warman. 2014. "Molding Messages: Analyzing the Reworking of 'Sleeping Beauty' in *Grimm's Fairy Tale Classics* and *Dollhouse*." In *Channeling Wonder: Fairy Tales on Television*, edited by Greenhill and Rudy, 144–62.

Kael, Pauline. 1985. "The Current Cinema: *The Purple Rose of Cairo*: Film Review." *The New Yorker*, March 25: 109.

Kalčik, Susan. 1975. "'. . . Like Ann's Gynecologist or the Time I Was Almost Raped': Personal Narratives in Women's Rap Groups." *Journal of American Folklore* 88 (347): 3–11.

Lull, James. 1980. "The Social Uses of Television." *Human Communication Research* 6 (3): 197–209.

Mechling, Jay. 1986. "Children's Folklore." In *Folk Groups and Folklore Genres: An Introduction*, edited by Elliott Oring, 91–120. Logan: Utah State UP.

Mittell, Jason. 2003a. "Audiences Talking Genre: Television Talk Shows and Cultural Hierarchies." *Journal of Popular Film and Television* 31 (1): 36–46.

———. 2003b. "The Great Saturday Morning Exile: Scheduling Cartoons on Television's Periphery in the 1960s." In *Prime Time Animation: Television Animation and American Culture*, edited by Carol A. Stabile and Mark Harrison, 33–54. New York: Routledge.

O'Connor, Jack. 1995. "Critic's Notebook: Setting Higher Sights for Animation." *New York Times*, March 23.

Propp, Vladimir. 1971. *Morphology of the Folktale.* 2nd ed. Austin: U Texas P.

Sawin, Patricia. 2014. "Things Walt Disney Didn't Tell Us (But at Which Rodgers and Hammerstein at Least Hinted): The 1965 Made-for-TV Musical of *Cinderella*." In *Channeling Wonder: Fairy Tales on Television*, edited by Greenhill and Rudy, 103–24.

Sutton-Smith, Brian. 1970. "Psychology of Childlore: The Triviality Barrier." *Western Folklore* 29 (1): 1–8.

———. 1981. *The Folkstories of Children.* Philadelphia: U Philadelphia P.

Whannel, Garry. 2004. "The Price Is Right but the Moments Are Sticky: Television, Quiz and Game Shows, and Popular Culture." In *Come On Down? Popular Media Culture in Post-War Britain*, edited by Dominic Strinati and Stephen Wagg, 179–201. New York: Routledge.

Wojcik-Andrews, Ian. 2000. *Children's Films: History, Ideology, Pedagogy, Theory.* New York: Routledge.

Zumwalt, Rosemary Lévy. 1999. "The Complexity of Children's Folklore." In *Children's Folklore: A Source Book*, edited by Brian Sutton-Smith, Jay Mechling, Thomas W. Johnson, and Felicia R. McMahon, 23–48. Logan: Utah State UP.

Mediagraphy

Backyardigans (TV). 2004–2010. Creator Janice Burgess. Canada/USA.

Cinderella (TV). 1965. Director Charles S. Dubin. USA.

Grimm Masterpiece Theatre, aka Grimm's Fairy Tale Classics (Gurimu Meisaku Gekijō, TV). 1987–1989. Creator Takaji Matsudo. Japan.

———. "Little Red Riding Hood [Akazukin]." 1987. Episode 1.05. November 18.

Happily Ever After: Fairy Tales for Every Child (TV). 1995–2000. Creator Donna Brown Guillaume. USA.

———. "Little Red Riding Hood." 1995. Episode 1.02. March 26.

Max and Ruby (TV). 2002–2013. Creator Rosemary Wells. Canada.

———. "Ruby Riding Hood." 2007. Episode 3.1121. May 9.
Rocky and His Friends (TV). 1959–1961. Creator Jay Ward. USA: NBC.
———. "Fractured Fairy Tales: Ridinghoods Anonymous." 1961. Episode 2.91. January 22.
Sesame Street (TV). 1969–. Creators Joan Ganz Cooney and Lloyd Morrisett. USA.
———. 1974. Episode 0691. December 9.
———. 1988a. Episode 2487. November 22.
———. 1988b. Episode 2503. December 14.
———. 1992. Episode 3006. November 9.
———. 1994. Episode 3231. April 4.
———. 1998. Episode 3741. March 16.
———. 2001. Episode 3973. March 21.
———. 2013. Episode 4318. February 14.
Super Why! (TV). 2007–. Creator Angela Santomero. Canada/USA.
———. "Momotarō the Peach Boy." 2008a. Episode 1.33. September 4.
———. "Tiddalick the Frog." 2008b. Episode 1.27. April 22.
Toopy and Binoo (Toupie et Binou, TV). 2005–. Creator Dominique Jolin. Canada.
Wolves, Witches and Giants (TV). 1995–1999. Creator Ed Welch. UK.
———. "Little Red Riding Hood." 1995. Episode 1.04. October 12.

50

CINEMA SCIENCE FICTION

John Rieder

According to the influential definition of science fiction as the literature of cognitive estrangement advanced in 1972 in Darko Suvin's "On the Poetics of the Science Fiction Genre," science fiction and the fairy tale are strictly incompatible forms. For Suvin, science fiction is "a literary genre whose necessary and sufficient conditions are the presence and interaction of estrangement and cognition" within the formal device of a non-empirical setting (375), and the mode of estrangement in fairy tale is not "cognitive" by his standards. The case against the "genological incest" of mixing fairy tale and science fiction was spelled out further by the Polish science fiction (SF) writer Stanislaw Lem in the inaugural issue of the journal *Science Fiction Studies* (1973, 26). According to Lem,

> If the depicted world is oriented positively toward man, it is the world of the classical fairy tale, in which physics is controlled by morality, [. . .] [but] it is the premise of SF that anything shown shall in principle be interpretable empirically and rationally. In SF there can be no inexplicable marvels.
>
> (28)

Lem goes on to lament, however, that much of what tries to pass itself off as SF is really fairy tale in disguise: "Since SF portrays the future or the extraterrestrial, the worlds of SF necessarily deviate from the real world, and the ways in which they deviate are the core and meaning of the SF creation. But what we usually find is not what may happen tomorrow but the forever impossible, not the real but the fairy-tale-like" (31).

Most contemporary genre theorists would take Lem's comment about "what we usually find" as evidence of a significant overlap of the two genres as seen, not through the lens of Lem's or Suvin's prescriptive formalism, but in light of their common usage in popular narrative practices. Eric S. Rabkin had made such a case already in his 1980 essay "Fairy Tales and Science Fiction," which argues for an "ample correspondence between science fiction and fairy tales [that] has led to frequent similarities in stylistic technique, audience attitude, character of the protagonist, choice of motif, and overall structure." He lays in evidence the two genres' common "propensity to externalize all inner states and to deal in extremes" (80), their "reliance on clarity, elemental colors, and cleanliness" (82), and the fact that both tend to be "highly formulaic" (84). Rabkin's argument about the formulaic qualities the genres share is consonant with Vivian Labrie's suggestion, in a paper first delivered at the International Society for Folk Narrative Research in Athens in 2009 (Labrie 2014), that the Aarne-Thompson-Uther (ATU) tale-type identifications that have long been used as a methodological tool in folklore studies could usefully be extended to popular SF films like Joss Whedon's *Serenity* (2005, ATU 707), Steven Soderbergh's *Solaris* (2002, ATU 652, based on a novel by none other than Stanislaw Lem), and George Lucas's *Star Wars* (1977, Lacourciére 305A).

The most significant overlapping of SF and fairy-tale motifs or formulas in recent SF film has occurred in stories concerning artificial humans. Holly Blackford (2007) has called attention to the childlike character of many of SF cinema's artificial beings, ranging from the computer HAL in Stanley Kubrick's *2001: A Space Odyssey* (1968) to the cyborg Data in *Star Trek: The Next Generation* (1987–1994), many of whom are driven, like so many Pinocchios, by their desire to become real people. The allusion to fairy-tale material in these "PC Pinocchios" is most extended and explicit in Steven Spielberg's *A.I.: Artificial Intelligence* (2001), which draws far more abundantly, both in terms of plot and tone, upon Carlo Collodi's 1883 novel than on the 1969 SF short story that the film's credits claim the script is based upon, Brian Aldiss's "Super-Toys Last All Summer Long" (also discussed by Sawers 2010).

An equally extensive engagement with the fairy tale "Bluebeard" (ATU 312) informs the 2015 film *Ex Machina*. Like *A.I.*, *Ex Machina* concerns a scientist's attempt to create an emotionally human artificial being, and the plots in both films turn upon testing the success of the experiment by setting the artificial beings into interaction with actual humans, on the one hand, and, on the other, on the cyborgs' desire to become or at least pass for real humans. The negative endings to these experiments point to the background presence of an authoritative, shared science fictional ancestor, Mary Shelley's *Frankenstein* (1818) with its myriad print, stage, and film adaptations, and behind *Frankenstein* stands a more fundamental mythic ancestor, the story of Prometheus (Shelley's novel is subtitled *The Modern Prometheus*). If, as Brian Attebery has argued, modern fantasy serves the function "of reconnecting [contemporary audiences] to traditional myths and the worlds they generate" (2014, 9), the similarities shared by this cluster of films about artificial humans point to the status of fantasy as a kind of master genre that subsumes science fiction and fairy tale as subsets within its general orientation to the repurposing or reimagining of mythic material.

Just as *A.I.* hybridizes and remixes its science fiction and fairy-tale hypotexts, *Ex Machina*, rather than performing a straightforward adaptation of "Bluebeard," hybridizes and melds a number of disparate sources and genres—the science fictional plot of the mad scientist and his neo-mythic attempt to steal the fire of the gods; the fairy-tale plot of the puppet who aspires to become real, mixed here with a heavy dose of romantic knight errantry in the view of the young man who tries to save the stunning female cyborg from the domineering, dark-bearded scientist; and the film noir motif of the femme fatale who uses her erotic attractions to manipulate a man into crimes on her behalf and then abandons him to the negative consequences of his actions while herself reaping all the rewards. *Ex Machina* thus stands as a thoroughgoing example of an SF film achieving the power of adult fairy-tale fiction in the mode of the generation of contemporary writers who have drawn their inspiration from Angela Carter.

It is also, unfortunately, a quite isolated example. There are some distinguished examples in Japanese anime of hybridizing SF and the tale of wonder, as in Mamoru Oshii's 1984 *Urusei Yatsura: Beautiful Dreamer*, described by Susan Napier as "an extraordinary fantasy film [. . .] [that mixes] elements of traditional Japanese folklore with apocalyptic visions" (2016, 174). More typically one finds only a sprinkling of fairy-tale elements or allusions in SF films—for example the Sleeping Beauty–like kiss by which Trinity (Carrie-Ann Moss) awakens Neo (Keanu Reeves) in *The Matrix* (1999)—or of science fictional elements in a predominantly fairy-tale film, like the cosmic clock and atomic bombs in John Korty and Charles Swenson's *Twice Upon a Time* (1983) (Zipes 2011, 103–105). Andrew Gordon argues convincingly that

Spielberg's *E.T. the Extra-Terrestrial* (1982) bears strong similarities to "The Frog Prince," but this is more a matter of drawing on a stereotypical version of the alliance between childhood innocence, openness to difference, and the aura of enchantment than of engaging in an interpretive dialogue with a specific version of the fairy tale.

It might be argued that *E.T.* owes more to the fairy-tale world associated with the films of the Disney corporation—the famous allusion of *E.T.*'s bike-riding-in-the-sky scene to Disney's *Peter Pan* (1953) would be a prime example—than it does to the tale of wonder in its oral or print traditions. The inclusion of *Star Wars*–related exhibits in Disney's Tomorrowland over the last thirty years, culminating in the purchase of the *Star Wars* franchise itself by Disney, suggests a different kind of affinity and a different point of departure for connecting fairy tale and cinema SF than the common ground of fantasy or the revision of mythic and folkloric material. Instead of tale types and motifs, we would be asking questions about commercially driven serial repetition, and these questions would lead ideas about the power and persistence of mythic images and narrative patterns into a differently focused analysis of the shaping of mass cultural narrative by its commercial investments and modes of distribution. For the affinity of *E.T.*, *Star Wars*, and the classic Disney fairy-tale films lies in their impressive commercial success as family entertainment, that is, their ability to appeal to a common audience within a common market and realm of production, that of mass-distributed, high-budget studio filmmaking.

The crucial point is that this is a historical and practical connection, not a formal one, for there is little similarity between the making and selling of Disney's *Snow White and the Seven Dwarfs* (1937) and Lucas's *Star Wars* other than the fact that both of these feature-length family entertainments achieved breakthrough commercial success for their respective genres, thereby transforming those genres into major investment vehicles, not only for further films in the same vein, but for the franchising of related products. This historical connection does not involve a rationality that imposes a certain kind of internal order on narratives, such as the reimagining of myth or, as Michael Saler has suggested about the "virtual reality" escapism offered by serialized popular fictions dating back to Arthur Conan Doyle's Sherlock Holmes stories, "the larger cultural project [. . .] of re-enchanting an allegedly disenchanted world" (2012, 6). Instead it depends upon an external rationality that selects for production and distribution whatever has proven in the past to be commercially successful and continues to select it for as long as it continues to produce profits. The generic and the formulaic emerge spontaneously and organically, so to speak, from the *raison d'etre* of mass cultural production itself, the identification and encouragement of habitual patterns of consumption. While the basis of those habits of consumption in collective, anonymous desires may in the end lead us back to questions about fantasy and its forms of expression, the entertainment industry aims at predictability, not wonder or enchantment. The intersection of fairy tale and science fiction at the Disney studios or in a Disney-like film such as *E.T.* simply extends the often lamented narrowing and normalizing Disneyfication of the tale of wonder to the genre of science fiction as well. Nonetheless the cultural power wielded by these vastly profitable films and franchises demands that they remain objects of critical and scholarly attention.

Within the context of such mass cultural production, the attribution of genre proceeds from several different sources that are quite distinct from the kind of formal genre definitions wielded by Suvin, Lem, or even Attebery. The generic associations given to a film by the marketing strategies of the studios, especially those evoked in pre-film publicity, may differ substantially from the generic analysis the films receive from critics or fans. Thus, as Jason Mittell has argued with respect to television genres, it is a mistake to consider genre as something determined solely by the text itself. Instead genre is a social construction that serves different purposes for different groups (2004, 1–19). I have argued that this is not a situation restricted to mass culture or contemporary media, but rather that the attribution of a generic identity to a text always constitutes an intervention in its distribution and reception. It helps to determine where, how, and how widely a text will be viewed or read, and it makes a promise or recommendation that it can be pleasurably or satisfactorily read within a certain, generically determined set of expectations and protocols (Rieder 2010, 200–201).

A film that strikingly illustrates the problems and possibilities attached to generic attribution, as well as another set of tensions regarding the connection between science fiction and the tale of wonder, is Helen Haig-Brown's 2009 short, *?E?ANX (The Cave)*. In a publicity release concerning the showcasing of the film at the Toronto International Film Festival as one of the top ten shorts of 2009, Haig-Brown says, "The Cave is the first ever indigenous science fiction film shot in Tsilhqot'in, my native language" (Rugged Media 2009). Since *The Cave* is also a fairly straightforward, beautifully made adaptation of an oral wonder tale told by Henry Solomon, Haig-Brown's great uncle, using Solomon's audio recording as its basis, one has to ask what it means to classify this film adaptation of a Tsilhqot'in traditional narrative as "[I]ndigenous science fiction"?

Part of the answer is that Haig-Brown is staking an epistemological claim about the science in science fiction. The story concerns a bear hunter who, after crawling into a cave on the trail of his prey, is transported into a different reality, named as the spirit world in the film's credits. Instead of the high-tech wonders normally associated with SF Haig-Brown offers in *The Cave* a story based on a different kind of technical expertise sometimes called TEK, or traditional ecological knowledge. Attaching the label of science fiction to this traditional wonder tale therefore amounts to a claim that "aboriginal sustainable practices constitute a science despite their lack of resemblance to taxonomic Western systems of thought" (Dillon 2012, 7). The oral tale qualifies as SF because of its basis in what Anishinaabe scholar Grace W. Dillon calls Indigenous scientific literacy. The generic labeling itself ought then to be considered an example of the kind of activist adaptation of the tale of wonder in the contemporary fairy-tale web analyzed at length by Cristina Bacchilega (2013).

One final, different point of departure for interrogating the connection between fairy tale and cinema SF is provided by the technical procedures of filmmaking itself. Both J. P. Telotte (2001) and Katherine A. Fowkes (2010) remark upon the similarity between cinematic SF and fantasy (not the fairy tale in particular) as genres that rely upon and foreground special effects and camera "trickery." According to Telotte, SF film's "concern with the technological engages us in a complex system of reflections on its own technological underpinnings" (2001, 24). Fowkes argues,

> As *film* genres, both science fiction and fantasy might be seen as expressions of the birth and evolution of cinema itself, and both genres can serve as barometers of technical innovation. If science fiction uses technology to tell stories about technology and science, we might say that fantasy harnesses cinema's ability to create illusions in order to tell stories about illusions themselves.
>
> (2010, 17)

A stronger connection between science fiction and the fairy tale, rather than fantasy in general, is provided in the work of the great pioneer of camera magic in filmmaking, Georges Méliès. Working out of a centuries-old tradition of stage illusionism and grand spectacle in the French *féerie*, Méliès explored both fairy tale and science fiction extensively in his prolific career (see Zipes 2011, 35–48; Bould 2012, 68–70). Other directors with especially pronounced visual styles whose work embraces both science fiction and the fairy tale would include the great Japanese animated filmmaker Hayao Miyazaki and Britain's Terry Gilliam.

At stake in taking this approach to the topic of fairy-tale and SF cinema is the status, not just of special effects, but of spectacle more broadly considered, as a more or less dominant component of making and viewing films. Mark Bould contends that "denunciations of the apparent ascendancy of spectacle at the expense of narrative and character psychology normalise a specific 'politics of taste'" based on restraint and delayed gratification. In contrast, the appeal of spectacle is its ability to generate "utopian feelings of abundance, energy, intensity, transparency and community" (2012, 68–69). Against a class-specific politics of taste, then, SF and fairy tale once again participate in what Bacchilega names the politics of wonder, here grasped, in different terms than Bacchilega's, as the immersive affective power of cinematic spectacle itself.

Related topics: Anime and Manga; Cinematic; Disney Corporation; Gender; Indigenous

References Cited and Further Reading

Aldiss, Brian. (1969) 2010. "Super-Toys Last All Summer Long." In *The Wesleyan Anthology of Science Fiction*, edited by Arthur B. Evans, Istvan Csicsery-Ronay Jr., Joan Gordon, Veronica Hollinger, Rob Latham, and Carol McGuirk, 443–51. Middletown, CT: Wesleyan UP.

Attebery, Brian. 2014. *Stories about Stories: Fantasy & the Remaking of Myth*. Oxford: Oxford UP.

Bacchilega, Cristina. 2013. *Fairy Tales Transformed? Twenty-First Century Adaptations & the Politics of Wonder*. Detroit: Wayne State UP.

Blackford, Holly. 2007. "PC Pinocchios: Parents, Children, and the Metamorphosis Tradition in Science Fiction." In *Folklore/Cinema: Popular Film as Vernacular Culture*, edited by Sharon R. Sherman and Mikel J. Koven, 74–92. Logan: Utah State UP.

Bould, Mark. 2012. *Science Fiction*. London: Routledge.

Dillon, Grace W. 2012. *Walking the Clouds: An Anthology of Indigenous Science Fiction*. Tucson: U Arizona P.

Fowkes, Katherine A. 2010. *The Fantasy Film*. Oxford: Blackwell.

Gordon, Andrew. 1983. "'E.T.' as Fairy Tale." *Science Fiction Studies* 10 (3): 298–305.

Labrie, Vivian. 2014. "*Serenity* (ATU 707), *This Boy's Life* (ATU 590), *Star Wars* (Lacourcière 305A), *Solaris* (ATU 652)? About Extending the Aarne-Thompson-Uther Tale-Type Identification Insight to Movies." In *Narratives across Space and Time: Transmissions and Adaptations*, edited by Aikaterini Polymerou-Kamilaki, Evangelos Karamanes, and Ioannis Plemmenos, 295–314. Athens: Academy of Athens, Publications of the Hellenic Folklore Research Centre, 31.

Lem, Stanislaw. 1973. "On the Structural Analysis of Science Fiction." *Science Fiction Studies* 1 (1): 26–33.

Mittell, Jason. 2004. *Genre and Television: From Cop Shows to Cartoons in American Culture*. London: Routledge.

Napier, Susan. 2016. "Not Always Happily Ever After: Japanese Fairy Tales in Cinema and Animation." In *Fairy-Tale Films Beyond Disney: International Perspectives*, edited by Jack Zipes, Pauline Greenhill, and Kendra Magnus-Johnston, 166–79. New York: Routledge.

Rabkin, Eric S. 1980. "Fairy Tales and Science Fiction." In *Bridges to Science Fiction*, edited by George E. Slusser, George E. Guffey, and Mark Rose, 78–90. Carbondale: Southern Illinois UP.

Rieder, John. 2010. "On Defining Science Fiction, or Not: Genre Theory, SF, and History." *Science Fiction Studies* 37 (2): 191–210.

Rugged Media. 2009. "The Cave: Tsilhqot'in Language Sci-Fi Short Film in TIFF's Top Ten Selection." *Vancouver Media Co-Op*, December 9. http://vancouver.mediacoop.ca/newsrelease/2235.

Saler, Michael. 2012. *As If: Modern Enchantment and the Literary Prehistory of Virtual Reality*. Oxford: Oxford UP.

Sawers, Naarah. 2010. "Building the Perfect Product: The Commodification of Childhood in Contemporary Fairy Tale Film." In *Fairy Tale Films: Visions of Ambiguity*, edited by Pauline Greenhill and Sidney Eve Matrix, 42–59. Logan: Utah State UP.

Shelley, Mary. 1818. *Frankenstein; or, the Modern Prometheus*. London: Lackington, Hughes, Harding, Mayor, and Jones.

Suvin, Darko. 1972. "On the Poetics of the Science Fiction Genre." *College English* 34 (3): 372–83.

Telotte, J. P. 2001. *Science Fiction Film*. Cambridge: Cambridge UP.

Zipes, Jack. 2011. *The Enchanted Screen: The Unknown History of Fairy-Tale Films*. New York: Routledge.

CINEMA SCIENCE FICTION

Mediagraphy

?E?ANX (The Cave). 2009. Director Helen Haig-Brown. Canada.

2001: A Space Odyssey. 1968. Director Stanley Kubrick. UK.

A. I.: Artificial Intelligence. 2001. Director Steven Spielberg. USA.

E.T. the Extraterrestrial. 1982. Director Steven Spielberg. USA.

Ex Machina. 2015. Director Alex Garland. USA.

The Matrix. 1999. Director The Wachowskis. USA.

Peter Pan. 1953. Directors Clyde Geronimo and Wilfred Jackson. USA.

Serenity. 2005. Director Joss Whedon. USA.

Snow White and the Seven Dwarfs. 1937. Directors William Cottrell, David Hand, Wilfred Jackson, Larry Morey, Perce Pearce, and Ben Sharpsteen. USA.

Solaris. 2002. Director Steven Soderbergh. USA.

Star Trek: The Next Generation (TV). 1987–1994. Creator Gene Rodenberry. USA.

Star Wars. 1977. Director George Lucas. Later Retitled *Star Wars: Episode IV: A New Hope*. USA.

Twice Upon a Time. 1983. Directors John Korty and Charles Swenson. USA.

Urusei Yatsura: Beautiful Dreamer. 1984. Director Mamoru Oshii. Japan.

51

CLASSICAL MUSIC

Pauline Greenhill and Danishka Esterhazy

The association of instrumental music with a fairy-tale character or title suggests its intent to convey specific images, scenes, events, and/or narratives. Such works with links to themes or stories are called "program music," in alleged contradistinction to "absolute music," which lacks external referents and is usually referred to as part of a sequence, such as "First Symphony." However, Leoš Janáček's *Fairy Tale* for cello and piano (1910), Frank Bridge's *Fairy Tale Suite* for piano (1917), Nikolay Medtner's 38 *Skazki* (fairy tales) for piano (1904–1915), and Robert Schumann's *Märchenbilder* (fairy-tale pictures) for viola and piano (1851) and *Märchenerzälungen* (fairy-tale tellings) for piano, clarinet, and viola (1853), among many others, have no musical connection to wonder tale, in the absence of any direct correlation between the notes and phrases of the former with the spoken/written language of the latter. Perhaps because of this difficulty of connecting the two, analytical literature on links between classical Western art instrumental music and fairy tales is surprisingly spotty. Histories of music or fairy tales may mention music linked with fairy tales, and a few musicologists examine specific fairy-tale pieces, but the connections between the musical forms and narrative content are not central to their examinations.[1]

Nevertheless, relevant work exists. Feminist musicologist Susan McClary punctuates her crucial work *Feminine Endings: Music, Gender, and Sexuality* with fairy-tale metaphors. She describes herself as Judith, the seventh wife in Béla Bartók's (1881–1945) opera *Bluebeard's Castle*, who insists on finding the truth. McClary's mentors "granted access [. . .] to an astonishing cultural legacy," yet, she says, though "I ought to be grateful [. . .] there has really only been one stipulation in the bargain—namely, that I never ask what any of it means, that I content myself with structural analysis and empirical research. Unfortunately, that is a stipulation I have never been able to accept" (1991, 4). Though the Bartók opera's story follows versions of ATU 312 like Charles Perrault's, with the explicit moral that women should not be curious, other fairy tales reward women's curiosity, like "The Robber Bridegroom" (ATU 955) or "Rescue by the Sister" (ATU 311) in which women not only survive but prosper, defeating the human and supernatural men who seek to marry and/or destroy them.

Like the latter stories, we seek an unconventional approach. As inspiration, we point to McClary's discussion of composer Janika Vandervelde, commissioned to write music for a "Jack and the Beanstalk" (ATU 328A) reading at a children's concert:

> Because this was a piece of program music, its sequence of images was designed to correspond to moments dictated by the fairy tale: the quality of thrust entered the serene landscape of the piece only with the beanstalk's dynamic tumescence, and the violent climax (both desired and dreaded) coincided with Jack's triumphant defeat of the giant.
>
> (1991, 112)

466

Dissatisfied with the frankly phallic Oedipal musical gendering of her composition, Vandervelde sought "to produce an alternative to the dominant discourse she had internalized in the course of her training" (McClary 1991, 116)—to undo the collusion of music and male gender. Writing non-violent, anti-patriarchal music counters traditional musical discursive expectations.

Looking at gender and the sexual politics of music, given the radical effect of feminist analysis on fairy-tale scholarship and application to this chapter's topic, inspired by McClary, we look at how fairy tales' mediation in audiovisual forms genders and sometimes also queers their presentation. We explore and reflect on transmediated classical music (tellings across platforms and formats) used in fairy-tale films disseminated via cinema theater, television, and home video. We begin with feminist filmmaker co-author Danishka's personal experiences of using music in her fairy-tale and other films.

Danishka on Working with Music

I started harp lessons, mostly classical at first, when I was twelve. I had to beg for music lessons for a long time before I got them. I practiced on concert harp, a classical instrument, and then I moved to Celtic harp, a folk instrument. An amazing part of musical training is that your inner sense of rhythm develops in a deep way. Most of the great film editors I've met started as musicians. That doesn't mean you have to cut to music. But you can pace things in a way that's time based that comes from a strong training in key signatures and other musical structures. And my background also helped me choose music and work with composers because I can speak musical language and talk about what I want. I think that all the weird things I've done in my life, including being a professional musician, have made me a better filmmaker because filmmaking is like opera as composer Richard Wagner described it, *Gesamtkunstwerk*, a total work of art. You need to know music, theater, visual arts, and performance. The more background you have in the fine arts, the better you are as a filmmaker. I approach screenwriting starting from a structural breakdown. I love to play with outlines for ages before I commit to scenes, and that's very much like music.

As a filmmaker, music enters my process at the earliest stage of creation. The public will know only the final film score, but directors often use playlists and temporary music as they work. My original concept is usually a set of images or a character. But when I sit down to write, I start with a musical playlist that evokes the emotional tone of the story I want to create. The tunes that I've chosen embody the tone and the mood of the piece. The playlist is not a document that I have planned to share or release. It is a private source of inspiration that helps me tap into the tone of my story. The selections are often classical or opera, contemporary or baroque, mixed with pop music by women performers and songwriters. I return to the playlist, adding more selections, as I revise my writing to the final draft. When I make the film, I've never actually used the playlist in the soundtrack, but I think that's definitely something on my wish list for future productions.

I've actually done some shooting to music. I've done some films without dialogue where we've played music while filming to help the actors get a sense of tone, to get me in the mood. That's hard to do, though, because music is so personal. I can use a piece that to me absolutely deeply represents the heart of the movie's tone but the actors don't like the music, and they're out of sync. It's more irritating to them than inspiring. So you can't always share that musical inspiration with someone, even with composers sometimes.

Music becomes important once again in post-production. Sometimes the music that you cut to and dream about and that inspires you to create, you actually can't use because of copyright restrictions. And so it's part of the creation; it's influenced the filmmaker deeply, but then it's not in the final work that the audience sees. Ideally, I engage a composer before I start my rough cut. I talk to the composer while the film is being shot and describe the scenes that I think will require score. I love being able to cut scenes to a (rough) original score. It avoids the disappointment and anguish of what filmmakers call "temp love," which is when we become deeply attached to music used during the rough cut edit that was only meant to be a temporary place filler for an original score that has yet to be composed. Often, this temp music cannot be licensed for film use or is too expensive for the filmmaker's production budget. Temp love can resemble a kind of addiction where the filmmaker can't imagine another musical track that will fit her scene. This conundrum can elicit creative anguish for the filmmaker.

But I love to cut to music. The rhythm and cadence of a well-scored or well-sourced piece of music can inspire the edit and help create the ideal tone. Collaboration with a composer can also bring surprise and discovery. If the filmmaker has been able to communicate her goals for the emotional tone, the composer can often create that feeling by using instruments and melody that that the filmmaker had never imagined. These new discoveries help elevate the storytelling and are a perfect example of the power of collaboration in filmmaking.

I've never used classical music or opera in any of my films as a score, which is strange because I love opera and classical music deeply, and there are many tunes I would use. I would love to use some baroque music. I'm a huge fan, constantly going to baroque music concerts, and I'm always thinking, how could I incorporate this music? The baroque period and our current culture have so much in common. That historical music could have an extra layer of meaning if I used it in a contemporary setting. For example, in my present-day fairy-tale film *H & G* (2013), a story about child neglect and abandonment, I could have used a stately baroque concerto grosso[2] for the scenes where the children wander through the depressed streets of Winnipeg. I used contemporary rap to underscore their innocence and lack of understanding. But I could have used elegant baroque music to show their disenfranchisement and the barriers to their participation in Canada's economic and cultural prosperity.

Music in my fairy-tale films has always been important. *Red Hood* (2009) was a partial collaboration with Alexis Cohen using music that she had already written, some of which was reinterpreted by Ken Gregory, my sound designer. For *H & G* I cleared—got permission to use—a song by CocoRosie, the wonderful independent band. There was a lot of tenacious begging! I paid for the rights, but they gave me an affordable price within my budget, so I was able to clear the song. Composer Joe Silva and I talked about each segment of music for *Black Field* (2009) and *The Singing Bones* (2016). I'd say, "Okay, here's what I'm thinking of for this segment of music. This is how I want it to perform dramatically, this is how I want it to interact with the scene." My notes to him would say things like, "I want something in a really slow tempo in a minor key with a heavy drone." But because he often works with directors who have no musical background, he really likes referential music. Directors who aren't musicians say things like, "I want something sad!" And that's very vague, so Joe will ask, "Okay, give me five kinds of music that you think are sad." And then he can translate, "Oh, you want something on a violin!" When he asked me, "Give me five pieces of music that sound like that to you," it became an interesting process gathering all these reference tracks for him. And it gave me a deeper understanding of the emotional elements in each scene. Like all filmmaking, fairy-tale films—even though their stories and references may be very familiar—always involve that kind of process of discovery, and music can be an essential element thereof.

Classical Music Incorporated in Fairy-Tale Film

When fairy tales are incorporated into operas and ballets, words and dance elaborate links between music and story. Not only do wonder tales provide plot contours, characters, and themes, but as with other adaptations, these narratives offer familiarity rather than an unknown quantity. Classical music is also integrated into films and television using fairy-tale narratives, characters, titles, images, plots, motifs, and themes.[3] Sometimes inclusions are obvious, as when Disney uses the "Garland Waltz" from Pyotr Ilyich Tchaikovsky's *Sleeping Beauty* ballet for the song "Once Upon a Dream" in the animated *Sleeping Beauty* (1959), then reprises it somberly in their live-action *Maleficent* (also based on ATU 410). For *Frozen* (2013), however, they used Southern Sámi composer Frode Fjellheim's "Eatnemen Vuelie"—not translated into English— as the title song. Not surprisingly, it was eclipsed in the popular imagination of the film by the more conventional pop song "Let It Go."

Many fairy-tale filmmakers use classical music to set a scene's mood or enhance narrative content. That music may be extradiegetic (background) or diegetic (part of the represented action). For example, Tarsem's live-action original fairy-tale film *The Fall* (2006) opens with a sepia-and-white-toned, slow-motion, multiple-cut sequence without diegetic sound; the somber A-minor second movement from Ludwig van Beethoven's Seventh Symphony provides the musical backdrop. Tarsem concludes with his main characters watching a film. *The Fall*'s frame story is set in the silent era, so a violinist within the scene riffs on Wagner's "Ride of the Valkyries." The Beethoven piece helps the audience recognize the seriousness of the depicted events; the diegetic Wagner performance underscores the historical setting, but also echoes the exciting stunts represented in the film-within-a-film (see Greenhill 2017). For very well-known films, once melodies and content become associated, it may be difficult for an audience member to disentangle their connections.

"The Sorcerer's Apprentice"

For example, for those who have seen Disney's *Fantasia* (1940), it could now be difficult to conceive of Paul Dukas's *The Sorcerer's Apprentice* (1896–1897, referencing ATU 325, "The Magician and his Pupil") without imagining the famous sequence with Mickey Mouse as the apprentice. Yet there is, of course, no necessary connection between music and film. Jack Zipes explains that Dukas was influenced by Johann Wolfgang von Goethe's 1797 short poem "Der Zauberlehrling" ("The Sorcerer's Apprentice")—subtitling his symphonic poem "Scherzo based on a ballad by Goethe." Goethe narrates the story of an apprentice (from his own perspective) who accidentally floods his absent sorcerer master's house. When the sorcerer returns, he banishes the ghosts his apprentice has called. Dukas's music backgrounds the *Fantasia* sequence featuring Mickey Mouse, "part of Disney's effort to resurrect [his] popularity [. . . that] had declined during the 1930s" (Zipes 2017, 16).[4]

The repetitive phrases in slow crescendo of the extradiegetic music undoubtedly link well with the continuing activity of trainee magician Mickey's futile battle with the cleaning equipment and water. But other musical pieces have similar repetition, including Maurice Ravel's *Bolero* (1928). Would that tune have served the story equally well? Perhaps. Further, Dukas is not the only composer of a "Sorcerer's Apprentice" piece. Number ten in Hungarian György Ligeti's piano etude series (1985–2001), "Der Zauberlehrling," has "continuous sound which is created by means of repeated patterns of greatest speed" (Can 2011, 206). Its crescendos recall the unremitting movement of water, with periodic intervening staccato phrases perhaps invoking the apprentice's attempts to control it. Like Dukas's piece, it ends abruptly, a loud note perhaps marking the sorcerer stopping the flowing water. Its movement toward a conclusion implicitly underscores the male sorcerer's phallic power—implicitly, the Goethe narrative is here too.

Several films from Czechoslovakia and successor states, East Germany, Japan, Canada, South Africa, the Soviet Union and successor states, and the United States use the theme of an apprentice or servant and his master magician. As Zipes points out, not all involve Goethe's/*Fantasia*'s hapless, powerless child taught a lesson by his betters—versions he calls "The Humiliated Apprentice." Some instead use what Zipes terms "The Rebellious Apprentice." This version involves a poor young man whose evil master seeks full control over him; these stories end in a duel between the two magicians—pupil and teacher—won when the apprentice tricks his master and kills or otherwise defeats him (2017). Such narratives suggest less repetitive musical themes than in the Dukas or Ligeti compositions—but whether culminating in the master's or servant's comeuppance, the story remains violent and phallic. Examination of how the music is rendered and gendered in "Rebellious Apprentice" films awaits further study.

Prélude à l'après-midi d'un faune

For those who have seen *Fantasia*, hearing Dukas invokes Mickey; for those who have seen David Kaplan's *Little Red Riding Hood* (1997, ATU 333), the beginning of Claude Debussy's *Prélude à l'après-midi d'un faune* (Prelude to the afternoon of a faun, 1894) calls up the opening Quentin Crisp voiceover, "Once there was a girl who went to take some bread and milk to her granny" and all that follows. This black-and-white short features Christina Ricci, who bears a striking resemblance to Red in a Gustave Doré illustration. Jennifer Orme links the music to the film's "queer invitation to reassess the relationship between the girl and the wolf" (2015, 87). *Faune*, now most familiar as a symphonic poem for orchestra, was originally composed for ballet. The multimediality of this work—fairy-tale hypotext (narrative source); (extradiegetic) music; voiceover; and visuals (including live action and puppetry)—repeatedly installs complex associations and meaning.

In Kaplan's film, the wolf's role is danced by Timour Bourtasenkov. What Orme calls "the celebrity intertexts," Crisp's location as "an important early gay celebrity" (100) and the ballet's association with bisexual choreographer and dancer Vaslav Nijinsky explicitly invoked in Bourtasenkov's performance, fuse "the wolf figure to the cultural image of [. . .] Nijinsky and the faun in the ballet as challengers of heteronormativity" (103). The film's visuals draw explicit links to the fairy tale, but reject the Grimms' rescuing huntsman and Charles Perrault's punitive consumption leaving grandmother and Red alike dead at the end (see Kohm and Greenhill 2014), choosing instead a lesser known version in which Red escapes through her own cunning. As Kaplan says, "What was striking about it was that it was a very resourceful young woman who does get out of trouble by herself. But more than that, she kind of wants to get into trouble in the first place!" (pers. comm.).[5] The filmmaker sees

> a story of sexual flirtation, of kind of walking the line between accepted behavior and taboo and the excitement and delight of that. And stepping over a little bit, but then stepping back. And I thought that was an experience that [is] also very universal; people growing up and coming into their sexuality and changes start to happen.
> (Kaplan 2012 pers. comm.)

McClary notes *Faune* as a work explicitly invoking sexuality. She argues that "because such pieces influence and constitute the way listeners experience and define some of their most intimate feelings, they participate actively in the social organization of sexuality" (1991, 9). She also notes how *Faune* "manages to shape itself only by moving as though toward climax, though that climax is ultimately refused" (1991, 146). Kaplan's choice of music follows his version of ATU 333's contours and conclusion:

I was actually very conflicted about using the piece of music because it is so well known. But it also seemed to just fit so perfectly. And I dreamed up the *mise en scene* listening to that song, and then was using it as a temporary track. But again, it just fit so perfectly that the producer and I just decided to go for it and leave it in. [. . .] It's also a very sensual piece of music which lent itself to the thematic element that I was going for. In particular with the wolf being a somewhat Nijinskyesque dancer, it also came to feel part and parcel of the same tone and approach; the idea from envisioning the wolf as a very sensual being, one that would elicit this kind of sensual pursuit on the part of Little Red Riding Hood, this sensual interest, this flirtation. The idea was to give the wolf a degree of beauty and elegance, coupled with the very real, practical nature of the film that there wasn't a tremendous amount of money for special effects and for makeup and CGI to create a monster wolf. So, that also pushed us toward a more theatrical approach in the whole thing, including the sets.

(Kaplan 2012 pers. comm.)

For Kaplan, as for Danishka, music is central to the filmmaking process.

"Tristan and Isolde"

In *Aria*, a 1987 British anthology film, ten directors created short works inspired by operatic arias. Directors including Nicolas Roeg, Jean-Luc Godard, and Derek Jarman created segments inspired by composers such as Giuseppe Verdi, Jean-Baptiste Lully, and Gustave Charpentier. Perhaps the most evocative segment is director Franc Roddam's short film using the "Liebestod" (Love/Death) from Wagner's opera *Tristan und Isolde*, a retelling of a much older Arthurian tale. The British legend dates to the early Middle Ages (McCann 2002, 3–35) and inspired the epic poem *The Romance of Tristan* by Béroul in the twelfth century, parts of Sir Thomas Malory's *Le morte d'Arthur* in the fifteenth century, and Lord Alfred Tennyson's *Idylls of the King* in the nineteenth century.

In the legend, a young Cornish knight, Tristan, travels to Ireland to fetch a new bride for his uncle King Mark: Isolde (or Iseult or Yseut). On the journey back to Cornwall, they fall in love as the result of a magic potion. Isolde marries King Mark, but the two young lovers cannot resist their mutual passion and continue their adulterous affair. When they are discovered, Tristan is forced to leave Cornwall and marry another woman. The lovers continue to pine for one another. Mortally wounded, Tristan sends word to Isolde, and she rushes to meet him. However, Tristan is tricked into believing that Isolde has abandoned him, and he dies of grief. Isolde sings the "Liebestod" as she finds Tristan's body and prepares to join him in death. Wagner's opera, for which he wrote both music and libretto, first performed in 1865, retells the lovers' full story. Roddam's film reimagines the doomed couple in a story of teenage angst in an unforgiving modern world. Two young lovers, played by Bridget Fonda and James Mathers, drive through the Nevada desert. They pass by a scene of police brutality: two young Indigenous men being arrested for no apparent reason. As they drive by, our Isolde locks eyes with one of the young men, and she is clearly moved by his despair. In the background, soprano Leontyne Price sings, "Seht ihr's, Freunde?/Seht ihr's nicht?" (Do you see it, friends?/Don't you see it?). The world is harsh and full of injustice.

The young lovers arrive in Las Vegas. As they drive through the night streets, they smile with a kind of innocent joy at the colorful sparkling lights that surround them. But then they begin to note the signs of crass commercialism and decay: aging gamblers, a quickie marriage at a chapel on the Strip. Everywhere, beauty dies and corruption triumphs. The couple check into a hotel and make love in the shadow of flashing neon lights. Their lovemaking is passionate, all consuming, a perfect union of body and soul that rises with the climax of the aria as Price sings "Soll ich atmen?" (Shall I breathe?).

Afterwards, the lovers share a bath. And then, slowly and deliberately, they use a shard from a broken liquor bottle to slit their wrists. They will die together before the world can spoil their love or corrupt their passion. They embrace as the aria ends. They have found the "höchste Lust" or "supreme delight" that concludes the Wagner "Liebestod"; their own Love Death. Roddam's film re-visions "Tristan and Isolde" in a remarkable cinematic short that demonstrates the powerful storytelling that can be achieved when traditional tale and music combine on screen. As Marcia J. Citron notes, "Roddam's 'Liebestod' stands as a magnificent realization of Wagner's music and text. I think of it as an ultimate, and ultimately appropriate, visual representation of the music. The orgasmic quality of the music is finally materialized, not merely expressed in sound, and we get to see literal 'Love-Death'" (2010, 65). It is the skillful interweaving of fable, opera, and modern filmmaking that makes this work so unforgettable.

Sex, Gender, Sexuality, and Fairy-Tale Music

The examples we've discussed in this chapter are by no means comprehensive or conclusive. Clearly, we've chosen ones that help us illustrate the ways that sex, gender, and sexuality are rendered in fairy-tale films with the support—collusion, even, as McClary suggests—of classical European music. The inherent multimediality of cinema, its use of collaboration and its embodiment of *Gesamtkunstwerk*, make it a rich source of meaning in the realm of gender and fairy-tale studies. When traditional tales and music combine on screen, they create complex associations that can give new meaning to the traditional stories that continue to haunt and inspire us.

Related topics: Cinematic; Disney Corporation; Gender; Intellectual Property; Musicals; Opera; Sexualities/Queer and Trans Studies

Notes

1. We thank research assistants Marcie Fehr and Baden Gaeke-Franz for their extensive work on background materials for this chapter.
2. In this musical form, a small group of players (in contrast to the [solo] concerto with a single instrument) take the main melody lines, accompanied by an orchestra.
3. For use of classical music in films see "Classical Music in Movies" (2016).
4. Zipes argues, "Disney and his collaborators seemingly copied many incidents and motifs from a 1930 film [*The Wizard's Apprentice*] directed by Sidney Levee and produced by William Carmen Menzies. They were the first to make use of Dukas's music to accompany their remarkable narrative" (2017, 16).
5. This and all further quotations from Kaplan are from Greenhill's telephone interview with him, May 11, 2012, transcribed by Marcie Fehr.

References Cited and Further Reading

Béroul. 12th C. *The Romance of Tristan*. France.

Can, Toros. 2011. "The Importance of Ligeti's Piano Etudes in Compositional and Pianistic Aspects: Why It Is Necessary to Analyze Ligeti Etudes Prior to Learning." *International Journal of Arts & Sciences* 4 (3): 201–7.

Citron, Marcia J. 2010. *When Opera Meets Film*. Cambridge: Cambridge UP.

Goethe, Johann Wolfgang von Goethe. 1797. *Der Zauberlehrling (The Sorcerer's Apprentice)* (Poem). Germany.

Greenhill, Pauline. 2017. "Fairy-Tale Films." In *Oxford Research Encyclopedia of Literature*, edited by Paula Rabinowitz. DOI 10.1093/acrefore/9780190201098.013.83

Kohm, Steven, and Pauline Greenhill. 2014. "Little Red Riding Hood Crime Films: Critical Variations on Criminal Themes." *Law, Culture and the Humanities* 10 (2): 257–78.

Malory, Thomas. 15th C. *Le morte d'Arthur*. London: Caxton.

McCann, W. J. 2002. "Tristan: The Celtic and Oriental Material Re-examined." In *Tristan and Isolde: A Casebook*, edited by Joan Tasker Gimbert, 3–35. New York: Routledge.

McClary, Susan. 1991. *Feminine Endings: Music, Gender, and Sexuality*. Minneapolis: U Minnesota P.

Orme, Jennifer. 2015. "A Wolf's Queer Invitation: David Kaplan's *Little Red Riding Hood* and Queer Possibility." *Marvels & Tales* 29 (1): 87–109.

Tennyson, Alfred. 1859–1885. *Idylls of the King*. England.

Zipes, Jack. 2017. *The Sorcerer's Apprentice: An Anthology of Magical Tales*. Princeton, NJ: Princeton UP.

Mediagraphy

Aria/Tristan und Isolde. 1987. Director Franc Roddam. UK.

Beethoven, Ludwig van. 1813. *Symphony No. 7*. Germany.

Black Field. 2009. Director Danishka Esterhazy. Canada.

Bluebeard's Castle (Opera). 1918. Music Béla Bartók; libretto Béla Balázs. Hungary.

Bridge, Frank. 1917. *Fairy Tale Suite*. England.

"Classical Music in Movies." 2016. *Naxos*. www.naxos.com/musicinmovies.asp.

Debussy, Claude. 1894. *Prélude à l'après-midi d'un faune*. France.

Dukas, Paul. 1896–1897. *The Sorcerer's Apprentice*. France.

The Fall. 2006. Director Tarsem Singh. India/USA.

Fantasia/The Sorcerer's Apprentice. 1940. Director James Algar. USA.

Fjellheim, Frode. 2013. *Eatnemen Vuelie*. Norway.

Frozen. 2013. Directors Jennifer Lee and Chris Buck. USA.

H & G. 2013. Director Danishka Esterhazy. Canada.

Janáček, Leoš. 1910. *Fairy Tale*. Czech.

"Let It Go" (Song). 2013. Artist Idina Menzel, album *Frozen*. USA.

Ligeti, György. 1985–2001. *Der Zauberlehrling*. Hungary.

Little Red Riding Hood. 1997. Director David Kaplan. USA.

Maleficent. 2014. Director Robert Stromberg. USA.

Medtner, Nikolay. 1904–1915. 38 *Skazki*. Russia.

"Once Upon a Dream" (Song). 1959. Artists Mary Costa and Bill Shirley, album *Sleeping Beauty*. USA.

———. 2014. Artist Lana Del Rey, album *Maleficent (Original Motion Picture Soundtrack)*. USA.

Ravel, Maurice. 1928. *Bolero*. France.

The Red Hood. 2009. Director Danishka Esterhazy. Canada.

Schumann, Robert. 1851. *Märchenbilder*. Germany.

———. 1853. *Märchenerzälungen*. Germany.

The Singing Bones. 2016. Director Danishka Esterhazy. USA.

Sleeping Beauty. 1959. Director Clyde Geronimi. USA.

The Snow Queen. 2005. Director Danishka Esterhazy. Canada.

Tchaikovsky, Pyotr Ilyich. 1890. "Garland Waltz." *TheSleeping Beauty* ballet. Russia.

Tristan und Isolde (Opera). 1865. Music and libretto Richard Wagner. Germany.

Wagner, Richard. 1870. "Ride of the Valkyries." *Die Walküre* opera. Germany.

The Wizard's Apprentice. 1930. Director Sidney Levee. USA.

52

COMICS AND GRAPHIC NOVELS

Fairy-Tale Graphic Narrative

Emma Whatman

Comics and graphic novels offer multimodal media for the adaptation of fairy-tale narratives, characters, motifs, and iconography. Many contemporary comics and graphic novels adapt classic literature such as fairy tales, myths, and legends in order to reimagine, expand, and update familiar, well-known stories. Wolfgang Mieder (2016) reminds us that "folktales and fairy tales have long inspired visual representations" (173). In a recent work, Jack Zipes traces fairy-tale graphic narratives back to "the broadsides and chapbooks of the eighteenth and nineteenth centuries as well as [. . .] [to] the single volume picture books that were widespread by the end of the nineteenth century." He argues that they are often "reproductions" of well-known stories and are frequently "highly experimental" where well-known tales are "sometimes drastically transformed and made into pastiches" (2015, 121–122). While some fairy-tale graphic narratives—that is, stories where fairy-tale characters, motifs, landscapes, or iconography are adapted to the comic or graphic novel medium—can be progressive because of this experimentation, others promote problematic ideologies that are often masked through experimental blurring of text and image, genre, style, and fairy tale.

"Graphic narrative" is the collective term first coined by David Kunzle (Peterson 2011, xv) and is used to encompass texts that utilize the comics form, whether short comic strips in the newspaper, collectable periodical comics, or novel-length graphic novels (see Chute and DeKoven 2006). According to Scott McCloud (1993) graphic narratives can be characterized as a "vessel" as they can hold any number of ideas, stories, and images (6). Indeed, they function as conduits for the shifting social, cultural, and political landscapes of the times and places in which they are produced. Although I refer to "graphic narratives" as a general term that includes comic books and graphic novels, it is important to discuss the specific differences between the two.

Comic books are traditionally identified as paperback texts produced as serials, released periodically, and typically targeted at a younger audience. The use of the term "graphic novel" emerged in the early 1960s as what Hilary Chute argues is a "marketing term" (2008, 453) that allowed publishers to bring out hardback (and thus more expensive) works of art for capitalist gains. Additionally, the term "graphic novel" had the implicit intention of persuading people, particularly scholars, to take the medium more seriously than comic books. Since that time, the graphic novel has become a popular and experimental medium that is generally longer than the comic book and targeted toward both young adults and adults. Zipes argues that it is more experimental in design and narrative than comics, tends to "borrow from different genres such as myth, legend, the Gothic story, and so on," and when specifically adapting fairy tales, makes a "greater change" in the traditional tale (2015, 122). While this may be the case in some instances, a number of the comic examples discussed here challenge these assertions, demonstrating that it is not graphic novels that are exclusively experimental in both form and content.

Graphic narratives are unique for the way that they visually represent temporality in comparison to other visual media. While animation, film, and picture books also present time sequentially, they are not "spatially *juxtaposed* as comics are" (McCloud 1993, 7). Chute contends that graphic narratives are compelling as they are "capacious, offering layers of words and images—as well as multiple layers of possible temporalities—on each page" (2010, 5). To extend this, I argue that the multimodal and temporal possibilities of comics and graphic novels are what make the media complex vessels for *both* the entrenchment and disruption of the conservative ideologies found in many fairy tales. The medium-specific conventions of many graphic narratives, such as the gutter (the space between each panel) and closure (the contextual meaning made by a reader in the gutter), require readers to bring their own knowledge to the experience in order to make and understand meaning.

For instance, readers must, as Duncan and Smith explain, use "an understanding of panel relations to combine panels mentally into events" (2009, 316). When well-known fairy tales are adapted to this form, iconography (such as Cinderella's glass slipper or Little Red Riding Hood's red cloak or cap) or motifs (such as talking animals and magical objects) ignite contextual knowledge of the relevant tale type for the reader. Furthermore, ideological meaning can be produced in different ways because a reader's understanding of a fairy tale can be purposefully satisfied or distorted by the conventions of the medium. Thus, I look specifically at the different ways that the fairy-tale graphic narrative draws on medium-specific conventions and different genres to adapt various tales to the form. I argue that these differences shape the ways each graphic narrative subscribes to, or transcends, the ideological origins of earlier versions.

In one of the only dedicated examinations of fairy-tale graphic narratives, B. Grantham Aldred proposes three categories: 1) direct retellings, 2) adaptations, and 3) pastiches (2016, 422). While these provide a broad umbrella to group these narratives, further clarification is needed. Aldred's "adaptation" encompasses comics or graphic novels that take "folktales or fairy beliefs as inspiration but adapt the setting or the characters in some way," often through the blending of "genre conventions of folktales and fairy tales with the conventions of other genres either in form or style" (423). While Aldred proposes adaptation as its own category, I suggest that *all* fairy-tale graphic narratives are in fact adaptations and that there are various categories under that large umbrella instead that I will go on to discuss.

Genre Blending

One subcategory is the blending of fairy or folktale conventions with those of other genres. Such blending is a common strategy in fairy-tale graphic narratives, and the oeuvre is diverse, encompassing many different genres from fantasy to horror to erotic.

A recent example is Matt Phelan's 2016 *Snow White* graphic novel that blends the ATU 709 tale type with the black-and-white film noir genre in a new cultural setting. The adaptation, set in 1928, combines the tale's motifs such as a poisoned apple and glass coffin with sepia and black-and-white watercolor illustrations to reference the oppositional glamor and desperation of depression-era New York City. Color is used sparingly yet effectively throughout.

The black-and-white washed-out illustrations doubly represent the desperation of late 1920s America and the murderous and jealous intent represented in the ATU 709 tale type. The color red is used as a symbol for blood and death, featuring in the blood Samantha White's mother coughs up before she dies, a heart the huntsman pretends belongs to Samantha, and the poisoned apple. Additionally, the final chapter titled "And they lived . . ." is illustrated in color and contains no text. However, it signals to readers a happy ending for the characters. While *Snow White* (2016) makes no substantial changes to the ideology of ATU 709, the medium adds an extra layer of meaning through its merging of genres, its art work, and its adaptation of setting.

Horror is a popular genre for graphic narrative adaptations. Many return to the darker themes of earlier fairy tales that expressed the "violence and brutality of everyday life" (Zipes 2006, 7–8) in order to challenge the notion of a "happily ever after." An example is Antarctic Press's *Zombie Fairy Tales*, four one-shot volumes (a volume with only a single issue that focuses on one specific storyline) from 2011 to 2015. The first, *Zombie Fairy Tales*, invited readers to "Sit down by the gravesite and with a big bowl of brain food!" (2011) with individual stories by different author-illustrators that turn fairy-tale characters into zombies, such as Rod Espinosa's *What Bloody Teeth You Have!* (2011) and David Hutchison's *Little Dead Riding Hood* (2011). Both are adaptations of "Little Red Riding Hood" (ATU 333). *What Bloody Teeth You Have!* shows Red threatening to eat the brains of the wolf, using the cannibalistic motifs of the French oral tradition of ATU 333, unlike Perrault's (1697) version of the tale.

These oral versions rely on the motif of "the blood and flesh of the grandmother" that "the little girl is invited to eat" (Soriano and Frey 1969, 27). The single-page comic shows a transformed cannibalistic zombie Red, identifiable by her cloak and basket, glaring at a frightened Wolf dressed as Red's grandmother. Perrault's famous lines, "'What big teeth you have, grandmother!', 'The better to eat you'" (1977) are transformed into "'W-what bloody teeth you have!', 'Hrrr. . . . The better to eat your brains with!!!'" (Espinosa 2011). Similarly, *Little Dead Riding Hood* ends with the skeletal protagonist and her grandmother feasting on the flesh of the wolf after she has clawed her way out of his stomach. This humorous horror comic is longer than *What Bloody Teeth You Have!* and includes the familiar journey into the forest and the wolf's consumption of Red.

The combination of humor and horror relies on a reader's contextual understanding of "Little Red Riding Hood"—much like the contextual knowledge a reader must bring to the graphic narrative form itself. Julie Cross elucidates that this kind of humor "relies on a sophisticated understanding of irony, parody, genre convention [. . .] and ultimate enjoyment and even acceptance of, incongruity" (2013, 58). Relying primarily on imagery, *Little Dead Riding Hood* shows the protagonist, Little Dead, journeying into a forest on her way to Grandma's house. This comic demonstrates how readers must use their contextual knowledge to understand the meaning made in the gutter between panels. Panel 10 shows the wolf looking down at Little Dead with gleaming teeth, but by panel 15, only the wolf remains with the word "Grumble" (Hutchinson 2011). Readers rely on their knowledge of ATU 333 to understand that the wolf has devoured her. However, *Little Dead Riding Hood* goes on to challenge the tale type's expectations by using incongruous humor in the closing illustration with Little Dead's hand popping through the wolf's stomach, intertextually referencing the image of a zombie rising from the dead.

Zenescope Entertainment's *Grimm Fairy Tales* (2005–) also adapts "Little Red Riding Hood" to the horror comic, along with other tales such as "Hansel and Gretel" (ATU 327A) and "Rumpelstiltskin" (ATU 500). In the ATU 333 adaptation, the unnamed teenage protagonist faces sexual pressure from her boyfriend before falling asleep reading a collection of fairy tales. Once again, readers rely on contextual knowledge to understand that the narrative has moved into a fairy-tale world as panel 18 shows the collection of fairy tales and panel 19 a figure cloaked in a red cape. The story loosely follows ATU 333 as Red begins a journey to visit her grandmother, meeting a previous lover on the way who also tries to pressure her into sex. The reader is positioned through the illustrations to understand that the lover (and Red) are from the "real world," as they are illustrated in the same way. Upon making it to her grandmother's house, Red is attacked by the wolf, who rips off her clothing to reveal her hypersexualized bare breasts as "the need for her sweet flesh consumes" him (2005).

The wolf is fatally injured by the huntsman and transforms into human form—Red's lover—stating, "I wanted you so badly. I couldn't control myself" (2005). It is here that the protagonist wakes up on her bed, with the dream prompting her to "kick Chad and his attitude to the curb" (2005). Although the illustrations of this comic conform to the overtly sexualized style common in fantasy comics of this style, it has subversive potential. The adaptation uses both the conventions of comics and the ATU 333 tale type to challenge narratives of sexual pressure and abuse. Through panel relations, readers are prompted to draw on their contextual knowledge of "Little Red Riding Hood" and apply it to the dream fairy-tale world the protagonist has entered. By confronting the sexual assault of Red in the fairy-tale world, readers are positioned to relate it to the situation in the "real" comic world where the teen protagonist is facing sexual pressure from her boyfriend. The protagonist wakes in the real world and breaks up with the boyfriend, which challenges the conservative morals of many "Little Red Riding Hood" versions where women are either murdered or blamed for their own sexual assault.

Direct Retellings

Along with the blending of genres, the other two categories, direct retellings and pastiche, are also forms of graphic narrative adaptations. Aldred suggests that direct retellings are the simplest, as "the setting and characters are the same as in the original source material" (2016, 423) but include differing accompanying images from the comics' illustrators and artists. However, I would argue that artists such as Camille Rose Garcia complicate the alleged simplicity of direct retellings. Garcia's *Snow White* (2012) and *Cinderella, or The Little Glass Slipper* (2015) employ the English translated text from the 1819 "Sneewittchen" (ATU 709) of the Brothers Grimm and Perrault's (1697) "Cendrillon, ou la petite pantoufle de verre" (ATU 510A) respectively. Garcia reimagines the tales by artistically transforming the size, shape, layout, and font of the original text and combining it with her unique art style, which produces hauntingly beautiful gothic imagery that experiments with contemporary understandings of female fairy-tale protagonists. Rather than a simplistic reimagining, Garcia transforms both the way the tale is read and how it is ideologically understood, creating a deliberate and effectual relationship between text and image.

Pastiche

Pastiche is when "characters from different folktales and fairy tales interact with each other, and in some cases with characters from other genres of folklore" (Aldred 2016, 423). Aldred's primary example is Bill Willingham's series *Fables* (2002–2016) as it "shows the most extensive use of folktale and fairy-tale material" (2016, 424). *Fables* is an adventure fantasy series that published 150 issues, with additional spinoffs based on popular characters such as Jack Horner (*Jack of Fables* [2006–2011]). It showcases an epic fairy-tale universe where various fairy-tale, folklore, and mythological characters are adapted to the pastiche graphic narrative form. Adam Zolkover argues that *Fables*' use of the medium is a "lens through which to comment on the fairy tales themselves" rather than using fairy tales to complement the graphic narrative (2008, 40).

The series also draws on different genres for specific story arcs, for example, "A Sharp Operation: Part One of a Two-Part Caper" (2003) and "Dirty Business: Part Two of a Two-Part Caper" (2003) pay homage to the caper-mystery genre. The Big Bad Wolf (known as Bigby) and Bluebeard use the skills of Briar Rose to capture and kill a mundy (non-magical folk) who threatens to expose the Fables' world. The illustrations draw on a 1950s film noir style, and the result represents the seedy underbelly of the *Fables* world that is featured in later story arcs and the spinoff video game, *The Wolf Among Us* (2013).

A further pastiche technique evident in the series is the unique grouping of "different folktales with similar characters" such as the way that "Snow White is implied to be from both 'Snow White and the Seven Dwarves' and 'Snow White and Rose Red'" (Aldred 2016, 424). Similarly, Prince Charming features as the Prince from "Cinderella," "Snow White and the Seven Dwarves," and "Sleeping Beauty"—explaining "his multiple marriages [. . .] by multiple divorces" (Aldred 2016, 423–424). Ultimately challenging the popular Disney conception of fairy-tale romance, the series is postmodern in its pastiche techniques and complication of well-known fairy-tale characters beyond their happy endings.

However, importantly, Karin Kukkonen reminds us that it doesn't boast "subversive and feminist agendas" (2016, 1103). Cinderella, a prominent figure in *Fables*, is a prime case study for exploring this contention. Cindy (as she is affectionately called) is the secret agent for Fabletown and first appeared in "Chapter Two: The (Un)Usual Suspects" (2002) and remained in the series until the final issue. In addition to her role in *Fables*, she is featured in her own spinoffs, *Cinderella: From Fabletown with Love* (2009–2010) and *Cinderella: Fables Are Forever* (2011) and had her own story arc in the notable *Fairest* (2012–2015) spinoff. *Fairest* had thirty-three issues in in its four-year life span, focusing on the female protagonists from the *Fables* world. The *Fairest* series does not stand separate from *Fables*, but rather occurs within the same time frame as its universe.

Fairest aims to provide *Fables* readers with the backstories of the female protagonists. As creator and writer Bill Willingham explained in an interview, while *Fables* "concentrates more on the larger, more epic stories," *Fairest* seeks to instead tell "modest" stories that focus on the "beautiful people" (2012). Volume 4 of *Fairest*, "Of Men and Mice" (2014), contains issues 21–26 and follows Cindy as she endeavors to capture those who have attempted to assassinate other female fairy-tale protagonists. Kukkonen argues that as a secret agent in the *Fables* universe, Cindy "is apt at spinning the stories she needs and at playing female stereotypes to her advantage," and while she appears as active and liberated in her role in the series, the *Fables* world "is a far cry from feminist storytelling" as she is represented "in a sexually exaggerated manner, with unnatural bodily proportions" (2013, 64).

In her illustrations and stories alike, Cindy encapsulates the postfeminist heroine who has commonly been represented in the history of comics with characters such as Wonder Woman and Cat Woman. Kerry Mallan argues that a common dilemma in contemporary popular culture productions of femininity (such as *Fairest* and *Fables*) is "how to establish female subjectivity while at the same time deconstructing patriarchal representations of femininity and the female subject" (2009, 20). In both series, this dilemma is left unresolved because, while on the surface they have elements of pseudo-agency, both the illustration and narrative trajectory of many female protagonists reinforce stereotypical and misogynist representations of femininity.

"Of Mice and Men" opens with Cindy in black lacy underwear bound to a chair, and the illustration is an up shot that draws attention to her accentuated breasts. Kukkonen comments that Cindy "relies on heavily sexist stereotypes to gain the upper hand" in her battles throughout the series, but also, as in more conservative versions of "Cinderella," "she waits for others to give her her cues [. . .] [with] no voice or agency of her own" (2013, 65). In order for Cindy to break free from her bondage in "Of Mice and Men," she is assisted by her male mouse companion, Dickory, who bites through the rope to free her. On the surface, Cindy may represent a reassuring fantasy to female readers as she battles her captors; however, her primary weapon is her naked body, which is regularly posed in compromising positions as the central focus in the fight scene panels. While fairy-tale graphic narratives such as *Fairest* and *Fables* represent hypersexualized female bodies and postfeminist or passive subjectivities, the following fairy-tale graphic narrative adaptations reject normative and limiting models of female subjectivity.

Subversive Fairy-Tale Graphic Narratives

Serena Valentino's *Nightmares & Fairy Tales* (2002–2008) is a gothic comic book series about the adventures of a doll named Annabelle; many of the story arcs involve fairy-tale characters and narratives. For example, issue 6, "Cinderella's Story" (2003), is a variation of ATU 510A that references aspects of both Perrault's (1697) "Cendrillon, ou la petite pantoufle de verre" and the Grimm brothers' 1812 "Aschenputtel." As in early versions of the tale, Cinderella is physically and emotionally abused by her stepfamily, but rather than Cinderella calling on a godmother as in "Cendrillon," the wicked stepmother makes a pact with a demon so that her daughters will be the most beautiful at the ball. The sisters sprout horns and hooves (as this is what the demon considers beautiful), and Cinderella rejects the Prince who has fallen in love with her. The end of the issue references "Aschenputtel" as one of the stepsisters slices off her toes to fit into the slipper. The Prince falls for this ploy and tortures the stepsister (thinking it is Cinderella) for rejecting him. Cinderella is left with perhaps a "true" happily ever after as she escapes both marriage and her abusive family, which Laurie Taylor reminds us is "a route not often offered even in revisionist tales" (2005, 131).

Issue 10, "Beauty and the Beast" (2004), is a lesbian reimagining of "Beauty and the Beast" (ATU 425C). Annabelle recounts how she was owned by a girl named Belle, who was physically abused and locked up by her father for her romantic and sexual relationship with another girl, Rose. The comic loosely follows Jeanne-Marie Leprince de Beaumont's 1757 "La Belle et la Bête" in that Belle's father picks a rose and is captured by a Beast in a castle. Belle is exchanged for her abusive father's life (he is then killed), and Belle overcomes Beast's monstrosity and falls in love, whereupon Beast turns back into Rose and the two women live happily ever after.

Through both the gothic style and rewriting of classic wonder tales, *Nightmares & Fairy Tales* subverts gendered power structures seen in more conservative fairy-tale graphic narratives such as the *Fables* and *Fairest* series. Through exploring trauma and abuse, and empowering female sexuality, *Nightmares & Fairy Tales* offers the potential to shift sexist and heteronormative ideologies seen in many conservative fairy-tale adaptations. Taylor argues that gothic comics, such as *Nightmares & Fairy Tales*, "rewrite the traditional comics trajectory by including tales that feature women main characters who are presented in visually non-hypersexualized ways due to the art style of Goth comics" (2005, 131). Thus, through its visual style, this fairy-tale graphic narrative alters the ideological impetus of familiar tales.

Alan Moore and Melinda Gebbie's three-volume erotic fantasy graphic novel *Lost Girls* (1991–2006) is another example of a subversive fairy-tale graphic novel as it offers a complex and nuanced representation of female sexuality and experience. *Lost Girls* adapts literary fairy tales by bringing together the female protagonists from *Alice's Adventures in Wonderland*

(1865), *Peter and Wendy* (1911), and *The Wonderful Wizard of Oz* (1900). In the pastiche style, Alice, Wendy, and Dorothy meet in 1913 in the "real world" as adults and offer the "true" stories from their well-known adventures, which involve and work through sexual abuse, drug use, trauma, and other life complexities. Eric Tribunella argues that *Lost Girls* pits "sexuality and imagination against violence and repression in complex and layered ways through both textual and visual material" (2012, 628). He points to the way that each protagonist is depicted in a different arrangement of panels to "visually represent the structure of each character's psyche" (639). The use of this specific graphic narrative convention enables complex exploration of histories of sexuality, sexual abuse, and trauma in a way that is unique to each character.

The series graphically represents and explores sexual encounters between the three women and represents female sexuality in nuanced and diverse ways. It problematizes the sexualization and treatment of many female characters in conservative fairy tales by directly addressing and responding to histories of sexual abuse and trauma. It simultaneously challenges the assumptions of childhood innocence that are often associated with children's literature and fairy tales by openly depicting sexually explicit acts regularly throughout the volumes. The graphic style of the series is notably different to the defined visual style seen in many fantasy comics. While *Lost Girls* uses similar bold colors such as blues and reds, the graphic style is reminiscent of Pre-Raphaelite and impressionist art movements, which functions as a historical marker that reminds readers of earlier time periods. By referencing specific art movements in the illustrations, the series presents classical renderings of the naked female body, which challenges the hypersexualized depiction of female bodies in other fairy-tale graphic narratives such as *Grimm Fairy Tales*, *Fables*, and *Fairest*. Through the multimodal combination of illustrations, comic conventions, and a focus on female sexuality and experiences, *Lost Girls* is a subversive fairy-tale graphic narrative that runs counter to others discussed in this chapter.

Webcomics

A final form of fairy-tale graphic narrative adaptations, which also have subversive potential, are webcomics. While many print graphic narratives are available online with the rise of E-reading culture, webcomics are produced and accessible solely online. Webcomics are often free of charge, and so they subvert capitalist driving forces surrounding the publishing industry. Two examples are Andrea L. Peterson's *No Rest for the Wicked* (2003–2013) series and Emily Carroll's range of fairy- and folktale-inspired webcomics such as *The Hare's Bride* (2010), *Anu Anulan & Yir's Daughter* (2011), *The Prince and the Sea* (2011), and *The Three Snake Leaves* (2013). Both collections alter the reading experience, as the act of turning the page is replaced by clicking the mouse to move to the next screen. In the case of Peterson's *No Rest for the Wicked* all 271 issues are available from the same page, along with extra links and resources to follow up with.

As has been evidenced in this chapter, the multimodal and temporal possibilities of comics and graphic novels allow for the media to become ideological vessels that facilitate both conservative and subversive ideologies found in many fairy-tale narratives. While some fairy-tale graphic narratives enable the reproduction of problematic ideologies—particularly surrounding gender and female subjectivity—many offer different ways to represent subversive discourses and offer a space to challenge and negotiate complex experiences.

Related topics: Adaptation and the Fairy-Tale Web; Anime and Manga; Chapbooks; Children's and Young Adult (YA) Literature; Children's Picture Books and Illustrations; Comic Cons; Gender; Horror; Pornography; Sexualities/Queer and Trans Studies

COMICS AND GRAPHIC NOVELS

References Cited and Further Reading

Aldred, B. Grantham. 2016. "Graphic Novel." In *Folktales and Fairy Tales: Traditions and Texts from around the World*, edited by Anne E. Duggan, Donald Haase, with Helen J. Callow, 422–4. 2nd ed. Santa Barbara, CA: Greenwood.

Barrie, James Matthew, and F. D. Bedford, illus. 1911. *Peter and Wendy*. London: Hodder & Stoughton.

Baum, Frank L., and W. W. Denslow, illus. 1900. *The Wonderful Wizard of Oz*. Chicago: G. M. Hill Co.

Carroll, Lewis, and Sir John Tenniel, illus. 1865. *Alice's Adventures in Wonderland*. London: Macmillan and Co, 1893.

Chute, Hillary. 2008. "Comics as Literature? Reading Graphic Narrative." *PMLA* 123 (2): 452–65.

———. 2010. *Graphic Women: Life Narrative and Contemporary Comics*. New York: Columbia UP.

Chute, Hillary L., and Marianne DeKoven. 2006. "Introduction: Graphic Narrative." *MFS: Modern Fiction Studies* 52 (4): 767–82.

Cross, Julie. 2013. "Frightening and Funny: Humour in Children's Gothic Fiction." In *The Gothic in Children's Literature: Haunting the Borders*, edited by Roderick McGillis, Anna Jackson, and Karen Coats, 57–76. New York: Taylor and Francis.

Duncan, Randy, and Matthew J. Smith. 2009. *The Power of Comics: History, Form and Culture*. London: A&C Black.

Grimm, Jacob, and Wilhelm Grimm. 1843a. "Aschenputtel." In *Kinder und- Hausmärchen*, edited by Jacob Grimm and Wilhelm Grimm, 308–19. P. Reclam.

———. 1843b. "Sneewittchen." In *Kinder und- Hausmärchen*. edited by Jacob Grimm and Wilhelm Grimm. 308–19. P. Reclam.

Kukkonen, Karin. 2013. *Contemporary Comics Storytelling*. Lincoln: U Nebraska P.

———. 2016. "Willingham, Bill (1956–)." In *Folktales and Fairy Tales: Traditions and Texts from around the World*, edited by Anne E. Duggan, Donald Haase, and Helen J. Callow, 1103. 2nd ed. Santa Barbara, CA: Greenwood.

Lees, Gavin. 2012. "Bill Willingham on Sex, Death and Politics." *Bleeding Cool*, April 3. www.bleedingcool.com/2012/04/03/bill-willingham-on-sex-death-and-politics/.

Leprince de Beaumont, Madame Jeanne-Marie. 1783. "Beauty and the Beast." In *The Young Misses Magazine, Containing Dialogues between a Governess and Several Young Ladies of Quality Her Scholars*, 45–67. 4th ed., Vol. 1. London: C. Nourse.

Mallan, Kerry. 2009. *Gender Dilemmas in Children's Fiction*. Hampshire: Palgrave Macmillan.

Massi, Elena. 2016. "Storytelling in Contemporary Fairy Tales: Little Lit, Folklore, and Fairy Tales Funnies by Art Spiegelman and Francoise Mouly." *Marvels & Tales* 30 (2): 309–27.

McCloud, Scott. 1993. *Understanding Comics: The Invisible Art*. New York: Harper Perennial.

Mieder, Wolfgang. 2016. "Cartoons and Comics." In *Folktales and Fairy Tales: Traditions and Texts from around the World*, edited by Anne E. Duggan, Donald Haase, and Helen J. Callow, 173–6. 2nd ed. Santa Barbara, CA: Greenwood.

Perrault, Charles. 1697. *Histories or, Tales of Past Times*. New York: Garland, 1977.

Petersen, Robert S. 2011. *Comics, Manga, and Graphic Novels: A History of Graphic Narratives*. Connecticut: Greenwood.

Soriano, Mark, and Julia Bloch Frey. 1969. "From Tales of Warning to Formulettes: The Oral Tradition in French Children's Literature." *Yale French Studies* 43: 24–43.

Taylor, Laurie N. 2005. "Goth Comics and Revisionist Fairytales." *Iowa Journal of Cultural Studies* 5: 130–2.

Tribunella, Eric L. 2012. "Literature for Us 'Older Children': *Lost Girls*, Seduction Fantasies, and the Re-Education of Adults." *The Journal of Popular Culture* 45 (3): 628–48.

Zipes, Jack. 2006. *Fairy Tales and the Art of Subversion: The Classical Genre for Children and the Process of Civilization*. 2nd ed. New York: Routledge.

———. 2015. "Comic Books and Graphic Novels." In *The Oxford Companion to Fairy Tales*, edited by Jack Zipes, 121–3. 2nd ed. Oxford: Oxford UP.

Zolkover, Adam. 2008. "Corporealizing Fairy Tales: The Body, the Bawdy, and the Carnivalesque in the Comic Book Fables." *Marvels & Tales* 22 (1): 38–51.

Mediagraphy

Anu Anulan & Yir's Daughter (Webcomic). 2011. Creator Emily Carroll. http://emcarroll.com/comics/anu/page01.html.

Cinderella: Fables Are Forever (Comic). 2011. Chris Roberson and Shawn McManus, illus. New York: DC Vertigo.

Cinderella: From Fabletown with Love (Comic). 2009–2010. Chris Roberson and Shawn McManus, illus. New York: DC Vertigo.

Cinderella, or The Little Glass Slipper (Graphic Novel). 2015. Charles Perrault and Camille Rose Garcia, illus. New York: Harper Collins.

Fables (Comic). 2002–2016. Creator Bill Willingham. New York: DC Vertigo.

———. 2002. "Chapter Two: The (Un)Usual Suspects." Vol. 1, Issue 2.

———. 2003a. "Dirty Business: Part Two of a Two-Part Caper." Vol. 1, Issue 13.

———. 2003b. "A Sharp Operation: Part One of a Two-Part Caper." Vol. 1, Issue 12.

Fairest (Comic). 2012–2015. Creator Bill Willingham. New York: DC Vertigo.

———. 2014. "Of Mice and Men." Vol. 4.

Grimm Fairy Tales (Comic). 2005–. Creators Ralph Tedesco and Joe Tyler. Pennsylvania: Zenescope Entertainment.

———. 2005. "Little Red Riding Hood." Issue 1.

The Hare's Bride (Webcomic). 2010. Creator Emily Carroll. http://emcarroll.com/comics/haresbride.html.

Jack of Fables (Comic). 2006–2011. Creators Bill Willingham and Lilah Sturges. New York: DC Vertigo.

Little Dead Riding Hood (Comic). 2011. Creator David Hutchison. Texas: Antarctic P.

Lost Girls (Graphic Novel). 1991–2006. Illustrators Alan Moore and Melinda Gebbie. Georgia: Top Shelf Productions.

Nightmares & Fairy Tales (Comic). 2002–2008. Illustrators Creator Serena Valentino and Foo Swee Chin. California: Slave Labor Graphics.

———. 2003. "Cinderella's Story." Issue 6.

———. 2004. "Beauty and the Beast." Issue 10.

No Rest for the Wicked (Webcomic). 2003–2013. Creator Andrea L. Peterson. www.forthewicked.net/archive/index.php.

The Prince and the Sea (Webcomic). 2011. Creator Emily Carroll. http://emcarroll.com/comics/prince/andthesea.html.

Snow White (Graphic Novel). 2012. Illustrators Brothers Grimm and Camille Rose Garcia. New York: Harper Collins.

——— (Graphic Novel). 2016. Creator Matt Phelan. Massachusetts: Candlewick P.

The Three Snake Leaves (Webcomic). 2013. Creator Emily Carroll. http://emcarroll.com/comics/snakeleaves/.

Through the Woods (Graphic Novel). 2014. Creator Emily Carroll. New York: Margaret K. McElderry Books.

What Bloody Teeth You Have! (Comic). 2011. Creator Rod Espinosa. Texas: Antarctic P.

The Wolf Among Us (Video Game). 2013. Developer Telltale Games, Producer Chris Schroyer. https://telltale.com/series/the-wolf-among-us/.

Zombie Fairy Tales, Issue 1 (Comic). 2011. Editors Doug Dlin and Robby Bevard. Texas: Antarctic P.

53

COMIC CONS

Fairy-Tale Culture and Comic Conventions: Perpetuating Storytelling Traditions

Emma Nelson

The historical and cultural prevalence of fairy tales makes them unique fodder for new and popular media. Comic conventions (cons), events catering to fans of popular culture, have evolved alongside modern iterations of the tales, creating expressive venues for fairy-tale media that echo the oral and literary customs of circulating the tales. Cons help perpetuate new media, creating an environment in which fans and creators interact face-to-face to retell familiar stories and create new narratives—much like storyteller and listener of fairy tales past—reshaping fairy tales for new audiences and inventing new outcomes for recognizable tropes.

Fairy-Tale Narratives: Familiar Tropes and Human Collaboration

Fairy-tale narratives, both folk (communal and oral) and literary (identifiable authors), contain patterns in which a "listener or reader is struck by their family resemblance to another story" (Warner 2014, xvi). Genre motifs anticipate audience familiarity to comment on some issues, while complicating or pointedly avoiding others—they "'work' because the reader comes to them with [an] understanding of what he or she is getting into beforehand" (Jenkins 2012, 138). Fairy tales' images, archetypes, and structures remain relevant to new audiences, as tales are reinvented to identify with different eras, genders, and social classes (inside *and* outside the tales) while maintaining the pieces that gave them life.

Fairy-tale narratives endure through human interactions, their longevity dependent on connecting tellers and listeners. Cons do this for the digital age in ways no other medium can by adapting to changing media and audiences. Where fairy tales, at times, catered to elite or literate minorities, cons reflect periods when commoners shared and recreated tales for enjoyment. Different circles appropriating the stories suggest fluid narratives and audiences, and cons intensify the settings through which "oral and literary fairy tales migrate into diverse media [. . .] [that] offer venues for their plots, themes, images, and characters" (Greenhill and Rudy 2014, 3). Cons perpetuate and reshape tales, with tellers and audiences mimicking performative, face-to-face storytelling. Just as oral tales engaged court crowds or peasants around campfires and sewing circles, conventions act as a gathering place to tell stories, strengthen and create fandoms, and reshape familiar tales.

Comic Conventions: Circulating Popular Media

Compared to today's standards, the first con in 1964 New York (NYCC) was small and comic focused, but it "would lay the groundwork for generations of continued engagement between fans and creators" (Q 2009). Today, rather than concentrating exclusively on comics, world-wide cons cater to popular culture and mass media—especially San Diego Comic-Con (SDCC or Comic-Con), which draws film studios, television networks, and publishers to become a springboard for all types of media, acting as a prototype for continually emerging conventions and serving as an "index to the Next Big Thing in popular culture" (Reid 2008, 4).

Because cons explore various forms of new and popular media, they are well suited to the circulation of fairy-tale adaptations. *Grimm* (2011–2017) and *Once Upon a Time* (*OUaT*, 2011–), television series centered on fairy-tale tropes, have especially capitalized on the con format to reveal characters and plot arcs, facilitate interactions with series actors, and garner viewer interest. Two of countless fairy-tale adaptations over the years, "'Grimm' a buddy-cop crime drama (with fairy-tale monsters)," and "'Once Upon a Time' a prime-time soap and romantic comedy (with fairy-tale heroes and villains)" (Hale 2011), illustrate how conventions intersect pop-culture fans with fairy-tale audiences, enlarging and enhancing both communities.

Although fairy tales are newer to the convention experience, "Comic book readers had been exploring the pleasures of multimodal serial storytelling for generations, following their favorite characters and narratives across installments, media, and industries" (Ryan and Thon 2014, 203). Fairy-tale narratives now have the same opportunities for growth and dispersion, but on a larger scale because the transcultural tales are more accessible to wider audience than some pop-culture niches. Cons create new ways—and echo old ways—of fairy-tale perpetuation through retellings, fan communities, and intertextual engagement.

Retellings: Dialogue, Panels, and Merchandising

Cons cater to the atmosphere of retellings, essential to spreading fairy-tale narratives since their beginning. According to Jack Zipes, the fairy tale "shaped and was shaped by the interactions of orality and print as well as other technological mediations and innovations" (2012, 21). Fairy tales have continually evolved from their inception, and cons, in many ways, intensify that movement as film, television, art, cosplay (costume play), comics, merchandise, and other media introduce new iterations of the longstanding tales.

One example of fairy-tale dialogue unique to cons is panel discussions, in which actors and creators sit before an audience as moderators and fans ask questions and comment on the retelling. The dialogues create distinctive layers to storytelling: writers, actors, and directors as storytellers and audience as listeners providing interpretations and feedback. Each interaction symbolizes the mingling of elites and peasants in the creation of story, where "every listener is potentially a new storyteller" (Warner 2014, 64). Panels become conversations that cannot be duplicated because all components will never again be the same.

Two moments from SDCC's 2015 *OUaT* panel illustrate why retellings are an important part of fairy-tale con culture. Fans, calling themselves "Oncers," pack Hall H (SDCC's largest venue, holding roughly 5 percent of attendees) for lively discussion interspersed with series scenes, character introductions, and a video dramatization of life in Storybrooke.

First, *OUaT*'s Wicked Witch of the West (Rebecca Mader) represents the fusion of fairy tales and stories with fairy-tale elements. Although L. Frank Baum's *The Wonderful Wizard of Oz* (1900) is traditionally considered classic literature, witches are iconic fairy-tale figures. *OUaT* merges both, allowing the Wicked Witch to influence backstories and outcomes of fairy-tale tropes. When panel moderator—actor Yvette Nicole Brown—asked about Mader's character portrayal, Mader said the witch "believes she's her own hero. Rather than trying to play awful, I trust in the fact that she needs to vindicate herself and find her own happy ending" ("*OUaT* Panel" 2015, 16:56). The convergence of the fairy-tale "happy ending" with the non-fairy-tale witch and Mader's interpretation layer the existing dynamic of *OUaT* as a retelling of Disney retellings. Evil as a common fairy-tale theme, Mader's take on the Wicked Witch's motives, and Brown's performance analysis lead to unique fairy-tale dialogue.

Second, panels bring storytellers face-to-face with audience reactions. On the same panel, Brown asked *OUaT* producers about a musical episode, and the audience erupted in cheers. Brown said, "Look at them—they want it!" Creator Edward Kitsis asked the cast, "You guys wanna sing?" The cast responded positively. Kitsis then addressed the audience, "Any songwriters out there? Any *OUaT* songwriters?" ("*OUaT* Panel" 2015, 34:10). Regardless of whether a musical episode happens, the point remains that fans voiced an idea, producers engaged with that idea, actors expressed enthusiasm, and creators solicited audience help to make it happen. The tone was playful, but this type of interchange, unique to cons, shows how storyteller, medium, and listener influence aspects of the story, rather than the storyteller (or corporation, such as Disney) maintaining sole ownership.

Retellings are also prevalent in con merchandising. Character reproductions, *Grimm*- and *OUaT*-decorated pedi-cabs and buses, show-inspired clothing, buttons, posters, artist renderings, and limited-edition items, such as Funko POP!'s *OUaT* Evil Queen at SDCC 2015—each adds a new viewpoint, reinterpreting and spreading stories to mass culture as items created for cons go public. Cons' written, oral, and new media interpretations play with fairy-tale motifs in new mediums, the fans offering feedback through con dialogue and where they spend their money. Convention and post-convention interactions become their own retellings of a retelling, perpetuating infinite storytelling cycles.

Fandoms: Community, Influence, and Diffusion

Cons are also significant to fairy tales because of unique fandoms. While online communities and social media play a role in storytelling, nothing can replace fans meeting in person to share ideas and demonstrate discipleship. Lynn Zubernis and Katherine Larsen in *Fandom at the Crossroads* suggest that fandoms matter because "we all strive to find those places—physical, psychological, social and emotional—where we feel most accepted and least different" (2012, 9). Cons are replete with fandoms of all types, lending to an atmosphere where tales are shared, compared, retold, and analyzed. Collaborative fandom coincides with Arthur Frank's theory that narratives are interdependent as well as universal because "stories depend on other stories: on recognizable plots, character types, conventional tropes, genre-specific cues [. . .] as resources for telling and expectations for hearing" (2010, 119). As a collaborative genre from inception, fairy tales epitomize con fodder, with limitless potential for discussion and an oral tradition few other genres have maintained.

Fairy tales are ripe for fan engagement, and cons cater to deeper participation. John L. Sullivan's *Media Audiences* explains that while fans and audiences are similar, fans "often spend a great deal of time with their favorite texts, reading them closely and often repeatedly, looking for greater nuance and detail. Fans spread their enthusiasm by interacting with their peers in

Internet chat groups, fan websites, and even informal and formal social gatherings" (2012, 195). Fandoms gravitate toward seeking fellow supporters and engaging with creators and actors, asking questions and giving feedback, sometimes influencing the adaptations they love. As fans' interpretations orbit "original" material, niches within fairy-tale culture reinvent tropes, just as generations of fairy-tale narratives have done.

Fans influencing tropes is seen in *OUaT* character Emma Swan (Jennifer Morrison) subverting fairy tales as an outsider. Because she doesn't initially believe the fairy-tale tropes audiences expect, she epitomizes normalcy as a reluctant hero, adding subtle commentary on viewer expectations, nuancing insider-versus-outsider tensions, and resonating with fans because of her pragmatic view of fairy-tale norms. *OUaT* researchers found viewers who connected with Swan were "more likely to become loyal fans" (Hay and Baxter 2014, 318). She pulls audiences into a magical world without forcing them to identify with the witch/princess types inherent to fairy tales, and focusing on her normalcy enables a contemporary, skeptical viewpoint of the magic she finds to be real.

OUaT fans are also credited with the show's renewal. Early critics suggested the series might fail because "everyone—from Morrison's hard-boiled bounty hunter to Parrilla's permanently enraged Queen—seems so miserable. This is a problem for the series, because viewers coming to the show for the light, good-will-prevail tone of fairy tales may be brought up short, and perhaps dismayed, by its dark fantasy" (Tucker 2011). But in the 2015 *OUaT* panel, Kitsis thanked fans for their devotion, recognizing them for the show's success.

Similarly, fandoms influenced *Beauty & the Beast* (*BATB*), which premiered at 2012's SDCC. Though the series has lower ratings than *OUaT* or *Grimm*, "Beasties" are a small but vocal group, with online forums, fan fiction, art, videos, and fan-made games and quizzes. Saveeachotherbatb.com (*SEA*), for example, petitioned The CW to send *BATB* actors to 2014's NYCC for more exposure, and Beasties worldwide rallied to create social media flyers, send letters to the network president, and tweet specific hashtags to help the show "trend." Although they were unsuccessful with NYCC, The CW president Mark Pedowitz credits "the engaged fanbase" (Thomas 2014) for the series' fourth and final season.

BATB fandoms demonstrate complex discussions about pop-culture fairy tales, with sites like *SEA* comparing *BATB* to other versions. User Darcy states, "I enjoy that their characters are more flawed, so we can relate so much more." Dickens said, "I love how they have turned mythology on its head and made an attractive man more of a beast than the original who literally looked like a beast," illustrating that fans think within fairy-tale frameworks, analyze modern portrayals, and make links between traditional and contemporary versions. Even *Beauty* actor Kristin Kreuk stated: "I think it'd be interesting if their fairy-tale ending is that Catherine forms half of her [. . .] darker beast side, and they can live together as half-beast, half-human" (Daley 2015)—a modern twist to the many retellings.

BATB premiered at SDCC, and fans fought for NYCC recognition; *OUaT* credits Comic-Con fans with series success; and *Grimm* actor Claire Coffee mentions her own SDCC fandoms, stating: "Getting to the point where I was on a show that was represented at Comic-Con [. . .] for me [. . .] I've made it" (quoted in Cay 2015). Reinventing the witch archetype based on her fandoms, Coffee layers *Grimm*'s retellings—and for her, contributing to cons was always the goal.

Comic conventions are audience focused, creating intimacy between fan, creator, and narrative. As fandoms add new ideas and formats to familiar tropes, they change the landscape of fairy-tale narratives and parallel oral storytelling histories where tellers emphasized their own interests and situations in connection with their audiences. Cons help maintain fairy-tale relevance as fans find their voices reflected in the stories they love, blurring genre lines for fairy-tale and pop-culture audiences. Fairy tales are "as fluid as a conversation taking place over centuries. The audience is not necessarily assembled in one place at one moment—the circle loops out across the centuries, forming a community across barriers of language and nation as well as time" (Warner 2014, 44). The fluidity and scope of the tales continue, and occasionally, beautifully, audiences converge to celebrate at cons worldwide.

Intertextuality: Cosplay, Genre Bending, and Social Media

Retellings, fandoms, and intertextuality work together to create "the complex ways in which fans interpret their favorite media texts but also the ability of these audiences to [produce] [. . .] both close readings of the primary text and the material production of creative texts that use the original as 'raw material' for brand-new narratives" (Sullivan 2012, 202). Where retellings and fandoms aren't specific to cons, some of the "raw material" used for intertextual connections are.

Fairy tales' longevity and transformative properties prove that literature and language are not set. "Fairy tales on the page invoke live voices, telling stories aloud. A memory of a living narrator reverberates in the genre, even when the story is manifestly a highly wrought literary text" (Warner 2014, 53). Perhaps more than any genre, fairy tales allow new generations to drive the story motifs. One essential way that cons foster new iterations is through cosplay— where fans interpret characters to invoke the voices that come from telling the stories aloud. Fairy-tale reenactments create a one-time-only event that can never be exactly repeated in context or execution, just like oral narrative.

Cons' propensity toward costume play is widely recognized, making cosplayers their own folkloric group using fairy-tale motifs. One example of the ubiquity of con cosplay meeting the ubiquity of fairy-tale tropes is a tweet by Margaret Atwood—known for fairy-tale novels—while participating in SDCC 2012, stating, "Now, off to #ComicCon #SDCC, in my little red Atwoodhood, with a bottle of wolves and a loaf of heads in my basket for many-fanged Granny." Atwood's tweet uses social media to pull her audience into the convention experience, while widely recognized fairy-tale images mixed with comic-convention expectations of fans cosplaying suggest intertextuality between fairy-tale tropes and con practices.

Another instance of con intertextuality is fan "mash-ups." For example, one mash-up trend is combining fairy-tale characters with elements of subcultures such as gothic, punk, and so forth to illustrate modern ideologies within a fairy-tale framework. The Salt Lake Comic Con (SLCC) fan in figure 53.1 blends Disney's iconic mermaid's (*The Little Mermaid*, 1989) red hair, clothing colors, and "dinglehopper" (fork) with skinny jeans, glasses, and "angst pose" to represent "hipster Ariel." Or fans wear T-shirts, such as in figure 53.2, which shows Disney's Anna and Elsa (*Frozen*, 2013), based on Hans Christian Andersen's "The Snow Queen," with the time machine from science fiction series *Doctor Who* (1963–). In the photo, fans of both the fairy tale and the series pose with the shirts' artist, Karen Hallion, at SLCC. Iterations like Atwood's tweet and mash-up shirts and costumes indicate fairy tales being discussed within other genres and tropes. Zipes asserts, "People told stories to communicate knowledge and experience in social contexts" (2012, 2), which is true of cons' cyclical nature. Creators create a retelling; fans reinterpret themes, stories, and characters and then often produce their own iterations as cosplay and other fan involvements.

Intertext discussions are also found in social media fandoms, including Twitter, Facebook, websites, and blogs that carry comic-con discussions beyond the convention. For instance, during the *OUaT* panel, Brown asked questions received on Twitter ahead of time. Shows and audiences interact in forums discussing meet-ups at conventions—bringing to life relationships

Figure 53.1 Comic-con fan Olivia McLaughlin dressed as hipster Ariel

made online—or bloggers recap con experiences on websites. *Once Upon a Blog*, for example, details fairy-tale-related discussions from various cons and speculates what they mean for the future of fairy tales. *OUaT*'s Facebook page shares teasers from SDCC and solicits fan comments. "Grimmsters" live-tweet SDCC panels for those unable to attend.

Intertextual innovations also occur as retellings merge fan bases. For example, Kristen Stewart appeared at SDCC from 2008–2012 for *Twilight* (2008). In 2011, she joined *Snow White and the Huntsman*'s panel, bringing *Twilight* fans along. Chris Hemsworth, the huntsman, drew crowds as Thor from Marvel films. *OUaT* creators Kitsis and Horowitz brought fans and expectations from writing science fiction series *Lost* (2004–2010). New iterations illustrate how "as types of fairy-tale telling evolved and became crystallized, the genre of the fairy tale borrowed and used motifs, themes, characters, expressions, and styles from other narrative forms and genres" (Zipes 2012, 14).

COMIC CONS

Figure 53.2 Artist Karen Hallion with fans wearing her design on T-shirts

Other retellings blend genres, like *Grimm* engaging fairy tales with police procedurals and the supernatural. Homicide detective turned monster hunter Nick Burkhardt (David Giuntoli) battles fairy-tale monsters that incorporate creatures from legend and myth. Each supernatural encounter is also infused with Portland, Oregon, crime-scene tactics, anchoring fantasy elements in reality. Endless examples of crossover illustrate that storytellers—both actors and creators—mix elements of science fiction, fantasy, superhero narratives, and more to create blended fairy-tale iterations.

Fairy-tale, social media, and genre interactions are enhanced through the comic-con dynamic. Face-to-face exchanges foster loyalties and crossover audiences, in which the fairy tale "continues to grow—embracing, if not swallowing, all types of genres, art forms, and cultural institutions, and adjusting itself to new environments through the human disposition to re-create relevant narratives, and via technologies that make its diffusion easier and more effective" (Zipes 2012, 22). Fairy tales, sometimes appropriated by the elite, have swung the pendulum to cater to the masses, incorporating images, themes, and archetypes into nuanced entertainment for all ages and social circles to find a spot in the heart of popular culture, in every conceivable medium.

Fairy Tales and Comic Conventions: A Perfect Pairing

Although fandoms may seem extreme and nonsensical to some, cons show fairy-tale relationships in which "the traffic does not only go one way, the fairy tale taking colour from real life. Real life is understood in light of the stories, too" (Warner 2014, 91). Just as oral tales were a shared experience between storytellers and listeners, cons act as modern gathering places for the same types of communication. Frank's "interdependent stories" are epitomized in con settings where zombies, superheroes, *Star Wars* fans, and princesses come together to celebrate, like the fairy tale, "fictional narratives that combine human and non-human protagonists with elements of wonder and the supernatural" (Greenhill and Matrix 2010, 1).

Cons offer intertextuality in ways that no other platform can, illustrating "a participatory culture which transforms the experience of media consumption into the production of new texts, indeed of a new culture and a new community" (Jenkins 2012, 46). Cons are face-to-face encounters where creators are on the spot, unable to avoid questions or redirect fans. They are bound by the social contract of the convention—and live audiences will react with cheers and applause, booing, or silence.

Cons matter to popular culture, especially to the malleability and preservation of fairy-tale narratives, because they provide space for visiting new and old meanings deeper into the texts. Returning once more to *OUaT*'s panel, a fan asked, "As someone who's made lifelong friends through the fandom, what do you think it is about this show that makes these strangers into a family?" Kitsis's response epitomizes the need for fairy-tale fan connections:

> This is a show for believers and people who want to believe. It united a lot of people who were tired of cynicism and believe in magic [. . .] the reason we created the show was to add a little hope to the world in any way we could.
> ("*OUaT* Panel" 2015, 25:00)

Fairy tales have run the gamut of oral and written tradition, so it seems appropriate they'd find a home in cons, where we see that "cultural evolution has taken off precisely because of this unique human ability to extract information from one context and manipulate it in another, which brings with it the possibility of new species emerging from the convergence of old ones" (Zipes 2012, 38). Like a modern campfire or sewing circle, cons create space to give new life and context to the tales, taking familiar arcs and expanding them as far as the imagination can go.

Referring to the Grimms' aim to collect "authentic" stories, Warner says the "stories were migrants, blow-ins, border-crossers, tunnellers" (2014, 59). The nostalgic image is applicable to cons, in which audiences from all over the world bring their own cultures and interpretations. Comic conventions play a role in shaping a new cultural identity for the tales that have been shaped so many times before, in every corner of the world.

Related topics: Adaptation and the Fairy-Tale Web; Convergence Culture; Digital; Disney Corporation; Fandom/Fan Culture; Fan Fiction; Material Culture; Storytelling; Video Games

References Cited and Further Reading

Cay, Callie. 2015. "Grimm: Claire Coffee on Hexenbiests and Hexenbabies." *The Fairy Tale Site*, September 9. http://thefairytalesite.net/2015/09/grimm-claire-coffee-on-hexenbiests-and-hexenbabies-video/.

Daley, Megan. 2015. "Beauty and the Beast." *Entertainment Weekly*, June 11. www.ew.com/article/2015/06/11/beauty-and-beast-cw-jay-ryan-season-three.

Frank, Arthur. 2010. *Letting Stories Breathe: A Socio-Narratology*. Chicago: U Chicago P.

Greenhill, Pauline, and Sidney Eve Matrix. 2010. "Introduction." In *Fairy Tale Films: Visions of Ambiguity*, edited by Pauline Greenhill and Sidney Eve Matrix, 1–22. Logan: Utah State UP.

Greenhill, Pauline, and Jill Terry Rudy. 2014. "Introduction." In *Channeling Wonder: Fairy Tales on Television*, edited by Pauline Greenhill and Jill Terry Rudy, 1–21. Detroit: Wayne State UP.

Hale, Mike. 2011. "The Enchanted Forest." *New York Times*, October 21. www.nytimes.com/2011/10/22/arts/television/grimm-on-nbc-and-once-upon-a-time-on-abc-review.html?_r=0.

Hay, Rebecca, and Christa Baxter. 2014. "Happily Never After: The Commodification of Fairy Tale in ABC's *Once Upon a Time*." In *Channeling Wonder: Fairy Tales on Television*, edited by Pauline Greenhill and Jill Terry Rudy, 316–25. Detroit: Wayne State UP.

Jenkins, Henry. 2012. *Textual Poachers: Television Fans and Participatory Culture*. New York: Routledge.

Q, Shathley. 2009. "The History of Comic Conventions." *Pop Matters*, June 17. www.popmatters.com/feature/95236-the-history-of-comic-conventions/.

Reid, Calvin. 2008. "Publishers Find Fans and Trends at Comic-Con." *Publishers Weekly*, August 4. www.publishersweekly.com/pw/by-topic/new-titles/adult-announcements/article/2006-publishers-find-fans-and-trends-at-comic-con.html.

Ryan, Marie-Laure, and Jan-Noël Thon. 2014. *Storyworlds across Media: Toward a Media-Conscious Narratology*. Lincoln: U Nebraska P.

Sullivan, John L. 2012. *Media Audiences: Effects, Users, Institutions and Power*. New York: Sage Publications.

Thomas, Kaitlin. 2014. "Why *Beauty and the Beast* Lives On." *TV*, July 18. www.tv.com/shows/the-100/community/post/tca-cw-mark-pedowitz-supernatural-spinoff-the-100-why-beauty-and-the-beast-was-renewed-140569917327/.

Tucker, Ken. 2011. "Did This Fairy-Tale Show Make Your Dreams Come True?" *Entertainment Weekly*, October 23. www.ew.com/article/2011/10/23/once-upon-a-time-jennifer-morrison-desperate-housewives.

Warner, Marina. 2014. *Once Upon a Time: A Short History of Fairy Tale*. Oxford: Oxford UP.

Zipes, Jack. 2012. *The Irresistible Fairy Tale: The Cultural and Social History of a Genre*. Princeton, NJ: Princeton UP.

Zubernis, Lynn, and Katherine Larsen. 2012. *Fandom at the Crossroads: Celebration, Fame, and Fan/Producer Relationships*. Newcastle: Cambridge Scholars Publishing.

Mediagraphy

Atwood, Margaret. 2012. "Now Off to #ComicCon." *Twitter*, July 14. https://twitter.com/MargaretAtwood/statuses/224172364986978304.

Beauty & the Beast (TV). 2012–2016. Creators Sherri Cooper-Landsman and Jennifer Levin. USA.

Doctor Who (TV). 1963–. Creators Sydney Newman, C. E. Webber, and D. Willson. UK.

Frozen. 2013. Directors Chris Buck and Jennifer Lee. USA.

Grimm (TV). 2011–2017. Creators Stephen Carpenter, David Greenwalt, and Jim Kouf. USA.

The Little Mermaid. 1989. Directors Ron Clements and John Musker. USA.

Lost (TV). 2004–2010. Creators Jeffrey Lieber, J. J. Abrams, and Damon Lindelof. USA.

Nelson, Emma. 2016. *Hipster Ariel*. Personal Photograph. USA.

Once Upon a Time (TV). 2011–. Creators Adam Horowitz and Edward Kitsis. USA.

"*OUaT* Comic Con Panel." 2015. Flicks and the City. *YouTube*. 11 July. www.youtube.com/watch?v=cKdssFOoVhI

Snow White and the Huntsman. 2012. Director Rupert Sanders. USA.

Tolman, Patrick. 2014. *Frozen/Tardis T-shirt*. Personal Photograph. USA.

Twilight. 2008. Director Catherine Hardwicke. USA.

54

CONTEMPORARY ART

Amanda Slack-Smith

Art has a long history of being used to tell stories. From early cave paintings through to today's art practices, art has provided an accessible way to transmit information to the viewer. The role of the artist throughout this history, and the how and why of the stories they've told, has largely reflected the cultural, political, and religious imperatives of their societies. In early Western art, a term broadly used to describe successive periods and art movements of Western Europe from classical Greek art of the fifth century BC through to the emergence of postmodernism in the late twentieth century, artists produced commissioned works for wealthy patrons such as the Catholic Church, telling stories primarily religious in nature and told through the use of template designs as handed down from teacher to student.

The role of the artist was one of a tradesperson, producing work in sculpture, painting, textiles, mosaics, metalwork, and architecture as required. While some artists gained prominence through their expertise, it wasn't until the late fifteenth century, during the High Renaissance period, that the perception of artists as manual laborers began to change. Artists such as Leonardo da Vinci, Michelangelo Buonarroti, Raphael Sanzio, Titian (Tiziano Vecellio), and Tintoretto (Jacopo Robusti) successfully challenged these creative boundaries and shifted the social perception to a more intellectual pursuit similar to poets, scholars, and philosophers.

The late eighteenth to early nineteenth centuries delivered fundamental changes in art and society when the industrial revolution introduced rapid advances in transportation technologies, manufacturing processes, science, and social sciences that transformed nearly every aspect of life. This radical social change, in conjunction with the decline of royal and religious power and the rise of private galleries and art dealers, offered an unprecedented opportunity for artists to choose to move away from the prescriptive nature of commissioned work and to instead create as independent practitioners exploring ideas, people, places, and subjects that personally resonated with them.

By the late nineteenth century artists were viewed as creative individuals who sought to translate through their work the impact of the immense social changes around them. Such was the creative energy ignited during this time that art movements developed and were subsequently overtaken at a speed previously unseen. Falling under the broad term "modern art," late-nineteenth-century movements such as impressionism and early to mid-twentieth-century movements such as cubism, Fauvism, Expressionism, Dadaism, Surrealism, and pop art, to name a small handful of movements identified as modernism, each in turn questioned the styles that came before them, driving artists to experiment with the way they approached materials and techniques, question the function of art itself, and respond to the social, political, and cultural rationale of the time.

While modernism was marked by a move away from traditional narrative storytelling to more abstract forms, this period also opened up a new way of thinking about the subconscious.

Surrealist artists Salvador Dali and André Breton in particular were greatly influenced by the publication of psychoanalyst Sigmund Freud's *The Interpretation of Dreams* in 1899 and its exploration into the unconscious fears and desires revealed through dreams and fairy tales. Their desire to reflect on the memories and motivations hidden within our unconscious mind, coupled with fellow psychoanalyst Carl Jung's belief in archetypes, forms, and symbolism, strongly influenced artistic work of the time and continues to underpin the work of many artists today.

By the 1950s and 1960s visual storytelling began to re-emerge as the influences of mass cultural sources such as cinema, advertising, illustration, music, and comic books saw the lines between high art and popular culture collapse. By the 1970s artists became dissatisfied with the single philosophical approach and began to shift away from any one dominant theoretical idea in favor of moving fluidly between all artistic styles, concepts, materials, and methods. This transitioned to "contemporary art," a term that broadly identifies works created in the present moment—a somewhat nebulous unit of time that still evokes discussions among art historians—a diverse reflection of the cultural and societal thoughts and concerns of today.

While only a brief overview of the emergence of contemporary art practice, this chapter offers some insight into the complex histories and influences at play when viewing fairy tales through the lens of contemporary art. Similarly to fairy tales, contemporary art defies a desire for a tidy classification; however, also similarly, its fluid and multifaceted nature shows us a rich and diverse reflection of the world around us. Both forms also offer a platform through which to consider a strong social consciousness toward local and global issues: in particular discussions surrounding gender and sexuality, environmental concerns, scientific and technological advancements, political conflicts, Indigeneity, as well as other cultural and social representations. It is little wonder, considering contemporary art fascination with popular culture and the ubiquitous nature of fairy tales within this environment, that artists are drawn to these tales and the polymorphic opportunities they represent. Not only do fairy tales provide paths to discuss the issues already inherent within them, but they also offer ways to help disseminate other difficult and complex issues underpinning an artist's existing practice.

For renowned fairy-tale scholar Jack Zipes, this assimilation of fairy-tale narratives within contemporary art practice demonstrates how expansive and mutable fairy tales have become, citing the connections between the "subversive and moral aspects of the whalelike fairy tale" (2012, 157) and its dissemination by artists in unexpected ways. Zipes describes this meeting as a "collision," an apt word to articulate the dynamic impact realized when these two robust forms combine to question and provoke social inertia and its reflexive acceptance of inherited beliefs.

When looked at more closely, these collisions are generally identified as falling into three tendencies. The first looks at how artists explicitly reference and re-create classic fairy tales in their work, often drawing on well-known tales such as "Little Red Riding Hood" (ATU 333), "Snow White" (ATU 709), "Cinderella" (ATU 510A), "Beauty and the Beast" (ATU 425C), "Bluebeard" (ATU 312), and "Hansel and Gretel" (ATU 327A). These engagements often involve a critical reevaluation and deconstruction of these narratives in light of current social concerns, particularly around issues of female representation and emergent sexuality and power dynamics. The second tendency considers the implicit fairy tale whereby artists are aware of, and draw upon, the atmosphere and wonder evoked by the fairy tale without referencing any one story. This allows artists to freely discuss a broad range of issues while still drawing on the familiarity of the fairy-tale vernacular. Finally, the third tendency looks at the unwitting use of the fairy tale. This perspective looks at works by artists who draw on the aesthetic pageantry of the fairy tale yet remain largely unaware, or disengaged, from the origin of these influences in their work. To better understand how these three tendencies interrelate, the following sections discuss these collisions in more detail.

The Explicit Tale: Classic Fairy Tales and Contemporary Art

When unpacking the ideas behind works by artists who explicitly reference and re-create classic or well-known fairy tales, an artist frequently cited is Kiki Smith (Germany, b. 1954). Celebrated for her love of narrative, Smith has produced large bodies of work exploring the fairy-tale realm, drawing on parallels between the issues within these tales and her own personal and social concerns. Like many artists working with fairy tales, Smith has melded these stories with elements of mythology, biblical narrative, spirituality, nature, and day-to-day experiences evidenced in her wider practice. By dipping in and out of this metaphorical toolbox of influences, styles, and techniques, she inserts her personal reflections and life experiences within the enchanted world and offers insights into the fairy-tale narrative.

Over the last four decades, Smith has delved into "Little Red Riding Hood," "Snow White," and "Alice in Wonderland" to unpack anxieties surrounding issues of nascent sexuality, physical vulnerability, abuse, and abandonment. Told through a wide range of media, including printmaking, drawing, and photography, these explorations run both parallel to, and interweave with, her wider explorations into the fragility and functions of the body and her concerns around the sexualized representation of the female form inherent throughout art history. Three of Smith's best-known life-size bronze nudes, *Rapture* (2001), *Born* (2002), and *Genevieve with May Wolf* (2002), found their initial inspiration from the realm of fairy tales; *Rapture* depicts a woman emerging from the corpse of a wolf, *Born* captures the final moments of a woman being birthed from the body of a deer, and *Genevieve with May Wolf* offers a striking moment of a woman standing beside a wolf, her hand outstretched with intent to comfort or command. Smith's foregrounding of feminine strength offers an empowering earthiness to the tableaux, made more so by her choice to draw her inspiration not from the prominent "Little Red Riding Hood" version of Charles Perrault but instead a lesser-known medieval story of Sainte Genevieve, the patron saint of Paris, who was often depicted surrounded by wolves and lambs.

For photographer Dina Goldstein (Israel, b. 1969), the fairy-tale retellings of well-known tales by the Walt Disney corporation focus a number of works in her practice. Goldstein's 2009 photographic series *Fallen Princesses* was one of many critical responses seen across all media forms responding to what many artists saw as problematic Middle American values that pulse throughout the various Disney productions. Consisting of ten works featuring well-known fairy-tale princesses, Goldstein challenges the notion of "happy ever after" by removing these women from their magical realms and placing them into real-life situations. Within this series we are confronted with a suburbanized Snow White co-parenting with a disinterested prince, *Beauty and the Beast*'s Belle seeking perfection under the plastic surgeon's knife, and a bald Rapunzel sitting on her hospital bed still clutching the remnants of her golden locks lost during her treatment for cancer. Drawing on the visual stylings of the Walt Disney animations and films, Goldstein's tableaux challenge the messages of eternal youth, beauty, and domestic bliss promoted by Disney, questioning a corporation's right to co-opt these stories with such a superficial and commercial agenda.

Perhaps the most controversial artist to rail against the fairy-tale depictions by the Walt Disney corporation is multidisciplinary provocateur Paul McCarthy (United States, b. 1945). Representing the outer edge of artists working with well-known tales, McCarthy's work draws on the aesthetics of Walt Disney animated films, children's stories, and other popular culture icons to deliver a scathing critique of American ideologies. A devotee of the grotesque, a strand of artistic practice that pushes the boundaries of conventional society by mixing popular culture with the profane, McCarthy combines drawing, performance art and video, multimedia installations, and sculpture with food, sex, scatological humor, art history, politics, and mass media.

McCarthy's most ambitious attack on the mythology of Walt Disney was held at the Park Avenue Armory New York in 2013. A mammoth-sized mixed media installation titled *WS*, an acronym for "White Snow," the work featured a three-quarter-scale replica of McCarthy's childhood home situated amidst an immense artificial forest. This highly theatrical installation was also the film set for a seven-hour video performance reincorporated within the space. The footage features McCarthy as the debauched caricature Walt Paul, alongside his muse Elyse Poppers as White Snow, with a range of extras including the prince, nine oversexed dwarves, and a cast of adult entertainers. Exhibited with a self-imposed NC-17 rating, often employed in cinema to denote films not suitable for children under seventeen, McCarthy's satire of Walt Disney, 1950s suburbia, corporate greed, and mass consumption was an explosion of exploitative sex, violent imagery, and malevolent destruction designed to rupture what he believes is the fascist symbol of the American entertainment-consumer economy, Walt Disney (Kennedy 2013).

The Implicit Tale: Fairy-Tale Fragments in Contemporary Art

In some ways McCarthy's fixation on the teller of the tale, rather than the fairy tale itself, cusps the implicit tale. Described by Zipes (2012, 174) as a "mosaic" of fairy-tale fragments interwoven into a single narrative, these works draw on the metaphors, motifs, and atmosphere of the fairy tale rather than retelling any one story. These commonly identifiable fairy-tale elements offer artists a way to broach awkward or disturbing issues through a more palatable vernacular of magic, wonder, and transformation.

In the collaborative works of sculptor Nathalie Djurberg (Sweden, b. 1978) and musician Hans Berg (Sweden, b. 1978), the moral lessons and happily ever afters widely associated with fairy tales are gleefully abandoned in favor of a carnivalesque ride through transgressive scenarios depicting hedonism, violence, jealousy, revenge, and greed. Featuring Djurberg's plasticine stop-motion animations and accompanied by Berg's affecting electronic scores, these works explore the darker side of the human psyche, blurring the lines between pleasure and perversion, victim and perpetrator, humor and the macabre. Echoing elements of the Brothers Grimm, Hans Christian Andersen, and Angela Carter, these discordant narratives are equal parts animalistic, transformative, and monstrous. In *Tiger Licking Girl's Butt* (2004) a young girl becomes aroused when a tiger licks her bare buttocks as she dries herself from her bath. As the text flashes "Why Do I Have This Urge To Do These Things Over And Over Again?" the girl embraces her desires and invites the beast into her bed. Similarly, a boy battles the externalization of his animalism when his conjoined twin, a wolf, continually thwarts him from preparing a meal in *We Are Not Two, We Are One* (2008). In a final example, *It's the Mother* (2008), the title figure undergoes a monstrous transformation when she allows her children to climb back into her womb. Exhausted and alone, her figure begins to distort as the absorbed bodies emerge again as fleshy appendages from her stomach, hips, back, and thighs.

Images of the anthropomorphized, the misshapen, or the magically transformed are not uncommon in the enchanted realm and speak to an ongoing need to find ways to process how we relate to Otherness in both our internal and external worlds. These challenges populate the practice of Patricia Piccinini (Sierra Leone, b. 1965), her works arising from our uneasy relationship with evolution, genetic engineering, advanced technologies, and bioethics. While she explores these ideas across photography, drawing, moving image, and installation, Piccinini is best known for her life-sized cross-species sculptures. Made from silicone, fiberglass, and human hair, these hyperrealistic anthropomorphized creations are both familiar and foreign, chimeras designed by the artist to explain the world she lives in but cannot totally understand or control (Piccinini 2007).

In *The Long Awaited* (2008), an aging mermaid-like creature lies on a bench, her head in the lap of a small boy who has fallen asleep while holding her. Similarly in *Eulogy* (2011) a kneeling man holds in his hands the body of an amorphous fish, its seemingly boneless head sporting a human-like face. For Piccinini, these beings, both human and hybrid, are equal in their need for comfort and compassion regardless of their genetic and biological histories (2007). She underscores this point by integrating, in *Eulogy*, the amorphous Blobfish, an inhabitant of the here and now, living in the deep waters off the coast of mainland Australia, Tasmania, and New Zealand. Unlike the confronting frankness in Djurberg and Berg's animations, Piccinini chooses to craft her creations to be both loveable and unthreatening, seeking to inspire conversations around Otherness rather than to distract with images of the monstrous. Intellectual discussions of what is good or bad, natural or artificial, are frequently tempered by incorporation of children, a technique often seen in fairy-tale narrative to reflect the curiosity, openness, and naivety they represent.

For collaborating artists Isobel Knowles (Australia, b. 1980) and Van Sowerwine (Australia, b. 1975), the role of the monstrous is integral to the telling of fairy tales, offering a place where the most dreadful, oppressive, and terrible things can be explored within relative safety. Inspired by Heinrich Hoffmann's *Struwwelpeter* (1845) and the fairy-tale anthologies of Andrew Lang, Knowles and Sowerwine interweave the monstrous with elements of mystery, vulnerability, curiosity, and the unexpected. In the interactive installation *Play With Me* (2002), the viewer is invited to enter a child-sized dollhouse to join animated eight-year-old "Flora" for tea. While the viewer is offered different ways to interact with the stop-motion animation, it soon becomes apparent that even the most innocuous of actions can escalate in horrifying ways as Flora responds by gouging out her eyes, cutting herself with broken china, or swapping her tea for poison. Reflecting on a common fairy-tale theme whereby children are abandoned to fend for themselves, Sowerwine sees Flora's actions as an assertion of her own desires above those of a controlling adult, even when she knowingly precipitates tragic consequences.

Elements of abandonment and self-reliance are explored again in the lush papercut stop-motion animation and interactive installation *You Were in My Dream* (2010). Seated at a console, the viewer is treated to the haunting sounds of the night as they watch a small child sleep on the jungle floor. Awakening the child with a click of a mouse, the viewer finds that their face has been imposed onto the animated figure through a live video feed. Prompted by pulsing stars throughout the landscape, the viewer is enticed on a magical journey that transforms the figure into a snake, bird, monkey, rabbit, or wolf. Echoing elements of the transformative chase in classic fairy tales, whereby a pursuit provokes the magical transformation of the protagonist through several forms, these changes are not without their own challenges in a world that tempts you to eat or be eaten. As the screen fades to black the viewer is once again returned to the sleeping child in the forest and the adventure begins anew.

For Knowles and Sowerwine, it is the tension found before the final conclusion of the fairy tale that inspires their work, particularly notions of transition and transformation that invite viewers to consider their personal vulnerabilities, an experience the artists amplify through the participatory nature of their interactive work. As meditations on the fairy-tale tropes of forbidding forests and childlike curiosity, alongside the lure of the prohibited, the artists explore complex notions of perception and identity, evolution and transformation that they invoke. For Knowles and Sowerwine the disquiet of interaction alongside the use of animation offer endless possibilities presented to blur the line between the real, the artificial, and the underpinning darkness found within these enchanted worlds.

The Unwitting Tale: The Ubiquitous Nature of Fairy Tales in Contemporary Art

Artists working with explicit and implicit tales do so with knowledge of the enchanted worlds upon which they draw. They engage mindfully with fairy-tale elements with the intent to provoke conversation surrounding the issues inherent in both in the work and the tale. While these engagements might be derived from tellings of a classic tale or interpretations several generations removed, these artists acknowledge through their artist's statements and interviews the inspirational foundation that underpins their work.

This conscious involvement, however, is not the case for all artists who draw on the fairy-tale realm. Skittering along the outer edges of the implicit tale are artists who draw on the aesthetic pageantry of these narratives yet are largely unaware, or disengaged, with the origin of these influences in their work. This disconnection can be attributed somewhat to Zipes's "whalelike fairy tale" and the ability of its narrative to penetrate the fabric of our social consciousness, moving through all cultural forms without attribution. Zipes cites academic Michael Drout's work on the power of memes in oral traditions, in particularly Drout's description that "a meme is the simplest unit of cultural replication; it is whatever is transmitted when one person imitates consciously or unconsciously, another" (2012, 88–90). This process can result in an unintentional association by the artist and features works that reflect a fairy-tale aesthetic but do not engage directly with the fairy-tale fragments they invoke, leaving it to viewers to reason with these associations they observe.

In his work *Living Together in Paradise* (2009–2012), painter and sculptor Nguyễn Mạnh Hùng (Vietnam, b. 1976) presents a towering apartment block, so tall only the top floors are visible as they break through clouds into the blissful peace of the upper atmosphere. The three-meter-high sculpture resembles a large diorama with its backdrop of painted hazy blue sky blending into a fluffy carpet of cumulus clouds, the minutiae of daily life captured in precise detail as lights glimmer behind window shutters, curtains appear to billow in the breeze, and washing hangs to dry on the makeshift balconies. The dreamy otherworldliness of the work invokes associations of an urban "Jack and the Beanstalk" (ATU 328A). In the place of magic beans are the roots of the community, the building created by hundreds of "Jacks" all scrambling to climb to the heavens to find their reward, a modern Tower of Babel, while the viewer takes on the role of giant observer.

While Hùng talks of the "otherworldly" in relation to this piece, his inspiration is rooted firmly in his own personal experiences growing up in a crowded apartment block in Hanoi, his work articulating the way a largely rural Vietnamese population copes within rapid urban change (Saioc 2014). The core of the sculpture reflects the Soviet-inspired architecture that proliferated in the major cities of North Vietnam during the 1960s to the late 1980s. Often housing multiple families, the cramped apartments forced residents to find creative ways to expand and improve their living environments, leading to their makeshift renovations and colonization of communal spaces for shelter, gardening, livestock, and social interaction, all the while hoping to hold onto their rural values within an urban surrounding. While these colorful editions of corrugated iron, mesh, and tarpaulin to Hùng's "vertical village" can be found in real life across Asia, the sculpture's toylike miniaturization offers a more playful, utopian appeal, inspiring the viewer to dream that perhaps paradise can be found within such communal living.

This outward allusion to play and serenity is reflected in the sculptural maze *My Monument: White Forest* (2008) by Kathy Temin (Australia, b. 1968). Made from white synthetic fur wrapped around steel and wood and surrounded by sky blue walls, this towering three-and-a-half-meter plush forest of bulbous forms invites the viewer to explore the large enchanting labyrinth within. Like the ostensibly kindly old woman inviting Hansel and Gretel into the gingerbread house, however, it is not until one looks beyond its serene embrace that the true meanings of the forest become apparent. As suggested by the title, Temin's forest is a monument: a memorial to loss, displacement, memory, and migration.

The daughter of a Nazi concentration camp survivor, her work *My Monument: White Forest* brings together Temin's interest in the abstract paintings of Frank Stella (United States, b. 1936), in particular *Arbeit macht frei* (1958), translated as "work will set you free," the phrase that adorned the entrances of several Nazi concentration camps, and a visit Temin made to Europe in 2008 as part of an organized tour for the children of Holocaust survivors. Struck by the intimidating size of the camps, designed to make those interned feel small and vulnerable, Temin was keen to replicate the physiological message of scale while still offering a way through these somber memories, literally through a maze, to a place of contemplation. Like Hùng, Temin describes her work as "other-worldly," an exploration of toys and games from childhood integrated with adult themes or art history. The allusion to fairy tale offers a disarming misdirection through the use of synthetic materials associated with crafts and toys and the work's homespun fabrication (Art Nation 2011).

While Temin's deceptively playful work deals with the ongoing intergenerational ramifications of the Nazi concentration camps, Abdul Abdullah (Australia, b. 1986) takes a more confrontational look at the dehumanization of the Muslim community in a post-9/11 world. The son of a sixth-generation Australian and a first-generation migrant mother from Malaysia, Abdullah was only fourteen when his Muslim family became the target of prejudice after the 2001 terrorist attack on the World Trade Center in the United States. With the rise of the nationalist beliefs that a utopian society can only be achieved through the exclusion of the minority by the power of majority, Abdullah began articulating the anxieties and frustrations of the Muslim community's religious and ethnic marginalization through painting, photography, video, installation, and performance.

In his photographic series *Siege* (2014), an extrapolation of his feelings of being constantly under siege in a traditional Western society, Abdullah created ten stark portraits each featuring a single figure that looms from the darkness, their shadowed faces veiled further by the mask of a monkey. A promotional prop from the film *The Planet of the Apes* (2001), the mask explicitly calls out the racism Abdullah and his family have endured, a literal externalization of his supposedly internal bestial form, a "damn dirty ape" as Charlton Heston's character George Taylor states in the original *Planet of the Apes* (1968).

Abdullah extends these associations further in the series *Coming to Terms* (2015), which sees the artist, with mask, holding a monkey he met on a trip to Malaysia. Within this same photographic series, Abdullah offers a series of wedding portraits featuring a bride and groom in full attire, their faces concealed with balaclavas dyed to match their outfits. In both series, the masks represent the monstrous, a modern beast without the beauty, an externalization of their perceived deceptiveness and criminality. While Abdullah's works are fixed within the realm of his specific community, the works also reflect the wider fairy-tale associations of monstrousness, mistrust, and misunderstanding of Otherness. As in many fairy tales, Abdullah's message is a call to arms of the marginalized to find their own destiny and happiness.

Fairy Tales and Contemporary Art

It is a tribute to the incredible resilience of fairy tales that a single fragment can provoke and enrich such a multitude of stories. When contemporary artists draw on the motifs, metaphors, and atmosphere of the fairy tale, they explore complex issues inherent within them while also reflecting concerns important to the artist's wider practice. Many move beyond the didactic to embrace a wider understanding of wonder, transformation, and magic, engaging with these tales as part of the metaphorical toolbox of influences, styles, and techniques at hand while drawing on the broad narrative options available. That not all artists understand, or desire to acknowledge, the stories on which they draw does not negate the use of the fairy tale or its ability to stimulate conversations around difficult subjects and provide a creative conduit between societal issues and the community.

Related topics: Children's Picture Books and Illustration; Disney Corporation; Material Culture; Photography; Pictorial; Sexualities/Queer and Trans Studies

References Cited and Further Reading

Anker, Suzanne, and Dorothy Nelkin. 2004. *The Molecular Gaze: Art in the Genetic Age.* Cold Spring Harbor, NY: Cold Spring Harbor Laboratory P.

"Art Nation—Kathy Temin." 2011. *ABC Arts,* October 28. www.abc.net.au/arts/stories/s3350782.htm.

Buttrose, Ellie. 2012. *Nguyen Manh Hung: Vertical village. APT7, the 7Th Asia Pacific Triennial of Contemporary Art.* Brisbane: Queensland Art Gallery/Gallery of Modern Art.

Callesen, Peter, and Angela Kingston. 2007. *Fairy Tale: Contemporary Art and Enchantment.* Walsall: New Art Gallery Walsall.

Duquenne, Olivier. 2012. *Pinocchio & Co: Fairy Tales and Contemporary Art.* Oostkamp: Stichting Kunstboek BVBA.

Fontenot, Elizabeth. 2013. "Kiki Smith Turns Everyday Objects into Mystical Creations." *The Art Studio, Inc.,* March. www.artstudio.org/kikismith/.

Freud, Sigmund. (1899) 1953. *The Interpretation of Dreams.* London: Hogarth P and the Institute of Psycho-Analysis.

Gombrich, Ernst H. 1995. *The Story of Art.* 16th revised ed. London: Phaidon P.

Gott, Ted, and Kathryn Weir. 2005. *Kiss of the Beast: From Paris Salon to King Kong.* Brisbane: Queensland Art Gallery.

Kennedy, Randy. 2013. "The Demented Imagineer." *New York Times,* May 10. www.nytimes.com/2013/05/12/magazine/paul-mccarthy-the-demented-imagineer.html.

Piccinini, Patricia. 2007. "The Naturally Artificial World: A Conversation with Patricia Piccinini." In *(Tender) Creatures.* Spain: ATRIUM, Basque Museum-Center of Contemporary Art.

Saioc, Andreea. 2014. "Could Angels Live Together in Paradise?: A Conversation with Vietnamese Artist Hung Nguyen Manh." http://theglobalpanorama.com/could-angels-live-together-in-paradise-a-conversation-with-vietnamese-artist-hung-nguyen-manh/.

Scala, Mark, ed. 2012. *Fairy Tales, Monsters, and the Genetic Imagination.* Nashville, TN: Frist Center for the Visual Arts, Vanderbilt UP.

Weitman, Wendy, and Kiki Smith. 2003. *Kiki Smith: Prints, Books & Things.* New York: Museum of Modern Art.

Zipes, Jack. 2012. *The Irresistible Fairy Tale: The Cultural and Social History of a Genre.* Princeton, NJ: Princeton UP.

Mediagraphy

Abdullah, Abdul. 2014. *Siege.* Photograph Series. Australia. http://abdulabdullah.com/section/387921-Siege.html.

———. 2015. *Coming to Terms.* Photograph Series. Australia. http://abdulabdullah.com/section/420196-Coming-to-terms.html.

Djurberg, Nathalie, and Hans Berg. 2004. *Tiger Licking Girl's Butt.* Clay Animation, Digital Video, Stereo Audio. Sweden. www.lissongallery.com/artists/nathalie-djurberg-hans-berg/gallery/3930.

———. 2008a. *It's the Mother.* Clay Animation, Digital Video. Sweden. http://arttattler.com/archivenathaliedjurberg.html.

———. 2008b. *We Are Not Two, We Are One.* Clay Animation, Digital Video. Sweden. http://fryemuseum.org/exhibition/3108/.

Goldstein, Dina. 2009. *Fallen Princesses*. Photograph Series. Canada. www.fallenprincesses.com.

Hùng, Nguyễn Mạnh. 2012. *Living Together in Paradise*. Sculpture; Wood, Paper, Plastic, Metal, Nylon, Foam, Wires, Lighting System. Vietnam. http://hung6776.com/web/index.php?id=50.

Knowles, Isobel, and Van Sowerwine. 2002. *Play With Me*. Interactive Installation and Exhibition. Australia. https://vimeo.com/161117385.

———. 2010. *You Were in My Dream*. Interactive Installation and Exhibition. Australia. www.youwereinmydream.com.

McCarthy, Paul. 2013. *WS*. Art Installation and Exhibition. Park Avenue Armory, New York. www.hauserwirth.com/artists/20/paul-mccarthy/images-clips/.

Piccinini, Patricia. 2008. *The Long Awaited*. Silicon, Fibreglass, Human Hair, Plywood, Leather, Clothing. Sierra Leone. www.patriciapiccinini.net/228/62.

———. 2011. *Eulogy*. Silicone, Fibreglass, Human Hair, Clothing. Sierra Leone. www.patriciapiccinini.net/68/101.

Planet of the Apes. 1968. Director Franklin J. Schaffner. USA.

———. 2001. Director Tim Burton. USA.

Smith, Kiki. 2001. *Rapture*. Bronze Statue. Germany.

———. 2002a. *Born*. Bronze Statue. Germany.

———. 2002b. *Genevieve with May Wolf*. Bronze Statue. Germany.

Stella, Frank. 1958. *Arbeit macht frei*. Painting. USA. http://artsearch.nga.gov.au/Detail.cfm?IRN=80688.

Temin, Kathy. 2008. *My Monument: White Forest*. Sculpture Exhibition. Australia. www.roslynoxley9.com.au/artists/37/Kathy_Temin/1134/41622/. DVD.

"Van Sowerwine." 2016. *VanSowerwine.Com*. www.vansowerwine.com.

55

CRITICISM

Vanessa Joosen

At first sight, it may seem awkward to locate an essay on "criticism" in a section on "expressive genres and venues." However, the concepts of criticism and creativity are by no means mutually exclusive. First, a number of hybrid forms mix elements traditionally assigned to either creative or critical responses to the fairy tale. Second, authors of both creative and critical works can feel inspired or compelled to respond to traditional fairy tales. As a result, both fiction and scholarship engage in interpreting and evaluating their meaning for contemporary society, and this situation produces compelling convergences between the two discourses. Rather than presenting an overview of current criticism on fairy-tale cultures and media, I discuss the interaction between fairy-tale retellings and criticism and the way they inspire, reflect on, and complement each other. After introducing the traditional features of expressive and critical discourse, I discuss a selection of hybrid media forms that mix features of the two. I then analyze the interaction between fairy-tale criticism and the creative response to fairy tales, focusing on one aspect of contemporary fairy-tale culture: the literary fairy-tale rewriting. The processes that I describe are, however, not unique to literature: fairy-tale adaptations in other media interact in similar ways with fairy-tale criticism, and various literary rewritings have been used as the basis for films and television programs.

Creative and Critical Discourse

As two different types of discourses, criticism and literature raise different reader expectations, and their quality is judged on different criteria. Academic writing manuals, for example, make explicit the norms for good criticism. For example, the evaluation scale that goes with *All Write: An Introduction to Writing in an Academic Context* (Van de Poel and Gasiorek 2007) invites students to assess the quality of their research papers. The questions include: Does my text have a transparent, logical structure? Did I cite the sources that I used? Could I say it more concisely? Literary critics use very diverse criteria to determine and describe the quality of fiction, more difficult to list in a tick-the-box type of evaluation scale like the one in *All Write*. Obviously, good literature does not have to refer to its sources of inspiration in detail, as a good scholar should. At most, these sources may be acknowledged with an overt intertextual reference or in an acknowledgment in an appendix, but more often than not, they go unreferenced. In scholarship, such practices would be considered sloppy or even plagiarism. Moreover, while concise and clear phrasing is a quality of some renowned authors' writing style (Ernest Hemingway and Benjamin Franklin come to mind), others are praised for their verbosity. Wordiness features as "The Third Deadly Sin" (N.d.) on the Hamilton University Writing Center's list of bad writing for essays and criticism, yet literary authors can use verbosity as their aesthetic hallmark (Charles Dickens, for example).

Literature and criticism also raise different expectations in their readership with regard to the information and opinions they formulate. Criticism ranks under non-fiction and as such is what Susan S. Lanser calls "attached." When readers encounter an "I" in an attached text, it is "conventionally assumed to be the author of the work." When they come upon an idea in criticism, they can assume it to be the author's truthful and well-researched opinion, "compromised perhaps by errors but not by lies" (2005, 208). In contrast, when readers encounter the same idea in fiction—for example, in a fairy-tale rewriting—they must form their own judgment about whether they can seriously attribute this idea to the author or not, whether it is perhaps used hyperbolically, as parody, to evoke criticism, whether the author has deliberately misrepresented or simplified the issue, and so forth.

What holds for opinions and ideas is also true for information. Non-fiction may contain speculative or even imagined parts, but they are clearly distinguished from the rest of the text. In fiction, by contrast, readers must assess what is imaginary and what is not. Gregory Maguire's novel *Confessions of an Ugly Stepsister* (1999), for example, rewrites the plot of "Cinderella" (ATU 510A) as a historical narrative. The novel was adapted to a television film, directed by Gavin Millar, in 2002. Both novel and film refer to cities and historical events, such as Haarlem and the 1637 Dutch tulip crash. It is less clear to what extent the characters are based on historical figures (some are and others are invented). Andy Tennant's fairy-tale film *Ever After* (1998) plays a similar game. As Jessica Tiffin argues, "By placing the Cinderella narrative within a deliberately historicized setting—that of sixteenth-century France—the film underlines its deliberate play with realism" (2008b, 314). While few viewers will believe that Leonardo Da Vinci ever played the role of fairy godmother, as the film suggests, they may wonder if other characters (e.g., Prince Henry) or events are rooted in reality. Similar questions arise in particular in the many biopics and theater plays that stage fairy-tale collectors and authors as characters and combine facts from their lives with imagined scenes and characters. Examples include the film *The Wonderful World of the Brothers Grimm* (1962) and *Grimm and Grimmer: The Misadventures of the Brothers Grimm* (2001), a comical play describing Jacob, Wilhelm, and their sister Lotte Grimm in their quest for fairy tales.

Ada Wildekamp, Ineke Van Montfoort, and Willem Van Ruiswijk use the term "indeterminate denotation" for such frequent uncertainties in fiction (1980, 549), which exist in addition to references with "null denotation," where the reader knows that characters or events are invented. Because of the so-called fictionality convention, the author and reader, or filmmaker and viewer, "play consciously accepted roles, which permits them to step outside their genuine feelings, opinions and the like" (1980, 555). As a result, authors of fiction—regardless of the medium or form—have freedom to use references that do not (accurately) correspond to the world outside the text, while authors of criticism are expected to make clear distinctions between the verifiable and the speculative or imaginary.

In practice, readers must assess whether a text is fictional or not on the basis of textual, paratextual, and contextual aspects. When criticism and fairy tales are published side by side, as in Maria Tatar's *The Classic Fairy Tales* (1999) or in the journal *Marvels & Tales*, chapter and section headings clearly demarcate the difference. The text's reception and the author's consequent comment or lack thereof can also be indicative when there is doubt.

Hybridity

Some books and journals go further than simply publishing fairy-tale criticism and fictional rewritings side by side, but offer hybrid forms to implement features of both. In postmodernism, traditional distinctions between fiction and criticism have become increasingly blurred into what Linda Hutcheon calls a "paraliterary space" (1988, 9–10), encompassing a wide range of practices that mix literary and critical aspects. Helen Flavell uses the label "fictocriticism" for texts that "blur the distinction between theory and fiction" (1998, 203). She mentions, among others, "mock criticism," which parodies critical discourse so that the reader may take a fictional text for being attached. A famous case of mock criticism in fairy-tale studies is Hans Traxler's *Die Wahrheit über Hänsel und Gretel* (The Truth about Hansel and Gretel, 1963), with which he sought to trick readers into believing that he had discovered the archeological remains of the gingerbread house from the Grimms' fairy tale (ATU 327A).

More recently, fairy-tale critics have experimented with various forms of hybridity. Sandra Gilbert and Susan Gubar's "The Further Adventures of Snow White," the closing chapter of their three-volume discussion of twentieth-century woman authors, *No Man's Land* (1994), opened with a critical analysis of "Snow White" (ATU 709) that has become a key text in feminist fairy-tale criticism. A survey of foundational feminist scholarship and literature is preceded by a section that mixes criticism and fiction into a dozen short tales that illustrate some of the evolutions discussed in the survey, from the liberation of the female libido (362), to the interest in "lesbianism, bisexuality, transvestism, and transsexuality" (364), to the indeterminacy of deconstruction theories (366). Gilbert and Gubar's retellings are influenced by renowned literary authors such as Margaret Atwood and Donald Barthelme, who are also referenced in the non-fictional parts of the text. The tales celebrate the diversity of female voices and stories that feminism has helped make possible and expressible, in both criticism and literature.

Not coincidentally, in a book called *Transcending Boundaries* (Beckett 1999), Roderick McGillis constructs his article about intertextuality as a dialogue between five historical figures, all of whom have written or illustrated fairy tales, and gives it the revealing heading "Ceci n'est pas un essai" (This is not an essay). He explores the boundaries of the fictional and the critical, introducing his characters to an anachronistic talk about recent theories on intertextuality and contemporary picture books, including *The Stinky Cheese Man* (Scieszka and Smith 1992), a picture book that itself brims with intertextual and metafictional games and invites readers to reflect on the narrative conventions of the fairy tale and the children's book. Throughout McGillis's article, the reader faces moments of Wildekamp, Van Montfoort, and Van Ruiswijk's indeterminate denotation. At one point, McGillis's Evelyn Sharp says: "We speak and in speaking hope to clarify what it means to be a subject by taking up a position in language. But every position is occupied and we can only sit in someone's lap" (1999, 124). Although it is clear that the combination of figures McGillis stages could not have occurred, it is unclear whether this quotation is from the real Evelyn Sharp or is McGillis's invention. To illustrate the concept of intertextuality, with its lack of overt referencing in fiction, McGillis deviates from the rules of criticism to engage in an experimental intertextual game, inviting the reader to play along.

Equally experimental and playful is "Extrapolating from Nalo Hopkinson's *Skin Folk*" (2008), in which Cristina Bacchilega visualizes a dialogue between various retellings by incorporating quotations and thoughts in text balloons that pop up in the margins of her argument. With this unusual layout, Bacchilega appears to imitate intertextual echoes heard through literary texts and includes afterthoughts and parallels that go far beyond the footnotes found in traditional critical discourse. It is left to the reader to choose which of these side thoughts to pursue and to make sense of the suggested parallels and remarks. With this approach, Bacchilega brings into practice the "hypertextuality" that she ascribes to the fictional texts that are her article's subjects.

VANESSA JOOSEN

The Critical Impulse in Fairy-Tale Rewritings

The texts in the prior section are all published within a critical context (a book, edited volume, or scholarly journal) by authors who have earned their merits predominantly as scholars. Such hybrids are relatively exceptional in fairy-tale criticism. Far more numerous are the fictional fairy-tale rewritings that share interpretations with fairy-tale criticism or, vice versa, fairy-tale criticism that refers to rewritings to support an argument. Various critics (Bacchilega 2013, 8; Benson 2008, 5; Zipes 2009, 122; Joosen 2011, 2) note the striking contemporaneity in the surging interest in fairy tales in fiction and scholarship—a surge that started in the 1970s with the so-called "fairy-tale renaissance." Several theoretical paradigms that have shaped the debate on fairy tales have their counterpart in the rewritings: both critical texts and fiction have been labeled as feminist, Marxist, psychoanalytic, postcolonial, and queer responses to the fairy tale.

Fictional texts use various textual strategies to express critical ideas about the traditional fairy tale. Mock criticism, as mentioned prior, contains explicit comments or interpretations, which must not be directly attributed to the author, but function as parodies of criticism. For example, in Linda Kavanagh's "The Princesses' Forum" (1985), female characters debate their own portrayal in the Grimms' fairy tales. In this fictional argument, conventions of critical discourse are exaggerated and exposed and its usual participants mocked—yet the reader is simultaneously introduced to some key issues that second-wave feminists had raised about fairy tales: the beauty contest as a patriarchal set up, for example, or the problematic trope of the damsel in distress who must be rescued by a man. Such examples are relatively rare compared to the many retellings in all media that revise fairy-tale plots and themes. In those, the critical evaluation of the traditional fairy tale is performed first, through exaggeration and exposure, and second, through the correction with a more positively valued ideal. In the YouTube video "Princess Rap Battle" (Avalon 2015), for example, Cinderella and Belle fight over who is the more successful fairy-tale heroine. Cinderella briefly refers to Freud in attacking Belle's "abnormality," a reproach understood as referencing Bruno Bettelheim's interpretation of "Beauty and the Beast." The two heroines battle over the preferred qualities of the fairy-tale heroine: beauty (Cinderella) or intelligence (Belle). Their verbal wit and numerous original arguments, however, mark both as a feminist response to Disney movies' traditional princesses.

A further literary example illustrates how the three practices of explicit comments, exaggeration, and correction can combine in fairy-tale retellings. In the 1970s, feminist critics including Marcia Lieberman, Karen E. Rowe, and Andrea Dworkin pointed out the lack of independent, active heroines in the best-known traditional fairy tales. On Kavanagh's princesses' forum, Red Riding Hood makes this observation explicitly: "Everyone assumes that in order to live happily ever after, we must each have a prince in tow" (1985, 6). Rather than addressing the problem directly, as Kavanagh does, many retellings correct it by providing an alternative, filling the gap with an active heroine who chooses not to conform to stereotypical gender patterns. Robert Munsch's *The Paperbag Princess* (1980), in which the heroine saves a prince from a dragon through cunning but refuses to marry him because he disdains her looks, offers a classic example. More recently, Disney's *Frozen*, loosely based on Hans Christian Andersen's "The Snow Queen," has been lauded for giving the relationship between two sisters priority over the heterosexual marriage plot (Hilton-Morrow and Battles 2015, 262).

Some writers exaggerate the traditional fairy-tale heroine's passivity to such a degree that it becomes a hyperbolic parody. In Anne Sexton's "Snow White," the narrator compares the eponymous heroine to a long list of inanimate, mainly fragile objects and thus creates the impression that she is barely alive, even when she is not lying in the glass coffin:

CRITICISM

No matter what life you lead
the virgin is a lovely number:
cheeks as fragile as cigarette paper,
arms and legs made of Limoges,
lips like Vin Du Rhone,
rolling her china-blue doll eyes
open and shut.

(1988, 149)

Snow White's passivity, romanticized in the Grimms' version of the tale, as feminist critics have pointed out, is here exaggerated to the extent that she becomes pitiable rather than admirable or desirable. Often two or even all three strategies—explicit comments, exaggeration, and correction—combine in one retelling. While a film like *Frozen* or a poem like Sexton's "Snow White" does not directly refer to feminist criticism, they share an awareness about the inaptness of passive fairy-tale heroines. Each, within its own generic conventions, promotes an alternative model.

Influence or Intertextual Dialogue?

In *Critical and Creative Perspectives on Fairy Tales* (Joosen 2011), I envision this interaction between retellings and criticism as an intertextual dialogue, which I prefer to a model of influence to explain convergences between fiction and criticism. I discuss, among others, Gillian Cross's *Wolf* (1990), a children's novel in which I see similarities to Bettelheim's psychoanalytic interpretation of "Little Red Riding Hood" (ATU 333): the link between fairy tales and dreams, for example, or the wolf figure as representation of the Id's wild and violent surges. Both question if repressed memories and desires can be fully mastered. Claiming that Cross was "influenced" by Bettelheim would presuppose that she was familiar with his work. That assertion is hard to make for fictional texts, unless an author has specifically so testified to that influence, something authors of fiction rarely do. The convergences with Bettelheim's theory that I read in *Wolf* may be Cross's own ideas or may stem from another source that she encountered. In the intertextual dialogue between fairy-tale retellings and literary criticism, it is usually difficult to trace where an idea appeared first or whether ideas were actually borrowed from each other. According to Maria Nikolajeva, "the question of who has borrowed the idea from whom" is "totally uninteresting" (1996, 183) if we apply M. M. Bakhtin's concept of intertextuality as dialogism. It is more worthwhile instead to explore the different uses that authors and critics make of the same idea in an intertextual dialogue.

Thus, in *Fairy Tales Transformed?* (2013), Bacchilega notes that Nalo Hopkinson's "Riding the Red" not only evokes intertextual links with "Little Red Riding Hood," but also with literary revisions by Robert Coover and Angela Carter and critical interpretations by Lutz Röhrich, Yvonne Verdier, and Jack Zipes (41). In *Fairy Tales, Myth, and Psychoanalytic Theory* (2014), Veronica L. Schanoes traces "the connections and correspondences between the stories told by second-wave feminist psychoanalytic theorists about what it means to be a woman and those told by their fairy-tale rewriting contemporaries" (141). Whereas I used criticism as a starting point for intertextual comparison, Schanoes advocates putting literature more centrally in the debate: "The fact that poets and novelists continue to work with ideas long after they have passed out of fashion in academia suggests that [. . .] criticism is a precondition, not the final word, but an early word" (142). Both retellings and criticism then build on each other to develop new meanings and keep relevant ideas alive.

VANESSA JOOSEN

Implicating New Audiences, Creating New Meanings

A further crucial difference between fiction and scholarship is the audience. For fairy-tale criticism, this audience is likely limited to those trained to read academic texts and literary analyses, although popularized criticism and essays may reach more readers. Nevertheless, even a well-received critical text will never have the vast audience that some books, films, television programs, and Internet productions reach. Moreover, fairy-tale retellings in various media have been aimed at specific groups who have not yet had academic training—children and adolescents in particular. Reader response research, such as that of Lawrence R. Sipe (2008), has shown that fairy-tale retellings can make children aware of ideological issues in the traditional versions, just as criticism can raise an awareness of these issues in its adult readers.

Literary theory has questioned if literature can ever be really effective in communicating critical interpretations and evaluations of other texts. In fiction, promoting ideology explicitly or foregrounding interpretations can easily have the opposite effect. Although simplistic parodies and role reversals may be rejected as one-dimensional and too moralistic, their very fictionality fosters a distance between author and narrator. The reader has the liberty to read even—or perhaps, especially—the most didactic retellings against the grain. Although the mixture of fiction and criticism has been welcomed by some, others claim that retellings fail both as literary and as critical texts. Some believe their literariness gets in the way of their clarity or that their overt didacticism obstructs their aesthetic qualities. Anna Altmann distinguishes between parody and poesis as two kinds of fairy-tale retellings: "parody is metafiction, a criticism of established forms. Criticism produces insight, but it does not necessarily make new use of the forms or create new meaning: it is not always poesis" (1994, 22). Because parody is a type of metafiction, it always looks back. Poesis, in contrast, "looks forward, creates new meaning." These poetic texts "use the form of the fairy tale without commenting on it. Or at least, commentary is not the main point" (23). Rather, poetic texts aesthetically explore the fairy-tale form.

Several rewritings have indeed been recognized for their literary qualities and complexity of form and meaning. The same is true for fairy-tale adaptations in other media. Neil Jordan's *The Company of Wolves* (1984), for example, based on Angela Carter's *The Bloody Chamber* (1979), "an intelligent and densely textured cinematic work" that supplements "Charles Perrault's 'Little Red Riding Hood' with psychological depth, Freudian significance, and a heightened sense of erotic menace" (Tiffin 2008a, 228). Poetic retellings like Carter's *Bloody Chamber* or Jordan's film account for an active exploration of the fairy tale's form and content, providing literary or filmic counterpoints to the reproach that criticism does not do justice to the fairy tale's aesthetic richness and multiple meanings. When the two discourses—fiction and criticism—are put side by side, they prove to be not only mutually influential, but also complementary in interpreting and evaluating the meanings of fairy tales and in keeping the interest in this form alive.

Related topics: Adaptation and the Fairy-Tale Web; Autobiography; Children's and Young Adult (YA) Literature; Cinematic; Gender; Hybridity; Poetry; Storyworlds/Narratology

References Cited and Further Reading

Altmann, Anna E. 1994. "Parody and Poesis in Feminist Fairy Tales." *Canadian Children's Literature* 73: 22–31.
Bacchilega, Cristina. 2008. "Extrapolating from Nalo Hopkinson's *Skin Folk*: Reflections on Transformation and Recent English-Language Fairy-Tale Fiction by Women." In *Contemporary Fiction and the Fairy Tale*, edited by Stephen Benson, 178–203. Detroit: Wayne State UP.
———. 2013. *Fairy Tales Transformed?: Twenty-First-Century Adaptations and the Politics of Wonder*. Detroit: Wayne State UP.
Beckett, Sandra L. 1999. *Transcending Boundaries: Writing for a Dual Audience of Children and Adults*. New York: Garland.

CRITICISM

Benson, Stephen, ed. 2008. *Contemporary Fiction and the Fairy Tale*. Detroit: Wayne State UP.

Carter, Angela. 1979. *The Bloody Chamber*. London: Victor Gollancz.

Cross, Gillian. 1990. *Wolf*. London: Puffin.

Dworkin, Andrea. 1974. *Woman Hating*. New York: Dutton.

Flavell, Helen. 1998. "Fictocriticism: The End of Criticism as We Write It?" *Paradoxa* 4 (10): 197–204.

Gilbert, Sandra M., and Susan Gubar. 1994. *Letters from the Front*, Vol. 3 of *No Man's Land: The Place of the Woman Writer in the Twentieth Century*. New Haven, CT: Yale UP.

Hilton-Morrow, Wendy, and Kathleen Battles. 2015. *Sexual Identities and the Media*. New York: Routledge.

Hutcheon, Linda. 1988. *A Poetics of Postmodernism: History, Theory, Fiction*. New York: Routledge.

Joosen, Vanessa. 2011. *Critical and Creative Perspectives on Fairy Tales*. Detroit: Wayne State UP.

Kavanagh, Linda. 1985. "The Princesses' Forum." In *Rapunzel's Revenge: Fairy Tales for Feminists*, edited by Anne Claffey, Linda Kavanagh, and Sue Russell, 5–11. Dublin: Attic.

Lanser, Susan. 2005. "The 'I' of the Beholder: Equivocal Attachments and the Limits of Structuralist Narratology." In *A Companion to Narrative Theory*, edited by James Phelan and Peter J. Rabinowitz, 206–19. Malden, MA: Blackwell.

Lieberman, Marcia K. (1972) 1989. "'Some Day My Prince Will Come': Female Acculturation through the Fairy Tale." In *Don't Bet On the Prince: Contemporary Feminist Fairy Tales in North America and England*, edited by Jack Zipes, 185–200. New York: Routledge.

Maguire, Gregory. 1999. *Confessions of an Ugly Stepsister*. New York: Regan.

McGillis, Roderick. 1999. "'Ages: All': Readers, Texts, and Intertexts in *The Stinky Cheese Man and Other Fairly Stupid Tales*." In *Transcending Boundaries: Writing for a Dual Audience of Children and Adults*, edited by Sandra L. Beckett, 111–26. New York: Garland.

Munsch, Robert. (1980) 1999. *The Paper Bag Princess*. New York: Scholastic.

Nikolajeva, Maria. 1996. *Children's Literature Comes of Age*. New York: Garland.

Rowe, Karen E. 1989. "Feminism and Fairy Tales." In *Don't Bet On the Prince: Contemporary Feminist Fairy Tales in North America and England*, edited by Jack Zipes, 209–26. New York: Routledge.

Schanoes, Veronica L. 2014. *Fairy Tales, Myth, and Psychoanalytic Theory: Feminism and Retelling the Tale*. Farnham: Ashgate.

Scieszka, Jon, and Lane Smith. 1992. *The Stinky Cheese Man and Other Fairly Stupid Tales*. London: Puffin.

Sexton, Anne. 1988. *The Selected Poems of Anne Sexton*, edited by Diane Wood Middlebrook and Diana Hume George. London: Virago.

Sipe, Lawrence R. 2008. *Storytime: Young Children's Literary Understanding in the Classroom*. New York: Teachers College.

Tatar, Maria. 1999. *The Classic Fairy Tales*. New York: Norton.

Tiffin, Jessica. 2008a. "*The Company of Wolves*." In *The Greenwood Encyclopedia of Folktales & Fairy Tales*, edited by Donald Haase, 228–30. Westport: Greenwood P.

———. 2008b. "Ever After." In *The Greenwood Encyclopedia of Folktales & Fairy Tales*, edited by Donald Haase, 313–14. Westport: Greenwood P.

Traxler, Hans. 1963. *Die Wahrheit über Hänsel und Gretel: Die Dokumentation des Märchens der Brüder Grimm*. Frankfurt am Main: Bärmeier.

Van de Poel, Kris, and Jessica Gasiorek. 2007. *All Write: An Introduction to Writing in an Academic Context*. Leuven: Acco.

Wildekamp, Ada, Ineke Van Montfoort, and Willem Van Ruiswijk. 1980. "Fictionality and Convention." *Poetics* 9: 547–67.

Zipes, Jack. 2009. *Relentless Progress: The Reconfiguration of Children's Literature, Fairy Tales, and Storytelling*. New York: Routledge.

Mediagraphy

Avalon, Whitney. 2015. "Cinderella vs. Belle: Princess Rap Battle." *YouTube*, March 11. www.youtube.com/watch?v=VeZXQf77hhk.

The Company of Wolves. 1984. Director Neil Jordan. UK.

Confessions of an Ugly Stepsister. 2002. Director Gavin Millar. Canada/Luxemburg.

Ever After: A Cinderella Story. 1998. Director Andy Tennant. USA.

Frozen. 2013. Directors Chris Buck and Jennifer Lee. USA.

Grimm and Grimmer: The Misadventures of the Brothers Grimm (Theater). 2001. Director Abigail Anderson. UK.

"The Third Deadly Sin: Wordiness." N.d. Hamilton Writing Center. www.hamilton.edu/writing/seven-sins-of-writing/the-third-deadly-sin-wordiness.

The Wonderful World of the Brothers Grimm. 1962. Director Henry Levin. USA.

56

FAN FICTION

Anne Kustritz

Fan fiction and fairy tales share some enemies. As the practice of writing new stories using public figures or previously published fictional characters, situations, and settings, fan fiction is often derided as hopelessly derivative. Fairy-tale history likewise traces promiscuous networks of retellings, across media forms, voiced by multiple, often unnamed authors and storytellers. For many academic and popular commentators, such conditions of anonymity, pseudonymity, and repetition mark both fan fiction and fairy tales as low culture with little artistic or political potential. That fan fiction is authored almost exclusively by women, and fairy tales often become gendered in their association with the home, childrearing, kinship, and romance, only appear to further consign both to frivolousness and obscurity (Coppa 2006; Coppa 2008; Jenkins 1992; Kustritz 2003; Lee 2008; Stone 1975).

Yet, while some theoretical traditions view repetition as a sign of stultifying cultural deadening associated with capitalist culture industries, others view it as the space of potential agency and critique. The ubiquity of fairy-tale themes and narratives throughout Western storytelling and popular culture make such stories profitable, but also powerful, as part of a shared pre-capitalist language that remains available for appropriation and retelling by anyone. On the one hand, it is a language of cultural reproduction in which brands and commodities are enunciated, reproducing economic, patriarchal, heteronormative, and racial hierarchies. However, feminist critics, academics, and fans can also enunciate fairy-tale language as an open and widely recognizable system of resonant signs, widely understood and easily circulated for critiques of the modern world. For example, because the fairy tale deals so often with coming of age and courtship, it offers fertile ground to feminist, queer, and trans appropriation. Thus, fan fiction that borrows fairy-tale themes, specifically fairy-tale alternate universes (AUs), occupies a complex crossroads between mass and folk culture and can offer a shared language wherein anyone can negotiate, discuss, and critique modern culture.

Repetition in Folk Culture, Fan Culture, and Shared Culture

Although each is steeped in repetition, fan fiction's prominent connection with popular culture and mass media creates potential political tensions with fairy tales. Investigating these relationships also connects to a longstanding conversation in which fairy tales have historically been a testing ground for questions swirling around the discipline of folklore about the relationship between oral, literary, and media forms, the nature of the folk, and the meaning of authenticity (Darnton 2009; Foster and Tolbert 2015). In much of Western culture repetition obscures the origins of folk narratives, which then become common property. As such, they need not be explicitly marked like recursive literary texts. Indeed, the Romantic conception of art and folklore is in direct opposition; folk narratives' value resides precisely in their lack of originality, that is, their status as survivals from an earlier age. These hierarchies of value downplay or disparage repetition and recursivity in literature as unoriginal and innovation in folk narrative as inauthentic (Bendix 1997; Tosenberger 2014).

Yet, while folktales' and fairy tales' status as allegedly authentic relics of pre-industrial traditional culture devalues them in comparison to high culture, it also rhetorically elevates and protects them from a much more pernicious force: the capitalist market. This tripartite system of cultural value thus rhetorically constructs one compromised and two "pure positions" (Clifford 1988) from which culture may be produced in the modern world: the market is opposed both to high culture, focused on unmarketably exclusive audiences, and to folk culture, with its demonstrable lineage connected to the pre-capitalist past and an artisan mentality that evades mass reproduction. Like salvage anthropology, which sought to document cultures untouched by modernity, such an approach for storytelling similarly inspires a salvage mentality, seeking to preserve any authentic expressions of folk culture before the influence of global mass media taints everything: what Barbara Kirshenblatt-Gimblett calls "eleventh hour" folklore scholarship (1998, 300). Thus J. Barre Toelken likewise notes that traditional folklorists "concerned themselves with the recording and study of customs, ideas, and expressions that were thought to be survivals of ancient cultural systems still existing in the modern world" (1979, 4). Faye Ginsburg and Fred Meyers note the unfairness and impracticality of basing authenticity on a stagnant definition of culture and argue for forms of storytelling about Aboriginal futures in a variety of technologies and media, accessing a hybrid intercultural space in which Native people often re-appropriate Western archival material and culture to create new critical meanings (2006). Their work points toward many forms of collage art, like fan fiction, that play at the juncture between cultural registers and trouble understandings of authenticity and genuine popular expression.

Fairy tales frequently become associated with particularly resonant and well-known versions, such as those by Disney or the Grimm brothers; yet even so, their strongest characteristic is a lack of any completely fixed form and a proliferation throughout culture in multiple media, described by Cristina Bacchilega as a "fairy tale web" (2013). Fan fiction likewise defines itself as a way to take familiar story elements and ask "what if?" How would the story be different if it continued, or were set in coffee shop, or all the characters were actually androids? The transformations, for fairy-tale stories and fan fiction stories, are as limitless as the storytellers' imaginations. Both also play across cultural registers, appearing in a variety of media and borrowing from high and low culture alike. Fairy-tale themes appear in the most revered forms of painting and literature, and although fan fiction is known almost exclusively for appropriating popular texts, fan fiction stories also exist for an almost limitless number of sources, including high-culture objects like Jane Austen (Steenhuyse 2011). Thus within the fairy-tale web, and within fan fiction, cultural artifacts from all across the spectrum intermingle.

Yet the repetitive nature of fairy-tale themes in Western culture, especially mass culture, and fans' consistent rereading of the same characters and situations with minor variations can sound less like populist freedom and the authentic culture of the people and more like the result of the market's cultural homogenization. Many theorists and critics following Frankfurt School scholars have argued that the mass media's reliance on formula and cliché are politically and aesthetically dangerous. For T. W. Adorno repetition lulls audiences into complacency through the pleasurable comfort of familiarity (Adorno and Horkheimer 1944). Such arguments have not been kind to the creative cultures and pleasures of women or minorities and would deride fan fiction as merely market-oriented false consciousness. This position has been critiqued from a number of fronts, with many questioning Adorno's entrenchment of elitist standards of cultural value, which associate literary and artistic accomplishment with the works preferred by wealthy Western men and deny the complexity and expressivity of art associated with historically oppressed people, including jazz and melodrama (Bourdieu 1984; Hall 1981). Similarly, others note that those who emphasize popular culture's reliance on repetition and formula underestimate the extent to which high-art objects like the plays of Shakespeare, for example, also rely on extensive borrowing from, and intertextuality with, a long history of other works. As a form of recursive literature, similar to the fairy tale, and as a women's writing community, fan fiction frequently comes under attack as inferior to original literature, due to its borrowing from published works, and inferior to folk creativity, due to its intimate imbrications with popular culture. That it primarily serves the pleasures of women, and forms the basis of relationships between women, only reaffirms its cultural status; yet these elements are precisely also why unique forms of aesthetic and political experimentation may also arise in fan fiction and via the language of fairy-tale tropes (Coppa 2008, 2011; Coppa and Tushnet 2011).

Perhaps contrary to expectations, the supposedly stultifying space of repetition can also become the space of critique. For many queer theorists drawing upon Michel Foucault, including Judith Butler and Judith/Jack Halberstam, it is in the moment that cultural norms and hierarchies must be translated into living bodies and repeatedly woven into the fabric of everyday life that individual people have the greatest agency and power to enact change (Halberstam 2011). As Butler argues, repetition is the moment when individuals may introduce variation, aberration, and dissonance into the system (1999). In Foucault's terms, these non-identical repetitions of social norms will not always become culturally meaningful. A revolution, according to Foucault (1978), and likewise Lauren Berlant (2011), is just a form of storytelling that narrates all these individual, often private instances of subversion, disruption, and failure into one unified public story about a "better good life." Psychoanalysis and cognitive psychology also invest in the potential therapeutic and liberatory power of narrative repetition (Johnson 1993). Analysis often seeks to transform the chaos of life into a coherent and affirmative story of self by narrating and renarrating events and emotions until arriving at a version that accommodates both the dictates of reality and the needs for self-esteem and agency. In remarkably similar language uniting the therapeutic and political models, Henry Jenkins described fan fiction as a way of "repairing the damage" wrought by living with the mass media and a culture of domination (2003). By repeating and renarrating mass media and collective forms of modern mythology, fan fiction authors intervene in the seemingly seamless process of cultural reproduction and thereby repair and re-envision damaging scripts by repeating them differently.

Fairy tales become especially fertile ground for this work because they form a shared cultural language that pre-exists modern mass media and cultural industries and thus offers a common cultural property that normalizes universal participation. Because the movement of fairy tales across media forms, cultural groups, and cultural registers throughout Bacchilega's "fairy tale web" began hundreds of years before the advent of mechanical reproduction and modern "transmedia storytelling," they manage to circulate widely without the limitations of copyright law (2013). Although certain versions of fairy tales become copyrighted property, and Disney has been especially aggressive in protecting its copyright claims (Hendenkamp 2002; Litman 1993; Sprigman 2002), fairy tales still offer a well-known, easily recognized set of tropes, characters, and iconography with which anyone may enter into an ongoing dialogue for the purpose of expression, critique, and community building.

These characteristics make fairy tales the epitome of what Jenkins, Sam Ford, and Joshua Green (2013) call a "spreadable" form: because nearly everyone recognizes fairy tales, new, independent, and amateur artists and authors can easily reach vast audiences by speaking their language, and cultural critiques can travel farther if enunciated through fairy-tale forms. This appears contrary to Jenkins's prognostications in *Convergence Culture*, wherein he argues that although participatory culture enables the involvement of more average people in the production of common culture, industrial mass-media products remain the touchstone around which amateur conversations and production are organized (2006); the participatory transmedia spreadability of fairy tales offers a different potential model of collective storytelling in the absence of one shared mass-media object, instead suggesting that participatory culture could include narrative worlds with their core content in the public domain, allowing both amateur and professional authors and artists to all add, critique, and collaborate with each other on more equal footing.

Fans Remix Fairy Tales

The open and collaborative nature of fairy-tale and fan fiction authorship means that numerous ideologies circulate under their aegeses, but both forms also support strong traditions of critique and counterculture. As an example, studying one point of intersection between fairy tales and fan fiction, the fairy-tale AU genre, can bring one particular tradition of critique based on gender and sexuality into focus. Although not all fairy tales include courtship plots, for feminist and queer artists, activists, authors, and academics, fairy tales have often become fruitful vehicles for intervention into modern mythologies about womanhood, marriage, reproduction, and heteropatriarchy. Indeed, these projects often overlap; as Vanessa Joosen (2011) has memorably demonstrated, the intertextuality of postmodern recursive fairy-tale retellings is also explicitly and implicitly in dialogue with fairy-tale scholarship, particularly well-known works of feminist scholarship such as that of Marsha P. Lieberman, Sandra Gilbert, and Susan Gubar. Bacchilega similarly argues that at this point in history, feminist critiques of fairy tales have gained enough cultural traction that most audience members can be expected to be aware that such critiques exist and to bring that awareness to their reading of any new fairy-tale text (2013). Thus, as demonstrated in the case studies that follow, fan fiction that borrows fairy-tale themes, specifically fairy-tale AUs, stages new versions as a form of repetition with a difference, and in so doing negotiates and critiques current conceptions of romance, sexuality, and gendered life.

The fan fiction site the Archive of Our Own currently contains 2,671 fairy-tale AU works, and authors and readers together collectively interpret and reinvent the form via several central themes (2015). Introducing erotic elements unearths long-acknowledged subtexts within fairy tales, allows readers the naughty pleasure of dirtying up stories associated with childhood, and enables a genre transposition, offering characters a new, magical means of addressing problems and inequalities. As I argue elsewhere, fairy tales, especially Disney versions, have become associated with idealism and lack of realism (Kustritz 2016). The phrase "this isn't a fairy tale" is often used to indicate this cultural value, suggesting that fairy tales are overly idealized and that what will follow contains a more grounded depiction of messy reality. Fan fiction fairy-tale AUs often serve as an interface for the collision between fantasy and reality by allowing fairy-tale story worlds and more realist story worlds to intersect. These links can provide opportunities to examine disparities between fantasy and material experience of cultural norms regarding romance, womanhood, motherhood, beauty, and goodness. Bringing together all these themes of eroticism, magic/wonder, and realism are stories addressing the happy ending. Chief among the reasons Disney versions of fairy tales promoted the preconception that fairy tales are not realistic is their inevitable happy ending of married, monogamous heterosexual privilege. This tendency has been roundly criticized on both feminist and queer grounds as enforcing marriage as the only welcome conclusion of a woman's life, making her story literally end in marriage, and silencing queer relationships and family structures (Kustritz 2003; Lee 2008; Stone 1975).

However, the feeling that once a fairy tale begins it will naturally and inevitably end in wedded bliss may also be turned to progressive political purposes when the couple (or threesome, or moresome) involved challenges dominant heteronormative assumptions. When the romantic couple or group (termed a "pairing") in a piece of fan fiction had little or no contact or were antagonistic in the source material, their romance may appear unlikely. However, when a pairing differs from cultural standards because of sexuality, age, class, deviation from beauty norms, and so on, some fan fiction authors may perceive that they had excellent screen chemistry, but dominant production codes for mass media made their romantic and erotic connection unlikely for structural reasons, whether due to cultural taboo or overt censorship. The fairy tale's ostensibly overwhelming momentum toward a happy ending can help overcome such cultural resistance. Once these characters are placed in a fairy-tale context, readers know the likely outcome. Getting to the happy ending thus requires rooting for this otherwise unlikely couple to overcome their differences and external social pressures so that they can be together and the story can arrive where many previous repetitions indicate is the correct point—with the couple together. Because audiences have seen this pattern repeated many times, the happy ending may feel like a satisfying return to a comfortably familiar place; however, by changing the players in this formula, an otherwise overwhelmingly heteronormative and patriarchal structure can serve very different ends, queering the fairy tale and the mass culture source material.

Two different fairy-tale AU versions of "Beauty and the Beast" (ATU 425C), with two very dissimilar couples, help demonstrate this effect. "Beauty and the Beast" by Imagineagreatadventure (2015) features a romance between Jaime Lannister and Brienne of Tarth from the dystopian quasi-medieval fantasy book and TV series *Game of Thrones* (2011–), while "The Beast" by Mangosong pairs *American Idol* singer contestants Adam Lambert and Kris Allen (2010). Imagineagreatadventure's version hews closely to the Disney version, which melds with the *Game of Thrones* story world as both include royalty, castles, and magic. The plot follows tightly as well, with Brienne's love transforming arrogant Jaime back from beast to prince. However, although she is called Brienne the Beauty in the *Game of Thrones* books (2005), the name sarcastically disparages her ugliness, and unlike Beauty, Brienne is more likely to be found sword fighting than reading. The "Beauty and the Beast" framework introduces romance into the book's friendship between Jaime and Brienne, but also challenges expectations about beauty standards, leading the audience to a happy ending involving a union between a tall, muscular, ugly woman and a golden, beautiful man—once their love breaks the curse, of course.

In Mangosong's "The Beast," the fairy-tale happy ending lends magical power to naturalizing same-sex attraction and relationships, as well as challenging fat phobia and, like Imagineagreatadventure's story, questioning dominant beauty standards. "The Beast," set in modern LA, depicts an Adam Lambert who never auditioned for *American Idol*. Insulting the wrong fan transforms him into his high school body, before weight loss and hair dye catapulted him into the cabaret and theater scene. He then has one year to find love and accept his body or the transformation will become permanent. Struggling musician Kris Allen becomes Adam's roommate, not his prisoner, and as Adam begins to accept his new-old body, they fall in love. Coming out, bashing, homophobia, body dysmorphia, poverty, and economics of the modern music industry are framed within a fairy-tale plot that pulls the audience toward the inevitable conclusion that Adam and Kris are meant for each other and should be happy together forever.

In both instances, the happy ending—in other circumstances one of the fairy tale's most conservative elements—becomes a tool for social critique, repeating the trope with players who challenge dominant assumptions about who deserves love and which kinds of relationships merit a blissful ever after. Fairy tales' pre-established momentum toward happy couple-dom structurally positions the audience in solidarity with pairs otherwise unthinkable in modern mass media: a physically imposing woman and a beautiful man, and a flamboyantly gay, overweight cabaret singer and his Southern, Christian roommate. Thus in these cases, the familiarity of fairy-tale romantic plots and happy endings helps naturalize non-normative sexual practices, pairings, and identities while simultaneously queering pop culture and the fairy tale.

Collective Authorship and Open Texts in Fan Fiction and Fairy-Tale Traditions

Fan fiction and fairy tales share similar origins, cultural tensions, narrative structures, and contemporary cultures of production. Stories that explicitly hybridize the two genres offer a fruitful space for studying current popular storytelling and its potential for addressing and representing average people's needs, desires, and critiques of modern life (Kustritz 2016). Both fan fiction and fairy tales are culturally marked by their association with women, courtship, repetition, and anonymous and collective authorship. Yet their origin in collective storytelling, especially among communities of women, opens a radical space for alternative forms of storytelling while cycles of narrative repetition in both genres create a shared symbolic language through which anyone can communicate with a potentially broad audience. Fan fiction stories that draw on fairy-tale tropes and traditions thus often mobilize repetition with a difference to make the familiar strange or to use genre conventions like the happy ending in the service of redefining cultural norms and ideals. Thus despite dour prognostications, repetition and romance can become spaces of radical queer possibility, and even forms of storytelling as shot through with mass culture complicity as fan fiction and the fairy tale can become vehicles for folk creativity, expression, and critique.

Related topics: Adaptation and the Fairy-Tale Web; Convergence Culture; Fandom/Fan Cultures; Fantasy; Fat Studies; Gender; Indigeneity; Intellectual Property; Romance; Sexualities/ Queer and Trans Studies; Storytelling

References Cited and Further Reading

Adorno, Theodor W., and Max Horkheimer. (1944) 2007. *Dialectic of Enlightenment*. Palo Alto, CA: Stanford UP.

Bacchilega, Cristina. 2013. *Fairy Tales Transformed?: Twenty-First Century Adaptations and the Politics of Wonder*. Detroit: Wayne State UP.

Bendix, Regina. 1997. *In Search of Authenticity: The Formation of Folklore Studies*. Madison: Wisconsin UP.

Berlant, Lauren. 2011. *Cruel Optimism*. Durham, NC: Duke UP.

Bourdieu, Pierre. 1984. *Distinction: A Social Critique of the Judgment of Taste*. Cambridge, MA: Harvard UP.

Butler, Judith. 1999. *Gender Trouble: Feminism and the Subversion of Identity*. New York: Routledge.

Clifford, James. 1988. *The Predicament of Culture: Twentieth-Century Ethnography, Literature, and Art*. Cambridge, MA: Harvard UP.

Coppa, Francesca. 2006. "A Brief History of Media Fandom." In *Fan Fiction and Fan Communities in the Age of the Internet: New Essays*, edited by Karen Hellekson and Kristina Busse, 41–59. Jefferson, NC: McFarland.

———. 2008. "Women, *Star Trek*, and the Early Development of Fannish Vidding." *Transformative Works and Cultures* 1.

———. 2011. "An Editing Room of One's Own: Vidding as Women's Work." *Camera Obscura* 26 (2): 123–30.

Coppa, Francesca, and Rebecca Tushnet. 2011. "How to Suppress Women's Remix." *Camera Obscura* 26: 131–8.

Darnton, Robert. 2009. *The Great Cat Massacre: And Other Episodes in French Cultural History*. New York: Basic Books.

Foster, Michael Dylan, and Jeffrey Tolbert. 2015. *The Folkloresque: Reframing Folklore in a Popular Culture World*. Boulder, CO: Utah UP.

Foucault, Michel. 1978. *History of Sexuality*. Vol. 1. New York: Pantheon Books.

Ginsburg, Faye, and Fred Meyers. 2006. "History of Aboriginal Futures." *Critique of Anthropology* 26 (1): 27–45.

Halberstam, Jack/Judith. 2011. *The Queer Art of Failure.* Durham, NC: Duke UP.

Hall, Stuart. 1981. "Notes on Deconstructing the Popular." In *People's History and Socialist Theory*, edited by Raphael Samuel, 227–40. London: Routledge.

Hendenkamp, Douglas A. 2002. "Free Mickey Mouse: Copyright Notice, Derivative Works, and the Copyright Act of 1909." *Virginia Sports & Entertainment Law Journal* 2: 254.

Jenkins, Henry. 1992. *Textual Poachers: Television Fans and Participatory Culture.* New York: Routledge.

———. 2003. "Quentin Tarantino's Star Wars?: Digital Cinema, Media Convergence and Participatory Culture." In *Rethinking Media Change*, edited by David Thorburn and Henry Jenkins, 281–314. Cambridge: MIT P.

———. 2006. *Convergence Culture.* New York: NYU P.

Jenkins, Henry, Sam Ford, and Joshua Green. 2013. *Spreadable Media: Creating Value and Meaning in a Networked Culture.* New York: NYU P.

Johnson, Mark. 1993. "The Narrative Context of Self and Action." In *Moral Imagination: Implications of Cognitive Science for Ethics*, 150–84. Chicago: U Chicago UP.

Joosen, Vanessa. 2011. *Critical and Creative Perspectives on Fairy Tales: An Intertextual Dialogue between Fairy-Tale Scholarship and Postmodern Retellings.* Detroit: Wayne State UP.

Kirshenblatt-Gimblett, Barbara. 1998. "Folklore's Crisis." *Journal of American Folklore* 111: 281–327.

Kustritz, Anne. 2003. "Slashing the Romance Narrative." *The Journal of American Culture* 6: 371–84.

———. 2016. "'They All Lived Happily Ever After Obviously': Realism and Utopia in Game of Thrones-Based Alternate Universe Fairy Tale Fan Fiction." *Humanities* 5 (2): 43.

Lee, Linda. 2008. "Guilty Pleasures: Reading Romance Novels as Reworked Fairy Tales." *Marvels & Tales* 22: 52–66.

Litman, Jessica. 1993. "Mickey Mouse Emeritus: Character Protection and the Public Domain." *University of Miami Entertainment & Sports Law Review* 11: 429.

Martin, George R. R. 2005. *A Feast for Crows.* New York: Bantam Books.

Sprigman, Chris. 2002. "The Mouse That Ate the Public Domain: Disney, the Copyright Term Extension Act and Eldred v. Ashcroft." FindLaw. http://writ.news.findlaw.com/commentary/20020305_sprigman.html.

Steenhuyse, Veerle Van. 2011. "Jane Austen Fan Fiction and the Situated Fantext: The Example of Pamela Aidan's Fitzwilliam Darcy, Gentleman." *English Text Construction* 4 (2): 165–85.

Stone, Kay. 1975. "Things Walt Disney Never Told Us." *The Journal of American Folklore* 88: 42–50.

Toelken, J. Barre. 1979. *The Dynamics of Folklore.* Boston: Houghton Mifflin Co.

Tosenberger, Catherine. 2014. "Mature Poets Steal: Children's Literature and the Unpublishability of Fanfiction." *Children's Literature Association Quarterly* 39 (1): 4–27.

Mediagraphy

American Idol (TV). 2002–2016. Creator Simon Fuller. USA.

Archive of Our Own. 2015. "'Alternate Universe—Fairy Tale' Tag." http://archiveofourown.org/tags/Alternate%20Universe%20-%20Fairy%20Tale/works.

Game of Thrones (TV). 2011–. Creators David Benioff and D. B. Weiss. USA.

Imagineagreatadventure. 2015. *Beauty and the Beast.* Archive of Our Own.

Mangosong. 2010. *The Beast.* Livejournal.

57
FANTASY
Ming-Hsun Lin

Fantasy has become familiar to today's public. It can be seen anywhere—in books, on screen, in games, and on canvas. Fantasy, especially fairy-tale-adapted literature and film, appears to be an unstoppable trend that has come to dominate the media. The popularization of fantasy indicates its significant influence in modern society. One cannot ignore fantasy when examining modern values, current issues, and their hidden connotations. However, the question of "what is fantasy?" has proven to be tremendously difficult to answer.

Links to reality play an important role in the study of fantasy. By looking at different interpretations of *real* and *unreal* in academia, this chapter shows how fantasy should be viewed as a literary impulse instead of as a homogeneous genre. Modern fantasy, labeled as a commercial genre, has been dismissed by some writers and scholars as merely a marketable commodity, not serious literature. Nevertheless, fantasy film has generated new interest in fairy tales by adapting and twisting classic narratives and has arguably broken the stereotypes of fairy tales and enabled new approaches for future studies.

Definitions of Fantasy

Fantasy might at first appear to be broadly indistinguishable from fairy tale. Both embrace wonders such as castles in the air, dragons and fairies, magic and witchcraft. Marina Warner defines fairy tales as "familiar stories" that consist "above all of acts of imagination, conveyed in a symbolic Esperanto," stories with "certain kinds of characters" and "certain recurrent motifs" that would strike "recognition in the reader or listener's body at a visceral depth" (2014, xvi–xix). This definition suggests that the audience recognizes fairy tales by their specific plots, characters, symbols, and motifs. However, unlike fairy tale, fantasy does not consist of stories that have been repeatedly revised through time and become a specific corpus.

How, then, can we differentiate fantasy from fairy tale? The notion of reality is often used to distinguish one from the other. Maria Nikolajeva (2000) remarks that fairy tales "take place in one magical world, detached from our own both in space and in time" while "the initial setting of fantasy" (152), such as Oxford in *Alice's Adventures in Wonderland* (Carroll 1865) and Kansas in *The Wonderful Wizard of Oz* (Baum 1900), "is reality" (Nikolajeva 2000, 152). She also suggests that the reader is not supposed to believe fairy tales, as they are set in a detached world with a hero who is given an impossible quest; fantasy, in contrast, is more believable, as it often portrays an ordinary character as the hero, who is "just like you" (2008, 331). This schema is useful yet exclusionary as it is easy to find fantasy with an unfamiliar setting, such as *The Lord of the Rings* (Tolkien 1954–5) and *A Wizard of Earthsea* (Le Guin 1968). Furthermore, the detached world of fairy tale in a sense reflects reality, as fairy tales originate from folktales

515

that "came directly from common experiences and beliefs" and have been revised according to sociohistorical transformations through time (Zipes 1994, 10).

It is not precisely the realistic setting, but rather how the reader approaches the fantastic narrative, that differentiates fantasy from fairy tale. As Nikolajeva states, "The most profound difference between fantasy and fairy tale is the position of the reader/listener toward what is narrated" (2008, 331). Magic is considered as normal in fairy tale, and readers are expected to take wonders in fairy tale for granted. Retold and adapted, for example, by Charles Perrault, the Grimm Brothers, and Disney films, classic fairy tales have developed a stereotypical image of magic. Cristina Bacchilega highlights the Grimms' influence in making fairy tale's "hegemonic association" with magic, which is "normalized as the mysterious ways in which the world works to produce immediate gratification" (2013, 5).

Nikolajeva notes that fantasy is an "eclectic genre" as it acquires elements from mythology, horror, science fiction, and other literary genres, resulting in the appearance of "incompatible elements," like "pagan and Christian images," in a single work (2000, 151). Early studies by scholars like Pierre-Georges Castex, Marcel Schneider, Roger Caillois, and Louis Vax tend to define literary fantasy by categorizing its recurring themes (Jackson 2003, 5). Vax, for example, in *L'art et la litterature fantastiques* (1960) defines fantasy based on its subject matter as literature that contains all sorts of abnormality, including "werewolves; vampires [. . .] and human degeneration" (Hume 2014, 13).

Another common method of classifying fantasy is using the concept of the secondary world, an idea normalized by J.R.R. Tolkien's "On Fairy-Stories." The readers are inside the secondary world of the fantastic as long as they believe it is true. However, once "disbelief arises, the spell is broken," and they are "out in the Primary World again, looking at the little abortive Secondary World from outside" (Tolkien 1965, 36–37). Fantasy, hence, can be viewed as the narrative integrating the primary and the secondary worlds. This idea is incorporated by Brian Attebery, who compares literary works created by American writers with European fairy tales and views fantasy as literature that introduces a secondary world that implies a sense of history beyond the presented story (1980). Unlike fantasy, traditional fairy tale does not depict a secondary world apart from the reader's primary world. Consequently, there is no connection to reality in fairy tales.

The most influential critical works of fantasy are those that focus on the essence of fantasy and its relationship with reality; above all, Tzvetan Todorov's *The Fantastic*, first published in 1970, is acknowledged as changing the direction of fantasy studies. Basing his definition on the notion of ambiguity, Todorov views fantasy as hesitancy experienced by the reader when confronted by supernatural events in the story. If the reader decides that the laws of reality remain intact and a rational explanation (such as psychological disorder) could be applied to the supernatural event, the work belongs to the uncanny, but if the reader accepts the supernatural phenomena in the story as magic, the work becomes the marvelous. The supernatural elements of the gothic novels of Clara Reeves and Ann Radcliffe are categorized as uncanny (Todorov 1975, 41), while the magic in fairy tales is considered as marvelous. For Todorov, the fantastic can only exist through the experience of hesitation, and once the story ends, the fantastic disappears.

Examining the psychological features of the fantastic, Rosemary Jackson further views fantasy as narrative that pulls "the reader from the apparent familiarity and security of the known and everyday world into something more strange" where "what is being seen and recorded as 'real' is constantly in question" (2003, 34). Similarly, Christine Brooke-Rose points out that the reader needs to define reality and examine the fantastic narrative on literal, allegorical, and moral levels (1983, 55–71). Fantasy, as Irène Bessière points out, is defined by reality instead of anti-rationality (1974). Consequently, "contradictions surface and are held anti-nomically in the fantastic text, as reason is made to confront all that it traditionally refuses to encounter" (Jackson 2003, 21). The nature of fantastic narrative is oxymoronic: it is the narrative that "plays the game of the impossible [. . .] it is the narrative result of transforming the condition contrary to fact into 'fact' itself" (Irwin 1976, 4).

Contemporary studies strive to provide a more inclusive definition of fantasy. Lucie Armitt highlights the need to liberate fantasy from the ghetto of genres (1996, 3), Kathryn Hume speaks of fantasy as "any departure from consensus reality" (2014, 21), and Jackson has gone so far as to claim that "all imaginary activity is fantastic, all literary works are fantasies" (2003, 13). Fantasy should not be viewed as a homogeneous genre or an exclusive form, but rather an urge created by human desire and social need. Hume eloquently argues that fantasy is an "impulse"—"the desire to change givens and alter reality—out of boredom, play, vision, longing for something lacking, or need for metaphoric images" (2014, 8, 20). Instead of constructing fantasy as a homogeneous genre, academics turn the focus of study to the theoretical connotations, social functions, and literary implications of fantasy. Among these, two of the main reoccurring notions, utopia and subversion, are applicable not only to fantasy but also to fairy tales.

Both fantasy and fairy tale are believed to depict utopia and fulfill utopian wishes through fantastic narrative. Armitt, for example, applies what Louis Marin views as utopia (1993, 411), "a vista onto unknowable promise," to the fantastic narrative and notes that fantasy can give the reader "a greater freedom from that overdetermination to order, organize, and package the chaotic set of experiences we call 'real life' than classical literary realism can" (Armitt 2005, 3–4). Similar ideas can be found in fairy-tale studies. Zipes points out that both Ernst Bloch and Tolkien use fairy tales to manifest "utopian visions of better worlds which human beings are capable of realizing" (2002, 149).

The utopian world in fantasy and fairy tale does not only offer escapism, but also the power of subversion. The power of subversion comes from the utopian function, which contains the "subversive element of revolutionary hope" and a common quest against "the same dragon of dehumanization" (Zipes 2002, 150). By making the unseen visible and addressing the inarticulate through metaphorical representation, fantasy and fairy tale give readers the chance to reflect, destroy, and reconstruct the norms and orders that cannot easily be violated in the real world. The fantastic narrative can "tell of, manifest or show desire" or "expel desire" and further can reveal "disorder" and "illegality" that are "outside dominant value systems" (Jackson 2003, 3–4). By questioning the boundary of the real and the normative, the limits of society are also challenged.

Fantasy in the Film Industry

Fantasy has been interpreted differently in the film industry. David Butler elucidates the changing meaning of the term and notes that before fantasy became a cinematic genre, the film industry viewed fantasy as a filmic technique and used it to indicate either fantasy violence or wonder (2009, 29–41). Once again, fantasy is considered as something unreal and less credible, resulting in the idea of fantasy violence as more appropriate screen violence for all ages, as it appears in a non-realistic setting and is thus considered less authentic by the film industry.

Fantasy is also recognized in Britain as an element of "wonder film"—a cinematic category containing spectacular effects that awed audiences in the 1920s and 1930s (Butler 2009, 34–36). Films like *The Thief of Bagdad* (1940) and *King Kong* (1933) are representative examples. Butler emphasizes that the term "wonder film" "seems to have been applied in relation to audience reaction—audiences, quite literally, wondered how these spectacles were achieved" (2009, 35).

The term "wonder" also refers to the elements and motifs of magic in the cinematic narrative, which are employed by fantasy and fairy-tale films. Jessica Tiffin notes: "fantasy films share with fairy tales not only the quest motif, but a continuing delight in the ability of cinema to visually embody the magical" (2016, 348). The global successes of Hollywood blockbusters *The Lord of the Rings* trilogy (2001–2003) and the *Harry Potter* series (2001–2011), Chinese kung-fu films like *Wo Hu Cang Long* (2000) and modern fairy-tale adaptations such as *Mei Ren Yu* (2016), and Japanese folkloric film adaptations by Miyazaki Hayao are evidence that fantasy has become a dominant cinematic genre today.

However, like its literary counterpart, fantasy film has been trivialized by the mainstream film industry for a long time. Both the film industry and critics have tended to deprecate fantasy by prioritizing other cinematic elements. For instance, *The Wizard of Oz* (1939) was advertised as a "Technicolor musical fantasy" (*Wizard of Oz* Pressbook 1939). As Butler states, there is "a sense in many contemporary reviews that fantasy is not something to be over-indulged," and the consequence of this notion is the marginalization of fantasy film, despite its popularity in the market, which has been underestimated by the film industry (2009, 36–37). This devaluation of fantasy film is due to a deep-rooted belief that fantasy is inferior to realistic mimesis, which is further reflected in the religious and genre-related criticisms of fantasy that remain contentious today.

Fantasy and Christianity

The debate between Christianity and fantasy is one of the most discussed and controversial issues of modern fantasy. Fantasy and Christianity share the same origin: the Old Testament. "Writings of the gods typically employ narrative modes," as Armitt points out, which could be called "fantasy" (2005, 13). However, although the Old Testament is full of fantastic elements, it "insists on realism, almost to the exclusion of any other mode of writing" (Armitt 2005, 14), and "Fathers of the Church developed a rhetoric of rejection that debarred" fantasy that depicts fantastic creatures and pagan faiths (Hume 2014, 6).

This focus remains a formidable feature of current Christianity and generates further debates in relation to modern fantasy. Philip Pullman's *His Dark Materials* trilogy (1995–2000) has been condemned as "a secular humanist attack on institutionalized religion" for its depiction of angels and hell and its ontology (Munt 2008, 198). J. K. Rowling's *Harry Potter* series (1997–2007) has been banned by several Christian schools around the world and was opposed by Pope Benedict XVI (2005) for its portrayal of sorcery and witchcraft.

Nevertheless, Christianity has also enabled the writing of works like C. S. Lewis's *The Chronicles of Narnia* (1950–6) and J.R.R. Tolkien's *The Lord of the Rings* (1954–5). Tolkien, "a devout Roman Catholic" (Carpenter 2000, 99), defines fantasy as a "natural human activity" that "does not seek delusion nor bewitchment and domination" (Tolkien 1966, 53). For Tolkien, fantasy can take the reader closer to the celestial creations that are not allowed or visible in mimetic works. Pullman also arguably uses fantasy as a subversive force to sanitize Christianity, and his fiction can be viewed as "a purification of false and idolatrous belief" (Kirwan 2015, 26). Fantasy can be an imaginary creation detached from reality or the embodiment of reality in an alternative world. It can be an attack on orthodoxies or a subversive force that reflects the desire to improve them.

Unlike fantasy, fairy tale is often criticized for the heavy Christian influence on its revisions. Zipes points out that the Grimm Brothers deleted "erotic and sexual elements" and inserted

Christian references according to the "patriarchal code of that time" (2003, xxxii). Interestingly, the paradoxical essence of fantasy in relation to Christianity can also be found in fairy tale, which is both conventional and subversive. On the one hand, fairy tale was often changed for children "to reinforce dominant religious and patriarchal attitudes about gender, mating, law, and order"; on the other hand, the magical narrative in fairy tale may give young readers "wild ideas" that their lives need not be governed by the "norms of society" (Zipes 2012, xi).

Fantasy as a Commercial Genre

Although the history of fantasy spans thousands of years, most studies of fantasy have appeared within the past two hundred. This dramatic development might be due to the phenomenon of marketing fantasy as a genre that began in the late nineteenth century. Brian Stableford notes that although fantasy should be considered "as old as literature" (2009, xliv), magic before the eighteenth century tended to mix supernatural elements with naturalistic ones, and what is considered modern fantasy "became firmly established as the label for a popular commercial genre of adult fiction in the 1970s" (xli).

When considering the thriving interest in fantastic writing, fairy tale, which has a long pedigree and a global presence, plays a crucial role. The rise of French fairy tale from the late seventeenth to the early eighteenth centuries built the first massive "corpus of tales," while Germany from the late eighteenth to the early nineteenth centuries further created collections by the Grimm brothers and kindled scholarly interest in the field (Haase 2008, xxxiii). However, it was also around the late nineteenth century when fairy tale became "firmly entrenched as children's literature" (Ashley 2010, vii). While fairy tales were reworked by writers like George MacDonald, praised by Colin Manlove as "the founder of much modern fantasy" (1994, 83), publishers endeavored to label works involving magic and heroic tales with the name "fantasy." Examining issues of the Ballantine Adult Fantasy Series, Jamie Williamson highlights the fact that fantasy abruptly appeared as a commercial genre because of the surge of interest in sword and sorcery (or heroic fantasy) in the early 1960s and the success of Tolkien's *The Lord of the Rings* on the market (2015, 1–7).

The thriving publication of fantasy, from Tolkien's books about Middle Earth, to Le Guin's *Earthsea* (1968–2001), William Goldman's *The Princess Bride* (1973), Terry Pratchett's *The Colour of Magic* (1983), George R. R. Martin's *A Song of Ice and Fire* (1996–2011), J. K. Rowling's *Harry Potter* (1997–2007), and others seems to show that fantasy is a rising force that cannot be stopped. Tom Shippey views fantasy literature as the "dominant literary mode of the twentieth century" and claims that "[b]y the end of the century, even authors deeply committed to the realist novel have often found themselves unable to resist the gravitational pull of the fantastic" (2000, vii–viii). Nevertheless, its massive commercial success has become both the crown and the shackle of fantasy. There is a constant uncertainty as to whether fantasy can be taken seriously or if it is merely a passing craze.

Fairy-Tale Fantasy Films: Where Do We Go From Here?

Fantasy film has walked a similar path as its literary coequal. Butler points out that "the film industry has followed in the footsteps of its counterpart in publishing" (2009, 41). "Since the late 1970s," as Ian Hunter notes, "the dominant genre of Hollywood blockbusters has been fantasy" (2007, 154). During the 1980s and 1990s, fantasy films fused with science fiction, such as the *Terminator* series (1984–2003) and *The Matrix* trilogy (1999–2003), were extremely popular, but the great success of *The Lord of the Rings* and the *Harry Potter* films since 2001 officially introduced the era of contemporary fantasy films, reflecting "a global hunger for fantasy" (Napier 2005, xi).

Its commercial success has also changed the target audience and story choice of fantasy films. There have been increasing numbers of fantasy films that have been adapted from children's literature in recent years, including: *Hauru no Ugoku Shiro* (*Howl's Moving Castle*) (2004), *The Chronicles of Narnia: The Lion, the Witch and the Wardrobe* (2005), *Gedo Senki* (*Tales from Earthsea*) (2006), *Stardust* (2007), *City of Ember* (2008), *Where the Wild Things Are* (2009), *Alice in Wonderland* (2010), *Hugo* (2011), *The Hunger Games* (2012), *Oz the Great and Powerful* (2013), *The Giver* (2014), and *Pan* (2015). Making a blockbuster fantasy film is expensive, and it is safer to use stories from successful pre-existing works. "A best-selling book may reach a million readers," Linda Hutcheon underlines, "but a movie or television adaptation will find an audience of many million more" (2013, 5). It is likely that more and more films are being adapted from fairy tales because they are well-known by both children and adults.

Despite fantasy's seeming departure from traditional fairy tale in the late nineteenth century, the two have never ceased to influence each other. Fantasy has played a significant role in reshaping the perception of magic in fairy tale. One of the methods authors often use when reworking a classic fairy tale is to change the nature of magic in the story: for example, the talking wolf from "Little Red Riding Hood" (ATU 333) is replaced by werewolves in Angela Carter's "The Company of Wolves" (1979). In Marissa Meyer's *Cinder* (2012), magic is transformed into technology, and Cinderella has become a cyborg in futuristic China. This retelling of fairy tale fused with fantastic elements has established a broad readership. Meanwhile, as Zipes notes, fairy-tale film adaptations have further generated a mass-media frenzy since the late twentieth century (2016, 6). The International Movie Database (IMDb) lists more than two hundred fairy-tale-related films, short movies, and television series that have been released under the label of fantasy since 2001. Notable examples are the *Shrek* fairy tale parodies (2001–2010), Hayao Miyazaki's Japanese adaptations such as *Sen to Chihiro no Kamikakushi* (*Spirited Away*) (2001), the award-winning *Pan's Labyrinth* (2006), blockbuster productions like *Enchanted* (2007), *Mirror Mirror* (2012), *Snow White and the Huntsman* (2012), *Jack the Giant Slayer* (2013), *Maleficent* (2014), *Into the Woods* (2014), *Cinderella* (2015), and the popular television series *Once Upon a Time* (2011–) and *Grimm* (2011–2017), to name but a few. While not all have been box office successes, fairy-tale fantasy films have flourished. Jen Bowden called 2012 the "year of the fairy tale blockbuster" (2012), and Molly Driscoll wondered three years later whether "anything [could] stop the fairy tale movie trend" (2015).

Popular interest in fairy tales has grown; nevertheless, some are concerned about the cultural connotations of this trend. Graeme McMillan points out that pop culture tends to "infantilize the audience"; since the market has "reached its zenith with Hollywood's reliance on superheroes," it may not be far-fetched to "draw parallels between the mainstreaming of superheroes and the apparent mainstreaming of fairy tales" (2012). McMillan explains the potential appeal of fairy tale for popular culture:

> First, they're firmly in the fantasy genre, and so provide a particularly successful kind of eye-candy-esque escapism [. . .] But what fairy tales have as a sub-genre that potentially gives them an edge over superheroes or Star Trek revivals is that they theoretically appeal to both genders equally thanks to the female leads and focus of the story and the male-centric appeal of violence, special effect spectacle and action.
>
> (2012)

Dazzling special effects, heroine-oriented plots, and familiar stories with violent action scenes seem to be the formula for success, the inference being that gender issues and twisted adaptations have become dominant in the most recent fairy-tale films. *Mirror Mirror* (2012), for instance, depicts the female rivalry and vanity generated by patriarchal values and focuses on the competition between Snow White and the Queen. *Snow White and the Huntsman* (2012), on the other hand, presents female suppression and enhancement through the heroine's quest.

Considering the target audience of fairy tale is children, the tone of most modern fairy-tale films is surprisingly darker than their literary versions. Some believe such adaptations allow the audience to explore authentic themes in fairy tale that were omitted or refined by the Grimms. For example, Andreea Șerban argues that the film *Red Riding Hood* (2011), with its twisted plot about adultery, werewolves, and supernatural inheritance, includes "references to domestic violence, youthful sexuality, incest and cannibalism, all of which featured in the oral tale of Red Riding Hood [. . .] [and touches] on issues that male writers (like the Grimms) deleted" (Șerban 2012, 130). Zipes, however, in reply to Emma Mustich's question "Are dark fairy tales more authentic?", dismisses the authenticity of such adaptations and looks instead at the economic influence: "They're trying to titillate you, to say that this is going to be the film that will expose the deep darkness, the profound darkness of these tales," Zipes says. "Hollywood, for the most part, has not really taken fairy tale seriously" (quoted in Mustich 2011). Kristiana Willsey also points out that the "rise of dark fairy tales" cannot be a return to authenticity, as "such purification projects are (at best) futile and (at worst) bad faith"; instead, one should note that "authentic remains a highly charged and marketable word" in this "fairy tale-saturated market" (2014, 225).

Certainly the fantasy trend has not only increased the public's interest in fairy tale, but has also invited discussion and debates around its value. Katherine Fowkes explains that fantasy films appealing to mature tastes cannot attract "the large youth demographic essential for recouping costs," yet those targeting only young audiences "won't be made unless [they are] relatively inexpensive" (2010, 33). Fairy-tale films with a darker tone might be made under such economic concerns, so as to appeal to both young and adult audiences. Zipes, however, believes that the "hundred different kinds of fairy-tale films produced in the twenty-first century [are a response to] the utopian longing of audiences" who fear the deluge of relentless changes (2016, 6). The unsettling tone of film adaptations, hence, could be seen as a reflection of modern anxiety. Either driven by economic concerns or cinematic values, the film industry is endeavoring to break with the stereotypes of classic fairy tales. Even Disney has tried to break its own magic spell by reworking its animation. Fantasy, consequently, has opened the door for the public to view fairy tales from a relatively novel viewpoint, instead of just as naive bedtime stories for children.

Fantasy exists as a literary impulse and a human desire that longs to understand, challenge, and better the normative reality. It is hard to tell if the enthusiasm for fantasy will continue or become just a passing craze. However, to some degree, fantasy has subverted the traditional values and perceptions of the world, especially the one in fairy tales. Whether or not it is merely commercial propaganda, the reinterpreted magic and so-called hidden truth behind the familiar stories in contemporary fairy-tale films have built a connection between the detached magical world and reality and have further linked traditional fairy tales with the world today. Because of that, fairy tale has never been closer to us.

Related topics: Adaptation and the Fairy-Tale Web; Anime and Manga; Children's and Young Adult (YA) Literature; Cinematic; Cinema Science Fiction; Gender; Musicals; Romance

References Cited and Further Reading

Armitt, Lucie. 1996. *Theorizing the Fantastic*. London: Arnold.

———. 2005. *Fantasy Fiction: An Introduction*. New York: Continuum.

Ashley, Mike. 2010. "Preface." In *Dreams and Wonder: Stories from the Dawn of Modern Fantasy*, edited by Mike Ashley, v–viii. Mineola: Dover Publications.

Attebery, Brian. 1980. *The Fantasy Tradition in American Literature: From Irving to Le Guin*. Bloomington: Indiana UP.

Bacchilega, Cristina. 2013. *Fairy Tales Transformed?: Twenty-First-Century Adaptations and the Politics of Wonder*. Detroit: Wayne State UP.

Baum, L. Frank. 1900. *The Wonderful Wizard of Oz*. Chicago: George M. Hill.

Bessière, Irène. 1974. *Le Récit Fantastique: La Poétique de l'incertain*. Paris: Larousse.

Bowden, Jen. 2012. "2012: The Year of the Fairy Tale Blockbuster." *Listfilm*, April 26. https://film.list.co.uk/article/41844-2012-the-year-of-the-fairy tale-blockbuster/.

Brooke-Rose, Christine. 1983. *A Rhetoric of the Unreal: Studies in Narrative and Structure, Especially of the Fantastic*. Cambridge: Cambridge UP.

Butler, David. 2009. *Fantasy Cinema: Impossible Worlds on Screen*. London: Wallflower.

Carpenter, Humphrey. 2000. *J. R. R. Tolkien: A Biography*. Boston: Houghton Mifflin Co.

Carroll, Lewis. 1865. *Alice's Adventures in Wonderland*. London: Macmillan.

Carter, Angela. 1979. "The Company of Wolves." In *The Bloody Chamber and Other Stories*, 110–18. London: Vintage.

Driscoll, Molly. 2015. "'Cinderella': Can Anything Stop the Fairy Tale Trend?" *The Christian Science Monitor*, March 2. www.csmonitor.com/The-Culture/Culture-Cafe/2015/0312/Cinderella-Can-anything-stop-the-fairy-tale-movie-trend.

Fowkes, Katherine. 2010. *The Fantasy Film*. West Sussex: Wiley-Blackwell.

Goldman, William. 1973. *The Princess Bride*. New York: Harcourt Brace Jovanovich.

Greenhill, Pauline, and Sidney Eve Matrix, eds. 2010. *Fairy Tale Films: Visions of Ambiguity*. Logan: Utah State UP.

Haase, Donald. 2008. "Introduction." In *The Greenwood Encyclopedia of Folktales and Fairy Tales*, edited by Donald Haase, xxxiii–xxxix. Vol. 1. Westport. CN: Greenwood P.

Hume, Kathryn. 2014. *Fantasy and Mimesis (Routledge Revivals): Responses to Reality in Western Literature*. Oxford: Routledge.

Hunter, Ian. 2007. "Post-Classical Fantasy Cinema: The Lord of the Rings." In *The Cambridge Companion to Literature on Screen*, edited by Deborah Cartmell and Imelda Whelehan, 154–66. Cambridge: Cambridge UP.

Hutcheon, Linda. 2013. *A Theory of Adaptation*. 2nd ed. Oxford: Routledge.

Irwin, William Robert. 1976. *The Game of the Impossible: A Rhetoric of Fantasy*. Urbana: U Illinois P.

Jackson, Rosemary. 2003. *Fantasy: The Literature of Subversion*. London: Routledge.

Kirwan, Michael. 2015. "Theology and Literature in the English-Speaking World." In *Poetry and the Religious Imagination: The Power of the Word*, edited by Francesca Bugliani Knox and David Lonsdale, 9–30. Farnham: Ashgate.

Le Guin, Ursula. 1968. *A Wizard of Earthsea*. New York: Parnassus P.

———. 1971. *The Tombs of Atuan*. New York: Atheneum.

———. 1972. *The Farthest Shore*. New York: Atheneum.

———. 1990. *Tehanu: The Last Book of Earthsea*. New York: Atheneum.

———. 2001a. *The Other Wind*. New York: Harcourt.

———. 2001b. *Tales from Earthsea*. New York: Harcourt.

Lewis, C. S. 1950–1956. *The Chronicles of Narnia* (Series). New York: HarperCollins.

Manlove, Colin. 1994. *Scottish Fantasy Literature: A Critical Survey*. Edinburgh: Canongate Academic.

Marin, Louis. 1993. "Frontiers of Utopia: Past and Present." *Critical Inquiry* 19 (3): 397–420.

Martin, George R. R. 1996–2011. *A Song of Fire and Ice* (Series). New York: Bantam Books.

McMillan, Graeme. 2012. "Another Bite of the Poisoned Apple: Why Does Pop Culture Love Fairy Tales Again?" *Time*, May 30. http://entertainment.time.com/2012/05/30/another-bite-of-the-poisoned-apple-why-does-pop-culture-love-fairy-tales-again/.

Meyer, Marissa. 2012. *Cinder (The Lunar Chronicles)*. New York: Feiwel and Friends.

Munt, Sally. 2008. *Queer Attachments: The Cultural Politics of Shame*. Aldershot: Ashgate.

Mustich, Emma. 2011. "Are Dark Fairy Tales More Authentic?" *Salon*, August 20. www.salon.com/2011/08/20/fairy_tale_movies/.

Napier, Susan. 2005. *Anime from Akira to Howl's Moving Castle: Experiencing Contemporary Japanese Animation*. New York: Palgrave.

Nikolajeva, Maria. 2000. "Fantasy Literature and Fairy Tales." In *The Oxford Companion to Fairy Tales*, edited by Jack Zipes, 150–4. Oxford: Oxford UP.

FANTASY

———. 2008. "Fantasy." In *The Greenwood Encyclopedia of Folktales and Fairy Tales*, edited by Donald Haase, 329–34. Vol. 1. Westport: Greenwood P.

"Pope Benedict Opposes Harry Potter Novels." 2005. *Life Site News*, June 27. www.lifesitenews.com/news/pope-benedict-opposes-harry-potter-novels.

Pratchett, Terry. 1983. *The Colour of Magic*. Gerrards Cross: Colin Smythe.

Pullman, Philip. 1995–2000. *His Dark Materials* (Trilogy). London: Scholastic.

Rowling, J. K. 1997–2007. *Harry Potter* (Series). London: Bloomsbury.

Şerban, Andreea. 2012. "(Little) Red Riding Hood: A British-American History of Undoing." In *Episodes from a History of Undoing: The Heritage of Female Subversiveness*, edited by Reghina Dasc l, 123–36. Newcastle upon Tyne: Cambridge Scholars Publishing.

Shippey, Tom. 2000. *J. R. R. Tolkien: Author of the Century*. New York: Houghton Mifflin Co.

Stableford, Brian. 2009. *The A to Z of Fantasy Literature*. Lanham, MD: Scarecrow P.

Tiffin, Jessica. 2016. "Film and Video." In *Folktales and Fairy Tales: Traditions and Texts from around the World*. 2nd ed., edited by Anne E. Duggan and Donald Haase, 342–9. Santa Barbara: ABC-CLIO.

Todorov, Tzvetan. (1970) 1975. *The Fantastic*. Ithaca, NY: Cornell UP.

Tolkien, J. R. R. 1954–1955. *The Lord of the Rings* (Trilogy). London: Allen & Unwin.

———. 1965. "On Fairy-Stories." In *Tree and Leaf*, 3–84. Boston: Houghton Mifflin.

———. 1966. *The Tolkien Reader*. New York: Ballantine.

Vax, Louis. 1960. *L'Art et la Litterature Fantastiques*. Paris: UP France.

Warner, Marina. 2014. *Once Upon a Time: A Short History of Fairy Tale*. Oxford: Oxford UP.

Williamson, Jamie. 2015. *The Evolution of Modern Fantasy: From Antiquarianism to the Ballantine Adult Fantasy Series*. New York: Palgrave Macmillan.

Willsey, Kristiana. 2014. "New Fairy Tales Are Old Again: Grimm and the Brothers Grimm." In *Channeling Wonder: Fairy Tales on Television*, edited by Pauline Greenhill and Jill Terry Rudy, 210–28. Detroit: Wayne State UP.

The Wizard of Oz Pressbook. 1939. British Film Institute microfiche.

Zipes, Jack. 1994. *Fairy Tales as Myth, Myth as Fairy Tale*. Lexington: UP Kentucky.

———. 2002. *Breaking the Magic Spell: Radical Theories of Folk and Fairy Tales*. Kentucky: UP Kentucky.

———. 2003. *The Complete Fairy Tales of the Brothers Grimm*. 3rd ed. London: Bantam Book.

———. 2011. *The Enchanted Screen: The Unknown History of Fairy-Tale Films*. New York: Routledge.

———. 2012. *Fairy Tales and the Art of Subversion: The Classical Genre for Children and the Process of Civilization*. 2nd ed. London: Routledge.

———. 2016. "The Great Cultural Tsunami of Fairy-Tale Films." In *Fairy-Tale Films Beyond Disney: International Perspectives*, edited by Jack Zipes, Pauline Greenhill, and Kendra Magnus-Johnston, 1–17. New York: Routledge.

Mediagraphy

Alice in Wonderland. 2010. Director Tim Burton. USA.

The Chronicles of Narnia: The Lion, the Witch and the Wardrobe. 2005. Director Andrew Adamson. USA/UK.

Cinderella. 2015. Director Kenneth Branagh. USA/UK.

City of Ember. 2008. Director Gil Kenan. USA.

Enchanted. 2007. Director Kevin Lima. USA.

Gedo Senki (Tales from Earthsea). 2006. Director Gorô Miyazaki. Japan.

The Giver. 2014. Director Philip Noyce. South Africa/Canada/USA.

Grimm (TV). 2011–2017. Creators Stephen Carpenter, David Greenwalt, and Jim Kouf. USA.

Harry Potter and the Chamber of Secrets. 2002. Director Chris Columbus. UK/USA/Germany.

Harry Potter and the Deathly Hallows: Part 1. 2010. Director David Yates. UK/USA.

Harry Potter and the Deathly Hallows: Part 2. 2011. Director David Yates. USA/UK.

Harry Potter and the Goblet of Fire. 2005. Director Mike Newell. UK/USA.

Harry Potter and the Half-Blood Prince. 2009. Director David Yates. UK/USA.

Harry Potter and the Order of the Phoenix. 2007. Director David Yates. UK/USA.

Harry Potter and the Prisoner of Azkaban. 2004. Director Alfonso Cuarón. UK/USA.

Harry Potter and the Sorcerer's Stone. 2001. Director Chris Columbus. UK/USA.

Hauru no Ugoku Shiro (Howl's Moving Castle). 2004. Director Hayao Miyazaki. Japan.

Hugo. 2011. Director Martin Scorsese. USA.

The Hunger Games. 2012. Director Gary Ross. USA.

Into the Woods. 2014. Director Rob Marshall. USA/UK/Canada.

Jack the Giant Slayer. 2013. Director Bryan Singer. USA.

King Kong. 1933. Directors Merian C. Cooper and Ernest B. Schoedsack. USA.

The Lord of the Rings: The Fellowship of the Ring. 2001. Director Peter Jackson. New Zealand/USA.

The Lord of the Rings: The Return of the King. 2003. Director Peter Jackson. USA/New Zealand.

The Lord of the Rings: The Two Towers. 2002. Director Peter Jackson. USA/New Zealand.

Maleficent. 2014. Director Robert Stromberg. USA/UK.

The Matrix. 1999. Director The Wachowskis. USA.

The Matrix Reloaded. 2003. Director The Wachowskis. USA/Australia.

The Matrix Revolutions. 2003. Director The Wachowskis. Australia/USA.

Mei Ren Yu. 2016. Director Stephen Chow. China.

Mirror Mirror. 2012. Director Tarsem Singh. USA/Canada.

Once Upon a Time (TV). 2011–. Creators Adam Horowitz and Edward Kitsis. USA.

Oz the Great and Powerful. 2013. Director Sam Raimi. USA.

Pan. 2015. Director Joe Wright. USA/UK/Australia.

Pan's Labyrinth. 2006. Director Guillermo del Toro. Spain/Mexico/USA.

Red Riding Hood. 2011. Director Catherine Hardwicke. USA/Canada.

Scared Shrekless. 2010. Directors Gary Trousdale and Raman Hui. USA.

Sen to Chihiro no Kamikakushi (Spirited Away). 2001. Director Hayao Miyazaki. Japan.

Shrek. 2001. Directors Andrew Adamson and Vicky Jenson. USA.

Shrek 2. 2004. Directors Andrew Adamson, Kelly Asbury, and Conrad Vernon. USA.

Shrek Forever After. 2010. Director Mike Mitchell. USA.

Shrek the Halls. 2007. Director Gary Trousdale. USA.

Shrek the Third. 2007. Directors Chris Miller and Raman Hui. USA.

Snow White and the Huntsman. 2012. Director Rupert Sanders. USA.

Stardust. 2007. Director Matthew Vaughn. UK/USA/Iceland.

The Terminator. 1984. Director James Cameron. UK/USA.

Terminator 2: Judgment Day. 1991. Director James Cameron. USA/France.

Terminator 3: Rise of the Machines. 2003. Director Jonathan Mostow. USA/Germany/UK.

The Thief of Bagdad. 1940. Directors Ludwig Berger, Michael Powell, and Tim Whelan. UK.

Where the Wild Things Are. 2009. Director Spike Jonze. Germany/Australia/USA.

The Wizard of Oz. 1939. Director Victor Fleming. USA.

Wo Hu Cang Long. 2000. Director Ang Lee. Taiwan/Hong Kong/USA/China.

58

FOOD

Sugar-Coated Fairy Tales and the Contemporary Cultures of Consumption

Natalia Andrievskikh

From the witch's infamous gingerbread residence in "Hansel and Gretel" (ATU 327A) to the poisonous apple that brought Snow White's demise, fairy tales abound with all things edible. Their emphasis on food fits well with the contemporary culture of consumption, so heavily focused on pleasure and immediate gratification. Western popular imagination construes fairy-tale foods as festive and sumptuous, if not outright decadent. Cookbooks often feature fairy-tale themed recipes, for example, *Fairy Tale Feasts* (Yolen and Stemple 2009); *Once Upon a Time in the Kitchen: Recipes and Tales from Classic Children's Stories* (Odell 2010); and *Fairytale Food: Enchanting Recipes to Bring a Little Magic to Your Table* (Cash 2014). Fairy tales are essential to candy-oriented children's holidays such as Halloween, with witches, gnomes, and Little Red Riding Hoods trick-or-treating their way into fantasyland. Modern adaptations of traditional stories often highlight descriptions of eating; for instance, Philip Pullman's retelling of the Grimms elaborates on the meals characters consume. In "One Eye, Two Eyes, and Three Eyes" (ATU 511), the heroine is saved from hunger by a magic goat who feeds the girl a delicious meal. Pullman, not satisfied with the generic description, furnishes the exact menu: "leek soup, roast chicken, and strawberries and cream" (2013, 333). The described meal's contemporariness—strawberries and cream being currently popular— is particularly striking.

Depictions of Food in Classic Fairy Tales

Fairy-tale food appears in celebrations for heroes who have returned victorious from a difficult journey, defeated a monster, or found a spouse. Most stories end with an immoderate feast; for example, standard expressions in Russian folktales are "Пир горой" (a mountain of a feast) and "пир на весь мир" (a feast for the whole world). The emphasis on food in many traditional stories was influenced by poverty and hunger, an ongoing reality for the peasants whose collective experience gave birth to the original tales (Tatar 1999). Wishful thinking thus shapes the motif of replenishable foods: a single loaf of bread feeds a kingdom; a magic table cloth provides food on demand; a pot keeps making porridge until told to stop. "The Magic Swan

525

Geese" (ATU 451) features a land with milk rivers and pudding shores (Afanasyev 2006, 349). In "Beauty and the Beast" (ATU 425C) enchanted dwellings hidden in the woods have tables laid with viands, and so on.

Vladimir Propp's *Morphology of the Folktale* (2009) ascribes to food the crucial function of magic helper. As the brother and sister in "The Magic Swan Geese" try to escape from the witch, they find help from an apple tree, an oven with freshly baked pies, and a milk river. The heroine of "One Eye, Two Eyes, and Three Eyes" also gets help from an apple tree, not to mention the magic goat that saves her from hunger (Zipes 2003, 428). Often the hero must eat a particular food to acquire supernatural abilities: "three beverages provide the drinker with unusual strength; the eating of a bird's giblets endows heroes with various magical qualities" (Propp 2009, 45). "The White Snake" (ATU 673) begins and ends with eating: a curious serv-ant tries the mysterious snake dish that his king has every day and discovers that tasting it gives him power to understand the language of animals (Zipes 2003, 62). This discovery sets him off on a journey where he finds an apple from the Tree of Life and shares it with his bride, who falls in love with him upon tasting the apple (64). More than mere sustenance, food has a pro-foundly transformative function. Tasting the forbidden dish is a transgressive act that facilitates a breakthrough in the servant's social standing; initially a secondary character, he becomes the protagonist/hero and marries a princess. Even when no magic happens, culinary motifs are important for plot development; for instance, in "All Fur" (ATU 510B), the disguised princess cooks soup for the king and hides her ring in it, helping him find her (Zipes 2003, 242).

Conception From Eating

Often, food in fairy tales is responsible for the miracle of life itself: in tales across cultures women become pregnant after eating a pea, an apple, or a fish or drinking water from a spring. While such stories might reflect a belief in Immaculate Conception, they even more obviously repre-sent women as exclusively responsible for procreation. The imagery of pregnancy and digestion form a homogenous cluster, resulting in the symbolic conflation of the two bodily functions.

The future mother is often unable to control her appetite and eats too much, resulting in a birth of an unusual or outright monstrous child. In the Norwegian story "Tatterhood" (ATU 711) a woman is warned by a witch to grow two flowers and eat the beautiful one, but not the other, dark and ugly one. Predictably, she disobeys and gives birth to one beautiful and one ugly daughter. Tatterhood, the ugly twin, is essentially an embodiment of the mother's sin of gluttony. However, the story does not deliver a didactic message about the dangers of transgression: instead, Tatterhood, like most fairy-tale children of miraculous origin, becomes the heroine and prevails over impossible obstacles (Phelps 1978, 1–6).

Jan Švankmajer's *Little Otik* (or *Greedy Guts*), on the contrary, features a truly monstrous child with appetite gone wild. The movie portrays a childless couple in contemporary Eastern Europe who, out of desperation, carve a baby from a log. The creature comes alive and soon develops a taste for human flesh, devouring several people, including his parents. The plot echoes the tale type of a devouring animal whose belly is eventually cut open (ATU 2028). The visual sequence juxtaposes repeated close-ups of a chewing mouth and imagery of pregnancy as Švankmajer explores the psychological fear of parturition and the all-consuming presence of a newborn.

Cannibalism: Tales of Hunger and Appetite

Cannibalism is common in classic fairy tales. While much actual cannibalism is ritual, rooted in cultural practices such as burial ceremonies or celebrations of victory, poor sustenance might account for many of the fairy-tale depictions of eating flesh. As Sheldon Cashdan puts it, "everywhere you look in fairy tales, someone is either looking for a meal or trying desperately not to become one" (1999, 63). "Hansel and Gretel" famously features the threat of starvation followed by the danger of being eaten by a witch, a proper nightmare in times of hunger. In most stories, the protagonist escapes, whether through magical means or through his or her own faculties. Jack in "Jack and the Beanstalk" (ATU 328A) confronts—and outwits—a giant who eats roasted little boys for breakfast (Opie and Opie 1980, 211). The hero of Charles Perrault's "Le petit Poucet" (ATU 327B, ATU 700) tricks the ogre into killing his own off-spring, thus saving his life (167). The folk wisdom and resilience embedded in fairy tales provide a recipe for fighting for one's life even in the direst circumstances.

Marina Warner offers a more allegorical interpretation of the cannibal motif, reading it as a fear of sex and its consequences. In tales that fall under the template of "Cupid and Psyche" (ATU 425), she explains, the "cannibal motif conveys a threefold incorporation: sexual union, by which a form of reciprocal devouring takes place, pregnancy, by which the womb encloses the growing child, and paternity, which takes over the infant after birth in one way or another" (1998, 165). Warner's analysis is consistent with psychoanalytic theory, which views appetite for food as sublimation of sexual desire. Language itself, mirror to our hidden fantasies and fears, reflects the close association between appetite for food and sexual desire: many words that denote eating can also metaphorically refer to sexual intercourse.

Jack Zipes (1993) discusses the double entendre of the wolf gobbling up Little Red Riding Hood, tracing the changed messages that different retellings of this well-known fairy tale deliver. Perrault, for example, accompanies his version with a moral directed at young women to warn them against sexual predators. In his story, the girl falls victim to the wolf's lust, while the Grimms' retelling supplies a happy ending in which a hunter kills the wolf and cuts the girl and her grandmother out of his belly. In contrast with the tamer Grimms' version, Perrault's story offers a more straightforward account of a sexual encounter between a predator male and an innocent young woman.

The Grimms' "The Robber Bridegroom" (ATU 955) also spotlights the motif of cannibalism with sexual undertones. In it, a young bride discovers her betrothed husband's cannibal inclinations before their wedding as she witnesses a sinister scene of what can be construed as a gang rape of another young woman: "They gave her wine to drink, three glasses full, one white, one red, and one yellow, and soon her heart burst in two. Then they tore off her fine clothes, put her on a table, chopped her beautiful body to pieces, and sprinkled the pieces with salt" (Zipes 2003, 143). At their wedding feast, the bride reveals to the guests what she witnessed, and the villain is convicted and executed. It is important that the woman rescues herself through sharing her own account of the events, as being able to tell her own story empowers her and renders her dangerous to the perpetrator. Many young girls in the best-known fairy tales have no agency in language: they never communicate the ills that are done to them, waiting in silence for somebody to remedy the situation. Unlike the quiet heroines destined to become victims of various fairy-tale predators, the young bride in this story flips the eat-or-be-eaten paradigm. Remarkably, she speaks up as she is feasting at the party, enjoying a meal instead of herself becoming the main dish at another feast.

Contemporary cinematic adaptations of fairy tales often flirt with the metaphoric con-flation of appetite and sexual desire. Catherine Breillat's *Bluebeard* (ATU 312) avoids openly erotic scenes; instead, the sexual tension between the monstrous groom and his young wife is portrayed through the scenes of them eating together. Alone at a large table laid with meat, eating in silence, they exchange glances that make us increasingly uncomfortable. The cam-era's focus in these visual sequences is on the wife as she unabashedly picks up large pieces of meat with her bare hands. In contrast to other instances in the movie when the heroine finds herself in danger, the eating sequences introduce another image—that of the couple mutually exploring their appetites. Breillat further complicates the traditional portrayal of the wife as a victim as the final scene offers an intertextual reference to Salome and the beheading of John the Baptist and the story of Judith and Holofernes: the young woman is holding a plate with her husband's head on it, slightly caressing his hair. Regrettably, the protagonist's only escape from the gendered economy of sexual consumption is through reciprocal violence. Like the young bride in "The Robber Bridegroom," she protects herself from the perpetrator, yet she is also aware of her role as an accomplice in the violent game of sexual consumption.

An even darker representation of the game appears in *Criminal Lovers*, a film by François Ozon loosely based on the plot of "Hansel and Gretel." It introduces viewers to a sinister world where reality blurs with imagination: a couple of young murderers on the run are held captive in the woods by an ogre-like figure who threatens to eat them. *Criminal Lovers*, shot through with erotic tension, exposes the violence inherent in desire. Ozon employs a polyphonic narrative strategy with intertextual references to fairy tales, the cinematic horror and film noir tradition, specifically *The Night of the Hunter* (1955) and movies of the *Bonnie and Clyde* type, to situate his characters in a culturally constructed context that reinforces sexual and social taboos. As the protagonists explore their sexualities, the movie's visual and narrative streaks parallel transgressive urges that propel the plot forward. Sex scenes are shot against the background of pots and pans and skinned animals, blurring the boundary between those who prey and those who are preyed upon.

Female Cannibal Cooks and the Devouring
Mother Archetype in Fairy Tales

While the examples discussed so far mostly focus on male cannibals, female cannibalism is a significant topic of numerous folktales, reminiscent of the Devouring Mother archetype described by Carl Jung (1968) and Erich Neumann (1974). The devouring mother eats her offspring, symbolically reversing the process of giving birth. Consumption seems an excellent metaphor to express power and subordination, as eating, sex, and mother-infant relations alike can be described in terms of devouring, appropriating, using the other.

Most women cannibals in fairy tales are, indeed, mother figures. The jealous stepmother in "Snow White" (ATU 709) orders the hunter to kill her beautiful stepdaughter and serve her lungs and liver at dinner (Zipes 2003, 182). Maria Tatar explains that the queen is hoping "that by incorporating her stepdaughter, she will also acquire her beauty" (2012, 83). Similarly, the queen in Perrault's "Sleeping Beauty" (ATU 410) orders Beauty and her children to be killed and cooked (Opie and Opie 1980, 115). Her hunger for their flesh indicates desire to overpower, asserting her dominant position as mother queen. Yet another evil stepmother from "The Juniper Tree" (ATU 720) kills her stepson, cuts him up, and makes pudding, which she serves to the boy's father (Zipes 2003, 158). Nietzchka Keene's adaptation of this story (*The Juniper Tree*, 1990, starring Björk) portrays the stepmother as a powerful witch who uses incantations to control the boy's father. After she kills her stepson, she sews his lips together, cuts off his finger, and puts it in a stew. Details aside, the most striking feature in these and other examples is the murderous woman's connection to cooking.

Arguably, it is her near singlehanded access to food production that inspires a fear of the cook. As queens of the domestic sphere, women can use their culinary abilities to reward as well as to punish those who depend on them for nourishment. Hiding in her "secret and solitary chamber where no one else ever [goes]," the evil queen makes a deadly poisonous apple to destroy Snow White (Zipes 2003, 186). Through cooking up her magic concoctions, the witch extends her power far beyond the kitchen, functioning not merely as a projection of the overbearing maternal figure, but, more importantly, as a manifestation of the widespread fear of women's control over the domestic realm.

Women, Food, and Fairy Tales in Feminist Criticism

Many cultures conventionally relegate both food (nurturing, cooking) and fairy tales (oral storytelling) to the female sphere.[1] Although Zipes dismisses the popular belief that fairy tales were traditionally disseminated exclusively by women (2001, 850), the popular association between women and oral storytelling is strong. Louis Marin emphasizes the storytelling role of the maternal nurturing figure, pointing out that Perrault "explicitly attributes the telling and reciting of the tale [. . .] to a young child's mother and, more frequently, his or her grandmother, governess, nurse, or godmother" (1997, 31). Women's relationship to both food and fairy tales is deemed ambivalent by feminist criticism that distinguishes normative/disciplinary uses and liberating/subversive potential of both. Food studies discuss disciplinary uses of food and often interpret food abstinence as symbolic suppression of agency. Fairy tales, too, fulfill the normative function, transmitting knowledge about prescribed feminine behavior.

As discussed prior, fairy-tale women who exhibit appetite are often cast in a negative light as bloodthirsty monsters; alternatively, they are disobedient girls who eventually get punished for their gluttony. Tatar analyzes the Italian story of Caterinella, who is chastised for her appetite (1992, 40), in a tale often interpreted as a cautionary one teaching proper behavior. Fairy-tale women are supposed to cook food, but not enjoy it: Cinderella is made to eat in the kitchen rather than dining with her family; Two Eyes only gets leftovers from her family's meals; All Fur cooks her mouthwatering dishes downstairs, remaining invisible, while the fruit of her labor is consumed by others. Prohibition against women indulging in gastronomic pleasures rules much of both the fairy-tale realm and the everyday world regulated through stereotypes of gendered eating habits. Confined to the kitchen and the nursery, women seemingly are banned from self-expression and exploration of desire, left to nurture and entertain others through "old wives' tales."

And yet, the presence of prohibition inevitably entails subversive potential. Many fairy-tale heroines use their appetites and cooking talents to their advantage, breaking the rules. The protagonist of "Clever Gretel" (ATU 1741), a cook who eats the food intended for her master, gets away without punishment (Zipes 2003, 264). Like all tricksters, Gretel is a transgressive character who oversteps the margins into the forbidden: instead of restricting her appetite to conform to existing norms, she defiantly eats away at the boundaries of the established social order. Cristina Bacchilega points out that the story was likely intended as an example of a working-class woman's unsuitable behavior (2012, 31); however, she continues, the protagonist ultimately embodies the triumphant subaltern breaking the normative script of accepted conduct. Bacchilega demonstrates how Gretel's sensual enjoyment of food is reserved solely for her own pleasure: "Counter to the imagery of the angel of the house and the self-sacrificing motherly figure, Gretel fulfills her desire by feeding herself exclusively" (33). The autoerotic indulgence in gastronomic pleasures positions Gretel outside the oppressive taxonomy of class and gender relationships.

Among the many fairy-tale crones and outcasts who exercise power in the kitchen, Baba Yaga of Slavic folklore is probably the most intriguing. Her description varies from tale to tale, but she consistently possesses some cannibal attributes. Baba Yaga lives in a house surrounded by a fence of skulls and bones; in "Vasilisa the Beautiful" (ATU 510A) she eats "human beings as if they were chickens" (Afanasyev 2006, 40). Baba Yaga follows the ancient laws of hospitality: a hero lost in the woods can always count on her for a savory dinner. However, the unfortunate hero might end up on the dinner table himself. Simultaneously life-affirming and destructive, Baba Yaga is an archetypal character who transcends all social paradigms. One of Yaga's recent appearances is in the *Harry Potter and the Prisoner of Azkaban* video game, where she is featured on the *Famous Witches and Wizards* collectible cards and is described as a cannibal who eats children for breakfast (*Harry Potter* 2004).

Eat Your Words: Food Consumption and Verbal Expression

Notably, eating is often linked to speech in folk imagination; for example, in many cultures and religions fasting is often accompanied by abstinence from talking. Marin explains the connection between consumption and verbal expression through their locus in the mouth: "from the moment that the first cry of want and hunger is released," an infant communicates its desire to consume (1997, 36). The mouth, therefore, is "a locus of need," as well as of expression through voice and, later, through language (36). Associated with the mouth, the oral functions of eating and verbal expression are symbolically interchangeable.

The prominent mouth is an attribute of monsters and liminal beings from the Cheshire Cat's mischievous grin to Maurice Sendak's monsters with sharp teeth. Dressed in a wolf costume, Sendak's Max is a "wild thing" threatening to eat up his mother, who then sends him to bed without supper (2012, 13). In the fantasy that follows, Max overpowers monsters who "roared their terrible roars and gnashed their terrible teeth" (25)—and also leaves them without food. Upon his return, Max finds his supper waiting for him. The consuming, roaring mouth functions as a tool of control, and the story is a symbolic negotiation of authority.

Fairy tales explicitly connect eating with power: the ogre in "Jack and the Beanstalk" has several oxen for breakfast (Opie and Opie 1980, 220), Baba Yaga can eat as much as ten men (Afanasyev 2006, 442), and so on. Simultaneously, Baba Yaga demonstrates agency in language: she curses, gives advice, often announces her appearance with formulaic chants, talks to herself, and uses magic incantations. Yaga's freedom of self-articulation and gastronomic potency are parallel strategies of oral gratification that account for much of her power.

The connection between language and consumption is highlighted in metaphors of language as food and reading as nurture. We talk about devouring books, greedy reading, eating words, digesting information, and so on. Fairy tales, then, are an early food consumed, symbolically, with mother's milk. Without doubt, the fantastic mode creates a perfect environment for the transformative and liberating power of language. Numerous literary traditions rely on exploration of the fantastic, allowing imagination to quench our thirst for wonder: baroque literature, folklore, fairy-tale, imagistic, and grotesque contexts offer the kind of comfort food that has healing powers. The carnivalesque orgy of hunger and satisfaction where reality no longer dictates its restrictive rules celebrates language as much as the body. Fairy tales heal shame, guilt, and the false sense of inadequacy; they are savory food steamed in a magic pot to fill the soul.

Related topics: Children's and Young Adult (YA) Literature; Cinematic; Fat Studies; Gender; Language; Material Culture; Sexualities/Queer and Trans Studies; Storytelling

Note

1. When cooking is approached as art, however, it is culturally marked as male territory. Men are chefs, cooking special dishes for display and pleasure, while women provide uninterrupted, day-to-day sustenance.

FOOD

References Cited and Further Reading

Afanasyev, Aleksandr. 2006. *Russian Fairy Tales*. New York: Pantheon Books.

Bacchilega, Cristina. 1999. *Postmodern Fairy Tales: Gender and Narrative Strategies*. Philadelphia: U Pennsylvania P.

———. 2012. "Whetting Her Appetite: What's a 'Clever' Woman to Do in the Grimms' Collection?" In *Transgressive Tales: Queering the Grimms*, edited by Kay Turner and Pauline Greenhill, 27–49. Detroit: Wayne State UP.

Cash, Lucie. 2014. *Fairytale Food: Enchanting Recipes to Bring a Little Magic to Your Table*. New York: Random House.

Cashdan, Sheldon. 1999. *The Witch Must Die: The Hidden Meaning of Fairy Tales*. New York: Basic Books.

Chernin, Kim. 1994. *The Hungry Self: Women, Eating and Identity*. New York: Harper Perennial.

Creed, Barbara. 1993. *Monstrous Feminine: Film, Feminism and Psychoanalysis*. New York: Routledge.

Gilbert, Sandra, and Susan Gubar. 2000. *The Madwoman in the Attic: The Woman Writer and the Nineteenth-Century Literary Imagination*. New Haven, CT: Yale UP.

Hallissy, Margaret. 1987. *Venomous Woman: Fear of the Female in Literature*. Westport: Greenwood P.

Jung, Carl. 1968. *Man and His Symbols*. New York: Dell Publishing.

Marin, Louis. 1997. *Food for Thought*. Baltimore: Johns Hopkins UP.

Neumann, Erich. 1974. *The Great Mother*. Princeton, NJ: Princeton UP.

Odell, Carol. 2010. *Once Upon a Time in the Kitchen: Recipes and Tales from Classic Children's Stories (Myths, Legends, Fairy and Folktales)*. Ann Arbor, MI: Sleeping Bear P.

Opie, Iona, and Peter Opie. 1980. *The Classic Fairy Tales*. Oxford: Oxford UP.

Phelps, Ethel Johnston. 1978. *Tatterhood and Other Tales*. New York: CUNY Feminist P.

Propp, Vladimir. 2009. *Morphology of the Folktale*. Austin: U Texas P.

Pullman, Philip. 2013. *Fairy Tales from the Brothers Grimm: A New English Version*. New York: Penguin Classics.

Sendak, Maurice. 2012. *Where the Wild Things Are*. Dunmore: Harper Collins.

Tatar, Maria. 1992. *Off with Their Heads! Fairy Tales and the Culture of Childhood*. Princeton, NJ: Princeton UP.

———. 1999. *The Classic Fairy Tales*. New York: W.W. Norton.

———. 2012. *The Annotated Brothers Grimm*. New York: W.W. Norton.

Warner, Marina. 1998. "Fee Fie Fo Fum: The Child in the Jaws of the Story." In *Cannibalism and the Colonial World*, edited by Francis Barker and Peter Hulme, 158–83. New York: Cambridge UP.

Yolen, Jane, and Heidi Stemple. 2009. *Fairy Tale Feasts: A Literary Cookbook for Young Readers and Eaters*. Northampton, MA: Interlink Publishing.

Zipes, Jack. 1993. *The Trials and Tribulations of Little Red Riding Hood*. New York: Routledge.

———. 2001. *The Great Fairy-Tale Tradition*. New York: W.W. Norton.

———. 2003. *The Complete Fairy Tales of the Brothers Grimm*. New York: Bantham.

Mediagraphy

Alice in Wonderland. 2010. Director Tim Burton. USA.

Bluebeard. 2009. Director Catherine Breillat. France.

Bonnie and Clyde. 1967. Director Arthur Penn. USA.

Criminal Lovers. 1999. Director François Ozon. France.

Harry Potter and the Prisoner of Azkaban (Computer Game). 2004. Windows PC. https://nicoblog.org/pc-games/harry-potter-and-the-prisoner-of-azkaban-usa/.

The Juniper Tree. 1990. Director Nietzchka Keene. Iceland/USA.

Little Otik. 2000. Director Jan Švankmajer. Czech Republic.

The Night of the Hunter. 1955. Director Charles Laughton. USA.

59

HORROR

Sue Short

Horror's kinship with fairy tales is especially apparent in providing a host of monsters (both supernatural and ostensibly human) to jangle our nerves and chill the blood. For centuries we have shared stories about diabolical characters committing atrocities such as murder and cannibalism, themes frequently reprised by modern filmmakers. The serial-killing fiend in "Bluebeard" (ATU 312) serves as a recognizable precursor of the countless psychos rampaging in the slasher, while a taste for human flesh—once the preserve of ogres and witches—has now been transposed to degenerate figures in such films as *The Texas Chainsaw Massacre* (1974), *Wrong Turn* (2003), and *The Descent* (2005). Both in terms of appearance and appetite these characters prove that they are not quite human, not subject to the same laws as ourselves, and the isolated territory where such encounters occur simply compounds the fear factor.

Monstrosity is not always readily discernible, however, confounding any assumptions about who we can trust, a salutary lesson often found in childhood tales. As Hansel and Gretel (in ATU 327A) discover, a seemingly kind stranger has sinister intentions, aiming to consume those who stray her way. Christopher Sharrett regards *The Texas Chainsaw Massacre* as basically recycling "the Hansel and Gretel story of apparently innocent youth stumbling upon unexplained and unimaginable evil" (1984, 257), and although its heroine is far less calculated in securing her escape, the comparison is clear. The shock of seemingly ordinary adults who prove to be dangerous finds its apotheosis in the ultimate fairy-tale fright: parents who turn out to be predators rather than protectors—an idea that has similarly provided fertile ground for filmmakers, resulting in a succession of flawed parents, from the smother mothers seen in *Psycho* (1960) and *Carrie* (1976) to deranged dad Jack Torrance in *The Shining* (1980), who tries to slaughter his family with an axe.

Horror's investment in such narratives affirms that what terrifies us as children often remains equally unnerving in adulthood: isolation, vulnerability, pursuit by hostile figures, the shock of realizing that appearances can be deceptive, and the sense of dread evoked in knowing there is no one to turn to for help. Contrasting theories have been employed to make sense of the purpose (and pleasure) of such tales. Do they provide a masochistic thrill in identifying with disempowered characters, or encourage a degree of sadism in witnessing their pain and terror? Is Carol Clover right to contend that both reactions may apply, arguing that we shift in our allegiances when we watch horror films—taking the role of "both Red Riding Hood *and* the wolf" (1996, 71)? The idea is similar to Marina Warner's observation that children enjoy imitating the ogre, as much as identifying with Jack, a strategy understood as mimicking what is monstrous, aiming to "internalize the aggressor in order to stave off the terror he brings" (2000, 169). Perhaps children simply relish adopting a position of power in such scenarios, taking unfettered delight in playing the monster and being mean. Or maybe there is something more to the ritual re-enactment of the grisliest bits of a tale, akin to watching a favorite horror film over again, mastering fear through repetition.

Are scary stories, whatever form they take, a means of controlling sublimated anxieties? Do they have therapeutic (perhaps even radical) value in expressing what may otherwise seem unsayable? Or are more sinister motivations apparent in terms of who tends to be made the object of fear, potentially mobilizing latent prejudices in identifying a perceived threat? What about variations that question our understanding of villainy, encouraging us to identify with apparent monsters? Does this reflect more liberal times, or is it another means of defusing dread? Clearly, there are no simple answers to these questions, with competing claims articulated in the effort to understand the pleasure taken in frightening narratives, pronounced differences of opinion expressed about whether they cause us harm or do us good, and dramatically different versions available of what may essentially seem to be the same tale.

The use of woods as a prime horror location replicates a common fairy-tale setting and its "otherworldly" possibilities. As Jack Zipes notes, woods are often a place of enchantment in fairy tales, the site of strange encounters and magical transformations "where society's conventions no longer hold true" (2002, 67), yet they are equally a synonym for danger and menace, an aspect horror films tend to foreground.[1] The heroine in *Pan's Labyrinth* (2006) may initially take comfort in being relocated to the woods, seeing fairies in the trees and a mysterious gateway to another world, yet she does not survive this move, like similar figures who find their way into the woods and fail to get out again. The fabled witch of *The Blair Witch Project* (1999) uses this liminal territory to trap her victims, divesting them of any control. In entering the woods they effectively leave modernity behind them, regressing as they do so, eventually emulating the fate of the lost children in "Babes in the Wood." The film's makers notably describe their intent as a means of evoking primordial fears: namely the dark—and the creatures we populate such darkness with—contending, "it's in the dark of the woods, when night falls, that something comes out in us that reminds us that once we were prey" (quoted in Mackenzie 1999, 15).

This comment sums up horror's ambivalent pleasure: recalling a time when we were vulnerable to a host of dangers yet also sought to entertain ourselves with tales of imperiled protagonists faced with the threat of death. What accounts for our continued fascination with such stories? For *Blair Witch* directors Daniel Myrick and Eduardo Sanchez, "fear is designed to protect us, to make us run away" (Mackenzie 1999, 15), yet we do not necessarily identify with characters seeking to escape the horror, but with those who stand and face their demons. Warner observes that "the condition of being scared is being increasingly sought after, not only as a source of pleasure but as a means of strengthening the sense of being alive, of having a command over self" (2000, 6). Perhaps humans have always craved a sense of excitement from scary stories, enjoying the adrenaline kick to be had from such narratives yet also drawing something positive from the steeling of our nerves required to put ourselves through such an ordeal. Maybe we need these tales more than ever, both to jolt us from our comparative complacency and in order to face our fears.

Many horror scenarios resemble cautionary tales in appearing to punish perceived transgression. Sexual activity and drug-taking typically incite murderous wrath in the slasher, while laziness, greed, and cruelty are the "sins" often punished in fairy tales (sometimes fatally). However, if death may result from ignoring approved strictures—"straying from the path"—a degree of independence is also commended in horror as an essential survival trait. Protagonists are forced to become self-reliant when parent figures or public officials let them down, and it is this trait, ultimately, that is their most vital asset, fostering the resilience and resourcefulness needed to survive. Some claim that children positively identify with fairy-tale characters who overcome the odds and evade oppressors, suggesting this situation replicates their perceived position with parents (and how they would like it to be), taking vicarious delight in turning the tables and acquiring sovereignty. Arguably, such tales remain intriguing in adulthood for much the same reason: because they both unsettle and inspire us, especially when a seemingly powerless figure survives. Are scary stories a means of alerting us to the potential hazards of life, warning about duplicitous strangers, as well as equally dangerous figures we might find ourselves related to? Do they provide salutary "life lessons" in admitting to such dangers yet also affirming our potential to survive them—an understanding that remains relevant, whatever our age?

Significantly, if woods are a source of danger in horror, the modern suburban home is equally a place of peril. Horror reminds us that bad things happen, even in the midst of apparent normality, and we cannot rely on others when it does. In *Halloween* (1978) a psychopath stages a murderous rampage in his hometown, notably choosing a night when all the parents are elsewhere. Similarly, *Elm Street*'s nightmarish Sandman, Freddy Krueger, enters teenagers' bedrooms and kills them as they sleep, unseen by adults. Following an established fairy-tale model, parents in horror are either absent, negligent, or appallingly abusive, even committing infanticide—although they rarely get away with such crimes. The *Ring* and *Grudge* franchises effectively reprise an age-old story: depicting murdered children who become vengeful spirits. Like "The Juniper Tree" (ATU 720), in which a dead child takes vengeance from beyond the grave, a degree of justice is enacted in such stories, yet they also exceed any boundaries in terms of who is killed, deriving their terror not only from a child's propensity for violence but the fact that the child learned such behavior from a parent.

Unhappy families are pivotal plot devices in many fairy tales, with murderous mothers and incestuous fathers featuring in a host of narratives around the world, provoking explanations that often seem equally distorted. Standard Freudian ideas are often uncritically reiterated, claiming incestuous fathers in tales such as "Donkey Skin" (ATU 510B) and "The Maiden without Hands" (ATU 706) actually reflect the daughter's subconscious desire for her father (see Dundes 1987), while the wicked stepmother, in examples like "Snow White" (ATU 709), is said to represent the resentment felt by daughters toward a figure seen as a rival for the father's affections (Bettelheim 1977). Even if we regard the latter trope as a means for children (of either sex) to displace any ill feeling toward mothers, the degree to which females are deemed blameworthy in such arguments is deeply alarming. Maria Tatar has noted a pronounced discrepancy in terms of which narratives have been popularized in print, with cases of maternal malevolence far outnumbering paternal wrongdoing—and being much more frequently punished (1992, 125–126). Research of this kind counters questionable psychoanalytic explanations and forces us to consider the sociocultural forces at work, not only in terms of the stories that have proliferated over the years, but the meanings they have generated and the changes they have undergone.

We might ask how modern narratives compare in terms of this apparent gender discrepancy in poor parenting. According to Barbara Creed (1996) the "monstrous-feminine" is a fundamental generic trait, asserting that horror is especially preoccupied with demonizing mothers, citing examples such as *Psycho* and *Carrie*. However, others claim the father is more frequently villainized in contemporary horror (see for example Tony Williams [1996] and Vivian Sobchack [1996], who contend that patriarchy is covertly targeted via malevolent father figures). Conflicting examples make it hard to reach any single conclusion, yet it seems the chief imperative is to defy and outlive the oppressive parent figure, irrespective of gender. An implicit narrative intent (in both fairy tales and horror cinema) is thus comparable to a rite of passage: aiming to make us dispense with innocence, realize the dangers that exist—both within the home and beyond—and applaud self-reliant protagonists who defy expectation and survive.

Some horror narratives have something else in mind, proving keen to subvert our usual understanding of villainy. *A Tale of Two Sisters* (2003) questions the validity of the wicked stepmother trope (and seems to parody ideas about an Electra complex), while *Dumplings* (2004) takes the cannibal theme of "Snow White" to new extremes, presenting an ordinary woman who becomes a baby-eating "ogress" in an effort to rejuvenate herself. The fact that she is propelled by an unfaithful husband and a career that has vetoed her right to age reiterates ideas raised by Sandra M. Gilbert and Susan Gubar (2000), highlighting patriarchy's role in creating monstrous insecurity, insisting female value is based on youthful good looks.[2] Although we do not condone her actions, we realize she is driven by external forces, a man-made monster, almost pitiable. An increasing number of examples similarly invite us to reconsider the nature of monstrosity and its cause, often depicting villains with increased ambivalence, if not outright sympathy. In such cases it seems that we do not necessarily summon the bogeyman in order to confront a threat but to question the source of our fears, with some narratives aiming to foster greater understanding rather than antipathy. While this may appear to be a relatively contemporary phenomenon, we might recall that some of the most intriguing fairy-tale villains are also somewhat ambivalent. The Russian witch, Baba Yaga, possesses both benign and malign powers, sometimes helping protagonists in some way (from ridding their home of adversaries to finding a consort), and thus serves as an interesting (albeit formidable) mentor.[3] Some Grimm tales contain equally unlikely benefactors, including the devil, who often grants otherwise outcast characters the means to progress in life.

If apparent villains can sometimes be shown in a better light, certain narratives aim to redeem them entirely. In fact, some recent children's films encourage greater affiliation with monsters than humans, portrayed as superficial and cruel by comparison. *The Boxtrolls* (2014) depicts trolls as endearing creatures who are unfairly demonized and destroyed by humans, a situation the young hero (a human raised by trolls) confronts. *ParaNorman* (2012) similarly targets prejudice and its consequence via a child hero whose ability to see the dead enables him to save his town, assuaging a girl's quest for revenge against the people who persecuted her as a witch. Classic fairy-tale foes are thus transformed into child-friendly "monsters," requiring help and understanding rather than posing a threat. In turn, an entire subgenre has emerged in which vampires have become allies and love interests for disaffected teens. The *Twilight* film franchise and TV series such as *The Vampire Diaries* expressly romanticize being undead, while *Let the Right One In* (2008) presents a vampire as the perfect playmate and protector for a lonely boy who is bullied by his peers and ignored by his parents. As these examples attest, although horror is often claimed to reinforce certain boundaries, these are also frequently tested, blurring any concrete distinctions about villainy through humans who behave inhumanely and apparent monsters with a soft side.

These variations result from a continuous process of transformation and renewal—a phenomenon fairy tales and horror perpetually undergo, reminding us of the ever-evolving nature of such tales and the multiple readings they offer. An angle may be adopted that tells a familiar story in a new way, or a backstory added that makes us regard former monsters from a new perspective. This muddying of the waters is consistent with some literary strategies adopted in the last few decades, aiming to "de-Grimm" fairy tales by confounding clichés and often redressing our understanding of former villains in the process. However, we might question whether a tendency to invite greater identification with monsters is necessarily progressive, as the likes of Robin Wood suggest, noting that a "postmodern" retelling of tales can equally entrench reactionary ideas.[4] In *Hansel and Gretel: Witch Hunters* (2013), for example, the "bad mother" of fairy-tale legend turns out to be well intentioned rather than cruel, sending her children into the woods to protect rather than kill them, yet the film nonetheless explicitly demonizes witches, affirming that "bad" ones are easily detected by their ugliness and murdering scores of women in gruesome fashion. Similarly, *Mama* (2013) may seek to tell a new version of the story, with two young girls (viciously rejected by their father) protected in the woods by a ghostly woman, yet she is ultimately shown to be equally threatening (her backstory affording little sympathy when we realize she is a child killer). Fairy-tale revisions are not necessarily improvements, in other words, and despite aiming to avoid telling the usual story, new versions may prove to be still more questionable.

It is in horror's depiction of ordinary people as killers that it becomes especially unnerving. The *Saw* franchise takes this scenario to a discomforting level, suggesting ruthless self-interest may make monsters of us all.[5] In other texts also some slippage is apparent in terms of who or what is deemed "monstrous," with humanity itself shown to be a precarious concept. While fairy tales often warn about the potential for dehumanization, with various figures adopting beastly form, horror has reworked the motif without necessarily undoing the "spell." Hit zombie series *The Walking Dead* asks tricky questions about what happens to our humanity when people fight to survive—and the fact that non-zombies behave even more ruthlessly suggests that the scariest threat we face is located within ourselves.

Our urge to externalize this negative side—transferring our worst instincts onto convenient Others—might be considered a key function both of horror and fairy tales: displacing what is too close to home, creating hate figures we can comfortably despise and thus vanquishing our fears, yet an alternative strategy is to internalize and accept, making monsters knowable, even lovable. Vampires can thus be romantically redeemed, irrespective of the death toll they have amassed, in shows like *Buffy the Vampire Slayer*, *True Blood*, and *The Vampire Diaries*—as long as there is a heroine willing to see the best in them. Equally, serial killers and cannibals serve as the unlikely heroes of *Dexter* and *Hannibal*, their threat apparently ameliorated by getting to know them. Bringing such characters out of the shadows and into our realm of understanding is a way of having it both ways: creating a monster who gives us a fright yet who we can observe up close, potentially even identify with on some level, although we might question whether any such allegiances are necessarily positive.

The modern world does not appear to have abated our taste for scary stories and frightening figures, proving as popular today as ever. Taking various forms, familiar tales are now embellished and remade for a variety of audiences, sometimes sanitizing contents for a younger audience or taking new extremes where adult viewers are in mind. Whatever means are found to give the audience a jolt, the popularity of certain themes suggests that we are not as different from our fairy tale-loving forebears as we might imagine. In fact, a sufficient number of examples affirm that the most unnerving aspect of the horrific in fairy tales transcends period, nationality, endless attempts at academic explanation, and the sentimentalizing endeavors of many current series and films—tapping into what appears to be a universal set of anxieties. Poor parent figures, inhuman predators in our midst, the inability to determine who we can trust, and the notion that evil can enter even our supposed sanctuary—our very homes—all remain conspicuous features. We might also note the prominence given to vampires, zombies, and cannibal killers in recent years, figures who were once human but have since radically altered and are now likely to perceive us (as directors Myrick and Sanchez put it) simply as prey. Despite the methods used to make such characters more understandable (often via the trope of a background that has damaged them in some way), their most disturbing feature lies in the fact that they are no longer human—as we would like to define the term—reminding us just how tenuous such an identity is. Ogres and devils may seem too supernatural to be deemed credible now, but monsters with a human face are a different proposition, continuing to both unnerve and intrigue us. While audiences still want to be entertained by such figures, horror's future is assured. As critics such as Carol Clover and Mikel J. Koven argue, it might even be seen as a form of folklore in new guise, recycling established motifs and archetypes and endlessly adapting itself for contemporary tastes. The late Wes Craven (quoted in Stratford 2015) made the parallel clear in one of his last interviews, noting that what draws us to be scared is elemental: "it's like boot camp for the psyche [. . .] the way humans deal with the horrific is to put it in a narrative and cloak it in character."

Related topics: Cinematic; Crime/Justice; Disability; Gender; Pornography

Notes

1. Forests are often inhabited by evil entities in horror cinema, including cannibal savages in *Wrong Turn*, dead witches in *The Woods* (2006) and *The Blair Witch Project*, demonic forces in *The Evil Dead* (1981), and a gang of murderous feral teens in *Eden Lake* (2008).
2. I refer here to Gilbert and Gubar's opening chapter, "The Queen's Looking Glass," in their book *The Madwoman in the Attic*, in which they argue that the "wicked" stepmother's vanity in "Snow White," her preoccupation with being "the fairest of them all," is a reflection of patriarchal expectation, claiming the king provides "the voice of the looking glass, the patriarchal voice of judgement that rules the queen's—and every woman's—self-evaluation" (2000, 38).
3. See Andreas Johns's *Baba Yaga: The Ambiguous Mother and Witch of the Russian Folk Tale* (2004)—the mere title of which sums up two contrasting sides to the character.
4. Wood (1984) contends that "the progressiveness of the horror film depends partly on the monster's capacity to arouse sympathy" (193), giving monsters a context rather than vilifying them as "simply evil." As my examples attest, a backstory will not necessarily result in a more enlightened approach.
5. The franchise takes the premise of a sadistic man, known as Jigsaw, who traps people and tests their will to live by seeing if they are willing to kill. Although often criticized as "torture porn," *Saw* has proved to be bewilderingly popular (with seven installments to date)—a fact which is almost as disturbing as its villain's belief that he is helping those he "tests."

References Cited and Further Reading

Bettelheim, Bruno. 1977. *The Uses of Enchantment: The Meaning and Importance of Fairy Tales.* New York: Vintage.
Clover, Carol. 1996. "Her Body, Himself: Gender in the Slasher Film." In *The Dread of Difference: Gender and the Horror Film*, edited by Barry Keith Grant, 66–113. Austin: U Texas P.
Creed, Barbara. 1996. "Horror and the Monstrous-Feminine: An Imaginary Abjection." In *The Dread of Difference: Gender and the Horror Film*, edited by Barry Keith Grant, 35–65. Austin: U Texas P.
Dundes, Alan. 1987. "The Psychoanalytic Study of the Grimm's Tales with Special Reference to 'The Maiden Without Hands (AT 706)'." *Germanic Review* 62: 50–65.
Gilbert, Sandra M., and Susan Gubar. 2000. *The Madwoman in the Attic: The Woman Writer in the Nineteenth Century Literary Imagination.* 2nd revised ed. New Haven, CN: Yale UP.
Johns, Andreas. 2004. *Baba Yaga: The Ambiguous Mother and Witch of the Russian Folk Tale.* Bern: Peter Lang.
Koven, Mikel J. 2007. *Film, Folklore and Urban Legends.* Lanham: Scarecrow P.
Mackenzie, Suzie. 1999. "Fear Be My Friend: Interviews with Wes Craven, Eduardo Sanchez and Daniel Myrick." *The Guardian* 'Weekend' supplement, October 23. www.theguardian.com/film/1999/oct/23/1.
Sharrett, Christopher. 1984. "The Idea of Apocalypse in *The Texas Chainsaw Massacre*." In *Planks of Reason: Essays on the Horror Film*, edited by Barry Keith Grant, 255–76. London: Scarecrow P.
Short, Sue. 2006. *Misfit Sisters: Screen Horror as Rite of Passage.* London: Palgrave Macmillan.
———. 2015. *Fairy Tale and Film: Old Tales with a New Spin.* London: Palgrave Macmillan.
Sobchack, Vivian. 1996. "Bringing It All Back Home: Family Economy and Generic Exchange." In *The Dread of Difference: Gender and the Horror Film*, edited by Barry Keith Grant, 143–63. Austin: U Texas P.
Stratford, Jennifer Juniper. 2015. "One Last Scream: The Definitive Interview with Wes Craven, the American Master of Horror." *The Front.* www.thefront.com/read/wes-craven-one-last-scream/.
Tatar, Maria. 1992. *Off with Their Heads! Fairy Tales and the Culture of Childhood.* Princeton, NJ: Princeton UP.
Warner, Marina. 2000. *No Go the Bogeyman: Scaring, Lulling and Making Mock.* London: Vintage.

Williams, Tony. 1996. "Trying to Survive the Darker Side: 1980's Family Horror." In *The Dread of Difference: Gender and the Horror Film*, edited by Barry Keith Grant, 164–80. Austin: U Texas P.

Wood, Robin. 1984. "Introduction to the American Horror Film." In *Planks of Reason: Essays on the Horror Film*, edited by Barry Keith Grant, 164–200. London: Scarecrow P.

Zipes, Jack. 2002. *The Brothers Grimm: From Enchanted Forests to the Modern World*. New York: Palgrave Macmillan.

Mediagraphy

The Blair Witch Project. 1999. Directors Daniel Myrick and Eduardo Sanchez. USA.

The Boxtrolls. 2014. Directors Graham Annable and Anthony Stacchi. USA.

Buffy the Vampire Slayer (TV). 1997–2003. Creator Joss Whedon. USA.

Carrie. 1976. Director Brian de Palma. USA.

The Descent. 2005. Director Neil Marshall. UK.

Dexter (TV). 2006–2013. Creator James Manos Jr. USA.

Dumplings. 2004. Director Fruit Chan. Hong Kong.

Eden Lake. 2008. Director James Watkins. UK.

The Evil Dead. 1981. Director Sam Raimi. USA.

The Grudge. 2004. Director Takashi Shimizu. USA.

Halloween. 1978. Director John Carpenter. USA.

Hannibal (TV). 2013–2015. Creator Brian Fuller. USA.

Hansel and Gretel: Witch Hunters. 2013. Director Tommy Wirkola. USA.

Let the Right One In. 2008. Director Tomas Alfredson. Sweden.

Mama. 2013. Director Andrés Muschietti. USA.

A Nightmare on Elm Street. 1984. Director Wes Craven. USA.

Pan's Labyrinth. 2006. Director Guillermo del Toro. Brazil.

ParaNorman. 2012. Directors Sam Fell and Chris Butler. USA.

Psycho. 1960. Director Alfred Hitchcock. USA.

The Ring. 2002. Director Gore Verbinski. USA.

Saw (Film Franchise). 2004–2010. Creators James Wan and Leigh Whannell. USA.

The Shining. 1980. Director Stanley Kubrick. UK/USA.

A Tale of Two Sisters. 2003. Director Kim Ji-Woon. South Korea.

The Texas Chainsaw Massacre. 1974. Director Tobe Hooper. USA.

True Blood (TV). 2008–2014. Creator Alan Ball. USA.

The Twilight Saga (Film Franchise). 2008–2012. Directors Catherine Hardwicke, Chris Weitz, David Slade, and Bill Condon. USA.

The Vampire Diaries (TV). 2009–. Creators Julie Pec and Kevin Williamson. USA.

The Walking Dead (TV). 2010–. Creator Frank Darabont. USA.

The Woods. 2006. Director Lucy McKee. USA.

Wrong Turn. 2003. Director Rob Schmidt. USA.

60

MOBILE APPS

Cynthia Nugent

Fairy tales are popular subjects with children's app developers because their well-known stories are readily adapted. This chapter looks at the range of expressions of fairy tales in children's picture book apps (also known as story apps) for the iPad, from little more than vehicles for advertising to creatively realized literary artworks. Thus, for example, Tab Tales advertises its apps as free, but they must be purchased if the player wishes to move beyond the first few screens. Fairy-tale apps are also one of the ways big media diversifies its assets, as in the case of Disney's *Frozen* (2013). But producers such as the successful children's publisher Nosy Crow, which specializes in both children's books *and* story apps, interpret fairy tales in entertaining, well-designed, and child-centered ways. As an example of the story app as literary artwork, I look at a remediation of the picture book *Caperucita Roja*, an interpretation of the 1924 poem by Nobel prizewinner Gabriela Mistral, by contemporary Chilean children's author-illustrator Paloma Valdivia.

I also use my own work to illustrate how picture book apps function. As a visual artist, story app maker, children's book author-illustrator, and student, fairy tales have been a rich source of inspiration. For my hybrid-creative MA in Children's Literature, I adapted the picture book *The King Has Goat Ears* (Jovanovic and Béhà 2008), a retelling of a traditional tale, as a story app, which I later published on the App Store. Working on this project gave me insights into the historical antecedents of the story app, the marketplace, the production process, popular and scholarly responses to the form, and the ways story app developers have interpreted fairy tales. And buying and playing over 100 story and toy apps gave me an overview of the range of artistic, literary, and multimodal sophistication of the story apps on the market.

In the traditional tale (ATU 782), as retold by Jovanovic, King Boyan never leaves the palace so no one will see his goat ears. Any barber who comes to cut his hair is never seen again. The last barber remaining in the kingdom faints from fear, and his apprentice volunteers to go in his place. Young Igor doesn't react to the king's ears but tells him he looks very handsome, so the king lets him go home. When the pressure of keeping the secret becomes too much, Igor shouts it into a hole in the ground and covers it. Reeds grow from the spot, which passing shepherds carve into flutes and sell. But instead of music, the flutes sing out, "The king has goat ears!" Igor convinces the king to venture out, but as he drives in his royal coach, children are blowing the talking flutes. When a guard seizes a child, the injustice forces the king to show his head and reveal his goat ears. In doing so, he learns that he is accepted by others and that he likes himself just the way he is.

To create *The King's Ears* (2016), I designed the interactions, edited sound effects and music, hired actors, and booked recording studios. I edited the story text to fit the iPad screen, created new art in the style of illustrator Philippe Béhà, made animations, and wrote detailed specifications for the two computer programmers who coded the project. Throughout the process, I was led by scholarship that defined the picture book as a marriage of the modes of words and pictures, seeking to extend this interrelationship to include the story app's sounds, animations, and interactions. My design was influenced by the idea that a picture book's words and illustrations "each speak[s] about matters on which the other is silent" (Nodelman 1988, 221); the modes should each tell aspects of the story with as little redundancy between modes as possible.

My design also benefited from research in sound semiotics and audiobooks and the fledgling field of children's app design theory, in particular, *Best Practices: Designing Touch Tablet Experiences for Preschoolers* (Sesame Workshop 2012). Another important source of insight were discussions of the story app from a literary perspective, such as Ture Schwebs on aesthetic considerations (2014). Krystina Madej's distinction between modes as incidental or integral to the narrative (2003, 9–12) was especially helpful in clarifying my design goals to myself and in discussions with the programmers, who were keen to add lots of action to each screen. Integral (or meaningful) interactions can "create tension between modes, move the story forward, add humour, and show alternate points of view or narrative outcomes" (Stichnothe 2014, 3) in the same way that words and pictures are interdependent in the picture book.

Interactive digital stories have been available on the web and as CD-ROMs for nearly thirty years, but the iPad's introduction in 2010 brought one critical difference: the touchscreen. It makes the iPad intuitively playable by even very young children (Buckleitner 2011, 36–37). When the finger touches the screen, the device detects electricity in the human body. The iPad allows up to eleven simultaneous touches (multitouch), so that several children can play on one iPad at the same time. Using the finger directly on the screen allows for "continuous interplay" (Schwebs 2014, 9) and intuitive, meaningful, and relatively unimpeded engagement, while a computer mouse, which you have to learn how to use, always keeps the player at a remove from what is happening on the screen. With the touchscreen, players may tap, drag, and pinch and spread their fingers; some gestures effectively mimic the sensation of touching a real object. For example, in the app *Moo, Baa, La La La* (2011), when a player drags back the dog, then lifts their finger off the screen, the dog flies off, giving the player a feeling uncannily similar to releasing a rubber band.

Inventive app designers, such as Nosy Crow, also employ the iPad's camera, microphone, speakers, and other sensors, including the accelerometer, which responds to rotating, tipping, and shaking the device. In their *The Three Little Pigs* (2011), blowing into the iPad's microphone when the wolf is huffing and puffing initiates an animation of the straw house falling down. In their *Snow White* (2013), the player can soothe a crying infant back to sleep by rocking the iPad. The iPad's camera simulates a mirror in other fairy tales by showing a live view of the player's face in a mirror frame (*Cinderella* 2011) or reflecting pond (*Little Red Riding Hood* 2013), creating an imaginary location of the child's body within the scene, opposite the characters. With narrative-related interactions such as these, "readers enter the fictional world as participants becoming [. . .] part of the fiction as well as its co-authors" (Frederico 2014, 148).

Some journalists writing about story apps do not distinguish between incidental and integral sounds, animations, and interactions, calling all of the playful elements in a story app diversions or "bells and whistles" (Quenqua 2014). Questions about whether touching the screen and listening to sounds interferes with reading comprehension prompted a number of studies comparing reading from the screen with reading a codex (paper book) (e.g., Chiong et al. 2012). Conscious of these concerns, most developers now add word highlighting synchronized with the narration to their story apps and use the word "educational" in their App Store descriptions. But picture book reading isn't just about word recognition, nor is reading the picture book an exclusively intellectual process. Margaret Mackey suggests that "we need to ask whether [. . .] the use of the hands engages the brain in ways that play a constitutive role in the reading processes" (2007, 113).

Although expensive and difficult to make, story apps are cheaper than eBooks in the App Store. Story apps are software written in computer code or built with app-authoring software like the *TigerCreate 2* app (2017) where sounds, text, and images can be dragged in. eBooks are document files, sometimes no more than faithful reproductions of picture book spreads with letter-boxing to preserve the book's proportions. Enhanced eBooks may have sound effects, narration, and simple animations. Warren Buckleitner suggests thinking of the relationship of the eBook to enhanced eBook to the story app as "a messy continuum between less and more interactivity" (2011, 10).

A sophisticated story app with narratologically rich sounds, animations, interactions, images, and words can be considered, like opera and cinema, a *Gesamtkunstwerk* (a total artwork) because it combines a number of art disciplines. *LittleRed App* (2014) is an example of combining beautiful and integral sound with technical and artistic innovation while encouraging playfulness and experimentation. Sophisticated picture books are artistically written and illustrated and the full meaning of the narrative only understood through an interplay between words and pictures:

> In a picture book, both the text and the illustration sequence would be incomplete without the other. They have a synergistic relationship in which the total effect depends not only on the union of the text and illustrations but also on the perceived interactions or transactions between these two parts.
>
> (Sipe 1998, 98–99)

But few story apps are sophisticated in this way. Many developers come to children's story app creation with a view of words and pictures as mere content. Their expertise is in video-game-derived technology, not with picture books and what constitutes a sophisticated multimodal story for children.

Popular and well-known, traditional fairy tales are a source of ready-made content, often with no copyright restrictions. For instance, *The Story of the Three Little Pigs* (1904) by L. Leslie Brooke is in the public domain and available on Project Gutenberg. It has been copied wholesale into apps such as *Three Little Pigs and the Secrets of a Popup Book* (2010) and *Three Little Pigs: The Story* (2013) by Russian developer Touchanka. While these two story apps are well made, and in some respects innovative, developers like Tab Tales use fairy tales as little more than vehicles for in-app sales and advertising. Interactivity is sparse and incidental, including the games players can open at any point during the progress of the story. Banners at the bottom of the screen advertise banks, cars, and other products, and the app uses the player's iPad's location detector to insert local advertising: my iPad had a local Kijiji sale ad for a van and another for an event advertised by my municipality. Many of their apps are free to download but must be purchased by the third story tableau or a big lock appears in the middle of the screen and the images become black and white (see figure 60.1). In Tab Tales' *Cinderella* (2011), there are four dress-up screens for choosing clothes for the sisters, the prince, and Cinderella. If a player doesn't pay for this option, Cinderella attends the ball in her underwear! Nevertheless, Tab Tales fairy tales have rhyming text that highlights along with the narration and so have some justification in describing their apps as "educational experiences."

Frozen Storybook Deluxe (2016) is one of the Disney Storybook Deluxe app series derived from their animated features. Based on Hans Christian Andersen's "The Snow Queen," it's about the struggle of an affectionate princess to reach her withdrawn sister, who is cursed with

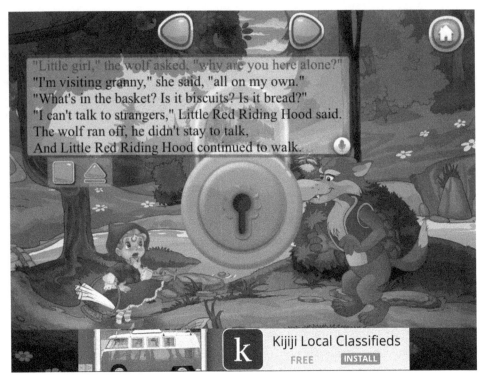

Figure 60.1 Locked screen of Tab Tales' *Little Red Riding Hood*

the power to freeze everything she touches. A nice aspect of the app is the choice of reading the story from one or the other sister's point of view by rotating the tablet. Video clips from the feature film are intercut with still artwork, purpose-written text, and games. The games do not affect the narrative, so there is no co-authoring by the player, and the non-interactive, embedded movie clips do not allow for a child-controlled experience.

Author-illustrator Jon Klassen, who started out in animation, notes, "One of the big differences between books and animation or film in general is that with books [. . .] the viewer is moving at their own speed through the story, whereas with film you are controlling their time" (quoted in Arrant 2011). In an app, a movie clip is a rectangular object with many things animating inside it. Generally it's non-interactive, which is significantly different from being able to cause different objects on the screen to animate separately (sprite animation—see figure 60.2). Short, replayable,

Figure 60.2 The four sprites of the parrot's flying cycle are played in a looping sequence of 1, 2, 3, 4, 3, 2; the flying cycle plays as long as the bird is touched

Figure 60.3 First story screen, *The King's Ears*

and child-controlled sprite animations better support what picture book scholarship describes as the hermeneutic process of reading the multimodal text: "we interpret the text in terms of the pictures and the pictures in terms of the texts in a potentially never-ending sequence" (Sipe 1998, 102)

In *The King's Ears*, I tried to make each sound, animation, and interaction integral to the story. In the beginning, the king is inside a picture frame—a metaphor for being kept prisoner in the palace by his fear of being judged. In contrast, the unselfconscious bird is free and can fly anywhere it wants, an experience players embody by dragging the flying bird. When the king's unhappy face is tapped, he cries. The child may deduce that the splashes they hear when tears drop off the bottom of the screen mean the king has been crying for so long that a puddle has formed. These discrete animations discovered at the child's own speed with their own body, and taken together with words, image, and sounds, help the reflective player gain a deeper understanding of the characters and story (see figure 60.3).

Nosy Crow, founded in 2011 in the UK, is one of the few story app publishers to combine expertise in children's publishing *and* video game programming in their fairy-tale apps. Publisher Kate Wilson says,

> We felt there was room to bring real publishing knowledge [. . .] into this technology space [. . .]. The thing about fairy tales is that [. . .] you can bend them and they don't break. You can do quite a lot with them and still retain the core Cindarellaness or Three Little Pigsness.
>
> (quoted in Dredge 2011)

The stories are narrated by the characters, with the words placed inside speech balloons. Characters can be dragged through scenes and made to run, walk, leap into the air, or change direction depending on the speed of the swipe. Ed Bryan's naturalistic art is attractive and enjoyably detailed without being fussy. The 3D is subtle and creates negotiable spaces for the movements of characters. Bryan's grounding in video games is evident in the innovative interactions, technical polish, and idle animations: characters are never completely at rest, gently and amusingly blinking and bouncing as if eager to get moving.

Nosy Crow's fairy-tale apps brilliantly exploit the affordances of the iPad, including taking advantage of the way tablets allow images to extend beyond the edge of the screen. Their *Cinderella* has an especially beautiful movable background in the nighttime garden scene where the player can help Cinderella find the objects and creatures that the fairy godmother will transform to take her to the ball. The impression of actually moving through a landscape, and the accompanying sensation of magical immersion in a garden at night, is heightened by the use of parallax. This animation effect is achieved by separating the background into three or more layers (i.e., foreground, midground, and background) and moving each at a different speed as the player moves a character or tilts the iPad. Parallax is also used to great effect in scenes of traveling through the forest, a setting for a number of their fairy tales.

The use of alternative paths through the story is one way Nosy Crow encourages deconstruction of well-known tales: in *Little Red Riding Hood*, the player, acting as Red Riding Hood, chooses at three forks in the road one of six possible routes to grandmother's house. Each choice has three encounters that endow Red Riding Hood with different tools to ultimately defeat the wolf. At any time, the player can choose a different route by touching the blue ribbon in the screen's upper right to open up the menu, which is in the shape of an interactive map. This option to step out of the forest may be particularly valuable for young players. Although getting lost in a dark forest is a common, symbolically rich fairy-tale motif, losing their way in the app's maze of alternate paths may uncomfortably intensify the story and cause anxiety in the young player. The interactive map with the overview of both the physical space and the narrative timeline supplies a reassuring structure to an unpredictable tale full of predators, darkness, and scary experiences. Because the stories are moved forward by the player, Nosy Crow decided to not kill the wolf in *The Three Little Pigs* or *Little Red Riding Hood*; they were concerned that the interactivity would make the child the agent of the killing, "implicated in the action" (Bonnick quoted in Dredge 2015).

Nosy Crow's fairy tales highlight manners and the importance of showing appreciation for the efforts of others. Ethnic diversity is reflected in the multiracial Goldilocks family and the South Asian prince in *Cinderella*, including an option to dance to Bhangra music at the ball. Wickedness is laughed at, and death doesn't exist. The fairy-tale world of Nosy Crow is middle class, heard in the accents of the child narrators, seen in the style of the family homes, and evident in the typical parental gender roles portrayed in *Goldilocks and Little Bear* (2015) and *Little Red Riding Hood*. Sometimes these same middle-class values are gently sent up by placing them anachronistically, as when Snow White replies as she takes the apple proffered by the disguised queen, "I'll accept this apple because fruit is a healthy snack."

The stories have an understated feminist sensibility. Characters are condemned for lack of character rather than appearance: the stepsisters are mean instead of ugly. Brave Red Riding Hood defeats the wolf with her wits, and a girl pig appears in *The Three Little Pigs*. Red Riding Hood's mother is attractively round, girl children don't have adult waists, and Red Riding Hood wears a red hooded sweatshirt, striped socks, and wellington boots.

Another example of the handful of publishers of both books and apps is Chilean Editorial Amanuta. Their *LittleRed App* (2014) is a thoughtful and artistic interpretation of *Caperucita*

Roja, a dark poem by Nobel Prize–winning Gabriela Mistral from her 1924 collection *Ternura*, with art and design by Chilean author-illustrator Paloma Valdivia. Much of Mistral's writing concerned the abuse of women and children, and in her poem the cruel wolf is transparently a man. In the last two heartbreaking lines the child is devoured and her heart discarded: "y ha molido las carnes, y ha molido los huesos/y ha exprimido como una cereza el corazón [and has ground the meat, and has ground the bones,/and has squeezed the heart like a cherry]" (Mistral 2014, 14–17). A two-page information section on Mistral's poetic interpretations of fairy tales is appended to both the codex and the eBook but is omitted in the app, a choice that perhaps reflects an attitude that sees the playful story app as entertainment and the non-interactive codex and eBook of the same story as literature.

While the *Caperucita Roja* picture book is true to Mistral's poem, the *LittleRed App* adds two alternate endings after the poem ends. One of two final wordless screens will appear depending on the time of day that the app is opened. During the day, the final screen shows a woodcutter departing after killing the wolf, leaving the grandmother and Red Riding Hood standing on the carcass and embracing. If the app is opened at night, the inexplicably alive grandmother and granddaughter are shown tossing the wolf into a pot on the stove in a celebratory manner—no transition from being eaten to cooking!

Most of the interaction in this app is arranging the lines of the poem. As each screen opens, a four-line stanza breaks into its constituent lines and falls into a disorderly heap at the bottom of the screen. The player must drag each line up to its proper place. As each line is positioned, a bit more of the image emerges, and when the entire stanza is in place the narration starts. This interaction places the emphasis on reading and understanding the text (see figure 60.4).

Figure 60.4 Story screen 2, *LittleRed App*, Gabriela Mistral and Paloma Valdivia

Red Riding Hood and the wolf, as well as small woodland creatures, can be touched to initiate a small movement, each accompanied by its signature instrumental sound as it animates. Valdivia's artwork is full of subtle allusions to Mistral's poem, from the phallic shape of the wolf's body and nose to the blood-red smoke rising from the chimney after the wolf eats the grandmother. The murders are only shown as shadow silhouettes.

In the codex spread, there's room for Valdivia's spot images of innocent woodland creatures opposite the main illustrations. Two of these allude to the abuse and murder of the child: in one a cat hides inside underwear, and in another a raccoon stands beside a tiny tomb (see figure 60.5). Unfortunately, the iPad's format doesn't allow for the placement of the vignettes, which provide rich elaboration and counterpoint in the codex and eBook versions. The words and pictures, expressive narration by actor María Izquierdo (Spanish version), and exciting original music make *LittleRed App* a rich multimodal literary artwork. Yet the final images, experienced either sequentially or separately, detract from Mistral's powerful statement and result in an app that is perhaps less successful artistically than the codex.

These examples show how the degree of embodiment may influence the version of the fairy tale chosen by the publisher. Nosy Crow, whose apps are intensely interactive, felt that the child would have to act as murderer and victim if a character is killed in one of their apps. In *LittleRed App*, however, the interactions are all to do with rearranging the words; the player watches the murderous events rather than acts them out, and even then only sees them in the shadows they cast, and so is not embodying something potentially traumatizing.

Story apps are very expensive to create, few make money, and demands by hardware companies for constant pricey updates to show off the latest device to its best advantage have caused many picture book app developers to shut up shop. However, a positive indicator for the future of the story app is that iPads are increasingly used in schools, even if the apps are almost exclusively non-fiction. In my own work developing a fairy-tale app, I experienced the work and expense involved in creating a quality story app, followed by the frustration and disappointment of trying to get reviews and sales. But I was heartened during classroom testing to discover how remarkably appealing story apps are to children and how engaging they can be for children with reading challenges, in particular. If this exciting format for children survives, and the technical and financial barriers come down, more literary artworks of great originality and appeal may result.

Figure 60.5 Two vignettes, *Caperucita Roja* codex, Gabriela Mistral and Paloma Valdivia

MOBILE APPS

Related topics: Adaptation and the Fairy-Tale Web; Children's and Young Adult (YA) Literature; Digital; Disney Corporation; Gender; Intellectual Property; Poetry; Video Games

References Cited and Further Reading

Arrant, Chris. 2011. "How Jon Klassen Leapt from Animation to Children's Books." *Cartoon Brew*, November 21. www.cartoonbrew.com/interviews/how-jon-klassen-made-the-leap-from-animation-to-childrens-books-52881.html.

Beckett, Sandra, ed. 2013. *Revisioning Red Riding Hood around the World: An Anthology of International Retellings.* Detroit: Wayne State UP.

Brooke, L. Leslie. 1904. *The Story of the Three Little Pigs.* Project Gutenberg.

Buckleitner, Warren. 2011. *Child Development 101 for the Developers of Interactive Media: An Overview of Influential Theories of Child Development, Applied to Practice.* Flemington, NJ: Active Learning Associates Inc.

———. 2013. "Thinking Outside the Page: Four Views of Children's eBooks." http://childrenstech.com/files/2013/09/ebooks-eel13.pdf.

Chiong, Cynthia, Jinny Ree, Lori Takeuchi, and Ingrid Erickson. 2012. *Print Books vs. E-Books: Comparing Parent-Child Co-Reading on Print, Basic, and Enhanced E-Book Platforms.* New York: The Joan Ganz Cooney Center at Sesame Workshop.

Dredge, Stuart. 2011. "Nosy Crow Talks Fairy Tales, Book-Apps and Making Your Own Machine." *The Guardian*, September 13. www.theguardian.com/technology/appsblog/2011/sep/13/nosy-crow-cinderella-book-apps.

———. 2015. "Snow White by Nosy Crow: 'Getting Children Sparkly-Eyed about Storytelling'." *The Guardian*, March 13. www.theguardian.com/technology/2015/mar/13/snow-white-nosy-crow-app-review.

Frederico, Aline. 2014. "Playfulness in E-Picture Books: How the Element of Play Manifests in Transmediated and Born-Digital Picture book Apps." MA thesis. Vancouver: U British Columbia.

Jovanovic, Katarina. 2008. *The King Has Goat Ears*, illustrated by Philippe Béhà. Vancouver: Tradewind Books.

Mackey, Margaret. 2007. *Literacies across Media: Playing the Text.* New York: Routledge.

Madej, Krystina. 2003. "Towards Digital Narrative for Children: From Education to Entertainment: A Historical Perspective." *ACM Computers in Entertainment* 1 (1): 1–17.

Mistral, Gabriela. (1924) 2014. *Caperucita Roja*, illustrated by Paloma Valdivia. Madrid: Diego Pun Ediciones.

Nodelman, Perry. 1988. *Words about Pictures: The Narrative Art of Children's Picture Books.* Athens: U Georgia P.

Quenqua, Douglas. 2014. "Is E-Reading to Your Toddler Story Time, or Simply Screen Time?" *The New York Times*, October 11. www.nytimes.com/2014/10/12/us/is-e-reading-to-your-toddler-story-time-or-simply-screen-time.html.

Schwebs, Ture. 2014. "Affordances of an App: A Reading of the Fantastic Flying Books of Mr. Morris Lessmore." *Nordic Journal of ChildLit Aesthetics* 5: 1–11.

Sesame Workshop. 2012. "Best Practices: Designing Touch Tablet Experiences for Preschoolers." www.sesameworkshop.org/wp_install/wp-content/uploads/2013/04/Best-Practices-Document-11-26-12.pdf.

Sipe, Lawrence R. 1998. "How Picture Books Work: A Semiotically Framed Theory of Text-Picture Relationships." *Children's Literature in Education* 29 (2): 97–107.

Stichnothe, Hadassah. 2014. "Engineering Stories? A Narratological Approach to Children's Book Apps." *Nordic Journal of ChildLit Aesthetics* 5: 1–9.

Mediagraphy

Cinderella (Mobile App). 2011. Nosy Crow. http://nosycrow.com/apps/cinderella/.

Frozen. 2013. Directors Chris Buck and Jennifer Lee. USA.

Frozen Storybook Deluxe (Mobile App). 2016. Disney LOL. http://lol.disney.com/games/frozen-storybook-deluxe-app.

Goldilocks and Little Bear (Mobile App). 2015. Nosy Crow. http://nosycrow.com/apps/goldilocks-and-little-bear/.

The King's Ears (Mobile App). 2016. Rascal Media. https://rascalmedia.com.

LittleRed App (Mobile App). 2014. Amanuta. https://itunes.apple.com/tn/app/littlered-app/id597592905?mt=8.

Little Red Riding Hood (Mobile App). 2013. Nosy Crow. http://nosycrow.com/apps/little-red-riding-hood/.

Moo, Baa, La La La (Mobile App). 2011. http://loudcrow.com/moo-baa-la-la-la/.

Snow White (Mobile App). 2013. Nosy Crow. http://nosycrow.com/apps/snow-white/.

The Three Little Pigs (Mobile App). 2011 Nosy Crow. http://nosycrow.com/apps/the-three-little-pigs/.

The Three Little Pigs and the Secrets of a Popup Book (Mobile App). 2010. Game Collage. http://gamecollage.com/three-little-pigs/.

Three Little Pigs: The Story (Mobile App). 2013. Touchanka. www.facebook.com/search/top/?q=touchanka.

TigerCreate 2 (Mac Desktop App). 2017. Tiger Media International GmbH. www.tigercreate.com/en/.

61

MUSIC VIDEOS AND POP MUSIC

Rebecca Hutton and Emma Whatman

Like oral, written, or filmic narratives, music videos form part of the ubiquitous and constantly evolving corpus of fairy-tale texts. In one of the few dedicated studies of the nature and typology of fairy-tale music videos, Kendra Magnus-Johnston argues that this form of adaptation protracts the "form and tradition" of the fairy tale while also reflecting the "sociocultural conditions in which [each] adaptation was produced and circulated" (2016, 681). Simultaneously, the music video as a medium finds "different ways of moving images or sounds into the social spaces of its users, and so places and displaces [audiences] differently" (Berland 1993, 27). Fairy-tale music videos thus constitute media conduits through which adaptations evidence shifting social, cultural, and political landscapes of the times and places in which they are produced. Yet these texts are also complicated by competing aesthetic and consumerist values, intensifying the complex matrix of significations and consequent ideologies that exist within, and are disseminated through, contemporary fairy-tale music videos.

The presence of fairy-tale intertexts within music videos is not unusual. The popularized and cross-cultural distribution of a number of fairy tales, coupled with an abundance of adaptations across modes and media, has meant that fairy tales have been adopted as a recurrent lyrical component of, or visual complement to, songs across myriad musical genres. Fairy-tale music videos—that is, videos where fairy-tale icons, motifs, characters, landscapes, storylines, or allusions are used as part of a short and usually self-contained audiovisual clip made to complement a single music track—are therefore distinct from, but still operate in relation to, the vast array of oral, written, and visual fairy-tale narratives and therefore contribute to the innumerable "hegemonic and counterhegemonic practices" that constitute the "twenty-first century fairy-tale web" (Bacchilega 2013, 36).

This type of fairy-tale text also operates in dialogue with the "multifarious set of cultural practices" and modes of representation that operate in and through the music video format (Railton and Watson 2011, 142). Music videos are simultaneously "artistic practice," "ideological apparatus" (Vernallis 2004, x), and a form of advertisement with an inherently "commercial agenda" (Railton and Watson 2011, 2). Within such a nexus the "danger" of the fairy tale becoming "instrumentalized and commercialized" (Zipes 1979, 2) becomes particularly entangled with conflicts between hegemony and subversion within a number of fairy-tale music videos. Fairy-tale music videos therefore require specific scrutiny of the multiple methods by which they place and displace their audiences rather than allowing the form to be overlooked or subsumed into larger bodies such as the fairy-tale film or musical. This specificity is particularly apparent in terms of excavating the ideological tensions between normative and subversive modes of gender and sexual representation.

A number of the music videos we discuss evidence an entrenchment in the values of predominantly patriarchal and heteronormative fairy-tale narratives that often runs counter to the overt ideological impetus of the lyrical and/or visual components. However, while the implementation of fairy tales in music videos cannot be easily separated from consumerist agendas, fairy-tale intertexts still offer sites through which resistance to, or the subversion of, normativity can be enacted through this consumer framework—namely, by disseminating counterhegemonic adaptations through a medium that is designed for mass and repeated consumption.

The fairy-tale music video oeuvre is modally diverse, favoring live action but also employing animation, CGI, or a combination of modalities. While animated and partially animated music videos are common as media tie-ins for fairy-tale films, some animated fairy-tale music videos have been produced independently of any film or television text. In the case of media tie-ins, the music video becomes doubly commercialized: not only as a tool of promoting the song, as all music clips are, but also selling the film from which the song is sourced. For example, American country singer Carrie Underwood's "Ever Ever After" (2007), written for the Disney film *Enchanted* (2007), has a title and lyrics that draw on fairy-tale motifs and a music video stylized to mirror the film's aesthetics through the interchanging of live action and animation. In addition to promoting the film, the clip simultaneously sells a fairy-tale romance script to viewers akin to the one in the film by having Underwood's animated avatar journey into the real (live action) world to find her own prince, just as Amy Adams's Princess Giselle does in *Enchanted*. Through this symmetry, viewers are enticed to enter, or re-enter, into an engagement with the patriarchal and heteronormative structures that the film and music video espouse.

The animated clip for British singer-songwriter Mika's 2007 pop song "Lollipop," in contrast, has no commercial relation to any animated fairy-tale film. The song and accompanying video were created to discourage sexual promiscuity for girls—namely, Mika's younger sister (see Hattenstone 2007). In this contemporary cautionary tale, a series of visual cues amalgamate the protagonist, Lollipop Girl, with Little Red Riding Hood. Before the music track commences, Lollipop Girl, drawn with a red bow and shoes, confronts a black screen that transforms into the intimidating shadow of a large wolf. This wolf then pursues Lollipop Girl as she makes her way along a Candyland-style landscape to meet with her mother and then grandmother, who caution her against the sexually suggestive behavior of "sucking too hard on your lollipop" ("Lollipop" 2007).

Fairy tales also appear as part of many live-action music videos designed to thematically complement songs across genres. In these videos, the implementation of each tale in the form of characterization, iconography, or closure often amplifies underlying ideological threads within the song and/or video. For example, a number of fairy-tale music videos seek to challenge gender hegemonies through revisions to the end of the expected fairy-tale script. In "Snow White" (ATU 709) themed videos, such as those of American pop star Katy Perry, American rapper Nicki Minaj, and German dance metal band Rammstein, the closure of each video attempts to break away from an entrenchment in female salvation through the intervention of a man. The 2012 video for Perry's hit song "Wide Awake" draws on ATU 709 and "Sleeping Beauty" (ATU 410) tale types and endeavors to dismantle heteronormative scripts found at the end of most versions of both tales. As with several other fairy-tale music videos, such as the American rock band Paramore's "Brick by Boring Brick" (2009) and American singer-songwriter Tori Amos's "Strange Little Girl" (2001), Perry's video includes a female child character who exists in the fairy-tale landscape alongside the adult woman. "Wide Awake" sees Perry wake up with the help of her younger self, who then leads her to punch the Prince Charming figure. In Minaj's "Va Va Voom" (2012), while the lyrics reinforce an expectation of conservative gender scripts where the prince rescues a passive and comatose Snow White, there is no resolution to Snow White's (played by Minaj) story as she is never awoken. Instead, halfway through the video Minaj swaps characters to play the evil queen, reorienting the visual narrative away from Snow White to the queen and unsettling the role of the prince within the narrative. Comparatively, in Rammstein's "Sonne" (2001), Snow White overdoses on gold (implied to be a drug akin to cocaine), and, rather than true love's kiss, an apple falling from a tree shatters the glass of her coffin and wakes her.

Continuing beyond the scope of primarily English-language examples, fairy-tale intertexts are prevalent in music videos across cultures and likewise evidence a matrix of aesthetic, ideological, and consumerist trends. German band Rammstein implements fairy-tale allusions and iconography in several of their music videos. They reconfigure tales such as "Snow White" in "Sonne" (as mentioned prior), "Little Red Riding Hood" (ATU 333) in the 1998 music video for "Du riechst so gut," and "Snow White and Rose Red" (ATU 426) in "Rosenrot" (2005) in ways that return them to "the genre's origin in darker adult tales" while also engaging these intertexts as "access point[s] for social commentary" concerning both national and transnational identities (Kahnke 2013, 189). Yet these commentaries are imbricated with misogynistic representations that permeate the band's work; in "Rosenrot," for example, "incarnations of female villain, victim, and protagonist are collapsed into the single word of 'Rosenrot' to signify female treachery and warn against the dangers that follow a loss of masculine social and sexual control" (Smith 2013, 153).

In Korean pop (K-pop) the aesthetics and tone of fairy-tale music videos are markedly different from that of a band like Rammstein and are employed to different ends. Where Rammstein's implementation of fairy-tale intertexts attempts to draw on (and at times subvert) their cultural heritage (Kahnke 2013), the use of traditional European fairy tales in K-pop videos often privileges idealized (and conservative) courtship and romance scripts. Music videos from K-pop boy bands such as 2pm (see the eclectic fairy-tale icons in "My House" [2015]), Boyfriend (see *Alice in Wonderland* motifs in "Bounce" [2015]), and CNBLUE (see "Cinderella" [2015]), for example, implement fairy tales as part of visual narratives where each male member of the band vies for the affection of a single girl who must choose between these suitors based on their embodiments of fairy-tale personas.

K-pop girl groups further exemplify a particular commerciality in the production of music videos where "the video [is] a signifier or a visualization [. . .] [that] overshadows the referent" because of intensive drives to "enhance marketability" (Unger 2015, 25–26). In a number of K-pop girl band fairy-tale music videos, fairy-tale personas are implicated in marketing female group members as idealized feminine figures. In enacting such roles, band members come to participate in affirming embedded patriarchal gender ideologies from tales such as "Red Riding Hood" and "Snow White" and literary examples such as *Alice in Wonderland* and *Peter Pan* (see for example Fiestar's "Apple Pie" [2016], Orange Caramel's "Aing" [2010], April's "Tinkerbell" [2016], and TINT's "Wolf is Stupid" [2014]). In contrast, Taiwanese pop star Jolin Tsai and Japanese pop star Namie Amuro's China pop (C-pop) song "I'm Not Yours" (2015) resists replicating conservative fairy-tale scripts that reward hyperfemininity and passivity and valorize heteronormative romance scripts. The song and accompanying music video simultaneously evoke and rewrite ATU 709 through the inclusion of lyrics such as "Mirror mirror on the wall, I don't need you anymore, I know I'm the smartest of them all" (2015). This revision is paired with a retelling of the Chinese folktale "The Three Illusions," a tale of two wealthy sisters who turn men into donkeys to serve as their slaves (see "Jolin" 2015). The video blends fairy-tale motifs and languages from both Eastern and Western cultures, interweaving visual allusions to "The Three Illusions" (such as artwork on the walls that comes to life to depict the transformation of the men into donkeys) and the verbal reference (in English) to "Snow White," as well as including lyrics in both Mandarin and English. This renders the adaptation both familiar and foreign across audiences while utilizing cross-cultural references to subvert assumptions of gender and sexual norms.

Magnus-Johnston (2016) identifies three forms of fairy-tale music videos based on the extent of the interrelationship between lyrics, video, and fairy-tale intertext: 1) music videos that reflect or subvert an already established intertextual relationship between the song's lyrics and specific tale(s); 2) videos that utilize fairy tales visually but not within the lyrics, so that fairy-tale intertexts operate as an enhancement or counterpoint to the words; and 3) videos that draw on tropes and archetypes rather than specific tales. We further distinguish fairy-tale music videos by the variegated manners in which they appropriate tales and argue that these differences are implicated in the ways each video subscribes to, or transcends, the ideological origins of its pre-texts. We suggest three subcategories: 1) videos where the music video engages with the characters, plot, or icons of a single tale or type; 2) videos that construct a composite of several tales through interweaving a number of characters, plots, and/or icons from different tales; and 3) videos where fairy-tale landscapes take precedence over specific tale types. The following suite of case studies exemplifies these subcategories and their intersections with the gender and sexual ideologies of five selected fairy-tale music videos.

The music video for American alternative group VAST's "Pretty When You Cry" (1998) subscribes to the second of Magnus-Johnston's categories, where videos employ fairy tales visually rather than in the lyrics, and the first of our subcategories in that it draws only on ATU 333. The video reproduces cautionary patriarchal ideologies through a combination of lyrics, motifs, and closure, all of which allow for a normalization of misogyny and sexual violence that runs counter to the surface female empowerment suggested visually. The video implies the abduction, rape, and murder of a young woman in a red hooded cloak by a middle-aged man. The clip suggests the sexual desires of a predator figure, and the visual "Red Riding Hood" intertexts enhance the lyrics and reflect Magnus-Johnston's assertion that fairy-tale music videos are often "adult-orientated" with a focus on sex, violence, murder, and misogyny (2016, 680). Sharon Johnson argues that in Perrault's version, "[r]epresentations of gender differences underpin the text's ideology" where the wolf represents social constructions of masculinity (intelligence, strength, aggression) and Red and her grandmother represent social constructions of femininity (pretty, passive, helpless) (2003, 331). Johnson asserts that "[w]hen interpreted symbolically instead of literally, the wolf's devouring of Little Red Riding Hood may be read as rape" (332).

ATU 333 has had specific didactic functions since its beginnings; the folktale has transformed over time from a warning to young women about getting lost in the forest into a rape narrative where women are too often condemned to accept responsibility for sexual violation (Zipes 1986, 227). VAST's video reproduces many of these patriarchal gender ideologies; however, rather than functioning symbolically, the clip delivers a literal representation of rape and murder. The music video (much like a selection of fairy-tale films analyzed by Greenhill and Kohm) "reference[s] the plot and/or central images of ATU 333, but offer[s] various twists," employing the thriller/drama genre and "current, realistic settings rather than magical, fantasied times and places" (2009, 37). The clip, set at night in a forest, begins with a woman asleep in the back seat of a man's car as they drive and then stop in a clearing. Her body, cloaked in the red hood, is draped over a tree stump, with the shot accompanied by the lyrics, "I enter/ through her eyes/she's losing her virginity/and all her will to compromise" (1998). These lyrics explicitly refer to both sex and a lack of consent and, when coupled with the visual intertext of the lifeless red-cloaked female figure, evoke the sexual violence often present in ATU 333.

After the implied rape and murder of Red, the clip shifts in setting to a house, where the visual narrative appears to subvert patriarchal ideologies as the grinning predator is attacked, stabbed, and almost drowned by a group of red amorphous figures and an older "hag" figure. Red is seen cutting her long hair off, and shots of her bruised and cut face highlight the abuse she has suffered. While this move could allude to a revenge narrative or reference other adaptations of ATU 333 where Red outwits the wolf, the overlaying lyrics of "I didn't want to hurt you baby/but you're pretty when you cry" (1998) sung by a male voice undo the visual narrative's subversive potential by returning to the pleasure taken in hurting the female protagonist. Furthermore, the closure returns to the opening scene of the woman asleep in the back of the car with the man smiling predatorily back at her, suggesting that this is a serial act.

In other ATU 333–themed videos, the overlap of fairy-tale personas and mise-en-scene similarly collapse back into—or even go so far as to emphasize and romanticize—representational models that normalize disempowerment and victimization of women and the policing of female sexuality. The video for American rock band Evanescence's 2006 "Call Me When You're Sober," for example, employs a revised ATU 333 script that on the surface appears to redress verbal and visual discourses of the passive woman. Yet tensions between empowerment and disempowerment in the mise-en-scene manifest for the three-minute-and-thirty-three-second clip. Frequent high camera angles force the band's lead singer, Amy Lee (costumed in red throughout the clip and often surrounded by wolves), to predominantly tilt her head upward as the camera looks down on her. This is reversed briefly when Lee is raised meters into the air and the camera alternates between high and low angles but is soon undercut by a return to high camera angles for the remainder of the clip. This includes the final shot, which sees Lee chuckle up at the camera in triumph only to revert to a demure figure at odds with the uncompromising woman who evolved throughout the clip.

In Tori Amos's video for "Strange Little Girl," in contrast, the artist's adoption of fairy-tale personas subverts the gendered binaries of many ATU 333 narratives where male/adult/predator threatens female/child/victim and in doing so destabilizes pervasive scripts that reinforce the disempowerment of women and children. The video for "Strange Little Girl" blurs the lines between adult and child, as well as human and wolf, through frequently interchanging Amos with both a female child and a wolf. Such transpositions deter audiences from being able to easily subscribe to a dichotomization of male as adult and predator versus female as child and victim while also excising the gendered violence of many versions. Both adult-Amos and child-Amos are victimized, yet the visual narrative reorients expectations regarding the threat, as well as the agency and power the female subject has in negotiating it.

Similar attempts to enact such subversions, however, often ultimately reinforce rather than resist conservative gender ideologies, as is evidenced by the music video for English singer Natalia Kills's 2011 pop song "Wonderland." The protagonist (played by Kills) is first seen in the opening of the video cloaked in a red hood as she is dragged by men in military garb. Through the amalgamation of different fairy-tale characters and motifs, "Wonderland" fits within our second subcategory as a composite of several tales through interweaving a number of characters and icons. The lyrics refer specifically to fairy-tale characters such as Snow White, Red Riding Hood, Cinderella, and Beauty and Beast. Additionally, both the lyrics and visual narration showcase associated fairy-tale motifs such as common settings—forest, Wonderland—and icons—the red cloak, a glass stiletto, a poisoned apple, a white rabbit, and the consumption of a human heart.

The consolidation of multiple female-focused fairy tales works to construct the patriarchal gender ideologies that underpin this music video. While the visual narrative flashes to scenes of resistance in the form of military protests, the intertextual references in the video's lyrical and visual components, and the beheading of the protagonist at the end, undo the attempt to dismantle conventional patriarchal fairy-tale ideologies. Some of the lyrics attempt to disassociate the song with notions of fairy-tale romance by saying, "I don't believe in fairy tales but I believe in you and me"; however, others such as "You be the Beast and I'll be the Beauty" (2011) explicitly position the subject as protagonist in tales that are often interpreted as patriarchal and centered in heteronormative romance. Jane Cummings argues that "'Beauty and the Beast' has always been in part a love story" (1995, 22), and Kills's later lyrics reinforce this through statements such as, "Who needs true love as long as you love me truly" (2011). In the accompanying visual narrative armed men force Kills to sit at a table with her hands bound with cable ties. As she consumes a live heart, licks an apple, and dances on the table, continuous flashes to these men highlight the constant surveillance she is under. While the video seems to construct scenes of resistance—to fairy tales, heteronormative romance, and systems of hierarchy—there is undoubtedly evidence of embedded patriarchal ideologies. Furthermore, scenes of resistance are quashed in the closure when Kills (who appears to be naked) is beheaded by a man in a white mask.

Alternatively, music videos where fairy-tale landscapes are employed, rather than specific tale types, evidence progressive potential in that they are less intimately bound to conservative ideological values. While many of the fairy-tale music videos we have addressed reveal a continuing subscription to patriarchal ideologies concerning gender and sexuality, some videos employ their format as a tool to resist or subvert hegemony. In effect, they reorient viewers to new ideological stances through both co-opting and re-deploying familiar motifs and scripts in novel ways or creating new narratives in unspecified fairy-tale landscapes. In 2015, for example, American YouTube blogger and reality TV personality Joey Graceffa released a music video for his song "Don't Wait," set in part in a generic fairy-tale forest landscape. The video was designed as an (abbreviated) semi-autobiographical account of Graceffa's life, with realist scenes of childhood bullying and parental alcoholism intercut with fairy-tale scenes featuring princes in full regalia, sword fights, the rescue of an entrapped male love interest, and a final kiss between the protagonist and his beloved that operate metaphorically to herald Graceffa's "coming out" as gay to a global audience (see Pittman 2015). By re-deploying a fairy-tale landscape, motifs, and the heroic script in the context of a romance between two princes (one played by Graceffa) rather than the familiar, and privileged, heterosexual courtship of most fairy-tale music videos, Graceffa's video capitalizes on the consumerist operations inherent in music videos to privilege a counterhegemonic representation of sexual orientation. The fairy-tale forest landscape of the video becomes a productive space where Graceffa's counterhegemonic fairy tale can be enacted. Additionally, Graceffa must battle traditional generic fairy-tale characters—trolls and a witch—before he can be with his Prince, suggesting that fairy-tale characters of the past serve as obstacles for a new ideological landscape in this adaptation.

As has been evidenced throughout this chapter, fairy tales often become a part of the ideological tapestry of a vast array of music videos spanning genres, decades, and cultures. The design of the music video—which sees fairy-tale adaptations condensed into short, self-contained audiovisual narratives meant to be consumed widely and repeatedly—means that they are powerful vehicles for the dissemination of overt and covert ideologies.

Related topics: Adaptation and the Fairy-Tale Web; Advertisement; Cinematic; Crime/ Justice; Disney Corporation; Gender; Horror; Musicals; Sexualities/Queer and Trans Studies; YouTube and Internet Video

REBECCA HUTTON AND EMMA WHATMAN

References Cited and Further Reading

Bacchilega, Cristina. 2013. *Fairy Tales Transformed? Twenty-First Century Adaptations and the Politics of Wonder*. Detroit: Wayne State UP.

Berland, Jody. 1993. "Sound, Image and Social Space: Music Video and Media Reconstruction." In *Sound and Vision: The Music Video Reader*, edited by Simon Frith, Andrew Goodwin and Lawrence Grossberg, 25–43. New York: Routledge.

Cummings, Jane. 1995. "Romancing the Plot: The Real Beast of Disney's *Beauty and the Beast*." *Children's Literature Association Quarterly* 20 (1): 22–8.

Greenhill, Pauline, and Steven Kohm. 2009. "Little Red Riding Hood and the Pedophile in Film: *Freeway, Hard Candy*, and *The Woodsman*." *Jeunesse: Young People, Texts, Cultures* 1 (2): 35–65.

Hattenstone, Simon. 2007. "Suddenly They All Wanted to Dance with Me." *The Guardian*, April 28. www.theguardian.com/music/2007/apr/28/popandrock.features.

Johnson, Sharon P. 2003. "The Toleration and Erotization of Rape: Interpreting Charles Perrault's 'Le Petit Chaperon Rouge' within Seventeenth- and Eighteenth-Century French." *Women's Studies* 32 (3): 325–52.

"Jolin Tsai Tells Boys 'I'm Not Yours' in Extravagant MV Feat. Namie Amuro." 2015. *Taipeimain*, February 5. www.taipeimain.com/jolin-tsai-tells-boys-im-not-extravagant-mv-feat-namie-amuro/.

Kahnke, Corinna. 2013. "Transnationale Teutonen: Rammstein Representing the Berlin Republic." *Journal of Popular Music Studies* 25 (2): 185–97.

Magnus-Johnston, Kendra. 2016. "Music Videos." In *Folktales and Fairy Tales: Traditions and Texts from around the World*, edited by Anne E. Duggan, Donald Haase, and Helen J. Callow, 679–83. 2nd ed. Santa Barbara: Greenwood.

Pittman, Taylor. 2015. "YouTube Star Joey Graceffa Comes Out as Gay in Magical Music Video." *The Huffington Post*, May 19. www.huffingtonpost.com.au/entry/joeygraceffacomes-out-in-music-video_n_7306218.

Railton, Diane, and Paul Watson. 2011. *Music Video and the Politics of Representation*. Edinburgh: Edinburgh UP.

Smith, Erin Sweeney. 2013. "Fear, Desire and the Fairy Tale *Femme Fatale* in Rammstein's 'Rosenrot'." In *Rammstein on Fire: New Perspectives on the Music and Performances*, edited by John T. Littlejohn and Michael T. Putnam, 150–72. Jefferson: McFarland & Company.

Unger, Michael A. 2015. "The Aporia of Presentation: Deconstructing the Genre of K-Pop Girl Group Music Videos in South Korea." *Journal of Popular Music Studies* 27 (1): 25–7.

Vernallis, Carol. 2004. *Experiencing Music Video: Aesthetics and Cultural Context*. New York: Columbia UP.

Zipes, Jack. 1979. *Breaking the Magic Spell: Radical Theories of Folk and Fairy Tales*. New York: Routledge.

———. 1986. *Don't Bet on the Prince: Contemporary Feminist Fairy Tales in North America and England*. New York: Methuen.

Mediagraphy

"Aing" (Music Video). 2010. Artist Orange Caramel. Pledis Entertainment. South Korea. www.youtube.com/watch?v=ITpV7hRQqw8.

"Apple Pie" (Music Video). 2016. Artist Fiestar. LOEN Entertainment. South Korea. www.youtube.com/watch?v=3BpnB47Fxts.

"Bounce" (Music Video). 2015. Artist Boyfriend. Starship Entertainment. South Korea. www.youtube.com/watch?v=hnum0Qie2rY.

"Brick by Boring Brick" (Music Video). 2009. Artist Paramore. Fueled by Ramen. USA. www.youtube.com/watch?v=A63VwWz1ij0.

"Call Me When You're Sober" (Music Video). 2006. Artist Evanescence. Wind-Up. USA. www.youtube.com/watch?v=_RrA-R5VHQs.

"Cinderella" (Music Video). 2015. Artist CNBLUE. FNC Entertainment. South Korea. www.youtube.com/watch?v=CkY8I7s_TOA.

"Du Riechst So Gut" (Music Video). 1998. Artist Rammstein. Motor Music. Germany. www.youtube.com/watch?v=rrmsJhf89MY.

Enchanted. 2007. Director Kevin Lima. USA.

"Ever Ever After" (Music Video). 2007. Artist Carrie Underwood. Arista. USA. www.youtube.com/watch?v=QAniOB1Ts4k.

Graceffa, Joey. 2015. "Don't Wait." *YouTube*, May 16, 2015. www.youtube.com/watch?v=Kcwo_mhyqTw.

"I'm Not Yours" (Music Video). 2015. Artist Jolin Tsai Featuring Namie Amuro. Warner Music Taiwan. Taiwan. www.youtube.com/watch?v=C7wRb9adQUc.

MUSIC VIDEOS AND POP MUSIC

"Lollipop" (Music Video). 2007. Artist Mika. Universal. USA. www.youtube.com/watch?v=6md5RSnVUuo.

"My House" (Music Video). 2015. Artist 2pm. JYP Entertainment. South Korea. www.youtube.com/watch?v=u2 pFB1dCSo4.

"Pretty When You Cry" (Music Video). 1998. Artist VAST. 2blossoms. USA. www.youtube.com/watch?v=IOZ 6ptqcbUc.

"Rosenrot" (Music Video). 2005. Artist Rammstein. Motor Music. Germany. www.youtube.com/watch?v=af59U 2BRRAU.

"Sonne"(Music Video). 2001. Artist Rammstein. Motor Music. Germany. www.youtube.com/watch?v=StZcUAPRRac.

"Strange Little Girl"(Music Video). 2001. Artist Tori Amos. Atlantic. USA. www.youtube.com/watch?v=ghGgycFEg64.

"Tinkerbell"(Music Video). 2016. Artist April. DSP Media. South Korea. www.youtube.com/watch?v=43Ai41L_UnI.

"Va Va Voom" (Music Video). 2012. Artist Nicki Minaj. Young Money. USA. www.youtube.com/watch?v=3U72 hzeBLOw.

"Wide Awake" (Music Video). 2012. Artist Katy Perry. Capitol. USA. www.youtube.com/watch?v=k0BWlvnBmIE.

"Wolf is Stupid" (Music Video). 2014. Artist TINT. GH Entertainment. South Korea. www.youtube.com/watch?v=7xfCvFIo68w.

"Wonderland" (Music Video). 2011. Artist Natalia Kills. will.i.am Music Group. USA. www.youtube.com/watch?v=ayVuQLT00v0.

62

MUSICALS

Jill Terry Rudy

Since singing transforms the speaking voice, and animation transforms the human body and the entire world to drawn- or computer-generated images, fairy-tale musicals after Walt Disney's *Snow White and the Seven Dwarfs* (1937) heighten the fairy tale's association with change. Transformation links fairy tale and song in nineteenth-century theatrical productions such as French *féeries* and British pantomimes, then with ensuing film and broadcast productions (Zipes 2011). Such change is not only thematic or ideological but an opportunity for special effects that envision wonder. Kristian Moen writes specifically of the cinema's apt association with fairy tale to highlight transformative possibilities. Connecting *féeries* and modern cinema, Moen acknowledges that French spectacular fairy plays "anticipated and in some respects moulded [. . .] vivid depictions of visual metamorphosis" (2013, 5). In addition to special effects, often the score and songs highlight thematic messages, express mood, and build memories with a metamusical savvy that involves thought and emotion. Thus, combining fairy tale and song signals an *aural* metamorphosis from talk to music that resonates with audiences.

The capacity to put together fairy tale, song, and a musical theater show creates wondrous cognitive and affective dimensions that may deepen or contradict what narrative alone accomplishes. Wonder here primarily "involves both awe and curiosity" (Bacchilega 2013, 5). Referring to René Descartes's placement of wonder as the first passion, Marguerite La Caze associates it with "a sudden surprise of the soul (or mind)" that "seems so worthy of attention that we are transfixed by it" (2013, 13). Music itself involves "a very broad range of mental processes and contents"; musical properties such as rhythm, tone, and pattern may be recognized and described, while preferences, feelings, and experiences elicited by music may be evaluated by listeners and scholars alike (Juslin and Sloboda 2001, 3–4). Therefore, musicals play with possibilities and work "to produce a utopian view of life" in order to acknowledge "the tensions, and their reconciliations, of everyday relations between individuals and society" (Filmer, Rimmer, and Walsh 1999, 382). Fairy tale accomplishes similar social work of expressing, and offering resolutions between, utopian aspirations and real-world tensions (Warner 2014; Zipes 2011; Tatar 2017). So, the musical combines with fairy tale to help producers and audiences navigate personal and collective social relations in pleasurable, instructive entertainments.

One way this happens and evokes wonder is to regularize singing as normal in the show. This regularizing effect sparks curiosity and surprise through the juxtaposition of song, dance, and showmanship with the storytelling and its enactment of life opportunities and troubles. Participants learn conventions of musical underscoring that may become integral to the storytelling while at other times may stand apart from the narrative trajectory as background, interlude, or distraction (Winters 2010).

The transition to singing in a musical often occurs without commentary on anything extraordinary happening, yet it still involves something remarkable with singing itself. Louis

Biancolli notes that "in a standard musical, you're not surprised when talk suddenly modulates into song" (Stempel 2010, 569). Yet musical comedy and other conventions may play up the "bump" that occurs in shifting into song; this admits, and often draws attention to, the distinction between talking and singing (268). In these ways of regularizing and surprising, song may nuance a tale and its telling while enhancing the fairy tale's "refusal to provide any sort of realistic detail or conventional causal logic to the worlds they describe" (Tiffin 2009, 4). Thus, fairy-tale musicals involve music with social life in marvelous, yet conventionalized, ways that combine theatrical art, sentimentality, or melodrama along with parody and play. This concerted effortlessness toward the fantastic effects wonder through juxtaposition and transformation.

Like other popular entertainments, musicals wax and wane in public favor; like fairy tales, whether highly popular or not, musicals remain culturally crucial (Stempel 2010, 655–656). Also like fairy tales, early exposure to musicals in childhood often initiates their lingering personal and cultural resonances (see Sawin 2014; Block 2003, xii–xiii). Anne Duggan links fairy tale with film and musicals, but she recognizes that film involves taking viewers "into an 'other' space" while a musical "transforms the everyday into a space of the marvelous through dance and song" (2013, 3). This makes fairy-tale musical films a fascinating site of transport and transformation involving the mundane and the spectacular, which also happens with the speaking, singing, and dancing of theatrical and broadcast shows (Stempel 2010, 3). Like fairy tales, musicals are intermedially adept especially because they involve "more than one medium—or sensory channel—in a given work" (Grishakova and Ryan 2010, 3).

Undeniably, fairy tale and musicals make a popular combination. The live-action remake of Disney's musical *Beauty and the Beast* (2017) took in over one billion dollars worldwide six weeks after its March 17 premiere (Google 2017). And a brief social media firestorm greeted word that the live-action *Mulan* movie (2019, dir. Niki Caro) would not include songs from the 1998 Disney animated version (Zeitchik 2017). Ranging from bright and breezy to terrifying and troubling, fairy-tale musicals help individuals and cultures navigate pivotal issues such as wealth, including social status; love (especially the romantic entwined with familial); and belonging, including social place. This chapter analyzes Disney and other fairy-tale musicals to study the wonder and important social work that happens when the spectacular juxtaposes with common, everyday occurrences.

Disney's First Classic Feature

Disney's *Snow White and the Seven Dwarfs* (1937) would be a dramatically different endeavor without the songs (words, Larry Morey, and music, Frank Churchill). The movie received a great deal of publicity as the "first feature-length cartoon film,"[1] while its status as a musical seems taken for granted (Holliss and Sibley 1987, 4). Yet, as Jack Zipes points out, fairy tale and music in film extend from earlier associations of "theater, vaudeville, and opera" that should not be underestimated (2011, 180). When analyzed for the music, this film demonstrates how the combination of fairy tale and song enacts the transformational and wondrous possibilities of each expressive mode by connecting them. *Snow White*'s songs and score tap into a musical and cultural spectrum of high- and lowbrow that Daniel Batchelder deftly identifies as both European and American inflected (2017). While not primarily billed as a musical, the film provides a metacommentary on the accomplishments of singing. Notably, the Queen/Witch (Lucille La Verne) never sings and is associated with melodramatic and classical underscoring, while Snow White (Adriana Caselotti) sings four songs in ways, such as "coloratura vocalise," that signal both the European operetta and her own sweetness (Batchelder 2017, 15–20).

Music not only works here to characterize the Evil Queen and Snow White but to influence audience reception of the characters and the story through the metamusical commentary and tight juxtapositions of talk and song.

Thematically, Snow White's four songs revolve around wishes, love, work, and singing. Her opening "I'm Wishing" song, where her voice echoes in the wishing well, is punctuated by the entrance of the Prince (Harry Stockwell). He sings the echo on "today" and then adds his own romantic "One Song," which expressly combines singing with the love and wishes Snow White has just expressed. He sings in the concluding lines, "One song/my heart keeps singing/of one love/only for you"; thus music and romance are combined in the song and embodied, through the animated drawings, by the Prince. His operetta singing style matches Snow White's, further linking them even in their initial encounter (Batchelder 2017, 19). Thus, the content of the song and its form reinforce fairy-tale conventions of the heroine being an apt match for the prince despite appearances since she is dressed in ragged work clothes.

In further metamusical commentary, after racing through the scary forest, to what Batchelder identifies as musical "German Expressionistic conventions," Snow White learns from the birds that singing "With a Smile and a Song" will help her recover from her fears (2017, 23). In tandem with the birds and woodland animals, she also asserts in "Whistle While You Work" that cleaning "won't take long/when there's a song/to help you set the pace." Tracey Mollet asserts that "Disney was one of the first to use song to tell his stories," since sound had only been part of motion pictures for ten years when *Snow White* premiered; he used "song to unite his audience around a common goal," such as overcoming the American Great Depression through the optimism of wishing and working (2013, 121).

Snow White set a standard for other Disney fairy-tale movies, with the regard and attachment for the story, songs, and movie fostered by publicity and confirmed by critics and the box office. This movie also claims to have the first soundtrack recording, which, along with sheet music and radio airtime, made the songs—as heard in the movie—available in everyday life (Kaufman 2012, 240). In reviews posted to the International Movie Database (IMDb), the most consistent response to *Snow White*'s music involves the words "classic" and "memorable," although some reviewers note that the operatic style is not appreciated decades later ("Reviews and Ratings" 2017). Disney's cultural and economic empire sparked by *Snow White* remains undeniably, or perhaps inexplicably, in tune with ways fairy-tale song appeals to global audiences (Zipes 2011, 180–181).

Because the songs are often about singing itself, in the film they keep music and singing indelibly connected with fairy-tale transformations involved in family life and human development. Disney's *Snow White* offers metamusical commentary on songs and singing as entwined with the fairy tale. Song aligns with the fairy tale's complex associations with reality, suspension of disbelief, wonder, and possibility. This happens because singing is a possible, but not typical, verbal communication that works in fairy-tale musicals, like Disney's *Snow White*, to express wishes, deal with the unexpected, handle mundane tasks like work and traumatic life situations like murderous stepmothers, and attract and retain viewing audiences.

Rodgers and Hammerstein's Broadway Musical on Television

Rodgers and Hammerstein's *Cinderella* (1957, dir. Ralph Nelson; 1965, dir. Charles S. Dubin; 1997, dir. Robert Iscove) basically maintains the ethos combining fairy tale and song to portray dreams, possibilities, love, and wonder but with the distinctive appeal of Broadway musical theater and the emerging and changing medium of television. The songs express these themes with memorable lyrics and music such as "Impossible/It's Possible," "Ten Minutes

Ago," and "Do I Love You Because You're Beautiful?" (Block 2003, 177). The writers and composers of many successful Broadway plays and film adaptations, Richard Rodgers and Oscar Hammerstein II became a blockbuster team who innovated the incorporation of song and story into a more seamless combination called a musical play or "book musical" (Filmer, Rimmer, and Walsh 1999, 382–383). *Cinderella* was Rodgers and Hammerstein's only overt fairy-tale musical and only play solely for television.[2] While live stage performance, history, location, and cultural cachet distinguish Broadway plays, television can at least replicate the live performance element and original casts and can introduce millions of viewers to the story and songs (Stempel 2010, 4). After the 1957 telecast, the television network, advertising sponsors, and critics all emphasized the magnitude of television's audience in trying to fathom over 100 million viewers at one time. One firm announced, "It would have taken an 80-year [Broadway] run—at eight performances a week—to reach an audience of the same size" (Messing 1957, 61–74). Many critics commented on television as a crucial component in the successful event, and all concurred on Julie Andrews's apt casting as Cinderella, with a few noting she was too polished for a cinder girl. This may have led to the more smudgy and "mousy" appearance of Leslie Ann Warren in the 1965 version (Zipes 2011, 180), although Brandy [Norwood] gave an assured stance in her 1997 role.

The 1957 production helped transform American entertainment and culture by bringing a Broadway-style show directly into homes while also solidifying the status of its production team and fairy tale itself.[3] Rodgers and Hammerstein's association with producer Richard Lewine of the Columbia Broadcasting System (CBS) and the availability of Andrews, the emerging star, linked Broadway musicals with television as it emerged as a cultural force. However, it was not the first televised musical in the United States, and not even the first fairy-tale musical, since the National Broadcasting Company (NBC) aired live productions with the Broadway cast of *Peter Pan* in 1955 and 1956 (Stempel 2010, 416). Yet *Peter Pan*'s 65 million viewers were surpassed soundly by *Cinderella*'s (Block 2003, 172–174). Culturally and technologically, the spectacle of combining fairy tale and musicals fostered event television and played well with millions of home viewers and emerging color television capabilities. Rodgers and Hammerstein's specific adjustments to the musical make less of the spectacle and more of the storytelling, with the contiguities of song and talk giving their plays a greater sense of narrative realism than productions based more on show-stopper song and dance numbers.

Not as overtly metamusical with song references to singing as in Disney's *Snow White*, every televised version of Rodgers and Hammerstein's *Cinderella* includes several songs that self-referentially explore, if not always transform, the characters' social and existential status by invoking a sense of wonder.[4] Cinderella's first song, "In My Own Little Corner," with its references to "little corner" and "little chair," rather easily reinforces the fairy-tale penchant for passive innocent female protagonists. Still, the song declares ownership that gets her off the floor and into her own imaginary world. Additionally, Cinderella asserts agency through singing, "I can be whatever I want to be." Rather than proclaiming certainties about love, the show's signature song between Cinderella and the Prince, "Do I Love You Because You're Beautiful?" provides no answers about love or the realities of beauty and identity—all favorite fairy-tale issues. Its conclusion remains the piercing question, "Or are you really as wonderful as you seem?" Musically, the song makes the less common closing shift from minor to major chord, which echoes the uncertainty (Block 2003, 183). The songs as musical numbers capsulize the characters' conundrums while expressing resonant life experiences of searching for a place in the world and for someone to love truly.

The number between Cinderella and the Fairy Godmother, "Impossible/It's Possible," also interrogates reality directly, at first asserting what isn't possible and then allowing what can be. The song plays with fairy-tale wonder by noting that "all the wishes in the world are poppycock and twaddle" to later affirm, "Impossible things are happening every day." Hammerstein's lyric, and the 1957 and 1997 staging, downplay the role of magic and the Fairy Godmother as Cinderella must work at wishing to have the impossible happen (Green 1957, 25). Yet singing sensation Whitney Houston, as the Fairy Godmother, makes the most metamusical and spectacular statement of the play when she closes the 1997 telecast and presides from a majestic height over the wedding scene singing, "Make a wish come true/ There's music in you."[5] The lyrics reinforce fairy-tale optimism by stating that music affects self-awareness and evokes magic. This deflects attention from the ways social position affects life opportunities, an issue, though, that is implied by the 1997 "matter-of-fact racial casting" that critic Caryn James juxtaposes with real life by saying "that this racial utopia exists in a fairy tale only emphasizes its distance from reality" (1997). The ideological and identity issues are visible and open for consideration because of the casting and production choices that exemplify how the combination of fairy tale and musical draws attention to issues of contingency and possibility.

Jacques Demy's Campy Homage

While Rodgers and Hammerstein's book musicals have garnered critical and public acclaim as "a serious contemporary form of music drama and theatre," the realism of tightly combining story and song tends to minimize the spectacle often associated with fairy-tale musical trans-formations (Filmer, Rimmer, and Walsh 1999, 382). The 1970 French film *Peau d'Âne* (dir. Jacques Demy) understands how fairy tale, musical, and spectacle inscribe camp aesthetics on Perrault's story of the same title, "Donkey Skin" (ATU 510B). This tale is a "Cinderella" story with an incestuous twist where the father seeks to marry his daughter after his wife's death; the daughter often requests three dresses to delay the marriage and then escapes dressed in animalistic rags, ends up as a scullery maid, and eventually meets and marries a prince. While not as widely known in the English-speaking world as Disney or Rodgers and Hammerstein, Demy's work is considered part of the French New Wave filmmaking and influences con-temporary filmmakers (Duggan 2013).[6] Duggan analyzes how traits of subversive sexuality, aesthetic incongruity, and "self-as-spectacle" challenge gender and sexuality norms through the camp that not only is read into the movie but infuses its production (2013, 47). While the analysis focuses more on thematic and ideological issues, Duggan also recognizes that the combination of fairy tale and musical serves the camp aesthetics as well.

The aural transformation involved when talk morphs, or bursts, into song signals the extraordinary aspects of the musical that play into fairy-tale wonder and navigations of the spectacular and the mundane. Duggan points out that Demy is unique among other French New Wave directors because "his films can seem strange, even laughable, in their use of sung dialogue" (1). The juxtaposition of speech and song is highlighted in Demy's movie, rather than minimized, to affirm the self-referential camp elements. According to Duggan, his direc-tion also brings "to the fore the inherent tensions and troubles that were always already present and never quite resolved in his source tales" (2). Demy was reflexive about the possibilities of the musical and his films, recognizing them as being "en-chantés" or "signifying both 'enchanted' and 'in song,'" which connects with his early fascination with fairy tale, theater, and Disney's *Snow White* (Duggan 2013, 2). His work manifests his ongoing fascination with Disney and Gene Kelly musicals through attention to the "very concrete form—with a focus on costume, music, and color" of the musical that keys gay aestheticism and camp (4–5). His *Peau d'Âne* makes full use of the troubling, transformative possibilities of the story through production choices that juxtapose the extraordinary and the ordinary to work through issues of love and social standing.

The combinatory, as well as transformative, elements of fairy tale and musical come to the fore in Demy's camp aesthetics. Duggan analyzes in depth how the film uses "incest as a trope for alternative sexualities" and makes "incongruous juxtapositions [. . .] which function to denaturalize accepted norms" (47). The "Love Cake" scene portrays some of these features especially as they combine with fairy-tale motifs, visual cues, and musical possibilities. Demy combines the dual identity of Donkey Skin as princess and scullery maid by having the actress Catherine Deneuve appear as both characters in the scene. Her sun-colored dress is subdued compared to the astonishing color used for most of the film's costuming, yet it portrays social status with the gold hues, sparkling gems, and petite, lofty crown. This fantastic costuming combines with the domestic actions because the princess expressly puts on the dress to start making the cake and begin to sing. The music, by Michel Legrand, becomes a whimsical duet. The princess sings the recipe, and the words are echoed in song by Donkey Skin following along with her recipe book. Because the shots switch back and forth, this is not a transformation of one being to another but an overt combination of the fairy-tale fantastic and mundane. *Peau d'Âne* does not have the global recognition of Disney fairy-tale musicals, yet it is Demy's most popular film and negotiates its thorny sexual and familial issues with heightened attention to the aesthetic display, visual and aural, afforded in the utopian longings of the fairy tale and musical put together.

Crazy Ex-Girlfriend, *Moana*, and the Social Work of Fairy-Tale Musical

The combination of fairy tale and musicals merits more study to better understand the interplay of the utopian and the contingent through wondrous stories, storytelling, showmanship, and music. This chapter has focused primarily on popular American productions and also considers Demy's film because it highlights negotiations of what is socially possible and what is a given. His film works through the "visual and emotional pleasures of all things fairy" and the "often tragic underseams that hold together conventional fairy-tale plots" (Duggan 2013, 12). Further investigations should address musicals in additional cultural traditions and follow the current uptick in fairy-tale musicals, which have significant box office success and still appear regularly on television.[7] Several are made-for-TV feature productions, while others are special episodes of ongoing series.

Once Upon a Time (2011–), created by Edward Kitsis and Adam Horowitz, features a musical episode where singing is associated with being cursed and combines with the wedding of the series' principal, Emma Swann (Jennifer Morrison), and Hook/Killian Jones (Colin O'Donoghue). *Crazy Ex-Girlfriend* (2015–), created and starring comedian Rachel Bloom, is a unique, critically acclaimed musical series that explores the implications of fairy-tale influence in personal decisions and cultural mores. In a platinum age of prestige TV built on very dark, violent, serious shows like *The Wire* (2002–2008) and *Game of Thrones* (2011–), *Crazy Ex-Girlfriend* exemplifies that a televised musical series can be significant by being light and funny and by dealing centrally with interpersonal relationships. This show emphasizes the important sociocultural work accomplished by the wondrous juxtaposition of everyday life with musical numbers to interrogate fairy-tale lessons on love and social standing. In ways, the comic tone and social implications compare interestingly with the musical series *Galavant*, created by Dan Fogelman, although it is set in medieval times but aired from 2015–2016.

Fairy-tale musical also affords greater consideration of intersectionality and decolonization, or the awareness of cultural and land sovereignty and "individuals' positions in the social world" intersecting issues of race, class, gender, sexuality, age, nation, and religion (Berger and Guidroz 2010, 1). Just months before millions of people saw Disney's live-action *Beauty and the Beast*, the company launched *Moana* (2016, dir. Ron Clements and John Musker). This is an animated musical-adventure film with songs by Lin-Manuel Miranda and Opetaia Foiʻi and music by Mark Mancina that features stories of Māui (Dwayne Johnson), a Polynesian god, and Moana (Auliʻi Cravalho), a lead character who proclaims she is not another princess.

As Disney's fifty-sixth animated feature, appearing almost eighty years after *Snow White*, the film both exemplifies and challenges the success of fairy-tale musicals—by doing well at the box office and in the Billboard 200 music chart while also suggesting the Eurocentrism of both expressive forms and their contingent and utopian values as a culture industry mainstay.[8] Wai Chee Dimock sees the "hybrid rhythm of alternation and imbrication, systemization and its residues" in *Moana*'s use of computer-generated and hand-drawn animation (2017). Tēvita O. Kaʻili finds, though, that such hybridity displaces symmetry, especially because the Disney movie omits Hina, a Polynesian goddess who usually appears with Māui (2016). By centering the story on Moana's coming of age, the movie minimizes Oceanian values and, according to Kaʻili, lacks "genealogy, symmetry, and indigeneity" (2017). Such disparities call for further research on fairy tale and musicals to consider more deeply the issues of story and music, transformation, combination, the spectacular, and common discussed here and to link with Indigenous and intersectional issues that imbricate traditional expression and popular culture conventions on local and global scales (Bacchilega 2013; Foster and Tolbert 2016; McDougall 2016). While the wondrous combination continues, the play and work of fairy-tale musical will reward full attention and attentiveness.

Related topics: Broadcast; Cinematic; Classical Music; Convergence Culture; Disney Corporation; Fantasy; Gender; Hybridity; Indigeneity; Language; Sexualities/Queer and Trans Studies; Theatrical; Traditional Song

Notes

1. As is often the case, the "first" designation may be contested. Zipes attributes "the first great animated [feature-length] films of the twentieth century" (2011, 82) to Lotte Reiniger's *The Adventures of Prince Achmed*, Die Abenteuer des Prinzen Achmed (1926), and Disney's *Snow White and the Seven Dwarfs* (1937). Quirino Cristiani also is recognized for *The Apostle*, El Apóstol (1917), and *Without a Trace*, Sin dejar rastros (1918), two now lost animated features (Osmond 2010).

2. Rodger's daughter Mary composed *Once Upon a Mattress* (1959), based on Hans Christian Andersen's "Princess and the Pea" (ATU 704), which appeared on Broadway and in three televised versions (Stempel 2010, 489). Their *Cinderella* did not become a Broadway musical until 2013.

3. While many movie producers were competing with television for cultural supremacy in the 1950s, live Broadway theater was collaborating by cross-promoting shows across media—as was Walt Disney, who used television to raise funds for and build interest in Disneyland, among other productions (Schickel 1997).

4. Block provides a helpful chart comparing all the songs in the three different versions (2003, 176–178).

5. The song is interpolated from the 1953 movie *Main Street to Broadway* (dir. Tay Garnett), which includes a cameo of Rodgers and Hammerstein writing it ("Adding More to Cinderella's Score" 1997).

6. *The Love Witch* (2016), directed and written by Anna Biller, expressly identifies with Demy's *Donkey Skin* in its working of fairy-tale tropes and issues.

7. Over 4.5 percent of 1,600 entries in the Fairy Tales on Television Visualizations (FTTV) database involve musicals: fttv.byu.edu. In May 2017, the Paley Center for Media and Playbill screened several television musicals, including Rodgers and Hammerstein's *Cinderella* (1957) and *Once Upon a Mattress* (1964). Among other notable musicals is the *Into the Woods* film (2014, dir. Rob Marshall) and its numerous theatrical incarnations.

8. In early January (2017), Keith Caulfield notes that the *Moana* (2016) soundtrack appeared at the number two spot on the Billboard 200 chart, which tracks popular U.S. albums by record sales, downloads, and streaming.

MUSICALS

References Cited and Further Reading

"Adding More to Cinderella's Score? It's Possible." 1997. *Rodgers and Hammerstein News*, October 1. www.rnh.com/news/554/Adding-More-To-Cinderella-s-Score-It-s-Possible.

Bacchilega, Cristina. 2007. *Legendary Hawai'i and the Politics of Place: Tradition, Translation, and Tourism*. Philadelphia: U Pennsylvania P.

———. 2013. *Fairy Tales Transformed? Twenty-First-Century Adaptations and the Politics of Wonder*. Detroit: Wayne State UP.

Batchelder, Daniel. 2017. "From Highbrow to Heigh-Ho: Musical Tropes in Disney's Snow White and the Seven Dwarfs." May 10. www.academia.edu/3164055/From_Highbrow_to_Heigh-Ho_Musical_Tropes_in_Disneys_Snow_White_and_the_Seven_Dwarfs.

Berger, Michele Tracy, and Kathleen Guidroz, eds. 2010. *The Intersectional Approach: Transforming the Academy through Race, Class, and Gender*. Chapel Hill: U North Carolina P.

Block, Geoffrey. 2003. *Richard Rodgers*. New Haven, CT: Yale UP.

Caulfield, Keith. 2017. "*The Weekend* Returns to No. 1 on Billboard 200, *Moana* Soundtrack Zooms to No. 2." *Billboard*, June 1. www.billboard.com/articles/columns/chart-beat/7647928/the-weeknd-returns-to-no-1-on-billboard-200-moana-soundtrack-no-2.

Dimock, Wai Chee. 2017. "Animating the Ocean." *Los Angeles Review of Books*, February 3. https://lareviewofbooks.org/article/animating-the-ocean/#!.

Duggan, Anne E. 2013. *Queer Enchantments: Gender, Sexuality, and Class in the Fairy-Tale Cinema of Jacques Demy*. Detroit: Wayne State UP.

Filmer, Paul, Val Rimmer, and Dave Walsh. 1999. "Oklahoma!: Ideology and Politics in the Vernacular Tradition of the American Musical." *Popular Music* 18 (3): 381–95.

Foster, Michael Dylan, and Jeffrey A. Tolbert, eds. 2016. *The Folkloresque: Reframing Folklore in a Popular Culture World*. Logan: Utah State UP.

Google. 2017. "Box office for Disney's *Beauty and the Beast*." April 26. www.google.com/search?q=beauty+and+the+beast&oq=beauty+and+the+beast&aqs=chrome.0.0l6.3041j0j7&sourceid=chrome&ie=UTF-8#q=beauty+and+the+beast+box+office.

Green, Stanley. 1957. "'Cinderella' on a Coaxial Cable." *Saturday Review* (March 30): 24–5.

Grishakova, Marina, and Marie-Laure Ryan, eds. 2010. *Intermediality and Storytelling*. Berlin: Walter de Gruyter.

Holliss, Richard, and Brian Sibley. 1987. *Walt Disney's* Snow White and the Seven Dwarfs *and the Making of the Classic Film*. London: Andre Deutsch.

James, Caryn. 1997. "TV Weekend; The Glass Slipper Fits with a 90's Conscience." *New York Times*, October 31. http://www.nytimes.com/1997/10/31/movies/tv-weekend-the-glass-slipper-fits-with-a-90-s-conscience.html.

Juslin, Patrik N., and John A. Sloboda, eds. 2001. *Music and Emotion: Theory and Research*. Oxford: Oxford UP.

Ka'ili, Tēvita O. 2016. "Goddess Hina: The Missing Heroine from Disney's *Moana*." *Huffington Post*, December 6. www.huffingtonpost.com/entry/goddess-hina-the-missing-heroine-from-disney%CA%A%BCs-moana_us_5839f343e-4b0a79f7433b6e5.

Kaufman, J. B. 2012. *Snow White and the Seven Dwarfs: The Art and Creation of Walt Disney's Classic Animated Film*. San Francisco: Walt Disney Family Foundation P.

La Caze, Marguerite. 2013. *Wonder and Generosity: Their Role in Ethics and Politics*. Albany: SUNY P.

McDougall, Brandy Nālani. 2016. *Finding Meaning: Kaona and Contemporary Hawaiian Literature*. Tucson: U Arizona P.

Messing, Harold. 1957. The CBS Television Production of Cinderella. MA Thesis. Stanford University.

Moen, Kristian. 2013. *Film and Fairy Tales: The Birth of Modern Fantasy*. London: I. B. Tauris.

Mollet, Tracey. 2013. "'With a Smile and a Song': Walt Disney and the Birth of the American Fairy Tale." *Marvels & Tales* 27 (1): 109–24.

Osmond, Andrew. 2010. *100 Animated Feature Films*. London: Palgrave.

"Reviews and Ratings for Snow White and the Seven Dwarfs." 2017. *International Movie Database (IMDb)*, May 22. www.imdb.com/title/tt0029583/reviews.

Sawin, Patricia. 2014. "Things Walt Disney Didn't Tell Us (But at Which Rodgers and Hammerstein at Least Hinted): The 1965 Made-for-TV Musical of *Cinderella*." In *Channeling Wonder: Fairy Tales on Television*, edited by Pauline Greenhill and Jill Terry Rudy, 103–24. Detroit: Wayne State UP.

Schickel, Richard. 1997. *The Disney Version: The Life, Times, Art, and Commerce of Walt Disney*. 3rd ed. Chicago: Ivan R. Dee.

Stempel, Larry. 2010. *Showtime: A History of the Broadway Musical Theater*. New York: Norton.

Tatar, Maria. 2017. *The Classic Fairy Tales: Texts, Criticism*. 2nd ed. New York: Norton.

Tiffin, Jessica. 2009. *Marvelous Geometry: Narrative and Metafiction in Modern Fairy Tale*. Detroit: Wayne State UP.

Warner, Marina. 2014. *Once Upon a Time: A Short History of Fairy Tale*. Oxford: Oxford UP.

Winters, Ben. 2010. "The Non-Diegetic Fallacy: Film, Music, and Narrative Space." *Music and Letters* 91 (2): 224–44.

Zeitchik, Steven. 2017. "A Music-Less *Mulan*?: It's Far From Written in Stone." *LA Times*, March 22. www.latimes.com/entertainment/movies/la-et-mn-mulan-songs-niki-caro-20170322-story.html.

Zipes, Jack. 2011. *The Enchanted Screen: The Unknown History of Fairy-Tale Films.* New York: Routledge.

Mediagraphy

The Adventures of Prince Achmed (Die Abenteuer des Prinzen Achmed). 1926. Directors Lotte Reiniger and Carl Koch. Germany.

The Apostle (El Apóstol). 1917. Director Quirino Cristiani. Argentina.

Beauty and the Beast. 2017. Director Bill Condon. USA.

Cinderella. 1950. Directors Clyde Geronimi, Hamilton Luske, and Wilfred Jackson. USA.

——— (TV). 1957. Director Ralph Nelson. USA.

——— (TV). 1965. Director Charles S. Dubin. USA.

——— (TV). 1997. Director Robert Iscove. USA.

——— (Musical). 2013. Lyrics by Oscar Hammerstein II, music by Richard Rodgers. Broadway. USA.

Crazy Ex-Girlfriend (TV). 2015–. Creators Rachel Bloom and Aline Brosh McKenna. USA.

"Do I Love You Because You're Beautiful?" (Song). 1957. Lyrics by Oscar Hammerstein II, music by Richard Rodgers, album *Cinderella Soundtrack.* USA.

Galavant (TV). 2015–2016. Creator Dan Fogelman. USA.

Game of Thrones (TV). 2011–. Creators David Benioff and D. B. Weiss. USA.

"Impossible/It's Possible" (Song). 1957. Lyrics by Oscar Hammerstein II, music by Richard Rodgers, album *Cinderella Soundtrack.* USA.

"I'm Wishing/One Song" (Song). 1938. Composed by Frank Churchill, Larry Morey, and Leigh Harline, album *Snow White and the Seven Dwarfs Soundtrack.* USA.

"In My Own Little Corner" (Song). 1957. Lyrics by Oscar Hammerstein II, music by Richard Rodgers, album *Cinderella Soundtrack.* USA.

Into the Woods. 2014. Director Rob Marshall. USA.

The Love Witch. 2016. Director Anna Biller. USA.

Main Street to Broadway. 1953. Director Tay Garnett. USA.

Moana. 2016. Directors Ron Clements and John Musker. USA.

Mulan. 1998. Directors Barry Crook and Tony Bancroft. USA.

———. 2019. Director Niki Caro. USA.

Once Upon a Mattress (Musical). 1959. Lyrics by Marshall Barer, music by Mary Rodgers. Broadway. USA.

——— (TV). 1964. Directed by Joe Layton and Dave Geisel. USA.

——— (TV). 1972. Directed by Ron Field and Dave Powers. USA.

——— (TV). 2005. Directed by Kathleen Marshall. USA.

Once Upon a Time (TV). 2011–. Creators Edward Kitsis and Adam Horowitz. USA.

Peau d'Âne (Donkey Skin). 1970. Directed by Jacques Demy. France.

Peter Pan (TV). 1955. Director Clark Jones. USA.

——— (TV). 1956. Director Jerome Robbins. USA.

Snow White and the Seven Dwarfs. 1937. Directors David Hand, William Cottrell, Wilfred Jackson, Larry Morey, Perce Pearce, and Ben Sharpsteen. USA.

"Ten Minutes Ago" (Song). 1957. Lyrics by Oscar Hammerstein II, music by Richard Rodgers, album *Cinderella Soundtrack.* USA.

"There's Music in You" (Song). 1997. Lyrics by Oscar Hammerstein II, music by Richard Rodgers, album *Cinderella Soundtrack.* USA.

"Whistle While You Work" (Song). 1938. Composed by Frank Churchill, Larry Morey, and Leigh Harline, album *Snow White and the Seven Dwarfs Soundtrack.* USA.

The Wire (TV). 2002–2008. Creator David Simon. USA.

"With a Smile and a Song" (Song). 1938. Composed by Frank Churchill, Larry Morey, and Leigh Harline, album *Snow White and the Seven Dwarfs Soundtrack.* USA.

Without a Trace (Sin dejar rastros). 1918. Director Quirino Cristiani. Argentina.

63
NOVELS
Christy Williams

The early twenty-first century has been an exciting time for lovers of fairy tales. Fairy tales have permeated practically every popular textual medium in production. They are everywhere, including in novels. Readers today may think of fairy-tale fantasy as the prime example, with novels by authors such as Patricia Wrede, Jane Yolen, Pamela Dean, Tanith Lee, Charles de Lint, Robin McKinley, and Gregory Maguire, among many others. But classic fairy tales retold in novel form, while encompassing an entire subgenre of fantasy literature, are only one way in which fairy tales are connected to the novel. One difficulty in discussing the topic is deciding what counts as a fairy-tale novel. Does Charlotte Brontë's *Jane Eyre* (1847), with its parallels to the plot of "Cinderella" (ATU 510A) and allusions to a variety of other fairy tales, count? What about J. R. R. Tolkien's *The Hobbit* (1937), which he famously referred to as a fairy story but is known today as a definitive text of the fantasy genre? Limiting ourselves to canonical fairy tales by well-known authors such as the Brothers Grimm, Charles Perrault, and Hans Christian Andersen and their retellings would certainly make identification easier, but it would fail to recognize the immense impact fairy tales have had on Western culture. Fairy tales are so important worldwide that they have pervaded every aspect of popular culture. Even sportscasters call on Cinderella to lend drama to between-play banter. Fairy tales are part of our shared language and the building blocks for a great many stories. Their plots, characters, and motifs are continually referenced and rewritten in novels both because fairy tales' multiplicity and variation invites continued use and because their ubiquity creates an easy shorthand for writers exploring human drama.

Part of the difficulty in discussing fairy tales and novels arises due to the slippery definitions that have been used for both terms. When readers think of fairy tales, the dominant form is that of (sometimes very) short stories with flat characters and vague settings. Folkloristic definitions typically affirm the form's short length, as Andrew Teverson's thorough discussion of the term demonstrates (2013, 33). Ruth Bottigheimer, in her argument for fairy tales as a literary genre, asserts that the short length is a defining feature (2009, 9). Tales that deviate from this typical form are usually referred to by qualifying language—fairy-tale novel or novella, postmodern fairy tale—to account for the way they differ from the stereotypical while still recognizing that they are identifiable as fairy tales. But as Elizabeth Wanning Harries shows, the extended form and complex techniques that are often associated with postmodern fairy tales have long been a part of tradition. Harries differentiates between compact fairy tales that conform to the dominant form through a "carefully constructed simplicity" that invokes an oral, folk origin and complex tales that deliberately "play with earlier romance patterns" and are "determinedly and openly 'intertextual'" (2001, 17). While extended length is not a requirement for complex tales, Harries's descriptive list of traits begins with it: "long, intricate, digressive, playful, self-referential, and self-conscious" (17). Gabrielle-Suzanne de Villeneuve's

"Beauty and the Beast" (1740), for example, is lengthy and narratively intricate. Despite being first published as part of a novel, *Les contes marins ou la jeune Américaine*, Villeneuve's tale is long enough to be called a novel itself (or at least a novella).

Historically, short-form fairy tales have been embedded in novels since at least the seventeenth century by French writers such as Marie-Catherine d'Aulnoy and Catherine Bernard, and today writers such as A. S. Byatt use the same technique. Another way fairy tales are embedded in longer works is through linking several together by a frame story. The early Italian fairy tales by Giovanni Francesco Straparola and Giambattista Basile were published in this form, but the most well-known text to use this technique is *The Arabian Nights* in which the narrator, Scheherazade, tells a new story to her husband every night. While this technique is less utilized today than embedding individual tales, writers like Emma Donoghue and Catherynne Valente have employed it with great success.

Novels that use fairy tales can be works of fantasy or realism, they can use whole tales or single motifs, or they might draw upon plot or particular details. Fairy tales can be embedded in a section of a novel or used throughout; they may be referenced implicitly or explicitly. There are retellings of single fairy tales in novel form (Gail Carson Levine, *Ella Enchanted*, 1997), novels that place fairy-tale motifs in a modern setting (Alice Hoffman, *Aquamarine*, 2001), novels that combine features of a variety of fairy tales in a single story or series (Jim C. Hines, *The Stepsister Scheme*, 2009), novels that contain short fairy tales within themselves (Jeanette Winterson, *Sexing the Cherry*, 1989), novels that reference fairy tales in realistic stories (Kurt Vonnegut, *Bluebeard*, 1987), and novels that entwine fairy tales with realistic narratives (Jane Yolen, *Briar Rose*, 1992). Some novels use traditional fairy-tale and narrative patterns; others experiment widely with both forms.

The variety of ways in which fairy tale and novel are brought together is further complicated by longstanding debates over how to define the novel. The early stages of the genre's history are a bit fuzzy. Some scholars locate it in the context of twelfth-century medieval French romances, others place it with the development of the printing press in fifteenth-century England, and many argue that it began with Miguel de Cervantes's *Don Quixote* (1605), Aphra Behn's *Oroonoko* (1688), or Daniel Defoe's *Robinson Crusoe* (1719). Still others point out that extended works of fictional prose existed much earlier, from second-century Greece to pre-modern China and Japan. These latter claims are increasingly important as they call attention to some of the problems with early efforts to distinguish the Western novel, which is what most scholars refer to when they use the term, from non-Western works of extended prose that may seem like novels, but whose inclusion of the fantastic or use of non-linear structure has traditionally marked them as different from their Western counterparts.

Much of the historical debate is about distinguishing novels from other extended works of fictional prose, like the romance, in Western narrative culture. The distinction between realism and romance, or wonder, is at the heart of this definitional debate. Fantastic and adventure- or love-driven plots were dubbed romances and separated from realistic novels to create a hierarchy with the latter judged as more serious works of literature. While these debates have continued, the novel is understood to be an extended work of fictional prose in today's common parlance. For contemporary examples, this debate has transferred to an issue of genre rather than of narrative form. There is no doubt that Gregory Maguire's *Mirror, Mirror* (2003) is a novel, but as a historicized fairy tale the question is in which section of the bookstore to place it. Maguire's novels are frequently sold in the literature section of bookstores despite the fairy-tale and magical elements that feature prominently in most of his work, while novels with similar treatment of fairy tales, such as ones by Juliet Marillier or Robin McKinley, are sold in the fantasy section. A critic of the politics of publishing genres might note that placement decisions can be implicitly based on gender, where works by men like Maguire have a greater chance than those of women like Marillier or McKinley to be considered serious and thus literature. But in any case, the inclusion of wonder may no longer preclude a work from being recognized as a novel.

For fairy-tale novels, this serious/non-serious distinction is less an issue because fairy tales have always been part of Western literary history. In addition to being nested in the sixteenth and seventeenth century works described prior, fairy tales and folk narratives are linked to the European medieval romance. Many romances use traditional motifs and would easily be recognized by modern readers as akin to fairy tales. The link to fairy tales is also evident in gothic novels and other prose romances that include a heavy dose of the fantastic and emphasize adventure and love in addition to drawing on well-known motifs. The turn of the twentieth century saw the publication of a great many children's fantasy novels, some of which were published as modern fairy tales (L. Frank Baum, *The Wonderful Wizard of Oz*, 1900), while others contain a great many fairy-tale motifs and are studied by fairy-tale scholars today (Lewis Carroll, *Alice's Adventures in Wonderland*, 1865; Carlo Collodi, *The Adventures of Pinocchio*, 1883; J. M. Barrie, *Peter Pan*, 1911). The term "novel" has expanded to include more works of wonder, although qualifying adjectives like "fantasy" or "children's" still denote a desire to emphasize literary realism over romance. So while the twentieth and twenty-first centuries have seen numerous novels marketed as fairy tales, the fairy-tale novel is not new.

Much critical discussion of fairy tales and novels is focused on the modes of retelling or inventiveness—what the novels do to the tales being retold—and interpretive readings. Definitions of fairy tales that emphasize their folkloric roots typically exclude novels based on length or inclusion of realism, but many fairy-tale scholars, such as Cristina Bacchilega and Jack Zipes, include novels alongside classic fairy tales in their analyses. Yet little attention is paid to the novel form as a venue or medium for fairy tales. Novels allow for extended development of specific features, such as plot or character, so scholars tend to explore what that extension does, not its relation to the novel form, style, or mode.

Many novels that use fairy tales follow traditional narrative structure; aside from the fairy-tale elements, they read much like any other example of the form. The fairy tale lends plot structure so that audiences familiar with the narrative contours have a set of expectations as to how events will unfold. A novel with a beautiful young female protagonist who has a wicked stepmother can be expected to involve the ingenue fleeing for her life but returning home triumphant at the end. That built-in structure allows authors to explore different elements of the fairy tales they draw upon. Fairy-tale references in otherwise realistic novels also offer a shorthand for complex ideas. The reference to a wicked stepmother brings with it vast reader knowledge and experience of that motif that the author can then build upon. The medium of the novel offers length. With it comes the space for complex development of character, plot, setting—all aspects that readers expect to be flattened in the compact fairy-tale form. Vanessa Joosen discusses these and other typical characteristics of fairy tales in terms of a "horizon of expectations" with which retellings of fairy tales can play (2011, 12–13). Short stories also provide an opportunity for writers to flesh out and develop these different elements, but the smaller word count imposes restrictions. Novels' greater size allows writers to experiment not only with characterization, plot, or setting, but also with form.

In 1978, American author Robin McKinley published her first novel, *Beauty: A Retelling of the Story of Beauty & the Beast*. For *Beauty*, the novel form provides an extended playground for exploring the gender issues of the eighteenth-century French fairy tale for a twentieth-century audience. McKinley's book, along with Angela Carter's short-story collection of fairy-tale retellings, *The Bloody Chamber* (1979), marks the beginning of an explosion of feminist adaptations in novels, poetry, and short-story collections. While the plot structure of *Beauty* closely mirrors the fairy tale, the characters are developed to show complex relationships and motivations. Beauty's submissive actions in the older tale, most notably agreeing to live with the beast to save her father's life, are given context in the novel. Her choices are shown to be part of a complex system of relationships. McKinley's is not a radical retelling, and it does not deviate from the fairy-tale plot, but in developing the characters of Beauty and her sisters, the novel explores why a practical, intelligent young woman might choose to go off with a beast.

Like McKinley, American postmodernist Robert Coover often draws upon fairy tales; however, he rarely follows traditional fairy-tale or novel structures and instead experiments with narrative form as part of his larger postmodern project. Coover's short novel *Briar Rose* (1996) is a good example of how the length provided by the form leads not to a traditional work but to a means of play. The novel's length allows for a cyclical repetition not possible in a short form. Through a series of passages focalized through three different characters—the princess, the prince, and the fairy—Coover repeats different motifs associated with different versions of "Sleeping Beauty" (ATU 410). The characters are trapped in the story(ies), unable to progress to the end. When one scene moves the plot, like the prince finding the princess or the princess waking up, subsequent disconnected scenes return the characters to moments of suspension so that they are right back where they started—asleep, trapped in the briar hedge, or waiting. The novel's length allows for this particular type of narrative exploration, but the final product does not provide the development one would expect of a work using traditional narrative methods. Readers do not better understand the princess's motivation, for example, as happens with a novel like *Beauty*. *Briar Rose* is particularly interesting because the scenes themselves are not fully connected. In fact, Robert Scholes created a hypertext version that allows readers to move between scenes in random orders. The stability of the novel form is undone by the repetition of the compact fairy-tale form and the invocation of multiple variants of "Sleeping Beauty." This type of narrative exploration is present in Coover's non-fairy-tale work as well and is a staple technique of postmodern writers. Fairy tales and well-known stories provide postmodernists with authoritative narratives and ideologies to critique and dismantle in addition to a conventional horizon of expectation with which to play.

Fairy-tale novels in the late twentieth and early twenty-first centuries also do a fair amount of genre blending. With fantasy novels, although there is room to argue that fairy tales are one of the forms from which the modern fantasy genre is derived, the form allows much room for experimenting and borrowing. Fairy-tale novels can also draw upon detective fiction, science fiction, and war narratives, among others. Fairy-tale themed romance novels are quite popular, with fairy tales that feature a "happily ever after" wedding dominating the form. Short fiction can mix genres as well, but the sustained form of the novel allows for extended genre blending. Marissa Meyer's *Cinder* (2012), a retelling of "Cinderella" set on a future Earth, blends science fiction tropes with those of fairy tale. The plot structure frames the novel's exploration of a dystopian future filled with political conflict, alien invasion, and deadly plague. The protagonist's status as a cyborg signals the novel's own hybrid form. As with other works, the fairy-tale structure creates a familiar frame to support readers through the unfamiliar dystopian content. *Cinder* is the first book in *The Lunar Chronicles* series, and each references multiple classic fairy tales. Meyer's series is just one among many in a fast-growing trend that has had particular success in books marketed to young adults and children. This development shows how the novel form can open up endless possibilities for fairy tales, not just by subverting, exploring, or playing with expectations, but by combining the narratives with other novel traditions in new and exciting ways.

The fairy-tale novel series has also gained great traction in recent years, and many blend elements from multiple fairy tales into a single storyworld to sustain multiple novels set in the same universe. In some cases, the novels are connected only by a shared setting (Gail Carson Levine's *Ella Enchanted*, 1997; *Fairest*, 2006) or by characters from one appearing in the background of another (Mercedes Lackey, *Tales of the Five Hundred Kingdoms* series, 2004–2011). Some series contain more episodic plots: each novel is a new, self-contained adventure featuring the series' characters (Jim C. Hines, *The Princess Series*, 2009–2011). Other series enframe these novel-centric adventures in a larger epic story so that each exploit builds upon the previous ones to conclude a plot arc for the entire series (Marissa Meyer, *The Lunar Chronicles* series, 2012–2015). Still others use a classic fairy tale as an entry point into the wider fantastic world (Juliet Marillier, *Sevenwaters* series, 1999–2012). Terry Pratchett's fairy-tale novel *Witches Abroad* (1991) appears as the twelfth book in his *Discworld* fantasy series (1983–2015). *The Fairy Tale Series* edited by Terri Windling (1987–2002) contains unconnected novels written by different authors, linked not by particular narratives but rather by a dedication to the fairy-tale form. Zipes explains that Windling's series "has as its major purpose to breathe new life into traditional material and show the diverse uses a modern storyteller can make out of the fairy-tale genre" (1994, 151).

The popularity of these series has led not only to the production of more series but also to the adaptation of novels across mediums, such as the 2004 film of *Ella Enchanted* and a graphic novel based on *The Lunar Chronicles* (*Wires and Nerve*, 2017). There are numerous fairy-tale graphic novel series as well, with Bill Willingham's *Fables* (2002–2015) as a prime example. The fairy-tale series is so popular in fact that Mattel commissioned two book series (Shannon Hale, 2013–2014; Suzanne Selfors, 2015–2016) and a web series (2013–) to support their *Ever After High* doll toy line. Many fairy-tale novels and series are marketed as young adult or children's literature; however, the popularity of Maguire's *The Wicked Years* series (1995–2011) demonstrates a wide adult audience as well. This trend of serialization reflects its success in fantasy publishing and on television (ABC's *Once Upon a Time* 2011–; CBS's *Grimm* 2011–2017) and film (Dreamworks' *Shrek*, 2001, and its sequels), all of which demonstrate audience interest in the extended narrative. The series structure allows for both epic and episodic plots and a further development of the fairy-tale features that can be explored in novel form. It enables writers to revisit the fairy-tale source material within the existing storyworld and add depth to or further complicate and disrupt the expected narratives. Audiences seemingly do not want fairy tales to end, and serialization defers the expected happy ending, allowing audiences and writers alike to spend more time exploring the stories and storyworlds they thought they once knew (see, e.g., Hay and Baxter 2014).

The popularity of fairy-tale novels—both long fairy tales and those that use fairy-tale motifs—suggests that this is a productive marriage of genre and form (even when the union is not harmonious, as in Coover's *Briar Rose*). The length provided by the medium of the novel allows writers to explore in depth characters, plots, and motifs of fairy tales and provides an opportunity for play. The familiarity of fairy-tale plots, motifs, and structure allows writers of novels to lead readers through new and difficult material and provides an opportunity to invoke or challenge conventional narratives and ideologies. The popularity of extended fairy-tale narratives enabled by novel form and serialization not only recognizes the genre's versatility, but demonstrates a desire to see just what the fairy tale and the novel can do. The difficulty in defining the fairy-tale novel due to definitions of the terms "fairy tale" and "novel" historically excluding each other offers scholars an opportunity to re-examine what these terms mean for a twenty-first-century audience and to chart the rich literary landscape of the fairy-tale novel.

Related topics: Blogs and Websites; Children's and Young Adult (YA) Literature; Cinema Science Fiction; Cinematic; Comics and Graphic Novels; Criticism; Gender; Print; TV Drama; Print

CHRISTY WILLIAMS

References Cited and Further Reading

The Arabian Nights. 1990. Translated by Husain Haddawy. New York: W. W. Norton & Company.

Bacchilega, Cristina. 1997. *Postmodern Fairy Tales: Gender and Narrative Strategies.* Philadelphia: U Pennsylvania P.

Barrie, J. M. (1911) 2012. *Peter Pan (Peter and Wendy).* Champaign, IL: Project Gutenberg.

Baum, L. Frank. (1900) 2008. *The Wonderful Wizard of Oz.* Champaign, IL: Project Gutenberg.

Behn, Aphra. (1688) 1994. *Oroonoko, and Other Writings,* edited by Paul Salzman. New York: Oxford University Press.

Benson, Stephen, ed. 2008. *Contemporary Fiction and the Fairy Tale.* Detroit: Wayne State UP.

Bottigheimer, Ruth B. 2009. *Fairy Tales: A New History.* Albany: SUNY P.

Bronte, Charlotte. (1847) 1962. *Jane Eyre.* New York: Harcourt, Brace & World.

Carroll, Lewis. (1865) 1993. *Alice's Adventures in Wonderland.* New York: Dover.

Carter, Angela. (1979) 1993. *The Bloody Chamber and Other Stories.* New York: Penguin.

Cervantes, Miguel de. (1605) 2015. *Don Quixote,* translated by John Ormsby. Champaign, IL: Project Gutenberg.

Collodi, Carlo. (1883) 2013. *The Adventures of Pinocchio,* translated by Carol Della Chiesa. Champaign, IL: Project Gutenberg.

Coover, Robert. 1996. *Briar Rose.* New York: Grove P.

Defoe, Daniel. (1719) 1994. *Robinson Crusoe: An Authoritative Text, Contexts, Criticism,* edited by Michael Shinagel. New York: W. W. Norton & Company.

Hale, Shannon. 2013–2014. *Ever After High* (Series). 3 vols. New York: Little, Brown and Company.

Harries, Elizabeth Wanning. 2001. *Twice Upon a Time: Women Writers and the History of the Fairy Tale.* Princeton, NJ: Princeton UP.

Hay, Rebecca, and Christa Baxter. 2014. "Happily Never After: The Commodification and Critique of Fairy Tales in ABC's *Once Upon a Time.*" In *Channeling Wonder: Fairy Tales on Television,* edited by Pauline Greenhill and Jill Terry Rudy, 316–34. Detroit: Wayne State UP.

Hines, Jim C. 2009. *The Stepsister Scheme.* New York: DAW Books.

———. 2009–2011. *The Princess Series.* 4 vols. New York: DAW Books.

Hoffman, Alice. 2001. *Aquamarine.* New York: Scholastic.

Joosen, Vanessa. 2011. *Critical and Creative Perspectives on Fairy Tales: An Intertextual Dialogue between Fairy-Tale Scholarship and Postmodern Retellings.* Detroit: Wayne State UP.

Lackey, Mercedes. 2004–2011. *Tales of the Five Hundred Kingdoms* (Series). 6 vols. New York: Luna.

Levine, Gail Carson. 1997. *Ella Enchanted.* New York: Harper Collins.

———. 2006. *Fairest.* New York: Harper Collins.

Maguire, Gregory. 1995–2011. *The Wicked Years* (Series). 4 vols. New York: HarperCollins.

———. 2003. *Mirror, Mirror.* New York: Regan Books.

Marillier, Juliet. 1999–2012. *Sevenwaters* (Series). 6 vols. Sydney: Pan Macmillan Australia.

McKinley, Robin. 1978. *Beauty: A Retelling of the Story of Beauty & the Beast.* New York: HarperCollins.

Meyer, Marissa. 2012. *Cinder.* New York: Square Fish.

———. 2012–2015. *The Lunar Chronicles* (Series). 4 vols. New York: Feiwel & Friends.

———. 2017. *Wires and Nerve.* New York: Feiwel & Friends.

Moretti, Franco, ed. 2006. *The Novel: Volume 1 History, Geography, and Culture.* Princeton, NJ: Princeton UP.

Prachett, Terry. 1983–2015. *Discworld* (Series). 41 vols. New York: HarperCollins.

———. (1991) 1992. *Witches Abroad.* London: Corgi Books.

Ross, Deborah L. 1991. *The Excellence of Falsehood: Romance, Realism, and Women's Contribution to the Novel.* Lexington: UP Kentucky.

Selfors, Suzanne. 2015–2016. *Ever After High* (Series). 5 vols. New York: Little, Brown and Company.

Teverson, Andrew. 2013. *Fairy Tale.* London: Routledge.

Tolkien, J.R.R. (1937) 2013. *The Hobbit, or There and Back Again.* Revised ed. New York: Del Rey.

Villeneuve, Gabrielle-Suzanne de. (1740) 1991. "Beauty and the Beast." In *Beauties, Beasts and Enchantment: Classic French Fairy Tales,* translated by Jack Zipes, 153–229. New York: Meridian.

Vonnegut, Kurt. 1987. *Bluebeard.* New York: Dell.

Willingham, Bill. 2002–2015. *Fables* (Series). 150 issues. New York: Vertigo.

Windling, Terri, ed. 1987–2002. *The Fairy Tale* (Series). 8 vols. New York: Tor.

Winterson, Jeanette. 1989. *Sexing the Cherry.* New York: Grove P.

Yolen, Jane. (1992) 2002. *Briar Rose.* New York: Tor.

Zipes, Jack. 1994. *Fairy Tale as Myth/Myth as Fairy Tale.* Lexington: UP Kentucky.

NOVELS

Mediagraphy

Coover, Robert. 2016. *Briar Rose* (Hypertext Version). Constructed by Robert Scholes. www.brown.edu/Departments/MCM/people/scholes/BriarRose/texts/BRhome.htm.

Ella Enchanted. 2004. Director Tommy O'Haver. USA.

Ever After High (Web Series). 2013–. Creator Mattel. USA.

Grimm (TV). 2011–2017. Creators Stephen Carpenter, David Greenwalt, and Jim Kouf. USA.

Once Upon a Time (TV). 2011–. Creators Edward Kitsis and Adam Horowitz. USA.

Shrek. 2001. Directors Andrew Adamson and Vicky Jenson. USA.

64

OPERA

Pauline Greenhill

Traditional and literary fairy tales supply material for operas (sung theatrical performances), including plot contours, themes, and characters. As with other adaptations, fairy tales provide a familiar story, with the attendant possibility of popularity or at least acceptance. Analytical work on the relationship of fairy tales and opera is rare; reference works usually offer little more than annotated lists of fairy-tale operas. While it is easy to think of opera onstage, fairy-tale opera gets disseminated in many audio or audiovisual forms, including cinema, television, radio, and home video. Thus, fairy-tale opera is simultaneously multimedia, in which one story takes many forms via a single channel (different composers make "Cinderella" [ATU 510A] operas); cross-media, in which a story appears via many channels ("Cinderella" operas appear on television, in theaters, on radio, and so on); and transmedia, in which one storyworld comprises tales in many forms via many channels (fairy-tale opera culture and context includes "Cinderella" on TV, HD in cinemas, and on home video, which may itself incorporate audiovisual media forms) (see Moloney 2014). Cross-media renderings of specific fairy-tale operas across platforms and formats often replicate live performances with surprising techniques borrowed from sports broadcasting and reality television. Looking at the broadcasting history of New York's Metropolitan Opera Company (the Met) foregrounds conventions that make the opera company a prime fairy-tale venue and producer. More specifically, production decisions and fairy-tale operas in the *Live in HD* series reveal how the arts institution can be both storyteller and purveyor of quintessential multimedia productions that promote tales and opera through transformative experience and performance.

The Metropolitan Opera *Live in HD*—Operatic Mediations

Founded in 1883, the Met first confined its activity almost exclusively to stage performances, though experiments with live radio broadcast began as early as 1910. However, in the 1930s, the Depression-threatened company, seeking larger audiences and more financial support, began concerted work toward the multiple mediations that have become an entertainment staple for many North Americans. The first complete opera the Met presented live on radio, Engelbert Humperdinck's (1854–1921) *Hänsel und Gretel* (premiere 1893) (ATU 327A), on Christmas Day, 1931, arguably installed the company's ongoing tradition of mediating fairy-tale opera, but also represented and reinforced the mediated fairy tale's European and North American association with the winter holiday season. The other full opera broadcast in that season was another fairy-tale-associated work, Richard Wagner's *Das Rheingold* (premiere 1869), in February 1932 (Dizikes 1993, 474–481). Live Saturday matinee radio broadcasts continue today, available across the world via free live audio streaming and online.

Undoubtedly, the popularity of fairy-tale operas explains their frequent presentation at the Met. Following several experiments beginning in 1948, the Met's television broadcast series was inaugurated in 1977 with Giacomo Puccini's highly popular non-fairy-tale melo-drama *La Bohème* (1896). However, the first presentation in its *Live in HD* series, simulcast in high-definition video mainly to movie theaters, was Wolfgang Amadeus Mozart's (1756–1791) *The Magic Flute* (premiere 1791) on December 30, 2006, continuing the holiday season/fairy tale association. Only one season had no fairy-tale operas, and five of the first ten seasons had two. From the beginning of this highly successful series (2015–2016 was its tenth year, and it continues in 2017–2018), it is clear that the Met learned about the possibilities of mediating opera from their earlier radio and television productions. Rather than simply trying to rep-licate a live performance on the big screen, *Live in HD* offers, as James Steichen argues, "a reality television–style organizational documentary that both capitalizes on and raises its own institutional stature." He understands live broadcast media as "much more than an innovation in cinematic opera, but a compelling new means through which prominent arts organizations such as the Met are learning to leverage new media to advance their institution-building agendas" (2009, 24).

The live opera experience, already multimodal, combines ritual and music with theater. In North America and Europe, (relatively) formal dress, use of opera glasses (binoculars) to closely view performers (and audience), chocolates and/or ice cream, a glass of wine during intermissions, and people-watching have become integral. From the outset, *Live in HD* quoted visual aspects of the latter, but also took advantage of the new medium. For Brianna Wells, "the HD series creates in its *audiences* a sense of doubling, of intellectual uncertainty, and strange recurrence within an experience of immediacy, and a sense of the familiar made alien: in other words, a sense of the uncanny" (2012, 193).

The radio broadcasts had already raised the problem of what to do with live opera's long intermissions. Interval features included facts about the work being performed, quizzes (some-times hosted by opera enthusiasts from other entertainment realms like actor Tony Randall), roundtables, and interviews with Met staff and stars. Intermission programming in the *Live in HD* productions, in keeping with opera's associations with elite culture, similarly focuses on education and information, perhaps seeking to democratize the medium but simultaneously rendering it a subject of arcane knowledge.

Each simulcast begins by mimicking the people-watching possibilities of live theater, showing the audience at the Metropolitan Opera House in New York's Lincoln Center for the Performing Arts, with a soundtrack of the orchestra warming up. The camera's many vantage points allow a much wider purview than would be available to individual audience members from their seats. Often the scene suggests narratives about the opera-goers, show-ing parents with excited children (a happy family outing), lone fans reading programs (the aficionada/o engrossed in the genre), and/or couples engaged in conversation (heterosexual courtship). But while the live audience must keep track of time—though a gong or bell in the lobby announces when the performance is imminent—a countdown clock runs in the upper right-hand corner of the movie screen, increasing anticipation. And while theatergo-ers have only a written program, sometimes supplemented by an announcement of a major cast change by a formally dressed company official before the curtain, the cinema audience has programs *plus* an opening welcome by the day's host, usually an American opera diva. Corporate sponsorship information precedes these announcements, but most additional programming for *Live in HD* is oriented toward merchandizing upcoming performances: explicit, like the rundown of forthcoming dates, or more subtle, like visits to rehearsals for the next event.

Barring technical glitches, common in the first seasons but now rare, careful camera work avoids drawing too much attention to itself or to the broad acting necessary in live theater. Medium shots with multiple performers are more common than close-ups, except during solos. Views covering the full stage are rare, and the conductor and orchestra are generally unseen except during the overture and at the beginning of an act—often established by a long shot zooming in from an upper-balcony vantage point—or at the end. A robotic dolly camera mounted behind the orchestra offers the possibility of a sequence of the entire stage from ground level. Adopted from sports videography, it gives a perspective looking up at the singers, a kind of orchestra-eye view.

Intermissions invariably begin with interviews of the star singers as they exit the stage. Other live or pre-recorded programming includes discussions with performers, directors, conductors, production designers, and other Met staff; vignettes and dates of upcoming presentations (including the "encores"—repeat broadcasts to movie theaters—which, unlike other parallel products like DVDs, include the entire show in its original sequence); and visits to dress rehearsals for the next production, to the prop and costume departments, and so on. Then another countdown clock begins, while cameras track the action backstage as sets are deployed and dressed. Additional programming follows that countdown. Except for the diva/o introductions, in the television broadcasts, this programming can be selectively shifted to the end, and the backstage set-moving portions greatly truncated or eliminated. The end of the opera focuses on curtain calls but also shots of the audience and recently backstage congratulations among performers and crew as the credits run.

As Wells suggests, "the stakes are so high in considering the opera simulcast because it is entangled in the meaning of liveness, and the impact of media technology on performance, repetition, and reception, and therefore the cultural distinctions of opera itself" (2012, 192). Steichen's reality TV analogy is telling, since the vagaries of live telecasts can increase apparently unscripted dramatic content. With viewers across five continents, and at least one "encore" performance and television rebroadcast, mistakes like a performer muffing lines while the subtitles continue, a prop sword breaking in half, or the prompter's singing are magnified by repetition and the large audience. Further unscripted elements included the orchestra wearing buttons to draw attention to their 2014 labor dispute; like the errors, such happenings are not something the Met's management would want to have in a more permanent record.

Yet the realities that support dramatic potential get as much attention as possible when time allows. For example, much was made of tenor Juan Diego Flórez's arrival a mere thirty-five minutes before the curtain rose on the performance of Gioachino Rossini's (1792–1868) *Le comte Ory* (premiere 1828) in 2011, after staying up all night as his wife gave birth to their son. In 2014, the last-minute replacement in the main role of Mimi in *La Bohème* of soprano Anita Hartig, suffering from the flu, by Kristine Opolais, provided nerve-wracking, suspenseful drama with an apparent "Cinderella" plot. Met general manager Peter Gelb announced from the stage that he had contacted Opolais in the early hours of the morning and that she would perform with only a few hours of sleep, having made her Met debut the night before in the main role of Cio-Cio-San in Puccini's *Madama Butterfly* (premiere 1904)! Cameras captured some of the frantic preparations only imagined by the live audience.

As infomercial (Steichen 2009, 25), the series represents not only opera, but the Met, with its extraordinary, lavishly expensive productions by directors and producers from film (Franco Zefferelli), Broadway theater (Bartlett Sher, Julie Taymor), and multimedia arts (Robert Lepage, William Kentridge), with international stars and featured American performers (underlined by the host diva/os). Each performance includes a direct appeal for donations and an exhortation that movie theater audiences should come to the Met or visit their local opera company.

OPERA

Live in HD Fairy-Tale Operas and Their Multiple Mediations

Fairy-tale associated operas' appearances are extensive. That in the first ten seasons *Cenerentola*, *Turandot*, and *Hoffman* have appeared twice, and that *Cenerentola*, *Hansel and Gretel*, *The Magic Flute*, *Rusalka*, *Turandot*, and the full Ring Cycle have been released on DVD, underlines their popularity as operas and fairy-tale texts' enduring appeal.

The Magic Flute

The Magic Flute (libretto [text] Emanuel Schikaneder) is often cited for its fairy-tale qualities, including a princess rescued by a prince and magical helper figures. Its many popular tunes include "heartfelt arias for Tamino and Pamina [. . .] fierce coloratura outbursts for the Queen of the Night [. . .] down-to-earth songs for Papageno and [. . .] two sublime arias for Sarastro" (Osborne 2004, 292, see 287–292). Scholars have linked the libretto to literary fairy tales: the seventeenth-century French "The Wizard King" (Abbate 2001, 62–70) and the eighteenth-century "Lulu oder die Zauberflöte" by J. A. Liebeskind (Spaethling 1975, 48).

Media using Mozart's opera and/or sharing its name are many: cinematic features, short films, TV movies, and TV episodes. Some offer productions of the work itself; some meditate on it; some have little connection beyond the title. Films include British director Kenneth Branagh's feature (2006), setting the story during WWI, and *Magic Flute Diaries* (2008), about a production in which the lives of the singers who play main characters Pamina and Tamino parallel their roles in the opera.

Swedish auteur Ingmar Bergman adapted the opera in 1975, originally for television (first shown on New Year's Day), but later released to cinema. Having created a puppet theater version of an Act I sequence for his *Hour of the Wolf* (1968), Bergman in the later film presents *The Magic Flute* as a utopian vision of humanity. Not a performance documentary, it offers cinematic exhibition of Bergman's holistic understanding of the opera. The overture sequence features extreme close-ups of audience members' faces—young and old, ethnically diverse. The production displayed is small, sparse, and whimsical. The arias' wise maxims about love, peace, and interpersonal harmony are punctuated by title cards, sometimes held by the actors. The intermission section shows the costumed singers' everyday behaviors and interactions— smoking, playing chess, and studying. The result is deeply moving.

By contrast, the *Live in HD* DVD of Julie Taymor's colorful Orientalist production of giant puppets, acrobatics, and dance opens not with the audience but with scenes of the performers dressing and being made up, documenting the spectacular artifice involved. The production mimics aspects of Kabuki theater, including Japanesque costuming, posing, and the performers representing the elite in whiteface, including the "Moor" Monostatos in a fat suit with a hook nose and Chinese operatic soprano Ying Huang as Pamina with the exaggerated eye makeup too often associated with stereotypes of Oriental(ist) characters.

Recently, opera's already multimediated form, combining music, acting, singing, and the-atrical presentation, is further mediated by mixing live performance with animated and live action projections. The Komische Oper Berlin's production of *The Magic Flute* offers an hom-age to early silent film: a Louise Brooks–like Pamina, a Nosferatu Monostatos, a spider Queen of the Night, and spoken dialogue replaced by text plates ("Die Zauberflöte" N.d.). William Kentridge's 2005 South African production, using his characteristic video projections, raises issues of colonialism and power, interpreting Sarastro as an Enlightenment despot. However, Kentridge incorporates the cinematograph—the motion picture camera, projector, and printer developed by the Lumière brothers—into the opera's diegesis, thus linking the story's magic with technology (see "Short" N.d.).

575

Hänsel und Gretel *(Hansel and Gretel)*

This opera (libretto Adelheid Wette), Humperdinck's best-known work, is often performed around Christmastime. Child viewers accustomed to picture book adaptations may be disappointed that the witch and gingerbread house do not appear until the third act. The chorus sings the well-known "Evening Prayer," underlining this version's link to the Christian elements found in later Grimm versions of ATU 327A. However, Humperdinck wrote other fairy-tale themed operas, including *The Seven Little Kids* (libretto Wette, premiere 1895), *The King's Children* (libretto Else Bernstein-Porges, premiere 1897), and *Sleeping Beauty* (libretto Elisabeth Ebeling and Bertha Lehrmann-Filhés, premiere 1902) (see Osborne 2004, 182–186). As with other fairy-tale operas, *Hansel and Gretel* has been multiply produced for television and often subsequently released in home video. The 2008–2009 Met *Live in HD* performance, issued on DVD, shows a move toward dark fairy tales, following early oral versions' focus on the family's hunger, but offering a remorseful biological mother at the conclusion.

La Cenerentola *(Cinderella)*

"Cinderella" has provided the subject matter for numerous operas. Rossini's *La Cenerentola* (libretto Jacopo Ferretti), presented twice in the same production with different stars on *Live in HD* (with the earlier offering released on DVD), is currently the most popular. The story accentuates Christian elements over magic: no supernatural transformations, but also no glass slipper. Predictably, the opera has been multiply presented on television and released on DVD, including productions from Austria, Germany, Italy, Norway, Spain, and the UK, from famous venues like La Scala, Milan, the Salzburg Opera House, and Glyndebourne.

Mécaniques célestes (Celestial Clockwork), a 1995 French/Belgian/Spanish film by Venezuelan-born Fina Torres, subverts the conventional "Cinderella" by offering a lesbian instead of a heterosexual love story, with the handsome prince–cum–fairy godmother a Parisian psychoanalyst and the innocent persecuted heroine an aspiring mezzo soprano who flees her Venezuelan wedding to fly to Paris, still in her wedding dress. The feminist plot also includes a male prince/seeker, the producer filming Rossini's *La Cenerentola* who hunts for the perfect lead. In further mediations on its "meta-filmic, intertextual swerve" (Soliño 2001, 68), Cinderella heroine Ana, unable to do a live audition, sends him a cassette tape of her singing, and wicked stepsister Celeste is frequently represented with animations that underline her role. In this enjoyable and satisfying movie, Torres not only "parodies and appropriates many of Disney's most memorable visual techniques" but also explores the "plight of the Latin American artist in the European world of high culture" (69; see also Burke Lawless 2015).

Turandot

The Puccini opera (libretto Giuseppe Adami and Renato Simoni), completed after the composer's death, sets ATU 851, "The Princess Who Cannot Solve the Riddle," in an exoticized, fictionalized China. Like its better-known Orientalist relative, Puccini's *Madama Butterfly* (libretto Luigi Illica and Giuseppe Giacosa), it quotes Asian-sounding music and is too often presented, as it is in Zeffirelli's production (used in both *Live in HD* broadcasts, with the earlier released to DVD), with White-identified singers in yellowface. However, the character Turandot, an all-powerful princess, contrasts with Butterfly's compliance, and the latter's suicide with the marriage that concludes in the former's opera (Ng 2006).

Turandot was one of six operas chosen for the first of the BBC series *Operavox* (1993), which offered thirty-minute animated versions in English. Representing the Chinese context in a style evocative of Chinese color wood-block printing, the visuals are impressive. Other full-length and short animated *Turandot* films have been produced in Italy. A documentary, *The Turandot Project*, follows Chinese film director Zhang Yimou and conductor Zubin Mehta in making a 1997 production of the opera in Beijing's Forbidden City.

Les contes d'Hoffman *(The Tales of Hoffman)*

This opera (libretto Jules Barbier) links fictionalized episodes from the life of literary fairy-tale author E.T.A. Hoffman (also an opera composer) while dramatizing aspects of his stories. *Tales's* four evil geniuses are adept in magic and science alike (see Osborne 2004, 300–304). Wells notes that the opera is "based in part on the very texts that Freud used to develop his psychoanalytic definition of the uncanny, invested in the disintegration of individual personality through multiple characters performed by one actor, as well as horrors of robotic and mechanical reproducibility standing in for and challenging the human" (2012, 194). She links the representations of science and the mechanical within the opera and Sher's production with the Act 1 representation of the automaton doll Olympia, whose famous coloratura aria suggests a preternatural vocal ability—one that may derive from science, magic, or both.

Wagner's Ring Cycle

This series of four operas, for which Wagner also wrote the libretti, incorporates elements of myth and legend, but also fairy tales (Osborne 2004, 500–594, especially 573–589). For example, *Siegfried* (premiere 1876) includes an explicit echo of ATU 326, "The Youth Who Wanted to Learn What Fear Is" (Syer 2014, 77–78, see also 30–79). The drama associated with the *Live in HD* broadcast increased with the *Siegfried* production when Texan Jay Hunter Morris replaced an ill Gary Lehman in the long, difficult title role only eight days before the recorded performance. Hunter Morris returned for the simulcast of *Götterdämmerung*.

Lepage's multimedia Met production, released on DVD, used projections as well as a common "machine" of aluminum beams that form different shapes in all four operas. It was controversial, from complaints about a lack of "overarching directorial concept" to "effusive praise [. . .] from websites devoted to Wagner" (Karlin 2013). As David Karlin notes, the production, though technically complex,

> is definitely traditional: [Lepage] and Met director Peter Gelb are on the record as having tried to imagine the Ring the way Wagner would have staged it if he had access to twenty-first century technology. The video projection and the use of "the machine" are true theatrical innovation and anything but traditional—but the underlying purpose is a purist Wagnerian one.
>
> (2013)

Productions like Lepage's underline not only the expense of opera production, but the imaginative ways in which magical happenings can be rendered onstage, for example, in projections, shadows, props, sets, and costumes. He has also been responsible for a Canadian Opera Company *Bluebeard's Castle*, and his fairy-tale theatrical adaptations and reimaginings include a solo show as author/adapter Hans Christian Andersen.

PAULINE GREENHILL

Rusalka

Dvořák wrote several musical works based on traditional ideas and characters, like the opera *The Cunning Peasant* (libretto Josef Otakar Veselý, premiere 1878, ATU 1030) and, based on the work of Czech folklore collector Karel Jaromír Erben, the symphonic poems *The Golden Spinning Wheel*, *The Noon Witch*, *The Water Goblin*, and *The Wild Dove*. His fairy-tale comic opera *The Devil and Kate* (libretto Adolf Wenig, premiere 1899), drawing on a story collected by Božena Němcová (ATU 812), included a ballet. *Rusalka* (libretto Jaroslav Kvapl), based on fairy tales from Erben and Němcová, recalls Friederich de la Motte Fouqué's novella *Undine* and Hans Christian Andersen's "The Little Mermaid." Its tragic story about a water nymph, who exchanges her power of speech for transformation into a human so she can wed a prince, offers leitmotifs for each character, as well as the famous first act aria "O Silver Moon" (see Osborne 2004, 122–125), featured in the DVD of the *Live In HD* production sung by Renée Fleming.

Bluebeard's Castle

Most fairy-tale operas draw on the form's conventionally light-hearted, happy-ever-after ethos—comic rather than dramatic works. A telling exception is *Bluebeard's Castle* (libretto Béla Balaz), Bartók's only opera (see Benson 2000; on an important Japanese production, see Ridgely 2013, 296–299). It loosely follows the traditional story (ATU 312), in which a newly married woman discovers her husband's murdered former wives, though the opera concludes with the current wife joining her predecessors, not with her rescue. The opening of successive doors behind which Bluebeard's victims are discovered punctuates the music and often the staging (see Osborne 2004, 4–6). Similarly, Paul Dukas's (French, 1865–1935) *Ariane et Barbe-Bleue* (libretto Maurice Maeterlinck, premiere 1907) has the antecedent wives imprisoned but not murdered (see Benson 2000). Ariane leaves at the end, and, as in Bartók's opera, Bluebeard remains alive.

Transmediating Fairy-Tale Opera

At least two picture books for young readers apparently seek to whet their appetites for the operatic theatrical experience, including illustrated short stories of *The Magic Flute* (Husain 1999, 15–26; Rosenberg 1989, 104–117), *Hansel and Gretel* (Husain 1999, 27–38; Rosenberg 1989, 82–91), *La Cenerentola* (Husain 1999, 49–58), and *The Tales of Hoffman* (Rosenberg 1989, 146–159). Making classical opera available on these different media platforms can be seen as an attempt to shore up a dying art and, in the case of the Met in particular, as working toward making a large, expensive, and unwieldy infrastructure viable. Yet these transmediations can also be seen as invitations to transformative experience in their performative (as well as financial) richness, just like other fairy-tale media. The cinema presentations attract regular attendees, and though their generally advanced age suggests to some that the medium is dying out, it also reflects opera's multigenerational appeal, along with its fairy-tale hypotexts.

Related topics: Broadcast; Classical Music; Orientalism; Theatrical

References Cited and Further Reading

Abbate, Carolyn. 2001. *In Search of Opera*. Princeton, NJ: Princeton UP.
Bendix, Regina. 1990. "Folk Narrative, Opera and the Expression of Cultural Identity." *Fabula* 31 (3–4): 297–303.

OPERA

Benson, Stephen. 2000. "'History's Bearer': The Afterlife of 'Bluebeard'." *Marvels & Tales* 14 (2): 244–67.

———. 2010. "Fairy-Tale Opera and the Crossed Desires of Words and Music." *Contemporary Music Review* 29 (2): 171–82.

Burke Lawless, Cecelia. 2015. "Inside-Out: A Socio-Spatial Reading of *Mécanicas celestes* (Fina Torres, 1995)." In *Despite All Adversities: Spanish-American Queer Cinema*, edited by Andrés Lema-Hincapié and Debra A. Castillo, 111–24. Albany: SUNY P.

Celenza, Anna Harwell. 2005. *Hans Christian Andersen and Music: The Nightingale Revealed*. Aldershot: Ashgate.

Dizikes, John. 1993. *Opera in America: A Cultural History*. New Haven, CT: Yale UP.

Husain, Shahrukh. 1999. *The Barefoot Book of Stories from the Opera*. New York: Barefoot Books.

Karlin, David. 2013. "Appraising the Full Cycle: Robert Lepage's *Ring* at the Met." *Bachtrack*, May 8. https://bachtrack.com/appraisal-wagner-ring-cycle-robert-lepage-metropolitan-opera

Moloney, Kevin. 2014. "Multimedia, Crossmedia, Transmedia . . . What's in a Name?" *Transmedia Journalism*, April 21. http://transmediajournalism.org/2014/04/21/multimedia-crossmedia-transmedia-whats-in-a-name/

Ng, Maria. 2006. "The Taming of the Oriental Shrew: The Two Asias in Puccini's *Madama Butterfly* and *Turandot*." In *A Vision of the Orient: Texts, Intertexts, and Contexts of Madame Butterfly*, edited by J. L. Wisenthal, 170–80. Toronto: U Toronto P.

Osborne, Charles. 2004. *The Opera Lover's Companion*. New Haven, CT: Yale UP.

Pisani, Michael V. 1997. "A *Kapustnik* in the American Opera House: Modernism and Prokofiev's *Love for Three Oranges*." *The Musical Quarterly* 81 (4): 487–515.

Ridgely, Steven C. 2013. "Terayama Shūji and Bluebeard". *Marvels & Tales* 27 (2): 290–300.

Rosenberg, Jane. 1989. *Sing Me a Story: The Metropolitan Opera's Book of Opera Stories for Children*. New York: Thames and Hudson.

Scholl, Tim. 2004. *"Sleeping Beauty," a Legend in Progress*. New Haven, CT: Yale UP.

"Short: William Kentridge: 'The Magic Flute'." N.d. *Art21*. www.art21.org/videos/short-william-kentridge-the-magic-flute.

Soliño, María Elena. 2001. "From Perrault Through Disney to Fina Torres: Cinderella Learns Spanish and Talks Back in *Celestial Clockwork*." *Letras Femeninas* 27 (2): 68–84.

Spaethling, Robert. 1975. "Folklore and Enlightenment in the Libretto of Mozart's *Magic Flute*." *Eighteenth-Century Studies* 9 (1): 45–68.

Steichen, James. 2009. "The Metropolitan Opera Goes Public: Peter Gelb and the Institutional Dramaturgy of *The Met: Live in HD*." *Music and the Moving Image* 2 (2): 24–30.

Syer, Katherine R. 2014. *Wagner's Visions: Poetry, Politics, and the Psyche in the Operas through Die Walküre*. Rochester, NY: U Rochester P.

Wells, Brianna. 2012. "'Secret Mechanism': 'Les Contes d'Hoffmann' and the Intermedial Uncanny in the Metropolitan Opera's Live in HD Series." *19th Century Music* 36 (2): 191–203.

Mediagraphy

Das Rheingold (*Live in HD* [DVD]). 2013. Conductor James Levine. USA.

Die Walküre (*Live in HD* [DVD]). 2013. Conductor James Levine. USA.

"Die Zauberflöte Trailer." N.d. *Komische Oper Berlin*. https://english.komische-oper-berlin.de/schedule/magic-flute/.

Götterdämerung (*Live in HD* [DVD]). 2013. Conductor Fabio Luisi. USA.

Hansel and Gretel (*Live in HD* [DVD]). 2008. Conductor Vladimir Jurowski. USA.

Hour of the Wolf (Vargtimmen). 1968. Director Ingmar Bergman. Sweden.

La Cenerentola (*Live in HD* [DVD]). 2010. Conductor Maurizio Benini. USA.

The Magic Flute. 2006. Director Kenneth Branagh. France/UK.

The Magic Flute (*Live in HD* [DVD]). 2006. Conductor James Levine. USA.

The Magic Flute (Trollflöjten). 1975. Director Ingmar Bergman. Sweden.

Magic Flute Diaries. 2008. Director Kevin Sullivan. Canada.

Mécaniques célestes (Celestial Clockwork). Director Fina Torres. France/Belgium/Spain.

Operavox. 2015. English Pocket Opera Company. UK. www.epoc.co/?q=content/animated-operas#Project4

Rusalka (*Live in HD* [DVD]). 2015. Conductor Yannick Nézet-Séguin. USA.

Siegfried (*Live in HD* [DVD]). 2013. Conductor Fabio Luisi. USA.

Turandot (*Live in HD* [DVD]). 2011. Conductor Andris Nelsons. USA.

The Turandot Project. 2000. Director Allan Miller. USA/Germany.

65

POETRY

Fairy-Tale Poems: The Winding Path to *Illo Tempore*

Michael Joseph

Within the tradition of fairy-tale poetry, "antiquity" functions to effect, heighten, or warrant impossible transformation and, in particular, conditions post-nineteenth-century poets' methodology. "If there is one 'constant' in the structure and theme of the wonder tale that was also passed on to the literary fairy tale, it is transformation—to be sure, miraculous transformation," writes Jack Zipes (2000, xvii). Margaret Atwood cites transformation when explaining why the most influential book she ever read was the Grimms' fairy tales (Baer 1988, 24). The symbolism of antiquity both conceals and expresses a unity of opposites: historical categories or specific periods for which we have records, spliced to a non-historical fairy-tale period, once upon a time.

The long history of fairy-tale poems is central to their efficacy. They entice us because they seem to have been around forever. The French salons' *précieuses* sometimes included verse insets for dramatic effect in their prose tales, as did Madame d'Aulnoy, who applied the term "fairy tale" to this genre in her *Contes des Fées*, published in 1697 (2000, 31). Charles Perrault included verse morals (*moralités*) at the end of his prose retellings in *Histoires ou contes du temps passé* (1697). In English *belles-lettres*, the Elizabethans wrote verse plays employing fairy-tale elements and motifs, as in Shakespeare's *The Tempest* (1610–1611) and *A Midsummer Night's Dream* (1590–1597), Ben Jonson's *Oberon, The Fairy Prince* (performed in 1611, published in 1616), and Spenser's *The Faerie Queene* (1590). They in turn were reworking the field broken by earlier English poets and poems, such as Geoffrey Chaucer's *Canterbury Tales* (1475), which draws on many fairy-tale characters and motifs—for example, "The Clerk's Tale" employs the same Griselda character as Perrault in his "Griseldis" (1671) (ATU 887).

Poetry about impossible transformation was already "antique" by Chaucer's time. It appears in the Old English epic *Beowulf* (eighth through eleventh centuries), which begins by evoking "once upon a time" (Staver 2005, 24). Predating *Beowulf* by a considerable span, *The Odyssey* (circa 1190 B.C.E.) showcases witches and a stone-throwing ogre, and *The Epic of Gilgamesh* (circa 2100 B.C.E.) includes a magical quest and a version of the witch or wicked queen/stepmother in the character of Ishtar. The familiar element of magical transformation comes when the serpent steals from Gilgamesh the boxthorn-like plant, with the fairy-tale name, "How-the-Old-Man-Once-Again-Becomes-A-Young-Man," and gains immortality at Gilgamesh's expense.

Gilgamesh followed the *Pyramid Texts* (ca. 2400–2300 B.C.E.), spells arguably in verse (Strudwick 2005, 6), which were designed to reanimate the corpse of the pharaoh and guide him into the afterlife (Allen 2005, 7). The pharaoh's ascent anticipates Gilgamesh's quest, as it

580

does that of Psyche, in the "Cupid and Psyche" chapters of Apuleius's second-century novel *The Golden Ass* (Asinus Aureus), and a host of fairy-tale protagonists, from the boy who climbs to Beanstalk land to the girl who flies to Neverland. The topos of the soul's transformation, or transportation to an otherworldly realm, occurs alongside the topos of the "happily ever after" castle—the feudalized paradise in numerous Grimms' tales. These elements even pre-date the *Pyramid Texts*, whose language was already somewhat archaic by the time of its first appearance in the tomb of Unas, the last pharaoh of the fifth dynasty (Allen 2005, 4). The *Pyramid Texts* may have been part of an oral tradition, and their projected effectiveness might have been warranted by their "antiquity," or a sense of divine order, even then (*Pyramid Texts* 1952, 1).

How far back can we trace fairy-tale poems? In *The Singing Neanderthals*, Steven Mithen conjectures that early hominin mothers, standing upright for the first time, needed to use their hands to gather food in the fields and therefore required a means other than the embrace to soothe and pacify their restless and cranky babies (2005, 202). In this necessity lies the very genesis of language, he argues. Is it impossible to imagine that if we were able to station our-selves in the tall grasses, and listen to those sweet, repetitive utterances, we might catch refer-ences to innocent girls who confront clever beasts, plants that reach to the clouds, and babies who sleep until awakened by a kiss? Perhaps the origin of language and of fairy-tale poems occurred simultaneously approximately two million years ago.

With this heuristic fiction I suggest how, as well as being an anthropological construct, the notion of "antiquity" acts as a religious construct and may act on readers and listeners as a myth—a notional reality invested by those prepared to experience it as such with a specific kind of explanatory power (Rennie 1996, 73). Fairy-tale myths usually take humble forms. For example, when we reference Hans Christian Andersen's "The Emperor's New Clothes" to describe a gullible politician or some other grandiose simpleton, we ascribe explanatory power to that tale—its ability to express a self-evident truth or an irreducible quiddity of human nature. The notion of "antiquity" has, under certain circumstances, mythic power of a larger, more existential scope; it can mediate a fundamental truth about the framework through which we comprehend our lives and the human condition.

Antiquity is central to the work of Mircea Eliade, a historian of religion, who writes that pre-modern (early or prehistoric) humanity lived in two kinds of time, "of which the most important, sacred time, appears under the paradoxical aspect of a circular time, reversible and recoverable, a sort of eternal mythical present that is periodically regenerated by means of rites" (1959, 70). Eliade also believed that pre-modern beliefs continued to operate, through symbols, in "camouflage," within the experience of modern humanity (Rennie 1996, 32, 59). I argue that the continuing importance of "sacred time," camouflaged within the secular term "antiq-uity," plays an integral role in the enduring appeal of fairy-tale poems to modern humanity. Antiquity's non-historical face, "once upon a time," is a modern day survival of Eliade's sacred time; and the nostalgia for "happily ever after" and "once upon a time" is a camouflaged ver-sion of the archaic nostalgia for the eternal mythic present. Thus, poetry lends the fairy tale a kind of illocutionary force. It acts as a spell. As well as attention, a fairy-tale poem commands action—not merely to suspend attention but also to prepare for renewal, regeneration, return to *illo tempore* (*That time*).

In the nineteenth century, even as doggerel versions of fairy tales were being published for children, Victorian poets including Alfred Tennyson, Bret Harte, John Greenleaf Whittier, James Whitcomb Riley, and Frances Sargent Osgood composed retellings in stanza form for adults. According to Jeanne Marie Beaumont and Claudia Carlson, these poems do not "chal-lenge or deeply reinvent the tales," but (notice the drift in terminology toward myth) express a "romantic vision and yearning for a golden age" (2003, xii). Instances of more "deeply reinvented tales" by nineteenth-century contemporaries include Christina Rossetti's "Goblin Market" (1862) and Robert Browning's "The Pied Piper of Hamelin" (1842).[1] Both poems draw on the temptation of Adam and Eve and evoke an unfallen world mediated by childhood. Browning's poem in particular expresses longing for an "unrecoverable" idyll, in Eliade's term. The loss of children and childhood sustains the impression of transcendence and gives poetic force. Rossetti's poem trades similarly in paradox, making childhood's end both repugnant and irresistible—a delectably spiked fruit. Both poems invoke a displaced serenity for which the fairy-tale poem's antiquity, rooted in a simultaneously actual and mythic symbolism, provides the ideal medium.

The yearning for a "golden age" Beaumont and Carlson ascribe to the pre-twentieth century operates in later poems, notwithstanding their aesthetic of nonconformism, fragmentation, and disenchantment. What Wolfgang Mieder (2000) calls "modern" fairy-tale poems (generally speaking, post-nineteenth century) moves toward a preoccupation with intertextuality and artistic representation, as it deliberates on the materiality of older texts. These poems directly confront fairy tales' seductiveness and engage with their usefulness in generating meanings from the historical flux of "unique [. . .] irreversible events of autonomous significance" (Rennie 1996, 90–91). Fairy-tale scholars acknowledge this characteristic, if obliquely. For example, when Mieder writes, "modern fairy tale poems concern themselves with *every imaginable* human problem" (2000, 472; italics added), he gestures at fairy tales' mythic function, shading into invocation and illocution via the statement's unfalsifiability: he assumes the truth of what he says is self-evident.

I turn now to the uses of "antiquity" to effect transformation in four twentieth-century poems, beginning with Amy Lowell's "A Fairy Tale" (1912). Generically titled, it narrates in two roughly equal stanzas of forty-nine lines of blank verse a tale of an ancient curse laid on the narrator at her christening. Lowell introduces the curse at the first stanza's close with the poem's only heroic couplet, a rhyming pair of lines in iambic pentameter (the traditional English verse form, itself materializing antiquity): "But always there was one unbidden guest/Who cursed the child and left it bitterness" (239). The bitterness curse is threefold. The child will never find love; her fascination with "semblances [and] cruel impostures" will always eventuate in disillusionment; and it will bar her from a life of deeper meaning and human affection: "And so, unlit,/Even by hope or faith, my dragging steps/Force me forever through the passing days" (239). Lowell's narrator's curse comments on the Sleeping Beauty's; to be forever surrounded by phantasms may be analogized to a nightmare.

Our knowledge of "Sleeping Beauty" (ATU 410) not only deepens the meaning of Lowell's text, but brings us into the presence of the very operation of meaning. We know from the Grimms that the prince should awaken the princess. And we expect the fairy tale to rise—to have a restorative value, to make dramaturgically satisfying and reassuring meaning of events. "A Fairy Tale" apparently does neither, scorning such "childish" or unsophisticated expectations as false and misleading—*merely* a fairy tale—and flinging us back into an incoherent universe: Pre-modern humanity's other kind of time, the history of autonomous significance.

The poet's lot, seemingly cast with a contracted world (the *Weltanschauung* of Browning and the Gilgamesh poet), denies transcendence. Lowell's failed fairy tale incriminates an entire genre. In this respect particularly, her poem anticipates a tradition of feminist fairy-tale poems denouncing the patriarchal ideology permeating conventional tales of betraying women. But the conclusions of Lowell's poem are set in productive tension with its formal brilliance. Although Lowell's narrator might lament the curse of poetry—the persistence of formal structure that, like the iambs homologous to "the one unbidden guest," misdirect her toward "semblances"—and force the reader to feel how painfully "dragging steps/Force me forever through the passing days," the poem's phonological elegance challenges its bitter allegations. The rough consonance precisely conveys the poet's alleged lack of control, just as the echoing iambs that heighten feeling become both a curse and a benefice: "my dragging steps [. . .]/[. . .] the passing days" endow her suffering with grace and dignity. The paradoxical "forever through passing days" suggests a moment both in and out of profane history, an oscillation in eternity, which marks the poem's implicit intent.

Although the narrator rejects the poetic fairy tale as an unstable epistemological tool, its artifice heightens her awareness of her liminal condition. But therein lies the poem's deeper irony. By rejecting the fairy tale's insubstantiality, the narrator leaves herself no means of knowing whether bitter fate is real or merely another unreliable perception. The insular, tautological ambiguity of her state—its dreaminess—indirectly implies the potential for external transformation. Dreamers and sleepers can awaken. For reader and writer, the outgrown and discarded medium of the fairy-tale poem, even childishness itself, may be the site of transcendence. While empiricism claims we occupy one profane time frame, we should be epistemologically nuanced enough to realize that we have no external warrant of its truth value. Our certainty may be no more and no less valid than a fairy tale. The ancient curse, or indeed the curse of antiquity, may be a blessing in disguise.

Mieder notes, "by composing their poems around fairy-tale motifs, these authors if only very indirectly seem to long for that miraculous transformation to bliss and happiness" (2000, 388). Nostalgia—the longing for miraculous transformation—still operates indirectly within the work of modernist poets: not in spite of but as a correlative function of their "demythologizing" project (Day 1998, 133). The ancient curse is also modernism's.

As Mieder observes, many twentieth-century poets "have written [. . .] fairy-tale poems that reinterpret the Grimm tales in a humorous, parodic, nonsensical, ironic, cynical, or satiric fashion, thereby turning the positive wisdom of the tales into so-called anti-fairy tales"— less a turnabout than a clarifying of subversive patterns implicit in tales that precede the Grimms (2004, 332). Positive wisdom, or the facility to make experience coherent, sustains. It is extracted from obsolescent literary models (wisdom no longer effectively communicated through traditional forms) and relies on irony and intersubjectivity. Anti-fairy tales, in anti-poetic forms, require readers to share the poet's conflicted feelings—disgust and desire— toward the fairy tale (and toward conventional formalisms) and to participate in its transformation. So the astute reader of "A Fairy Tale" finds herself transformed, her existential situation a re-actualization of the condition mirrored by Sleeping Beauty. The poet's strategy shifts the fairy-tale poem's ontological footing away from naive realism toward transcendental realism, in which transcendence also concerns the poet's exemplary struggle with the constraints of traditional poetic form.

If it rejects nostalgia's outward appeal, this strategy emulates its method of operation, seeking new means to an old end. The reader's interpretive struggle with an enigmatic (shading toward oracular) text, which re-actualizes the poet's creative struggle—even to an extent supersedes it—implies an imaginatively original vision. In its re-creation, the tale affords the reader an experience of its initial creation in the time of the archetypes, in *illo tempore*. Eliade identifies the fundamental contradiction vis-à-vis nostalgia as determinative in the condition of modern—historical or nontraditional—man [sic]: "Myth still persists in his [sic] life. But the answer to his [sic] problems is given in secular terms" (1959, 204–205).

Among mid-twentieth-century poets who composed anti-fairy-tale poems, none worked with greater attention to the disjuncture between the fairy tale's inherent optimism and our experience of daily life than Randall Jarrell. Mieder notes that Jarrell's fairy-tale poems "capture frustrations that modern people experience in a world void of happy endings" (Mieder 2004, 390). Jarrell revisits the terms if not the actual text of Lowell's "A Fairy Tale" in "The Sleeping Beauty: Variation of the Prince" (2003), six stanzas of unrhymed lines of tetrameter (a line of four measures or metrical feet), save for four concluding lines of pentameter (a line with five measures). Stephen Burt cites psychologists Melanie Klein and Joseph Smith, and poet Alan Williamson, to help him characterize the poem's dilemma as Jarrell's desire to re-merge with the mother confounded by a dread of losing subjectivity (Burt 2002, 89). Whether directly or indirectly, "The Sleeping Beauty" addresses the riddle of truth and artifice that Lowell proposed in "A Fairy Tale." Jarrell's first-person narrator finds his way into the castle in which Sleeping Beauty lies

> just under the dust
> That was roses once—the steady lips
> Parted between a breath and a breath
> In love, for the kiss of the hunter, Death.
>
> (175)

Like the "unravished bride" in Keats's *Ode on a Grecian Urn*, Sleeping Beauty is poised to receive a deferred kiss, not from a love-struck prince, but from an angel of death. Adopting one of the *Ode*'s central themes, Jarrell reframes Lowell's curse of semblances affirmatively as the defeat of death through artistic representation. Jarrell's narrator wishes not to disturb the image. He stretches out beside the princess, vowing to wait with her, even though the span of years "will never end." (The tale is without horizon; it begins in "antiquity" or in a past-less past and will end in its mirror image, a futureless future.) But prophetically, miraculously, the narrator foresees the moment the impossible occurs, by definition, out of time. He promises that when it does, he will stir from his "long light sleep" and (as the metrical pattern swells to five beats per line to mark this miraculous transformation) stop Death from claiming Sleeping Beauty. In a poetic trance, he envisions drawing Death into their stateless sleep. Indirectly, in the subjunctive, art conquers death.

Like Lowell, Jarrell looks beyond the material tale on the page and its historical context of conventional interpretations, implicitly claiming a greater fidelity to an occulted truth. Jarrell demonstrates how poetry can free the lost original from the clutches of an outworn language and restore its lost vitality. His poem enables readers to re-experience "our world void of happy endings" while also igniting "a nostalgia for a regeneration of a sacred time" (Rennie 2006, 124). Nostalgia for a belief in the transcendent power of poetry, for a child's first sense of magic and meaning in the world, is as crucial to understanding the poem as Jarrell's a priori desire to save Sleeping Beauty. It is part of the poet's birthright, the poesis, without which there is no poem. Thus Jarrell begins with inflexible conditions: "After the thorns I came to the first page" (175). He must save Beauty from the domain ruled by "the hunter." To do so he cannot bring her into his world, for that would mean submitting to desire, to lethal kisses; he must enter hers, an overdetermined fairyland separate from the life–death timeline, a poetic evocation, once again, of sacred time.

To recontextualize Burt's reading of Jarrell's psychological dilemma, the poet must refresh his personal struggle within the smothering flesh of text, epitomized by the smelly, old fairy tale, despite knowing that such an embrace will crush him. To express oneself wholly, in any genre, requires a self-sacrifice to the conventions of representation, and self-expression is to become something other than what one knows oneself to be, a unique, ineffable, historical being. For the modernist poet, the fairy-tale poem becomes an analogue for every type of artistic representation. Yeats yearns to become a nightingale "to set upon a golden bough" because he has license from the traditional ontology of wondrous transformation and from poetic precedent. His aesthetic fairyland echoes Tennyson's: "Yet all experience is an arch wherethro'/Gleams that untravell'd world whose margin fades/For ever and for ever when I move" ("Ulysses," 19–21). But this is an aesthetic that poets mistrustful, if not contemptuous, of semblances, of non-historical categories, cannot accept. Nevertheless, Jarrell, recapitulating the crisis articulated in the Lowell poem, incrementally recovers the intentional attitude of faith in poetry's transformative power, on which he insists with childlike puns and riddles referencing stories and books.

"Transformation," "rising," or flight in fairy tales assumes transcendence, resurrection, and initiation: "The tale takes up and continues 'initiation' on the level of the imaginary. [. . .] In the deep psyche initiation scenarios preserve their seriousness and continue to transmit their message, to produce mutation" (Eliade 1963, 202). In anti-fairy-tale poems, mutation follows Ezra Pound's clarion call to make it new (1934). The paradox of modernism perhaps lies with the "it"—the old—which, to retain, the modernist or postmodernist poet must make new, transform. (It is that toward which, however disgusting, the reader experiences desire.) The old embodies the seeds of transformation. In Jarrell's "Sleeping Beauty," the old, in the guise of the text's materiality, acquires the function of the archetypal helper. Jarrell signals this reading, both by adopting the fairy tale—the example par excellence of art—and by the self-aware bookishness of his opening lines: "After the thorns, I came to the first page./He lay there grey in his fur of dust" (175). The pun on "page" insinuates a reading of "dust" as book dust. The poem reasserts the reading on line 6: "and the sentry's cuirass was red with rust" (175) With a second pun (red/read), the concluding poetical iambs, and the pedantic "cuirass," the line asserts the text's antiquity, the poem's tangible corpus available only through the accretions of time, the mortal source of disgust but also miraculous change. The justification for the fairy tale, and for poetry, is its link to the past. The supremely real treasure the text conceals must be reclaimed from time's spoilage, the historical pileup of riddles, puns, tales, and poems. "Dust" reoccurs in all but one stanza, making it, if not a metaphor, then a marker, of text. Its final appearance occurs in the concluding phrase, "and close with the tips of the dust of my hand/The lips of the steady—/ Look, He is fast asleep!" (176). The broken last line identifies Death as the sleeper—its curse removed from history by the poet's self-sacrificing touch—with a typically Jarrellian twist. "Look, he is fast asleep!" parents comment, looking in on a beloved child who perhaps only a moment earlier had been cranky. Death, miraculously reimagined as a darling child, a cupid, might allude to "Cupid and Psyche" in which Apuleius transforms Psyche's husband from "a dire mischief, viperous and fierce" to the God of Love (Apuleius 1950, 100).

The almost-liturgical repetition of "dust" makes us weigh reiterations carefully, including that of "hand" in this stanza, calling to mind its use in stanzas 2–4: "Children play inside: the dirty hand/Of the little mother an inch from the child/That has worn out" (175). The earlier entropic depiction, redeemed by a mother, no longer worn out, beaming affection upon a sleeping child, no longer worn out, offers an immutable image of Eliade's eternal mythical present, suggesting a quickening of the text and psyche alike. The text or book (aspects of materiality) moving toward magical transformation flare out in another pun. "The tips of the dust of my hand" suggests the poem's words or letterpress (tip/type), contrasting with "lips of the steady," which suggests breath or spirit. The poet frees the fairy tale's spirit from the clutches of a dead material text, but only with the compliance of the text—the physical expression or fabrication required of the poet.

Similar strategies prevail among feminist fairy-tale authors, which Beaumont and Carlson term "The Grimm Sisterhood," including Enid Dame, Robin Morgan, Olga Broumas,

Margaret Atwood, and Julia Alvarez. Beaumont and Carlson acknowledge Anne Sexton's priority; her book *Transformations* (1971) "inspired countless other poets to revisit the tales as a powerful poetic source" (Beaumont and Carlson 2003, xii). Shawn Jarvis credits *Transformations* as having "recognized the impact of the socialization process on women and focused on the socio-cultural context of received tradition" (2000, 157). Mieder notes "these [. . .] transfigured tales in which questions of sexuality, sexual politics, and emancipation all add up to a feministic statement against gender stereotypes" (2000, 389).

With their insistent focus on the sociocultural context, feminists' fairy-tale poems ostensibly resist nostalgia. This aversion comports with the attitude of skepticism that surfaces in Lowell, the rigorous insistence on secular terms and, correspondingly, weariness with the formulaic reifications of transcendence in nineteenth-century fairy-tale poems. For "modern humans, historical realities [are] the only source of significance, meaning, truth, and power" (Rennie 2006, 15). We modern humans deny "effective agency to [Eliade's] 'sacred categories which lack historical autonomy'" (15). In order to achieve the impossible task of reconciling nostalgia for paradise with contemporary historicism, feminist ideology provides a solution.

A feminist poet can configure an attitude of belief toward the effective agency of the same sacred categories she dismisses by attacking history as hegemonic narrative. The alternative feminist history, desacralized from phallogocentric patriarchy, reinscribes the transcendent paradisiacal antithesis without forfeiting historical autonomy. Feminism makes paradise a historical possibility. As Elizabeth Keyser observes, "although the most polemical and thesis-ridden of these new tales do perpetrate what Charles Dickens called a 'fraud on the fairies,' the best [. . .] entice the disenchanted to reenter" (1989, 157).

Anne Sexton's "The Twelve Dancing Princesses" (1971) exemplifies feminist logic. The marriage of soldier and eldest princess is given a critical reading: in marriage, the commonplace has abolished the ethereal:

> He had won. The dancing shoes would dance
> no more. The princesses were torn from
> their night life like a baby from its pacifier.
> At the wedding the princesses averted their eyes
> and sagged like old sweatshirts.
>
> (92)

The patriarchal wedding is an ideological construct that draws on the Fall as the source of mortal cares, the curse of childbirth, and manual labor adumbrated in the poem's first seven stanzas. The truth of feminism replaces the dissimulations of patriarchal historians who have imposed the quotidian on the ecstatic and condemned women to the prosaic. The twelve dancing princesses become a metaphor for a self-replenishing cycle and the loss of their "eldest"—a symbol of the Beginning—an outcry for "a regeneration of time," or mythic return (Rennie 2006, 124).

Feminism touches more lightly on some work of later poets, such as Rachel Hadas, who turns to "Little Red Riding Hood" (ATU 333) in "The Wolf in the Bed" (1995). As with Lowell's and Jarrell's, this poem does not simply allude to Little Red Cap, but seeks to re-actualize it as "a structure of exemplary behavior" available to human experience (Zipes 1994, 2). Hadas conjoins historical and non-historical categories within four poetic moves that transition from actuality to antiquity.

The poem begins in our time with an injunction to a blind other to remember the Gustav Doré print illustrating Red Riding Hood in bed. In it, Red is wide-eyed, but not innocent.

She regards the wolf in Grandma's bonnet beside her with intelligent curiosity. Doré illustrates the exchange beginning, "Grandmother, what big eyes you have," perhaps the best-known fairy-tale dialogue, archly inverted in the pop-novelty song "Li'l Red Riding Hood" by Sam the Sham and the Pharaohs, in which it is the wolf who remarks to Red, "What big eyes you have/The kind of eyes that drive wolves mad." Hadas's text similarly reverses agency with the conceit "wide-eyed" signifying both Red and the disguised wolf caught out by his eyes (his hunger). This fusion of identities is compounded: "Recall the sidelong/look that links the child/and the shaggy monster" (253). Blind, the figure in bed can only recall sight (or look backward). Thus the poem moves into a conjectural realm. The encompassing moment constitutes a mise-en-abyme. "Red Riding Hood" shimmers through several displacements within the print being recollected within the narrative. The displaced moment symbolizes the lost, eclipsed, visually unavailable beginning, a surrogate of antiquity, of *illud tempus*. Hadas then turns to the unmade, the not-yet imagined, contemplating what the blankets, under which wolf and girl cozily lie, might conceal. Identifying herself with the blind other (since both can imagine), Hadas invokes the tradition of Homer and Tiresias, granting ontological weight to the unseen, in which the boundaries of past, present, and future are perhaps more porous. She envisions under the blankets:

> A secret region, shadowy deep forest
> Through which a covered basket
> Is being carried, bread and wine
> And books to the sick one's bedside.
> (253)

In the Grimms' version, Red carries a basket filled with *cake* and wine. Hadas perhaps recollects Edward FitzGerald's translation of *Rubáiyát of Omar Khayyám*:

> Here with a loaf of bread beneath the Bough,
> A Flask of Wine, a Book of Verse—and Thou
> Beside me singing in the Wilderness—
> And Wilderness is Paradise enow.
> (Khayyám 1990, 5)

Hadas draws attention to her own intertextual play, with her Jarrell-like addition of "books." The Grimms' Red of course carried no books, but most subsequent authors have discovered her through that medium.

At this juncture, the poem returns, temporarily, to the actual, only to demonstrate how reality is attenuated—how antiquity is more real than the actual moment in whose constraints the narrator becomes confused: "You are the girl in bed beside the beast/or you're the grandmother, I visit you—/but no, since it's my mother, too, who's dying" (253). The narrator is deceived not by semblances, but by their lack of purchase in ordinary life, which cannot contain poetic experience's complexity, just as sight cannot encompass the realities of a life richly and imaginatively lived.

The recollection that her mother, too, is dying disturbs the narrator's rational mode of consciousness, and she asks, "Is she [mother] in bed with you, since both are breathed on,/ crowded, jostled by the restless wolf?" (253). Her question hammers upon the constraints of identity and legitimizes the poem's myth-ward trajectory to the goblin market in which contradictory semblances may coexist, although to enter it entails a sacrifice. Hadas, like Jarrell

MICHAEL JOSEPH

(and unlike Lowell), is prepared. Climbing into bed with friend/mother/wolf, the narrator embraces the otherness:

> [I] cradle you in my arms, my friend, my mother,
> and read you stories of children
> walking unattended through dark woods.
>
> (253)

As in Jarrell's "Sleeping Beauty," blind friend/mother/poet/narrator/reader become unmade by surrendering their identity to myth. But nobody is permanently lost; the unmade can be made again. Without the implied circular time of *illo tempore*, the final act of reading children's stories would lose its meaning. The dark woods in which we cannot be attended (seen) are the crucible of rebirth and re-creation. As in "A Sleeping Beauty," "The Wolf in the Bed" concludes with the iconic conceit of mother and child, although unconventionally reversed. The poem's playful transposition is a token of the liberties it takes with the fairy tale, as well as its accommodations to creative reinvention.

The four poems discussed here demonstrate the flexibility and power of fairy-tale poetry to translate subjective states into communal myth. Their celebration of magical transformation reflects our deepest intuitions of the world; our most intimate, meaningful relationships; and our incompletely historicized selves, which balance with one foot in the library and one on the path to *illo tempore*.

Related topics: Criticism; Language; Oral Tradition; Translation

Note

1. Rossetti's "Goblin Market" appears in Guillermo del Toro's *Hellboy II: The Golden Army* (2008); films based on "The Pied Piper" include Jiří Barta's *Krysař* (1985), Jacques Demy's *The Pied Piper* (1972), and Atom Egoyan's *The Sweet Hereafter* (1997) (see *International Fairy-Tale Filmography* 2013–).

References Cited and Further Reading

Allen, James P. 2005. *The Ancient Egyptian Pyramid Texts*. Atlanta: Society of Biblical Literature.

Apuleius. 1950. *The Golden Ass*, translated by Robert Graves. London: Penguin Classics.

Baer, Elizabeth R. 1988. "Pilgrimage Inward: Quests and Fairy Tale Motifs in *Surfacing*." In *Margaret Atwood: Visions and Forms*, edited by Kathryn VanSpanckeren and Jan Garden Castro, 24–34. Carbondale: Southern Illinois UP.

Beaumont, Jeanne Marie, and Claudia Carlson, eds. 2003. *The Poets' Grimm: 20th Century Poems from Grimm Fairy Tales*. Ashland, OR: Story Line P.

Beowulf. 1996. Internet Archive, June 19. http://web.archive.org/web/20020702025807/http://etext.lib.virginia.edu/etcbin/toccer-new2?id=AnoBeow.sgm&images=images/modeng&data=/texts/english/modeng/parsed&tag=public&part=2&division=div1.

Bottigheimer, Ruth. 2002. *Fairy Godfather: Straparola, Venice, and the Fairy Tale Tradition*. Philadelphia: U Pennsylvania P.

Browning, Robert. 2016. "The Pied Piper of Hamelin." *Poetry Foundation*, May 1. www.poetryfoundation.org/poems-and-poets/poems/detail/45818.

Burt, Stephen. 2002. *Randall Jarrell and His Age*. New York: Columbia UP.

Chaucer, Geoffrey. 1993. *The Canterbury Tales*. Oxford Text Archive, June 19. http://quod.lib.umich.edu/cgi/t/text/text-idx?c=cme;idno=CT.

Day, Aidan. 1998. *Angela Carter: The Rational Glass*. Manchester: Manchester UP.

Eliade, Mircea. 1959. *The Sacred and the Profane*, translated by Willard R. Trask. New York: Harcourt.

———. 1963. *Myth and Reality*, translated by Willard R. Trask. New York: Harper.

The Epic of Gilgamesh. 2002. Translated by Andrew George. New York: Penguin.

Hadas, Rachel. 2003. "The Wolf in the Bed." In *The Poets' Grimm: 20th Century Poems from Grimm Fairy Tales*, 253. Ashland, OR: Story Line P.

Homer. 2002. *The Odyssey*, translated by Rodney Merrill. Ann Arbor: U Michigan.

Jarrell, Randall. 2003. "The Sleeping Beauty: Variation of the Prince." *The Poets' Grimm: 20th Century Poems from Grimm Fairy Tales*, 175–6. Ashland, OR: Story Line.

Jarvis, Shawn. 2000. "Feminism and Fairy Tales." In *The Oxford Companion to Fairy Tales*, edited by Jack Zipes, 155–8. New York: Oxford UP.

Jonson, Ben. 2003. *Oberon, the Fairy Prince.* Anniina Jokinen of Luminarium, June 19. www.luminarium.org/editions/oberon.htm.

Keats, John. 2016. "Ode on a Grecian Urn." *Poetry Foundation*, June 19. www.poetryfoundation.org/poems-and-poets/poems/detail/44477.

Keyser, Elizabeth. 1989. "Feminist Revisions: Frauds on the Fairies?" *Children's Literature* 17: 156–70.

Khayyám, Omar. 1990. *The Rubáiyát of Omar Khayyám*, translated by Edward FitzGerald, 5. 1st and 5th ed. New York: Dover.

Lowell, Amy. 2003. "A Fairy Tale." In *The Poets' Grimm: 20th Century Poems from Grimm Fairy Tales*, 239. Ashland, OR: Story Line.

Mieder, Wolfgang, ed. 1985. *Disenchantments: An Anthology of Modern Fairy Tale Poetry.* Lebanon, NH: UP New England.

———. 2000. "Poetry and Fairy Tales." In *The Oxford Companion to Fairy Tales*, edited by Jack Zipes, 388–91. New York: Oxford UP.

———. 2004. "The Poets' Grimm: 20th Century Poems from Grimm Fairy Tales (Review)." *Marvels & Tales* 18 (2): 331–5.

Mithen, Steven J. 2005. *The Singing Neanderthals: The Origins of Music, Language, Mind and Body.* Cambridge, MA: Harvard UP.

Perrault, Charles. 1697. *Histoires ou contes du temps passé.* Paris: Claude Barbin.

Pound, Ezra. 1935. *Make It New: Essays.* New Haven, CN: Yale UP.

Pyramid Texts. 1952. Translated by Samuel A. B. Mercer. New York: Longmans, Green.

Rennie, Bryan. 1996. *Reconstructing Eliade: Making Sense of Religion.* Albany: SUNY P.

———. 2006. "The Life and Work of Mircea Eliade." In *Mircea Eliade: A Critical Reader*, edited by Bryan Rennie, 5–16. London: Equinox.

Rossetti, Christina. 2016. "Goblin Market." *Poetry Foundation*, May 1. www.poetryfoundation.org/poems-and-poets/poems/detail/44996.

Saliba, John A. 2006. "*Homo Religiosus* in the Thought of Mircea Eliade." In *Mircea Eliade: A Critical Reader*, edited by Bryan Rennie, 122–30. London: Equinox.

Seifert, Lewis C. 2000. "Aulnoy, Marie-Catherine Le Jumel de Barneville, Baronne d'." In *The Oxford Companion to Fairy Tales*, edited by Jack Zipes, 29–32. New York: Oxford UP.

Sexton, Anne. 1971. "The Twelve Dancing Princesses." In *Transformations*, 87–92. New York: Houghton Mifflin.

Shakespeare, William. 1993. *The Complete Works of William Shakespeare.* MIT, June 19. http://shakespeare.mit.edu.

Spenser, Edmund. 1995. *The Faerie Queene.* Risa S. Bear for Luminarium, June 19. www.luminarium.org/renascence-editions/queene1.html.

Staver, Ruth Johnston. 2005. *A Companion to Beowulf.* Westport, CN: Greenwood.

Strudwick, Nigel. 2005. *Texts from the Pyramid Age (Writings from the Ancient World).* Atlanta, GA: Society of Biblical Literature.

Tennyson, Alfred Lord. 2016. "Ulysses." *Poetry Foundation*, June 19. www.poetryfoundation.org/poems-and-poets/poems/detail/45392.

Zipes, Jack. 1994. *Fairy Tale as Myth, Myth as Fairy Tale.* Lexington: UP Kentucky.

———. 2000. "Introduction: Toward a Definition of the Literary Fairy Tale." In *The Oxford Companion to Fairy Tales*, edited by Jack Zipes, xv–xxxii. New York: Oxford UP.

Mediagraphy

Hellboy II: The Golden Army. 2008. Director Guillermo del Toro. USA.

International Fairy-Tale Filmography. 2013–. Creators Jack Zipes, Pauline Greenhill, and Kendra Magnus-Johnston. http://iftf.uwinnipeg.ca.

Krysař (The Pied Piper of Hamelin). 1985. Director Jirí Barta. Czechoslovakia/West Germany.

"Li'l Red Riding Hood" (Song). 1966. Artist Sam the Sham and the Pharaohs, album *Li'l Red Riding Hood*. USA.

The Pied Piper. 1972. Director Jacques Demy. France.

The Sweet Hereafter. 1997. Director Atom Egoyan. Canada.

66
REALITY TELEVISION
Vanessa Nunes

Fairy tales are particularly attractive to specific types of reality television imbricated in the trope that "dreams come true." Our familiarity with fairy tales helps us naturalize promises of true love and makeover when we see them in reality television, a venue whose alliances supposedly lie with "the real." Quests, transformation, and romance are found alike in both genres, but certain specific types of reality television programs such as *The Bachelor* (2002–) and *The Swan* (2004) might further be considered as reiterations of popular fairy tales. Either way, many reality television shows have both built upon and expanded the world of fairy tales to the point that there is an entire subgenre of fairy-tale-oriented reality shows.

By the latter, I refer specifically to series that draw on fairy-tale motifs and structures in documenting "real people" (rather than actors in fictional roles) in what are assumed to be real-life situations. This chapter focuses on those specific forms, rather than on the entire broad category of reality television, which comprises many and distinct formats from hidden cameras and talent contests to job searching and court shows. While acknowledging the "complicated" relationship between fairy tale and reality television (Lee 2014, 276), this chapter examines examples mostly from dating and makeover programs and follows Susan Murray and Laurie Ouellette's definition of reality television as "an unabashedly commercial genre united less by aesthetic rules or certainties than by the fusion of popular entertainment with a self-conscious claim to the discourse of the real" (2009, 3). The illusion that reality television deals with the real has to do with the assumption that these shows require minimal script and use non-actors. However, not only do participants attend situations that are out of the ordinary and explicitly contrived to be televised, but also the way these "real people" who participate are perceived depends on editing and tailoring storylines.

Background

Reality television's roots have been associated with a European tradition, an interesting similarity with the development of literary fairy tales. Toby Miller traces the origins of reality television back to the propaganda activities of the Nazi Party in the 1930s with a reference to a television show discussing unsolved police cases with participation of police officers and the audience. In North America, Allen Funt's *Candid Camera*, which debuted in 1948, introduced "the notion of surveillance as a source of fun, information, and narcissism" (Miller 2010, 162). Many shows of the mid-twentieth century, including *Candid Camera*, started out on radio (as *The Candid Microphone*) and then moved to a televised version.

Richard Huff notes "the 1950s wave of game shows" (2006, 17), including *Queen for a Day* (1945–1964), which featured homemakers telling stories about how miserable their lives were. The contestant with the saddest story (determined by the audience's applause meter) won prizes and was crowned and covered with a sable-trimmed robe. *Queen for a Day* was one of the earliest reality shows to directly link with fairy tales, from its title to the tropes of transformation and wishes that come true. From its foundation in staged pranks and quiz games, reality television changed and grew significantly during the 1990s, with the rise of European-based companies specialized not only in creating and selling concept rights of reality shows but also in aiding local markets in adapting these productions to their situations (McMurria 2009).

American television, which has helped popularize fairy tales with Disney's cartoons, has done the same for reality television. For instance, MTV's debut of *The Real World* (1992–) was a landmark because it trained "a new generation of young viewers in the language of reality TV" (Murray and Ouellette 2009, 3) by introducing features that define the genre today, including the intentional casting of young adults in such a way as to generate conflict and storyline, the use of settings filled with cameras and microphones, editing tricks, and serial format. But it was by the turn of the millennium that "[r]eality television became a 'phenomenon,'" as Ouellette notes (2003, 1), thanks to the debut in the United States of popular prime time franchises such as *Survivor* (2000–) and *Big Brother* (2000–), both with their origins in European formats. New ways of audience interaction and lower production costs have also contributed to the proliferation of reality television in the 2000s. As Chad Raphael (2009) explains, reality television's "ability to sell abroad" has attracted producers and network investors with the opportunity to sell or license the concept of show for local production with local contestants (134). The result is the existence of reality series that share a core structure but appear in different local versions, which bears certain similarity with the universe of fairy tales.

Intersection With Fairy Tales

As a subgroup of folk narratives, fairy tales "tend to exist in multiple versions" (Oring 1986, 123), and the same holds true for reality shows, especially if we consider each season of a reality television series as a different narrative that shares a common structure. Elliott Oring states that folk narratives "must be re-created with each telling" because they are reflections of their societies (1986, 123). The stories told on reality television are also re-created with each season and location. The notion that fairy tales change—in both form and content—is crucial to thinking about their intersection with reality television. On the one hand, reality television functions as one more medium for fairy tales among options that include, for instance, film, comic books, and opera. Some reality television series might be approached as iterations of popular fairy tales, as in the case of *The Bachelor*, which shares crucial features with Cinderella stories. On the other hand, some reality series remind us of fairy tales even though they do not function as retellings of particular stories. In this case, they share some qualities or motifs that we associate mostly with the world of fairy tales, such as the search for an enchanted prince/husband.

As Linda J. Lee (2014) notes, most of the scholarship about fairy tales and reality television has been limited to what Mikel J. Koven labels motif spotting, which means studies that "seek to enumerate folklore types and motifs when they occur in popular media" (2008, 9). This approach is tempting because reality shows offer so many references to fairy tales; indeed, contestants often frame their experience in fairy-tale terms. Remarks about "finding true love," "fairy-tale wedding," and "being like a princess" have become clichés not only in reality television but also in popular culture in general.

In their discussion of legends, Linda Dégh and Andrew Vázsonyi (1983) use the concept of ostension in reference to stories that are enacted rather than narrated. Certainly, one can argue that for contestants in reality television shows such as *The Bachelor*, their experience is ostensive. As Lee puts it, "In their efforts to transform into a 'swan' or to marry 'a real-life Prince

Charming,' participants enact fairy tales through, on, and with their bodies." Lee frames this experience as repurposing fairy tales, saying that these shows function as "postmodern fairy tales or fairy-tale pastiches" (2014, 276) because they reproduce and transform some classic fairy tales "for ideological and economic purposes" (277). Lee's emphasis on the instability of genre conventions aligns with Cathy Lynn Preston's (2004) reading of *Who Wants to Marry a Multi-Millionaire* (2000) among postmodern texts that break or blur genre frames. Lee's argument is that "[n]one of these programs recreates the source fairy tale whole cloth" (2014, 276). Considering, though, that fairy tales are not static but narratives that change through time, space, culture, and media, one could contend that certain reality television shows might be read as variants too. While viewers are not themselves enacting a role in a fairy tale by watching reality shows, they can use folklore—in this case, their knowledge of fairy tales—as a tool to make sense of these programs.

A test case for this argument comes from those many dating reality shows that follow scripts that viewers know well from the world of fairy tales. Series such as *The Bachelor* and *Joe Millionaire* (2003) might be read as "Cinderella" (ATU 510A) stories as they feature women's competition as suitors for an "enchanted prince" and the promise of "true love" with a happy ending for the chosen bride. Scholars have discussed "Cinderella" in the context of "a bride-show custom," a practice in which rich and powerful men seeking a bride gather a group of eligible candidates among whom to choose (Bourboulis 1988).

Reality shows such as *The Bachelor* resonate not only with the tradition of bride-show contests, but also with the false impression that love stories are universal and timeless. The enduring appeal of love stories such as "Cinderella" sheds light onto the success of shows like *The Bachelor*, in which women dispute for the love interest of an eligible man, who eliminates a candidate per episode. In the finale, the bachelor is supposed to propose marriage to the remaining girl, the chosen Cinderella. Initially launched in 2002, this show has spawned spinoffs, including notably *The Bachelorette* (2003–2005; 2008–), a gender-reversed format in which a woman chooses her "true love" from a pool of male participants, and international versions of both have reached countries in Latin America, Oceania, and Europe.

The characterization of weddings as indicative of "happily ever after" is not limited to Cinderella stories. Russian formalist Vladimir Propp (1968) enumerates recurring plot devices in folk narratives, noting that many fairy tales end with a wedding. Despite the current popular idea that a fairy-tale wedding is a celebration of true love, marriage is often approached as a business affair in folk narratives. For instance, after the hero completes his quest or task—for instance, killing a dragon—the king gives him the hand of the princess in return. In reality shows, the contestants are also often more driven by monetary prizes than by the search for true love. As Jennifer L. Pozner states, "That's the thing about fairytales [. . .] they're not real. [. . .] After all the happily-ever-after build up, after all the pathetic pandering to be picked, nearly every dating show hero has dumped his chosen 'princess'" (2010, 58). She argues that dating shows are a "subgenre where commerce is the key to the fairytale" (39). For instance, *Extreme Makeover* (2002–2007) has a wedding episode set in Disneyland, whose theme parks have the slogan "where dreams come true," and one cannot forget that Disney owns ABC, which airs this show. As June Deery affirms, "The fairy-tale analogy is therefore a matter not just of engaging the audience's imagination but also of keeping business options open" (2012, 110). In other words, fairy tales help "sell" reality television, just as reality series help circulate fairy tales.

Much of the scholarly scrutiny toward reality shows, especially *The Bachelor*, is informed by second-wave feminist criticism about fairy tales. Dating shows are blamed for reinforcing the patriarchal status quo by emphasizing notions of female beauty and heterosexual marriage. Gust Yep and Ariana Ochoa Camacho claim that *The Bachelor* "normalizes heterogendered relations in contemporary US society" through its connections with fairy tales (2004, 338). One argument is that reality television reinforces the view of marriage as women's primary goal in life, echoing Karen E. Rowe's criticism that marriage is celebrated in fairy tales as "an enchantment which will shield [women] against harsh realities outside the domestic realm and guarantee everlasting happiness" (1979, 250).

The reality show *Joe Millionaire*, aired in 2003, featured female contestants arriving via horse and carriage to the castle that was the production's setting. In her feminist critique, Alison Graham-Bertolini affirms that "*Joe Millionaire* perpetuates problematic stereotypical images of appropriate female demeanors and goals" (2004, 342), a parallel with some fairy tales' view of courtship "magnified into the most important and exciting part of a girl's life" (Lieberman 1972, 394). It is no coincidence that the show aired a participant remarking, "We are living in a fairy tale. It will be interesting to see how this plays out. Will we have a fairy-tale ending?" In this context, to have a happy ending is to marry a millionaire bachelor. Graham-Bertolini points out that the winner of *Joe Millionaire* was precisely the contestant "portrayed as sexually pure, submissive, and domestic" (2004, 343). This analysis reinforces Marcia Lieberman's argument that fairy tales "serve to acculturate women to traditional social roles" since good temper and beauty are rewarded (1972, 383).

Interestingly, though, the man was a working-class construction worker, information revealed only to the last remaining girl in the finale, a development that resonates with another key theme in fairy tales: the notion that true love must go beyond appearances—in fact, disguise is also a common motif in fairy-tale romance (*Peau d'Asne*, ATU 510B, for instance). Like fairy tales, reality television can be cruel. Jonathan Gray suggests that the show's twist invited "viewers to enjoy the [sight] of 'gold diggers' being 'put in their place' [. . .] setting the entire season up to punish the ultimate 'winner'" (2009, 264). This commentary seems to indicate the assumption that this woman was never a true Cinderella looking for love, but rather someone only seeking marriage to enhance her financial situation. Like fairy tales, reality TV rarely makes its morals explicit.

The Power of Transformation

While shows such as *Joe Millionaire* and *The Bachelor* franchise emphasize the illusion of happy ending through true love and marriage, other reality series such as *The Swan*, *Extreme Makeover*, and *The Biggest Loser* (2004–) focus on notions of beauty and transformation, also a standard feature in fairy tales. Transfiguration is even one of the functions in Propp's scheme of folk narratives. In many cases, a hero gets a new appearance "by means of the magical action of a helper" (1968, 62). A classic example is Cinderella's transformation thanks to the help of her fairy godmother. An entire category of reality shows focuses on makeovers, in which contestants get the help of doctors, stylists, and other professionals. For instance, *The Swan*, which had two seasons (both in 2004), featured women competing to receive extreme makeovers, including plastic surgery, while *The Biggest Loser* is a competition to lose weight in which the participants face not only challenges but also temptations.

Heike Steinhoff (2015) states that makeover shows "suggest that they transform insecure and desperate beings into self-confident and self-loving" (70). Writing about *The Swan*, Steinhoff notes that each episode features "a revelation scene that resonates with Hollywood as well as fairy tale imagery and positions the previously 'ordinary person,' but now transformed woman, as a media star and princess" (2015, 70). The appeal of transformation goes beyond fairy tales. Diet changes, workouts, piercing, tattooing, sex-change procedures, cosmetic surgery, and popular culture's growing interest in werewolves, vampires, and superheroes all contribute to

Steinhoff's argument that "[t]ransformations of the body take center stage in American culture at the turn of the twenty-first century" (2015, 3). Drawing on theories of performativity, Steinhoff suggests that transformation can operate in paradoxical ways, as a form of empowerment and as a form of subjugation to societal standards. In particular, she discusses *The Swan*, a show whose title alludes to Hans Christian Andersen's fairy tale "The Ugly Duckling," but this fairy tale also resonates with other shows like *The Biggest Loser* and *Extreme Makeover*.

Andersen's fairy tale is about a bird despised and scorned as an ugly duckling who later learns that he is in fact a beautiful swan. In her psychoanalytic reading of *The Swan*, Pamela Orosan-Weine argues that this reality show is "partly about beauty and partly about change" (2007, 17). Her analysis addresses Bruno Bettelheim's negative reading of Andersen's "The Ugly Duckling" as a story that offers "no active solution to the problem of feeling left out, different, and unloved. The duckling just waits to be discovered as a superior bird; no talent or effort on his part is required" (1977, 105). Orosan-Weine points out that the lack of physical change in the tale differs from *The Swan*, which "oversells its dramatic transformation and minimizes the hard work" (2007, 25). She adds that the concerns of the majority of the participants of the show "are not very different from normative female body discontent" (2007, 20). Makeover shows thereby rely on viewers' familiarity with fairy tales about personal growth to naturalize cosmetic surgery. In this context, it is worth noting the findings of Julie Albright's research on the effects of the makeover shows *The Swan* and *Extreme Makeover* on body image and dissatisfaction among college students. While her sample from Buffalo, New York, considered the achievement of beauty ideals as a form of upward social mobility, her sample from Los Angeles, California, perceived body image as a status symbol. According to Albright's conclusion, in both perspectives the class factor "is a prominent subtext not lost on these audiences" (2007, 123).

In her analysis of *Extreme Makeover*, Cressida Heyes makes the point that these programs rely on fairy tales because these narratives "evoke culturally familiar and reassuring developmental trajectories and archetypes" (2007, 24). Gareth Palmer considers *Extreme Makeover: Home Edition* as "part of a growing number of television programmes that are not simply recording or reflecting on society but becoming active elements, working practically and ideologically to change the world" (2007, 174). This show aired from 2003 to 2012 in the United States, providing home improvements to families facing some type of hardship. Lee sees further connections between fairy tales and reality television because both "serve as a means for communicating cultural values. When both vehicles combine in a single venue, the message is intensified and naturalized" (2014, 291). In Jack Bratich's view, fairy tales are an antecedent of reality television because both are about "the powers of transformation" (2007, 17). Whether in the realm of fairy tales or in real life, this power is not necessarily positive. Transformation is cruel in the case of Cinderella's stepsisters in versions of the tale in which their feet are mutilated to fit into the slipper, as are the body-shaming tactics of makeover reality shows.

In fairy tales, transformation goes beyond the idea of getting a new physical appearance. The same could be said about reality shows such as *Beauty and the Geek*, which had five seasons in the United States (2005–2008) and gained more than twenty international versions. This show does not frame itself as a dating show but rather as "a social experiment," pairing a group of beautiful women with men considered to be highly intelligent but lacking social skills. In each episode the contestants are tested in their new skills, and the couple that learns the most receives a monetary reward in the end. The references to fairy tales start with the show's title. "Beauty and the Beast" (ATU 425C) is one of the tales cast under the "Disney spell" (Zipes 1999, 333) thanks to the 1991 film based on the version penned by Madame de Beaumont in the eighteenth century. While the fairy tale is more about self-sacrifice and love,

Beauty and the Geek appeals to the idea of personal transformation, yet it does so by drawing on stereotypes, associating men's brains with social awkwardness and women's beauty with superficiality.

The finale of the fourth season of this series in Australia (2012) made explicit fairy-tale references in a thematic episode framed as an opportunity for the contestants to "fulfill [their] destiny as princes and princesses" in order to learn "who is going to get their fairy tale ending?" The episode featured a medieval-like setting and included three challenges from "old times." In the first task, male participants, dressed as knights in armor, had to joust. In the second, the women dressed as princesses had to grab a frog, recite a love poem, and then kiss the amphibian. The idea that kissing can transform a frog into a prince is a powerful fairy-tale trope, despite the fact that in narratives such as the Brothers Grimm's "The Frog Prince; or Iron Henry," the spell is broken when the princess throws the frog against a wall in disgust (ATU 440, Zipes 2003). The third challenge required the male contestants to slay a toy dragon, described as "very cute" by one of the women, and then scale a tower to rescue the princess—following the damsel in distress trope. Elizabeth Warner (2002) states that "the kidnapping, requisitioning, or seducing of women" to be eaten or become the creature's wives are the actions that most define the function of dragons in Russian fairy tales (70). But the dragon-slayer (ATU 300) is a tale type found in numerous countries. In addition, the participants of *Beauty and the Geek Australia* (2009–2014), dressed as princes and princesses, went to a ball in a horse-drawn carriage. The references to fairy tales in this episode were further emphasized by the contestants' remarks, including phrases such as, "This is my dream coming true," "This is like a fairy tale," and "I feel like a princess" (2012).

Connections with the world of fairy tales can also be found in shows that do not follow an obvious fairy-tale structure, as does *The Bachelor*, or have explicit references, such as *Beauty and the Geek*. Consider, for instance, *Undercover Boss* (2010–), which originated in 2009 in the United Kingdom and received franchises in more than ten countries, including the United States. In each episode, a person in an upper-management position works undercover as an entry-level employee in his/her company. The executive goes in disguise (through the use of wigs, for instance) as a way to get information about what it is really going on in the company and to get to know the employees. The boss's rewards for his or her employees have a dynamic that may remind viewers of "The Kind and the Unkind Girl" (ATU 480), a tale type in which good girls are rewarded while ill-manner girls are punished by a powerful figure who masquerades as a weak old woman.

Much has been said about the voyeuristic appeal of reality television (Calvert 2000; Hill 2005), and the association of this genre with fairy tales further underlines what Lee has called "television's potential to offer a vehicle for wish fulfillment" (2014, 277). Moreover, reality television provides insights about our fascination with fairy tales and the potential to reinvent these narratives through new venues. After all, series such as *The Bachelor*, *The Swan*, and *Beauty and the Geek* put a spotlight onto fairy tales' fit for survival and change. Ultimately, fairy tales attract and connect viewers to certain types of reality shows while also gaining a more pervasive circulation thanks to these shows to the extent that some reality series might even be read as one of the many different variants in which fairy tales exist. Even though some programs discussed in this chapter are no longer on air, reality television seems far from breaking away from the fairy-tale spell as long as it continues to be a strong, mutually beneficial relationship.

Related topics: Broadcast; Disney Corporation; Fat Studies; Gender; Romance; Sexualities/ Queer and Trans Studies

VANESSA NUNES

References Cited and Further Reading

Albright, Julie M. 2007. "Impossible Bodies: TV Viewing Habits, Body Image, and Plastic Surgery Attitudes among College Students in Los Angeles and Buffalo, New York." *Configurations* 15: 103–23.

Bettelheim, Bruno. 1977. *The Uses of Enchantment: The Meaning and Importance of Fairy Tales.* New York: Vintage Books.

Bourboulis, Photeine P. 1988. "The Bride-Show Custom and the Fairy Story of Cinderella." In *Cinderella: A Casebook*, edited by Alan Dundes, 98–109. Madison: Wisconsin UP.

Bratich, Jack Z. 2007. "Programming Reality: Control Societies, New Subjects and the Powers of Transformation." In *Makeover Television: Realities Remodelled*, edited by Dana Heller, 6–22. London: I.B. Tauris.

Calvert, Clay. 2000. *Voyeur Nation: Media, Privacy, and Peeping in Modern Culture.* Boulder, CO: Westview P.

Deery, June. 2012. *Consuming Reality: The Commercialization of Factual Entertainment.* New York: Palgrave.

Dégh, Linda, and Andrew Vázsonyi. 1983. "Does the Word 'Dog' Bite? Ostensive Action: A Means of Legend Telling." *Journal of Folklore Research* 20 (1): 5–34.

Graham-Bertolini, Alison. 2004. "*Joe Millionaire* as Fairy Tale: A Feminist Critique." *Feminist Media Studies* 4 (3): 341–4.

Gray, Jonathan. 2009. "Cinderella Burps: Gender, Performativity, and the Dating Show." In *Reality TV: Remaking Television Culture*, edited by Susan Murray and Laurie Ouellette, 260–77. New York: NYU P.

Heyes, Cressida J. 2007. "Cosmetic Surgery and the Televisual Makeover." *Feminist Media Studies* 7 (1): 17–32.

Hill, Annette. 2005. *Reality TV: Audiences and Popular Factual Television.* New York: Routledge.

Huff, Richard M. 2006. *Reality Television.* Westport: Praeger.

Koven, Mikel J. 2008. *Film, Folklore, and Urban Legends.* Lanham, MD: Scarecrow.

Lee, Linda J. 2014. "Ugly Stepsisters and Unkind Girls: Reality TV's Repurposed Fairy Tales." In *Channeling Wonder: Fairy Tales on Television*, edited by Pauline Greenhill and Jill Terry Rudy, 275–93. Detroit: Wayne State UP.

Lieberman, Marcia. 1972. "'Some Day My Prince Will Come': Female Acculturation through the Fairy Tale." *College English* 34 (3): 383–95.

McMurria, John. 2009. "Global TV Realities: International Markets, Geopolitics, and the Transcultural Contexts of Reality TV." In *Reality TV: Remaking Television Culture*, edited by Susan Murray and Laurie Ouellette, 179–202. New York: NYU P.

Miller, Toby. 2010. *Television Studies: The Basics.* New York: Routledge.

Murray, Susan, and Laurie Ouellette. 2009. "Introduction." In *Reality TV: Remaking Television Culture*, edited by Susan Murray and Laurie Ouellette, 1–20. New York: NYU P.

Oring, Elliott. 1986. "Folk Narratives." In *Folk Groups and Folklore Genre: An Introduction*, edited by Elliott Oring, 121–45. Logan: Utah State UP.

Orosan-Weine, Pamela. 2007. "*The Swan*: The Fantasy of Transformation Versus the Reality of Growth." *Configurations* 15 (1): 17–32.

Ouellette, Laurie. 2013. "Introduction." In *A Companion to Reality Television*, edited by Laurie Ouellette, 1–8. Malden, MA: Wiley-Blackwell.

Palmer, Gareth. 2007. "*Extreme Makeover: Home Edition*: An American Fairy Tale." In *Makeover Television: Realities Remodelled*, edited by Dana Heller, 165–76. London: I.B. Tauris.

Pozner, Jennifer L. 2010. *Reality Bites Back: The Troubling Truth about Guilty Pleasure TV.* Berkeley: Seal P.

Preston, Cathy Lynn. 2004. "Disrupting the Boundaries of Genre and Gender: Postmodernism and Fairy Tale." In *Fairy Tales and Feminism: New Approaches*, edited by Donald Haase, 197–212. Detroit: Wayne State UP.

Propp, Vladímir. 1968. *Morphology of the Folktale.* Austin: Texas UP.

Raphael, Chad. 2009. "The Political Economic Origins of Reali-TV." In *Reality TV: Remaking Television Culture*, edited by Susan Murray and Laurie Ouellette, 123–40. New York: NYU P.

Rowe, Karen E. 1979. "Feminism and Fairy Tales." *Women's Studies: An Interdisciplinary Journal* 6: 237–57.

Steinhoff, Heike. 2015. *Transforming Bodies: Makeovers and Monstrosities in American Culture.* New York: Palgrave.

Warner, Elizabeth. 2002. *Russian Myths.* Austin: Texas UP.

Yep, Gust, and Ariana Ochoa Camacho. 2004. "The Normalization of Heterogendered Relations in *The Bachelor*." *Feminist Media Studies* 4 (3): 338–41.

Zipes, Jack. 1999. "Breaking the Disney Spell." In *The Classic Fairy Tales*, edited by Maria Tatar, 332–52. New York: Norton.

———, ed. and trans. 2003. *The Complete Fairy Tales of the Brothers Grimm.* New York: Bantam.

Mediagraphy

The Bachelor (TV). 2002–. Creator Mike Fleiss. USA.

The Bachelorette (TV). 2003–2005, 2008–. Creator Mike Fleiss. USA.

REALITY TELEVISION

Beauty and the Beast. 1991. Directors Gary Trousdale and Kirk Wise. USA.

Beauty and the Geek (TV). 2005–2008. Producers Ashton Kutcher, Jason Goldberg, and Nick Santora. USA.

Beauty and the Geek Australia (TV). 2009–. Australia.

———. 2012. Episode 4.9. November 29.

Big Brother (TV). 2000–. Directors Mark W. Roden, Anthony Gonzales, Quinn Saunders, Philip Abatecola, and Danny Roew. USA.

The Biggest Loser (TV). 2004–. Creator Dave Broome. USA.

Candid Camera (TV). 1948–1954. Creators Allen Funt. USA.

Extreme Makeover (TV). 2002–2007. Creator Howard Schultz. USA.

Extreme Makeover: Home Edition (TV). 2003–2012. Creator Tom Forman. USA.

Joe Millionaire (TV). 2003. Producers Chris Cowan and Jean-Michel Michenaud. USA.

Queen for a Day (Radio and TV). 1945–1964. Creator John Masterson. USA.

The Real World (TV). 1992–. Creators Mary-Ellis Bunim and Jonathan Murray. USA.

Survivor (TV). 2000–. Creator Charlie Parsons. USA.

The Swan (TV). 2004. Producers Arthur Smith and Nely Galán. USA.

Undercover Boss (TV). 2010–. Creator Stephen Lambert. USA.

Who Wants to Marry a Multi-Millionaire? (TV). 2000. Director Don Weiner. USA.

67

ROMANCE

The Transmedial Romance of "Beauty and the Beast"

Tomasz Z. Majkowski and Agata Zarzycka

Fairy tales' adaptability to various aesthetic conventions and media affects depictions of romantic love. Our interest lies in both fairy tale and romance, as well as the dynamics between their respective frameworks. We focus on the case study of "Beauty and the Beast" (ATU 425C), which not only features a couple of lovers exceptionally susceptible to enthusiastic appropriation and medialization, but also highlights the theme of courting, thus lending itself to romance-oriented interpretation. Specifically, we trace changes in Beauty and the Beast's relationship with regard to their story's chronology and the media of selected adaptations. Some employments of the fairy-tale romance rely on transgressing or subverting seemingly rigid literary formulas, while others make those formulas connect with contemporary popular culture and serve as efficient and surprisingly innovative tools for addressing a broad scope of issues relevant for contemporary audiences.

Faeries and Docile Daughters

The oldest version of "Beauty and the Beast" is inserted as a *conte de fées* within the novel *La jeune Américaine ou les contes marins* by Gabrielle-Suzanne Barbot de Villeneuve (2008), originally published in 1740 in Paris. Introduced in Marie-Catherine d'Aulnoy's 1690 *Story of Hypolite* (2013) as a tale of the impossible and magical embedded within a conventional baroque romance novel, *conte de fées* became an independent narrative form around 1697. De Villeneuve encountered the genre already in decline, but also rich in formulas and motifs she was able to reuse. The world of *contés de fées* was marvelous and fanciful, as aristocratic authors freely combined parts borrowed from oral folk tradition, Italian *novella*, classic literature, and chivalric romance to compose narratives both entertaining and didactic (Zipes 2012, 13). Therefore, they were simultaneously conventionalized and innovative, showing the author's wit and originality (16). Moreover, such ironic, witty tales can be also interpreted as women's literature of the period, dealing with rigid rules imposed on highborn women and the paradox of the need and reluctance to get married (Harries 2003, 39; Seifert 2004, 92–93).

De Villeneuve's tale can be perceived as the swan song of adult-oriented *contes de fées*, so popular fifty years earlier. Belle, whose main virtues are obedience, common sense, and mercy, differs from resourceful, aristocratic heroines capable of outwitting an ogre as in Marie-Catherine d'Aulnoy's tale from 1698, "Finette-Cendron," or driving off an unwanted suitor with an axe as in Marie-Jeanne L'Héritier de Villandon's 1696 "The Discreet Princess" (1989). Moreover, Belle's impact on the Beast's fate is diminished since the main reason behind the fortunate finale turns out to be a good fairy's intrigue. This way, the tale meets the *contes de fées* requirements: it deals with matrimonial issues of the nobility, depicted as a playground for powerful, older women secretly tricking youngsters into fruitful unions. Court-related metaphors are, however, absent from the second variant of the story, first published in 1757 by Jeanne-Marie Leprince de Beaumont (1989)—the version regarded as the canonic rendition of "Beauty and the Beast" (Short 2015, 34; Zipes 2012, 54).

While de Villeneuve was a member of the aristocracy, brought to financial ruin by her husband's extravagances, and after his death associated with Académie Française, de Beaumont came from a bourgeois family. As a very successful governess, she started an educational journal, *Le Magasin des Enfants* (Waksmund 1998, 23–26), in which her version of "Beauty and the Beast" was published as a didactic text, adapted for the needs of children's moral education (Zipes 2012, 55–56). The new version focuses on Belle's kindness, courage, and humbleness. The Beast's transformation into a prince becomes a reward for a girl who desires only to be good and obedient and understands that spiritual qualities are more important than appearance or social standing. Marriage is a prize for the worthy, achieved through self-sacrifice and appealing because it signifies elevation into higher social strata; that spouses are actually fond of each other is just a happy coincidence. Interestingly, de Beaumont's Belle expresses dissatisfaction with the Beast's transformation: when confronted with a handsome prince, she asks about her bestial companion.

Apart from the target audience and social reality, the medium also changes between the two early versions of "Beauty and the Beast." De Villeneuve's story is included in an even larger novel imitating court romance literature of the seventeenth century. De Beaumont published her version in a magazine, which makes her streamline the narrative and concentrate on a single thread—the one best suited to produce a moral lesson of female humility. Thus, the simplified tale appears to have more in common with the nineteenth-century *Märchen* poetics and can easily enter the unofficial canon of Western fairy tale. Throughout the eighteenth and nineteenth centuries, the shortened variant of the text is subject to numerous translations and publications, as well as adaptations to different media, including a 1771 opéra comique, *Zémire et Azor*. It also suits the ideological climate of the epoch, swapping de Villeneuve's preoccupation with an aristocratic marriage game for a clear message of bourgeois female virtues (Zipes 2012, 56). Unsurprisingly, it is this very message that will attract the attention of the twentieth-century authors seeking to update de Beaumont's story.

Beauty Unleashed

Stepping into the twentieth century, "Beauty and the Beast's" path toward becoming a fairy-tale classic testifies to the story's shifting political significance and cultural productivity, encouraging artists to retrieve the narrative for various aesthetic and interpretative purposes. Significant directions of such retellings are demarcated by feminist explorations of Beauty's agency and development—conventionally subordinated to the dynamics of the Beast's curse—as well as problematizations of the male protagonist's Otherness.

An emblematic example of such subversion is provided by Angela Carter's double take on "Beauty and the Beast" in two short stories from her seminal collection, *The Bloody Chamber* (1979): "The Courtship of Mr. Lyon" and "The Tiger's Bride." According to Anny Crunelle-Vanrigh, both narratives employ the romantic thread to build up a zone of fluidity encompassing binary oppositions that define conventional gendered identities (2001, 132–133, 136–137). Moreover, by focusing on Beauty's changes, which provide her with various degrees of bestiality, Carter's stories work against the operative function of the female character in the Beast's release from the curse (132, 138–139). A similar complication of the nonhuman factor in the romantic context occurs in "Beast" by Francesca Lia Block, where the male protagonist's monstrosity provides Beauty with a gateway to the natural world and nonverbal communication. Those two spheres of experience are irrevocably lost to more mundane routine of the "happily ever after," making the heroine "wis[h] that he would have remained a Beast" (2011, 363).

Subtle yet profound interventions into fairy-tale depictions of romance, such as those offered by Carter or Block, characterize a broader wave of retellings that developed in the 1970s, inspired mostly by the cultural impact of feminism (Joosen 2011, 4–5). The rise of the feminist fairy tale is a mostly literary phenomenon that occurs, however, in an intermedial environment. The relevance of the latter is confirmed in the case of "The Courtship of Mr. Lyon," argued by Crunelle-Vanrigh to embrace a "cinematic structure" (2001, 130) and allude in its imagery to Jean Cocteau's famous movie, *La belle et la bête* (1946). Cocteau's classic seems to bridge subversion-oriented approaches to "Beauty and the Beast" with adaptations driven less by the renegotiation of romance or characters' identities than by aesthetic experiments, especially spectacular when it comes to the Beast's appearance. As those two tendencies in cultural appropriations of the tale are by no means mutually exclusive, the results of their interplay are explored in the further parts of this chapter.

Romancing the Beast

A claim might be risked that the entirety of *Beauty and the Beast*'s transmedial legacy is indebted, in one way or another, to Cocteau's adaptation. Among its formal and aesthetic aspects that have gained critical recognition, the Beast's function in the romantic axis of the plot is the one crucial for our analysis. The French director is responsible for giving the hero the characteristic lion aura (Crunelle-Vanrigh 2001, 130) that affects his look in subsequent visualizations and for imbuing the character with subtle erotization. According to Anne E. Duggan, in the director's vision "the Beast is positioned as the object of desire" (2016, 69), thus paving the way for the renegotiation of Otherness in the already mentioned feminist retellings. Such a depiction of the "monster" is accompanied by the introduction of Belle's other suitor, enjoying a far more conventionally attractive physique (Duggan 2016, 78). While Duggan focuses on queerness in the French adaptation, the impact of Cocteau's rendering of the Beast exceeds the frames of a singular thematic reading by opening the tale to the practice of reconsidering beauty standards and constructions of desire.

Another influential adaptation of "Beauty and the Beast" is Disney's animation from 1991. It combines the legacy of Cocteau's version, confirmed by the Beast's lion-like mane and the presence of his rival, Gaston the Hunter, with significant innovations concerning Beauty's character and the construction of romance. The animated medium that allows much freedom in creating movement reinforces the animalistic features of the cursed prince. Consequently, his transformation is gradual: before he regains his human features, he starts to move, dress, and talk in a less savage fashion, and that process brings about the greatest alteration to the original story: it is the Beast who learns to love Belle. The tale of the vain, self-absorbed prince gradually changing to meet high standards set by a female intellectual can be perceived as more in line with modern sensibilities and gender policies (Short 2015, 28, 54–55), especially if contrasted with de Villeneuve's and de Beaumont's versions.

Simultaneously, however, that innovation results in a more general reinforcement of romance elements in the story. As Jane Cummins points out, the whole movie is strikingly preoccupied with the romance tropes (1995), even though its heroine is by no means a passive or docile love object. Accordingly, the main source of Belle's social stigmatization shifts from the financial crisis of her family to its intellectualism. Thus, the dynamic of exclusion echoes high school teenage drama of the 1980s, posing maladjusted nerds against popular jocks. Still, in contrast to those modernizations stands the gothicization of the romantic plot. As Suzan Z. Swan observes, the story of a strong-willed girl arriving to a gloomy castle with a harsh and uncultured host, just to see his softer side and learn how to love him, is very characteristic of the late-eighteenth- and early nineteenth-century British romance novel (Swan 1999, 353–356). Thus, in an attempt to create a love story for the 1990s (Downey 1996), Disney produces a narrative straight from the 90s of the eighteenth century.

Cocteau's and Disney's contributions to the fairy-tale topoi, resonating with subsequent big-screen visions, bring a transmedial consolidation of the story's romantic potential. The latter is, however, verified by its first major confrontation with the formula of a TV series, which triggered a genre-related controversy. As Henry Jenkins observes, referring also to John Tulloch's *Television Drama: Agency, Audience and Myth* (1990), the economic conditioning of television, closely related with viewership statistics, results in the practice of mixing cultural conventions in order to expand the potential appeal of the given production (Jenkins 1992, 124–125). Ron Koslow's three-season TV show *Beauty and the Beast* (1987–1990) complies with the demands of its medium by locating the plot in 1980s New York, where the "beauty" character works as a lawyer and the "beast" lives among social outcasts forming a secret commune in the city's labyrinthine underground. Thus, the series embraces a whole scope of themes and stylizations, from personal drama to social criticism (Jenkins 1992, 133).

Nevertheless, the show's genre-related flexibility turned out to be problematic, leading to its termination after three seasons. While the growth of the protagonists' relationship—promised by the series' original inspiration—attracted the most intense and active interest of the viewers (Jenkins 1992, 121–152), the predictable romantic theme became violated with the "beauty's" death and the "beast's" temporary surrender to a mourning-triggered rage. Jenkins highlights the context of gender politics around the series' development and the resultant frustration of its fans by summing up statistics-based TV policies: "Crudely put, romance-centered episodes meant more female fans, while action plots held the prospect of enlarging its share of male viewership" (1992, 128). Simultaneously, the confusion of the audience reveals the significant friction generated between the cultural functions of genre and medium. However motivated, Koslow's controversial but daring challenge posed to fairy-tale and romance formulas may have foreshadowed a need for reinventing the thematic and aesthetic impact of "Beauty and the Beast." By the beginning of the twenty-first century such efforts became more visible, their crossing point being the image of the Beast.

Beautiful Beasts

The animalistic charm and impressive aura of Koslow's "beast," performed by Ron Perlman, balances the visual monstrosity of the character as envisioned by Cocteau against modern standards of male attractiveness. Such aesthetization is taken a step further in the cinematic adaptation of *Beastly* (2007), a novel-length retelling of *Beauty and the Beast* by Alex Flinn, addressed to young adult readers and combining fairy-tale fantasy with an exploration of contemporary American high school culture. In Flinn's book, the jock-nerd axis is far more explicit than in Disney's animation, although this time it is the Beast himself who embodies the rich, handsome, and popular type before being cursed. In order to punish his vanity and contempt for others, a goth witch gives him a monstrous appearance and two years to undo the spell with a kiss of true love (Flinn 2007, 47–50). The Beauty's part is taken up by a socially disadvantaged bookworm. *Beastly* shares with the Disney classic both Beauty's intellectualism and the Beast's appearance resembling a human-animal hybrid (Flinn 2007, 47).

However, Daniel Barnz's novel-based movie (2011) replaces furry bestiality with a characterization of the Beast actor that changes his looks from conventionally attractive to modeled by exaggerated attributes of subcultural stylization, such as tattoo, piercing, or scarification. The created image embraces alternative aesthetic standards rather than explicit signs of monstrosity. Turning to goth-like body modification rather than classic fairy-tale imagery, that striking alternation of the character's screen appearance may point to the cinematic pressure for a new visual solution.

An even more symbolic presentation of monstrosity, reducing the Beast's deformation to a scar, is chosen by an Italian director, Fabrizio Costa. In commentaries available on YouTube (2015, 2016), he describes his 2014 TV mini-series, *La bella e la bestia*, as replacing the story's fantastic elements with the aesthetics of gothicized historical romance. The deformation of Prince Leon's face is a token of his psychological damage that, as Costa clarifies, becomes an equivalent of the magical curse and needs to be healed with Bella's involvement. Simultaneously, as Luca Bernabei, the producer of *La bella e la bestia*, underlines in the commentary from 2016, the characterization is hardly able to ruin Preziosi's appearance, which makes the mini-series subscribe to the visual trope of an attractive Beast.

While the romantic model in Costa's adaptation bears resemblance to that of *Beastly*, featuring the faulty male character improving and developing under the steady influence of the heroine's goodness, it diversifies the gender dynamics of the relationship by introducing rivals of both protagonists. Bella's agreeable suitor poses no threat to Leon and gracefully accepts the eventual rejection. The prince's obsessive cousin Helene, determined to become his wife, proves, in turn, to be the main villain and, indirectly, the cause of Leon's bestial transformation. That development is relevant for the theme of domestic violence, definitely more prominent than in other adaptations. It is Leon's emotional volatility and the alleged part in his former wife's death that is the source of Bella's doubts. Consequently, his redemption comes with the revelation of Helene as the actual killer. The abusive tendencies of the prince affect also his position as a whimsical landowner, eventually pushing local farmers to a violent reaction. Thus, *La bella e la bestia* constitutes another example of an uneasy fusion of a generic fairy-tale romance with more specific, socially involved themes.

Social issues may also be seen as important for *La belle et la bête*, the 2014 production of French director Christophe Gans, "which plays on the cute woodland creatures found in Disney only to undermine the class message of the tale at the film's conclusion" (Duggan 2016, 78). Indeed, its romantic thread leads to an innovative happy ending in which the saved prince joins Belle and her father in their countryside cottage. Still, Gans's work seems dedicated, first and foremost, to depicting the tale's full phantasmagoric glory by means of impressive visuals. Their illustrative function is emphasized by the movie's frame: Belle reading the story to her (and the Beast's) children from a beautifully designed storybook, whose pictures come alive to introduce the viewer into particular stages of the plot. Thus, the history of transmedial adaptations of "Beauty and the Beast" draws a self-aware spiral curve, humbly turning toward its literary roots.

A Transmedial Romance

In de Villeneuve's original narrative the Beast's return to his human form does not conclude the plot, but leads to several new threads matching the larger storyworld of *contes de fées*. Thus, the tale foreshadows a contemporary tendency to expand storytelling beyond a single plot or medium, a process labelled as "transmedia storytelling" (Jenkins 2006), or "transmedia narrative" (Ryan 2004). This process relies on the given tale's ability to move through different media and focuses on mapping a fictive world capable of hosting different stories, yet identified as a single, coherent universe.

The most successful Disney movies tend to spawn plenty of hypertexts seared across various media, and "Beauty and the Beast," residing currently at the center of numerous narratives, is no exception. Apart from the possibly most influential among them, the Broadway musical, there are two animated sequels, *Beauty and the Beast: The Enchanted Christmas* (1997) and *Beauty and the Beast: Belle's Magical World* (1998), a live-action TV show featuring Belle as a hostess, several picture books, video games, and two theme restaurants. Although all those products tell the same story in different ways, they also introduce some medium-specific alterations. For instance, *Disney's Sing Me a Story with Belle* (1995–1997), the aforementioned TV show with a *Sesame Street* aesthetic, erases the romantic subplot by not featuring the Beast at all. It depicts Belle as a bookshop keeper educating a bunch of modern-looking children and bearing similarity to Wise Governess narrating the story of "Beauty and the Beast" in de Beaumont's magazine (Waksmund 1998, 25).

The Disney video games can also be divided into those adapting the movie plot and those expanding the world. The former allow the player to control either Beauty or the Beast struggling to win their partner's love. In both games featuring the Beast avatar—*Beauty and the Beast: Roar of the Beast* (1993) and *Disney's Beauty and the Beast* (1994)—the player overcomes obstacles and fights enemies. In *Beauty and the Beast: Belle's Quest* (1993) the Belle avatar explores the Beast's castle and dances with the host. There is less combat, but some enemies need to be avoided. Both games therefore use a court-romance frame, as the player has to accomplish a series of quests to be rewarded with love. *Disney's Beauty and the Beast Magical Ballroom* (2000), in turn, expands the original narrative: the player acts as Beauty's assistant, helping prepare a surprise party for the cursed prince. Consequently, the game makes Belle use the same courting techniques that the Beast employs in the movie.

In the *Kingdom Hearts* (2002–2015) video game series created by Square Enix and set in a crossover world filled with Disney characters, the Beast is depicted in his monstrous form, affirming it as an iconic aspect of the couple's relationship. In contrast, ABC's TV series *Once Upon a Time* (2011–) makes the trademark male protagonist disappear completely. While Belle shares several traits with her counterpart from the animated movie, from the love of books to the cut of the dress, her love interest is Mr. Gold/Rumpelstiltskin, the series' primary villain. Thus, her ability to see past appearances turns out to be pure naivety: Mr. Gold quite frequently preys on her love to hide his various misdeeds, although he undoubtedly loves Belle back.

While the Disney narratives presented here avoid the exploration of Belle and the Beast's relationship after the curse has been lifted, by either revisiting earlier parts of the story or removing the Beast from the narrative, the "happily ever after" period becomes a subject of another transmedial narrative composed of Bill Willingham's *Fables* comic series (2002–2015) and the video game *The Wolf Among Us* (2013) by Telltale Games. The story's main plot revolves around various fairy-tale characters living in modern New York City after their homeland has been destroyed. Beauty and the Beast are among the survivors, struggling in the new reality to maintain the lifestyle they are used to. Although the plot takes place years after the original tale's ending, the Beast's monstrosity is retrieved: when Beauty is angry at her husband, he gradually turns back to a more animalistic form that closely resembles Disney's design. What eventually alters the curse to allow the Beast voluntary transformation is the affirmation of his wife's domesticated status as she becomes a mother.

The overall *noir* convention of *Fables* reframes *Beauty and the Beast* as a detective story, the wife's faithfulness being the central object of investigation. Belle has to turn down the advances of her boss, Prince Charming, and hide them from her husband, who might kill the rival. *The Wolf Among Us* makes the detective plot even more prominent, combining it with the adventure game formula, reliant on the interpretation of clues and proper navigation through dialogues, aimed to collect necessary information (Apperley 2006; Karhulahti 2011). The investigation leads the player from suspecting that Beauty is having an affair, or works as a prostitute, to discovering that she moonlights as a receptionist to support her husband's lifestyle. Eventually, the Beast accuses the player's avatar, Bigby the Wolf, of being Belle's lover and needs to be proved wrong.

Still, it turns out that while Beauty is not cheating on the Beast, their relationship does rely on a mystery. Similarly to her husband, Belle hides a monstrous nature that occasionally takes over, sending the unaware heroine on a killing spree. The Beast's task is, therefore, to guard her and her secret, while Beauty's virtue becomes deconstructed as a façade for monstrosity. Simultaneously, the Beast is provided with a nurturing and sacrificial nature, conventionally ascribed to Belle. Their romance, in turn, stays in line with the *noir* convention, as the strength of couple's bond is drawn from a shared secret.

Beauty and the Beast's Transmedial Dance

The selection of "Beauty and the Beast" adaptations, appropriations, and rewritings presented here, while undoubtedly incomplete, has been guided by a twofold goal. First, we have aimed to show the impressive scale and diversity of the cultural influence exerted by the eponymous characters' dynamic and moldable romance. Whether provoking scrutiny of gender relations, aesthetic standards, and images of Otherness within the fairy-tale formula or offering a fixed, familiar frame for introducing and investigating specific new issues—such as domestic violence, class consciousness, and peer pressure—the story of the unlikely lovers has been inspiring noteworthy artistic efforts for over three centuries and does not seem to be wearing out its potential. Second, we argue that a significant part of such potential comes from the sheer acts of remediation. They affect the story itself—by changing the points of narrative emphasis or bringing some motifs from the background into the limelight, as is the case with the issue of the Beast's visualization. Furthermore, they sustain productive tension between formal characteristics and modes of storytelling—by questioning and redefining cultural functions of the fairy tale and romance, exposing internal conflicts within the genre construction, or simply activating new aesthetic and experiential dimensions. And so, Beauty and the Beast continue their graceful dance around both genre- and medium-based petrification.

Related topics: Animal Studies; Broadcast; Cinematic; Disney Corporation; Fan Fiction; Fantasy; Gender; Reality TV; Storytelling

References Cited and Further Reading

Apperley, Thomas H. 2006. "Genre and Game Studies: Toward a Critical Approach to Video Game Genres." *Simulation & Gaming* 37 (1): 6–23.

Block, Francesca Lia. 2011. *Roses and Bones: Myths, Tales and Secrets*. New York: HarperTeen.

Carter, Angela. (1979) 1993. *The Bloody Chamber and Other Stories*. Harmondsworth: Penguin Books.

Craven, Allison. 2016. *Fairy Tale Interrupted: Feminism, Masculinity, Wonder Cinema*. Bern: Peter Lang.

Crunelle-Vanrigh, Anny. 2001. "The Logic of the Same and Difference: The Courtship of Mr. Lyon." In *Angela Carter and the Fairy Tale*, edited by Danielle Marie Roemer and Cristina Bacchilega, 128–44. Detroit: Wayne State UP.

ROMANCE

Cummins, June. 1995. "Romancing the Plot: The Real Beast of *Disney's Beauty and the Beast*." *Children's Literature Association Quarterly* 20 (1): 22–8.

d'Aulnoy, Marie-Catherine Le Jumel de Barneville. (1690) 2013. *Histoire d'Hyppolite, Comte de Douglas*. Geneve: Slatkine Reprints.

———. (1698) 1989. "Finette Cendron." In *Beauties, Beasts, and Enchantment: Classic French Fairy Tales*, translated by Jack David Zipes, 400–16. Maidstone: Dutton Adult.

de Villeneuve, Gabrielle-Suzanne Barbot Gallon. (1740) 2008. *La jeune américaine et les contes marins:(la belle et la bête); Les belles solitaires*, edited by Élisa Biancardi. Paris: Honoré Champion.

Downey, Sharon D. 1996. "Feminine Empowerment in Disney's *Beauty and the Beast*." *Women's Studies in Communication* 19 (2): 185–212.

Duggan, Anne E. 2016. "The Fairy-Tale Film in France: Postwar Reimaginings." In *Fairy-Tale Films Beyond Disney: International Perspectives*, edited by Jack. Zipes, Pauline Greenhill, and Kendra Magnus-Johnston, 64–79. New York: Routledge.

Flinn, Alex. 2007. *Beastly*. New York: Harper Teen.

Harries, Elizabeth Wanning. 2003. *Twice Upon a Time: Women Writers and the History of the Fairy Tale*. Princeton, NJ: Princeton UP.

Jenkins, Henry. 1992. *Textual Poachers: Television Fans and Participatory Culture*. New York: Routledge.

———. 2006. *Convergence Culture: Where Old and New Media Collide*. New York: NYU P.

Joosen, Vanessa. 2011. *Critical and Creative Perspectives on Fairy Tales: An Intertextual Dialogue between Fairy-Tale Scholarship and Postmodern Retellings*. Detroit: Wayne State UP.

Karhulahti, Veli-Matti. 2011. "Mechanic/Aesthetic Videogame Genres: Adventure and Adventure." Proceedings of the 15th International Academic MindTrek Conference: Envisioning Future Media Environments, 71–4. New York: ACM.

Lawrence, Rachel Louise, ed. 2014. *Madame de Villeneuve's "The Story of the Beauty and the Beast."* Ilminster: Blackdown Publications.

Leprince de Beaumont, Jeanne-Marie. (1757) 1989. "The Story of Beauty and the Beast." In *Beauties, Beasts, and Enchantment: Classic French Fairy Tales*, translated by Jack David Zipes. 233–45. Maidstone: Dutton Adult.

L'Héritier de Villandon, Marie-Jeanne. (1696) 1989. "The Discreet Princess, or the Adventures of Finette." In *Beauties, Beasts, and Enchantment: Classic French Fairy Tales*, translated by Jack David Zipes. 77–94. Maidstone: Dutton Adult.

Ryan, Marie-Laure, ed. 2004. *Narrative across Media: The Languages of Storytelling*. Lincoln: U Nebraska P.

Seifert, Lewis C. 2004. "On Fairy Tales, Subversion, and Ambiguity: Feminist Approaches to Seventeenth-Century Contes de Fées." In *Fairy Tales and Feminism: New Approaches*, edited by Donald Haase, 53–71. Detroit: Wayne State UP.

Short, Sue. 2015. *Fairy Tale and Film*. London: Palgrave Macmillan.

Swan, Susan Z. 1999. "Gothic Drama in Disney's *Beauty and the Beast*: Subverting Traditional Romance by Transcending the Animal-Human Paradox." *Critical Studies in Media Communication* 16 (3): 350–69.

Tulloch, John. 1990. *Television Drama: Agency, Audience and Myth*. New York: Routledge.

Waksmund, Ryszard. 1998. *Gabinet wróżek: Antologia baśni francuskiej XVII—XVIII wieku*. Wrocław: Wydawnictwo Wacław Bagiński.

Willingham, Bill, and Lan Medina. 2002–2015. *Fables*. New York: Vertigo.

Zipes, Jack. 1997. *Beauty and the Beast: And Other Classic French Fairy Tales*. New York: Signet Classics.

———. 2012. *Fairy Tales and the Art of Subversion*. New York: Routledge.

Mediagraphy

Beastly. 2011. Director Daniel Barnz. USA.

Beauty and the Beast (TV). 1987–1990. Creator Ron Koslow. USA.

———. 1991. Directors Gary Trousdale and Kirk Wise. USA.

——— (Performance). 1994. Linda Woolverton (book), Alan Menken (music), Howard Ashman, and Tim Rice (lyrics). New York. USA.

Beauty and the Beast: Belle's Magical World. 1998. Director Cullen Blaine Bob Kline, Dale Kase, Mitch Rochon, Burt Medall, Barbara Dourmashkin, Daniel De La Vega. USA.

Beauty and the Beast: Belle's Quest (Video Game). 1993. Sunsoft Inc. USA. www.letsplaysega.com/play-beauty-the-beast-belles-quest-online/.

Beauty and the Beast: Roar of the Beast (Video Game). 1993. Sunsoft Inc. USA.

Beauty and the Beast: The Enchanted Christmas. 1997. Director Andy Knight. USA.

Disney's Beauty and the Beast (Video Game). 1994. The Walt Disney Company/Hudson Soft. USA.

Disney's Beauty and the Beast Magical Ballroom (Video Game). 2000. Disney Interactive Studios. www.mobygames.com/game/disneys-beauty-and-the-beast-magical-ballroom.

Disney's Sing Me a Story with Belle (TV). 1995–1999. Director Steve Purcell. USA.

Kingdom Hearts (Video game). 2002–2015. Square Enix. www.kingdomhearts.com/home/gb/.

La bella e la bestia (Beauty and the Beast) (TV). 2014. Director Fabrizio Costa. Italy/Spain.

La belle et la bête (Beauty and the Beast). 1946. Director Jean Cocteau. France.

——— (Beauty and the Beast). 2014. Director Christophe Gans. France/Germany.

Lina NoPlaceForSanity. 2015. "Fabrizio Costa Talks 'Beauty and the Beast'." *YouTube*, December 20. www.youtube.com/watch?v=q6l1_ouFIT8.

———. 2016. "On the Set of 'The Beauty and the Beast' 2014 Miniseries." *YouTube*, January 19. www.youtube.com/watch?v=9p-pF68hxTU.

Once Upon a Time (TV). 2011–. Creators Edward Kitsis and Adam Horowitz. USA.

The Wolf Among Us (Video Game). 2013. Telltale Games. USA. https://telltale.com/series/the-wolf-among-us/.

Zémire et Azor (Music Album). (1771) 2011. Artist André Ernest Modeste Grétry, recorded by Bournemouth Symphony Orchestra, conducted by Sir Thomas Beecham. UK.

68

STORYTELLING

Fairy Tales in Contemporary American and European Storytelling Performance

Joseph Sobol and Csenge Virág Zalka

Fairy tales (or "wonder tales") continue to play an essential part in the repertoire of many contemporary storytellers, much as they have in historic oral traditions, despite the fact that personal stories—crafted autobiographical narratives—have superseded traditional folktales as the dominant storytelling genre in many contemporary American performance sites (as opposed to European sites, as we discuss in the following). But the rise of personal storytelling is a relatively recent development. We speak here of organized storytelling venues as distinct from traditional folkloric storytelling contexts, which have become ever more habitat-challenged as the world continues to knit itself into a single web of literate, digital communications. The traditional isolation of folk communities, bridged perhaps by mobile bands of traditional story-bearers such as the traveling people of the British Isles, has been largely supplanted by communities of affinity and voluntary association, such as intentional storytelling revivalist, conservationist, and story slam groups. The first two types of group and venue are closely linked and we discuss them in tandem; the third, the story slam, now in the ascendant in urban storytelling scenes, is almost entirely the province of oral personal narratives, and thus beyond the scope of this article; we discuss it only elliptically in order to draw necessary distinctions.

Storytelling revivalism and preservationism are as old as the rise of print and the widespread internalization of literacy, which as both Walter Benjamin and Walter Ong have pointed out, at once strip oral folklore of its primary role in the imaginative economy and make it "possible to see a new beauty in what is vanishing" (Benjamin 2006, 87). In this retrospective light, the self-conscious creation of venues for storytelling performances illumined through the prism of a theorized and nostalgia-tinted past becomes a duty assumed by generations of cultural activists. Just as the tales have migrated across languages, cultures, and regions and so become hosts for a diversity of media, meanings, and messages, so wonder tales in contemporary performance take on a range of aesthetics and agendas.

The preservationist urge as expressed in such writer/collectors as Charles Perrault and the Grimm brothers resulted in the paradoxical emergence of a literary genre with its own subtextual palette of nationalist and idealist aesthetics, which continue to color the work of contemporary story performers. Some express primarily imaginative, escapist, or entertainment objectives; others mirror the educational and cultural programs of institutions such as schools and libraries that typically sponsor their performances; while others frame their tellings in terms of idealistic agendas, including peace-making, psychological integration, ecumenical spiritual explorations, or projection of nationalist and regionalist political identities. For each of these, the archetypal narrative blueprints of fairy tales can provide familiar yet flexible narrative platforms.

There have been two major waves of storytelling revivalist or preservationist activity in the United States since the late nineteenth century. The first, as Richard Alvey (1974) pointed out, grew out of the ideas of Friedrich Froebel and the Kindergarten movement that he brought to the U.S. from Germany—which sprang in turn from the cultural agendas of the Grimms and their followers. It took root institutionally via the Carnegie library movement, starting in Pittsburgh and New York in the 1880s, which began training young librarians in storytelling techniques as part of the standard professional equipment of children's library work. The other institutional pillars of organized storytelling activity in the U.S. were in schools and urban parks and recreation centers. Schools were influenced by the educational philosophies of John Dewey, which strongly emphasizing storytelling in children's intellectual and emotional development, while parks and recreation began to be organized in urban areas to help assimilate the influx of immigrant children. The recommended story repertoires for each of these institutional settings featured fairy tales—from both the folkloristically derived volumes of the Grimms, Peter Christen Asbjørnsen and Jørgen Engebretsen Moe, Joel Chandler Harris, and similar national or regional collections and the literary fairy tales of Hans Christian Andersen, Oscar Wilde, Eleanor Farjeon, and others. Important early twentieth-century storytellers such as Marie Shedlock, Ruth Sawyer, Richard Thomas Wyche, and Gudrun Thorne-Thompson did much of their work under these institutional auspices.

The difference between a revivalist and preservationist ethos can be identified principally in the element of missionary fervor that animates a revivalist milieu. Wyche, who founded the National Storytellers' League in 1903, possessed (or was possessed by) this kind of fervor, as evidenced in early publications of the League and in Wyche's book *Some Great Stories and How to Tell Them* (1910). The spate of books on storytelling published between 1900 and WWI (Wyche 1910; Bryant 1910; Shedlock 1915) are full of a crusading spirit that makes large claims for the cultural and spiritual efficacy of storytelling and story-listening—mainly focused on children, but also for the benefit of tellers and teachers. One sees similar fervor in the same period in the works of Irish storytelling revivalists of the "Celtic Twilight" movement in Ireland, where such figures as W. B. Yeats, James Stephens, Seumas MacManus, and Pamela Coleman-Smith used the oral as well as the literary performance of fairy tales in such venues as salons, university lecture halls, and the Lyceum circuit to further a broad range of artistic and ideological programs.

After the boom-and-bust cycle of the 1920s and 1930s this fervor largely recedes from the cultural fabric, although Sawyer's majestic 1942 *The Way of the Storyteller* remains as an artifact of the author's experience as a young storytelling revivalist in New York and Boston in the first decades of the century. The storytellers of the Carnegie and New York Public Library lineages, such as Frances Jenkins Olcott, Anna Cogswell Tyler, Frances Clarke Sayers, Mary Gould Davis, Anne Pellowski, and Augusta Baker, helped library-based storytelling establish and reproduce itself in centers of training, employment, and practice and so formed a bridge between the storytelling revivalist periods of the early and late twentieth century.[1] These librarian-storytellers, however, took pains to foreground not the storytelling event itself, but the primary goal of promoting the reading of books in which their fairy tales and related children's stories were contained. Storytelling events that foregrounded orality as a good in itself emerged later, during the next outbreak of storytelling revivalism in the 1970s.

Two figures who helped extend cultural authority for the performance of fairy tales in the inter-revival period were Richard Chase (1900–1984) and Joseph Campbell (1904–1987). Chase was a young performer and teacher of Appalachian ballad singing in 1935 when he met Marshall Ward from Beech Mountain, North Carolina, who introduced him to the story-telling tradition of that isolated section of the Blue Ridge. Chase's collections based on those encounters, *The Jack Tales* (1943), *Grandfather Tales* (1948), and *American Folk Tales and Songs* (1956), became important popular sources for naturalized American wonder tales. Although Chase's ethics and aesthetics have come under harsh critical scrutiny in recent years (Perdue 1987; Lindahl 2001; Sobol 2006), and subsequent collections have hewn much more faithfully to their Appalachian oral sources (Roberts 1964; Roberts 1974; Emrich 1972; Lindahl 2004; McCarthy 1994), his literary versions were notable in being strongly shaped by his experience as not just a collector and writer but a public performer of folktales, in schools, colleges, folk festivals, and adult education settings, for children and adults. His work was also marked by its effort to construe its Anglo-American wonder tales as emblems of authentic American folklore—a project that was very much in the intellectual tradition of the Grimms, but which during and after WWII became redolent with nationalist, nativist, even racialist implications. Chase's work demonstrated yet again the ways that wonder tales could be spun into colorful cloaks to cover complex ideological agendas.

Campbell's signature work, *The Hero with a Thousand Faces*, sought to construct a popular synthesis of literature, folklore, psychology, and cross-cultural mythology. After retirement from college teaching in 1972, Campbell took his narrative seminars on the road, team-ing up with an influential supporting cast of poets (Robert Bly, Coleman Barks), storytellers (Gioia Timpanelli, Diana Wolkstein, Michael Meade), and Jungian analytical psychologists (Marie-Louise von Franz, James Hillman) to make the case for myth—which he characteristi-cally conflated with wonder tales and other folktale genres, as well as literary narratives such as *Finnegan's Wake* (Joyce 1939) and *The Magic Mountain* (Mann 1944) as psychological blueprints for living authentic lives. Campbell was not a performer in any extroverted or theatrical way, but his mode of telling stories in his seminars while framing them with extensive commentary and exegesis, although ethnographically questionable, proved powerful for making narratives palatable for modern adults. Instead of seeming childlike fantasies, the retellings of Campbell and his cohort in their seminar and workshop contexts and in Bill Moyers's popular television series *The Power of Myth* (1988) imbued the stories with passionate symbolic superstructures, spiritual substance, and the promise of psychological boon.

Bruno Bettelheim's popular book *The Uses of Enchantment* (1977) performed a similar task from a Freudian perspective, as did the more nuanced and esoteric works of Marie-Louise von Franz from the Jungian. Continuing to mine the Campbell-Jung synthesis of storytelling and archetypal psychology, Bly (1990) and Meade (1994) elaborated fairy tales such as "Iron John" (ATU 502) and "The Water of Life" (ATU 551) into full-fledged initiatory rituals in workshops and retreats for groups of adult men, while Jean Shinoda Bolen (1984) and Clarissa Pinkola Estés (1992) followed suit with myth- and folktale-based therapeutic events for women.

Campbell's late-life entrance into the 1970s counter-cultural cavalcade coincided with and at many points helped inspire a revitalized interest among alienated members of the post-Vietnam generation in storytelling performance for its own sake. After the chaotic street theater of 1960s protest movements, the 1970s saw an inward turn toward Eastern meditation forms and humanistic psychological pursuits. At the same time a network of storytelling festivals sprang up in widening circles from a self-styled National Storytelling Festival founded in Jonesborough, Tennessee, in 1973. These worked as popular showcases and proving grounds for new breeds of professional performers, as well as settings where older and younger performers from folkloric, library, theatrical, or folk music worlds could fruitfully interact.

The most influential and iconic of the elder traditional storytellers was Ray Hicks, a member of the same Beech Mountain extended family whose repertoires had been featured in Chase's collections. His grandfather, John Benjamin Hicks, was one of the source tellers cited in both *The Jack Tales* and *Grandfather Tales*. Chase had striven to control the frame for transmitting the Appalachian tale-telling tradition within literary discourse, but in the electronically mediated environment of the new storytelling festivals, Ray Hicks's image was more powerful and televisually potent than Chase's. Hicks was invited to the inaugural National Festival in 1973 and then annually until his death in 2003. His deeply personal versions of well-known Appalachian *Märchen* solidified his status as the festival's "official" traditional teller.

While many story genres have been represented at the National Storytelling Festival, in their first decade or so the two genres that were portrayed metonymically as signature types were, on the one hand the tall tale, standing in popular discourse for American storytelling as a whole, and on the other hand the wonder tale, Appalachian Jack tales in particular. Their representative power was drawn in part from Chase's foundational work, magnified through the iconic figure of Hicks. His striking beanpole torso and long waving arms were featured on festival brochures for decades as a visual metonym for the festival and for the storytelling art. Many younger tellers, including Barbara Freeman and Connie Regan-Blake (who toured for many years as The Folktellers), Doug Lipman, Elizabeth Ellis, Jim May, and Ed Stivender, learned repertoire, but also an oral traditional approach to memory and story-speaking, from Ray's fluid, digressive, rhetorically elevated conversational approach.

A significant transitional figure in the American storytelling movement, with considerable influence in both traditional wonder tale telling and the creation of a certain style of performed autobiographical narrative, is Donald Davis. Originally from Haywood County in the Blue Ridge Mountains of North Carolina (about seventy miles southwest of the Hicks home place), Davis grew up with rich repertoires of wonder tales, tall tales, and trickster/numbskull stories from family and community sources (Davis 1992). Early in his career as a performer on festival stages he began to mix these traditional stories with crafted personal stories about his relatives and neighbors. The increasing popularity of Davis's autobiographical stories with large, middle-class festival crowds helped move the gravitational center of storytelling festival repertoires in the 1990s away from traditional stories and into the direction of "personal stories." Other important tellers who made their festival marks telling wonder tales, animal tales, or ghost legends (such as Elizabeth Ellis, Laura Simms, and the late Jackie Torrence [1944–2004] and Kathryn Windham [1918–2011]) also made notable shifts toward personal tales in this period—or in Simms's case toward framing traditional tales with personal anecdotes to weave together the contrasting fabrics of literal and imaginative worlds. Still other tellers, such as Diane Wolkstein (1942–2013) and Margaret Read MacDonald, never shifted their repertoires toward personal tales, and their collections of folktales, fairy tales, and mythic tales (Wolkstein 1980, 1983; MacDonald 1993, 1999) are examples of the fruitful interchange between oral and literary arts and ethnographically informed scholarship.

The rise of a network of live urban venues for the telling of autobiographical stories, such as The Moth and other so-called "Story Slams," modeled on performance poetry competitions, has significantly extended the genre's range and prominence. The Moth was founded in 1997 in the New York City living room of poet and novelist George Dawes Green. It has since become an international phenomenon, with dozens of franchised and related events monthly in New York, Los Angeles, Chicago, Detroit, and many other cities across the United States. As of 2016, Moth venues have sprung up in London, Dublin, Sydney, and Melbourne as well. The term "digital storytelling" entered the American storytelling scene through the work of the Center for Digital Storytelling in Berkeley, California, founded in 1993. In their definition, it refers to the sharing of personal narratives through digital media, such as audio and video recordings. Many other projects and organizations have adopted this understanding of digital stories—among them, the Moth Radio Hour, the "Just Stories" online storytelling festival, RaceBridges Studio, and StoryCorps.

For all that, the telling of fairy tales remains an important foundational genre of contemporary story performance. In a recent (unpublished) survey of members of the National Storytelling Network (the principal storytelling revival organization in the U.S., dating back to the founding of the storytelling festival movement), nearly half estimated the percentage of folk and fairy tales in their repertoires at 75 percent or more; nearly one-third estimated the percentage at 90 percent or more. Fully 97 percent of the sample group have at least some percentage of fairy tales in their repertoires and perform them in venues ranging from schools and libraries, to festivals and senior centers, for audiences from pre-school age to centenarians. The use of digital media has expanded beyond personal narratives and has made the dissemination of fairy-tale-related works easier, more visible, and more popular. Storytellers record and share their performances on YouTube, Facebook, and other social platforms. Fairy tale and folktale podcasts have proliferated, and Twitter has seen a rise of trending storytelling- and folklore-related hashtags such as #FolkloreThursday and #StorySat, allowing people around the wired world to share their sources, ideas, adaptations, and enthusiasm for folk and fairy tales.

Tellers from African American and Native American backgrounds seem especially inclined to value ancestral or archetypal folktale voices above the mainstream American first-person. Both communities have generated their own networks of storytelling organizations and venues—the National Association of Black Storytellers (NABS) for African American tellers and audiences and reservation schools and inter-tribal pow-wows among Native Americans—with numerous professional performers who work across cultural lines. Traditional African American and Native American folktales tend to show somewhat different formal characteristics than the classic European wonder tale, yet hybrid traditional stories like the Gullah "Jack and Mary and the Devil" and "Jack and Mary and the Three Dogs" have made their way onto contemporary tellers' repertoires through recordings by Janie Hunter of St. John's Island, South Carolina (*Been in the Storm So Long* 1990). NABS co-founder the late Mary Carter Smith (1919–2007) made a signature tale out of "Cindy Ellie," a pitch-perfect transposition of ATU 510A to the African American neighborhoods of East Baltimore. Native American Coyote tales, which blend formal and contextual aspects of myths, magic tales, and animal trickster tales, have become popular with mixed and mainstream tellers and audiences—despite concerns over appropriation and loss of cultural integrity. Perhaps the most popular tale ascribed to Native American traditions to have crossed over into contemporary performance venues is "The Burnt-Faced Girl," commonly known as "The Algonquin Cinderella," originally published by Charles Leland in 1884 and since adapted by a host of tellers (Shah 1979; Martin 1992; San Souci 1997) as a generic Native American story—yet likely prized both for its pre-conquest setting and its formal congruence with the ubiquitous European wonder tale.

In England, Scotland, Wales, Ireland, and on the European continent, traditional wonder tales seem to be holding firmly to their pride of place in the storytelling scene. Tellers from the lineage of Scottish traveling people such as Willie McPhee, Betsy Whyte, Alex and Sheila Stewart, Stanley Robertson, and Duncan Williamson have played dominant roles in the British Isles storytelling revivals. Those from succeeding generations such as Robin Williamson and

David Campbell in Scotland; Ben Haggarty, Hugh Lupton, and Sally Pomme Clayton in England; Daniel Morden and Michael Harvey in Wales; and Liz Weir, Niall De Burca, and Claire Murphy in Ireland have followed them in basing their repertoires on traditional wonder tale stocks, either from their particular regions or from global cultures (Wilson 2005). Folk- and fairy tales still predominate within European storytelling and form an integral part of storytellers' identities.

Following on the rise of national and local folktale collections in the eighteenth and nineteenth centuries, European nations have undergone what Jack Zipes (2000, xxvii) calls the institutionalization of traditional wonder tales as official signifiers of national heritage. Many contemporary European storytellers specialize in keeping the oral tradition alive, referring to themselves as "tale tellers" or even "fairy tale tellers" in their respective languages. There is an ongoing debate surrounding how close one should keep as a contemporary performer to the alleged original (e.g., first recorded) text—and the answers vary from verbatim recitation of the Grimms' texts all the way to modernized, "fractured" fairy tales replete with comic anachronisms.

In Europe, the umbrella organization for professional storytelling is called FEST (Federation for European Storytelling), conceived in 2008 at a conference in Norway and incorporated as a non-profit organization in Belgium in 2012. One of the first collaborations FEST facilitated was *Project Grimm*, celebrating the 200th anniversary of the first publication of the Grimms' fairy tales, in 2012. Storytellers all over Europe recorded a selection of the Grimms' tales in their respective languages, making them freely available online. The project's goal was to promote the creative live telling of the classic Grimm brothers' tales, as well as versions of the same folktale types from across Europe. Numerous European organizations and events make it their specific goal to celebrate and promote the telling of traditional stories—examples include the Kea Island Folktale Festival in Greece, the Stories Today Festival (Festival Pravljice Danes) in Slovenia, and the annual Day of the Hungarian Folktale (Népmese Napja) in Hungary. Recent decades have seen the opening of several "story museums," designed to house live storytelling events, folk- and fairy-tale libraries, and exhibitions, giving a physical home to many expressions of the contemporary storytelling movement. One of the oldest is the German Museum of Tales and Local Legends (*Deutsches Märchen- und Wesersagenmuseum*) in Bad Oeynhausen, Germany, founded in 1973 by historian and author Karl Paetow with the donation of his own private library. The Museum of Legends (*Sagomuseet*) in Ljungby, Sweden, not only houses exhibitions, but is also the home venue of the Ljungby International Storytelling Festival since 1990 and offers guidance to the region's legend-filled landscape. Storyteller Michal Malinowski opened the Storyteller Museum (*Muzeum Bajek Baśni i Opowieści*) of Krakow, Poland, in 2002 to preserve and promote the world's oral traditions and narrative heritage through digital exhibitions and storytelling events. The Story Museum in Oxford, England, opened its gates in 2003; the Scottish Storytelling Centre opened on Edinburgh's Royal Mile in 2006; the Story Museum (*Mesemúzeum*) of Budapest, Hungary, opened in 2012. Storytellers also frequently work with local and national institutions during events such as the International Museum Day, International Archaeology Day, or the Night of the Museums movement.

The strong connection between tales and landscape in most European traditions found new forms of presentation with the rise of the contemporary storytelling movement. One of the best-known examples, the German Fairy Tale Route (*Deutsche Märchenstraße*), was established in 1975 and is one of the country's main tourist attractions. It covers almost 400 miles from Hanau (the birthplace of Jacob and Wilhelm Grimm) to Bremen; the route is lined with tourist attractions, museums, UNESCO World Heritage sites, guided tours, and storytelling events. Similarly, major cities around Europe—Prague, Rome, Vienna, and Edinburgh, to name a few—have experienced a boom in storytelling walks and tours. Some focus on the eerie and the supernatural (ghost story walks), while others build on local tales and legends tied to certain spaces (e.g., legends of the Golem in the Prague ghetto). By participating in these tours, visitors not only immerse themselves in oral cultural heritage, but also physically move through spaces imbued with traditional tales. A prime example of a contemporary conjunction of storytelling and landscape is the project *Seeing Stories*, brought to life in 2013 with the help of an EU grant and the participation of storytellers from four cities: Aachen, Florence, Lisbon, and Edinburgh. During the two years of its existence, the participants gathered local wonder tales, legends, and other genres from their respective cities and used them to trace the landscape of oral tradition on their physical coordinates. The results were storytelling events, festival performances, and story walks—several of which remain to enrich the array of local culture.

International collaborations such as this are not uncommon in the European storytelling movement. One of the largest in recent years was the 2012 Mysteries of Europe (*Misterios de Europa*) conference in Guadalajara, Spain. Also born from an EU grant, it gathered storytellers and story-researchers from thirty different countries to share tales of mystery, secrets, and riddles from their respective oral traditions. The event's focus helped connect it structurally with the story slam movement, which also relies on thematic tags to give coherence to personal story evenings; this in turn has led to the hybridizing of story slam events with folk and fairy-tale performances. The slam format can easily be applied to folktales, fairy tales, or mythology while keeping the competitive element and the interactive, adult-oriented atmosphere that draws new audiences to storytelling. MassMouth Inc., a non-profit organization dedicated to increasing the visibility of the art form, staged a six-part monthly Folk and Fairy Tale Slam series in 2012–2013. The event was advertised specifically for adults, with invited featured storytellers and a different monthly theme. As they have throughout their immemorial engagement with the oral and literate cultures of humankind, wonder tales continue to adapt to changing social realities, finding new ways to bestow elixirs of imagination and to restore the communal spirit.

Related topics: Blogs and Websites; Broadcast; Children's Museums; Comic Cons; Fandom/Fan Cultures; Fan Fiction; Food; Oral Tradition; Pedagogy; Romance; Storyworlds/Narratology

Note

1. The battle over appropriate repertoires between proponents of fairy tales and other imaginative literature and proponents of purpose-written, sociologically literal story texts is detailed in Alvey (1974).

References Cited and Further Reading

Alvey, Richard. 1974. *The Historical Development of Organized Storytelling for Children in the United States.* Philadelphia: U Pennsylvania P.

Benjamin, Walter. (1968) 2006. *Illuminations.* New York: Harcourt, Brace, World.

Bettelheim, Bruno. 1977. *The Uses of Enchantment.* New York: Vintage.

Bly, Robert. 1990. *Iron John.* New York: Vintage.

Bolen, Jean Shinoda. 1984. *Goddesses in Everywoman.* New York: Harper and Row.

Bryant, Sara Cone. 1910. *How to Tell Stories to Children.* London: Harap.

Campbell, Joseph. 1948. *The Hero with a Thousand Faces.* Princeton, NJ: Bollingen.

Campbell, Joseph, and Bill Moyers. 1988. *The Power of Myth.* New York: Doubleday.

Center for Digital Storytelling. 2016. www.storycenter.org.

Chase, Richard. 1943. *The Jack Tales.* Boston: Houghton.

———. 1948. *Grandfather Tales.* Boston: Houghton.

———. 1956. *American Folk Tales and Songs*. New York: New American Library.

Davis, Donald. 1992. *Jack Always Seeks His Fortune*. Little Rock: August House.

Deutsches Märchen- und Wesersagenmuseum. 2016. www.badoeynhausen.de.

Deutsche Märchenstraße. 2016. www.deutsche-maerchenstrasse.com/.

Emrich, Duncan. 1972. *Folklore on the American Land*. Boston: Little Brown.

Estés, Clarissa Pinkola. 1992. *Women Who Run With the Wolves*. New York: Ballantine.

The Fairy Tale Lobby. 2016. https://fairytalelobby.wordpress.com/.

Federation for European Storytelling (FEST). 2015. www.fest-network.eu/.

Folklore Thursday. 2016. http://folklorethursday.com.

Forest, Heather. 1996. *Wonder Tales from around the World*. Little Rock: August House.

Joyce, James. 1939. *Finnegan's Wake*. New York: Viking.

Legends, Myths and Whiskey. 2016. https://legendsmythsandwhiskey.com.

Leland, Charles. 1884. *The Algonquin Legends of New England*. Boston: Houghton Mifflin.

Lindahl, Carl. 2001. *Perspectives on the Jack Tales: And Other North American Märchen*. Bloomington: Special Publications of the Folklore Institute.

———. 2004. *American Folktales from the Collections of the Library of Congress*. Armonk, NY: Sharpe.

MacDonald, Margaret Read. 1993. *The Storyteller's Start-Up Book*. Little Rock: August House.

———. 1999. *Traditional Storytelling Today: An International Sourcebook*. Chicago: Fitzroy-Dearborn.

Mann, Thomas. 1944. *The Magic Mountain*. New York: Knopf.

Martin, Rafe. 1992. *The Rough-faced Girl*. New York: Putnam.

McCarthy, William, ed. 1994. *Jack in Two Worlds*. Chapel Hill: U North Carolina P.

Meade, Michael. 1994. *Men and the Water of Life*. San Francisco: Harper.

Mesemúzeum, Budapest. 2016. www.mesemuzeum.hu.

The Moth. 2016. https://themoth.org.

Muzeum Bajek Baśni i Opowieści. 2016. www.mubabao.pl.

National Storytelling Network. 2016. www.storynet.org/.

Ong, Walter. 1982. *Orality and Literacy*. London: Routledge.

Perdue, Charles. 1987. *Outwitting the Devil: Jack Tales from Wise County, Virginia*. Santa Fe: Ancient City Press.

Project Grimm. 2012. http://projectgrimm.blogspot.com.

RaceBridges Studio. 2016. http://racebridgesstudio.com.

Roberts, Leonard. 1964. *South from Hell-fer-Sartin'*. Welch, WV: Council of the Southern Mountains.

———. 1974. *Sang Branch Settlers*. Pikeville, KY: Pikeville College P.

Sagomuseet, Ljungby. 2016. www.sagobygden.se.

San Souci, Robert. 1997. *Sootface*. New York: Dragonfly.

Sawyer, Ruth. 1942. *The Way of the Storyteller*. New York: Viking.

Scottish Storytelling Centre. 2016. www.tracscotland.org/scottish-storytelling-centre.

Seeing Stories. 2015. http://seeingstories.eu.

Shah, Idries. 1979. *World Tales*. New York: Harcourt Brace.

Shedlock, Marie. 1915. *The Art of the Story-Teller*. New York: Appleton.

Sobol, Joseph D. 1999. *The Storytellers' Journey: An American Revival*. Urbana: U Illinois P.

———. 2006. "Whistlin' Down Towards the Devil's House." *Oral Tradition* 21 (1): 3–43.

StoryCorps. 2016. https://storycorps.org.

Story Museum. 2014. www.storymuseum.org.uk.

von Franz, Marie-Louise. 1996. *The Interpretation of Fairy Tales*. Boston: Shambhala.

Wilson, Michael. 2005. *Storytelling and Theatre*. London: Palgrave Macmillan.

Wolkstein, Diane. 1980. *The Magic Orange Tree*. New York: Schocken.

———. 1983. *Inanna, Queen of Heaven and Earth*. New York: Harper.

Wyche, Richard Thomas. 1910. *Some Great Stories and How to Tell Them*. New York: Newsom.

Zalka, Csenge V. 2013. *Tales of Superhuman Powers: 55 Traditional Stories from around the World*. Jefferson: McFarland.

Zipes, Jack. 2000. "Introduction." In *The Oxford Companion to Fairy Tales*, edited by Jack Zipes, xv–xxxii. Oxford: Oxford UP.

Mediagraphy

acousticfiddle. 2012. "A Love Like Salt (excerpt)." *YouTube*, January 19. www.youtube.com/watch?v=9AaEosbCO3o.

American Storytelling (Video). 1986. 8 vols. Wilson. USA.

STORYTELLING

BarbaraElektraDroth. 2013. "Grimm Tales . . . 3 Drops of Blood." *YouTube*, April 26. www.youtube.com/watch?v=t6sNzt91LE0.

Been in the Storm So Long (Music Album). 1967/1990. Artist Guy Carawan. USA.

Best-Loved Stories Told at the National Storytelling Festival (Audio Book). 1994. Jonesborough, TN: National Storytelling P.

By Word of Mouth: Storytelling in America (Video). 1982. Discovery Education. USA.

Diangle. 2010. "Robin Williamson in Concert 1990—Part 1/8." *YouTube*, August 12. www.youtube.com/watch?v=zSmZ1Mlz5k8.

Fat Cat and Friends (Music Album). 2003. Artist Margaret Read McDonald. USA.

The Fisherman's Son and the Gruagach of Tricks (Music Album). 1981. Artist Robin Williamson. USA.

Fixin' to Tell about Jack: Ray Hicks, Storyteller from Beech Mountain, North Carolina. 1975. Director Elizabeth Barret. USA.

Folktales of Strong Women (Music Album). 1983. Artist Doug Lipman. USA.

A Glint at the Kindling/Five Bardic Mysteries (Music Album). 1994. Artist Robin Williamson. USA.

Grandma's Lap Stories (Music Album). 1995. Artist Donald Davis. USA.

Groundhogs Meet Grimm (Music Album). 2002. Artist Megan Hicks. USA.

Homespun Tales (Audio Book). 1988. Jonesborough, TN: National Storytelling P.

Jack and Granny Ugly (Music Album). 2006. Artist Donald Davis. USA.

JustStoriesVideo. 2012. "SuddenStorybyLauraSimms."*YouTube*, July 23. www.youtube.com/watch?v=Yw2JLf2CZIY.

Like Meat Loves Salt (Audio Book). 1989. Author Elizabeth Ellis. National Storytelling Network. USA.

Live & Thriving at the 30th National Storytelling Festival (Audio Book). 2003. Jonesborough, TN: National Storytelling P.

Lupton, Hugh. 2013. "Who Takes the Most Pleasure from the Act of Love?" *YouTube*, January 29. www.youtube.com/watch?v=lfVzd9IUQVk&index=2&list=PLVYl7BPfaylL0h8UEL0KV9P6q6ZdViao0.

Mataharifilms. 2012. "Robert Bly & Friends: Reviving the Oral Tradition." *YouTube*, October 15. www.youtube.com/watch?v=PbX_yrNnus8.

Milk from the Bull's Horn: Tales of Nurturing Men (Music album). 1983. Artist Doug Lipman. USA.

Mr. Gutenberg and Other Tales (Music Album). 2003. Artist Niall De Burca. Ireland.

Myths and Legends (Podcast). 2016. Written, produced, and hosted by Jason Weiser. www.mythpodcast.com.

No Tricks, Just Magic (Music Album). 2013. Artist Megan Hicks. USA.

The Power of Myth (TV). 1988. Starring Joseph Campbell and Bill Moyers. USA.

The Power of Story, Vol. 1–4. 2014. Artist Laura Simms. BetterListen. USA.

Ray Hicks Tells Four Traditional Jack Tales (Music Album). 1962. Artist Ray Hicks. USA.

Scottish Traditional Tales (Audio Book). 2000. East Lothian, Scotland: Greentrax.

Smith, Mary Carter. 1986. "Cindy Ellie." In *American Storytelling* (Video), Vol. 5. Wilson. USA.

Tellin' Time (Music Album). 2001. Artist Ed Stivender. Klarity. USA.

Tell Me a Story (Vol. 1–3). 1995. Director David Coggeshall. USA.

Travellers' Tales, Vol. 1–2 (Music Album). 2002. Artists Stanley Robertson and Duncan Williamson. Scotland.

69

TRADITIONAL SONG

Pauline Greenhill and Jill Terry Rudy

Undeniably, fairy tale and song make a powerful and popular combination.[1] Consider the box office receipts for the live-action remake of Disney's musical *Beauty and the Beast*, over one billion U.S. dollars worldwide six weeks after the March 17, 2017, premiere (Google). Also remember the social media flurry, and some fury, that surrounded word that the live-action *Mulan* (2019) movie, directed by Niki Caro (who also directed *Whale Rider* 2002), would not include songs from the 1998 Disney animated version (Zeitchik 2017).[2] Lest it seem that Disney alone recognizes the valuable combination of fairy tale and song, this chapter historicizes and expands these popular associations by tracing intermedial instances linking song and fairy tale from other centuries and locations. For example, Christine Jones and Jennifer Schacker include the lai "Le Fresne" (The Ash Tree), a mistaken-bride story of twin sisters separated at birth, in their *Marvelous Transformations* anthology (2013, 69–83). The term "lai," or "lay," indicates song associated with narrative. Told in rhyming couplets, this lyric narrative poem, often sung and/or accompanied by music, is attributed to Marie de France in the twelfth century. Sometimes affiliated with the Cinderella cycle, this engaging tale confirms the longstanding combination of fairy tale and song (Heiner N.d.).

The addition of music to speech indicates song's intermediality, involving more than one expressive medium, with the body (via the voice) as the expressive means—sometimes including instrument accompaniment. William A. Wilson associates the imperatives of music-making with the wider, and deeper, necessity of "combin[ing] words, sounds, colors, shapes, and movements into aesthetically satisfying patterns" (2006, 13). To speech, music adds "pitch, tempo, timbre and volume," making the ensuing expression similar to and yet drastically different from the spoken word or story (Frontczak 1995, 238). Yet the popular tradition that combines fairy tale with song in the cante fable (folktales that incorporate song) and ballad (traditional narrative songs), and in theatrical productions, film, and broadcasts, also indicates a wide range of intermedial and technological involvements. With folklorist Edward D. Ives's observation (1985) that music is universal, then, we add that singing is utterly normal but still distinct from more quotidian communication and that it often brings aesthetic pleasure through a variety of expressive forms.

We consider here the transformative aspects of song and the fairy tale as oral expression that may be part of large- or small-scale entertainments. This chapter focuses on traditional song, or folksong, which "picks up the colorations, nuances, and styles of the group among whom it circulates, and gets continually rephrased to suit their responses to time, place, rhetoric, and performance" (Toelken 1986, 147). In addition to distinguishing informal singing from commercial production, folklorists like Barre Toelken acknowledge the "dynamic change" that leads to "constant interaction between formal and informal music" (1986, 149). Given the persisting popularity of tales and song together, these crucial connections merit analysis in terms of their transformations within the tales and adaptations across versions and media. We emphasize, therefore, this multifaceted popular tradition of folksong that instructs, entertains, and provides metamusical commentary on the power of song with fairy tale to share knowledge and effect justice.

Fairy Tales in Ballads: The Cante Fable

Folklorists have documented the cante fable, a "story interspersed with song," in Africa, Asia, Europe, and North America (see Harris and Reichl 1997). Not all such folktales are fairy tales per se. For example, versions of "Old Hildebrand" (ATU 1360C), a tale type about an unfaithful wife whose machinations against her husband are disclosed in song, have been found, for example, in New Jersey (Halpert 1942), New Brunswick (Ives 1963; Greenhill 1985), and Newfoundland (Widdowson 2009). The cante fable is already multimedia, linking prose and poetry, spoken and sung elements. However, as the following example shows, the form also appears in film versions of fairy tales, further extending its intermediation.

W. H. F. Nicolaisen (1997) enumerates the Grimms' tales that include verses (which, in performance, can be sung) and finds twenty-one. He notes that apart from animal rhymsters/singers,

> all the speakers[/singers] are either supernatural beings or humans temporarily enchanted [. . .] by supernatural beings. Non-prosaic language is the language of non-prosaic speakers; rhymes and formulas convey magic and are therefore appropriate for those who have the power of magic or for those who address beings in possession of such power [. . .], or [who] by stealth and deceit usurp such power [. . .]. This does not mean that ordinary language is never employed by supernatural creatures or the purveyors of magic but when humans encounter the world of magic they must also be prepared for a change in language, as ordinary language may not suffice.
>
> (186)

The sources on which Nicolaisen draws are written, not performed versions, but he notes the undeniable link of what appears as written verse to singing:

> Much of [the verse] must originally have been sung as the many references to singing indicate. In some instances, the actual tunes of the sung portions have been recorded or otherwise preserved. Much of the singing is envisaged as very pleasant and sweet, almost seductive, and has effects which ordinary spoken prose could not have achieved [. . .]. [The song is] part of an oral performance in which sung verse is felicitously used to interrupt spoken prose at appropriate points in the narrative [. . .] making its occasional employment all the more startling and effective.
>
> (194)

Nicolaisen also notes that the "substance, content, and meaning" of the incorporated songs take the form of "requests, either to the magically powerful, or by those magically enchanted to associated human beings [. . .], warnings, advice, or revelations [. . .] [and] other types of utterance" (186–188). He concludes that "within the framework of the European folk-narrative tradition, the occurrence of verse[/song] within prose [. . .] is closely associated with, in fact dependent on, connections with the other world, especially its magic power" (194). Songs may be "employed for structuring purposes, in some instances facilitating an incremental

PAULINE GREENHILL AND JILL TERRY RUDY

movement or retardation of the plot" (194). Thus, song interacts with tales ontologically and epistemologically, indexing other worlds and pacing the audience's knowledge of what is happening.

One example of cante fable, "The Juniper Tree" (ATU 720), Maria Tatar calls "probably the most shocking of all fairy tales" (2004, 209), singling it out despite her inventory of the Grimm tales' "murder, mutilation, cannibalism, infanticide, and incest" (1987, 3). In the traditional narrative:

> A boy is born but his mother dies. The little boy is slain by his cruel stepmother who closes the lid of an apple chest on him [. . .]. She cooks him and serves him to his father who eats him unwittingly [. . .]. The boy's stepsister gathers up his bones and puts them under a juniper tree [. . .]. *A bird comes forth and sings about what happened.* It brings presents to the father and the sister and drops a millstone on the stepmother, killing her [. . .]. The boy is resuscitated [our emphasis].
>
> (Uther 2004, 1, 389)

In the Grimms' version translated by Jack Zipes, the bird sings identical lyrics no less than eight times. The first time, the bird, who "landed on a goldsmith's house" (2003, 161), intones:

> My mother, she killed me.
> My father, he ate me.
> My sister, Marlene, she made sure to see
> my bones were all gathered together,
> bound nicely in silk, as neat as can be,
> and laid beneath the juniper tree.
> *Tweet, tweet!* What a lovely bird I am!
>
> (161–162)

The goldsmith hears the song, comes out holding a golden chain, and asks the bird to sing again, but the creature replies, "I never sing twice for nothing. Give me the golden chain, and I'll sing it for you again" (162). The bird collects the chain, reprises his song, and moves on to a shoemaker, sings again for a pair of red shoes, and then on to a mill where he exchanges his song for a millstone. He goes to "his father's house" (164), where he sings and gives the gold chain to his father, then sings again and gives the shoes to Marlene. He does not sing to his stepmother; he simply "threw the millstone down on her head, and she was crushed to death." When the father and Marlene go outside, "Smoke, flames, and fire were rising from the spot, and when it was over, the little brother was standing there." The three enter the house, "sat down at the table, and ate" (166). The bird/(dead) boy magically becomes a living human once more.

Nicolaisen categorizes the song in "The Juniper Tree" with "warnings, advice, or revelations" (187), but it also serves as a coded request "by those magically enchanted to associated human beings" (186). That is, the bird/boy picks specific individuals/groups and locations for singing, and though his lyrics explicitly outline what has happened to him, the hearers only note how beautifully the bird sings and ask for a reprise. They fail to recognize the words as literal truth-telling. Of course, such a reaction is by no means peculiar. Though the hearers do not appear discomfited by the presence of Nicolaisen's "non-prosaic speaker," a bird singing actual lyrics (in addition to the more expected "*tweet, tweet*") in "non-prosaic language," they see the song as mere story (implicitly fictional), rather as a twenty-first-century listener does not assume that every song is autobiographical for the singer.

The repetitions of the lyrics combine truth-telling with a structural reiteration that not only works in the narrative, but also extends the story and defers its ending in an overtly aesthetic move. The reiterations also mark the song as a kind of incantation, perhaps even a magical spell to restore the bird to boy form. That the song combines with—indeed is the literal instrument facilitating—the gathering of significant objects, and then marks the donation of gifts to the deserving, supports this reading. The elements of just desserts to the undeserving, and the millstone dropped on the mother, lack song accompaniment in the Grimms' version. Of course, she (unlike Marlene and the father) knows the full truth of what the bird sings to others, but also the song's absence marks a time of the metamorphosis to human/living from the magical enchantment. Thus, singing aestheticizes even as it recaps the gruesome plot developments in "The Juniper Tree," and it also prepares for, and in part effects, the crucial narrative transformation.

Three feature films by women directors draw on "The Juniper Tree." American writer, director, editor, and producer Nietzchka Keene's *The Juniper Tree* (1990) is a German version made in Iceland with Icelandic actors speaking English. It explores fraught family relations in a pre-modern Icelandic setting, incorporating elements of local traditional magic, invoking issues of heterosexual and sibling love and jealousy within what would now be called a blended family. The thematic links to the traditional tale type's exploration of kinship and its discontents clearly manifest (see Greenhill and Brydon 2010). While this film is currently known primarily because it was Icelandic popular singer Björk's first movie, it does not use or refer to the bird/boy's song.

Micheline Lanctôt's *Le piège d'Issoudun* (English title Juniper Tree, 2003) addresses the inchoate desperation of an early twenty-first-century privileged woman. Metafictionally, it juxtaposes the explicit incorporation of a stylized theatrical performance directly based on a Brothers Grimm version of "The Juniper Tree" with a social realist evocation of the same narrative set in suburban Quebec, Canada (see Greenhill 2014).

On a wintry day, Esther (played by Sylvie Drapeau) jumps into her backyard pool with her two children. The kids drown, but when Esther's suicide attempt fails, she speeds along a highway, distraught, trying again to kill herself. Police officer Laurier (played by Frédérick De Grandpré) stops her at the Issoudun exit and eventually agrees to drive her home. Their intense interactions en route, during which Esther repeatedly taunts Laurier, reveal some of her personal background, but little about her motivation for the murders beyond her extreme fears. The divorced Laurier is forthcoming about his life; he has not seen his three boys for five months but plans to meet them to explain why the marriage ended. His love for children and his horror when he discovers the murders leads to the film's conclusion.

Like ATU 720, the realist plot of *Issoudun* is about a murdering mother and an unknowing father. Drapeau and De Grandpré enact the primary characters in the realistic narrative, Esther and Laurier, and the stepmother and father respectively. The staged drama includes the young daughter, Marlene; the murdered son; and his mother, as well as the bird's interlocutors. The song appears in the theatrical performance, but not in the realist portion. It is repeated three times, as the bird gathers his gifts and millstone, with actual bird calls sounding as background.

In the theater piece, Pierre-Luc Lafontaine, playing the boy, manipulates a large puppet bird so that its wings flap. The actor is clearly visible during the puppet bird's appearances but does not sing the song. Instead, an acapella high-voiced solo echoes spookily in the background. The director chose not to present the first time the song is sung for each donor, but instead when it is reprised, marking the song's part in an exchange of artistry for material objects that serve the bird/boy. The bird's transformation to human is directly represented when Lafontaine appears after the stepmother's death. The realist narrative has no such happy ending.

Canadian director Mary Harron's *The Moth Diaries* (2011), closely based upon the book by Rachel Klein (2002), focuses on interactions in a girls' boarding school. Though *Moth* offers various references to fairy tales, the primary link to "The Juniper Tree" happens when the pre-ternatural suspect sings a version of the bird's song. In the film, sixteen-year-old Rebecca (played by Sarah Bolger) returns to her boarding school two years after her poet father has committed suicide. She particularly looks forward to seeing her best friend, Lucy (played by Sarah Gadon), but mysterious new student Ernessa Bloch (played by Lily Cole), also an outsider to the Christian school who is Jewish like Rebecca, and whose father also committed suicide, supplants Rebecca in Lucy's affections. Rebecca blames Ernessa when members of the school community leave or die (including Lucy, who becomes Ernessa's lover and succumbs to anorexia). Rebecca finds in the school basement an old stone coffin on which Ernessa's name is engraved and documents suggesting that she killed herself many years ago. Rebecca returns to pour kerosene on the coffin, with Ernessa in it, and set it afire. As Rebecca is driven to the police station, she drops out the car window a razor blade Ernessa gave her with which to commit suicide.

The sequence in which Ernessa sings the "Juniper Tree" bird's song overdetermines the relationship between Ernessa and Rebecca in terms of suicidality and blood. In the previous scene, Rebecca recalls walking into her home bathroom and discovering her father's dead body—he has slit his wrists. She leans against a doorframe and cries as she remembers. Ernessa and Rebecca's confrontation takes place in a circular, ornate room, the school library, where Rebecca sits at a desk, studying. Ernessa appears and tells Rebecca that books, her writing, the past, and teacher Mr. Davies won't save her and that "Daddy can't save you." Rebecca affirms that her father loved her, but Ernessa says, "He's the one who caused you all this trouble in the first place." Rebecca says, "You're wrong," recalling "walks we took, the fairy tales he read to me." Ernessa counters, "He read you other fairy tales that you forgot."

Ernessa then sings,

> My mother, she butchered me
> My father, he ate me
> My sister, little Anne-Marie
> She gathered up the bones of me
> And tied them in a silken cloth.
> To lay under the juniper.
> Tweet, tweet What a pretty bird am I.

She raises her left sleeve to show cuts on her wrist. "It's time to free yourself." She makes an additional slice with a razor, and blood spurts into Rebecca's face and on an open book. Blood then rains down on Ernessa, splashing on Rebecca's table. Then, abruptly, Rebecca is in an unspoiled library; she looks down onto the table and reaches for a razor now lying in front of her open book. She takes it, turns it over, and closes her hands around it.

With a single shot in the entire sequence wherein the audience sees anything that Rebecca could not have seen—a view of Ernessa's hands and arm in the foreground with Rebecca in the background—multiple reverse shots suggest Ernessa being seen from Rebecca's point of view. Ernessa reminds Rebecca of the forgotten "Juniper Tree" tale, with its explicit violence underlined by the copious blood in the scene. Though the tale does not apparently deal with suicide, the Grimms' version suggests, echoed in *Issoudun*, that the mother knows her dire fate when she says, "I feel as if the world were coming to an end." Yet her decision to go where the bird and millstone await comes because she thinks, "Maybe I'd feel better if I went outside" (Zipes 2003, 166). She does not court death, unlike *Issoudun*'s Esther.

Throughout the film, Rebecca has an ambivalent relationship to suicide. But Ernessa's blood/bird song scene underlines the extent to which she may not be coping as well as everyone thinks. The song in *Moth* again marks an aestheticizing—of Ernessa's and Rebecca's experiences and their associations with blood and death. Crucially, the scene also leads directly to Rebecca's resolve to get rid of Ernessa and implicitly of her own suicidality. Again, the song marks metamorphosis and deep affect, but a sole song performance suffices.

Fairy Tales as Ballads/Ballads as Fairy Tales

Often the motifs, ideas, characters, and themes popularly associated with fairy tales also appear in ballad form. Unlike a cante fable where the song intersperses the story, a ballad is the story told through singing. Traditional ballads can include figures like a wicked mother-in-law, not unlike the one who appears in the traditional tale type "The Maiden Who Seeks Her Brothers" (ATU 451). A woman whose mother-in-law steals her child/children accuses her of eating it/them. Initially, the woman cannot defend herself because she must avoid speaking in order to disenchant her brothers (see Jorgensen 2012). Similarly, in one of the 305 classic ballads in Francis James Child's anthology (1882–1898), "Willie's Lady" (Child 6),

> Willie travels to woo and wed a wife. His mother, not approving of the bride, casts spells to ensure that she will [remain pregnant but] never bear a child. Willie tricks his mother into believing the baby has been born, and the mother blurts out the way to lift the spell.
>
> (Waltz and Engle 2017c)

Ballads can include supernatural narrative elements that might appear fairy-tale like to some listeners. "Tam Lin" (Child 39) narrates the story of a woman who meets Tam Lin, has sex with him, and becomes pregnant. So he can marry her, "she must rescue him from thralldom to the Elven queen. With difficulty, she does so" (Waltz and Engle 2017a). Ballad and tale scholar Martin Lovelace suggests:

> Tam Lin, the character, is like any enchanted prince in a fairy tale who must be disenchanted by the resoluteness of the young woman who loves him. They are obviously right for each other, being both young, and human, unlike the Queen of Fairy who is not a fit consort for Tam Lin. This ballad, in relation to fairy tale, is another instance of the unspelling of an enchanted person; the victim is under the thrall of someone who is not a fit partner (too old? not human?) and that person has to be restored by someone who IS their right partner.
>
> (pers. comm.)

Where many twenty-first-century folks might see fairy abductions like that of Tam Lin as entirely fantastical and fictitious, fairy belief can be serious. For example, in 1895, in Ireland, Bridget Cleary was murdered by her husband, Michael, because he believed she was a changeling, abducted by the fairies and left in place of his wife (see Bourke 1999). The horror film *Tam Lin* (aka *The Devil's Widow*; *The Ballad of Tam Lin*), directed by Roddy McDowell (1970), has Ava Gardner as an older woman who seeks to maintain hold over her younger lover, played by Ian McShane. As in the ballad, the male protagonist's attraction to a woman closer to his age leads to the film's denouement.

PAULINE GREENHILL AND JILL TERRY RUDY

However, a few fairy tales have closer narrative/plot connections with ballads. "The Singing Bone" (ATU 780) has "a brother (sister) [who] kills his (her) brother (sister) and buries him (her) in the earth. From the bones a shepherd makes an instrument (harp, violin, flute) which brings the secret to light" (Uther 2004, 439). In the Grimms, "the little bone began to sing on its own accord":

Oh, shepherd, shepherd, don't you know
you're blowing on my bone!
My brother killed me years ago,
buried me by the brook that flows,
carried off the dead wild boar,
and married the king's fine daughter.

(Zipes 2003, 100)

The shepherd goes to the king, not because of the lyrics' content but because the horn is "remarkable" when it "sings by itself." "The little horn began to sing its song again." Unlike the "Juniper" characters, the king recognizes the song's telling as real and truthful; he "understood it well and had the ground [. . .] dug up." The result is not the good brother's resuscitation, but instead his bones being "laid to rest in a beautiful grave in a churchyard" (Zipes 2003, 100).

Though this version does not reprise the lyrics, one can imagine a performer singing the verses again when the bone gets to the king. But instead of aestheticizing the song as in "Juniper," "The Singing Bone" makes the bone itself appealing—it's "a little bone, as white as snow" that "would make a good mouthpiece"—in addition to its aforementioned "remarkable" magical properties. The Grimms' "Singing Bone," gathered from Dortchen Wild, who married Wilhelm Grimm in 1825 (Zipes 2003, 733), is little more than a precis of the story, taking only two pages in Zipes's translation. In contrast, the extended "Juniper Tree" that comes from a text provided by artist and writer Philipp Otto Runge (Zipes 2003, 734) covers nine pages. The similarity of purpose with the bird's song in "The Juniper Tree" is striking—and Nicolaisen places "The Singing Bone" in the same category. It is clearly more unusual that a bone would sing than that a bird would do so—however, a bird's using human language as in "Juniper" is clearly marked and strange.

"The Singing Bone" is one of the stories represented in *The Wonderful World of the Brothers Grimm* (directed by Henry Levin 1962; see Magnus-Johnston 2016), but we focus on its alternative mediation in the classic ballad called "The Twa Sisters" (see Child 1882, 118–141). In it, "a knight woos two (three) sisters, choosing the younger. The older drowns the younger. Her body is recovered and made into an instrument by a passing miller/musician. As the knight prepares to wed the older sister, the instrument sings out the truth" (Waltz and Engle 2017b). Child says that (even in the nineteenth century), "this is one of the very few old ballads which are not extinct as tradition in the British Isles" (1882, 118) and notes its popularity in Scandinavia and Eastern Europe. Perhaps the song's overlaps with the fairy tale kept it current; since the ballad is not extinct, clearly Child associates singing with ongoing tradition.

In the ballad version, also called "The Cruel Sister," the murdered and murderous siblings are women. In a 1656 broadside version, the younger sister begs the older to save her, but she replies:

O sister, O sister, that may not bee,
Till salt and oatmeale grow both of a tree.

(Child 1882, 126)

The sister's refusal is aestheticized. The construction of the harp is considerably more grue-some than the shepherd's bleached-bone creation in "Singing": the miller makes her breast-bone into a "violl," with her fingers as pegs, her nose ridge as bridge, and her veins as strings. Her eyes, tongue, and shins also participate. The treble string identifies the "my father the king," the second string "my mother the queen," but all three "my sister that drowned mee." The viol[l] finally instructs that the miller be paid "for his payne,/And let him bee gone in the divel's name" (Child 1882, 126). The sister is perhaps understandably cross at the desecration of her corpse. Versions of the ballad by folk bands Old Blind Dogs and Pentangle, on YouTube, include a "Fa la la la la la la la la la la" refrain that in its lilting tune and "Deck the Halls" associations belies the murderous sister's dark plot and reinforces song's affective and cognitive transformations when combined with the tale.

With cante fable and ballads, the songs are not merely ornamentation but a deeper way of telling and experiencing a fairy tale. In most situations analyzed here, singing accumulates and shares knowledge through narrative and tangible, material objects that are then used and/or exchanged in order to bring about justice for the wronged family member in the tale. Because of collecting work by the Brothers Grimm and anthology-making by Francis James Child, these songs attributed to oral tradition acquire literary and scholarly status where they may be studied as printed verse (Wilgus 1959; McLane 2008). Marked in the text as verse or sung as part of storytelling performance in informal and mass-mediated contexts, intermedial versions allude to or may actually effect the transformations of spoken, printed, and heard words into song. If listeners and viewers participate in the singing, according to Toelken, they "share more than verbal information" but also "provide a living voice for the concerns of others (who may be far distant in time or space) who have also sung the songs" (1986, 169). While not tangible, song creates a nearly palpable transformation of the mundane that matches and conveys fairy-tale wonder.

Related topics: Cinematic; Crime/Justice; Disney Corporation; Language; Oral Tradition

Notes

1. Some material in this chapter comes from Greenhill (2014).
2. For information on Mulan films from China, see Li (2016).

References Cited and Further Reading

Bourke, Angela. 1999. *The Burning of Bridget Cleary: A True Story*. New York: Penguin.

Child, Francis James. 1882–1898. *The English and Scottish Popular Ballads*. 5 vols. Boston: Houghton Mifflin.

Frontczak, Susan Marie. 1995. "An Oral Tradition Perspective on Fairy Tales." *Marvels & Tales* 9 (2): 237–46.

Google. 2017. "Box office for Disney's *Beauty and the Beast*." April 26. http://bit.ly/2w8aCCJ.

Greenhill, Pauline. 1985. *Lots of Stories: Maritime Narratives from the Creighton Collection*. Ottawa: National Museums of Canada.

———. 2014. "Le piège d'Issoudun: Motherhood in Crisis." *Narrative Culture* 1 (1): 49–70.

Greenhill, Pauline, and Anne Brydon. 2010. "Mourning Mothers and Seeing Siblings: Feminism and Place in *The Juniper Tree*." In *Fairy Tale Films: Visions of Ambiguity*, edited by Pauline Greenhill and Sidney Eve Matrix, 116–36. Logan: Utah State UP.

Halpert, Herbert. 1942. "The Cante Fable in New Jersey." *Journal of American Folklore* 55 (217): 133–43.

———. 1962. "The Cante Fable in Decay." In *Folklore in Action: Essays for Discussion in Honor of MacEdward Leach*, edited by Horace P. Beck, 139–50. Philadelphia: American Folklore Society.

Harris, Joseph, and Karl Reichl, eds. 1997. *Prosimetrum: Crosscultural Perspectives on Narrative in Prose and Verse*. Cambridge: D. S. Brewer.

Heiner, Heidi Ann. N.d. "History of Cinderella." www.surlalunefairytales.com/cinderella/history.html.

Ives, Edward D. 1963. *Eight Folktales from Miramichi: As Told by Wilmot MacDonald*. Orono, ME: Northeast Folklore Society.

———. 1985. "'The Teamster in Jack McDaniel's Crew': A Song in Context and Its Singing." In *Folklife Annual*, edited by Alan Jabbour and James Hardin, 74–85. Washington, DC: American Folklife Center at the Library of Congress.

Jones, Christine A., and Jennifer Schacker, eds. 2013. *Marvelous Transformations: An Anthology of Fairy Tales and Contemporary Critical Perspectives*. Peterborough, ON: Broadview P.

Jorgensen, Jeana. 2012. "Queering Kinship in 'The Maiden Who Seeks Her Brothers'." In *Transgressive Tales: Queering the Grimms*, edited by Kay Turner and Pauline Greenhill, 69–89. Detroit: Wayne State UP.

Klein, Rachel. 2002. *The Moth Diaries*. Washington, DC: Counterpoint.

Li, Jing. 2016. "The Love Story, Female Images, and Gender Politics: Folktale Films in the People's Republic of China." In *Fairy-Tale Films Beyond Disney: International Perspectives*, edited by Jack Zipes, Pauline Greenhill, and Kendra Magnus-Johnston, 180–95. New York: Routledge.

Magnus-Johnston, Kendra. 2016. "'My Life as a Fairy Tale': The Fairy-Tale Author in Popular Cinema." In *Fairy-Tale Films Beyond Disney: International Perspectives*, edited by Jack Zipes, Pauline Greenhill, and Kendra Magnus-Johnston, 18–33. New York: Routledge.

McLane, Maureen. 2008. *Balladeering, Minstrelsy, and the Making of British Romantic Poetry*. Cambridge: Cambridge UP.

Nicolaisen, W. H. F. 1997. "The *Cante Fable* in Occidental Folk Narrative." In *Prosimetrum: Crosscultural Perspectives on Narrative in Prose and Verse*, edited by Joseph Harris and Karl Reichl, 183–211. Cambridge: D. S. Brewer.

"Tam Lin." N.d. Roud Folksong Index, Vaughan Williams Memorial Library. www.vwml.org/roudnumber/35.

Tatar, Maria. 1987. *The Hard Facts of the Grimm's Fairy Tales*. Princeton, NJ: Princeton UP.

———. 2004. *The Annotated Brothers Grimm*. New York: Norton.

Toelken, Barre. 1986. "Ballads and Folksongs." In *Folk Groups and Folklore Genres: An Introduction*, edited by Elliott Oring, 147–74. Logan: Utah State UP.

"The Twa Sisters." N.d. Roud Folksong Index, Vaughan Williams Memorial Library. www.vwml.org/roudnumber/8.

Uther, Hans-Jörg. 2004. *The Types of International Folktales: A Classification and Bibliography*. 3 vols. Helsinki: Academia Scientiarum Fennica.

Waltz, Robert B., and David G. Engle. 2017a. "Tam Lin [Child 39]." The Ballad Index. www.fresnostate.edu/folklore/ballads/C039.html.

———. 2017b. "Twa Sisters, The [Child 10]." The Ballad Index. www.fresnostate.edu/folklore/ballads/C010.html.

———. 2017c. "Willie's Lady [Child 6]." The Ballad Index. www.fresnostate.edu/folklore/ballads/C006.html.

Widdowson, J. D. A. 2009. "Folktales in Newfoundland Oral Tradition: Structure, Style, and Performance." *Folklore* 120 (1): 19–35.

Wilgus, D. K. 1959. *Anglo-American Folksong Scholarship since 1898*. New Brunswick, NJ: Rutgers UP.

"Willie's Lady." N.d. Roud Folksong Index, Vaughan Williams Memorial Library. www.vwml.org/roudnumber/220.

Wilson, William A. 2006. "The Deeper Necessity: Folklore and the Humanities." In *The Marrow of Human Experience: Essays on Folklore*, edited by Jill Terry Rudy with Diane Call, 9–22. Logan: Utah State UP.

Zeitchik, Steven. 2017. "A Music-Less *Mulan*? It's Far From Written in Stone." *LA Times*, March 22. www.latimes.com/entertainment/movies/la-et-mn-mulan-songs-niki-caro-20170322-story.html.

Zipes, Jack, ed. 2003. *The Complete Fairy Tales of the Brothers Grimm*. New York: Bantam Books.

Mediagraphy

Beauty and the Beast. 2017. Director Bill Condon. USA.

"The Cruel Sister" (Song). 1990. Artist Pentangle, album *Cruel Sister*. www.youtube.com/watch?v=P3S2brPXjEM

———. (Song). 1993. Artist Old Blind Dogs, album *Close to the Bone*. www.youtube.com/watch?v=yPbCi7eY5TM.

The Juniper Tree. 1990. Director Nietzchka Keene. Iceland/USA.

Le piège d'Issoudun (Juniper Tree). 2003. Director Micheline Lanctôt. Canada.

The Moth Diaries. 2011. Director Mary Harron. Canada/Ireland/USA.

Mulan. 1998. Directors Barry Crook and Tony Bancroft. USA.

———. 2018. Director Niki Caro. USA.

Snow White and the Seven Dwarfs. 1937. Directors David Hand, William Cottrell, Wilfred Jackson, Larry Morey, Perce Pearce, and Ben Sharpsteen. USA.

Tam Lin. 1970. Director Roddy McDowell. UK.

Whale Rider. 2002. Director Niki Caro. New Zealand/Germany.

The Wonderful World of the Brothers Grimm. 1962. Directors Henry Levin and George Pal. USA.

70

TELEVISION DRAMA
Fairy Tales and American TV Drama

Mikel J. Koven

Fairy tales appear to be everywhere today; in our cinemas and on our television screens. The success of series like *Once Upon a Time* (ABC, 2011–) and *Grimm* (NBC, 2011–2017) attests to their popularity. I explore how Cristina Bacchilega's (1997) "magic mirror" analogy can be used as a tool for analyzing contemporary American television dramas: these narratives (to some extent) *reflect* our experiential reality while also *refracting* that reflection through its implicit (occasionally explicit) metatextual commentary and *framed* as a simple fiction—merely an amusement. Specifically, I explore *Once Upon a Time* and *Grimm*, but also the earlier television series *Beauty and the Beast* (CBS, 1987–1990) and its recent reboot, *Beauty and the Beast* (The CW, 2012–2017).

Beauties and Beasts

In *Beauty and the Beast* (1987–1990), "Beauty" is Catherine Chandler (Linda Hamilton), a crusading assistant district attorney who works in the office towers and lives in the condos of mid-1980s Manhattan—a world of privilege, money, and power. Vincent (Ron Perlman), the series' "Beast," lives in an alternate world below the New York City streets—a subaltern world of poetry, music, philosophy, and kindness. Vincent rescues Catherine one evening and the two are instantly drawn to one another, despite their different worlds and Vincent's bestial leonine appearance (see figure 70.1).

Vincent's subterranean world is a fantasy-distorted commentary on contemporary (mid-1980s) New York. The series' city is a land of chrome and glass skyscrapers, a yuppie paradise for the elite. Catherine is this world's veritable princess, who turns her back on a successful law career at her father's prestigious law firm to work for the nearly bankrupt District Attorney's Office. Vincent's world is the opposite: a place in which the humanities are prized above material wealth. It is a land of art, music, literature, honor, and beauty, in marked contrast to the *in*humanities of the 1980s business world. All the detritus that New York throws away, that it devalues, finds its way into Vincent's world, including the people who can't, or won't, survive in the last years of Mayor Ed Koch's city. But like the world above, and despite the series' pretense of a romanticized utopia, the world below is actually a dictatorship (albeit a benevolent one) under the gentle, learned, and fair hand of Jacob Wells (Roy Dotrice), whom everyone calls "Father"—quite literally a patriarchy. Very few female characters are given storylines in this world, beyond Catherine's own.

625

Figure 70.1 Beauty and the Beast's (1987–1990) Linda Hamilton and Ron Perlman

Applying Bacchilega's "magic mirror" paradigm, *Beauty and the Beast* reflects (superficially) the social and political issues of the day via the generic requirements of an episodic crime series: crime, drugs, political corruption, slum landlords, and the like make up most plotlines. And like most television crime shows, the divide between good and bad tends to be simplistically polar and, as such, is not that different from fairy tales. The show's cultural critique seems to hope that although our world appears removed from the Enlightenment and Renaissance humanities, we have not *lost* such scholarship, despite its apparent absence and irrelevance to our (postmodern) age. The fantasy is that Vincent's world is a veritable ark of knowledge and art, a subaltern bricolage waiting out the deluge of corporate exploitation. *Beauty and the Beast* articulates the refracted desire to balance urban wealth and the human soul. The circular entryways that connect Vincent's utopia with Catherine's commercial dystopia (via subway tunnels and storm drains), and in particular the oft-repeated image of the spiral staircase, suggests the harmony between these two worlds.

While CBS produced a third season of *Beauty and the Beast* as a mid-season replacement in 1990, due primarily to pressure on the network and its advertisers by the series' legion of fans, that final (half) season disappointed many. In an effort to attract more male viewers, more emphasis was placed on action than on the romance between Vincent and Catherine. Viewers tuned out. Jump ahead twenty-two years, and the American cable network The CW brings *Beauty and the Beast* (2012–2016) back to television screens. The CW itself, known for its teenage and young adult audiences (and advertising demographic), was a corporate marriage between CBS and Time Warner, so the ownership of the series is still held effectively by the same parent company.

Beauty and the Beast (2012–2016) (to distinguish it from the 1987 series) keeps little of the original but the characters' names. Catherine "Cat" Chandler (Kristin Kreuk) is now a plucky New York cop whose life was saved when she was a little girl by a mysterious defender whom she later recognizes as Vincent (Jay Ryan) (see figure 70.2). Vincent, in this reboot, is a

Figure 70.2 Beauty and the Beast's (2012–2016) Kristin Kreuk and Jay Ryan

genetically modified super-soldier, officially declared dead on the Afghanistan battlefields; his bestial qualities of super-strength, agility, and speed come out when he is in a heightened state of fear or arousal. And unlike Perlman's cat-like makeup, the 2012 Vincent gets veiny and his eyes glow yellow when in beast mode. The other beasts in this fantasy New York, genetically modified individuals who are "Fireproof" or otherwise "Upgraded," offer worthy opponents for Vincent to fight to protect his Cat.

The transformation of "Beauty and the Beast" (ATU 425C) from fairy tale to young adult (YA) fantasy is awkward, particularly as the production shifted further away from the 1987 series. While the latter appealed to a more mainstream (presumed) adult audience, the 2012 series aims for a younger demographic. The show's action/detective frame remains, but unlike the earlier *Beauty and the Beast*, the 2012 series relies less on stand-alone episodic structure in favor of more serial storytelling with narrative arcs spanning entire seasons, as well as across seasons, in what Jason Mittell (2015) calls "Complex TV." This change of narrative structure is due, in large part, to the changes in television consumption. In the late 1980s, viewers watched a television show on a regular basis, week by week, as it was broadcast. Now viewers tend to "binge watch" entire seasons over a few days through DVD box sets and streaming media platforms such as Netflix and other on-demand services. This change in consumption impacts series storytelling, by enabling television shows to develop more complicated narrative arcs, because of the expectation that several episodes will be watched consecutively in an evening (see Mittell 2015).[1]

The change to the physical frame (in Bacchilega's sense of the structure and shape that hold the "magic mirror") is not the only divergence from the 1987 CBS series. While adults over The CW's key age demographic can certainly binge watch a contemporary television series, the move to more serial storytelling suggests calculated programming policies reflecting how producers believe YA audiences consume television shows. By changing its structure and shape, they make *Beauty and the Beast* a different television narrative in 2012 than it was in 1987.

Beauty and the Beast (2012–2016) better reflects contemporary television aesthetics (faster paced editing, prettier people), at least for that all-important YA consumer market. Unlike the subterranean world Vincent inhabited in 1987, the 2012 iteration takes place entirely in a vague facsimile of the present day. Instead of 1987 creator Ron Koslow's "Ark of Humanities" waiting out the deluge of consumer capitalism (but not patriarchy), Sherri Cooper-Landsman and Jennifer Levin's 2012 reboot posits the secret agency Muirfield working within the U.S. military-industrial complex as the locus of the series' fantasy; in Claudia Schwabe's terms (2014), both "Father" Jacob's underground (patriarchal) utopia and the murky machinations of Muirfield function as second realities. In *Beauty and the Beast's* (2012–2016) reflection of the (televised) real world, while it's far from *realistic*, the (first) reality reflects what contemporary audiences expect from a representation of reality on television as established by countless other series' images of New York (see Trifonova 2007, 261–306). In this regard, the magic mirror's reflection is an extension of the frame's generic demands: an (apparently correct) assumption that a successful television drama, even with overtones of fantasy, must be rooted within the external reality of audience expectation. Even a fantastic corporate conspiracy narrative needs to be vaguely plausible, at least for the series' YA demographic. A subterranean world of poetry and art, in the bowels of a great metropolis, is no longer an acceptable locus for believable fantasy, an oxymoron that seems to reflect The CW's main audience's expectations.

The larger ideological resonances to *Beauty and the Beast* (2012–2016) take this argument further: showrunners (television producer/writers) Cooper-Landsman and Levin have ostensibly adapted Koslow's television property for the twenty-first century; however, in doing so, they've removed much of the fantasy world that presumably was the draw of the series in the first place. There's very little recognizable from the fairy tale itself; science fiction replaces anything potentially enchanted. *Beauty and the Beast* (2012–2016) is less a fairy-tale television show than it is a superhero show with bestial Vincent a kind of Incredible Hulk for The CW audience: rugged, hunky, and shallow. A New York City firefighter before 9/11 (his brother died in one of the towers), he went to medical school to become a doctor before being shipped out to Afghanistan (where Muirfield began experimenting on him). Vincent is more or less able to control his beast mode, except when he is emotionally (or sexually) aroused. Vincent becomes even more sexy in beast mode, suggesting viewers will find him that much more hunky with a streak of danger to him. As played by Ryan, Vincent is a super-hunk genetically modified to be the ultimate YA pin-up; even when in full beast mode, he retains this pheromonal attractiveness. Magic and wonder have been replaced by a thin layer of science fiction and bodice-ripping romance. For the YA audience, passion, romance, and nefarious government subcontractors are as mysterious as man-beasts and true-love's kiss.

Once Upon a Grimm

Once Upon a Time (2011–) takes place in two different worlds, an enchanted kingdom of fairy tales come to life ("Land with Magic") and a small Maine town, Storybrooke, in what is ostensibly our world ("Land without Magic"), connected by magical portals. Emma Swan (Jennifer Morrison) is a bail bonds collector brought to Storybrooke by ten-year-old Henry Mills (Jared Gilmore), who claims to be her relinquished birth son. Henry believes that everyone in Storybrooke is actually a fairy-tale character (Snow White, Gepetto, Prince Charming, Rumpelstiltskin, and so on) under a forgetting spell cast by the Evil Queen and mayor of Storybrooke, his adopted mother, Regina (Lana Parrilla). The first season is more or less concerned with breaking that spell. Once the spell is broken, various curses, imprisonments, coups, usurpations, and other narrative contrivances justify movement between these two worlds to fuel the series' narrative across (to date) six seasons (see Hay and Baxter 2014; Schwabe 2014).

To be sure, one key pleasure of *Once Upon a Time* is the anachronistic play of setting fairy-tale characters in our modern experienced world and, conversely, bringing our logic and contemporary style to the enchanted kingdom. Snow White (Ginnifer Goodwin) has become a school teacher, the Evil Queen is the mayor, Rumpelstiltskin (Robert Carlyle) (see figure 70.3) is the town's pawnbroker, and Granny (Beverley Elliott) owns the town restaurant where Red Riding Hood/Ruby Lucas (Meghan Ory) works. Although the narrative is contrived, as Bacchilega's mirror is phenomenologically reflective, the series creates new adventures for familiar characters while inviting comparisons of idealized character types with lived experiences. Presumably, one watches *Once Upon a Time* to become involved in the serialized narrative (the frame) with characters known since the nursery, experiencing new stories and adventures (the reflection).

In addition to the stable of fairy-tale protagonists one would expect to see in this "Land with Magic," *Once Upon a Time* includes additional characters whose familiarity derives from the movies: Mulan (Jamie Chung) fights among the heroes of fairyland, Princess Aurora (Sarah Bolger) does her *Sleeping Beauty* bit (a la Disney's 1959 version), the Evil Queen's sister is Maleficent (Kirstin Bauer van Straten), and Tinker Bell (Rose McIver) makes an appearance, as does Captain Hook (Colin O'Donoghue). Season 4 brought *Frozen* (2013) to life with live-action

Figure 70.3 *Once Upon a Time*'s (2011–) Robert Carlyle as Rumpelstiltskin

Elsa (Georgina Haig) and Anna (Elizabeth Lail) moving between the two lands, and Season 5 introduces Merida (Amy Manson) from *Brave* (2012). In many respects, *Once Upon a Time* reflects our familiarity with the Disney fairy-tale film (see Zipes 2011) by including these figures within the televisual narrative.

Once Upon a Time can be so disarmingly benign we lose sight of the magic mirror's *refraction*, of what the series *actually* says underneath the sweet candy exterior. To begin with, since 1996, the American Broadcasting Company (operating since 1943 as ABC) has been owned by Disney. At no point in the series is Disney, or its immediately associated iconography (such as Mickey Mouse), mentioned in the show. ABC Studios is given full and sole credit for producing the series; Disney is never mentioned. And yet, particularly in the "Land with Magic," the traditional fairy-tale characters, where possible, are the *authorized* Disney versions, in yet another attempt for the Company to try and lay claim to these creations of the folk imagination. The costumes, magical attributes, histories, and narratives all specifically ape the Disney film versions. Characters crop up, seemingly out of nowhere, serving primarily to further demonstrate Disney's hegemony throughout this "Land with Magic." By furthering Disney's claim on the folktale characters, *Once Upon a Time* becomes the smiling, happy, benign face of what is essentially an extension of copyright ownership of (mostly European) intangible heritage. By ABC Studios (that is, Disney) producing a show titled *Once Upon a Time*, which further extends copyright into normalized representations of the characters, Disney may also seek to copyright, and therefore lay ownership to, the phrase "once upon a time" itself.

Grimm is another story altogether (see figure 70.4). Nick Burkhardt (David Giuntoli), a Portland detective, discovers he is a Grimm, a line of assassins who trace their history back to Central European origins. Grimms kill Wesen, a diverse species of animal/human hybrids who can hide their bestial natures and countenances from most people. Grimms see them for what they are and historically simply killed them: wolf-like Blutbads, fox-like Fuchsbaus, ogre Hexenbiests, and dozens of others. Jacob and Wilhelm, the Brothers Grimm, weren't *named*

Figure 70.4 Members of the *Grimm* (2011–2017) cast

Grimm, they *were* Grimms, and their *Kinder- und Hausmärchen* was a guide to these "monsters" (see Willsey 2014; Schwabe 2014).

Grimm features a strong central cast: Nick's partner, Hank (Russell Hornsby), and fiancée, Juliette (Bitsie Tulloch), are human, but he is assisted in understanding the Wesen world by Blutbad Monroe (Silas Weir Mitchell) and Fuchsbau Rosalee (Bree Turner). Nick's captain, Sean Renard (Sasha Roiz), is half-Zauberbiest, a Hexenbiest who can work magic. While *Grimm* offers story arcs that reach across entire and multiple seasons, the series is more episodic than *Once Upon a Time* or *Beauty and the Beast* (2012–2016). In the first season, each episode introduced a different kind of Wesen and how it could be killed, in a kind of monster-of-the-week form of televisual storytelling. As the series progressed, the narrative became more serial while maintaining the frame of a police procedural mixed with supernatural fantasy. Folkloric elements do not reach much beyond the series' premise, that Grimms' fairy tales are guides to the Wesen who walk among us. With the frame of the hour-long prime time drama, the series' reflection is both generic (police procedural meets supernatural fantasy) and largely mimetic in that the action occurs within our recognizable world.

Despite the series' mimetic cinematography (see Lukasiewicz 2010), monstrous Hexenbiest do not walk among us. The world of the Wesen is the refraction in the magic mirror, a self-conscious artificial construction that enables the series to comment on contemporary America. Fantasy as a genre, when used well, can be a subversive voice, just like fairy tales (see Warner 1995; Zipes 1983). Grimm and Wesen folklore is filled with stories that make monstrous the fantastical Other and narrate their adversarial relationship. Yet Nick fulfills his duties as a police officer, sworn to protect and serve, and as a Grimm, punishing Wesen who break the law, but equally trying to reassure their law-abiding counterparts that he is no threat to them, despite what the stories say. *Grimm* becomes an analogy for racial/ethnic harmony in America, where humans, Grimms, and Wesen can live peacefully together. While some Wesen are violent and drawn to criminality, often the attraction toward the wrong side of the law for others, particularly young Wesen, results from their socio-economic deprivation. Monroe practices an extensive regime of yoga and vegetarianism to keep his wolf-self at bay. He and Rosalee become models for ethnic/racial assimilation; they have pride in and openly celebrate their Wesen culture while also mixing freely with non-Wesen.

As refracted discourse, a fantasy series like *Grimm* can raise issues about cultural diversity without the inclusive sentiments always coming across as preachy or cloying. In one episode in particular, "One Night Stand" (3.04), *Grimm* explores Naiad fundamentalism: Dominic (Derek Ray) and Jessie (Coltron James) want to retain their old world traditions, separate from human beings. Within their worldview, any Wesen who tries to join mainstream (that is, human) society has betrayed their race. Their Naiad neighbor, Elly (Stephanie Nogueras), who demonstrates love and affection for humans, deserves to be "cut," having the telae between the fingers and toes severed.[2] While an attempt is made to justify Dominic and Jesse's fundamentalism based on a Wesen fear of difference in a human world, Nick dismisses that as rationalization, suggesting that Wesen need to get over their fear. None of the social commentary is particularly sophisticated or subtle; fantasy doesn't have to be in order to work. And that's what this fairy-tale television ultimately does; it enables its audience to discuss social issues in the context of plausible deniability of its inherent subversion.

Converging Realities

Schwabe (2014) distinguishes between a first reality (the world as we experience it mediated by conventional narrative television) with a second reality (the fantasy realm). The narrative spaces these two realities share are those moments when the fantastic bleeds into the everyday, thereby creating a third reality, a magical realist space where the marvelous coexists with the banal. *Beauty and the Beast* (1987–1990) bifurcates the worlds explicitly, with Catherine's suggestive of the first reality, Vincent's the second reality, and the spiral and circular openings that join the two worlds as the spaces of that third reality. *Once Upon a Time* also has a distinct separation between the first two realities—the (idealized) experiential reality of contemporary Maine and the fantasy world of the fairy-tale land. Storybrooke itself is that third reality where the two converge, a place of "neomagical realism" (Lukasiewicz 2010) where the fantastic unproblematically coexists with the banal.

Beauty and the Beast (2012–2016) exists entirely in the third reality; while Cat's life before meeting Vincent may be a kind of first reality, and the secretive world of Muirfield a second, the series is based around the third where the two realities converge. *Grimm*, too, exists in this third reality: Hank and Sergeant Wu (Reggie Lee) exist in an idealized yet recognizable facsimile of our world (the first reality), and the Wesen suggest a second, while the series as a whole also occupies that third reality wherein they interact with our world. In fact, reading ideologically, *Grimm*'s third reality suggests that Wesen have always existed in the first reality and that, like humans, most are fine, law-abiding individuals; Wesen may be different, but apparently we've always used the same toilets, and everything is okay. Whether Wesen suggest immigrants, transgender folks, or non-Christians, *Grimm*'s third reality destabilizes the homogeneity of its first reality by infusing its second reality/fantasy.

Bacchilega developed her "magic mirror" analogy to discuss contemporary women's fiction that made free and provocative use of fairy-tale narratives. While not advanced to study popular television, the model is particularly well suited for it. The live-action cinematography and location shooting create a degree of mimetic reflection; in addition, genre conventions (like police procedurals) suggest familiarity with the narrative and the expectations of a viewing audience. Their highly conservative narrative frames and banal address to our experienced world enable the fairy-tale television show to be studied, for example, for its implicit copyright control of the folk narratives on which it is based or to discuss issues of race/ethnicity in an increasingly culturally complex North America. While my examples explicitly reference fairy-tale conventions, future research could apply Bacchilega's magic mirror to other television drama to see what ideas of the folk imagination are refracted in them.

Related topics: Advertising; Broadcast; Cinematic; Crime/Justice; Disney Corporation; Intellectual Property; Reality TV; Romance

Notes

1. This transformation began in the late 1990s with shows like *Buffy the Vampire Slayer* (The WB/UPN, 1997–2003), *Angel* (The WB, 1999–2004), and *The X-Files* (Fox, 1993–2002), series that were not only watched compulsively week to week, but also through fan consumption of video box sets.
2. While Naiads are not mermaids, per se, Elly is deaf in a nod to Hans Christian Andersen's mute mermaid. While Andersen's mermaid is never named, Elly is not too different from Ariel, Disney's *The Little Mermaid* (1989). Deaf and mute are not the same, and Elly and Ariel are not identical names, but each has an echo of the other. Vague references can also be meaningful, in what Jorgensen calls fairy-tale "fragments" (2007) and Michael Dylan Foster calls "fuzzy allusions" (2016).

References Cited and Further Reading

Bacchilega, Cristina. 1997. *Postmodern Fairy Tales: Gender and Narrative Strategies.* Philadelphia: U Pennsylvania P.
Foster, Michael Dylan. 2016. "The Folkloresque Circle: Toward a Theory of Fuzzy Allusion." In *The Folkloresque*, edited by Foster and Tolbert, 41–63.

Foster, Michael Dylan, and Jeffrey A. Tolbert, eds. 2016. *The Folkloresque: Reframing Folklore in a Popular Culture World.* Logan, UT: Utah State UP.

Greenhill, Pauline, and Sidney Eve Matrix, eds. 2010. *Fairy Tale Films: Visions of Ambiguity.* Logan: Utah State UP.

Greenhill, Pauline, and Jill Terry Rudy, eds. 2014. *Channeling Wonder: Fairy Tales on Television.* Detroit: Wayne State UP.

Hay, Rebecca, and Christa Baxter. 2014. "Happily Never After: The Commodification and Critique of Fairy Tale in ABC's *Once Upon a Time.*" In *Channeling Wonder*, edited by Greenhill and Rudy, 318–35.

Jorgensen, Jeana. 2007. "A Wave of the Magic Wand: Fairy Godmothers in Contemporary American Media." *Marvels & Tales* 21 (2): 216–27.

Lukasiewicz, Tracie D. 2010. "The Parallelism of the Fantastic and the Real: Guillermo del Toro's *Pan's Labyrinth/El Laberinto del fauno* and Neomagical Realism." In *Fairy Tale Films*, edited by Greenhill and Matrix, 60–78.

Mittell, Jason. 2015. *Complex TV: The Poetics of Contemporary Television Storytelling.* New York: NYU P.

Schwabe, Claudia. 2014. "Getting Real with Fairy Tales: Magic Realism in *Grimm* and *Once Upon a Time.*" In *Channeling Wonder*, edited by Greenhill and Rudy, 294–315.

Trifonova, Temenuga. 2007. *The Image in French Philosophy.* Amsterdam: Rodopi.

Warner, Marina. 1995. *From the Beast to the Blonde: On Fairy Tales and their Tellers.* New York: Vintage.

Willsey, Kristiana. 2014. "New Fairy Tales are Old Again: *Grimm* and the Brothers Grimm." In *Channeling Wonder*, edited by Greenhill and Rudy, 210–28.

Zipes, Jack. (1983) 2006. *Fairy Tales and the Art of Subversion.* London: Routledge.

———. 2011. *The Enchanted Screen: The Unknown History of the Fairy-Tale Film.* London: Routledge.

Mediagraphy

Angel (TV). 1999–2004. Creator Joss Whedon and David Greenwalt. USA.

Beauty and the Beast (TV). 1987–1990. Creator Ron Koslow. USA.

——— (TV). 2012. Creators Sherri Cooper-Landsman and Jennifer Levin. Canada.

Brave. 2012. Directors Mark Andrews, Brenda Chapman and Steve Purcell. USA.

Buffy the Vampire Slayer (TV). 1997–2003. Creator Joss Whedon. USA.

Frozen. 2013. Directors Chris Buck and Jennifer Lee. USA.

Grimm (TV). 2011–2017. Creators Stephen Carpenter, David Greenwalt, and Jim Kouf. USA.

The Little Mermaid. 1989. Directors Ron Clements and John Musker. USA.

Mulan. 1998. Directors Tony Bancroft and Barry Cook. USA.

Once Upon a Time (TV). 2011. Creators Adam Horowitz and Edward Kitsis. USA.

Sleeping Beauty. 1959. Director Clyde Geronimi. USA.

The X-Files (TV). 1993–2002. Creator Chris Carter. USA.

71

VIDEO GAMES

Emma Whatman and Victoria Tedeschi

Over the past forty years, fairy tales have proven to be easily adaptable to the medium of video games. Like other forms of digital media, video games draw on fairy-tale narratives, motifs, and iconography to form part of the diverse body of fairy-tale media texts. However, unlike many other such texts, fairy-tale video games offer the medium-specific affordances of the form that often rely on player interactivity and decision making. Video game studies is still in its youth, having only emerged in the 1980s (see Egenfeldt-Nielsen, Smith, and Tosca 2015); however, it already boasts a range of approaches including, but not limited to, narratology, theories of representation, postmodernism, and art theory (see Wolf and Perron 2003). Not only is the video game industry a "financial juggernaut" (Egenfeldt-Nielson, Smith, and Parajes 2015, 7) worthy of attention, but video games also demand critical analysis of their cultural, aesthetic, and ideological affordances and limitations. Our focus here is on how fairy-tale video games adapt their source narratives and motifs to the medium and, as a result, how ideological concerns—such as gender, trauma, and abuse—are entangled within these constructs. This chapter identifies a current rising trend of revisionist fairy-tale video games that offer a virtual space for players to explore the darker undercurrents of the fairy-tale form through player interactivity and culpability. Many fairy-tale video games seek to romanticize or sensationalize their source narratives, yet fairy-tale video games can also offer a space of catharsis, exposing the transformative power and wish-fulfillment potential that the fairy tale has to offer.

Video games have largely been omitted from previous studies on fairy-tale media, featuring, for example, only briefly in the section "digital fairy tales" by Joellyn Rock in the 2015 *Oxford Companion to Fairy Tales*. In one of the only pieces specifically dedicated to fairy-tale video games, B. Grantham Aldred includes them with board games and card games under a broader section on fairy-tale games in the 2016 *Folktales and Fairy Tales: Traditions and Texts from around the World*, highlighting that games based on folktales and fairy tales have been present "since at least the nineteenth century" (392). He argues that folktales and fairy tales cannot be easily adapted into the game form as they are "noted for linear narratives, while games require interactivity to create dramatic tension" (392), and proposes a number of methods that enable this to happen. These include, 1) protagonist insertion, 2) morphological division, 3) genre blending, 4) fairy-tale pastiche, and 5) point-of-view development (392). These are necessary distinctions, and we expand on them to demonstrate how fairy-tale video games constitute a new media vessel that evidences shifting social, cultural, and political ideologies.

Indeed, as Donald Haase argues, burgeoning new media and technology have turned fairy tales "into an un-manageable and un-imaginable universe of stories" that has "no borders, no limits," and thus, the increasing "digitization of the folktale and fairy-tale corpus also challenges us to develop new modes of analysis" (2016, 77–78). Fairy tales are cultural placeholders; their inclusion in video games relies on their ability to transfer cultural and ideological information to the player. As such, fairy-tale video games require specific scrutiny of ideological function through the aesthetics, conventions, and interactive capabilities of a medium that often requires users to make decisions, fulfill tasks, and participate in role-playing scenarios. Video games often move away from typically linear representations, such as those in oral tales, books, and films, and can instead introduce forms of non-linear *interactivity* where players are positioned as implicit in the outcome and ideological closure of a game. Ultimately, the affordances of this medium, such as interactivity, player culpability, and character representation, which shape the messages circulated through video games, merit specific and close examination, rather than being subsumed under broader categories such as digital media or games.

A number of the video games we discuss here evidence these notions while also demonstrating a move to the darker traditions of earlier fairy tales and oral folktales. Such tales were powerful as they "presented the stark realities of power politics without disguising the violence and brutality of everyday life" by expressing the "abandonment of children, rape, corporeal punishment, ruthless exploitation" (Zipes 2006a, 7–8), and death. The fairy tale also has the potential to offer "future vistas for the possibility of transformation" (Zipes 2006b, 100), as it is a "broad arena" that "takes the form of a mammoth discourse" to represent and explore ideological and sociopolitical power (Zipes 1997, 7). As Jacquelyn Morie and Celia Pearce indicate in their discussion of fairy-tale computer games, these transformations suggest possibilities that cannot be explored or tested in the "real world, a place where imagination must succumb to the exigencies of survival" (2008, 10). Thus, we argue that fairy-tale video games offer a virtual space for players to both explore the "violence and brutality of everyday life" (Zipes 2006a, 7) and experience the transformative potentials the fairy tale offers.

Since Nintendo's *The Legend of Zelda* (1986–2017) and Square Enix's *Final Fantasy* series (1987–2016), video games have capitalized on fantasy narratives and Campbellian monomyths. While video games featuring distressed damsels and knight errantry have thrived, games showcasing fairy-tale plots, patterns, and iconography have abounded since the early 1990s. Sierra On-Line's *Mixed-Up Fairy Tales* (1992) is an early adventure and object-acquiring game targeted at young users. The game uses both protagonist insertion and morphological division—where tales are broken into parts, "often based on motifs, functions, characters, or objects" (Aldred 2016, 392)—as an unnamed child protagonist (the player) is inserted into a fairy-tale world where he or she must seek out specific iconography from classic fairy tales. The game begins to recount a version of a classical tale, such as "Cinderella" (ATU 510A), when it is noted that tale-specific objects (such as the pumpkin) have gone missing. The player is then tasked with finding the object so that the tale, and the game, can be completed. Similarly, PlayPond's *Mystery Legends: Beauty and the Beast* (2011) is a dark fantasy object-acquiring puzzle game. Situated within the world of "Beauty and the Beast" (ATU 425C), players must seek specific objects, such as a dagger and a pitchfork, and complete puzzles in order to find "soul shards" of Beast and complete the tale. Both games are linear as they "prioritize the structure of the original stories" (Aldred 2016, 394) yet rely on player interactivity to reach narrative closure.

Unlike *Mixed-Up Fairy Tales* and *Mystery Legends*, many fairy-tale video games are targeted at older players and incorporate violence and non-linear interactivity. Playlogic Game Factory's 2009 *Fairytale Fights* is a fairy-tale pastiche (Aldred 2016, 392) combat action game—specifically a hack-and-slash game—where users play as either Jack ("Jack and the Beanstalk," ATU 328), the Naked Emperor (from "The Emperor's New Clothes," ATU 1620), "Little Red Riding Hood" (ATU 333), or "Snow White" (ATU 709). The characters have lost their fame and wish to reclaim it, and as the press release for the game boasts, "Luckily, many different weapons lay strewn throughout the fairytale kingdom, which players can use to slice and dice their way through swathes of cute fluffy bunnies and imposing enemies" (Playlogic 2009).

Fairytale Fights functions simplistically as a combat game, enabling players to indeed hack, slash, and kill opponents with the added bonus of a "volumetric liquid system" (Playlogic 2009) that provides realistic properties, meaning players can skid and slip through puddles of blood.

With its history and ties to sexuality and violence, "Little Red Riding Hood" is a marketable choice for game developers. Rather than proliferating the image of the protagonist as a child *ingénue*, the titular character is often remodeled into a violent avatar. Harking back to Roald Dahl's "Little Red Riding Hood and the Wolf" (1982) in which the child protagonist kills and skins the wolf predator, Capcom's gothic-horror *Darkstalkers* series (1994–2013) recasts Little Red Riding Hood as a skilled fighter and mercenary. Set with the task of hunting down otherworldly monsters, Baby Bonnie Hood is outfitted with a submachine gun, land mines, Molotov cocktail, knives, and apple-shaped grenades. She carries her artillery in her picnic basket, which also functions as a rocket launcher. Among her array of attacks, she can summon the spirit of her grandmother to deliver fatal blows and can fire heavy artillery with the help of two huntsmen. Despite being set in a pastiche gothic-horror universe, Baby Bonnie Hood's pet dog and the flock of birds that circle around her function as cultural markers of the heroine's saccharine past, contrasting the normative image of the child ideal with the mercenary's penchant for explosive devices. Baby Bonnie Hood subverts the "damsel in distress" trope, which is used to motivate the agency of male characters. She is not a passive protagonist who is killed as in Perrault's "Le Petit Chaperon Rouge" (1697), or who otherwise must be saved via male intervention as the Grimms' "Rotkäppchen" (1812) suggests. On the contrary, through her acquired supernatural powers, independence, and agency, Baby Bonnie Hood serves as an ironic and reflexive character who subverts the archetype of the innocent child.

EnjoyUp and Gammick Entertainment's *Little Red Riding Hood's Zombie BBQ* (2008) features a similar interpretation of the classic fairy-tale character. Classified as a standard combat rail-shooter—in which the player's control of the avatar is limited to firing and dodging oncoming attacks—the gameplay follows Red "Ready to Rock" Riding Hood as she defends Storyland from a hoard of ravenous zombies. The outbreak has a devastating effect on popular fairy-tale characters such as Pinocchio, Sleeping Beauty, and Gretel, who appear as demonic versions of their more familiar selves. The distortion of these pre-textual characters "serve[s] as a carnival mirror, concurrently parodying the saccharine-sweet retellings of the stories that turn characters into facile, mindless, pleasure-seeking creatures while also recovering the original violence and sexuality original to the tales" (Keebaugh 2013, 592).

To prevent the townsfolk from further corruption, Red is equipped with a machine gun, a flame thrower, and a laser beam. According to game designer Julio Moruno, Red's proficiency with firearms, alongside her sexualized representation, offers an intoxicating image for the player "who would have imagined this cute little girl pulling the trigger like this to defend [t]his land from such evil creatures!" (Keebaugh 2013, 593). In this way, Red resembles fictional characters such as Buffy Summers (*Buffy the Vampire Slayer*, 1997–2003) and Vanessa Lutz (*Freeway*, 1996) who have long subverted the trope of the distressed damsel. In *Little Red Riding Hood's Zombie BBQ*, Red is no longer the "little" darling from her village. On the contrary, the child is supplanted with a shapely woman who flaunts an exposed *derrière*. While comparatively Baby Bonnie Hood is not a visual manifestation for the male gaze, her "win quotes" (the phrase spoken by a victorious character after defeating an opponent) are certainly suggestive. One of the phrases superimposed on an image of her winking face reads, "Wanna play with an innocent girl like me? You bad boy!" (*Darkstalkers 3* 1997), a concerning sentiment given that Baby Bonnie Hood is reportedly ten to fourteen years old. Both the *Darkstalkers* series and *Little Red Riding Hood's Zombie BBQ* are dependent on the associative power of the Red Riding Hood tale type, as each video game seeks to subvert the trope of the innocuous, obedient child with a pugnacious, sexually provocative woman. Rather than regulating gender roles, both video games seek to transform the traditional tale type by replacing the sexual predator (the infamous wolf) with a sexualized female protagonist.

While the previous games employ strategies such as fairy-tale pastiche and genre blending, point-of-view development happens when games "turn normally third person folktales and fairy tales into first person narratives" (Aldred 2016, 392). This practice is common in a number of fairy-tale video games; however, it is important to further distinguish between games that simply feature first-person narratives where players see through the eyes of the protagonist and games that require players to make choices and perform actions that make them implicit in both the narratological and ideological outcome of the game. For example, MoaCube's indie game *Cinders* (2012) is a visual novel game where players are faced with up to 120 decision points and over 300 options to choose from that lead to one of four endings. The player acts as the first-person protagonist, Cinders, who is adapted from the innocent persecuted heroine tale type (ATU 510).

The game's creators and developers argue that they chose the tale type because the protagonist is passive and their aim with this game was to create a "clever, active woman who makes her own choices" (Grochowiak 2011), who "is not afraid of taking fate into her own hands. Even if it means breaking the rules" (MoaCube 2012). This assertion suggests that players have the ability to take Cinders's fate into their own hands and break the rules of ATU 510. Each of the four endings has different categories, with different variants of each category built in. For example, if players pursue "The Fairytale Ending" (2012), the result of choosing to marry the Prince, they can become a "Fair Queen," "Evil Queen," "Machiavellic Queen," or "Good Queen." To become the Evil Queen, the player follows a path that relates to lying and being rude, lazy, and seductive. If players pursue the "Independent Woman," they must become the head of the house by either choosing to seek the stepmother's support, break her spirit, murder her, or imprison her. As such, players are held responsible for their choices and for building or dismantling relationships in order to get the outcome they desire.

LabLabLab's *A Tough Sell* (2014) is a natural language conversational game where players are cast as the Evil Queen of the "Snow White" tale, charged with the task of persuading Snow White to take a bite of a poisoned apple. Natural language conversational games involve players partaking in a conversation with a game that is designed to respond to what the user types, thus making it "natural" conversation between the player and software. Jonathan Lessard explains that the game "revolves on an economy of 'trust'" (2016, 4) where a progress bar fills or empties depending on what the user types to Snow White. The game also uses a "patience" bar that when emptied, means the player has lost and Snow White closes the door.

The game appears to be specifically modeled from the Grimms' "Schneewittchen" (1812); when the game begins, Snow White is reluctant to talk to strangers, as there have been previous attempts on her life. The challenge of the game is then for players to "build an understanding of Snow White's personality on the basis of her answers to devise and test trust-building approaches" (Lessard 2016, 4). If the trust bar fills, Snow White will eat the apple and the game finishes with, "Congratulations, you've murdered an innocent woman to satisfy your vanity" (*A Tough Sell* 2014). The game requires players to be invested in poisoning Snow White, as persuasion is the sole task of the game. Furthermore, rather than selecting a prewritten answer, as in *Cinders*, users must create and type their own response, making them more culpable in the attempt on Snow's life. Thus, when they "win" the game, they are explicitly implicated in the murder and are reminded that it is because of their own vain motives (as the stepmother from ATU 709).

Interactive gameplay and point-of-view development are also used to explore the limits of player culpability in Tale of Tales' psychological thriller *The Path* (2009). Based on ATU 333, the game features six playable protagonists (sisters aged from nine to nineteen) named after various shades of red. Once players have selected an avatar, they are instructed to "go to Grandmother's house and stay on the path" (*The Path* 2009). Should players adhere to these rules, the game ends abruptly with the selected avatar kneeling at the bed of her ailing grandmother. The result screen that follows informs players that they have failed, as players can only advance the narrative if they disobey and stray from the path.

Through their disobedience, players can explore locations, interact with grim objects, and decipher their avatar's past. Moreover, it is also in the woods where each girl can encounter a different wolf. Whether in the form of a human or an animal, the wolf perpetuates the child avatar's trauma and abuse. Each girl is ignorant of the imminent danger that lies in wait, leading to an interaction with the predator. After the encounter, the scene fades to black and each child is pictured lying on the path outside her grandmother's house. Upon entering the house, the camera angle reverts to first-person perspective, and the character moves independently through a series of long corridors. When she arrives in Grandmother's room, a sequence of broken images flash on the screen, depicting each girl being attacked by her wolf. The character selected is no longer playable, and the process repeats with the remaining sisters.

The Path rejects standard modes of gameplay that typically operate on the player's ability to follow instructions. The player is figuratively (and literally) placed in the position of Little Red Riding Hood, who is similarly punished for disobeying orders from an authoritative figure. Having made the decision to disobey, the player is "forced to watch the consequences with the helplessness that is characteristic of horror and tragedy" (Ryan and Costello 2012, 121). This is the paradox of the anti-game: it coerces the player to disregard instructions to advance the plot. By making players complicit in their avatar's demise, *The Path* effectively demonstrates the powerlessness felt by victims of childhood trauma and underscores themes of sexual violence prevalent in the tale's oral and literary tradition.

Similarly, sexual and emotional abuse are the fulcrum of cause and effect in Spicy Horse's third-person action-adventure video game *Alice: Madness Returns* (2011), which details trauma and recovery through the lens of a child protagonist. Set after the events of *American McGee's Alice* (2000), Alice Liddell is sent to an orphanage after witnessing the death of her parents and sister in a house fire. Unbeknownst to her, Alice's psychologist, Doctor Angus Bumby, caused the fire in an effort to silence her younger sister, Lizzy, the victim of his sexual abuse. As the sole survivor, Doctor Bumby must groom Alice into believing that she is responsible for the death of her family. Under Doctor Brumby's influence, Alice succumbs to "mournful catatonia, hallucinations, suicidal self-loathing and aggressive rage" (Kérchy 2016, 114). As a coping mechanism, Alice journeys to her mental retreat, Wonderland. It is only within this space of play that Alice can identify her family's murderer and reveal his secret child prostitution ring. Wonderland is both a manifestation of Alice's delusions and a site of recovery: it is a "psychogeographic realm simultaneously associated with trauma and remedy, a [site] of dangerous self-risking and empowering revenge which provide therapeutic release from suicidous passivity and remote while facing fatal annihilation" (116). Through reclaiming her selfhood in Wonderland, *Alice: Madness Returns* allows the child protagonist to regain social agency and acquire "vicarious catharsis, the clichéd resolution of a trauma narrative" (Fawcett 2016, 501). Both *The Path* and *Alice: Madness Returns* demonstrate how the fairy-tale video game can offer a virtual space to explore both physical and psychological trauma, along with the transformative and wish-fulfillment potential the fairy tale offers.

In video games, fairy-tale characters typically rebel against their sanitized counterparts. Their resistance to Disneyfication allows players to explore the deeper implications of the source material from which they have derived. Fairy-tale video games rarely present watered-down narratives with the intent of making the subject matter more pleasant or easily grasped. On the contrary, rather than rehashing idyllic outcomes, video games often showcase traditional fairy-tale characters as antiheroes with tragic backstories. "Blood and Wine," the final add-on adventure to CD Projekt RED's *The Witcher 3: Wild Hunt* (2015–2016), explores the ambivalence of human nature by featuring fairy-tale characters with devastating storylines.

As children, the Duchess of Toussaint, Anna Henrietta, and her older sister, Syanna, were able to enter "the land of a thousand fables" (2015–2016) by opening an enchanted book and reciting the correct incantation. Upon entering the fantastical realm, the sisters were able to interact and play with the iconic fairy-tale characters who dwelt there. However, as they grew older, Anna Henrietta and Syanna's relationship became strained, and they neglected to visit the fairy-tale world. Without their supervision and intervention, fairy-tale characters began to stray from their traditional storylines. For example, the Big Bad Wolf develops a drinking problem as he is stuck in a cyclic loop in which Little Red Riding Hood and the Huntsmen repeatedly brutalize him. Seeking to escape this cruel fate, the wolf "repay[s] the little imp for all her loving labour" by throwing her down a well (*The Witcher 3* 2016).

The protagonist, Geralt, must retrieve the famed red cloak from the girl's dead corpse in order to advance the plot. This reference to Little Red Riding Hood's demise certainly signals to fairy-tale tradition, particularly Charles Perrault's "Le Petit Chaperon Rouge," in which the titular character does not survive her encounter with the bestial predator. Additionally, Long-locks (modeled from "Rapunzel," ATU 310) also meets a tragic fate. Unbeknownst to her, the prince has died from attempting to scale her tower. Driven by loneliness, Longlocks commits suicide by hanging herself with her hair. Similarly, business is not booming for Hans Christian Andersen's Little Match Girl, who resorts to selling cigars, fisstech (a drug similar to amphet-amine), and "all sorts of fun things" to make ends meet (*The Witcher 3*, 2016). Interestingly, Geralt does not seek to rectify these tragic backstories. On the contrary, as a Witcher, Geralt's priority is in hunting monsters (such as the Big Bad Wolf and Longlocks's tortured spirit) for monetary gain. Such violent, revisionist tales hark back to a fairy-tale tradition that had the propensity to punish selected characters for the moral benefit of the implied child reader.

While some fairy-tale characters suffer from a traumatic past in video games, others are placed in dystopian settings in order to emphasize the graphic themes that underscore the source material. Telltale Games' *The Wolf Among Us* (2013) is a prime example of revisionism steeped in the neo-noir tradition, complete with a cynical detective protagonist and femmes fatales. Based on Bill Willingham's *Fables* comic book series (2002–2015), *The Wolf Among Us* follows the chain-smoking sheriff Bigby Wolf (modeled from ATU 333) as he investigates a murder of a prostitute named Faith (modeled from "Donkey Skin," ATU 510B). In order to decipher the murderer, Bigby must navigate around Fabletown's criminal underbelly, which is comprised of con-artists, embezzlers, standover men, drug dealers, and procurers.

The Wolf Among Us also involves interactive gameplay in which the player—having limited control over Bigby—is presented with a set of narratological choices in order to advance the plot. The video game is tailored to player activity and, consequently, player culpability. For example, during a bar brawl, the player has the option to dismember Grendel's arm, linking back to the monster's fatal wound inflicted by the protagonist in the Anglo-Saxon epic poem *Beowulf* (700–1000 C.E.). While Grendel survives the attack, the player loses the public's favor after the encounter, which affects the narrative later in the game. Moreover, after selecting specific dialogue options with certain characters, the game informs the player that the character in question will "remember that," thereby reinforcing player culpability (*The Wolf Among Us* 2013). The consequences of Bigby's actions are amplified, as they are the result of the player's decision making. In this way, "the player is not just an observer, [he or she] must accept some of the responsibility for the outcome" (Ryan and Costello 2012, 112). *The Wolf Among Us* uses the fairy-tale form as a means of self-reflection, as players are faced with an ethical quandary and are given the opportunity to consider and reflect upon their own morality.

Ever since Nintendo's *Mario* (1981–2016) franchise capitalized on the "damsel in distress" quest narrative, fairy tales have abounded in video games. Since then, protagonists have completed the hero's journey in Big Blue Box and Lionhead Studios' *Fable* (2004), have explored underwater cities in 2K Boston and 2K Australia's *BioShock* (2007), and have even battled Baba Yaga in Crystal Dynamics' *Rise of the Tomb Raider* (2013). Within their potential to stimulate the imagination, fairy-tale games offer a rich and immersive experience for players to explore the darker undercurrents of the fairy tale and negotiate ideological concerns such as gender, trauma, and abuse. By romanticizing or sensationalizing conventions of the fairy tale, video games provide a wealth of revisionist adaptations that expose the transformative power and wish-fulfillment potential that the fairy tale has to offer.

Related topics: Adaptation and the Fairy-Tale Web; Crime/Justice; Digital; Fantasy; Gender; Horror; Mobile Apps; Sexualities/Queer and Trans Studies; Storyworlds/Narratology

References Cited and Further Reading

Aldred, B. Grantham. 2016. "Games." In *Folktales and Fairy Tales: Traditions and Texts from Around the World*, edited by Anne E. Duggan, Donald Haase, and Helen J. Callow, 392–6. 2nd ed. Santa Barbara: Greenwood.

Dahl, Roald. 1982. "Little Red Riding Hood and the Wolf." In *Revolting Rhymes*, 36–40. London: Jonathan Cape.

Egenfeldt-Nielsen, Simon, Jonas Heide Smith, and Susana Pajares Tosca. 2015. *Understanding Video Games: The Essential Introduction.* 3rd ed. New York: Routledge.

Fawcett, Christina. 2016. "*American McGee's Alice: Madness Returns* and Traumatic Memory." *The Journal of Popular Culture* 49 (3): 492–521.

Grimm, Jacob, and Wilhelm Grimm. (1812) 1987. *The Complete Fairy Tales of the Brothers Grimm*, translated by Jack Zipes. New York: Bantam Books.

Grochowiak, Tom. 2011. "So What's Cinders About?" *MoaCube*, June 27. http://moacube.com/news/so-whats-cinders-about/.

Haase, Donald. 2016. "Challenges of Folktale and Fairy-Tale Studies in the Twenty-First Century." *Fabula* 75 (2–1): 73–85.

Keebaugh, Cari. 2013. "'The Better to Eat You[r Brains] With, My Dear': Sex, Violence, and *Little Red Riding Hood's Zombie BBQ* as Fairy Tale Recovery Project." *Journal of Popular Culture* 46 (3): 589–603.

Kérchy, Anna. 2016. *Alice in Transmedia Wonderland: Curiouser and Curiouser New Forms of a Children's Classic.* Jefferson, NC: McFarland.

Lessard, Jonathan. 2016. "Designing Natural-Language Game Conversations." Proceedings of the First International Joint Conference of DiGRA and FDG 1 (13). Dundee, Scotland.

MoaCube. 2012. "Cinders." *MoaCube.* http://moacube.com/games/cinders/.

Morie, Jacquelyn, and Celia Pearce. 2008. "Uses of Digital Enchantment: Computer Games as the New Fairy Tales." Proceedings of the Vienna Games Conference 2008: The Future of Reality and Gaming (FROG). Vienna, Austria.

Perrault, Charles. 1697. *Histories; or, Tales of Past Times.* New York: Garland, 1977.

Playlogic Entertainment Inc. 2009. "Playlogic Announces 'Fairytale Fights' . . . a Fairytale Unlike Any Other." *Market Wired*, April 28. www.marketwired.com/press-release/playlogic-announces-fairytale-fights-a-fairytale-unlike-any-other-1230596.htm.

Rock, Joellyn. 2015. "Digital Fairy Tales." In *The Oxford Companion to Fairy Tales*, edited by Jack Zipes, 153–4. Oxford: Oxford UP.

Ryan, Malcolm, and Brigid Costello. 2012. "My Friend Scarlet: Interactive Tragedy in the Path." *Games and Culture* 7 (2): 111–26.

VIDEO GAMES

Wolf, Mark J. P., and Bernard Perron. 2003. "Introduction." In *The Video Game Theory Reader*, edited by Mark J. P. Wolf and Bernard Perron, 1–24. New York: Routledge.

Zipes, Jack. 1997. *Happily Ever After: Fairy Tales, Children, and the Culture Industry*. New York: Routledge.

———. 2006a. *Fairy Tales and the Art of Subversion: The Classical Genre for Children and the Process of Civilization*. 2nd ed. New York: Routledge.

———. 2006b. *Why Fairy Tales Stick: The Evolution and Relevance of a Genre*. New York: Routledge.

Mediagraphy

Alice: Madness Returns (Video Game). 2011. Developer Spicy Horse, Director American McGee. http://www2.ea. com/alice.

American McGee's Alice (Video Game). 2000. Developer Rogue Entertainment, Director American McGee.

BioShock (Video Game). 2007. Developer 2K Games. www.2k.com/games/bioshock-the-collection.

Buffy the Vampire Slayer (TV). 1997–2003. Creator Joss Whedon. USA.

Cinders (Video Game). 2012. Developer MoaCube. http://moacube.com/games/cinders/.

Darkstalkers (Video Game). 1994–2003. Developer Capcom.

Fable (Video Game). 2004. Developer Big Blue Box Studios and Lionhead Studios.

Fables (Comics). 2002–2015. New York: Vertigo.

Fairytale Fights (Video Game). 2009. Developer Playlogic Game Factory, Director Olivier Lhermite. www.playlogicgames. com/game/fairytale-fights/.

Final Fantasy (Video Game). 1987–2016. Developer Square Enix.

Freeway. 1996. Director Matthew Bright. USA.

The Legend of Zelda (Video Game). 1986–2017. Creators Shigeru Miyamoto and Takashi Tezuka, Developer Nintendo. www.zelda.com/.

Little Red Riding Hood's Zombie BBQ (Video Game). 2008. Developer Enjoy Up and Gimmick Entertainment, Producer Jose M. Iñiguez, Designer Julio Moruno. www.nintendo.com/games/detail/5azEvG-3KHWZsBXLEiXRlEyU3j7 W2qHK.

Mario (Video Game). 1981–2016. Developer Nintendo, Creator Shigeru Miyamoto. http://mario.nintendo.com/.

Mixed-Up Fairy Tales (Video Game). 1992. Developer Sierra On-Line.

Mystery Legends: Beauty and the Beast (Video Game). 2011. Developer PlayPond.

The Path (Computer Game). 2009. Developer Tale of Tales. http://tale-of-tales.com/ThePath/.

Rise of the Tomb Raider (Video Game). 2013. Developer Crystal Dynamics, Producer Rose Hunt. http://buyrottr. com/us/.

A Tough Sell (Computer Game). 2014. Developer LabLabLab. www.lablablab.net/?page_id=33&lang=en.

The Witcher 3: Wild Hunt (Video Game). 2015–2016. Developer CD Projekt RED, Producers Piotr Krzywonosiuk and Jędrzej Mróz. http://thewitcher.com/en/witcher3.

The Wolf Among Us (Computer Game). 2013. Developer Telltale Games, Producer Chris Schroyer. https://telltale. com/series/the-wolf-among-us/.

72

YOUTUBE AND INTERNET VIDEO

Brittany Warman

The website YouTube (www.youtube.com) has become such an enormous part of Western online experiences that one would be hard pressed to find someone unfamiliar with it, but Michael Miller provides a concise, helpful overview:

> YouTube is a video sharing site that lets users upload and view all sorts of video clips online. The site has become a repository for literally millions of movie clips, TV clips (both current and classic), music videos, and home videos. The most popular YouTube videos quickly become "viral," getting passed around from email to email and linked to from other sites and blogs on the web. If a YouTube video is particularly interesting, you'll see it pop up virtually everywhere, from TV's *The Daily Show* to the front page of your favorite website.
>
> (2007, 7)

Conceived of by three friends, former PayPal employees Chad Hurley, Steven Chen, and Jawed Karim, YouTube launched in December 2005. It achieved almost instant popularity and was named Invention of the Year by *Time* magazine only a year after its initial appearance. In October 2006, the site was purchased by Google (Miller 2007, 9) and, as of 2013, streams "1.2 billion videos a day" (Vernallis 2013, 24). To "YouTube" something has become an acceptable and understood way of indicating that one is looking for a video on the site (Strangelove 2010, 5). Setting aside the commercial material that illegally makes its way online, I explore the presence of the fairy tale on YouTube.

The world of online video is admittedly "vast and uncharted", but "part of what separates YouTube [etc.] from other media are the clips' brevity and the ways they're often encountered through exchange with other people: a clip's interest derives from its associations with colleagues, family, friends, and contexts within communities" (Vernallis 2013, 10). YouTube and similar websites are not solely hosts for video material, they are also social networks—communities generated by their users. In posting a video on YouTube and/or similar websites, a user invites critique and praise in the comments section, asking for the video to be shared across the Internet for an uncountable number of reasons. Perhaps most importantly, posting invites viewers to take part in a collaborative watching experience that theatrical film and television viewing simply does not and cannot provide.

This communal aspect has likely contributed to the popularity of clips that play with intertextuality; in the way that it is fun for people to enjoy an inside joke, intertextual content in YouTube videos promotes sharing and commentary from those with esoteric knowledge and thus contributes to the feeling of being part of a group that is so essential to the site. Carol Vernallis identifies intertextuality as one of the key components for popular YouTube clips (2013, 11) and fairy tales—"intertexts par excellence" according to Pauline Greenhill and Sidney Eve Matrix (2010, 2)—often work well as familiar starting points.

Searching "fairy tale" on YouTube's website in September 2015 resulted in over 298,000 results. This number does not count the numerous videos categorized by fairy-tale titles alone—for example, "Cinderella" (ATU 510A) prompts almost 2.5 million results. Overall, fairy-tale YouTube clips tend to involve music prominently in some way. Vernallis argues that online video, due to what she sees as a largely universal turn to intensified "audiovisual aesthetics" across visual media, often mimics the traditional music video format that began in the 1980s and has developed since (2013, 6–7). Even clips that are "not quite music videos" frequently "function similarly" (7). While it is impossible and/or impractical to document every YouTube clip having to do with fairy tales, I highlight several of the most well-known and/or critically important videos recently available there.

Parody Videos

By far the most popular fairy-tale videos on YouTube are parodies: creations meant to humorously exaggerate and comment on stereotypical aspects of a popular genre (like the fairy tale itself), creator (like Disney), or even cultural object (like a generic fairy-tale princess.) As Vernallis notes,

> Parody and the sardonic response occur partly because technology makes it possible; adding a second layer that circumvents, undercuts, or makes ridiculous the original object is one of the easiest things to do. In the anonymity of the web, YouTube makers are in search of a ground—your sarcastic take immediately places you in relation to a select group of viewers as well as producers and fans of the original material. Your parody, now tied to original content, piggybacks on an already accrued attention.
>
> (2013, 146)

Fairy tales, particularly Disney's well-known versions, are especially ripe content to explore in video format via parody. As parody is considered "fair use" under American copyright laws (Stim N.d.), this practice has continued to be allowed under YouTube's guidelines. Indeed, one of the most popular fairy-tale YouTube parody videos, Eric Faden's "A Fair(y) Use Tale" (2007), is actually about this issue; Faden cuts famous Disney cartoons into tiny segments and then weaves them together to talk about fair use in copyright law.

As Cristina Bacchilega observes, the preponderance of such parodies "point[s] to how Disney is key to the image of the fairy tale in popular cultural memory, and also how people are questioning the authority (on their lives) of the Disneyfied fairy tales that sugarcoated the Brothers Grimm and Charles Perrault's tales to produce a romantically enchanting happily ever after" (2013, 11). A quite famous Disney fairy-tale parody, for example, is the two-video set of song satires by Jon Cozart (pseudonym "Paint" on YouTube): "After Ever After" (2013) and "After Ever After 2" (2014). In them, Cozart sings versions of Disney fairy-tale "happily ever afters" in terms of the mundane realities of twenty-first-century life—for example, Ariel from *The Little Mermaid* (1989) has to cope with "fishing and oil spills."

The messages of the Disney princesses are also popular subjects for parody. The comedy group Second City, for example, produced a series of shorts entitled "Advice for Young Girls from a Cartoon Princess" in which fairy-tale princesses offer questionable instruction to children based exclusively on the Disney versions of their stories. In "Advice for Young Girls from

Belle" (2010), for example, the heroine from Disney's *Beauty and the Beast* (1991) urges girls to "find a man who wants to imprison you with his love" and to "never settle for something that doesn't feel like it's a challenge."

In the same vein, the "Princess Rap Battles" by actor, writer, and producer Whitney Avalon feature Disney princesses singing about each other's numerous shortcomings. The "rap battle" parody video, a common trend online, offers a humorous way of imagining what two characters, or even real people, might say to deride each other. In "Cinderella vs. Belle: Princess Rap Battle" (2015), for example, Belle (Avalon) notes Cinderella's "gold-digging," while Cinderella (played by well-known *Buffy the Vampire Slayer* [1997–2003] actor Sarah Michelle Geller) retorts that Belle suffers from "Stockholm Syndrome." Major youth-targeted comedy websites known for funny videos and amusing lists have also latched on to the popularity of Disney parodies: BuzzFeed's contributions include "If Disney Princes Were Real" (2014a), "If Disney Princesses Wore Realistic Makeup" (2015), and "Things Disney Characters Do That'd Be Creepy If You Did Them" (2014b), and Cracked has produced, among others, the horrifying "If Disney Cartoons Were Historically Accurate" (2013).

Fairy-tale parodies on YouTube need not depend on Disney exclusively, however. College Humor's "Tinderella: A Modern Fairy Tale" (2014), for example, with over eight million views, does not rely on the Disney "Cinderella" beyond a few subtle visual clues. In this parody, Tinderella, a frequent user of the dating web app "Tinder," meets up with her "prince" for an extremely brief romance. Also notable is "Granny O'Grimm's Sleeping Beauty" (2009), by Brown Bag Films, nominated for an Academy Award in 2010 for best animated short. In it, an elderly woman offers her own unique, cantankerous interpretation of the classic story to a terrified child.

Fairy-tale parody on YouTube can also function as activism. As Bacchilega explores, the "transformative poetics and politics of the fairy tale are emerging" (2013, 36) and resulting in adaptations decidedly meant to respond, critique, and present "a politicized challenge to the hegemonic tropes of the genre" (70). As an example, former *American Idol* contestant Todrick Hall—now a director, choreographer, entertainer, and maker of several extremely popular Disney parody videos including "Beauty and the Beat" (2013a), "Disney Dudez" (2013b), and "Spell Block Tango" (2013c)—released "Cinderfella" on YouTube on May 5, 2014. The film, in which a male Cinderella (Hall) dreams of going to a ball and meeting a handsome prince, was designed explicitly in support of gay marriage.

The video "Frozen—A Musical feat. Disney Princesses" by Antonius and Vijay Nazareth (pseudonym "AVbyte" on YouTube) (2014), although less unequivocal, still has a clear political message supporting feminist thinking and women who take charge of their own lives. Thus, "YouTube is not merely a new window on the frontlines of regional and global conflicts," but rather "a battleground, a contested ground where amateur [and professional] videographers try to influence how events [and subjects] are represented and interpreted" (Strangelove 2010, 4). Fairy tales, ripe with subversive potential, are particularly apt for such endeavors. Their ability to be told and retold in a huge variety of different ways gives them the potential to become, to use Bacchilega's phrase, "activist adaptations," that is, "retellings in different media that take a questioning stance towards their pre-texts, and/or take an activist stance towards the fairy tale's hegemonic uses in popular culture, and/or instigate readers/viewers/listeners to engage with the genre as well as with the world with a transformed sense of possibility" (2015, 80).

Retellings

More straightforward retellings of fairy tales also appear on YouTube, often designed with children in mind. The organization Smart Kids TV, for example, has produced several short animated adaptations of classic fairy tales. Their version of "The Bremen Town Musicians" (ATU 130, 2014) features colorful animation, amusing voices, and a storyteller as guide and remains close to the Grimms' version. YouTube channel "Cool School" does similar productions in a slightly sillier style, often taking great liberties with the source material. In their version of "Rapunzel" (ATU 310, 2014), for example, the title character spends her days doing jigsaw puzzles, and, once rescued, she and her prince enjoy square dancing. Later Cool School fairy-tale videos include a teacher named Ms. Booksy who serves as a storyteller but also enters into her stories as various characters. Many of these videos are meant to be educational, calling to mind the structures and modes of similar programs on television such as *Super Why!* (2007–; see Brodie and McDavid 2014).

YouTube serves as a repository for "book trailers," as well, a relatively new concept developed to promote new works of literature in a fashion similar to film advertising. These clips are both officially released by publishing houses and unofficially made by fans. Young adult novels seem most likely to receive this treatment, including a number of fairy-tale retellings. One of the most impressive of these is the official book trailer by Harper Teen for Heather Dixon's *Entwined*, based on "The Twelve Dancing Princesses" (ATU 306, 2011).

Similarly, unofficial fan videos use images from well-known, copyrighted productions, re-edited and set to music in clips sometimes also known as "vids" (Russo 2009, 126). Julie Levin Russo argues that creating these mash-ups has become a popular pastime due to the ease of making and posting them and the "digitalization of mass media," which has "made commercial texts more readily available for appropriation and manipulation" (125). Most highlight a specific aspect of a TV show or film—often the romantic relationship (or wished-for romantic relationship) between two characters—set to a famous song that is meant to reveal their inner thoughts. Although owners of intellectual property often pursue such makers, questioning their legality (125–126), as parody they fall into the category of fair use in American law. Further, fans of commercial fairy-tale films and television shows like *Once Upon a Time* (2011–) often express their appreciation for these other media by making these kinds of videos and posting them to YouTube (see Hay and Baxter 2014).

Commercials and music videos, including those by famous artists, also often appear on YouTube, both legally and illegally. YouTube makes these videos accessible beyond a few brief showings on television, and they should therefore be considered part of the YouTube community. Many of these clips draw from fairy tales. For example, the Sky Broadband Internet commercial, posted by user "Chris P," comically uses "The Princess and the Pea" (ATU 704, 2010), and the music videos for both Tori Amos's "Strange Little Girl" (Alternative Music 2013) and Katy Perry's "Wide Awake" (KatyPerryVEVO 2012) use strong fairy-tale imagery. The Amos video focuses, for example, on a wolf in the woods chasing a little girl home, while the Perry video features a vine-covered labyrinth, mirrors, and even a unicorn-riding prince (whom Perry punches). The fairy-tale-inspired music videos of less famous artists are often posted exclusively on YouTube. Polly Paulusma's "The Woods" (MPaulusma 2007), made with paper cut-outs and other work created by noted fairy-tale artist Rima Staines, recalls Lotte Reiniger's fairy-tale films. Overall, music videos tend to rely more on fairy-tale imagery and motifs than on plots, but still distinctly draw on the form for their primary source material.

Contemporary Storytelling

Contemporary storytellers have begun using YouTube as a resource as well, posting everything from previews to full recordings of their performances. Often a simple video of a live performance on a stage or even in a more intimate setting, they usually feature the storyteller alone, without props. Some, like the UK-based Crick Crack Club, use YouTube videos as a means of promoting their live-action storytelling productions. Their mission statement—to "recreat[e] storytelling as a contemporary performance art in the UK" and "unleash the rich metaphorical content of international fairytales, epics and myths on the imaginations of contemporary audiences" (*Crick Crack Club* 2014), results in a variety of fairy-tale-based performances, including the 2012–2013 "Festival of Fairytales for Grown-ups," for which they posted a trailer (2014) featuring several individual storytelling performances from the show. Storytellers also upload videos of performances specifically designed to be watched via the Internet, and accordingly, as Anthony Buccitelli argues, "folklorists must stop thinking of digital technologies as simply media that record or transmit offline folklore. Instead, we must think of them as *places of performance*" as well (2011, 73). Storytelling artists, many of whom work with traditional fairy tales, have begun taking advantage of YouTube in this way, and it is key that those who study these performances take their method and media into consideration.

Other Online Video Websites

Numerous other websites offer online videos for web surfers to peruse, but most of their material ultimately makes its way to YouTube, particularly if they achieve any level of popularity. Vimeo (www.vimeo.com) may be the main exception to this rule, as it features no advertisements and tends to promote higher quality content (some of which viewers must pay for). Vimeo is thus often the choice for independent, longer, more professional films. For example, Tom Davenport's critically acclaimed *From the Brothers Grimm* series of films, which includes American versions of popular Brothers Grimm stories like "Bearskin" (ATU 361) and "Hansel and Gretel" (ATU 327A), appears in full for free on the site (2011a; 2011b).

Other bigger productions on Vimeo that draw from traditional fairy tales include a documentary by EyeSteelFilm Distribution entitled "The Frog Princes" about several people with developmental disabilities who mount a production of the classic tale (ATU 440, 2014) and an artistic short by Cale Atkinson based on "Little Red Riding Hood" (ATU 333) called "Lil' Red" (2012). Original films inspired by fairy tales also appear on Vimeo, including the enchanting animated shorts "The Song for Rain" by Yawen Zheng (2012) and "The Alchemist's Letter" by Carlos Stevens (2015). While posting exclusively on Vimeo lends an air of legitimacy to the production, YouTube is still by far the more popular website, and the drawback is that Vimeo does not tend to generate the numbers of views possible on YouTube. That said, views on Vimeo do tend to be from people genuinely interested in fairy-tale film, not just those casually surfing for content.

Vine (www.vine.co, active 2012–2016, now online only in archival form) was a website that offered a slightly different experience, exclusively presenting extremely short user-uploaded looped videos as part of a social network. None were more than six seconds long. The most popular of the fairy-tale themed Vines, with over 20 million recorded loops as of July 2016, is a parody of the "happily ever after" ending by Thomas Sanders in which the prince and the male villain declare their love and run off together to the delight of the left-behind princess (2014).

Considering the Importance of YouTube

Having established the healthy presence of fairy-tale inspired videos on YouTube and other sites, one can ask why these clips—so often short, funny, low-budget, and relatively amateur—

merit attention. The first and most significant reason is that YouTube is phenomenally popular—as Jean Burgess and Joshua Green put it, "part of the mainstream media landscape, and a force to be reckoned with in contemporary popular culture" (2009, vii). It is both "a platform that provides access to culture" and "a platform that enables consumers to participate as producers" (14). From a specifically Western perspective, YouTube also offers a way for viewers to watch fairy-tale-related video from around the world, thereby broadening the definition of what fairy tale is and can be. As Jack Zipes points out, websites like YouTube have been a large part of what has allowed Western audiences to view previously "excluded, neglected, censored, poorly dubbed, or blocked" international fairy-tale material, both legally and illegally, forever changing the global scope of what is considered as such (2011, 322).

Along the same lines, digital media of all kinds—video included—has contributed and continues to contribute to new ways of thinking about the fairy-tale form and its uses; "the new media landscape [. . .] allows a person to think more creatively. New relations are constructed" (Vernallis 2013, 29). Although materials like Disney fairy-tale parodies and critiques continue to be the most popular and circulated videos currently (again revealing how mainstream those versions of the tales still are), digital media resources like YouTube have the potential to be paths to new understanding as well—even when they begin with something as old as a traditional fairy tale.

Related topics: Activism; Adaptation and the Fairy-Tale Web; Advertising; Blogs; Convergence Culture; Digital; Disney Corporation; Fandom/Fan Cultures; Fan Fiction; Intellectual Property; Music Videos and Pop Music; Pornography; Reality TV; Sexualities/Queer and Trans Studies; Storytelling; Television Drama; Video Games

References Cited and Further Reading

Bacchilega, Cristina. 2013. *Fairy Tales Transformed? Twenty-First-Century Adaptation and the Politics of Wonder.* Detroit: Wayne State UP.

———. 2015. "Fairy-Tale Adaptations and Economies of Desire." In *The Cambridge Companion to Fairy Tales*, edited by Maria Tatar, 79–96. Cambridge: Cambridge UP.

Brodie, Ian, and Jodi McDavid. 2014. "Who's Got the Power? *Super Why!*, Viewer Agency, and Traditional Narrative." In *Channeling Wonder: Fairy Tales on Television*, edited by Pauline Greenhill and Jill Terry Rudy, 25–44. Detroit: Wayne State UP.

Buccitelli, Anthony. 2011. "Performance 2.0: Observations toward a Theory of the Digital Performance of Folklore." In *Folk Culture in the Digital Age: The Emergent Dynamics of Human Interaction*, edited by Trevor J. Blank, 60–84. Logan: Utah State UP.

Burgess, Jean, and Joshua Green. 2009. *YouTube: Online Video and Participatory Culture.* Cambridge, UK: Polity P.

"Crick Crack Club—About Us." 2014. *Crick Crack Club.* http://crickcrackclub.com/MAIN/CLUBE.HTM.

Dixon, Heather. 2012. *Entwined.* New York: Greenwillow Books.

Greenhill, Pauline, and Sidney Eve Matrix. 2010. "Introduction: Envisioning Ambiguity: Fairy Tale Films." In *Fairy Tale Films: Visions of Ambiguity*, edited by Pauline Greenhill and Sidney Eve Matrix, 1–22. Logan: Utah State UP.

Hay, Rebecca, and Christa Baxter. 2014. "Happily Never After: The Commodification and Critique of Fairy Tale in ABC's *Once Upon a Time*." In *Channeling Wonder: Fairy Tales on Television*, edited by Pauline Greenhill and Jill Terry Rudy, 316–35. Detroit: Wayne State UP.

Miller, Michael. 2007. *YouTube 4 You.* Indianapolis: Pearson Education Que Publishing.

Russo, Julie Levin. 2009. "User-Penetrated Content: Fan Video in the Age of Convergence." *Cinema Journal* 48 (4): 125–30.

Stim, Rich. N.d. "What Is Fair Use?" Stanford U. http://fairuse.stanford.edu/overview/fair-use/what-is-fair-use/.

Strangelove, Michael. 2010. *Watching YouTube: Extraordinary Videos by Ordinary People.* Toronto: U Toronto P.

Vernallis, Carol. 2013. *Unruly Media: YouTube, Music Video, and the New Digital Cinema.* New York: Oxford UP.

Zipes, Jack. 2011. *The Enchanted Screen: The Unknown History of Fairy-Tale Films.* New York: Routledge.

BRITTANY WARMAN

Mediagraphy

Alternative Music. 2013. "Tori Amos—Strange Little Girl (Official Video)." *YouTube*, September 27. www.youtube.com/watch?v=ghGgycFEg64.

American Idol (TV). 2002–2016. Creator Simon Fuller. USA.

Atkinson, Cale. 2012. "Lil' Red." *Vimeo*, June 15. https://vimeo.com/44122539.

Avalon, Whitney. 2015. "Cinderella vs. Belle: Princess Rap Battle." *YouTube*, March 11. www.youtube.com/watch?v=VeZXQf77hhk.

AVbyte (Antonius and Vijay Nazareth). 2014. "Frozen: A Musical feat. Disney Princesses." *YouTube*. 11 February. www.youtube.com/watch?v=CtyOC6ayKoU.

Beauty and the Beast. 1991. Directors Gary Trousdale and Kirk Wise. USA.

Brown Bag Films. 2009. "Granny O'Grimm's Sleeping Beauty." *YouTube*, December 1. www.youtube.com/watch?v=cIDv1jJhoxY.

Buffy the Vampire Slayer (TV). 1997–2003. Creator Joss Whedon. USA.

BuzzfeedInc. 2014a. "If Disney Princes Were Real." *YouTube*, September 6. www.youtube.com/watch?v=ct-CdyT4HkM.

———. 2014b. "Things Disney Characters Do That'd Be Creepy If You Did Them." *YouTube*, April 4. www.youtube.com/watch?v=ItRm7p3mL88.

———. 2015. "If Disney Princesses Wore Realistic Makeup." *YouTube*, August 4. www.youtube.com/watch?v=qg0RLhouTbQ.

Chris P. 2010. "Sky Broadband: The Princess and the Pea TV Advert." *YouTube*, June 28. www.youtube.com/watch?v=3e-g37aP4TE.

CollegeHumor Media. 2014. "Tinderella: A Modern Fairy Tale." *YouTube*, January 29. www.youtube.com/watch?v=bLoRPielarA.

Cool School. 2014. "Rapunzel Gets Tangled Up—Fairy Tales for Kids." *YouTube*, February 13. www.youtube.com/watch?v=xY-2K-N3IS0.

Cracked. 2013. "If Disney Cartoons Were Historically Accurate—Disney Musical Parody—With Rachel Bloom." *YouTube*, June 5. www.youtube.com/watch?v=jwA1VeYpvaM.

CrickCrackClub. 2014. "The Festival of Fairytales for Grown-Ups." *YouTube*, June 19. www.youtube.com/watch?v=gm9d9Sb4zM8.

The Daily Show (TV). 1996. Creators Lizz Winstead and Madeleine Smithberg. USA.

Davenport, Tom. 2011a. "Bearskin." *Vimeo*, April 12. https://vimeo.com/22313540.

———. 2011b. "Hansel and Gretel." *Vimeo*, April 12. https://vimeo.com/22313796.

EyeSteelFilm Distribution. 2014. "The Frog Princes." *Vimeo*, April 28. https://vimeo.com/ondemand/thefrogprinces/92967451.

Faden, Eric. 2007. "A Fair(y) Use Tale." Jas A. *YouTube*, May 18. www.youtube.com/watch?v=CJn_jC4FNDo.

Hall, Todrick. 2013a. "Beauty and the Beat by Todrick Hall." *YouTube*, March 1. www.youtube.com/watch?v=AJzds6fRfjM.

———. 2013b. "Disney Dudez." *YouTube*, June 25. www.youtube.com/watch?v=MWdFrw5DoJU.

———. 2013c. "Spell Block Tango by Todrick Hall." *YouTube*, October 28. www.youtube.com/watch?v=GAUZIw95ueM.

———. 2014. "Cinderfella by Todrick Hall." *YouTube*, May 5. www.youtube.com/watch?v=F9ZA7bn5ujk.

Harper Teen. 2011. "ENTWINED by Heather Dixon Book Trailer." Harper Collins. *YouTube*, April 28. www.youtube.com/watch?v=f_Ydp0sga5g.

KatyPerryVEVO. 2012. "Katy Perry—Wide Awake." *YouTube*, June 18. www.youtube.com/watch?v=k0BWlvnBmIE.

The Little Mermaid. 1989. Directors Ron Clements and John Musker. USA.

MPaulusma. 2007. "Polly Paulusma—The Woods." *YouTube*, March 27. www.youtube.com/watch?v=hTDlmvY7MKM.

Once Upon a Time (TV). 2011. Creators Adam Horowitz and Edward Kitsis. USA.

Paint (Jon Cozart). 2013. "After Ever After—DISNEY Parody." *YouTube*, March 12. www.youtube.com/watch?v=diU70KshcjA.

———. 2014. "After Ever After 2—DISNEY Parody." *YouTube*, June 24. www.youtube.com/watch?v=diU70KshcjA.

Sanders, Thomas. 2014. "A Fairy Tale Ending." *Vine*, December 15. https://vine.co/v/OgZxi7W9tqD.

The Second City Network. 2010. "Advice for Young Girls from Belle." *YouTube*, August 30. www.youtube.com/watch?v=Uuk-h2ZYNJU.

Smart Kids TV. 2014. "Bremen Town Musicians | Fairy Tales Bedtime Stories 4 | Fairy Stories and Songs for Kids." *YouTube*, May 21. www.youtube.com/watch?v=K5gr-A03RFM.

Stevens, Carlos. 2015. "The Alchemist's Letter." *Vimeo*, April 20. https://vimeo.com/125527643.

Super Why! (TV). 2007. Creator Angela Santomero. USA.

Zheng, Yawen. 2012. "The Song for Rain." *Vimeo*, September 2. https://vimeo.com/48717374.

CONTRIBUTORS

B. Grantham Aldred is a subject librarian at Loyola University Chicago. He received his PhD in Folklore and American Studies from Indiana University in 2009 and has contributed to numerous reference works on fairy tales and media.

Leah Claire Allen is Assistant Professor of Gender, Women's, and Sexuality Studies at Grinnell College. She received her PhD in Literature and a Graduate Certificate in Feminist Studies from Duke University in 2014.

Natalia Andrievskikh is a Russian-born writer working as a language lecturer at the Expository Writing Program at NYU. She holds a PhD in Comparative Literature from SUNY Binghamton, and her research interests include contemporary British and Anglophone literature, digital writing, and media and culture.

Cristina Bacchilega teaches at the University of Hawai'i–Mānoa. She co-edits *Marvels & Tales: Journal of Fairy-Tale Studies*; her recent essays appear in *Fairy Tale Films Beyond Disney: International Perspectives*; *The Cambridge Companion to the Fairy Tale*; *Narrative Culture*; *Folktales and Fairy Tales: Traditions and Texts from around the World*; and *Revista d'Etnologia de Catalunia*.

Meredith A. Bak is an Assistant Professor in the Department of Childhood Studies at Rutgers University–Camden. She writes on historical and contemporary children's media, visual, and material culture and is working on projects about pre-cinematic children's media and the history and theory of animate toys.

Balaka Basu is Assistant Professor of English Literature at the University of North Carolina at Charlotte where she specializes in children's and young adult literature, popular culture, fan studies, and the digital humanities.

Lauren Bosc's research interests include feminist and queer representations of bodies—particularly fat bodies—in the context of film, television, and other media. She currently works as a Research Coordinator and as Managing Editor for *Jeunesse* at the University of Winnipeg.

Ian Brodie is Associate Professor of Folklore at Cape Breton University and the author of *A Vulgar Art: A New Approach to Stand-up Comedy* (2014). He is also the co-editor of *Contemporary Legend*, the journal of the International Society for Contemporary Legend Research.

Lindsay Brown is a graduate of the Master of Arts in Cultural Studies, Texts and Cultures program at the University of Winnipeg. She also holds a BA and a BEd and has taught English Language Arts in the Seven Oaks School Division for over a decade.

Folklorist and storyteller **Milbre Burch** teaches for the Office of Graduate Studies at the University of Missouri. Her publications on narrative performance include "Learning to Listen

CONTRIBUTORS

to an All-Day Talker: First-, Second- and Third-Hand Hearing of an Oral Performance by Ray Hicks" (2013).

Molly Clark Hillard is Associate Professor of English at Seattle University, where she teaches Victorian literature. She is the author of *Spellbound: The Fairy Tale and the Victorians* (2014).

Allison Craven is a Senior Lecturer in English and Screen Studies at James Cook University, North Queensland, Australia. She publishes on Disney media and Australian cinema. She has published *Fairy Tale Interrupted: Feminism, Masculinity, Wonder Cinema* (2017) and *Finding Queensland in Australian Cinema* (2016).

Anne E. Duggan is Professor of French at Wayne State University, author of *Queer Enchantments: Gender, Sexuality, and Class in the Fairy-Tale Cinema of Jacques Demy* (2013), co-editor with Donald Haase of *Folktales and Fairy Tales: Traditions and Texts from around the World* (2016), and co-editor with Cristina Bacchilega of *Marvels & Tales*.

Bill Ellis is Professor Emeritus of English and American Studies at Penn State University. A Fellow of the American Folklore Society and past President of AFS's Folk Narrative Section, he has written on contemporary legends, Jack Tales, and Japanese manga/anime.

Filmmaker **Danishka Esterhazy** is often inspired by fairy tales. Her feature films *Black Field* and *H & G* (based on the fairy tale "Hansel and Gretel") are beautifully rendered tales of gothic intrigue. Her films have shown at Vancouver International Film Festival, Kölner Filmhaus, and many women's film festivals.

William Gray is retired Professor of Literary History and Hermeneutics at the University of Chichester, United Kingdom. He founded the Sussex Centre for Folklore, Fairy Tales and Fantasy. His publications include *Fantasy, Art and Life* (2011), and more about his work can be found at williamgray.org.

Pauline Greenhill is Professor of Women's and Gender Studies at the University of Winnipeg. Her recent books include *Fairy-Tale Films Beyond Disney* (co-editors Jack Zipes and Kendra Magnus-Johnston, 2016); *Unsettling Assumptions* (co-editor Diane Tye, 2014); *Channeling Wonder* (co-editor Jill Terry Rudy, 2014); and *Transgressive Tales* (co-editor Kay Turner, 2012).

Lynda Haas teaches rhetoric and composition at the University of California, Irvine. She began watching and writing about Disney films when her children were young and co-edited *From Mouse to Mermaid: The Politics of Film, Gender, and Culture* in 1995.

Naomi Hamer is Assistant Professor in English at Ryerson University. She is co-editor of *More Words About Pictures: Current Research on Picture Books and Visual/Verbal Texts for Young People* (with Perry Nodelman and Mavis Reimer, 2017). She is President of the Association for Research in the Cultures of Young People and editor for the journal *Jeunesse: Young People, Texts, Cultures*.

Martine Hennard Dutheil de la Rochère is Professor of English and Comparative Literature at the University of Lausanne. She is the author of *Reading, Translating, Rewriting: Angela Carter's Translational Poetics* (2013). She guest-edited *Angela Carter traductrice—Angela Carter en traduction* (2014) and co-edited *Cinderella across Cultures: New Directions and Interdisciplinary Perspectives* (2016).

kuʻualoha hoʻomanawanui is an Associate Professor of Hawaiian Literature, English Department, University of Hawaiʻi at Mānoa. Her first book is *Voices of Fire—Reweaving the Lei of Pele and Hiʻiaka Literature* (2014).

650

CONTRIBUTORS

Rebecca Hutton teaches children's and young adult literature at Deakin University, Australia. Her recent publications include an article on the intersections between music and sexuality in young adult literature and a co-authored chapter (with Clare Bradford) on gender in Arthurian television and film for children.

Vanessa Joosen is Professor of English Literature and Children's Literature at the University of Antwerp, Belgium. She is the author of *Critical and Creative Perspectives on Fairy Tales* (2011) and co-editor of *Grimm's Tales Around the Globe* (2014, with Gillian Lathey).

Michael Joseph, the Rare Book Librarian at Rutgers University, has published extensively in the fields of children's literature, book arts, and Robert Graves and is the author of *The Teaching Guide to the Norton Anthology of Children's Literature* and several published adaptations of seventeenth-century fairy tales.

Maria Kaliambou is Senior Lector at the Hellenic Studies Program at Yale University. In 2015 she published the *Routledge Modern Greek Reader: Greek Folktales for Learning Modern Greek*. Her research interests are folktales, popular literature, book history, migration literature, and foreign language pedagogy.

Anna Kérchy is an Associate Professor at the English Department of the University of Szeged, Hungary. Her research interests include gender studies, fantastic imagination, and children's/YA literatures. She authored two books: *Alice in Transmedia Wonderland* and *Body-Texts in Angela Carter*.

Mikel J. Koven is Senior Lecturer in Film Studies at the University of Worcester. He is the author of *La Dolce Morte: Vernacular Cinema and the Italian Giallo Film* (2006), *Film, Folklore and Urban Legends* (2008), and *Blaxploitation Films* (2010).

Anne Kustritz is an Assistant Professor in the Media and Culture Studies Department and the ICON research institute at Utrecht University. She specializes in fan culture and digital ethnography. Her work appears in *Camera Obscura* and *Feminist Media Studies*.

Vivian Labrie, an independent scholar and member of the Quebec research group ÉRASME, has navigated in the past forty years between formal folktale research and her personal involvement, both as a researcher and a citizen, in social justice issues, mainly about poverty and economic inequalities.

John Laudun is Professor of English at the University of Louisiana. His PhD in folklore studies is from the Folklore Institute at Indiana University (1999). For more information, see johnlaudun.org.

Ming-Hsun Lin is Assistant Professor at Feng Chia University in Taiwan. She received her PhD in Drama from the University of Manchester, UK. Her research interests include gender studies, film studies, fairy tales, children's literature, and fantasy.

Carl Lindahl, Martha Gano Houstoun Research Professor of English at the University of Houston, has published *American Folktales from the Collections of the Library of Congress* (2004), *Perspectives on the Jack Tales and Other North American Märchen* (2001), and (with Maida Owens and C. Renée Harvison) *Swapping Stories: Folktales from Louisiana* (1997).

Martin Lovelace taught Folklore at Memorial University of Newfoundland from 1980 until his retirement in 2016. With Anita Best and Pauline Greenhill he is preparing a collection of magic tales recorded from recent oral tradition in Newfoundland.

CONTRIBUTORS

Tomasz Z. Majkowski is an Assistant Professor at Jagiellonian University in Cracow. His research deals with game studies, pop-culture studies, and literary theory. He has published on fantasy fiction and video games. Researching fairy tales is one of his favorite pastimes.

Jodi McDavid is a folklorist at McDavid Brodie Consulting. Her research interests include children's and adolescent folklife and counter-clericalism in Atlantic Canada, and she is currently working on a book on children's television and legend.

Lynne S. McNeill is an Assistant Professor of Folklore in the English Department at Utah State University. Her research interests include legend, belief, and digital culture, and she is the author of the popular textbook *Folklore Rules*.

Mayako Murai is a Professor in the English Department at Kanagawa University, Japan. Her publications include *From Dog Bridegroom to Wolf Girl: Contemporary Japanese Fairy-Tale Adaptations in Conversation with the West* (2015).

Sadhana Naithani is Professor at the Centre of German Studies, Jawaharlal Nehru University. Her recent publications are *Folklore Theory in Postwar Germany* (2014), two ethnographic films: *Village Tales 1 & 2* (2013; 2016), and *Elephantine, A Novella* (2016).

Emma Nelson received her MA in American Literature from Brigham Young University, where she focused on folklore and cultural studies, including fairy tales and popular culture. She has published in *Channeling Wonder: Fairy Tales on Television*.

Cynthia Nugent is a children's author-illustrator and the founder of Rascal Media, a studio for animated picturebook trailers and apps. Her MA in Children's Literature (University of British Columbia) focused on the application of picturebook theory to the creation and assessment of story apps.

Vanessa Nunes is a PhD candidate in the Department of English, Film, and Theatre at University of Manitoba. She is also a Social Sciences and Humanities Research Council of Canada Doctoral Scholar.

Jessie Riddle is an MA student in the Folklore Department at Indiana University. She graduated with a BA in English from Brigham Young University and participated in the creation of the Fairy Tales on Television Visualizations Database while at BYU.

John Rieder is Professor of English at the University of Hawai'i–Mānoa, editor of the science fiction studies journal *Extrapolation*, and author of *Science Fiction and the Mass Cultural Genre System* (2017), *Colonialism and the Emergence of Science Fiction* (2008), and essays on many subjects including genre theory and fairy-tale film.

Jill Terry Rudy, Associate Professor of English, Brigham Young University, publishes on American folklore history, fairy tale and folk narratives, intermediality, family folklore, and foodways. She edited *The Marrow of Human Experience* by William A. Wilson and co-edited *Channeling Wonder*.

Folklorist **Patricia Sawin** is Associate Professor in the Department of American Studies, University of North Carolina, Chapel Hill. Her publications on narrative performance include "Performance at the Nexus of Gender, Power, and Desire" (2002) and *Listening for a Life* (2004).

Jennifer Schacker is Associate Professor of English and Theatre Studies, University of Guelph. She is author of *National Dreams: The Remaking of Fairy Tales in Nineteenth-Century*

England and many articles on the histories of folklore, fairy tale, and pantomime, as well as co-editor of two fairy-tale anthologies.

Veronica Schanoes is an Associate Professor in the Department of English at Queens College–City University of New York. Her first book, *Fairy Tales, Myth, and Psychoanalytic Theory: Feminism and Retelling the Tale*, was published in 2014.

Ann Schmiesing is Professor of German at the University of Colorado–Boulder. She is the author of the books *Disability, Deformity, and Disease in the Grimms' Fairy Tales* and *Norway's Christiania Theatre, 1827–1867: From Danish Showhouse to National Stage.*

Claudia Schwabe, Assistant Professor of German at Utah State University, co-edited *New Approaches to Teaching Folk and Fairy Tales* (2016) and is currently working on her monograph *Craving Supernatural Creatures: German Fairy-Tale Figures in American Pop Culture.*

Karen Seago is Programme Director for Translation Studies at City University of London. She has published widely on folk and fairy tales, feminist and literary revisions of fairy tales especially in the work of Angela Carter, proto-feminist translations of fairy tales, and the reception/translation of the Grimms' fairy tales in England.

Sue Short is a Research Fellow at Birkbeck College, University of London. Her publications include *Fairy Tale and Film: Old Tales with a New Spin* (2015) and *Misfit Sisters: Screen Horror as Rite of Passage* (2007).

Amanda Slack-Smith is an Associate Curator at the Queensland Art Gallery & Gallery of Modern Art, Brisbane, Australia. Specializing in film, video, and new media, she received a Masters of Arts from the Royal Melbourne Institute of Technology in 2006.

Joseph Sobol is Coordinator of the Graduate Program in Storytelling at East Tennessee State University, where he is a tenured Professor in the Department of Communication and Performance. He is author of *The Storytellers' Journey: An American Revival* and is co-founder and co-editor of the journal *Storytelling, Self, Society.*

Victoria Tedeschi is a PhD candidate in English and Theatre Studies in the School of Culture and Communication at the University of Melbourne, Australia. Her research is published in international, peer-reviewed journals and received accolades such as the Australian Postgraduate award, the Gwenda Ford English Literature award, and the Percival Serle prize.

Andrew Teverson is Professor of English Literature and Head of Humanities at Kingston University, London. His recent work includes *The Edinburgh Critical Edition of the Selected Writings of Andrew Lang* (2015, co-edited with Alexandra Warwick and Leigh Wilson), shortlisted for the Folklore Society's Katharine Briggs Folklore Award, and *Fairy Tale* for the Routledge New Critical Idiom series (2013).

Catherine Tosenberger is Associate Professor of English at the University of Winnipeg, where she is attached to the Centre for Research in Young People's Texts and Cultures. Her areas of research include folklore, fandom studies, adolescent literature, and Neo-Paganism.

Shaina Trapedo teaches literature and composition in both traditional and online settings, most recently at Seneca College. Since relocating to New York, she continues to explore the connections between literacy, cultural identity, and social engagement as an Instructional Design consultant.

CONTRIBUTORS

Francisco Vaz da Silva lectures in Anthropology and Folklore at University Institute of Lisbon (ISCTE-IUL). He has published extensively on symbolism in *Märchen*, folklore, and popular culture. He is the author of *Metamorphosis: The Dynamics of Symbolism in European Fairy Tales* (2002) and *Archeology of Intangible Heritage* (2008).

Brittany Warman is a PhD candidate in English and Folklore at The Ohio State University. Her main interests are folkloric retellings, fairy tales, nineteenth-century literature (particularly the gothic and fantastic), supernatural folklore, feminist and queer theory, speculative literature, experimental literature, and digital media.

Olivia Weigeldt is a PhD student at McMaster University in the Department of English and Cultural Studies.

Emma Whatman is a PhD candidate and teaches children's literature and digital media at Deakin University, Australia. Her research focuses on representations of female subjectivities in contemporary fairy-tale adaptations. She recently completed a research fellowship at the University of Winnipeg and has presented her research both nationally and internationally.

Christy Williams is an Assistant Professor of English at Hawai'i Pacific University. Her research focuses on the interplay between gender and narrative in contemporary fairy tales and retellings. She co-edited *Beyond Adaptation: Essays on Radical Transformations of Original Works* (2010).

Jenny Heijun Wills is Associate Professor of English at the University of Winnipeg. Her research and teaching focus on Ethnic American literatures, including African American and Asian/American texts. Specifically, her work analyzes representations of transnational and transracial adoption, biologism, and liberalism.

Ida Yoshinaga (University of Hawai'i) uses labor theory, cultural studies, production history, and anticolonial feminism to analyze creative industry. Her dissertation historicizes screenwriters' use of fantastic modes in teleplays; deconstructs Disney's transmedial "Cinderellagemony"; and theorizes training scriptwriters in cultural forms.

Katharine Young is an independent scholar, writer, and visiting lecturer at the University of California, Berkeley, and San Francisco State University in folklore, anthropology, and rhetoric. Her early work examined the phenomenology of narrative and the body; she now researches folklore and aesthetics, anthropology of the senses, folklore of disability, and the film body.

Csenge Virág Zalka is a professional storyteller, author, and culture studies scholar from Hungary. She researches role-playing games and digital narratives for her dissertation in American Culture Studies at Bowling Green State University, Ohio. She serves on the Executive Committee of the Federation for European Storytelling.

Agata Zarzycka is an Assistant Professor at the University of Wrocław. Her research deals with popular culture, gothic studies, participatory culture, and self-fashioning. She has published on role-playing games, fantasy literature, Goths, and video games.

INDEX

1001 Nights 17–18, 83, 86, 342; illustration and 139, 445–6; influence of 76–7, 300, 339–40; Orientalism and 133–7; translation and 302

Aarne, Antti 189; *see also* Aarne-Thompson-Uther tale type numbers
Aarne-Thompson-Uther tale type numbers (ATU) 15–16, 20–1, 57, 460–1; animals and 226–7; criticism of 21
Abdullah, Abdul 498
Aboriginal Australian 328
actantial model (Greimas) 23
activism 50–1, 93–102, 162–3, 165, 242, 644; fat 258–60
adaptation 145–51; linguistic 266–8
Adorno, Theodor 49–50, 70, 509–10
advertising 154–9, 369, 430
Africa 51–3
African American 16, 68, 183–4; sexualizing 208; storytelling 611
age 228, 352, 413; in adaptations 180, 207; audience and 61, 236, 368, 430, 578, 611; binary 23; coming of 193, 239, 241, 372, 508, 562; gender and 535; romance and 621
agency 206; children's 235, 237–8, 454; comics and 478–9; in consumer culture 162, 164–8, 333–4; creative 312, 314, 420–1; fan fiction and 241, 508, 510; gender and 67, 106, 113–15, 118, 323, 409; language and 527, 530, 559, 587; nonhuman 384–5; nostalgia and 586; victim 173; video games and 214
Agnes Weld as "Little Red Riding Hood" (Charles Dodgson) 348–50
A.I. Artificial Intelligence (dir. Steven Spielberg) 461–2
"Aladdin" (ATU 561) 133–8, 174, 341
Aladdin (dir. Ron Clements & John Musker) 137–8, 183
"Ali Baba and the Forty Thieves" (ATU 954) 136, 174–5, 177n5
Alice in Tumblr-land (Tim Manley) 376, 380–2, 386
Alice in Wonderland (Lewis Carroll) 236, 254, 410, 444, 480, 550; in contemporary art 494
Alice: Madness Returns (video game) 638

amants criminels, Les (dir. François Ozon) *see Criminal Lovers*
American Dream 178
anchors, linguistic 264–70, 276, 367, 370
Andersen, Hans Christian 106, 303, 342; authorship of 200–1, 403; autobiography and 411; canon and 113, 116, 286, 367, 421, 495; endings of 231; House museum 435–8; illustration and 444; language and 253; Orientalism and 138–41; sexuality of 293–4; translation and 305–6; *see also* titles of specific tales
"Animal Bride, The" (ATU 402) 230
"Animal Bridegroom, The" (ATU 425A) 230
animal studies 225–32, 354–5
animal tale 12, 21, 226, 412, 610
animation 557–8; development of 179–81; *see also* film
anime 391–7
anthologies 8, 12–15, 35, 176n3, 399–407; broadcast media and 369, 372–3, 453–4; children and 135; colonialism and 84–7, 134–8; context and 314; genre and 76; nationalism and 41; pedagogy and 284, 286; performance and 58; socioeconomic class and 115
Arabian Nights see 1001 Nights
archetype 6, 20–1, 184, 248–9, 551; child 636; female 43–4, 286, 486, 528–30; helper 165, 227; Jungian 40–1, 493; Orientalism and 137–8
architecture 497
Aria/Tristan und Isolde (dir. Franc Roddam) 471–2
art, visual 118–19, 126, 139–40, 219–20, 320–6, 423; chapbooks and 429; high *vs.* low 342; picture books and 443–9; *see also* contemporary art
artificial intelligence 384–6, 461
Asbjørnsen, Peter Christen, and Jørgen Moe 303, 403, 608
Asia 138–41; *see also* Orientalism
atheism 420
ATU *see* Aarne-Thompson-Uther tale type numbers
audience 523; accountability 637–8; assumptions 421–2; children as 206 (*see also* children's literature); gendered 205–6
authenticity 351, 386, 446, 508–9, 521; anthologies and 149, 401, 490; and voice 60, 312–13, 333

INDEX

authorial instruction 215, 219–20, 276
authorship 197–203, 249, 275–6, 311–12, 317–18;
 broadcast media and 368–9; chapbooks and 428–9;
 collective 513; *see also* anthologies; Grimm brothers,
 editorship; intellectual property
autobiography 408–17, 422–5; storytelling and 610–11

Baba Yaga 529–30, 535
Bachelor, The (2002–) 590–3
Bae, Chan-Hyo 353–4
ballad, traditional 621–3
ballet 341–3, 470–1
Barthes, Roland 155
Basile, Giambattista 114, 273, 300, 401–2; theater and
 339
Bauman, Richard 56–7
"Bear, The" (ATU 510B) 158
Beastly (dir. Daniel Barnes) 601–2
Beaumont, Jeanne-Marie Leprince de 113, 182, 282,
 302, 410, 599; *see also* "Beauty and the Beast"
 (ATU 425C)
beauty 185, 239–40, 559, 593–5; male 600–2; *see also*
 fat studies
"Beauty and the Beast" (ATU 425C) 113, 598–604;
 adaptations of 146, 229–30, 341; fan fiction and
 512–13; feminism and 76; in photography 353–4,
 423; pornography and 207–8; in print 318, 410,
 479, 565–8, 601–2; in video games 635; in visual art
 447, 493
Beauty and the Beast (dir. Gary Trousdale & Kirk Wise)
 52, 68, 108, 182–3, 600–1; transmedia and 603
Beauty and the Beast (the 2012–2017 & 1987–1990 TV
 series) 486, 601, 625–8, 632
Beauty and the Geek (2005–2008) 595
bella e la bestia, La (dir. Fabrizio Costa) 602
belle endormie, La (dir. Catherine Breillat) 116, 294–5
belle et la bête, La (dir. Christophe Gans) 602
belle et la bête, La (dir. Jean Cocteau) 413, 600–1
Benfey, Theodor 134
Benjamin, Walter 47–8, 70
Berg, Hans 495
Bettelheim, Bruno 40–5, 192, 504–5, 594, 609;
 influence of 337, 391–3, 412; language and 265–6;
 reality and 285
Big Fat Mermaid 256
Biggest Loser, The (2004–) 593–4
"Big World" phenomenon 439
binary opposition 9n1, 20, 23, 226, 311, 600
bisexuality 291, 293, 360, 470, 503
Blind (dir. Tamar van den Dop) 110
Bloch, Ernst 47–50
blogs 126, 415, 418–24; critique and 104–5, 107–10;
 travel 436–7
"Bluebeard" (ATU 312) 172–3, 461, 466, 527–8;
 feminism and 23, 76–7; in horror 360, 532; in
 theater 341, 578; in visual art 493
Bluebeard's Castle (Béla Bartók) 578

bodies 304–5; discomfort with 392; female 348–52;
 see also fat studies
Bollywood 86
book trailers 645
Brave (dir. Mark Andrews, Brenda Chapman & Steve
 Purcell) 151
Bread Crumbs (dir. Mike Nichols) 209, 357
bricolage 377
broadcast media 367–73; anthologies 403–5; opera and
 572–8; self-identity and 414; television 451–7, 590–5,
 601, 625–32; *see also* specific programs by title
"Brushwood Boy, The" (Rudyard Kipling) 50
Burne-Jones, Edward 320–6
Burne-Jones, Georgiana 322
Butler, Judith 247, 510

Calvino, Italo 149
Campbell, Joseph 609–13, 635
Canada 93–102, 197, 273–9, 463, 617
cannibalism 53, 187, 210, 359, 526–9; *see also* "Hansel
 and Gretel"; "The Juniper Tree"
canon 113–19, 166–7, 239, 286, 451–2, 457; feminist
 66; fidelity to 147–8; mashups and 403–5;
 Orientalism and 135, 141; translation and 299;
 see also conteuses; d'Aulnoy, Marie-Catherine; Disney
 Corporation; Grimm brothers; Perrault, Charles
cante fable 617–21
capacities (metapoetics) 369–71, 373
capitalism 150, 247–8, 253–4, 508–9; colonialism and
 83–5; communicative 162–3, 165–6; criticism of
 47–54; *see also* advertising; economy; socioeconomic
 class
Cardcaptor Sakura (1996–2000) 395–6
Carroll, Lewis 348–50; *see also Alice in Wonderland*
Carter, Angela 240; canon and 17–18, 317, 505–6;
 critical writings of 76–8, 278, 412; influence of 461,
 495; radio and 148; tales by 44, 66, 116, 520, 567–8,
 599–600; translation and 301
cartoons, newspaper 269
celebrity 317–18, 435–9; culture 201–2; intertext 470
Celestial Clockwork (dir. Fina Torres) *see Mécaniques
 célestes*
Cenerentola, La (Gioachino Rossini) 576
censorship 291, 413
chapbooks 135, 302, 312–13, 426–33; "new" 314–17;
 oral tales and 17
Chase, Richard 609
children: abuse of 171–2, 358–60, 638–9; broadcast
 media and 451–7; film for 645 (*see also* Disney and
 specific titles); horror and 532–3, 535; literature for
 (*see* children's literature); mobile apps and 539–46;
 museums for 435–41; psychology of 41–3, 239;
 sexuality and 348–50; in tales 13, 175; theater for
 343–4
children's literature 235–42, 301, 443–9; autobiography
 in 413; realism in 42, 350; translation and 304–5
China 139–40, 283–4, 322, 324–5

INDEX

Chinoiserie 133, 139–40, 320, 324

Chronicles of Narnia, The (C.S. Lewis) 241, 518, 520

Cinder (Marissa Meyers) 240, 520, 568–9

"Cinderella" (ATU 510A) 5–6, 15–16, 52, 113; adaptations of 29, 145; in broadcast media 592; in comics 478–9; in marketing 253–4; in photography 353–4; print history of 322; video games and 635, 637–8; visual representations of 320–6; *see also* specific adaptations by title

Cinderella (dir. Clyde Geronimi, Wilfred Jackson & Hamilton Lake) 67, 115, 178, 447

Cinderella (Edward Burne-Jones) 320–2

Cinderella (Rogers and Hammerstein) 343, 558–60

Cinders (video game) 637

cinema *see* film

cinematography 159, 207, 255, 277, 350–2; *see also* film

class *see* socioeconomic class

"Clever Else" (ATU 1450) 291

"Clever Gretel" (ATU 1741) 291, 529

coding, queer 293–6, 314

colonialism 7–8, 40–1, 50, 83–9, 150, 575; settler 85, 129–31; *see also* decolonization; Indigenous, studies; Orientalism; postcolonialism

coloniality 85

Columbus, Christopher 85

comedy 255–6, 338–44, 557, 643–4; horror and 358–9; in pornography 208, 210–11; romantic 165, 484

comic conventions 483–90; *see also* cosplay

comics 86–7, 107, 117–18, 412, 474–80; *see also* manga

coming of age *see* age, coming of; children's literature

Commedia dell'Arte 338–40

community expression 164–6; *see also* grassroots media

Company of Wolves, The (dir. Neil Jordan) 77–8, 148, 227, 240, 286, 506

conservatism *see* twin laws of folklore

consumption: economic 75, 141, 154, 462; of food (*see* food); media 59, 490, 495, 549, 628

contemporary art 492–9

contes de fées 337–8, 598–9, 602

contes d'Hoffman, Les (Jacques Offenbach) 571, 577

conteuses 8, 74, 205, 300–2, 305, 410

context 26–7, 149–50, 171–2; ignoring 42–3

convergence culture 75, 150–1, 161–8, 484–5; *see also* fan fiction

Coover, Robert 76–7

Coraline (Neil Gaiman) 237–8

copyright: adaptation and 444, 467–8; authorship and 311–12; fair use 65, 247–50, 643, 645; profit and 151, 630; public domain and 368–9, 376, 510, 541, 543; *see also* intellectual property

cosplay 238, 487–90

C-pop 550–1

Crazy Ex-Girlfriend (2015–) 561

creolization 166–8

crime 171–7, 360–3, 625–8

Criminal Lovers (dir. François Ozon) 362–3, 528

crisis management 235, 239

criticism 501–6; *see also under* blogs; social media

Cross, Sarah 383

Cruikshank, George 18, 314, 317

cultural appropriation 124, 129–30, 136–8; *see also* *Moana*

cultures of production 70–1, 311–12, 370

"Cupid and Psyche" (ATU 425B) 14, 272, 527

cyclic time 190–1

Darkest Desire, The (Anthony Schmitz) 240

Darkstalkers series 636–7

d'Aulnoy, Marie-Catherine 11–12, 273, 300–1, 402, 566; gender and 113–15; non-fairy tale work of 410; translation and 341

Davis, Donald 610

decolonization 83–9, 122–4

Demy, Jacques 291; *see also Peau d'Âne*

diachrony 33

Dickens, Charles 198, 314, 323, 349, 411

digital media 376–7, 411–15; (hash)tagging in 381, 383, 611; webcomics 480

disability 104–10, 240, 413

Disney, Walt 178–80

Disney Corporation 24, 44–5, 52, 178–85, 357–8; canon and 114, 178, 494–5, 629–30, 643; colonialism and 87; feminism and 67–71, 118; grassroots media and 164–8; intellectual property and 196, 203; Ladybird storybooks 314–17; Orientalism and 446–7; pornography and 205–6; science fiction and 462; transmedia and 592; *see also* individual films by title

Djurberg, Nathalie 495

Doctor Who (1963–) 487

doha dhani 87

domestication 354–5; of incest 396–7; of tales 428

domesticity, cult of 323–4

domestic violence 602; *see also* children, abuse against; sex, violence and

"Donkey Skin" (ATU 510B) 42–3, 219, 228–9, 391–7, 526; in film 360, 560–1; in horror 534; in photography 351; in video games 639

Donoghue, Emma 116, 238, 413, 566

Doré, Gustav 18, 145–6, 470, 586–7

doxxing 420–1

drag, animal 226–9

dynamism 264–6; *see also* twin laws of folklore

ecocriticism 225, 232

economy 69–70, 95–6; of knowledge 151; of profit 151; *see also* capitalism; socioeconomic class

Edison, Thomas 202

editorship 399; *see also* Grimm brothers

education 273; *see also* pedagogy

emic 84, 88, 101, 383, 386

empathy 62, 242, 361

employment 97–8; *see also* poverty; socioeconomic class

Enchanted (dir. Kevin Lima) 5–6, 68, 79, 185, 549

INDEX

enchantment 188, 215, 237; *see also* wonder, ethics of

England 114, 197, 283; Victorian 320–6, 348–50; *see also* United Kingdom

Esterhazy, Danishka (autoethnography of) 467–8

estrangement 460

Ever After: A Cinderella Story (dir. Andy Tennant) 69, 343, 502

Ex Machina (dir. Alex Garland) 461–2

expert (as opposed to fan) 246–7

Extreme Makeover (2002–2007) 593–4

fable 84, 292

Fables (Bill Willingham) 117–18, 268, 477–9, 603–4, 639–40

"Fairy Fables" 384–6

Fairy Godmother, The (Mercedes Lackey) 165

fairy tale: definitions of 11–15, 20–7, 83–4, 337–8; 565–6, 634–5; utility in psychology 49; web 150–1, 163–4, 249, 508–11

Fairy Tale Fights (video game) 635–6

Fall, The (dir. Tarsem) 357, 469

family: business 428; exonerating 304–5; in horror 534; storytelling 274–5; *see also* fatherhood; marriage; motherhood

famine 53; *see also* food

fan art 238, 486, 645

fandom 245–50, 377–80; *see also* comic conventions; cosplay; fan art; fan fiction

fan fiction 241, 249, 377, 486, 508–13

Fantasia see "Sorcerer's Apprentice, The"

fantasy 16, 62, 147–8, 163, 515–21; advertising and 154, 156; male 116; Orientalism and 136, 138–9; about parents 43, 45; and reality 5–6; *see also* happily ever after

fatherhood 534

Fat Princess 256–7

fat studies 252–60, 593–4

female 113–14; autobiography 408–13; agency 478–9, 559, 599–600, 636–7; crime and 172–3, 175–6; cycles and 190–4; desire 116; domesticity and 115, 155–9; food and 526–30; kinship 172–3; monstrous 534–5; strength and 494

feminism 53, 65–71, 150, 166–8, 381, 503–5; and canon 114–15; children and 41–2, 544; novels and 567–8; personal *vs.* radical 69; poetry and 585–8; post- 67; and psychology 43–5

film 51–3, 104–10, 126, 357–64; animation (*see* animation); animation *vs.* live action 70–1, 79; fantasy 517–18; female creators of 70 (*see also* production, cultures of); Indian 87; industry 202–3 (*see also* Disney Corporation); music and 467–72, 495; science fiction 460–4; *see also* specific films by title; YouTube

Finding Nemo (dir. Andrew Stanton & Lee Unkrich) 110

"Fisherman and His Wife, The" (ATU 555) 13, 227

"Fitcher's Bird" (ATU 311) 173, 229, 291, 304, 350, 409

folkloresque 350–1, 383–6

folksonomy 381, 385, 386n1

food 208–9, 255–6, 258, 525–30; abundance and 95–6; animals and 228–9; family and 53; *see also* cannibalism

forests 363–4, 371, 476, 530, 533

form 20–7, 37–8

formalism 31–8; *see also* function

Fractured Fairy Tales (1959–1964) 6, 80, 230, 404, 454–5

"Frau Trude" (ATU 334) 291

Freudian analysis 40–1, 237, 391, 393–4, 397, 493; horror and 533–4; *see also* Bettelheim, Bruno

"Frog Prince, The" (ATU 440) 159, 230, 595, 646

Frozen (dir. Jennifer Lee & Chris Buck) 104–5, 106–10, 151, 184–5, 295–6; material culture and 328–9, 331; mobile app 541–2; music of 469

function: of language 31, 33; Proppian 22–3, 34–6, 106, 188, 276–7, 384

Gaiman, Neil 237, 317–18, 438; *see also Coraline*

Galland, Antoine 83, 300, 302, 339–41, 445; *see also 1001 Nights*

Game of Thrones (2011–) 368, 512, 561

Game of Thrones, A (George R. R. Martin) 519

Gaskell, Anna 351

gay 230–1, 291, 512–13, 553; *see also* lesbian; queer; sex/sexuality

gaze 66–7, 159, 277, 350–1; adult 452–3; male 116–18, 325, 348–50, 636–7

gender 113–21, 305; marketing and 295–6; music and 466–7, 549–53; psychoanalysis and 43–5; roles 353 (*see also* domesticity, cult of); time and 452; violence and 106–7, 148–9, 157–9; *see also* feminism; intersex; queer/queer studies; sex

genre 33, 84, 86–8; blending 150, 475–8, 487–90, 568–9, 601; marketing and 566–7

Germany 15, 284–5, 405, 469–70, 519; *see also* Grimm brothers; Nazism

Gesamtkunstwerk 467, 472, 541

ghost stories 86–7

Gift, The (dir. Sam Raimi) 172

Gilbert, Sandra and Susan Gubar 66, 503, 535

Girl Who Circumnavigated Fairyland in a Ship of Her Own Making, The (Catherynne M. Valente) 238–9

Goldstein, Dina 353, 494

"Goose Girl, The" (ATU 870) 218, 227

Gozzi, Carlo 339

graphic novels 474–80

grassroots media 162

Grimm (2011–2017) 69, 227, 404–5, 630–2; beginnings for 370–1; comic conventions and 484, 486; genre 489

Grimm brothers: editorship of 58, 181, 199–200, 403; in film 502; translations of 303–4; *see also Kinder- und Hausmärchen*; specific tales by title

Grimm Masterpiece Theatre (1987–1989) 395, 453

Grudge, The (dir. Takashi Shimizu) 172

INDEX

Hadas, Rachel 586–8

Hans Christian Andersen: My Life as a Fairy Tale (dir. Philip Saville) 293–4, 436

"Hansel and Gretel" (ATU 327A) 171–2, 174, 527; in criticism 503; in film 357–64, 535–6, 646; in horror 532; in opera 572, 576; in pornography 208–11; in print 440, 476; in visual art 493

Hänsel und Gretel (Engelbert Humperdinck) 572, 576

"Hans My Hedgehog" (ATU 441) 108, 230, 291

happily ever after 115, 157, 166–8, 178, 183; bodily 253–4, 258–60; in broadcast media 371–3, 485; definition of fairy tale 44–5, 86; linguistic anchor 26, 38; *see also* heteronormativity

Happily Ever After: Fairy Tales for Every Child (1995–2000) 404, 453–4

Happyland (2014) 167–8

Harry Potter series 241–2, 421, 518

Haven, Kendall 61–2

Hawai'i 84, 85, 130

helper archetype 165, 227

heteroglossia 400, 402, 405

heteronormativity 69, 115–16, 151, 292, 504, 511; reality television and 592–3; *see also* queer

H & G (dir. Danishka Esterhazy) 357, 360, 468

Hicks, Ray 610

His Dark Materials (Phillip Pullman) 518

historic-geographic method 15–16

Hoffman, E. T. A. 342, 577, 578

Holdsworth, Ethel Carnie 53

holiday 340–1

Holocaust, the 239–40, 411–12, 498

homosexuality *see* gay; lesbian; queer

"Hop o' My Thumb" (ATU 327B) 173, 527

horror 172–3, 209, 360–2, 405, 476–7, 532–7

"How Six Made Their Way Through the World" (ATU 513B) 97, 253, 258; *see also* "Land and Water Ship, The"

human/nonhuman animal kinship 225–7, 231–2, 354–5

humor 256–8; *see also* comedy

Hùng, Nguyễn Mạnh 497

Hutcheon, Linda 75, 145–6, 149, 503, 520

hybridity 188–94, 502–5

hypotext, fairy-tale 24, 146–7, 157, 264

identity: autobiography and 420–1; storytelling and 510; *see also* disability; gender; Indigenous; Orientalism

imagination: popular 268–70; reason and 283; as tool 237–8, 241–2, 286

incest 171, 177n6, 216, 392–7; *see also* "Donkey Skin"

India 86–8, 278

Indigenous: film 463; studies 88, 122–31

individualism 51–2

industrialization 48, 115, 239, 283

intellectual property 196–203; *see also* copyright

intermediality 3–9, 31–2, 148–50, 161–2; broadcast media and 368–9, 372; film and music 165, 292, 328, 471–4, 548–53, 616; novels and 569

Internet 418–24, 642–7; fan fiction and 511–13; intellectual property and 203; pedagogy and 287; *see also* blog; social media

intersectional theory 65

intersex 207–8, 290, 296n1

intertextuality 25, 76–80, 145–8, 503, 505–6; in broadcast media 372, 456; fandom and 489–90; in music videos 551–3; in picture books 447

Into the Woods (musical play & film) 146, 185, 188, 337, 405

Inupiat 127–9

"Jack and the Beanstalk" (ATU 328A) 78, 174, 466–7, 497; language of 265; in video games 635

Jack Tales (American) 16, 609–10

Jameson, Fredric 31–4, 74–5, 421

Jane the Virgin (2014–) 167–8

Japan 140–1, 337, 394; *see also* anime

Jarrell, Randall 583–5

Jefferson, Thomas 198, 203n2

Jenkins, Henry 75, 150, 161–2, 245–6, 248; *see also* convergence culture

Joe Millionaire (2003) 592–3

"Juniper Tree, The" (ATU 720) 16, 171–2, 218–19, 230, 528, 618–22; in film 360, 534

Juniper Tree, The (dir. Nietzchka Keene) 619

justice 171–7, 239, 316, 619

Kare Kare Zvako (dir. Tsitsi Dangarembga) 53

katha 87

Kentridge, William 574–5

Kenya 89

kernel narrative 456–7

Kill Bill (dir. Quentin Tarantino) 172–3

"Kind and the Unkind Girls, The" (ATU 480) 115–16, 193–4, 595

Kinder- und Hausmärchen 11–12, 149, 394; broadcast media and 630–1; children and 282–3; print history of 443–5; *see also* editorship; Grimm brothers

"King Has Goat Ears, The" (ATU 782) 539–40, 543

knowledge 200–1; dominant/subservient 101; ways of gaining 236–7

Knowles, Isobel 496–7

Komische Oper Berlin 575

K-pop 550

labor *see* work

Ladybird storybooks 314–17

"Land and Water Ship, The" (ATU 513B) 113, 148

Lang, Andrew 220, 301, 403, 496

language 263–70, 330; of chapbooks 428; dialect 199; food and 530; instruction 285–7; video games and 637; *see also* translation

Latinas/os/x 167–8

lesbian 292–6, 377–80, 479, 576, 620; in film 116, 207; *see also* gay; queer; sex/sexuality

Let's Pretend (1934–1954) 367, 373

659

INDEX

"Liebestod" (Richard Wagner) 471–2
liminality 13, 60–1, 157, 188, 530, 533
Between the Lines (Jodi Picoult) 258
linguistic dynamism/stasis 264–6
literacy 430, 608–9
"Little Mermaid, The" (Hans Christian Andersen) 106, 231, 253, 332, 578
Little Mermaid, The (dir. Ron Clements) 182, 254, 487; merchandise and 332
Little Otik (dir. Jan Švankmajer) 255, 526
LittleRed App 544–5
Little Red Riding Hood (dir. David Kaplan) 146, 227–8, 291, 470
Little Red Riding Hood's Zombie BBQ (video game) 228, 636
Lost Girls (Alan Moore and Melinda Gebbre) 479–80
love: romantic (*see* heteronormativity; marriage; sex); sibling 109, 184, 328–9, 619–21
"Love Like Salt" (ATU 923) 228, 291
Lowell, Amy 582–3
Lüthi, Max 189–90

"Magic Flight, The" (ATU 313) 276
Magic Flute, The (dir. Ingmar Bergman) 575
Magic Flute, The (Wolfgang Amadeus Mozart) 573, 575
"Maiden Without Hands, The" (ATU 706) 104–5, 108–9
Maleficent (dir. Robert Stromberg) 44–5, 67, 109, 184–5, 191–2, 469
manga 391–7
Manley, Tim *see Alice in Tumblr-land*
Maori 124–7
marriage 109, 205–6, 295–6, 471–2; heteronormative 116, 182–3; nonnormative 291–2, 396, 511, 644; patriarchal 228–9, 323–4, 353, 410, 586; Proppian 23, 36, 205, 277, 592–3; unequal 230, 272, 274 (*see also* "Cupid and Psyche"); Victorian 323; weddings and 118
Marxism 47–54
masculinity 114, 116, 119n6, 156; animal 227; fatness and 257; threatened 207–8; toxic 182
mash-ups 33, 372, 495–7; broadcast media and 403–5; fan 65, 487–90, 645; video games and 635–7
material culture 138, 325, 328–35, 377; *see also* cosplay; merchandise
Max and Ruby (2002–2013) 455–6
McCance, Dawn 226
McCarthy, Paul 494–5
McClary, Susan 466–7, 471–2
McGillis, Roderick 235, 503
McKinley, Robin 317–18, 565–8
McMullin, Dan Taulapapa 88, 151, 292
Mécaniques célestes (*Celestial Clockwork*; dir. Fina Torres) 292, 576
media: broadcast 367–73, 590–5; digital 124, 376–87, 418–24, 539–47, 642–7 (*see also* social media); film 357–64, 460–4; material 328–35; photography

348–55; pictorial 118–19, 148, 320–6; print 311–18, 443–9; theater 337–44
meme: analysis of 20, 24–5, 161–2; motifs as 4, 249; orality and 497
menstruation 190
merchandise 295–6, 328–9, 331–3, 484–5, 569
metaphysical constants 216–19
metapoetics 367–73
Metropolitan Opera *Live in HD, The* 572–8
micronarrative 384–6; *see also* Tumblr; Twitter
Middle East, the 133–8
Mirror, Mirror (Katherine Noll) 258–61, 266, 521
Mirror Mirror (dir. Tarsem Singh) 69, 70, 79, 110, 266, 520–1
Mixed-Up Fairy Tales (video game) 635
Miyazawa Kenji Dowa Mura (Village of Fairy Tales) 438–9
Moana (dir. Ron Clements & John Musker) 130–1, 166, 168, 562
mobile apps 436, 448, 539–46; *see also Fat Princess*
Moby Dick (Herman Melville) 125
modernity 84–5, 123, 255, 410, 509
monster of the week 369, 631
mo'olelo 84, 124–7
Moon, Sarah 350
Moth, The 610–11
Moth Diaries, The (dir. Mary Harron) 620–1
Mother Goose: in film 210; in print 11, 301, 401, 430; in theater 340
motherhood 114, 117–18, 176n2, 587–8, 603–4; and daughters 44–5, 107; food and 526, 528–9; global 67; Oedipus complex and 41; true 99
mother-in-law 272, 621
motif: advertising and 154–7, 159; anthologies and 286, 301, 303; decontextualized 78, 110, 240, 268, 324, 377; fairy-tale structure and 12, 20–1, 32, 36–7, 93–4; index 22, 189 (*see also* Aarne-Thompson-Uther tale type numbers); recurring 24–6, 272; repertoire of 102
Mulan (dir. Tony Bancroft & Barry Cook) 183, 291
murder 172–4, 546, 619; *see also* "Bluebeard"; cannibalism; "Juniper Tree, The"
museums 205, 435–41, 612
music: broadcast media and 370; classical 466–72; film and 180–1, 295; online videos and 643; pop 230, 548–53; traditional 616–23; videos 548–53, 645; *see also* musicals; opera
musicals 204–5, 343–4, 556–62

narratology 9, 35–7, 213–20; transmedia and 164–6; video games and 634, 637, 639; *see also* formalism
nationalism 7, 14–16, 282, 403, 445–7
Native Americans 58, 85, 124, 353, 611
Nazism 54n8, 179, 284, 412, 498, 590
Nervous Conditions (Tsitsi Pangaremga) 51–3
Never Alone (video game) 127–30
New Criticism 32–4, 36–7; *see also* formalism

INDEX

Nicolaisen, W. H. F. 617–18, 622

"Nightingale, The" (Hans Christian Andersen) 134, 138–41

Nightmares and Fairy Tales (Serena Valentino) 479

Night of the Hunter, The (dir. Charles Laughton) 360–2, 528

nostalgia 421, 581, 583–6; Orientalism and 445; pornography and 206

Nosy Crow 448, 539–40, 543–4, 546

Nothing (Jane Teller) 240–1

novels 565–9, 601–2; French salons and 598–9; *see also* specific books by title

Olrik, Axel 276–7

Once Upon a Blog (InkGypsy) 423–4

Once Upon a Mattress 267

Once Upon a Time (2011–) 45, 69, 78, 117–18, 268, 372, 629–32; beginnings for 370–1; comic conventions 484–6; mashup 404–5; romance and 603; sexuality in 291; Swan Queen ship 377–80

"One Eye, Two Eyes, Three Eyes" (ATU 511) 525–6

opera 230, 292, 339–40, 466–8, 471–2, 572–8

oral tradition 14–15, 25, 56–63, 272–9; contemporary 87, 101, 266, 607–13, 645–6; and literature 4–9, 16–17, 31, 272–4, 277, 402, 430

Orientalism 83, 133–41, 302, 413, 445–7; in photography 353–4; in theater 339, 575–7

originality 60, 77, 149, 189, 312

origin of tales 15, 42, 117, 134

Otherness 252, 495–6, 536, 631–2; compassion and 239, 498, 587–8; internal 237; and sexuality 291, 599–600, 604; wonder and 241–2; *see also* Orientalism

Oxford Story Museum 437–8

Pacific Islands 122–31; *see also* Hawai'i; Maori

Paikea 125–7

Panchatantra 134, 272, 282, 299–300

pantomime (British) 148, 230, 323, 337–41, 343

parody 75–6, 78–9, 206–7, 338, 340, 454–5; critique and 506, 643–4

passing 106, 108

pastiche 68, 74–6, 78–9, 267–8, 477–80; *see also* mash-up

Path, The (online game) 228, 638

patriarchy 66, 116, 184, 552–3, 625; capitalist 156; history and 586; White 129; *see also* marriage, patriarchal

Peau d'Âne (dir. Jacques Demy) 18, 393, 414, 560–1

pedagogy 37, 179, 235–6, 281–7, 441; *see also* children's literature; young adult literature

pedophilia 240, 292, 350, 358–60

"Peg Bearskin" 291

Penelope (dir. Mark Palmsky) 240

performance 6, 56–63, 328, 334, 607–13; mediated 58–9, 369; public model of 452; theatrical 337–44

performative context 27, 273

Perrault, Charles 16, 113, 149, 273, 300–2, 402; canon and 8, 367, 404–5, 421, 516, 565; influence of 428;

language and 476–7, 580; nationalism and 607–8; portrayals of women 11, 401, 527–9, 551, 643; in theater 339, 341–3; translation and 12, 341, 430; *see also* specific tales by title

"Persinette" 190–3, 317

Peter Pan (J. M. Barrie) 165, 317, 357, 438, 462, 480

petit récits 75

photography 258, 348–55, 498

Piccinini, Patricia 495–6

pictorial media 320–6; *see also* art, visual; photography

piège d'Issoudun, Le (dir. Micheline Lanctôt) 230, 619

Pinocchio (dir. Ben Sharpsteen & Hamilton Luke) 178

plot genotype 22–3

Pocahauntas (Dina Goldstein) 353

poesis 506

poetry 25, 218–19, 401, 580–8, 617–21

"Poiluse, La" 291

point-of-view development 636–7

politics 96–7; *see also* activism

poor theory 89

popular culture 414, 493–5; *see also* comic conventions; fandom; music (pop)

porcelain 139, 320, 324–5

pornography 205–11

postcolonialism 83–9; *see also* colonialism

posthumanism 225, 495–6

postmodernism 74–82, 268–9, 377, 448; definitions of 74

poverty 94–102, 497; defense for crime 174–5

pregnancy 172, 190, 254, 295, 424, 621; conception and 304, 526–7; teen 184; *see also* motherhood

Prélude à l'après-midi d'un faune (Claude Debussy) 470–1

Princess and the Frog, The (dir. Ron Clements & John Musker) 68, 168, 183–4

"Princess and the Pea, The" (ATU 708) 267

princesses: Disney 179–85, 295, 643–4; fatness and 256–60; passivity and 181, 504–5; photography and 351–4; video games and 296

print 382; anthologies 443–9; digital media and 540–1; history 114, 311–18; picture books 443–9; *see also* chapbooks; novels

production: of chapbooks 428–9; culture of 70–1, 513

Propp, Vladimir *see* function

pseudonym 408, 420–1, 429, 508

psychoanalysis *see* Freudian analysis

psychology 40–5; photography and 351; storytelling and 60–1; therapeutic 533, 638

public domain 181, 200–2, 311, 451, 511, 541; *see also* copyright; intellectual property

"Puss in Boots" (ATU 545B) 79, 113, 218, 227, 257, 299–300

queer/queer studies 118–19, 165, 228, 231–2, 290–7, 470; anime and 391–7; in autobiography 413–14; creators 360; fan fiction and 511–13; in theater 342–3; time 190–1; *see also* feminism; gender

INDEX

racial casting 208, 560

racism 159, 226, 241, 284, 362, 631; in broadcast media 167; in film 138; personal 498; in tales 351, 357; *see also* colonialism; cultural appropriation

rap battle 644

rape 171–3, 176n1, 305; *see also* sex, violence and

"Rapunzel" (ATU 310) 184, 189–93; in autobiography 413; online 645; in print 317; in video games 639

reality television 414, 590–5

"Red Riding Hood" (ATU 333) 148, 227–30, 301, 527; in broadcast media 79, 451, 453–6; canon and 13, 113; fatness and 258; in film 21, 24, 70, 358, 521; justice and 175; language and 263–5, 267; in music videos 549–52; in photography 348–50; in poetry 586–8; in pornography 205; in print 149, 240; translation and 37; in video games 635–9; *see also* specific titles of adaptations

religion 281–5, 295, 304, 359, 361; art and 492; chapbooks and 427, 429; fantasy and 518–19

retellings 644–5; visual 77–8; *see also* specific titles of retellings

Ring, The (dir. Gore Verbinski) 172

Ring Cycle, The (Richard Wagner) 577

rites of passage 13, 190, 534

ritual 13–14, 16, 59, 573, 609; cannibalism and 526–7; digital 377; horror and 533

riturain 87

"Robber Bridegroom, The" (ATU 955) 172–3, 357, 466, 527–8

role-playing games 414–15

romance 598–604; family 45; at first sight 184–5; literary 11; over time 182–3; *see also* heteronormativity; marriage; sex/sexuality

Romanticism 84, 311–13

Rosemary's Baby (dir. Roman Polanski) 172, 176n1

Rossetti, Dante Gabriel 322, 325

"Rumpelstiltskin" (ATU 500) 420–1, 476

Rusalka (Antonín Dvořák) 578

Russia 284, 341–2, 421, 525; formalism and 22, 31–4, 592; Soviet Union 369, 469

salons, French 8, 115, 282, 300–2, 402, 580

Sasami: Magical Girls Club (2006–2007) 396

science fiction 240, 359, 460–4, 489; *see also* comic conventions

script (cognitive narratology) 24

Seifert, Lewis 113, 191, 225, 282, 290–1

semiotics 24, 31, 35–7, 147, 447, 540

Sendak, Maurice 236, 412, 440, 447, 530

Serenity (dir. Joss Whedon) 461

serial publication 313–14

sex/sexuality 560–1; children and 348–50; female 479–80 (*see also* female, desire; lesbian); food and 208–11, 226, 527–8; horror and 533–4; interracial 208; marketing and 628, 636–7; teenage 180, 190, 241, 362–3, 471–2, 549; translation 304–5; violence and 171–3, 175–6,

210, 477, 551–2, 638; *see also* gender; intersex; queer; transgender

Sexton, Anne 16, 145, 414, 504–5, 530, 586

shapeshifting 316; *see also* drag, animal

Sheldon v. Metro-Goldwyn 202–3

Sherman, Cindy 350–1

"Shift of Sex, The" (ATU 514) 291, 301

shipping (in fandom) 377–80

Shirley Temple's Storybook 404

Shrek: (dir. Andrew Adamson & Vicky Jenson) 78–9, 108, 256, 268, 317, 520; in print (William Stieg) 317; *Shrek 2* (dir. Andrew Adamson, Kelly Asbury & Conrad Vernon) 114, 165; *Shrek Forever After* (dir. Mike Mitchell) 257

simulacrum 74, 136–7, 139, 421

"Singing Bone, The" (ATU 780) 622–3

"Six Swans, The" (ATU 451) 116, 230

"Sleeping Beauty" (ATU 410) 78, 113, 148, 171, 189–93, 528; in digital media 383; in poetry 583–4; in print 316–17, 383, 428, 477, 568, 582; queered 291; in translation 304–5

Sleeping Beauty (dir. Clyde Geronimi) 184, 191–2, 469

Smith, Kiki 494

"Snow Queen, The" (Hans Christian Andersen) 104–5, 184, 292–6

Snow Queen (dir. David Wu) 294

Snow White and the Huntsman (dir. Rupert Sanders) 44–5, 110, 266, 488, 521

"Snow White and the Seven Dwarfs" (ATU 709) 148, 252, 403, 503, 528; in broadcast media 372; feminism and 76, 113; language and 269; in music videos 549–50; in photography 351–5; in print 106, 315–16, 475–6; in translation 304–5; in video games 635, 637; in visual art 493; *see also* titles of specific adaptations

Snow White and the Seven Dwarfs (dir. David Hand et al.) 115, 178–81, 205, 315, 557–8; book tie-in 315

social justice 48, 50, 161; *see also* activism

social media 162, 164–5, 256, 489–90; critique and 328; *see also* Tumblr; Twitter; YouTube

socioeconomic class 47, 94–102, 115, 167–8, 199–201; middle 323, 353, 544

Solaris (dir. Steven Soderbergh) 461

Sondheim, Stephen 337

song, traditional 616–23

"Son of the Witch" (ATU 425B) 272

"Sorcerer's Apprentice, The" 469–70

Sowerwine, Van 496–7

Stallings, Fran 61

Star Wars series 331, 461–2

Stein, Amy 354–5

"Stone Soup, The" (ATU 1548) 95

"Story of the Three Bears, The" (Robert Southey) 217–18

Storyrealm 26–7

StoryTeller, The (1988) 108, 227–30

INDEX

storytelling 8, 16–18, 53, 59–63, 122–31, 215–17; contemporary 607–13, 645–6; expectations of 385; festival 60; gendered 508–10; participatory 245–50, 484–7, 490; professional 59–60, 273–4; repertoires 401; *see also* performance

storyworld 213–22, 164–6, 439–40

Stowe v. Thomas 198

Straparola, Giovanni 113, 272–3, 300, 311, 401–2

structuralism 32, 35–7; *see also* formalism

subscription 429–30

subversive: children 237, 454–8; graphic narratives 479–80; reading 391, 410; writing 208, 239, 242, 274

suicide 230, 413, 576, 619–21, 639

supercripples 105–10

superheroes 117

Supernatural (2005–) 69, 377–80

Swan, The (2004) 590, 593–4

synchrony 32–3

"Table, the Donkey, and the Stick, The" (ATU 563) 95–6

Tab Tales 539, 541–2

Tales of Faerie (Kristin) 287, 420–4

tale type *see* Aarne-Thompson-Uther tale type numbers

taleworld 26, 57

"Tam Lin" (Child 39; Roud 35) 621

Tangled (dir. Nathan Greno & Byron Howard) 184, 193; in print 317

Tatar, Maria 173, 176, 235, 502, 618; criticism of Bettelheim 42–3; discussion of print history 272–3, 534; feminism and 528–9; on imagination 4, 286, 330; influence of 318

"Tatterhood" (ATU 711) 526

Taymor, Julie 574–5

Tchaikovsky, Pyotr Ilyich 316, 342, 469

technology 461–4; fetishism 162–3; *see also* blogs; Internet; social media

television 367–73, 451–7, 558–60; commercials 155; digital media and 628; long-arc serial 626–8 (*see also Once Upon a Time, Grimm*); reality (*see* reality television); *see also* broadcast media

Temin, Kathy 498

Texas Chainsaw Massacre, The (dir. Tobe Hooper) 532

texture, fairy-tale 26, 383–4

theater 337–44, 619; *see also* musicals; opera

theft 13, 173–5; of children 621; mythic 461

"Three Doctors, The" (ATU 660) 231

Three Fat Men (Yuri Olesha) 255

"Three Golden Children, The" (ATU 707) 99–100, 461

Three Little Pigs, The (1933) 179–80, 269

"Three Little Pigs, The" (ATU 124) 266, 540–1, 543–4

"Three Wishes, The" (ATU 675) 300

"Thumbling" (ATU 700) 109, 114, 173–5

time 421–2, 452, 582–3, 580–1, 584

Tinder 415, 644

Todorov, Tzvetan 215, 516

Tolkien, J. R. R. 236–7, 241, 312, 439, 515–19, 565

topological analysis 26, 93–4, 101–2

Tough Spell, A (video game) 637

tourism 75, 85, 167, 435–7, 612–13

trailers 370

trance, listening 60–1, 215

trans, animal 226–7, 229–31, 240, 495–7; *see also* "Beauty and the Beast" (ATU 425C)

transbiology 225–7; *see also* trans, animal

transformation 67–8, 154–9, 176, 247–50; marketing of 253; medium and 556–9; personal 302, 325, 593–5; poetry and 580–8

transgender 165, 207–8, 231–2, 360

translation 135–7, 299–306, 394; *see also* d'Aulnoy, Marie-Catherine; Galland, Antoine; Grimm brothers; Perrault, Charles

transmediality 164–6, 237–8, 572–8, 598–604; *see also* intermediality

trauma 45, 167, 410–13, 479–80, 546, 638–40; *see also* psychology

"Treasure Finders Who Murder One Another, The" (ATU 763) 175

Tristan and Isolde (Richard Wagner) 471–2

Tsilhqot'in 463

Tumblr 376–86, 419

Turandot (Gioachino Rossini) 576–7

Turner, Kay 191, 226–7, 291

Twain, Mark 198–9, 420

"Twa Sisters, The" (Child 10, Roud 8) 622–3

"Twelve Brothers, The" (ATU 451) 227, 291

twin laws of folklore 377, 400, 452–3

Twitter 382, 384–5, 487–8, 611

typology 93–4, 101–2

"Ugly Duckling, The" (Hans Christian Andersen) 381, 411, 436, 594

United Kingdom 611–12, 646; broadcast media and 595; copyright in 197–8; print in 426–8, 566; theater in 338, 340–1; translations in 114, 300; *see also* England

Uther, Hans-Jörg 20, 57, 106

utopia 50–2, 99–100, 205–6, 517

"Vasilisa the Beautiful" (ATU 510A) 421, 529–30

veganism 226

video games 127–30, 603–4, 634–40; Indigenous 127–30

Viehmann, Dorothy 199–200

villains 95, 109, 202, 350, 534–6; Disney 182, 192, 254, 603; female 294, 550, 602; horror and 533–5; metaphoric 253, 312; Orientalism and 137; in print 237

Villeneuve, Gabrielle-Suzanne Barbot de 598–9; *see also* "Beauty and the Beast" (ATU 425C)

Vimeo 646

Vine 646

violence 636–8; *see also* crime; murder; sex, violence and

INDEX

Wagner, Richard 467–9, 471–2, 572, 577
washing machine 157–9
"Water of Life" (ATU 551) 96–7
Weems, Carrie Mae 351
well-made film 23–4
Whale Rider (Witi Ihimaera) 125–6
Wicked (Gregory Macguire) 240
What Lies Beneath (dir. Robert Zemeckis) 172
"White Cat, The" (Marie-Catherine d'Aulnoy) 114
"White Snake, The" (ATU 673) 526
Wild Woman archetype 43–4
"Willie's Lady" (Child 6) 621
Witcher 3: Wild Hunt, The (video game) 639
Wolf Among Us, The (video game) 639–40
Wolves, Witches and Giants (1995–1999) 454
women: as-image 66; and intellectual property 199–201; *see also* female
wonder, ethics of 236
Wonderful Wizard of Oz, The (Frank L. Baum) 480, 485

wonder tale: colonialism and 84, 86; Indigenous 122–31; institutionalization of 612; Russian 34
work 183–4, 574; gendered 157–9

Yamamoto, Takayuki 440
Yanagi, Miwa 351–2
Yeats, William Butler 584–5, 608
young adult literature 235–42, 383, 412
"Youth Who Wanted to Know What Fear Is, The" (ATU 326) 577
YouTube 504, 642–7

Zipes, Jack: adaptation and 146–7, 266, 474–5; autobiography and 409, 422–4; definition of fairy tale 20, 484, 517; Disney and 67–8, 105, 179–80, 269, 469–70; the Grimms and 181, 359, 445, 518–19; Marxism and 47–53, 239; memetic theory and 4, 24–5, 281, 497; Orientalism and 134–5; subversion and 174, 235, 334, 493; well-made film and 23, 294, 357, 520